**RAND McNALLY**

PREMIER
WORLD ATLAS

President and CEO, Rand McNally & Company

Michael K. Hehir

Senior Vice President and General Manager, Consumer Travel Solutions

Victoria Donnowitz

Director, Local Travel

Leslie H. Hoadley

Editors

Brett R. Gover
Ann T. Natunewicz
Jane K. Soung

Art Direction and Design

John C. Nelson
Jamie O'Neal

Cartography (U.S.)

V. Patrick Healy
Jon M. Leverenz
Robert K. Argersinger
Barbara Benstead-Strassheim
Kerry B. Chambers
Marzee L. Eckhoff
Winifred V. Farbman
Susan K. Hudson
Gwynn A. Lloyd
Nina Lusterman
John M. McAvoy
Robert L. Merrill
Patty A. Porter
James A. Purvis
David R. Simmons
Thomas F. Vitacco

Cartography (U.K.)

Craig Asquith

Cartography (Italy)

Giovanni Baselli
Ubaldo Uberti

Manufacturing

Michele Smith

Marketing

JoEllen A. Klein

Photo Research

Feldman and Associates, Inc.

Photo Credits

(l=left, r=right, c=center, t=top, b=bottom)

Jacket/cover

Tony Stone Images: © Sally Mayman (volcano); © Art Wolfe (penguin); © John Beatty (desert); © Michael Busselle (Masai warrior); © William J Hebert (mountain and field); © Demetrio Carrasco (geishas)

Contents

© North Wind Picture Archives, iv (figures 4, 6, and 7)

Tony Stone Images: © Nicholas Parfitt, x (background); © Christopher Arnesen, x (t r); © Johnny Johnson, x (b l); © Warren Jacobs, xi (background); © Nicholas DeVore, xi (t r), xv (background); © Stephen Studd, xi (b r); © Tony Stone Images, xii (background); © Kevin Schafer, xii (m); © Joel Bennett, xiii (background and t l); © Fred Felleman, xiii (b r); © Tony Stone Images, xiv (background); © Paul Harris, xiv (t r); © Keren Su, xiv (b l); © Sylvain Grandadam, xv (t l); © Anthony Cassidy, xv (b r); © Oliver Strewe, xvi (background); © Paul Chesley, xvi (t r); © Penny Tweedie, xvi (b l); © Stuart Westmorland, xvii (background); © Chad Ehlers, xvii (t l); © Fred Bavendam, xvii (b r); © Art Wolfe, xviii (background); © Joe Cornish, xviii (b l), xix (t l); © David Hiser, xviii (t r); © David Paterson, xix (background); © David Sutherland, xix (b r); © Richard During, xx (background); © John Running, xx (t r); © Tim Davis, xx (b l); © Darrell Gulin, xxi (background); © Robert Frerck, xxi (t l)

© 1997 PhotoDisc: iii (t), vi (figure 3), viii (background), ix (background and t l), xxi (b r), xxiv (Energy)

Copyright © Corel Corp.: xxii (background, t r, and b l), xxiii (background, t l, and b r), xxiv (Land, Population, and Growth)

Satellite photo, iv (figure 1), provided by Wally Jansen, WTJ Software Series

Premier World Atlas

Copyright © 2000 by Rand McNally and Company
2002 Revised Printing

randmcnally.com

This product is protected under copyright law. It is illegal to reproduce or transmit it in whole or in part, in any form or by any means (including mechanical, photographic, or electronic methods), without the written permission of Rand McNally.

Published and printed in the United States of America

Rand McNally and Company.
    Rand McNally premier world atlas.
        p.   cm.
    Includes index.
    ISBN 0-528-83893-8 (hardback). - - ISBN 0-528-83894-6 (paperback)
        1. Atlases. I. Title.   II. Title: Premier world atlas
  G1021 .R45   1997   <G&M>
  912- - DC21

97-11900
CIP
MAPS

Contents

INTRODUCTORY SECTION

Understanding Maps & Atlases . . . . iv - v
How to Use the Atlas . . . . vi-vii
The World & Its Seven Continents . viii - xxiv

MAPS

Index Map and Legend 1

World 2-5

World, Political 2-3
World, Physical 4-5

Europe 6-23

Europe, Political 6-7
Northern Europe 8-9
Scandinavia and the Baltic States 10-11
Northwest Europe 12-13
Mediterranean Lands 14-15
Southwest Europe 16-17
Southern Europe 18-19
Central and Eastern Europe 20-21
Eastern Europe 22-23

Asia 24-45

Asia, Political 24-25
Northern Eurasia 26-27
China, Mongolia, Korea, and Japan 28-29
Eastern China 30
Japan 31
Southeast Asia 32-33
Mainland Southeast Asia and the Philippines . . 34-35
Malaysia, Singapore, and Indonesia 36-37
Southwest Asia 38-39
India 40-41
The Middle East 42-43
Turkey and Transcaucasia 44-45

Africa 46-57

Africa, Political 46-47
Northern Africa 48-49

West Africa 50-51
Central and Southern Africa 52-53
Central Africa 54-55
Southern Africa and Madagascar 56-57

Australia and Oceania 58-63

Australia and Oceania, Political 58-59
Western Australia 60-61
Eastern Australia and New Zealand 62-63

Pacific and Indian Oceans 64-65
Atlantic Ocean 66

Antarctica 67

South America 68-74

South America, Political 68
Southern South America 69
Northern South America 70-71
Central South America 72-73
Northeast Brazil 74

North America 75-143

North America, Political 75
Mexico, Central America, and the Caribbean . . 76-77
Mexico 78-79
Central America and the Caribbean 80-81
Canada and Alaska 82-83
Canadian Province Maps 84-91
United States 92-93
U.S. State Maps 94-143

Arctic Region 144

INDEX

Index to the Reference Maps . . . . I•1-I•80

Understanding Maps & Atlases

figure 1

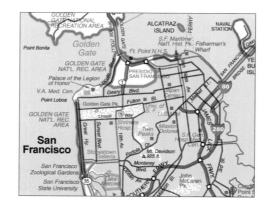

San Francisco

figure 2

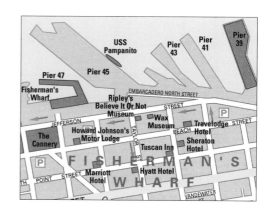

figure 3

What is a map?

A map is a representation, usually at a much-reduced size, of the location of things or places relative to one another. There are many different types of maps, including maps of the world, its regions or countries, cities, neighborhoods, and buildings. Figure 1 is a satellite image of California's San Francisco Bay area; figure 2 shows the same area represented on a road map; and figure 3 provides street-level detail of one of the city's neighborhoods.

figure 4

A set of maps bound together is called an atlas. Abraham Ortelius' *Theatrum orbis terrarum*, published in 1570, is considered to be the first modern "atlas," although it was not referred to as such for almost 20 years. In 1589, Gerardus Mercator (figure 4) coined the term when he named his collection of maps after the mythological titan Atlas, who carried the Earth on his shoulders as punishment for warring against Zeus. Since then, the definition of "atlas" has been expanded, and atlases often include additional geographic information in diagrams, tables, and text.

History of Cartography

Around 500 B.C., on a tiny clay tablet the size of a hand, the Babylonians inscribed the Earth as a flat disk (figure 5) with Babylon at the center. Geographic knowledge was also highly developed among the Egyptians, who drew maps on papyrus and carved them into temple walls. Ancient Greek philosophers and scientists debated endlessly the nature of the Earth and its place in the universe; Ptolemy, the influential geographer and astronomer, made an early attempt to map the known world (figure 6). Roman maps most often depicted boundaries, physical features, and the infrastructure of the Roman Empire. Over the following centuries, territorial expansion directly increased geographic knowledge, which in turn greatly enhanced the cartography, or map-making, of the time.

figure 5

As trade and navigation grew, maps were developed to guide merchants and explorers. The Cantino map of 1502 (figure 7) is an example of a *portolan* (sea) chart used by mariners traveling to the newly discovered Americas. Information gained from the past expeditions of John Cabot, Christopher Columbus, and Ferdinand Magellan led to great advances in the content and structure of world maps. As a result, many maps produced between 1600 and 1800, including the colored woodcut shown in figure 8, were works of art as well as geographical representations.

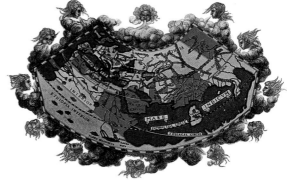

figure 6

figure 8

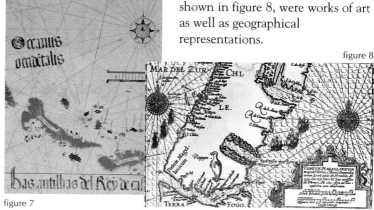

figure 7

Over the past three centuries, cartography throughout the world has become extremely precise, aided most recently by satellites which provide images of the Earth and, within the last 25 years, have led to the development of global positioning systems. Sophisticated computers now manage large amounts of geographic information used to produce maps for a variety of purposes, including business, science, government, and education.

Latitude and Longitude

The imaginary horizontal line that circles the Earth exactly halfway between the North and South poles is called the Equator, which represents 0° latitude and lies 90° from either pole. The other lines of latitude, or parallels, measure the distance from the Equator, either north or south (figure 9). The imaginary vertical line that measures 0° longitude runs through the Greenwich Observatory in the United Kingdom, and is called the Prime Meridian. The other lines of longitude, or meridians, measure distances east and west of the Prime Meridian (figure 10), up to a maximum of 180°. Lines of latitude and longitude cross each other, forming a pattern called a grid system (figure 11). Any point on Earth can be located by its precise latitude and longitude coordinates.

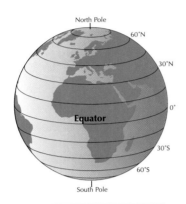

figure 9

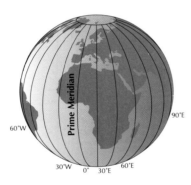

figure 10

figure 11

Map projections

Spherical representations of the Earth are called globes, while flat representations are called maps. Because globes are round and three-dimensional, they can show the continents and oceans undistorted and unbroken; therefore, they represent the Earth and its various features more correctly than do maps. Maps, however, generally feature larger scales and higher levels of detail.

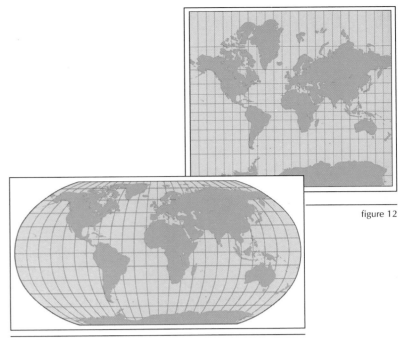

figure 12

figure 13

With the help of mathematics, cartographers are able to depict the curvature of the Earth on a two-dimensional surface. This process is called projecting a map, or creating a map projection. The size, shape, distance, area, and proportion of map features can be distorted, however, when the curves of a globe become the straight lines of a map. Distortion occurs because the Earth's spherical surface must be stretched and/or broken in places as it is flattened. Different map projections have specific properties that make them useful, and a cartographer must select the projection best-suited to the map's purpose.

The Mercator (figure 12) and the Robinson (figure 13) projections are commonly chosen for maps of the entire world. In this atlas, the Robinson is used along with four additional projections—the Lambert Azimuthal Equal Area, the Lambert Conformal Conic, the Sinusoidal, and the Azimuthal Equidisant.

Map scale

The scale of a map is the relationship between distances or areas shown on the map and the corresponding distances or areas on the Earth's surface. Large-scale maps generally show relatively small areas in greater detail than do small-scale maps, such as those of the world or the continents.

There are three different ways to express scale. Most often it is given as a fraction, such as 1:10,000,000, which means that the ratio of map distances to actual Earth distances is 1 to 10,000,000 (figure 14). Scale also can be expressed as a word phrase, such as, "One inch represents approximately 150 miles" (figure 15). Lastly, scale can be illustrated as a scale bar, labeled with miles on one side and kilometers on the other (figure 16). Any of these three scale expressions can be used to calculate distances on a map.

1:10 000 000

figure 14

One inch represents approximately 150 miles

figure 15

figure 16

How to Use the Atlas

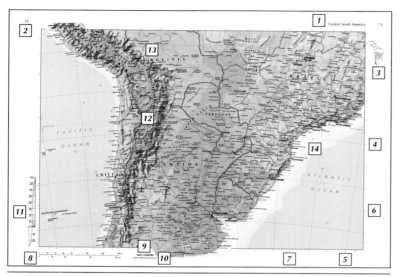

figure 1

[1] Map title	[9] Scale ratio
[2] Page number	[10] Map projection
[3] Locator map	[11] Hypsometric/bathymetric scale bar
[4] Latitude	[12] Shaded relief
[5] Longitude	[13] Hypsometric tints
[6] Index reference letter	(to show elevation)
[7] Index reference number	[14] Bathymetric tints
[8] Scale bar	(to show water depths)

figure 2

[1] International boundary	[9] City/town
[2] Mountain peak/elevation	[10] Swamp
[3] Hypsometric elevation tints	[11] River
[4] International airport	[12] Mountain range
[5] Urban area	[13] Railroad
[6] National capital	[14] Lake
[7] Country name	[15] Bathymetric tints
[8] Road	[16] Depth of water (in meters)

What the *Premier World Atlas* includes

At the core of the *Premier World Atlas* is a collection of regional maps covering the entire world. The maps were designed to be as easy as possible to understand and use. Figure 1 is an example of a map spread contained in this atlas. The boxed numbers on this map, which correspond to items listed below it, highlight the features and information found on each map page—such as the map title, the locator map showing the area of the world depicted on the map, and the map scale.

Figure 2 is an enlarged section from the same map. As in figure 1, a few of the most common feature symbols have been highlighted. A more complete list of the map symbols used in this atlas can be found on page 1.

The atlas opens with a 17-page photographic essay devoted to the world and the continents (figure 3). Each of the seven continents is featured on two pages with photos and descriptive text. Fact blocks (figure 4) provide vital information about each continent's most notable characteristics and features.

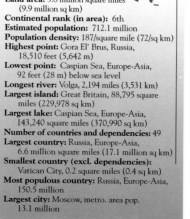

figure 4

Europe Facts

Land area: 3.8 million square miles (9.9 million sq km)
Continental rank (in area): 6th
Estimated population: 712.1 million
Population density: 187/square mile (72/sq km)
Highest point: Gora El' Brus, Russia, 18,510 feet (5,642 m)
Lowest point: Caspian Sea, Europe-Asia, 92 feet (28 m) below sea level
Longest river: Volga, 2,194 miles (3,531 km)
Largest island: Great Britain, 88,795 square miles (229,978 sq km)
Largest lake: Caspian Sea, Europe-Asia, 143,240 square miles (370,990 sq km)
Number of countries and dependencies: 49
Largest country: Russia, Europe-Asia, 6.6 million square miles (17.1 million sq km)
Smallest country (excl. dependencies): Vatican City, 0.2 square miles (0.4 sq km)
Most populous country: Russia, Europe-Asia, 150.5 million
Largest city: Moscow, metro. area pop. 13.1 million

figure 3

The World & its Seven Continents

Following the regional maps are individual maps of each of the United States, and the Canadian provinces (figure 5).

The last section of the *Premier World Atlas* is an 80-page index with entries for approximately 45,000 places and geographic features that appear on the maps.

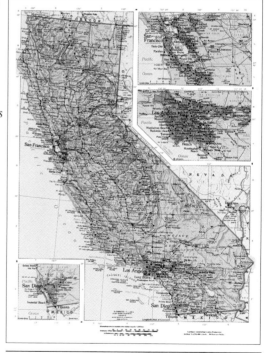

figure 5

Physical and Political Maps

The two main types of maps that appear in this atlas are physical maps and political maps. Physical maps, like the one shown in figure 6 (see next page), emphasize terrain, landforms, and elevation. Political maps, as in figure 7, emphasize countries and other political units over topography. The state and province maps found on pages 84-91 and pages 94-143 are both political and physical: they feature political coloration but also include shaded relief to depict landforms.

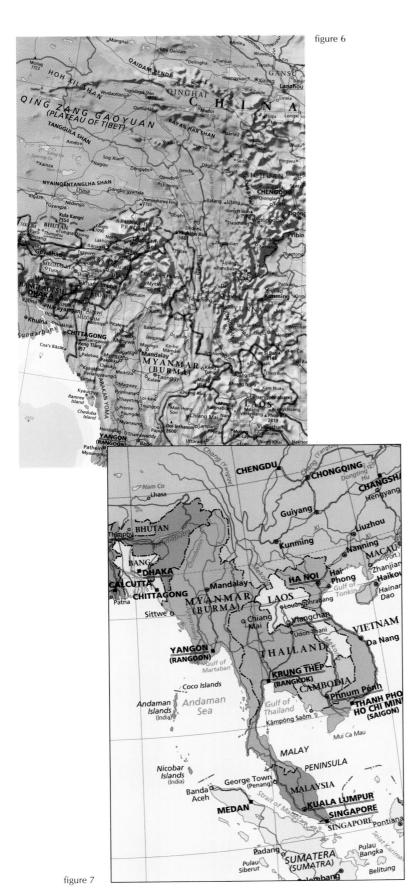

figure 6

figure 7

figure 8

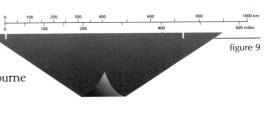

figure 9

between the 400-mile mark and the unlabeled 500-mile mark, indicating that the distance separating the two cities is approximately 450 miles (figure 9).

3) To confirm this measurement, make a third pencil mark (shown in red in figure 9) at the 400-mile mark. Slide the paper to the left so that the red mark lines up with 0. The white Sydney mark now falls very close to the 50-mile mark, which is unlabeled. Thus, Melbourne and Sydney are indeed approximately 450 (400 plus 50) miles apart.

Using the Index to Find Places

One of the most important purposes of an atlas is to help the reader locate places or features. In this atlas, each map is bordered by a letter and number grid. In the index, found in the back of the atlas on pages I•1 through I•80, every entry is assigned a map reference key, which consists of a letter and a number that correspond to a letter and a number on the grid. To locate places or features, follow the steps outlined in this example for Palembang, Indonesia:

P

Pālanpur, India	F5	40
Palaoa Point, C., Hi., U.S.	C4	104
Palapye, Bots.	F5	56
Palatine, Il., U.S.	A5	106
Palatka, Fl., U.S.	C5	102
Palau, ctry., Oc.	B8	37
Palawan, i., Phil.	B5	37
Pālayankottai, India	E8	41
Palembang, Indon.	D2	36
Palencia, Spain	G6	17
Palermo, Italy	D5	18
Palestine, Ar., U.S.	C5	97
Palestine, Il., U.S.	D6	106
Palestine, Tx., U.S.	D5	136

figure 10

1) Look up Palembang in the index. The entry (figure 10) contains the following information: the feature name (Palembang), an abbreviation for the country (Indon.) in which Palembang is located, the map reference key (D2) that corresponds to Palembang's location on the map, and the page number (36) of the map on which Palembang can be found.

2) Turn to page 36. Look along either the left or right margin for the letter "D" —the letter code given for Palembang. The "D" denotes a narrow horizontal band, roughly 1½" wide, in which Palembang is located. Then, look along either the top or bottom margin for the number "2" —the numerical part of the code given for Palembang. The "2" denotes a narrow vertical band, also roughly 1½" wide, in which Palembang is located.

3) Using your finger, follow the "D" band and the "2" band to the area where they meet (figure 11). Palembang can be found within the darker shaded square where the bands overlap.

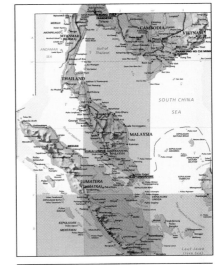

figure 11

Measuring Distances

Using a map scale bar, it is possible to calculate the distance between any two points on a map. To find the approximate distance between Melbourne and Sydney, Australia, for example, follow these steps:

1) Lay a piece of paper on the right-hand page of the "Eastern Australia and New Zealand" map found on pages 62-63, lining up its edge with the city dots for Melbourne and Sydney. Make a mark on the paper next to each dot (figure 8).

2) Place the paper along the scale bar found below the map, and position the first mark at 0. The second mark falls about halfway

The World & its Seven Continents

The world we humans inhabit—a world that sustains, inspires, and challenges us—is Planet Earth, a massive ball of rock spinning through the darkness of space.

On a human scale the Earth is immense, but on the incomprehensibly vast scale of the universe, it is no more significant than a grain of sand in a desert. Along with its companion planets, the Earth orbits a relatively small star we call the Sun, which is but one of 260 billion stars clustered in a great spiral-shaped galaxy known as the Milky Way, which is but one of billions of known galaxies.

Water dominates the surface of our planet; land covers only slightly more than a quarter of it. We arbitrarily call the largest pieces of land "continents": North America, South America, Africa, Antarctica, Australia, and Europe and Asia, which share a single landmass. All of the other pieces of land, from enormous Greenland to minuscule parcels of sand and rock breaking the ocean's surface, are considered islands.

Although life first appeared on the Earth perhaps 3.5 billion years ago, our own human species, Homo sapiens, has walked the planet for only 300,000 to 400,000 years—the blink of an eye in geologic time. Our distant ancestors led nomadic lives as hunters and gatherers, constantly on the move in search of prey and edible plants, fruits, and nuts. Over time they spread to every continent except Antarctica, even crossing wide seas to colonize Australia.

About 10,000 years ago, shortly after the end of the great Ice Age, a dramatic change swept through some areas of the world: humans began to cultivate crops—wheat and barley were probably the first—and to keep herds of domesticated animals, such as sheep, goats, and pigs. With the advent of agriculture came the first permanent settlements and ultimately the first civilizations.

Prior to these developments, the world's population had grown very slowly, and probably never exceeded ten million. But agriculture brought a much greater and more reliable supply of food, and the population began a climb that in modern times has reached explosive proportions. At the beginning of the first millennium A.D., perhaps 250 million people inhabited the planet. By 1850, this number had quadrupled to roughly 1.2 billion. Since then, it has nearly quintupled: today the world holds a whopping 5.8 billion people.

Nevertheless, large parts of each continent remain unpopulated or only sparsely populated. Most such areas are hostile to human life: some are too hot and dry (deserts such as the Sahara and the Gobi); some are too cold or do not have adequate growing seasons (Antarctica and the northern regions of Asia, Europe, and North America); some are too densely vegetated (the rain forests of South America and central Africa); and some are too mountainous or poor in soil (western North America and western Asia). This leaves only a small part of the Earth's surface to support all of its people.

Until the last five or so centuries, the world's peoples and civilizations were largely isolated from one another, either by great distances or by natural barriers such as mountains, deserts, and seas. As a result, a myriad of languages and cultures arose, and inhabitants of one region or continent differed greatly from those of another. Recent advances in transportation and communication have reversed this situation, and now many local languages and traditions are slowly being replaced by an emerging global culture. Suddenly, our vast world is beginning to feel very small.

World Facts

Land area: 57.9 million square miles (150.1 million sq km)
Estimated population: 5.8 billion
Population density: 99/square mile (38/sq km)
Highest point: Mt. Everest, China (Tibet)-Nepal, 29,028 feet (8,848 m)
Lowest point: Dead Sea, Israel-Jordan, 1,339 feet (408 m) below sea level
Longest river: Nile, Africa, 4,145 miles (6,671 km)
Largest island: Greenland, North America, 840,000 square miles (2.2 million sq km)
Largest lake: Caspian Sea, Asia-Europe, 143,240 square miles (371,000 sq km)
Number of countries and dependencies: 246
Largest country: Russia, Asia-Europe, 6.6 million square miles (17.1 million sq km)
Smallest country (excl. dependencies): Vatican City, Europe, 0.2 square miles (0.4 sq km)
Most populous country: China, Asia, 1.2 billion
Largest city: Tokyo, Japan, Asia, metro. area pop. 31.3 million

Africa

Africa is a land of vast spaces and infinite variety. Across its great length and breadth are found tropical rain forests, savannas teeming with wildlife, sun-scorched deserts, sprawling modern cities, and a kaleidoscope of peoples and cultures.

The Sahara, largest of the world's deserts, dominates the northern half of the continent. Reaching from the Atlantic Ocean to the Red Sea, the Sahara covers an area nearly as large as the entire continent of Europe. Few people inhabit this inhospitable landscape of shifting sand dunes, gravel-covered plains, and bare mountains, where rain seldom falls and hot, dust-laden winds blow relentlessly.

Southern Africa also contains large arid regions, most notably the Namib and Kalahari deserts. Along the equator, however, rain falls in abundance. Verdant rain forests blanket much of this region, alive with monkeys, gorillas, wild pigs, and countless species of birds and insects. Between the deserts and the rain forests lie the broad swaths of grassland known as savannas. Herds of zebras, wildebeests, giraffes, elephants, and many other animals graze on the savannas, always on the alert for lions, hyenas, and other predators. Poaching and destruction of habitat have decimated animal populations in many parts of Africa, but enormous concentrations still exist in places such as northern Botswana and the Serengeti Plain of Tanzania.

Africa's greatest rivers are the Congo, the Zambezi, the Niger, and of course the Nile, the longest river in the world. From its headwaters in Burundi, the Nile flows northward more

Left page: Acacia trees on the Serengeti Plain, Tanzania; Samburu girls, Kenya; African elephant.

Right page: Sahara near Arak, Algeria; brightly painted hut and its occupants, Lesotho; avenue of sphinxes, Luxor, Egypt.

than four thousand miles —through rugged mountains and highlands, the beautiful lake country of East Africa, and the wide marshy plain known as the Sudd—before spilling into the Mediterranean Sea.

Humans have farmed the fertile land of the Nile Delta from time immemorial, and it was here that the great civilization of the ancient Egyptians sprang up more than five thousand years ago. The marvelous archaeological legacies of this civilization include the Pyramids, the Sphinx, and the temples of Karnak and Luxor.

Among Africa's seven hundred million people there is tremendous ethnic and cultural diversity. More than eight hundred languages are spoken across the continent, and scores of distinct ethnic groups can be identified—groups such as the Tuareg and Berbers of Saharan Africa, the Masai and Kikuyu of the eastern savannas, the Fang and Bateke of the rain forests. Not surprisingly, few African countries are ethnically homogeneous.

Tremendous change has swept through Africa in the twentieth century. As recently as the 1940s, nearly the entire continent was controlled by colonial powers. In the wake of the Second World War, independence movements gathered strength, and by the end of the 1970s all of Africa's countries had shaken off their colonial shackles. For the first time in centuries, the continent was free to seek its own identity and destiny.

Africa Facts

Land area: 11.7 million square miles (30.3 million sq km)
Continental rank (in area): 2nd
Estimated population: 722.2 million
Population density: 62/square mile (24/sq km)
Highest point: Kilimanjaro, Tanzania, 19,340 feet (5,895 m)
Lowest point: Lac Assal, Djibouti, 515 feet (157 m) below sea level
Longest river: Nile, 4,145 miles (6,671 km)
Largest island: Madagascar, 226,658 square miles (587,041 sq km)
Largest lake: Lake Victoria, 26,820 square miles (69,463 sq km)
Number of countries and dependencies: 61
Largest country: Sudan, 967,500 square miles (2,505,813 sq km)
Smallest country (excl. dependencies): Seychelles, 175 square miles (453 sq km)
Most populous country: Nigeria, 102.9 million
Largest city: Cairo, metro. area pop. 13.4 million

Antarctica

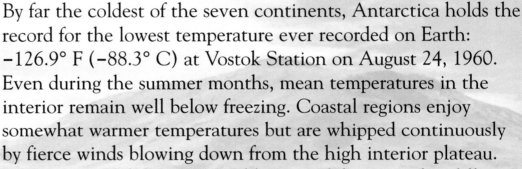

The frozen continent of Antarctica lies at the very bottom of the world, buried beneath a great sheet of ice and encircled by frigid seas crowded with towering icebergs.

By far the coldest of the seven continents, Antarctica holds the record for the lowest temperature ever recorded on Earth: −126.9° F (−88.3° C) at Vostok Station on August 24, 1960. Even during the summer months, mean temperatures in the interior remain well below freezing. Coastal regions enjoy somewhat warmer temperatures but are whipped continuously by fierce winds blowing down from the high interior plateau.

Because of the extreme cold, most of the snow that falls over Antarctica's interior does not melt; instead, it accumulates and gradually compacts. Over the course of millions of years, this process has formed the ice sheet that now covers nearly the entire continent. Almost inconceivably massive, the sheet has an average thickness as great as the depth of the Grand Canyon; its maximum thickness is three times greater. It holds some ninety percent of all the ice on Earth, and seventy percent of the fresh water.

As the ice sheet slowly spreads outward under its own crushing weight, its edges spill into the surrounding seas, forming immense shelves that in some places extend hundreds of miles from the shore. The largest of these, the Ross Ice Shelf, covers an area as large as the entire country of France. Enormous pieces continuously break off, or "calve," from the margins of the shelves and drift northward as icebergs.

If all of Antarctica's ice were to melt, the consequences would be disastrous. Ocean levels would rise dramatically, flooding coastal regions around the world. Florida, for example, would disappear under water, as would southeast Asia's Malay Peninsula and the Low Countries of Europe. More than half of the world's people would be forced to relocate.

Antarctica's coasts, islands, and seas are as full of life as its interior is barren. Clamorous penguin rookeries, some containing tens of thousands of individuals, dot the coastline. Petrels, albatrosses, and cormorants sail the coastal skies, searching the sea for fish and crustaceans. Seven species of seal, including leopard seals, elephant seals, and crabeaters, swim the nutrient-rich Antarctic waters along with squid, octopuses, killer whales, blue whales, and more than a dozen other whale species.

To whom does Antarctica belong? This question has provoked a great deal of controversy in the twentieth century, as numerous countries have explored the continent, made territorial claims, or established research stations. The possibility of rich mineral deposits adds urgency to the question.

In 1959, twelve countries drafted and signed the Antarctic Treaty, which declares Antarctica a natural reserve to be used only for peaceful purposes, especially scientific investigation. So far, the treaty has met with great success, and today Antarctica enjoys a spirit of international cooperation unknown elsewhere in the world.

Left page: Sled and dog team; Emperor penguins.
Right page: Iceberg and ice floes; research ship anchored along sea ice; killer whale.

Antarctica Facts

Land area: 5.4 million square miles (14 million sq km)

Continental rank (in area): 5th

Estimated population: No permanent population

Highest point: Vinson Massif, 16,066 feet (4,897 m)

Lowest point: Deep Lake, 184 feet (56 m) below sea level

Longest river: Antarctica has no true rivers

Largest island: Berkner Island, 20,005 square miles (51,829 sq km)

Number of countries with territorial claims: 7

Number of countries with research stations: 18

Asia

Three out of five people on Earth live in Asia, by far the world's largest and most heavily populated continent. With its myriad of landscapes, peoples, and historical treasures, and its swelling population, Asia represents a microcosm of the entire world.

Mountain systems—some ancient, some young and still rising—are the continent's signature landform. The Himalayas, which run through Pakistan, China, India, Nepal, and Bhutan, form the loftiest range in the world. Reaching more than five miles into the heavens, Mount Everest is the world's highest mountain, but nearby Kanchenjunga, Dhawalāgiri, Annapurna, and the peak known simply as K2 are hardly less formidable.

Seemingly endless expanses of semiarid grassland, or steppes, blanket much of the vast continental interior. Just north of the Himalayas lies the remote Tibetan Plateau, nicknamed the "Rooftop of the World": its average elevation is nearly half the height of Mount Everest.

The northern third of the continent is occupied by the region known as Siberia. Its name evokes images of a bitterly cold wasteland of snow and tundra, but visitors also discover vast, pristine forests, grassy plains, and extensive marshlands.

A long belt of desert stretches from the Arabian peninsula to eastern China. Most of this arid region is virtually uninhabited, and life is harsh for the few residents. The parched landscape of the Gobi, Asia's largest desert, contains little more than tough scrub vegetation and brackish lakes.

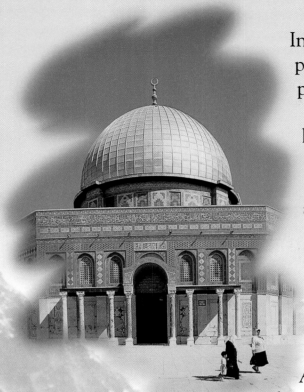

In the far west, the Arabian peninsula is a sea of sand dunes, punctuated by an occasional oasis where tall palm trees provide the desert's only shade.

In sharp contrast to these barren landscapes, the tropical lands and islands of Southeast Asia are awash in greenery. Crops and rain forests thrive in this wet region, where seasonal monsoon rains saturate the land for months at a time.

For centuries, rivers have been a lifeline for the people of the continent. Nestled between the Tigris and Euphrates rivers is the fertile land of Mesopotamia, which supported an advanced society that flourished as early as 4000 B.C. Ruins found in the lush Indus River valley of Pakistan tell of an advanced culture dating back to around 3000 B.C. And, almost 4,000 years ago, the ancient Chinese civilization developed along the banks of the Huang (Yellow) River.

Irrigation networks are vital to Asia because rocky terrain and minimal precipitation make much of the continent ill-suited for agriculture, and all arable land must be farmed intensively. The fertile valleys and coasts of eastern and southern Asia already strain to meet the demands of Asia's soaring population.

Recent economic and technological development has allowed Japan, Singapore, Indonesia, and Korea to rise to international prominence. It is likely that this trend will continue for these and other Asian countries into the 21st century, which many observers are already referring to as "the Asian Century." It will be a time for the countries of the continent to flex their collective muscle. Since Asia represents such a large percentage of the Earth's population, what happens there might dictate what the future brings to the rest of the world.

Left page: Mount Fuji and tea fields, Japan; Kazak man with hunting eagle, Mongolia; giant panda.

Right page: Mount Everest; Dome of the Rock, Omar Mosque, Jerusalem, Israel; schoolboys in Nāgaur, India.

Asia Facts

Land area: 17.3 million square miles (44.9 million sq km)

Continental rank (in area): 1st

Estimated population: 3.5 billion

Population density: 203/square mile (78/sq km)

Highest point: Mt. Everest, China (Tibet)-Nepal, 29,028 feet (8,848 m)

Lowest point: Dead Sea, Israel-Jordan, 1,339 feet (408 m) below sea level

Longest river: Yangtze (Chang), 3,900 miles (6,300 km)

Largest island: New Guinea, 309,000 square miles (800,000 sq km)

Largest lake: Caspian Sea, Asia-Europe, 143,240 square miles (370,990 sq km)

Number of countries and dependencies: 50

Largest country: Russia, Asia-Europe, 6.6 million square miles (17.1 million sq km)

Smallest country (excl. dependencies): Maldives, 115 square miles (298 sq km)

Most populous country: China, 1.2 billion

Largest city: Tokyo, metro. area pop. 31.3 million

Australia
& Oceania

The continent of Australia, along with its island neighbor New Zealand, is often classified as part of Oceania, a larger region that includes more than 25,000 islands, volcanic peaks, and coral atolls scattered across the southern Pacific Ocean.

The first European explorers to Australia came ashore near present-day Sydney and were so awed by the profusion of unfamiliar vegetation that they named the area Botany Bay. Today, eucalyptus and acacia trees, fuschias, and spear lilies thrive alongside exotic animal species such as kangaroos, wallabies, koala bears, kookaburras, and platypuses in Australia's warm climate.

Low, semiarid plateaus cover much of western Australia, taking in the Great Sandy Desert, the Gibson Desert, and the Great Victoria Desert. Here, scrubby grasses and spiky bushes break up stretches of pebble-covered land. This barren, largely uninhabited region is the Outback, whose harsh beauty and remoteness have come to epitomize "The Land Down Under" for many non-Australians.

Australia's indigenous people, called the Aborigines, arrived and settled the Outback and other parts of the continent perhaps 35,000 years prior to the Europeans. The complex Aboriginal society is based on kinship and the belief that humans, the environment, and time are intimately associated. Aborigines hold sacred numerous sites across Australia, including Uluru, or Ayers Rock, the world's largest monolith.

Left page: Dirt road through Australia's Outback; Aboriginal man, northern Australia; koala bear, Australia.

Right page: Rock Islands, Palau; Mount Cook, New Zealand's highest peak; school of sweetips.

Among Australia's most valuable natural resources are its vast grasslands, dotted with woolly herds of grazing sheep and fenced in by the paddocks of great ranches, or stations. Australia is a major world producer and exporter of wool, veal, and mutton.
Sheep herding and grazing also dominate the economy of New Zealand, where sheep outnumber humans fourteen to one.

In this century, New Zealand has aggressively developed its own resources and now ranks among the world's most economically advanced countries. Cascading rivers provide water power for burgeoning industrial development, and rich reserves of minerals, natural gas, and timber drive a strong economy. With this wealth of resources, New Zealand has become a world leader in trade, much of which passes through the superb natural harbor of Wellington, the capital city.

New Zealand has two main islands, both of which are mountainous and ruggedly beautiful. On South Island, icy glaciers cut through the Southern Alps, and dazzling fjords such as Milford Sound indent the southwestern coast. The smaller North Island, home to three-quarters of the country's population, is dominated by a central volcanic plateau over which tower three impressive peaks: Ruapehu, Ngauruhoe, and Tongariro.

Papua New Guinea, on the eastern half of the island of New Guinea, is an uneven mixture of lush rain forests, swamplands, and steep volcanic mountains. Along with many of the smaller islands of Oceania, it lies on the southwestern section of the Ring of Fire—a band of active volcanoes that encircles the Pacific Ocean.

Every year, thousands of winter-weary tourists escape to Oceania's tropical island paradises, such as Tahiti, Fiji, and Guam. Here, they revel in the endless stretches of sandy beaches, secluded coves, and absolute isolation, half a world away from their homes.

Australia & Oceania Facts

Land area: 3.3 million square miles (8.5 million sq km)
Continental rank (in area): 7th
Estimated population: 29.0 million
Population density: 8.8/square mile (3.4/sq km)
Highest point: Mt. Wilhelm, Papua New Guinea, 14,793 feet (4,509 m)
Lowest point: Lake Eyre, South Australia, 52 feet (16 m) below sea level
Longest river: Murray-Darling, 2,330 miles (3,750 km)
Largest island: New Guinea, Oceania-Asia, 309,000 square miles (800,000 sq km)
Largest lake: Lake Eyre, 3,700 square miles (9,500 sq km)
Number of countries and dependencies: 33
Largest country: Australia, 3 million square miles (7.7 million sq km)
Smallest country (excl. dependencies): Nauru, 8.1 square miles (21 sq km)
Most populous country: Australia, 18.4 million
Largest city: Sydney, metro. area pop. 3.5 million

Europe

Human settlements and civilizations have flourished in Europe for more than four thousand years, benefiting from the generally mild climate and the abundance of arable land, navigable rivers, and natural resources. The continent today ranks with East Asia and South Asia as one of the three greatest population centers in the world.

The northern half of Europe bears dramatic evidence of past ice ages. During the Pleistocene epoch, immense sheets and rivers of ice plowed across the region, rounding the mountains of Scandinavia and Scotland, scouring river valleys to create Norway's deep fjords, and depositing a thick layer of sand, gravel, and boulder-filled clay across the landscape. This glacial deposition played a major part in the formation of the Great European Plain, which stretches in an arc from western France to the Urals. The western part of the plain is Europe's most intensively farmed region as well as its most densely populated, home to such great cities as Paris, Amsterdam, Berlin, Stockholm, Warsaw, and Moscow.

Uplands and mountain systems dominate the southern half of the continent. The Pyrenees, Alps, and Carpathians together form a nearly unbroken band of mountains stretching from the Atlantic to central Romania. Until the advent of modern transportation, this formidable natural barrier impeded overland travel between the Mediterranean region and the rest of Europe, especially when winter snows fell on the mountain passes. As a result, a distinct Mediterranean culture evolved, and it remains strong today.

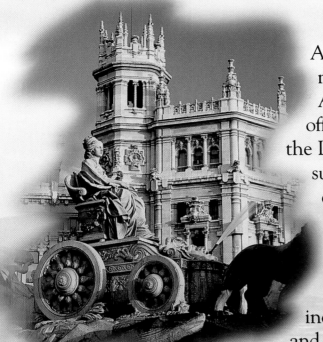

Thanks to a warm ocean current called the North Atlantic Drift, northwestern Europe enjoys a climate far milder than those of lands at similar latitudes in North America and Asia. The current warms and moistens offshore air masses, which then flow across the British Isles, the Low Countries, France, Denmark, Germany, and surrounding lands. As this maritime air moves into eastern Europe, its effects become weaker and weaker, and climates become increasingly extreme. Mountain systems block the air masses from the Mediterranean region, which has a hotter, drier climate.

Europe has been home to many great civilizations, including those of the Minoans, Mycenaeans, Greeks, and Romans. With the collapse of the Roman Empire, Europe plunged into a period of relative decline and darkness, but emerged roughly one thousand years later into the light of the Renaissance, a glorious rebirth that pervaded nearly every field of human endeavor but especially art and science.

The Renaissance also marked the beginning of an era of exploration and expansion. Great powers such as England, Spain, Portugal, and France explored, conquered, and colonized lands all over the world—Africa, the Americas, Australia, India, and other parts of Asia. As gold, silver, and other riches poured into Europe, emigrants poured out, spreading European ideas, languages, and cultures to nearly every part of the globe. The Industrial and Agricultural revolutions further increased the continent's wealth and dominance. Through the first part of the 20th century, Europe held sway over the world as no continent had ever done before or is likely to do in the future.

Left page: Ibexes on mountainside above lake, Interlaken, Switzerland; farmer picking grapes, Italy; Big Ben, London.

Right page: Highlands of Scotland; Cibeles Fountain, Madrid; St. Basil's Cathedral, Moscow.

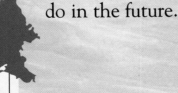

Europe Facts

Land area: 3.8 million square miles (9.9 million sq km)

Continental rank (in area): 6th

Estimated population: 712.9 million

Population density: 188/square mile (72/sq km)

Highest point: Gora El'brus, Russia, 18,510 feet (5,642 m)

Lowest point: Caspian Sea, Europe-Asia, 92 feet (28 m) below sea level

Longest river: Volga, 2,194 miles (3,531 km)

Largest island: Great Britain, 88,795 square miles (229,978 sq km)

Largest lake: Caspian Sea, Europe-Asia, 143,240 square miles (370,990 sq km)

Number of countries and dependencies: 49

Largest country: Russia, Europe-Asia, 6.6 million square miles (17.1 million sq km)

Smallest country (excl. dependencies): Vatican City, 0.2 square miles (0.4 sq km)

Most populous country: Russia, Europe-Asia, 150.5 million

Largest city: Moscow, metro. area pop. 13.1 million

North America

Almost 30,000 years ago, the first North Americans arrived on the continent after crossing the Bering land bridge from Asia. Before them lay a rich land of dense forests, virgin streams and lakes, and prairies where great herds of bison roamed.

These same treasures beckoned the first European settlers to North America in the early 16th century. For nearly 500 years, emigrants from all corners of the globe have been pouring onto the continent in search of a better life. Many have realized their dreams, and along the way North America has become the world's wealthiest and most influential continent.

Among its richest resources are vast tracts of arable land. The farmland of the Great Plains is so productive that this region has been called "the Breadbasket of the World." The United States and Canada are world leaders in food production, harvesting so much wheat, corn, barley, soybeans, oats, sugar, and fruit each year that thousands of surplus tons can be exported.

Sweeping mountain systems frame the plains in the east and west. Eastern North America is traversed by the ancient, well-weathered Appalachian Mountains, which stretch from Newfoundland south through Georgia. The soaring Rockies extend from western Canada into New Mexico, showcasing some of

Left page: Jasper National Park, Canadian Rockies, Alberta; Tarahumara man, Mexico; red-eyed tree frog, Central America.

Right page: farmhouse and fields near Moscow, Idaho; El Tajin, a Mayan temple in Veracruz, Mexico; spikes of wheat.

North America Facts

Land area: 9.5 million square miles (24.7 million sq km)

Continental rank (in area): 3rd

Estimated population: 459.6 million

Population density: 48/square mile (19/sq km)

Highest point: Mt. McKinley, Alaska, U.S., 20,320 feet (6,194 m)

Lowest point: Death Valley, California, U.S., 282 feet (84 m) below sea level

Longest river: Mississippi-Missouri, 3,740 miles (6,019 km)

Largest island: Greenland, 840,000 square miles (2,175,600 sq km)

Largest lake: Lake Superior, Canada-U.S., 31,700 square miles (82,100 sq km)

Number of countries and dependencies: 38

Largest country: Canada, 3.8 million square miles (10 million sq km)

Smallest country (excl. dependencies): St. Kitts and Nevis, 104 square miles (269 sq km)

Most populous country: United States, 265.1 million

Largest city: Mexico City, metro. area pop. 18.4 million

the continent's most dramatic landscapes. Mexico's greatest mountain ranges, the Sierra Madres, collide to form a spiny, volcanic backbone that continues into Central America.

Fed by hundreds of tributaries, the Mississippi-Missouri river system—North America's longest—cuts a path through the center of the continent. The mighty river both embraces and disregards those who settle along its banks, providing fertile farmland and access to a vital transport corridor, but also periodically flooding adjacent farms and towns.

Canada, the United States, and Mexico comprise almost 90% of North America. The United States and Canada have diversified, service-oriented economies, and increasingly urban populations. Mexico, although poorer than its northern neighbors, has in recent decades become a key manufacturing center and a popular tourist destination.

Brilliant tropical vegetation and exotic wildlife abound in the seven countries of Central America, which occupy a slender isthmus connecting Mexico and South America. Unlike the rest of North America, Central America has a population that is both dispersed and predominantly rural.

Many people in Mexico and Central America are of mixed Spanish and Indian ancestry, a rich heritage defined by a proud culture. This blending is less evident in remote areas, where Indian villages have remained virtually unchanged for centuries. In the cities, however, a strong Indian influence intermingles with architectural remnants of the colonial era and dramatic evidence of modern development.

To the east lie the balmy islands of the Caribbean Sea, including Cuba, Hispaniola, the West Indies, Jamaica, and Puerto Rico. Each boasts a colorful culture that reflects the diverse mix of peoples—Europeans, Africans, and Indians—who found themselves thrown together during the colonial past.

South America

South America is a land of untamed beauty and tremendous diversity—in its landscapes, plant and animal life, and people.

Large parts of the continent remain as wild and pristine as they were when the first humans arrived more than eleven millennia ago. Human movement and settlement have been hindered by the rugged Andes mountains and the nearly impenetrable Amazonian rain forest.

The Andes, which curve along the continent's western edge from Venezuela in the north to Tierra del Fuego in the south, form the longest mountain system in the world. The loftiest Andean peaks reach greater heights than any others in the Western Hemisphere.

High in the Andes, clear, cold streams wander among moss-covered boulders, merge with one another, and eventually tumble out of the mountains as the Marañon and Ucayali rivers. These are the principal tributaries of the world's mightiest river, the Amazon. Crossing nearly the entire breadth of the continent, the Amazon carries one-fifth of all of the world's flowing water.

The rain forest that covers much of the Amazon's vast drainage basin holds an astonishing abundance and variety of life. Still largely unexplored, the rain forest is a torrid, watery realm of slow-moving rivers and sloughs, of colorful birds, insects, and flowers, and of trees growing so densely that little sunlight

Left page: Incan ruins, Machupicchu, Peru;
Quechua woman and child, Peru;
great blue heron, Galapagos Islands.

Right page: Iguassu Falls, Argentina-Brazil;
colonial buildings, Bahia, Brazil;
bird of paradise flower, Amazonia.

reaches the forest floor. Most of Amazonia's animals and insects live high up in the forest canopy and rarely descend to the ground.

Archaeologists believe that the first humans to reach South America were groups of hunters and gatherers migrating southward from North America some 11,000 to 14,000 years ago. Thousands of years later, the descendants of these first arrivals built several great civilizations on the continent, including the magnificent Inca Empire, which reached its maximum extent during the period AD 1100—1350. The city of Cusco, in present-day Peru, served as the Incas' capital, and today tourists are drawn to the many splendid ruins in and around the city.

The arrival of Europeans in the early 1500s, and their subsequent conquest and colonization of the continent, were disastrous to the indigenous peoples: it is estimated that three-quarters of the population died as a result of European diseases, warfare, and forced labor.

Although the colonial period came to an end in the 1800s, its architectural legacy endures in cathedrals, plazas, houses, and government buildings found in cities throughout the continent.

Nine out of ten South Americans live within 150 miles of the coast; much of the interior is only sparsely settled. For this reason, South America is sometimes spoken of as "the hollow continent." In recent decades, millions of people have abandoned their small farms and villages in search of a better life in the city.

This trend has greatly swollen the populations of many of the largest cities, including São Paulo, Rio de Janeiro, Buenos Aires, and Caracas. As a new millennium begins, the crowding and frenzy of such cities stand in sharp contrast to remote interior villages, where the people live just as they have for centuries and time seems to stand still.

South America Facts

Land area: 6.9 million square miles (17.8 million sq km)

Continental rank (in area): 4th

Estimated population: 319.5 million

Population density: 46/square mile (18/sq km)

Highest point: Cerro Aconcagua, Argentina, 22,831 feet (6,959 m)

Lowest point: Salinas Chicas, Argentina, 138 feet (42m) below sea level

Longest river: Amazon, 4,000 miles (6,400 km)

Largest island: Tierra del Fuego, 18,600 square miles (48,200 sq km)

Largest lake: Lake Titicaca, Bolivia-Peru, 3,200 square miles (8,300 sq km)

Number of countries and dependencies: 15

Largest country: Brazil, 3.3 million square miles (8.5 million sq km)

Smallest country (excl. dependencies): Suriname, 63,251 square miles (163,820 sq km)

Most populous country: Brazil, 161.7 million

Largest city: São Paulo, metro. area pop. 16.7 million

Land

The Earth has a total surface area of 197 million square miles (510.2 million sq km). Water, including oceans, seas, lakes, and rivers, covers nearly three-quarters of this area; land only one-quarter.

The largest landmass is Eurasia, shared by the continents of Europe and Asia. Eurasia represents 36.5% of the Earth's total land area (but only 10.7% of the total surface area). The largest continent is Asia, which accounts for 30% of the total land area. Africa ranks second, with 20% of the total land area.

The smallest continent by far is Australia, which holds only 5.1% of the world's land. When it is grouped with New Zealand and the other islands of Oceania, the figure rises only slightly, to 5.7%.

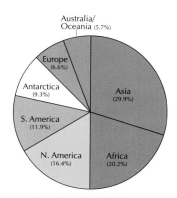

Percentage of world land area

Energy

A large percentage of the world's energy is used for manufacturing. This fact helps explain the great variances among the continents in the consumption of energy. Highly developed North America, with only 8% of the world's population, consumes nearly 30% of the world's energy, and more than five times as much as Africa and South America combined.

For two continents, energy consumption exceeds production: North America produces roughly nine-tenths of the energy it consumes, and Europe only three-fifths. In contrast, Africa consumes less than two-fifths of the energy it produces.

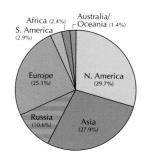

Percentage of world energy consumption

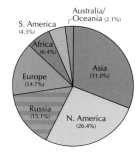

Percentage of world energy production

Population

Asia is the world's most populous continent, and has been for at least two millennia. Its current population of 3.5 billion represents an astonishing 60% of the world's people, nearly five times as much as any other continent. It is home to the world's two most populous countries: China, with nearly 1.2 billion people, and India, with 900 million. Four other Asian countries rank among the ten most populous in the world: Indonesia (4th), Pakistan (7th), Japan (8th), and Bangladesh (9th).

Europe and Africa each contain roughly 700 million people. Europe, however, has only one-third the land area of Africa, so its population density is three times greater. Antarctica has no permanent population and therefore does not appear on the graph.

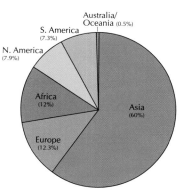

Percentage of world population

Population Growth

The world's population is growing at a rapid pace: at present, the annual rate of natural increase (births minus deaths) is 1.5%. Today, the world holds 5.8 billion people; some experts predict that by the year 2050 this number will have increased by two-thirds, to 9.8 billion.

The largest part of the growth is taking place in Asia, which already is home to three-fifths of the world's people. Of every hundred people added to the Earth's population each year, 65 are Asian. Africa is also gaining a larger share of the world total: the continent's current population represents 12% of the world total, but its growth accounts for more than 19% of the annual world increase.

Europe, on the other hand, is seeing its share of the world population erode. Although Europe is the second most populous continent, its annual growth represents less than 2% of the world total.

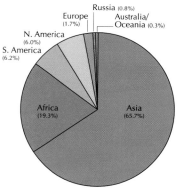

Percentage of world population growth

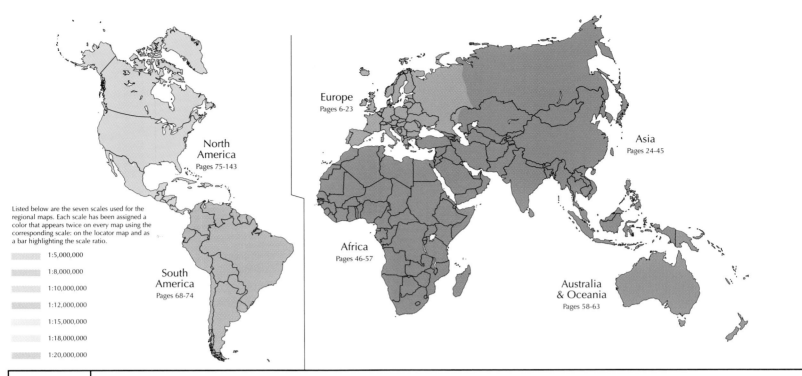

Europe
Pages 6-23

North
America
Pages 75-143

Asia
Pages 24-45

Listed below are the seven scales used for the regional maps. Each scale has been assigned a color that appears twice on every map using the corresponding scale: on the locator map and as a bar highlighting the scale ratio.

1:5,000,000

1:8,000,000

1:10,000,000

1:12,000,000

1:15,000,000

1:18,000,000

1:20,000,000

Africa
Pages 46-57

South
America
Pages 68-74

Australia
& Oceania
Pages 58-63

Legend

World and Regional Maps

Hydrographic Features

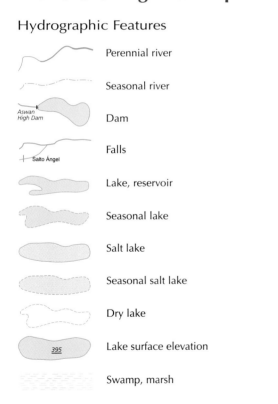

Perennial river

Seasonal river

Aswan High Dam — Dam

Salto Ángel — Falls

Lake, reservoir

Seasonal lake

Salt lake

Seasonal salt lake

Dry lake

395 — Lake surface elevation

Swamp, marsh

Reef

Glacier/ice sheet

Topographic Features

Elevations and depths are given in meters.

754 ▼ — Depth of water

2278 ▲ — Elevation above sea level

1700 ▼ — Elevation below sea level

⨯ — Mountain pass

Huo Shan 1774 — Mountain peak/elevation

The highest elevation on each continent is underlined.
The highest elevation in each country is shown in boldface.

Transportation Features

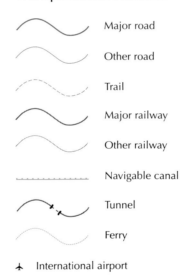

Major road

Other road

Trail

Major railway

Other railway

Navigable canal

Tunnel

Ferry

✈ International airport

✦ Other airport

Political Features

International Boundaries (First-order political unit)

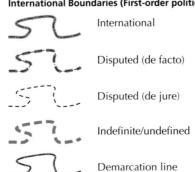

International

Disputed (de facto)

Disputed (de jure)

Indefinite/undefined

Demarcation line

Internal Boundaries

State/province

 NORMANDIE
(Denmark)

Cultural/historic region
Administering country

Cities and Towns

The size of symbol and type indicates the relative importance of the locality.

■ **LONDON**

▣ **CHICAGO**

◉ **Milwaukee**

◎ Tacna

⊙ Iquitos

○ Old Crow

∘ Mettawa

Urban area

Capitals

MEXICO CITY
Bratislava — Country, dependency

RIO DE JANEIRO
Perth — State, province

MANCHESTER
Chester — County

Cultural Features

or ▪ National park

▪ Point of interest

Wall

∴ Ruins

State and Province Maps

Pages 84-91 and Pages 94-143

⊙ Capital

∘ County seat

▲ Military installation

△ Point of interest

+ Mountain peak

International boundary

State/province boundary

County boundary

Road

Railroad

Urban area

ARCTIC OCEAN

GREENLAND
(Den.)

ARCTIC OCEAN
Ellesmere
Island
Thule
Greenland
Baffin Bay
Baffin Island
Godhavn
Angmagssalik
Godthåb
Reykjavík   ICELAND   Norwe
FAROE ISLANDS
(Den.)

RUSSIA
Bering Strait
Nome
Anchorage
Fairbanks
Juneau
Inuvik
Victoria
Island
Yellowknife
Great Bear
Lake
Great Slave
Lake
Churchill
Hudson
Bay

UNITED
STATES
Arctic Circle
Yukon
Gulf of
Alaska

Beaufort Sea
Mackenzie

Davis Strait
Denmark Strait

Glasgow
Dublin
IRELAND
UNI
KIN
LOND
FRANC

Bering Sea

Aleutian Islands

Vancouver
Seattle
Portland

Edmonton
Calgary
Winnipeg

CANADA
ROCKY MTS.

Lake
Winnipeg
Lake Superior
Missouri

Québec
Ottawa
MONTREAL
TORONTO
Lake Huron
Lake
Michigan
Lake Ontario
Lake Erie
Detroit

St. Lawrence
Newfoundland
St. John's
Boston
NEW YORK
PHILADELPHIA
WASHINGTON
Halifax

Acores
(Port.)
Porto
PORTUGAL
LISBOA
SPA

Salt Lake
City
Minneapolis
CHICAGO

Denver
St. Louis

UNITED STATES
SAN FRANCISCO
LOS ANGELES
San Diego
Phoenix
El Paso
DALLAS
HOUSTON
Atlanta
BERMUDA
(U.K.)

MIDWAY ISLANDS
(U.S.)
Tropic of Cancer

New
Orleans
Monterrey
Gulf of Mexico
Miami
Bahamas

Arquipélago
da Madeira
(Port.)
CASABLANCA
MOROCCO
Ra
Islas Canarias
(Sp.)
El Aaiún
WESTERN
SAHARA

Honolulu
Hawaiian Islands
(U.S.)

MEXICO
GUADALAJARA
CIUDAD DE
MÉXICO
(MEXICO CITY)
LA HABANA
(HAVANA)
CUBA
Port-au-Prince
HAITI
JAMAICA
DOMINICAN
REPUBLIC
PUERTO RICO (U.S.)
San Juan
Santo
Domingo
GUADELOUPE (Fr.)
DOMINICA

ATLANTIC
OCEAN

Nouakchott
MAURITANIA
CAPE VERDE   DAKAR
SENEGAL
Bamako

Johnson Atoll
(U.S.)

GUATEMALA
Guatemala
EL SALVADOR
San Salvador
BELIZE
HONDURAS
Tegucigalpa
NICARAGUA
Managua
San José
COSTA RICA
Panamá
PANAMA
Caribbean Sea
BARBADOS
GRENADA
Port of Spain
TRINIDAD AND TOBAGO
CARACAS
VENEZUELA
Georgetown
Paramaribo
GUYANA
SURI-
NAME
FRENCH GUIANA

THE GAMBIA
GUINEA-BISSAU
Conakry
Freetown
SIERRA LEONE
Monrovia
LIBERIA
Ouagadou
GUINEA
COT
D'IVO
ABI

Île Clipperton
(Fr.)

PACIFIC

OCEAN

Archipiélago de Colón
(Galapagos Islands)
(Ec.)
Equator

MEDELLÍN
BOGOTÁ
CALI
COLOMBIA
QUITO
ECUADOR
GUAYAQUIL
Iquitos
Trujillo
MANAUS
Amazon
Belém
Madeira
BRAZIL
Fortaleza
Cabo de Sao Roque
RECIFE

POLYNESIA

OCEAN
Íles
Marquises

Íles
Tuamotu

Phoenix
Islands
KIRIBATI
TOKELAU
TUVALU
WALLIS
AND
FUTUNA
SAMOA
AMER.
SAMOA
FIJI
TONGA
NIUE
(N.Z.)
COOK ISLANDS
(N.Z.)
FRENCH
POLYNESIA

LIMA
PERU
Arequipa
BOLIVIA
LA PAZ
Sucre
Goiânia
BRASÍLIA
BELO HORIZONTE
RIO DE JANEIRO
SÃO PAULO
Santos
Curitiba
SALVADOR

ST. HELE
(U.K.)

ANDES

Tropic of Capricorn

PITCAIRN
(U.K.)

Isla de Pascua
(Easter Island)
(Chile)

Isla San Ambrosio
(Chile)

Antofagasta
PARAGUAY
Asunción
ANDES

PORTO ALEGRE
URUGUAY

Chatham Islands
(N.Z.)

Archipiélago
Juan Fernandez
(Chile)

CHILE
Córdoba
Rosario
SANTIAGO
BUENOS AIRES
Concepción
ARGENTINA
Mar del Plata
Bahía Blanca
MONTEVIDEO

FALKLAND ISLANDS
(U.K.)
South Georgia
(U.K.)

Punta Arenas
Cabo de Hornos
Drake Passage

South Orkney
Islands
(U.K.)

Antarctic Circle

Bellingshausen
Sea

Weddell Sea

Ross Sea

A N T

West of Greenwich

M-DRJ1010-P1-   -4°
Copyright © Rand McNally & Co.

0	1000	2000	4000	6000	8000	10000 km
0	1000	2000		4000		6000 miles

Scale 1 : 90 000 000

Robinson Projection

ARCTIC OCEAN

Barents Sea

more Laptevyh

Novosibirskie ostrova

Vostočno-Sibirskoe more

Zemlja Franca-Iosifa

pitsbergen

Novaja Zemlja

Karskoe more

Tiksi

ALBARD (Nor.)

Igarka

Narvik

Hammerfest

Murmansk

Vorkuta

Jakutsk

Arctic Circle

SWEDEN

Arhangel'sk

FINLAND
Helsinki

adožskoe ozero

NIŽNIJ
NOVGOROD

Perm'

Ekaterinburg

Omsk

Krasnojarsk

Čita

Magadan

Bering Sea

slo

Stockholm

SANKT-PETERBURG

Samara

Čeljabinsk

Novosibirsk

Irkutsk

Sea of Okhotsk

Kamčatka

København

ESTONIA

LATVIA

MOSKVA
(MOSCOW)

Volgograd

Astana

ozero Bajkal

Amur

Habarovsk

Petropavlovsk-Kamčatskij

MARK

LITH.

ostrov Sahalin

ostrova Kuril'skie

GERMANY

BELARUS

KAZAKHSTAN

Irtyš

Ulaanbaatar

Harbin

BERLIN

POLAND

WARSZAWA

KYIV

ozero Balhaš

Sapporo

WIEN

UKRAINE

Aral Sea

MONGOLIA

Vladivostok

Hokkaidō

BUDAPEST

ROMANIA

UZBEKISTAN

ALMATY

Urūmqi

BEIJING

SHENYANG

NORTH KOREA

Sea of Japan

Sendai

MILANO

Beograd

Sofia

TAŠKENT

TIEN-SHAN

Hohhot

Dalian

P'yŏngyang

JAPAN

ROMA

ITALY

BULGARIA

GEORGIA

AZER.

BAKI

TAJIKISTAN

GOBI

TIANJIN

SOUTH KOREA

SŎUL

TŌKYŌ

ZAIR

GREECE

ISTANBUL

ANKARA

ARM.

TURKMENISTAN

KABOL

Huang

CHINA

Xi'an

Qingdao

Yellow Sea

PUSAN

Honshū

ŌSAKA

Fukuoka

ERS)

ATHINAI

Izmir

TURKEY

CYPRUS

SYRIA

TEHRĀN

Esfahān

AFGHANISTAN

Islāmābād

Rāwalpindi

LAHORE

Lhasa

Chengdu

Chang

Nanjing

SHANGHAI

WUHAN

PACIFIC

OCEAN

Tunis

BAGHDĀD

LEBANON

ISRAEL

Ammān

IRAQ

JORDAN

IRAN

Ābadān

KUWAIT

PAKISTAN

DELHI

New Delhi

HIMALAYAS

NEPAL

Kāthmāndau

BNGL.

Chongqing

Changsha

Kunming

GUANGZHOU

Nansei-shotō

Tropic of Cancer

TUNISIA

Tarābulus
(Tripoli)

EL-ISKANDARĪYA
(ALEXANDRIA)

EL-QÂHIRA
(CAIRO)

AR-RIYĀD
(RIYADH)

Abū
Zaby

Masqat

Ahmadābād

KARĀCHI

DHAKA

XIANGGANG
(HONG KONG)

T'AIPEI

WAKE ISLAND
(U.S.)

GERIA

LIBYA

EGYPT

SAUDI
ARABIA

QATAR

U.A.E.

INDIA

Ganges

KOLKATA

MYANMAR
(BURMA)

LAOS

HA NOI

TAIWAN

nghest

OMAN

MUMBAI

HYDERĀBĀD

YANGON
(RANGOON)

Viangchan

VIETNAM

South China

Sea

PHILIPPINES

Philippine

NORTHERN
MARIANA
ISLANDS
(U.S.)

NIGER

CHAD

Al-Khartūm

ERITREA

YEMEN

Arabian

Pune

BANGALORE

CHENNAI

Andaman
Islands
(India)

THAILAND

KRUNG THEP
(BANGKOK)

CAMBODIA

Luzon

MANILA

GUAM (U.S.)

MARSHALL
ISLANDS

Kano

N'Djamena

Asmera

San'ā

Sea

Kochi

Nicobar
Islands
(India)

Phnum
Pênh

THANH PHO
HO CHI MINH
(SAIGON)

Davao

FEDERATED STATES OF
MICRONESIA

NIGERIA

Abuja

SUDAN

ĀDĪS ĀBEBA

DJIBOUTI

Djibouti

SRI LANKA

Mindanao

PALAU

rto-Novo

LAGOS

CENTRAL AFRICAN
REPUBLIC

ETHIOPIA

MALDIVES

Colombo

Medan

BRUNEI

MICRONESIA

CAMEROON

Yaoundé

Bangui

UGANDA

Kampala

Gees Gwardafuy

Kuāla Lumpur

MALAYSIA

Equator

EQUAT. GUIN.

GABON

DEM. REP. OF
THE CONGO
(ZAIRE)

KENYA

SINGAPORE

Borneo

PAPUA NEW
GUINEA

NAURU

KIRIBATI

Libreville

CONGO

Kigali

RWANDA

NAIROBI

Banjarmasin

Sulawesi

New
Guinea

Brazzaville

BURUNDI

Bujumbura

Lake
Victoria

Sumatera

Ujungpandang

TUVALU

KINSHASA

TANZANIA

Zanzibar

JAKARTA

INDONESIA

Jawa

Surabaya

EAST TIMOR

Port Moresby

SOLOMON
ISLANDS

LUANDA

Lake
Tanganyika

Dodoma

SEYCHELLES

MELANESIA

Lubumbashi

Dar es Salaam

Lake Nyasa

Darwin

Cape York

VANUATU

FIJI

Lobito

ANGOLA

ZAMBIA

MALAWI

Lilongwe

COMOROS

INDIAN

Cairns

Suva

NAMIBIA

Lusaka

Hārare

ZIMBABWE

MOZAMBIQUE

MADAGASCAR

Antananarivo

OCEAN

Rockhampton

NEW
CALEDONIA
(Fr.)

Nouméa

Windhoek

BOTSWANA

Moçambique Channel

MAURITIUS

Alice Springs

Coral Sea

Tropic of Capricorn

Walvis Bay

Gaborone

Pretoria

Maputo

REUNION
(Fr.)

AUSTRALIA

Brisbane

JOHANNESBURG

SWAZILAND

SOUTH
AFRICA

LESOTHO

Durban

Perth

Darling

Adelaide

SYDNEY

Tasman Sea

Auckland

Cape Town

Port Elizabeth

Canberra

North Island

Cape of Good Hope

MELBOURNE

NEW ZEALAND
Wellington

Tasmania

Hobart

South Island
Christchurch

Îles Kerguélen
(Fr.)

SOUTHERN   OCEAN

Antarctic Circle

CTICA

ENDERBY LAND

WILKES LAND

East of Greenwich

4

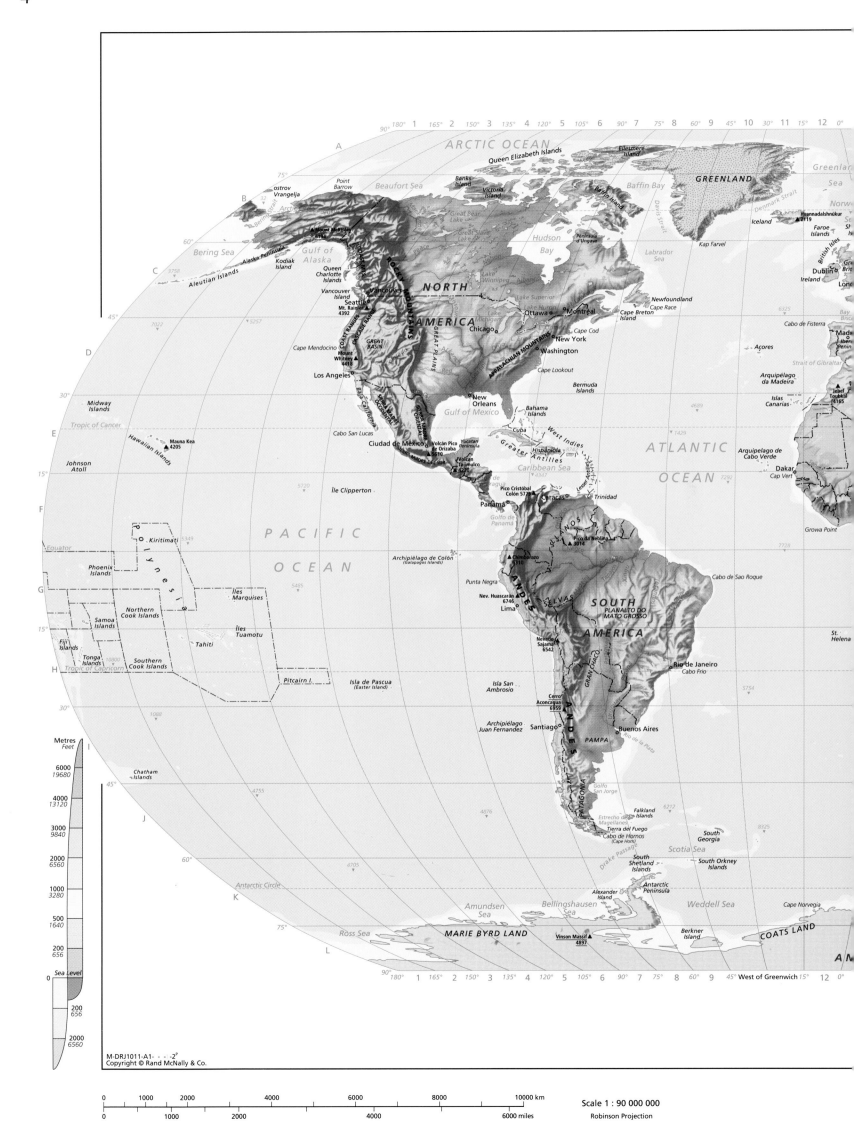

ARCTIC OCEAN

Queen Elizabeth Islands

Ellesmere Island

GREENLAND

Greenland Sea

Norw

Point Barrow

Beaufort Sea

Banks Island

Victoria Island

Baffin Bay

Davis Strait

Denmark Strait

Iceland

Hvannadalshnúkur ▲2119

Faroe Islands

St

ostrov Vrangelja

Bering Strait

Arctic

Great Bear Lake

Baffin Island

Bering Sea

Gulf of Alaska

Mount McKinley 6194 ▲

Great Slave Lake

Hudson Bay

Peninsula d'Ungava

Labrador Sea

British Isles

Dublin

Ireland

Lon

3758

Aleutian Islands

Alaska Peninsula

Kodiak Island

Queen Charlotte Islands

Lake Athabasca

ROCKY MOUNTAINS

COAST RANGES

CASCADE RANGE

NORTH

Lake Winnipeg

Peace

NORTH AMERICA

Lake Superior

Lake Huron

Ottawa

Montreal

Cape Breton Island

Newfoundland

Cape Race

6325

Cabo de Fisterra

Mad

Ib Penin

Vancouver Island

Vancouver

Seattle

Mt. Rainier 4392

7022

5257

Chicago

Lake Michigan

New York

Cape Cod

Washington

Açores

Cape Mendocino

Mount Whitney ▲ 4418

GREAT BASIN

GREAT PLAINS

APPALACHIAN MOUNTAINS

Bermuda Islands

Strait of Gibraltar

Arquipélago da Madeira

Los Angeles

SIERRA MADRE OCCIDENTAL

Baja California

Red

Cape Lookout

Islas Canarias

Jebel Toubkal ▲4165

Midway Islands

New Orleans

Gulf of Mexico

Bahama Islands

4689

Tropic of Cancer

Cabo San Lucas

Cuba

West Indies

Greater Antilles

ATLANTIC

Hawaiian Islands

Mauna Kea ▲ 4205

Ciudad de México

Volcán Pico de Orizaba 5610

Yucatán Peninsula

Hispaniola

OCEAN

Arquipélago de Cabo Verde

Johnson Atoll

Cabo San Lucas

SIERRA MADRE DEL SUR

Volcán Tajumulco 4220

Caribbean Sea

Lesser Antilles

Dakar

Cap Vert

7292

4347

Equator

5720

Île Clipperton

de Nicaragua

Pico Cristóbal Colón 5775 ▲

Caracas

Trinidad

Panamá

Golfo de Panamá

Pico da Neblina ▲ 3014

Growa Point

Kiritimati

6349

PACIFIC

Archipiélago de Colón (Galápagos Islands)

Chimborazo ▲ 6310

LLANOS

7728

Phoenix Islands

OCEAN

5485

Punta Negra

ANDES

SOUTH

Cabo de São Roque

Polynesia

Northern Cook Islands

Îles Marquises

Nev. Huascarán 6746 ▲

Lima

SELVAS

AMERICA

PLANALTO DO MATO GROSSO

St. Helena

Samoa Islands

Íles Tuamotu

Tahiti

Nevado Sajama 6542 ▲

Rio de Janeiro

Cabo Frio

Fiji Islands

Tonga Islands

10800

Southern Cook Islands

Tropic of Capricorn

Cerro Aconcagua 6959 ▲

GRAN CHACO

ANDES

5754

Pitcairn I.

Isla de Pascua (Easter Island)

Isla San Ambrosio

Santiago

PAMPA

Buenos Aires

Rio de la Plata

1088

Archipiélago Juan Fernández

PATAGONIA

Golfo San Jorge

Chatham Islands

4755

6212

Falkland Islands

4876

Estrecho de Magallanes

Tierra del Fuego (Cape Horn)

Cabo de Hornos

South Georgia

8325

Antarctic Circle

4705

South Shetland Islands

Scotia Sea

South Orkney Islands

Amundsen Sea

Bellingshausen Sea

Alexander Island

Antarctic Peninsula

Weddell Sea

Cape Norvegia

Ross Sea

MARIE BYRD LAND

Vinson Massif ▲ 4897

Berkner Island

COATS LAND

A

West of Greenwich

Metres Feet

6000 19680

4000 13120

3000 9840

2000 6560

1000 3280

500 1640

200 656

Sea Level 0

200 656

2000 6560

0   1000   2000   4000   6000   8000   10000 km

0   1000   2000   4000   6000 miles

Scale 1 : 90 000 000

Robinson Projection

14 *30°* 15 *45°* 16 *60°* 17 *75°* 18 *90°* 19 *105°* 20 *120°* 21 *135°* 22 *150°* 23 *165°* 24 *180°* *90°*

ARCTIC OCEAN

Zemlja Franca-Iosefa
Severnaja Zemlja
Novosibirskie ostrova
75°

sbergen
Barents Sea
Nordkapp
Novaja Zemlja
Karskoe more
more Laptevyh
Vostočno-Sibirskoe more

A

B

Kol'skij poluostrov
ZAPADNO-SIBIRSKAJA
RAVNINA
gora Kamen 1701
SIBIR' (SIBERIA)
gora Pobedy 3147
60°

Gällapiggen 2469
L
URAL'SKIE GORY
Nižnaja Tunguska
Ob'
Bering sea
C

Ladožkoe ozero
Ekaterinberg
Ob'
Ishim
ASIA
Sea of Okhotsk
mys Lopatka
Berlin
Moskva
Irtyš
ostrov Sahalin
45°

ROPE
CARPATHIAN
PS
Aral Sea
ozero Balhaš
Ikrutsk
Kuril'skie ostrova
D

APPENNINO
gora El'brus 5642
Syr Darja
Mt. Kujtun 4374
Peak Pobedy 7439
Ulaanbaatar
Hokkaidō
orse
Roma
Balkan Peninsula
CAUCASUS
TIEN SHAN
ALTAI
GOBI
Sea of Japan
Honshū
degna
Black Sea
5005
Qolleh-ye Damavand 5604
HINDU KUSH
KUNLUN SHAN
Beijing
Fuji-san 3776
Tōkyō
Sicilia
Istanbul
Tehran
Qing Zàng Gaoyuan
Shanghai
Shikoku
Kyūshū
292
Kriti
Cyprus
DASHT-E KAVIR
HIMALAYAS
Song Shan 5596
Yellow Sea
Nansei-shotō
9595
30°

Mediterranean Sea
El-Qahira
KUHHA-YE ZAGROS
Delhi
Mount Everest 8848
East China Sea
PACIFIC
HAGGAR
Persian Gulf
Gulf of Oman
Taiwan
OCEAN
Tropic of Cancer
HARA
Red Sea
ARABIAN PENINSULA
AR-RUB AL-KHALI
DECCAN
Yu Shan 3997
15°

Tahat 2908
Émi Koussi 3415
NUBIAN DESERT
Gulf of Aden
WESTERN GHATS
EASTERN GHATS
2359
Mumbai
Hainan Dao
Luzon
Mariana Islands
E

TIBESTI
AFRICA
Arabian Sea
Andaman Islands
Krung Thep
South China Sea
Manila
Philippine Islands
Philippine Sea
Marshall Islands
10915
6674
F

Lake Chad
Chari
Suquṭrā
Gees Gwardafuy
INDOCHINA
M i c r o n e s i a
10057

gos
Cape Comorin
Pidurutalagala 2524
Nicobar Islands
Gulf of Thailand
Palawan
Mindanao
Palau Islands
Caroline Islands
Equator

mé
Margherita Peak 5109
Ras Dashen Terara 4620
Adis Abeba
Maldive Islands
Sri Lanka 5423
Andaman Sea
Malay Peninsula
165
Gunong Kinabalu 4101
Celebes Sea
Halmahera
New Britain
G

nea
CONGO BASIN
Kilimanjaro 5895
Kilimanjaro 5199
Zanzibar
Seychelles
Sumatera
BORNEO
Sulawesi
MALUKU
Seram
NEW GUINEA
Mount Wilhelm 4509
8940
Solomon Islands
15°

RIFT VALLEY
Lake Tanganyika
Les Amirantes
5340
Greater Sunda Islands
Jakarta
Laut Jawa
Laut Banda
Melanesia
New Hebrides
Fiji Islands

Tanjona Bobaomby
Maromokotro 2875
INDIAN
Jawa
Timor
Arafura Sea
Cape York
Nouvelle-Calédonie
Tropic of Capricorn
5303
H

Cape Fria
KALAHARI DESERT
NAMIB DESERT
Mozambique Channel
MADAGASCAR
Reunion
Mauritius
OCEAN
6090
1706
125
Timor Sea
Gulf of Carpentaria
Kimberley Plateau
Cape York Peninsula
Coral Sea
6658

North West Cape
Great Sandy Desert
Mount Meharry 1253
AUSTRALIA
Mount Woodroffe 1435
GREAT DIVIDING RANGE
Sydney
North Cape
I

Thabana-Ntlenyana 3482
DRAKENSBERG
Tanjona Vohimena
6400
Île Amsterdam
Cape Leeuwin
GREAT VICTORIA DESERT
Great Australian Blight
Darling
Mount Kosciusko 2229
5267
Tasman Sea
497
North Island
Mount Ruapehu 2797
30°

Cape of Good Hope
Cape Town
5536
Mount Ossa 1617
Tasmania
South East Cape
South Island
Mount Cook 3754
45°

Prince Edward Islands
3079
Archipel Crozet
Îles Kerguélen
2690
South West Cape
J

5124
Heard Island
6089
SOUTHERN OCEAN
Macquarie Island
60°

4425

Cape Poinsett
Antarctic Circle
K

ENDERBY LAND
WILKES LAND
VICTORIA LAND
Cape Adare
75°

EN MAUD LAND
TICA
Ross Sea
L

st of Greenwich *45°* 16 *60°* 17 *75°* 18 *90°* 19 *105°* 20 *120°* 21 *135°* 22 *150°* 23 *165°* 24 *180°* *90°*

Scale 1 : 15 000 000

Equidistant Conic Projection

West of Greenwich 0° East of Greenwich

M-DRJ3014-P1
Copyright © Rand McNally & Co.

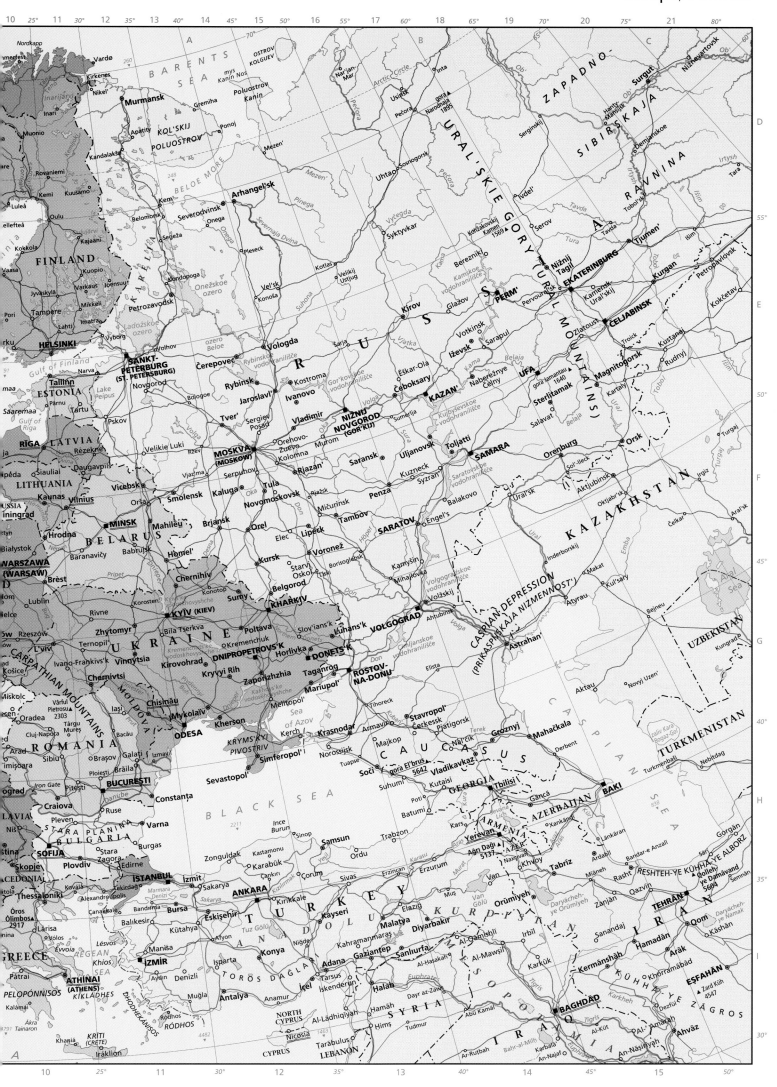

Scale 1 : 10 000 000

Lambert Conformal Conic Projection

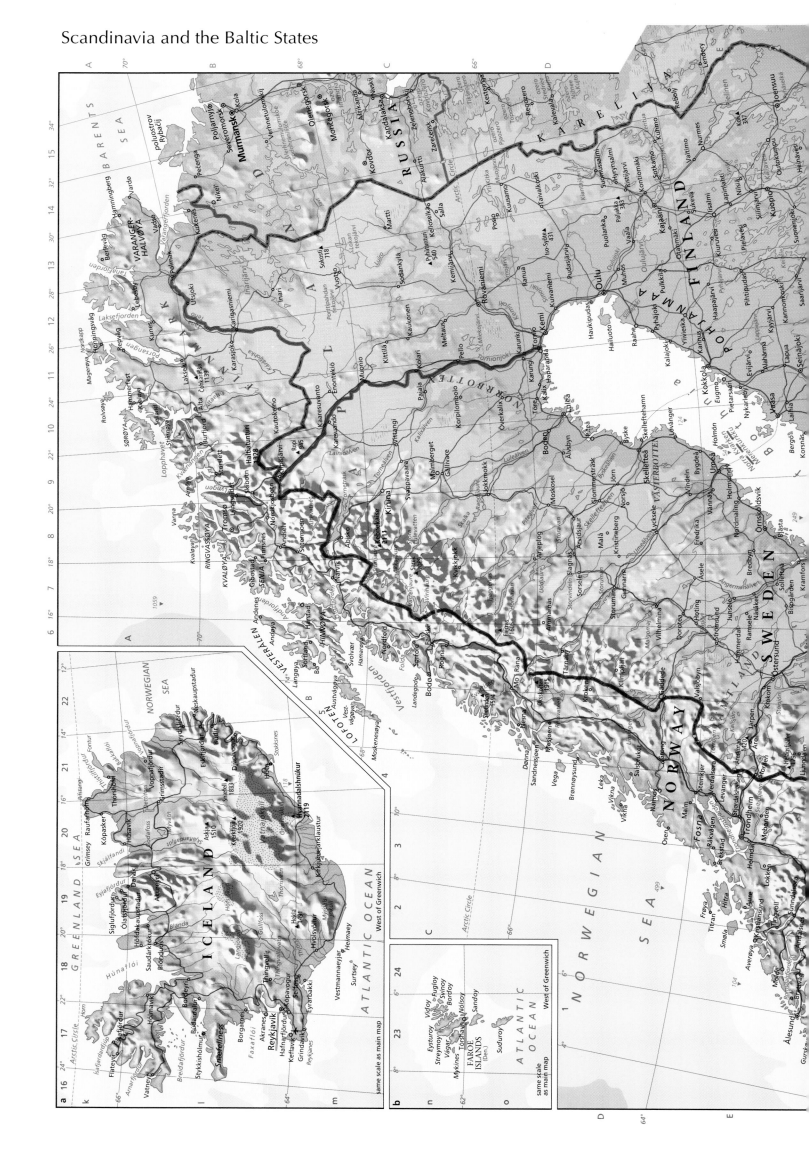

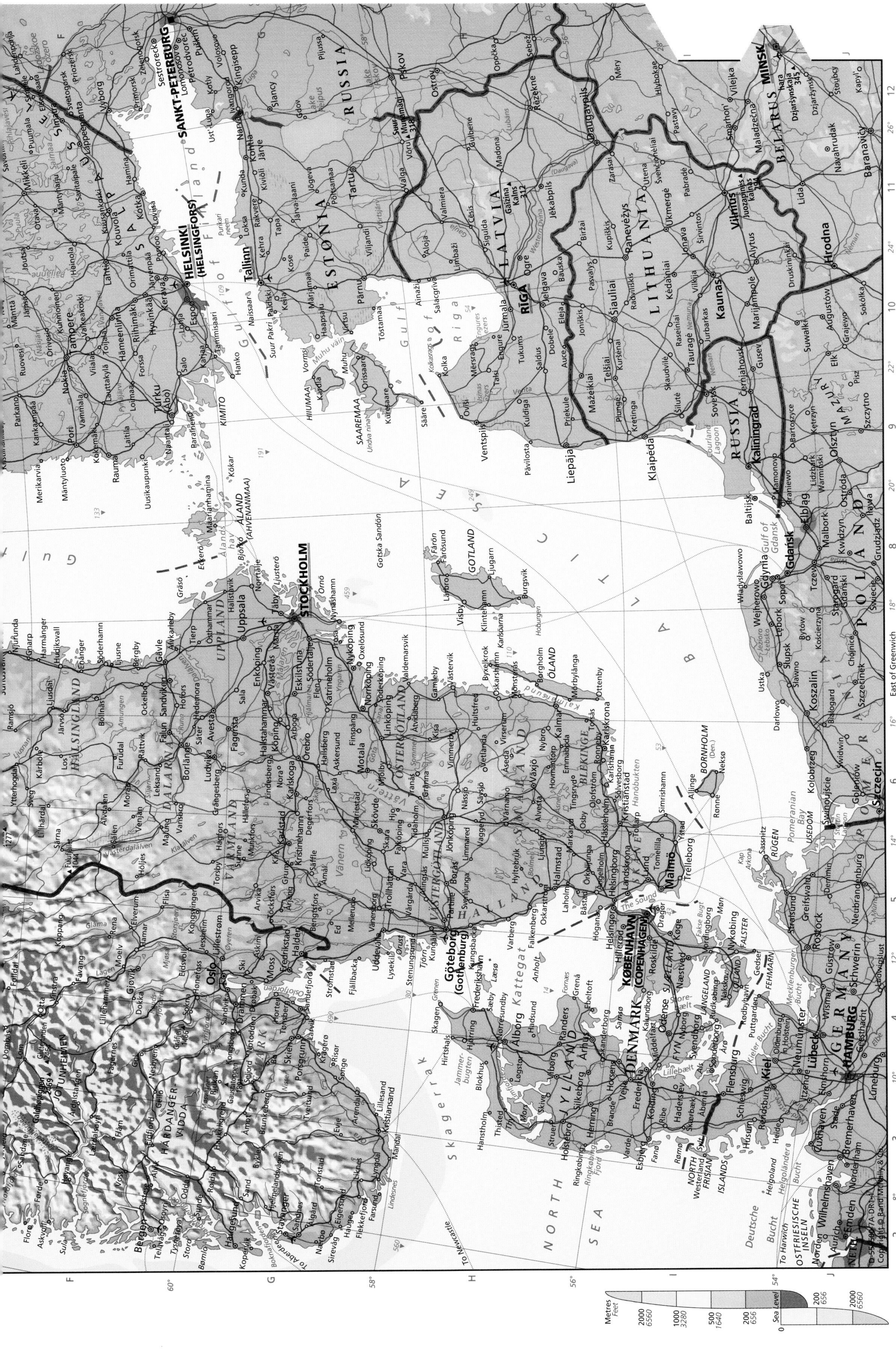

Scale 1 : 5 000 000

Lambert Conformal Conic Projection

East of Greenwich

Metres	Feet
2000	6560
1000	3280
500	1640
200	656
Sea level	0
200	656
2000	6560

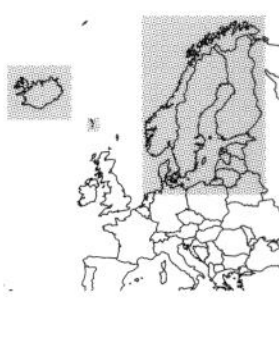

SHETLAND ISLANDS (U.K.)

Unst
To Torshavn
Fetlar
Yell
Whalsay
St. Magnus Bay
MAINLAND
Foula
Lerwick
Bressay

18   19

h

ATLANTIC OCEAN

60°

Fair Isle

NORTH SEA

Westray
Rousay
Sanday
Stronsay
MAINLAND
Kirkwall **ORKNEY ISLANDS**
Hoy
South Ronaldsay
Pentland Firth
Thurso Duncansby Head
John o' Groats

i

West of Greenwich

12°   1°   10°   2°   8°   3°   2°   8°   3°

A

Flannan Islands
Butt of Lewis
OUTER HEBRIDES
ISLE OF LEWIS
Stornoway
St. Kilda
North Uist
Benbecula
South Uist
Lochboisdale
Barra
The Little Minch
Portree
ISLAND OF SKYE
Kyle of Lochalsh

Cape Wrath
Duncansby Head
Durness John o' Groats
Thurso
Pentland Firth
Kirkwall
ORKNEY ISLANDS
Hoy South Ronaldsay

To Lerwick

MAINLAND

To Bressay
Stronsay

146

B

58°

The Minch
Ullapool
Lochinver
Ben More Assynt 998
Helmsdale
Brora
Dornoch

Wick

Sea of the Hebrides
Rùm
Eigg
Coll
Tobermory
ISLAND OF MULL
Tiree

NORTHWEST HIGHLANDS
Dingwall
Moray Firth
Inverness
Carn Eige 1182
Loch Ness
Ben Macdui 1309
Fort William
Ben Nevis 1343

Elgin
Nairn
Portsoy
Fraserburgh
Kinnaird Head
Peterhead

Aberdeen
Stonehaven

GRAMPIAN MOUNTAINS
BALMORAL CASTLE
Montrose

2487

C

56°

INNER HEBRIDES
Colonsay
ISLAY
Port Ellen
JURA
Oban
Firth of Lorn
Inveraray
Greenock
GLASGOW

Perth
Dundee
Arbroath
SCOTLAND
Glenrothes St. Andrews
Kirkcaldy Fife Ness
Dunfermline
Firth of Forth
EDINBURGH

GREAT

Malin Head
GIANT'S CAUSEWAY
Rathlin Island
Kintyre
ISLAND OF ARRAN
Ayr
Kilmarnock
Motherwell
Firth of Clyde
Campbeltown

Berwick-upon-Tweed

NO
S

Rocky Point
Buncrana
Errigal Mountain 752
Londonderry
Coleraine
Ballymena
Larne
SOUTHERN UPLANDS
Girvan
843
Dumfries
Moffat
Galashiels
Alnwick

UNITED

D

54°

Erris Head
Donegal
Strabane
NORTHERN IRELAND
Omagh
Lower
Lough Neagh
Belfast
Portadown
Newry
Bangor
Downpatrick

HADRIAN'S WALL
Stranraer
Gatehouse of Fleet
Solway Firth
Carlisle
Whitehaven
Penrith
Lake District
Scafell Pikes 978
Kendal

Tyne
NEWCASTLE UPON TYNE
Sunderland
Durham Hartlepool
Darlington **Middlesbrough**
Scarborough

KINGDOM

Achill Head
Ballina
Castlebar
Clew Bay
Mweelrea 817
Clifden
Carrick on Shannon
Sligo
Lough Conn
Lough Gill
Dundalk
Drogheda
CONNAUGHT
Roscommon
Longford
Ballymote

Isle of Man (U.K.)
Douglas
Barrow-in-Furness
Lancaster
Morecambe Bay
Blackpool
Preston
Bradford
Blackburn
Bolton

Ripon
York
Bridlington

LEEDS
Kingston upon Hull
Huddersfield
Grimsby

BRITAIN

10

E

52°

ARAN ISLANDS
Galway
Galway Bay
Lough Corrib
Lough Mask
Lough Ree
Athlone
Royal Canal
Grand Canal
DUBLIN (BAILE ÁTHA CLIATH)
Dún Laoghaire
Kildare
Port Laoise
IRELAND
LEINSTER

Holyhead
ANGLESEY
Caernarfon
Bangor
Wrexham
Chester
LIVERPOOL
MANCHESTER
Sheffield
Stoke-on-Trent
Mansfield
Lincoln
Skegness

Ennistimon
CLIFFS OF MOHER
Loop Head
Mouth of the Shannon
Kilkee
Lough Derg
Limerick
MUNSTER
Newcastle West
Shannon
Killarney
Tralee
Carrantuohill 1038
Cahersiveen
Kenmare
Bantry
Skull
Mizen Head
Bantry Bay

Snowdon 1085
CAMBRIAN MOUNTAINS
Pwllheli
Braich y Pwll
Cardigan Bay
Aberystwyth
New Quay
Cardigan
Fishguard
St. David's Head
WALES
Carmarthen
Milford Haven
Pembroke

Telford
Shrewsbury
Stafford
Wolverhampton
Walsall
Dudley
BIRMINGHAM
Coventry
Derby
Nottingham
Leicester
Boston
The Wash
King's Lynn
Peterborough
Norwich
Cromer
Great Yarmouth
Lowestoft

Carnsore Point
Carlow
Kilkenny
Clonmel
Mallow
Blackwater
Cork
Kinsale
Old Head of Kinsale
Youghal
Dungarvan
Waterford
Enniscorthy
Wexford
Rosslare

128

Llandovery
Hereford
Worcester
Banbury
Northampton
Bedford
Milton Keynes
Cambridge
Bury Saint Edmunds
Ipswich
ENGLAND

's-Grave (The
RO

F

50°

CELTIC SEA

St. George's Channel

110

Merthyr Tydfil
Builth Wells
Gloucester
Cheltenham
Oxford
Luton
Harlow
Colchester
Harwich
Clacton-on-Sea

**'s-Grave (The
ROT**

Swansea
Port Talbot
Cardiff
Newport
Bristol
Bath
Swindon
Reading
Basingstoke
Guildford
LONDON
Slough
Chelmsford
Southend-on-Sea
Vlissingen
Oostende
Brugge
RO

Lundy
Bristol Channel
Weston-super-Mare
Bridgwater
Barnstaple
Taunton
Bude
STONEHENGE
Winchester
Southampton
Worthing
Reigate
Crawley
Canterbury
Dover
Folkestone
Ramsgate
Calais
Dunkerque
Roeselare
**BRU
(Br**

LILLE
**BRU
(B**
To

Newquay
Redruth
Penzance
ISLES OF SCILLY
Land's End
Lizard Point
St. Austell
Falmouth
CORNWALL
Plymouth
Torquay
Exeter
Dorchester
Lyme Bay
Weymouth
Bill of Portland
Poole
Bournemouth
ISLE OF WIGHT
Portsmouth
Eastbourne
Brighton
Hastings
Boulogne-sur-Mer
Berck
COLLINS DE L'ARTOIS
Lens
Arras
Valencie
Maube
Camb

120

Start Point
128

English Channel

Strait of Dover
Abbeville
Albert
Saint-Quen

G

48°

ATLANTIC

OCEAN

Alderney
Cap de la Hague
Pointe de Barfleur
GUERNSEY (U.K.)
St. Peter Port
CHANNEL ISLANDS
Cherbourg
Baie de la Seine
Bolbec
Yvetot
Dieppe
Fécamp
Neufchâtel-en-Bray
Chauny
Amiens
PICARDIE

JERSEY (U.K.)
St. Helier
Sark
Carentan
Bayeux
Le Havre
Lisieux
Rouen
Beauvais
Creil
Compiègne
Oise
Soiss

Île d'Ouessant
Lannion
Saint-Pol-de-Léon
Morlaix
Guingamp
Saint-Malo
Granville
Coutances
Saint-Lô
Caen
Vire
Argentan
Évreux
Dreux
Mantes
ÎLE-DE-FRANCE
Meaux
Rambouillet
Chantilly
Étampes
Sens
Tre

Landerneau
BRETAGNE
Brest
Pointe Saint-Mathieu
Douarnenez
Iroise
Quimper
Pointe du Raz
Concarneau
Pointe de Penmarc'h
Dinan
Saint-Brieuc
Loudéac
Châteaulin
Fougères
Mayenne
Mont-Saint-Michel
Golfe de Saint-Malo
Sillon de Talbert
Rennes
Vitré
Laval
Sablé-sur-Sarthe
Le Mans
Nogent-le-Rotrou
Chartres
Châteaudun
Fontainebleau
Melun
Provi
PARIS
Versailles
Corbeil-Essonnes
Saint-Denis
Étampes

H

46°

Lorient
Hennebont
Quimperlé
Île de Groix
Vannes
Redon
Châteaubriant
Ancenis
Angers
Saumur
Tours
FRANCE
Blois
Orléans
Auxerre
Romorantin-Lanthenay
Vierzon
Bourges
Cosne-sur-Loire

Carnac
Quiberon
Le Palais
Belle-Île
Muzillac
La Baule-Escoublac
Saint-Nazaire
Blain
Rezé
Nantes
Cholet
Loire
ANJOU
TOURAINE
Vendôme
La Flèche
Ségré
Mauron
Châteauroux
Liguiel
Issoudun
Nevers

Noirmoutier
Île de Noirmoutier
Île d'Yeu
Saint-Jean-de-Monts
Machecoul
Thouars
Bressuire
Châtellerault

To Santander, Barakaldo

150

Copyright © Rand McNally & Co.

2°   8°   3°   6°   4°   4°   5°   2°   6° West of Greenwich 0° East of Greenwich 7°   2°   8°

Metres / Feet

3000 / 9840
2000 / 6560
1000 / 3280
500 / 1640
200 / 656
0 / Sea Level
200 / 656
2000 / 6560

0   50   100   150   200   300   400   500 km
0   50   100   200   300 miles

Scale 1 : 5 000 000

Lambert Conformal Conic Projection

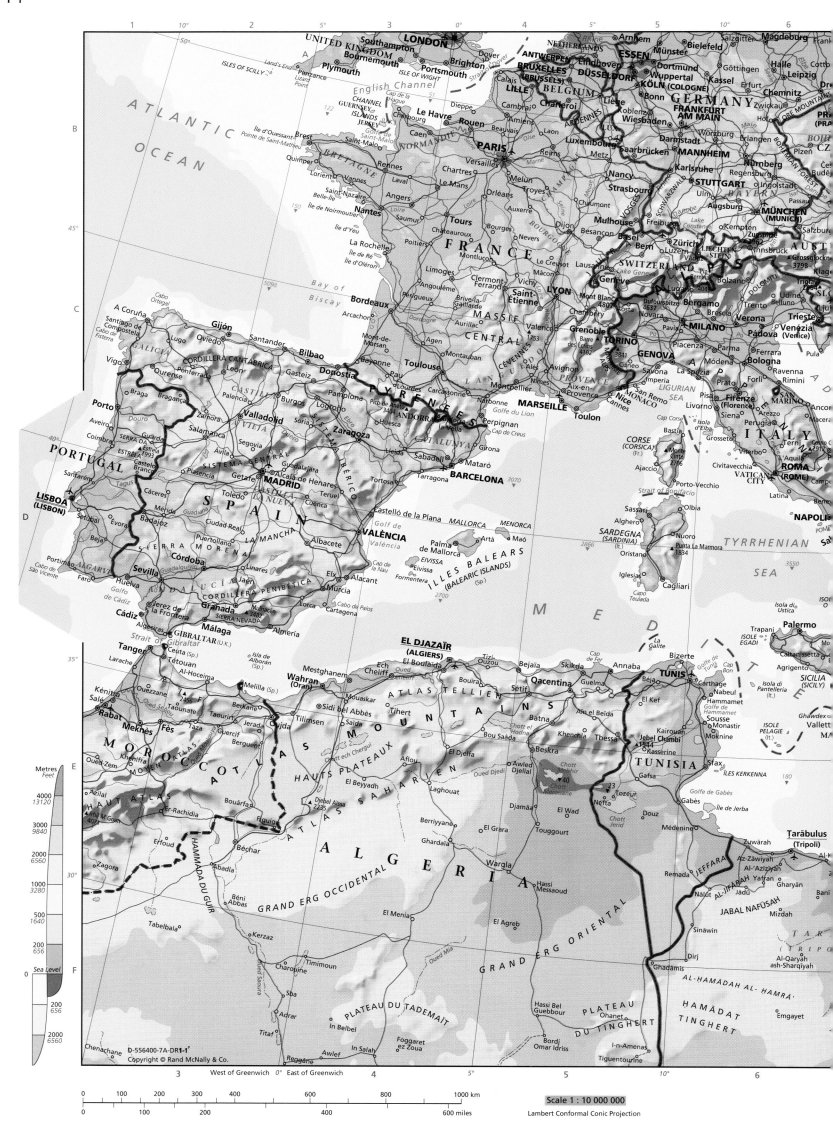

14

D-556400-7A-DR1-1
Copyright © Rand McNally & Co.

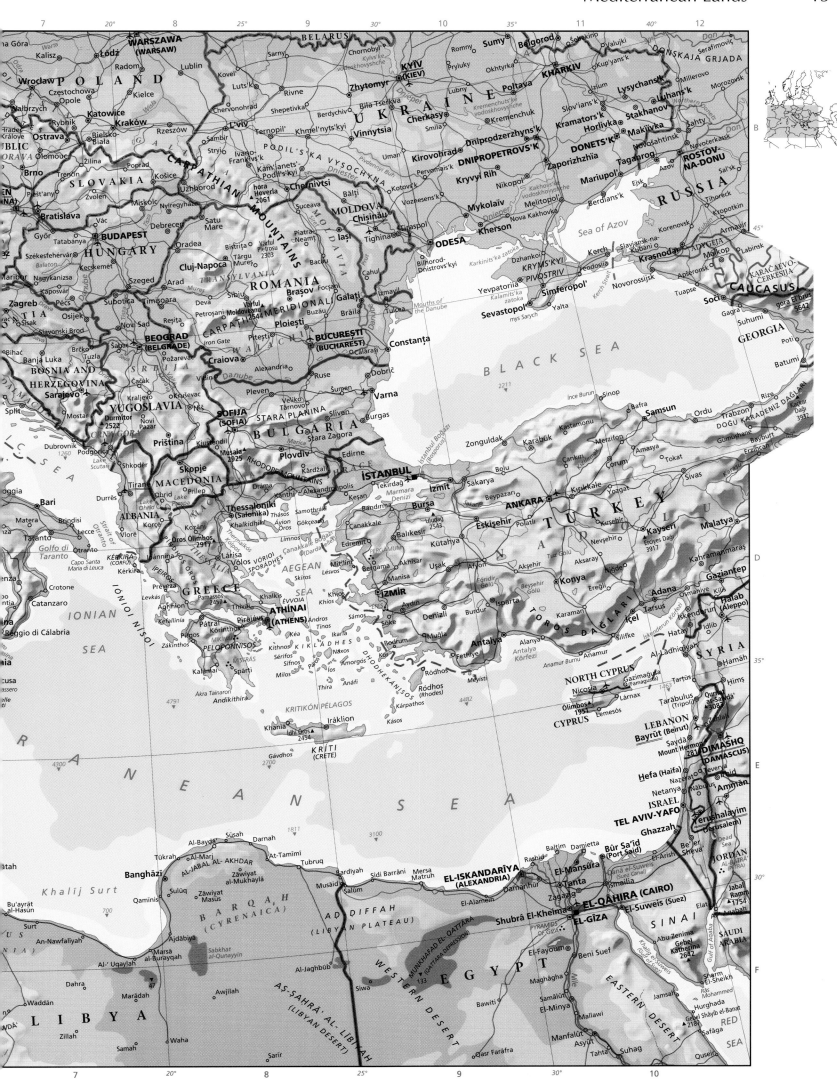

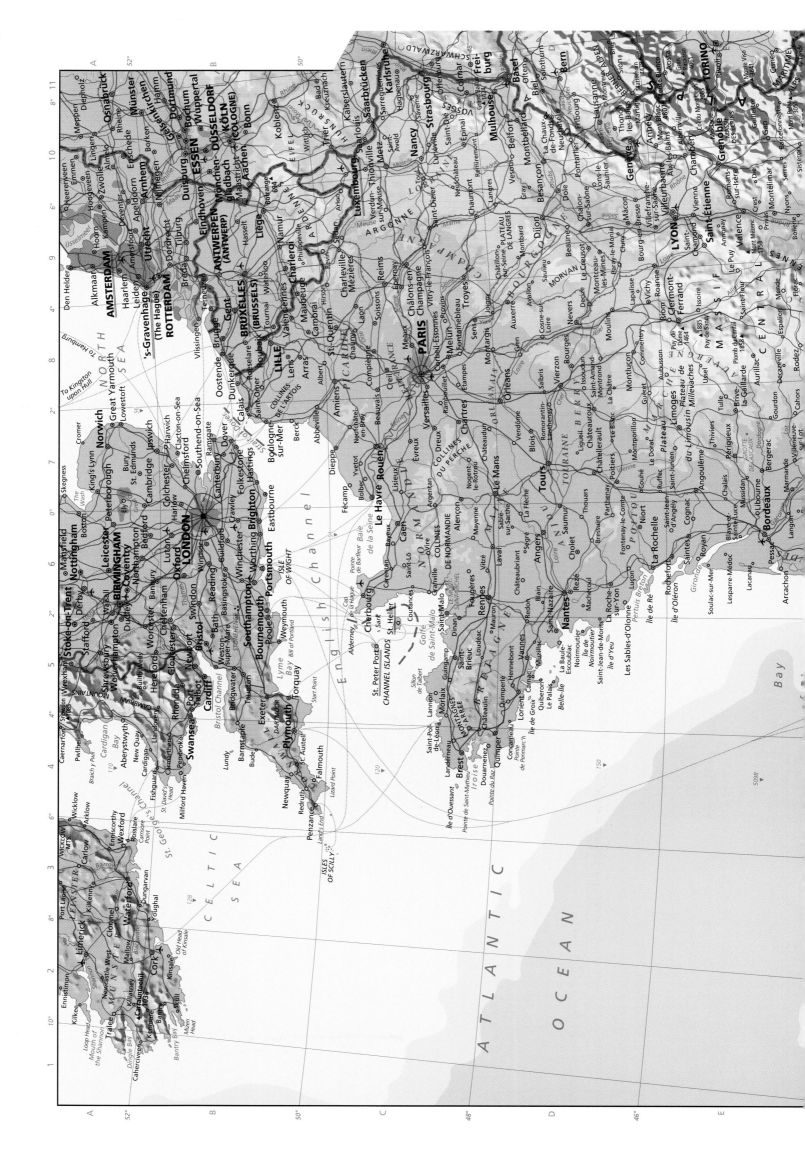

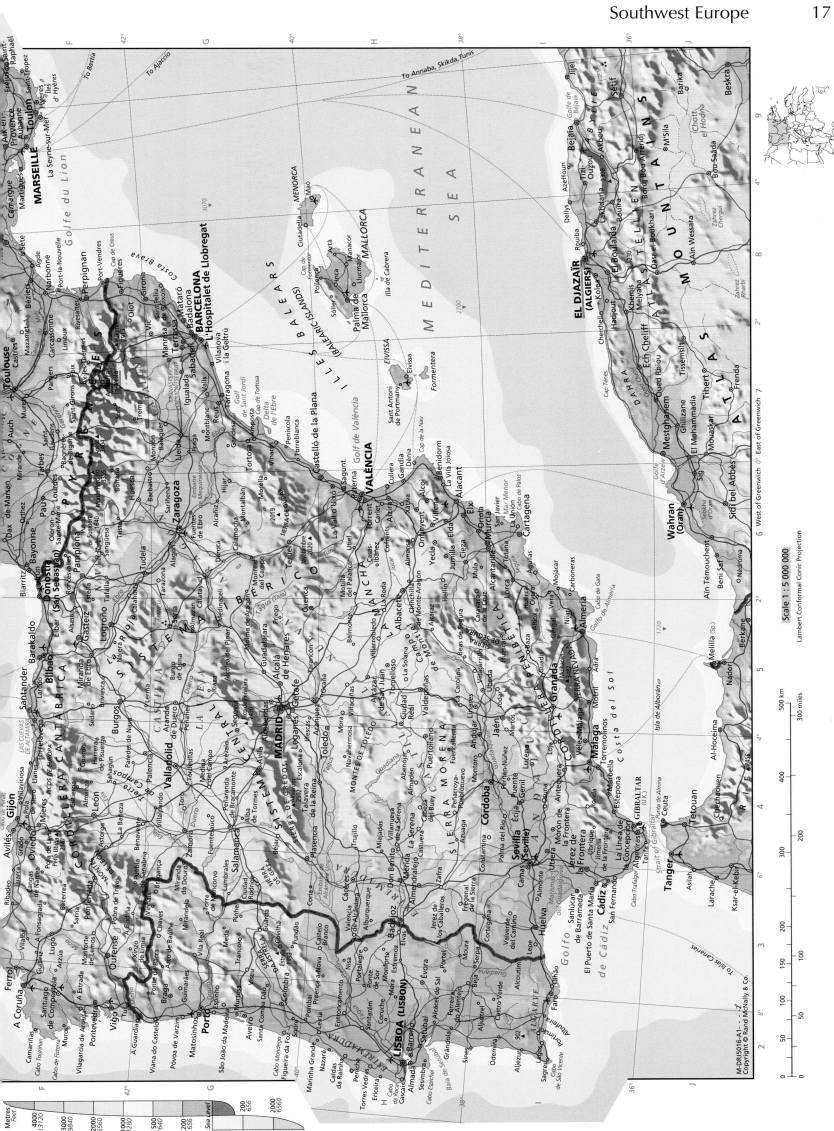

Scale 1 : 5 000 000

Lambert Conformal Conic Projection

500 km

300 miles

Metres
Feet

4000
13120

3000
9840

2000
6560

1000
3280

500
1640

200
656

0   Sea Level

200
656

2000
6560

0   50   100   150   200   300   400   500 km

0   50   100   200   300 miles

Scale 1 : 5 000 000

Lambert Conformal Conic Projection

D-556082-7A-DR-1-1
Copyright © Rand McNally & Co.

Scale 1 : 5 000 000

Lambert Conformal Conic Projection

D-559592-7A-DR1-1'
Copyright © Rand McNally & Co.

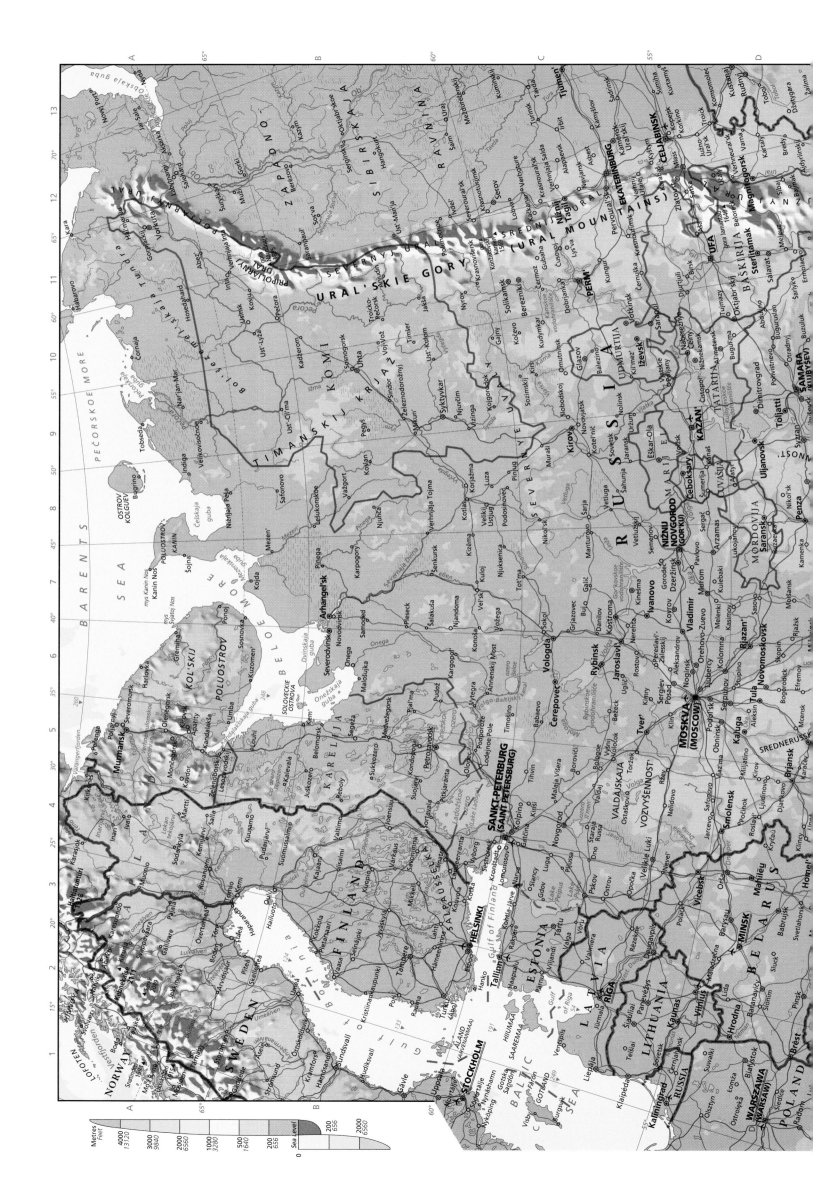

A · 65° · B · 60° · C · 55° · D

13
70°
12
65°
11
60°
10
55°
9
50°
8
45°
7
40°
6
35°
5
30°
4
25°
3
20°
2
15°
1
60°

NORWAY
SWEDEN
FINLAND
NORWAY
SWEDEN

LOFOTEN
Vestfjorden
Smölla
Vega

Kirkenes
Karasjok
Haltiatunturi
Inari
Ivalo
Sodankylä

Rovaniemi
Kemijärvi
Salla

Kuusamo
Suomussalmi
Kajaani

Oulu
Raahe
Kokkola
Pietarsaari
Vaasa
Seinäjoki

Tampere
Hämeenlinna
Lahti
Kouvola
Kotka

HELSINKI
Espoo
Turku

Pori
Rauma

Mariehamn
ÅLAND
(AHVENANMAA)
HIIUMAA
SAAREMAA

STOCKHOLM
Uppsala
Gävle
GOTLAND
Visby

ESTONIA
Tallinn
Haapsalu
Pärnu
Tartu
Viljandi
Valga
Võru

LATVIA
RIGA
Jūrmala
Ventspils
Liepāja
Jelgava

LITHUANIA
Šiauliai
Panevėžys
Kaunas
Vilnius
Klaipėda
Kaliningrad
Telšiai

BELARUS
MINSK
Baranavičy
Hrodna
Hrodna
Brest

POLAND
WARSZAWA
(WARSAW)
Białystok
Łomża
Olsztyn

RUSSIA

BARENTS SEA
PEČORSKOE MORE
BELOE MORE

OSTROV KOLGUEV
KANIN
POLUOSTROV
Bugrino

KOL'SKIJ POLUOSTROV
Murmansk
Severomorsk
Monchegorsk
Apatity
Kandalakša

KARELIJA
Belomorsk
Kem'
Segeža
Medvežegorsk
Petrozavodsk
Kondopoga

SANKT-PETERBURG
(SAINT PETERSBURG)
Gatčina
Kingisepp
Vyborg
Luga
Pskov
Novgorod
Staraja Russa
Velikie Luki

Arhangel'sk
Severodvinsk
Novodvinsk
Onega

Mezen'
Pinega

KOMI
Syktyvkar
Uhta
Pečora
Vorkuta
Inta
Usinsk
Narjan-Mar

ZAPADNO-SIBIRSKAJA RAVNINA
Salehard
Labytnangi
Ob'

PRIPOLJARNYJ URAL
POLJARNYJ URAL
SEVERNYJ URAL
URAL'SKIE GORY
(URAL MOUNTAINS)
SREDNIJ URAL
JUŽNYJ URAL

TIMANSKIJ KRJAŽ
BOL'ŠEZEMEL'SKAJA TUNDRA

Kirov
Slobodskoj

PERM'
Solikamsk
Berezniki
Krasnovišersk

EKATERINBURG
Nižnij Tagil
Pervoural'sk
Kamensk-Ural'skij

ČELJABINSK
Zlatoust
Magnitogorsk

UFA
BAŠKIRIJA
Sterlitamak
Salavat

UDMURTIJA
Iževsk
Glazov

TATARIJA
KAZAN'
Nabereznye Čelny
Dimitrovgrad

MARIJ EL
Joškar-Ola

ČUVAŠIJA
Čeboksary

NIŽNIJ NOVGOROD
(GOR'KIJ)
Dzeržinsk
Arzamas

MORDOVIJA
Saransk

SAMARA
KUJBYŠEV
Toljatti
Syzran'

Uljanovsk

Penza

MOSKVA
(MOSCOW)
Ljubercy
Podol'sk
Serpuhov
Kolomna

Tver'
Vyšnij Voloček

Jaroslavl'
Rybinsk
Uglič

Vologda
Čerepovec

Kostroma
Ivanovo
Vladimir

Rjazan'
Kasimov
Novomoskovsk

Tula
Kaluga

Brjansk

Smolensk

VALDAJSKAJA VOZVYŠENNOST'

SREDNERUSSKAJA VOZVYŠENNOST'

GULF OF FINLAND
Lake Peipus
Lake Ladožskoe ozero
Onežskoe ozero
ozero Beloe

BALTIC SEA

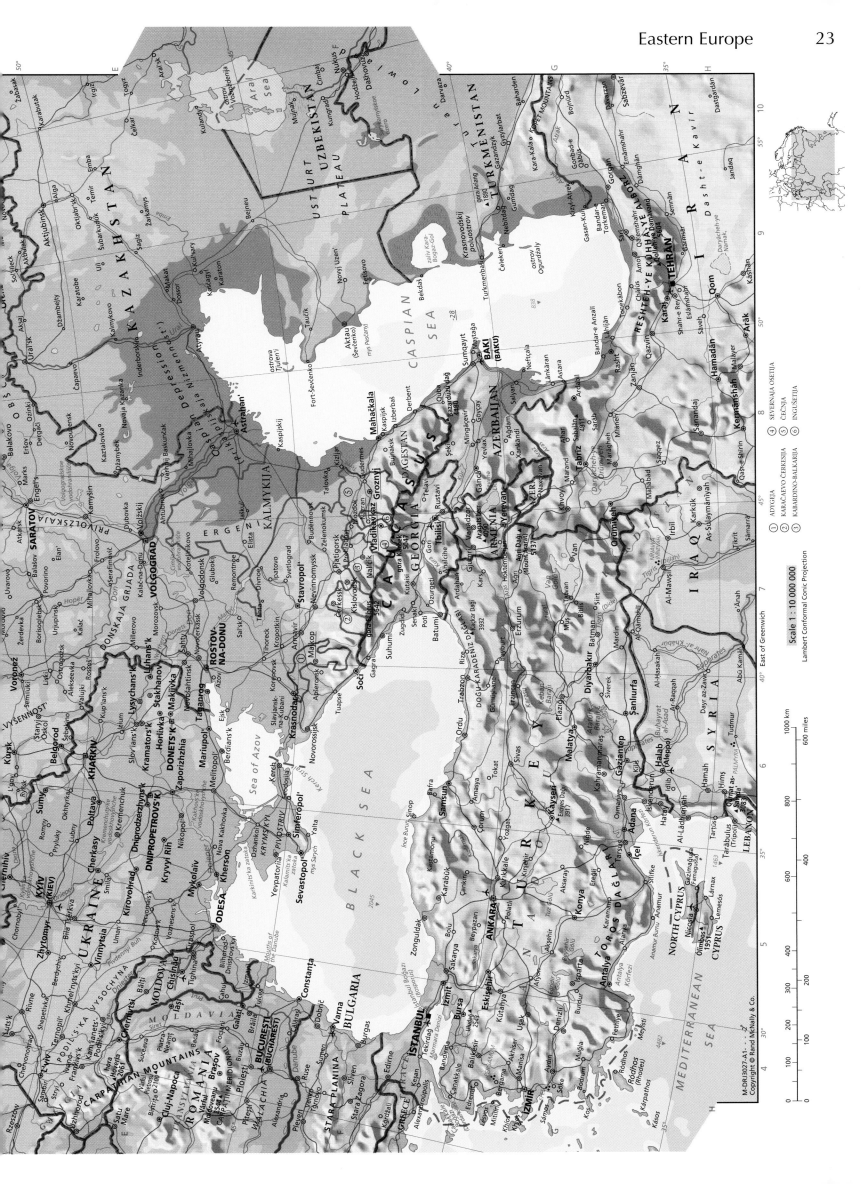

SEVERNAJA OSETIJA
ČEČNIJA
INGUŠETIJA
ADYGEJA
KARAČAEVO ČERKESIJA
KABARDINO-BALKARIJA

Scale 1 : 10 000 000
Lambert Conformal Conic Projection

East of Greenwich

M-DRI3D27-A1- - - -2
Copyright © Rand McNally & Co.

1000 km
600 miles

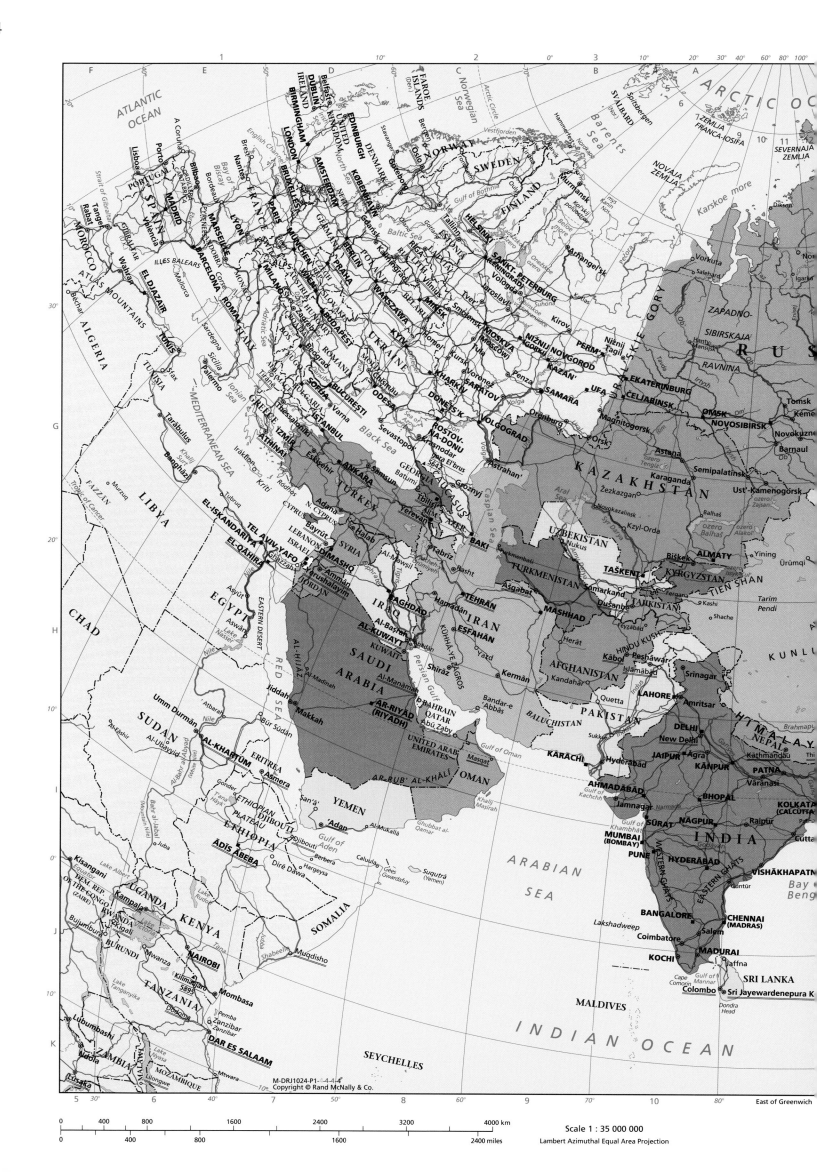

24

Scale 1 : 35 000 000

East of Greenwich

| 0 | 400 | 800 | 1600 | 2400 | 3200 | 4000 km |
| 0 | 400 | 800 | 1600 | | 2400 miles | |

Lambert Azimuthal Equal Area Projection

A 18 17 16 15

150° 160° 170° 19 20

B 170° C D E F 30°

PACIFIC OCEAN

Arctic Circle

Tropic of Cancer

more Laptevyh

NOVOSIBIRSKIE OSTROVA

Vostočno-Sibirskoe more

proliv Longa

mys Ožugorskij

Uelkal'

Anadyr'

Bering Sea

ALEUTIAN ISLANDS (U.S.)

Attu Island

Cape Wrangell

170°

G

ONESIBIRSKOE OSKOGOR'E

Ambarčik

Alazeja

Kolyma

Omolon

Markovo

Olenëk

Anabar

Kazače

POLUOSTROV KAMČATKA

ostrov Karaginskij

zaliv Šelihova

21

Anga

Olenëk

HREBET ČERSKOGO

VERHOJANSKIJ HREBET

Lena

Verhojansk

Jana

Indigirka

Magadan

Ojmjakon

Seimčan

Petropavlovsk-Kamčatskij

mys Lopatka

20°

SIBIR'

SIBERIA

Vitim

Vilyj

Jakutsk

Aldan

STANOVOJ HREBET

Skovorodino

Komsomol'sk-na-Amure

SREDINNYJ HREBET

Sea of Okhotsk

Ajan

Ohotsk

ostrov Ona

mys Elizavety

OSTROV SAHALIN (SAKHALIN)

Aleksandrovsk-Sahalinskij

Tatarskij proliv

mys Terpenija

KURIL'SKIE OSTROVA (KURIL ISLANDS)

180°

20

Angara

Bratskoe vodohranilišče

Irkutsk

ozero Bajkal

Čita

Šilka

Ulan-Ude

HANGAYN NURUU

Hövsgöl nuur

Us

HREBET

Hailar

Amur

Habarovsk

Skovorodino

Argun (Ergun)

Blagoveščensk

SIHOTE-ALIN'

Vladivostok

Komsomol'sk-na-Amure

Južno-Sahalinsk

Asahikawa

HOKKAIDO

Sapporo

Hakodate

Aomori

Sea of Japan

Sendai

HONSHŪ

10°

Enisej

Krasnojarsk

HÖVSGÖL NUUR

Ulaanbaatar

Kerulen

QIQIHAR

HARBIN

Jilin

CHANGCHUN

SHENYANG FUSHUN

NORTH KOREA

Dandong

P'yongyang

Niigata

Kanazawa

KYOTO

TOKYO YOKOHAMA

NAGOYA

OSAKA

JAPAN

H

MONGOLIA

GOBI

Hohhot

Zhangjiakou

BEIJING

DALIAN

SOUTH KOREA

SŎUL (SEOUL)

PUSAN

Taegu

HIROSHIMA

FUKUOKA

Shikoku

Mokp'o

KYŪSHŪ

Kagoshima

Amami-ō-shima

NANSEI-SHOTŌ (RYUKYU ISLANDS)

Okinawa-jima

Naha

Farallon de Pajaros

Agrihan

Anatahan

NORTHERN MARIANA ISLANDS (U.S.)

Saipan

Rota

Tinian

GUAM (U.S.)

10°

TIANJIN

TAIYUAN

Yinchuan

Shijiazhuang

JINAN

Qingdao

Bo Hai

Yellow Sea

Korea Strait

Cheju-do

East China Sea

Qinghai Hu

Lanzhou

XI'AN

Zhengzhou

Kaifeng

NANJING

SHANGHAI

Hangzhou

Ningbo

Wenzhou

Philippine Sea

I

CHINA

Huang (Yellow)

Chang (Yangtze)

CHENGDU

CHONGQING

Dongting Hu

WUHAN

CHANGSHA

Nanchang

Fuzhou

Xiamen

T'AIPEI

T'ainan

TAIWAN

KAOHSIUNG

Hengyang

FEDERATED STATES OF MICRONESIA

Lhasa

HAN

Guiyang

Guilin

Liuzhou

GUANGZHOU

XIANGGANG (HONG KONG)

Aomen (Macau)

Zhanjiang

Luzon Strait

0°

TIAN

Brahmaputra

Kunming

Nanning

Haikou

Hainan Dao

Baguio

LUZON

PHILIPPINES

MANILA

Naga

Koror

PALAU

New Ireland

New Britain

HAKA

TAGONG

Mandalay

HA NOI

Hai Phong

Gulf of Tonkin

Samar

Masbate

Sibuyan Sea

Mindoro

Panay

Iloilo

Negros

Cebu

MINDANAO

Davao

Kavieng

Rabaul

ttwe

MYANMAR (BURMA)

LAOS

Louangphrabang

Chiang Mai

VIETNAM

Da Nang

South China Sea

Palawan

Sulu Sea

Zamboanga

Moro Gulf

Cape San Agustin

Tinaca Point

Bismarck Sea

Madang

Wewak

Lae

New Britain

10°

YANGON (RANGOON)

Gulf of Martaban

THAILAND

Udon Thani

Viangchan

Mekong

KRUNG THEP (BANGKOK)

CAMBODIA

Phnum Pénh

THANH PHO HO CHI MINH (SAIGON)

Morotai

HALMAHERA

Manado

Celebes Sea

Jayapura

NEW GUINEA

PAPUA NEW GUINEA

Port Moresby

Gulf of Papua

Coco Islands

Kâmpóng Saôm

Gulf of Thailand

Mui Ca Mau

Gunong Kinabalu 4101

Bandar Seri Begawan

BRUNEI

Puncak Jaya 5030

Biak

Torres Strait

Cape York

J

Andaman Sea

Nicobar Islands (India)

MALAY PENINSULA

Kuching

MALAYSIA

BORNEO (KALIMANTAN)

SULAWESI (CELEBES)

Teluk Tomini

Teluk Tolo

Pulau Taliabu

Buru

Pulau Seram (Ceram)

Laut Seram

Pulau Yos Sudarso

Cape Wessel

CAPE YORK PENINSULA

Gulf of Carpentaria

Cairns

Coral Sea

Naman Islands (India)

Banda Aceh

George Town (Penang)

MALAYSIA

KUALA LUMPUR

SINGAPORE

Strait of Malacca

Pontianak

Balikpapan

Kapuas

Selat Makasar

Teluk Bone

Pulau Buton

Laut Banda

Laut Flores

Cape Arnhem

Arafura Sea

AUSTRALIA

K

MEDAN

Padang

Pulau Siberut

SUMATERA (SUMATRA)

Palembang

Bandar Lampung

Pulau Bangka

Belitung

Tanjung Karimata

Banjarmasin

Laut Jawa

Ujungpandang

Tanjung Selatan

INDONESIA

Laut Sawu

EAST TIMOR

Timor

Melville Island

Darwin

Timor Sea

20°

JAKARTA

BANDUNG

SURABAYA

JAWA (JAVA)

Madura

Selat Sunda

Laut Bali

Bali

Sumbawa

Lombok

Sumba

Flores

Dili

12

100°

43

110°

14

120°

15

16

130°

17

140°

150°

12

Scale 1 : 20 000 000

Lambert Conformal Conic Projection

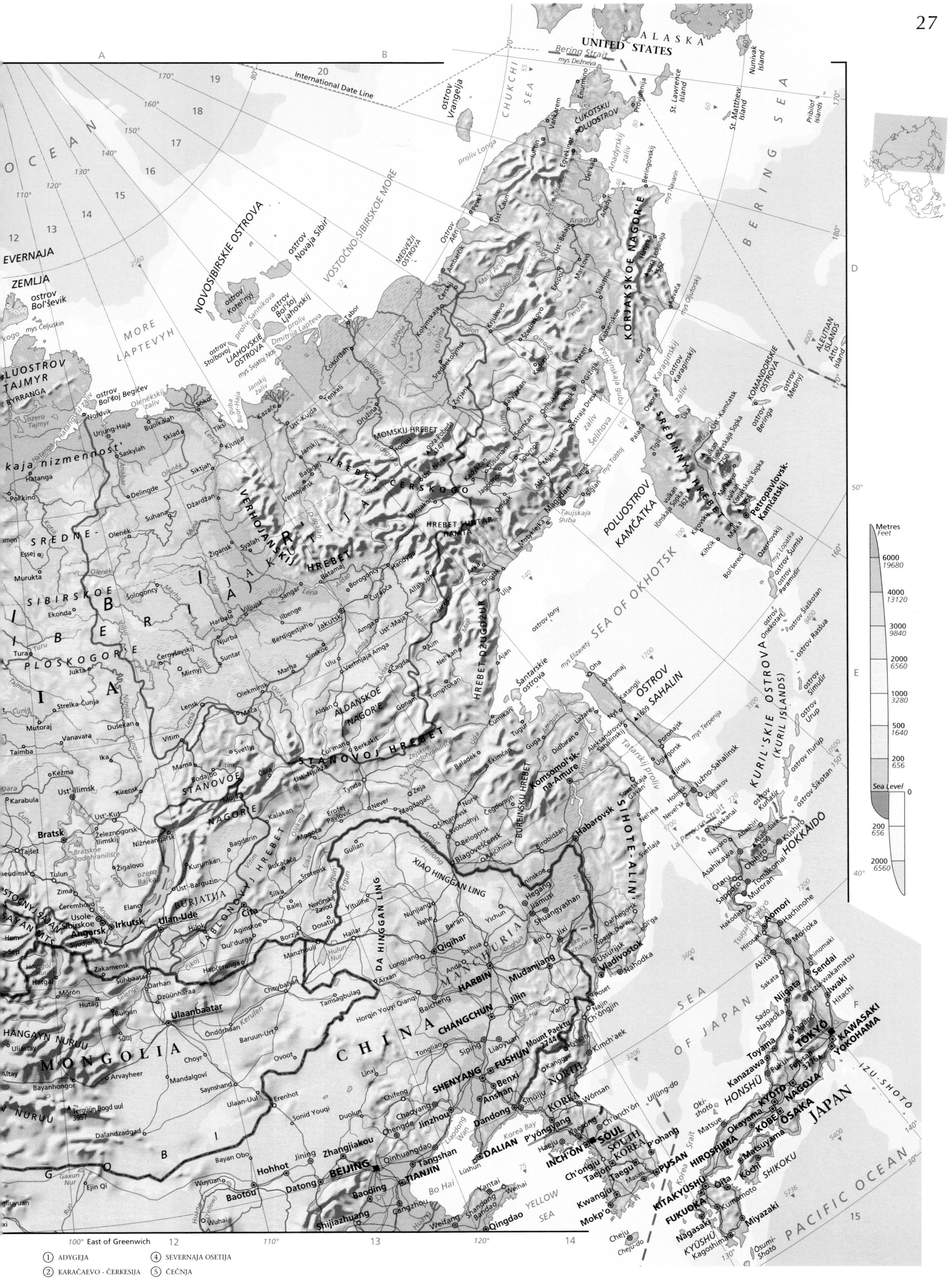

27

ALASKA
UNITED STATES
Bering Strait
mys Dežneva
CHUKCHI SEA
BERING SEA
Nunivak Island
St. Lawrence Island
St. Matthew Island
Pribilof Islands

SEVERNAJA ZEMLJA
ostrov Bol'ševik
mys Čeljuskin
NOVOSIBIRSKIE OSTROVA
ostrov Novaja Sibir'
LJAHOVSKIE OSTROVA
MORE LAPTEVYH
VOSTOČNOSIBIRSKOE MORE
proliv Longa
ostrov Vrangelja
ČUKOTSKIJ POLUOSTROV

POLUOSTROV TAJMYR
gory Byrranga
KORJAKSKOE NAGOR'E
SREDINNYJ HREBET
POLUOSTROV KAMČATKA
Petropavlovsk-Kamčatskij
ALEUTIAN ISLANDS
Attu Island
KOMANDORSKIE OSTROVA

SEVERO-SIBIRSKOE PLOSKOGOR'E
SREDNE-SIBIRSKOE PLOSKOGOR'E
SIBERIA / SIBIRIJA
VERHOJANSKIJ HREBET
HREBET ČERSKOGO
MOMSKIJ HREBET
HREBET SUNTAR-HAJATA
ALDANSKOE NAGOR'E
HREBET DŽUGDŽUR
STANOVOJ HREBET
STANOVOE NAGOR'E
JABLONOVYJ HREBET
Jakutsk
Irkutsk
Bratsk
Ust'-Ilimsk
Angarsk
Ulan-Ude
Čita

SEA OF OKHOTSK
OSTROV SAHALIN
Južno-Sahalinsk
Aleksandrovsk-Sahalinskij
KURIL'SKIE OSTROVA (KURIL ISLANDS)
Tatarskij proliv
La Perouse Strait
HOKKAIDO
Sapporo
Asahikawa
Hakodate
Aomori

SIHOTE-ALIN'
Habarovsk
Komsomol'sk-na-Amure
Vladivostok
Nahodka
BUREINSKIJ HREBET
Blagoveščensk
DA HINGGAN LING
XIAO HINGGAN LING
MANCHURIA
HARBIN
Qiqihar
Mudanjiang
Jilin
CHANGCHUN
SHENYANG FUSHUN
Anshan
Benxi

BURJATIJA
MONGOLIA
Ulaanbaatar
HANGAYN NURUU
GOBI
CHINA
BEIJING
TIANJIN
Baotou
Hohhot
Datong
Zhangjiakou
Tangshan
Shijiazhuang
Baoding
Qingdao
YELLOW SEA
Bo Hai
DALIAN
DANDONG

NORTH KOREA
P'yŏngyang
SOUTH KOREA
SŎUL
INCH'ŎN
PUSAN
Taegu
Taejŏn
Kwangju
Mokp'o
Cheju-do

SEA OF JAPAN
JAPAN
HONSHŪ
TŌKYŌ
YOKOHAMA
KAWASAKI
NAGOYA
KYŌTO
ŌSAKA
KŌBE
HIROSHIMA
KITAKYŪSHŪ
FUKUOKA
NAGASAKI
KYŪSHŪ
SHIKOKU
Kagoshima
Sendai
Niigata
Kanazawa
Toyama
IZU-SHOTŌ
OSUMI-SHOTŌ

PACIFIC OCEAN

International Date Line
100° East of Greenwich

Metres / Feet
6000 / 19680
4000 / 13120
3000 / 9840
2000 / 6560
1000 / 3280
500 / 1640
200 / 656
Sea Level 0
200 / 656
2000 / 6560

① ADYGEJA   ④ SEVERNAJA OSETIJA
② KARAČAEVO - ČERKESIJA   ⑤ ČEČNJA
③ KABARDINO-BALKARIJA   ⑥ INGUŠETIJA

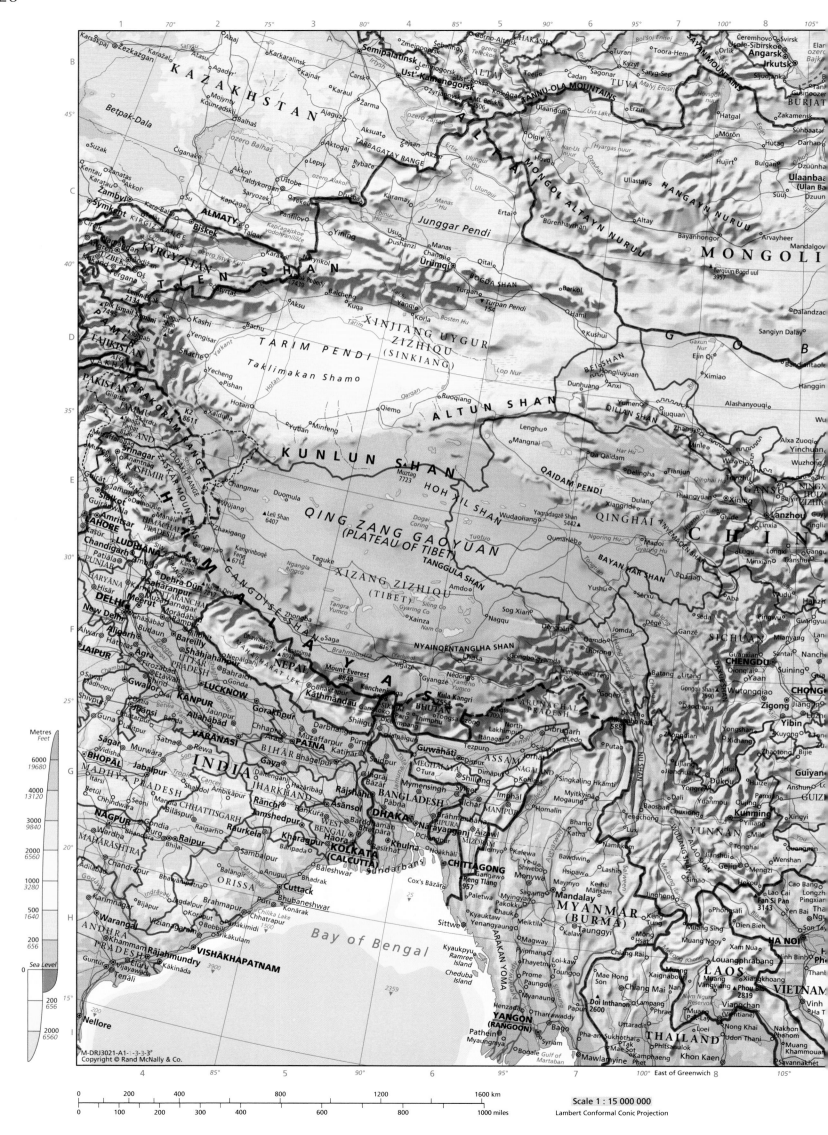

28

Scale 1 : 15 000 000

Lambert Conformal Conic Projection

M-DRJ3021-A1-1-3-3-3'
Copyright © Rand McNally & Co.

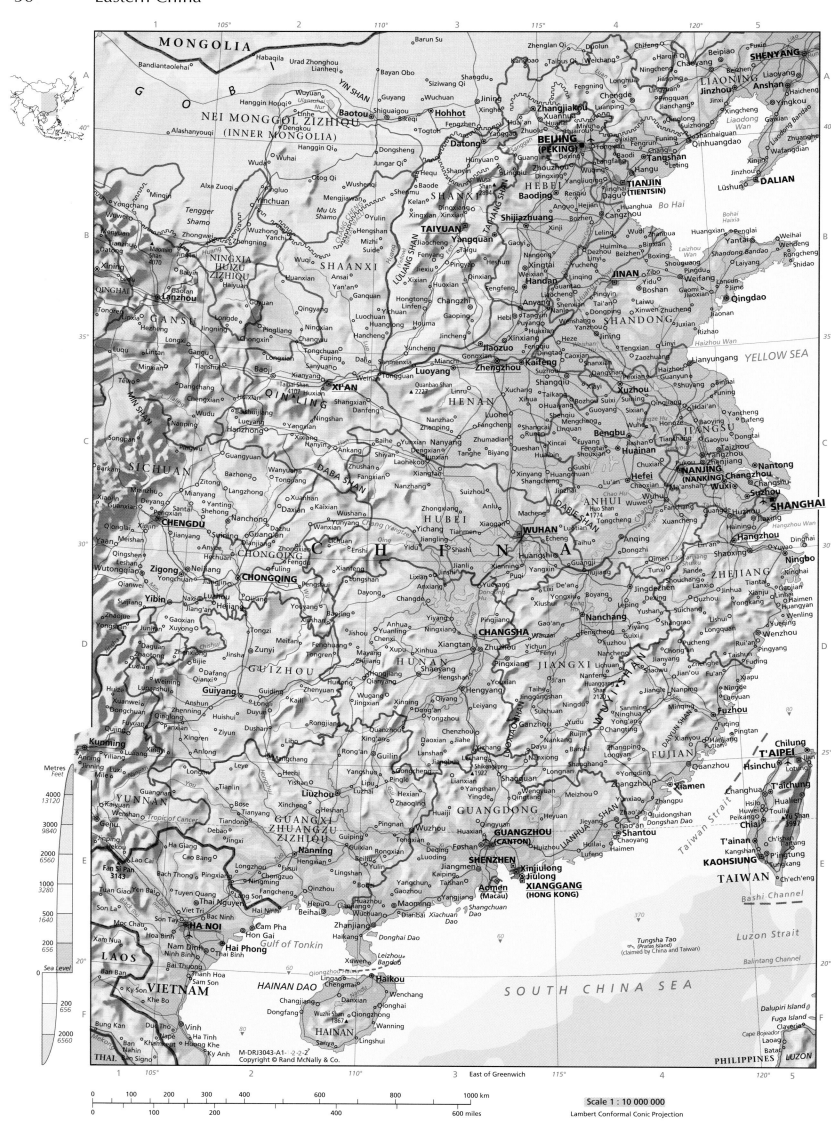

Scale 1 : 10 000 000
Lambert Conformal Conic Projection

M-DRJ3043-A1- -2-2-2°
Copyright © Rand McNally & Co.

1 130° 2 135° 3 140° 4 145° 5

XIAO HINGGAN LING
Yichun
Luobei
RUSSIA
Leninskoe
Korfovskij

Tieli
Nancha
Hegang
Amur
Heilong
Tongjiang
Vjazemskij
Hor

Dailing Heli
Tangyuan
Fujin
Nel'ma
Tatarskij
proliv
Iljinskij
Tomari
Čehov

Fangzheng
Jiamusi Shuangyashan
Raohe
Bikin
Adimi
1100
Dolinsk
OSTROV SAHALIN
(SAKHALIN)
Holmsk
Južno-Sahalinsk

MANCHURIA
Yilan
Huanan
Baoqing
Burlit
Svetlaja
Nevel'sk
Korsakov

HEILONGJIANG
Boli
Didao
Dal'nerečensk
gora Vysokaja
1745
Gornozavodsk
zaliv
Aniva

ZHANGGUANGCAI
Hailin
Mishan
Lake
Khanka
Kirovskij
Ariadnoe
Velikaja Kema
Dal'naja
Wakkanai
SEA OF
OKHOTSK
3282

CHINA
45°
Haibai
Jixi
Spassk-
Dal'nij
Svetlaja
Ternej
Rebun-tō
Rishiri-tō
Formerly part of Japan, Malaja
Kuril'skaja, Šikotan, Kunašir,
and Iturup, occupied by Russia
since 1945, are claimed by Japan
pending a final peace treaty.
KURIL'SKIE OSTROVA
(KURIL ISLANDS)

JILIN
Ning'an
Dongjingcheng
Suiyang
Pograničnyj
Sibircevo
Mihajlovka
Dal'negorsk
Rudnaja Pristan'
Teshio
Nayoro
Mombetsu
Abashiri
ostrov
Iturup
(Etorofu-tō)

Liangbingtai
Wangqing
Laohelshan
Razdol'noe
Ussurijsk
Arsenev
gora Oblačnaja
1855
Rumoi
Asahikawa
Asahi-dake
3190
Takikawa
Kitami
ostrov
Šikotan
(Shikotan-tō)

Yanji
Hunchun
Vladivostok
Art'em
Lazo
Ol'ga
Otaru
HOKKAIDŌ
Nemuro
ostrov
Kunašir
(Kunashiri-tō)

B
Hoeryŏng-ŭp
Musan-ŭp
Tumen
Aojiri
Poset
Slavjanka
Kamen
Nahodka
Petra
Velikogo
Okushiri-tō
Ebetsu
Yūbari
Sapporo
Chitose
Date
Tomakomai
Horoshiri-dake
2052
Obihiro
Kushiro
B
MALAJA KURIL'SKAJA GRJADA

Ch'ŏngjin
Kwanmo-bong
2540
Najin
Muroran
Urakawa
Erimo-misaki

Kilchu-ŭp
Kyŏngsŏng-ŭp
Yakumo
Uchiura-wan

NORTH
KOREA
3685
Oshima-hantō
Hakodate

Kimch'aek
Mutsu
Mutsu-wan

40°
Tanch'ŏn-ŭp
Tsugaru-kaikyō
Aomori
40°

SEA OF JAPAN
Hirosaki
Hachinohe

Noshiro
Ninohe
7586

244
Akita
Iwate-san
2041
Miyako
Morioka

(EAST SEA)
Honjō
Hanamaki
Kamaishi

Yokote
Mizusawa

Sakata
Kesennuma
OU-SAMMYAKU

Tsuruoka
Ishinomaki

Murakami
Yamagata
Sendai

C
Sado
Niigata
JAPAN
Yonezawa
Fukushima
5759
C

Samch'ŏk
Ullŭng-do
(S. Korea)
Sanjo
Aizu-wakamatsu

Noto-hantō
Nagaoka
Kōriyama

Ulchin
Nanao
Joetsu
Tōkamachi
HONSHŪ
Iwaki

SOUTH
KOREA
Takaoka
Itoigawa
Nagano
Nikkō
Kitaibaraki

P'ohang
Kanazawa
Hotaka-dake
3190
Toyama
Ueda
Utsunomiya
Hitachi

Kyŏngju
Kaga
Matsumoto
Takasaki
Maebashi
Mito
Ashikaga

Ulsan
Fukui
Okaya
Kumagaya

PUSAN
130°
Kōfu
Hachiōji
TŌKYŌ
Chōshi

Matsue
Tottori
Miyazu
Ōtsu
Gifu
NAGOYA
Shizuoka
YOKOHAMA
KAWASAKI

35°
Yonago
suyama
Maizuru
KYŌTO
Takatsuki
Toyota
Okazaki
Fuji
Fuji-san
3776
Yokosuka
35°

Taisha
Wakasa-wan
Nara
Tsu
Ise
Numazu

HIROSHIMA
CHŪGOKU-SANCHI
Hamada
Masuda
Miyoshi
Okayama
KŌBE
ŌSAKA
Kishiwada
Toyohashi
Hamamatsu
Ō-shima

Yamaguchi
Hagi
Fukuyama
Kurashiki
Himeji
Takamatsu
Wakayama
Nii-jima

KITAKYŪSHŪ
Ube
Izuka
Imabari
Niihama
Tokushima
Enshū-
nada
Miyake-jima

FUKUOKA
Karatsu
Usa
Hita
Beppu
Matsuyama
Ishizuchi-san
1982
Anan
Gobō
Mikura-jima

Sasebo
Saga
Kurume
Ōita
Kōchi
SHIKOKU
Tanabe
Shingū
Shiono-misaki
PACIFIC

Ōmura
Ōmuta
Kuju-san
1787
Uwajima
Saiki
Sukumo
Muroto
Aoga-shima

Nagasaki
Kumamoto
Yatsushiro
Nobeoka
Hitoyoshi

Akune
KYŪSHŪ

Kagoshima
Miyazaki
Miyakonojō
Nichinan

Sata-misaki
Kanoya

Tanega-shima
OSUMI-
SHOTŌ
NANSEI-SHOTŌ
(RYUKYU ISLANDS)

Yaku-shima
5011

Nakano-shima
1495
Sumisu-jima

Suwanose-jima

AMAMI-
SHOTŌ
Naze
Kikai-shima

Kikai-shima

130° 2 135° *East of Greenwich* 3 140°

Scale 1 : 8 000 000
Lambert Conformal Conic Projection

0 100 200 300 400 600 800 km
0 50 100 150 200 300 400 500 miles

Metres
Feet
3000
9840
2000
6560
1000
3280
500
1640
200
656
Sea Level 0
200
656
2000
6560

W-561500-7A-DR1-1
Copyright © Rand McNally & Co.

a same scale as main map
147
EAST CHINA SEA
(DONG HAI)
Yūwan-dake
694
Amami-
Ō-shima
Naze
Kikai-shima

Tokuno-shima
AMAMI-SHOTŌ

JAPAN

Okino-Erabu-shima
Yoron-jima

NANSEI-SHOTŌ (RYUKYU ISLANDS)
Iheya-shima

Kume-jima
Nago
Okinawa
Okinawa
OKINAWA-SHOTŌ
Naha
PACIFIC
OCEAN

28°
30°
130° 6 7

Metres / Feet

4000	13120
3000	9840
2000	6560
1000	3280
500	1640
200	656
Sea Level	0
200	656
2000	6560

M-DRJ3022-A1-❘-3-3-4"
Copyright © Rand McNally & Co.

Scale 1 : 15 000 000

0 200 400 800 1200 1600 km

0 100 200 300 400 500 600 800 1000 miles

East of Greenwich

Sinusoidal Projection

KISHIMA-SHOTO (Japan)
Hirara
Miyako-jima
iomote-ma

25°

Tropic of Cancer

8649

20°

Farallon de Pajaros
Maug Islands
Asuncion Island

MARIANA ISLANDS

Agrihan

NORTHERN MARIANA ISLANDS (U.S)

Pagan
Alamagan   ▼8700
Guguan

C

Sarigan

Anatahan   Farallon de Medinilla

P H I L I P P I N E

S E A

15°

Tinian

Saipan

ILIPPINES

Catanduanes Island
Naga   Virac
Mayon Volcano 2462
Legaspi
lal   Sorsogon
Catarman   Laoang
asbate

Rota
Hagåtña   GUAM
(U.S)

P A C I F I C

D

Taclobar
Bogo
colod   Ormoc
CEBU   San Carlos   LEYTE
bu   Libagon

SAMAR
Catbalogan

O C E A N

10°

3500

Dinagat Island
Bohol   Siargao Island
Surigao
umaguete   Tandag
Bislig
Dipolog   Butuan
Cagayan de Oro
Oliian   Bislig
Malaybalay
tabato   MINDANAO
Davao
Mount Apo   Davao
2954   Gulf   Cape San
Agustin
Kiamba
6200
Tinaca Point

Yap   8527

Fais

FEDERATED STATES OF MICRONESIA

E

Palau Islands
Koror   Babelthuap
Beliliou
Ngeaur   6800

Eauripik   Pulap

Kepulauan Nanusa

Sonsorol Islands

PALAU

5°

Pulau
Karakelong   KEPULAUAN
TALAUD
Tahuna
Pulau Sangihe

C a r o l i n e   I s l a n d s

Pulau Siau   KEPULAUAN
Pulau Tahulandang   SANGIHE
Pulau Biaro

F

Morotai

do (Menado)   Bitung
Gunung Klabat
2022
MINAHASA   Kotamobagu
arontalo

Galela

HALMAHERA

Pulau
Waigeo

Equator   0°

6920

Jailolo

Laut Maluku   Weda

Pulau Gebe

Selat Damper

4600

Manokwari

Biak

Ninigo Group   Kaniet Islands

G

Pulau
Kasiruta   Labuha
yuk   Pulau
Peleng
Pulau   Pulau   Pulau Obi
Taliabu   Mangole
KEPULAUAN   Laiwui
GGAI   KEPULAUAN
SULA   OBI
Pulau
Sanana

Sorong   JAZIRAH
Salawati   DOBERAI   Ransiki
Pulau
Misool   Pulau
Yapen

Bosnik   Hermit Islands   Manus
Island
Sarmi   ADMIRALTY
ISLANDS   Mussau Island

New
Hanover

Wuvulu Island   Kavieng

BISMARCK ARCHIPELAGO

Pulau
Manui
5700   Namlea
Buru   Piru
Amahai   SERAM
(CERAM)
Wahai
Pulau
Wowoni

Inanwatan   Bintuni   Babo
Teluk Berau   Waren
Teluk   Nabire
Cenderawasih
Bula   Fakfak   Wasior
1400

PEGUNUNGAN VAN REES   Demta
Jayapura
Vanimo
Aitape
Wewak

Demta   NEW
IRELAND

Angoram   Manam Island   Talasea

G

Pulau
Buton   KEPULAUAN
SULA
Karufa

Modowi   Puncak Jaya   Puncak Trikora
5030   4750
Kokenau

PEGUNUNGAN MAOKE

Ambunti   Karkar Island
Sepik   Madang
Umboi
Island   Witu Islands

Wabag

Rabaul

KEPULAUAN
TUKANGBESI   Laut Banda   7440   Kepulauan
Kai   Tual   Nuhu
Cut   Dobo
Kepulauan
Banda
Kepulauan
Watubela   Kepulauan
Adi

Pulau Wokam   NEW
GUINEA   Wabag   Mount Wilhelm
4509   New Britain
Mendi   Hagen
Garoka   Lae

Pulau Binongko   Pulau Nila   Pulau
Yamdena   Pulau Kobroor   PAPUA NEW
GUINEA   Huon Gulf

Tanahmerah   Lake
Murray   Mapi
Digul

Balimo   Kikori   Morobe

Solomon
Sea

Pulau Damar

Pulau Romang   KEPULAUAN
ARU

Pulau Wetar   Ilwaki   Kepulauan
Babar   Pulau Yos
Sudarso   Fly   Daru

Gulf of
Papua

H

Pulau
omblen   Pulau
Alor   Kalabahi   Pulau Kisar
rantuka   Pulau Ataura   Tutuala   Kepulauan
Leti   Saumlaki   Tanjung Vals
Dili
Soe   3300   EAST TIMOR
Kupang   TIMOR
Pulau Roti

Pulau Selaru   Merauke   Okaba

Mount Victoria
4035   Popondetta
Kokoda
Kulumadau   Murua
Island
Wanigela
Banara   D'ENTRECASTEAUX ISLANDS

STANLEY RANGE

Port Moresby
Rigo
Abau   Esa'ala

10°

ARAFURA SEA

Saibai Island

Torres Strait

Thursday Island
Cape York

Samarai

Timor Sea

Melville
Island   Cape Croker   Wessel
Islands   Cape Wessel   70   Prince of Wales Island

Bamaga
CAPE YORK
PENINSULA

I

13

125°   8   Bathurst
Island   Van Diemen
Gulf   Goulburn
Islands   A U S T R A L I A   145°   12   150°
130°   Darwin   9   Arnhem Land   135°   10   140°   11   Cape
Iron
Range   Cape
Greville

| 1 | 90° | 2 | 95° | 3 | 100° | 4 | 105° | 5 |

SIKKIM
Pünäkha Kula Kangri 7554
Paro Thimphu Tongsa Dzong
BHUTAN
Shliguri Kälimpang
Koch Bihar Barpeta
Jalpaigurī Dhuburi Goalpara
Pürnia Katihār Saidpur Rangpur Dipur
BIHAR Bhagalpur Raiganj Dinājpur
Balurghāt Ingrāj Bāzār
JHARKHAND Maldah
Navadwip Kishnanagar
WEST BENGAL Bhātpāra
Hāora KOLKATA (CALCUTTA)
Medinipur Diamond Harbour
Sundarbans
Mouths of the Ganges

ARUNACHAL PRADESH
Itānagar Bomdila
Tezpur
Lakhimpur
Jorhat
Golāghāt Mokokchūng
NĀGĀLAND
Dimāpur NAGA HILLS
Kohīma
MANIPUR
Imphāl
MIZORAM
Āīzawl

Dibrugarh
Tinsukia
Digboi Ledo
Shingbwiyang
Hkamti

SICHUAN
Xichang

BANGLADESH
Rājshāhī Sirājganj
Pabna
DHAKA
Nārāyanganj
Comilla
Khulna Noākhāli
Barisāl
Nazir Hāt
Maiskhāl Island
Cox's Bāzār

INDIA
ASSAM
Shillong
MEGHĀLAYA
Mymensingh
Sylhet
Karimganj Silchar
TRIPURA
Agartala
Brahmanbaria

Buthidaung

Bay of Bengal

ARAKAN YOMA

MYANMAR (BURMA)

THAILAND

Bangkok

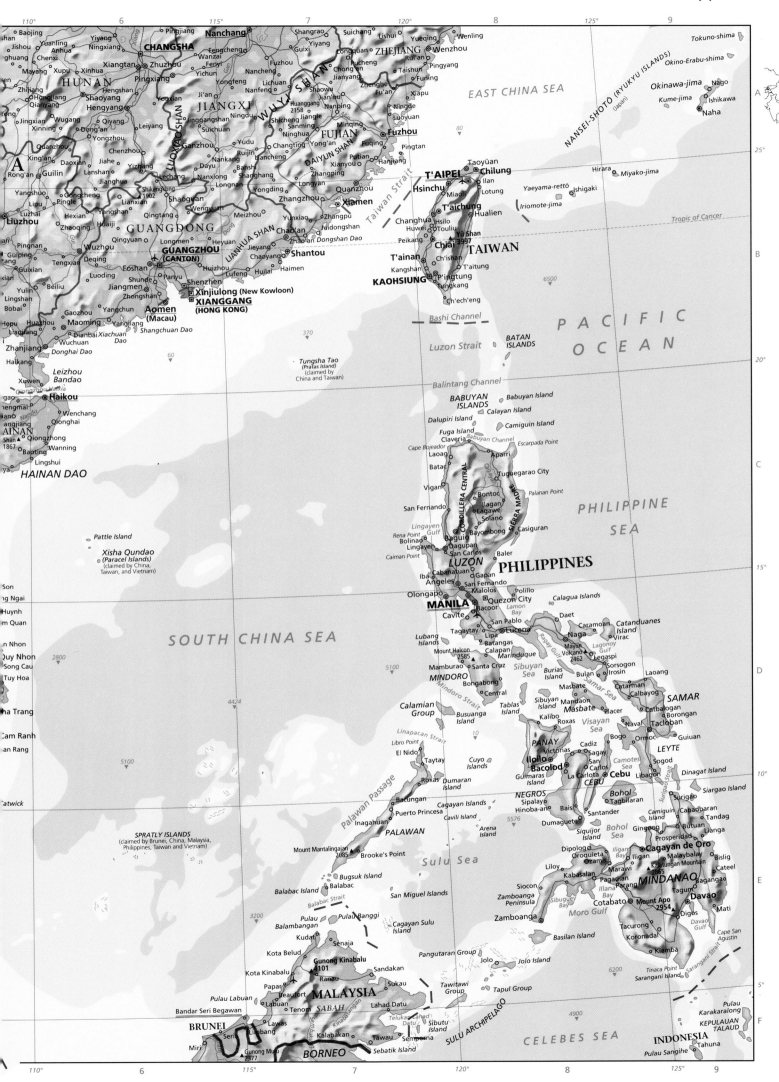

A

110°   6   115°   7   120°   8   125°   9

CHANGSHA

Baojing   Yuanling   Yiyang   Pingjiang   **Nanchang**   Shangrao   Suichang   Lishui   Yueqing   Wenling
Jishou   Anhua   Ningxiang   Ningxiang   Fengcheng   Wanzai   Fenyi   Guixi   Yiyang   Longquan   Jianou   Wenzhou
ghuang   Chenxi   Xinhua   Xiangtan   Zhuzhou   **ZHEJIANG**   Rui'an   Pingyang
Mayang   Xupu   Yichun   Nanfeng   Lichuan   Jianyang   Fuding
Zhijiang   **HUNAN**   **JIANGXI**   Huanggang   Nanping   Xiapu
Hongjiang   Qianyang   Shaoyang   Hengshan   Ji'an   2158   Shicheng   Jiangle   Minqing   **Fuzhou**
    Hengyang   Jinggangshan   Ningdu   Sanming   Yong'an   Pingtan
Jingxian   Youxian   Yongfeng   **FUJIAN**   Changting   **Fuzhou**
Qianyang   Wugang   Qiyang   Leiyang   Ruijin   Longyan   **Xiamen**   Pingtan

GUANGDONG   **GUANGZHOU (CANTON)**

Xinjiulong (New Kowloon)
XIANGGANG (HONG KONG)

Aomen (Macau)

Haikou

HAINAN DAO

SOUTH CHINA SEA

Pattle Island
Xisha Qundao (Paracel Islands) (claimed by China, Taiwan, and Vietnam)

SPRATLY ISLANDS (claimed by Brunei, China, Malaysia, Philippines, Taiwan and Vietnam)

EAST CHINA SEA

NANSEI-SHOTŌ (RYUKYU ISLANDS) (Japan)   Tokuno-shima   Okino-Erabu-shima   Nago
Okinawa-jima   Ishikawa
Kume-jima   Naha

Tropic of Cancer

Yaeyama-rettō   Hirara   Miyako-jima
Iriomote-jima   Ishigaki

T'AIPEI   **Chilung**
Hsinchu   Ilan   Lotung
T'aichung   Hualien
Changhua   Hsilo   Touliu   Yū Shan 3997
TAIWAN
T'ainan   Chiai
Kangshan   Ch'ishan   T'aitung
KAOHSIUNG   P'ingtung   Yungkang   6500
Ch'ech'eng

Taiwan Strait
Bashi Channel

PACIFIC OCEAN

Luzon Strait   **BATAN ISLANDS**
Balintang Channel

BABUYAN ISLANDS   Babuyan Island
Dalupiri Island   Calayan Island
Fuga Island   Camiguin Island
Claveria   *Babuyan Channel*   Escarpada Point
Cape Bojeador   Aparri
Laoag   Tuguegarao City
Batac
Vigan   Bontoc   *Palanan Point*
San Fernando   Ilagan   Solano   Casiguran
Rena Point   Lagawe   Bayombong
Bolinao   Baguio   Casiguran
Lingayen   San Carlos   Baler
Caiman Point   Dagupan
LUZON   Cabanatuan   **PHILIPPINES**
Iba   Angeles   Gapan
    San Fernando
Olongapo   Malolos   Polillo
    Quezon City   *Calagua Islands*
MANILA   Bacoor   *Lamon Bay*
    Cavite   San Pablo   Daet   *Catanduanes Island*
Lubang   Tagaytay   Lucena   Naga   Virac
Islands   Lipa   *Ragay Gulf*   *Lagonoy Gulf*
    Batangas   Mayon   Legaspi   *PHILIPPINE SEA*
Mount Halcon   Calapan   Volcano   Sorsogon
2585   Marinduque   2462   Irosin   Laoang
Mamburao   Santa Cruz   *Sibuyan Sea*   Catarman
MINDORO   Bongabong   Burias   Bulan   Calbayog
    Central   Island   Masbate   **SAMAR**
    Tablas   *Sibuyan*   Mandaon   *Samar Sea*
Calamian   Island   Island   **Masbate**   Placer   Catbalogan
Group   Busuanga   Kalibo   Naval   Borongan
    Island   Roxas   *Visayan Sea*   Tacloban
Linapacan Strait   10   **PANAY**   Bogo   Ormoc   Guiuan
Libro Point   Victorias   Cadiz   San   *Camotes*   **LEYTE**
El Nido   Sagay   Carlos   *Sea*   Sogod   Dinagat Island
Taytay   *Cuyo Islands*   **Iloilo**   La Carlota   **Cebu**   Libagon
Roxas   Dumaran   **Bacolod**   *Guimaras*   **CEBU**   Surigao   Siargao Island
    Island   Cagayan Islands   Island   *NEGROS*   **Bohol**   Tagbilaran
Bacungan   Cavili Island   Sipalay   Santander   Camiguin   Cabadbaran
Puerto Princesa   Arena   Hinoba-an   Bais   *Bohol*   Island   Tandag
    Island   Dumaguete   Siquijor   *Sea*   Gingoog   Butuan   Bislig
PALAWAN   5576   Island   Dipolog   Prosperidad   Cateel
Mount Mantalingajan   Brooke's Point   *Sulu Sea*   Oroquieta   Iligan   **Cagayan de Oro**
2085   Liloy   Ozamiz   *Iligan*   Malaybalay
    Bugsuk Island   Kabasalan   Marawi   *Bay*   Kaputungan Mountain
Balabac Island   Balabac   Pagadian   Parang   2865   Gingoog
        Siocon   *Illana*   **MINDANAO**   Bagangga
    San Miguel Islands   Zamboanga   *Bay*   Digos   Mati
Pulau   Pulau Banggi   Peninsula   *Sibugue*   Cotabato   Mount Apo   **Davao**
Balambangan   Cagayan Sulu   Zamboanga   *Bay*   2954   Digos
3200   Island   *Moro Gulf*   Tacurong   *Davao Gulf*
Kudat   Senaja   Koronadal   Cape San Agustin
Kota Belud   *Pangutaran Group*   Jolo   Jolo Island   Kiamba
Gunong Kinabalu   Sandakan   Tinaca Point   *Sarangani Strait*
4101   Ranau   *Tawi-Tawi Group*   6200   Sarangani Islands
Kota Kinabalu   *Tapul Group*   *SULU ARCHIPELAGO*
Papar   Beaufort   Sukau   Lahad Datu   Basilan Island   *Pulau Karakaralong*
Labuan   Tenom   *Telukan*   Sibutu Island   4900   *KEPULAUAN TALAUD*
Bandar Seri Begawan   **SABAH**   Lahad Datu   **INDONESIA**
MALAYSIA   Lawas   *Kinabatangan*   Tawau   Tahuna
BRUNEI   Seria   Kalabakan   *SULU ARCHIPELAGO*   **CELEBES SEA**   Pulau Sangihe
Miri   **Gunung Mulu**   Semporna   Sebatik Island
2377   **BORNEO**

2800   *5100*   *5100*   *4424*

36

MYANMAR (BURMA)

Myinmoletkat Taung ▲ 2075

MERGUI
ARCHIPELAGO
Bentinck Island
Letsôk-aw Kyun
Kannaw Kyun
Kadan Kyun
Lanbi Kyun

ANDAMAN SEA

Nakhon Pathom
Chachoengsao
Samut Prakan
Samut Sakhon
KRUNG THEP (BANGKOK)
Si Racha
Phetchaburi
Cha-am
Rayong
Hua Hin
Chanthaburi
Prachuap Khiri Khan
Palaw
Mergui
Chumphon

Gulf of Thailand

Ko Chang
Ko Kut
Trat

CAMBODIA
Bătdâmbâng
Poŭthĭsăt
Phnum Aôral 1813
Krŏng Kaôh Kŏng
Phumĭ Chhnăng
Phumĭ Chămbăk
Phumĭ Chhuk
Kâmpóng Saôm
Kâmpôt

Tônlé Sap
ANGKOR WAT

Kâmpóng Thum
Kâmpóng Chhnăng
Krâchéh
Kâmpóng Cham
Phumĭ Dâk Dăm
Svay Riĕng
Long Xuyen
Sa Dec
Can Tho
Vinh Long
Rach Gia

Lumphăt
Buon Ma Thuot
Loc Ninh
Tay Ninh
Bao Loc
Phnum Pénh (Phnom Penh)

VIETNAM
Song Cau
Tuy Hoa
Nha Trang
Da Lat
Cam Ranh
Phan Rang
Bien Hoa
Phan Thiet
THANH PHO HO CHI MINH (SAIGON)
My Tho Vung Tau
Soc Trang
Îles Catwick

THAILAND
Isthmus of Kra
Ranong
Ko Tao
Ko Phangan
Ko Samui
Surat Thani
Nakhon Si Thammarat
Pak Phanang
Phangnga
Trang
Kantang
Phatthalung
Ko Phuket
Phuket
Songkhla
Hat Yai
Pattani
Yala
Narathiwat

Quan Dao Nam Du
Ca Mau
Bac Lieu
Mui Ca Mau
Hon Khoai
Con Son

SPRATLY ISLANDS

SOUTH CHINA SEA

Satun
Kangar
Pulau Langkawi
Alor Setar
Sungai Kolok
Kota Bharu
Pasir Mas
Kuala Krai
Betong

MALAY PENINSULA
Sungai Petani
George Town (Penang)
Butterworth

Taiping
Ipoh
Kampar
Kuala Kangsar
Gunong Tahan 2187
Kuala Lipis
Teluk Intan
Raub
Gunong Benum 2107
Bentung
Kuala Terengganu
Cukai
Kuantan

MALAYSIA

KEPULAUAN NATUNA BESAR
Natuna Besar
Pulau Laut

KEPULAUAN ANAMBAS
Pulau Midai
Pulau Subi
Pulau Serasan
KEPULAUAN NATUNA SELATAN

MALAYSIA
Miri
Niah
Bintulu
SARAWAK
Mukah

KUALA LUMPUR
SEMENANJUNG MALAYSIA
Shah Alam
Klang
Seremban
Kajang
Kuala Pilah
Segamat
Melaka
Labis
Keluang
Mersing
Batu Pahat
SINGAPORE
Johor Bahru

Banda Aceh
Pulau We
Lhokseumawe
Langsa
Gunung Abongabong 2985
Gunung Bandahara 3012
Meulaboh
Gunung Leuser 3381
Binjai
MEDAN
Tebingtinggi
Gunung Sinabung 2451
Tapaktuan
Tanjungbalai
Pematangsiantar
Danau Toba
Kisaran

Strait of Malacca

Pulau Tioman
Mempawah
Sambas
Singkawang
Serian
Kuching
Sarikei
Sibu
Rajang
Betong
PEG. KAPUAS HULU
Putussibau
Semitau
Bukit Raya 2278

Pulau Simeule
Sinabang
Pulau Babi
Tarutung
Bagansiapiapi
Pulau Rupat
Dumai
Pulau Tuangku
Pulau Mursala
Sibolga
Bantauprapat
Padangsidempuan
Pulau Bengkalis
Pekanbaru
SINGAPORE
Padang
Pulau Tebingtinggi
Pulau Batam
Pulau Kundur
Pulau Bintan
Tanjungpinang
KEPULAUAN RIAU

Pontianak
Sanggau
Sintang
Kapuas
Melawi
Gunung Saran 1758
PEGUNUNGAN M

BORNEO (KALIMANTA

Pulau Nias
Gunungsitoli
Pulau Pini
Pulau Tanahmasa
KEPULAUAN BATU
Pulau Tanahbala
Talu
Bangkinang
SUMATERA (SUMATRA)
Kampar Kanan

Equator

Bukittinggi
Payakumbuh
Pulau Basu
Pulau Sebangka
Pulau Lingga
KEPULAUAN LINGGA
Pulau Singkep
Telukbatang
Sukadana
Nangatayap
Ketapang
Pulau Karimata
Pangkalanbuun
Kumai
Pulau Siberut
Padangpanjang
Pariaman
Taluk
Rengat
Tembilahan
Padang
Painan
Muarabungo
Gunung Kerinci 3800
Bangko
Jambi
Selat Berhala
Tanjung Jabung

KEPULAUAN MENTAWAI
Pulau Sipura
Sungaidareh
Selat Mentawai
PEGUNUNGAN BARISAN
Surulangun
Mukomuk
Pulau Pagai Utara
Pulau Pagai Selatan
Lubuklinggau
Gresik
Muntok
Pangkalpinang
Pulau Bangka
Tanjungpandan
Manggar
Selat Bangka
Tanjungsambar
Sukaraja
Kendawangan
Kualakapua
Sampit
Banjarmasin
Teluk Sampit

Lais
Lahat
Muaraenim
Palembang
Kayuagung
Perabumulih
Pulau Lepar
Belitung
Pulau Gelasa
Tanjung Lumut
Bengkulu
Gunung Dempo 3159
Baturaja
Ulangbawang
Martapura
Manna
Menggala
Kotabumi
Bintuhan

Tanjung Puting

G R E A T E R   S U N

Laut Jawa (Java Sea)

Tanjung S

I N D O N

Krui
Pulau Enggano
Metro
Kotaagung
Bandar Lampung
Panjang

6000

Pulau Masalembu Besar
Pulau Bawean

INDIAN OCEAN

Selat Sunda
Tanjung Cina
Serang
Bekasi
JAKARTA
Karawang
Indramayu
Cirebon
Pulau Karimunjawa
Kudus
Rembang
Tuban
MADURA
Bangkalan
Gresik
Pamekasan
Selat Madura

Tanjung Cangkuang
Bogor
Purwakarta
Cianjur
Sukabumi
Sumedang
BANDUNG
Pekalongan
Tegal
Batang
Kudus
Purwokerto
Garut
Gunung Slamet 3428
Magelang
SEMARANG
Surakarta
SURABAYA
Pasuruan
Ujunggenteng
Sindangbarang
Cilacap
Gunung Lawu 3265
Kediri
Malang
Yogyakarta
Gunung Lawu
Jember
Probolinggo
Banyuw
Blitar
Tulungagung

7000

7125

JAWA (JAVA)

⚓ **CHRISTMAS ISLAND** (Austl.)

Metres Feet

3000 / 9840
2000 / 6560
1000 / 3280
500 / 1640
200 / 656
0 / Sea Level
200 / 656
2000 / 6560

M-DRJ3044-A1-1-2-2-3°
Copyright © Rand McNally & Co.

| 0 | 100 | 200 | 300 | 400 | 600 | 800 | 1000 km |

| 0 | 100 | 200 | 300 | 400 | 500 | 600 miles |

Scale 1 : 10 000 000
Sinusoidal Projection

East of Greenwich

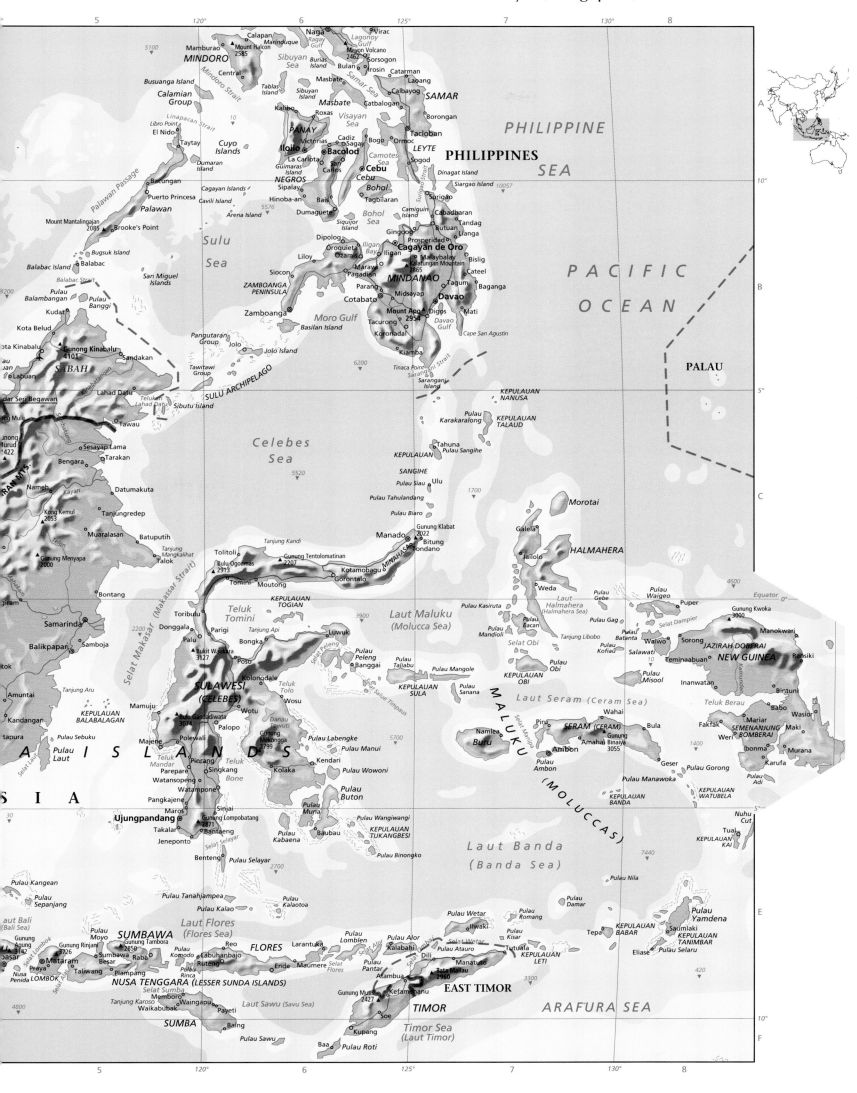

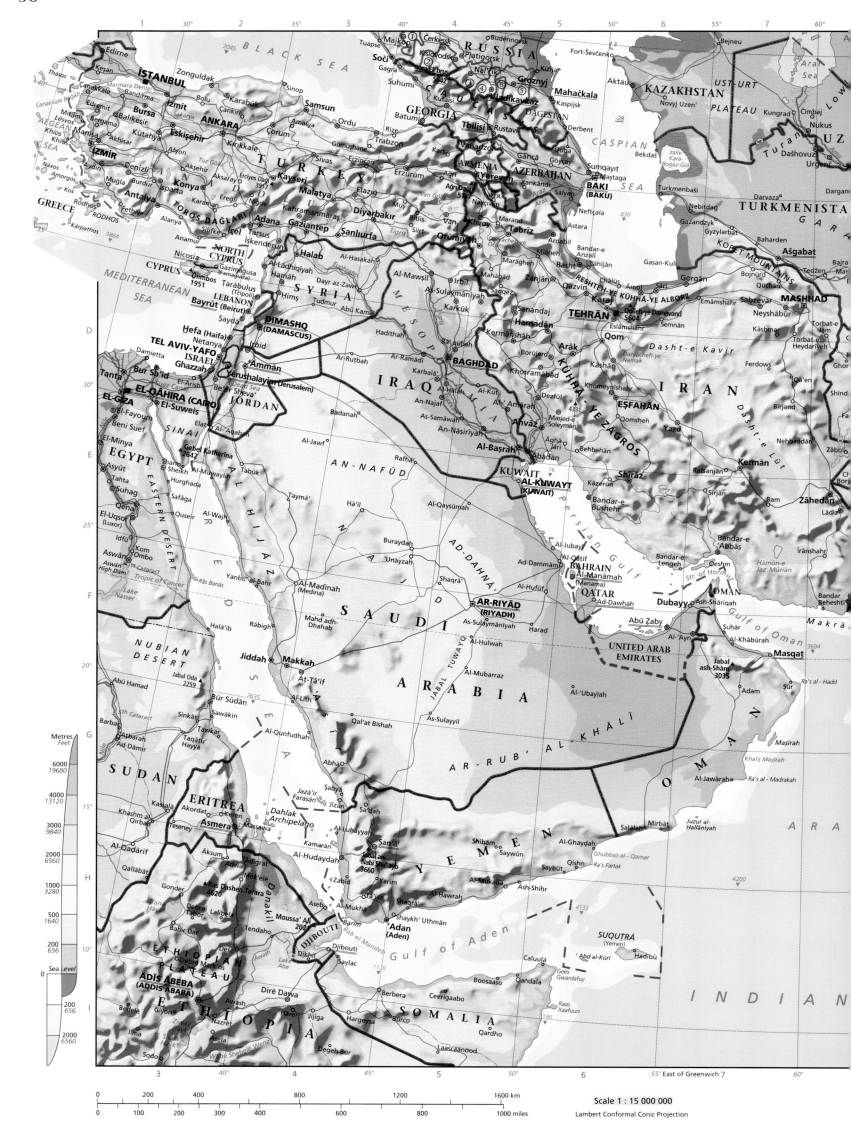

Scale 1 : 15 000 000

Lambert Conformal Conic Projection

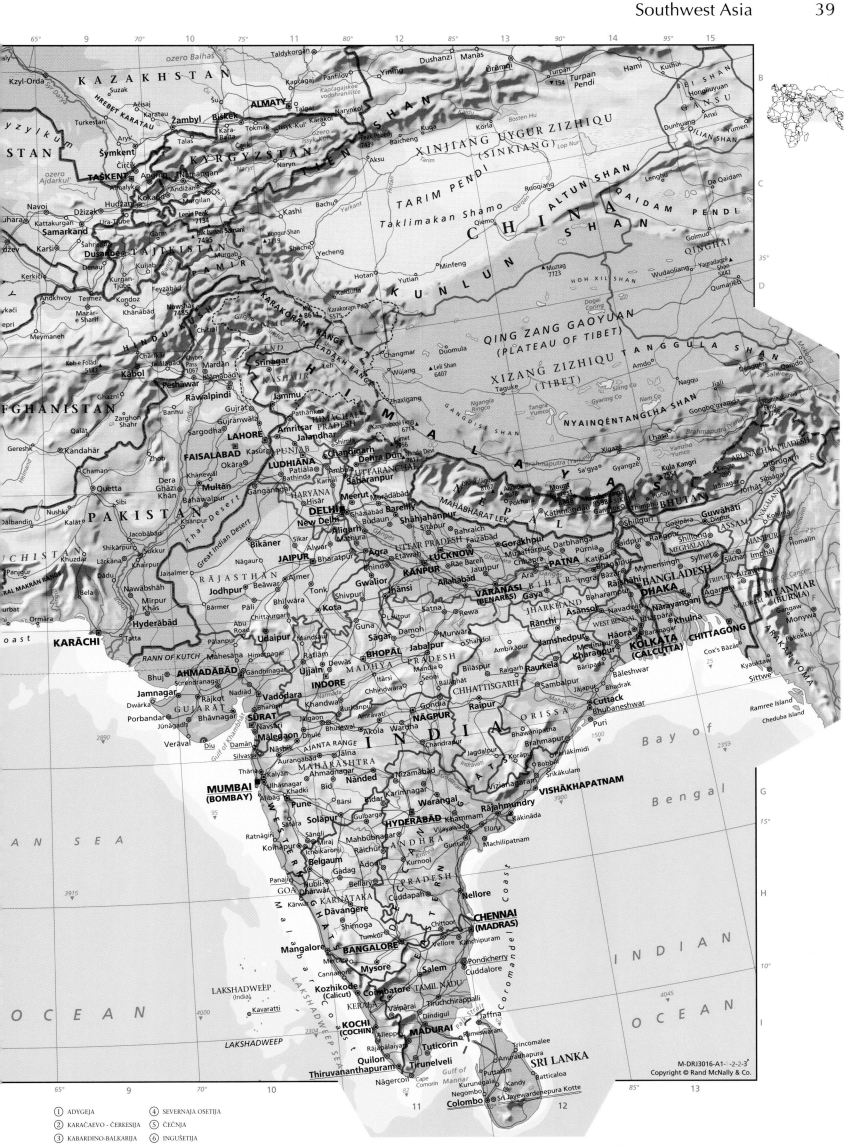

① ADYGEJA   ④ SEVERNAJA OSETIJA
② KARAČAEVO - ČERKESIJA   ⑤ ČEČNJA
③ KABARDINO-BALKÁRIJA   ⑥ INGUŠETIJA

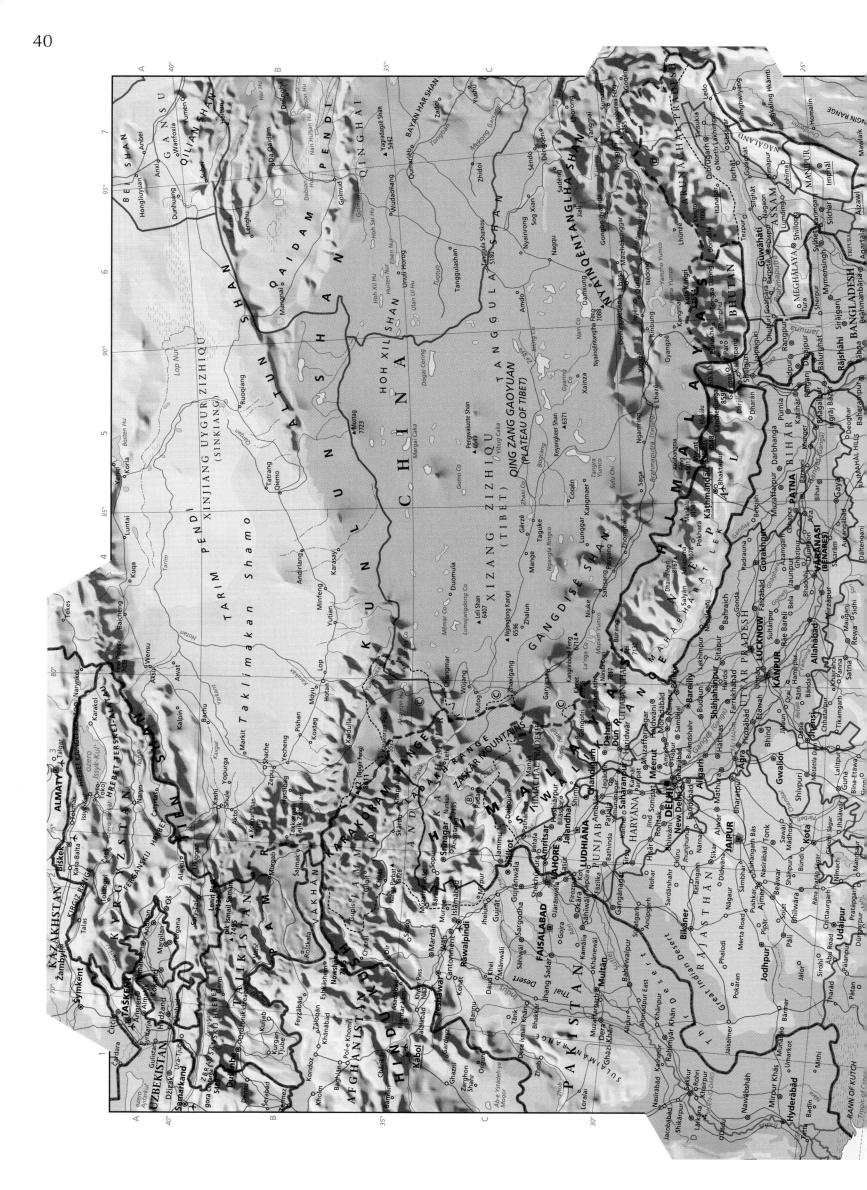

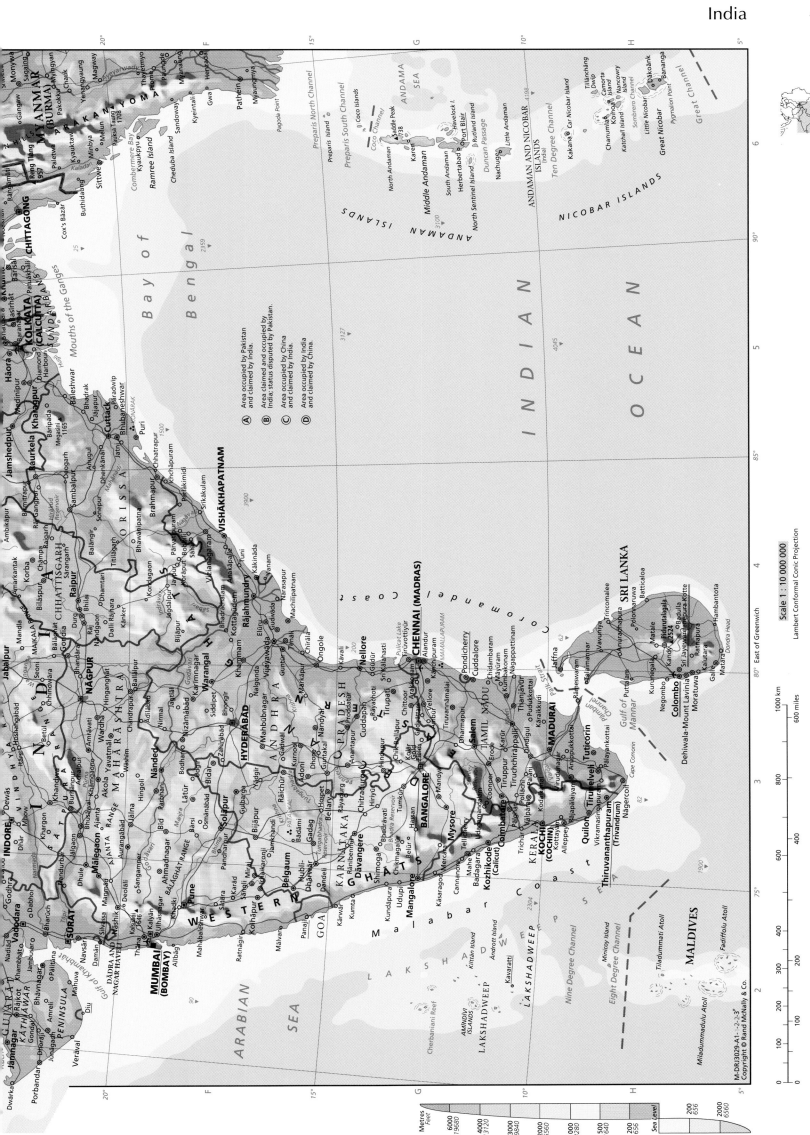

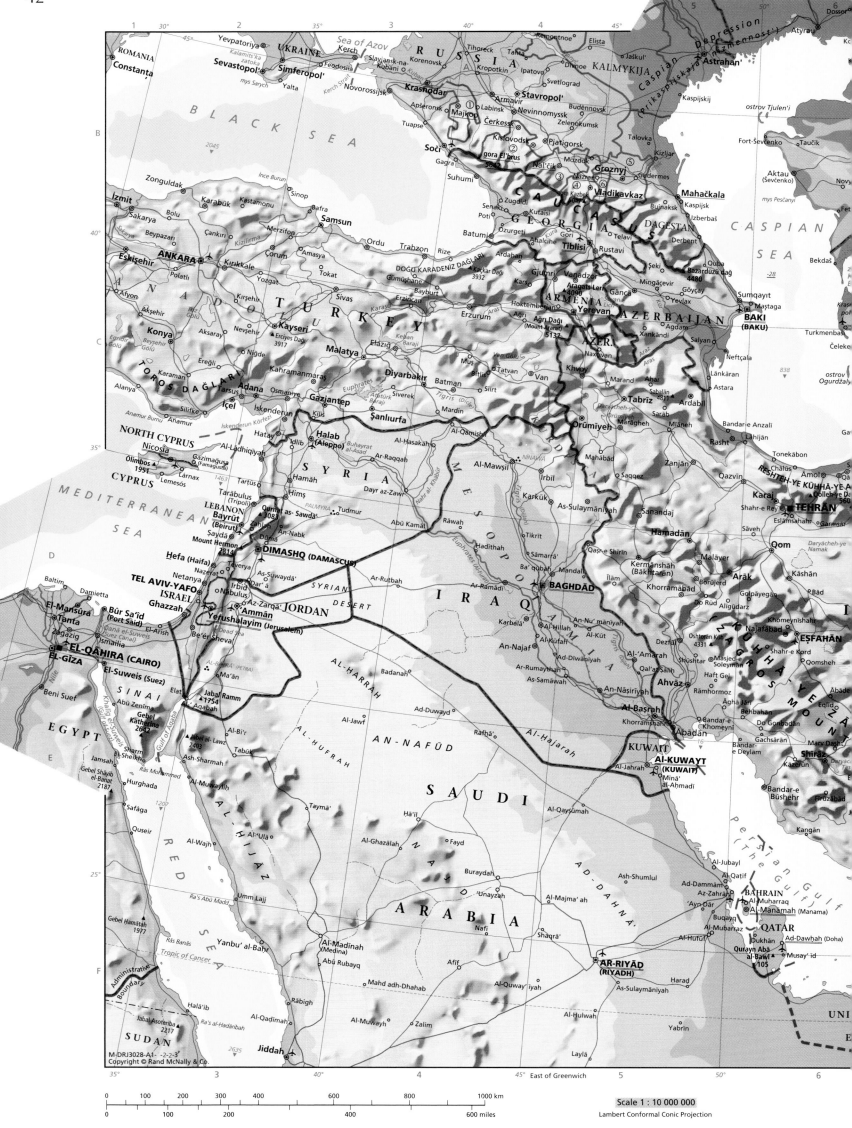

42

BLACK SEA

MEDITERRANEAN SEA

CASPIAN SEA

RUSSIA

UKRAINE
ROMANIA
Constanța

Sea of Azov

KALMYKIJA

Yevpatoriya
Sevastopol'
Simferopol'
Yalta
Feodosia
Kerch
Slavjansk-na-
Kerch Strait
Novorossijsk
Kubani
Korenovsk
Krasnodar
Tuapse
Soči
Gagra
Suhumi

Tihoreck
Tahta
Kropotkin
Armavir
Apšeronsk
Majkop
Labinsk
Čerkessk
Nevinnomyssk
gora El'brus
Kislovodsk

Elista
Ipatovo
Dinoe
Svetlograd
Budennovsk
Stavropol'
Pjatigorsk
Talovka
Mozdok
Nal'čik
Zelenokumsk

Astrahan'
Atyrau
Dossor
Kaspijskij
Kizljar
Groznyj
Vladikavkaz
Nazran'
Mahačkala
Kaspijsk
Izberbaš

ostrov Tjulen'i

Fort-Ševčenko
Taučik
Aktau
(Ševčenko)
mys Pesčanyj
Bekdaš

CAUCASUS
DAGESTAN
GEORGIA
Zugdidi
Senaki
Poti
Batumi
Kutaisi
Ozurgeti
Ahalcihe
Tiblisi
Telavi
Rustavi
Derbent
Quba
Bazardüzü dağ
4480
Šeki
Mingäçevir
Göyçay

İzmit
Zonguldak
Karabük
Kastamonu
Sinop
Bafra
İstasyon
Samsun
Ordu
Trabzon
Rize
Ardahan
DOĞU KARADENİZ DAĞLARI
Gümüşhane
Bayburt
Kačkar Dağı 3932
Kars
Hoktemberjan
Ağrı
Erzurum
Erzincan
Ardabil

ANKARA
Eskişehir
Kırıkkale
Çankırı
Çorum
Amasya
Tokat
Yozgat
Sivas
Kayseri
Erciyes Dağı 3917
Malatya
Elazığ
Keban Baraji
Muş
Bitlis
Tatvan
Van
Van Gölü
Khvoy
Marand
Ahar
Tabriz
Sabalan 4811
Ardabil

Polatlı
Kırşehir
Afyon
Akşehir
Tuz Gölü
Nevşehir
Niğde
Aksaray
Ereğli
Kahramanmaraş
Adıyaman
Diyarbakır
Batman
Siirt
Mardin
Al-Hasakah
Al-Qamishli
Orümiyeh
Orümiyeh
Marägheh
Miändoäb
Zanjän

Konya
Karaman
Ereğli
TOROS DAĞLARI
Tarsus
Adana
Osmaniye
Gaziantep
Kilis
Şanlıurfa
Euphrates
Atatürk Baraji
Siverek
Halab (Aleppo)
Ar-Raqqah
Al-Mawsil
NINAWA
Irbil
Karkük
As-Sulaymaniyah
Sanandaj
Saqqez
Zanjän
Qazvin

Alanya
Anamur
Silifke
İçel
İskenderun
Hatay
İdlib
İskenderun Körfezi
Anamur Burnu
NORTH CYPRUS
Nicosia
Olimbos 1951
Gazimağusa (Famagusta)
Lárnax
Lemesós
CYPRUS
Al-Ladhiqiyah
Tartüs
Hamäh
Himş
Tarábulus (Tripoli)
SYRIA
Hamäh
Dayr az-Zawr
Mardin
Nahr al-Khabür
Al-Mawsil
Buhayrat al-Asad
Ar-Raqqah
Khäbür
Euphrates (Al Furät)
Rawah
Abü Kamäl
Tudmur
PALMYRA
MESOPOTAMIA
Tigris (Dijlah)
Tikrit
Sämarrä'
Karkük (Oilah)
As-Sulaymaniyah
Qaşr-e Shirin
Kermänshäh (Bäkhtarän)
Iläm
Hamadän
Maläyer
Boründjerd
Aräk

LEBANON
Bayrüt (Beirut)
Şaydä
Qurnat as-Sawdä 3083
Zahlón
An-Nabk
Düma
Mount Hermon 2814
DIMASHQ (DAMASCUS)
Yabrüd
As-Suwaydä'
Dar'ä
SYRIAN DESERT
Ar-Rutbah
Ar-Ramädi
Haditha
Ba'qübah
Mandali
BAGHDAD
Khorramäbäd
Do Rüd
Golpäyegän
Bäd
Käshän
Qom

Hefa (Haifa)
Netanya
TEL AVIV-YAFO
ISRAEL
Ghazzah
El-'Arish
Nazerat
Teverya
Irbid
Nablus
Az-Zarqä'
Amman
JORDAN
Karbalä'
An-Najaf
An-Nu'mäniyah
Al-Hillah
Al-Küfah
Ad-Diwäniyah
Al-Kut
Al-'Amärah
Qal'at Säliḥ
Dezfül
Oshtorän Küh 4331
Shüshtar
Ahvaz
Masjed-e Soleymän
Qomsheh
ESFAHAN
Najafäbäd

El-Mansüra
Bür Sa'id (Port Said)
Tanta
Zagazig
Ismailia
Qanä el-Suweis (Suez Canal)
Yerushalayim (Jerusalem)
Be'ér Sheva'
Dead Sea
Ma'än
AL-BATRÄ' (PETRA)
Ar-Rumaythah
As-Samäwah
An-Näşiriyah
An-Nu'mäniyah
Haft Gel
Äghä Järi
Rämhormoz
Do Gonbadän
Gachsärän
Behbahän

EL-QAHIRA (CAIRO)
EL-GIZA
El-Suweis (Suez)
Beni Suef
SINAI
Abü Zenima
Gebel Katherina 2642
Elat
Jabal Ramm 1754
Aqabah
Al-Bi'r
Al-Jawf
Badanah
AL-HARRAH
Al-Harrah
Ad-Duwayd
Rafhä'
Al-Hajarah
An-Nu' mäniyah
Al-Basrah
Khorramshahr
Äbädän
KUWAIT
AL-KUWAYT (KUWAIT)
Al-Jahrah
Mînä' al-Ahmadi
Bandar-e Khomeyni
Bandar-e Deylam
Marv Dasht
SHIRÄZ
Käzerün

EGYPT
Jamsah
Gebel Shâyib el-Banat 2187
Hurghada
Al-Muwaylih
Tabük
Ash-Sharmah
Jabal al-Lawz 2403
Taymä'
AN-NAFÜD
SAUDI
Al-Jubayl
Al-Qatif
Ad-Dammäm
Az-Zahrän
BAHRAIN
Al-Muharraq
Al-Manamah (Manama)
QATAR
Bandar-e Büshehr
Firüzäbäd
Kangän

RED SEA
Safäga
Quseir
AL-HIJAZ
Al-Wajh
Al-'Ulä
Al-Ghazälah
Hä'il
Fayd
NAJD
Buraydah
'Unayzah
Al-Majma' ah
Ash-Shumlul
AD-DAHNÄ'
'Ayn Där
Buqayq
Al-Mubarraz
Al-Hufüf
Dukhän
Qurayn Abä al-Bawl 105
Musay' id

Gebel Hamätäh 1977
Räs Banäs
Umm Lajj
Yanbu' al-Bahr
Al-Madinah (Medina)
Abü Rubayq
Tropic of Cancer
ARABIA
Afif
Mahd adh-Dhahab
Al-Quway' iyah
Shaqrä'
AR-RIYÄD (RIYADH)
Nafi
Harad
As-Sulaymäniyah
Ad-Dawhah (Doha)

Halä'ib
Ra's al-Hadäribah
Gebel Hamätäh
Jabal Asoteriba 2217
Ra's al-Hadäribah
Al-Qadimah
Al-Muwayh
Zalim
Layla'
Yabrin
SUDAN
Jiddah
Räbigh
Administrative Boundary

0 100 200 300 400   600   800   1000 km
0 100   200   400   600 miles

East of Greenwich

Scale 1 : 10 000 000
Lambert Conformal Conic Projection

Scale 1 : 5 000 000

Lambert Conformal Conic Projection

In November 1983 Turkish Cypriots unilaterally declared their independence as the Turkish Republic of Northern Cyprus. A United Nations buffer zone now runs across the island.

Area occupied by Israel since June 1967
(A) Golan Heights: occupied by Israel
(B) West Bank: parts occupied by Israel

CASPIAN SEA

RUSSIA

KARAČAEVO-ČERKESIJA
Soči
Adler
Gagra
Gudauta
Suhumi
Očamčira
Gali
Tkvarčeli
Zugdidi
gora Psiš 3789
gora El'brus 5642
KABARDINO-BALKARIJA
Nal'čik
Terek
Beslan
Nazran'
INGUŠETIJA
ČEČNJA
Alagir
Vladikavkaz
SEVERNAJA OSETIJA
gora Šahara 5068
pereval Mamisonskij 2829
gora Kazbek 5047
gora Tebulosmta 4492
Itum-Kale
Botlih
Bujnaksk
Mahačkala
Kaspijsk
Izberbaš
Levaši
Sergokala
Gunib
Bežta
Vači
Mädžalis
Derbent
DAGESTAN
-28
-788

GEORGIA
Senaki
Poti
Ozurgeti
Samtredia
Kutaisi
Zestafoni
Čiatura
Boržomi
Gori
Kaspi
Chinvali
Džava
Dušeti
Telavi
Kvareli
Zaqatala
Rutul
Usuhžaur'
Quba
Xaçmaz
Yalama
Kasumkent
Qonaqkänd

Batumi
Hopa
Pazar
Rize
Artvin
Posof
Ahalcihe
Bakuriani
Ahalkalaki
Bolnisi
Dmanisi
Tbilisi
Rustavi
Calka
Dedoplis Ckaro
Zemo-Kedi
Gürdžaani
Şäki
Oğuz
Bazardüzü dağ 4480
Siyäzän
Ismayıllı
Altıağac
İsmayıllı
Märäzä
Şamaxı
Maştağa
Sumqayıt
BAKI (BAKU)
Suiti burnu

Trabzon
Akçaabat
Of
Maçka
Gümüşhane
Bayburt
Ispir
Yusufeli
Ardahan
Çıldır
Çıldır Gölü
Arpaçay
Göle
Gümri
Vanadzor
Artik
Aragats Lerr 4090
Ashtarak
Sevan
Sevana Lich
Martuni
Kamo
ARMENIA
Yerevan
Artashat
Ararat
Gäncä
Şämkir
Mingäçevir
Mingäçevir su anbarı
Göyçay
Ucar
Kürdämir
Bärdä
Tärtär
Ağdam
Xankändi
Füzuli
Naxçıvan
AZER.
AZERBAIJAN
Sabirabad
İmişli
Saatlı
Äli Bayramlı
Salyan
Neftçala
Biläsuvar
Qazımämmäd

DOĞU KARADENİZ DAĞLARI
KEŞİŞ DAĞLARI
Kaçkar Dağı 3932
Mescit Tepe 3230
ALLAHÜEKBER DAĞLARI
Kars
Narman
Sarıkamış
Kağızman
Iğdır
Ağrı Dağı (Mount Ararat) 5137
Ararat
Vike
Sürür
Mäkü
Qazangöldağ 3829
Culfa
Mehgri
Bälän Şäfar 'Ali
Cäbrayıl
Garmi
Mišali
Yardımlı
Länkäran
Astara
Namin

Refahiye
Erzincan
Kemah
Tercan
Çat
Tekman
Erzurum
Aşkale
Kop Geçidi 2430
Pasinler
Horasan
Ağrı
Tutak
Doğubayazıt
Tendürek Dağı 3533
Khvoy
Marand
Ahar
Meshgin Shahr
Sabalan 4814
Sofian
Sarab
Ardabil
Haviq
Astärä
KÜHHÄ-YE TAVÄLEŞ

MUNZUR DAĞLARI
Ovacik
Tunceli
Nazimiye
Kiği
Karlıova
BİNGÖL DAĞLARI
Hınıs
Bulanık
Malazgirt
Erciş
Muradiye
Zürabad
Qotur
Salmas
Oskü
Tabrīz
Kūh-e Sahand 3712
Azär Shahr
Marägheh
Miäneh
Zanjan
Keban Baraji
Elazığ
Palu
Maden
Genç
Muş
Tatvan
Süphan Dağı 4058
Ahlat
Van Gölü 1646
Van
Gevaş
Gürpınar
Daryächeh-ye Orümiyeh 1275
Orümiyeh
Ajab Shir
Benäb
Malek Kandi
Miändoab
Khalkhäl
Bandar-e Anzali
Fowman
Rasht
Qezel Owzan

Hankendi
Sivrice
Ergani
Lice
Hazro
Silvan
HACRES DAĞLARI
Bitlis
Bafkale
Ǧilo Dağı 4168
Salmäs
Naqadeh
Mahäbäd
Piran Shahr
Sardasht
Saqqez
Bükän
Takäb
Saʼidiyeh

Malatya
Diyarbakır
Bismil
Çınar
Karaca Dağ 1957
Savur
Kurtalan
Siirt
Pervari
Çatak
Hakkâri
Eruh
Findik
Şırnak
Zakho
Çukurca
Uromiyeh
Silvänen
3607
Ränyah
Rawändoz
Aqrah
Divandarreh
Bijär
Hoseynäbäd
Razan
Hamadän
Bahär
Asadäbäd
Kangävar
Tüysärkän
Malayer

Adıyaman
Hilvan
Bozova
Şanlıurfa
Sürüç
Akçakale
Viranşehir
Kızıltepe
Derik
Mardin
Midyat
İdil
Cizre
Nusaybin
Al-Qamishli
'Aamüdah
Al-Amädiyah
Dahük
Tall Küjik
Ra's al-'Ayn
Tall Tamir
Al-Hasakah
Ash-Shaddädah
JABAL SINJÄR
Şinjär
Tall 'Afar
NÎNAWÄ (NINEVEH)
Al-Mawsil (Mosul)
Irbil
Altun Kupri
Karkük
As-Sulaymäniyah
Halabjah
Päveh
Sırwän
Sanandaj
Qorveh
Kabüdarähang
Oorveh
Bahär

JABAL 'ABD AL-'AZIZ
Ar-Raqqah
Suwaydah
As-Suwär
Dayr az-Zawr
Al-Mayädin
Abū Kamāl
JABAL BISHRI
Al-Hadr
Ash-Sharqät
Täwüq
Tuz
Kifri
Tikrit
Samarrä'
Kirkük
Khänaqin
Qasr-e Shirin
Gilän-e Gharb
Eslämäbäd
Sümär
Kermänshäh (Bakhtaran)
Harsin
Nahävand
Oshtorinän
Boruljerd
Khorramäbäd
ILÄM
KÜHHÄ-YE ZAGROS
KABIR KÜH

SYRIA
Buhayrat ath-Tharthär
Sabkhat Albü Gharz
Wädi Hawran
Khän al-Baghdädi
Hit
Euphrates (Al-Furät)
Balad
Al-Khäls
Al-Mqdädiyah
Mandali
Ba'qübah
BAGHDÄD
Ar-Ramädi
Al-Fallüjah
Buchayrat al-Habbäniyah
Mehrän
Äbdänän
Dehloran
Andimeshk
Dezfül
Shüsh
Gatvand

SYRIAN DESERT
'Akäshät
Al-Qä'im
'Änah
Jabal 'Unayzah 940
Al-Hamäd
Ar-Rutbah
Wädi al-Ghudäf
An Nukhayb
Wädi al-Ubayyid
Bahr al-Milh
Shithäthah
An-Najaf
Al-Küfah
Al-Kifl
Al-Hindiyah
Al-Hillah
Karbalä'
Al-Musayyib
 Ad-Dīwäniyah
Al-Hayy
Al-Küt
Shaykh Sa'd
Qal'at Sälih
Al-'Amärah
Bostan
Süsangerd
Ahväz
Hüzgän

SAUDI ARABIA
Al-Jalamid
Mirah
An Nukhayb
Ash-Shinäfiyah
Ash-Shämiyah
Qal' at Sukkar
As-Samäwah
Ar-Rumaythah
An-Näsiriyah
Ash-Shatrah
Al-Halfäyah
Al-Qurnah
IRAQ
MESOPOTAMIA
Tigris (Dijlah)
Euphrates
Hawr al-Hammär

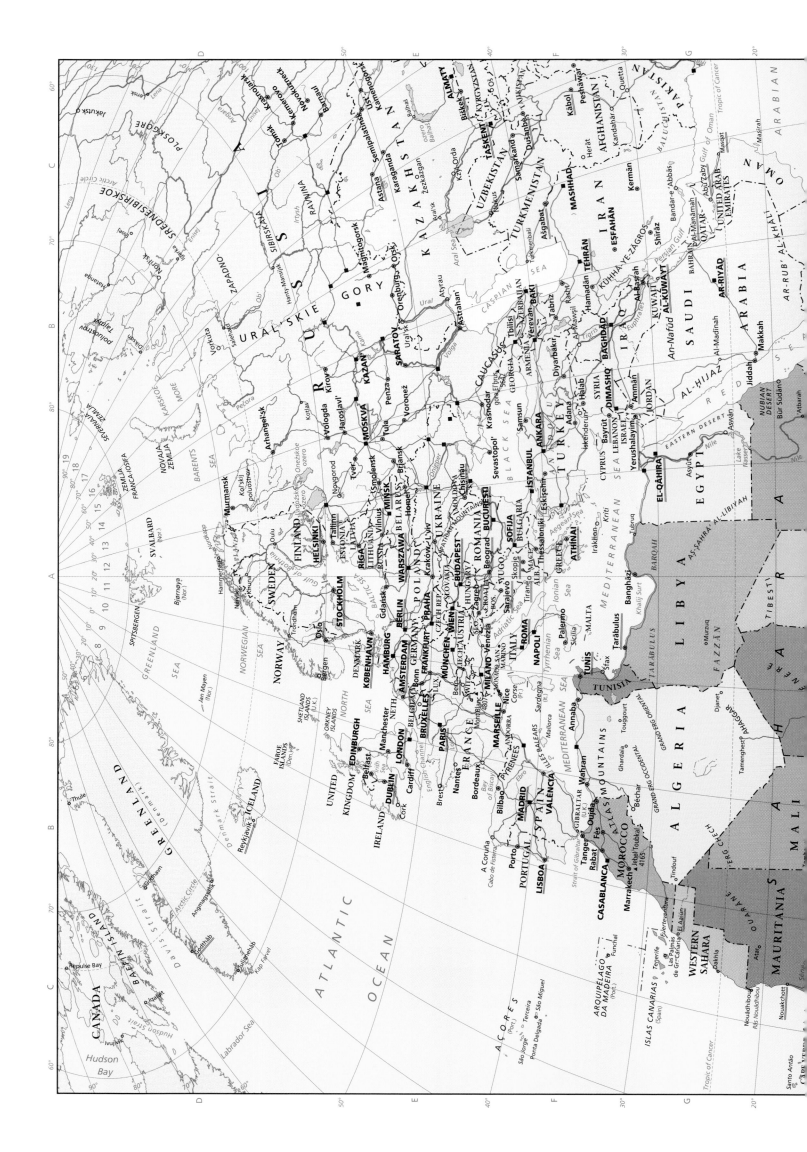

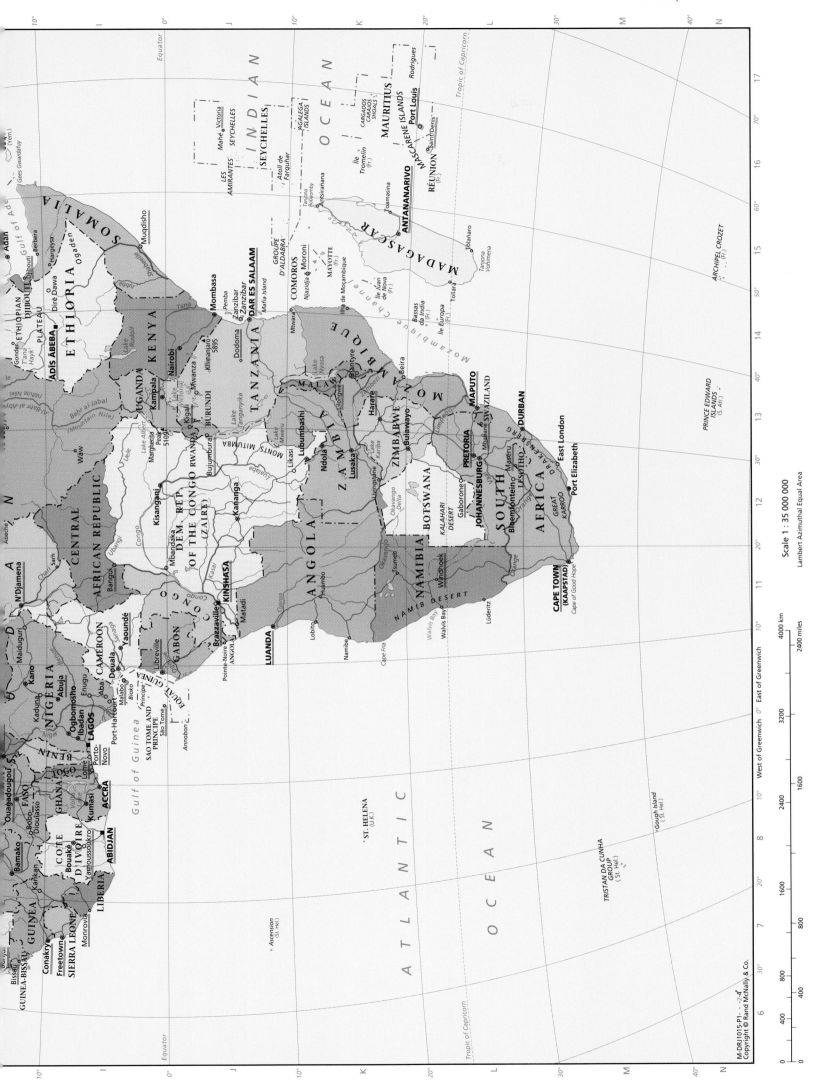

Scale 1 : 35 000 000

Lambert Azimuthal Equal Area

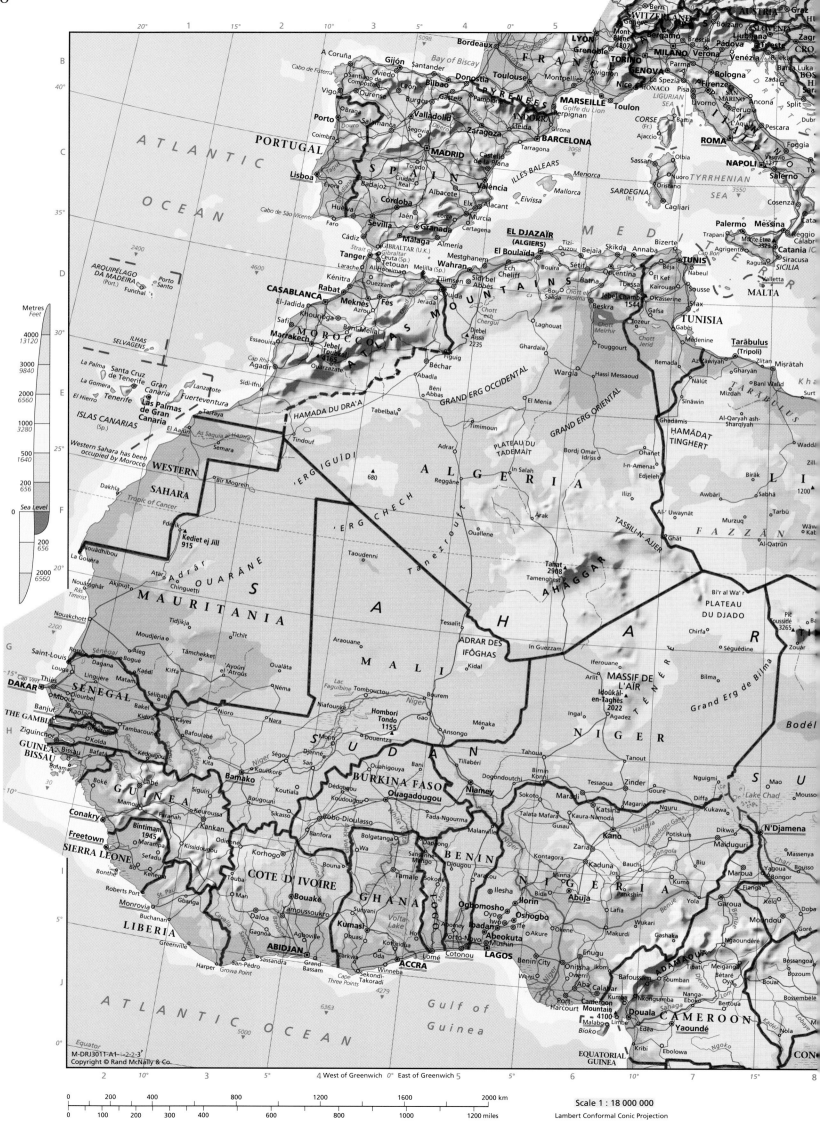

ATLANTIC

OCEAN

PORTUGAL

SPAIN

Lisboa

MADRID

BARCELONA

ILLES BALEARS

CASABLANCA

Rabat

MOROCCO

Marrakech

Agadir

WESTERN

SAHARA

ISLAS CANARIAS
(Sp.)

Las Palmas
de Gran
Canaria

ARQUIPÉLAGO
DA MADEIRA
(Port.)

ILHAS
SELVAGENS

Western Sahara has been
occupied by Morocco

Tropic of Cancer

MAURITANIA

Nouakchott

DAKAR

SENEGAL

THE GAMBIA

GUINEA-
BISSAU

GUINEA

Conakry

Freetown

SIERRA LEONE

LIBERIA

Monrovia

COTE D'IVOIRE

GHANA

ABIDJAN

ACCRA

MALI

SUDAN

BURKINA FASO

Ouagadougou

Bamako

ALGERIA

SAHARA

GRAND ERG OCCIDENTAL

GRAND ERG ORIENTAL

EL DJAZAÏR
(ALGIERS)

Wahran

ATLAS

MOUNTAINS

TUNIS

TUNISIA

Tarābulus
(Tripoli)

NIGER

NIGERIA

Abuja

LAGOS

Lagos

BENIN

Porto-Novo

Cotonou

CAMEROON

Yaoundé

Douala

Malabo

EQUATORIAL
GUINEA

N'Djamena

Lake Chad

Gulf of
Guinea

ATLANTIC OCEAN

Equator

M-DRJ301T-A1-1-2-2-3
Copyright © Rand McNally & Co.

Metres
Feet

4000
13120

3000
9840

2000
6560

1000
3280

500
1640

200
656

Sea Level

0

200
656

2000
6560

West of Greenwich   East of Greenwich

0   200   400   800   1200   1600   2000 km

0   100 200 300 400   600   800   1000   1200 miles

Scale 1 : 18 000 000

Lambert Conformal Conic Projection

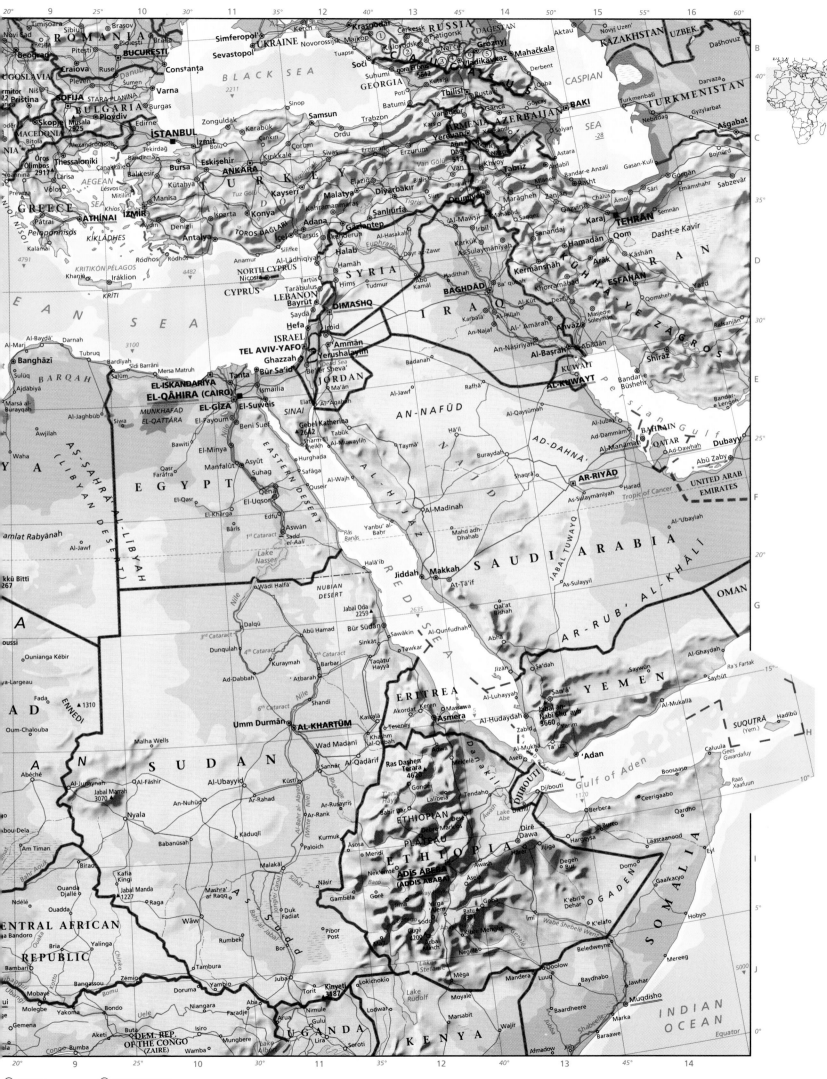

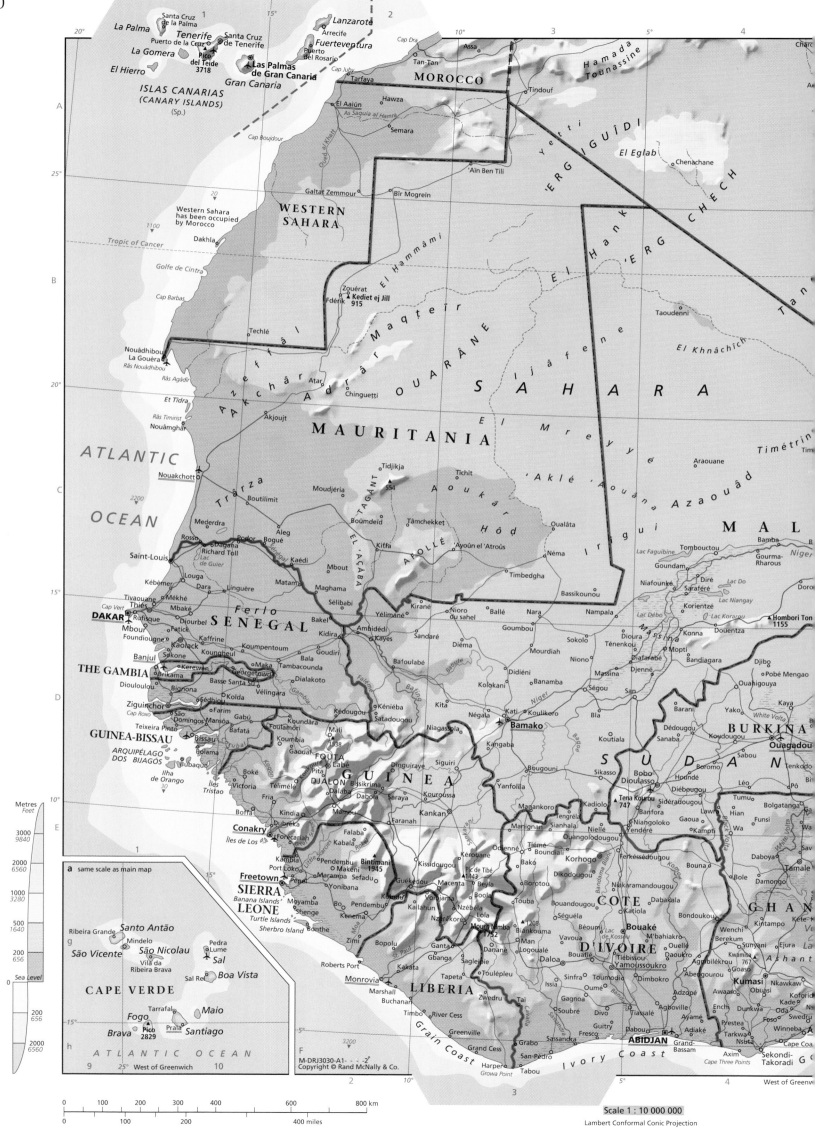

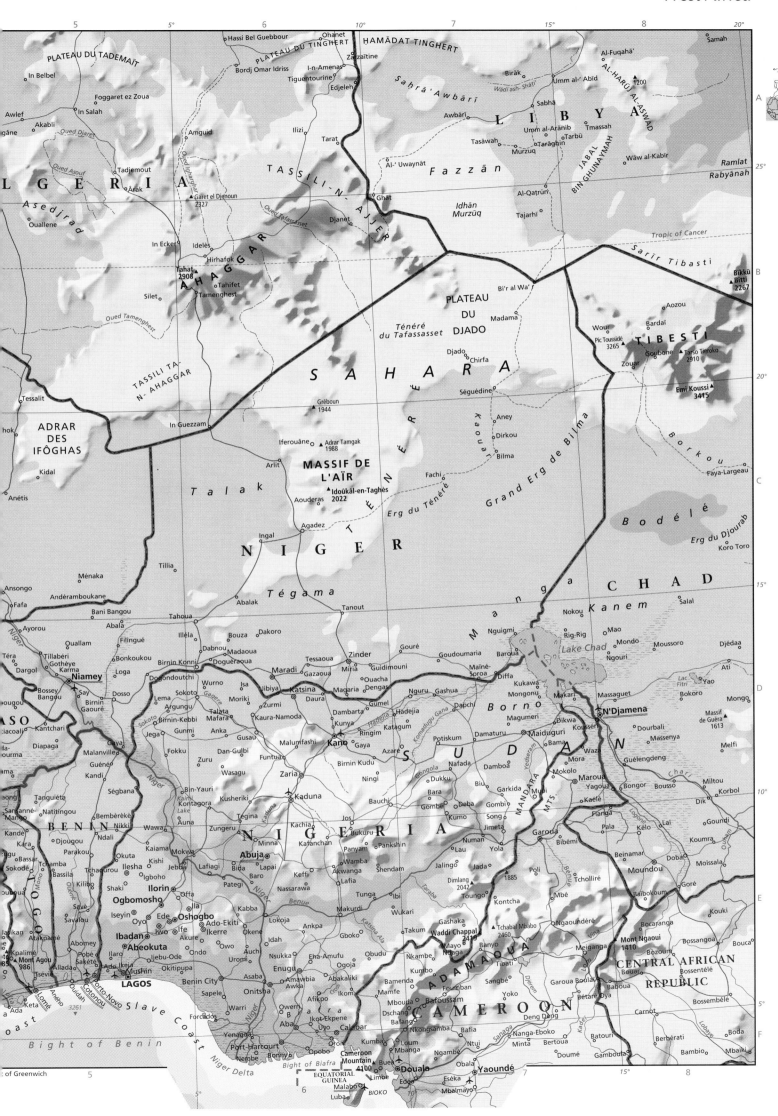

Scale 1 : 18 000 000

Lambert Conformal Conic Projection

D-589200-7A-DR1-1°
Copyright © Rand McNally & Co.

ETHIOPIA

SOMALIA

Kibre Mengist
Negēlē
Mēga
oyale
rsabit
Ilmi
K'elafo
Doolow
Beledweyne
Mandera
Luuq
Baydhabo
Baardheere
Jilib
Garissa
Kismaayo
Jamaame
Baraawe
Marka
Muqdisho
Jawhar
Mereeg
Hobyo
Gaalkacyo

YA
Mado Gashi
(Kenya)
Afmadow
Wajir
Buur Gaabo
Garsen
Lamu
Malindi
Mombasa
Chake Chake
Pemba
Zanzibar
Zanzibar
DAR ES SALAAM
Mafia Island
Kilindoni
Kilwa Kivinje
Lindi
Palma
Mocímboa
da Praia
Masasi
Pemba
Nacala-a-Velha
Ilha de
Moçambique
Angoche
Moma
Namapa
Lhrio
Mogincual

Equator

SEYCHELLES
Praslin
Victoria
Mahé
LES
Poivre
Atoll
AMIRANTES
Île
Plate
Alphonse
Coëtivy

INDIAN

OCEAN

SEYCHELLES

GROUPE
D'ALDABRA
ATOLL DE
COSMOLEDO
Île au Cerf
Atoll de
Farquhar

AGALEGA
ISLANDS

COMOROS
Njazidja
Moroni
Nzwani
Mwali
Mutsamudu
Dzaoudzi
MAYOTTE
(Fr.)
ARCHIPEL DES COMORES

ÎLES GLORIEUSES
(Fr.)
Tanjona
Bobaomby
Antsirañana
Ambilobe
Ambanja
Maromokotro
2876
Analalava
Sambava
Bealanana
Antalaha
Antsohihy
Maroantsetra
Mahajanga
Mananara Avaratra
Île Tromelin
(Fr.)
Mampikony

Île Juan
de Nova
(Fr.)
Besalampy
Soalala
Maevatanana
Tsaratanana
Nosy
Sainte Marie
CARGADOS
CARAJOS
SHOALS
Morafenobe
Ambatondrazaka
Maintirano
MADAGASCAR
Toamasina
Tsiroanomandidy
ANTANANARIVO
MAURITIUS
Miandrivazo
Ambatolampy
Vatomandry
Morondava
Antsirabe
Mahanoro
assas da India
(Fr.)
Ambositra
MA S C A R E N E   I S L A N D S
Rodrigues
Manja
Mandabe
Ambohimahasoa
Port Louis
Île Europa
(Fr.)
Morombe
Fianarantsoa
Mananjary
Saint-Denis
Mauritius
Ankazoabo
Ihosy
Ambalavao
Saint-Pierre
RÉUNION
(Fr.)
Manakara
Toliara
Farafangana
Bekily
Betroka
Tropic of Capricorn
Ampanihy
Tôlañaro
Tsiombe
Ambovombe
Tanjona
Vohimena

Mombasa
Zanzibar
DAR ES SALAAM
ANTANANARIVO
Port Louis

5340
4406
6402
5300
4300
4200

Mozambique Channel

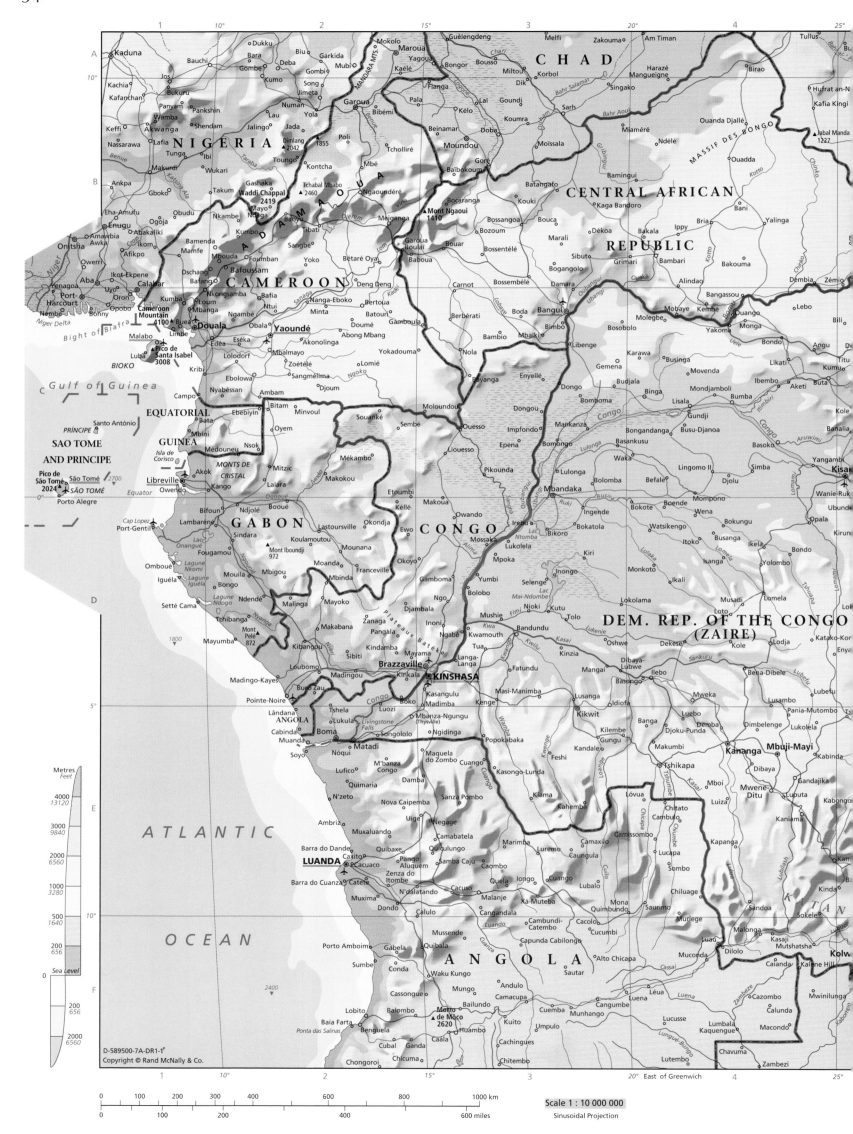

ATLANTIC

OCEAN

Metres	Feet
4000	13120
3000	9840
2000	6560
1000	3280
500	1640
200	656
0	Sea Level
200	656
2000	6560

D-589500-7A-DR1-1"
Copyright © Rand McNally & Co.

| 0 | 100 | 200 | 300 | 400 | 600 | 800 | 1000 km |

| 0 | 100 | 200 | 400 | 600 miles |

Scale 1 : 10 000 000
Sinusoidal Projection

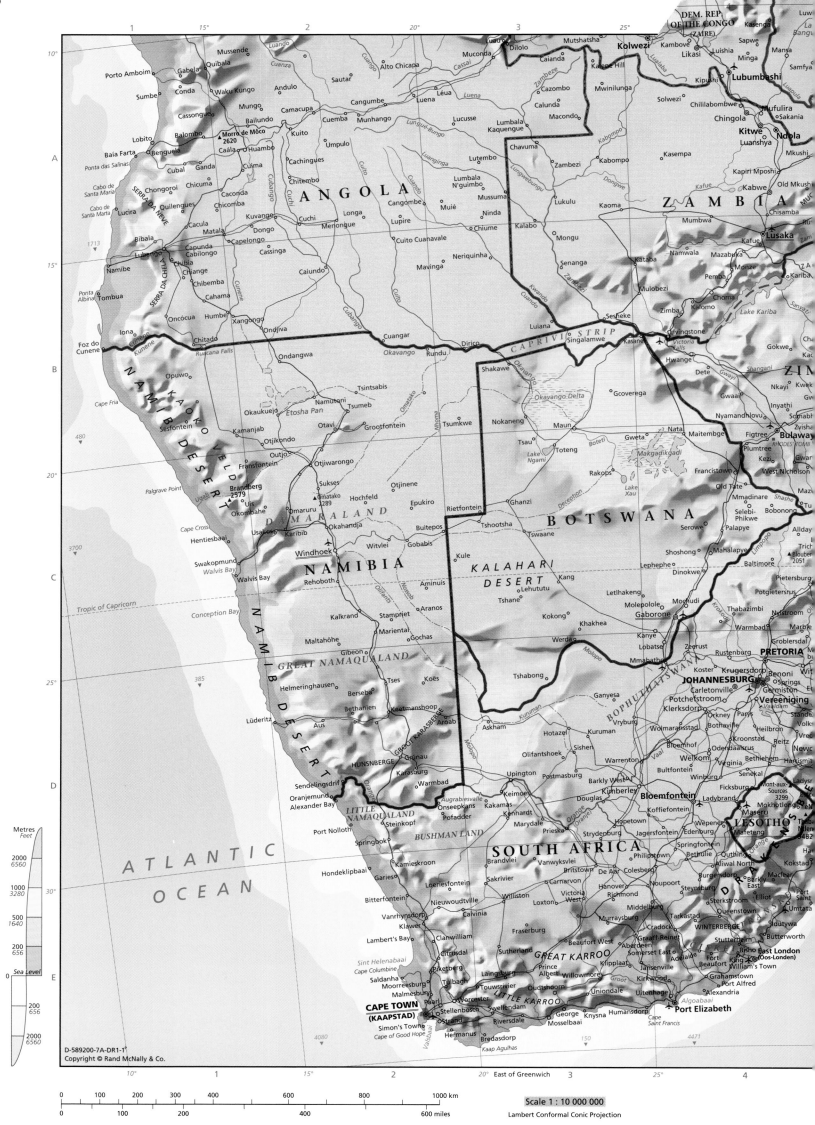

ANGOLA

ZAMBIA

NAMIBIA

BOTSWANA

SOUTH AFRICA

LESOTHO

ATLANTIC OCEAN

NAMIB DESERT

KALAHARI DESERT

KAOKOVELD

DAMARALAND

GREAT NAMAQUALAND

GROOT KARASBERGE

BOPHUTHATSWANA

LITTLE NAMAQUALAND

BUSHMAN LAND

GREAT KARROO

LITTLE KARROO

DRAKENSBERGE

WINTERBERGE

CAPRIVI STRIP

DEM. REP. OF THE CONGO (ZAIRE)

ZIMBABWE

Tropic of Capricorn

Metres
Feet

2000
6560

1000
3280

500
1640

200
656

0 Sea Level

200
656

2000
6560

D-589200-7A-DR1-1
Copyright © Rand McNally & Co.

Scale 1 : 10 000 000

Lambert Conformal Conic Projection

East of Greenwich

0   100   200   300   400   600   800   1000 km

0   100   200   400   600 miles

TANZANIA

Kasama · Isoka · Chilumba · Manda · Lindi
Chinsali · NYIKA PLATEAU 2608 · Nyamtumbo · Nachingwea · Mtama
Livingstonia · Mbinga · Songea · Masasi · Newala · Mtwara
Rumphi · Mzuzu · Mbamba Bay · Tunduru · Mikindani
Mpika · Nkhata Bay · Mzimba 474 · Chamba · Ruvuma · Cabo Delgado · Palma
Mpulungu · Lake Nyasa (Lake Malawi) · Olivença · Diaca · Quiterajo · Mucojo
Chipata · MALAWI · Cóbuè · Mecula · Nantulo · Macomia · Quissanga
Katete · Mchinji · Metangula · Márrupa · Montepuez · Ancuabe · Pemba
Lundazi · Salima · Catur · Belém · Maúa · Balama
Lilongwe · Liwonde · Lúrio · Namapa · Memba
Zâmbue · Fíngoè · Kazula · Zomba · SERRA NAMULI · Malema · Ribauè · Nacala-a-Velha · Nacala
Furancungo · Ulóngue · Blantyre · Sapitwa 3002 · Milange · Alto Molócuè · Mecubúri · Monapo · Ilha do Moçambique
ARPMENT · Moatize · Thyolo · Chiromo · Namarrói · Errego · Nametil · Lumbo
MAVURADONHA MTS · Chioco · Tete · Tambara · Dôa · Chiperone 2054 · Lugela · Mulevala · Mogincual
Shamva · Mazowe · Changara · Chemba · Morrumbala · Mocuba · Mocubela · Larde
Bindura · Mutoko · Manica · Vila Fontes · Namacurra · Pebane · Angoche
Murewa · MOZAMBIQUE · Inhaminga · Mopeia · Quelimane · Moma
Rusape · Serra da Gorongosa 1856 · Marromeu · Chinde
Chivhu · Manica · Monte Binga 2437 · Dondo · Beira
Chipinge · Chibabava · Sofala
Espungabera · Nova Mambone
Mwenezi · Massangena · Inhassoro · Ilha do Bazaruto
Mabote · Vilankulo
Malvèrnia · Mapinhane
Chigubo · Funhalouro · Massinga
Mabalane · Morrumbene · Ponta da Barra
Phalaborwa · Chibuto · Panda · Maxixe · Inhambane
Chókwè · Xinavane · Quissico · Inharrime
Macia · Chidenguele
Moamba · Xai-Xai
Komatipoort · Baia de Maputo
Nelspruit · MAPUTO · Ilha da Inhaca
Barberton · Bela Vista
SWAZILAND · Zitundo
Mbabane · Manzini
Lavumisa
Piet Retief
Vryheid · Nongoma · Lake Saint Lucia
Ulundi · Mtubatuba · Cape Saint Lucia 1306
Empangeni
Richards Bay
...maritzburg · Pinetown
DURBAN
Umzinto
Port Shepstone

ZIMBABWE · Inyangani 2592 · Mutare

COMOROS
Njazidja · Moroni · Kartala 2361 · ÎLES GLORIEUSES (Fr.)
Mwali · Nzwani · Mutsamudu · ATOLL DE COSMOLEDO (Sey.)
Fomboni · Mamoudzou
MAYOTTE (Fr.)
ARCHIPEL DES COMORES

MADAGASCAR
Antsiranana · Tanjona Bobaomby
Nosy Be · Antsohihy · Ambilobe · Iharana
Andoany · Ambanja · Antalaha
Maromokotro 2876 · TSARATANANA · Sambava
Analalava · Maromandia · Bealanana · Andapa
Mahajanga · Soalala · Marovoay · Tsaratanana · Mandritsara · Maroantsetra
Besalampy · Madirovalo · Mampikony · Mananara Avaratra · Cap Masoala
Île Juan de Nova (Fr.) · Bekodoka · Mahabe · Andriamena · Ambodifototra
Tamboraho · Morafenobe · Kandreho · Andilamena · Nosy Sainte Marie
Maintirano · Antsalova · Ankazobe · Farihy Alaotra · Fenoarivo Atsinanana
Nosy Barren · Ankavandra · Tsiroanomandidy · Ambatondrazaka
Bekopaka · Arivonimamo · ANTANANARIVO · Toamasina
Belo Tsiribihina · Miandrivazo · Soavinandriana · Ampasimanolotra
Morondava · Mahabo · Manjakandriana · Moramanga
Belo sur Mer · Malaimbandy · Ambatofinandrahana · Ambatolampy · Vatomandry
Andranopasy · Mandabe · Tsiafajavona 2643 · Betafo · Antsirabe
Manja · Ambositra · Mahanoro
Morombe · Ambohimahasoa · Nosy-Varika
Befandriana Atsimo · Fianarantsoa · Ifanadiana
Ankazoabo · Ranohira · Ambalavao · Manakara
Manombo Atsimo · Sakaraha · Ihosy · Pic Boby 2658 · Ivohibe · Vohipeno
Bezaha · Betroka · Vondrozo · Farafangana
Toliara · Onilahy · Midongy Atsimo · Vangaindrano
Ejeda · Bekily · Beraketa · Manantenina
Itampolo · Ampanihy · Amboasary · Androka
Tsiombe · Ambovombe · Tôlañaro
Tanjona Vohimena

INDIAN OCEAN

Mozambique Channel

Bassas da India (Fr.)
Île Europa (Fr.)

MASCARENE ISLANDS

INDIAN OCEAN
Port Louis · MAURITIUS
Piton de la Petite Rivière Noire 828 · Curepipe · Mahébourg
Saint-Denis
Saint-Paul · Piton des Neiges 3070
Saint-Pierre · RÉUNION (Fr.)
MASCARENE ISLANDS
55° East of Greenwich

INDIAN OCEAN
SEYCHELLES
Saint Pierre
GROUP D'ALDABRA · ATOLL DE COSMOLEDO
Astove · ATOLL DE FARQUHAR · AGALEGA ISLANDS (Maur.)
50° East of Greenwich

SEYCHELLES
Praslin · La Digue
Silhouette · Victoria · Mahé
Poivre Atoll · Desroches · Île Plate
LES AMIRANTES
Alphonse
Coëtivy Island

58

Scale 1 : 35 000 000
Lambert Azimuthal Equal Area Projection

| 0 | 400 | 800 | 1600 | 2400 | 3200 | 4000 km |

| 0 | 400 | 800 | 1600 | 2400 miles |

M-DRJ1018-P1- - -2-4°
Copyright © Rand McNally & Co.

170°   11   180°   12   170°   13   160°   14   150°   15   140°   16   130°   17

A

30°

MIDWAY
ISLANDS
(U.S.)

B

HAWAIIAN ISLANDS   Tropic of Cancer

Kauai
Oahu   Molokai
Honolulu   Maui   UNITED STATES
Mauna Kea 4205 ▲ Hilo
Ka Lae   HAWAII   20°

AKE ISLAND
(U.S.)

P   A   C   I   F   I   C   O   C   E   A   N

MARSHALL
ISLANDS   C

Bikar

ngelap

Maloelap   10°

Ailinglaplap   Majuro

Butaritari

AURU   Tarawa   KIRIBATI
Abemama   Kiritimati
Banaba   (Christmas Island)

KIRIBATI   Jarvis   D
Island
NESIA   PHOENIX ISLANDS   (U.S.)
Rawaki   P
OMON ISLANDS   O   Malden
Nui   L   Starbuck
TUVALU   Funafuti   TOKELAU   Y
Niulakita   (N.Z.)   N   Penrhyn   E

Santa Cruz Islands   E
SAMOA AMERICAN   Nassau Island   S   Vostok   Caroline   ÎLES
s Banks   WALLIS AND FUTUNA   SAMOA   NORTHERN COOK   I   Flint   MARQUISES
NEW   (Fr.)   SAMOA ISLANDS   ISLANDS   A
HEBRIDES   Îles Wallis   Saval'i Apia
spiritu   FIJI   Île Futuna   Upolu Tutuila   Suwarrow   FRENCH POLYNESIA
Santo   10°
Malakula   Vanua Levu   Pago Pago
Ambrym   COOK ISLANDS   ÎLES TUAMOTU   Îles du Désappointement
Éfaté   Viti   Suva   (N.Z.)
Port Vila   Levu   Koro   Maupihaa Anaa   Raraka
Erromango   Sea   Vava'u   NIUE   Palmerston
WELLE-   Lifou   (N.Z.)   SOUTHERN Aitutaki ARCHIPEL DE LA SOCIÉTÉ   Marutea
DONIE   Îles Loyauté   TONGA   COOK Manuae Tahiti
uméa   Tongatapu Nuku'alofa   ISLANDS Takutea Papeete
'Eua   Atiu
Îles Maria

NORFOLK ISLAND   Rarotonga   20°
(Austl.)
Kermadec   Tubuai   Îles Gambier
Islands
(N.Z.)   Tropic of Capricorn

PITCAIRN   Henderson Island
NEW   (U.K.)   G
North Cape
Auckland   Bay of
NORTH ISLAND   Plenty   East Cape
New Plymouth Mount Ruapehu 2797
Cape Egmont   Hawke Bay
Napier
Cape Farewell   **Wellington**
EALAND   P   A   C   I   F   I   C
UTH ISLAND   Cook Strait
Mount Cook ▲   **Christchurch**   30°
3754   Canterbury
Bight   Chatham
Dunedin   Islands
rt Island Invercargill   (N.Z.)
West Cape   O   C   E   A   N   H

Auckland Islands
(N.Z.)

Campbell Island
(N.Z.)   50°

0   East of Greenwich   11   180°   12   West of Greenwich 13   160°   14   150°   15   140°   16   130°   17   120°   18   110°

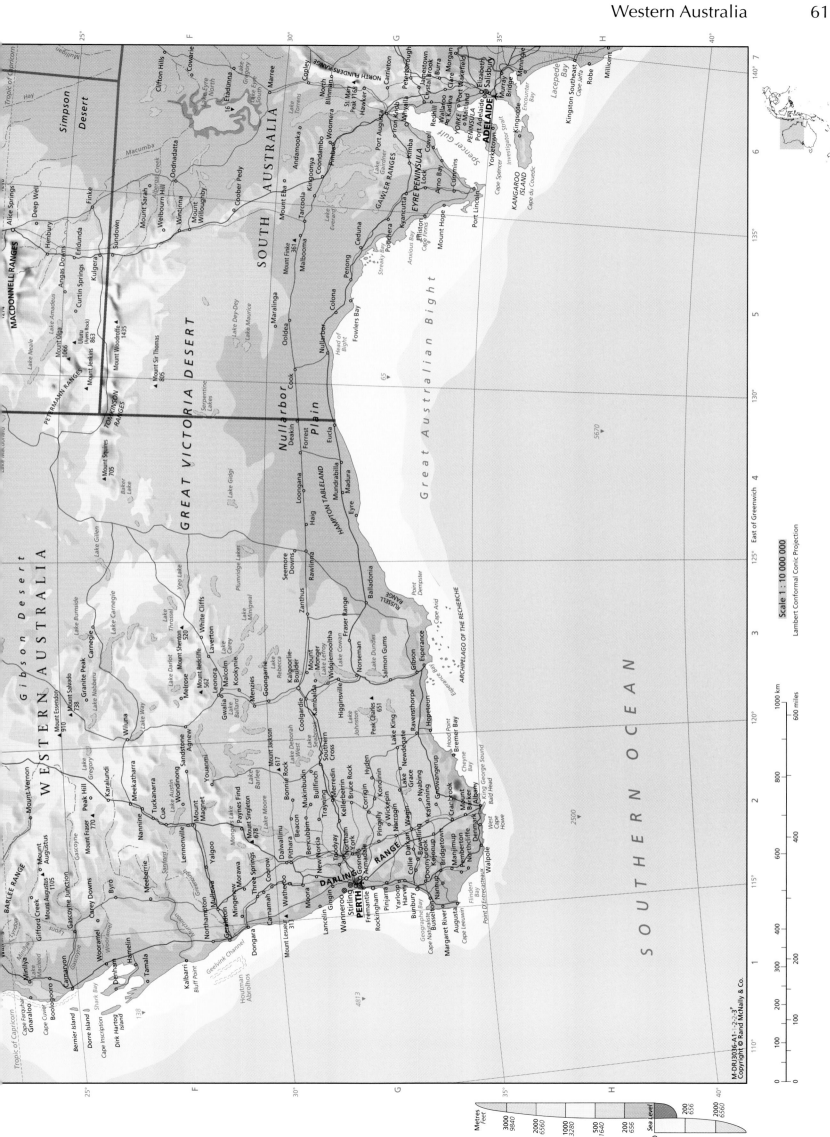

SOUTHERN OCEAN

Great Australian Bight

WESTERN AUSTRALIA

SOUTH AUSTRALIA

GREAT VICTORIA DESERT

Gibson Desert

Simpson Desert

MACDONNELL RANGES

PETERMANN RANGES

TOMKINSON RANGES

BARLEE RANGE

DARLING RANGE

STIRLING RANGE

RUSSELL RANGE

NORTH FLINDERS RANGE

GAWLER RANGES

EYRE PENINSULA

YORKE PENINSULA

KANGAROO ISLAND

ARCHIPELAGO OF THE RECHERCHE

Nullarbor Plain

HAMPTON TABLELAND

Tropic of Capricorn

Scale 1 : 10 000 000
Lambert Conformal Conic Projection

1000 km
600 miles

M-DR3036-A1-¹-2-2-3⁹
Copyright © Rand McNally & Co.

Metres Feet
3000 / 9840
2000 / 6560
1000 / 3280
500 / 1640
200 / 656
Sea Level
200 / 656
2000 / 6560

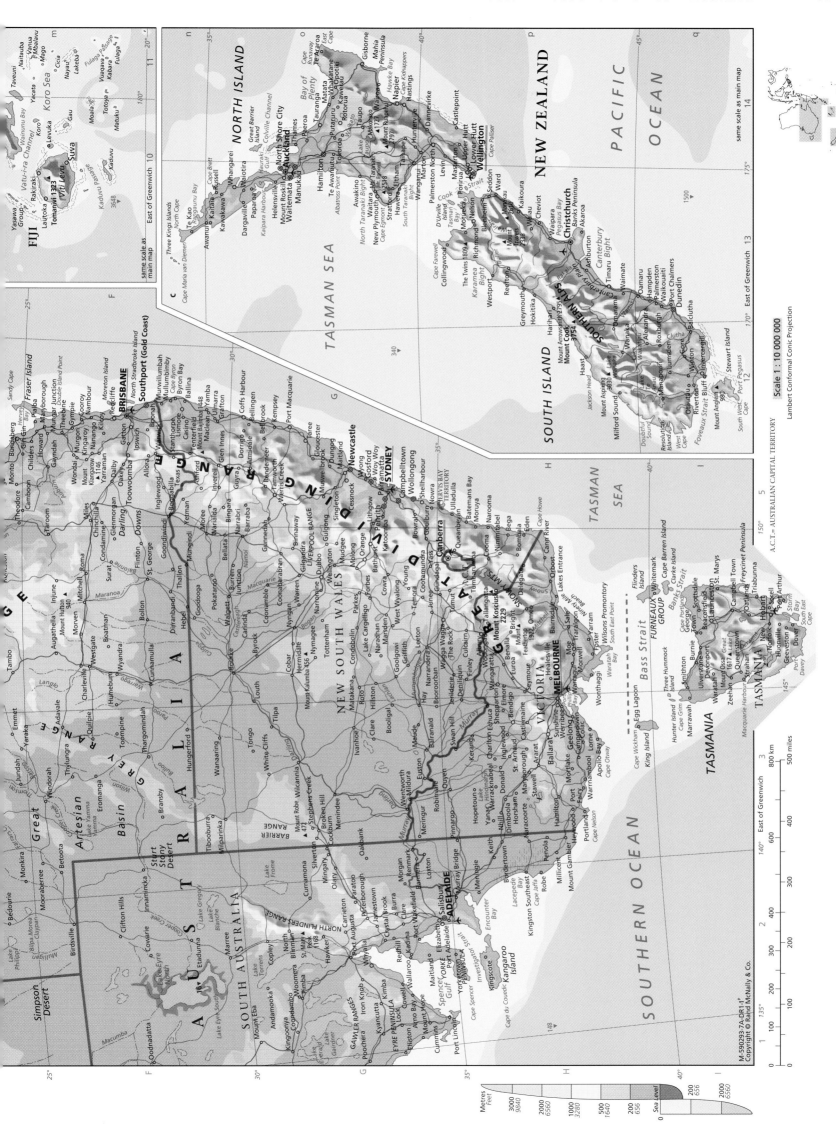

FIJI

Yasawa Group
Vanua Mbalavu
Tavueni
Natauba
Mago
Yacata
Nayau
Cicia
Koro Sea
Lakeba
Rakiraki
Vatu-i-ra Channel
Laitoka
Tomanivi 1323
Viti Levu
Suva
Levuka
Ovalau
Koro
Moala
Totoya
Matuku
Kaduvu
Vuaqava Passage
Fulaga Passage
Kabara
Fulaga
3648

East of Greenwich

same scale as main map

NORTH ISLAND

Three Kings Islands
Cape Maria van Diemen
Te Kao
North Cape
Te Paki
Cape Reinga
Te Araroa
Cape Runaway
East Cape
Awanui
Kaitaia
Cape Brett
Russell
Whangarei
Kawakawa
Dargaville
Paparoa
Helensville
Cape Colville
Coromandel Channel
Great Barrier Island
Little Barrier Island
Hauraki Gulf
Waihi
Tauranga
Whakatane
Matata
Opotiki
Gisborne
Mahia Peninsula
Hawke Bay
Napier
Hastings
North Shore City
Auckland
Manukau
Waitemata
Mount Roskill
Thames
Paeroa
Hamilton
Te Awamutu
Cambridge
Putaruru
Rotorua
Taupo
Lake Taupo
Mokai
Wairoa
Cape Kidnappers
Dannevirke
Kawerau
Ruapehu 2797
Taihape
New Plymouth
Waitara
Stratford
Mt. Taranaki 2518
Cape Egmont
Hawera
Eltham
Mount Ruapehu
Mokau
Waitomo
Raetihi
Ohakune
Wanganui
Marton
Palmerston North
Castlepoint
Feilding
Levin
Masterton
Foxton
Upper Hutt
Lower Hutt
Paraparaumu
Porirua
Wellington
Cook Strait
Cape Palliser
South Taranaki Bight
North Taranaki Bight
Albatross Point

NEW ZEALAND

TASMAN SEA

SOUTH ISLAND

Cape Farewell
D'Urville Island
Collingwood
Golden Bay
Motueka
Nelson
Richmond
Blenheim
Seddon
Ward
Kaikoura
Cheviot
Waipara
Amberley
Rangiora
Christchurch
Akaroa
Banks Peninsula
Pegasus Bay
Cook Strait
The Twins 1804
Karamea Bight
Karamea
Westport
Reefton
Murchison
Greymouth
Hokitika
Harihari
Mount Cook 3754
Mount Tasman 3498
Mount Aspiring 3030
Jackson Head
Haast
Arthur's Pass
Ashburton
Methven
Geraldine
Timaru
Temuka
Waimate
Oamaru
Hampden
Palmerston
Waikouaiti
Port Chalmers
Dunedin
SOUTHERN ALPS
Canterbury Plain
Canterbury Bight
Mount Arrowsmith 2795
Lake Tekapo
Lake Pukaki
Twizel
Lake Ohau
Lake Hawea
Wanaka
Lake Wanaka
Cromwell
Alexandra
Roxburgh
Clutha
Milford Sound
Te Anau
Lake Te Anau
Lake Manapouri
Manapouri
Doubtful Sound
Resolution Island
West Cape
Mossburn
Lumsden
Gore
Balclutha
Winton
Riverton
Invercargill
Bluff
Foveaux Strait
Port Pegasus
South West Cape
Stewart Island
Mount Anglem 980

PACIFIC OCEAN

1500

340

same scale as main map

Scale 1 : 10 000 000
Lambert Conformal Conic Projection

East of Greenwich

A.C.T. = AUSTRALIAN CAPITAL TERRITORY

Sandy Cape
Fraser Island
Hervey Bay
Bundaberg
Gin Gin
Childers
Howard
Maryborough
Pialba
Gympie
Tiaro
Mungar Junction
Kingaroy
Theebine
Cooroy
Nambour
Redcliffe
Moreton Island
Caboolture
Moreton Bay
BRISBANE
Ipswich
Southport (Gold Coast)
North Stradbroke Island
Beenleigh
Gatton
Toowoomba
Nanango
Murwillumbah
Murrumbimby
Kilcoy
Cape Byron
Byron Bay
Ballina
Lismore
Casino
Yamba
Maclean
Grafton
Tenterfield
Warwick
Stanthorpe
Glen Innes
Inglewood
Texas
Bang, Bebo
Mount Barney
Woodenbong
Tabulam
Coffs Harbour
Bellingen
Dorrigo
Armidale
Uralla
Walcha
Macksville
Nambucca Heads
Kempsey
Wauchope
Port Macquarie
Taree
Gloucester
Wingham
Forster
Bulahdelah
Nelson Bay
Newcastle
Maitland
Cessnock
Singleton
Muswellbrook
Scone
Murrurundi
Quirindi
Gunnedah
Tamworth
Manilla
Barraba
Bingara
Inverell
Moree
Narrabri
Wee Waa
Boggabri
Werris Creek
Coonabarabran
Gilgandra
Dubbo
Wellington
Mudgee
Gulgong
Lithgow
Bathurst
Orange
Katoomba
Penrith
Parramatta
SYDNEY
Wollongong
Campbelltown
Woy Woy
Gosford
Wyong

GREAT DIVIDING RANGE
LIVERPOOL RANGE

NEW SOUTH WALES

AUSTRALIA

Theodore
Cracow
Cameron
Taroom
Monto
Eidsvold
Mundubbera
Gayndah
Wondai
Murgon
Goomeri
Proston
Wandoan
Miles
Chinchilla
Dalby
Jandowae
Oakey
Pittsworth
Allora
Clifton
Millmerran
Goondiwindi
Moonie
Surat
St. George
Dirranbandi
Mungindi
Thallon
Boomi
Collarenebri
Walgett
Lightning Ridge
Brewarrina
Bourke
Byrock
Nyngan
Narromine
Trangie
Peak Hill
Parkes
Forbes
Condobolin
Cowra
Young
Grenfell
Temora
West Wyalong
Barmedman
Ardlethan
Ariah Park
Junee
Cootamundra
Wagga Wagga
Gundagai
Tumut
The Rock
Culcairn
Holbrook
Henty
Albury
Corowa
Jerilderie
Finley
Berrigan
Deniliquin
Tocumwal
Barooga
Mathoura
Moama
Echuca

Mount Hutton 940
Injune
Augathella
Mitchell
Roma
Morven
Muckadilla
Amby
Yuleba
Wallumbilla
Condamine

Tambo
Augathella
Blackall
Isisford
Charleville
Wyandra
Cunnamulla
Eulo
Hungerford
Wanaaring
Brindingabba
Bollon
Nebine
Angellala
Langlo

Quilpie
Eromanga
Thargomindah

GREY RANGE

Great Artesian Basin

Lake Yamma Yamma

Windorah
Jundah
Stonehenge

GREAT DIVIDING RANGE

QUEENSLAND

Mount Hutton

Bedourie
Birdsville
Betoota
Clifton Hills
Monkira
Mooraberree

Simpson Desert
Sturt Stony Desert

Cooper Creek
Lake Eyre North
Marree
Lake Eyre South
Etadunna
Dulkaninna
Muloorina
Innamincka

Lakes Philippi
Billa Moona
Clayton R.
Lake Gregory
Mulligan

Oodnadatta
Macumba

Lake Blanche
Lake Callabonna
Lake Frome

Copley
Leigh Creek
Beltana
Blinman
Hawker
Quorn
Wilpena
St. Mary Peak 1168
Orroroo
Peterborough
Jamestown
Crystal Brook
Port Pirie
Port Augusta
Whyalla
Iron Knob
Iron Baron
Kimba
Cowell
Cleve
Arno Bay
Port Neill
Tumby Bay
Port Lincoln
Cummins
Elliston
Lock
Cowell
Wudinna
Kyancutta
Minnipa
Poochera
Streaky Bay
Ceduna
Penong

SOUTH AUSTRALIA

NORTH FLINDERS RANGE

GAWLER RANGES
EYRE PENINSULA

Andamooka
Roxby Downs
Olympic Dam
Woomera
Pimba
Coober Pedy

SPENCER GULF
Spencer Gulf

Kingoonya
Tarcoola

Cowarie

Darling River
Culgoa
Birrie
Bokhara
Narran
Bogan
Castlereagh
Macquarie
Namoi
Gwydir
Barwon
Culgoa

Goodooga
Weilmoringle
Enngonia
Louth
Tilpa
Wilcannia
White Cliffs
Cobar
Nymagee
Hillston
Mount Hope
Roto
Ivanhoe
Booligal
Hay
Carrathool
Darlington Point
Griffith
Leeton
Narrandera
Coleambally
Jerilderie
Tooleybuc
Balranald
Euston
Robinvale
Wentworth
Mildura
Red Cliffs
Ouyen
Manangatang
Swan Hill
Kerang

Lake Cargelligo
Lake Brewster
Rankins Springs
Goolgowi

Tibooburra
Milparinka
Cameron Corner
Noccundra
Hungerford
Wanaaring
Bransby
Dowling
Tongo
Packsaddle
Broken Hill
Silverton
Menindee
Lake Menindee
Pooncarie
Ivanhoe

Olary
Mannahill
Yunta
Terowie
Peterborough
Burra
Morgan
Waikerie
Barmera
Berri
Renmark
Loxton
Karoonda
Lameroo
Pinnaroo
Tailem Bend
Murray Bridge
Mannum

BARRIER RANGE
Mount Robe 456
Mount Darling
Stephens Creek
Cockburn

Salisbury
Elizabeth
ADELAIDE
Port Adelaide

Wallaroo
Kadina
Moonta
Maitland
Ardrossan
Port Wakefield
Balaklava
Clare
Riverton
Gawler
Two Wells
Nuriootpa
Tanunda
Angaston
Kapunda
Freeling

YORKE PENINSULA
Edithburgh
Yorketown
Stansbury
Port Victoria

Investigator Strait
Cape Spencer

Kangaroo Island
Kingscote
Penneshaw
Cape Borda
Cape du Couedic

Encounter Bay
Victor Harbor
Goolwa
Port Elliot
Cape Jervis

The Coorong
Meningie
Tintinara
Keith
Bordertown
Naracoorte
Kingston Southeast
Lacepede Bay
Robe
Beachport
Millicent
Mount Gambier
Penola
Cape Jaffa

Lake Alexandrina
Lake Albert

VICTORIA

Mildura
Robinvale
Ouyen
Hopetoun
Birchip
Donald
Charlton
St. Arnaud
Stawell
Ararat
Horsham
Nhill
Dimboola
Warracknabeal
Jeparit
Rainbow
Yaapeet
Murtoa
Minyip
Beulah
Sea Lake
Wycheproof
Boort
Kerang
Cohuna
Echuca
Rochester
Elmore
Bendigo
Castlemaine
Maryborough
Clunes
Ballarat
Bacchus Marsh
Geelong
Queenscliff
Torquay
Anglesea
Lorne
Apollo Bay
Cape Otway
Colac
Camperdown
Terang
Mortlake
Warrnambool
Port Fairy
Portland
Heywood
Hamilton
Casterton
Coleraine
Cape Nelson
Port Campbell

Shepparton
Mooroopna
Tatura
Kyabram
Numurkah
Nathalia
Cobram
Yarrawonga
Benalla
Wangaratta
Beechworth
Myrtleford
Bright
Mount Buffalo
Wodonga
Rutherglen
Chiltern
Euroa
Seymour
Nagambie
Mansfield
Alexandra
Yea
Kilmore
Broadford
Healesville
Lilydale
Ringwood
Dandenong
MELBOURNE
Sunshine
Werribee
Frankston
Mornington
Port Phillip
Western Port
Phillip Island
French Island
Wonthaggi
Korumburra
Leongatha
Foster
Wilsons Promontory
Yarram
Traralgon
Morwell
Moe
Warragul
Drouin
Pakenham
Sale
Maffra
Bairnsdale
Orbost
Lakes Entrance
Ninety Mile Beach
Cann River
Nowa Nowa

MOUNT KOSCIUSKO MTS
Mount Kosciusko 2229
Mount Buller
SNOWY MTS
Corryong
Khancoban
Tumbarumba
Batlow
Adelong
Tumut
Talbingo
Cabramurra
Jindabyne
Dalgety
Berridale
Cooma
Nimmitabel
Bombala
Delegate
Cann River
Bemboka
Bega
Candelo
Eden

Canberra
AUSTRALIAN CAPITAL TERRITORY
Yass
Goulburn
Crookwell
Boorowa
Harden
Gunning
Queanbeyan
Cooma
Braidwood
Araluen
Bungendore
Captains Flat
Tarago
Bungonia
Moss Vale
Bowral
Mittagong
Berrima
Goulburn
Marulan
Nowra
Nowra
JERVIS BAY TERRITORY
Jervis Bay
Kiama
Shellharbour
Ulladulla
Milton
Batemans Bay
Moruya
Narooma
Bermagui
Cobargo
Merimbula
Tathra

Cape Howe

Mount River

TASMAN SEA

Bass Strait

FURNEAUX GROUP
Flinders Island
Cape Barren Island
Clarke Island
Whitemark
Lady Barron
Banks Strait
Swan Island

King Island
Currie
Grassy
Egg Lagoon
Cape Wickham

Three Hummock Island
Hunter Island
Cape Grim
Marrawah
Smithton
Stanley
Wynyard
Burnie
Ulverstone
Devonport
Latrobe
Sheffield
Deloraine
Westbury
Longford
Launceston
George Town
Beaconsfield
Beauty Point
Scottsdale
Bridport
St. Marys
St. Helens
Fingal
Avoca
Campbell Town
Ross
Oatlands
Bothwell
Hamilton
New Norfolk
Triabunna
Sorell
HOBART
Kingston
Huonville
Geeveston
Dover
Port Arthur
Nubeena
South East Cape
Strahan
Queenstown
Zeehan
Rosebery
Waratah
Tullah
Lake St. Clair
Great Lake
Mount Ossa 1617
Cradle Mountain
Strathgordon
Lake Pedder
Macquarie Harbour
Port Davey
South West Cape

TASMANIA

SOUTHERN OCEAN

East of Greenwich

M-590293-7A-DR1-1°
Copyright © Rand McNally & Co.

Metres   Feet
3000   9840
2000   6560
1000   3280
500   1640
200   656
Sea level
0   0
200   656
2000   6560

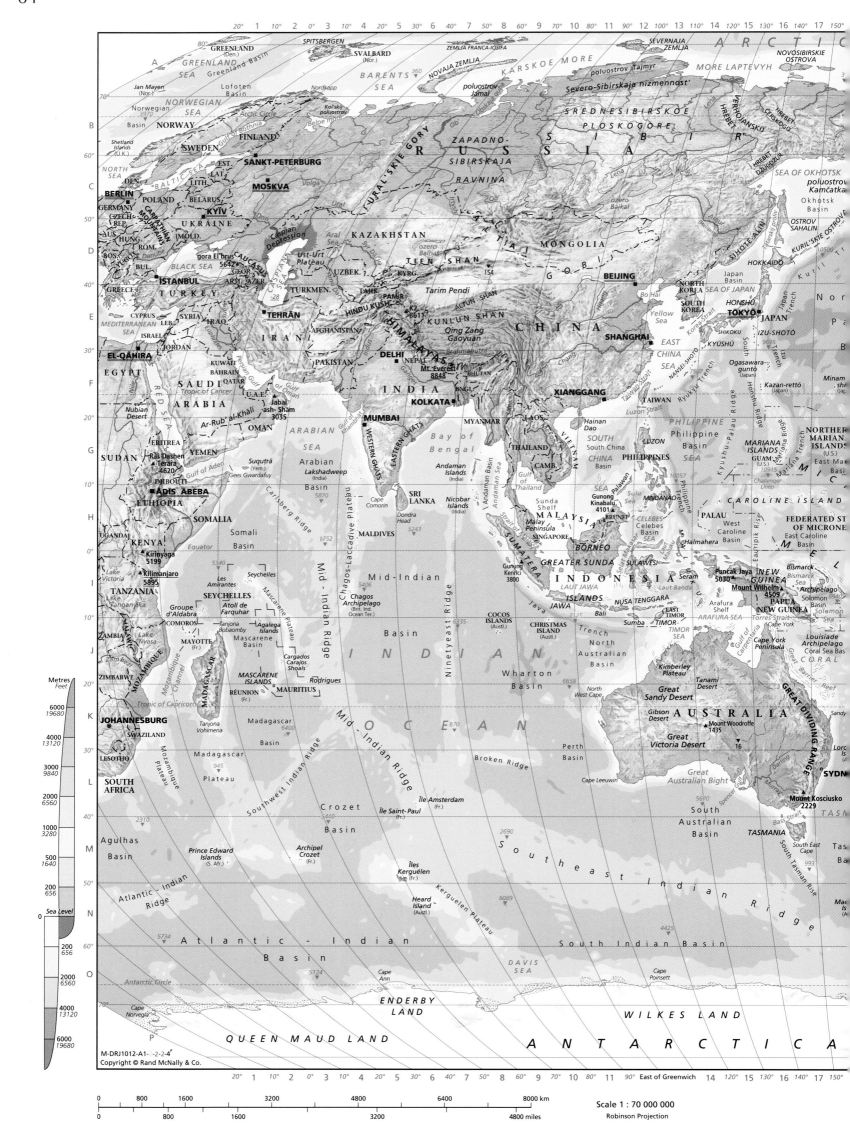

Metres Feet
6000 19680
4000 13120
3000 9840
2000 6560
1000 3280
500 1640
200 656
0 Sea Level
200 656
2000 6560
4000 13120
6000 19680

M-DRJ1012-A1- -2-2-4°
Copyright © Rand McNally & Co.

0   800   1600   3200   4800   6400   8000 km
0   800   1600   3200   4800 miles

Scale 1 : 70 000 000
Robinson Projection

OCEAN
ČNO-SKOE ORE
ostrov Vrangelja
CHUKCHI SEA
Bering Strait
Point Barrow
BEAUFORT SEA
Canada Basin
Prince Patrick Island
Melville Island
Banks Island
Amundsen Gulf
Victoria Island
Axel Heiberg Island
QUEEN ELIZABETH ISLANDS
North Magnetic Pole (1975)
Devon Island
Prince of Wales Island
Somerset Island
ELLESMERE ISLAND
Baffin Bay
Baffin Basin
Southampton Island
GREENLAND (Den.)
Gunnbjørn Field 3700
80°
70°
Arctic Circle

Anadyrskij zaliv
BROOKS RANGE
ALASKA (U.S.)
Mount McKinley 6194
ALASKA RANGE
Yukon
Mount Logan 5959
MACKENZIE MOUNTAINS
Great Bear Lake
Great Slave Lake
Lake Athabasca
CANADA
Foxe Basin
Hudson Strait
Péninsule d'Ungava
Belcher Islands
Hudson Bay
LABRADOR
LABRADOR SEA
Kap Farvel
Irminger Basin
NEW-FOUNDLAND
60°
B

Komandorskie Ostrova
BERING SEA
Aleutian Basin
Aleutian Peninsula
Kodiak Island
Gulf of Alaska
COAST MTS
QUEEN CHARLOTTE ISLANDS
Mount Waddington 3994
VANCOUVER ISLAND
ROCKY MOUNTAINS
Lake Winnipeg
Nelson
Lake Superior
Lake Michigan
Lake Huron
Ottawa
Montréal
Lake Ontario
Lake Erie
Cape Cod
50°
C

ALEUTIAN ISLANDS
Aleutian Trench
International Date Line
CASCADE RANGE
Columbia
COAST RANGES
Cape Mendocino
GREAT PLAINS
Great Salt Lake
CHICAGO
Mississippi
Missouri
Arkansas
Ohio
APPALACHIAN MOUNTAINS
NEW YORK
Washington
North
ATLANTIC
40°
D

Emperor Seamounts
PACIFIC OCEAN
Mendocino Fracture Zone
Mount Whitney 4418
Great Basin 86
UNITED STATES
Red
Rio Grande
LOS ANGELES
HOUSTON
Cape Lookout
Blake Plateau
BERMUDA (U.K.)
American Basin
30°
E

MIDWAY ISLANDS (U.S.)
Murray Fracture Zone
Hawaiian Ridge
Musicians Seamounts
Isla Guadalupe (Mex.)
3008
Moloka'i Fracture Zone
SIERRA MADRE OCCIDENTAL
Baja California
Cabo San Lucas
Gulf of Mexico
Mexico Basin
Straits of Florida
BAHAMAS
WEST INDIES
Tropic of Cancer
OCEAN
F

HAWAIIAN ISLANDS (U.S.)
Oahu
Hawaii
6298
292
WAKE ISLAND (U.S.)
Pacific Mountains
Johnston Atoll (U.S.)
859
Clarion Fracture Zone
4809
MEXICO
Islas Revillagigedo (Mex.)
CIUDAD DE MÉXICO
Yucatán Peninsula
Volcán Pico de Orizaba 5610
SIERRA MADRE DEL SUR
BELIZE
CUBA
GREATER
HAITI
DOM. REP.
JAMAICA
ANTILLES
20°
G

SHALL ANDS
Central
POLY
Pacific Basin
Christmas Ridge
Kiritimati
5720
Île Clipperton (Fr.)
Middle America Trench
6600
GUAT.
EL SALV.
HONDURAS
NICARAGUA
Guatemala Basin
Lago de Nicaragua
CARIBBEAN SEA
10°

Ralik Chain
Ratak Chain
KIRIBATI
Howland Island (U.S.)
Baker Island (U.S.)
Jarvis Island (U.S.)
5349
LINE ISLANDS
COSTA RICA
Isla del Coco (C.R.)
Cocos Ridge
PANAMA
Panama Basin
COLOMBIA
BOGOTÁ
VEN.
Golfo de Maracaibo
H

NAURU
PHOENIX ISLANDS
KIRIBATI
5029
NE
Equator
Archipiélago de Colón (Galapagos Islands) (Ec.)
ECUADOR
Chimborazo 6310
0°
I

SOLOMON ISLANDS
TUVALU
TOKELAU (N.Z.)
Northern Cook Islands
5485
5249
Punta Pariñas
PERU
Nevado Huascarán 6746
BRAZIL
ANDES
10°

Santa Cruz Islands
WALLIS AND FUTUNA (Fr.)
SAMOA
AMERICAN SAMOA
COOK ISLANDS (N.Z.)
Archipel de la Société
FRENCH POLYNESIA
Îles Marquises
Peru Basin
Lima
Peru–Chile Trench
Nazca Ridge
J

North Fiji Basin
FIJI
Suva
TONGA
Tonga Ridge
Tonga Trench
Tahiti
ÎLES TUAMOTU
Tuamotu Ridge
8000
NEW HEBRIDES
NORFOLK ISLAND (Austl.)
NIUE (N.Z.)
Southern Cook Islands
Austral Seamounts
Îles Gambier
PITCAIRN (U.K.)
ÎLES AUSTRALES
Pitcairn Island
5537
Isla Sala y Gómez (Chile)
Sala y Gomez Ridge
Isla de Pascua (Easter Island) (Chile)
Tropic of Capricorn
Cerro Aconcagua 6959
20°
K

New Hebrides Trench
Kermadec Islands (N.Z.)
Lau Ridge
Kermadec Trench
10047
International Date Line
Louisville Ridge
Southwest
PACIFIC OCEAN
Archipiélago Juan Fernández (Chile)
SANTIAGO
CHILE
PAMPA
PATAGONIA
30°
L

NORTH ISLAND
Cook Strait
NORTH CAPE
497
South Fiji Basin
North Caledonia Ridge
Norfolk Ridge
NEW ZEALAND
Mount Cook 3754
Chatham Rise
Chatham Islands (N.Z.)
Pacific
Basin
4755
1447
Isla Grande de Chiloé
ARGENTINA
Golfo San Jorge
ATLANTIC
Argentine Basin
40°
M

Campbell Plateau
Bounty Trough
Bounty Islands (N.Z.)
Antipodes Islands (N.Z.)
4876
FALKLAND ISLANDS (U.K.)
Strait of Magellan
TIERRA DEL FUEGO
OCEAN
50°
N

Campbell Island (N.Z.)
5249
Pacific–Antarctic Ridge
5240
Cabo de Hornos (Cape Horn)
Drake Passage
5036
South Shetland Islands (U.K.)
South Orkney Islands (U.K.)
SCOTIA SEA
Antarctic Circle
60°
O

alleny Islands
Cape Adare
Scott Island
4706
Southeast Pacific Basin
Alexander Island
ANTARCTIC PENINSULA
Atlantic–Indian Basin
70°
ROSS SEA
Roosevelt Island
Ross Ice Shelf
MARIE BYRD LAND
Vinson Massif 4897
AMUNDSEN SEA
Thurston Island
BELLINGSHAUSEN SEA
Ronne Ice Shelf
BERKNER ISLAND
WEDDELL SEA
80°
P

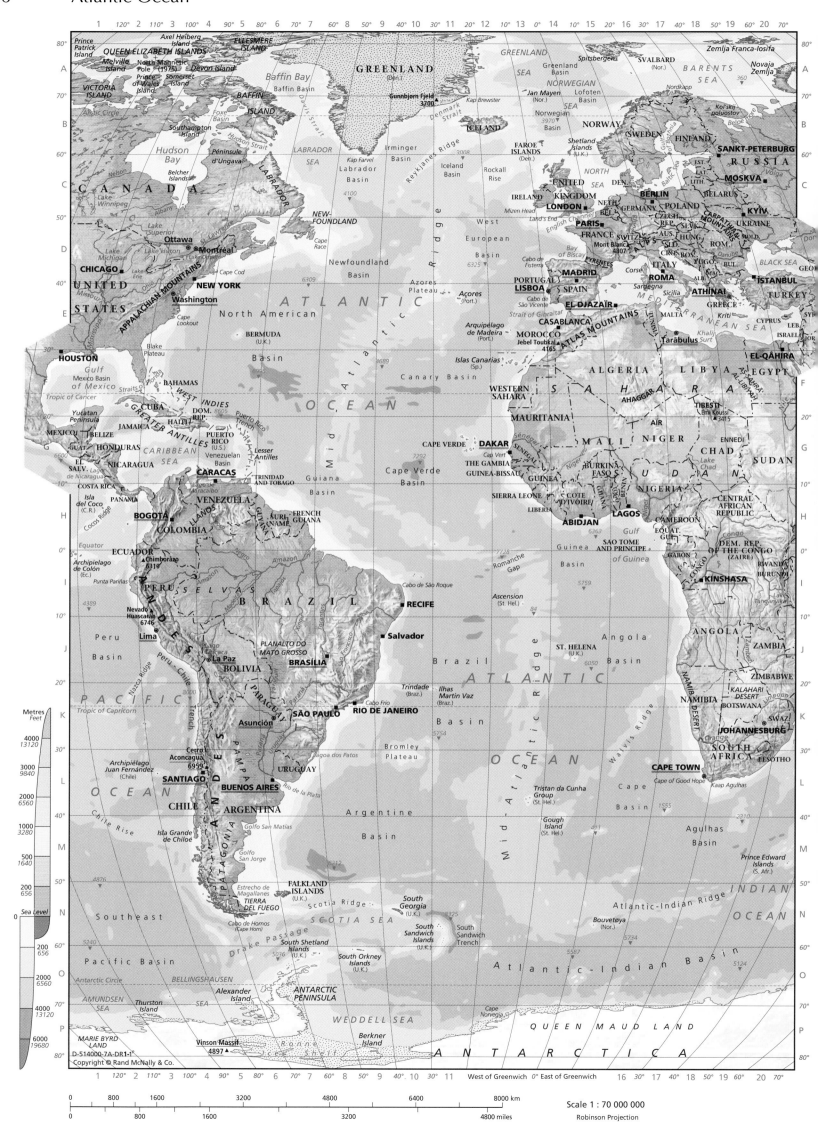

Metres	Feet
4000	13120
3000	9840
2000	6560
1000	3280
500	1640
200	656
0	Sea Level
200	656
2000	6560
4000	13120
6000	19680

0   800   1600   3200   4800   6400   8000 km

0   800   1600   3200   4800 miles

Scale 1 : 70 000 000

Robinson Projection

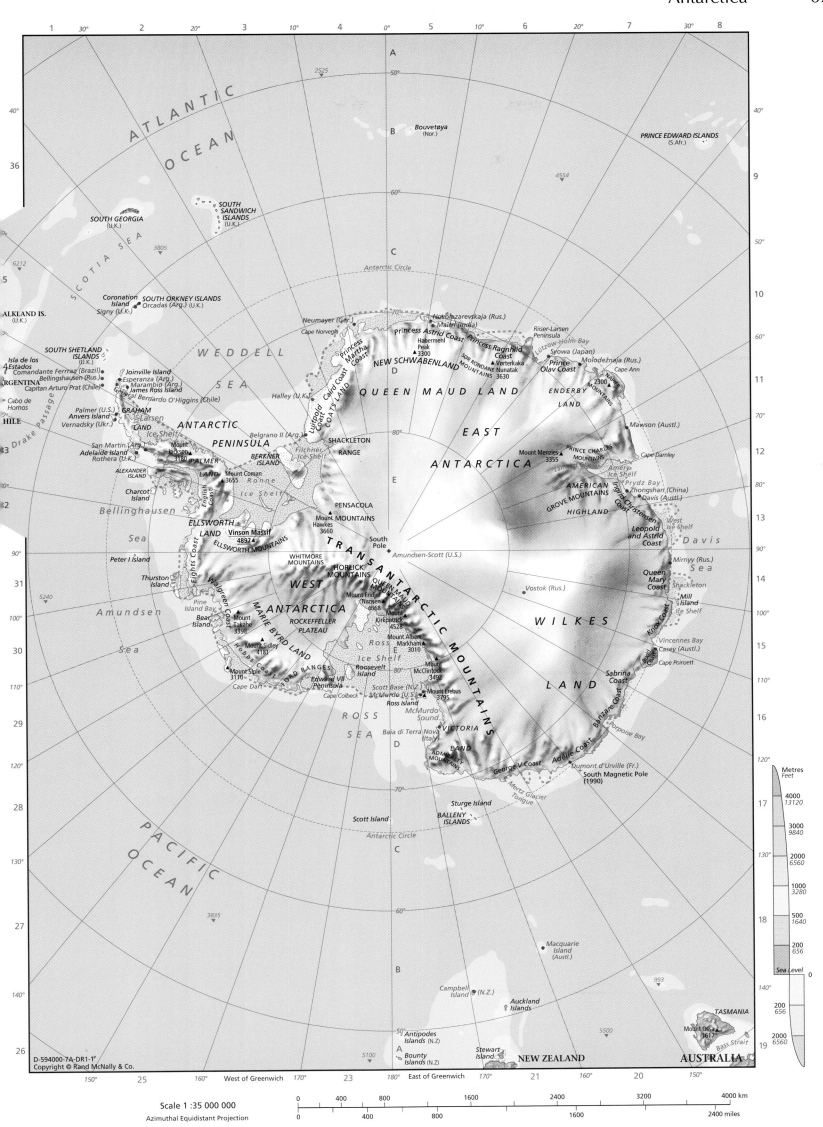

ATLANTIC OCEAN

Bouvetøya (Nor.)

PRINCE EDWARD ISLANDS (S.Afr.)

2525

4554

SOUTH GEORGIA (U.K.)

SOUTH SANDWICH ISLANDS (U.K.)

3805

6212

SCOTIA SEA

Antarctic Circle

ALKLAND IS. (U.K.)

Coronation Island
Signy (U.K.)

SOUTH ORKNEY ISLANDS
Orcadas (Arg.) (U.K.)

Neumayer (Ger.)
Cape Norvegia

Novolazarevskaja (Rus.)
Maitri (India)

Riiser-Larsen Peninsula

Lützow-Holm Bay
Syowa (Japan)

WEDDELL SEA

Princess Martha Coast

Princess Astrid Coast

Princess Ragnhild Coast

Habermehl Peak 3300

Prince Olav Coast

Molodežnaja (Rus.)

Cape Ann

Isla de los Estados

SOUTH SHETLAND ISLANDS (U.K.)

Comandante Ferrraz (Brazil)

RGENTINA

Bellingshausen (Rus.)

Capitan Arturo Prat (Chile)

Joinville Island
Esperanza (Arg.)
Marambio (Arg.)
James Ross Island
Gral Bernardo O'Higgins (Chile)

Halley (U.K.)

Caird Coast

COATS LAND

NEW SCHWABENLAND

SØR RONDANE MOUNTAINS

Vörterkaka Nunatak 3630

QUEEN MAUD LAND

ENDERBY LAND

NAPIER MOUNTAINS 2300

Mawson (Austl.)

HILE

Palmer (U.S.)
Anvers Island
Vernadsky (Ukr.)

GRAHAM LAND

Larsen Ice Shelf

Cabo de Hornos

Mount Jackson 3180

Belgrano II (Arg.)

SHACKLETON RANGE

EAST ANTARCTICA

Mount Menzies 3355

PRINCE CHARLES MOUNTAINS

Cape Darnley

San Martin (Arg.)

ANTARCTIC PENINSULA

BERKNER ISLAND

Filchner Ice Shelf

South Pole

AMERICAN HIGHLAND

Amery Ice Shelf

Prydz Bay
Zhongshan (China)
Davis (Austl.)

Adelaide Island
Rothera (U.K.)

PALMER LAND

Mount Coman 3655

Ronne Ice Shelf

GROVE MOUNTAINS

Ingrid Christensen Coast

ALEXANDER ISLAND

English Coast

Leopold and Astrid Coast

Charcot Island

Pensacola Mountains

West Ice Shelf

Davis

Bellinghausen Sea

ELLSWORTH LAND

Mount Hawkes 3660

Amundsen-Scott (U.S.)

Sea

Peter I Island

Vinson Massif 4897

ELLSWORTH MOUNTAINS

TRANSANTARCTIC MOUNTAINS

Mirnyy (Rus.)

Thurston Island

Eights Coast

WHITMORE MOUNTAINS

HORLICK MOUNTAINS

QUEEN MAUD MOUNTAINS

Queen Mary Coast

Shackleton

5240

Amundsen Sea

Pine Island Bay

Walgreen Coast

WEST ANTARCTICA

Mount Fridtjof (Nansen) 4868

Vostok (Rus.)

WILKES LAND

Mill Island

Mill Ice Shelf

Bear Island

Mount Takahe 3398

MARIE BYRD LAND

ROCKEFFELLER PLATEAU

Mount Kirkpatrick 4528

Ross Ice Shelf

Knox Coast

Mount Sidley 4181

FORD RANGES

Mount Albert Markham 3010

Vincennes Bay
Casey (Austl.)
Cape Poinsett

Mount Siple 3110

Hobbs Coast

Edward VII Peninsula

Roosevelt Island

Mount McClintock 3492

Sabrina Coast

Cape Dart

Cape Colbeck

Scott Base (N.Z.)

McMurdo (U.S.)

Mount Erebus 3795

Banzare Coast

ROSS SEA

Ross Island

McMurdo Sound

Porpoise Bay

Scott Island

Baia di Terra Nova (Italy)

VICTORIA LAND

ADMIRALTY MOUNTAINS

George V Coast

Adélie Coast

Dumont d'Urville (Fr.)

South Magnetic Pole (1990)

PACIFIC OCEAN

Mertz Glacier Tongue

3835

Sturge Island

BALLENY ISLANDS

Antarctic Circle

Macquarie Island (Austl.)

Campbell Island (N.Z.)

Auckland Islands

993

TASMANIA

Mount Ossa 1617

Bass Strait

5500

Antipodes Islands (N.Z.)

Stewart Island

Bounty Islands (N.Z.)

5100

NEW ZEALAND

AUSTRALIA

West of Greenwich

East of Greenwich

Scale 1:35 000 000

Azimuthal Equidistant Projection

Metres Feet	
4000	13120
3000	9840
2000	6560
1000	3280
500	1640
200	656
Sea Level	0
200	656
2000	6560

0   400   800   1600   2400   3200   4000 km

0   400   800   1600   2400 miles

Scale 1 : 35 000 000
Lambert Azimuthal Equal Area Projection

M-540000-2A-DR1-1
Copyright © Rand McNally & Co.

ATLANTIC

OCEAN

PACIFIC

OCEAN

FALKLAND ISLANDS
(U.K.)

Jason Islands

WEST
FALKLAND

Mount Usborne
705

Stanley

EAST
FALKLAND

SOUTH
GEORGIA
(U.K.)

Shag Rocks

Black Rock

Annenkov Island
Cape Disappointment

Metres Feet	
4000 13120	
3000 9840	
2000 6560	
1000 3280	
500 1640	
200 656	
Sea Level	0
200 656	
2000 6560	

BOLIVIA

PARAGUAY

BRAZIL

ARGENTINA

CHILE

URUGUAY

MATO GROSSO
DO SUL

SÃO
PAULO

MINAS GERAIS

PARANÁ

SANTA CATARINA

RIO GRANDE
DO SUL

GRAN CHACO

PATAGONIA

ANDES

TIERRA DEL
FUEGO

M-549200-7A-DR1-1°
Copyright © Rand McNally & Co.

Scale 1 : 15 000 000
Lambert Conformal Conic Projection

West of Greenwich

0	200	400	600	800	1200	1600 km

0	100	200	300	400	600	800	1000 miles

CARIBBEAN SEA

PACIFIC OCEAN

ARCHIPIÉLAGO DE COLÓN (GALAPAGOS ISLANDS) (Ec.)

NICARAGUA

COSTA RICA

PANAMA

COLOMBIA

VENEZUELA

ECUADOR

PERU

BOLIVIA

CHILE

ARGENTINA

AMAZONAS

SELVA

LLANOS

ANDES

CORDILLERA OCCIDENTAL

CORDILLERA ORIENTAL

CORDILLERA CENTRAL

CORD. DE MERIDA

CORDILLERA REAL

Metres Feet	
6000 19680	
4000 13120	
3000 9840	
2000 6560	
1000 3280	
500 1640	
200 656	
0 Sea Level	
200 656	
2000 6560	

M-549100-7A-DR1-1
Copyright © Rand McNally & Co.

| 0 | 200 | 400 | 800 | 1200 | 1600 km |
| 0 | 100 | 200 | 300 | 400 | 600 | 800 | 1000 miles |

Scale 1 : 15 000 000
Sinusoidal Projection

West of Greenwich

Tropic of Capricorn
Equator

ATLANTIC

OCEAN

Equator

Tropic of Capricorn

GRENADA
t George's
Scarborough
Tobago
Port of Spain
TRINIDAD AND TOBAGO
San Fernando
Trinidad

Morawhanna
Charity
Spring Garden
Parika Georgetown
Bartica
Rockstone Linden
New Amsterdam
Corriverton
Paramaribo
Nieuw Amsterdam
Nieuw Nickerie
Saint-Laurent
du Maroni
Île du Diable
Kourou
Kwakoegron
Brokopondo Saint-Élie Cayenne
FRENCH
GUIANA
Mount Roraima
2875
GUYANA
Lethem
Brokopondo Stuwmeer
SURINAME
Juliana Top
1230
Regina
Saint-Georges
Oiapoque
Saül
Cunani
Calçoene
Amapá
Ilha de Maracá
TÛMUCUMAC MTS.
AMAPÁ
ACARAÍ MTS.
Caracaraí
Serra do
Navio
4200
Vista
Ilha Janaucu
Ilha Caviana de Fora
Ilha Mexiana
Macapá
5450
ANAUS
Oriximiná
Alenquer
Porto de Moz
Belém
Bragança
Carutapera
Cururupu
São Luís
Rosário
Parnaíba
Acaraú
Camocim
FORTALEZA
Maranguape
Baturité
Aracati
Areia Branca
Macau
Ceará-Mirim
Natal
apuru
Faro Óbidos
Monte Alegre
Breves
Abaetetuba
Camiranga
Pinheiro
Viana
Monção
Itapecuru-Mirim
Brejo
Sobral
Ipu
Quixadá
Mossoró
RIO GRANDE
DO NORTE
Careiro
Itacoatiara
Santarém
Cametá
Portel
Bacabal
Codó
Barras
Campo
Maior
Crateús
Iguatu
Senador
Pompeu
Sousa
Caicó
Currais Novos
Novo Aripuanã
Maués
Altamira
Tucuruí
PARÁ
Marabá
Imperatriz
MARANHÃO
Caxias
Teresina
Floriano
Oeiras
Picos
Juazeiro
do Norte
Patos
PARAÍBA
Rio Tinto
João Pessoa
Campina Grande
Manicoré
Borba
Itaituba
São João do
Araguaia
Araguatins
Grajaú
Barra do Corda
Colinas
Mirador
Amarante
Benedito Leite
Balsas
PIAUÍ
Paulistana
São Raimundo
Nonato
PERNAMBUCO
Serra
Talhada
Sertânia
Caruaru
Garanhuns
Olinda
RECIFE
Barreiros
BRAZIL
Prainha Nova
SERRA DO CACHIMBO
Gradaús
Conceição do Araguaia
Carajás
Carolina
Loreto
Alto Parnaíba
Santa Filomena
Gilbués
Parnaguá
Remanso
Juazeiro
Petrolina
Paulo
Afonso
Jeremoabo
ALAGOAS
Arapiraca
Propriá
Maceió
SERGIPE
Itabaiana
Estância
Aracaju
S
Novo Aripuanã
SERRA DOS APIACÁS
Araguacema
Pedro Afonso
Pium
XÍMU
TOCANTINS
Natividade
Dianópolis
Morro do Chapéu
Serrinha
Inhambupe
Alagoinhas
Candeias
SALVADOR
Valença
aná
Roosevelt
SERRA FORMOSA
Cristalândia
Ilha do
Bananal
Palmas
Porto Nacional
Gurupi
Paranã
Arraias
Barreiras
Represa de
Sobradinho
Jacobina
Tucano
Santo Amaro
Feira de Santana
Santo Antônio
de Jesus
Vilhena
MATO GROSSO
PLANALTO DO
MATO GROSSO
Utiariti
Diamantino
Rosário Oeste
São Miguel
do Araguaia
Porangatu
Posse
Bom Jesus
da Lapa
Paramirim
Caetité
Guanambi
BAHIA
Mucujé
Jequié
Ipiaú
Itabuna
Ibicaraí
Ilhéus
3600
Porto Esperidião
San Ignacio
de Velasco
Cuiabá
Cáceres
Poxoréu
Aruanã
GOIAS
DISTRITO
FEDERAL
Formosa
BRASÍLIA
Luziânia
São Francisco
Januária
Pedra Azul
Monte Azul
Vitória da
Conquista
Itapetinga
Canavieiras
Belmonte
4500
Laguna Concepción
San José de Chiquitos
Roboré
Pantanal de
são Lourenço
Rosário Oeste
Rondonópolis
Alto Araguaia
Ipora
Anápolis
GOIÂNIA
Pires do Rio
Catalão
MINAS
Corinto
Diamantina
Governador
Valadares
Almenara
Prado
Alcobaça
Caravelas
 dos
zog
Puerto Suárez
MATO GROSSO
DO SUL
Corumbá
Pantanal do
Rio Negro
Coxim
Rio Verde
Jataí
Morrinhos
Itumbiara
Araguari
Ituiutaba
GERAIS
Curvelo
Araxá
Ibiá
Sete Lagoas
Pirapora
Montes Claros
Araçuaí
SERRA DO ESPINHAÇO
Nanuque
São Mateus
ESPÍRITO
SANTO
Porto Seguro
4900
Porto
Esperança
Campo Grande
Santa Fé do Sul
Três Lagoas
Uberaba
Represa de
Água Vermelha
Uberlândia
Ibiá
Represa de
Três Marias
BELO
HORIZONTE
Divinópolis
Itaúna
Conselheiro
Lafaiete
Caratinga
Ponte Nova
Itaquari
Colatina
Aracruz
Vitória
Vila Velha
Cachoeiro de Itapemirim
Cabo de São Tomé
Aquidauana
São José
do Rio Preto
Franca
Barretos
Passos
Formiga
Represa de
Furnas
Guaxupé
Poços de
Caldas
Juiz de
Fora
Itaparuna
Campos
PARAGUAY
Porto Murtinho
Bela Vista
Dourados
Presidente
Prudente
Marília
Araçatuba
Ribeirão
Preto
Rio Claro
São
Paulo
Rio de Janeiro
Nova Iguaçu
Niterói
Volta Redonda
RIO DE JANEIRO
fiscal
ribia
Pedro Juan
Caballero
Ponta Porã
Amambaí
Concepción
Umuarama
Maringá
Apucarana
Londrina
Bauru
Sorocaba
CAMPINAS
São José dos
Campos
SÃO PAULO
GRAN CHACO
PARANÁ
4600
110
40
5200
4000
60°   55°   50°   45°   40°   35°
8   9   10   11   12   13

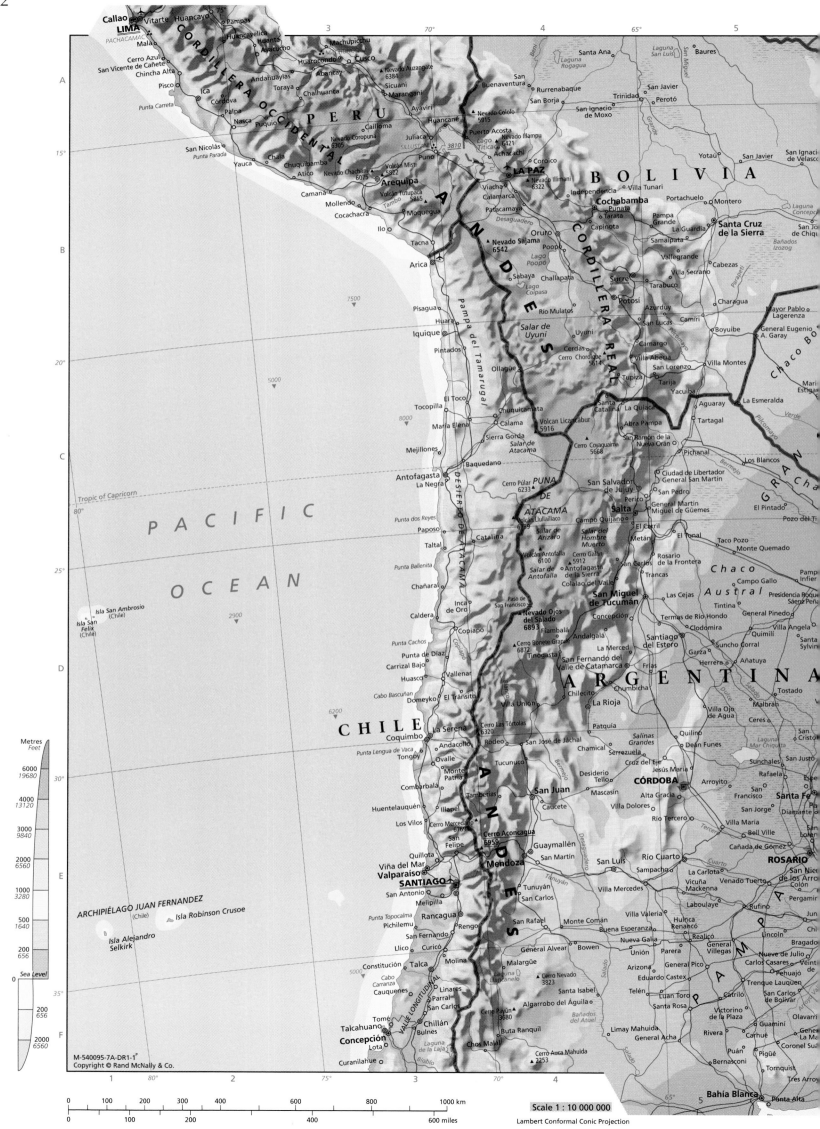

Callao • Vitarte Huancayo
LIMA
PACHACAMAC
Cerro Azul
San Vicente de Cañete
Chincha Alta
Pisco
Ica
Córdova
Palpa
Nasca
Punta Carreta
San Nicolás
Punta Parada
Yauca
Chala
Atico
Camaná
Mollendo
Cocachacra
Ilo
Tacna
Arica
Pisagua
Iquique
Pintados
Huara

CORDILLERA OCCIDENTAL
PERU
Andahuaylas
Abancay
Toraya
Chalhuanca
Puquio
Chuquibamba
Volcán Misti
5822
Nevado Chachani
6075
Volcán Tutupaca
5815
Tambo
Moquegua

Machupicchu
MA HERO
Huarocondo
Cusco
Sicuani
Marangani
Ayaviri
Cailloma
Juliaca
SILLUSTANI
Puno
Volcán
Nevado Coropuna
6305
Arequipa

Huancavelica
Huanta
Ayacucho
Pampas
75

Nevado Auzangate
6384
Huancané
Puerto Acosta
Nevado Cololo
5915
3810
Lago Titicaca
Achacachi
Coroico
LA PAZ
Nevado Illampu
6421
Nevado Illimani
6322
Viacha
Calamarca
Patacamaya
Desaguadero

BOLIVIA
Santa Ana
Laguna San Luis
San Baures
Buenaventura
Rurrenabaque
San Borja
Trinidad
San Javier
Peroto
San Ignacio de Moxo
Yotaú
San Javier
San Juan de Velasco

Independencia
Villa Tunari
Cochabamba
Punata
Tarata
Pampa Grande
La Guardia
Capinota
Samaipata
Portachuelo
Montero
Santa Cruz de la Sierra
San Jo de Chiqu
Laguna Concep

ANDES

Nevado Sajama
6542
Oruro
Poopó
Lago Poopó
Sabaya
Challapata
Lago Coipasa
Potosí
Río Mulatos
Azurduy
Sucre
Tarabuco
Villa Serrano
Cabezas
Vallegrande

CORDILLERA REAL

Salar de Uyuni
Uyuni
Cerdas
Cerro Chorolque
5614
Ollagüe
Chuquicamata
Santa Catalina
La Quiaca
Abra Pampa
San Ramón de la Nueva Orán
Tartagal
Aguaray
Yacuiba
La Esmeralda
Villa Montes
San Lorenzo
Tupiza
Tarija
Camargo
San Lucas
Camiri
Boyuibe
Charagua
Mayor Pablo Lagerenza
General Eugenio A. Garay

CHACO BO
GRA
Mari
Estiga
Verde

El Toco
Tocopilla
María Elena
Sierra Gorda
Mejillones
Antofagasta
La Negra
Baquedano
Calama
Volcán Licancabur
5916
Salar de Atacama
Cerro Coyaguaima
5668
Pichanal
Ciudad de Libertador General San Martín
San Salvador de Jujuy
San Pedro
Perico
General Martin Miguel de Güemes
El Pintado
Pozo del Ti
Los Blancos

PACIFIC
OCEAN

Tropic of Capricorn
80°

Punta dos Reyes
Paposo
Taltal
Punta Ballenita
Chañaral
Isla San Ambrosio (Chile)
Isla San Félix (Chile)

7500

5000

8000

DESIERTO DE ATACAMA

Cerro Púlar
6233
PUNA DE
ATACAMA
Volcán Llullaillaco
6739
Salar de Arizaro
Volcán Antofalla
6100
Salar de Antofalla
Cerro Galán
5912
Antofagasta de la Sierra
Colalao del Valle
Salar del Hombre Muerto
Campo Quijano
El Carril
Salta
Metán
El Tunal
Rosario de la Frontera
Trancas
San Carlos
Taco Pozo
Monte Quemado
Campo Gallo
General Pinedo
Chaco Austral
Las Cejas
Termas de Río Hondo
Tintina
Quimilí
Presidencia Roque Sáenz Peña
Villa Angela
Santa Sylvin

2900

Inca de Oro
Caldera
Copiapó
Paso de San Francisco
Nevado Ojos del Salado
6893
Fiambalá
Andalgalá
Concepción
San Miguel de Tucumán
Santiago del Estero
Clodomira
Suncho Corral
Garza
Añatuya
Tostado

Punta Cachos
Carrizal Bajo
Huasco
Vallenar
Cabo Bascuñán
Domeyko
El Tránsito
Villa Unión
Cerro Bonete Grande
6872
Tinogasta
San Fernando del Valle de Catamarca
La Merced
Frías
Herrera
Chilecito
Chumbicha
La Rioja
Patquía
Quilino
Dean Funes
Salinas Grandes
Malbrán
Ceres
San Cristo

6200

CHILE
Coquimbo
La Serena
Cerro Las Tórtolas
6320
Rodeo
San José de Jáchal
Chamical
Serrezuela
Cruz del Eje
Jesús María
Laguna Mar Chiquita
Sunchales
San Justo

Punta Lengua de Vaca
Tongoy
Andacollo
Ovalle
Monte Patria
Combarbalá
Tamberías
San Juan
Caucete
Mascasín
Desiderio Tello
Villa Dolores
Río Tercero
CÓRDOBA
Alta Gracia
Arroyito
San Francisco
San Jorge
Rafaela
Santa Fe
Espe

Huentelauquén
Illapel
Los Vilos
Cerro Mercedario
6769
Cerro Aconcagua
6959
San Felipe
Tucunuco
Guaymallén
San Martín
San Luis
Sampacho
Río Cuarto
La Carlota
Venado Tuerto
Villa María
Bell Ville
Cañada de Gómez
ROSARIO
San Nic de los Arro
Colón

Quillota
Viña del Mar
Valparaíso
SANTIAGO
San Antonio
Melipilla
ANDES
Tunuyán
San Carlos
Villa Mercedes
Vicuña Mackenna
Laboulaye
Rufino
Pergamin

ARCHIPIÉLAGO JUAN FERNANDEZ
(Chile)
Isla Robinson Crusoe
Isla Alejandro Selkirk

Punta Topocalma
Pichilemu
Rancagua
Rengo
San Fernando
Llico
Curicó
Constitución
Punta Carranza
Cauquenes
Linares
Parral
San Carlos
Talca
Molina
Malargüe
San Rafael
Monte Comán
Buena Esperanza
General Alvear
Bowen
Nueva Galia
Realicó
Unión
Parera
Villa Valeria
Huinca Renancó
General Villegas
Lincoln
Bragado
Nueve de Julio

5000
Laguna Llancanelo
Cerro Nevado
3823
Telén
Santa Isabel
Luan Toro
Santa Rosa
Arizona
Eduardo Castex
General Pico
Catriló
Trenque Lauquen
Carlos Casares
Pehuajó
Veinti

Tomé
Talcahuano
Concepción
Lota
Bulnes
Chillán
Buta Ranquil
Chos Malal
Curanilahue
Laguna de la Laja
Biobío
VALLE LONGITUDINAL
Cerro Payún
3680
Cerro Auca Mahuida
2253
Limay Mahuida
Rivera
General Acha
Victorino de la Plaza
Carhué
La Ma
Coronel Su
Puán
Guaminí
Pigüé
Bernasconi
Tornquist
Tres Arroy
Bahía Blanca
Punta Alta
Olavarr
La

M-540095-7A-DR1-1°
Copyright © Rand McNally & Co.

Metres
Feet
6000 / 19680
4000 / 13120
3000 / 9840
2000 / 6560
1000 / 3280
500 / 1640
200 / 656
Sea Level
0
200 / 656
2000 / 6560

	3	70°		4	65°	5

15°
20°
Tropic of Capricorn
25°
30°
35°

A
B
C
D
E
F

Scale 1 : 10 000 000
Lambert Conformal Conic Projection

0 100 200 300 400 600 800 1000 km
0 100 200 400 600 miles

1 80° 2 75° 3 70° 4 65° 5

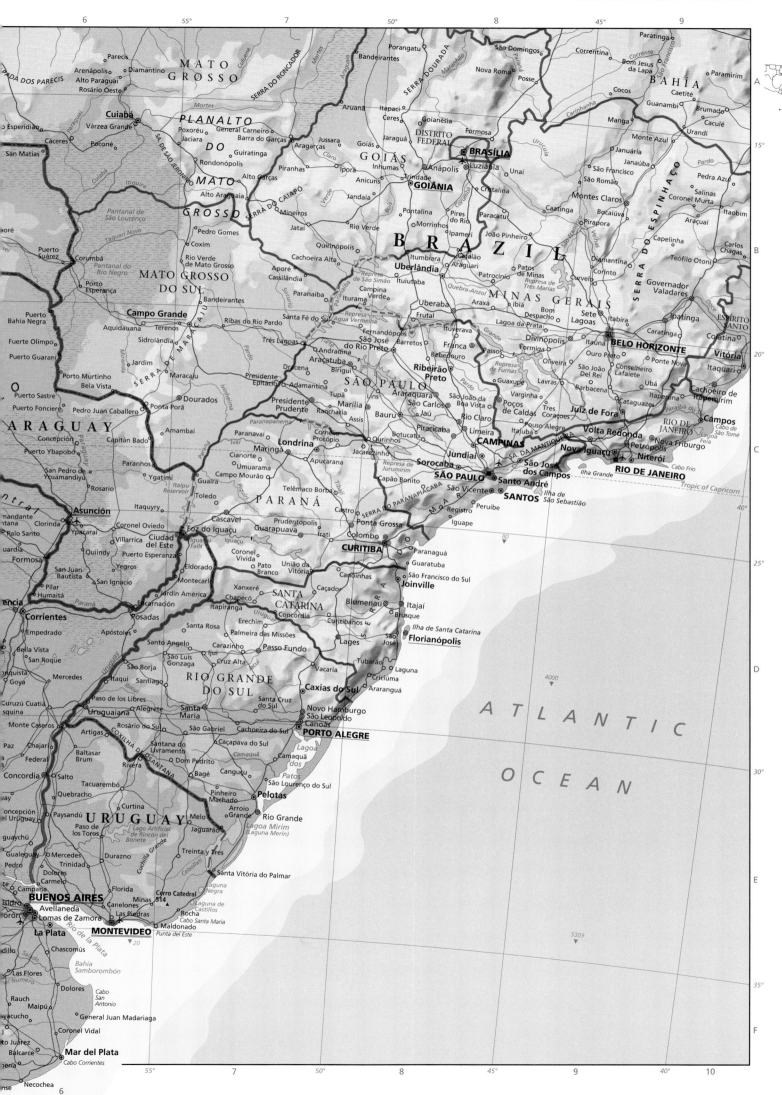

MATO GROSSO

PLANALTO DO MATO GROSSO

SERRA DO RONCADOR

Parecis
Arenápolis
Alto Paraguaí
Diamantino
DADOS PARECIS
Esperidão
Cuiabá
Várzea Grande
Rosário Oeste
Cáceres
Poconé
San Matías

BRAZIL

Porangatu
Bandeirantes
São Domingos
Nova Roma
Posse
Correntina
Bom Jesus da Lapa
Paramirim
BAHIA
Caetité
Cocos
Manga
Guanambi
Brumado
Caculé
Urandi
Monte Azul
Januária
Pedra Azul
Coronel Murta
Itaobim
Salinas
Jananúba
Itaberaba

Aruana
Itapaci
Ceres
Goianésia
Formosa
Goiás
Jussara
Aragarças
Jaraguá
DISTRITO FEDERAL
BRASÍLIA
Luziânia
Unaí
Cristalina
Carinhanha

MATO GROSSO DO SUL
Pantanal de São Lourenço
Taquari Novo
Porto Esperança
Corumbá
Pantanal do Rio Negro
Puerto Suárez
Puerto Bahía Negra
Fuerte Olimpo
Puerto Guaraní
Porto Murtinho
Bela Vista
Campo Grande
Aquidauana
Terenos
Sidrolândia
Maracaju
Jardim
Dourados
Ponta Porã
Amambaí

GOIÁS
Inhumas
Anápolis
Trindade
GOIÂNIA
Anicuns
Jandaia
Pontalina
Morrinhos
Pires do Rio
Ipameri
Paracatu
João Pinheiro
Coromandel
Monte Carmelo

MINAS GERAIS
Ibiá
Bom Despacho
Lagoa da Prata
Formiga
Divinópolis
Oliveira
BELO HORIZONTE
Itaúna
Sete Lagoas
Curvelo
Diamantina
Corinto
SERRA DO ESPINHAÇO
Governador Valadares
Teófilo Otoni
Carlos Chagas
Capelinha
Araçuaí

PARAGUAY
Concepción
Puerto Ybapobó
San Pedro de Ycuamandiyú
Rosario
Asunción
Ypacaraí
Villarrica
Ciudad del Este

URUGUAY
Montevideo

ATLANTIC OCEAN

BUENOS AIRES
Avellaneda
Lomas de Zamora
La Plata
Mar del Plata

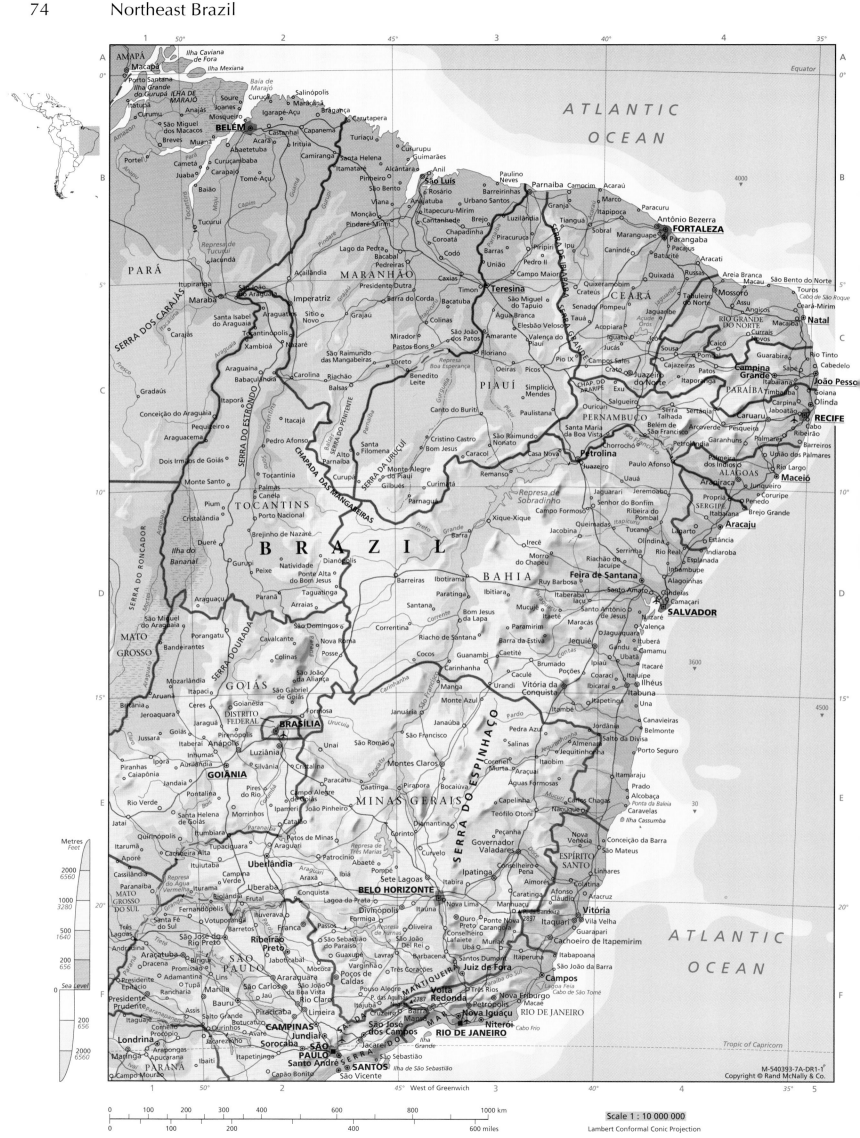

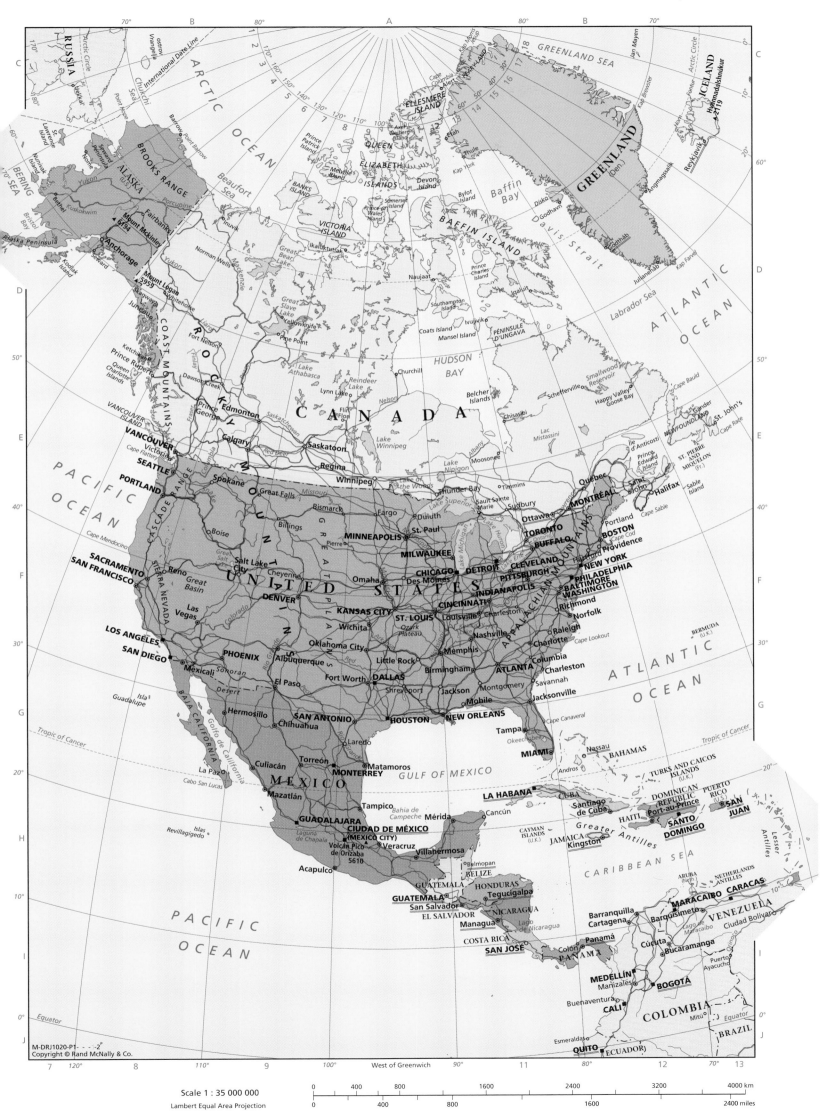

RUSSIA

ARCTIC OCEAN

ostrov Vrangelja

International Date Line

Arctic Circle

Chukchi Sea

Point Hope

Point Barrow

GREENLAND SEA

Kap Morris Jesup

Cape Columbia

Alert

17 18

16

15

14

ELLESMERE ISLAND

GREENLAND (Den.)

Kap York

Thule

ICELAND

Reykjavík

Hvannadalshnúkur 2119

BEAUFORT SEA

BROOKS RANGE

ALASKA (U.S.)

Mount McKinley 6194

Fairbanks

Anchorage

Seward

Kodiak Island

Alaska Peninsula

Bristol Bay

Bethel

Nome

Kuskokwim

Seward Peninsula

Yukon

Nunivak Island

St. Lawrence Island

BERING SEA

Uelkal'

Prince Patrick Island

Melville Island

BANKS ISLAND

QUEEN ELIZABETH ISLANDS

Prince of Wales Island

Somerset Island

VICTORIA ISLAND

Devon Island

Bylot Island

Baffin Bay

Disko

Godhavn

Davis Strait

Julianehåb

Kap Farvel

Jan Mayen

Arctic Circle

ATLANTIC OCEAN

Angmagssalik

Godthåb

COAST MOUNTAINS

Mount Logan 5959

Skagway

Whitehorse

Juneau

Ketchikan

Prince Rupert

Queen Charlotte Islands

VANCOUVER ISLAND

Cape Flattery

PACIFIC OCEAN

Cape Mendocino

ROCKY MOUNTAINS

Fort Nelson

Yukon

Inuvik

Norman Wells

Mackenzie

Great Bear Lake

Ikaluktutiak

Naujaat

Coats Island

Mansel Island

Ivujivik

PÉNINSULE D'UNGAVA

Labrador Sea

Cape Bauld

NEWFOUNDLAND

Cape Race

Gander

St. John's

Dawson Creek

Finlay

Peace

Prince George

Edmonton

Calgary

Red Deer

Saskatoon

Regina

Great Slave Lake

Yellowknife

Pine Point

Lake Athabasca

Reindeer Lake

Lynn Lake

Churchill

Nelson

Flin Flon

Lake Winnipeg

HUDSON BAY

Southampton Island

Belcher Islands

Chisasibi

Smallwood Reservoir

Schefferville

Happy Valley Goose Bay

Cape Harrison

Île d'Anticosti

PRINCE EDWARD ISLAND

ST. PIERRE AND MIQUELON (Fr.)

C A N A D A

Lake Winnipegosis

Lake of the Woods

Winnipeg

Thunder Bay

Timmins

Lac Mistassini

Lake Nipigon

Moosonee

Albany

Lake Superior

Sault Sainte Marie

Sudbury

Ottawa

QUÉBEC

MONTRÉAL

SAINT JOHN

Halifax

Sable Island

VANCOUVER

Victoria

SEATTLE

PORTLAND

CASCADE RANGE

Spokane

Great Falls

Billings

Missouri

Bismarck

Fargo

Duluth

St. Paul

MINNEAPOLIS

MILWAUKEE

Lake Michigan

Lake Huron

TORONTO

BUFFALO

Lake Ontario

Lake Erie

DETROIT

CLEVELAND

Portland

BOSTON

Hartford

Providence

Cape Cod

NEW YORK

PHILADELPHIA

BALTIMORE

WASHINGTON

SACRAMENTO

SAN FRANCISCO

Reno

SIERRA NEVADA

Great Basin

Salt Lake City

Great Salt Lake

Cheyenne

Omaha

Des Moines

CHICAGO

Pierre

U N I T E D   S T A T E S

G R E A T   P L A I N S

DENVER

Colorado

KANSAS CITY

ST. LOUIS

CINCINNATI

INDIANAPOLIS

PITTSBURGH

APPALACHIAN MOUNTAINS

Richmond

Norfolk

Las Vegas

Wichita

Louisville

Charleston

Nashville

Raleigh

Charlotte

Cape Lookout

BERMUDA (U.K.)

LOS ANGELES

SAN DIEGO

PHOENIX

Albuquerque

Oklahoma City

Red

Little Rock

Memphis

Birmingham

ATLANTA

Columbia

Charleston

Savannah

ATLANTIC OCEAN

Mexicali

Sonoran Desert

El Paso

Fort Worth

DALLAS

Shreveport

Jackson

Montgomery

Mobile

Jacksonville

Ozark Plateau

Rio Grande

Arkansas

BAJA CALIFORNIA

Golfo de California

Hermosillo

Chihuahua

SAN ANTONIO

HOUSTON

NEW ORLEANS

Tampa

Cape Canaveral

Okeechobee

MIAMI

Nassau

BAHAMAS

Andros

TURKS AND CAICOS ISLANDS (U.K.)

Tropic of Cancer

Isla Guadalupe

La Paz

Cabo San Lucas

Culiacán

Torreón

Laredo

Matamoros

GULF OF MEXICO

M E X I C O

Mazatlán

Tampico

Bahía de Campeche

Mérida

Cancún

LA HABANA

CUBA

Santiago de Cuba

CAYMAN ISLANDS (U.K.)

JAMAICA

Kingston

HAITI

Port-au-Prince

DOMINICAN REPUBLIC

SANTO DOMINGO

PUERTO RICO (U.S.)

SAN JUAN

Greater Antilles

Lesser Antilles

Revillagigedo

Islas

GUADALAJARA

CIUDAD DE MÉXICO (MEXICO CITY)

Veracruz

Villahermosa

Laguna de Chapala

Volcán Pico de Orizaba 5610

Acapulco

Belmopan

BELIZE

GUATEMALA

GUATEMALA

San Salvador

EL SALVADOR

HONDURAS

Tegucigalpa

NICARAGUA

Managua

Lago de Nicaragua

COSTA RICA

SAN JOSÉ

PANAMA

Colón

Panamá

CARIBBEAN SEA

ARUBA (Neth.)

NETHERLANDS ANTILLES

Barranquilla

Cartagena

Barquisimeto

MARACAIBO

Lago de Maracaibo

CARACAS

VENEZUELA

Ciudad Bolívar

Cúcuta

Bucaramanga

Puerto Ayacucho

PACIFIC OCEAN

MEDELLÍN

Manizales

BOGOTÁ

Buenaventura

CALI

COLOMBIA

Mitú

Equator

Esmeraldas

QUITO

ECUADOR

BRAZIL

Scale 1 : 35 000 000

Lambert Equal Area Projection

M-DRJ1020-P1-
Copyright © Rand McNally & Co.

0   400   800   1600   2400   3200   4000 km

0   400   800   1600   2400 miles

B

115°

110°

105°

100°

95°

90°

Oceanside
SAN DIEGO
Tijuana
Mexicali
PHOENIX
Escondido
El Centro
Tempe
Mesa
Globe
Gila Bend
CALIF
Salton Sea
Socorro
Vaughn
Clovis
Childress
OKLAHOMA
McAlester
Fort Smith
Little Rock
Memphis
Ensenada
ARIZONA
Tucson
NEW MEXICO
Baldy Peak
Silver City
Elephant Butte Reservoir
Alamogordo
Roswell
Artesia
Llano Estacado
Plainview
Wichita Falls
Altus
Lawton
Duncan
Denton
Sherman
Hope
Texarkana
Camden
El Dorado
Greenville
ARKANSAS
Hot Springs
Cleveland
Tupelo
MISSISSIPPI

Pico del Diablo
San Felipe
Puerto Peñasco
Sonoran Desert
Nogales
Nogales
Agua Prieta
El Paso
Ciudad Juárez
Deming
Las Cruces
Pecos
Midland
Odessa
San Angelo
Abilene
Fort Worth
DALLAS
Corsicana
Tyler
Palestine
Nacogdoches
Lufkin
Temple
LOUISIANA
Natchez
Jackson
Canton

Ensenada
2500
BAJA CALIFORNIA
335
3100
Caborca
Cananea
TEXAS
Killeen
Bryan
Alexandria
Baton Rouge

Isla Guadalupe
Isla Ángel de la Guarda
Santa Ana
Magdalena de Kino
Ures
SONORA
Nuevo Casas Grandes
Buenaventura
Ahumada
Stockton Plateau
Edwards Plateau
Kerrville
Austin
Houston
Beaumont
Port Arthur
Opelousas
Lafayette
New Iberia
NEW ORLEANS

Punta Eugenia
Isla Cedros
Bahía Sebastián Vizcaíno
Isla Tiburón
HERMOSILLO
Empalme
Guaymas
Ciudad Obregón
Moctezuma
CHIHUAHUA
Ojinaga
Ciudad Acuña
Del Rio
Uvalde
San Marcos
SAN ANTONIO
Victoria
Bay City
Galveston
Texas City
Freeport
Morgan City
Houma

C

30°

25°

Tropic of Cancer

20°

Isla San José
Santa Rosalía
Huatabampo
Guerrero
Chihuahua
Meoqui
Delicias
Camargo
Jiménez
Ciudad Camargo
Piedras Negras
Allende
Nueva Rosita
Sabinas
Allende
Beeville
Corpus Christi
Kingsville
Laguna Madre
5203

La Paz
Isla Carmen
Topolobampo
Guasave
Los Mochis
SINALOA
Santa Bárbara
Hidalgo del Parral
Santiago Papasquiaro
COAHUILA
Monclova
Nueva
Laredo
Laredo
Lampazos de Naranjo
Raymondville
Brownsville
Matamoros
Reynosa
MONTERREY
Matamoros

Isla Santa Magdalena
Isla Santa Margarita
BAJA CALIFORNIA SUR
Culiacán
SIERRA MADRE OCCIDENTAL
Gómez Palacio
Torreón
Saltillo
Matamoros
NUEVO LEÓN
McAllen
San Fernando
Laguna Madre

Isla San José
Isla Cerralvo
2599
Altata
Concepción del Oro
ZACATECAS
Matehuala
Linares
Montemorelos
Ciudad Victoria
TAMAULIPAS
Gulf of Mexico

D

Cabo San Lucas
San José del Cabo
San Lucas
DURANGO
MAZATLÁN
Villa Unión
Escuinapa de Hidalgo
Durango
Fresnillo
Zacatecas
San Luis Potosí
SAN LUIS POTOSÍ
Ciudad del Maíz
Ciudad Mante
Tula
Laguna de Tamiahua

Tropic of Cancer

Acaponeta
NAYARIT
Tuxpan
Aguascalientes
AGUASCALIENTES
Lagos de Moreno
León
Guanajuato
GUANAJUATO
Río Verde
Valles
Tamazunchale
Tuxpan de Rodríguez Cano
Tampico
Pánuco
2700
Progreso
Temax

20°

ISLAS REVILLAGIGEDO
Tepic
GUADALAJARA
Puerto Vallarta
JALISCO
Laguna de Chapala
Salamanca
Irapuato
Celaya
QUERÉTARO
Querétaro
Pachuca
Tulancingo
HIDALGO
Nautla
Bahía de Campeche
30
Campeche
Mérida
YUCATÁN
Hopelchén
CAMPECHE
YUCATÁN PENINSULA
QUINTANA ROO

E

15°

Isla Socorro
Autlán de Navarro
Colima
COLIMA
Guzmán
CIUDAD DE MÉXICO (MEXICO CITY)
Toluca
Morelia
MICHOACÁN
Uruapan
Ciudad Hidalgo
Apatzingán del Progreso
Cuernavaca
Tecomán
Manzanillo
PUEBLA
Córdoba
Orizaba
Volcán Pico de Orizaba 5610
Xalapa
Veracruz
San Andrés Tuxtla
Coatzacoalcos
TABASCO
Ciudad del Carmen
Jonuta
Villahermosa
BELIZE

Lázaro Cárdenas
SIERRA MADRE DEL SUR
Balsas
GUERRERO
Chilpancingo
Iguala
Minatitlán
Tecpan de Galeana
Zihuatanejo
Petatlán
Acapulco de Juárez
Chilapa
OAXACA
Oaxaca
Istmo de Tehuantepec
Jesús Carranza
Teapa
Tenosique
San Cristóbal de las Casas
La Libertad

F

10°

Ometepec
Miahuatlán de Porfirio Díaz
Santiago Jamiltepec
Juchitán de Zaragoza
Salina Cruz
Tonalá
Tuxtla Gutiérrez
CHIAPAS
Puerto Barrios
Puerto Ángel
Golfo de Tehuantepec
5450
Huehuetenango
Huixtla
Tapachula
Mazatenango
Volcán Tajumulco 4220
GUATEMALA
GUATEMALA
San Pedro Sula
Santa Ana
San Salvador
6600
Sonsonate
EL SALVADOR

5°

PACIFIC OCEAN

G

0°

3500

Equator

H

3667

ARCHIPIÉLAGO DE COLÓN (GALAPAGOS ISLANDS) (Ec.)
Isla Fernandina
Isla Santiago
Isla Santa Cruz
Isla San Cristóbal
Isla Isabela
Puerto Villamil
Puerto Baquerizo Moreno

I

Isla Santa María

Metres
Feet

4000
13120

3000
9840

2000
6560

1000
3280

500
1640

200
656

Sea Level
0

200
656

2000
6560

M-530000-7A-DR1-1
Copyright © Rand McNally & Co.

110°

105°

100°

95°

West of Greenwich

90°

0   200   400   800   1200   1600 km
0 100 200 300 400 500 600 700 800 1000 miles

Scale 1 : 15 000 000
Lambert Conformal Conic Projection

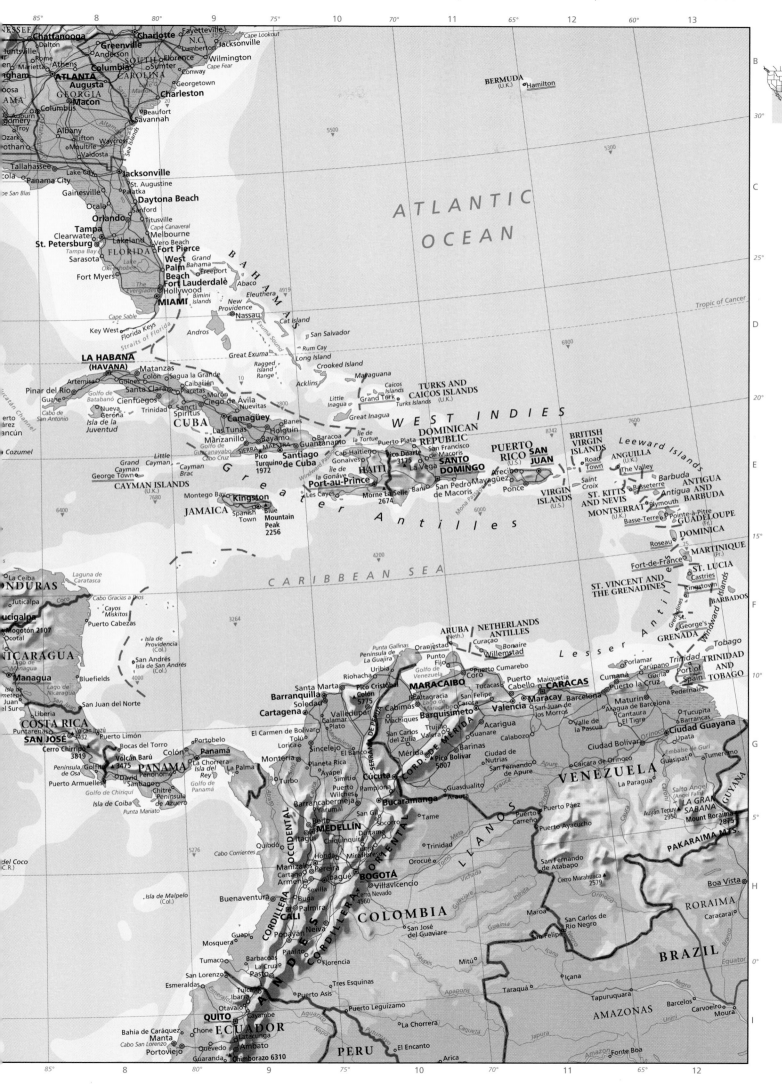

SAN DIEGO
El Cajon
Chula Vista
El Centro
CALIFORNIA
Tijuana
Mexicali
Yuma
San Luis Rio Colorado
Descanso
El Sauzal
Ensenada
Santo Tomás
Punta Colnett
Pico del Diablo
3100
San Felipe
BAJA CALIFORNIA
Rosario de Arriba
Laguna Salada
Cabo San Quintín
Isla Guadalupe
Isla Ángel de la Guarda
Isla Tiburón
Bahía Kino
Hermosillo
Isla Cedros
Bahía Sebastián Vizcaíno
Guerrero Negro
Punta Eugenia
Punta San Roque
San Ignacio
Santa Rosalía
Mulegé
BAJA CALIFORNIA SUR
SIERRA DE LA GIGANTA
Loreto
Isla Carmen
Liguí
Escollos Alijos
Isla Santa Magdalena
Ciudad Constitución
Isla San José
2599
Cabo San Lázaro
Isla del Espíritu Santo
Isla Santa Margarita
Isla Cerralvo
La Paz
Tropic of Cancer
Las Casitas
2164
Punta Arena
Santiago
Cabo San Lucas
San Lucas
San José del Cabo

ARIZONA
Tucson
Casa Grande
Gila Bend
Green Valley
Nogales
Bisbee
Douglas
Sonoyta
Puerto Peñasco
Enchiladas
Caborca
Magdalena de Kino
Santa Ana
Benjamín Hill
Puerto Libertad
SONORA
Moctezuma
Carbó
Ures
Presa Plutarco Elías Calle
Sahuaripa
Ortiz
Empalme
Guaymas
Esperanza
Presa Álvaro Obregón
Ciudad Obregón
Vícam
Navojoa
Huatabampo
Los Mochis
Topolobampo
General Juan José Ríos
Guasave
SINALOA
Guamúchil
Pericos
Culiacán
Costa Rica
Altata
Quilá
Higuera de Abuya
Mazatlán
Villa Unión
Rosario
Escuinapa de Hidalgo
Acaponeta
Tecuala
Tuxpan
Ruiz
Santiago Ixcuintla
NAYARIT
Tepic
Compostela
Las Varas
Ahuacatlán
Punta de Mita
Puerto Vallarta
Cabo Corrientes

ISLAS TRES MARÍAS

ISLAS REVILLAGIGEDO
(Mex.)
Isla San Benedicto
Isla Roca Partida
Isla Socorro
Isla Clarión
1668
4134

P A C I F I C   O C E A N
4616

San Carlos
Clifton
Whitewater Baldy
3321
Truth or Consequences
Elephant Butte Reservoir
Roswell
Llan
Estaca
Brown
Mount Graham
3267
Silver City
Deming
Las Cruces
NEW MEXICO
Alamogordo
Artesia
Hobbs
Carlsbad
Ar
Willcox
Chiricahua Peak
2986
Lordsburg
El Paso
Ciudad Juárez
Del City
Guadalupe Peak
2667
Van Horn
Odessa
McCar
Agua Prieta
Cananea
Samalayuca
Pecos
Ascensión
Marfa
Fort Stockton
Alpine
Nacozari de García
Nuevo Casas Grandes
Ahumada
Presidio
Sanderson
Las Varas
Buenaventura
El Sueco
Madera
Temósachic
CHIHUAHUA
Ojinaga
Guerrero
Chihuahua
Aldama
Herrera
Creel
Cuauhtémoc
Meoqui
Delicias
Cerro El Nopal
3060
Ciudad Camargo
COAHU
Valle de Olivos
Hidalgo del Parral
Jiménez
Ciudad Jiménez
Bolsón de Mapimí
Laguna del Guaje
San Francisco del Oro
Morelos
Santa Bárbara
Ceballos
Indé
Tlahualilo de Zaragoza
Cerro Iglesias
Cerro Ocotes
3150
Bermejillo
Topia
Tepehuanes
Gómez Palacio
Nazas
Matamoros
San Ped de la Colonia
Torreón
Santiago Papasquiaro
DURANGO
Cuencamé de Ceniceros
Cerro La Bandera
3230
San Pec
Otinapa
Miguel Auza
Juan Aldana
El Salto
Durango
Sombrerete
Rio Gran
ZACATECAS
Fresni
Zacatecas
Jerez de García Salinas
Ojocalie
Rincón de
AC
Aguascaliente
Calvilo
San Fra
del
SIERRA MADRE OCCIDENTAL
Colima
Manzanillo
Tecomán
Apatzingán de Constitución
Lázaro Cárden
COLIMA
GUADALA
Zapopan
Tlaquepa
Ameca
JALISCO
Sayula
Laguna
Ocotlán
Autlán de Navarro
Guzmán
La
Zar
del Progr
Uruap
San
Fra

Metres
Feet
4000
13120
3000
9840
2000
6560
1000
3280
500
1640
200
656
0
Sea Level
200
656
2000
6560

0   100   200   300   400   600   800 km
0   50   100   150   200   300   400   500 miles

Scale 1 : 8 000 000
Lambert Conformal Conic Projection

West of Greenwich

Gulf of Mexico

Caribbean Sea

Bahía de Campeche

Golfo de Tehuantepec

ATLANTIC OCEAN

Tropic of Cancer

6900

BAHAMAS
Samana Cay
Crooked Island
Cay
Acklins
Mayaguana
Little Inagua
Caicos Islands
North Caicos
Middle Caicos
East Caicos
Grand Turk
Turks Islands
TURKS AND CAICOS ISLANDS (U.K.)
Matthew Town
Great Inagua
Baracoa
Punta de Quemado

7600

HISPANIOLA
Manzanillo Bay
Cabo Isabela
Cap-Haïtien
Puerto Plata
Cabo Francés Viejo
8742

LESSER

PUERTO RICO (U.S.)
SAN JUAN
Arecibo
Bayamón
Caguas
Charlotte Amalie
St. Thomas
St. John
Virgin Gorda
Anegada
Road Town
BRITISH VIRGIN ISLANDS
VIRGIN ISLANDS (U.S.)
Virgin Islands
St. Croix

ANTILLES

ANGUILLA (U.K.)
The Valley
Saint Martin (Fr.-Neth.)
St. Christopher (St. Kitts)
Basseterre
Saba (Neth.)
Barbuda
ANTIGUA AND BARBUDA
St. John's
Antigua
ST. KITTS AND NEVIS
Nevis
MONTSERRAT (U.K.)
Plymouth

LEEWARD ISLANDS

Guadeloupe Passage
Grande-Terre
Basse-Terre
Soufrière 1467
Pointe-à-Pitre
GUADELOUPE (Fr.)
Marie Galante
Basse-Terre
Morne Diablotins 1447
Roseau
DOMINICA
Montagne Pelée 1397
Martinique Passage
Fort-de-France
MARTINIQUE (Fr.)
St. Lucia Channel
Mount Gimie 950
Castries
ST. LUCIA
St. Vincent Passage
Soufrière 1234
ST. VINCENT AND THE GRENADINES
St. Vincent
Kingstown
Mount Hillaby 340
Bridgetown
BARBADOS
Grenadines

WINDWARD ISLANDS

HAITI
Limbé
Cap à Foux
Gonaïves
Golfe de la Gonâve
Île de la Gonâve
Jérémie
Les Cayes
Jacmel
Pointe Abacou
Île à Vache
Saint-Marc
Pétion-Ville
Port-au-Prince
Morne La Selle 2674
LA CITADELLE
Pico Duarte 3175
San Juan de la Maguana
Barahona
Enriquillo
Isla Beata
Cabo Beata

Mao
Moca
Santiago de los Caballeros
San Francisco de Macorís
Cabo Samaná
La Vega
Sánchez
Yuna
Alto Bandera 2630
Higüey
SANTO DOMINGO
Azua
Bani
San Cristóbal
San Pedro de Macorís
La Romana
Isla Saona
Cabo Engaño
DOMINICAN REPUBLIC
Bahía de Ocoa

Mona Passage
Isla de Mona
Cabo Rojo
Mayagüez
Cerro de Punta 1338
Ponce
Isla de Vieques

6000

4200

BEAN SEA

ANTILLES

LESSER ANTILLES

Isla Blanquilla
Isla de Margarita
La Asunción
Tobago
Scarborough

ARUBA (Neth.)
Oranjestad
NETHERLANDS ANTILLES
Curaçao
Bonaire
Kralendijk
Willemstad
Punta Gallinas
Cabo de La Vela
Punta Espada
Península de La Guajira
Uribia
Punta Fijo
Península de Paraguaná
Islas Los Roques
Islas de Aves
Isla La Orchila

Puerto Bolívar
Riohacha
Maicao
Santa Marta
Barranquilla
Soledad
Ciénaga
Pico Cristóbal Colón 5775
MARACAIBO
La Concepción
Santa Rita
Cabimas
Ciudad Ojeda
Machiques
Lago de Maracaibo
Mene Grande
Valera
Trujillo
Bocono
Valledupar
Agustín Codazzi
El Banco
Ciénaga de Zapatosa
Ocaña
Aguachica
Simití
San Juan de Colón
Cúcuta
Pamplona
San Cristóbal
Bucaramanga
Floridablanca
Piedecuesta
Málaga
San Gil
Socorro
Barbosa
Chiquinquirá
La Dorada
Honda
Tunja
Duitama
Sogamoso
Miraflores
Yopal
BOGOTÁ
Villavicencio
Puerto López
San Martín
Granada

Dabajuro
Altagracia
Churuguara
Coro
San Rafael
Cerrón 1990
Carora
San Felipe
Barquisimeto
Chivaco
Tinaquillo
San Carlos
Tinaco
Acarigua
Guanare
Barinas
Santa Bárbara
Mérida
Pico Bolívar 5007
Ciudad de Nutrias
San Fernando de Apure
Elorza
Santa Rosa
Arauca
Arauquita
Tame
Casanare
Trinidad
Puerto Rondón
Nueva Antioquia
Puerto Carreño
Puerto Páez
Puerto Ayacucho
Arabelo
San Fernando de Atabapo
Puerto Inírida
Puerto Nariño
Orinoco

Tucacas
Puerto Cabello
Maiquetía
CARACAS
Maracay
Valencia
La Victoria
Cúa
Ocumare del Tuy
Guarenas
Guatire
Puerto la Cruz
Barcelona
Pozuelos
VENEZUELA
El Sombrero
Calabozo
Valle de la Pascua
Chaguaramas
Aragua de Barcelona
San José de Guanipa
El Tigre
Cantaura
Anaco
Caripito
Maturín
Barrancas
Cumaná
Carúpano
Güiria
Pen. de Paria
Punta Peñas
Port of Spain
Arima
TRINIDAD AND TOBAGO
San Fernando
Río Claro
Point Fortin
Boca de la Serpiente
Gulf of Paria
Pedernales
Temblador
DELTA DEL ORINOCO
Tucupita
Barrancas
Boca Grande
Corocoro Island
Morawhanna
Ciudad Guayana
Upata
Cerro Bolívar 802
Ciudad Piar
Guasipati
El Callao
Tumeremo
Matthews Ridge
El Dorado
GUYANA
Ciudad Bolívar
Cerro Mato 1863
Caicara de Orinoco
Cabruta
Aragua de Apure
La Urbana
La Paragua
Canaima
Salto Ángel (Angel Falls)
Auyán Tepuy 2950
Cerro Yaví 2441
Arabelo
La Gran Sabana
Cerro Uquía 2500
Irú Tepuy 2620
Mount Roraima 2875
PAKARAIMA MOUNTAINS
RORAIMA
BRAZIL

COLOMBIA
LLANOS

Puerto Wilches
Rionegro
Barrancabermeja

10°

5°

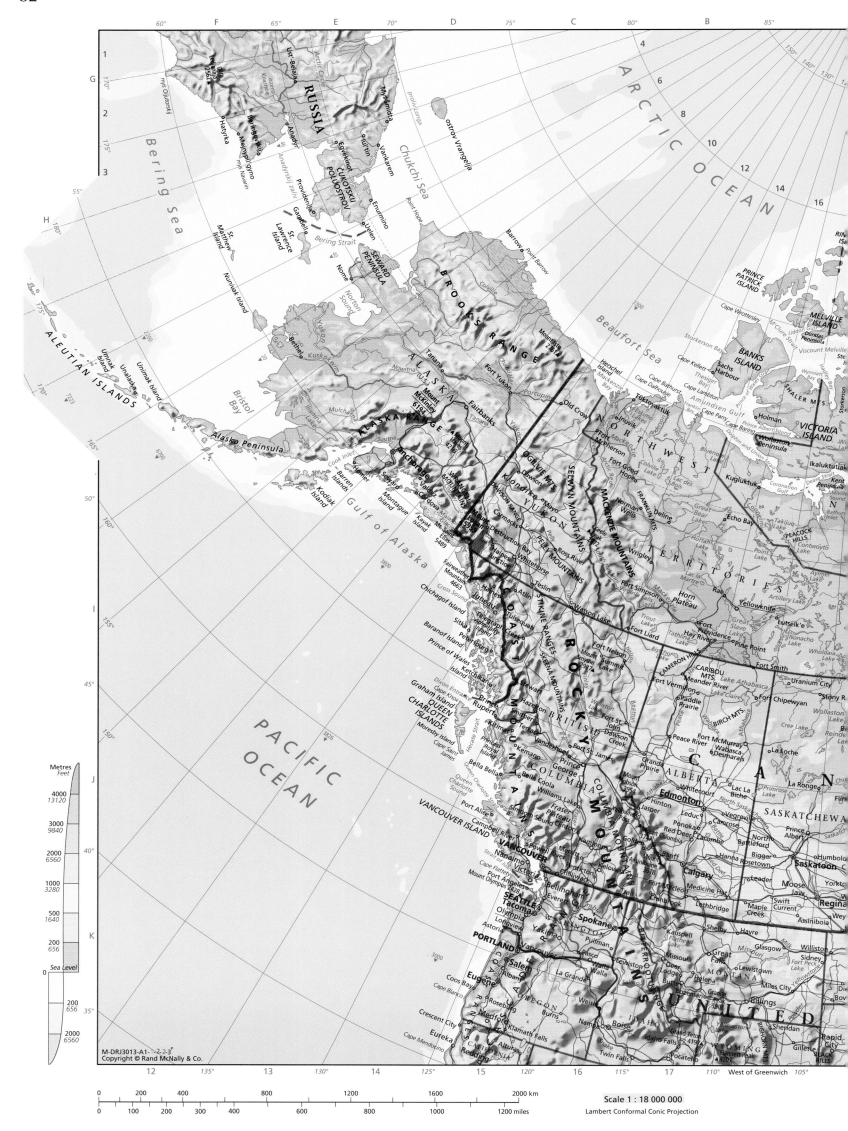

ARCTIC OCEAN

RUSSIA

Bering Sea

ALEUTIAN ISLANDS

Chukchi Sea

Beaufort Sea

BROOKS RANGE

ALASKA

ALASKA RANGE

Gulf of Alaska

PACIFIC OCEAN

Mount McKinley 6194

Anchorage

Fairbanks

NORTHWEST

YUKON

MACKENZIE MOUNTAINS

TERRITORIES

BRITISH COLUMBIA

ROCKY MOUNTAINS

ALBERTA

SASKATCHEWAN

COAST MOUNTAINS

VANCOUVER ISLAND

VANCOUVER

Victoria

SEATTLE

Tacoma

Olympia

PORTLAND

Salem

Eugene

WASHINGTON

OREGON

Spokane

Calgary

Edmonton

MONTANA

IDAHO

WYOMING

UNITED

Regina

Saskatoon

CANADA

Metres / Feet

Metres	Feet
4000	13120
3000	9840
2000	6560
1000	3280
500	1640
200	656
0	Sea Level
200	656
2000	6560

West of Greenwich

Scale 1 : 18 000 000

Lambert Conformal Conic Projection

0   200   400   800   1200   1600   2000 km

0   100   200   300   400   500   600   800   1000   1200 miles

GREENLAND
(Den.)

ICELAND
Reykjavík

FAROE ISLANDS
(Den.)
Tórshavn

Greenland Sea

Denmark Strait

ATLANTIC OCEAN

Labrador Sea

Baffin Bay

Davis Strait

ELLESMERE ISLAND

Peary Land

Cape Columbia
Barbeau Peak 2616
Alert

AXEL HEIBERG ISLAND

DEVON ISLAND

BAFFIN ISLAND

Thule (Qaanaaq)
Kap York
Upernavik
Umanak
Disko
Godhavn
Jakobshavn
Holsteinsborg
Sukkertoppen
Søndre Strømfjord
Gotthåb (Nuuk)
Egedesminde
Frederikshåb
Ivigtut
Julianehåb
Kap Farvel

Etah

SOMERSET ISLAND

BOOTHIA PENINSULA

MELVILLE PENINSULA

Foxe Basin

FOXE PENINSULA

SOUTHAMPTON ISLAND

Hudson Bay

All islands within Hudson Bay, James Bay, and Ungava Bay lie within Nunavut.

Churchill
Cape Churchill

NUNAVUT

Baker Lake
Arviat

York Factory
Fort Severn

PENINSULE D'UNGAVA

Ungava Bay

Kuujjuaq
Kangiqsualujjuaq

NEWFOUNDLAND AND LABRADOR

Nain
Hopedale
Cartwright
Battle Harbour
St. Anthony

Happy Valley Goose Bay
Labrador City
Schefferville
Gagnon
Sept-Iles

Smallwood Reservoir

QUÉBEC

MONTS OTISH

Lac Mistassini

ÎLE D'ANTICOSTI

Gulf of St. Lawrence

NEWFOUNDLAND
Gander
Bonavista
St. John's
Cape Race
Grand Bank
Corner Brook
Stephenville
Channel-Port aux Basques

SAINT PIERRE AND MIQUELON (Fr.)
Saint-Pierre

CAPE BRETON ISLAND
Sydney
Glace Bay
PRINCE EDWARD ISLAND
Charlottetown

NOVA SCOTIA
Halifax
Dartmouth
Yarmouth
Liverpool

NEW BRUNSWICK
Fredericton
Saint John
Moncton
Bathurst
Edmundston

ONTARIO

MANITOBA

Winnipeg
Lake Winnipeg
Norway House
Grand Rapids
Berens River
Gimli
Selkirk

Red Lake
Sioux Lookout
Dryden
Kenora
Thunder Bay
Atikokan
Fort Frances
International Falls

Lake Superior

Moosonee
Fort Albany
Attawapiskat
Pickle Lake

Kapuskasing
Hearst
Cochrane
Timmins
Geraldton
Marathon
Wawa
Sault Sainte Marie
Sudbury
North Bay
Pembroke

Ottawa
Hull
Gatineau

MONTREAL
Trois-Rivières
Shawinigan
Sherbrooke
Québec
Chicoutimi
Jonquière
Alma
Baie-Comeau
Rimouski
Matane

LAURENTIDE MOUNTAINS
APPALACHIAN MOUNTAINS

TORONTO
Hamilton
London
Kitchener
Windsor
Sarnia
Barrie
Peterborough
Belleville
Kingston
Brockville
Cornwall

Lake Huron
Lake Erie
Lake Ontario
Lake Michigan

UNITED STATES

MINNESOTA
MINNEAPOLIS
St. Paul
St. Cloud
Duluth
Fargo
Grand Forks
Bemidji
Brookings
Aberdeen
Sioux Falls
Rochester

WISCONSIN
MICHIGAN
Green Bay
Appleton
Eau Claire
Wausau
La Crosse
Madison
MILWAUKEE
Sheboygan

DETROIT
Flint
Lansing
Grand Rapids
Traverse City
Marquette
Escanaba
Alpena
Petoskey
Iron Mountain
Ironwood

CHICAGO
Gary
Rockford
Elgin

BOSTON
Providence
NEW YORK
Newark
PHILADELPHIA
Trenton
Albany
Syracuse
Rochester
Buffalo
Scranton
Binghamton
New Haven
Hartford
Portland
Portsmouth

NEW YORK
PENNSYLVANIA
NEW JERSEY
MASS.
NEW HAMPSHIRE
MAINE
Bangor
Augusta
Lewiston

Gulf of Maine
Cape Cod
Sable Island

Note: Map colors do not reflect elevation.

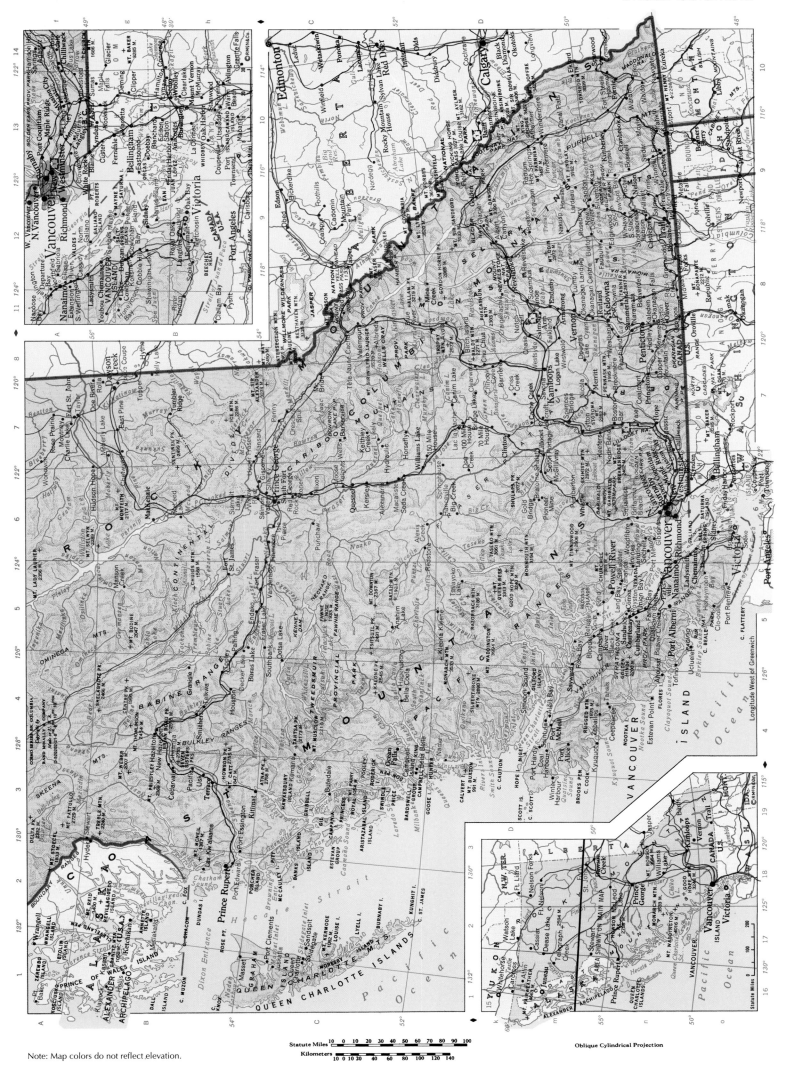

Note: Map colors do not reflect elevation.

Statute Miles 10 0 10 20 30 40 50 60 70 80 90 100
Kilometers 10 0 10 20 40 60 80 100 120 140

Oblique Cylindrical Projection

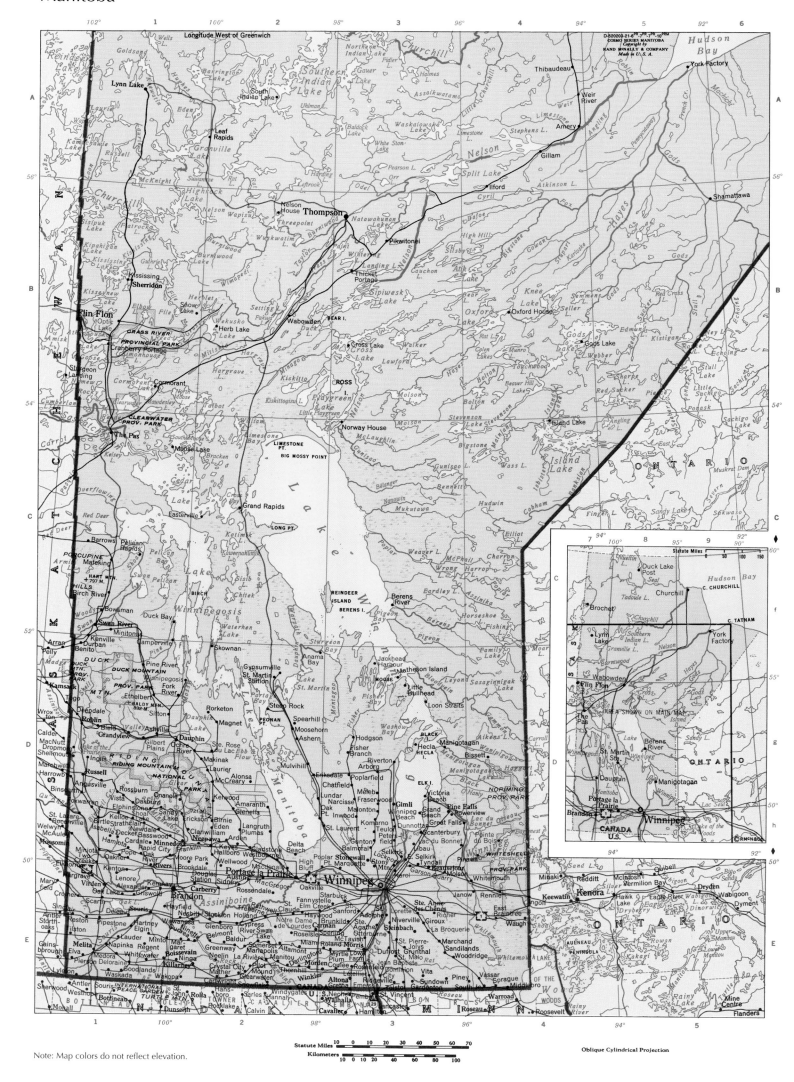

Longitude West of Greenwich

D-520203-21-6 PR.-7R-10 PM
COSMO SERIES MANITOBA
Copyright by
RAND McNALLY & COMPANY
Made in U.S.A.

Note: Map colors do not reflect elevation.

Statute Miles
10 0 10 20 30 40 50 60 70
Kilometers
10 0 10 20 40 60 80 100

Oblique Cylindrical Projection

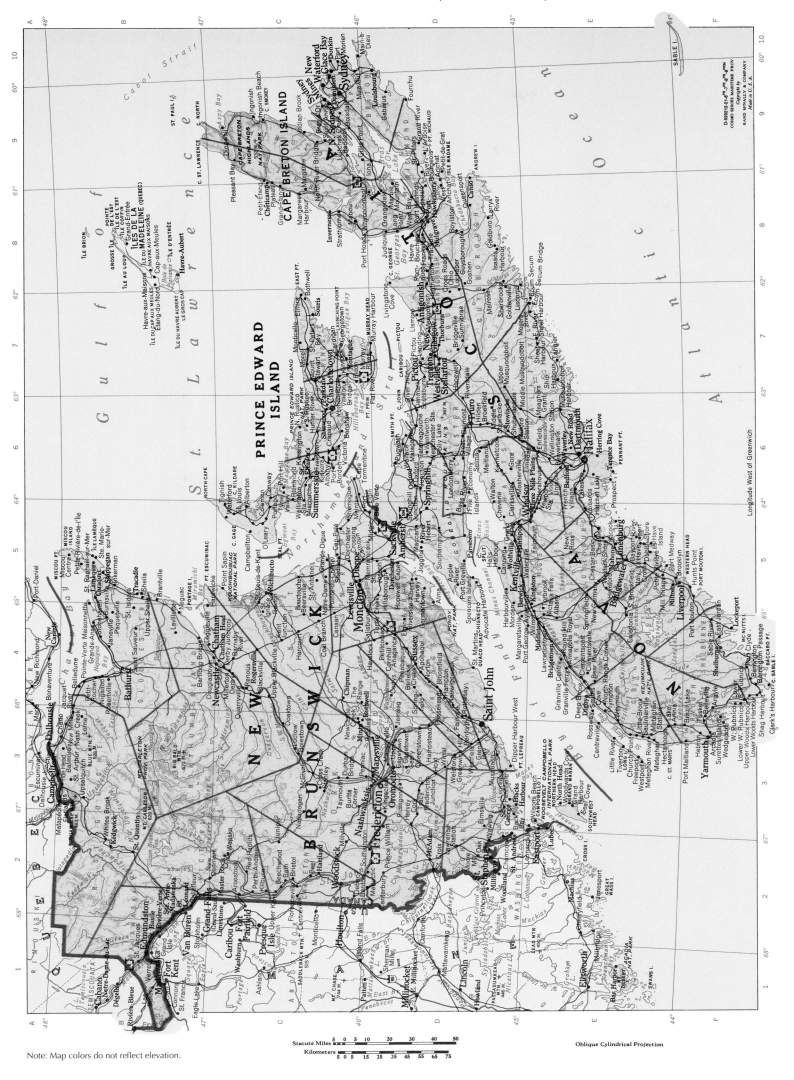

Note: Map colors do not reflect elevation.

Statute Miles 5 0 5 10   20   30   40   50

Kilometers 5 0 5 15 25 35 45 55 65 75

Oblique Cylindrical Projection

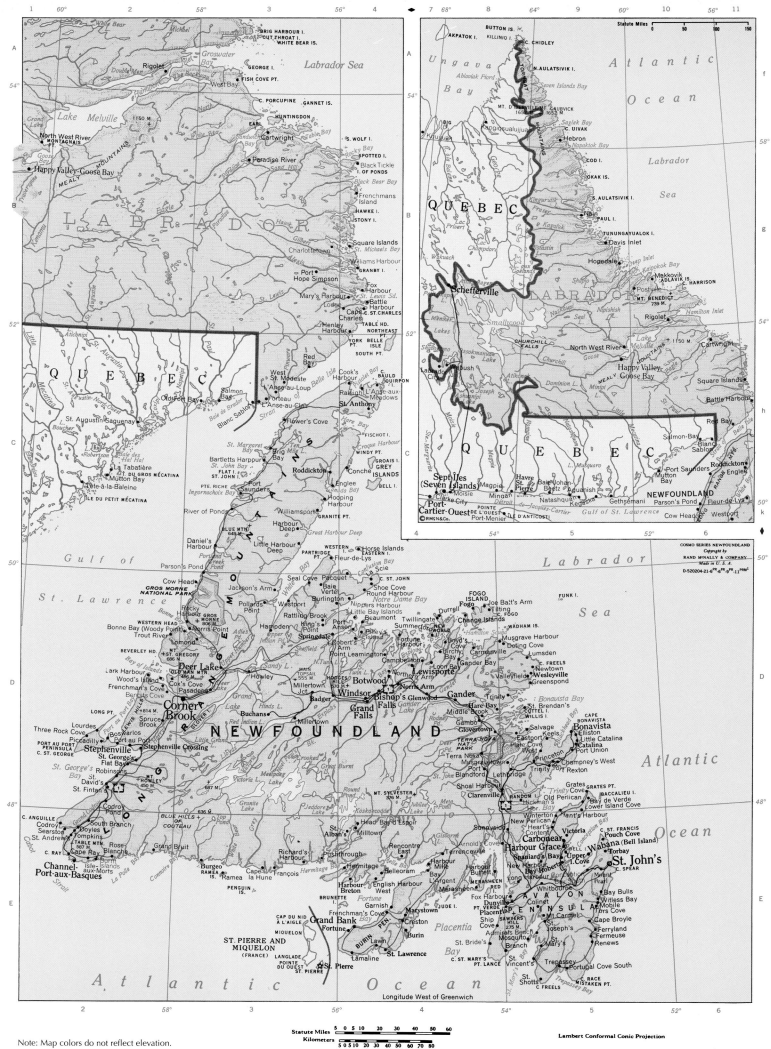

Note: Map colors do not reflect elevation.

Statute Miles
Kilometers

Lambert Conformal Conic Projection

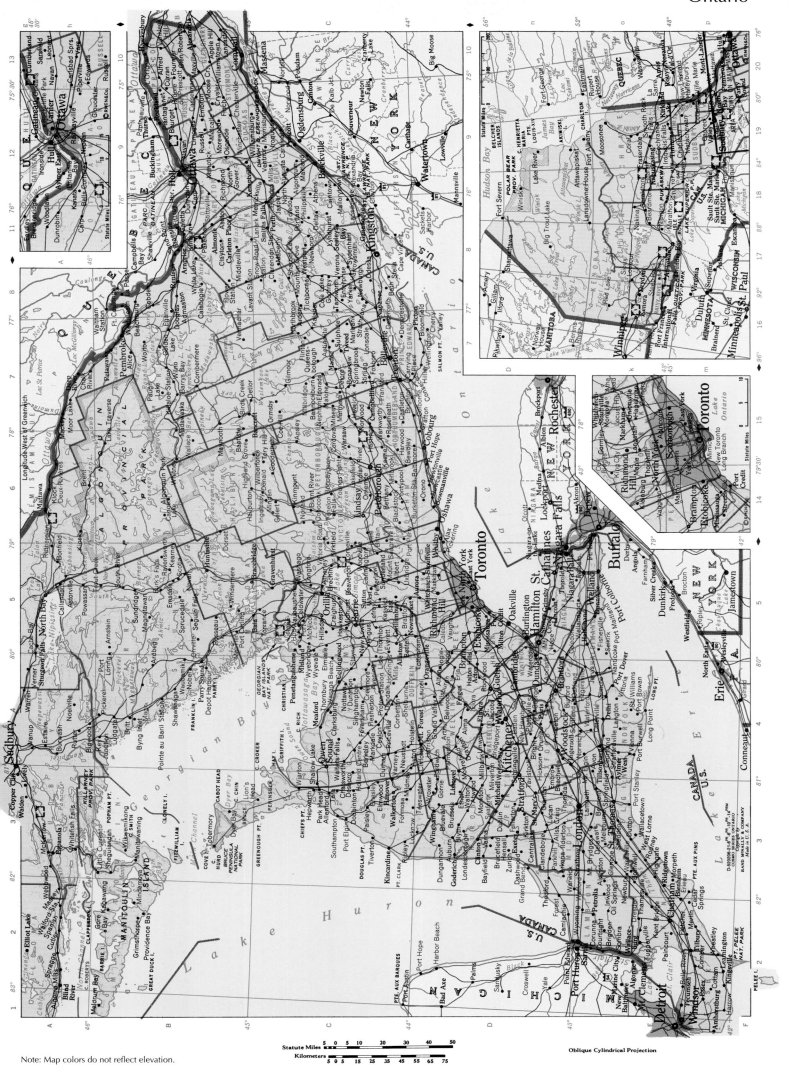

Note: Map colors do not reflect elevation.

Statute Miles
Kilometers

Oblique Cylindrical Projection

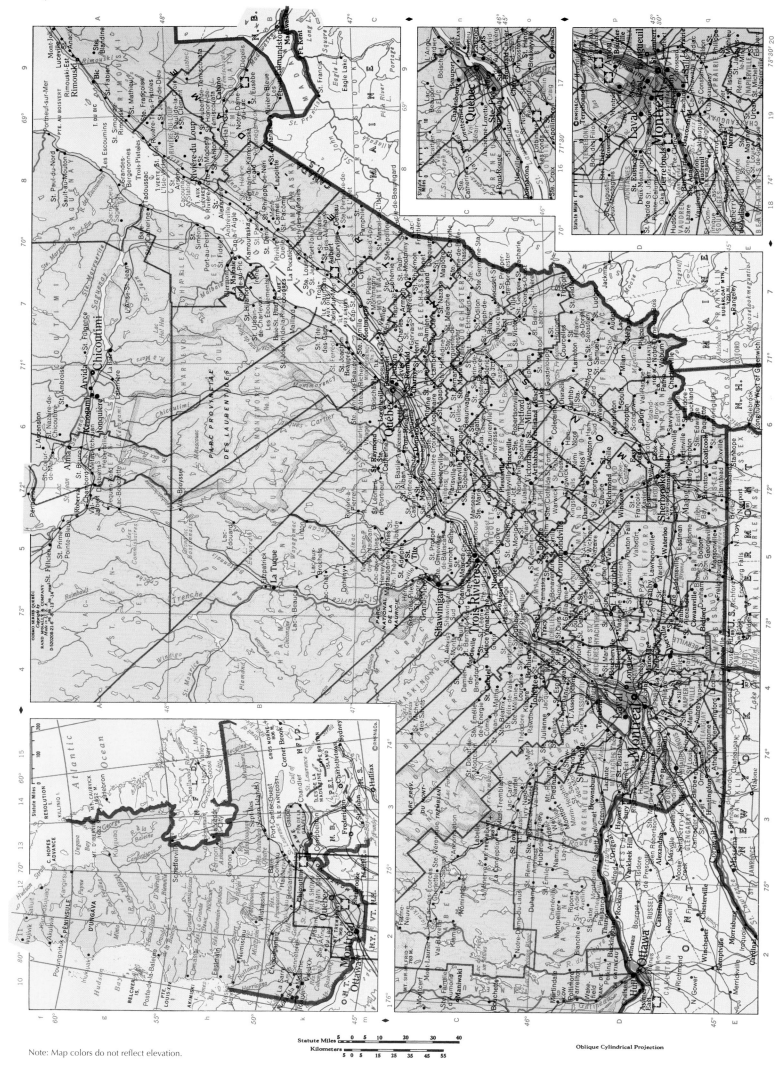

Statute Miles 5 0 5 10 20 30 40
Kilometers 5 0 5 15 25 35 45 55

Oblique Cylindrical Projection

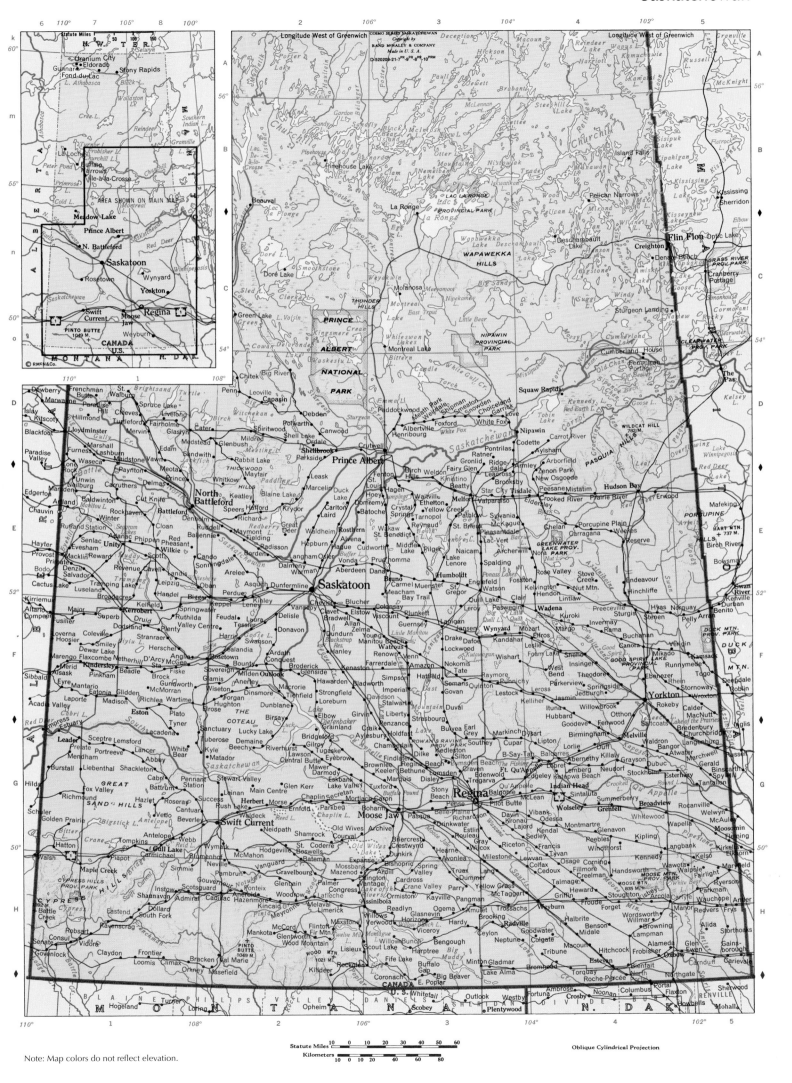

Note: Map colors do not reflect elevation.

Statute Miles 10   0   10   20   30   40   50   60
Kilometers 10 0 10 20   40   60   80

Oblique Cylindrical Projection

Scale 1 : 12 000 000
Lambert Conformal Conic Projection

	0	200	400		800		1200 km

0	100	200		400		600	800 miles

Metres
Feet

4000
13120

3000
9840

2000
6560

1000
3280

500
1640

200
656

Sea Level 0

200
656

2000
6560

M-520500-7A-DR1-1
Copyright © Rand McNally & Co.

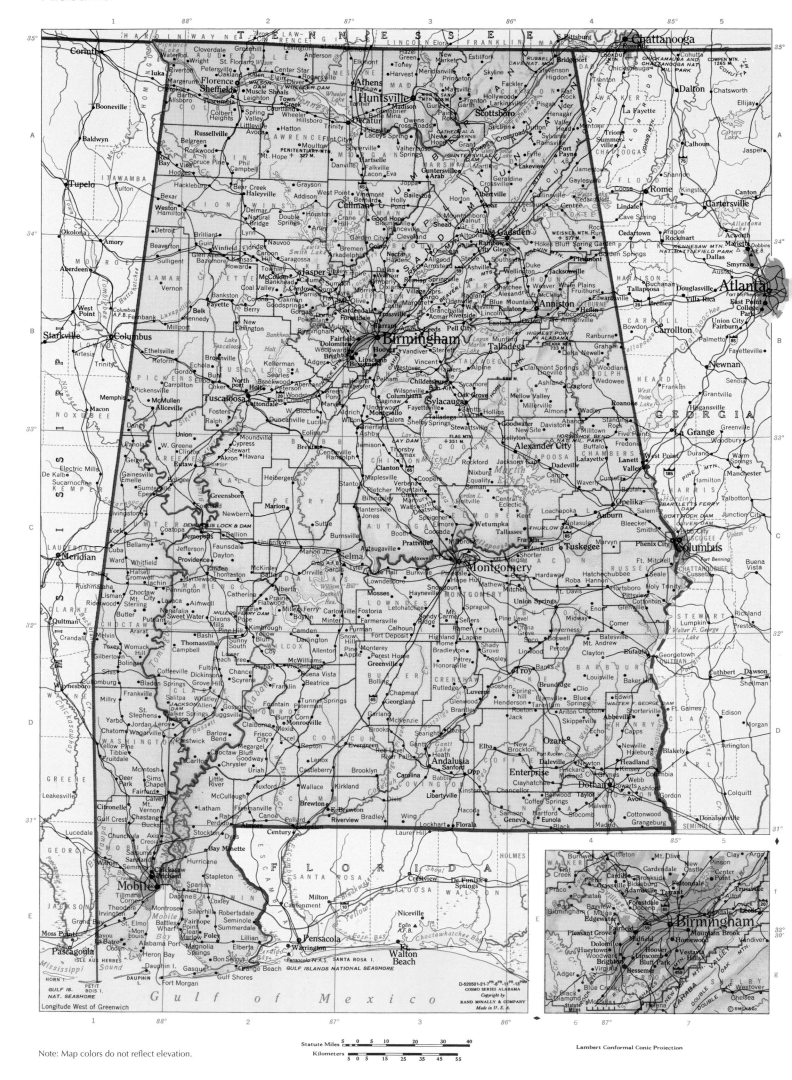

Note: Map colors do not reflect elevation.

Longitude West of Greenwich

Gulf of Mexico

Statute Miles
Kilometers

Lambert Conformal Conic Projection

D-520501-21-7 COSMO SERIES ALABAMA
Copyright by
RAND McNALLY & COMPANY
Made in U.S.A.

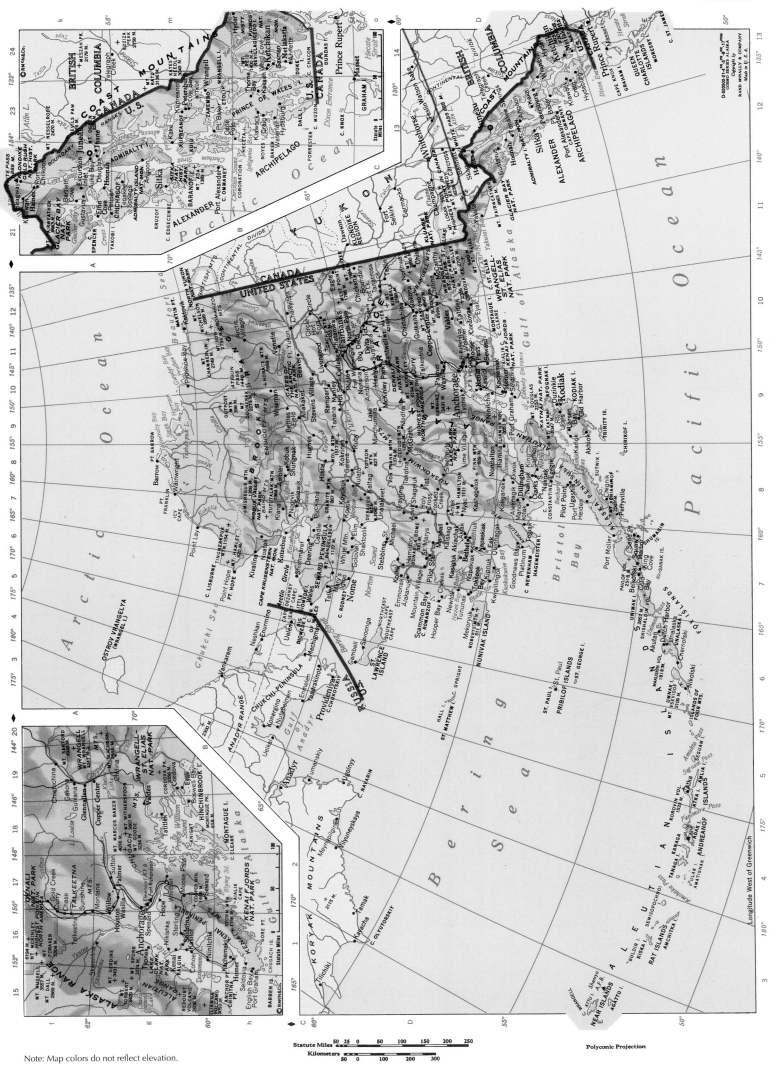

Note: Map colors do not reflect elevation.

Statute Miles
Kilometers

Polyconic Projection

D-500500-21-4-P³ ₂P ₂P² 1¹⁷PM
COSMOPOLITAN SERIES: ALASKA
Copyright by
RAND McNALLY & COMPANY
Made in U. S. A.

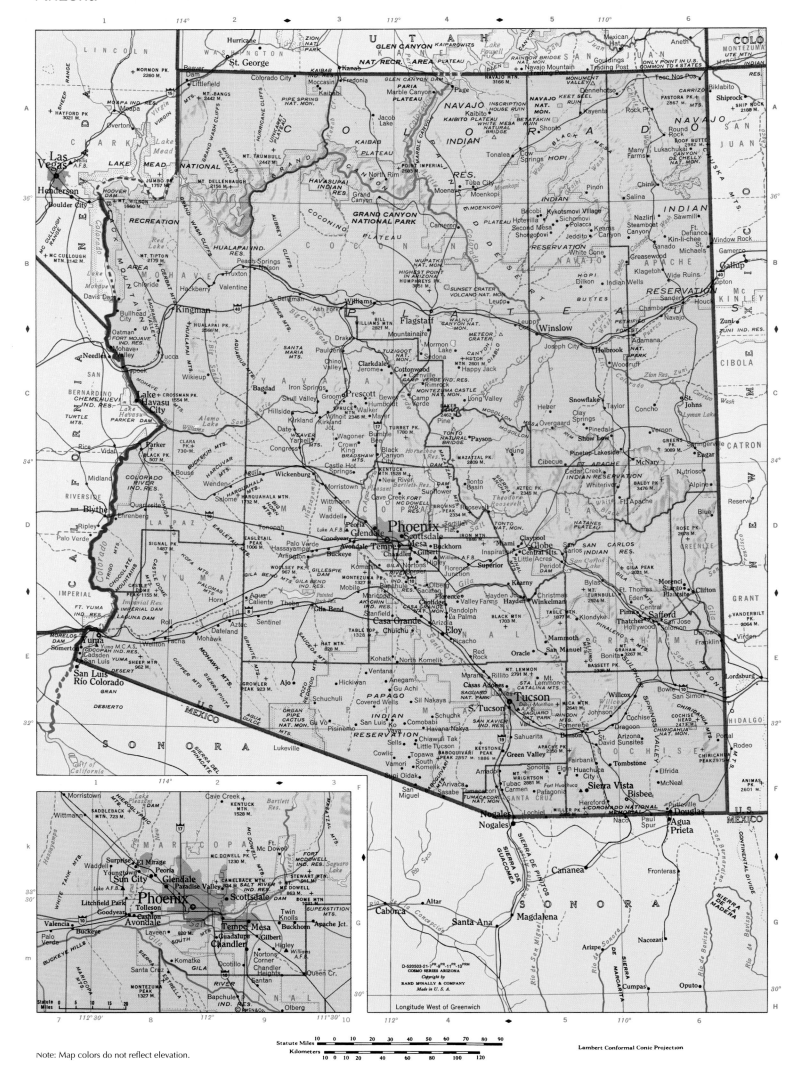

Note: Map colors do not reflect elevation.

Statute Miles 10 0 10 20 30 40 50 60 70 80 90

Kilometers 10 0 10 20 40 60 80 100 120

Lambert Conformal Conic Projection

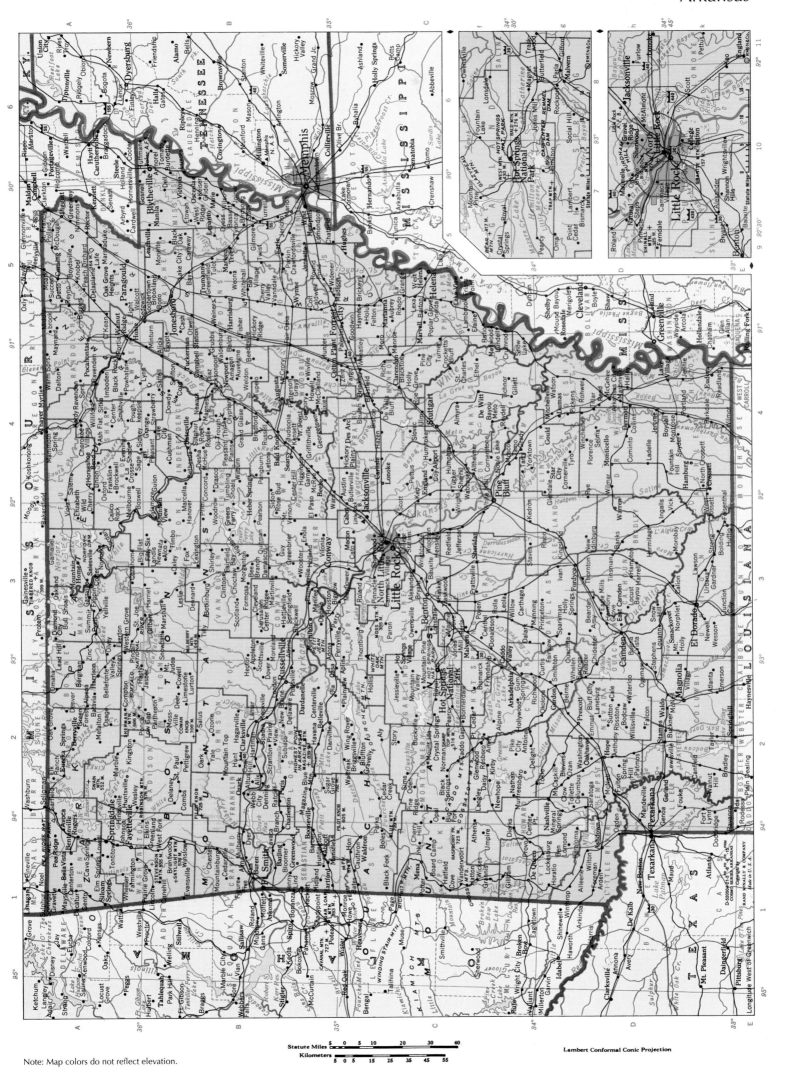

Note: Map colors do not reflect elevation.

Statute Miles   5 0 5   10   20   30   40
Kilometers   5 0 5   15   25   35   45   55

Lambert Conformal Conic Projection

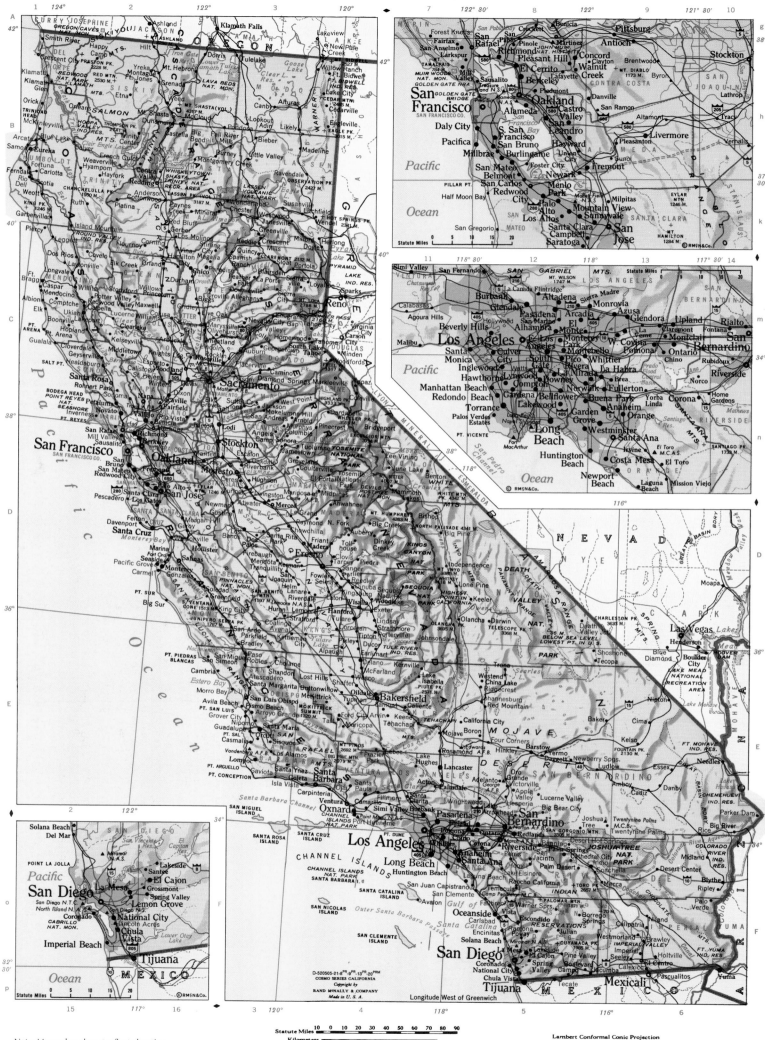

Note: Map colors do not reflect elevation.

Statute Miles
Kilometers

Lambert Conformal Conic Projection

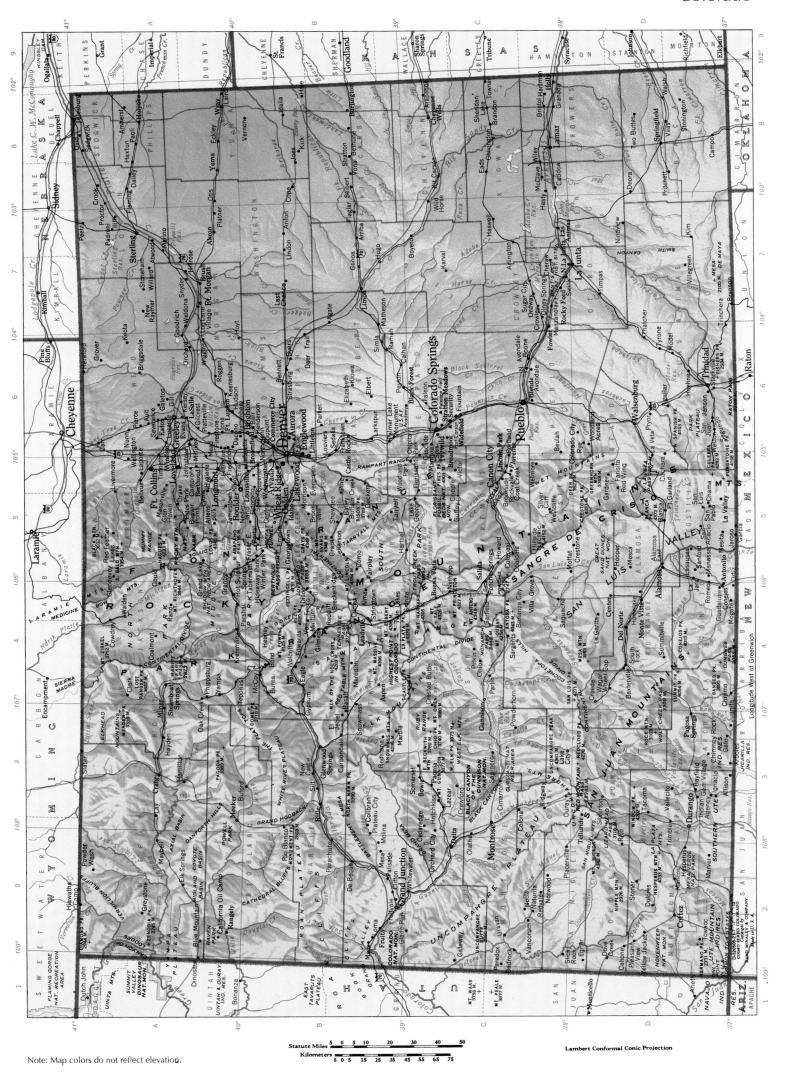

Note: Map colors do not reflect elevation.

Statute Miles 5 0 5 10 20 30 40 50
Kilometers 5 0 5 15 25 35 45 55 65 75

Lambert Conformal Conic Projection

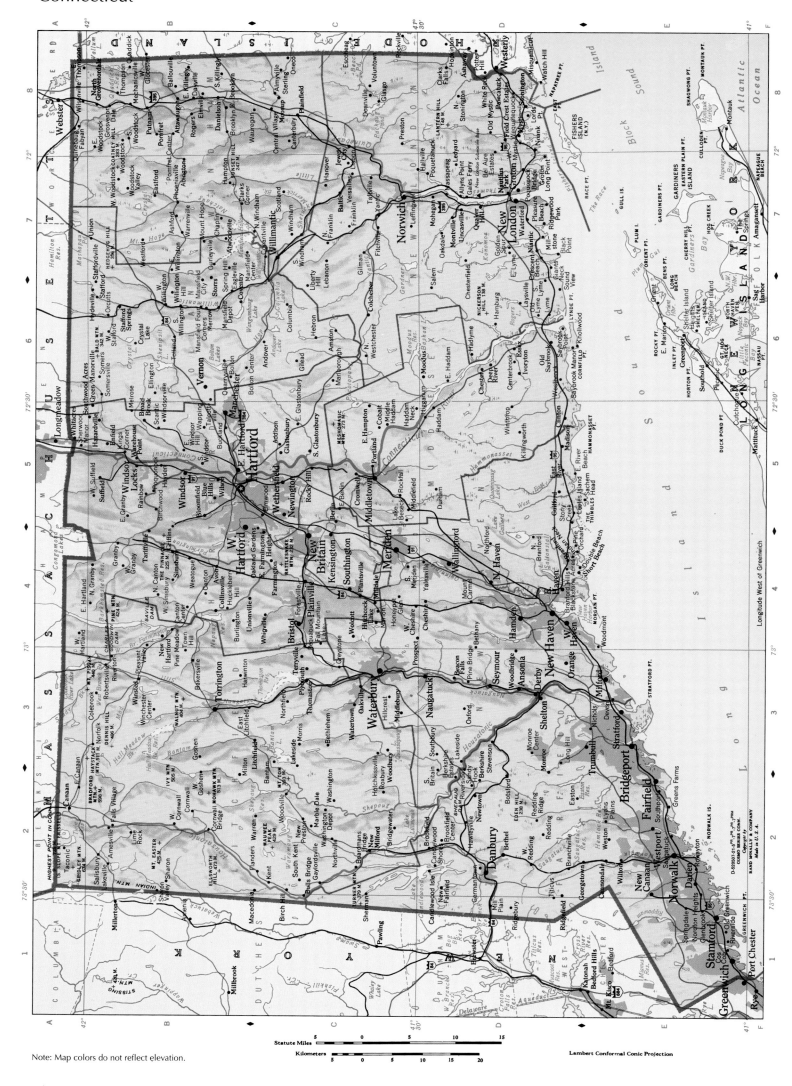

Note: Map colors do not reflect elevation.

Statute Miles

5　　0　　5　　10　　15

Kilometers

5　　0　　5　　10　　15　　20

Lambert Conformal Conic Projection

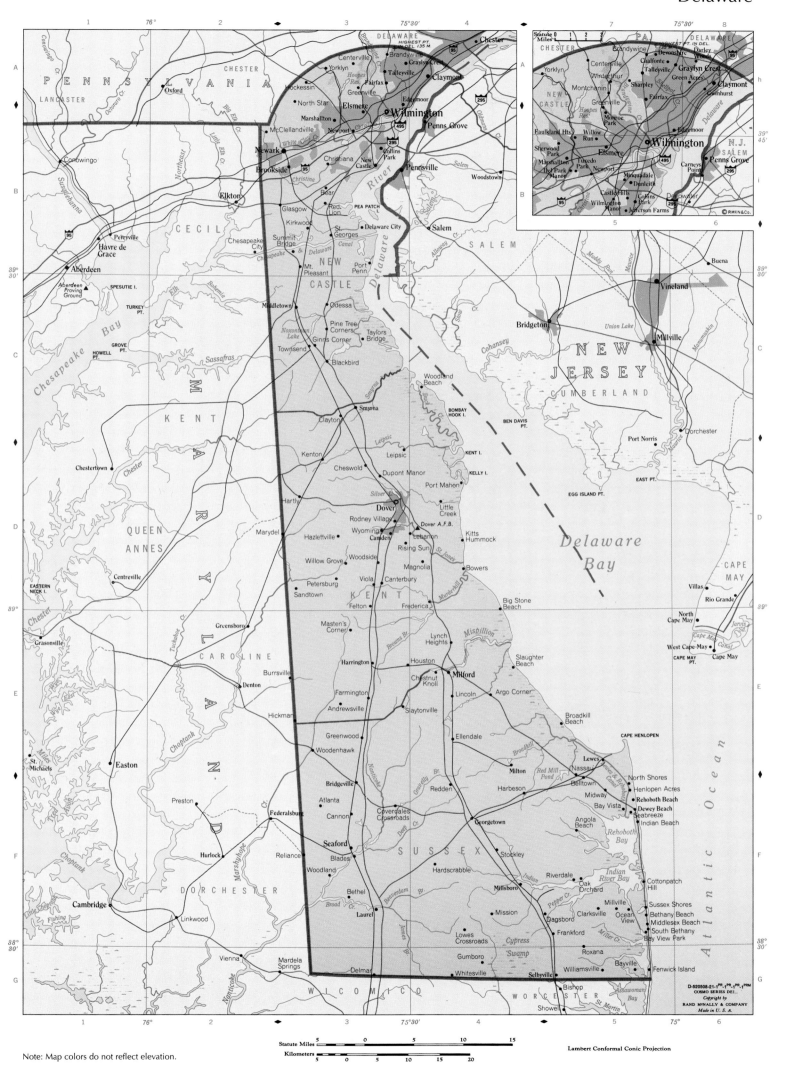

Note: Map colors do not reflect elevation.

Statute Miles
Kilometers

Lambert Conformal Conic Projection

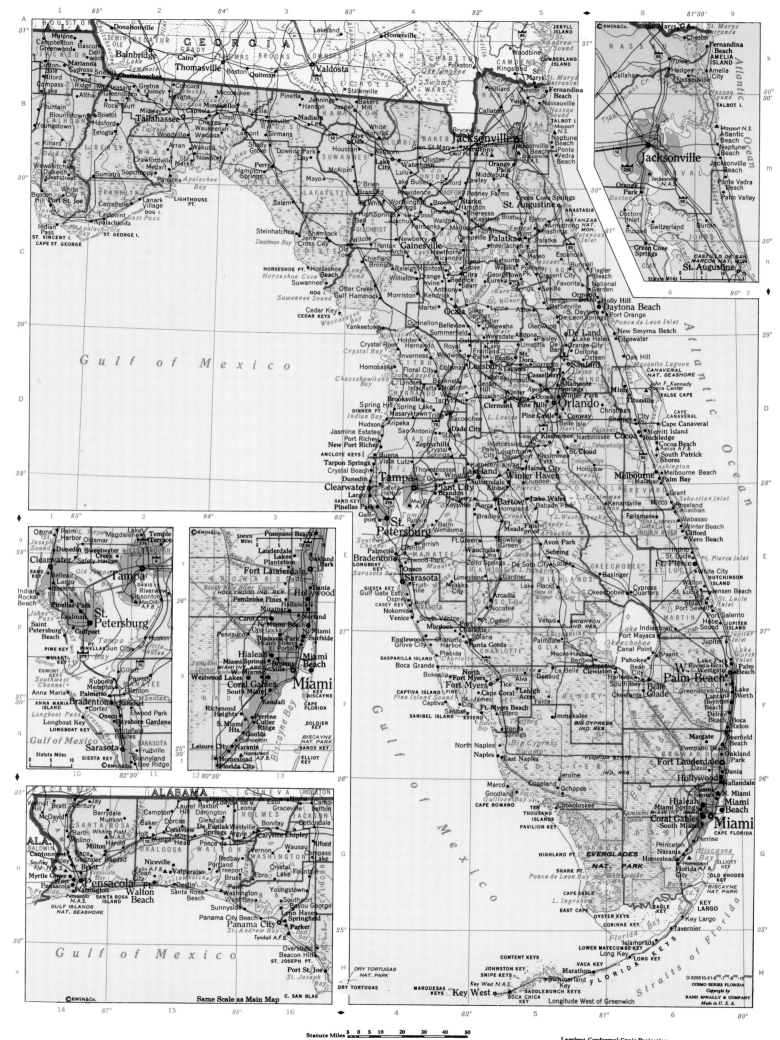

Note: Map colors do not reflect elevation.

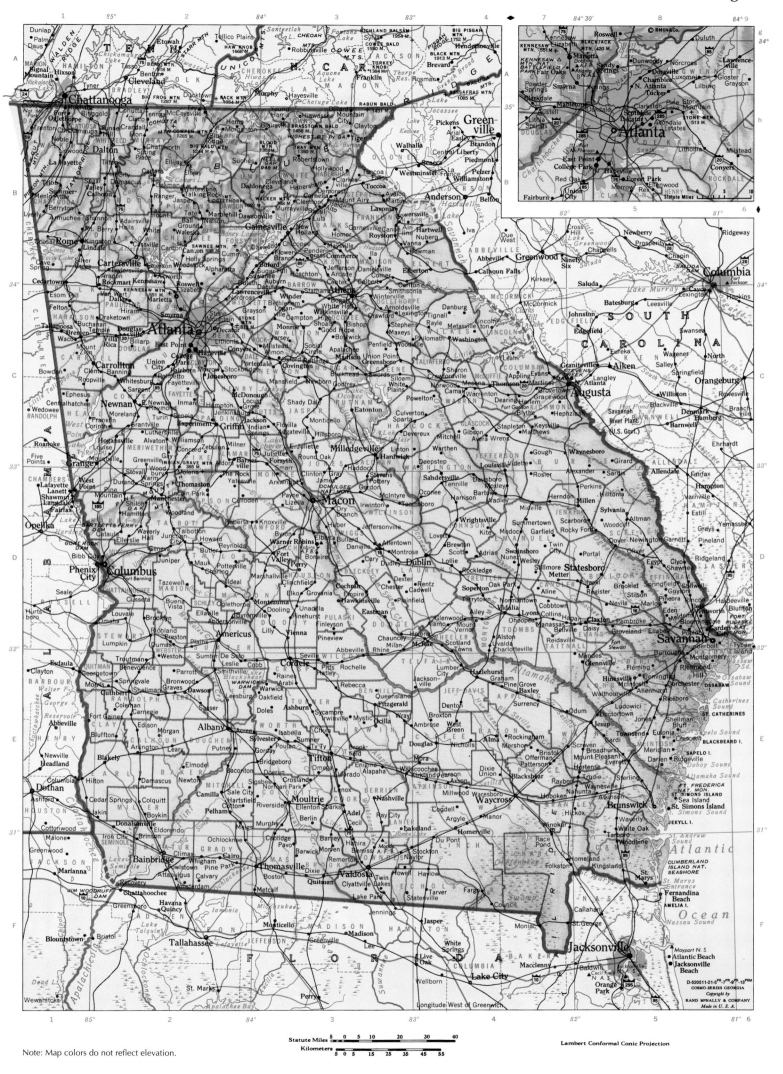

Statute Miles
Kilometers
Lambert Conformal Conic Projection

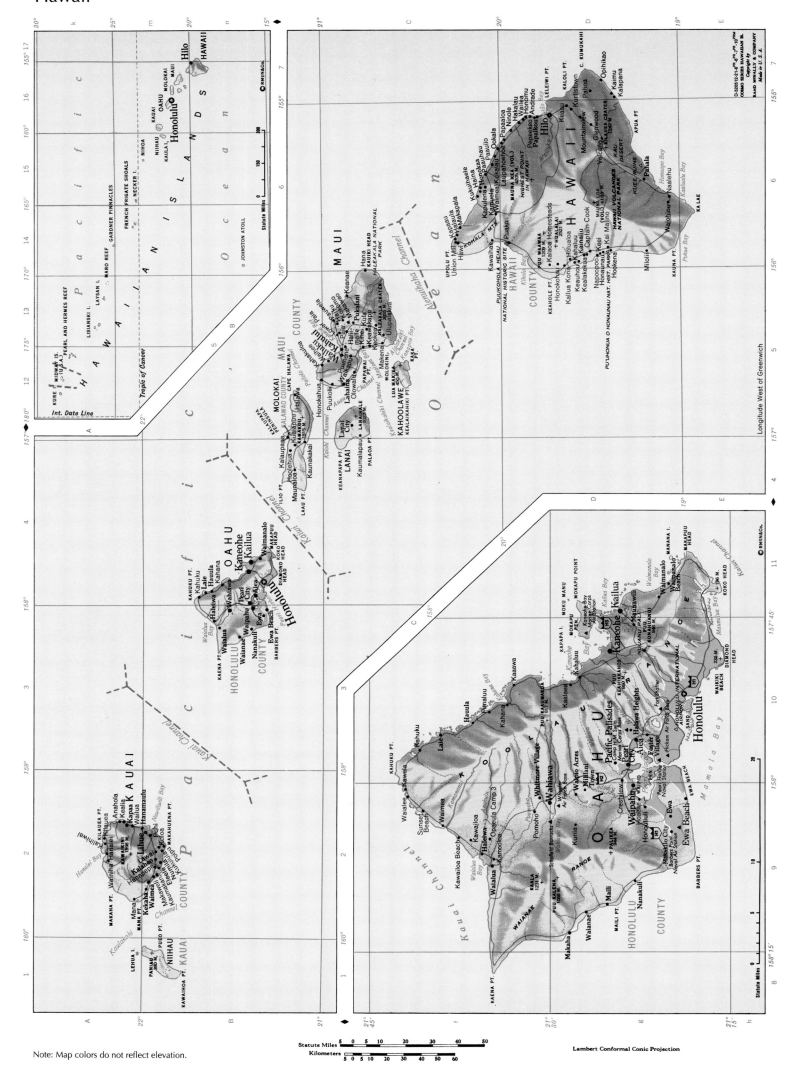

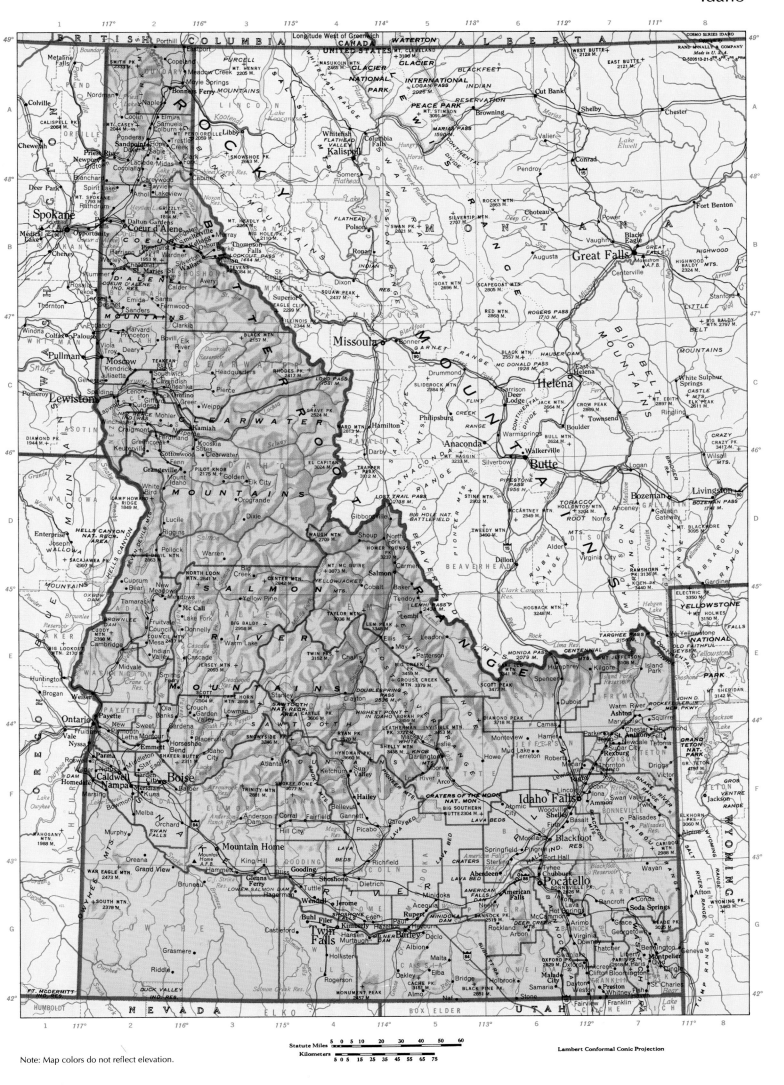

Note: Map colors do not reflect elevation.

Statute Miles 5 0 5 10   20   30   40   50   60
Kilometers 5 0 5 15 25 35 45 55 65 75

Lambert Conformal Conic Projection

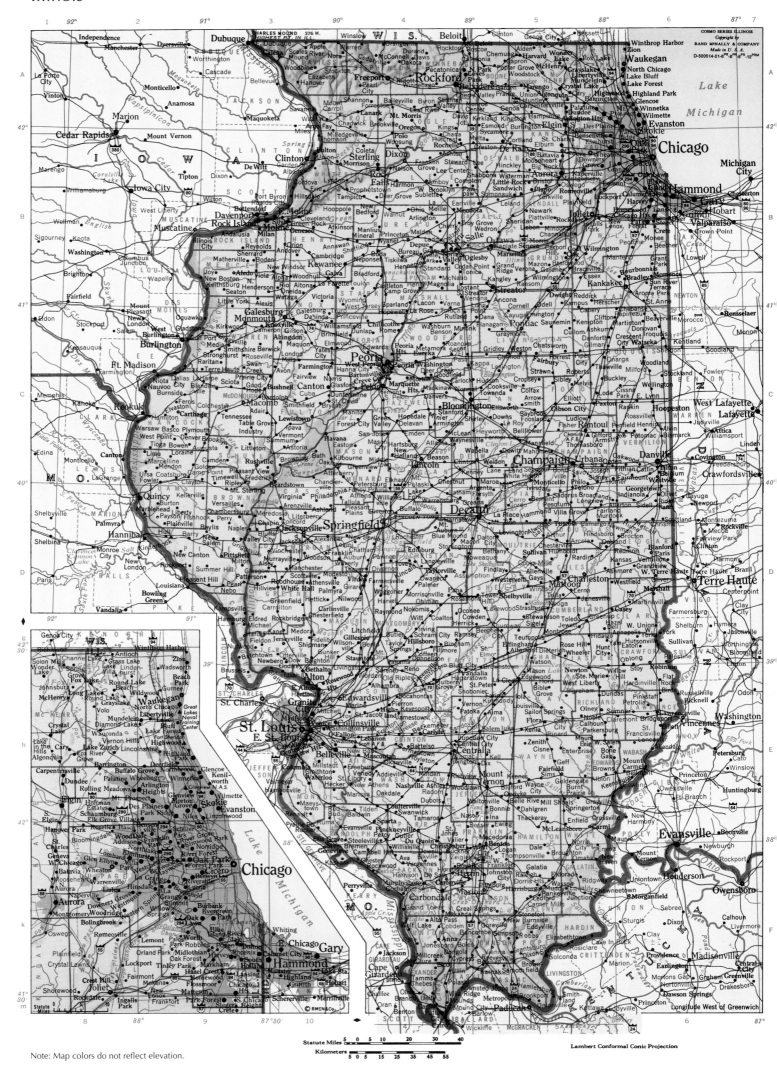

Note: Map colors do not reflect elevation.

Statute Miles   5 0 5   10   20   30   40

Kilometers   5 0 5 15 25 35 45 55

Lambert Conformal Conic Projection

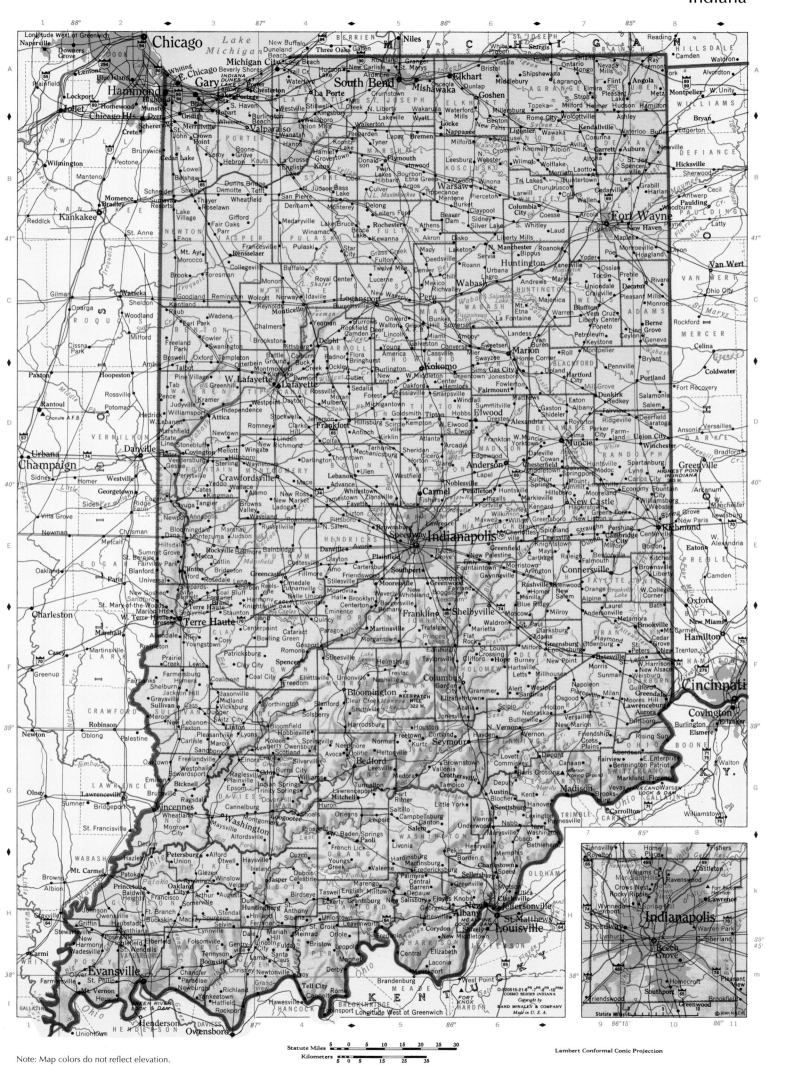

Note: Map colors do not reflect elevation.

Statute Miles 5 0 5 10 15 20 25 30
Kilometers 5 0 5 15 25 35

Lambert Conformal Conic Projection

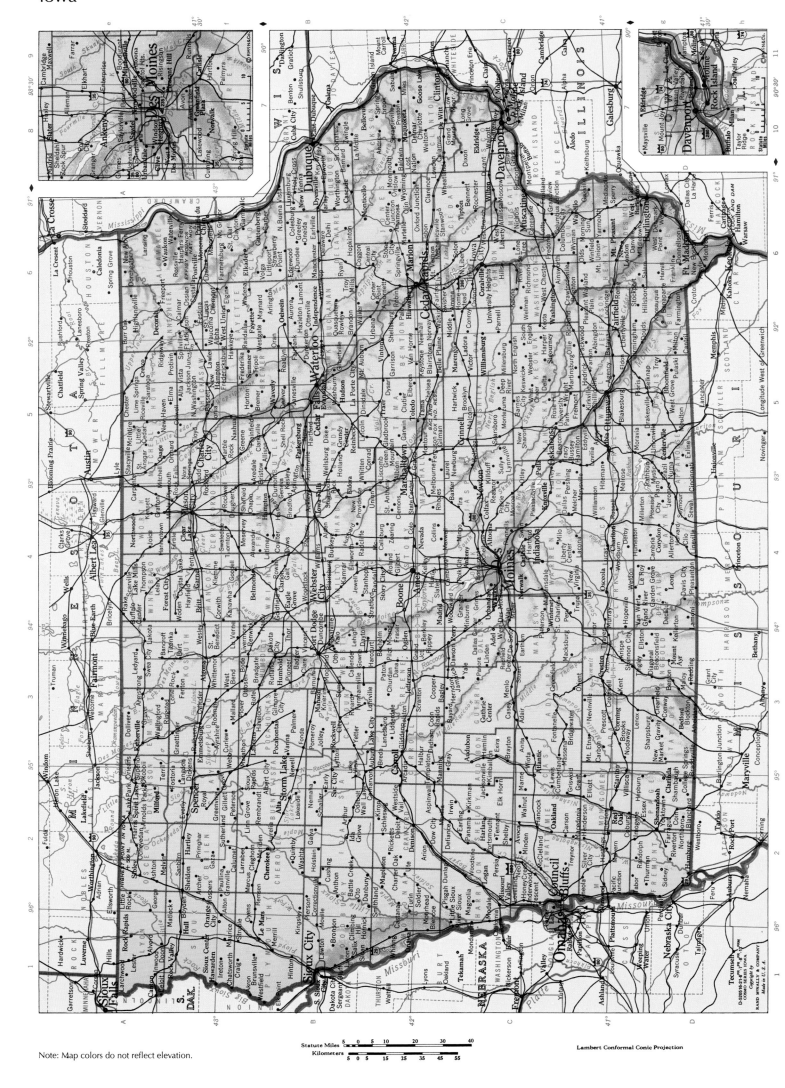

Note: Map colors do not reflect elevation.

Statute Miles 5 0 5 10   20   30   40

Kilometers 5 0 5   15   25   35   45   55

Lambert Conformal Conic Projection

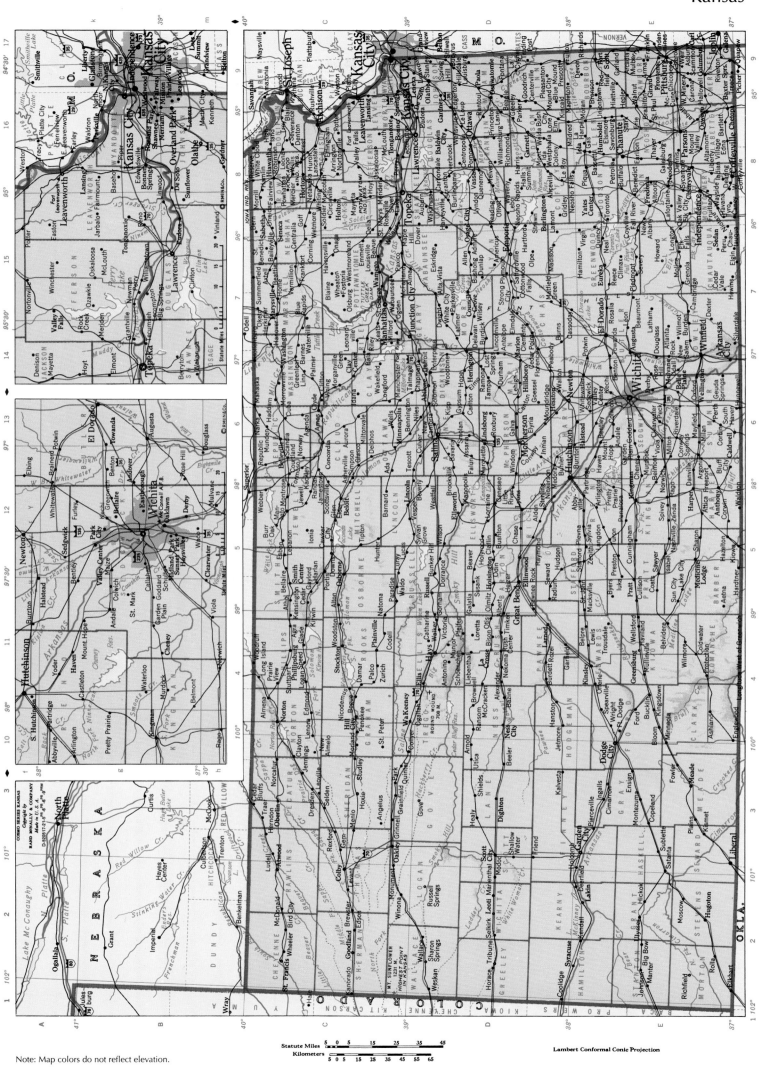

Note: Map colors do not reflect elevation.

Statute Miles 5 0 5 15 25 35 45

Kilometers 5 0 5 15 25 35 45 55 65

Lambert Conformal Conic Projection

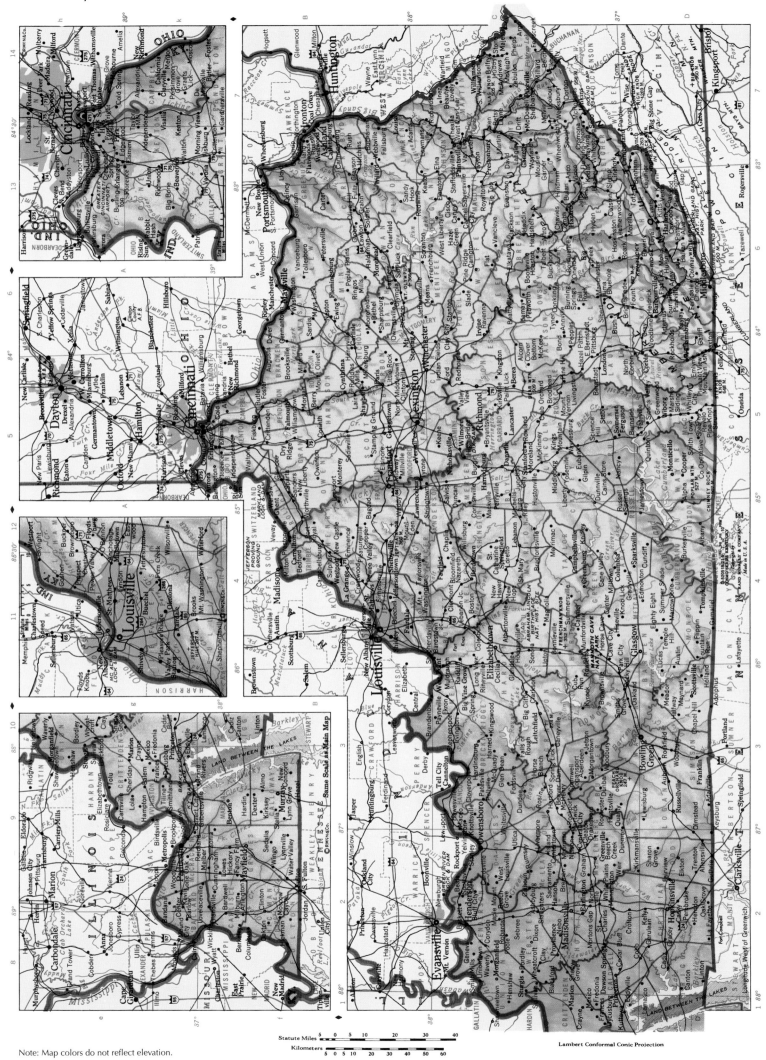

Note: Map colors do not reflect elevation.

Statute Miles 5 0 5 10 20 30 40

Kilometers 5 0 5 10 20 30 40 50 60

Lambert Conformal Conic Projection

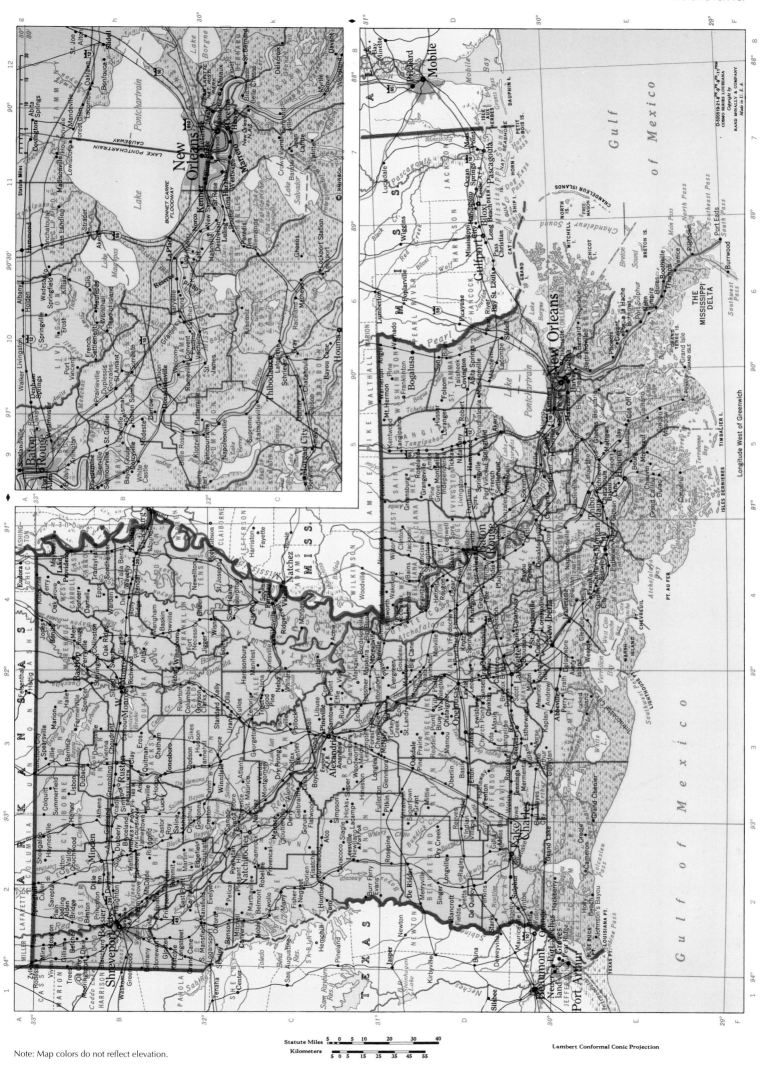

Note: Map colors do not reflect elevation.

Statute Miles   5 0 5 10   20   30   40
Kilometers   5 0 5   15 25   35   45   55

Lambert Conformal Conic Projection

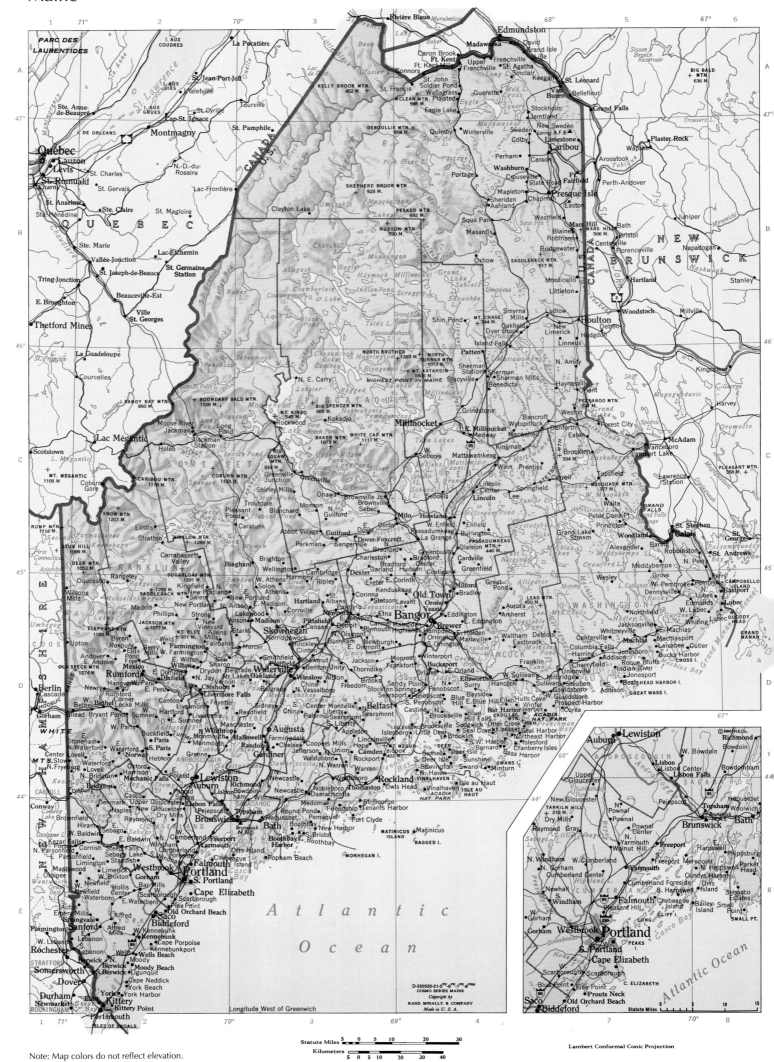

Note: Map colors do not reflect elevation.

Statute Miles
Kilometers

D-520520-21-5TH·8TH·7TH·PRM
COSMO SERIES MAINE
Copyright by
RAND McNALLY & COMPANY
Made in U.S.A.

Lambert Conformal Conic Projection

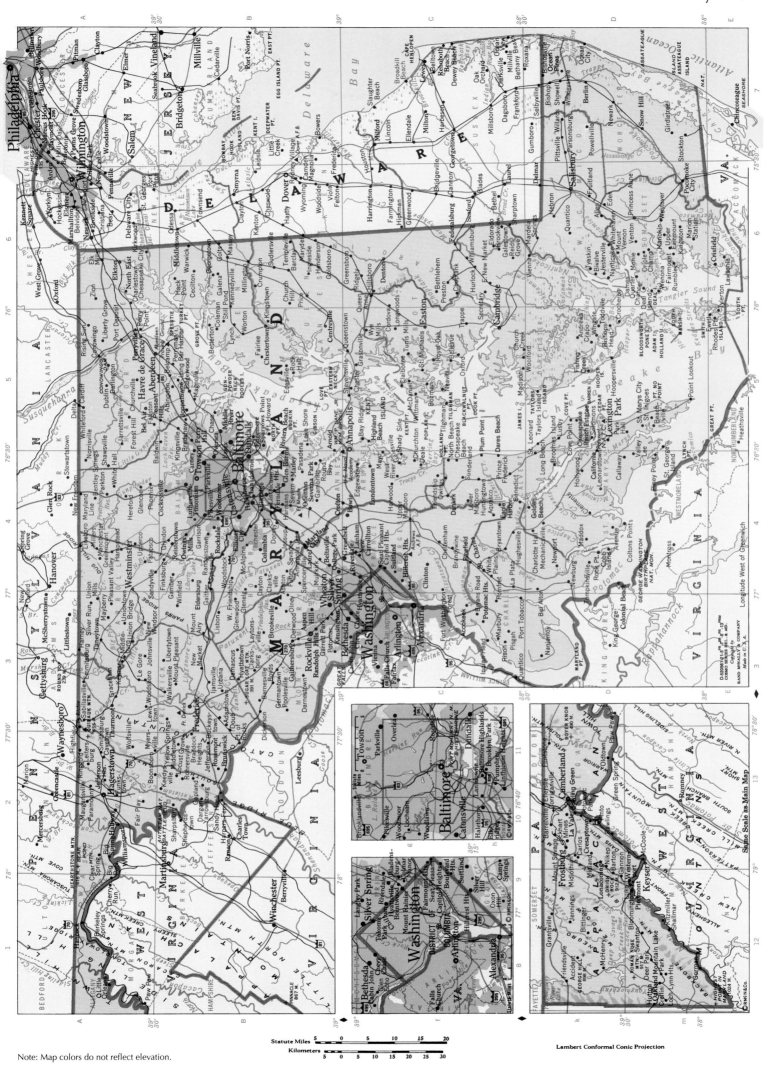

Note: Map colors do not reflect elevation.

Statute Miles 5 0 5 10 15 20
Kilometers 5 0 5 10 15 20 25 30

Lambert Conformal Conic Projection

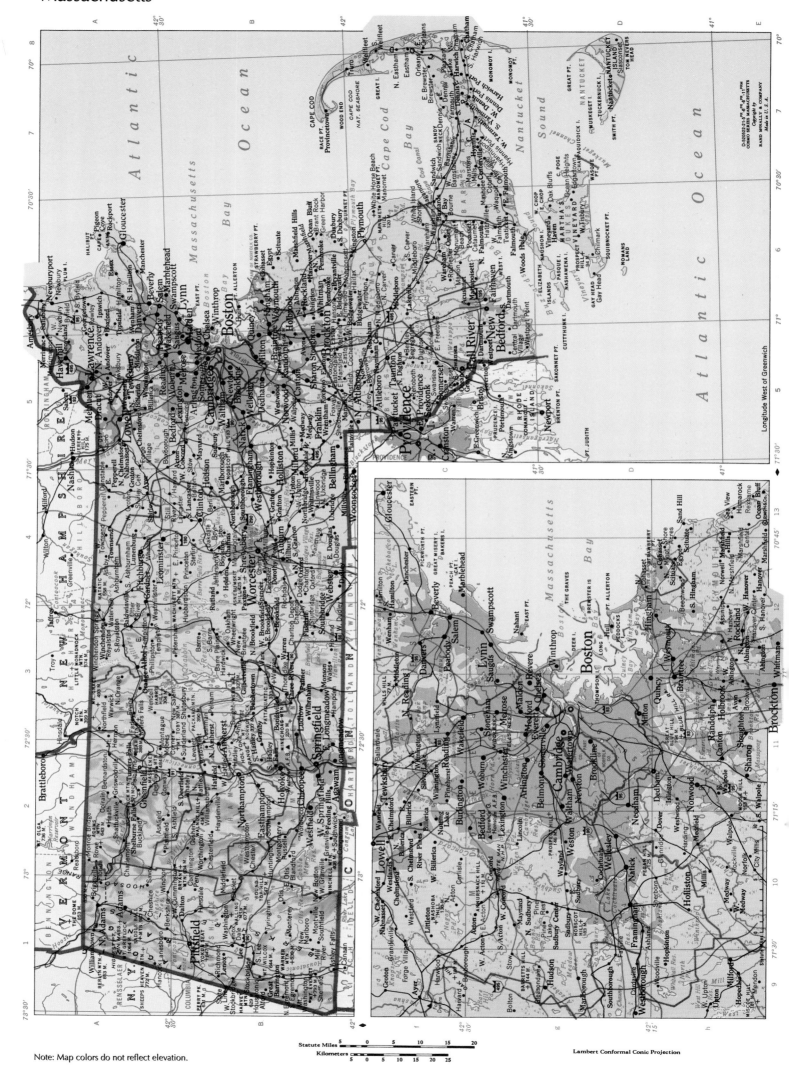

Note: Map colors do not reflect elevation.

Statute Miles

Kilometers

Lambert Conformal Conic Projection

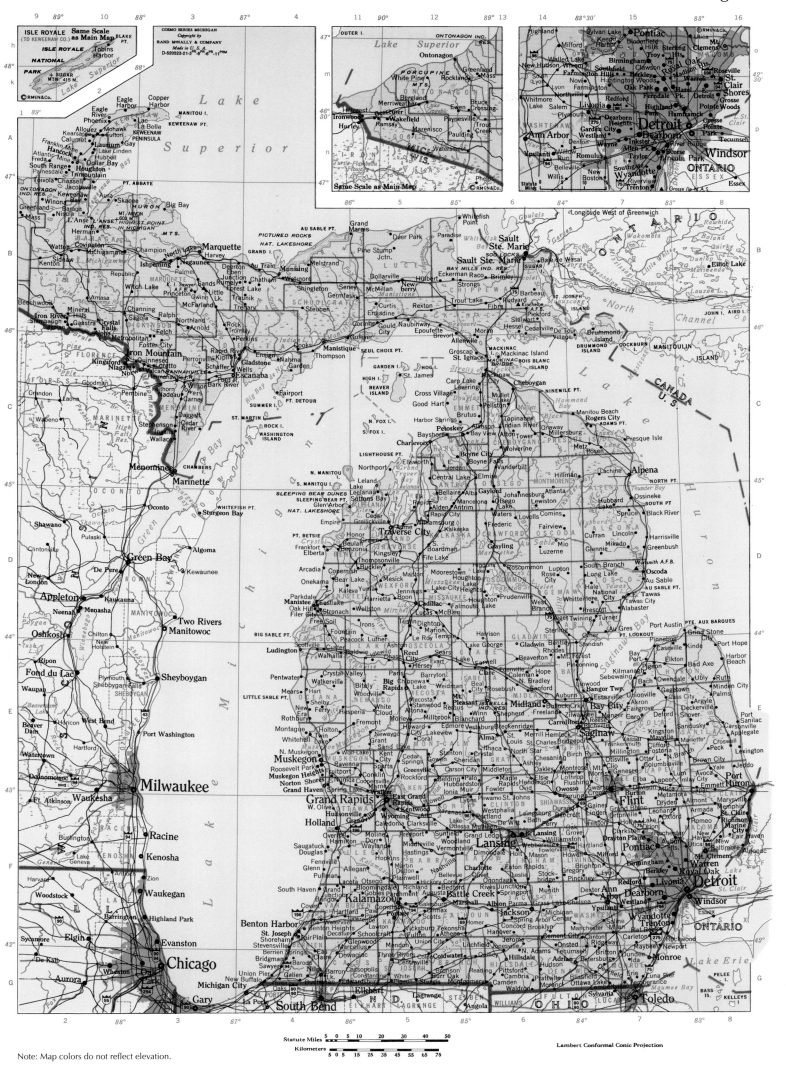

Note: Map colors do not reflect elevation.

Statute Miles 5 0 5 10 20 30 40 50
Kilometers 5 0 5 15 25 35 45 55 65 75

Lambert Conformal Conic Projection

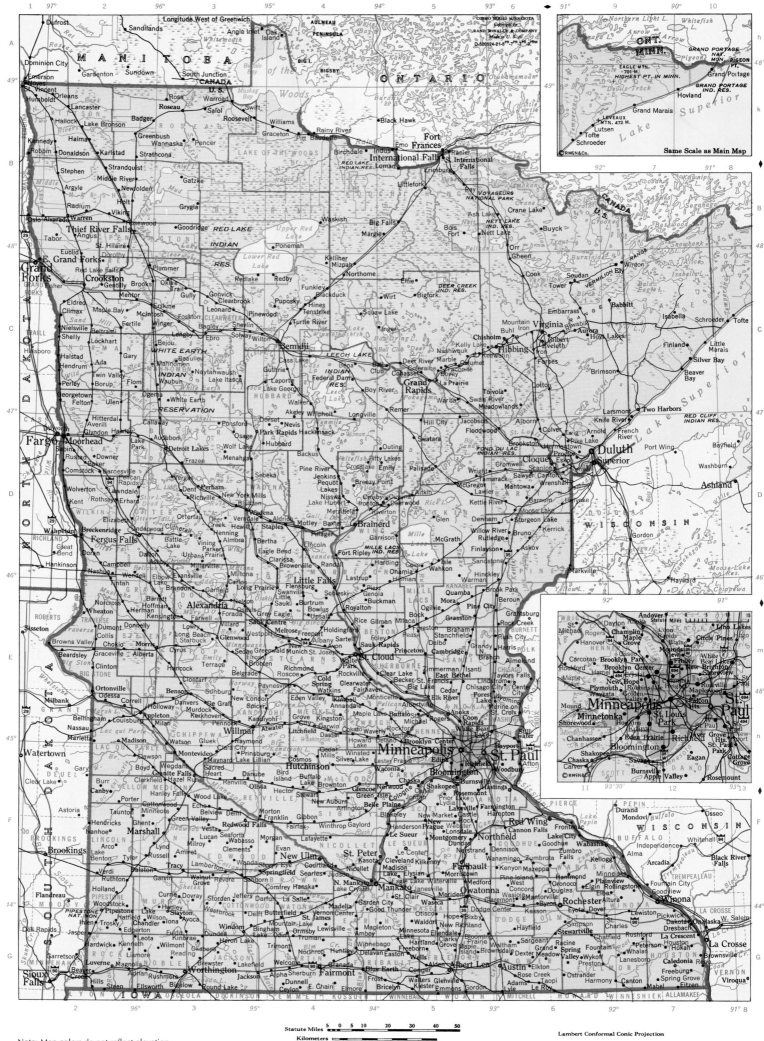

Note: Map colors do not reflect elevation.

Statute Miles   5   0   5   10   20   30   40   50
Kilometers   5   0   5   15   25   35   45   55   65

Lambert Conformal Conic Projection

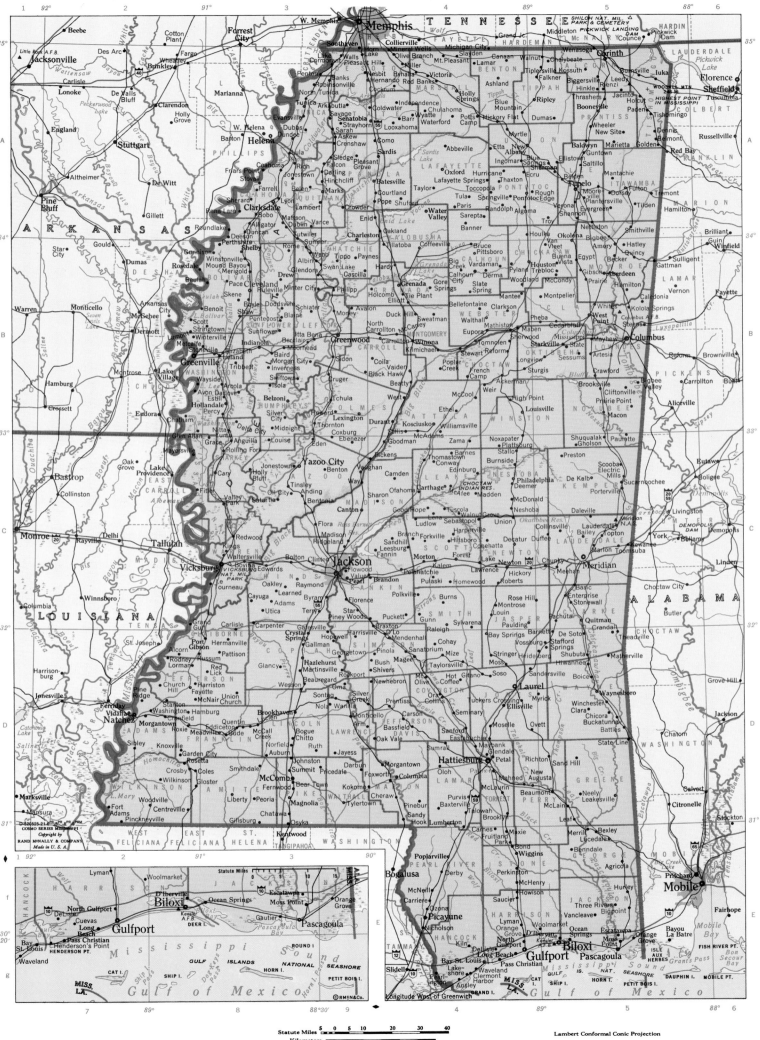

Note: Map colors do not reflect elevation.

Statute Miles 5 0 5 10 20 30 40
Kilometers 5 0 15 25 35 45 55

Lambert Conformal Conic Projection

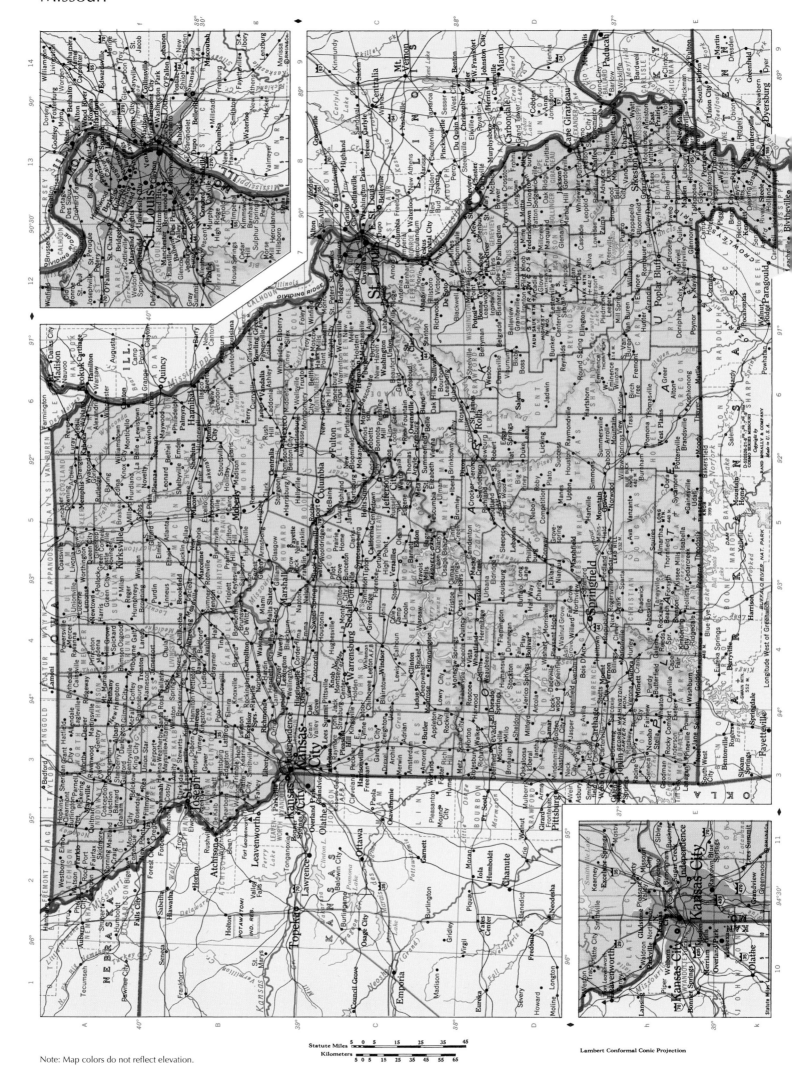

Note: Map colors do not reflect elevation.

Statute Miles 5 0 5   15   25   35   45
Kilometers 5 0 5 15 25 35 45 55 65

Lambert Conformal Conic Projection

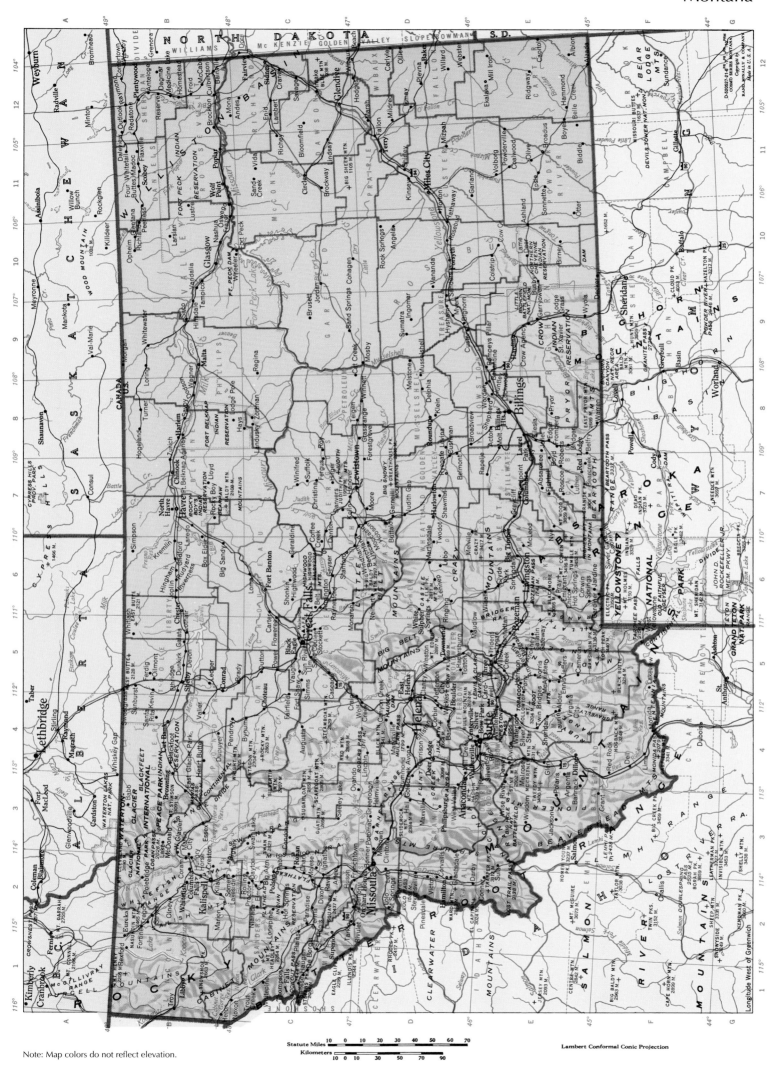

Note: Map colors do not reflect elevation.

Statute Miles   10   0   10   20   30   40   50   60   70
Kilometers   10   0   10   30   50   70   90

Lambert Conformal Conic Projection

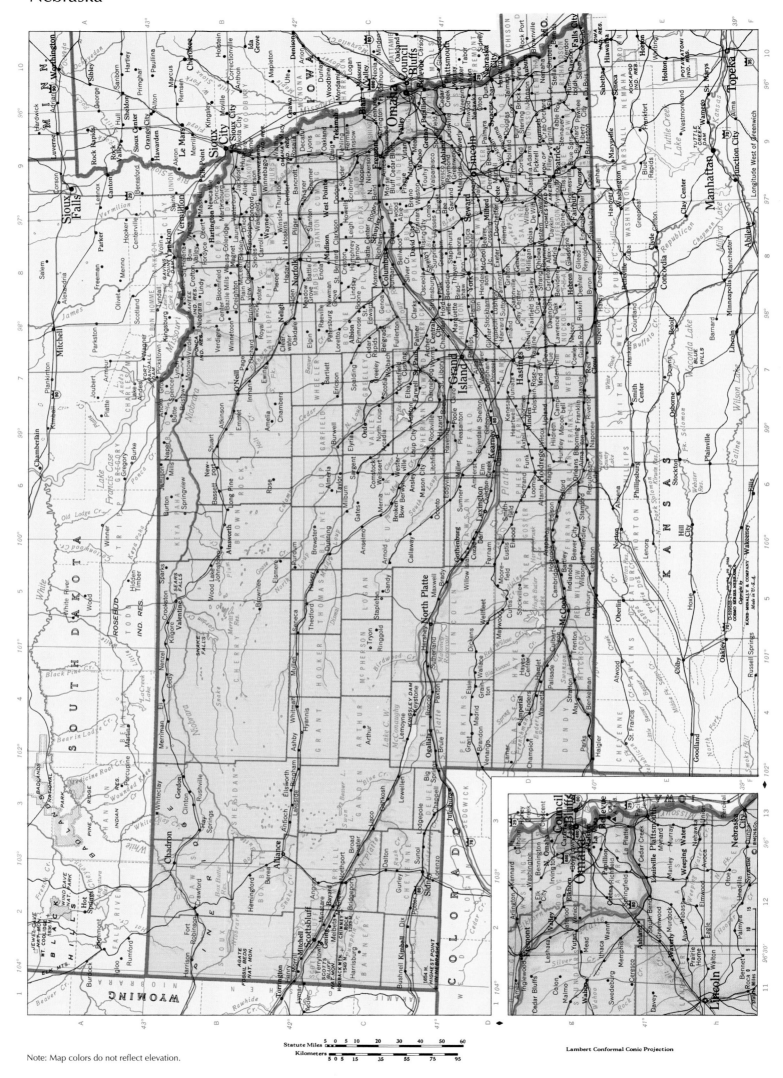

Note: Map colors do not reflect elevation.

Statute Miles   5 0 5 10   20   30   40   50   60
Kilometers   5 0 5 15   35   55   75   95

Lambert Conformal Conic Projection

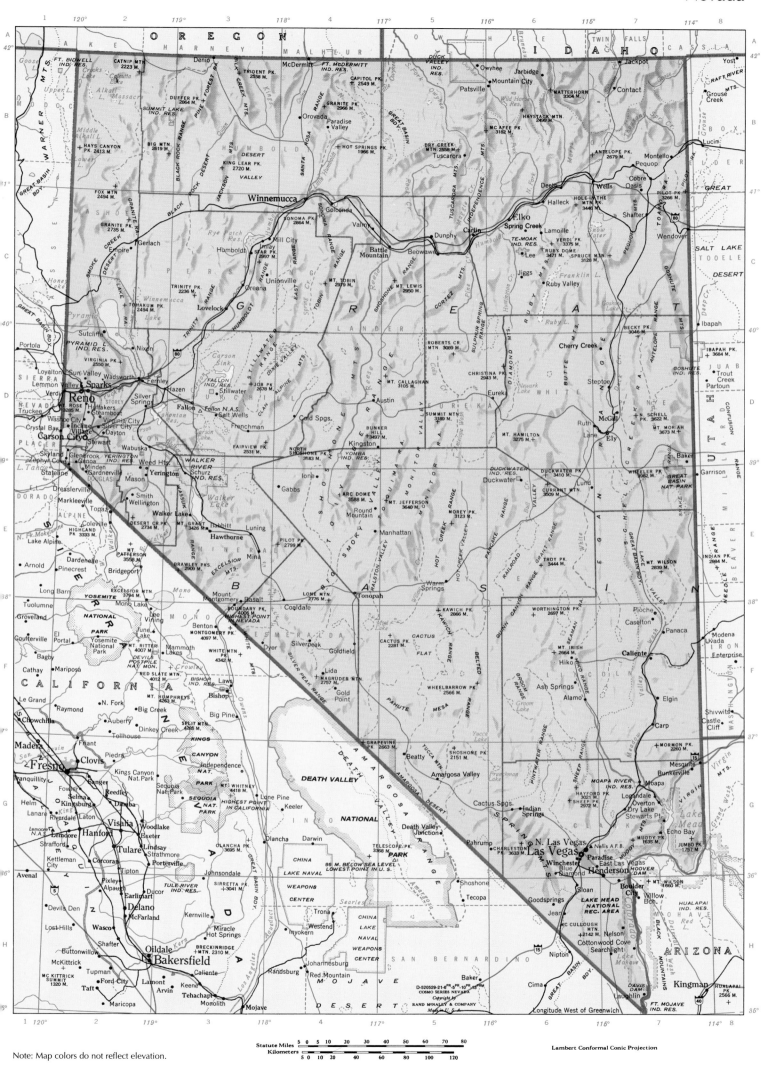

Note: Map colors do not reflect elevation.

Statute Miles 5 0 5 10   20   30   40   50   60   70   80
Kilometers 5 0 10 20   40   60   80   100   120

Lambert Conformal Conic Projection

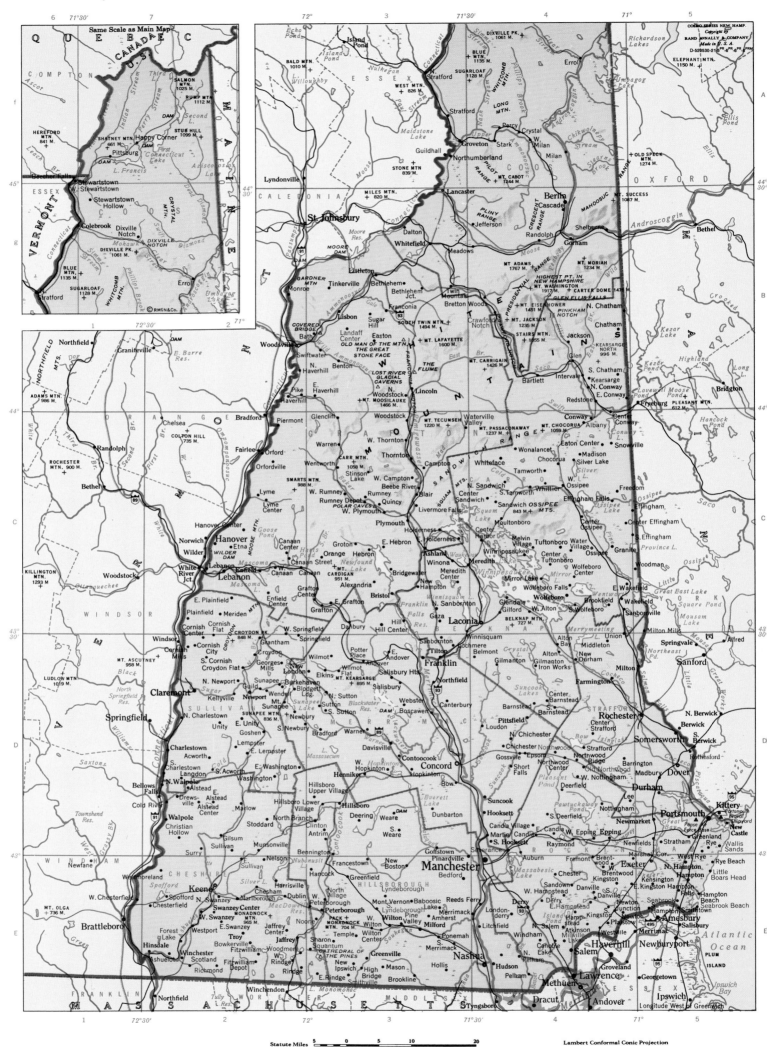

Note: Map colors do not reflect elevation.

Statute Miles   5   0   5   10   20

Kilometers   5   0   5   10   15   20   25

Lambert Conformal Conic Projection

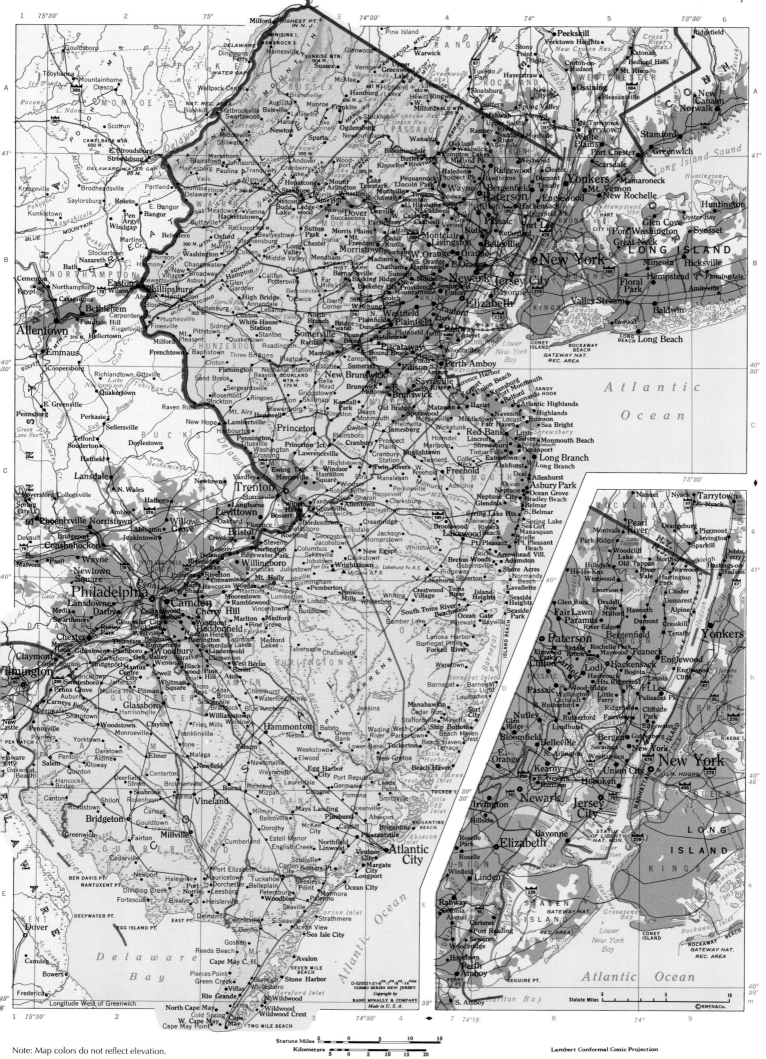

Note: Map colors do not reflect elevation.

Longitude West of Greenwich

Statute Miles
Kilometers

D-520531-21-6 7^P-8^P-14^P-M
Copyright by
RAND M?NALLY & COMPANY
Made in U.S.A.

Lambert Conformal Conic Projection

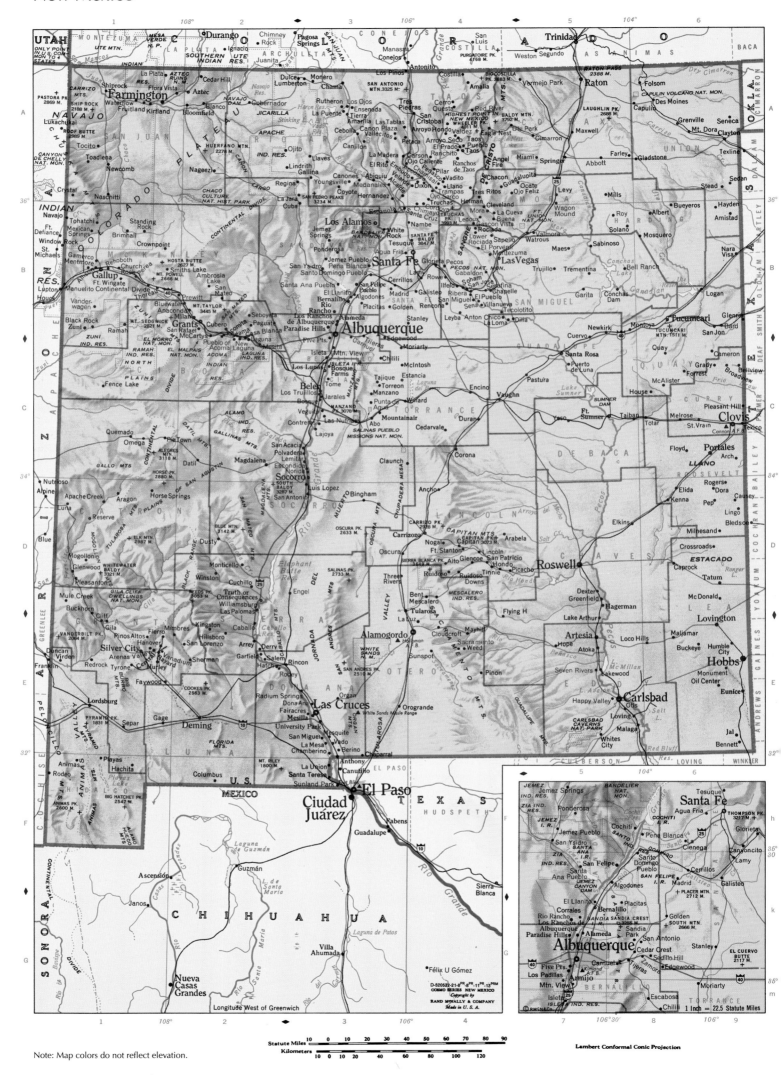

Note: Map colors do not reflect elevation.

Statute Miles
10 0 10 20 30 40 50 60 70 80 90

Kilometers
10 0 10 20 40 60 80 100 120

Lambert Conformal Conic Projection

1 Inch = 22.5 Statute Miles

D-520532-21-8᠎ᴾᴹ-8᠎ᴾᴹ-11᠎ᴾᴿ-13᠎ᴾᴿᴹ
COSMO SERIES NEW MEXICO
Copyright by
RAND McNALLY & COMPANY
Made in U.S.A.

Longitude West of Greenwich

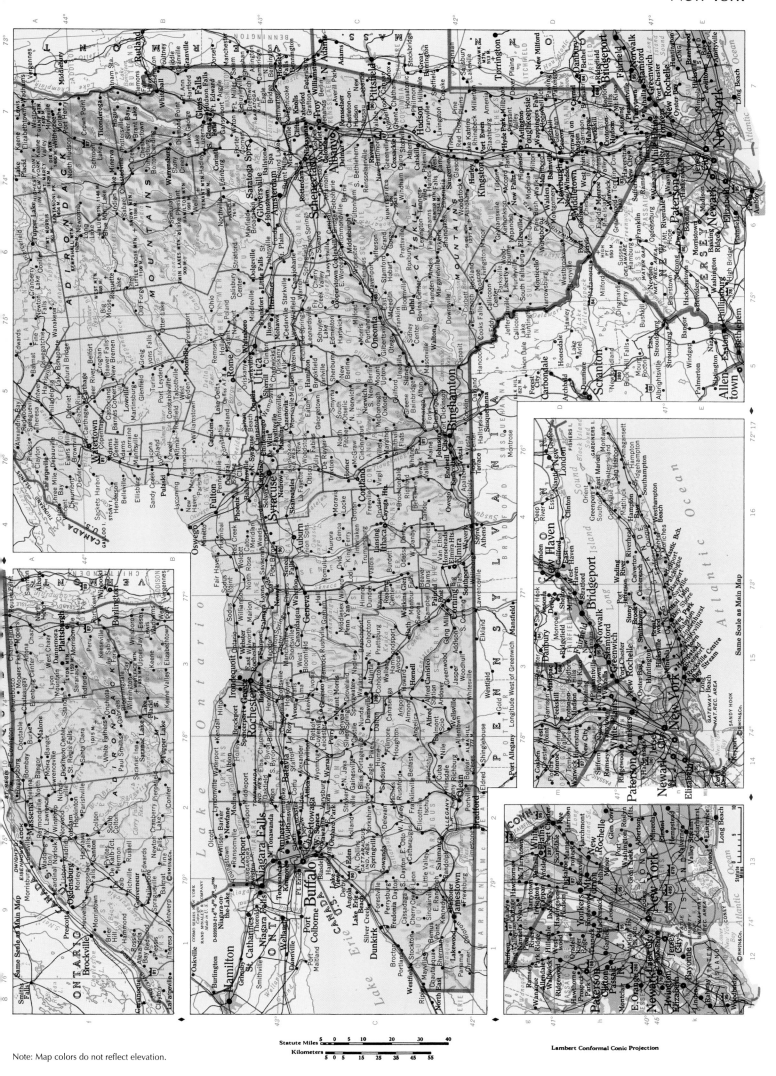

Note: Map colors do not reflect elevation.

Statute Miles 5 0 5 10   20   30   40
Kilometers 5 0 5   15   25   35   45   55

Lambert Conformal Conic Projection

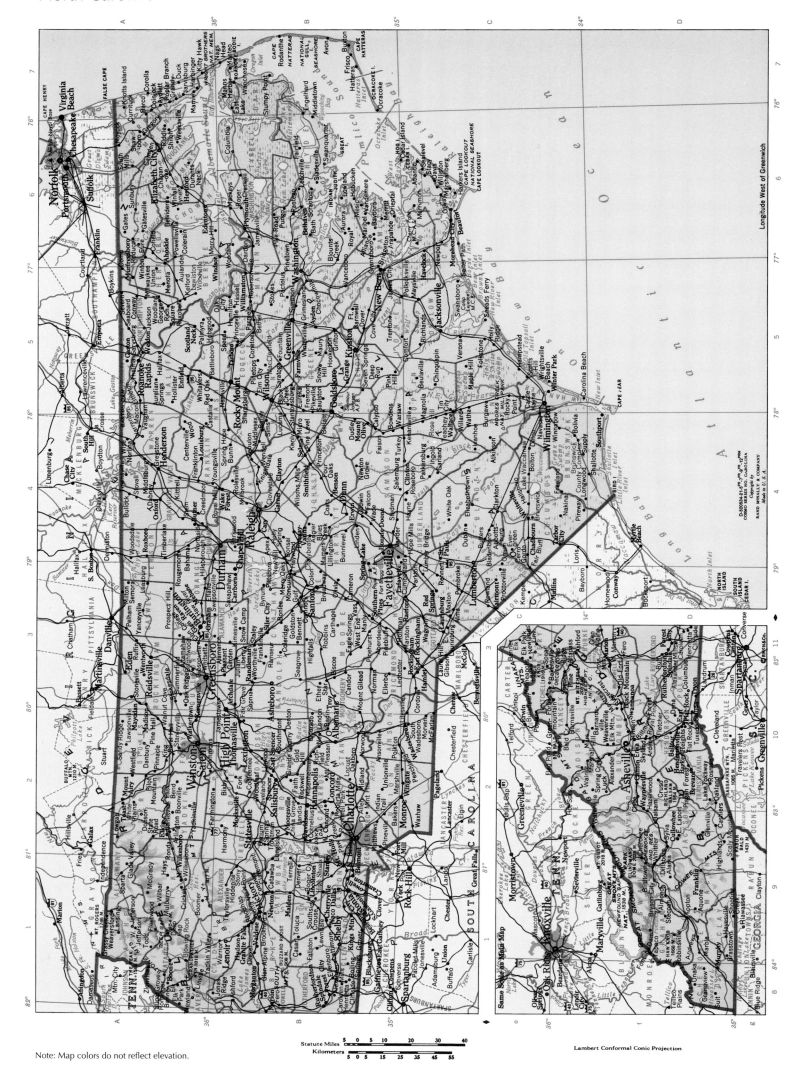

Note: Map colors do not reflect elevation.

Statute Miles
Kilometers

Lambert Conformal Conic Projection

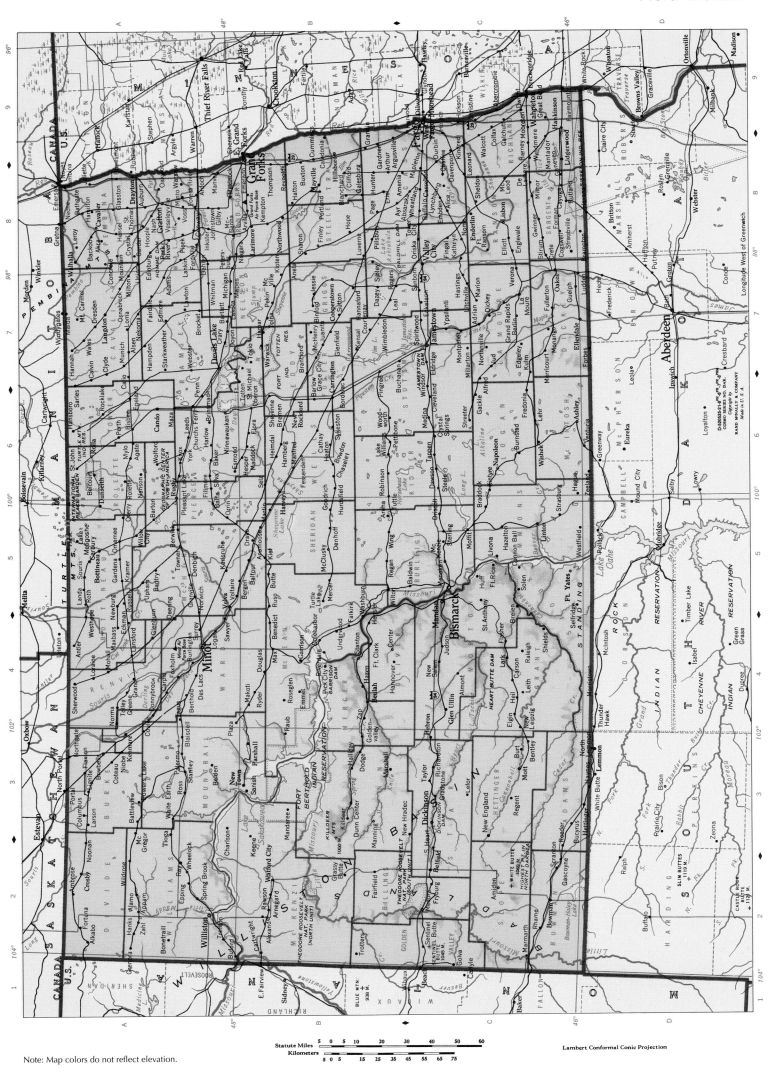

Note: Map colors do not reflect elevation.

Statute Miles 5 0 5 10 20 30 40 50 60

Kilometers 5 0 5 15 25 35 45 55 65 75

Lambert Conformal Conic Projection

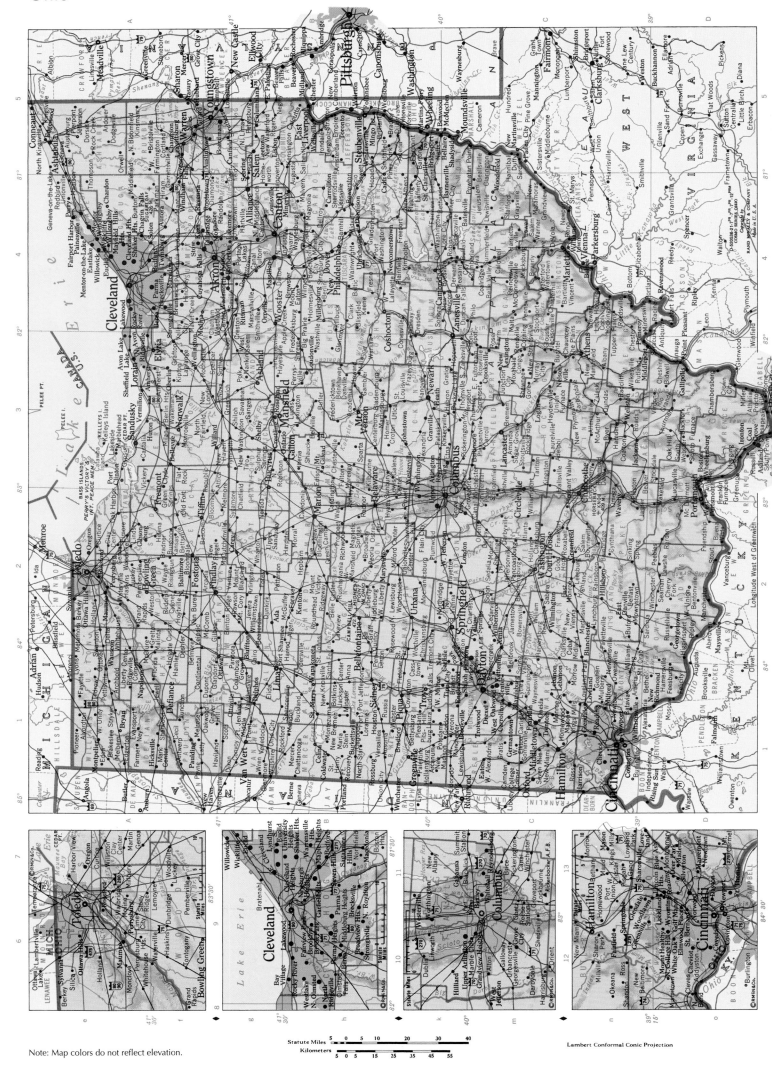

Note: Map colors do not reflect elevation.

Statute Miles 5 0 5 10 20 30 40

Kilometers 5 0 5 15 25 35 45 55

Lambert Conformal Conic Projection

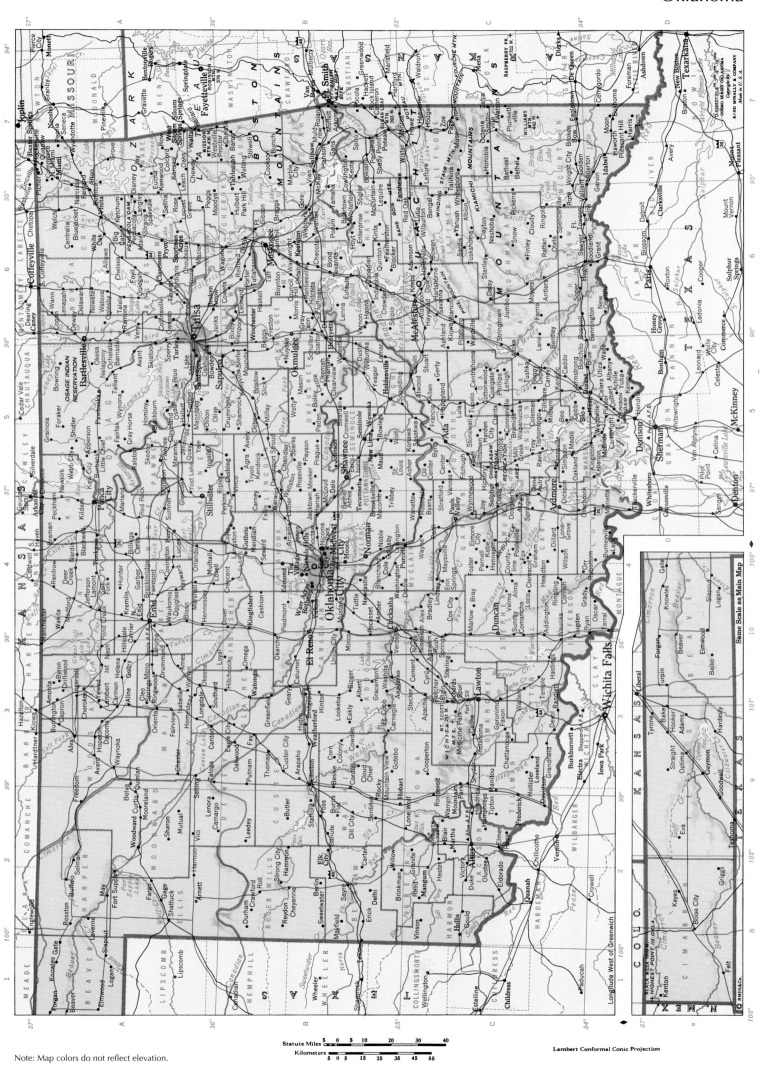

Note: Map colors do not reflect elevation.

Statute Miles 5 0 5 10 20 30 40
Kilometers 5 0 5 15 25 35 45 55

Lambert Conformal Conic Projection

Same Scale as Main Map

© RMM&Co.

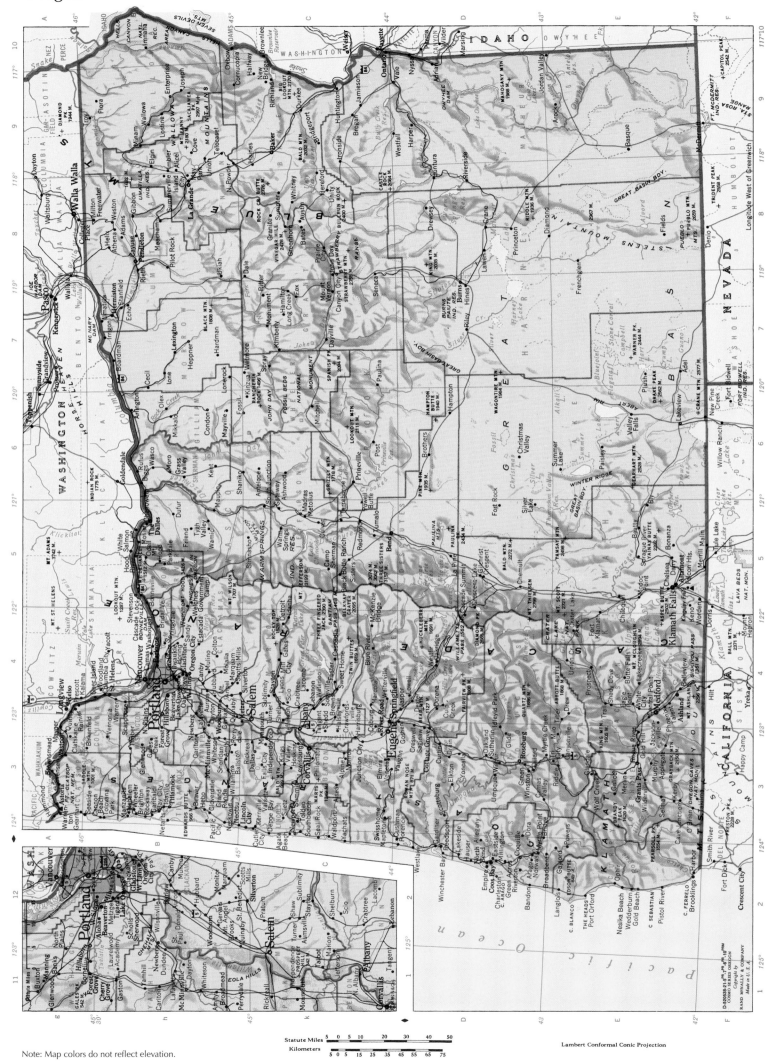

Note: Map colors do not reflect elevation.

Statute Miles   5 0 5 10   20   30   40   50
Kilometers   5 0 5 15   25   35   45   55   65 75

Lambert Conformal Conic Projection

D-580538-21-575_JPR_JPR_10^PRM
COSMO SERIES OREGON
Copyright by
RAND MCNALLY & COMPANY
Made in U.S.A.

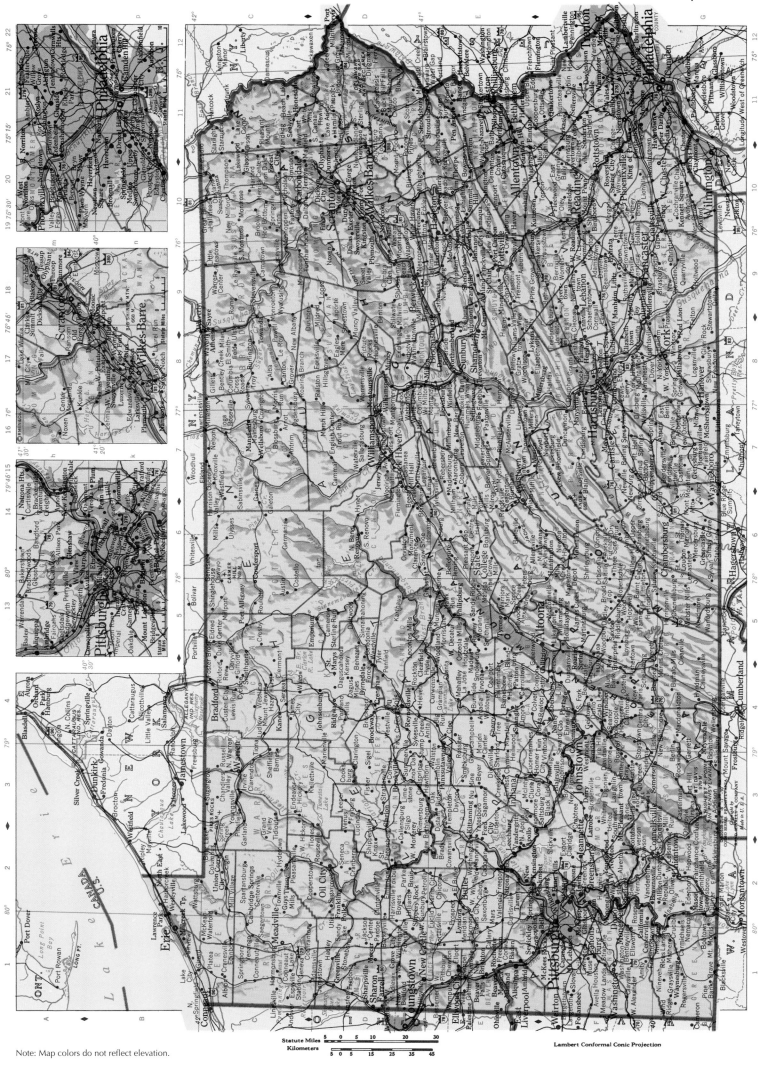

Note: Map colors do not reflect elevation.

Statute Miles
Kilometers

Lambert Conformal Conic Projection

WORCESTER

NORFOLK

Franklin

Wrentham

Foxboro

North Easton

South Easton

Mansfield

Whitin Reservoir

East Douglas

Uxbridge

Millville

Lake Chaubunagungamaug

Blackstone

Blackstone

Grants Mills

Diamond Hill Reservoir

North Attleboro

Norton Reservoir

Norton

Wallum Lake

Branch Village

Woonsocket

Diamond Hill

Slatersville

Forestdale

Union Village

Cumberland Hill

Arnold Mills Reservoir

Arnold Mills

Attleboro

Lake Sabbatia

Mohegan

Nasonville

Slatersville Reservoir

Manville

Lippitt Estate

Abbott Run Valley

Ashton

Harrisville

Glendale

Oakland

Primrose

Albion

Berkeley

Valley Falls

Pascoag

Mapleville

Woonsocket Res. No. 3

Quinnville

Limerock

Lonsdale

Saylesville

Taunton

BRISTOL

Tarkiln

Stillwater Reservoir

Central Falls

Pawtucket

Pascoag Reservoir

Bowdish Reservoir

Chepachet

Spragueville

West Greenville

Esmond

North Providence

North Dighton

Thompson

West Glocester

Smith and Sayles Reservoir

Harmony

Waterman Reservoir

Greenville

Providence

East Providence

Seekonk

Dighton

Ponaganset Reservoir

Stack Reservoir

Johnston

Middle Reservoir

HIGHEST POINT IN RHODE ISLAND + JERIMOTH HILL 248 M.

Moswansicut Pond

North Scituate

Cranston

Somerset

Ballouville

South Foster

Saundersville

West Barrington

Ocean Grove

WINDHAM

Scituate Reservoir

Waterman Four Corners

Barrington

Warren

Touisset

Fall River

Foster

Clayville

Warwick

South Swansea

Danielson

Westconnaug Reservoir

Jackson

Conimicut Pt.

Rumstick Pt.

North Watuppa Pond

Hope

Arkwright

Harris

PROVIDENCE

Moosup Valley

West Warwick

Anthony

Quidnick

Greenwich Bay

Providence Pt.

Bristol

South Watuppa Pond

Moosup

Coventry Center

Summit

Coventry

Tiogue Lake

East Greenwich

Patience I.

Common Fence Point

North Tiverton

Greene

Stump Pond

Flat River Reservoir

Potowomut

Hog I.

Hummocks

Stafford Pd.

Nannaquaket Pd.

Sandy Pd.

Hopkins Hollow

Quidnick Reservoir

Nooseneck

Mount View

Bristol Ferry

Island Park

Tiverton

West Greenwich Center

BALD HILL 192 M.

Quidnessett

Yorktown Manor

Naragansett Bay

Prudence Island

Portsmouth

KENT

Davisville

Hope I.

PRUDENCE ISLAND

Escoheag

Beach Pond

Austin

Exeter

La Fayette

Shores Acres

Conanicut Pt.

Quonset Pt.

DYER I.

RHODE ISLAND

Fogland Pt.

Tiverton Four Corners

Voluntown

North Kingstown

Belleville

Fox I.

CONANICUT ISLAND

Adamsville

WASHINGTON

Arcadia

Liberty

Belleville Pond

Hamilton

Secret Lake

Allenton

GOULD I.

Nonquit Pd.

Patchet Brook Reservoir

Rockville

Moscow

Wyoming

Slocum

Plum Point

Plum Beach

COASTERS HARBOR I.

Middletown

Quicksand Pond

Little Compton

Centerville

Usquepaug

Hundred Acre Pond

Saunderstown

Hope Valley

West Kingston

DUTCH I.

Jamestown

Briggs Marsh

Canonchet

Indian Lake Shores

GOAT I.

Newport

Hopkinton

Woodville

Kingston

Indian Lake

Pettaquamscutt Lake Shores

SACHUEST PT.

Carolina

Shannock

Great Swamp

Peace Dale

BEAVERTAIL PT.

BRENTON PT.

LANDS END

Sakonnet

Warren Point

SAKONNET PT.

Alton

Kenyon

Wakefield

Ashaway

Wood River Junction

Worden Pond

Narragansett

Burdickville

South Hopkinton

Perryville

Pt. Judith Pond

Rhode Island Sound

White Rock

Potter Hill

Bradford

Charlestown

East Matunuck

Jerusalem

Galilee

Pawcatuck

Westerly

Green Hill Pond

Matunuck

Point Judith

Chapman Pond

Watchaug Pond

Trustom Pd.

POINT JUDITH

Wequetequock

Ninigret Pond

Green Hill

Dunns Corners

Haversham

Shelter Harbor

Quonochontaug

Avondale

Weekapaug

Quonochontaug Pond

Misquamicut

Watch Hill

NAPATREE PT.

WATCH HILL PT.

Block Island Sound

Atlantic Ocean

NEW LONDON

CONNECTICUT

Quaddick Reservoir

Fivemile

Wallum Lake

Moosup

Flat

Wood

Pachaug

Yawgoog Pond

Wincheck Pond

Green Fall

Beaver

Queen

Pawcatuck

Wyassup

Shunock

Note: Map colors do not reflect elevation.

D-520540-21-1PR-1PR-1PR-1PRM
COSMO SERIES RHODE ISLAND
Copyright by
RAND McNALLY & COMPANY
Made in U.S.A.

Statute Miles 1 0 1 2 3 4 5 6 7 8 9 10
Kilometers 1 0 1 2 3 4 5 6 7 8 9 10 11 12 13 14 15

Lambert Conformal Conic Projection

Same Scale as Main Map

Block Island Sound

SANDY PT.

Block Island

(WASHINGTON COUNTY, R.I.)

Great Salt Pond

BLOCK ISLAND

SOUTHWEST PT.

SOUTHEAST PT.

Atlantic Ocean

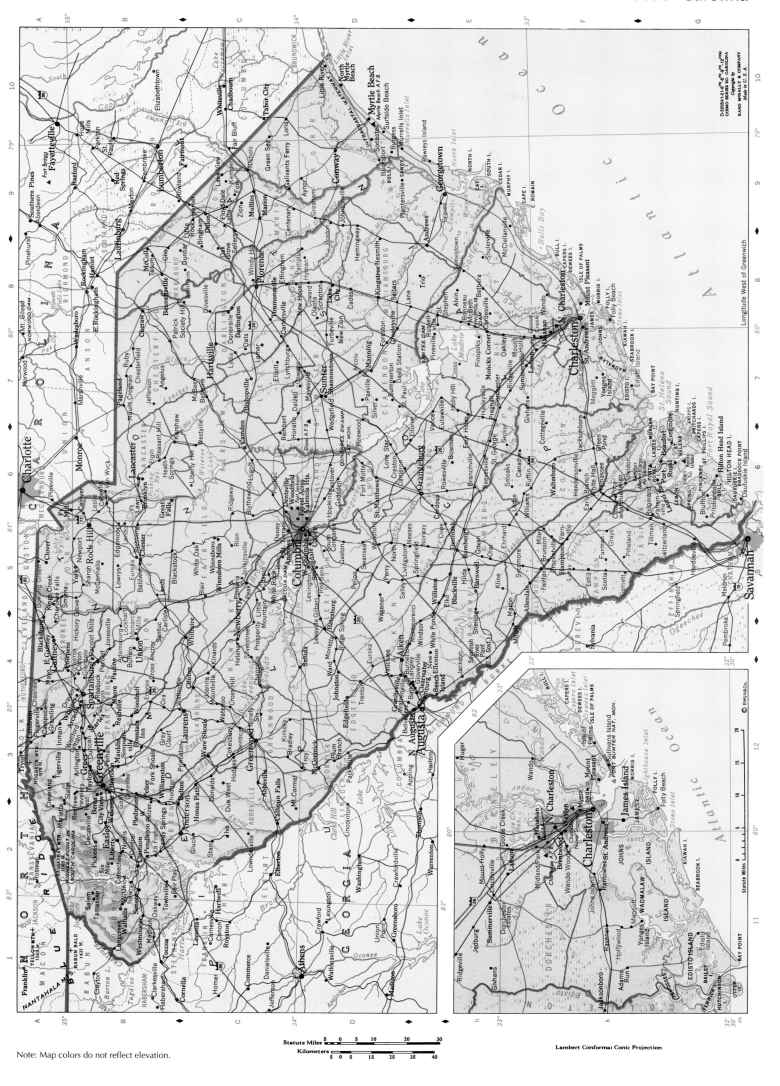

Note: Map colors do not reflect elevation.

Statute Miles
Kilometers

Lambert Conformal Conic Projection

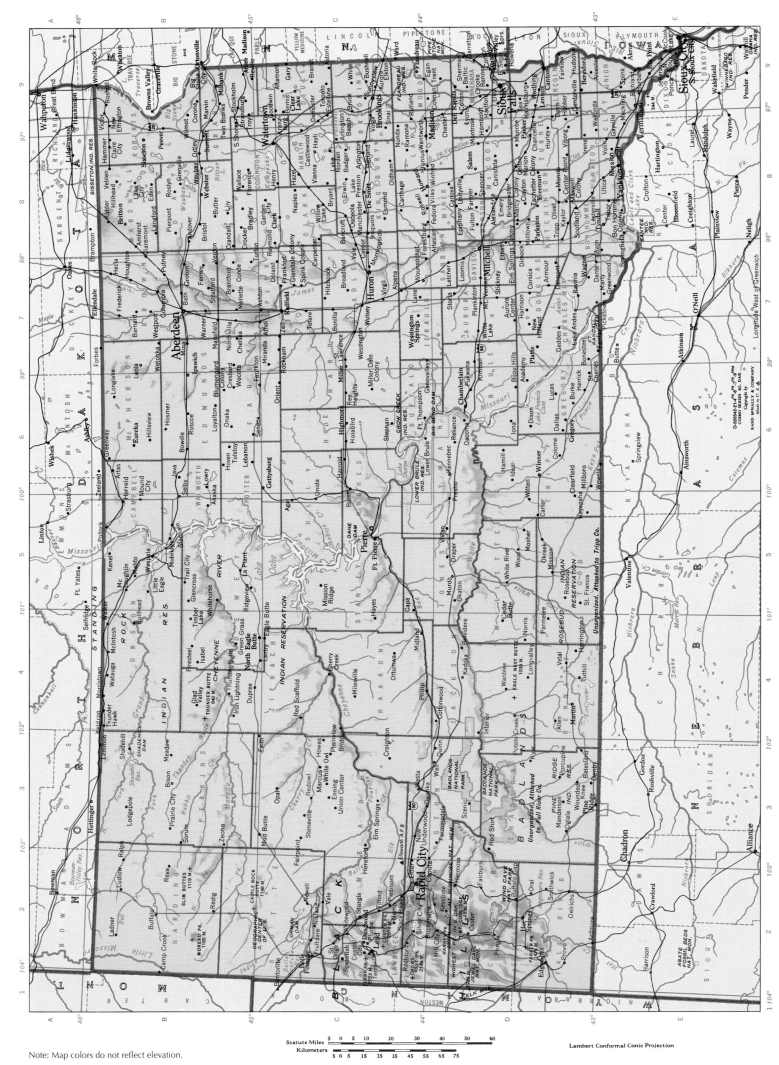

Note: Map colors do not reflect elevation.

Statute Miles   5 0 5 10   20   30   40   50   60
Kilometers   5 0 5 15   25   35   45   55   65   75

Lambert Conformal Conic Projection

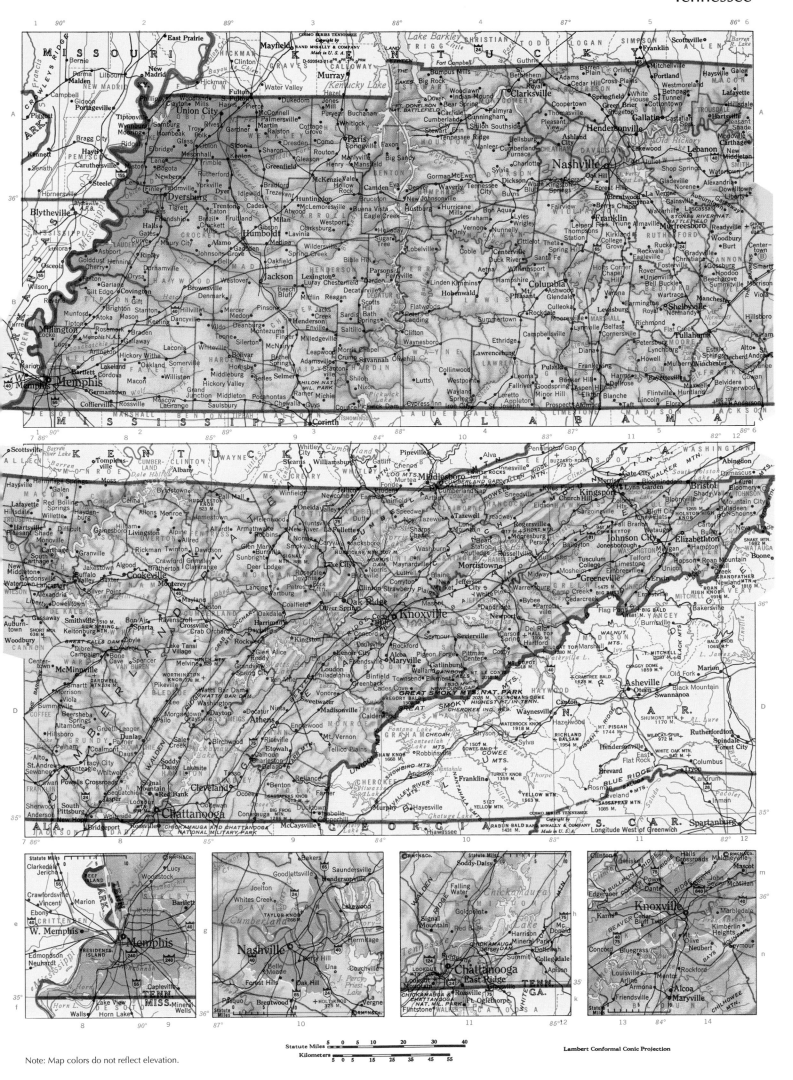

Note: Map colors do not reflect elevation.

Statute Miles 5 0 5 10   20   30   40
Kilometers 5 0 5 15   25   35   45   55

Lambert Conformal Conic Projection

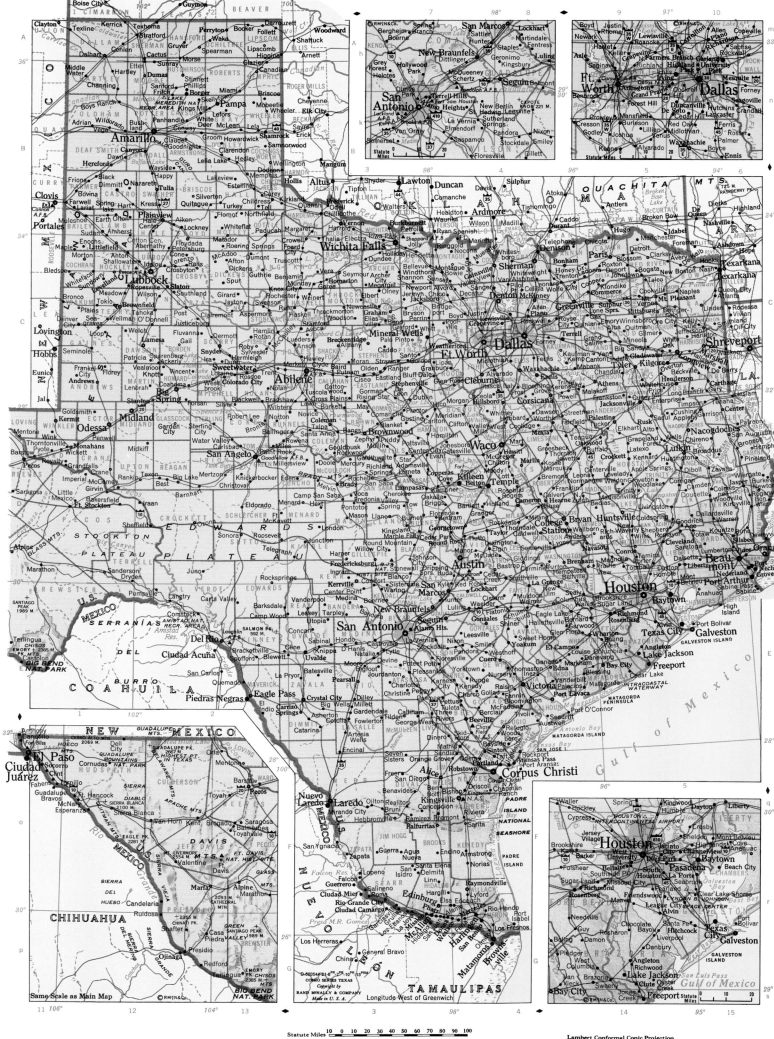

Note: Map colors do not reflect elevation.

Statute Miles
10 0 10 20 30 40 50 60 70 80 90 100

Kilometers
10 0 10 20 40 60 80 100 120 140

Lambert Conformal Conic Projection

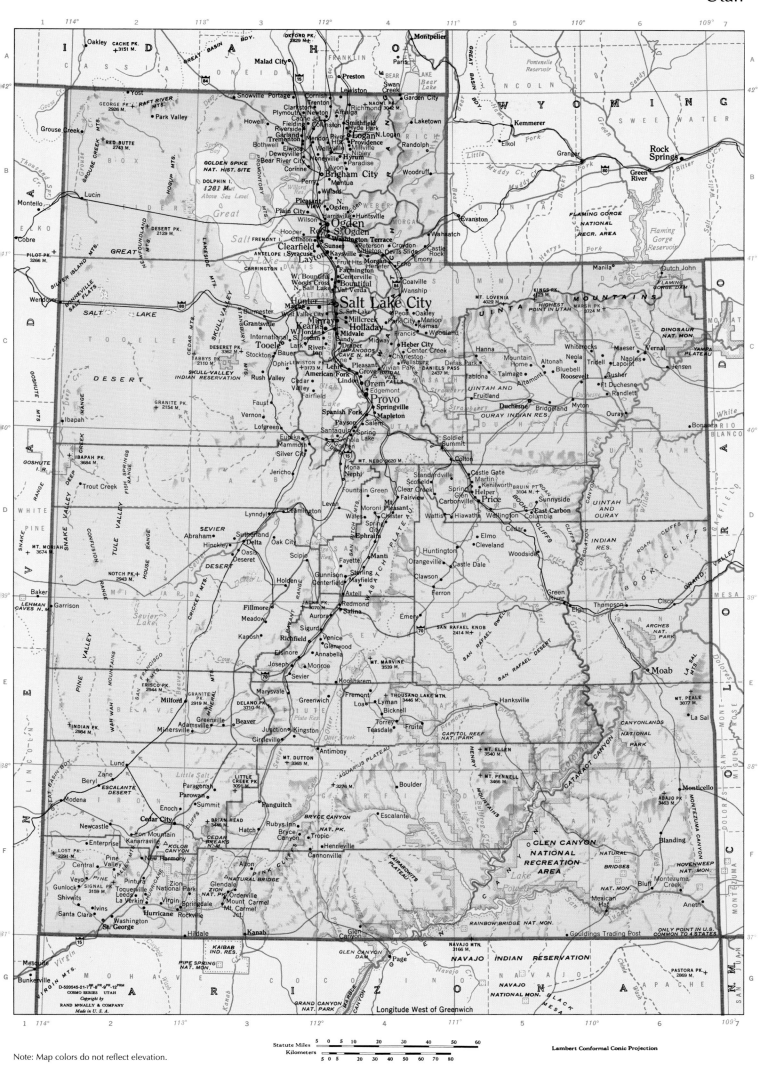

Note: Map colors do not reflect elevation.

Statute Miles
Kilometers

Lambert Conformal Conic Projection

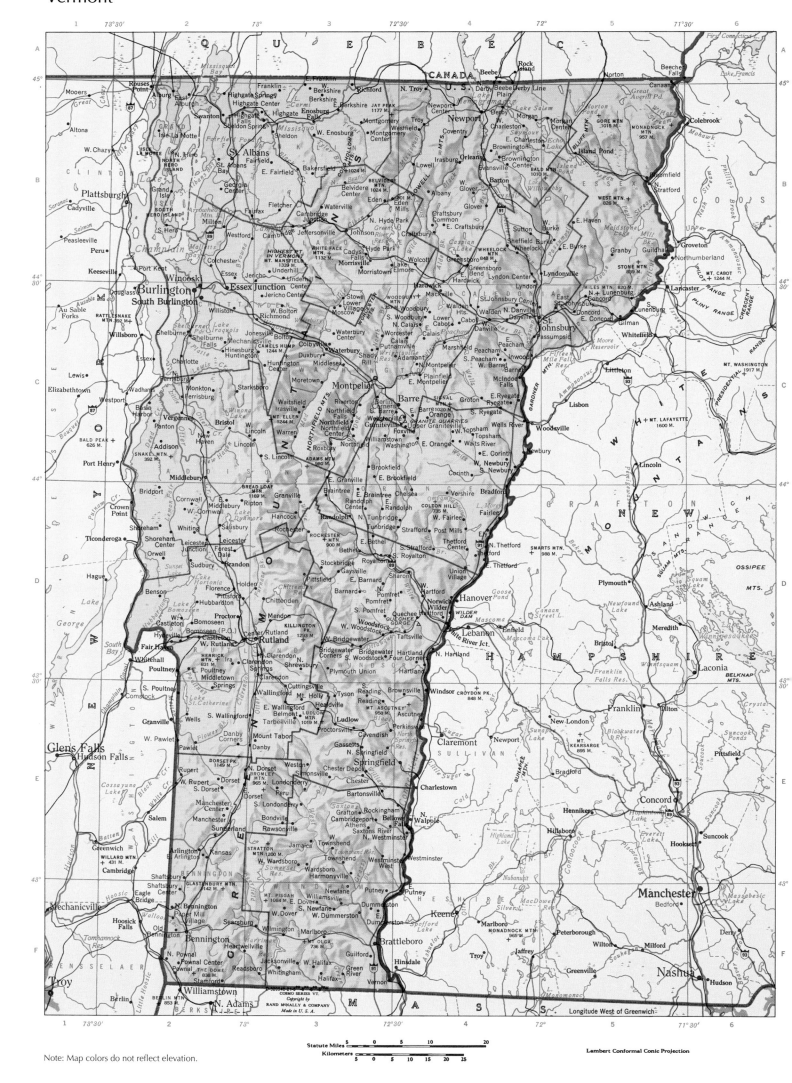

Note: Map colors do not reflect elevation.

Statute Miles   0   5   10   20

Kilometers   5   0   5   10   15   20   25

Lambert Conformal Conic Projection

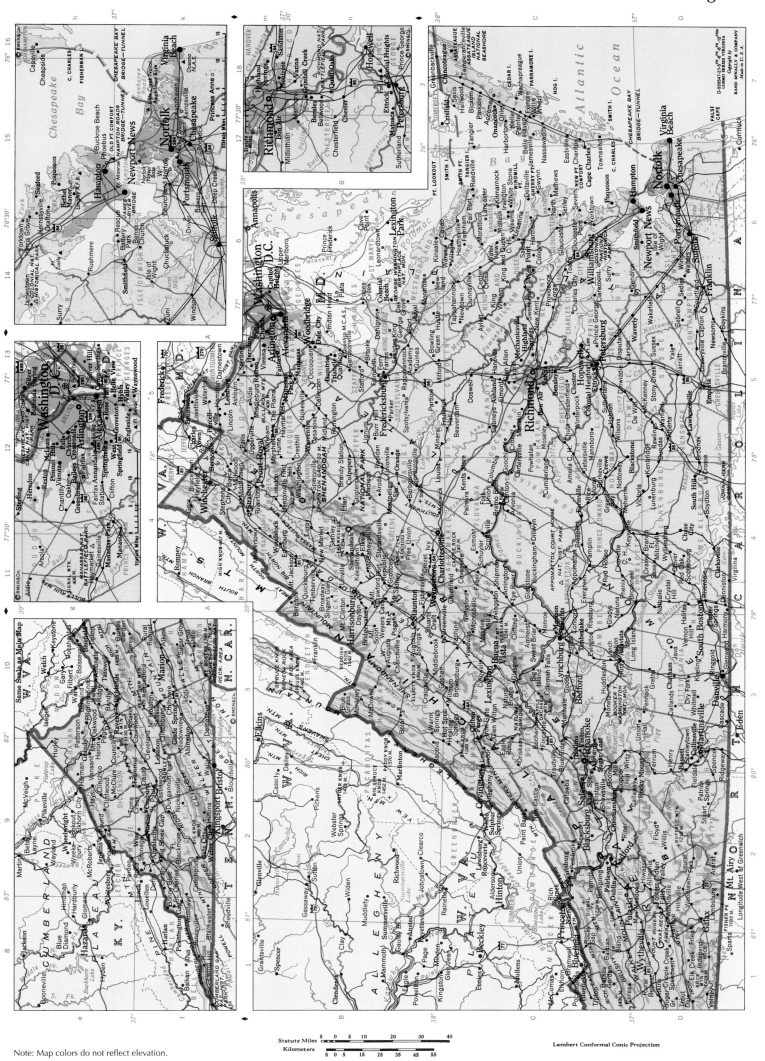

Note: Map colors do not reflect elevation.

Statute Miles
Kilometers

Lambert Conformal Conic Projection

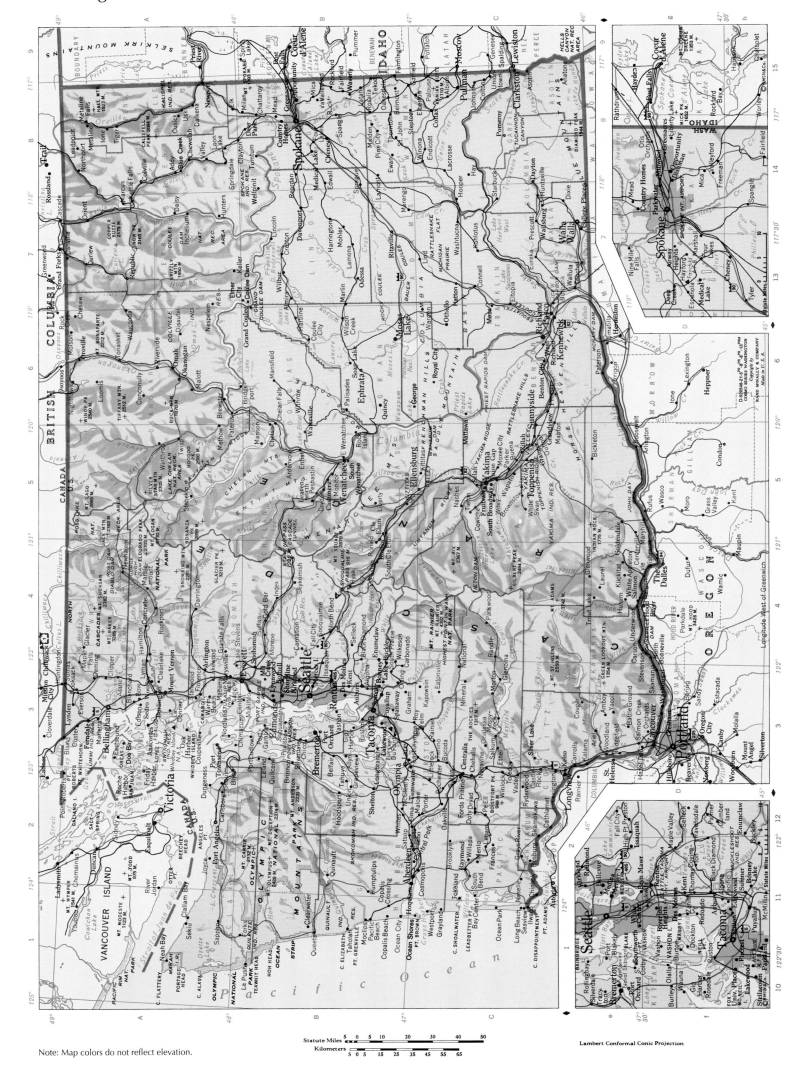

Note: Map colors do not reflect elevation.

Statute Miles 5 0 5 10 20 30 40 50
Kilometers 5 0 5 15 25 35 45 55 65

Lambert Conformal Conic Projection

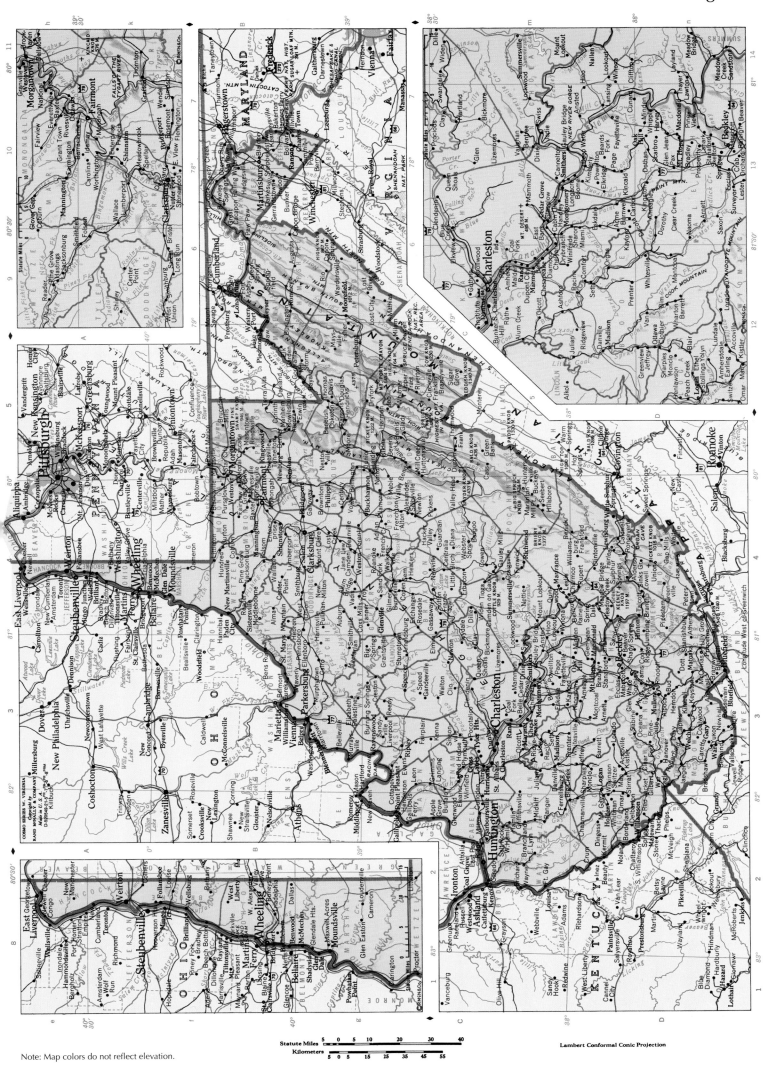

Note: Map colors do not reflect elevation.

Statute Miles
Kilometers

Lambert Conformal Conic Projection

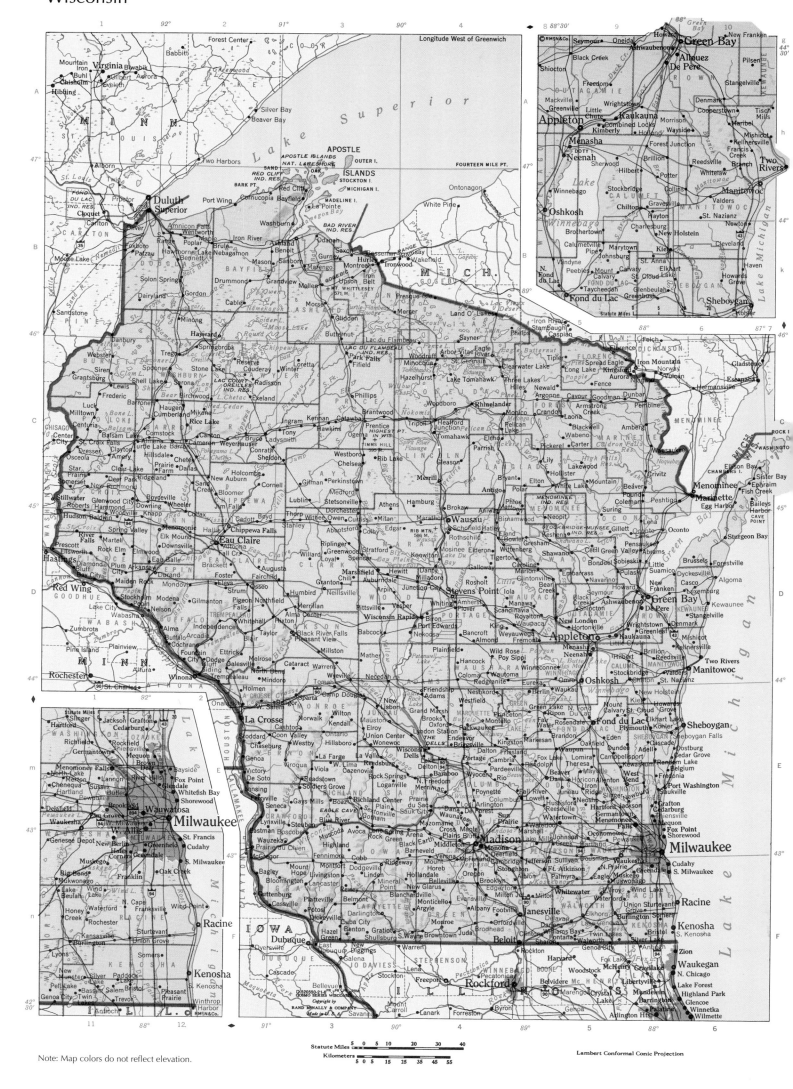

Note: Map colors do not reflect elevation.

Statute Miles 5 0 5 10   20   30   40
Kilometers 5 0 5 15 25 35 45 55

Lambert Conformal Conic Projection

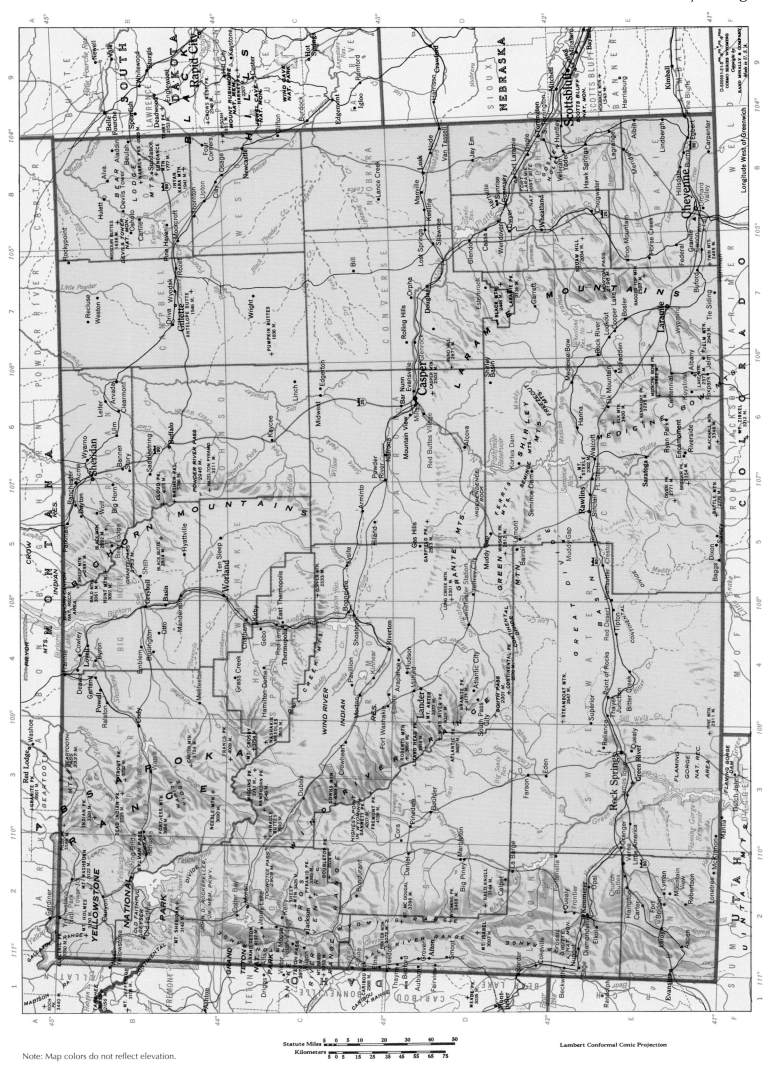

Note: Map colors do not reflect elevation.

Statute Miles 5 0 5 10   20   30   40   50
Kilometers 5 0 5 15   25   35   45 55 65 75

Lambert Conformal Conic Projection

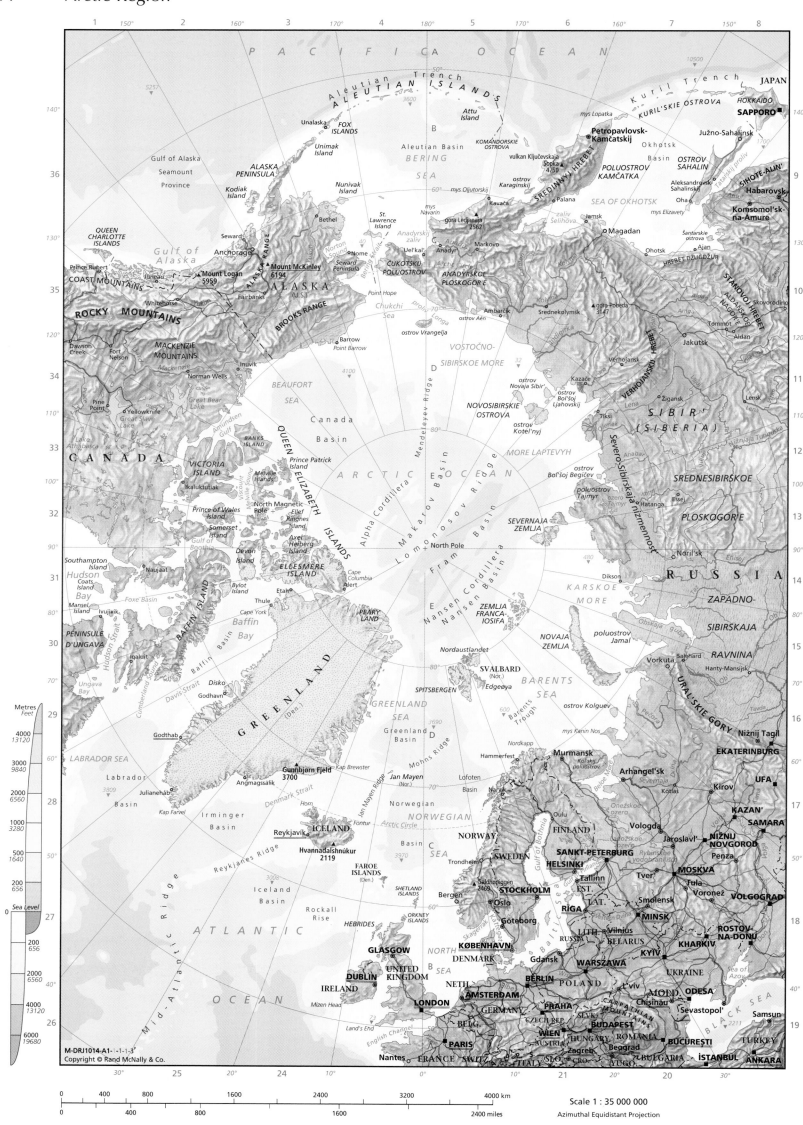

Scale 1 : 35 000 000
Azimuthal Equidistant Projection

Metres					
Feet					
4000	13120				
3000	9840				
2000	6560				
1000	3280				
500	1640				
200	656				
Sea Level					
200	656				
2000	6560				
4000	13120				
6000	19680				

0   400   800   1600   2400   3200   4000 km

0   400   800   1600   2400 miles

Index to World Reference Maps

Introduction to the Index

This index includes in a single alphabetical list approximately 45,000 names of features that appear on the reference maps. Each name is followed by the name of the country or continent in which it is located, a map reference key, and a page reference.

Names The names of cities appear in the index in regular type. The names of all other features appear in *italics*, followed by descriptive terms (hill, mtn., state) to indicate their nature.

Abbreviations of names on the maps have been standardized as much as possible. Names that are abbreviated on the maps are generally spelled out in full in the index.

Country names and names of features that extend beyond the boundaries of one country are followed by the name of the continent in which each is located. Country designations follow the names of all other places in the index. The locations of places in the United States, Canada, and the United Kingdom are further defined by abbreviations that indicate the state, province, or political division in which each is located.

All abbreviations used in the index are defined in the List of Abbreviations below.

Alphabetization Names are alphabetized in the order of the letters of the English alphabet. Spanish *ll* and *ch*, for example, are not treated as distinct letters. Furthermore, diacritical marks are disregarded in alphabetization—German or Scandinavian *ä* or *ö* are treated as *a* or *o*.

The names of physical features may appear inverted, since they are always alphabetized under the proper, not the generic, part of the name, thus: "Gibraltar, Strait of". Otherwise every entry, whether consisting of one word or more, is alphabetized as a single continuous entity. "Lakeland", for example, appears after La Crosse" and before "La Salle". Names beginning with articles (Le Havre, Den Helder, Al-Manāmah) are not inverted. Names beginning "St.", "Ste." and "Sainte" are alphabetized as though spelled "Saint".

In the case of identical names, towns are listed first, then political divisions, then physical features. Entries that are completely identical are listed alphabetically by country name.

Map Reference Keys and Page References The map reference keys and page references are found in the last two columns of each entry.

Each map reference key consists of a letter and number. The letters appear along the sides of the maps. Lowercase letters indicate reference to inset maps. Numbers appear across the tops and bottoms of the maps.

Map reference keys for point features, such as cities and mountain peaks, indicate the locations of the symbols. For other features, such as countries, mountain ranges, or rivers, locations are given for the names.

The page number generally refers to the main map for the country in which the feature is located. Page references to two-page maps always refer to the left-hand page.

Ab., Can.	Alberta, Can.
Afg.	Afghanistan
Afr.	Africa
Ak., U.S.	Alaska, U.S.
Al., U.S.	Alabama, U.S.
Alb.	Albania
Alg.	Algeria
Am. Sam.	American Samoa
And.	Andorra
anch.	anchorage
Ang.	Angola
Anguilla	Anguilla
Ant.	Antarctica
Antig.	Antigua and Barbuda
Ar., U.S.	Arkansas, U.S.
Arg.	Argentina
Arm.	Armenia
Aruba	Aruba
Asia	Asia
Aus.	Austria
Austl.	Australia
Az., U.S.	Arizona, U.S.
Azer.	Azerbaijan
b.	bay, gulf, inlet, lagoon
Bah.	Bahamas
Bahr.	Bahrain
Barb.	Barbados
B.C., Can.	British Columbia, Can.
Bdi.	Burundi
Bel.	Belgium
Belize	Belize
Bela.	Belarus
Benin	Benin
Ber.	Bermuda
Bhu.	Bhutan
B.I.O.T.	British Indian Ocean Territory
Bngl.	Bangladesh
Bol.	Bolivia
Bos.	Bosnia and Herzegovina
Bots.	Botswana
Braz.	Brazil
Br. Vir. Is.	British Virgin Islands
Bru.	Brunei
Bul.	Bulgaria
Burkina	Burkina Faso
c.	cape, point
Ca., U.S.	California, U.S.
Camb.	Cambodia
Cam.	Cameroon
Can.	Canada
C.A.R.	Central African Republic
Cay. Is.	Cayman Islands
Chad	Chad
Chile	Chile
China	China
Christ. I.	Christmas Island
C. Iv.	Cote d'Ivoire
clf.	cliff, escarpment
Co., U.S.	Colorado, U.S.
co.	county, parish
Cocos Is.	Cocos (Keeling) Islands
Col.	Colombia
Com.	Comoros
Congo	Congo
cont.	continent
Cook Is.	Cook Islands
C.R.	Costa Rica
crat.	crater
Cro.	Croatia
Ct., U.S.	Connecticut, U.S.
ctry.	independent country
Cuba	Cuba
C.V.	Cape Verde
Cyp.	Cyprus
Czech Rep.	Czech Republic
D.C., U.S.	District of Columbia, U.S.
De., U.S.	Delaware, U.S.
Den.	Denmark
dep.	dependency, colony
depr.	depression
dept.	department, district
des.	desert
Dji.	Djibouti
Dom.	Dominica
Dom. Rep.	Dominican Republic
D.R.C.	Democratic Republic of the Congo
Ec.	Ecuador
Egypt	Egypt
El Sal.	El Salvador
Eng., U.K.	England, U.K.
Eq. Gui.	Equatorial Guinea
Erit.	Eritrea
Est.	Estonia
est.	estuary
Eth.	Ethiopia
Eur.	Europe
Falk. Is.	Falkland Islands
Far. Is.	Faroe Islands
Fiji	Fiji
Fin.	Finland
Fl., U.S.	Florida, U.S.
for.	forest, moor
Fr.	France
Fr. Gu.	French Guiana
Fr. Poly.	French Polynesia
Ga., U.S.	Georgia, U.S.
Gabon	Gabon
Gam.	Gambia
Gaza Str.	Gaza Strip
Geor.	Georgia
Ger.	Germany
Ghana	Ghana
Gib.	Gibraltar
Golan Hts.	Golan Heights
Grc.	Greece
Gren.	Grenada
Grnld.	Greenland
Guad.	Guadeloupe
Guam	Guam
Guat.	Guatemala
Guernsey	Guernsey
Gui.	Guinea
Gui.-B.	Guinea-Bissau
Guy.	Guyana
Haiti	Haiti
Hi., U.S.	Hawaii, U.S.
hist.	historic site, ruins
hist. reg.	historic region
Hond.	Honduras
Hung.	Hungary
i.	island
Ia., U.S.	Iowa, U.S.
Ice.	Iceland
ice	ice feature, glacier
Id., U.S.	Idaho, U.S.
Il., U.S.	Illinois, U.S.
In., U.S.	Indiana, U.S.
India	India
Indon.	Indonesia
I. of Man	Isle of Man
Iran	Iran
Iraq	Iraq
Ire.	Ireland
Isr.	Israel
is.	islands
Italy	Italy
Jam.	Jamaica
Japan	Japan
Jersey	Jersey
Jer.	Jericho Area
Jord.	Jordan
Kaz.	Kazakstan
Kenya	Kenya
Kir.	Kiribati
Ks., U.S.	Kansas, U.S.
Kuw.	Kuwait
Ky., U.S.	Kentucky, U.S.
Kyrg.	Kyrgyzstan
l.	lake, pond
La., U.S.	Louisiana, U.S.
Laos	Laos
Lat.	Latvia
Leb.	Lebanon
Leso.	Lesotho
Lib.	Liberia
Libya	Libya
Liech.	Liechtenstein
Lith.	Lithuania
Lux.	Luxembourg
Ma., U.S.	Massachusetts, U.S.
Mac.	Macedonia
Macau	Macau
Madag.	Madagascar
Malay.	Malaysia
Mald.	Maldives
Mali	Mali
Malta	Malta
Marsh. Is.	Marshall Islands
Mart.	Martinique
Maur.	Mauritania
May.	Mayotte
Mb., Can.	Manitoba, Can.
Md., U.S.	Maryland, U.S.
Me., U.S.	Maine, U.S.
Mex.	Mexico
Mi., U.S.	Michigan, U.S.
Micron.	Micronesia, Federated States of
Mid. Is.	Midway Islands
mil.	military installation
Mn., U.S.	Minnesota, U.S.
Mo., U.S.	Missouri, U.S.
Mol.	Moldova
Mon.	Monaco
Mong.	Mongolia
Monts.	Montserrat
Mor.	Morocco
Moz.	Mozambique
Mrts.	Mauritius
Ms., U.S.	Mississippi, U.S.
Mt., U.S.	Montana, U.S.
mth.	river mouth or channel
mtn.	mountain
mts.	mountains
Mwi.	Malawi
Myan.	Myanmar
N.A.	North America
Nauru	Nauru
N.B., Can.	New Brunswick, Can.
N.C., U.S.	North Carolina, U.S.
N. Cal.	New Caledonia
N. Cyp.	Cyprus, North
N.D., U.S.	North Dakota, U.S.
Ne., U.S.	Nebraska, U.S.
Nepal	Nepal
Neth.	Netherlands
Neth. Ant.	Netherlands Antilles
Nf., Can.	Newfoundland and Labrador, Can.
N.H., U.S.	New Hampshire, U.S.
Nic.	Nicaragua
Nig.	Nigeria
Niger	Niger
N. Ire., U.K.	Northern Ireland, U.K.
Niue	Niue
N.J., U.S.	New Jersey, U.S.
N. Kor.	Korea, North
N.M., U.S.	New Mexico, U.S.
N. Mar. Is.	Northern Mariana Islands
Nmb.	Namibia
Nor.	Norway
Norf. I.	Norfolk Island
N.S., Can.	Nova Scotia, Can.
N.T., Can.	Northwest Territories, Can.
Nu., Can.	Nunavut, Can.
Nv., U.S.	Nevada, U.S.
N.Y., U.S.	New York, U.S.
N.Z.	New Zealand
Oc.	Oceania
Oh., U.S.	Ohio, U.S.
Ok., U.S.	Oklahoma, U.S.
Oman	Oman
On., Can.	Ontario, Can.
Or., U.S.	Oregon, U.S.
Pa., U.S.	Pennsylvania, U.S.
Pak.	Pakistan
Palau	Palau
Pan.	Panama
Pap. N. Gui.	Papua New Guinea
Para.	Paraguay
P.E., Can.	Prince Edward Island, Can.
pen.	peninsula
Peru	Peru
Phil.	Philippines
Pit.	Pitcairn
pl.	plain, flat
plat.	plateau, highland
Pol.	Poland
Port.	Portugal
P.Q., Can.	Quebec, Can.
P.R.	Puerto Rico
prov.	province, region
Qatar	Qatar
Reu.	Reunion
reg.	physical region
res.	reservoir
rf.	reef, shoal
R.I., U.S.	Rhode Island, U.S.
Rom.	Romania
Russia	Russia
Rw.	Rwanda
S.A.	South America
S. Afr.	South Africa
Samoa	Samoa
Sau. Ar.	Saudi Arabia
S.C., U.S.	South Carolina, U.S.
sci.	scientific station
Scot., U.K.	Scotland, U.K.
S.D., U.S.	South Dakota, U.S.
Sen.	Senegal
Sey.	Seychelles
S. Geor.	South Georgia and the South Sandwich Islands
Sing.	Singapore
Sk., Can.	Saskatchewan, Can.
S. Kor.	Korea, South
S.L.	Sierra Leone
Slvk.	Slovakia
Slvn.	Slovenia
S. Mar.	San Marino
Sol. Is.	Solomon Islands
Som.	Somalia
Spain	Spain
Sp. N. Afr.	Spanish North Africa
Sri L.	Sri Lanka
state	state, republic, canton
St. Hel.	St. Helena
St. K./N.	St. Kitts and Nevis
St. Luc.	St. Lucia
stm.	stream (river, creek)
St. P./M.	St. Pierre and Miquelon
strt.	strait
S. Tom./P.	Sao Tome and Principe
St. Vin.	St. Vincent and the Grenadines
Sudan	Sudan
Sur.	Suriname
Swaz.	Swaziland
sw.	swamp, marsh
Swe.	Sweden
Switz.	Switzerland
Syria	Syria
Tai.	Taiwan
Taj.	Tajikistan
Tan.	Tanzania
T./C. Is.	Turks and Caicos Islands
ter.	territory
Thai.	Thailand
Tn., U.S.	Tennessee, U.S.
Togo	Togo
Tok.	Tokelau
Tonga	Tonga
Trin.	Trinidad and Tobago
Tun.	Tunisia
Tur.	Turkey
Turk.	Turkmenistan
Tuvalu	Tuvalu
Tx., U.S.	Texas, U.S.
U.A.E.	United Arab Emirates
Ug.	Uganda
U.K.	United Kingdom
Ukr.	Ukraine
Ur.	Uruguay
U.S.	United States
Ut., U.S.	Utah, U.S.
Uzb.	Uzbekistan
Va., U.S.	Virginia, U.S.
val.	valley, watercourse
Vanuatu	Vanuatu
Vat.	Vatican City
Ven.	Venezuela
Viet.	Vietnam
V.I.U.S.	Virgin Islands (U.S.)
vol.	volcano
Vt., U.S.	Vermont, U.S.
Wa., U.S.	Washington, U.S.
Wake I.	Wake Island
Wales, U.K.	Wales, U.K.
Wal./F.	Wallis and Futuna
W.B.	West Bank
Wi., U.S.	Wisconsin, U.S.
W. Sah.	Western Sahara
wtfl.	waterfall
W.V., U.S.	West Virginia, U.S.
Wy., U.S.	Wyoming, U.S.
Yemen	Yemen
Yk., Can.	Yukon Territory, Can.
Yugo.	Yugoslavia
Zam.	Zambia
Zimb.	Zimbabwe

Name	Map Ref.	Page

A

Name	Map Ref.	Page
Aachen, Ger.	E10	12
Aali, Sadd el-, Egypt	F11	48
Äänekoski, Fin.	E11	10
Aba, China	E8	28
Aba, Nig.	E6	50
Abaco, i., Bah.	C9	76
Ābādān, Iran	D5	42
Ābādeh, Iran	D6	42
Abadla, Alg.	D4	48
Abaeté, Braz.	E2	74
Abaetetuba, Braz.	B2	74
Abag Qi, China	C10	28
Abaj, Kaz.	B2	28
Abajo Peak, mtn., Ut., U.S.	F6	137
Abakaliki, Nig.	E6	50
Abakan, Russia	D11	26
Abala, Niger	D5	50
Abancay, Peru	F5	70
Abashiri, Japan	B4	31
Abau, Pap. N. Gui.	I12	32
Ābay see Blue Nile, stm., Afr.	H11	48
Ābaya Hāyk', l., Eth.	B7	54
Abaza, Russia	D11	26
Abbaye, Point c., Mi., U.S.	B2	115
Abbeville, Fr.	B7	16
Abbeville, Al., U.S.	D4	94
Abbeville, Ga., U.S.	E3	103
Abbeville, La., U.S.	E3	111
Abbeville, S.C., U.S.	C3	133
Abbeville, co., S.C., U.S.	C2	133
Abbotsford, Wi., U.S.	D3	142
Abbott Butte, mtn., Or., U.S.	E4	130
Abbott Run, stm., U.S.	B4	132
Abbott Run Valley, R.I., U.S.	B4	132
Ābdānān, Iran	F12	44
Abdulino, Russia	D9	22
Abe, Lake, l., Afr.	H13	48
Abéché, Chad	H9	48
Abengourou, C. Iv.	I3	50
Åbenrå, Den.	I3	10
Abeokuta, Nig.	E5	50
Aberdeen, Scot., U.K.	B5	12
Aberdeen, Id., U.S.	G6	105
Aberdeen, Md., U.S.	A5	113
Aberdeen, Ms., U.S.	B5	117
Aberdeen, N.C., U.S.	B3	126
Aberdeen, Oh., U.S.	D2	128
Aberdeen, S.D., U.S.	B7	134
Aberdeen, Wa., U.S.	C2	140
Aberdeen Lake, l., N.T., Can.	E20	82
Abernathy, Tx., U.S.	C2	136
Abert, Lake, l., Or., U.S.	E6	130
Abert Rim, clf., Or., U.S.	E6	130
Aberystwyth, Wales, U.K.	D4	12
Abez', Russia	A11	22
Abhā, Sau. Ar.	G4	38
Abhar, Iran	D13	44
Abidjan, C. Iv.	E4	50
Abilene, Ks., U.S.	D6	109
Abilene, Tx., U.S.	C3	136
Abingdon, Il., U.S.	C3	106
Abingdon, Md., U.S.	B5	113
Abingdon, Va., U.S.	f10	139
Abington, Ma., U.S.	B6	114
Abington [Township], Pa., U.S.	o21	131
Abinsk, Russia	G15	20
Abisko, Swe.	B8	10
Abita Springs, La., U.S.	D5	111
Abitibi, stm., On., Can.	H23	82
Åbo see Turku, Fin.	F10	10
Abomey, Benin	E5	50
Abongabong, Gunung, mtn., Indon.	C1	36
Abong Mbang, Cam.	C2	54
Abou-Deïa, Chad	H8	48
Abraham Lake, res., Ab., Can.	C2	84
Abraham Lincoln Birthplace National Historic Site, hist., Ky., U.S.	C4	110
Abra Pampa, Arg.	C4	72
Absaroka Range, mts., U.S.	F7	143
Absarokee, Mt., U.S.	E7	119
Absecon, N.J., U.S.	E4	123
Absecon Inlet, b., N.J., U.S.	E4	123
Abu Dhabi see Abū Ẓaby, U.A.E.	F6	42
Abū Ḩamad, Sudan	G11	48
Abuja, Nig.	E6	50
Abū Kamāl, Syria	E9	44
Abū Madd, Ra's, c., Sau. Ar.	F3	42
Abū Maţāriq, Sudan	A5	54
Abunã, Braz.	E6	70
Abū Road, India	E2	40
Abū Ẓaby (Abu Dhabi), U.A.E.	F6	42
Abu Zenîma, Egypt	F10	14
Abyad, Al-Baḩr al- (White Nile), stm., Sudan	H11	48
Abyei, Sudan	B5	54
Academia, Oh., U.S.	B3	128
Acadia, co., La., U.S.	D3	111
Acadia National Park, Me., U.S.	D4	112
Açailândia, Braz.	B2	74
Acámbaro, Mex.	C4	78
Acaponeta, Mex.	C3	78
Acapulco, Mex.	D5	78
Acarai Mountains, mts., S.A.	C8	70
Acaraú, Braz.	B3	74
Acarigua, Ven.	B6	70
Acayucan, Mex.	D5	78
Accomack, co., Va., U.S.	C7	139
Accoville, W.V., U.S.	D3	141
Accra, Ghana	E4	50
Achacachi, Bol.	B4	72
Achalpur, India	E3	40
Acheng, China	B13	28
Acı Göl, l., Tur.	D3	44
Ačinsk, Russia	D11	26
Acireale, Italy	F5	18
Ačisaj, Kaz.	B9	42
Ackerman, Ms., U.S.	B4	117
Ackley, Ia., U.S.	B4	108
Acklins, i., Bah.	D10	76
Acoma Indian Reservation, N.M., U.S.	C2	124
Aconcagua, Cerro, mtn., Arg.	E4	72
Acopiara, Braz.	C4	74
Açores, is., Port.	F7	46
A Coruña, Spain	F2	16
Acre, state, Braz.	E5	70
Acton, Ma., U.S.	B5	114
Acton Vale, P.Q., Can.	D5	90
Acushnet, Ma., U.S.	C6	114
Acworth, Ga., U.S.	B2	103
Ada, Ghana	E5	50
Ada, co., Id., U.S.	F2	105
Ada, Mn., U.S.	C2	116
Ada, Oh., U.S.	B2	128
Ada, Ok., U.S.	C5	129
Ada, Mount, mtn., Ak., U.S.	m22	95
Adair, Ia., U.S.	C3	108
Adair, co., Ia., U.S.	C3	108
Adair, co., Ky., U.S.	C4	110
Adair, co., Mo., U.S.	A5	118
Adair, Ok., U.S.	A6	129
Adair, co., Ok., U.S.	B7	129
Adairsville, Ga., U.S.	B2	103
Adairville, Ky., U.S.	D3	110
Adak Island, i., Ak., U.S.	E4	95
Adak Naval Station, mil., Ak., U.S.	E4	95
Adam, Oman	F7	38
Adamantina, Braz.	F1	74
Adamaoua, mts., Afr.	B2	54
Adamaoua, state, Cam.	E7	50
Adamawa see Adamaoua, mts., Afr.	B2	54
Adam Island, i., Md., U.S.	D5	113
Adams, co., Co., U.S.	B6	99
Adams, co., Ia., U.S.	C3	108
Adams, co., Id., U.S.	E2	105
Adams, co., Il., U.S.	D2	106
Adams, co., In., U.S.	C8	107
Adams, Ma., U.S.	A1	114
Adams, Mn., U.S.	G6	116
Adams, co., Ms., U.S.	D2	117
Adams, co., N.D., U.S.	C3	127
Adams, co., Ne., U.S.	D7	120
Adams, N.Y., U.S.	B4	125
Adams, co., Oh., U.S.	D2	128
Adams, co., Pa., U.S.	G7	131
Adams, co., Wa., U.S.	B7	140
Adams, Wi., U.S.	E4	142
Adams, co., Wi., U.S.	D4	142
Adams, Mount, mtn., N.H., U.S.	B4	122
Adams, Mount, mtn., Wa., U.S.	C4	140
Adams Point, c., Mi., U.S.	C7	115
Adams Run, S.C., U.S.	k11	133
Adamstown, Pa., U.S.	F9	131
Adamsville, Al., U.S.	f7	94
Adamsville, R.I., U.S.	E6	132
Adamsville, Tn., U.S.	B3	135
Adamsville Brook, stm., R.I., U.S.	E6	132
'Adan (Aden), Yemen	H5	38
Adana, Tur.	D6	44
Adare, Cape, c., Ant.	D22	67
Adda, stm., Italy	B2	18
Ad-Dabbah, Sudan	G11	48
Ad-Dahnā', des., Sau. Ar.	E5	38
Ad-Dāmir, Sudan	G2	38
Ad-Dammām, Sau. Ar.	E5	38
Ad-Dawḩah (Doha), Qatar	E6	42
Ad-Diffah (Libyan Plateau), plat., Afr.	E9	14
Addis, La., U.S.	D4	111
Addis Ababa see Ādīs Ābeba, Eth.	B7	54
Addison, Al., U.S.	A2	94
Addison, Ct., U.S.	C5	100
Addison, Il., U.S.	k8	106
Addison, N.Y., U.S.	C3	125
Addison, co., Vt., U.S.	C2	138
Ad-Dīwānīyah, Iraq	D5	42
Addyston, Oh., U.S.	o12	128
Adel, Ga., U.S.	E3	103
Adel, Ia., U.S.	C3	108
Adelaide, Austl.	G2	62
Adelaide, S. Afr.	E4	56
Adelaide Island, i., Ant.	C33	67
Adelaide River, Austl.	C5	60
Adelanto, Ca., U.S.	E5	98
Adèle Island, i., Austl.	D3	60
Adélie Coast, Ant.	C19	67
Aden see 'Adan, Yemen	H5	38
Aden, Gulf of, b.	H5	38
Adi, Pulau, i., Indon.	D8	36
Adiaké, C. Iv.	E4	50
Adige, stm., Italy	B3	18
Ādīgrat, Eth.	H3	38
Ādilābād, India	F3	40
Adimi, Russia	B15	28
Adirondack Mountains, mts., N.Y., U.S.	A6	125
Ādīs Ābeba (Addis Ababa), Eth.	B7	54
Adıyaman, Tur.	D8	44
Adjuntas, Presa de las see Vicente Guerrero, Presa, res., Mex.	C5	78
Adler, Russia	A8	44
Admiralty Bay, b., Ak., U.S.	A9	95
Admiralty Gulf, b., Austl.	C4	60
Admiralty Inlet, b., N.T., Can.	D22	82
Admiralty Island, i., Ak., U.S.	m22	95
Admiralty Islands, is., Pap. N. Gui.	G12	32
Admiralty Mountains, mts., Ant.	D21	67
Ado, Nig.	E5	50
Adobe Creek Reservoir, res., Co., U.S.	C7	99
Ado-Ekiti, Nig.	E6	50
Ādoni, India	F3	40
Adour, stm., Fr.	F6	16
Adra, Spain	I5	16
Adrar, Alg.	E4	48
Adrâr, reg., Maur.	B2	50
Adrian, Ga., U.S.	D4	103
Adrian, Mi., U.S.	G6	115
Adrian, Mn., U.S.	G3	116
Adrian, Mo., U.S.	C3	118
Adrianople see Edirne, Tur.	B2	44
Adriatic Sea, s., Eur.	C5	18
Adusa, D.R.C.	B5	54
Advance, Mo., U.S.	D8	118
Ādwa, Eth.	H12	48
Aix, Mount, mtn., Wa., U.S.	C4	140
Aix-en-Provence, Fr.	F9	16
Aix-les-Bains, Fr.	E9	16
Aegean Sea, s.	E10	18
Aën, ostrov, i., Russia	C18	26
A Estrada, Spain	F2	16
Afadjoto, mtn., Ghana	E5	50
Afars and Issas see Djibouti, ctry., Afr.	H13	48
Afghanistan, ctry., Asia	D8	42
Afgooye, Som.	C9	54
Afikpo, Nig.	E6	50
Aflou, Alg.	C5	48
Afmadow, Som.	J13	48
Afognak Island, i., Ak., U.S.	D9	95
Africa, cont.	E14	4
Afşin, Tur.	C7	44
Afton, Ia., U.S.	C3	108
Afton, Mn., U.S.	F6	116
Afton, Ok., U.S.	A7	129
Afton, Wy., U.S.	D2	143
Afyon, Tur.	C4	44
Agadez, Niger	C6	50
Agadir, Mor.	D2	48
Agadyr', Kaz.	E9	26
Agalak, Sudan	A6	54
Agalega Islands, is., Mrts.	E11	52
Agana see Hagåtña, Guam	D11	32
Agartala, India	E6	40
Agate Fossil Beds National Monument, Ne., U.S.	B2	120
Agattu Island, i., Ak., U.S.	E2	95
Agawam, Ma., U.S.	B2	114
Agboville, C. Iv.	E4	50
Agde, Fr.	F8	16
Agen, Fr.	E7	16
Agency, Ia., U.S.	D5	108
Agency, Mo., U.S.	B3	118
Āghā Jārī, Iran	D5	42
Aginskoe, Russia	D13	26
Agnew, Austl.	F3	60
Agnibilékrou, C. Iv.	E4	50
Agou, Mont, mtn., Togo	E5	50
Agoura Hills, Ca., U.S.	m11	98
Āgra, India	D3	40
Ağrı Dağı, mtn., Tur.	C11	44
Agrigento, Italy	F4	18
Agrihan, i., N. Mar. Is.	C12	32
Agrínion, Grc.	E8	18
Agrópoli, Italy	D5	18
Água Branca, Braz.	C3	74
Aguachica, Col.	D5	80
Aguadas, Col.	D4	80
Aguadulce, Pan.	D3	80
Agua Fria, stm., Az., U.S.	D3	96
Agua Fria, N.M., U.S.	B3	124
Aguán, stm., Hond.	B2	80
Agua Prieta, Mex.	A3	78
A Guardia, Spain	G2	16
Aguarico, stm., S.A.	D4	70
Aguascalientes, state, Mex.	C4	78
Aguascalientes, Mex.	C4	78
Águas Formosas, Braz.	E3	74
Água Vermelha, Represa de, res., Braz.	G9	70
Aguelhok, Mali	C5	50
Águilas, Spain	I6	16
Aguja, Cabo, c., Col.	C5	80
Agulhas, Kaap, c., S. Afr.	E3	56
Agulhas Basin	M15	66
Agustín Codazzi, Col.	C5	80
Ahaggar, mts., Alg.	B5	50
Ahaggar, Tassili ta-n-, plat., Alg.	B5	50
Ahalcihe, Geor.	B10	44
Ahalkalaki, Geor.	B10	44
Ahklun Mountains, mts., Ak., U.S.	D7	95
Ahlat, Tur.	C10	44
Ahmadābād, India	E2	40
Ahmadnagar, India	F2	40
Ādīs Ābeba (Addis Ababa), Eth.	B7	54
Ahmar Mountains, mts., Eth.	B8	54
Ahoskie, N.C., U.S.	A6	126
Ahtanum Creek, stm., Wa., U.S.	C5	140
Ahtubinsk, Russia	E6	26
Ahuacatlán, Mex.	C4	78
Ahumada, Mex.	A3	78
Ahvāz, Iran	D5	42
Ahvenanmaa see Åland, is., Fin.	G9	10
Aialik, Cape, c., Ak., U.S.	D10	95
Aiea, Hi., U.S.	B4	104
Aiken, S.C., U.S.	D4	133
Aiken, co., S.C., U.S.	D4	133
Ailao Shan, mts., China	G8	28
Aileron, Austl.	E5	60
Ailinglaplap, atoll, Marsh. Is.	D10	58
Ailsa Craig, On., Can.	D3	89
Aim, Russia	D15	26
Aimorés, Braz.	E3	74
Aïn el Beïda, Alg.	D5	14
Ainslie Lake, l., N.S., Can.	C8	87
Ainsworth, Ne., U.S.	B6	120
Aïn Témouchent, Alg.	J6	16
Aïn Wessara, Alg.	J8	16
Aïr, Massif de l', mts., Niger	C6	50
Airdrie, Ab., Can.	D3	84
Aïssa, Djebel, mtn., Alg.	D4	48
Aitape, Pap. N. Gui.	G11	32
Aitkin, Mn., U.S.	D5	116
Aitkin, co., Mn., U.S.	D5	116
Aitutaki, at., Cook Is.	F14	58
Aiud, Rom.	F7	20
Aix, Mount, mtn., Wa., U.S.	C4	140
Āk'ak'ī Besek'a, Eth.	B7	54
'Akāshāt, Iraq	F8	44
Akbou, Alg.	I9	16
Akbulak, Russia	D10	22
Akçaabat, Tur.	B8	44
Akçadağ, Tur.	C7	44
Akçakale, Tur.	D8	44
Akçakoca, Tur.	B4	44
Akchâr, reg., Maur.	C1	50
Ak-Chin Indian Reservation, Az., U.S.	E3	96
Akdağmadeni, Tur.	C6	44
Aketi, D.R.C.	C4	54
Akhḍar, Al-Jabal al-, mts., Oman	F7	42
Akhisar, Tur.	C2	44
Akiachak, Ak., U.S.	C7	95
Akita, Japan	D16	28
Akjoujt, Maur.	C2	50
Akkajaure, l., Swe.	C7	10
Akkol', Kaz.	E9	26
Akkol', Kaz.	B10	42
'Aklé ('Aouâna), reg., Afr.	C3	50
Akmola see Astana, Kaz.	D9	26
Akok, Gabon	C1	54
Akola, India	E3	40
Akonolinga, Cam.	C2	54
Akordat, Erit.	G12	48
Akranes, Ice.	l17	10a
Akron, Co., U.S.	A7	99
Akron, Ia., U.S.	B1	108
Akron, In., U.S.	B5	107
Akron, N.Y., U.S.	B2	125
Akron, Oh., U.S.	A4	128
Akron, Pa., U.S.	F9	131
Aksaj, Kaz.	D9	22
Aksaray, Tur.	C6	44
Aksarka, Russia	A12	22
Akşehir, Tur.	C4	44
Akşehir Gölü, l., Tur.	C4	44
Akseki, Tur.	D4	44
Aksu, China	C4	28
Aksuat, Kaz.	E10	26
Āksum, Eth.	H3	38
Aktau, Kaz.	E7	26
Aktjubinsk, Kaz.	D7	26
Akto, China	B3	40
Aktogaj, Kaz.	E9	26
Akune, Japan	D1	31
Akure, Nig.	E6	50
Akureyri, Ice.	l19	10a
Akwanga, Nig.	E6	50
Akžar, Kaz.	B4	28
Alabama, stm., Al., U.S.	D2	94
Alabama, state, U.S.	C3	94
Alabaster, Al., U.S.	B3	94
Alaca, Tur.	B6	44
Alaçam, Tur.	B6	44
Alacant, Spain	H6	16
Alachua, Fl., U.S.	C4	102
Alachua, co., Fl., U.S.	C4	102
Aladža manastir, rel., Blg.	C12	18
Alagir, Russia	A11	44
Alagoas, state, Braz.	C4	74
Alagoinhas, Braz.	D4	74
Alagón, Spain	G6	16
Alahärmä, Fin.	E10	10
Alajuela, C.R.	C3	80
Alakanuk, Ak., U.S.	C7	95
Alakol', ozero, l., Kaz.	E10	26
Alalakeiki Channel, strt., Hi., U.S.	C5	104
Al-'Amādīyah, Iraq	D10	44
Alamagan, i., N. Mar. Is.	C12	32
Alamance, co., N.C., U.S.	B3	126
Al-'Amārah, Iraq	D5	42
Alameda, Ca., U.S.	h8	98
Alameda, co., Ca., U.S.	D3	98
Alameda, N.M., U.S.	B3	124
Alameda Naval Air Station, mil., Ca., U.S.	h8	98
Alamito Creek, stm., Tx., U.S.	p12	136
Alamo, Ga., U.S.	D4	103
Alamo, Nv., U.S.	F6	121
Alamo, Tn., U.S.	B2	135
Alamo, Tx., U.S.	F3	136
Alamogordo, N.M., U.S.	E4	124
Alamo Heights, Tx., U.S.	E3	136
Alamo Hueco Mountains, mts., N.M., U.S.	F1	124
Alamo Indian Reservation, N.M., U.S.	C2	124
Alamo Lake, res., Az., U.S.	C2	96
Alamosa, Co., U.S.	D5	99
Alamosa, stm., Co., U.S.	D4	99
Alamosa, co., Co., U.S.	D5	99
Alamosa Creek, stm., N.M., U.S.	D2	124
Alamosa East, Co., U.S.	D5	99
Åland, is., Fin.	G9	10
Ålands hav, s., Eur.	F8	10
Alandur, India	G4	40
Alanya, Tur.	D4	44
Alapaevsk, Russia	C11	22
Alapaha, Ga., U.S.	E3	103
Alapaha, stm., U.S.	E3	103
Al-'Aqabah, Jord.	E3	42
Alas, Selat, strt., Indon.	E5	36
Alaşehir, Tur.	C3	44
Alashanyouqi, China	C8	28
Alaska, state, U.S.	C5	95
Alaska, Gulf of, b., Ak., U.S.	D10	95
Alaska Peninsula, pen., Ak., U.S.	D8	95
Alaska Range, mts., Ak., U.S.	C9	95
Alatna, stm., Ak., U.S.	B9	95
Alatyr', Russia	D8	22
Alava, Cape, c., Wa., U.S.	A1	140
Alavus, Fin.	E10	10
Al-'Ayn, U.A.E.	F7	42
Al-'Azīzīyah, Libya	E6	14
Alba, Italy	B2	18
Al-Bāb, Syria	D7	44
Albacete, Spain	H6	16
Alba Iulia, Rom.	F7	20
Albania, ctry., Eur.	D7	18
Albano Laziale, Italy	D4	18
Albany, Austl.	G2	60
Albany, stm., On., Can.	o18	89
Albany, Ga., U.S.	E2	103
Albany, Il., U.S.	B3	106
Albany, In., U.S.	D7	107
Albany, Ky., U.S.	D5	110
Albany, La., U.S.	g10	111
Albany, Mn., U.S.	E4	116
Albany, Mo., U.S.	A3	118
Albany, N.Y., U.S.	C7	125
Albany, co., N.Y., U.S.	C6	125
Albany, Or., U.S.	C3	130
Albany, Tx., U.S.	C3	136
Albany, Wi., U.S.	F4	142
Albany, co., Wy., U.S.	E7	143
Al-Başrah, Iraq	D5	42
Al-Batrā' (Petra), sci., Jord.	D3	42
Al-Batrūn, Leb.	E6	44
Al-Baydā', Libya	D9	48
Albemarle, N.C., U.S.	B2	126
Albemarle, co., Va., U.S.	C4	139
Albemarle Island see Isabela, Isla, i., Ec.	D1	70
Albemarle Lake, l., Ms., U.S.	C2	117
Albemarle Sound, strt., N.C., U.S.	A6	126
Albert, Fr.	B8	16
Albert, Lake, l., Afr.	C6	54
Alberta, prov., Can.	C4	84
Alberta, Mount, mtn., Ab., Can.	C2	84
Albert City, Ia., U.S.	B3	108
Albert Lea, Mn., U.S.	G5	116
Albert Markham, Mount, mtn., Ant.	E22	67
Albert Nile, stm., Ug.	C6	54
Alberton, P.E., Can.	C6	87
Albertson, N.Y., U.S.	k13	125
Albertville see Kalemie, D.R.C.	E5	54
Albertville, Fr.	E10	16
Albertville, Al., U.S.	A3	94
Albertville, Mn., U.S.	E5	116
Albi, Fr.	F8	16
Albia, Ia., U.S.	C5	108
Albion, Il., U.S.	E5	106
Albion, In., U.S.	B7	107
Albion, Mi., U.S.	F6	115
Albion, Ne., U.S.	C7	120
Albion, N.Y., U.S.	B2	125
Albion, Pa., U.S.	C1	131
Albion, R.I., U.S.	B4	132
Albion, Wa., U.S.	C8	140
Al-Biqā', val., Leb.	F6	44
Alborán, Isla de, i., Spain	J5	16

Name	Map Ref.	Page
Ålborg, Den.	H3	10
Alborz, Reshteh-ye Kūhhā-ye, mts., Iran	C6	42
Albox, Spain	I5	16
Ālbū Gharz, Sabkhat, pl., Asia	E9	44
Albuquerque, N.M., U.S.	B3	124
Alburquerque, Spain	H3	16
Alburtis, Pa., U.S.	F10	131
Albury, Austl.	H4	62
Alcalá de Henares, Spain	G5	16
Alcalde, N.M., U.S.	A3	124
Alcamo, Italy	F4	18
Alcañiz, Spain	G6	16
Alcántara Uno, Embalse de, res., Spain	H3	16
Alcantarilla, Spain	I6	16
Alcázar de San Juan, Spain	H5	16
Alcazarquivir see Er-Rachidia, Mor.	E3	14
Alcester, S.D., U.S.	D9	134
Alchevs'k, Ukr.	E15	20
Alcoa, Tn., U.S.	D10	135
Alcobaça, Braz.	G12	70
Alcobendas, Spain	G5	16
Alcoi, Spain	H6	16
Alcolu, S.C., U.S.	D7	133
Alcona, co., Mi., U.S.	D7	115
Alcorn, co., Ms., U.S.	A5	117
Aldabra, Groupe d', i., Sey.	i11	57b
Aldama, Mex.	B3	78
Aldan, Russia	D14	26
Aldan, stm., Russia	C15	26
Aldan Plateau see Aldanskoe nagor'e, plat., Russia	D14	26
Aldanskoe nagor'e, plat., Russia	D14	26
Alden, Ia., U.S.	B4	108
Alden, Mn., U.S.	G5	116
Alden, N.Y., U.S.	C2	125
Alder Brook, stm., Vt., U.S.	B4	138
Alderney, i., Guern.	F5	12
Alderson, W.V., U.S.	D4	141
Aldrich, Al., U.S.	B3	94
Aledo, Il., U.S.	B3	106
Aleg, Maur.	C2	50
Alegres Mountain, mtn., N.M., U.S.	C2	124
Alegrete, Braz.	D6	72
Alejandro Selkirk, Isla, i., Chile	E1	72
Alejsk, Russia	D10	26
Aleksandrov, Russia	C6	22
Aleksandrovsk-Sahalinskij, Russia	D16	26
Alekseevka, Russia	D15	20
Aleksin, Russia	B14	20
Aleksinac, Yugo.	C8	18
Alençon, Fr.	C7	16
Alenquer, Braz.	D9	70
Alenuihaha Channel, strt., Hi., U.S.	C5	104
Aleppo see Ḥalab, Syria	D7	44
Alert Bay, B.C., Can.	D4	85
Alès, Fr.	E9	16
Alessándria, Italy	B2	18
Ålesund, Nor.	E6	10
Aleutian Basin	B4	144
Aleutian Islands, is., Ak., U.S.	E3	95
Aleutian Range, mts., Ak., U.S.	D9	95
Aleutian Trench	B4	144
Aleutka, Russia	B18	38
Alex, Ok., U.S.	C4	129
Alexander, co., Il., U.S.	F4	106
Alexander, co., N.C., U.S.	B1	126
Alexander, Lake, l., Mn., U.S.	D4	116
Alexander Archipelago, is., Ak., U.S.	D12	95
Alexander Bay, S. Afr.	D2	56
Alexander City, Al., U.S.	C4	94
Alexander Island, i., Ant.	C33	67
Alexandra, N.Z.	q12	63c
Alexandretta see İskenderun, Tur.	D7	44
Alexandria, On., Can.	B10	89
Alexandria see El-Iskandarîya, Egypt	E9	48
Alexandria, Rom.	H8	20
Alexandria, S. Afr.	E4	56
Alexandria, In., U.S.	D6	107
Alexandria, Ky., U.S.	B5	110
Alexandria, La., U.S.	C3	111
Alexandria, Mn., U.S.	E3	116
Alexandria, Tn., U.S.	A5	135
Alexandria, Va., U.S.	B5	139
Alexandroúpolis, Grc.	D10	18
Alexis, Il., U.S.	B3	106
Alfalfa, co., Ok., U.S.	A3	129
Al-Fallūjah, Iraq	F10	44
Al-Fāshir, Sudan	H10	48
Alföld, pl., Hung.	F6	20
Alfred, On., Can.	B10	89
Alfred, N.Y., U.S.	C3	125
Al-Fujayrah, U.A.E.	E7	42
Al-Furāt see Euphrates, stm., Asia	D4	42
Alga, Kaz.	E10	22
Algarrobo del Águila, Arg.	F4	72
Algarve, hist. reg., Port.	I2	16
Algeciras, Spain	I4	16
Alger, co., Mi., U.S.	B4	115
Alger, Oh., U.S.	B2	128
Algeria, ctry., Afr.	E5	48
Al-Ghaydah, Yemen	G6	38
Al-Ghazālah, Sau. Ar.	E4	42
Alghero, Italy	D2	18
Algiers see El Djazaïr, Alg.	C5	48
Algoabaai, b., S. Afr.	E4	56
Algoma, Wi., U.S.	D6	142
Algona, Ia., U.S.	A3	108
Algona, Wa., U.S.	B3	140
Algonac, Mi., U.S.	F8	115
Algonquin, Il., U.S.	A5	106
Algonquin Provincial Park, On., Can.	B6	89
Algood, Tn., U.S.	C8	135
Al-Hajarah, reg., Asia	E5	42
Al-Halfāyah, Iraq	G12	44
Al-Hamād, pl., Sau. Ar.	G8	44
Alhambra, Ca., U.S.	m12	98
Al-Harrah, lav., Sau. Ar.	D3	42
Al-Harrah, reg., Asia	E5	42
Al-Harūj al-Aswad, Libya	A8	50
Al-Hasakah, Syria	D9	44
Al-Hawrah, Yemen	H5	38
Al-Hayy, Iraq	F12	44
Al-Hijāz, reg., Sau. Ar.	E3	38
Al-Hillah, Iraq	D4	42
Al-Hoceima, Mor.	C4	48
Al-Hudaydah, Yemen	H4	38
Al-Hufrah, reg., Sau. Ar.	E3	42
Al-Hufūf, Sau. Ar.	E5	38
Al-Hulwah, Sau. Ar.	F5	38
Aliağo, Tur.	C2	44
'Alī al-Gharbī, Iraq	F12	44
Alībāg, India	F2	40
Äli Bayramlı, Azer.	C13	44
Alicante see Alacant, Spain	H6	16
Alice, Tx., U.S.	F3	136
Alice Lake, l., Mn., U.S.	C7	116
Alice Springs, Austl.	E5	60
Aliceville, Al., U.S.	B1	94
Alīgarh, India	D3	40
Aligūdarz, Iran	D5	42
Alingsås, Swe.	H5	10
Alīpur, Pak.	E10	42
Aliquippa, Pa., U.S.	E1	131
Aliwal North, S. Afr.	E4	56
Alix, Ab., U.S.	C4	84
Al-Jaghbūb, Libya	E9	48
Al-Jahrah, Kuw.	E5	42
Al-Jalāmīd, Sau. Ar.	G9	44
Al-Jawārah, Oman	G7	38
Al-Jawf, Libya	F9	48
Al-Jawf, Sau. Ar.	E3	38
Al-Jubayl, Sau. Ar.	E5	38
Al-Junaynah, Sudan	H9	48
Aljustrel, Port.	I2	16
Alkali Lake, l., Nv., U.S.	B2	121
Alkali Lake, l., Or., U.S.	E6	130
Alkaline Lake, l., N.D., U.S.	C6	127
Al-Karak, Jord.	G6	44
Al-Khābūrah, Oman	F7	38
Al-Khalīl (Hebron), W.B.	G6	44
Al-Khartūm, Sudan	G11	48
Al-Khasab, Oman	E7	42
Al-Khums, Libya	E6	14
Al-Kifl, Iraq	F11	44
Alkmaar, Neth.	D9	12
Al-Kūfah, Iraq	D4	42
Al-Kūt, Iraq	D5	42
Al-Kuwayt (Kuwait), Kuw.	E5	42
Al-Lādhiqīyah, Syria	E6	44
Allagash, stm., Me., U.S.	B3	112
Allagash Lake, l., Me., U.S.	B3	112
Allahābād, India	D4	40
Allah-Jun', Russia	C15	26
Allamakee, co., Ia., U.S.	A6	108
Allan, Sk., Can.	F2	91
Allanmyo, Mya.	C3	34
Allardt, Tn., U.S.	C9	135
Allatoona Lake, res., Ga., U.S.	B2	103
Alldays, S. Afr.	C4	56
Allegan, Mi., U.S.	F5	115
Allegan, co., Mi., U.S.	F5	115
Allegany, co., Md., U.S.	k13	113
Allegany, N.Y., U.S.	C2	125
Allegany, co., N.Y., U.S.	C2	125
Allegany Indian Reservation, N.Y., U.S.	C2	125
Alleghany, co., N.C., U.S.	A1	126
Alleghany, co., Va., U.S.	C2	139
Allegheny, co., Pa., U.S.	E2	131
Allegheny, stm., U.S.	E2	131
Allegheny Reservoir, res., U.S.	B4	131
Allemands, Lac Des, l., La., U.S.	E5	111
Allen, co., In., U.S.	B7	107
Allen, co., Ks., U.S.	E8	109
Allen, co., Ky., U.S.	D3	110
Allen, co., La., U.S.	D3	111
Allen, co., Oh., U.S.	B1	128
Allen, Ok., U.S.	C5	129
Allen, Mount, mtn., Ak., U.S.	C11	95
Allendale, N.J., U.S.	A4	123
Allendale, S.C., U.S.	E5	133
Allendale, co., S.C., U.S.	F5	133
Allende, Mex.	B4	78
Allen Park, Mi., U.S.	p15	115
Allenton, R.I., U.S.	E4	132
Allenton, Wi., U.S.	E5	142
Allentown, Pa., U.S.	E11	131
Alleppey, India	H3	40
Allerton, Point, c., Ma., U.S.	B6	114
Alliance, Ne., U.S.	B3	120
Alliance, Oh., U.S.	B4	128
Allier, stm., Fr.	D8	16
Alligator, stm., N.C., U.S.	B6	126
Alligator Lake, l., Me., U.S.	D4	112
Allison, Ia., U.S.	B5	108
Allison, Pa., U.S.	G2	131
Allison Park, Pa., U.S.	h14	131
Alliston [Beeton Tecumseth and Tottenham], On., Can.	C5	89
Al-Līth, Sau. Ar.	F4	38
Allouez, Wi., U.S.	h9	142
Alloway Creek, stm., N.J., U.S.	D2	123
Al-Luhayyah, Yemen	G4	38
Allumette Lake, l., Can.	B7	89
Allyn, Wa., U.S.	B3	140
Alma, P.Q., Can.	A6	90
Alma, Ar., U.S.	B1	97
Alma, Ga., U.S.	E4	103
Alma, Ks., U.S.	C7	109
Alma, Mi., U.S.	E6	115
Alma, Ne., U.S.	D6	120
Alma, Wi., U.S.	D2	142
Alma-Ata see Almaty, Kaz.	E9	26
Almada, Port.	H2	16
Almadén, Spain	H4	16
Al-Madīnah (Medina), Sau. Ar.	F3	38
Al-Mafraq, Jord.	F7	44
Almalyk, Uzb.	E8	26
Al-Manāmah (Manama), Bahr.	E6	42
Almanor, Lake, l., Ca., U.S.	B3	98
Almansa, Spain	H6	16
Al-Marj, Libya	D9	48
Almaty, Kaz.	E9	26
Al-Mawşil, Iraq	C4	42
Al-Mayādīn, Syria	E9	44
Almelo, Neth.	D10	12
Almenara, Braz.	E3	74
Almendralejo, Spain	H3	16
Almería, Spain	I5	16
Almería, Golfo de, b., Spain	I5	16
Al'metevsk, Russia	D7	26
Al-Mijlad, Sudan	A5	54
Al-Miqdādīyah, Iraq	F11	44
Almirante, Pan.	D3	80
Almont, Mi., U.S.	F7	115
Almonte, On., Can.	B8	89
Almonte, Spain	I3	16
Al-Mubarraz, Sau. Ar.	E5	42
Al-Mubarraz, Sau. Ar.	F5	38
Al-Muharraq, Bahr.	E6	42
Al-Mukallā, Yemen	H5	38
Al-Mukhā, Yemen	H4	38
Al-Muwaylih, Sau. Ar.	E3	38
Alnön, i., Swe.	E7	10
Alnwick, Eng., U.K.	C6	12
Aloha, Or., U.S.	h12	130
Alor, Pulau, i., Indon.	D7	36
Alor Setar, Malay.	B2	36
Alpena, Mi., U.S.	C7	115
Alpena, co., Mi., U.S.	D7	115
Alpha Cordillera	E33	144
Alpharetta, Ga., U.S.	B2	103
Alphonse, i., Sey.	i12	57b
Alpine, Az., U.S.	D6	96
Alpine, co., Ca., U.S.	C4	98
Alpine, Tx., U.S.	D1	136
Alpine, Ut., U.S.	C4	137
Alps, mts., Eur.	B5	14
Al-Qadārif, Sudan	H12	48
Al-Qā'im, Iraq	E9	44
Al-Qāmishlī, Syria	D9	44
Al-Qaryah ash-Sharqīyah, Libya	D7	48
Al-Qaryatayn, Syria	E7	44
Al-Qaţīf, Sau. Ar.	E6	38
Al-Qaţrūn, Libya	F7	48
Al-Qaysūmah, Sau. Ar.	E5	38
Al-Quds see Jerusalem, Isr.	G6	44
Al-Qunayţirah, Syria	F6	44
Al-Qunfudhah, Sau. Ar.	G4	38
Al-Qurnah, Iraq	G12	44
Al-Quţayfah, Syria	F7	44
Als, i., Den.	I3	10
Alsace, hist. reg., Fr.	C10	16
Alsasua, Spain	F5	16
Alta, Nor.	B10	10
Alta, Ia., U.S.	B2	108
Altadena, Ca., U.S.	m12	98
Alta Gracia, Arg.	E5	72
Altagracia, Ven.	C5	80
Altai, mts., Asia	B5	28
Altai, mts., Asia	B5	28
Altaj, state, Russia	A5	28
Altamaha, stm., Ga., U.S.	E4	103
Altamira, Braz.	D9	70
Altamont, Il., U.S.	D5	106
Altamont, Ks., U.S.	E8	109
Altamont, Or., U.S.	E5	130
Altamont, Tn., U.S.	D8	135
Altamonte Springs, Fl., U.S.	D5	102
Altamura, Italy	D6	18
Altata, Mex.	C3	78
Altavista, Va., U.S.	C3	139
Altay, Mong.	B7	28
Altay Mountains see Altai, mts., Asia	B5	28
Altay Mountains see Altai, mts., Asia	B5	28
Altevatnet, l., Nor.	B8	10
Altheimer, Ar., U.S.	C4	97
Alto, Ga., U.S.	B3	103
Alto, N.M., U.S.	D4	124
Alto Araguaia, Braz.	G9	70
Alton, Ia., U.S.	B2	108
Alton, Il., U.S.	E3	106
Alton, Mo., U.S.	E6	118
Alton, N.H., U.S.	D4	122
Altona, Mb., Can.	E3	86
Altona, Il., U.S.	B3	106
Alton Bay, N.H., U.S.	D4	122
Altoona, Al., U.S.	A3	94
Altoona, Fl., U.S.	D5	102
Altoona, Ia., U.S.	C4	108
Altoona, Pa., U.S.	E5	131
Altoona, Wi., U.S.	D2	142
Alto Paraguai, Braz.	A6	72
Alto Parnaíba, Braz.	E10	70
Alto Río Senguer, Arg.	G2	69
Altun Shan, mts., China	D5	28
Alturas, Ca., U.S.	B3	98
Altus, Ok., U.S.	C2	129
Altus Air Force Base, mil., Ok., U.S.	C2	129
Altus Reservoir, res., Ok., U.S.	C2	129
Alucra, Tur.	B8	44
Al-'Ubaylah, Sau. Ar.	F6	38
Al-Ubayyid, Sudan	H10	48
Alum Bank, Pa., U.S.	F4	131
Alum Creek, stm., Oh., U.S.	k11	128
Alupka, Ukr.	G13	20
Al-'Uqaylah, Libya	E7	14
Alushta, Ukr.	G13	20
Al-'Uwaynāt, Libya	E7	48
Alva, Fl., U.S.	F5	102
Alva, Ok., U.S.	A3	129
Alvarado, Mex.	D5	78
Alvarado, Tx., U.S.	C4	136
Álvaro Obregón, Presa, res., Mex.	B3	78
Älvdalen, Swe.	F6	10
Alvin, Tx., U.S.	E5	136
Alvinston, On., Can.	E3	89
Älvkarleby, Swe.	F7	10
Alvord Lake, l., Or., U.S.	E8	130
Al-Wajh, Sau. Ar.	E3	38
Alwar, India	D3	40
Alxa Zuoqi, China	D9	28
Alzira, Spain	H6	16
Ama, La., U.S.	k11	111
Amacuro, stm., S.A.	D7	80
Amadeus, Lake, l., Austl.	E5	60
Amador, co., Ca., U.S.	C3	98
Amagansett, N.Y., U.S.	n16	125
Amahai, Indon.	D7	36
Amakusa-nada, s., Japan	D1	31
Amakusa Sea see Amakusa-nada, s., Japan	D1	31
Åmål, Swe.	G5	10
Amalfi, Col.	D4	80
Amalfi, Italy	D5	18
Amaliás, Grc.	F8	18
Amambaí, Braz.	H8	70
Amami-Ō-shima, i., Japan	E1	31
Amami-shotō, is., Japan	g6	31a
Amana, Ia., U.S.	C6	108
Amapá, Braz.	C9	70
Amapá, state, Braz.	C9	70
Amarante, Braz.	E11	70
Amarapura, Mya.	B3	34
Amargosa, stm., U.S.	D5	98
Amargosa Desert, des., U.S.	G5	121
Amargosa Range, mts., U.S.	G5	121
Amargosa Valley, Nv., U.S.	G5	121
Amarillo, Tx., U.S.	B2	136
Amarkantak, India	E4	40
Amasya, Tur.	B6	44
Amatignak Island, i., Ak., U.S.	E4	95
Amawbia Awka, Nig.	E6	50
Amazon (Solimões) (Amazonas), stm., S.A.	D9	70
Amazonas see Amazon, stm., S.A.	D9	70
Ambāla, India	C3	40
Ambalavao, Madag.	C8	56
Ambanja, Madag.	A8	56
Ambarčik, Russia	C18	26
Ambato, Ec.	D4	70
Ambatofinandrahana, Madag.	C8	56
Ambatolampy, Madag.	B8	56
Ambatondrazaka, Madag.	B8	56
Amberg, Ger.	F12	12
Ambikāpur, India	E4	40
Ambilobe, Madag.	A8	56
Ambler, Pa., U.S.	F11	131
Amboasary, Madag.	C8	56
Ambodifototra, Madag.	B8	56
Ambon, Indon.	D7	36
Ambon, Pulau, i., Indon.	D7	36
Ambositra, Madag.	C8	56
Ambovombe, Madag.	D8	56
Amboy, Il., U.S.	B4	106
Ambridge, Pa., U.S.	E1	131
Ambriz, Ang.	E2	54
Ambrym, i., Vanuatu	k9	62a
Ambunti, Pap. N. Gui.	G11	32
Āmbūr, India	G3	40
Amchitka Island, i., Ak., U.S.	E3	95
Amchitka Pass, strt., Ak., U.S.	E4	95
Amderma, Russia	C8	26
Amdo, China	E6	28
Ameca, Mex.	C4	78
Amelia, La., U.S.	E4	111
Amelia, Oh., U.S.	C1	128
Amelia, co., Va., U.S.	C4	139
Amelia Court House, Va., U.S.	C5	139
Amelia Island, i., Fl., U.S.	k9	102
American, stm., Ca., U.S.	C3	98
American Falls, Id., U.S.	G6	105
American Falls Dam, Id., U.S.	G6	105
American Falls Reservoir, res., Id., U.S.	F5	105
American Fork, Ut., U.S.	C4	137
American Highland, plat., Ant.	D12	67
American Samoa, dep., Oc.	F12	58
Americus, Ga., U.S.	D2	103
Americus, Ks., U.S.	D7	109
Amersfoort, Neth.	D9	12
Amery, Wi., U.S.	C1	142
Amery Ice Shelf, ice, Ant.	C12	67
Ames, Ia., U.S.	B4	108
Amesbury, Ma., U.S.	A6	114
Amfilokhía, Grc.	E8	18
Amga, Russia	C15	26
Amga, stm., Russia	C14	26
Amgun', stm., Russia	D15	26
Amherst, Ma., U.S.	B2	114
Amherst, N.H., U.S.	E3	122
Amherst, N.Y., U.S.	C2	125
Amherst, Oh., U.S.	A3	128
Amherst, Va., U.S.	C3	139
Amherst, co., Va., U.S.	C3	139
Amherst, Wi., U.S.	D4	142
Amherstburg, On., Can.	E1	89
Amherstdale, W.V., U.S.	n12	141
Amiens, Fr.	C8	16
Aminuis, Nmb.	C2	56
Amirantes, Les, is., Sey.	i12	57b
Amisk Lake, l., Sk., Can.	C4	91
Amistad, Presa de la (Amistad Reservoir), res., N.A.	B4	78
Amistad National Recreation Area, Tx., U.S.	E2	136
Amistad Reservoir (Amistad, Presa de la), res., N.A.	B4	78
Amite, La., U.S.	D5	111
Amite, stm., La., U.S.	D5	111
Amite, co., Ms., U.S.	D3	117
Amity, Or., U.S.	B3	130
Amityville, N.Y., U.S.	E7	125
Amlia Island, i., Ak., U.S.	E5	95
'Ammān, Jord.	D3	42
Ammon, Id., U.S.	F7	105
Ammonoosuc, stm., N.H., U.S.	B3	122
Āmol, Iran	C6	42
Amorgós, i., Grc.	F10	18
Amory, Ms., U.S.	B5	117
Amos, P.Q., Can.	k11	90
Åmot, Nor.	G2	10
Amoy see Xiamen, China	G11	28
Ampanihy, Madag.	C7	56
Ampasimanolotra, Madag.	B8	56
Amposta, Spain	G7	16
Amrāvati, India	E3	40
Amreli, India	E2	40
Amritsar, India	C2	40
Amroha, India	D3	40
Amsterdam, Neth.	D9	12
Amsterdam, N.Y., U.S.	C6	125
Amstetten, Aus.	F14	12
Am Timan, Chad	A4	54
Amu Darya, stm., Asia	B8	42
Amukta Pass, strt., Ak., U.S.	E5	95
Amundsen Gulf, b., N.T., Can.	D15	82
Amundsen Sea, s., Ant.	C30	67
Amuntai, Indon.	D5	36
Amur (Heilong), stm., Asia	D16	26
Amvrakikós Kólpos, b., Grc.	E8	18
Anaa, at., Fr. Poly.	F15	58
Anaco, Ven.	D7	80
Anacoco, La., U.S.	C2	111
Anaconda, Mt., U.S.	D4	119
Anaconda Range, mts., Mt., U.S.	E3	119
Anacortes, Wa., U.S.	A3	140
Anacostia, stm., Md., U.S.	C4	113
Anacostia, Northwest Branch, stm., Md., U.S.	B3	113
Anadarko, Ok., U.S.	B3	129
Anadolu, hist. reg., Tur.	C6	44
Anadyr', Russia	C19	26
Anadyr', stm., Russia	C19	26
Anadyr, Gulf of see Anadyrskij zaliv, b., Russia	C20	26
Anadyrskij zaliv, b., Russia	C20	26
'Ānah, Iraq	E9	44
Anaheim, Ca., U.S.	F5	98
Anahola, Hi., U.S.	A2	104
Anahuac, Tx., U.S.	E5	136
Anakāpalle, India	F4	40
Analalava, Madag.	A8	56
Ana María, Golfo de, b., Cuba	A4	80
Anambas, Kepulauan, is., Indon.	C3	36
Anamosa, Ia., U.S.	B6	108
Anamur, Tur.	D5	44
Anan, Japan	D2	31
Anan'ïv, Ukr.	F11	20
Anantapur, India	E3	40
Anantnāg, India	C3	40
Anapa, Russia	G14	20
Anápolis, Braz.	E2	74
Anastasia Island, i., Fl., U.S.	C5	102
Anatahan, i., N. Mar. Is.	C12	32

Name	Map Ref.	Page
Anatolia see Anadolu, hist. reg., Tur.	C6	44
Anatom, i., Vanuatu	I9	62a
Añatuya, Arg.	D5	72
Anbei, China	A7	40
Ancaster, On., Can.	D4	89
Ancha, Sierra, mts., Az., U.S.	D4	96
Anchorage, Ak., U.S.	C10	95
Anchorage, Ky., U.S.	g11	110
Anchor Point, Ak., U.S.	D9	95
Anchor Point, c., Ak., U.S.	h15	95
Ancienne-Lorette, P.Q., Can.	C6	90
Anclote Keys, is., Fl., U.S.	D4	102
Ancona, Italy	C4	18
Ancud, Chile	F2	69
Anda, China	B13	28
Andacollo, Chile	E3	72
Andalgalá, Arg.	D4	72
Åndalsnes, Nor.	E2	10
Andalucía, hist. reg., Spain	I4	16
Andalusia, Al., U.S.	D3	94
Andalusia, Il., U.S.	B3	106
Andaman and Nicobar Islands, ter., India	G6	40
Andaman Basin	H12	64
Andaman Islands, is., India	G6	40
Andaman Sea, Asia	G6	40
Andamooka, Austl.	G2	62
Andapa, Madag.	A8	56
Andéramboukane, Mali	C5	50
Anderson, Ak., U.S.	C10	95
Anderson, Ca., U.S.	B2	98
Anderson, In., U.S.	D6	107
Anderson, Mo., U.S.	E3	118
Anderson, S.C., U.S.	B2	133
Anderson, co., Ks., U.S.	D8	109
Anderson, co., Ky., U.S.	C4	110
Anderson, co., S.C., U.S.	B2	133
Anderson, co., Tn., U.S.	C9	135
Anderson, co., Tx., U.S.	D5	136
Anderson, stm., N.T., Can.	E14	82
Anderson, In., U.S.	H4	107
Anderson, Mount, mtn., Wa., U.S.	B2	140
Anderson Ranch Reservoir, res., Id., U.S.	F3	105
Andes, mts., S.A.	B4	72
Andes, Lake, l., S.D., U.S.	D7	134
Andfjorden, strt., Nor.	B7	10
Andhra Pradesh, prov., India	F3	40
Andīmeshk, Iran	F13	44
Andirlang, China	B4	40
Andižan, Uzb.	E9	26
Andkhvoy, Afg.	C9	42
Andoany, Madag.	A8	56
Andong, S. Kor.	D13	28
Andorra, ctry., Eur.	F7	16
Andorra-la-Vella, And.	F7	16
Andover, Ks., U.S.	g12	109
Andover, Ma., U.S.	A5	114
Andover, Mn., U.S.	m12	116
Andover, Oh., U.S.	A5	128
Andover Lake, res., Ct., U.S.	C6	100
Andøya, i., Nor.	B6	10
Andradina, Braz.	F1	74
Andreanof Islands, is., Ak., U.S.	E4	95
Andrew, co., Mo., U.S.	B3	118
Andrew Island, i., N.S., Can.	D9	87
Andrews, In., U.S.	C6	107
Andrews, N.C., U.S.	f9	126
Andrews, S.C., U.S.	E8	133
Andrews, Tx., U.S.	C1	136
Andrews, co., Tx., U.S.	C1	136
Andrews Air Force Base, mil., Md., U.S.	C4	113
Andria, Italy	D6	18
Andriamena, Madag.	B8	56
Androka, Madag.	D7	56
Andropov see Rybinsk, Russia	D5	26
Andros, i., Bah.	D9	76
Ándros, i., Grc.	F10	18
Androscoggin, co., Me., U.S.	D2	112
Androscoggin, stm., Me., U.S.	D2	112
Androscoggin Lake, l., Me., U.S.	D2	112
Āndrott Island, i., India	G2	40
Andudu, D.R.C.	C5	54
Andújar, Spain	H4	16
Andulo, Ang.	F3	54
Anegada, i., Br. Vir. Is.	B7	80
Anegada Passage, strt., N.A.	B7	80
Aného, Togo	E5	50
Aneto, mtn., Spain	F7	16
Aney, Niger	C7	50
Ang'angxi, China	B12	28
Angara, stm., Russia	D11	26
Angarsk, Russia	D12	26
Änge, Swe.	E6	10
Ángel, Salto (Angel Falls), wtfl., Ven.	B7	70
Ángel de la Guarda, Isla, i., Mex.	B2	78
Angeles, Phil.	C8	34
Angeles Point, c., Wa., U.S.	A2	140
Angel Falls see Ángel, Salto, wtfl., Ven.	B7	70
Ängelholm, Swe.	H5	10
Angelina, co., Tx., U.S.	D5	136
Angels Camp, Ca., U.S.	C3	98
Ångermanälven, stm., Swe.	E7	10
Angers, Fr.	D6	16
Angier, N.C., U.S.	B4	126
Angkor Wat, hist., Camb.	D4	34
Anglesey, i., Wales, U.K.	D4	12
Angleton, Tx., U.S.	E5	136
Angmagssalik, Grnld.	E32	82
Ango, D.R.C.	C5	54
Angoche, Moz.	B6	56
Angol, Chile	E2	69
Angola, In., U.S.	A8	107
Angola, N.Y., U.S.	C1	125
Angola, ctry., Afr.	F3	54
Angola Basin	J14	66
Angola Swamp, sw., N.C., U.S.	C5	126
Angoon, Ak., U.S.	D13	95
Angora see Ankara, Tur.	C5	44
Angoram, Pap. N. Gui.	G11	32
Angostura see Ciudad Bolívar, Ven.	B7	70
Angostura, Presa de la, res., Mex.	D6	78
Angostura Reservoir, res., S.D., U.S.	D2	134
Angoulême, Fr.	E7	16
Angren, Uzb.	E9	26
Angu, D.R.C.	C4	54
Anguilla, Ms., U.S.	C3	117
Anguilla, dep., N.A.	E12	76
Anguille, Cape, c., Nf., Can.	E2	88
Anguo, China	B4	30
Anholt, i., Den.	H4	10
Anhua, China	D3	30
Anhui, state, China	E11	28
Aniak, Ak., U.S.	C8	95
Anil, Braz.	B3	74
Animas, stm., U.S.	D3	99
Animas Mountains, mts., N.M., U.S.	F1	124
Animas Peak, mtn., N.M., U.S.	F2	124
Animas Valley, val., N.M., U.S.	F1	124
Anina, Rom.	G6	20
Anita, Ia., U.S.	C3	108
Aniva, zaliv, b., Russia	B16	28
Aniwa, i., Vanuatu	I9	62a
Anjār, India	E2	40
Anjou, P.Q., Can.	p19	90
Anjou, hist. reg., Fr.	D6	16
Anjouan see Nzwani, i., Com.	A7	56
Anjudin, Russia	B10	22
Ankang, China	E9	28
Ankara, Tur.	C5	44
Ankavandra, Madag.	B8	56
Ankazoabo, Madag.	C7	56
Ankazobe, Madag.	B8	56
Ankeny, Ia., U.S.	C4	108
Anking see Anqing, China	E11	28
Ankoro, D.R.C.	C5	54
Anlong, China	D2	30
Anlu, China	D10	28
Ann, Cape, c., Ma., U.S.	A6	114
Anna, Russia	D16	20
Anna, Il., U.S.	F4	106
Anna, Oh., U.S.	B1	128
Anna, Lake, res., Va., U.S.	B5	139
Annaba, Alg.	C6	48
An-Nabk, Syria	E7	44
An-Nafūd, des., Sau. Ar.	E4	38
An-Najaf, Iraq	D4	42
An-Najaf, state, Iraq	G11	44
Anna Maria, Fl., U.S.	p10	102
Anna Maria Island, i., Fl., U.S.	q10	102
Annandale, Mn., U.S.	E4	116
Annandale, Va., U.S.	g12	139
Anna Plains, Austl.	D3	60
Annapolis, Md., U.S.	C5	113
Annapolis, stm., N.S., Can.	E4	87
Annapolis Junction, Md., U.S.	B4	113
Annapolis Royal, N.S., Can.	E4	87
Annapūrṇa, mtn., Nepal	D4	40
Ann Arbor, Mi., U.S.	F7	115
An-Nāṣirīyah, Iraq	D5	42
Annawan, Il., U.S.	B4	106
Anne Arundel, co., Md., U.S.	B4	113
Annecy, Fr.	E10	16
Annenkov Island, i., S. Geor.	H9	69
Annette, Ak., U.S.	n24	95
An Nhon, Viet.	D5	34
Anning, China	E1	30
Anniston, Al., U.S.	B4	94
Annobón, i., Eq. Gui.	C1	52
An-Nuhūd, Sudan	H10	48
An Nukhayb, Iraq	F10	44
Annville, Pa., U.S.	F8	131
Anoka, Mn., U.S.	E5	116
Anoka, co., Mn., U.S.	E5	116
Anori, Braz.	D7	70
Anqing, China	E11	28
Ansai, China	B2	30
Ansbach, Ger.	F12	12
Anshan, China	C12	28
Anshun, China	F9	28
Anson, Me., U.S.	D3	112
Anson, Tx., U.S.	C3	136
Anson, co., N.C., U.S.	B2	126
Ansongo, Mali	C5	50
Ansonia, Ct., U.S.	D3	100
Ansonia, Oh., U.S.	B1	128
Ansted, W.V., U.S.	C3	141
Antalaha, Madag.	A9	56
Antalya, Tur.	D4	44
Antalya, Gulf of see Antalya Körfezi, b., Tur.	D4	44
Antalya Körfezi, b., Tur.	D4	44
Antananarivo, Madag.	B8	56
Antarctica	L13	4
Antarctic Peninsula, pen., Ant.	D35	67
Antelope, co., Ne., U.S.	B7	120
Antelope Creek, stm., Wy., U.S.	C7	143
Antelope Island, i., Ut., U.S.	B3	137
Antelope Peak, mtn., Nv., U.S.	B7	121
Antelope Range, mts., Nv., U.S.	D7	121
Antelope Reservoir, res., Or., U.S.	E9	130
Antelope Wash, val., U.S.	D5	121
Antequera, Spain	I4	16
Antero, Mount, mtn., Co., U.S.	C4	99
Antero Reservoir, res., Co., U.S.	C5	99
Anthon, Ia., U.S.	B2	108
Anthony, Fl., U.S.	C4	102
Anthony, Ks., U.S.	E5	109
Anthony, N.M., U.S.	F3	124
Anthony, R.I., U.S.	D3	132
Anthony, Tx., U.S.	o11	136
Anthony Creek, stm., W.V., U.S.	D4	141
Aomen (Macau), China	B6	34
Antibes, Fr.	F10	16
Anticosti, Île d', i., P.Q., Can.	k14	90
Antietam National Battlefield, hist., Md., U.S.	B2	113
Antigo, Wi., U.S.	C4	142
Antigua, i., Antig.	B7	80
Antigua and Barbuda, ctry., N.A.	E12	76
Antioch see Hatay, Tur.	D7	44
Antioch, Ca., U.S.	h9	98
Antioch, Il., U.S.	A5	106
Antioquia, Col.	D4	80
Antipodes Islands, is., N.Z.	N20	64
Antlers, Ok., U.S.	C6	129
Antofagasta, Chile	B2	69
Antofalla, Salar de, pl., Arg.	D4	72
Anton, Tx., U.S.	C1	136
Antongila, Helodrano, b., Madag.	B8	56
Antônio Bezerra, Braz.	B4	74
Antonito, Co., U.S.	D5	99
Antora Peak, mtn., Co., U.S.	C4	99
Antrim, N.H., U.S.	D3	122
Antrim, co., Mi., U.S.	C5	115
Antsalova, Madag.	B7	56
Antsirabe, Madag.	B8	56
Antsirañana, Madag.	A8	56
Antsohihy, Madag.	A8	56
Antwerp see Antwerpen, Bel.	E9	12
Antwerp, Oh., U.S.	A1	128
Antwerpen (Antwerp), Bel.	E9	12
Anugul, India	E5	40
Anūpgarh, India	D2	40
Anuradhapura, Sri L.	H4	40
Anxi, China	C7	28
Anxiang, China	D3	30
Anyang, China	D10	28
A'nyêmaqên Shan, mts., China	D7	28
Anyue, China	C2	30
Anžero-Sudžensk, Russia	D10	26
Anzio, Italy	D4	18
Aoga-shima, i., Japan	E15	28
Aoji-ri, N. Kor.	B2	31
Aomen (Macau), China	B6	34
Aomori, Japan	C16	28
Aoral, Mount see Aôral, Phnum, mtn., Camb.	D4	34
Aôral, Phnum, mtn., Camb.	D4	34
Aosta, Italy	B1	18
'Aouâna ('Aklé), reg., Afr.	C3	50
Aouderas, Niger	C6	50
Aouk, stm., Afr.	I9	48
Aoukâr, reg., Maur.	C3	50
Aozou, Chad	B8	50
Apache, Ok., U.S.	C3	129
Apache, co., Az., U.S.	B6	96
Apache Junction, Az., U.S.	m9	96
Apache Peak, mtn., Az., U.S.	F5	96
Apalachee Bay, b., Fl., U.S.	B2	102
Apalachicola, Fl., U.S.	C2	102
Apalachicola, stm., Fl., U.S.	B1	102
Apalachicola Bay, b., Fl., U.S.	C2	102
Apaporis, stm., S.A.	C5	70
Aparri, Phil.	C8	34
Apatity, Russia	C5	26
Apatzingán de la Constitución, Mex.	D4	78
Apeldoorn, Neth.	D9	12
Apennines see Appennino, mts., Italy	C4	18
Apex, N.C., U.S.	B4	126
Apia, Samoa	F12	58
Apiacás, Serra dos, plat., Braz.	E8	70
Apishapa, stm., Co., U.S.	D6	99
Aplington, Ia., U.S.	B5	108
Apo, Mount, mtn., Phil.	E9	34
Apollo, Pa., U.S.	E2	131
Apopka, Fl., U.S.	D5	102
Apopka, Lake, l., Fl., U.S.	D5	102
Apostle Islands, is., Wi., U.S.	A3	142
Apostle Islands National Lakeshore, Wi., U.S.	A3	142
Apóstoles, Arg.	D6	72
Apostolove, Ukr.	F12	20
Appalachia, Va., U.S.	f9	139
Appalachian Mountains, mts., N.A.	D11	92
Appanoose, co., Ia., U.S.	D5	108
Appennino, mts., Italy	C4	18
Appennino Ligure, mts., Italy	B2	18
Apple, stm., Wi., U.S.	C1	142
Apple Creek, Oh., U.S.	B4	128
Applegate, Or., U.S.	E3	130
Applegate, stm., Or., U.S.	E3	130
Appleton, Mn., U.S.	E2	116
Appleton, Wi., U.S.	D5	142
Appleton City, Mo., U.S.	C3	118
Apple Valley, Ca., U.S.	E5	98
Apple Valley, Mn., U.S.	n12	116
Appling, Ga., U.S.	C4	103
Appling, co., Ga., U.S.	E4	103
Appomattox, Va., U.S.	C4	139
Appomattox, co., Va., U.S.	C4	139
Appomattox, stm., Va., U.S.	C4	139
Appomattox Court House National Historical Park, Va., U.S.	C4	139
Apšeronsk, Russia	B3	42
Apua Point, c., Hi., U.S.	D6	104
Apucarana, Braz.	F1	74
Apure, stm., Ven.	B6	70
Apurímac, stm., Peru	F5	70
Aqaba, Gulf of, b.	E2	42
'Aqrah, Iraq	D10	44
Aquarius Mountains, mts., Az., U.S.	C2	96
Aquidauana, Braz.	H8	70
Ara, India	D4	40
Arab, Al., U.S.	A3	94
'Arab, Baḥr al-, stm., Sudan	A4	54
Arabi, La., U.S.	k11	111
Arabian Basin	G9	64
Arabian Desert see Eastern Desert, des., Egypt	E11	48
Arabian Gulf see Persian Gulf, b., Asia	E6	42
Arabian Sea, Asia	G8	38
Aracaju, Braz.	D4	74
Aracati, Braz.	B4	74
Araçatuba, Braz.	F1	74
Aracruz, Braz.	E3	74
Araçuaí, Braz.	E3	74
Arad, Rom.	F6	20
Arafura Sea	E7	58
Arafura Shelf	I16	64
Aragac, gora see Aragats Lerr, mtn., Arm.	B11	44
Aragarças, Braz.	G9	70
Aragats Lerr, mtn., Arm.	B11	44
Arago, Cape, c., Or., U.S.	D2	130
Aragon, Ga., U.S.	B1	103
Aragón, hist. reg., Spain	G6	16
Araguacema, Braz.	E10	70
Aragua de Barcelona, Ven.	B7	70
Araguaia, stm., Braz.	E10	70
Araguaína, Braz.	C2	74
Araguari, Braz.	E2	74
Araguatins, Braz.	C2	74
'Arak, Alg.	E5	48
Arāk, Iran	D5	42
Arakan Yoma, mts., Myan.	B2	34
Arakkonam, India	G3	40
Araks (Aras) (Araz), stm., Asia	B10	44
Aral see Aral'sk, Kaz.	E8	26
Aral Sea, Asia	B7	42
Aral'sk, Kaz.	E8	26
Aranda de Duero, Spain	G5	16
Aranos, Nmb.	C2	56
Aranjuez, Spain	G5	16
Aransas, co., Tx., U.S.	E4	136
Aransas Bay, b., Tx., U.S.	E4	136
Aransas Pass, Tx., U.S.	F4	136
Aranyaprathet, Thai.	D4	34
Araouane, Mali	C4	50
Arapaho, Ok., U.S.	B3	129
Arapahoe, Ne., U.S.	D6	120
Arapahoe, co., Co., U.S.	B6	99
Arapiraca, Braz.	C4	74
Arapkir, Tur.	C8	44
Arapongas, Braz.	F1	74
Araranguá, Braz.	D8	72
Araraquara, Braz.	F2	74
Ararat, Arm.	C11	44
Ararat, Austl.	H3	62
Ararat, Mount see Ağrı Dağı, mtn., Tur.	C11	44
Aras (Araks) (Araz), stm., Asia	C12	44
Arauca, Col.	D5	80
Arauquita, Col.	D5	80
Araxá, Braz.	E2	74
Araz (Araks) (Aras), stm., Asia	C12	44
Ārba Minch', Eth.	B7	54
Arboga, Swe.	G6	10
Arborg, Mb., Can.	D3	86
Arbroath, Scot., U.K.	B5	12
Arbuckle, Lake, l., Fl., U.S.	E5	102
Arbuckle Mountains, mts., Ok., U.S.	C4	129
Arbuckles, Lake of the, res., Ok., U.S.	C5	129
Arcachon, Fr.	E6	16
Arcade, Ga., U.S.	B3	103
Arcade, N.Y., U.S.	C2	125
Arcadia, Ca., U.S.	m12	98
Arcadia, Fl., U.S.	E5	102
Arcadia, In., U.S.	D5	107
Arcadia, La., U.S.	B3	111
Arcadia, Mo., U.S.	D7	118
Arcadia, S.C., U.S.	B4	133
Arcadia, Wi., U.S.	D2	142
Arcanum, Oh., U.S.	C1	128
Arcata, Ca., U.S.	B1	98
Arc Dome, mtn., Nv., U.S.	E4	121
Archangel see Arhangel'sk, Russia	C6	26
Archbald, Pa., U.S.	m18	131
Archbold, Oh., U.S.	A1	128
Archdale, N.C., U.S.	B3	126
Archer, Fl., U.S.	C4	102
Archer, co., Tx., U.S.	C3	136
Archer City, Tx., U.S.	C3	136
Arches National Park, Ut., U.S.	E6	137
Archie, Mo., U.S.	C3	118
Archuleta, co., Co., U.S.	D3	99
Arco, Id., U.S.	F5	105
Arcola, Il., U.S.	D5	106
Arcoverde, Braz.	C4	74
Arctic Ocean	E36	144
Ardabīl, Iran	C5	42
Ardahan, Tur.	B10	44
Ārdakān, Iran	D6	42
Årdalstangen, Nor.	F2	10
Ardennes, reg., Eur.	B9	16
Ardeşen, Tur.	B9	44
Ardmore, Al., U.S.	A3	94
Ardmore, Ok., U.S.	C4	129
Ardmore, Tn., U.S.	B5	135
Ardsley, N.Y., U.S.	g13	125
Areia Branca, Braz.	B4	74
Arena, Point, c., Ca., U.S.	C2	98
Arena, Punta, c., Mex.	C3	78
Arenac, co., Mi., U.S.	D7	115
Arenápolis, Braz.	A6	72
Arenas, Cayo, i., Mex.	C6	78
Arendal, Nor.	G3	10
Arequipa, Peru	G5	70
Arévalo, Spain	G4	16
Arezzo, Italy	C3	18
Argenta, Il., U.S.	D5	106
Argentan, Fr.	C6	16
Argentina, ctry., S.A.	E3	69
Argentino, Lago, l., Arg.	H2	69
Argentine Basin	L9	66
Argeş, stm., Rom.	G8	20
Arghandāb, stm., Afg.	D9	42
Argolikós Kólpos, b., Grc.	F9	18
Argonne, reg., Fr.	C9	16
Árgos, Grc.	F9	18
Argos, In., U.S.	B5	107
Argostólion, Grc.	E8	18
Argun (Ergun), stm., Asia	A12	28
Argungu, Nig.	D5	50
Argyle, Mn., U.S.	B2	116
Argyle, Wi., U.S.	F4	142
Arhangel'sk, Russia	C6	26
Arhangel'skoe, Russia	C14	20
Arhéa Epídavros, hist., Grc.	F9	18
Århus, Den.	H4	10
Arica, Chile	A2	69
Arica, Col.	D5	70
Arichat, N.S., Can.	D8	87
Arid, Cape, c., Austl.	G3	60
Arīḥā (Jericho), Gaza Str.	G6	44
Arikaree, stm., U.S.	B8	99
Arima, Trin.	C7	80
Arinos, stm., Braz.	F8	70
Ariquemes, Braz.	E7	70
Aristazabal Island, i., B.C., Can.	C3	85
Ariton, Al., U.S.	D4	94
Arivonimamo, Madag.	B8	56
Arizaro, Salar de, pl., Arg.	D4	72
Arizona, Arg.	F4	72
Arizona, state, U.S.	C4	96
Arizona Sunsites, Az., U.S.	F6	96
Arjay, Ky., U.S.	D6	110
Arjeplog, Swe.	C7	10
Arjona, Col.	C4	80
Arka, Russia	C16	26
Arkabutla Lake, res., Ms., U.S.	A4	117
Arkadelphia, Ar., U.S.	C3	97
Arkalyk, Kaz.	D8	26
Arkansas, co., Ar., U.S.	C4	97
Arkansas, state, U.S.	C3	97
Arkansas, stm., U.S.	E9	92
Arkansas City, Ks., U.S.	E6	109
Arkoma, Ok., U.S.	B7	129
Arktičeskogo Instituta, ostrova, is., Russia	B10	26
Arles, Fr.	F9	16
Arlington, Ga., U.S.	E2	103
Arlington, Ma., U.S.	B5	114

Name	Map Ref.	Page
Arlington, Mn., U.S.	F4	116
Arlington, N.C., U.S.	A2	126
Arlington, Ne., U.S.	C9	120
Arlington, N.Y., U.S.	D7	125
Arlington, Oh., U.S.	B2	128
Arlington, S.C., U.S.	B3	133
Arlington, S.D., U.S.	C8	134
Arlington, Tn., U.S.	B2	135
Arlington, Tx., U.S.	n9	136
Arlington, Va., U.S.	B5	139
Arlington, Vt., U.S.	E2	138
Arlington, Wa., U.S.	A3	140
Arlington, co., Va., U.S.	g12	139
Arlington, Lake, res., Tx., U.S.	n9	136
Arlington Heights, Il., U.S.	A5	106
Arlit, Niger	C6	50
Arlon, Bel.	F9	12
Arma, Ks., U.S.	E9	109
Armada, Mi., U.S.	F8	115
Armadale, Austl.	G2	60
Armagh, P.Q., Can.	C7	90
Armagnac, hist. reg., Fr.	F7	16
Armavir, Russia	B4	42
Armenia, Col.	C4	70
Armenia, ctry., Asia	B11	44
Armians'k, Ukr.	F12	20
Armidale, Austl.	G5	62
Armijo, N.M., U.S.	k7	124
Armour, S.D., U.S.	D7	134
Armstrong, B.C., Can.	D8	85
Armstrong, Ia., U.S.	A3	108
Armstrong, co., Pa., U.S.	E2	131
Armstrong, co., Tx., U.S.	B2	136
Armstrong Creek, stm., W.V., U.S.	m13	141
Arnaudville, La., U.S.	D4	111
Arnett, W.V., U.S.	D3	141
Arnhem, Neth.	E10	12
Arnhem, Cape, c., Austl.	C6	60
Arnhem Bay, b., Austl.	C6	60
Arnhem Land, reg., Austl.	C5	60
Arno, stm., Italy	C3	18
Arnold, Mn., U.S.	D6	116
Arnold, Mo., U.S.	C7	118
Arnold, Ne., U.S.	C5	120
Arnold, Pa., U.S.	h14	131
Arnold Mills, R.I., U.S.	B4	132
Arnold Mills Reservoir, res., R.I., U.S.	B4	132
Arnold's Cove, Nf., Can.	E4	88
Arnolds Park, Ia., U.S.	A2	108
Arnøya, Nor.	A9	10
Arnprior, On., Can.	B8	89
Aroab, Nmb.	D2	56
Aroostook, co., Me., U.S.	B4	112
Ar-Rahad, Sudan	H11	48
Arraias, Braz.	F10	70
Ar-Ramādī, Iraq	D4	42
Arran, Island of, i., Scot., U.K.	C4	12
Ar-Rank, Sudan	H11	48
Ar-Raqqah, Syria	E8	44
Arras, Fr.	B8	16
Arrecife, Spain	A2	50
Arriaga, Mex.	D6	78
Ar-Riyāḍ (Riyadh), Sau. Ar.	F5	38
Arroio Grande, Braz.	E7	72
Arrowhead Mountain Lake, res., Vt., U.S.	B2	138
Arrowrock Reservoir, res., Id., U.S.	F3	105
Arrowwood Lake, res., N.D., U.S.	B7	127
Arroyito, Arg.	E5	72
Arroyo Grande, Ca., U.S.	E3	98
Ar-Rub' al-Khālī, des., Asia	G6	38
Ar-Rumaythah, Iraq	D4	42
Ar-Ruṣayriṣ, Sudan	H11	48
Ar-Ruṭbah, Iraq	D4	42
Arsenev, Russia	C14	28
Árta, Grc.	E8	18
Artà, Spain	H8	16
Artašat (Artashat), Arm.	C11	44
Artashat (Artašat), Arm.	C11	44
Art'em, Russia	C14	28
Artemisa, Cuba	A3	80
Artemivs'k, Ukr.	E14	20
Artëmovsk, Russia	D11	26
Artemus, Ky., U.S.	D6	110
Arter, Mount, mtn., Wy., U.S.	D4	143
Artesia, N.M., U.S.	E5	124
Arthabaska, P.Q., Can.	C6	90
Arthur, On., Can.	D4	89
Arthur, Il., U.S.	D5	106
Arthur, co., Ne., U.S.	C4	120
Arthur, Lake, l., La., U.S.	D3	111
Arthur, Lake, res., Pa., U.S.	E1	131
Arthur Kill, stm., N.J., U.S.	k8	123
Artigas, Ur.	E6	72
Artik, Arm.	B10	44
Artsyz, Ukr.	F10	20
Artvin, Tur.	B9	44
Aru, Kepulauan, is., Indon.	H10	36
Aru, Tanjung, c., Indon.	D5	36
Arua, Ug.	C6	54
Aruanã, Braz.	G9	70
Aruba, dep., N.A.	C6	80
Arunāchal Pradesh, prov., India	D6	40
Aruppukkottai, India	H3	40
Arusha, Tan.	D7	54
Aruwimi, stm., D.R.C.	C4	54
Arvada, Co., U.S.	B5	99
Arvayheer, Mong.	B8	28
Arvidsjaur, Swe.	D8	10
Arvika, Swe.	G5	10
Arvin, Ca., U.S.	E4	98
Arvon, Mount, mtn., Mi., U.S.	B2	115
Arvonia, Va., U.S.	C4	139
Arxan, China	B11	28
Arys', Kaz.	E8	26
Arzamas, Russia	C7	22
Arzew, Golfe d', b., Alg.	J6	16
Aša, Russia	D10	22
Asaba, Nig.	E6	50
Asad, Buḥayrat al-, res., Syria	D8	44
Asad, Lake see Asad, Buḥayrat al-, res., Syria	D8	44
Asadābād, Afg.	C10	42
Asadābād, Iran	E13	44
Asahi-dake, vol., Japan	B4	31
Asahikawa, Japan	C16	28
Āsānsol, India	E5	40
Asbest, Russia	C11	22
Asbestos, P.Q., Can.	D6	90
Asbury Park, N.J., U.S.	C4	123
Ascensión, Mex.	A3	78
Ascension, co., La., U.S.	D5	111
Ascension, i., St. Hel.	J8	46
Ascoli Piceno, Italy	C4	18
Aseb, Erit.	H13	48
Āseda, Swe.	H6	10
Āsela, Eth.	B7	54
Āsele, Swe.	D7	10
Aşgabat, Turk.	F7	26
Ashanti, prov., Ghana	E4	50
Ashaway, R.I., U.S.	F1	132
Ashburn, Ga., U.S.	E3	103
Ashburton, N.Z.	p13	63c
Ashburton, stm., Austl.	E2	60
Ashcroft, B.C., Can.	D7	85
Ashdod, Isr.	G6	44
Ashdown, Ar., U.S.	D1	97
Ashe, co., N.C., U.S.	A1	126
Asheboro, N.C., U.S.	B3	126
Ashepoo, stm., S.C., U.S.	F6	133
Ashern, Mb., Can.	D2	86
Asherton, Tx., U.S.	E3	136
Asheville, N.C., U.S.	f10	126
Ash Flat, Ar., U.S.	A4	97
Ashford, Al., U.S.	D4	94
Ashford, W.V., U.S.	m12	141
Ash Grove, Mo., U.S.	D4	118
Ashikaga, Japan	C3	31
Ashkhabad see Aşgabat, Turk.	F7	26
Ashland, Al., U.S.	B4	94
Ashland, Il., U.S.	D3	106
Ashland, Ks., U.S.	E4	109
Ashland, Ky., U.S.	B7	110
Ashland, Ma., U.S.	g10	114
Ashland, Me., U.S.	B4	112
Ashland, Mo., U.S.	C5	118
Ashland, Ne., U.S.	C9	120
Ashland, N.H., U.S.	C3	122
Ashland, Oh., U.S.	B3	128
Ashland, Or., U.S.	E4	130
Ashland, Pa., U.S.	E9	131
Ashland, Va., U.S.	C5	139
Ashland, Wi., U.S.	B3	142
Ashland, co., Oh., U.S.	B3	128
Ashland, co., Wi., U.S.	B3	142
Ashland, Mount, mtn., Or., U.S.	E4	130
Ashland City, Tn., U.S.	A4	135
Ashland Reservoir, res., Ma., U.S.	h10	114
Ashley, In., U.S.	A7	107
Ashley, N.D., U.S.	C6	127
Ashley, Oh., U.S.	B3	128
Ashley, Pa., U.S.	n17	131
Ashley, co., Ar., U.S.	D4	97
Ashley, stm., S.C., U.S.	F7	133
Ashley Creek, stm., Ut., U.S.	C6	137
Ashmore, Il., U.S.	D5	106
Ashmore Islands, is., Austl.	C3	60
Ashokan Reservoir, res., N.Y., U.S.	D6	125
Ash-Shaddādah, Syria	D9	44
Ash-Shāmīyah, Iraq	F11	44
Ash-Shāriqah, U.A.E.	E7	42
Ash-Sharqāt, Iraq	E10	44
Ash-Shaṭrah, Iraq	G12	44
Ash-Shiḥr, Yemen	H5	38
Ash-Shināfīyah, Iraq	G11	44
Ashtabula, Oh., U.S.	A5	128
Ashtabula, co., Oh., U.S.	A5	128
Ashtabula, Lake, res., N.D., U.S.	B8	127
Ashtarak, Arm.	B11	44
Ashton, Id., U.S.	E7	105
Ashton, Il., U.S.	B4	106
Ashton, Md., U.S.	B3	113
Ashton, R.I., U.S.	B4	132
Ashuanipi Lake, l., Nf., Can.	h8	88
Ashuelot, stm., N.H., U.S.	E2	122
Ashville, Al., U.S.	B3	94
Ashville, Oh., U.S.	C3	128
Ashwaubenon, Wi., U.S.	D5	142
Asi, stm., Asia	D7	44
Asilah, Mor.	J3	16
Asinara, Golfo dell', b., Italy	D2	18
Asinara, Isola, i., Italy	D2	18
Asino, Russia	D10	26
Asipovičy, Bela.	C10	20
'Asīr, reg., Sau. Ar.	G4	38
Aşkale, Tur.	C9	44
Askersund, Swe.	G6	10
Askham, S. Afr.	D3	56
Asmara see Asmera, Erit.	G12	48
Asmera, Erit.	G12	48
Āsosa, Eth.	A6	54
Asotin, Wa., U.S.	C8	140
Asotin, co., Wa., U.S.	C8	140
Asotin Creek, stm., Wa., U.S.	C8	140
Aspen, Co., U.S.	B4	99
Aspen Butte, mtn., Or., U.S.	E4	130
Aspendos, hist., Tur.	D4	44
Aspermont, Tx., U.S.	C2	136
Aspinwall, Pa., U.S.	k14	131
Aspy Bay, b., N.S., Can.	C9	87
Assa, Mor.	A3	50
Assabet, stm., Ma., U.S.	g9	114
As-Safīrah, Syria	D7	44
As-Salṭ, Jord.	F6	44
Assam, prov., India	D6	40
As-Samāwah, Iraq	D5	42
Assateague Island, i., U.S.	D7	113
Assateague Island National Seashore, U.S.	D7	113
Assawoman Bay, b., Md., U.S.	D7	113
Assiniboine, stm., Can.	E2	86
Assiniboine, Mount, mtn., Can.	D3	84
Assis, Braz.	F1	74
Assu, Braz.	C4	74
As-Sudd, reg., Sudan	I11	48
As-Sulaymānīyah, Iraq	C5	42
As-Sulaymānīyah, Sau. Ar.	F5	38
As-Sulayyil, Sau. Ar.	F5	38
As-Sumayḥ, Sudan	B5	54
Assumption, Il., U.S.	D4	106
Assumption, co., La., U.S.	E4	111
As-Suwaydā', Syria	F7	44
Astana, Kaz.	D9	26
Astara, Azer.	C13	44
Āstārā, Iran	C13	44
Asti, Italy	B2	18
Astipálaia, i., Grc.	F11	18
Astorga, Spain	F3	16
Astoria, Il., U.S.	C3	106
Astoria, Or., U.S.	A3	130
Astove, i., Sey.	j11	57b
Astrahan', Russia	E6	26
Asunción, Para.	D6	72
Asuncion Island, i., N. Mar. Is.	C12	32
Aswân, Egypt	F11	48
Aswan High Dam see Aali, Sadd el-, Egypt	F11	48
Asyūṭ, Egypt	E11	48
'Ata, i., Tonga	G12	58
Atacama, Desierto de, des., Chile	C2	69
Atacama, Puna de, plat., S.A.	C4	72
Atacama, Salar de, pl., Chile	B3	69
Atakpamé, Togo	E5	50
Atambua, Indon.	E6	36
Aṭar, Maur.	B2	50
Atascadero, Ca., U.S.	E3	98
Atascosa, co., Tx., U.S.	E3	136
Atasu, Kaz.	E9	26
Atatürk Baraji, res., Tur.	D8	44
Atauro, Pulau, i., E. Timor	E6	36
'Aṭbarah, Sudan	G11	48
Atbasar, Kaz.	D8	26
Atchafalaya, stm., La., U.S.	D4	111
Atchafalaya Bay, b., La., U.S.	E4	111
Atchison, Ks., U.S.	C8	109
Atchison, co., Ks., U.S.	C8	109
Atchison, co., Mo., U.S.	A2	118
Athabasca, Ab., Can.	B4	84
Athabasca, stm., Ab., Can.	A5	84
Athabasca, Lake, l., Can.	G17	82
Athena, Or., U.S.	B8	130
Athens see Athínai, Grc.	E9	18
Athens, On., Can.	C9	89
Athens, Al., U.S.	A3	94
Athens, Ga., U.S.	C3	103
Athens, Il., U.S.	D4	106
Athens, Mi., U.S.	F5	115
Athens, N.Y., U.S.	C7	125
Athens, Oh., U.S.	C3	128
Athens, Pa., U.S.	C8	131
Athens, Tn., U.S.	D9	135
Athens, Tx., U.S.	C5	136
Athens, W.V., U.S.	D3	141
Athens, Wi., U.S.	C3	142
Athens, co., Oh., U.S.	C3	128
Atherton, Austl.	D4	62
Athi, stm., Kenya	D7	54
Athínai (Athens), Grc.	E9	18
Athol, Ma., U.S.	A3	114
Athos, mtn., Grc.	D10	18
Ati, Chad	D8	50
Atiak, Ug.	C6	54
Atik Lake, l., Mb., Can.	B4	86
Atikonak Lake, l., Nf., Can.	h8	88
Atiu, i., Cook Is.	G14	58
Atka, Russia	D8	22
Atkarsk, Russia	D8	22
Atkins, Ar., U.S.	B3	97
Atkins, Va., U.S.	D1	139
Atkinson, Il., U.S.	B3	106
Atkinson, Ne., U.S.	B7	120
Atkinson, N.H., U.S.	E4	122
Atkinson, co., Ga., U.S.	E4	103
Atlanta, Ga., U.S.	C2	103
Atlanta, Il., U.S.	C4	106
Atlanta, In., U.S.	D5	107
Atlanta, Mi., U.S.	C6	115
Atlanta, Tx., U.S.	C5	136
Atlantic, Ia., U.S.	C2	108
Atlantic, N.C., U.S.	C6	126
Atlantic, co., N.J., U.S.	E3	123
Atlantic Beach, Fl., U.S.	m9	102
Atlantic City, N.J., U.S.	E4	123
Atlantic Highlands, N.J., U.S.	C4	123
Atlantic-Indian Basin	O12	66
Atlantic-Indian Ridge	N14	66
Atlantic Ocean	E9	66
Atlantic Peak, mtn., Wy., U.S.	D3	143
Atlas Mountains, mts., Afr.	D4	48
Atlas Saharien, mts., Alg.	E3	14
Atlas Tellien, mts., Alg.	D4	14
Atlin Lake, l., Can.	G13	82
Atmore, Al., U.S.	D2	94
Atna Peak, mtn., B.C., Can.	C3	85
Atoka, Ok., U.S.	C5	129
Atoka, Tn., U.S.	B2	135
Atoka, co., Ok., U.S.	C5	129
Atoka Reservoir, res., Ok., U.S.	C5	129
Atrak (Atrek), stm., Asia	C7	42
Atrato, stm., Col.	B4	70
Atrek (Atrak), stm., Asia	C6	42
Aṭ-Ṭā'if, Sau. Ar.	F4	38
Attala, co., Ms., U.S.	B4	117
Attalla, Al., U.S.	A3	94
Attapu, Laos	D5	34
Attawapiskat, stm., On., Can.	n18	89
Attica, In., U.S.	D3	107
Attica, Ks., U.S.	E5	109
Attica, N.Y., U.S.	C2	125
Attica, Oh., U.S.	A3	128
Attleboro, Ma., U.S.	C5	114
Attu Island, i., Ak., U.S.	E2	95
Atuel, Bañados del, sw., Arg.	F4	72
Ātvidaberg, Swe.	G7	10
Atwater, Mn., U.S.	E4	116
Atwood, On., Can.	D3	89
Atwood, Il., U.S.	D5	106
Atwood, Ks., U.S.	C2	109
Atwood, Tn., U.S.	B3	135
Atwood Lake, res., Oh., U.S.	B4	128
Atyrau, Kaz.	E7	26
Auau Channel, strt., Hi., U.S.	C5	104
Aubagne, Fr.	F9	16
Auberry, Ca., U.S.	D4	98
Auburn, Al., U.S.	C4	94
Auburn, Ca., U.S.	C3	98
Auburn, Ga., U.S.	B3	103
Auburn, Il., U.S.	D4	106
Auburn, In., U.S.	B7	107
Auburn, Ks., U.S.	D8	109
Auburn, Ky., U.S.	D3	110
Auburn, Ma., U.S.	B4	114
Auburn, Me., U.S.	D2	112
Auburn, Mi., U.S.	E6	115
Auburn, Ne., U.S.	D10	120
Auburn, N.Y., U.S.	C4	125
Auburn, Wa., U.S.	B3	140
Auburndale, Fl., U.S.	D5	102
Auburn Heights, Mi., U.S.	F7	115
Aubusson, Fr.	E8	16
Auch, Fr.	F7	16
Auchi, Nig.	E6	50
Aucilla, stm., Fl., U.S.	B3	102
Auckland, N.Z.	o13	63c
Auckland Islands, is., N.Z.	J10	58
Audrain, co., Mo., U.S.	B6	118
Audubon, Ia., U.S.	C3	108
Audubon, N.J., U.S.	D2	123
Audubon, co., Ia., U.S.	C2	108
Augathella, Austl.	F4	62
Auglaize, co., Oh., U.S.	B1	128
Auglaize, stm., Oh., U.S.	A1	128
Augrabiesvalle, wtfl, S. Afr.	D3	56
Au Gres, Mi., U.S.	D7	115
Augsburg, Ger.	F12	12
Augusta, Austl.	G1	60
Augusta, Italy	F5	18
Augusta, Ar., U.S.	B4	97
Augusta, Ga., U.S.	C5	103
Augusta, Ks., U.S.	E7	109
Augusta, Ky., U.S.	B6	110
Augusta, Me., U.S.	D3	112
Augusta, Mi., U.S.	F5	115
Augusta, Wi., U.S.	D2	142
Augusta, co., Va., U.S.	B3	139
Augustów, Pol.	C7	20
Augustus, Mount, mtn., Austl.	E2	60
Aulander, N.C., U.S.	A5	126
Aulneau Peninsula, pen., On., Can.	E4	86
Ault, Co., U.S.	A6	99
Aumsville, Or., U.S.	k12	130
Aurangābād, India	F3	40
Aurangābād, India	E4	40
Aure, Nor.	E3	10
Aurelia, Ia., U.S.	B2	108
Aurich, Ger.	D10	12
Aurillac, Fr.	E8	16
Aurora, On., Can.	C5	89
Aurora, Co., U.S.	B6	99
Aurora, Il., U.S.	B5	106
Aurora, In., U.S.	F8	107
Aurora, Mn., U.S.	C6	116
Aurora, Mo., U.S.	E4	118
Aurora, Ne., U.S.	D7	120
Aurora, Oh., U.S.	A4	128
Aurora, S.D., U.S.	C9	134
Aurora, Ut., U.S.	E4	137
Aurora, co., S.D., U.S.	D7	134
Aus, Nmb.	D2	56
Au Sable, Mi., U.S.	D7	115
Au Sable, stm., Mi., U.S.	D6	115
Ausable, stm., N.Y., U.S.	f11	125
Au Sable Forks, N.Y., U.S.	f11	125
Au Sable Point, c., Mi., U.S.	D7	115
Au Sable Point, c., Mi., U.S.	B4	115
Austell, Ga., U.S.	h7	103
Austin, In., U.S.	G6	107
Austin, Mn., U.S.	G6	116
Austin, Nv., U.S.	D4	121
Austin, Tx., U.S.	D4	136
Austin, co., Tx., U.S.	E4	136
Austintown, Oh., U.S.	A5	128
Austinville, Va., U.S.	D2	139
Australia, ctry., Oc.	G7	58
Australia, i., Austl.	H21	4
Australian Capital Territory, ter., Austl.	H4	62
Austral Seamounts	K23	64
Austria, ctry., Eur.	G14	12
Autauga, co., Al., U.S.	C3	94
Autaugaville, Al., U.S.	C3	94
Autlán de Navarro, Mex.	D4	78
Auvergne, hist. reg., Fr.	E8	16
Auxerre, Fr.	D8	16
Auxier, Ky., U.S.	C7	110
Auxvasse, Mo., U.S.	B6	118
Auyán Tepuy, mtn., Ven.	B7	70
Auzangate, Nevado, mtn., Peru	F5	70
Ava, Mo., U.S.	E5	118
Avallon, Fr.	D8	16
Avalon, Ca., U.S.	F4	98
Avalon, Pa., U.S.	h13	131
Avalon, Lake, res., N.M., U.S.	E5	124
Avalon Peninsula, pen., Nf., Can.	E5	88
Avaré, Braz.	F2	74
Aveiro, Port.	G2	16
Avella, Pa., U.S.	F1	131
Avellaneda, Arg.	E6	72
Avellino, Italy	D5	18
Avenal, Ca., U.S.	E3	98
Avery, co., N.C., U.S.	e11	126
Aves, Islas de, is., Ven.	C6	80
Avesta, Swe.	F7	10
Avezzano, Italy	C4	18
Avignon, Fr.	F9	16
Ávila, Spain	G4	16
Avilés, Spain	F4	16
Avilla, In., U.S.	B7	107
Avis, Pa., U.S.	D7	131
Aviston, Il., U.S.	E4	106
Avoca, Ia., U.S.	C2	108
Avoca, Pa., U.S.	m18	131
Avola, Italy	F5	18
Avon, Ct., U.S.	B4	100
Avon, Il., U.S.	C3	106
Avon, Ma., U.S.	B5	114
Avon, Mn., U.S.	E4	116
Avon, N.Y., U.S.	C3	125
Avon, Oh., U.S.	A3	128
Avondale, Az., U.S.	D3	96
Avondale, Co., U.S.	C6	99
Avondale, Pa., U.S.	G10	131
Avondale Estates, Ga., U.S.	h8	103
Avon Lake, Ia., U.S.	e8	108
Avon Lake, Oh., U.S.	A3	128
Avonmore, Pa., U.S.	E3	131
Avon Park, Fl., U.S.	E5	102
Avoyelles, co., La., U.S.	C3	111
Awaaso, Ghana	E4	50
Awarē, Eth.	B8	54
Āwasa, Eth.	B7	54
Āwash, Eth.	B8	54
Āwash, stm., Eth.	H13	48
Awbārī, Libya	E7	48
Awbārī, Ṣaḥrā', reg., Libya	A7	50
Awjilah, Libya	E9	48
Awled Djellal, Alg.	E6	14
Awlef, Alg.	F4	14
Axim, Ghana	F4	50
Axiós (Vardar), stm., Eur.	D9	18
Axis, Al., U.S.	E1	94
Axtell, Ne., U.S.	D7	120
Ayacucho, Arg.	F6	72
Ayacucho, Peru	F4	70
Ayamé, C. Iv.	E4	50
Ayancık, Tur.	B6	44
Ayapel, Col.	D4	70
Ayaviri, Peru	F5	70
Ayden, N.C., U.S.	B5	126
Aydın, Tur.	D2	44
Ayer, Ma., U.S.	A4	114
Ayers Cliff, P.Q., Can.	D5	90
Ayeyarwady, stm., Myan.	C3	34
Áyios Nikólaos, Grc.	G10	18
Áyíou Órous, Kólpos, b., Grc.	D10	18
Aylesford, N.S., Can.	D5	87

Name	Map Ref.	Page
Aylmer, Mount, mtn., Ab., Can.	D3	84
Aylmer East, P.Q., Can.	D2	90
Aylmer West, On., Can.	E4	89
'Ayn Dār, Sau. Ar.	E5	42
Ayorou, Niger	D5	50
Ayr, Austl.	D4	62
Ayr, Scot., U.K.	C4	12
Ayvalık, Tur.	C2	44
Āzamgarh, India	D4	40
Azaouâd, reg., Mali	C4	50
Azare, Nig.	D7	50
Āzar Shahr, Iran	D11	44
Azdavay, Tur.	B5	44
Azeffâl, dunes, Afr.	B2	50
Azerbaijan, ctry., Asia	B12	44
Azilal, Mor.	E2	14
Aziscohos Lake, l., Me., U.S.	C1	112
Azle, Tx., U.S.	n9	136
Azogues, Ec.	D4	70
Azores see Açores, is., Port.	F7	66
Azores Plateau	D10	66
Azov, Russia	F15	20
Azov, Sea of, Eur.	F14	20
Azraq, Al-Baḥr al- see Blue Nile, stm., Afr.	H11	48
Azrou, Mor.	D3	48
Aztec, N.M., U.S.	A2	124
Aztec Peak, mtn., Az., U.S.	D5	96
Aztec Ruins National Monument, N.M., U.S.	A1	124
Azua, Dom. Rep.	B5	80
Azuaga, Spain	H4	16
Azuero, Península de, pen., Pan.	D3	80
Azul, Arg.	F6	72
Azurduy, Bol.	B5	72
Azusa, Ca., U.S.	m13	98
Aẓ-Ẓahrān, Sau. Ar.	E5	42
Az-Zarqā', Jord.	D3	42
Az-Zāwiyah, Libya	D7	48

B

Name	Map Ref.	Page
Baa, Indon.	F6	36
Baardheere, Som.	J13	48
Babadag, Rom.	G10	20
Babaeski, Tur.	B2	44
Babaevo, Russia	C6	22
Babanūsah, Sudan	H10	48
Babar, Kepulauan, is., Indon.	E7	36
Babb Creek, stm., Pa., U.S.	C7	131
Babbitt, Mn., U.S.	C7	116
Babbitt, Nv., U.S.	E3	121
Bab el Mandeb see Mandeb, Bab el, strt.	H4	38
Babelthuap, i., Palau	E9	32
Bābil, Aṭlāl (Babylon), hist., Iraq	F11	44
Babine, stm., B.C., Can.	B4	85
Babine Lake, l., B.C., Can.	B5	85
Babine Range, mts., B.C., Can.	B4	85
Babo, Indon.	D8	36
Baboquivari Mountains, mts., Az., U.S.	F4	96
Baboquivari Peak, mtn., Az., U.S.	F4	96
Babrujsk, Bela.	C10	20
Babuškin, Russia	A9	28
Babuyan Channel, strt., Phil.	C8	34
Babuyan Island, i., Phil.	C8	34
Babuyan Islands, is., Phil.	C8	34
Babylon see Bābil, Aṭlāl, hist., Iraq	F11	44
Babylon, N.Y., U.S.	n15	125
Baca, co., Co., U.S.	D8	99
Bacabal, Braz.	B3	74
Bacan, Pulau, i., Indon.	D7	36
Bacău, Rom.	F9	20
Bachu, China	D3	28
Back, stm., S.C., U.S.	h12	133
Bačka Palanka, Yugo.	B7	18
Backbone Mountain, mtn., U.S.	m12	113
Bac Lieu, Viet.	E5	34
Bac Ninh, Viet.	B5	34
Bacolod, Phil.	D8	34
Bacon, co., Ga., U.S.	E4	103
Baconton, Ga., U.S.	E2	103
Bacoor, Phil.	D8	34
Bād, Iran	D6	42
Bad, stm., S.D., U.S.	C5	134
Bad, stm., Wi., U.S.	B3	142
Badagara, India	G3	40
Badajoz, Spain	H3	16
Badalona, Spain	G8	16
Bādāmi, India	F3	40
Badanah, Sau. Ar.	D4	42
Bad Axe, Mi., U.S.	E8	115
Baddeck, N.S., Can.	C9	87
Baden, Aus.	G14	12
Baden, On., Can.	D4	89
Baden, Pa., U.S.	E1	131
Baden-Baden, Ger.	F11	12
Badger, Nf., Can.	D3	88
Bad Hersfeld, Ger.	E11	12
Badīn, Pak.	F9	42
Badin, N.C., U.S.	B2	126
Badin Lake, res., N.C., U.S.	B2	126
Bad Kreuznach, Ger.	F10	12
Badlands, S.D., U.S.	D3	134
Badlands, reg., U.S.	C2	127
Badlands National Park, S.D., U.S.	D3	134
Bad Reichenhall, Ger.	G13	12
Bad River Indian Reservation, Wi., U.S.	B3	142
Bad Tölz, Ger.	G12	12
Badulla, Sri L.	H4	40
Badwater Creek, stm., Wy., U.S.	C5	143
Bafang, Cam.	B2	54
Bafatá, Gui.-B.	D2	50
Baffin Basin	C29	144
Baffin Bay, b., N.A.	D26	82
Baffin Bay, b., Tx., U.S.	E4	136
Baffin Bugt see Baffin Bay, b., N.A.	D26	82
Baffin Island, i., Can.	D24	82
Bafia, Cam.	C2	54
Bafing, stm., Afr.	D2	50
Bafoulabé, Mali	D2	50
Bafoussam, Cam.	B2	54
Bafra, Tur.	B6	44
Bafwasende, D.R.C.	C5	54
Bagaces, C.R.	C2	80
Bagamoyo, Tan.	E7	54
Baganga, Phil.	E9	34
Bagansiapiapi, Indon.	C2	36
Bagdad see Baghdād, Iraq	D4	42
Bagdad, Az., U.S.	C2	96
Bagdad, Fl., U.S.	u14	102
Bagdarin, Russia	D13	26
Bagé, Braz.	E7	72
Baggs, Wy., U.S.	E5	143
Baghdād, Iraq	D4	42
Bagheria, Italy	E4	18
Baghlān, Afg.	C9	42
Bagley, Mn., U.S.	C3	116
Bagnères-de-Bigorre, Fr.	F7	16
Bago, Mya.	C3	34
Baguio, Phil.	C8	34
Bahamas, ctry., N.A.	C9	76
Bahār, Iran	E13	44
Baharampur, India	E5	40
Baharden, Turk.	C7	42
Bahardok, Turk.	C7	42
Bahāwalpur, Pak.	E10	42
Bahçe, Tur.	D7	44
Bahia, state, Braz.	D3	74
Bahía, Islas de la, is., Hond.	B2	80
Bahía Blanca, Arg.	F5	72
Bahir Dar, Eth.	H12	48
Bahraich, India	D4	40
Bahrain, ctry., Asia	E6	42
Bahta, Russia	C10	26
Bāhū Kalāt, Iran	E8	42
Baía Farta, Ang.	F2	54
Baia Mare, Rom.	F7	20
Baicheng, China	C4	28
Baicheng, China	B12	28
Baidoa see Baydhabo, Som.	J13	48
Baie-Comeau, P.Q., Can.	k13	90
Baie-d'Urfé, P.Q., Can.	q19	90
Baie-Saint-Paul, P.Q., Can.	B7	90
Baie Verte, Nf., Can.	D3	88
Baihe, China	C3	30
Baikal, Lake see Bajkal, ozero, l., Russia	D12	26
Baile Átha Cliath see Dublin, Ire.	D3	12
Băileşti, Rom.	G7	20
Bailey, co., Tx., U.S.	B1	136
Bailey Island, Me., U.S.	g8	112
Bailey Island, i., S.C., U.S.	k11	133
Baileys Crossroads, Va., U.S.	g12	139
Bailundo, Ang.	F3	54
Bainbridge, Ga., U.S.	F2	103
Bainbridge, In., U.S.	E4	107
Bainbridge, Oh., U.S.	C2	128
Bainbridge Island, i., Wa., U.S.	e10	140
Baing, Indon.	F6	36
Baird, Tx., U.S.	C3	136
Bairdford, Pa., U.S.	h14	131
Baird Inlet, b., Ak., U.S.	C7	95
Baird Mountains, mts., Ak., U.S.	B7	95
Bairin Zuoqi, China	C11	28
Bairnsdale, Austl.	H4	62
Bais, Phil.	E8	34
Baishuijiang, China	C2	30
Baitou Shan see Paektu, Mount, mtn., Asia	C13	28
Baiyin, China	D8	28
Baja, Hung.	F5	20
Baja California, pen., Mex.	B2	78
Baja California, state, Mex.	A1	78
Baja California Norte see Baja California, state, Mex.	A1	78
Baja California Sur, state, Mex.	B2	78
Bajestān, Iran	D7	42
Bajkal, ozero, l., Russia	D12	26
Bajkit, Russia	C11	26
Bajkonur, Kaz.	E8	26
Bajmak, Russia	D10	22
Bajo Boquete, Pan.	D3	80
Bajramaly, Turk.	C8	42
Bakala, C.A.R.	B4	54
Bakanas, Kaz.	B11	42
Bakel, Sen.	D2	50
Baker, co., Fl., U.S.	B4	102
Baker, co., Ga., U.S.	E2	103
Baker, La., U.S.	D4	111
Baker, Mt., U.S.	D12	119
Baker, stm., N.H., U.S.	C3	122
Baker, co., Or., U.S.	C9	130
Baker, Or., U.S.	C9	130
Baker, Mount, mtn., Wa., U.S.	A4	140
Baker Air Force Base, mil., Ar., U.S.	B6	97
Baker Butte, mtn., Az., U.S.	C4	96
Baker Island, i., Oc.	H21	64
Baker Island, i., Ak., U.S.	n22	95
Baker Lake, l., Austl.	F4	60
Baker Lake, l., Me., U.S.	B3	112
Baker Lake, res., Wa., U.S.	A4	140
Bakersfield, Ca., U.S.	E4	98
Bakers Island, i., Ma., U.S.	f12	114
Bakerstown, Pa., U.S.	h14	131
Bakhmach, Ukr.	D12	20
Bakī (Baku), Azer.	B13	44
Bako, Eth.	B7	54
Bakouma, C.A.R.	B4	54
Baku see Bakī, Azer.	B13	44
Bala, Sen.	D2	50
Balabac Island, i., Phil.	E7	34
Balabac Strait, strt., Asia	E7	34
Ba'labakk, Leb.	F7	44
Balaḍëk, Russia	D15	26
Bālāghāt, India	E4	40
Balaguer, Spain	G7	16
Balakliia, Ukr.	E14	20
Balakovo, Russia	D6	26
Balama, Moz.	A6	56
Balambangan, Pulau, i., Malay.	B5	36
Bālā Morghāb, Afg.	C8	42
Balāngīr, India	E4	40
Balašov, Russia	D6	26
Balassagyarmat, Hung.	F5	20
Balaton, l., Hung.	F4	20
Balaton, Mn., U.S.	F3	116
Balbina, Represa, res., Braz.	D8	70
Balcad, Som.	A6	56
Balcarce, Arg.	F6	72
Balcarres, Sk., Can.	G4	91
Balclutha, N.Z.	p12	63c
Bald Eagle Lake, l., Mn., U.S.	m12	116
Bald Eagle Lake, l., Mn., U.S.	C7	116
Baldhill Dam, N.D., U.S.	B7	127
Bald Knob, Ar., U.S.	B4	97
Bald Knoll, mtn., Wy., U.S.	D2	143
Bald Mountain, mtn., Or., U.S.	D5	130
Bald Mountain, mtn., Or., U.S.	C9	130
Bald Mountain, mtn., Wy., U.S.	B5	143
Bald Mountains, mts., N.C., U.S.	f10	126
Baldwin, co., Al., U.S.	E2	94
Baldwin, Fl., U.S.	B5	102
Baldwin, Ga., U.S.	B3	103
Baldwin, co., Ga., U.S.	C3	103
Baldwin, La., U.S.	E4	111
Baldwin, Mi., U.S.	E5	115
Baldwin, Pa., U.S.	k14	131
Baldwin, S.C., U.S.	B5	133
Baldwin, Wi., U.S.	D1	142
Baldwin City, Ks., U.S.	D8	109
Baldwinsville, N.Y., U.S.	B4	125
Baldwinville, Ma., U.S.	A3	114
Baldwyn, Ms., U.S.	A5	117
Baldy Mountain, mtn., B.C., Can.	D7	85
Baldy Mountain, mtn., Mb., Can.	D1	86
Baldy Mountain, mtn., Mt., U.S.	B7	119
Baldy Mountain, mtn., N.M., U.S.	A4	124
Baldy Peak, mtn., Az., U.S.	D6	96
Balearic Islands see Balears, Illes, is., Spain	H7	16
Balears, Illes (Balearic Islands), is., Spain	H7	16
Baleia, Ponta da, c., Braz.	E4	74
Baleine, Rivière à la, stm., P.Q., Can.	g13	90
Balej, Russia	D13	26
Baler, Phil.	C8	34
Bāleshwar, India	E5	40
Balezino, Russia	C9	22
Balfate, Hond.	B2	80
Balfour, N.C., U.S.	f10	126
Balhaš, Kaz.	E9	26
Balhaš, ozero, l., Kaz.	E9	26
Bali, i., Indon.	E5	36
Bali, Laut (Bali Sea), Indon.	E5	36
Balıkesir, Tur.	C2	44
Balikpapan, Indon.	D5	36
Balimo, Pap. N. Gui.	H11	32
Balintang Channel, strt., Phil.	C8	34
Bali Sea see Bali, Laut, Indon.	E5	36
Balkan Mountains see Stara Planina, mts., Eur.	C9	18
Balkaria see Kabardino-Balkarija, state, Russia	E6	26
Balkh, Afg.	C9	42
Balkhash, Lake see Balhaš, ozero, l., Kaz.	E9	26
Ball, La., U.S.	C3	111
Ballālpur, India	F3	40
Ballarat, Austl.	H3	62
Ballard, co., Ky., U.S.	e8	110
Ball Club Lake, l., Mn., U.S.	C5	116
Balleny Islands, is., Ant.	C21	67
Ballina, Austl.	F5	62
Ballina, Ire.	C2	12
Ballinger, Tx., U.S.	D3	136
Ball Mountain Lake, res., Vt., U.S.	E3	138
Ballston Spa, N.Y., U.S.	B7	125
Ballwin, Mo., U.S.	f12	118
Bally, Pa., U.S.	F10	131
Ballymena, N. Ire., U.K.	C3	12
Balmoral, N.B., Can.	B3	87
Balmoral Castle, hist., Scot., U.K.	B5	12
Balmville, N.Y., U.S.	D6	125
Balombo, Ang.	F2	54
Balqash Köli see Balhaš, ozero, l., Kaz.	E9	26
Balş, Rom.	G8	20
Balsam Lake, Wi., U.S.	C1	142
Balsam Lake, l., Wi., U.S.	C1	142
Balsas, Braz.	E10	70
Balsas, stm., Mex.	D4	78
Balta, Ukr.	F10	20
Baltasar Brum, Ur.	E6	72
Bălţi, Mol.	F9	20
Baltic, Ct., U.S.	C7	100
Baltic, S.D., U.S.	D9	134
Baltic Sea, Eur.	I7	10
Baltijsk, Russia	B5	20
Baltim, Egypt	E10	14
Baltimore, Md., U.S.	B4	113
Baltimore, co., Md., U.S.	B4	113
Baltimore, Oh., U.S.	C3	128
Baltimore Highlands, Md., U.S.	h11	113
Baluchistan, hist. reg., Asia	E8	42
Bālurghāt, India	D5	40
Balygyčan, Russia	C17	26
Bam, Iran	E7	42
Bama, Nig.	D7	50
Bamako, Mali	D3	50
Bamba, Mali	C4	50
Bambari, C.A.R.	B4	54
Bamberg, Ger.	F12	12
Bamberg, S.C., U.S.	E5	133
Bamberg, co., S.C., U.S.	E5	133
Bambesi, Eth.	B6	54
Bamenda, Cam.	B2	54
Bāmīān, Afg.	D9	42
Bamingui, C.A.R.	B4	54
Bampūr, Iran	E8	42
Banaba, i., Kir.	E10	58
Banalia, D.R.C.	C5	54
Banamba, Mali	D3	50
Bananal, Ilha do, i., Braz.	D1	74
Banana River, b., Fl., U.S.	D6	102
Bananga, India	J15	40
Banās, Rās, c., Egypt	F12	48
Banaz, Tur.	C3	44
Banbury, Eng., U.K.	D6	12
Bancroft, On., Can.	B7	89
Bancroft, Ia., U.S.	A3	108
Bancroft see Chililabombwe, Zam.	A4	56
Bānda, India	D4	40
Banda, Kepulauan, is., Indon.	D7	36
Banda, Laut (Banda Sea), Indon.	E7	36
Banda Aceh, Indon.	B1	36
Bandama, stm., C. Iv.	E4	50
Bandar Beheshtī, Iran	E8	42
Bandar-e 'Abbās, Iran	E7	42
Bandar-e Anzalī, Iran	C5	42
Bandar-e Būshehr, Iran	E6	42
Bandar-e Deylam, Iran	E6	42
Bandar-e Khomeynī, Iran	D5	42
Bandar-e Lengeh, Iran	E6	42
Bandar-e Torkeman, Iran	C6	42
Bandar Lampung, Indon.	E3	36
Bandar Seri Begawan, Bru.	C4	36
Banda Sea see Banda, Laut, Indon.	E7	36
Banded Peak, mtn., Co., U.S.	D4	99
Bandeira, Pico da, mtn., Braz.	F3	74
Bandeirantes, Braz.	B7	72
Bandelier National Monument, N.M., U.S.	B3	124
Bandera, co., Tx., U.S.	E3	136
Bandiagara, Mali	D4	50
Bandiantaolehai, China	C8	28
Bandırma, Tur.	B2	44
Bandon, Or., U.S.	D2	130
Bandundu, D.R.C.	C3	54
Bandung, Indon.	E3	36
Bāneh, Iran	E11	44
Banes, Cuba	A4	80
Banff National Park, Ab., Can.	D2	84
Banfora, Burkina	D4	50
Bangalore, India	G3	40
Bangassou, C.A.R.	C4	54
Banggai, Indon.	D6	36
Banggai, Kepulauan, is., Indon.	D7	36
Banggi, Pulau, i., Malay.	B5	36
Banghāzī, Libya	D9	48
Bangka, Pulau, i., Indon.	D3	36
Bangka, Selat, strt., Indon.	D3	36
Bangkalan, Indon.	E4	36
Bangkinang, Indon.	C2	36
Bangko, Indon.	D2	36
Bangkok see Krung Thep, Thai.	D4	34
Bangladesh, ctry., Asia	B2	34
Bang Mun Nak, Thai.	C4	34
Ban Gnômmarat Kèo, Laos	C5	34
Bangor, N. Ire., U.K.	C4	12
Bangor, Wales, U.K.	D4	12
Bangor, Me., U.S.	D4	112
Bangor, Mi., U.S.	F4	115
Bangor, Pa., U.S.	E11	131
Bangor, Wi., U.S.	E3	142
Bangor Township, Mi., U.S.	E7	115
Bangs, Mount, mtn., Az., U.S.	A2	96
Bangui, C.A.R.	C3	54
Bangweulu, Lake, l., Zam.	A4	56
Ban Houayxay, Laos	B4	34
Bani, Burkina	D4	50
Baní, Dom. Rep.	B5	80
Baniara, Pap. N. Gui.	B4	62
Banister, stm., Va., U.S.	D4	139
Banī Walīd, Libya	D7	48
Bāniyās, Syria	E6	44
Banja Luka, Bos.	B6	18
Banjarmasin, Indon.	D4	36
Banjul, Gam.	D1	50
Banka Banka, Austl.	D5	60
Bankhead Lake, res., Al., U.S.	B2	94
Banks, co., Ga., U.S.	B3	103
Banks, Îles, is., Vanuatu	j9	62a
Banks Island, i., B.C., Can.	C2	85
Banks Lake, res., Wa., U.S.	B6	140
Banks Strait, strt., Austl.	I4	62
Bānkura, India	E5	40
Ban Nalè, Laos	C4	34
Banner, co., Ne., U.S.	C2	120
Banner Elk, N.C., U.S.	A1	126
Banning, Ca., U.S.	F5	98
Bannock, co., Id., U.S.	G6	105
Bannock Peak, mtn., Id., U.S.	F6	105
Bannock Range, mts., Id., U.S.	G6	105
Bannu, Pak.	D10	42
Ban Pong, Thai.	D3	34
Ban Signo, Laos	C5	34
Banská Bystrica, Slvk.	E5	20
Bānswāra, India	E2	40
Bantaeng, Indon.	E6	36
Bantam, stm., Ct., U.S.	B3	100
Bantam Lake, l., Ct., U.S.	C3	100
Banyo, Cam.	B2	54
Banyuwangi, Indon.	E4	36
Banzare Coast, Ant.	C17	67
Baode, China	D10	28
Baodi, China	B4	30
Baoding, China	D11	28
Bao Ha, Viet.	B4	34
Baoji, China	E9	28
Baojing, China	D2	30
Bao Lac, Viet.	D5	34
Baoqing, China	A2	31
Baoshan, China	F7	28
Baoting, China	H9	28
Baotou, China	C9	28
Baoying, China	E11	28
Ba'qūbah, Iraq	D4	42
Baquedano, Chile	B2	69
Bara, Nig.	D2	54
Baraawe, Som.	J13	48
Baraboo, stm., Wi., U.S.	E3	142
Baraboo, Wi., U.S.	E4	142
Baracoa, Cuba	A5	80
Baraga, Mi., U.S.	B2	115
Baraga, co., Mi., U.S.	B2	115
Barahona, Dom. Rep.	B5	80
Barakaldo, Spain	F5	16
Baram, stm., Malay.	C4	36
Bāramūla, India	C2	40
Baranagar, India	E5	40
Baranavičy, Bela.	C9	20
Barani, Burkina	D4	50
Baranof Island, i., Ak., U.S.	m22	95
Barataria, La., U.S.	E5	111
Barataria Bay, b., La., U.S.	E6	111
Barauni, India	D5	40
Barbacena, Braz.	F3	74
Barbacoas, Col.	C4	70
Barbados, ctry., N.A.	F12	76
Barbar, Sudan	G11	48
Barbas, Cap, c., W. Sah.	B1	50
Barbastro, Spain	F7	16
Barber, co., Ks., U.S.	E5	109
Barbers Point, mtn., U.S.	B3	104
Barbers Point Naval Air Station, mil., Hi., U.S.	g9	104
Barberton, S. Afr.	D5	56
Barberton, Oh., U.S.	A4	128
Barbour, co., Al., U.S.	D4	94
Barbour, co., W.V., U.S.	B4	141
Barboursville, W.V., U.S.	C2	141
Barbourville, Ky., U.S.	D6	110
Barbuda, i., Antig.	B7	80
Barcaldine, Austl.	E4	62
Barcelona, Spain	G8	16
Barcelona, Ven.	B6	70
Barcelos, Braz.	D7	70

Name	Map Ref.	Page
Barcroft, Lake, res., Va., U.S.	g12	139
Bärdä, Azer.	B12	44
Bardaï, Chad	B8	50
Bardawîl, Sabkhet el-, b., Egypt	G5	44
Bardejov, Slvk.	E6	20
Barden Reservoir, res., R.I., U.S.	C2	132
Bardīyah, Libya	D10	48
Bardstown, Ky., U.S.	C4	110
Bardwell, Ky., U.S.	f9	110
Bardwell Lake, res., Tx., U.S.	C4	136
Bareilly, India	D3	40
Barents Sea, Eur.	B6	26
Barents Trough	D20	144
Bargersville, In., U.S.	E5	107
Bar Harbor, Me., U.S.	D4	112
Bari, Italy	D6	18
Barika, Alg.	J9	16
Barillas, Guat.	B1	80
Barīm, i., Yemen	H4	38
Barinas, Ven.	B6	70
Bāripada, India	E5	40
Bârîs, Egypt	F11	48
Barisāl, Bngl.	E6	40
Barisan, Pegunungan, mts., Indon.	D2	36
Barkam, China	C1	30
Barker Heights, N.C., U.S.	f10	126
Barkhamsted Reservoir, res., Ct., U.S.	B3	100
Barkley, Lake, res., U.S.	f10	110
Barkley Sound, strt., B.C., Can.	E5	85
Barkly East, S. Afr.	E4	56
Barkly Tableland, plat., Austl.	D6	60
Barkol, China	C6	28
Bark Point, c., Wi., U.S.	B2	142
Barksdale Air Force Base, mil., La., U.S.	B2	111
Bârlad, Rom.	F9	20
Barlee, Lake, l., Austl.	F2	60
Barletta, Italy	D6	18
Barling, Ar., U.S.	B1	97
Barlow, Ky., U.S.	e8	110
Bärmer, India	D2	40
Barmera, Austl.	G3	62
Barnaul, Russia	D10	26
Barnegat Bay, b., N.J., U.S.	D4	123
Barnegat Inlet, b., N.J., U.S.	D4	123
Barnes, co., N.D., U.S.	B7	127
Barnesboro, Pa., U.S.	E4	131
Barnes Sound, strt., Fl., U.S.	G6	102
Barnesville, Ga., U.S.	C2	103
Barnesville, Mn., U.S.	D2	116
Barnesville, Oh., U.S.	C4	128
Barnhart, Mo., U.S.	C7	118
Barnsdall, Ok., U.S.	A5	129
Barnstable, Ma., U.S.	C7	114
Barnstable, co., Ma., U.S.	C7	114
Barnstaple, Eng., U.K.	E4	12
Barnwell, S.C., U.S.	E5	133
Barnwell, co., S.C., U.S.	E5	133
Baro, Nig.	E6	50
Barpeta, India	D6	40
Barqah (Cyrenaica), hist. reg., Libya	E8	14
Barques, Pointe aux, c., Mi., U.S.	D8	115
Barquisimeto, Ven.	A6	70
Barra, Braz.	F6	74
Barra, i., Scot., U.K.	D3	12
Barra, Ponta da, c., Moz.	C6	56
Barrackville, W.V., U.S.	B4	141
Barra do Corda, Braz.	C2	74
Barra do Cuanza, Ang.	E2	54
Barra do Dande, Ang.	E2	54
Barra do Garças, Braz.	B7	72
Barra Mansa, Braz.	F3	74
Barranca, Peru	F4	70
Barrancabermeja, Col.	B5	70
Barrancas, Ven.	D7	80
Barranquilla, Col.	A5	70
Barras, Braz.	B3	74
Barre, Vt., U.S.	C4	138
Barre, Lake, l., La., U.S.	E5	111
Barre Falls Reservoir, res., Ma., U.S.	B4	114
Barreiras, Braz.	D3	74
Barreiro, Port.	H2	16
Barreiros, Braz.	C4	74
Barren, stm., Ky., U.S.	C3	110
Barren, co., Ky., U.S.	D4	110
Barren, Nosy, is., Madag.	B7	56
Barren Island, i., Md., U.S.	D5	113
Barren Islands, is., Ak., U.S.	h15	95
Barren River Lake, res., Ky., U.S.	D3	110
Barretos, Braz.	F2	74
Barrett, W.V., U.S.	D3	141
Barrhead, Ab., Can.	B3	84
Barrie, On., Can.	C5	89
Barrie Island, i., On., Can.	B2	89
Barrière, B.C., Can.	D7	85
Barrier Range, mts., Austl.	G3	62
Barrington, Il., U.S.	A5	106
Barrington, N.J., U.S.	D2	123
Barrington, R.I., U.S.	D5	132
Barrington, stm., R.I., U.S.	C5	132
Barron, Wi., U.S.	C2	142
Barron, co., Wi., U.S.	C2	142
Barron Lake, Mi., U.S.	G4	115
Barrow, Ak., U.S.	A8	95
Barrow, co., Ga., U.S.	B3	103
Barrow, Point, c., Ak., U.S.	A8	95
Barrow Creek, Austl.	E5	60
Barrow-in-Furness, Eng., U.K.	C5	12
Barrow Island, i., Austl.	E2	60
Barry, Il., U.S.	D2	106
Barry, co., Mi., U.S.	F5	115
Barry, co., Mo., U.S.	E4	118
Barrys Bay, On., Can.	B7	89
Bārsi, India	F3	40
Barstow, Ca., U.S.	E5	98
Bartholomew, co., In., U.S.	F6	107
Bartholomew, Bayou, stm., U.S.	D4	97
Bartica, Guy.	B8	70
Bartın, Tur.	B5	44
Bartlesville, Ok., U.S.	A6	129
Bartlett, N.H., U.S.	B4	122
Bartlett, Tn., U.S.	B2	135
Bartlett, Tx., U.S.	D4	136
Bartlett Reservoir, res., Az., U.S.	D4	96
Bartletts Ferry Dam, U.S.	C4	94
Barton, co., Ks., U.S.	D5	109
Barton, co., Mo., U.S.	D3	118
Barton, Oh., U.S.	B5	128
Barton, Vt., U.S.	B4	138
Barton, stm., Vt., U.S.	B4	138
Bartonville, Il., U.S.	C4	106
Bartoszyce, Pol.	B6	20
Bartow, Fl., U.S.	E5	102
Bartow, co., Ga., U.S.	B2	103
Barú, Volcán, vol., Pan.	D3	80
Barun Su, China	A3	30
Baruun-Urt, Mong.	B10	28
Barysau, Bela.	B10	20
Basalt, Co., U.S.	B3	99
Basankusu, D.R.C.	C3	54
Bascuñán, Cabo, c., Chile	D3	72
Basehor, Ks., U.S.	k16	109
Basel, Switz.	G10	12
Bashan Lake, l., Ct., U.S.	D6	100
Bashaw, Ab., Can.	C4	84
Bashi Channel, strt., Asia	B8	34
Basilan Island, i., Phil.	E8	34
Basile, La., U.S.	D3	111
Basin, Wy., U.S.	B4	143
Basingstoke, Eng., U.K.	E6	12
Basīrhāt, India	E5	40
Baskahegan Lake, l., Me., U.S.	C5	112
Başkale, Tur.	C10	44
Basking Ridge, N.J., U.S.	B3	123
Baškirija, state, Russia	D7	26
Basoko, D.R.C.	C4	54
Basra see Al-Baṣrah, Iraq	D5	42
Bassano, Ab., Can.	D4	84
Bassar, Togo	E5	50
Bassein see Pathein, Mya.	C2	34
Basse Santa Su, Gam.	D2	50
Basse-Terre, Guad.	B7	80
Basse-Terre, i., Guad.	B7	80
Basseterre, St. K./N.	B7	80
Bassett, Ne., U.S.	B6	120
Bassett, Va., U.S.	D3	139
Bassett Peak, mtn., Az., U.S.	E5	96
Bassikounou, Maur.	C3	50
Bass Islands, is., Oh., U.S.	A3	128
Bass Lake, In., U.S.	B4	107
Bass Strait, strt., Austl.	H4	62
Basswood Lake, l., Mn., U.S.	B7	116
Båstad, Swe.	H5	10
Bastia, Fr.	C2	18
Bastrop, La., U.S.	B4	111
Bastrop, Tx., U.S.	D4	136
Bastrop, co., Tx., U.S.	D4	136
Basu, Pulau, i., Indon.	D2	36
Basutoland see Lesotho, ctry., Afr.	D4	56
Bata, Eq. Gui.	C1	54
Batabanó, Golfo de, b., Cuba	A3	80
Batac, Phil.	C8	34
Batagaj, Russia	C15	26
Batala, India	C3	40
Batamaj, Russia	C14	26
Batang, China	E7	28
Batang, Indon.	E3	36
Batangafo, C.A.R.	B3	54
Batangas, Phil.	D8	34
Batan Islands, is., Phil.	B8	34
Batanta, Pulau, i., Indon.	D8	36
Batavia see Jakarta, Indon.	E3	36
Batavia, Il., U.S.	B5	106
Batavia, N.Y., U.S.	C2	125
Batavia, Oh., U.S.	C1	128
Batchelor, Austl.	C5	60
Batchelor Bay, b., N.C., U.S.	B6	126
Bătdâmbâng, Camb.	D4	34
Batemans Bay, Austl.	H5	62
Bates, co., Mo., U.S.	C3	118
Batesburg, S.C., U.S.	D4	133
Batesville, Ar., U.S.	B4	97
Batesville, In., U.S.	F7	107
Batesville, Ms., U.S.	A4	117
Bath, N.B., Can.	C2	87
Bath, On., Can.	C8	89
Bath, Eng., U.K.	E5	12
Bath, co., Ky., U.S.	B6	110
Bath, Me., U.S.	E3	112
Bath, N.Y., U.S.	C3	125
Bath, Pa., U.S.	E11	131
Bath, S.C., U.S.	D4	133
Bath, co., Va., U.S.	B3	139
Bathinda, India	C3	40
Bathurst, Austl.	G4	62
Bathurst, N.B., Can.	B4	87
Bathurst see Banjul, Gam.	D1	50
Bathurst Island, i., Austl.	C5	60
Batiscan, stm., P.Q., Can.	B5	90
Batman, Tur.	D9	44
Batna, Alg.	C6	48
Baton Rouge, La., U.S.	D4	111
Batouri, Cam.	C2	54
Batsto, stm., N.J., U.S.	D3	123
Batten Kill, stm., U.S.	E2	138
Batticaloa, Sri L.	H4	40
Battle, stm., Can.	H17	82
Battle Creek, Ia., U.S.	B2	108
Battle Creek, Mi., U.S.	F5	115
Battle Creek, Ne., U.S.	C8	120
Battle Ground, In., U.S.	C4	107
Battle Ground, Wa., U.S.	D3	140
Battle Lake, Mn., U.S.	D2	116
Battle Mountain, Nv., U.S.	C5	121
Battle Mountain, mtn., Wy., U.S.	E5	143
Batu, mtn., Eth.	B7	54
Batu, Kepulauan, is., Indon.	D1	36
Batu Pahat, Malay.	C2	36
Baturaja, Indon.	D2	36
Baturité, Braz.	B4	74
Baubau, Indon.	E6	36
Bauchi, Nig.	D6	50
Baudette, Mn., U.S.	B4	116
Bauld, Cape, c., Nf., Can.	C4	88
Baures, Bol.	A5	72
Bauru, Braz.	F2	74
Bauska, Lat.	H11	10
Bautzen, Ger.	E14	12
Bavispe, stm., Mex.	A3	78
Bawdwin, Mya.	B3	34
Bawean, Pulau, i., Indon.	E4	36
Bawiti, Egypt	E10	48
Baxley, Ga., U.S.	E4	103
Baxter, co., Ar., U.S.	A3	97
Baxter, Ia., U.S.	C4	108
Baxter, Mn., U.S.	D4	116
Baxter, Tn., U.S.	C8	135
Baxter Springs, Ks., U.S.	E9	109
Bay, Ar., U.S.	B5	97
Bay, co., Fl., U.S.	u16	102
Bay, co., Mi., U.S.	E6	115
Bayamo, Cuba	A4	80
Bayamón, P.R.		
Bayan Har Shan, mts., China	E7	28
Bayanhongor, Mong.	B8	28
Bayano, Lago, res., Pan.	D4	80
Bayan Obo, China	C10	28
Bayard, Ne., U.S.	C2	120
Bayard, N.M., U.S.	E1	124
Bayboro, N.C., U.S.	B6	126
Bay Bulls, Nf., Can.	E5	88
Bayburt, Tur.	B9	44
Bay City, Mi., U.S.	E7	115
Bay City, Or., U.S.	B3	130
Bay City, Tx., U.S.	E5	136
Bay de Verde, Nf., Can.	D5	88
Baydhabo, Som.	J13	48
Bayeux, Fr.	C6	16
Bayfield, On., Can.	D3	89
Bayfield, Co., U.S.	D3	99
Bayfield, Wi., U.S.	B3	142
Bayfield, co., Wi., U.S.	B2	142
Baylor, co., Tx., U.S.	C3	136
Bay Mills Indian Reservation, Mi., U.S.	B6	115
Bay Minette, Al., U.S.	E2	94
Bayombong, Phil.	C8	34
Bayonne, Fr.	F5	16
Bayonne, N.J., U.S.	B4	123
Bayou Bodcau Reservoir, res., La., U.S.	B2	111
Bayou D'Arbonne Lake, res., La., U.S.	B3	111
Bayou George, Fl., U.S.	u16	102
Bayou Goula, La., U.S.	D4	111
Bayou La Batre, Al., U.S.	E1	94
Bayovar, Peru	E2	70
Bay Point, c., S.C., U.S.	G7	133
Bayport, Mn., U.S.	E6	116
Bayport, N.Y., U.S.	n15	125
Bayreuth, Ger.	F12	12
Bay Ridge, Md., U.S.	C5	113
Bay Roberts, Nf., Can.	E5	88
Bayrūt (Beirut), Leb.	F6	44
Bays, Lake of, l., On., Can.	B5	89
Bay Saint Louis, Ms., U.S.	E4	117
Bay Shore, N.Y., U.S.	E7	125
Bayshore Gardens, Fl., U.S.	q10	102
Bayside, Wis.	m12	142
Bay Springs, Ms., U.S.	D4	117
Bayt Laḥm, W.B.	G6	44
Baytown, Tx., U.S.	E5	136
Bayview, Al., U.S.	f7	94
Bay Village, Oh., U.S.	h9	128
Baza, Spain	I5	16
Bazardjuzju, gora see Bazardüzü dağ, mtn., Azer.	B12	44
Bazardüzü dağ, mtn., Azer.	B12	44
Bazaruto, Ilha do, i., Moz.	C6	56
Bazhong, China	C2	30
Be, Nosy, i., Madag.	A8	56
Beach, N.D., U.S.	C1	127
Beachburg, On., Can.	B8	89
Beach City, Oh., U.S.	B4	128
Beach Haven Inlet, b., N.J., U.S.	D4	123
Beach Pond, res., U.S.	C8	100
Beachville, On., Can.	D4	89
Beachwood, N.J., U.S.	D4	123
Beacon, Austl.	G2	60
Beacon, N.Y., U.S.	D7	125
Beacon Falls, Ct., U.S.	D3	100
Beaconsfield, P.Q., Can.	q19	90
Beadle, co., S.D., U.S.	C7	134
Beagle Gulf, b., Austl.	C4	60
Bealanana, Madag.	A8	56
Beale, Cape, c., B.C., Can.	E5	85
Beale Air Force Base, mil., Ca., U.S.	C3	98
Bear, De., U.S.	B3	101
Bear, stm., U.S.	B3	137
Bear Creek, Al., U.S.	A2	94
Bear Creek, stm., Or., U.S.	E4	130
Bear Creek, stm., Wy., U.S.	E8	143
Bear Creek, stm., U.S.	E2	109
Bearden, Ar., U.S.	D3	97
Beardstown, Il., U.S.	C3	106
Bear Inlet, b., N.C., U.S.	C5	126
Bear Island see Bjørnøya, i., Nor.	B3	26
Bear Lake, co., Id., U.S.	G7	105
Bear Lake, l., Wi., U.S.	C2	142
Bear Lake, l., U.S.	A4	137
Bear Lake, l., U.S.	C5	92
Bear Lodge Mountains, mts., Wy., U.S.	B8	143
Bear Mountain, mtn., Or., U.S.	D4	130
Bearpaw Mountains, mts., Mt., U.S.	B7	119
Bear River, N.S., Can.	E4	87
Bear River City, Ut., U.S.	B3	137
Beartooth Pass, Wy., U.S.	E8	143
Beartooth Range, mts., U.S.	E7	119
Bear Town, Ms., U.S.	D3	117
Beas, stm., India	C3	40
Beata, Isla, i., Dom. Rep.	B5	80
Beatrice, Ne., U.S.	D9	120
Beatrice, Cape, c., Austl.	C2	62
Beatty, Nv., U.S.	G5	121
Beattyville, Ky., U.S.	C6	110
Beaufort, N.C., U.S.	C6	126
Beaufort, co., N.C., U.S.	B5	126
Beaufort, S.C., U.S.	G6	133
Beaufort, co., S.C., U.S.	G6	133
Beaufort Marine Corps Air Station, mil., S.C., U.S.	F6	133
Beaufort Sea, N.A.	D12	82
Beaufort West, S. Afr.	E3	56
Beauharnois, P.Q., Can.	D4	90
Beau Lake, l., Me., U.S.	A3	112
Beaumont, Ab., Can.	C4	84
Beaumont, Ms., U.S.	D5	117
Beaumont, Tx., U.S.	D5	136
Beaune, Fr.	D9	16
Beauport, P.Q., Can.	n17	90
Beaupré, P.Q., Can.	B7	90
Beauregard, co., La., U.S.	D2	111
Beausejour, Mb., Can.	D3	86
Beauvais, Fr.	C8	16
Beauval, Sk., Can.	B2	91
Beaver, stm., Can.	B2	91
Beaver, stm., N.Y., U.S.	B5	125
Beaver, co., Ok., U.S.	e10	129
Beaver, Ok., U.S.	A1	129
Beaver, Pa., U.S.	E1	131
Beaver, co., Pa., U.S.	E1	131
Beaver, stm., R.I., U.S.	E2	132
Beaver, Ut., U.S.	E3	137
Beaver, co., Ut., U.S.	E2	137
Beaver, W.V., U.S.	D3	141
Beaver, stm., U.S.	A2	129
Beaverbank, N.S., Can.	E6	87
Beaver Brook, stm., U.S.	E4	122
Beaver City, Ne., U.S.	D6	120
Beaver Creek, stm., N.D., U.S.	C1	127
Beaver Creek, stm., N.D., U.S.	C5	127
Beaver Creek, stm., Ok., U.S.	C3	129
Beaver Creek, stm., Tn., U.S.	m13	135
Beaver Creek, stm., Wy., U.S.	D4	143
Beaver Creek, stm., U.S.	C8	143
Beaver Creek, stm., U.S.	E4	120
Beaverdale, Pa., U.S.	F4	131
Beaver Dam, Ky., U.S.	C3	110
Beaver Dam, Wi., U.S.	E5	142
Beaverdam Branch, stm., De., U.S.	F3	101
Beaverdam Lake, res., Wi., U.S.	E5	142
Beaverhead, co., Mt., U.S.	E3	119
Beaverhead Mountains, mts., U.S.	D5	105
Beaverhill Lake, l., Ab., Can.	C4	84
Beaver Lake, res., Ar., U.S.	A2	97
Beaverlodge, Ab., Can.	B1	84
Beaver Meadows, Pa., U.S.	E10	131
Beaver Run Reservoir, res., Pa., U.S.	F2	131
Beavertail Point, c., R.I., U.S.	F4	132
Beaverton, Mi., U.S.	E6	115
Beaverton, Or., U.S.	B4	130
Beāwar, India	D2	40
Bebedouro, Braz.	C8	72
Bécancour, P.Q., Can.	C5	90
Bečej, Yugo.	B8	18
Béchar, Alg.	D4	48
Becharof Lake, l., Ak., U.S.	D8	95
Bechuanaland see Botswana, ctry., Afr.	C3	56
Beckemeyer, Il., U.S.	E4	106
Becker, Mn., U.S.	E5	116
Becker, co., Mn., U.S.	D3	116
Beckham, co., Ok., U.S.	B2	129
Beckley, W.V., U.S.	D3	141
Becky Peak, mtn., Nv., U.S.	D7	121
Bedelē, Eth.	B7	54
Bedford, P.Q., Can.	D5	90
Bedford, Eng., U.K.	D6	12
Bedford, Ia., U.S.	D3	108
Bedford, In., U.S.	G5	107
Bedford, Ky., U.S.	B4	110
Bedford, Ma., U.S.	B5	114
Bedford, N.H., U.S.	E3	122
Bedford, Oh., U.S.	A4	128
Bedford, Pa., U.S.	F4	131
Bedford, co., Pa., U.S.	G4	131
Bedford, co., Tn., U.S.	B5	135
Bedford, Va., U.S.	C3	139
Bedford, co., Va., U.S.	C3	139
Bedford Hills, N.Y., U.S.	D7	125
Bee, co., Tx., U.S.	E4	136
Beebe, P.Q., Can.	D5	90
Beebe, Ar., U.S.	B4	97
Beecher, Il., U.S.	B6	106
Beech Fork, stm., Ky., U.S.	C4	110
Beech Grove, In., U.S.	E5	107
Beech Island, S.C., U.S.	E4	133
Beemer, Ne., U.S.	C9	120
Bee Ridge, Fl., U.S.	q11	102
Beersheba see Be'ér Sheva', Isr.	D2	42
Be'ér Sheva', Isr.	D2	42
Beeton (part of Alliston Beeton Tecumseth and Tottenham), On., Can.	C5	89
Beeville, Tx., U.S.	E4	136
Befale, D.R.C.	C4	54
Befandriana Atsimo, Madag.	C7	56
Bega, Austl.	H4	62
Beggs, Ok., U.S.	B5	129
Behbahān, Iran	D6	42
Behm Canal, strt., Ak., U.S.	n24	95
Bei'an, China	B13	28
Beigi, Eth.	B6	54
Beihai, China	G9	28
Beijing, China	D11	28
Beiliu, China	E3	30
Beipiao, China	C12	28
Beira, Moz.	B5	56
Beirut see Bayrūt, Leb.	F6	44
Bei Shan, mts., China	C7	28
Beitbridge, Zimb.	C5	56
Beizhen, China	B4	30
Beizhen, China	A5	30
Beja, Port.	I3	16
Béja, Tun.	C6	48
Bejaïa, Alg.	C6	48
Bejaïa, Golfe de, b., Alg.	I9	16
Béjar, Spain	G4	16
Bejneu, Kaz.	E7	26
Bekaa Valley see Al-Biqā', val., Leb.	F6	44
Bekabad, Uzb.	B9	42
Bekasi, Indon.	E3	36
Bekdaš, Turk.	B6	42
Békéscsaba, Hung.	F6	20
Bekily, Madag.	C8	56
Bekodoka, Madag.	B8	56
Bela, India	D4	40
Bela, Pak.	E9	42
Bela Crkva, Yugo.	B8	18
Bel Air, Md., U.S.	A5	113
Bel Alton, Md., U.S.	D4	113
Belarus, ctry., Eur.	C9	20
Belau see Palau, ctry., Oc.	F10	32
Bela Vista, Braz.	H8	72
Bela Vista, Moz.	D5	56
Belcamp, Md., U.S.	B5	113
Belchatów, Pol.	D5	20
Belchertown, Ma., U.S.	B3	114
Belcourt, N.D., U.S.	A6	127
Belding, Mi., U.S.	E5	115
Belden, Ms., U.S.	A5	117
Beledweyne, Som.	J13	48
Belém, Braz.	B2	74
Belém, Moz.	A6	56
Belém de São Francisco, Braz.	C4	74
Belen, N.M., U.S.	C3	124
Belëv, Russia	C14	20
Belfair, Wa., U.S.	B3	140
Belfast, S. Afr.	D5	56
Belfast, N. Ire., U.K.	C4	12
Belfast, Me., U.S.	D3	112
Belfield, N.D., U.S.	C2	127
Belford Roxo, Braz.	C4	74
Belfort, Fr.	D10	16
Belgaum, India	F2	40
Belgium, ctry., Eur.	B9	16
Belgium, Wi., U.S.	E6	142

Name	Map Ref.	Page

Belgium, ctry., Eur. B9 16
Belgorod, Russia D5 26
Belgrade, Mn., U.S. E3 116
Belgrade, Mt., U.S. E5 119
Belgrade see Beograd, Yugo. B8 18
Belhaven, N.C., U.S. B6 126
Beliliou, i., Palau E9 32
Belington, W.V., U.S. B5 141
Belitung, i., Indon. D3 36
Belize, ctry., N.A. B2 80
Belize City, Belize B2 80
Belknap, co., N.H., U.S. . . . C3 122
Belknap Crater, crat., Or., U.S. C5 130
Bell, co., Ky., U.S. D6 110
Bell, co., Tx., U.S. D4 136
Bella Coola, stm., B.C., Can. C4 85
Bellaire, Ks., U.S. g12 109
Bellaire, Mi., U.S. D5 115
Bellaire, Oh., U.S. C5 128
Bellaire, Tx., U.S. r14 136
Bellamy, Al., U.S. C1 94
Bellary, India F3 40
Bella Vista, Arg. D6 72
Bellavista, Peru E4 70
Bella Vista, Arg., U.S. A1 97
Bellbrook, Oh., U.S. C1 128
Belle, Mo., U.S. C6 118
Belle, W.V., U.S. C3 141
Belle, stm., La., U.S. k9 111
Belleair, Fl., U.S. p10 102
Belle Bay, b., Nf., Can. . . . E4 88
Belle Chasse, La., U.S. . . . E5 111
Bellefontaine, Oh., U.S. . . . B2 128
Bellefonte, Pa., U.S. E6 131
Belle Fourche, S.D., U.S. . . C2 134
Belle Fourche, stm., U.S. . . C3 134
Belle Fourche Reservoir, res., S.D., U.S. C2 134
Belle Glade, Fl., U.S. F6 102
Belle-Île, i., Fr. D5 16
Belle Isle, i., Fl., U.S. D5 102
Belle Isle, i., Nf., Can. C4 88
Belle Isle, Strait of, strt., Nf., Can. C3 88
Belle Meade, Tn., U.S. g10 135
Belle Plaine, Ia., U.S. C5 108
Belle Plaine, Ks., U.S. E6 109
Belle Plaine, Mn., U.S. F5 116
Belle River, On., Can. E2 89
Belle Rose, La., U.S. D4 111
Belle Vernon, Pa., U.S. . . . F2 131
Belleview, Fl., U.S. C4 102
Belle View, Va., U.S. g12 139
Belleville, On., Can. C7 89
Belleville, Il., U.S. E4 106
Belleville, Ks., U.S. C6 109
Belleville, Mi., U.S. p15 115
Belleville, N.J., U.S. B4 123
Belleville, Pa., U.S. E6 131
Belleville, Wi., U.S. F4 142
Belleville Pond, l., R.I., U.S. E4 132
Bellevue, Ia., U.S. B7 108
Bellevue, Id., U.S. F4 105
Bellevue, Ky., U.S. h13 110
Bellevue, Mi., U.S. F5 115
Bellevue, Ne., U.S. C10 120
Bellevue, Oh., U.S. A3 128
Bellevue, Pa., U.S. F1 131
Bellevue, Wa., U.S. e11 140
Bellflower, Ca., U.S. n12 98
Bellingham, Ma., U.S. B5 114
Bellingham, Wa., U.S. A3 140
Bellingshausen Sea, Ant. . . C32 67
Bellinzona, Switz. A2 18
Bell Island, i., Nf., Can. . . . C4 88
Bellmawr, N.J., U.S. D2 123
Bello, Col. B4 70
Bellows Falls, Vt., U.S. . . . E4 138
Bellport, N.Y., U.S. n16 125
Bells, Tn., U.S. B2 135
Bells Creek, stm., W.V., U.S. m13 141
Belluno, Italy A4 18
Bell Ville, Arg. E5 72
Bellville, Oh., U.S. B3 128
Bellville, Tx., U.S. E4 136
Bellwood, Il., U.S. k9 106
Bellwood, Pa., U.S. E5 131
Bellwood, Va., U.S. n18 139
Belmar, N.J., U.S. C4 123
Belmond, Ia., U.S. B4 108
Belmont, On., Can. E3 89
Belmont, Ca., U.S. h8 98
Belmont, Ma., U.S. g11 114
Belmont, Ms., U.S. A5 117
Belmont, N.C., U.S. B1 126
Belmont, N.H., U.S. D4 122
Belmont, W.V., U.S. B3 141
Belmont, Wi., U.S. F3 142
Belmont, co., Oh., U.S. . . . C4 128
Belmonte, Braz. G12 70
Belmopan, Belize B2 80
Bel-Nor, Mo., U.S. f13 118
Beloe, ozero, l., Russia . . . C5 26
Beloe more, Russia C5 26
Belogorsk, Russia D14 26
Belo Horizonte, Braz. E3 74
Beloit, Ks., U.S. C5 109
Beloit, Oh., U.S. B5 128
Beloit, Wi., U.S. F4 142
Belomorsk, Russia C5 26
Beloreck, Russia D10 22

Belorussia see Belarus, ctry., Eur. C9 20
Belo Tsiribihina, Madag. . . . B7 56
Belpre, Oh., U.S. C4 128
Belt, Mt., U.S. C6 119
Belted Range, mts., Nv., U.S. F5 121
Belton, Mo., U.S. C3 118
Belton, S.C., U.S. B3 133
Belton, Tx., U.S. D4 136
Belton Lake, res., Tx., U.S. D4 136
Beltrami, co., Mn., U.S. . . . B3 116
Beltsville, Md., U.S. B4 113
Beluha, gora, mtn., Asia . . B5 28
Belūr, India G3 40
Belvedere, S.C., U.S. D4 133
Belvidere, Il., U.S. A5 106
Belvidere, N.J., U.S. B2 123
Belyj, ostrov, i., Russia . . . B8 26
Belyj Jar, Russia D10 26
Belzoni, Ms., U.S. B3 117
Bembèrèkè, Benin D5 50
Bement, Il., U.S. D5 106
Bemidji, Mn., U.S. C4 116
Bemidji, Lake, l., Mn., U.S. C4 116
Benāb, Iran D11 44
Bena-Dibele, D.R.C. D4 54
Benalla, Austl. H4 62
Benares see Vārānasi, India D4 40
Benavente, Spain F4 16
Benavides, Tx., U.S. F3 136
Benbecula, i., Scot., U.K. . . B3 12
Benbrook Lake, res., Tx., U.S. n9 136
Bencubbin, Austl. G2 60
Bend, Or., U.S. C5 130
Ben Davis Point, c., N.J., U.S. E2 123
Bendeleben, Mount, mtn., Ak., U.S. B7 95
Bendigo, Austl. H3 62
Benedict, Md., U.S. C4 113
Benedito Leite, Braz. E11 70
Benewah, co., Id., U.S. . . . B2 105
Bengal, Bay of, b., Asia . . F5 40
Bengbu, China E11 28
Benghazi see Banghāzī, Libya D9 48
Bengkalis, Pulau, i., Indon. C2 36
Bengkulu, Indon. D2 36
Bengtsfors, Swe. G5 10
Benguela, Ang. F2 54
Bengweulu Swamps, sw., Zam. A5 56
Benham, Ky., U.S. D7 110
Ben Hill, co., Ga., U.S. . . . E3 103
Beni, D.R.C. C5 54
Beni, stm., Bol. F6 70
Béni Abbas, Alg. D4 48
Benicia, Ca., U.S. C2 98
Benidorm, Spain H6 16
Beni-Mellal, Mor. D3 48
Benin, ctry., Afr. D5 50
Benin, Bight of, b., Afr. . . . E5 50
Benin City, Nig. E6 50
Beni Saf, Alg. J6 16
Beni Suef, Egypt E11 48
Benjamin Constant, Braz. . . D5 70
Benkelman, Ne., U.S. D4 120
Benld, Il., U.S. D4 106
Bennett, Co., U.S. B6 99
Bennett, co., S.D., U.S. . . . D4 134
Bennettsville, S.C., U.S. . . . B8 133
Bennington, N.H., U.S. D3 122
Bennington, Vt., U.S. F2 138
Bennington, co., Vt., U.S. . . E2 138
Benoit, Ms., U.S. B2 117
Benoni, S. Afr. D4 56
Bénoué see Benue, stm., Afr. E6 50
Bensenville, Il., U.S. B6 106
Bensheim, Ger. F11 12
Bensley, Va., U.S. C5 139
Benson, Az., U.S. F5 96
Benson, Mn., U.S. E3 116
Benson, N.C., U.S. B4 126
Benson, co., N.D., U.S. . . . A6 127
Bent, co., Co., U.S. D7 99
Benteng, Indon. E6 36
Bentinck Island, i., Austl. . . D2 62
Bentinck Island, i., Myan. . . D3 34
Bentley, Ab., Can. C3 84
Bentleyville, Pa., U.S. F1 131
Benton, Ar., U.S. C3 97
Benton, Il., U.S. E5 106
Benton, Ky., U.S. f9 110
Benton, La., U.S. B2 111
Benton, Pa., U.S. D9 131
Benton, Tn., U.S. B7 135
Benton, Wi., U.S. F3 142
Benton, co., Ar., U.S. A1 97
Benton, co., Ia., U.S. B5 108
Benton, co., In., U.S. C3 107
Benton, co., Mn., U.S. E4 116
Benton, co., Ms., U.S. A4 117
Benton, co., Or., U.S. C3 130
Benton, co., Tn., U.S. A3 135
Benton, co., Wa., U.S. C6 140
Benton City, Wa., U.S. C6 140
Benton Harbor, Mi., U.S. . . F4 115

Benton Heights, Mi., U.S. . . F4 115
Bentonville, Ar., U.S. A1 97
Ben Tre, Viet. D5 34
Bent's Old Fort National Historic Site, hist., Co., U.S. C7 99
Bentung, Malay. C2 36
Benue, stm., Afr. E6 50
Benwood, W.V., U.S. f8 141
Benxi, China C12 28
Benzie, co., Mi., U.S. D4 115
Beograd (Belgrade), Yugo. . B8 18
Béoumi, C. Iv. E3 50
Beppu, Japan D2 31
Beraketa, Madag. C8 56
Berat, Alb. D7 18
Berau, Teluk, b., Indon. . . . D8 36
Berazino, Bela. C10 20
Berbera, Som. H14 48
Berbérati, C.A.R. C3 54
Berck, Fr. B7 16
Berdians'k, Ukr. F14 20
Berdigestjah, Russia C14 26
Berdychiv, Ukr. E10 20
Berea, Ky., U.S. C5 110
Berea, Oh., U.S. A4 128
Berea, S.C., U.S. B3 133
Berehove, Ukr. E7 20
Berekum, Ghana E4 50
Berens, stm., Can. C3 86
Beresford, S.D., U.S. D9 134
Berettyóújfalu, Hung. F6 20
Berezhany, Ukr. E8 20
Berezivka, Ukr. F11 20
Berezniki, Russia D7 26
Berëzovo, Russia C8 26
Berg, Swe. F7 10
Bergama, Tur. C2 44
Bergamo, Italy B2 18
Bergen, Ger. D12 12
Bergen, Nor. F1 10
Bergen, co., N.J., U.S. A4 123
Bergenfield, N.J., U.S. B4 123
Bergerac, Fr. E7 16
Bergland, Mi., U.S. m12 115
Berguent, Mor. E3 14
Berhala, Selat, strt., Indon. D2 36
Beringa, ostrov, i., Russia . D18 26
Beringovskij prol see Bering Strait, strt. F6 82
Beringovskij, Russia C19 26
Bering Sea G3 82
Bering Strait, strt. F6 82
Berkakit, Russia D14 26
Berkane, Mor. E3 14
Berkeley, Ca., U.S. D2 98
Berkeley, Mo., U.S. f13 118
Berkeley, R.I., U.S. B4 132
Berkeley, co., S.C., U.S. . . . E8 133
Berkeley, co., W.V., U.S. . . B6 141
Berkeley Heights, N.J., U.S. B4 123
Berkeley Springs, W.V., U.S. B6 141
Berkley, Mi., U.S. F7 115
Berks, co., Pa., U.S. F9 131
Berkshire, co., Ma., U.S. . . B1 114
Berkshire Hills, hills, Ma., U.S. B1 114
Berlevåg, Nor. A13 10
Berlin, Ger. D13 12
Berlin, Ct., U.S. C5 100
Berlin, Md., U.S. D7 113
Berlin, N.H., U.S. B4 122
Berlin, N.J., U.S. D3 123
Berlin, Pa., U.S. G4 131
Berlin, Wi., U.S. E5 142
Berlin Lake, res., Oh., U.S. A4 128
Bermejo, stm., S.A. C5 72
Bermuda, dep., N.A. B12 76
Bern, Switz. A1 18
Bernalillo, N.M., U.S. B3 124
Bernalillo, co., N.M., U.S. . C3 124
Bernardsville, N.J., U.S. . . . B3 123
Bernasconi, Arg. F5 72
Berne see Bern, Switz. A1 18
Berne, In., U.S. C8 107
Berner Alpen, mts., Switz. . A1 18
Bernese Alps see Berner Alpen, mts., Switz. A1 18
Bernice, La., U.S. B3 111
Bernie, Mo., U.S. E8 118
Bernier Island, i., Austl. . . . E1 60
Bernina, Piz, mtn., Eur. . . . A2 18
Beroroha, Madag. C8 56
Berriane, co., Ga., U.S. . . . E3 103
Berrien, co., Mi., U.S. G4 115
Berrien Springs, Mi., U.S. . . G4 115
Berry, Al., U.S. B2 94
Berry, hist. reg., Fr. D7 16
Berryessa, Lake, res., Ca., U.S. C2 98
Berry Hill, Tn., U.S. g10 135
Berryville, Ar., U.S. A2 97
Berryville, Va., U.S. A5 139
Berseba, Nmb. D2 56
Bershad', Ukr. E10 20
Berthierville, P.Q., Can. . . . C4 90
Berthoud, Co., U.S. A5 99
Berthoud Pass, Co., U.S. . . B5 99
Bertie, co., N.C., U.S. A5 126
Bertoua, Cam. C2 54
Bertrand, Mo., U.S. E8 118
Bertrand, Ne., U.S. D6 120
Berwick, Ia., U.S. e8 108
Berwick, La., U.S. E4 111

Berwick, Me., U.S. E2 112
Berwick, Pa., U.S. D9 131
Berwick-upon-Tweed, Eng., U.K. C6 12
Berwyn, Ab., Can. A2 84
Berwyn, Il., U.S. k9 106
Berwyn, Pa., U.S. o20 131
Besalampy, Madag. B7 56
Besançon, Fr. D9 16
Beskids, mts., Eur. E5 20
Beskra, Alg. D6 48
Beslan, Russia A11 44
Besni, Tur. D7 44
Bessemer, Al., U.S. B3 94
Bessemer, Mi., U.S. n11 115
Bessemer, Pa., U.S. E1 131
Bessemer City, N.C., U.S. . . B1 126
Bétaré Oya, Cam. B2 54
Betatakin Ruin, hist., Az., U.S. A5 96
Bethalto, Il., U.S. E3 106
Bethanien, Nmb. D2 56
Bethany, Ct., U.S. D4 100
Bethany, Il., U.S. D5 106
Bethany, Mo., U.S. A3 118
Bethany, Ok., U.S. B4 129
Bethany, W.V., U.S. A4 141
Bethany Beach, De., U.S. . . F5 101
Bethel, Ak., U.S. C7 95
Bethel, Ct., U.S. D2 100
Bethel, Me., U.S. D2 112
Bethel, N.C., U.S. B5 126
Bethel, Oh., U.S. D1 128
Bethel, Vt., U.S. D3 138
Bethel Park, Pa., U.S. k14 131
Bethel Springs, Tn., U.S. . . B3 135
Bethesda, Md., U.S. C3 113
Bethesda, Oh., U.S. B4 128
Bethlehem, S. Afr. D4 56
Bethlehem, Ct., U.S. C3 100
Bethlehem, N.H., U.S. B3 122
Bethlehem, Pa., U.S. E11 131
Bethlehem see Bayt Lahm, W.B. G6 44
Bethulie, S. Afr. E4 56
Betong, Malay. C4 36
Betong, Thai. E4 34
Betoota, Austl. F3 62
Betpak-Dala, des., Kaz. . . . E8 26
Betroka, Madag. C8 56
Betsiboka, stm., Madag. . . . B8 56
Betsie, Point, c., Mi., U.S. . D4 115
Betsy Layne, Ky., U.S. C7 110
Bettendorf, Ia., U.S. C7 108
Bettiah, India D4 40
Betūl, India E3 40
Betwa, stm., India D3 40
Betzdorf, Ger. E10 12
Beulah, Co., U.S. C6 99
Beulah, N.D., U.S. B4 127
Beulah, Lake, l., Ms., U.S. . B3 117
Beulaville, N.C., U.S. C5 126
Beverley Head, c., Nf., Can. D2 88
Beverly, Ma., U.S. A6 114
Beverly, N.J., U.S. C3 123
Beverly, Oh., U.S. C4 128
Beverly, W.V., U.S. C5 141
Beverly Hills, Ca., U.S. m12 98
Beverly Shores, In., U.S. . . A4 107
Bexar, co., Tx., U.S. E3 136
Bexley, Oh., U.S. m11 128
Beyla, Gui. E3 50
Beypazari, Tur. B4 44
Beyşehir, Tur. D4 44
Beyşehir Gölü, l., Tur. D4 44
Bežeck, Russia C6 22
Béziers, Fr. F8 16
Bhadohi, India D4 40
Bhadrachalam, India F4 40
Bhadrak, India E5 40
Bhadra Reservoir, res., India G3 40
Bhadrāvati, India G3 40
Bhāgalpur, India D5 40
Bhāgirathi see Ganges, stm., India D5 40
Bhakkar, Pak. D10 42
Bhaktapur, Nepal D5 40
Bhamo, Myan. B3 34
Bhandāra, India E3 40
Bharatpur, India D3 40
Bharūch, India E2 40
Bhātpāra, India E5 40
Bhāvnagar, India E2 40
Bhawānipatna, India F4 40
Bhilai, India E4 40
Bhīlwāra, India D3 40
Bhīma, stm., India F3 40
Bhind, India D3 40
Bhiwāni, India D3 40
Bhongīr, India F3 40
Bhopāl, India E3 40
Bhubaneshwar, India E5 40
Bhuj, India E1 40
Bhusāwal, India E3 40
Bhutan, ctry., Asia D6 40
Bia, Mount see Bia, Phou, mtn., Laos C4 34
Bia, Phou, mtn., Laos C4 34
Biafra, Bight of, Afr. C1 54
Biak, i., Indon. G10 32
Biała Podlaska, Pol. D7 20
Białogard, Pol. B4 20

Białystok, Pol. C7 20
Bianco, Monte (Blanc, Mont), mtn., Eur. B1 18
Biankouma, C. Iv. E3 50
Biaora, India E3 40
Biaro, Pulau, i., Indon. C7 36
Biarritz, Fr. F6 16
Bibala, Ang. A1 56
Bibb, co., Al., U.S. C2 94
Bibb, co., Ga., U.S. D3 103
Bibémi, Cam. B2 54
Biberach an der Riss, Ger. . F11 12
Bic, P.Q., Can. A9 90
Bic, Île du, i., P.Q., Can. . . A9 90
Biche, Lac la, l., Ab., Can. . B4 84
Bicknell, In., U.S. G3 107
Bīd, India F3 40
Bida, Nig. E6 50
Bīdar, India F3 40
Biddeford, Me., U.S. E2 112
Bidwell, Mount, mtn., Ca., U.S. B3 98
Biel, Switz. A1 18
Bielefeld, Ger. E11 12
Biella, Italy B2 18
Bielsko-Biała, Pol. E5 20
Bielsk Podlaski, Pol. C7 20
Bien Hoa, Viet. D5 34
Bienville, co., La., U.S. . . . B2 111
Bienville, Lac, l., P.Q., Can. g12 90
Big, stm., Mo., U.S. c7 118
Biga, Tur. B2 44
Big Bald, mtn., Ga., U.S. . . B2 103
Big Bald Mountain, mtn., N.B., Can. B3 87
Big Baldy, mtn., Id., U.S. . . E3 105
Big Baldy Mountain, mtn., Mt., U.S. D6 119
Big Bay De Noc, b., Mi., U.S. C4 115
Big Bear City, Ca., U.S. . . . E5 98
Big Belt Mountains, mts., Mt., U.S. D5 119
Big Bend, Wi., U.S. n11 142
Big Bend Dam, S.D., U.S. . C6 134
Big Bend National Park, Tx., U.S. E1 136
Big Birch Lake, l., Mn., U.S. E4 116
Big Black, stm., U.S. B3 112
Big Blue, stm., Ms., U.S. . . C3 117
Big Blue, stm., In., U.S. . . . E6 107
Big Burro Mountains, mts., N.M., U.S. E1 124
Big Cabin Creek, stm., Ok., U.S. A6 129
Big Coal, stm., W.V., U.S. . C3 141
Big Costilla Peak, mtn., N.M., U.S. A4 124
Big Creek, stm., Tn., U.S. . . e8 135
Big Creek Lake, res., Al., U.S. E1 94
Big Creek Peak, mtn., Id., U.S. E5 105
Big Cypress Indian Reservation, Fl., U.S. F5 102
Big Cypress Swamp, sw., Fl., U.S. F5 102
Big Darby Creek, stm., Oh., U.S. C2 128
Big Delta, Ak., U.S. C10 95
Big Duke Dam, N.C., U.S. . B2 126
Big Eau Pleine, stm., Wi., U.S. D3 142
Big Eau Pleine Reservoir, res., Wi., U.S. D4 142
Big Escambia Creek, stm., U.S. D2 94
Big Flats, N.Y., U.S. C4 125
Bigfork, Mt., U.S. B2 119
Big Fork, stm., Mn., U.S. . . B5 116
Biggs, Ca., U.S. C3 98
Big Hatchet Peak, mtn., N.M., U.S. F1 124
Big Hole, stm., Mt., U.S. . . E4 119
Big Hole National Battlefield, hist., Mt., U.S. E3 119
Big Horn, co., Mt., U.S. . . . E9 119
Big Horn, co., Wy., U.S. . . . B4 143
Bighorn Canyon National Recreation Area, U.S. . . . F8 119
Bighorn Lake, res., U.S. . . . E8 119
Big Horn Mountains, mts., Az., U.S. D2 96
Bighorn Mountains, mts., U.S. C6 92
Bighorn Mountains, mts., U.S. B5 143
Bight, Head of, b., Austl. . . G5 60
Big Kandiyohi Lake, l., Mn., U.S. E4 116
Big Lake, Mn., U.S. E5 116
Big Lake, Tx., U.S. D2 136
Big Lake, l., Me., U.S. C5 112
Biglerville, Pa., U.S. G7 131
Big Lookout Mountain, mtn., Or., U.S. C9 130
Big Lost, stm., Id., U.S. . . . F5 105
Big Mossy Point, c., Mb., Can. C2 86
Big Mountain, mtn., Nv., U.S. B2 121
Big Muddy, stm., Il., U.S. . . F4 106
Big Nemaha, stm., Ne., U.S. D10 120
Bignona, Sen. D1 50

Name	Map Ref.	Page
Big Otter, stm., Va., U.S.	C3	139
Big Pine Lake, l., Mn., U.S.	D3	116
Big Pine Mountain, mtn., Ca., U.S.	E4	98
Big Piney, Wy., U.S.	D2	143
Big Piney, stm., Mo., U.S.	D5	118
Bigpoint, Ms., U.S.	E5	117
Big Rapids, Mi., U.S.	E5	115
Big Rib, stm., Wi., U.S.	C3	142
Big River, Sk., Can.	D2	91
Big Sable Point, c., Mi., U.S.	D4	115
Big Sandy, Mt., U.S.	B6	119
Big Sandy, Tx., U.S.	C5	136
Big Sandy, stm., Az., U.S.	C2	96
Big Sandy, stm., Tn., U.S.	B3	135
Big Sandy, stm., Wy., U.S.	D3	143
Big Sandy, stm., U.S.	C2	141
Big Sandy Creek, stm., W.V., U.S.	C3	141
Big Sandy Lake, l., Mn., U.S.	D5	116
Big Sandy Reservoir, res., Wy., U.S.	D3	143
Big Sheep Mountain, mtn., Mt., U.S.	C11	119
Big Sioux, stm., U.S.	E9	134
Big Smoky Valley, val., Nv., U.S.	E4	121
Big Snowy Mountains, mts., Mt., U.S.	D7	119
Big Southern Butte, mtn., Id., U.S.	F5	105
Big South Fork, stm., Ky., U.S.	k13	110
Big Spring, Tx., U.S.	C2	136
Big Stone, co., Mn., U.S.	E2	116
Big Stone City, S.D., U.S.	B9	134
Big Stone Gap, Va., U.S.	f9	139
Big Stone Lake, l., U.S.	E2	116
Big Sunflower, stm., Ms., U.S.	B3	117
Big Thompson, stm., Co., U.S.	A5	99
Big Timber, Mt., U.S.	E7	119
Big Trout Lake, l., On., Can.	n17	89
Big Walnut Creek, stm., Oh., U.S.	m11	128
Big Wood, stm., Id., U.S.	F4	105
Bihać, Bos.	B5	18
Bīhar, India	D5	40
Bihār, prov., India	E5	40
Biharamulo, Tan.	D6	54
Bijagós, Arquipélago dos, is., Gui.-B.	D1	50
Bijāpur, India	F3	40
Bījār, Iran	E12	44
Bijeljina, Bos.	B7	18
Bijie, China	F9	28
Bijsk, Russia	D10	26
Bīkāner, India	D2	40
Bikar, atoll, Marsh. Is.	C10	58
Bikeqi, China	C10	28
Bikin, Russia	B14	28
Bikini, atoll, Marsh. Is.	C10	58
Bīkkū Bīttī, mtn., Libya	F8	48
Bikoro, D.R.C.	D3	54
Bilāspur, India	A4	40
Bilāspur, India	E4	40
Biläsuvar, Azer.	C13	44
Bila Tserkva, Ukr.	E11	20
Bilauktaung Range, mts., Asia	D3	34
Bilbao, Spain	F5	16
Bilecik, Tur.	B4	44
Biłgoraj, Pol.	D7	20
Bilhorod-Dnistrovs'kyi, Ukr.	F11	20
Bili, D.R.C.	C5	54
Bilk Creek Mountains, mts., Nv., U.S.	B3	121
Billerica, Ma., U.S.	A5	114
Billings, Mo., U.S.	D4	118
Billings, Mt., U.S.	E8	119
Billings, co., N.D., U.S.	B2	127
Billings Heights, Mt., U.S.	E8	119
Bill Williams, stm., Az., U.S.	C1	96
Bill Williams Mountain, mtn., Az., U.S.	B3	96
Bilma, Niger	C7	50
Bilohirs'k, Ukr.	G13	20
Bilopillia, Ukr.	D13	20
Biloxi, Ms., U.S.	E5	117
Biloxi, stm., Ms., U.S.	E4	117
Biloxi Bay, b., Ms., U.S.	f8	117
Biltmore Forest, N.C., U.S.	f10	126
Bimbo, C.A.R.	C3	54
Bimini Islands, is., Bah.	C9	76
Bīna-Etāwa, India	E3	40
Bindura, Zimb.	B5	56
Binga, D.R.C.	C4	54
Binga, Monte, mtn., Afr.	B5	56
Bingamon Creek, stm., W.V., U.S.	k10	141
Bingara, Austl.	F5	62
Bingen, Wa., U.S.	D4	140
Binger, Ok., U.S.	B3	129
Bingham, Me., U.S.	C3	112
Bingham, co., Id., U.S.	F6	105
Binghamton, N.Y., U.S.	C5	125
Bingöl, Tur.	C9	44
Binhai, China	E12	28
Binh Son, Viet.	C5	34
Binjai, Indon.	C1	36
Binongko, Pulau, i., Indon.	E6	36
Bintan, Pulau, i., Indon.	C2	36
Bintimani, mtn., S.L.	E2	50
Bintuhan, Indon.	D2	36
Bintulu, Malay.	C4	36
Bintuni, Indon.	D8	36
Binxian, China	B4	30
Binyang, China	B5	30
Bin-Yauri, Nig.	D5	50
Binzert see Bizerte, Tun.	C6	48
Biobío, stm., Chile	F3	72
Bioko, i., Eq. Gui.	C1	54
Birāk, Libya	E7	48
Bi'r al Wa'r, Libya	F7	48
Birao, C.A.R.	A4	54
Birch, stm., W.V., U.S.	C4	141
Birch Island, i., Mb., Can.	C2	86
Birch Lake, l., Mn., U.S.	C7	116
Birch River, Mb., Can.	C1	86
Birch Run, Mi., U.S.	E7	115
Birchy Bay, Nf., Can.	D4	88
Bird Creek, stm., Ok., U.S.	A6	129
Bird Island, Mn., U.S.	F4	116
Bird Island, i., N.C., U.S.	D4	126
Birdsboro, Pa., U.S.	F10	131
Birdum, Austl.	D5	60
Birecik, Tur.	D8	44
Birigui, Braz.	F1	74
Bīrjand, Iran	D7	42
Birmingham, Eng., U.K.	D6	12
Birmingham, Al., U.S.	B3	94
Birmingham, Mi., U.S.	F7	115
Birmitrapur, India	E4	40
Bīr Mogreïn, Maur.	A2	50
Birnin-Kebbi, Nig.	D5	50
Birnin Konni, Niger	D6	50
Birnin Kudu, Nig.	D6	50
Birobidžan, Russia	E15	26
Biron, Wi., U.S.	D4	142
Birsk, Russia	C10	22
Birtle, Mb., Can.	D1	86
Biržai, Lith.	H11	10
Bisbee, Az., U.S.	F6	96
Biscay, Bay of (Gascogne, Golfe de), b., Eur.	E5	16
Biscayne, Key, i., Fl., U.S.	s13	102
Biscayne Bay, b., Fl., U.S.	G6	102
Biscayne National Monument, Fl., U.S.	G6	102
Biscayne Park, Fl., U.S.	s13	102
Biscoe, N.C., U.S.	B3	126
Bishkek see Biškek, Kyrg.	E9	26
Bishop, Ca., U.S.	D4	98
Bishop, Tx., U.S.	F4	136
Bishop's Falls, Nf., Can.	D4	88
Bishopville, S.C., U.S.	C7	133
Biškek, Kyrg.	E9	26
Bislig, Phil.	E9	34
Bismarck, Il., U.S.	C6	106
Bismarck, Mo., U.S.	D7	118
Bismarck, N.D., U.S.	C5	127
Bismarck Archipelago, is., Pap. N. Gui.	G12	32
Bismarck Range, mts., Pap. N. Gui.	H11	32
Bismarck Sea, Pap. N. Gui.	G12	32
Bismil, Tur.	D9	44
Bison Peak, mtn., Co., U.S.	B5	99
Bissau, Gui.-B.	D1	50
Bissikrima, Gui.	D2	50
Bistineau, Lake, res., La., U.S.	B2	111
Bistriţa, Rom.	F8	20
Bitam, Gabon	C2	54
Bitlis, Tur.	C10	44
Bitola, Mac.	D8	18
Bitou, Burkina	D4	50
Bitter Creek, stm., Wy., U.S.	E4	143
Bitterfontein, S. Afr.	E2	56
Bitter Lake, l., S.D., U.S.	B8	134
Bitterroot, stm., Mt., U.S.	D2	119
Bitterroot Range, mts., Mt.	B4	92
Bitterroot Range, mts., U.S.	B3	105
Bitung, Indon.	C7	36
Biu, Nig.	D7	50
Biwabik, Mn., U.S.	C6	116
Biwa-ko, l., Japan	C3	31
Bixby, Ok., U.S.	B6	129
Biyang, China	C3	30
Bizerte, Tun.	C6	48
Bjala, Bul.	C10	18
Bjarëzina, stm., Bela.	C10	20
Bjelovar, Cro.	B6	18
Bjørnøya, i., Nor.	B3	26
Bla, Mali	D3	50
Black, stm., Ire.	D2	12
Black, stm., Ar., U.S.	B4	97
Black, stm., Az., U.S.	D5	96
Black, stm., La., U.S.	C4	111
Black, stm., Mi., U.S.	E8	115
Black, stm., N.C., U.S.	C4	126
Black, stm., N.Y., U.S.	B4	125
Black, stm., S.C., U.S.	D8	133
Black, stm., Vt., U.S.	E3	138
Black, stm., Wi., U.S.	D3	142
Blackall, Austl.	E4	62
Black Bear Creek, stm., Ok., U.S.	A4	129
Blackbeard Island, i., Ga., U.S.	E5	103
Blackburn, Mount, mtn., Ak., U.S.	C11	95
Black Butte, mtn., Mt., U.S.	F5	119
Black Butte Lake, res., Ca., U.S.	C2	98
Black Canyon, val., Co., U.S.	C3	99
Black Canyon City, Az., U.S.	C3	96
Black Canyon of the Gunnison National Monument, Co., U.S.	C3	99
Black Creek, B.C., Can.	E5	85
Black Creek, Wi., U.S.	D5	142
Black Creek, stm., S.C., U.S.	B7	133
Black Creek, stm.,	B1	124
Black Diamond, Ab., Can.	D3	84
Black Diamond, Wa., U.S.	B4	140
Blackduck, Mn., U.S.	C4	116
Black Eagle, Mt., U.S.	C5	119
Blakely, Ga., U.S.	E2	103
Blakely, Pa., U.S.	m18	131
Blackfalds, Ab., Can.	C4	84
Blackfeet Indian Reservation, Mt., U.S.	B4	119
Blackfoot, Id., U.S.	F6	105
Blackfoot, stm., Mt., U.S.	C3	119
Blackfoot Mountains, mts., Id., U.S.	F7	105
Blackfoot Reservoir, res., Id., U.S.	G7	105
Blackford, co., In., U.S.	D7	107
Black Forest, Co., U.S.	C6	99
Black Forest see Schwarzwald, mts., Ger.	F11	12
Blackhall Mountain, mtn., Wy., U.S.	E6	143
Black Hawk, S.D., U.S.	C2	134
Black Hawk, co., Ia., U.S.	B5	108
Black Hills, mts., U.S.	C2	134
Blackjack Mountain, mtn., Ga., U.S.	h8	103
Black Lake, P.Q., Can.	C6	90
Black Lake, l., Mi., U.S.	C6	115
Black Lake, l., N.Y., U.S.	f9	125
Black Lick, Pa., U.S.	F3	131
Black Mesa, mtn., Ok., U.S.	e8	129
Black Mingo Creek, stm., S.C., U.S.	D9	133
Blackmore, Mount, mtn., Mt., U.S.	E6	119
Black Mountain, N.C., U.S.	f10	126
Black Mountain, mtn., Az., U.S.	E4	96
Black Mountain, mtn., Co., U.S.	A5	99
Black Mountain, mtn., Id., U.S.	C3	105
Black Mountain, mtn., Mt., U.S.	D4	119
Black Mountain, mtn., Or., U.S.	B7	130
Black Mountain, mtn., Wy., U.S.	B5	143
Black Mountain, mtn., Wy., U.S.	D7	143
Black Mountain, mtn., U.S.	D7	110
Black Mountains, mts., Az., U.S.	B1	96
Black Peak, mtn., Az., U.S.	C1	96
Black Pine Peak, mtn., Id., U.S.	G5	105
Blackpool, Eng., U.K.	D5	12
Black Range, mts., N.M., U.S.	D2	124
Black River Falls, Wi., U.S.	D3	142
Black Rock, Ar., U.S.	A4	97
Black Rock, N.M., U.S.	B1	124
Black Rock, rock, S. Geor.	H8	69
Black Rock Desert, des., Nv., U.S.	B3	121
Black Rock Range, mts., Nv., U.S.	B3	121
Blacksburg, S.C., U.S.	A4	133
Blacksburg, Va., U.S.	C2	139
Black Sea	F5	22
Blacks Fork, stm., U.S.	E3	143
Blacks Harbour, N.B., Can.	D3	87
Blackshear, Ga., U.S.	E4	103
Blackstone, Ma., U.S.	B4	114
Blackstone, Va., U.S.	C5	139
Blackstone, stm., R.I., U.S.	B4	132
Black Thunder Creek, stm., Wy., U.S.	C8	143
Blackville, N.B., Can.	C4	87
Blackville, S.C., U.S.	E5	133
Black Volta, stm., Afr.	D4	50
Blackwalnut Point, c., Md., U.S.	C5	113
Black Warrior, stm., Al., U.S.	C2	94
Blackwater, stm., Ire.	D2	12
Blackwater, stm., Fl., U.S.	u15	102
Blackwater, stm., Md., U.S.	D5	113
Blackwater, stm., N.H., U.S.	D3	122
Blackwater, stm., Va., U.S.	D6	139
Blackwater Reservoir, res., N.H., U.S.	D3	122
Blackwell, Ok., U.S.	A4	129
Blackwood, N.J., U.S.	D2	123
Bladen, co., N.C., U.S.	C4	126
Bladenboro, N.C., U.S.	C4	126
Bladensburg, Md., U.S.	f9	113
Blades, De., U.S.	F3	101
Blagoevgrad, Bul.	D9	18
Blagoveščensk, Russia	D14	26
Blaine, Me., U.S.	B5	112
Blaine, Mn., U.S.	m12	116
Blaine, Tn., U.S.	C10	135
Blaine, Wa., U.S.	A3	140
Blaine, co., Id., U.S.	F4	105
Blaine, co., Mt., U.S.	B7	119
Blaine, co., Ne., U.S.	C6	120
Blaine, co., Ok., U.S.	B3	129
Blaine Lake, Sk., Can.	E2	91
Blair, Ne., U.S.	C9	120
Blair, Ok., U.S.	C2	129
Blair, W.V., U.S.	n12	141
Blair, Wi., U.S.	D2	142
Blair, co., Pa., U.S.	E5	131
Blairstown, Ia., U.S.	C5	108
Blairsville, Pa., U.S.	F3	131
Blake Island, i., Wa., U.S.	e11	140
Blakely, Ga., U.S.	E2	103
Blakely, Pa., U.S.	m18	131
Blake Plateau	E6	66
Blake Point, c., Mi., U.S.	h10	115
Blanc, Cap see Nouâdhibou, Râs, c., Afr.	B1	50
Blanc, Mont (Bianco, Monte), mtn., Eur.	B1	18
Blanca Peak, mtn., Co., U.S.	D5	99
Blanchard, La., U.S.	B2	111
Blanchard, Ok., U.S.	B4	129
Blanchard, stm., Oh., U.S.	A1	128
Blanchardville, Wi., U.S.	F4	142
Blanchester, Oh., U.S.	C2	128
Blanco, Tx., U.S.	D3	136
Blanco, co., Tx., U.S.	D3	136
Blanco, Cape, c., Or., U.S.	E2	130
Bland, Mo., U.S.	C6	118
Bland, co., Va., U.S.	C1	139
Blanding, Ut., U.S.	F6	137
Blandinsville, Il., U.S.	C3	106
Blanquilla, Isla, i., Ven.	C7	80
Blantyre, Mwi.	B5	56
Blasdell, N.Y., U.S.	C2	125
Blawnox, Pa., U.S.	k14	131
Bleckley, co., Ga., U.S.	D3	103
Bledsoe, co., Tn., U.S.	D8	135
Blekinge, hist. reg., Swe.	H6	10
Blende, Co., U.S.	C6	99
Blenheim, On., Can.	E3	89
Blenheim, N.Z.	p13	63c
Blennerhassett, W.V., U.S.	B3	141
Blind, stm., La., U.S.	h10	111
Blind River, On., Can.	A2	89
Blissfield, Mi., U.S.	G7	115
Blitar, Indon.	E4	36
Block Island, R.I., U.S.	h7	132
Block Island, i., R.I., U.S.	h7	132
Block Island Sound, strt., U.S.	G2	132
Bloemfontein, S. Afr.	D4	56
Bloemhof, S. Afr.	D4	56
Blois, Fr.	D7	16
Blommestein Meer see Brokopondo Stuwmeer, res., Sur.	C8	70
Blönduós, Ice.	l18	10a
Blood Mountain, mtn., Ga., U.S.	B3	103
Bloodsworth Island, i., Md., U.S.	D5	113
Bloodvein, stm., Can.	D3	86
Bloomer, Wi., U.S.	C2	142
Bloomfield, On., Can.	D7	89
Bloomfield, Ct., U.S.	B5	100
Bloomfield, Ia., U.S.	D5	108
Bloomfield, In., U.S.	F4	107
Bloomfield, Ky., U.S.	C4	110
Bloomfield, Mo., U.S.	E8	118
Bloomfield, Ne., U.S.	B8	120
Bloomfield, N.J., U.S.	h8	123
Bloomfield, N.M., U.S.	A2	124
Bloomfield Hills, Mi., U.S.	o15	115
Bloomingdale, Ga., U.S.	D5	103
Bloomingdale, Il., U.S.	k8	106
Bloomingdale, N.J., U.S.	A4	123
Bloomingdale, Tn., U.S.	C11	135
Blooming Prairie, Mn., U.S.	G6	116
Bloomington, Il., U.S.	C4	106
Bloomington, In., U.S.	F4	107
Bloomington, Mn., U.S.	F5	116
Bloomington, Tx., U.S.	E4	136
Bloomington, Wi., U.S.	F3	142
Bloomington, Lake, res., Il., U.S.	C5	106
Bloomsburg, Pa., U.S.	E9	131
Bloomville, Oh., U.S.	A2	128
Blossburg, Pa., U.S.	C7	131
Blossom, Tx., U.S.	C5	136
Blount, co., Al., U.S.	B3	94
Blount, co., Tn., U.S.	D10	135
Blountstown, Fl., U.S.	B1	102
Blountsville, Al., U.S.	A3	94
Blountville, Tn., U.S.	C11	135
Blowing Rock, N.C., U.S.	A1	126
Blue, stm., In., U.S.	H5	107
Blue, stm., Mo., U.S.	k10	118
Blue, stm., Ok., U.S.	C5	129
Blue Ash, Oh., U.S.	o13	128
Blue Buck Point, c., La., U.S.	E2	111
Blue Creek, W.V., U.S.	m13	141
Blue Creek, stm., W.V., U.S.	m13	141
Blue Cypress Lake, l., Fl., U.S.	E6	102
Blue Diamond, Nv., U.S.	G6	121
Blue Earth, Mn., U.S.	G4	116
Blue Earth, co., Mn., U.S.	G4	116
Blue Earth, stm., Mn., U.S.	G4	116
Bluefield, Va., U.S.	C1	139
Bluefield, W.V., U.S.	D3	141
Bluefields, Nic.	C3	80
Blue Grass, Ia., U.S.	C7	108
Blue Hill, Me., U.S.	D4	112
Blue Hill, Ne., U.S.	D7	120
Blue Hill Range, hills, Ma., U.S.	h11	114
Blue Hills, Ct., U.S.	B5	100
Blue Island, Il., U.S.	B6	106
Bluejoint Lake, l., Or., U.S.	E7	130
Blue Lake, Ca., U.S.	B2	98
Blue Mesa Reservoir, res., Co., U.S.	C3	99
Blue Mound, Il., U.S.	D4	106
Blue Mountain, Ms., U.S.	A4	117
Blue Mountain, mtn., Mt., U.S.	C12	119
Blue Mountain, mtn., N.M., U.S.	D2	124
Blue Mountain, mtn., Pa., U.S.	F6	131
Blue Mountain Lake, res., Ar., U.S.	B2	97
Blue Mountain Peak, mtn., Jam.	B4	80
Blue Mountains, mts., U.S.	B4	92
Blue Nile, stm., Afr.	H11	48
Blue Point, Me., U.S.	g7	112
Blue Rapids, Ks., U.S.	C7	109
Blue Ridge, Va., U.S.	C3	139
Blue Ridge, mts., U.S.	D11	92
Blue Ridge Summit, Pa., U.S.	G7	131
Blue Springs, Mo., U.S.	h11	118
Bluestone, stm., W.V., U.S.	D3	141
Bluestone Lake, res., U.S.	D4	141
Bluewell, W.V., U.S.	D3	141
Bluff, N.Z.	q12	63c
Bluff City, Tn., U.S.	C11	135
Bluff Creek, stm., Ok., U.S.	A4	129
Bluff Lake, res., Ms., U.S.	B5	117
Bluff Park, Al., U.S.	g7	94
Bluffs, Il., U.S.	D3	106
Bluffton, In., U.S.	C7	107
Bluffton, Oh., U.S.	B2	128
Bluffton, S.C., U.S.	G6	133
Blumenau, Braz.	D8	72
Bly, Or., U.S.	E5	130
Blying Sound, strt., Ak., U.S.	h17	95
Blyth, On., Can.	D3	89
Blythe, Ca., U.S.	F6	98
Blytheville, Ar., U.S.	B6	97
Bo, S.L.	E2	50
Boaco, Nic.	C2	80
Boa Esperança, Represa, res., Braz.	E11	70
Boalsburg, Pa., U.S.	E6	131
Boardman, Oh., U.S.	A5	128
Boardman, Or., U.S.	B7	130
Boa Vista, Braz.	C7	70
Boa Vista, i., C.V.	g10	50a
Boaz, Al., U.S.	A3	94
Bobai, China	E2	30
Bobaomby, Tanjona, c., Madag.	A8	56
Bobbili, India	F4	40
Bobcaygeon, On., Can.	C6	89
Bobo-Dioulasso, Burkina	D4	50
Bobonong, Bots.	C4	56
Bobrov, Russia	D16	20
Bobrynets', Ukr.	E12	20
Bobtown, Pa., U.S.	G2	131
Boby, mtn., Madag.	C8	56
Boca Chica Key, i., Fl., U.S.	H5	102
Boca Ciega Bay, b., Fl., U.S.	p10	102
Boca do Acre, Braz.	E6	70
Boca Grande, Fl., U.S.	F4	102
Bocaiúva, Braz.	E3	74
Bocaranga, C.A.R.	B3	54
Boca Raton, Fl., U.S.	F6	102
Bocas del Toro, Pan.	D3	80
Bochnia, Pol.	E6	20
Bochum, Ger.	E10	12
Boconó, Ven.	D5	80
Bocşa, Rom.	G6	20
Bodajbo, Russia	D13	26
Bodega Head, c., Ca., U.S.	C2	98
Bodélé, reg., Chad	C8	50
Boden, Swe.	D9	10
Bodhan, India	F3	40
Bodie Island, i., N.C., U.S.	B7	126
Bodkin Point, c., Md., U.S.	B5	113
Bodø, Nor.	C6	10
Bodrum, Tur.	D2	44
Boende, D.R.C.	C4	54
Boerne, Tx., U.S.	E3	136
Boeuf, stm., La., U.S.	C4	111
Boeuf, Lake, l., La., U.S.	k10	111
Boffa, Gui.	D2	50
Bogale, Myan.	C3	34
Bogalusa, La., U.S.	D6	111
Bogangolo, C.A.R.	C3	54
Bogart, Ga., U.S.	C3	103
Bogata, Tx., U.S.	C5	136
Boğazlıyan, Tur.	B6	44
Bogda Shan, mts., China	C5	28
Boger City, N.C., U.S.	B1	126
Bogo, Phil.	D8	34
Bogor, Indon.	E3	36
Bogorodick, Russia	C15	22
Bogotá, Col.	C5	70
Bogota, N.J., U.S.	h8	123
Bogué, Maur.	A2	50
Bogue Chitto, Ms., U.S.	D3	117
Bogue Chitto, stm., U.S.	D5	117
Bogue Inlet, b., N.C., U.S.	C5	126
Bogue Phalia, stm., Ms., U.S.	B3	117
Bo Hai, b., China	D11	28

Name	Map Ref.	Page
Bohai Haixia, strt., China	D12	28
Bohemia, hist. reg., Czech Rep.	E3	20
Bohodukhiv, Ukr.	D13	20
Bohol, i., Phil.	E8	34
Bohol Sea, Phil.	E8	34
Bohuslav, Ukr.	E11	20
Boiling Springs, N.C., U.S.	B1	126
Boiling Springs, Pa., U.S.	F7	131
Bois Blanc Island, i., Mi., U.S.	C6	115
Bois Brule, stm., Wi., U.S.	B2	142
Boischâtel, P.Q., Can.	C6	90
Bois-des-Filion, P.Q., Can.	p19	90
Bois de Sioux, stm., Mn., U.S.	E2	116
Boise, Id., U.S.	F2	105
Boise, co., Id., U.S.	F3	105
Boise City, Ok., U.S.	e8	129
Boissevain, Mb., Can.	E1	86
Boissevain, Va., U.S.	e10	139
Boistfort Peak, mtn., Wa., U.S.	C2	140
Bojeador, Cape, c., Phil.	C8	34
Bojnūrd, Iran	C7	42
Boké, Gui.	D2	50
Boknafjorden, strt., Nor.	G1	10
Boko, Congo	D2	54
Bokoro, Chad	D8	50
Bokungu, D.R.C.	D4	54
Bolama, Gui.-B.	D1	50
Bolbec, Fr.	C7	16
Bole, Ghana	E4	50
Bolesławiec, Pol.	D3	20
Boley, Ok., U.S.	B5	129
Bolgatanga, Ghana	D4	50
Bolhov, Russia	C14	20
Boli, China	B14	28
Bolingbrook, Il., U.S.	k8	106
Bolivar, Mo., U.S.	D4	118
Bolivar, Oh., U.S.	B4	128
Bolivar, Tn., U.S.	B3	135
Bolivar, W.V., U.S.	B7	141
Bolivar, co., Ms., U.S.	B3	117
Bolívar, Cerro, mtn., Ven.	B6	70
Bolivar, Lake, l., Ms., U.S.	B3	117
Bolívar, Pico, mtn., Ven.	B5	70
Bolivia, ctry., S.A.	G7	70
Bollinger, co., Mo., U.S.	D7	118
Bollnäs, Swe.	F7	10
Bolnisi, Geor.	B11	44
Bolobo, D.R.C.	D3	54
Bologna, Italy	B3	18
Bologoe, Russia	C5	22
Bolomba, D.R.C.	C3	54
Bol'šaja Murta, Russia	D11	26
Bolsena, Lago di, l., Italy	C3	18
Bol'šereck, Russia	D17	26
Bol'ševik, ostrov, i., Russia	B12	26
Bol'šezemel'skaja Tundra, reg., Russia	A9	22
Bol'šoj Begičev, ostrov, i., Russia	B13	26
Bol'šoj Enisej, stm., Russia	A7	28
Bol'šoj Kamen', Russia	B2	31
Bol'šoj Ljahovskij, ostrov, i., Russia	B16	26
Bolton, Eng., U.K.	D5	12
Bolton, Ms., U.S.	C3	117
Bolton Lakes, l., Ct., U.S.	B6	100
Bolton Landing, N.Y., U.S.	B7	125
Bolu, Tur.	B4	44
Bolvadin, Tur.	C4	44
Bolzano, Italy	A3	18
Boma, D.R.C.	E2	54
Bombay see Mumbai, India	F2	40
Bomberai, Semenanjung, pen., Indon.	D8	36
Bom Despacho, Braz.	B8	72
Bomdila, India	D6	40
Bom Jesus da Lapa, Braz.	D3	74
Bomongo, D.R.C.	C3	54
Bomoseen, Lake, l., Vt., U.S.	D2	138
Bomu, stm., Afr.	C4	54
Bon, Cap, c., Tun.	C7	48
Bon Accord, Ab., Can.	C4	84
Bon Air, Va., U.S.	C5	139
Bonaire, Ga., U.S.	D3	103
Bonaire, i., Neth. Ant.	C6	80
Bonanza Peak, mtn., Wa., U.S.	A5	140
Bonaparte, Mount, mtn., Wa., U.S.	A6	140
Bonasila Dome, mtn., Ak., U.S.	C7	95
Bonaventure, P.Q., Can.	A4	87
Bonavista, Nf., Can.	D5	88
Bonavista, Cape, c., Nf., Can.	D5	88
Bonavista Bay, b., Nf., Can.	D5	88
Bond, co., Il., U.S.	E4	106
Bondo, D.R.C.	C4	54
Bondo, D.R.C.	D4	54
Bondoukou, C. Iv.	E4	50
Bondsville, Ma., U.S.	B3	114
Bonduel, Wi., U.S.	D5	142
Bondurant, Ia., U.S.	C4	108
Bône see Annaba, Alg.	C6	48
Bone, Gulf of see Bone, Teluk, b., Indon.	D6	36
Bone, Teluk, b., Indon.	D6	36
Bone Lake, l., Wi., U.S.	C1	142
Bongandanga, D.R.C.	C4	54
Bongka, Indon.	D6	36
Bongo, Massif des, mts., C.A.R.	B4	54
Bongor, Chad	D8	50
Bonham, Tx., U.S.	C4	136
Bon Homme, co., S.D., U.S.	D8	134
Bonifacio, Strait of, strt., Eur.	D2	18
Bonifay, Fl., U.S.	u16	102
Bonin Islands see Ogasawara-guntō, is., Japan	F16	64
Bonita Springs, Fl., U.S.	F5	102
Bonkoukou, Niger	D5	50
Bonn, Ger.	E10	12
Bonneauville, Pa., U.S.	G7	131
Bonne Bay, b., Nf., Can.	D3	88
Bonner, co., Id., U.S.	A2	105
Bonners Ferry, Id., U.S.	A2	105
Bonner Springs, Ks., U.S.	C9	109
Bonnet Carre Floodway, La., U.S.	h11	111
Bonne Terre, Mo., U.S.	D7	118
Bonneville, co., Id., U.S.	F7	105
Bonneville Dam, U.S.	B4	130
Bonneville Peak, mtn., Id., U.S.	F6	105
Bonneville Salt Flats, pl., Ut., U.S.	C2	137
Bonney Lake, Wa., U.S.	B3	140
Bonnie Doone, N.C., U.S.	B4	126
Bonnie Rock, Austl.	G2	60
Bonny, Nig.	F6	50
Bonny Reservoir, res., Co., U.S.	B8	99
Bonnyville, Ab., Can.	B5	84
Bono, Ar., U.S.	B5	97
Bon Secour, Al., U.S.	E2	94
Bonthe, S.L.	E2	50
Bontoc, Phil.	C8	34
Booker, Tx., U.S.	A2	136
Booker T. Washington National Monument, Va., U.S.	C3	139
Boola, Gui.	E3	50
Boolaloo, Austl.	E2	60
Boomer, W.V., U.S.	C3	141
Boone, Ia., U.S.	B4	108
Boone, N.C., U.S.	A1	126
Boone, co., Ar., U.S.	A2	97
Boone, co., Ia., U.S.	B3	108
Boone, co., Il., U.S.	A5	106
Boone, co., In., U.S.	D4	107
Boone, co., Ky., U.S.	B5	110
Boone, co., Mo., U.S.	B5	118
Boone, co., Ne., U.S.	C7	120
Boone, co., W.V., U.S.	C3	141
Boone, stm., Ia., U.S.	B4	108
Boone Lake, res., Tn., U.S.	C11	135
Booneville, Ar., U.S.	B2	97
Booneville, Ms., U.S.	A5	117
Boonsboro, Md., U.S.	A2	113
Boonton, N.J., U.S.	B4	123
Boonville, In., U.S.	H3	107
Boonville, Mo., U.S.	C5	118
Boonville, N.C., U.S.	A2	126
Boonville, N.Y., U.S.	B5	125
Boosaaso, Som.	H14	48
Boothbay Harbor, Me., U.S.	E3	112
Boothia, Gulf of, b., Nu., Can.	D21	82
Booths Creek, stm., W.V., U.S.	h11	141
Boothville, La., U.S.	E6	111
Bophuthatswana, hist. reg., S. Afr.	D4	56
Bopolu, Lib.	E2	50
Bor, Sudan	I11	48
Bor, Tur.	C4	44
Bor, Yugo.	B9	18
Borah Peak, mtn., Id., U.S.	E5	105
Borås, Swe.	H5	10
Borba, Braz.	D8	70
Bordeaux, Fr.	E6	16
Borden, co., Tx., U.S.	C2	136
Bordentown, N.J., U.S.	C3	123
Bordj Bou Arreridj, Alg.	J9	16
Bordj Omar Idriss, Alg.	E6	48
Bordoy, i., Far. Is.	n23	10a
Borgarnes, Ice.	l17	10a
Borger, Tx., U.S.	B2	136
Borgholm, Swe.	H7	10
Borgne, Lake, b., La., U.S.	D6	111
Borisoglebsk, Russia	D7	22
Borken, Ger.	E10	12
Borkou, reg., Chad	C8	50
Borlänge, Swe.	F6	10
Borneo (Kalimantan), i., Asia	D4	36
Bornholm, i., Den.	I6	10
Borno, prov., Nig.	D7	50
Borogoncy, Russia	C15	26
Boromo, Burkina	D4	50
Boron, Ca., U.S.	E5	98
Borongan, Phil.	D9	34
Boroviči, Russia	D5	26
Borrego Springs, Ca., U.S.	F5	98
Borroloola, Austl.	C6	62
Borşa, Rom.	B8	20
Borūjerd, Iran	D5	42
Boryslav, Ukr.	E7	20
Boryspil', Ukr.	D11	20
Borzja, Russia	D13	26
Boržomi, Geor.	B10	44
Bosanski Novi, Bos.	B6	18
Boscobel, Wi., U.S.	E3	142
Bose, China	G9	28
Boshan, China	D11	28
Bosna, stm., Bos.	B6	18
Bosnia and Herzegovina, ctry., Eur.	B6	18
Bosnik, Indon.	G10	32
Bosobolo, D.R.C.	C3	54
Bosporus see İstanbul Boğazı, strt., Tur.	B3	44
Bosque, co., Tx., U.S.	D4	136
Bossangoa, C.A.R.	B3	54
Bossembélé, C.A.R.	B3	54
Bossentélé, C.A.R.	B3	54
Bossier, co., La., U.S.	B2	111
Bossier City, La., U.S.	B2	111
Bostān, Iran	G13	44
Bosten Hu, l., China	C5	28
Boston, Eng., U.K.	D6	12
Boston, Ga., U.S.	F3	103
Boston, Ma., U.S.	B5	114
Boston Bay, b., Ma., U.S.	B6	114
Boston Mountains, mts., Ar., U.S.	B2	97
Boswell, In., U.S.	C3	107
Boswell, Ok., U.S.	C6	129
Boswell, Pa., U.S.	F3	131
Botetourt, co., Va., U.S.	C3	139
Bothell, Wa., U.S.	B3	140
Bothnia, Gulf of, b., Eur.	F8	10
Bothwell, On., Can.	E3	89
Botkins, Oh., U.S.	B1	128
Botlih, Russia	A12	44
Botoşani, Rom.	F9	20
Bo Trach, Viet.	C5	34
Botswana, ctry., Afr.	C3	56
Bottineau, N.D., U.S.	A5	127
Bottineau, co., N.D., U.S.	A4	127
Botucatu, Braz.	F2	74
Botwood, Nf., Can.	D4	88
Bouaflé, C. Iv.	E3	50
Bouaké, C. Iv.	E3	50
Bouar, C.A.R.	B3	54
Bouarfa, Mor.	E3	14
Bouca, C.A.R.	B3	54
Boucherville, P.Q., Can.	D4	90
Bouctouche, N.B., Can.	C5	87
Boudreaux, Lake, l., La., U.S.	E5	111
Bougainville, i., Pap. N. Gui.	B6	62
Bougainville, Détroit de, strt., Vanuatu	k9	62a
Bougie see Bejaïa, Alg.	C6	48
Bougouni, Mali	D3	50
Bouïra, Alg.	C5	48
Boujdour, Cap, c., W. Sah.	A2	50
Boulder, Co., U.S.	A5	99
Boulder, Mt., U.S.	D4	119
Boulder, co., Co., U.S.	A5	99
Boulder City, Nv., U.S.	H7	121
Boulevard Heights, Md., U.S.	f9	113
Boulia, Austl.	E2	62
Boulogne-sur-Mer, Fr.	B7	16
Boulsa, Burkina	D4	50
Bouna, C. Iv.	E4	50
Boundary, co., Id., U.S.	A2	105
Boundary Bay, b., Wa., U.S.	A3	140
Boundary Peak, mtn., Nv., U.S.	F3	121
Bound Brook, N.J., U.S.	B3	123
Boundiali, C. Iv.	E3	50
Bountiful, Ut., U.S.	C4	137
Bounty Islands, is., N.Z.	M21	64
Bounty Trough	M20	64
Bourail, N. Cal.	l9	62a
Bourbeuse, stm., Mo., U.S.	C6	118
Bourbon, In., U.S.	B5	107
Bourbon, Mo., U.S.	C6	118
Bourbon, co., Ks., U.S.	E9	109
Bourbon, co., Ky., U.S.	B5	110
Bourbonnais, Il., U.S.	B6	106
Bourem, Mali	C4	50
Bourg, La., U.S.	E5	111
Bourg-en-Bresse, Fr.	D9	16
Bourges, Fr.	D8	16
Bourgogne, hist. reg., Fr.	D9	16
Bourke, Austl.	G4	62
Bournemouth, Eng., U.K.	E5	12
Bou Saâda, Alg.	C5	48
Bousso, Chad	D8	50
Boutilimit, Maur.	C2	50
Boutte, La., U.S.	k11	111
Bouvetøya, i., Ant.	B5	64
Bouza, Niger	D6	50
Bovey, Mn., U.S.	C5	116
Bovina, Tx., U.S.	B1	136
Bow, N.H., U.S.	D3	122
Bow, stm., Ab., Can.	D4	84
Bowden, Ab., Can.	D4	84
Bowdish Reservoir, res., R.I., U.S.	B1	132
Bowdon, Ga., U.S.	C1	103
Bowen, Austl.	D4	62
Bowen, Il., U.S.	C2	106
Bowie, Az., U.S.	E6	96
Bowie, Md., U.S.	C4	113
Bowie, Tx., U.S.	C4	136
Bowie, co., Tx., U.S.	C5	136
Bow Island, Ab., Can.	E5	84
Bow Lake, l., N.H., U.S.	D4	122
Bowling Green, Fl., U.S.	E5	102
Bowling Green, Ky., U.S.	D3	110
Bowling Green, Mo., U.S.	B6	118
Bowling Green, Oh., U.S.	A2	128
Bowling Green, S.C., U.S.	A5	133
Bowling Green, Va., U.S.	B5	139
Bowling Green, Cape, c., Austl.	D4	62
Bowman, Ga., U.S.	B3	103
Bowman, N.D., U.S.	C2	127
Bowman, S.C., U.S.	E6	133
Bowman, co., N.D., U.S.	C2	127
Bowman Creek, stm., Pa., U.S.	m16	131
Bowman-Haley Lake, res., N.D., U.S.	C2	127
Bowral, Austl.	G5	62
Bowron, stm., B.C., Can.	C7	85
Bowstring Lake, l., Mn., U.S.	C5	116
Box Butte, co., Ne., U.S.	B2	120
Box Butte Reservoir, res., Ne., U.S.	B2	120
Box Elder, S.D., U.S.	C2	134
Box Elder, co., Ut., U.S.	B2	137
Boxford, Ma., U.S.	A6	114
Boxing, China	B4	30
Boyabat, Tur.	B6	44
Boyang, China	D4	30
Boyce, La., U.S.	C3	111
Boyceville, Wi., U.S.	C1	142
Boyd, Tx., U.S.	C4	136
Boyd, co., Ky., U.S.	B7	110
Boyd, co., Ne., U.S.	B7	120
Boyden, Ia., U.S.	A2	108
Boyd Lake, l., Me., U.S.	C4	112
Boyer, stm., Ia., U.S.	C2	108
Boyertown, Pa., U.S.	F10	131
Boykins, Va., U.S.	D5	139
Boyle, Ab., Can.	B4	84
Boyle, Ms., U.S.	B3	117
Boyle, co., Ky., U.S.	C5	110
Boyne City, Mi., U.S.	C6	115
Boynton Beach, Fl., U.S.	F6	102
Boyoma Falls see Stanley Falls, wtfl, D.R.C.	C5	54
Boysen Reservoir, res., Wy., U.S.	C4	143
Boys Town, Ne., U.S.	g12	120
Bozeman, Mt., U.S.	E5	119
Bozeman Pass, Mt., U.S.	E6	119
Bozhen, China	D11	28
Bozhou, China	C4	30
Bozoum, C.A.R.	B3	54
Bozova, Tur.	D8	44
Bozüyük, Tur.	C3	44
Bra, Italy	B1	18
Bracebridge, On., Can.	B5	89
Bräcke, Swe.	E6	10
Bracken, co., Ky., U.S.	B5	110
Brackenridge, Pa., U.S.	h15	131
Brackettville, Tx., U.S.	E2	136
Brad, Rom.	F7	20
Braddock, Pa., U.S.	k14	131
Braddock Heights, Md., U.S.	B2	113
Braddock Point, c., S.C., U.S.	G6	133
Bradenton, Fl., U.S.	E4	102
Bradenville, Pa., U.S.	F3	131
Bradford, Eng., U.K.	D5	12
Bradford, Ar., U.S.	B4	97
Bradford, Oh., U.S.	B1	128
Bradford, Pa., U.S.	C4	131
Bradford, R.I., U.S.	F2	132
Bradford, Tn., U.S.	A3	135
Bradford, Vt., U.S.	D4	138
Bradford, co., Fl., U.S.	C4	102
Bradford, co., Pa., U.S.	C8	131
Bradford [West Gwillimbury], On., Can.	C5	89
Bradfordwoods, Pa., U.S.	h13	131
Bradley, Il., U.S.	B6	106
Bradley, Me., U.S.	D4	112
Bradley, W.V., U.S.	D3	141
Bradley, co., Ar., U.S.	D3	97
Bradley, co., Tn., U.S.	D9	135
Bradley Beach, N.J., U.S.	C4	123
Bradner, Oh., U.S.	A2	128
Bradshaw, Md., U.S.	B5	113
Bradshaw Mountains, mts., Az., U.S.	C3	96
Brady, Tx., U.S.	D3	136
Braga, Port.	D2	16
Bragado, Arg.	F5	72
Bragança, Braz.	B2	74
Bragança, Port.	G3	16
Braham, Mn., U.S.	E5	116
Brāhmanbāria, Bngl.	E6	40
Brahmapur, India	F4	40
Brahmaputra (Yarlung), stm., Asia	D6	40
Braidwood, Il., U.S.	B5	106
Brăila, Rom.	G9	20
Brainerd, Mn., U.S.	D4	116
Braintree, Ma., U.S.	B5	114
Brampton, On., Can.	D5	89
Bramwell, W.V., U.S.	D3	141
Branch, co., Mi., U.S.	G5	115
Branch, stm., R.I., U.S.	B3	132
Branch, stm., Wi., U.S.	h10	142
Branch Lake, l., Me., U.S.	D4	112
Branch Village, R.I., U.S.	B3	132
Branchville, S.C., U.S.	E6	133
Branco, stm., Braz.	C7	70
Brandberg, mtn., Nmb.	C1	56
Brandenburg, Ger.	D13	12
Brandenburg, Ky., U.S.	C3	110
Brandon, Mb., Can.	E2	86
Brandon, Fl., U.S.	E4	102
Brandon, Ms., U.S.	C4	117
Brandon, S.C., U.S.	B3	133
Brandon, S.D., U.S.	D9	134
Brandon, Vt., U.S.	D2	138
Brandon, Wi., U.S.	E5	142
Brandvlei, S. Afr.	E3	56
Brandy Peak, mtn., Or., U.S.	E3	130
Brandywine, Md., U.S.	C4	113
Brandywine Creek, stm., U.S.	A3	101
Branford, Ct., U.S.	D4	100
Branford Hills, Ct., U.S.	D4	100
Branson, Mo., U.S.	E4	118
Brantford, On., Can.	D4	89
Brantley, Al., U.S.	D3	94
Brantley, co., Ga., U.S.	E4	103
Brant Rock, Ma., U.S.	B6	114
Brantville, N.B., Can.	B5	87
Bras d'Or Lake, l., N.S., Can.	D9	87
Brasil, ctry., S.A.	D2	74
Brasiléia, Braz.	F6	70
Brasília, Braz.	E2	74
Braşov, Rom.	G8	20
Brasstown Bald, mtn., Ga., U.S.	B3	103
Brassua Lake, res., Me., U.S.	C3	112
Bratenahl, Oh., U.S.	g9	128
Bratislava, Slvk.	E4	20
Bratsk, Russia	D12	26
Bratskoe vodohranilišče, res., Russia	D12	26
Bratsk Reservoir see Bratskoe vodohranilišče, res., Russia	D12	26
Brattleboro, Vt., U.S.	F3	138
Braunau am Inn, Aus.	F13	12
Braunschweig, Ger.	D12	12
Brava, i., C.V.	h10	50a
Bravo (Rio Grande), stm., N.A.	B5	78
Brawley, Ca., U.S.	F6	98
Brawley Peaks, mts., Nv., U.S.	E3	121
Braxton, co., W.V., U.S.	C4	141
Bray, Ok., U.S.	C4	129
Braymer, Mo., U.S.	B4	118
Brazeau, stm., Ab., Can.	C2	84
Brazil, In., U.S.	E3	107
Brazil, ctry., S.A.	D5	68
Brazil Basin	J11	66
Brazoria, Tx., U.S.	r14	136
Brazoria, co., Tx., U.S.	E5	136
Brazos, co., Tx., U.S.	D4	136
Brazos, stm., Tx., U.S.	D4	136
Brazzaville, Congo	D3	54
Brčko, Bos.	B7	18
Brea, Ca., U.S.	n13	98
Breakenridge, Mount, mtn., B.C., Can.	E7	85
Breathitt, co., Ky., U.S.	C6	110
Breaux Bridge, La., U.S.	D4	111
Breckenridge, Co., U.S.	B4	99
Breckenridge, Mi., U.S.	E6	115
Breckenridge, Mn., U.S.	D2	116
Breckenridge, Tx., U.S.	C3	136
Breckinridge, co., Ky., U.S.	C3	110
Brecksville, Oh., U.S.	A4	128
Břeclav, Czech Rep.	E4	20
Breda, Neth.	E9	12
Bredasdorp, S. Afr.	E3	56
Bredy, Russia	D11	22
Breese, Il., U.S.	E4	106
Breidafjördur, b., Ice.	l17	10a
Brejo, Braz.	D11	70
Bremen, Ger.	D11	12
Bremen, Ga., U.S.	C1	103
Bremen, In., U.S.	B5	107
Bremen, Oh., U.S.	C3	128
Bremer, co., Ia., U.S.	B5	108
Bremer Bay, Austl.	G2	60
Bremerhaven, Ger.	D11	12
Bremerton, Wa., U.S.	B3	140
Bremond, Tx., U.S.	D4	136
Brenham, Tx., U.S.	D4	136
Brenner Pass, Eur.	A3	18
Brent, Al., U.S.	C2	94
Brent, Fl., U.S.	u14	102
Brentwood, Ca., U.S.	h9	98
Brentwood, Md., U.S.	f9	113
Brentwood, Mo., U.S.	f13	118
Brentwood, N.Y., U.S.	E7	125
Brentwood, Pa., U.S.	k14	131
Brentwood, S.C., U.S.	k11	133
Brentwood, Tn., U.S.	A5	135
Brescia, Italy	B3	18
Breslau see Wrocław, Pol.	D4	20
Bressuire, Fr.	D6	16
Brèst, Bela.	C7	20
Brest, Fr.	C4	16
Bretagne, hist. reg., Fr.	C5	16
Breton, Pertuis, strt., Fr.	D6	16
Breton Islands, is., La., U.S.	E6	111
Breton Sound, strt., La., U.S.	E6	111
Breueh, Pulau, i., Indon.	E1	32
Brevard, N.C., U.S.	f10	126
Brevard, co., Fl., U.S.	E6	102
Breves, Braz.	B1	74
Brevoort Lake, l., Mi., U.S.	B6	115
Brewer, Me., U.S.	D4	112
Brewster, Ma., U.S.	C7	114

Name	Map Ref.	Page
Brewster, N.Y., U.S.	D7	125
Brewster, Oh., U.S.	B4	128
Brewster, Wa., U.S.	A6	140
Brewster, co., Tx., U.S.	E1	136
Brewster, Kap, c., Grnld.	D35	82
Brewster Islands, is., Ma., U.S.	g12	114
Brewton, Al., U.S.	D2	94
Brezhnev see Naberežnye Čelny, Russia	D7	26
Bria, C.A.R.	B4	54
Brian Boru Peak, mtn., B.C., Can.	B4	85
Brian Head, mtn., Ut., U.S.	F3	137
Briceville, Tn., U.S.	C9	135
Brick [Township] N.J., U.S.	C4	123
Bridal Veil Falls, wtfl, Ut., U.S.	C4	137
Bridgehampton, N.Y., U.S.	n16	125
Bridgeport, Al., U.S.	A4	94
Bridgeport, Ct., U.S.	E3	100
Bridgeport, Il., U.S.	E6	106
Bridgeport, Mi., U.S.	E7	115
Bridgeport, Ne., U.S.	C2	120
Bridgeport, Oh., U.S.	B5	128
Bridgeport, Pa., U.S.	o20	131
Bridgeport, Tx., U.S.	C4	136
Bridgeport, W.V., U.S.	B4	141
Bridgeport, Wa., U.S.	B4	140
Bridger, Mt., U.S.	E8	119
Bridger Peak, mtn., Wy., U.S.	E5	143
Bridger Range, mts., Mt., U.S.	E6	119
Bridgeton, Mo., U.S.	C7	118
Bridgeton, N.J., U.S.	E2	123
Bridgetown, Austl.	G2	60
Bridgetown, Barb.	C7	80
Bridgetown, N.S., Can.	E4	87
Bridgeville, De., U.S.	F3	101
Bridgeville, Pa., U.S.	k13	131
Bridgewater, Ma., U.S.	C6	114
Bridgewater, N.J., U.S.	B3	123
Bridgewater, Va., U.S.	B4	139
Bridgman, Mi., U.S.	G4	115
Bridgton, Me., U.S.	D2	112
Bridgwater, Eng., U.K.	E5	12
Bridlington, Eng., U.K.	C6	12
Brielle, N.J., U.S.	C4	123
Brigantine, N.J., U.S.	E4	123
Brigantine Beach, N.J., U.S.	E4	123
Brigden, On., Can.	E2	89
Briggs Marsh, sw., R.I., U.S.	F6	132
Brigham City, Ut., U.S.	B3	137
Bright, Austl.	H4	62
Brighton, On., Can.	C7	89
Brighton, Eng., U.K.	E6	12
Brighton, Al., U.S.	B3	94
Brighton, Co., U.S.	B6	99
Brighton, Ia., U.S.	C6	108
Brighton, Il., U.S.	D3	106
Brighton, Mi., U.S.	F7	115
Brighton, N.Y., U.S.	B3	125
Brighton, Tn., U.S.	B2	135
Brighton Indian Reservation, Fl., U.S.	E5	102
Brikama, Gam.	D1	50
Brilliant, Al., U.S.	A2	94
Brilliant, Oh., U.S.	B5	128
Brillion, Wi., U.S.	D5	142
Brimfield, Il., U.S.	C4	106
Brindisi, Italy	D6	18
Brinkley, Ar., U.S.	C4	97
Brinnon, Wa., U.S.	B3	140
Brisbane, Austl.	F5	62
Briscoe, co., Tx., U.S.	B2	136
Bristol, N.B., Can.	C2	87
Bristol, Eng., U.K.	E5	12
Bristol, Ct., U.S.	C4	100
Bristol, In., U.S.	A6	107
Bristol, N.H., U.S.	C3	122
Bristol, R.I., U.S.	D5	132
Bristol, Tn., U.S.	C11	135
Bristol, Va., U.S.	f9	139
Bristol, Vt., U.S.	C2	138
Bristol, co., Ma., U.S.	C5	114
Bristol, co., R.I., U.S.	D5	132
Bristol Bay, b., Ak., U.S.	D7	95
Bristol Channel, strt., U.K.	E5	12
Bristol [Township], Pa., U.S.	F12	131
Bristow, Ok., U.S.	B5	129
British Columbia, prov., Can.	C6	85
British Guiana see Guyana, ctry., S.A.	B8	70
British Honduras see Belize, ctry., N.A.	B2	80
British Indian Ocean Territory, dep., Afr.	I10	64
British Isles, is., Eur.	C12	4
British Virgin Islands, dep., N.A.	E12	76
Britstown, S. Afr.	E3	56
Britt, Ia., U.S.	A4	108
Brittany see Bretagne, hist. reg., Fr.	C5	16
Britton, S.D., U.S.	B8	134
Brive-la-Gaillarde, Fr.	E7	16
Brjansk, Russia	D5	26
Brjuhoveckaja, Russia	G15	20
Brno, Czech Rep.	E4	20
Broad, stm., S.C., U.S.	C5	133
Broad Brook, Ct., U.S.	B5	100
Broadkill, stm., De., U.S.	E4	101
Broadkill Beach, De., U.S.	E5	101
Broad Run, stm., Va., U.S.	g11	139
Broad Sound, b., Austl.	E4	62
Broadus, Mt., U.S.	E11	119
Broadview Heights, Oh., U.S.	h9	128
Broadwater, co., Mt., U.S.	D5	119
Broadway, N.C., U.S.	B3	126
Broadway, Va., U.S.	B4	139
Brockman, Mount, mtn., Austl.	E2	60
Brockport, N.Y., U.S.	B3	125
Brockton, Ma., U.S.	B5	114
Brockton Reservoir, res., Ma., U.S.	h11	114
Brockville, On., Can.	C9	89
Brockway, Pa., U.S.	D4	131
Brodhead, Ky., U.S.	C5	110
Brodhead, Wi., U.S.	F4	142
Brodheadsville, Pa., U.S.	E11	131
Brodnica, Pol.	C5	20
Brody, Ukr.	D8	20
Broken Arrow, Ok., U.S.	A6	129
Broken Bow, Ne., U.S.	C6	120
Broken Bow, Ok., U.S.	C7	129
Broken Bow Lake, res., Ok., U.S.	C7	129
Broken Hill, Austl.	G3	62
Broken Hill see Kabwe, Zam.	A4	56
Broken Ridge,	L12	64
Brokopondo, Sur.	C8	70
Brokopondo Stuwmeer, res., Sur.	C8	70
Brome, Lac, l., P.Q., Can.	D5	90
Bromley Plateau	K10	66
Bromptonville, P.Q., Can.	D6	90
Bronson, Fl., U.S.	C4	102
Bronte, Tx., U.S.	D2	136
Bronson, Mi., U.S.	G5	115
Bronx, co., N.Y., U.S.	E7	125
Bronxville, N.Y., U.S.	h13	125
Brook, In., U.S.	C3	107
Brooke, co., W.V., U.S.	A4	141
Brookfield, N.S., Can.	D6	87
Brookfield, Ct., U.S.	D2	100
Brookfield, Il., U.S.	k9	106
Brookfield, Mo., U.S.	B4	118
Brookfield, Wi., U.S.	m11	142
Brookfield Center, Ct., U.S.	D2	100
Brookhaven, Ms., U.S.	D3	117
Brookhaven, W.V., U.S.	h11	141
Brookings, Or., U.S.	E2	130
Brookings, S.D., U.S.	C9	134
Brookings, co., S.D., U.S.	C9	134
Brookland, Ar., U.S.	B5	97
Brooklandville, Md., U.S.	g10	113
Brooklet, Ga., U.S.	D5	103
Brookline, Ma., U.S.	B5	114
Brooklyn, N.S., Can.	E5	87
Brooklyn, Ct., U.S.	B8	100
Brooklyn, Ia., U.S.	C5	108
Brooklyn, In., U.S.	E5	107
Brooklyn, Mi., U.S.	F6	115
Brooklyn, Ms., U.S.	D4	117
Brooklyn, Oh., U.S.	h9	128
Brooklyn, S.C., U.S.	B6	133
Brooklyn, Wi., U.S.	F4	142
Brooklyn Center, Mn., U.S.	E5	116
Brooklyn Park, Md., U.S.	h11	113
Brooklyn Park, Mn., U.S.	m12	116
Brookneal, Va., U.S.	C4	139
Brook Park, Oh., U.S.	h9	128
Brookport, Il., U.S.	F5	106
Brooks, Ab., Can.	D5	84
Brooks, Ky., U.S.	g11	110
Brooks, co., Ga., U.S.	F3	103
Brooks, co., Tx., U.S.	F3	136
Brooks Air Force Base, mil., Tx., U.S.	k7	136
Brookshire, Tx., U.S.	E5	136
Brookside, Al., U.S.	f7	94
Brookside, De., U.S.	B3	101
Brooks Range, mts., Ak., U.S.	B9	95
Brookston, In., U.S.	C4	107
Brooksville, Fl., U.S.	D4	102
Brooksville, Ky., U.S.	B5	110
Brooksville, Ms., U.S.	B5	117
Brookville, In., U.S.	F8	107
Brookville, Oh., U.S.	C1	128
Brookville, Pa., U.S.	D3	131
Brookville Lake, res., In., U.S.	E7	107
Brookwood, Al., U.S.	B2	94
Brookwood, N.J., U.S.	C4	123
Broomall, Pa., U.S.	p20	131
Broome, Austl.	D3	60
Broome, co., N.Y., U.S.	C5	125
Broomfield, Co., U.S.	B5	99
Brossard, P.Q., Can.	q20	90
Broussard, La., U.S.	D4	111
Broward, co., Fl., U.S.	F6	102
Browerville, Mn., U.S.	D4	116
Brown, co., Il., U.S.	D3	106
Brown, co., In., U.S.	F5	107
Brown, co., Ks., U.S.	C8	109
Brown, co., Mn., U.S.	F4	116
Brown, co., Ne., U.S.	B6	120
Brown, co., Oh., U.S.	D2	128
Brown, co., S.D., U.S.	B7	134
Brown, co., Tx., U.S.	D3	136
Brown, co., Wi., U.S.	D6	142
Brown, Point, c., Wa., U.S.	C1	140
Brown City, Mi., U.S.	E8	115
Brown Deer, Wi., U.S.	m12	142
Brownfield, Tx., U.S.	C1	136
Browning, Mt., U.S.	B3	119
Brownlee Dam, U.S.	E2	105
Brownlee Reservoir, res., U.S.	C10	130
Browns, stm., Vt., U.S.	B2	138
Browns Branch, stm., De., U.S.	E3	101
Brownsburg, P.Q., Can.	D3	90
Brownsburg, In., U.S.	E5	107
Brownsdale, Mn., U.S.	G6	116
Browns Inlet, b., N.C., U.S.	C5	126
Browns Mills, N.J., U.S.	D3	123
Browns Peak, mtn., Az., U.S.	D4	96
Brownstown, In., U.S.	G5	107
Browns Valley, Mn., U.S.	E2	116
Brownsville, Fl., U.S.	s13	102
Brownsville, Ky., U.S.	C3	110
Brownsville, Or., U.S.	C4	130
Brownsville, Pa., U.S.	F2	131
Brownsville, Tn., U.S.	B2	135
Brownsville, Tx., U.S.	G4	136
Brownton, Mn., U.S.	F4	116
Brownville Junction, Me., U.S.	C3	112
Brownwood, Tx., U.S.	D3	136
Brownwood, Lake, res., Tx., U.S.	D3	136
Broxton, Ga., U.S.	E4	103
Bruce, Ms., U.S.	B4	117
Bruce, Wi., U.S.	C2	142
Bruce, Mount, mtn., Austl.	E2	60
Bruce National Park, On., Can.	B3	89
Bruce Peninsula, pen., On., Can.	B3	89
Bruce Rock, Austl.	G2	60
Bruceton, Tn., U.S.	A3	135
Bruderheim, Ab., Can.	C4	84
Brugge, Bel.	E8	12
Bruin Point, mtn., Ut., U.S.	D5	137
Brule, co., S.D., U.S.	D6	134
Brule, stm., U.S.	C5	142
Brule Lake, l., Mn., U.S.	k9	116
Brumado, Braz.	D3	74
Brundidge, Al., U.S.	D4	94
Bruneau, stm., U.S.	G3	105
Brunei see Bandar Seri Begawan, Bru.	C4	36
Brunei, ctry., Asia	F6	34
Bruno, Sk., Can.	E3	91
Brunswick see Braunschweig, Ger.	D12	12
Brunswick, Ga., U.S.	E5	103
Brunswick, Md., U.S.	B2	113
Brunswick, Me., U.S.	E3	112
Brunswick, Oh., U.S.	A4	128
Brunswick, co., N.C., U.S.	C4	126
Brunswick, co., Va., U.S.	D5	139
Brunswick, Península, pen., Chile	H2	69
Brunswick Naval Air Station, mil., Me., U.S.	E3	112
Brush, Co., U.S.	A7	99
Brushy Mountains, mts., N.C., U.S.	B1	126
Brusly, La., U.S.	D4	111
Brusque, Braz.	D8	72
Brussels see Bruxelles, Bel.	E9	12
Brussels, On., Can.	D3	89
Bruxelles (Brussels), Bel.	E9	12
Bryan, Oh., U.S.	A1	128
Bryan, Tx., U.S.	D4	136
Bryan, co., Ga., U.S.	D5	103
Bryan, co., Ok., U.S.	D5	129
Bryans Road, Md., U.S.	C3	113
Bryant, Ar., U.S.	C3	97
Bryantville, Ma., U.S.	B6	114
Bryce Canyon National Park, Ut., U.S.	F3	137
Bryn Mawr, Wa., U.S.	e11	140
Bryson City, N.C., U.S.	f9	126
Brzeg, Pol.	D4	20
Bua Yai, Thai.	C4	34
Bu'ayrat al-Hasun, Libya	E7	14
Bubaque, Gui.-B.	D1	50
Bucak, Tur.	D4	44
Bucaramanga, Col.	B5	70
Buccaneer Archipelago, is., Austl.	D3	60
Buchanan, Lib.	E2	50
Buchanan, Ga., U.S.	C1	103
Buchanan, Mi., U.S.	G4	115
Buchanan, Va., U.S.	C3	139
Buchanan, co., Ia., U.S.	B6	108
Buchanan, co., Mo., U.S.	B3	118
Buchanan, co., Va., U.S.	e9	139
Buchans, Nf., Can.	D3	88
Bucharest see București, Rom.	G9	20
Buckatunna, Ms., U.S.	D5	117
Buckeye, Az., U.S.	D3	96
Buckeye Lake, Oh., U.S.	C3	128
Buckhannon, W.V., U.S.	C4	141
Buck Hill Falls, Pa., U.S.	D11	131
Buckhorn Lake, res., Ky., U.S.	C6	110
Buckingham, P.Q., Can.	D2	90
Buckingham, co., Va., U.S.	C4	139
Buckingham Indian Reservation, Fl., U.S.	E5	102
Buckley, Wa., U.S.	B3	140
Bucklin, Ks., U.S.	E4	109
Bucklin, Mo., U.S.	B5	118
Buck Mountain, mtn., Wa., U.S.	A6	140
Buckner, Mo., U.S.	h11	118
Bucks, co., Pa., U.S.	F11	131
Buckskin Mountains, mts., Az., U.S.	C2	96
Bucksport, Me., U.S.	D4	112
Bucksport, S.C., U.S.	D9	133
Buco Zau, Ang.	D2	54
București (Bucharest), Rom.	G9	20
Bucyrus, Oh., U.S.	B3	128
Buda, Tx., U.S.	D4	136
Budapest, Hung.	F5	20
Budaun, India	D3	40
Budd Lake, l., N.J., U.S.	B3	123
Bude, Ms., U.S.	D3	117
Budënnovsk, Russia	B4	42
Budjala, D.R.C.	C3	54
Buea, Cam.	C1	54
Buechel, Ky., U.S.	B4	110
Buena, N.J., U.S.	D3	123
Buena, Wa., U.S.	C5	140
Buena Esperanza, Arg.	E4	72
Buena Park, Ca., U.S.	n12	98
Buenaventura, Col.	C4	70
Buenaventura, Mex.	B3	78
Buena Vista, Co., U.S.	C4	99
Buena Vista, Fl., U.S.	D4	102
Buena Vista, Ga., U.S.	D2	103
Buena Vista, Va., U.S.	C3	139
Buena Vista, co., Ia., U.S.	B2	108
Buenos Aires, Arg.	E6	72
Buffalo, Ia., U.S.	C7	108
Buffalo, Mn., U.S.	E5	116
Buffalo, Mo., U.S.	D4	118
Buffalo, N.Y., U.S.	C2	125
Buffalo, Ok., U.S.	A2	129
Buffalo, S.C., U.S.	B4	133
Buffalo, Tx., U.S.	D5	136
Buffalo, W.V., U.S.	C3	141
Buffalo, Wi., U.S.	D2	142
Buffalo, Wy., U.S.	B6	143
Buffalo, co., Ne., U.S.	D6	120
Buffalo, co., S.D., U.S.	C6	134
Buffalo, co., Wi., U.S.	D2	142
Buffalo, stm., Ar., U.S.	B3	97
Buffalo, stm., Mn., U.S.	D2	116
Buffalo, stm., Tn., U.S.	B4	135
Buffalo, stm., Wi., U.S.	D2	142
Buffalo Bill Reservoir, res., Wy., U.S.	B3	143
Buffalo Center, Ia., U.S.	A4	108
Buffalo Creek, stm., W.V., U.S.	h10	141
Buffalo Creek, stm., W.V., U.S.	n12	141
Buffalo Creek, stm., U.S.	f8	141
Buffalo Grove, Il., U.S.	h9	106
Buffalo Lake, Mn., U.S.	F4	116
Buffalo Lake, l., Ab., Can.	C4	84
Buffalo Lake, res., Tx., U.S.	B1	136
Buffalo Lake, res., Wi., U.S.	E4	142
Buffumville Lake, res., Ma., U.S.	B4	114
Buford, Ga., U.S.	B2	103
Bug, stm., Eur.	C6	20
Buga, Col.	C4	70
Bugsuk Island, i., Phil.	E7	34
Bugt, China	B12	28
Bugul'ma, Russia	D9	22
Buguruslan, Russia	D9	22
Buhara, Uzb.	F8	26
Buhl, Id., U.S.	G4	105
Buhl, Mn., U.S.	C6	116
Buhler, Ks., U.S.	D6	109
Buies Creek, N.C., U.S.	B4	126
Buitepos, Nmb.	C2	56
Buj, Russia	C7	22
Bujnaksk, Russia	A12	26
Bujumbura, Bdi.	D5	54
Bukačača, Russia	D13	26
Bukama, D.R.C.	E5	54
Bukavu, D.R.C.	D5	54
Bukeya, D.R.C.	F5	54
Bukittinggi, Indon.	D2	36
Bukoba, Tan.	D6	54
Bula, Indon.	D8	36
Bulan, Phil.	D8	34
Bulan, Ky., U.S.	C6	110
Bulancak, Tur.	B8	44
Bulandshahr, India	D3	40
Bulanık, Tur.	C10	44
Bulawayo, Zimb.	C4	56
Buldan, Tur.	C3	44
Bulgan, Mong.	B8	28
Bulgaria, ctry., Eur.	C10	18
Bulkley, stm., B.C., Can.	B4	85
Bullaxaar, Som.	A8	54
Bull Creek, stm., S.D., U.S.	B3	134
Bullfinch, Austl.	G2	60
Bullfrog Creek, stm., Ut., U.S.	F5	137
Bullhead City, Az., U.S.	B1	96
Bull Island, i., S.C., U.S.	D9	133
Bull Island, i., S.C., U.S.	F8	133
Bull Island, i., S.C., U.S.	G6	133
Bullitt, co., Ky., U.S.	C4	110
Bull Mountain, mtn., Mt., U.S.	D4	119
Bulloch, co., Ga., U.S.	D5	103
Bullock, co., Al., U.S.	C4	94
Bullock Creek, Mi., U.S.	E6	115
Bull Run, stm., Va., U.S.	g11	139
Bullrun Rock, mtn., Or., U.S.	C8	130
Bulls Bay, b., S.C., U.S.	F8	133
Bulls Gap, Tn., U.S.	C10	135
Bull Shoals, Ar., U.S.	A3	97
Bull Shoals Lake, res., U.S.	A3	92
Bull Shoals Lake, res., U.S.	A3	97
Bully Creek Reservoir, res., Or., U.S.	C9	130
Bultfontein, S. Afr.	D4	56
Bumba, D.R.C.	C4	54
Bumping, stm., Wa., U.S.	C4	140
Buna, Tx., U.S.	D6	136
Bunbury, Austl.	G2	60
Buncombe, co., N.C., U.S.	f10	126
Bundaberg, Austl.	E5	62
Būndi, India	D3	40
Bungoma, Kenya	C6	54
Búðir, Ice.	I21	10a
Bungo-suidō, strt., Japan	E14	28
Bunia, D.R.C.	C6	54
Bunker Hill, Il., U.S.	D4	106
Bunker Hill, In., U.S.	C5	107
Bunker Hill, W.V., U.S.	m12	141
Bunker Hill, W.V., U.S.	B6	141
Bunker Hill, mtn., Nv., U.S.	D4	121
Bunkerville, Nv., U.S.	G7	121
Bunkie, La., U.S.	D3	111
Bunnell, Fl., U.S.	C5	102
Buntok, Indon.	D4	36
Bünyan, Tur.	C6	44
Buolkalah, Russia	B13	26
Buon Ma Thuot, Viet.	D5	34
Buor-Haja, guba, b., Russia	B15	26
Buqayq, Sau. Ar.	E5	42
Bura, Kenya	D7	54
Burang, China	C4	40
Buras, La., U.S.	E6	111
Buraydah, Sau. Ar.	E4	38
Burbank, Ca., U.S.	E4	98
Burbank, Il., U.S.	k9	106
Burbank, Wa., U.S.	C7	140
Burco, Som.	I14	48
Burdickville, R.I., U.S.	F2	132
Burdur, Tur.	D4	44
Burdur Gölü, l., Tur.	D4	44
Bureau, co., Il., U.S.	B4	106
Bureinskij hrebet, mts., Russia	D15	26
Büренhayrhan, Mong.	B6	28
Burfjord, Nor.	B10	10
Burgas, Bul.	C11	18
Burgaski Zaliv, b., Bul.	C11	18
Burgaw, N.C., U.S.	C5	126
Burgeo, Nf., Can.	E3	88
Burgersdorp, S. Afr.	E4	56
Burgettstown, Pa., U.S.	F1	131
Burgin, Ky., U.S.	C5	110
Burgo de Osma, Spain	G5	16
Burgos, Spain	F5	16
Burgundy see Bourgogne, hist. reg., Fr.	D9	16
Burhaniye, Tur.	C2	44
Burhānpur, India	B3	40
Burias Island, i., Phil.	D8	34
Burin, Nf., Can.	E4	88
Burin Peninsula, pen., Nf., Can.	E4	88
Buri Ram, Thai.	C4	34
Burjatija, state, Russia	D13	26
Burkburnett, Tx., U.S.	B3	136
Burke, S.D., U.S.	D6	134
Burke, co., Ga., U.S.	C4	103
Burke, co., N.C., U.S.	B1	126
Burke, co., N.D., U.S.	A3	127
Burke Channel, strt., B.C., Can.	C4	85
Burkesville, Ky., U.S.	D4	110
Burketown, Austl.	D2	62
Burkina Faso, ctry., Afr.	D4	50
Burk's Falls, On., Can.	B5	89
Burleigh, co., N.D., U.S.	C5	127
Burleson, Tx., U.S.	n9	136
Burleson, co., Tx., U.S.	D4	136
Burley, Id., U.S.	G5	105
Burlingame, Ca., U.S.	h8	98
Burlingame, Ks., U.S.	D8	109
Burlington, On., Can.	D5	89
Burlington, Co., U.S.	B8	99
Burlington, Ia., U.S.	D6	108
Burlington, Ks., U.S.	D8	109
Burlington, Ky., U.S.	A5	110
Burlington, Ma., U.S.	f11	114
Burlington, N.C., U.S.	A3	126
Burlington, N.D., U.S.	A4	127
Burlington, N.J., U.S.	C3	123
Burlington, Vt., U.S.	C2	138
Burlington, Wa., U.S.	A3	140
Burlington, Wi., U.S.	F5	142
Burlington, co., N.J., U.S.	D3	123
Burlington Beach, In., U.S.	B3	107
Burlington Junction, Mo., U.S.	A2	118
Burlit, U.S.	A2	31
Burma see Myanmar, ctry., Asia	B3	34
Burnaby, B.C., Can.	E6	85
Burnet, Tx., U.S.	D3	136
Burnet, co., Tx., U.S.	D3	136
Burnett, co., Wi., U.S.	C1	142
Burney, Ca., U.S.	B3	98
Burnham, Pa., U.S.	E6	131
Burnie, Austl.	I4	62
Burns, Or., U.S.	D7	130
Burns, Tn., U.S.	A4	135
Burns, Wy., U.S.	E8	143
Burns Flat, Ok., U.S.	B2	129
Burnside, Ky., U.S.	D5	110
Burns Lake, B.C., Can.	B5	85

Name	Map Ref.	Page

Burns Paiute Indian Reservation, Or., U.S. . **D7** 130
Burnsville, Mn., U.S. **F5** 116
Burnsville, Ms., U.S. **A5** 117
Burnsville, N.C., U.S. **f10** 126
Burnsville Lake, res., W.V., U.S. **C4** 141
Burnt Islands, Nf., Can. . . **E2** 88
Burnt Mills, Lake, l., Va., U.S. **k14** 139
Burntside Lake, l., Mn., U.S. **C6** 116
Burntwood, stm., Mb., Can. **B2** 86
Burra, Austl. **G2** 62
Burrel, Alb. **D8** 18
Burr Oak, Mi., U.S. **G5** 115
Burr Oak Reservoir, res., Oh., U.S. **C3** 128
Burrton, Ks., U.S. **D6** 109
Bursa, Tur. **B3** 44
Bûr Sa'îd, Egypt **D11** 48
Bûr Sûdân, Sudan **G12** 48
Burt, co., Ne., U.S. **C9** 120
Burt Lake, l., Mi., U.S. . . . **C6** 115
Burton, Mi., U.S. **F7** 115
Burton, Oh., U.S. **A4** 128
Burtts Corner, N.B., Can. . . **C3** 87
Buru, i., Indon. **D7** 36
Burullus, Buheirat el-, l., Egypt **G4** 44
Burundi, ctry., Afr. **D5** 54
Burwell, Ne., U.S. **C6** 120
Bury Saint Edmunds, Eng., U.K. **D7** 12
Busanga, D.R.C. **D4** 54
Bushman Land, hist. reg., S. Afr. **D2** 56
Bushnell, Fl., U.S. **D4** 102
Bushnell, Il., U.S. **C3** 106
Bush River, b., Md., U.S. . **B5** 113
Busia, Ug. **C6** 54
Businga, D.R.C. **C4** 54
Busira, stm., D.R.C. **D3** 54
Busko-Zdrój, Pol. **D6** 20
Buşrá ash-Shām, Syria . . **F7** 44
Busselton, Austl. **G2** 60
Busuanga Island, i., Phil. . **D8** 34
Busu-Djanoa, D.R.C. **C4** 54
Buta, D.R.C. **C4** 54
Butare, Rw. **D5** 54
Butaritari, atoll, Kir. **D11** 58
Bute Inlet, b., B.C., Can. . . **D5** 85
Butembo, D.R.C. **C5** 54
Butere, Kenya **C6** 54
Buthidaung, Myan. **B2** 34
Butiaba, Ug. **C6** 54
Butler, Al., U.S. **C1** 94
Butler, Ga., U.S. **D2** 103
Butler, In., U.S. **B8** 107
Butler, Ky., U.S. **B5** 110
Butler, Mo., U.S. **C3** 118
Butler, N.J., U.S. **B4** 123
Butler, Oh., U.S. **B3** 128
Butler, Pa., U.S. **E2** 131
Butler, Wi., U.S. **m11** 142
Butler, co., Al., U.S. **D3** 94
Butler, co., Ia., U.S. **B5** 108
Butler, co., Ks., U.S. **E7** 109
Butler, co., Ky., U.S. **C3** 110
Butler, co., Mo., U.S. **E7** 118
Butler, co., Ne., U.S. **C8** 120
Butler, co., Oh., U.S. **C1** 128
Butler, co., Pa., U.S. **E2** 131
Butner, N.C., U.S. **A4** 126
Buton, Pulau, i., Indon. . . . **D6** 36
Butrint, hist., Alb. **E8** 18
Buttahatchee, stm., U.S. . **B5** 117
Butte, Mt., U.S. **E4** 119
Butte, co., Ca., U.S. **C3** 98
Butte, co., Id., U.S. **F5** 105
Butte, co., S.D., U.S. **C2** 134
Butte des Morts, Lake, l., Wi., U.S. **D5** 142
Butte Mountains, mts., Nv., U.S. **D6** 121
Butternut Lake, l., Wi., U.S. **C5** 142
Butterworth, Malay. **B2** 36
Buttonwillow, Ca., U.S. . . . **E4** 98
Butts, co., Ga., U.S. **C3** 103
Butuan, Phil. **E9** 34
Buturlinovka, Russia **D16** 22
Buulobarde, Som. **C9** 54
Buur Gaabo, Som. **D8** 54
Buxton, N.C., U.S. **B7** 126
Büyük Ağrı Dağı see Ağrı Dağı, mtn., Tur. **C11** 44
Büyükmenderes, stm., Tur. **D2** 44
Buzuluk, Russia **D9** 22
Buzzards Bay, Ma., U.S. . . **C6** 114
Buzzards Bay, b., Ma., U.S. **C6** 114
Bwendi, D.R.C. **C5** 54
Bydgoszcz, Pol. **C5** 20
Byelorussia see Belarus, ctry., Eur. **C9** 20
Byers, Co., U.S. **B6** 99
Byesville, Oh., U.S. **C4** 128
Byhalia, Ms., U.S. **A4** 117
Bybaụ, Bela. **C11** 20
Bylas, Az., U.S. **D5** 96
Byng, Ok., U.S. **C5** 129
Byrdstown, Tn., U.S. **C8** 135
Byro, Austl. **F2** 60
Byron, Ga., U.S. **D3** 103
Byron, Il., U.S. **A4** 106
Byron, Mn., U.S. **F6** 116
Byron, Wy., U.S. **B4** 143

Byron, Cape, c., Austl. **F5** 62
Byron Bay, Austl. **F5** 62
Byrranga, gory, mts., Russia **B12** 26
Bytom, Pol. **D5** 20
Bytów, Pol. **B4** 20
Byzantium see İstanbul, Tur.**B3** 44

C

Caála, Ang. **F3** 54
Caatinga, Braz. **B8** 72
Cabadbaran, Phil. **E9** 34
Cabaiguán, Cuba **A4** 80
Caballo Mountains, mts., N.M., U.S. **E2** 124
Caballo Reservoir, res., N.M., U.S. **E2** 124
Cabanatuan, Phil. **C8** 34
Cabano, P.Q., Can. **B9** 90
Cabarrus, co., N.C., U.S. . . **B2** 126
Cabbage Swamp, sw., Fl., U.S. **m9** 102
Cabedelo, Braz. **C5** 74
Cabell, co., W.V., U.S. . . . **C2** 141
Cabeza del Buey, Spain . . **H4** 16
Cabimas, Ven. **A5** 70
Cabin Creek, W.V., U.S. . . **m13** 141
Cabin Creek, stm., W.V., U.S. **m13** 141
Cabinda, Ang. **E2** 54
Cabinet Gorge Reservoir, res., U.S. **B1** 119
Cabinet Mountains, mts., Mt., U.S. **B1** 119
Cabin John, Md., U.S. **C3** 113
Cabo, Braz. **C4** 74
Cabo Blanco, Arg. **G3** 69
Cabonga, Réservoir, res., P.Q., Can. **I24** 82
Cabool, Mo., U.S. **D5** 118
Caborca, Mex. **C2** 78
Cabot, Ar., U.S. **C3** 97
Cabot, Mount, mtn., N.H., U.S. **A4** 122
Cabot Head, c., On., Can. . **B3** 89
Cabrayıl, Azer. **C12** 44
Cabri, Sk., Can. **G1** 91
Cabrillo National Monument, Ca., U.S. . . **o15** 98
Caçador, Braz. **D7** 72
Čačak, Yugo. **C8** 18
Caçapava do Sul, Braz. . . . **E7** 72
Cacapon, stm., W.V., U.S. . **B6** 141
Cáceres, Braz. **G8** 70
Cáceres, Spain **H3** 16
Cache, Ok., U.S. **C3** 129
Cache, co., Ut., U.S. **B4** 137
Cache, stm., Ar., U.S. . . . **C4** 97
Cache, stm., Il., U.S. **F4** 106
Cache Bay, On., Can. **A5** 89
Cache Creek, B.C., Can. . . **D7** 85
Cache la Poudre, stm., Co., U.S. **A5** 99
Cache Mountain, mtn., Ak., U.S. **B10** 95
Cache Peak, mtn., Id., U.S. **G5** 105
Cachimbo, Serra do, mts., Braz. **E8** 70
Cachingues, Ang. **F3** 54
Cachoeira do Sul, Braz. . . **E7** 72
Cachoeiro de Itapemirim, Braz. **F8** 70
Cacolo, Ang. **F3** 54
Caconda, Ang. **A2** 56
Cactus Flat, pl., Nv., U.S. . **F5** 121
Cactus Peak, mtn., Nv., U.S.**F5** 121
Cacuaco, Ang. **E2** 54
Caculé, Braz. **A9** 72
Čadan, Russia **D11** 26
Caddo, Ok., U.S. **C5** 129
Caddo, co., La., U.S. **B2** 111
Caddo, co., Ok., U.S. **B3** 129
Caddo, stm., Ar., U.S. . . . **C2** 97
Caddo Creek, stm., Ok., U.S. **C4** 129
Caddo Lake, res., U.S. . . . **B2** 111
Cadillac, Mi., U.S. **D5** 115
Cadillac Mountain, mtn., Me., U.S. **D4** 112
Cadiz, Phil. **D8** 34
Cádiz, Spain **I3** 16
Cadiz, Ky., U.S. **D2** 110
Cadiz, Oh., U.S. **B4** 128
Cádiz, Golfo de, b., Eur. . . **I3** 16
Cadiz, Gulf of see Cádiz, Golfo de, b., Eur. **I3** 16
Cadott, Wi., U.S. **D2** 142
Čaek, Kyrg. **A2** 40
Caen, Fr. **C6** 16
Caernarfon, Wales, U.K. . . **D4** 12
Caesar Creek Lake, res., Oh., U.S. **C2** 128
Caetité, Braz. **D3** 74
Cagayan de Oro, Phil. **E8** 34
Cagayan Islands, is., Phil. . **E8** 34
Cagayan Sulu Island, i., Phil.**E7** 34
Čagda, Russia **D15** 26
Cagles Mill Lake, res., In., U.S. **F4** 107
Cagliari, Italy **E2** 18
Cagliari, Golfo di, b., Italy . **E2** 18
Caguas, P.R. **B6** 80
Cahaba, stm., Al., U.S. . . . **C2** 94
Cahama, Ang. **B1** 56
Cahokia, Il., U.S. **E3** 106

Cahora Bassa, Albufeira, res., Moz. **B5** 56
Cahors, Fr. **E7** 16
Cahul, Mol. **G10** 20
Caiapó, Serra do, mts., Braz.**B7** 72
Caibarién, Cuba **A4** 80
Caicara de Orinoco, Ven. . . **D6** 80
Caicó, Braz. **C4** 74
Caicos Islands, is., T./C. Is. **A5** 80
Caicos Passage, strt., N.A. . **A5** 80
Cailloma, Peru **B3** 72
Caillou Bay, b., La., U.S. . . **E5** 111
Caillou Lake, l., La., U.S. . . **E5** 111
Caimanera, Cuba **B4** 80
Cairnbrook, Pa., U.S. **F4** 131
Cairns, Austl. **A4** 62
Cairo see El-Qâhira, Egypt . **D11** 48
Cairo, Ga., U.S. **F2** 103
Cairo, Il., U.S. **F4** 106
Cairo, Ne., U.S. **D7** 120
Caiundo, Ang. **B3** 56
Cajamarca, Peru **E4** 70
Cajazeiras, Braz. **C4** 74
Calabar, Nig. **F6** 50
Calabozo, Ven. **B6** 70
Calagua Islands, is., Phil. . . **D8** 34
Calahorra, Spain **F6** 16
Calais, Fr. **B7** 16
Calais, Me., U.S. **C5** 112
Calama, Chile **B3** 69
Calamian Group, is., Phil. . . **D7** 34
Calamus, stm., Ne., U.S. . . **B6** 120
Calapan, Phil. **D8** 34
Călărași, Mol. **F10** 20
Călărași, Rom. **G9** 20
Calatayud, Spain **G6** 16
Calaveras, co., Ca., U.S. . . **C3** 98
Calayan Island, i., Phil. . . . **C8** 34
Calbayog, Phil. **D8** 34
Calcasieu, co., La., U.S. . . **D2** 111
Calcasieu, stm., La., U.S. . **D2** 111
Calcasieu Lake, l., La., U.S. **E2** 111
Calcasieu Pass, strt., La., U.S. **E2** 111
Calcutta see Kolkata, India . **E5** 40
Calcutta, Oh., U.S. **B5** 128
Calcutta Lake, l., Nv., U.S. . **B2** 121
Caldas da Rainha, Port. . . . **H2** 16
Caldera, Chile **C2** 69
Calderwood, Tn., U.S. **D10** 135
Caldron Falls Reservoir, res., Wi., U.S. **C5** 142
Caldwell, Id., U.S. **F2** 105
Caldwell, Ks., U.S. **E6** 109
Caldwell, N.J., U.S. **B4** 123
Caldwell, Oh., U.S. **C4** 128
Caldwell, Tx., U.S. **D4** 136
Caldwell, co., Ky., U.S. . . . **C2** 110
Caldwell, co., La., U.S. . . . **B3** 111
Caldwell, co., Mo., U.S. . . . **B3** 118
Caldwell, co., N.C., U.S. . . **B1** 126
Caldwell, co., Tx., U.S. . . . **E4** 136
Caledon, On., Can. **D5** 89
Caledonia, Mi., U.S. **F5** 115
Caledonia, Mn., U.S. **G7** 116
Caledonia, Ms., U.S. **B5** 117
Caledonia, N.Y., U.S. **C3** 125
Caledonia, co., Vt., U.S. . . **C4** 138
Calera, Al., U.S. **B3** 94
Calera, Ok., U.S. **D5** 129
Calexico, Ca., U.S. **F6** 98
Calgary, Ab., Can. **D3** 84
Calhoun, Ga., U.S. **B2** 103
Calhoun, Ky., U.S. **C2** 110
Calhoun, co., Al., U.S. . . . **B4** 94
Calhoun, co., Ar., U.S. . . . **D3** 97
Calhoun, co., Fl., U.S. . . . **B1** 102
Calhoun, co., Ga., U.S. . . . **E2** 103
Calhoun, co., Ia., U.S. . . . **B3** 108
Calhoun, co., Il., U.S. **D3** 106
Calhoun, co., Mi., U.S. . . . **F5** 115
Calhoun, co., Ms., U.S. . . . **B4** 117
Calhoun, co., S.C., U.S. . . **D6** 133
Calhoun, co., Tx., U.S. . . . **E4** 136
Calhoun, co., W.V., U.S. . . **C3** 141
Calhoun City, Ms., U.S. . . . **B4** 117
Calhoun Falls, S.C., U.S. . . **C2** 133
Cali, Col. **C4** 70
Cametá, Braz. **B2** 74
Calico Rock, Ar., U.S. **A3** 97
Calicut see Kozhikode, India **G3** 40
Caliente, Nv., U.S. **F7** 121
California, Mo., U.S. **C5** 118
California, Pa., U.S. **F2** 131
California, state, U.S. **D4** 98
California, Golfo de, b., Mex. **B2** 78
California, Gulf of see California, Golfo de, b., Mex. **B2** 78
California Aqueduct, Ca., U.S. **E4** 98
Calipatria, Ca., U.S. **F6** 98
Calispell Peak, mtn., Wa., U.S. **A8** 140
Calistoga, Ca., U.S. **C2** 98
Callaghan, Mount, mtn., Nv., U.S. **D5** 121
Callahan, co., Tx., U.S. . . . **C3** 136
Callao, Peru **F4** 70
Callaway, co., Mo., U.S. . . **C6** 118
Calling Lake, l., Ab., Can. . **B4** 84
Calloway, co., Ky., U.S. . . . **f9** 110
Calmar, Ab., Can. **C4** 84

Calmar, Ia., U.S. **A6** 108
Caloosahatchee, stm., Fl., U.S. **F5** 102
Caltanissetta, Italy **F4** 18
Calulo, Ang. **E2** 54
Calumet, P.Q., Can. **D3** 90
Calumet, Mi., U.S. **A2** 115
Calumet, co., Wi., U.S. . . . **D5** 142
Calumet, Lake, l., Il., U.S. . **k9** 106
Calumet City, Il., U.S. **B6** 106
Calunda, Ang. **F4** 54
Caluula, Som. **H15** 48
Calvert, Tx., U.S. **D4** 136
Calvert, co., Md., U.S. . . . **C4** 113
Calvert City, Ky., U.S. **e9** 110
Calverton Park, Mo., U.S. . **f13** 118
Calvillo, Mex. **C4** 78
Calvinia, S. Afr. **E2** 56
Camabatela, Ang. **E3** 54
Camaçari, Braz. **D4** 74
Camacupa, Ang. **F3** 54
Camagüey, Cuba **A4** 80
Camaná, Peru **G5** 70
Camanche, Ia., U.S. **C7** 108
Camano Island, i., Wa., U.S.**A3** 140
Camaquã, Braz. **E7** 72
Camará, Braz. **D7** 70
Camargo, Bol. **C4** 72
Camargue, reg., Fr. **F9** 16
Camarones, Arg. **F3** 69
Camas, Spain **I3** 16
Camas, Wa., U.S. **D3** 140
Camas, co., Id., U.S. **F4** 105
Ca Mau, Viet. **E5** 34
Ca Mau, Mui, c., Viet. **E4** 34
Cambodia, ctry., Asia **D4** 34
Cambrai, Fr. **B8** 16
Cambria, Ca., U.S. **E3** 98
Cambria, Wi., U.S. **E4** 142
Cambria, co., Pa., U.S. . . . **E4** 131
Cambridge, On., Can. **D4** 89
Cambridge, Eng., U.K. . . . **D7** 12
Cambridge, Ia., U.S. **C4** 108
Cambridge, Il., U.S. **B3** 106
Cambridge, Ma., U.S. **B5** 114
Cambridge, Md., U.S. **C5** 113
Cambridge, Mn., U.S. **E5** 116
Cambridge, Ne., U.S. **D5** 120
Cambridge, N.Y., U.S. **B7** 125
Cambridge, Oh., U.S. **B4** 128
Cambridge, Wi., U.S. **F4** 142
Cambridge City, In., U.S. . . **E7** 107
Cambridge Reservoir, res., Ma., U.S. **g10** 114
Cambridge Springs, Pa., U.S. **C1** 131
Cambulo, Ang. **E4** 54
Cambundi-Catembo, Ang. . **F3** 54
Camden, Al., U.S. **D2** 94
Camden, Ar., U.S. **D3** 97
Camden, De., U.S. **D3** 101
Camden, In., U.S. **C4** 107
Camden, Me., U.S. **D3** 112
Camden, N.J., U.S. **D2** 123
Camden, N.Y., U.S. **B5** 125
Camden, Oh., U.S. **C1** 128
Camden, S.C., U.S. **C6** 133
Camden, Tn., U.S. **A3** 135
Camden, co., Ga., U.S. . . . **F5** 103
Camden, co., Mo., U.S. . . . **C5** 118
Camden, co., N.C., U.S. . . **A6** 126
Camden, co., N.J., U.S. . . . **D3** 123
Camdenton, Mo., U.S. . . . **D5** 118
Camelback Mountain, mtn., Az., U.S. **k9** 96
Cameron, Az., U.S. **B4** 96
Cameron, La., U.S. **E2** 111
Cameron, Mo., U.S. **B3** 118
Cameron, Tx., U.S. **D4** 136
Cameron, W.V., U.S. **B4** 141
Cameron, Wi., U.S. **C2** 142
Cameron, co., La., U.S. . . . **E2** 111
Cameron, co., Pa., U.S. . . . **D5** 131
Cameron, co., Tx., U.S. . . . **F4** 136
Cameron Hills, hills, Can. . . **G16** 82
Cameroon, ctry., Afr. **J7** 48
Cameroon Mountain, vol., Cam. **C1** 54
Cametá, Braz. **B2** 74
Çamiçi Gölü, l., Tur. **D2** 44
Camiguin Island, i., Phil. . . **C8** 34
Camiguin Island, i., Phil. . . **E8** 34
Camilla, Ga., U.S. **E2** 103
Camino, Ca., U.S. **C3** 98
Camiranga, Braz. **D10** 70
Camiri, Bol. **C5** 72
Camissombo, Ang. **E4** 54
Cammack Village, Ar., U.S. **C3** 97
Camocim, Braz. **B3** 74
Camooweal, Austl. **D2** 62
Camorta Island, i., India . . **H6** 40
Camotes Sea, Phil. **D8** 34
Camp, co., Tx., U.S. **C5** 136
Campana, Arg. **E6** 72
Campbell, Ca., U.S. **k8** 98
Campbell, Fl., U.S. **D5** 102
Campbell, Mo., U.S. **E7** 118
Campbell, Oh., U.S. **A5** 128
Campbell, co., Ky., U.S. . . **B5** 110
Campbell, co., S.D., U.S. . **B5** 134
Campbell, co., Tn., U.S. . . **C9** 135
Campbell, co., Va., U.S. . . **C3** 139
Campbell, co., Wy., U.S. . . **B7** 143
Campbellford, On., Can. . . **C7** 89

Campbell Hill, hill, Oh., U.S. **B2** 128
Campbell Island, i., N.Z. . . **J10** 58
Campbell Lake, l., Or., U.S. **E7** 130
Campbell Plateau **M20** 64
Campbellsburg, In., U.S. . . **G5** 107
Campbellsburg, Ky., U.S. . . **B4** 110
Campbells Creek, stm., W.V., U.S. **m13** 141
Campbellsport, Wi., U.S. . . **E5** 142
Campbellsville, Ky., U.S. . . **C4** 110
Campbellton, N.B., Can. . . **A3** 87
Campbellton, Nf., Can. . . . **D4** 88
Campbelltown, Austl. **G5** 62
Campbeltown, Scot., U.K. . **C4** 12
Campeche, Mex. **D6** 78
Campeche, state, Mex. . . . **D6** 78
Campeche, Bahía de, b., Mex. **D6** 78
Campeche, Gulf of see Campeche, Bahía de, b., Mex. **D6** 78
Camperdown, Austl. **H3** 62
Camperville, Mb., Can. . . . **D1** 86
Cam Pha, Viet. **B5** 34
Camp Hill, Al., U.S. **C4** 94
Camp Hill, Pa., U.S. **F8** 131
Camp H. M. Smith Marine Corps Base, mil., Hi., U.S. **g10** 104
Camp Howard Ridge, mtn., Id., U.S. **D2** 105
Câmpina, Rom. **G8** 20
Campina Grande, Braz. . . . **C4** 74
Campinas, Braz. **F2** 74
Campina Verde, Braz. **E2** 74
Camp Lejeune Marine Corps Base, mil., N.C., U.S. **C5** 126
Campo, Cam. **C1** 54
Campobasso, Italy **D5** 18
Campobello Island, i., N.B., Can. **E3** 87
Campo de la Cruz, Col. . . . **C5** 80
Campo Formoso, Braz. . . . **D3** 74
Campo Gallo, Arg. **D5** 72
Campo Grande, Braz. **H9** 70
Campo Maior, Braz. **B3** 74
Campo Mourão, Braz. **F1** 74
Campos, Braz. **F3** 74
Campos Sales, Braz. **C3** 74
Camp Pendleton Marine Corps Base, mil., Ca., U.S. **F5** 98
Camp Point, Il., U.S. **C2** 106
Camp Springs, Md., U.S. . . **f9** 113
Campti, La., U.S. **C2** 111
Campton, N.H., U.S. **C3** 122
Câmpulung, Rom. **G8** 20
Câmpulung Moldovenesc, Rom. **F8** 20
Camp Verde, Az., U.S. . . . **C4** 96
Camp Verde Indian Reservation, Az., U.S. . . **C4** 96
Cam Ranh, Viet. **D5** 34
Camrose, Ab., Can. **C4** 84
Çan, Tur. **B2** 44
Canaan, Ct., U.S. **A2** 100
Canaan, N.H., U.S. **C2** 122
Canaan, stm., N.B., Can. . . **C4** 87
Canada, ctry., N.A. **G17** 82
Canada Basin **D1** 144
Canada Bay, b., Nf., Can. . **C3** 88
Cañada de Gómez, Arg. . . . **E5** 72
Canada Falls Lake, res., Me., U.S. **C2** 112
Canadensis, Pa., U.S. **D11** 131
Canadian, Tx., U.S. **B2** 136
Canadian, co., Ok., U.S. . . **B3** 129
Canadian, stm., U.S. **D7** 92
Canaima, Ven. **D7** 80
Canajoharie, N.Y., U.S. . . . **C6** 125
Çanakkale, Tur. **B2** 44
Çanakkale Boğazı (Dardanelles), strt., Tur. **C1** 44
Canal Flats, B.C., Can. . . . **D10** 85
Canal Fulton, Oh., U.S. . . . **B4** 128
Canal Winchester, Oh., U.S.**C3** 128
Canandaigua, N.Y., U.S. . . **C3** 125
Canandaigua Lake, l., N.Y., U.S. **C3** 125
Cananea, Mex. **A2** 78
Canarias, Islas (Canary Islands), is., Spain **A1** 50
Canary Basin **F10** 66
Canary Islands see Canarias, Islas, is., Spain **A1** 50
Cañasgordas, Col. **D4** 80
Canastota, N.Y., U.S. **B5** 125
Canaveral, Cape, c., Fl., U.S. **D6** 102
Canaveral National Seashore, Fl., U.S. . . . **D6** 102
Canavieiras, Braz. **E4** 74
Canberra, Austl. **H4** 62
Canby, Mn., U.S. **F2** 116
Canby, Or., U.S. **B4** 130
Cancún, Mex. **C7** 78
Candeias, Braz. **D4** 74
Candia see Iráklion, Grc. . . **G10** 18
Candiac, P.Q., Can. **q19** 90
Candle Lake, l., Sk., Can. . **D3** 91
Candler, co., Ga., U.S. . . . **D4** 103
Candlewood, Lake, l., Ct., U.S. **D1** 100

Name	Map Ref.	Page

Candlewood Isle, Ct., U.S. . D2 100
Candlewood Shores, Ct., U.S. . D2 100
Cando, N.D., U.S. . A6 127
Candor, N.C., U.S. . B3 126
Cane, stm., La., U.S. . C2 111
Canelones, Ur. . E6 72
Caney, Ks., U.S. . E8 109
Caney, stm., Ok., U.S. . A5 129
Caney Creek, stm., Tx., U.S. r14 136
Caney Fork, stm., Tn., U.S. C8 135
Canfield, Oh., U.S. . A5 128
Cangas de Narcea, Spain . F3 16
Cangkuang, Tanjung, c., Indon. . E3 36
Cangombe, Ang. . A2 56
Canguçu, Braz. . E7 72
Cangumbe, Ang. . F3 54
Cangyuan, China . B3 34
Cangzhou, China . D11 28
Caniapiscau, stm., P.Q., Can. . g13 90
Canicattì, Italy . F4 18
Canindé, Braz. . B4 74
Canistear Reservoir, res., N.J., U.S. . A4 123
Canisteo, N.Y., U.S. . C3 125
Canisteo, stm., N.Y., U.S. . C3 125
Canistota, S.D., U.S. . D8 134
Çankırı, Tur. . B5 44
Canmore, Ab., Can. . D3 84
Cannanore, India . G3 40
Cannelton, In., U.S. . I4 107
Cannes, Fr. . F10 16
Canning, N.S., Can. . D5 87
Cannon, co., Tn., U.S. . B5 135
Cannon, stm., Mn., U.S. . F5 116
Cannon Air Force Base, mil., N.M., U.S. . C6 124
Cannonball, stm., N.D., U.S. C5 127
Cannon Beach, Or., U.S. . B3 130
Cannondale, Ct., U.S. . E2 100
Cannon Falls, Mn., U.S. . F6 116
Cannonsburg, Ky., U.S. . B7 110
Cannonsville Reservoir, res., N.Y., U.S. . C5 125
Canoas, Braz. . D7 72
Canoinhas, Braz. . D7 72
Canon, Ga., U.S. . B3 103
Canon City, Co., U.S. . C5 99
Canonsburg, Pa., U.S. . F1 131
Cantabrian Mountains see Cantábrica, Cordillera, mts., Spain . F4 16
Cantábrica, Cordillera, mts., Spain . F4 16
Cantaura, Ven. . B7 70
Canterbury, Eng., U.K. . E7 12
Canterbury, De., U.S. . D3 101
Canterbury Bight, b., N.Z. . p13 63c
Can Tho, Viet. . E5 34
Canton see Guangzhou, China . C3 30
Canton, Ct., U.S. . B4 100
Canton, Ga., U.S. . B2 103
Canton, Il., U.S. . C3 106
Canton, Ks., U.S. . D6 109
Canton, Ma., U.S. . B5 114
Canton, Mo., U.S. . A6 118
Canton, Ms., U.S. . C3 117
Canton, N.C., U.S. . f10 126
Canton, N.Y., U.S. . f9 125
Canton, Oh., U.S. . B4 128
Canton, Ok., U.S. . A3 129
Canton, Pa., U.S. . C8 131
Canton, S.D., U.S. . D9 134
Canton, Tx., U.S. . C5 136
Canton Lake, res., Ok., U.S. A3 129
Cantonment, Fl., U.S. . u14 102
Canutama, Braz. . E7 70
Çanutillo, Tx., U.S. . o11 136
Çany, ozero, l., Russia . D9 26
Canyon, Tx., U.S. . B2 136
Canyon, co., Id., U.S. . F2 105
Canyon City, Or., U.S. . C8 130
Canyon de Chelly National Monument, Az., U.S. . A6 96
Canyon Ferry Lake, res., Mt., U.S. . D5 119
Canyon Lake, Tx., U.S. . E3 136
Canyon Lake, res., Tx., U.S. E3 136
Canyonlands National Park, Ut., U.S. . E6 137
Canyonville, Or., U.S. . E3 130
Cao Bang, Viet. . B5 34
Caoxian, China . C4 30
Çapac, Mi., U.S. . F8 115
Çapaevo, Kaz. . D9 22
Cap-à-l'Aigle, P.Q., Can. . B7 90
Capanema, Braz. . B2 74
Capão Bonito, Braz. . F4 72
Cap-aux-Meules, P.Q., Can. B8 87
Cap-de-la-Madeleine, P.Q., Can. . C5 90
Cape Barren Island, i., Austl. I4 62
Cape Basin . L14 66
Cape Breton Highlands National Park, N.S., Can. . C9 87
Cape Breton Island, i., N.S., Can. . C9 87
Cape Broyle, Nf., Can. . E5 88
Cape Canaveral, Fl., U.S. . D6 102
Cape Charles, Va., U.S. . C6 139
Cape Coast, Ghana . E4 50

Cape Cod Bay, b., Ma., U.S. C7 114
Cape Cod Canal, Ma., U.S. C6 114
Cape Cod National Seashore, Ma., U.S. . C7 114
Cape Coral, Fl., U.S. . F5 102
Cape Elizabeth, Me., U.S. . E2 112
Cape Fear, stm., N.C., U.S. C4 126
Cape Girardeau, Mo., U.S. D8 118
Cape Girardeau, co., Mo., U.S. . D8 118
Cape Hatteras National Seashore, N.C., U.S. . B7 126
Cape Horn Mountain, mtn., Id., U.S. . E3 105
Cape Island, i., S.C., U.S. . E9 133
Capelinha, Braz. . E3 74
Capelongo, Ang. . A2 56
Cape Lookout National Seashore, N.C., U.S. . C6 126
Cape May, N.J., U.S. . F3 123
Cape May, co., N.J., U.S. . E3 123
Cape May Court House, N.J., U.S. . E3 123
Capers Inlet, b., S.C., U.S. . k12 133
Capers Island, i., S.C., U.S. F8 133
Capers Island, i., S.C., U.S. G6 133
Cape Sable Island, i., N.S., Can. . F4 87
Cape Town (Kaapstad), S. Afr. . E2 56
Cape Verde Basin . G10 66
Cape Verde, ctry., Afr. . g9 50a
Cape York Peninsula, pen., Austl. . C3 62
Cap-Haïtien, Haiti . B5 80
Capinota, Bol. . B4 72
Capitan, N.M., U.S. . D4 124
Capitan Mountains, mts., N.M., U.S. . D4 124
Capitan Peak, mtn., N.M., U.S. . D4 124
Capitol Heights, Ia., U.S. . e8 108
Capitol Heights, Md., U.S. . C4 113
Capitol Peak, mtn., Nv., U.S. . B4 121
Capitol Reef National Park, Ut., U.S. . E4 137
Çaplygin, Russia . C15 20
Cap-Pelé, N.B., Can. . C5 87
Capreol, On., Can. . p19 89
Capri, Isola di, i., Italy . D5 18
Capricorn Channel, strt., Austl. . E5 62
Capricorn Group, is., Austl. E5 62
Caprivi Strip, hist. reg., Nmb. . B3 56
Cap-Rouge, P.Q., Can. . n17 90
Cap-Saint-Ignace, P.Q., Can. B7 90
Captain Cook, Hi., U.S. . D6 104
Captiva, Fl., U.S. . F4 102
Captiva Island, i., Fl., U.S. . F4 102
Capulin Volcano National Monument, N.M., U.S. A6 124
Capunda Cabilongo, Ang. . F2 54
Caquetá (Japurá), stm., S.A. D5 70
Çara, Russia . D13 26
Caracal, Rom. . G8 20
Caracaraí, Braz. . C7 70
Caracas, Ven. . A6 70
Carajás, Braz. . E9 70
Carajás, Serra dos, hills, Braz. . E9 70
Carangola, Braz. . F3 74
Caransebeş, Rom. . G7 20
Caraquet, N.B., Can. . B5 87
Caratasca, Laguna de, b., Hond. . B3 80
Caratinga, Braz. . E3 74
Carauari, Braz. . D6 70
Caravaca de la Cruz, Spain . H6 16
Caravelas, Braz. . G12 70
Caraway, Ar., U.S. . B5 97
Carazinho, Braz. . D7 72
Carberry, Mb., Can. . E2 86
Carbon, co., Mt., U.S. . E7 119
Carbon, co., Pa., U.S. . E10 131
Carbon, co., Ut., U.S. . D5 137
Carbon, co., Wy., U.S. . E5 143
Carbondale, Co., U.S. . B3 99
Carbondale, Il., U.S. . F4 106
Carbondale, Ks., U.S. . D8 109
Carbondale, Pa., U.S. . C10 131
Carbonear, Nf., Can. . E5 88
Carbon Hill, Al., U.S. . B2 94
Carbonia, Italy . E2 18
Carcassonne, Fr. . F8 16
Çardara, Kaz. . B9 42
Cárdenas, Cuba . A3 80
Cárdenas, Mex. . D6 78
Cardiff, Wales, U.K. . E5 12
Cardigan, Wales, U.K. . D4 12
Cardigan Bay, b., P.E., Can. C7 87
Cardigan Bay, b., Wales, U.K. . D4 12
Cardinal, On., Can. . C9 89
Cardington, Oh., U.S. . B3 128
Cardston, Ab., Can. . E4 84
Cardwell, Mo., U.S. . E7 118
Çardžev, Turk. . F8 26
Carei, Rom. . F7 20
Careiro, Braz. . D8 70
Carelia see Karelia, hist. reg., Eur. . C12 6
Carencro, La., U.S. . D3 111
Carentan, Fr. . C6 16

Caretta, W.V., U.S. . D3 141
Carey, Id., U.S. . F5 105
Carey, Oh., U.S. . B2 128
Carey Downs, Austl. . F2 60
Cargados Carajos Shoals, is., Mrts. . F11 52
Caribbean Sea . C4 80
Cariboo Mountains, mts., B.C., Can. . C7 85
Caribou, Me., U.S. . B5 112
Caribou, co., Id., U.S. . G7 105
Caribou Island, i., N.S., Can. D7 87
Caribou Lake, l., Me., U.S. . C3 112
Caribou Mountain, mtn., Id., U.S. . F7 105
Caribou Mountains, mts., Ab., Can. . f7 84
Caribou Range, mts., Id., U.S. . F7 105
Caripito, Ven. . C7 80
Carl Blackwell, Lake, res., Ok., U.S. . A4 129
Carlet, Spain . H6 16
Carleton, Mi., U.S. . F7 115
Carleton, Mount, mtn., N.B., Can. . B3 87
Carleton Place, On., Can. . B8 89
Carletonville, S. Afr. . D4 56
Carlin, Nv., U.S. . C5 121
Carlinville, Il., U.S. . D4 106
Carlisle, Eng., U.K. . C5 12
Carlisle, Ar., U.S. . C4 97
Carlisle, Ia., U.S. . C4 108
Carlisle, In., U.S. . G3 107
Carlisle, Ky., U.S. . B5 110
Carlisle, Oh., U.S. . C1 128
Carlisle, Pa., U.S. . F7 131
Carlisle, co., Ky., U.S. . f8 110
Carl Junction, Mo., U.S. . D3 118
Carlos Casares, Arg. . F5 72
Carlos Chagas, Braz. . E3 74
Carlow, Ire. . D3 12
Carlsbad see Karlovy Vary, Czech Rep. . D2 20
Carlsbad, Ca., U.S. . F5 98
Carlsbad, N.M., U.S. . E5 124
Carlsbad Caverns National Park, N.M., U.S. . E5 124
Carlsberg Ridge . H8 64
Carlstadt, N.J., U.S. . h8 123
Carlton, Mn., U.S. . D6 116
Carlton, Or., U.S. . B3 130
Carlton, co., Mn., U.S. . D6 116
Carlyle, Il., U.S. . E4 106
Carlyle Lake, res., Il., U.S. . E4 106
Carman, Mb., Can. . E2 86
Carmanville, Nf., Can. . D4 88
Carmarthen, Wales, U.K. . E4 12
Carmaux, Fr. . F9 16
Carmel, Ca., U.S. . D3 98
Carmel, In., U.S. . E5 107
Carmel, N.Y., U.S. . D7 125
Carmelo, Ur. . E6 72
Carmen, Isla, i., Mex. . D6 78
Carmen, Isla del, i., Mex. . D6 78
Carmen de Patagones, Arg. F4 69
Carmi, Il., U.S. . E5 106
Carmi, Lake, l., Vt., U.S. . B3 138
Carnamah, Austl. . F2 60
Carnarvon, Austl. . E1 60
Carnarvon, S. Afr. . E3 56
Carnation, Wa., U.S. . B4 140
Carnegie, Ok., U.S. . B3 129
Carnegie, Pa., U.S. . F1 131
Carnegie, Lake, l., Austl. . E3 60
Carneys Point, N.J., U.S. . D2 123
Carnic Alps, mts., Eur. . C7 18
Car Nicobar Island, i., India H6 40
Carnot, C.A.R. . C3 54
Carol City, Fl., U.S. . s13 102
Caroleen, N.C., U.S. . B1 126
Carolina, Braz. . C2 74
Carolina, R.I., U.S. . F2 132
Carolina, W.V., U.S. . k10 141
Carolina Beach, N.C., U.S. . C5 126
Caroline, co., Md., U.S. . C6 113
Caroline, co., Va., U.S. . C5 139
Caroline, atoll, Kir. . E15 58
Caroline Islands, is., Oc. . D8 58
Caroní, stm., Ven. . C7 70
Carora, Ven. . C5 80
Carpathian Mountains, mts., Eur. . E6 20
Carpaţii Meridionali, mts., Rom. . G7 20
Carpentaria, Gulf of, b., Austl. . F7 58
Carpenter Dam, Ar., U.S. . g7 97
Carpentersville, Il., U.S. . A5 106
Carpentras, Fr. . E9 16
Carpina, Braz. . C4 74
Carpinteria, Ca., U.S. . E4 98
Carrabelle, Fl., U.S. . C2 102
Carranza, Cabo, c., Chile . F3 72
Carrara, Italy . B3 18
Carrauntoohil, mtn., Ire. . D2 12
Carrboro, N.C., U.S. . B3 126
Carreta, Punta, c., Peru . F4 70
Carrick on Shannon, Ire. . C3 12
Carrie, Mount, mtn., Wa., U.S. . B2 140
Carriere, Ms., U.S. . E4 117
Carrier Mills, Il., U.S. . F5 106
Carrington, N.D., U.S. . B6 127

Carrington Island, i., Ut., U.S. . C3 137
Carrizal Bajo, Chile . C2 69
Carrizo Creek, stm., U.S. . A1 136
Carrizo Mountain, mtn., N.M., U.S. . D4 124
Carrizo Mountains, mts., U.S. . A6 96
Carrizozo, N.M., U.S. . D4 124
Carroll, Ia., U.S. . B3 108
Carroll, co., Ar., U.S. . A2 97
Carroll, co., Ga., U.S. . C1 103
Carroll, co., Ia., U.S. . B3 108
Carroll, co., Il., U.S. . A4 106
Carroll, co., In., U.S. . C4 107
Carroll, co., Ky., U.S. . B4 110
Carroll, co., Md., U.S. . A3 113
Carroll, co., Mo., U.S. . B4 118
Carroll, co., Mn., U.S. . D4 116
Carroll, co., Ms., U.S. . B4 117
Carroll, co., N.H., U.S. . C4 122
Carroll, co., Oh., U.S. . B4 128
Carroll, co., Tn., U.S. . B3 135
Carroll, co., Va., U.S. . D2 139
Carrollton, Al., U.S. . B1 94
Carrollton, Ga., U.S. . C1 103
Carrollton, Il., U.S. . D3 106
Carrollton, Ky., U.S. . B4 110
Carrollton, Mi., U.S. . E7 115
Carrollton, Mo., U.S. . B4 118
Carrollton, Oh., U.S. . B4 128
Carrolltown, Pa., U.S. . E4 131
Carrot, stm., Can. . D4 91
Carry Falls Reservoir, res., N.Y., U.S. . f10 125
Çarşamba, Tur. . B7 44
Carsk, Kaz. . B4 28
Carson, Ia., U.S. . C2 108
Carson, Wa., U.S. . D4 140
Carson, co., Tx., U.S. . B2 136
Carson, stm., Nv., U.S. . D2 121
Carson City, Mi., U.S. . E6 115
Carson City, Nv., U.S. . D2 121
Carson Lake, l., Nv., U.S. . D3 121
Carson Sink, l., Nv., U.S. . D3 121
Carson Spring, Tn., U.S. . D10 135
Carstairs, Ab., Can. . D3 84
Cartagena, Col. . A4 70
Cartagena, Spain . I6 16
Cartago, C.R. . D3 80
Cartago, Col. . E3 70
Carter, co., Ky., U.S. . B6 110
Carter, co., Mo., U.S. . E7 118
Carter, co., Mt., U.S. . E12 119
Carter, co., Ok., U.S. . C4 129
Carter, co., Tn., U.S. . C11 135
Carter Lake, Ia., U.S. . C2 108
Carter Mountain, mtn., Wy., U.S. . B3 143
Carteret, N.J., U.S. . B4 123
Carteret, co., N.C., U.S. . C6 126
Cartersville, Ga., U.S. . B2 103
Carterville, Il., U.S. . F4 106
Carterville, Mo., U.S. . D3 118
Carthage, Tun. . F3 18
Carthage, Il., U.S. . C2 106
Carthage, In., U.S. . E6 107
Carthage, Mo., U.S. . D3 118
Carthage, Ms., U.S. . C4 117
Carthage, N.C., U.S. . B3 126
Carthage, N.Y., U.S. . B5 125
Carthage, Tn., U.S. . C8 135
Carthage, Tx., U.S. . C5 136
Carthage, hist., Tun. . F3 18
Cartier Islands, is., Austl. . C3 60
Cartwright, Nf., Can. . B3 88
Cartwright, Ok., U.S. . D5 129
Caruaru, Braz. . C4 74
Carúpano, Ven. . A7 70
Carutapera, Braz. . D10 70
Caruthersville, Mo., U.S. . E8 118
Carver, Ma., U.S. . C6 114
Carver, Mn., U.S. . F5 116
Carver, co., Mn., U.S. . F5 116
Carville, La., U.S. . h9 111
Carvoeiro, Braz. . D7 70
Cary, Il., U.S. . A5 106
Cary, N.C., U.S. . B4 126
Caryville, Tn., U.S. . C9 135
Casablanca, Mor. . D3 48
Casa Grande, Az., U.S. . E4 96
Casa Grande National Monument, Az., U.S. . E4 96
Casa Nova, Braz. . C3 74
Casas Adobes, Az., U.S. . E5 96
Cascade, Co., U.S. . C6 99
Cascade, Ia., U.S. . B6 108
Cascade, Id., U.S. . E2 105
Cascade, Mt., U.S. . C5 119
Cascade, co., Mt., U.S. . C5 119
Cascade Locks, Or., U.S. . B5 130
Cascade Range, mts., N.A. . C3 92
Cascade Reservoir, res., Id., U.S. . E3 105
Cascade Tunnel, Wa., U.S. . B4 140
Cascais, Port. . H2 16
Cascavel, Braz. . D7 72
Caserta, Italy . D5 18
Caseville, Mi., U.S. . E7 115
Casey, Il., U.S. . D6 106
Casey, co., Ky., U.S. . C5 110
Casey, Mount, mtn., Id., U.S. . A2 105
Casey Key, i., Fl., U.S. . E4 102

Cashion, Az., U.S. . m8 96
Cashmere, Wa., U.S. . B5 140
Cashton, Wi., U.S. . E3 142
Casino, Austl. . F5 62
Casper, Wy., U.S. . D6 143
Casper Mountain, mtn., Wy., U.S. . D6 143
Caspian, Mi., U.S. . B2 115
Caspian Depression (Prikaspijskaja nizmennost'), pl. . E8 22
Caspian Lake, l., Vt., U.S. . B4 138
Caspian Sea . F9 22
Cass, co., Ia., U.S. . C3 108
Cass, co., Il., U.S. . D3 106
Cass, co., In., U.S. . C5 107
Cass, co., Mi., U.S. . G4 115
Cass, co., Mn., U.S. . D4 116
Cass, co., Mo., U.S. . C3 118
Cass, co., N.D., U.S. . C8 127
Cass, co., Ne., U.S. . D9 120
Cass, co., Tx., U.S. . C5 136
Cass, stm., Mi., U.S. . E7 115
Cassai (Kasai), stm., Afr. . F4 54
Cass City, Mi., U.S. . E7 115
Casselberry, Fl., U.S. . D5 102
Casselman, On., Can. . B9 89
Casselman, stm., U.S. . k12 113
Casselton, N.D., U.S. . C8 127
Cassia, co., Id., U.S. . G5 105
Cassiar, B.C., Can. . m17 85
Cassilândia, Braz. . E1 74
Cassino, Italy . D4 18
Cass Lake, Mn., U.S. . C4 116
Cass Lake, l., Mn., U.S. . C4 116
Cassongue, Ang. . F2 54
Cassopolis, Mi., U.S. . G4 115
Cassville, Ga., U.S. . B2 103
Cassville, Mo., U.S. . E4 118
Cassville, Wi., U.S. . F3 142
Castalia, Oh., U.S. . A3 128
Castanea, Pa., U.S. . D7 131
Castanhal, Braz. . B2 74
Castellammare, Golfo di, b., Italy . E4 18
Castelló de la Plana, Spain . H6 16
Castelo Branco, Port. . H3 16
Castelsarrasin, Fr. . F7 16
Castelvetrano, Italy . F4 18
Castilla, Peru . E3 70
Castilla la Nueva, hist. reg., Spain . H4 16
Castilla la Vieja, hist. reg., Spain . G5 16
Castillo de San Marcos National Monument, Fl., U.S. . n9 102
Castine, Me., U.S. . D4 112
Castlebar, Ire. . D2 12
Castleberry, Al., U.S. . D2 94
Castle Dale, Ut., U.S. . D4 137
Castle Dome Mountains, mts., Az., U.S. . D1 96
Castle Dome Peak, mtn., Az., U.S. . m1 96
Castlegar, B.C., Can. . E9 85
Castle Hayne, N.C., U.S. . C5 126
Castle Hills, De., U.S. . i7 101
Castlemaine, Austl. . H3 62
Castle Mountains, mts., Mt., U.S. . D6 119
Castle Peak, mtn., Co., U.S. B4 99
Castle Peak, mtn., Id., U.S. . E4 105
Castle Point, Mo., U.S. . f13 118
Castle Rock, Co., U.S. . B6 99
Castle Rock, Wa., U.S. . C3 140
Castle Rock, mtn., Or., U.S. C8 130
Castle Rock Lake, res., Wi., U.S. . E4 142
Castleton, Vt., U.S. . D2 138
Castlewood, Va., U.S. . f9 139
Castor, Ab., Can. . C5 84
Castor, stm., Mo., U.S. . D7 118
Castres, Fr. . F8 16
Castries, St. Luc. . C7 80
Castro, Braz. . C7 72
Castro, Chile . F2 69
Castro, co., Tx., U.S. . B1 136
Castro Valley, Ca., U.S. . h8 98
Castrovillari, Italy . E6 18
Castroville, Tx., U.S. . E3 136
Castuera, Spain . H4 16
Caswell, co., N.C., U.S. . A3 126
Cataguazes, Braz. . F3 74
Catahoula, co., La., U.S. . C4 111
Catahoula Lake, l., La., U.S. C3 111
Catalão, Braz. . E2 74
Catalina, Nf., Can. . D5 88
Catalina, Chile . C2 69
Catalunya, hist. reg., Spain . F7 16
Catanduanes Island, i., Phil. D8 34
Catania, Italy . F5 18
Catanzaro, Italy . E6 18
Cataouatche, Lake, l., La., U.S. . k11 111
Catarino Rodríguez, Mex. . C4 78
Catarman, Phil. . D8 34
Catasauqua, Pa., U.S. . E11 131
Cataumet, Ma., U.S. . C6 114
Catawba, co., N.C., U.S. . B1 126
Catawba, stm., S.C., U.S. . B6 133
Catawba, South Fork, stm., N.C., U.S. . B1 126

Name	Map Ref.	Page

Catawissa, Pa., U.S. E9 131
Catbalogan, Phil. D8 34
Catete, Ang. E2 54
Cathance, Lake, l., Me.,
  U.S. D5 112
Cathedral City, Ca., U.S. . .F5 98
Cathedral of the Pines, rel.,
  N.H., U.S. E3 122
Catherine, Lake, res., Ar.,
  U.S. C3 97
Cat Island, i., Bah. D9 76
Cat Island, i., Ma., U.S. . . .f12 114
Cat Island, i., Ms., U.S. . . .E4 117
Cat Island, i., S.C., U.S. . . .E9 133
Catlettsburg, Ky., U.S. B7 110
Catlin, Il., U.S. C6 106
Catnip Mountain, mtn., Nv.,
  U.S. B2 121
Catoche, Cabo, c., Mex. . . .C7 78
Catonsville, Md., U.S. B4 113
Catoosa, co., Ga., U.S. B1 103
Catoosa, Ok., U.S. A6 129
Catriló, Arg. F5 72
Catron, co., N.M., U.S. D1 124
Catskill, N.Y., U.S. C7 125
Catskill Mountains, mts., N.Y.,
  U.S. C6 125
Catt, Mount, mtn., B.C., Can. B3 85
Cattaraugus, co., N.Y., U.S. .C2 125
Cattaraugus Creek, stm., N.Y.,
  U.S. C2 125
Cattaraugus Indian Reservation,
  N.Y., U.S. C2 125
Čatyrtaš, Kyrg. A3 40
Caubvick, Mount (Mont
  d'Iberville), mtn., Can. . .f9 88
Cauca, stm., Col. B5 70
Caucasia, Col. D4 80
Caucasus, mts. A10 49
Caucete, Arg. E4 72
Caucomgomoc Lake, l., Me.,
  U.S. B3 112
Caungula, Ang. E3 54
Cauquenes, Chile E2 69
Caura, stm., Ven. B7 70
Cavalier, N.D., U.S. A8 127
Cavalier, co., N.D., U.S. . . .A7 127
Cave City, Ar., U.S. B4 97
Cave City, Ky., U.S. C4 110
Cave Creek, Az., U.S. D4 96
Cave Junction, Or., U.S. . . .E3 130
Cave Point, c., Wi., U.S. . . .D6 142
Cave Run Lake, res., Ky.,
  U.S. B6 110
Cave Spring, Ga., U.S. B1 103
Cave Spring, Va., U.S. C2 139
Cavetown, Md., U.S. A2 113
Caviana de Fora, Ilha, i.,
  Braz. A2 74
Cavite, Phil. D8 34
Cawood, Ky., U.S. D6 110
Cawston, B.C., Can. E8 85
Caxias, Braz. B3 74
Caxias do Sul, Braz. D7 72
Caxito, Ang. E2 54
Cayambe, vol., Ec. C4 70
Cayce, S.C., U.S. D5 133
Cayenne, Fr. Gu. C9 70
Cayman Brac, i., Cay. Is. . . .E8 80
Cayman Islands, dep., N.A. . .E8 76
Cayuga, In., U.S. E3 107
Cayuga, co., N.Y., U.S. C4 125
Cayuga Heights, N.Y., U.S. .C4 125
Cayuga Lake, l., N.Y., U.S. .C4 125
Cazenovia, N.Y., U.S. C5 125
Cazombo, Ang. F4 54
Ceará, state, Braz. C4 74
Ceará-Mirim, Braz. C4 74
Ceballos, Mex. B4 78
Čeboksary, Russia D6 26
Cebu, i., Phil. D8 34
Cebu, Phil. D8 34
Cecil, co., Md., U.S. A6 113
Cecil Field Naval Air Station,
  mil., Fl., U.S. B5 102
Cecilia, Ky., U.S. C4 110
Cecina, Italy C3 18
Čečnja, state, Russia E6 26
Cedar, co., la., U.S. C6 108
Cedar, co., Mo., U.S. D4 118
Cedar, co., Ne., U.S. B8 120
Cedar, stm., Wa., U.S. B4 140
Cedar, stm., U.S. C6 108
Cedar Bluff, Al., U.S. A4 94
Cedar Bluff Reservoir, res.,
  Ks., U.S. F3 137
Cedar Bluff Two, Tn., U.S. .D9 135
Cedar Breaks National
  Monument, Ut., U.S. . . .F3 137
Cedarburg, Wi., U.S. E6 142
Cedar City, Ut., U.S. F2 137
Cedar Creek, stm., N.D.,
  U.S. C3 127
Cedar Creek, stm., N.J.,
  U.S. D4 123
Cedar Creek, stm., Oh.,
  U.S. e7 128
Cedar Creek Lake, res.,
  Tx., U.S. C4 136
Cedar Crest, N.M., U.S. . . .k8 124
Cedaredge, Co., U.S. C3 99
Cedar Falls, Ia., U.S. B5 108
Cedar Grove, N.J., U.S. B4 123
Cedar Grove, Wi., U.S. E6 142

Cedar Grove, W.V., U.S. . . .C3 141
Cedar Hill, Mo., U.S. g12 118
Cedar Hill, Tx., U.S. n10 136
Cedarhurst, N.Y., U.S. k13 125
Cedar Island, i., N.C., U.S. . .C6 126
Cedar Island, i., S.C., U.S. . .E9 133
Cedar Island, i., Va., U.S. . . .C7 139
Cedar Key, Fl., U.S. C3 102
Cedar Keys, is., Fl., U.S. . . .C3 102
Cedar Lake, res., Mb., Can. .C1 86
Cedar Lake, l., Il., U.S. F4 106
Cedar Lake, In., U.S. B3 107
Cedar Mountain, mtn., Ca.,
  U.S. B3 98
Cedar Point, c., Md., U.S. . .D5 113
Cedar Point, c., Oh., U.S. . .e7 128
Cedar Point, c., Oh., U.S. . .A3 128
Cedar Rapids, la., U.S. C6 108
Cedar Springs, Mi., U.S. . . .E5 115
Cedartown, Ga., U.S. B1 103
Cedar Vale, Ks., U.S. E7 109
Cedarville, Oh., U.S. C2 128
Cedros, Isla, i., Mex. B1 78
Ceduna, Austl. G5 60
Ceerigaabo, Som. H14 48
Cefalonia see Kefallinía, i.,
  Grc. E8 18
Cefalù, Italy F5 18
Čegdomyn, Russia D15 26
Cegléd, Hung. F5 20
Čehov, Russia A4 31
Čehov, Russia B14 20
Çekerek, stm., Tur. C6 44
Çekerek, Tur. B6 44
Celaya, Mex. C4 78
Celebes see Sulawesi, i.,
  Indon. D6 36
Celebes Basin H15 64
Celebes Sea, Asia C6 36
Čeleken, Turk. C6 42
Celina, Oh., U.S. B1 128
Celina, Tn., U.S. C8 135
Celina, Tx., U.S. C4 136
Čeljabinsk, Russia D8 26
Celje, Slvn. A5 18
Čeljuskin, mys, c., Russia . .B12 26
Čelkar, Kaz. E7 26
Celle, Ger. D11 12
Celtic Sea, Eur. B3 16
Cement, Ok., U.S. C3 129
Cementon, Pa., U.S. E10 131
Cenderawasih, Teluk, b.,
  Indon. G10 32
Cenderawasih Bay see
  Cenderawasih,
  Teluk, b., Indon. G10 32
Centennial Mountains, mts.,
  Id., U.S. E7 105
Center, Co., U.S. D4 99
Center, N.D., U.S. B4 127
Center, Tx., U.S. D5 136
Centerbrook, Ct., U.S. D6 100
Centerburg, Oh., U.S. B3 128
Centereach, N.Y., U.S. n15 125
Centerfield, Ut., U.S. D4 137
Center Hill Lake, res., Tn.,
  U.S. C8 135
Center Moriches, N.Y., U.S. .n16 125
Center Mountain, mtn., Id.,
  U.S. D3 105
Center Point, Al., U.S. f7 94
Center Point, Ia., U.S. B6 108
Centerville, Ia., U.S. D5 108
Centerville, In., U.S. E8 107
Centerville, La., U.S. E4 111
Centerville, Ma., U.S. C7 114
Centerville, Oh., U.S. C1 128
Centerville, Pa., U.S. F2 131
Centerville, S.D., U.S. D9 134
Centerville, Tn., U.S. B4 135
Centerville, Ut., U.S. C4 137
Central, Phil. D8 34
Central, N.M., U.S. E1 124
Central, S.C., U.S. B2 133
Central, Cordillera, mts.,
  Col. E4 80
Central, Cordillera, mts.,
  Peru E4 70
Central, Massif, mts., Fr. . . .E8 16
Central, Sistema, mts.,
  Spain G4 16
Central African Republic,
  ctry., Afr. B3 54
Central City, Co., U.S. B5 99
Central City, Ia., U.S. B6 108
Central City, Il., U.S. E4 106
Central City, Ky., U.S. C2 110
Central City, Ne., U.S. C7 120
Central City, Pa., U.S. F4 131
Central Falls, R.I., U.S. B4 132
Central Heights, Az., U.S. . .D5 96
Centralia, Il., U.S. E4 106
Centralia, Mo., U.S. B5 118
Centralia, Wa., U.S. C3 140
Central Islip, N.Y., U.S. . . .n15 125
Central Lake, Mi., U.S. C5 115
Central Makrān Range, mts.,
  Pak. E8 42
Central Pacific Basin G21 64
Central Park, Wa., U.S. C2 140
Central Point, Or., U.S. E4 130
Central Siberian Uplands see
  Srednesibirskoe ploskogor'e,
  plat., Russia C12 26
Central Square, N.Y., U.S. . .B4 125

Central Valley, Ca., U.S. . . .B2 98
Central Valley, N.Y., U.S. . . .D6 125
Central Village, Ct., U.S. . . .C8 100
Centre, Al., U.S. A4 94
Centre, co., Pa., U.S. E6 131
Centre Hall, Pa., U.S. E6 131
Centreville, Al., U.S. C2 94
Centreville, Il., U.S. E3 106
Centreville, Md., U.S. B5 113
Centreville, Mi., U.S. G5 115
Centreville, Ms., U.S. D2 117
Centuria, Wi., U.S. C1 142
Century, Fl., U.S. u14 102
Ceos see Kéa, i., Grc. F10 18
Ceram see Seram, i., Indon. .D7 36
Ceram Sea see Seram, Laut,
  Indon. D7 36
Cerbat Mountains, mts., Az.,
  U.S. B1 96
Cerdas, Bol. C4 72
Ceredo, W.V., U.S. C2 141
Čeremhovo, Russia D12 26
Čerepovec, Russia D5 26
Ceres, Arg. D5 72
Ceres, Braz. E2 74
Ceres, Ca., U.S. D3 98
Ceresco, Ne., U.S. C9 120
Cerignola, Italy D5 18
Čerkessk, Russia A5 44
Čerlak, Russia D9 26
Čermoz, Russia C10 22
Cernavodă, Rom. G10 20
Černjahovsk, Russia B6 20
Černjanka, Russia D14 22
Černobyl', Ukr. D11 20
Černuška, Russia C10 22
Černyševskij, Russia C13 26
Cerralvo, Isla, i., Mex. C3 78
Cerritos, Mex. E6 111
Cerro Azul, Peru A2 72
Cerro de Pasco, Peru F4 70
Cerro Gordo, co., Ia., U.S. . .A4 108
Cerro Gordo, Il., U.S. D5 106
Čerskij, Russia C18 26
Čerskogo, hrebet, mts.,
  Russia C15 26
Červen', Bela. C10 20
Cervino see Matterhorn, mtn.,
  Eur. C1 18
Cesena, Italy B4 18
Cēsis, Lat. H11 10
České Budějovice, Czech
  Rep. E3 20
Çeşme, Tur. C2 44
Češskaja guba, b., Russia . .A8 22
Cetinje, Yugo. G2 20
Ceuta, Sp. N. Afr. J4 16
Cévennes, reg., Fr. E8 16
Ceyhan, stm., Tur. D6 44
Ceyhan, Tur. D6 44
Ceylanpinar, Tur. D9 44
Ceylon see Sri Lanka, ctry.,
  Asia H4 40
Cha-am, Thai. D3 34
Chachani, Nevado, vol.,
  Peru G5 70
Chachapoyas, Peru E4 70
Chachoengsao, Thai. D4 34
Chaco, stm., N.M., U.S. . . .A1 124
Chaco Austral, reg., Arg. . . .D5 72
Chaco Boreal, reg., Para. . . .C5 72
Chaco Central, reg., Arg. . . .C5 72
Chaco Culture National
  Historic Park, N.M., U.S. .A2 124
Chacon, Cape, c., Ak., U.S. .n24 95
Chad, ctry., Afr. G8 48
Chad, Lake, l., Afr. D7 50
Chadbourn, N.C., U.S. C4 126
Chadds Ford, Pa., U.S. . . .G10 131
Chadron, Ne., U.S. B3 120
Chadwicks, N.Y., U.S. B5 125
Chaffee, co., Co., U.S. C4 99
Chaffee, Mo., U.S. D8 118
Chaffin, Ma., U.S. B4 114
Chaghcharān, Afg. D9 42
Chagos Archipelago, is.,
  B.I.O.T. I10 64
Chagos-Laccadive Plateau . .I10 64
Chagrin Falls, Oh., U.S. A4 128
Chaguaramas, Ven. D6 80
Chai Nat, Thai. D4 34
Chaiyaphum, Thai. C4 34
Chajarí, Arg. E6 72
Chakachamna Lake, l., Ak.,
  U.S. g15 95
Chakari, Zimb. B4 56
Chakasija, state, Russia A5 28
Chala, Peru B3 72
Chalatenango, El Sal. C2 80
Chalbi Desert, des., Kenya . .C7 54
Chalcidice see Khalkidhikí,
  hist. reg., Grc. D9 18
Chalcis see Khalkís, Grc. . . .E9 18
Chaleur Bay, b., Can. B4 87
Chalfonte, De., U.S. h7 101
Chalk River, On., Can. B7 89
Challapata, Bol. B4 72
Challenger Deep G17 64
Challis, Id., U.S. E4 105
Chalmette, La., U.S. E6 111
Châlons-en-Champagne, Fr. .C9 16
Chalon-sur-Saône, Fr. D9 16
Chālūs, Iran C6 42
Chama, N.M., U.S. A3 124

Chama, Rio, stm., N.M.,
  U.S. A3 124
Chaman, Pak. D9 42
Chambal, stm., India D3 40
Chamberlain, S.D., U.S. . . .D6 134
Chamberlain Lake, l., Me.,
  U.S. B3 112
Chamberlin, Mount, mtn., Ak.,
  U.S. B10 95
Chambers, co., Al., U.S. . . .C4 94
Chambers, co., Tx., U.S. . . .E5 136
Chambersburg, Pa., U.S. . .G6 131
Chambers Island, i., Wi.,
  U.S. C6 142
Chambéry, Fr. E9 16
Chambi, Jebel, mtn., Tun. . .C6 48
Chamblee, Ga., U.S. h8 103
Chambly, P.Q., Can. D4 90
Chamical, Arg. E4 72
Chamisal, N.M., U.S. A4 124
Chāmpa, India E4 40
Champagne, hist. reg., Fr. . .C9 16
Champaign, Il., U.S. C5 106
Champaign, co., Il., U.S. . . .C5 106
Champaign, co., Oh., U.S. . .B2 128
Champasak, Laos D5 34
Champion, Oh., U.S. A5 128
Champlain, Lake, l., N.A. . .C13 92
Champlin, Mn., U.S. m12 116
Champotón, Mex. D6 78
Chañaral, Chile C2 69
Chance, Md., U.S. D6 113
Chanchelulla Peak, mtn., Ca.,
  U.S. B2 98
Chandalar, stm., Ak., U.S. .B10 95
Chandeleur Islands, is., La.,
  U.S. E7 111
Chandeleur Sound, strt., La.,
  U.S. E6 111
Chandīgarh, India C3 40
Chandler, P.Q., Can. k14 90
Chandler, Az., U.S. D4 96
Chandler, In., U.S. H3 107
Chandler, Ok., U.S. B5 129
Chandler, Tx., U.S. C5 136
Chandler Heights, Az., U.S. .m9 96
Chāndpur, Bngl. E6 40
Chandrapur, India F3 40
Chang (Yangtze), stm.,
  China E9 28
Chang, Ko, i., Thai. D4 34
Changane, stm., Moz. C5 56
Changara, Moz. B5 56
Chang Cheng (Great Wall),
  China B2 30
Changchun, China C13 28
Changde, China F10 28
Changhua, Tai. E5 30
Changji, China C5 28
Changjiang, China H9 28
Changli, China B4 30
Changmar, China E3 28
Changning, China B3 34
Changsha, China F10 28
Changshu, China C5 30
Changting, China F11 28
Changwu, China B2 30
Changzhi, China D10 28
Changzhou, China E12 28
Chanhassen, Mn., U.S. . . .n11 116
Channahon, Il., U.S. B5 106
Channel Islands, is., Eur. . . .C5 16
Channel Islands National Park,
  Ca., U.S. F4 98
Channel Lake, Il., U.S. H8 106
Channel-Port-aux-Basques, Nf.,
  Can. E2 88
Channelview, Tx., U.S. r14 136
Chanthaburi, Thai. D4 34
Chantilly, Va., U.S. g12 139
Chanute, Ks., U.S. E8 109
Chao'an, China G11 28
Chao Hu, l., China E11 28
Chaoxian, China C4 30
Chaoyang, China E4 30
Chaoyang, China C12 28
Chapadinha, Braz. B3 74
Chapala, Laguna de, l.,
  Mex. C4 78
Chaparral, Col. E4 80
Chapecó, Braz. D7 72
Chapel Hill, N.C., U.S. B3 126
Chapel Hill, Tn., U.S. B5 135
Chaplin, stm., Ky., U.S. C4 110
Chaplin, l., Sk., Can. G2 91
Chaplynka, Ukr. F12 20
Chapman, Ks., U.S. D6 109
Chapman Pond, l., R.I., U.S. .F1 132
Chapmanville, W.V., U.S. . . .D2 141
Chappaquiddick Island, i.,
  Ma., U.S. D7 114
Chappell, Ne., U.S. C3 120
Charagua, Bol. B5 72
Charcas, Mex. C4 78
Chardon, Oh., U.S. A4 128
Charenton, La., U.S. E4 111
Chari, stm., Afr. H8 48
Chārīkār, Afg. C9 42
Charity, stm., Ky., U.S. C4 110
Charleroi, Bel. E9 12
Charleroi, Pa., U.S. F2 131

Charles, stm., Ma., U.S. . . .B5 114
Charles, co., Md., U.S. C3 113
Charles, Cape, c., Va., U.S. .C6 139
Charles A. Goodwin Dam,
  Ct., U.S. B3 100
Charlesbourg, P.Q., Can. . .n17 90
Charles City, la., U.S. A5 108
Charles City, co., Va., U.S. . .C5 139
Charles Mill Lake, res., Oh.,
  U.S. B3 128
Charles Mix, co., S.D., U.S. .D7 134
Charles Mound, Il., U.S. . . .A3 106
Charleston, Ar., U.S. B1 97
Charleston, Il., U.S. D5 106
Charleston, Mo., U.S. E8 118
Charleston, Ms., U.S. A3 117
Charleston, Or., U.S. D2 130
Charleston, co., S.C., U.S. . .F8 133
Charleston, S.C., U.S. F8 133
Charleston, Tn., U.S. D9 135
Charleston, W.V., U.S. C3 141
Charleston Air Force Base,
  mil., S.C., U.S. k11 133
Charleston Naval Shipyard,
  mil., S.C., U.S. k12 133
Charleston Peak, mtn., Nv.,
  U.S. G6 121
Charlestown, In., U.S. H6 107
Charlestown, N.H., U.S. . . .D2 122
Charlestown, R.I., U.S. F2 132
Charles Town, W.V., U.S. . . .B7 141
Charleville, Austl. F4 62
Charleville-Mézières, Fr. . . .C9 16
Charlevoix, Mi., U.S. C5 115
Charlevoix, co., Mi., U.S. . . .C5 115
Charlevoix, Lake, l., Mi.,
  U.S. C5 115
Charlo, N.B., Can. B3 87
Charlotte, co., Fl., U.S. F5 102
Charlotte, Mi., U.S. F6 115
Charlotte, N.C., U.S. B2 126
Charlotte, Tn., U.S. A4 135
Charlotte, Tx., U.S. E3 136
Charlotte, co., Va., U.S. C4 139
Charlotte Amalie, V.I.U.S. . .B6 80
Charlotte Hall, Md., U.S. . . .D4 113
Charlotte Harbor, Fl., U.S. . .F4 102
Charlotte Harbor, b., Fl.,
  U.S. F4 102
Charlottesville, Va., U.S. . . .B4 139
Charlottetown, P.E., Can. . .C6 87
Charlton, co., Ga., U.S. F4 103
Charmco, W.V., U.S. C4 141
Charny, P.Q., Can. C6 90
Charters Towers, Austl. E4 62
Chartres, Fr. C7 16
Chascomús, Arg. F6 72
Chase, B.C., Can. D8 85
Chase, co., Ks., U.S. D7 109
Chase, Md., U.S. B5 113
Chase, co., Ne., U.S. D4 120
Chase City, Va., U.S. D4 139
Chaska, Mn., U.S. F5 116
Chassahowitzka Bay, b., Fl.,
  U.S. D4 102
Chassell, Mi., U.S. B2 115
Châteaubriant, Fr. D6 16
Châteaudun, Fr. C7 16
Châteauguay, P.Q., Can. . . .D4 90
Château-Richer, P.Q., Can. . .C6 90
Châteauroux, Fr. D7 16
Châtellerault, Fr. D7 16
Chatfield, Mn., U.S. G6 116
Chatham, N.B., Can. B4 87
Chatham, On., Can. E2 89
Chatham, co., Ga., U.S. E5 103
Chatham, Il., U.S. D4 106
Chatham, La., U.S. B3 111
Chatham, Ma., U.S. C8 114
Chatham, co., N.C., U.S. . . .B3 126
Chatham, N.J., U.S. B4 123
Chatham, N.Y., U.S. C7 125
Chatham, Va., U.S. D3 139
Chatham Islands, is., N.Z. . .I12 58
Chatham Rise M21 3
Chatham Strait, strt., Ak.,
  U.S. m22 95
Châtillon-sur-Seine, Fr. D9 16
Chatom, Al., U.S. D1 94
Chatsworth, Ga., U.S. B2 103
Chatsworth, Il., U.S. C5 106
Chatsworth Reservoir, res., Ca.,
  U.S. m11 98
Chattahoochee, Fl., U.S. . . .B2 102
Chattahoochee, co., Ga.,
  U.S. D2 103
Chattahoochee, stm., U.S. . .E1 103
Chattanooga, Tn., U.S. D8 135
Chattaroy, W.V., U.S. D2 141
Chattooga, co., Ga., U.S. . . .B1 103
Chattooga, stm., U.S. B1 133
Chatuge Lake, res., U.S. . . .g9 126
Chaudière, stm., P.Q., Can. . .C6 90
Chauk, Mya. B2 34
Chaumont, Fr. C9 16
Chauncey, Oh., U.S. C3 128
Chauny, Fr. C8 16
Chautauqua, co., Ks., U.S. . .E7 109
Chautauqua, co., N.Y.,
  U.S. C1 125
Chautauqua Lake, l., N.Y.,
  U.S. C1 125
Chauvin, La., U.S. E5 111
Chaves, Port. G3 16
Chaves, co., N.M., U.S. D5 124

Name	Map Ref.	Page

Cheaha Mountain, mtn., Al., U.S. ...B4 94
Cheat, Shavers Fork, stm., W.V., U.S. ...B5 141
Cheatham, co., Tn., U.S. ...A4 135
Cheb, Czech Rep. ...D2 20
Chebanse, Il., U.S. ...C6 106
Cheboygan, Mi., U.S. ...C6 115
Cheboygan, co., Mi., U.S. ...C6 115
Chech, 'Erg, des., Afr. ...B4 50
Chechaouen, Mor. ...J4 16
Chechnya see Čečnja, state, Russia ...E6 26
Checotah, Ok., U.S. ...B6 129
Chedabucto Bay, b., N.S., Can. ...D8 87
Cheduba Island, i., Mya. ...C2 34
Cheektowaga, N.Y., U.S. ...C2 125
Cheeseman Lake, res., Co., U.S. ...B5 99
Chehalem Mountains, mts., Or., U.S. ...h12 130
Chehalis, Wa., U.S. ...C3 140
Chehalis, stm., Wa., U.S. ...C2 140
Cheju, S. Kor. ...E13 28
Cheju-do, i., S. Kor. ...E13 28
Chekhov see Čehov, Russia ...A4 31
Chekhov see Čehov, Russia ...B14 20
Chelan, Wa., U.S. ...B5 140
Chelan, co., Wa., U.S. ...B4 140
Chelan, Lake, l., Wa., U.S. ...A5 140
Chelan Mountains, mts., Wa., U.S. ...A5 140
Chelif, Oued, stm., Alg. ...D4 14
Chełm, Pol. ...D7 20
Chełmno, Pol. ...C5 20
Chelmsford, Eng., U.K. ...E7 12
Chelmsford, Ma., U.S. ...A5 114
Chelsea, P.Q., Can. ...D2 90
Chelsea, Al., U.S. ...g7 94
Chelsea, Ma., U.S. ...B5 114
Chelsea, Mi., U.S. ...F6 115
Chelsea, Ok., U.S. ...A6 129
Cheltenham, Eng., U.K. ...E5 12
Cheltenham, Md., U.S. ...C4 113
Chelyabinsk see Čeljabinsk, Russia ...D8 26
Chelyan, W.V., U.S. ...C3 141
Chemba, Moz. ...B5 56
Chemehuevi Indian Reservation, Ca., U.S. ...E6 98
Chemnitz, Ger. ...E13 12
Chemquasabmticook Lake (Ross Lake), l., Me., U.S. ...B3 112
Chemung, co., N.Y., U.S. ...C4 125
Chemung, stm., Pa., U.S. ...C8 131
Chemung Lake, l., On., Can. ...C6 89
Chenāb, stm., Asia ...C2 40
Chenango, stm., N.Y., U.S. ...C5 125
Chenango, co., N.Y., U.S. ...C5 125
Chenango Bridge, N.Y., U.S. ...C5 125
Chenes, River Aux, b., La., U.S. ...k12 111
Chénéville, P.Q., Can. ...D2 90
Cheney, Ks., U.S. ...E6 109
Cheney, Wa., U.S. ...B8 140
Cheney Reservoir, res., Ks., U.S. ...E6 109
Cheneyville, La., U.S. ...C3 111
Chengde, China ...C11 28
Chengdu, China ...E8 28
Chengmai, China ...F2 30
Chengshan Jiao, c., China ...D12 28
Chengxian, China ...C2 30
Chennai (Madras), India ...G4 40
Chenoa, Il., U.S. ...C5 106
Chenoweth, Or., U.S. ...B5 130
Chenxi, China ...D3 30
Chenzhou, China ...F10 28
Chepachet, R.I., U.S. ...B2 132
Chepachet, stm., R.I., U.S. ...B2 132
Chequamegon Bay, b., Wi., U.S. ...B3 142
Cher, stm., Fr. ...D7 16
Cheraw, S.C., U.S. ...B8 133
Cherbaniani Reef, rf., India ...G2 40
Cherbourg, Fr. ...C6 16
Cherchell, Alg. ...I8 16
Chergui, Chott ech, l., Alg. ...D5 48
Cherkasy, Ukr. ...E11 20
Cherkessia see Karačaevo-Čerkesija, state, Russia ...E6 26
Cherniakhiv, Ukr. ...D10 20
Chernihiv, Ukr. ...D11 20
Chernivtsi, Ukr. ...E8 20
Chernobyl see Černobyl', Ukr. ...D11 20
Cherokee, co., Al., U.S. ...A2 94
Cherokee, co., Al., U.S. ...A4 94
Cherokee, co., Ga., U.S. ...B2 103
Cherokee, Ia., U.S. ...B2 108
Cherokee, co., Ia., U.S. ...B2 108
Cherokee, co., Ks., U.S. ...E9 109
Cherokee, Ks., U.S. ...E9 109
Cherokee, co., N.C., U.S. ...f8 126
Cherokee, Ok., U.S. ...A3 129
Cherokee, co., Ok., U.S. ...B6 129
Cherokee, co., S.C., U.S. ...A4 133
Cherokee, co., Tx., U.S. ...D5 136
Cherokee Indian Reservation, N.C., U.S. ...f9 126
Cherokee Lake, res., Tn., W.V., U.S. ...C10 135
Cherokees, Lake O' The, res., Ok., U.S. ...A7 129

Cherokee Village, Ar., U.S. ...A4 97
Cherry, co., Ne., U.S. ...B4 120
Cherry Creek, stm., S.D., U.S. ...C3 134
Cherry Hill, N.J., U.S. ...D2 123
Cherry Point, c., Va., U.S. ...C6 139
Cherry Point Marine Corps Air Station, mil., N.C., U.S. ...C6 126
Cherryvale, Ks., U.S. ...E8 109
Cherry Valley, Ar., U.S. ...B5 97
Cherry Valley, Il., U.S. ...A5 106
Cherryville, N.C., U.S. ...B1 126
Cherskiy Mountains see Čerskogo, hrebet, mts., Russia ...C15 26
Chervonohrad, Ukr. ...D8 20
Chesaning, Mi., U.S. ...E6 115
Chesapeake, Oh., U.S. ...D3 128
Chesapeake, Va., U.S. ...D6 139
Chesapeake, W.V., U.S. ...C3 141
Chesapeake and Delaware Canal, U.S. ...A3 101
Chesapeake Bay, b., U.S. ...D12 92
Chesapeake Bay Bridge-Tunnel, Va., U.S. ...D7 139
Chesapeake Beach, Md., U.S. ...C4 113
Chesapeake City, Md., U.S. ...A6 113
Chesdin, Lake, res., Va., U.S. ...C5 139
Chesha Bay see Češskaja guba, b., Russia ...A8 22
Cheshire, Ct., U.S. ...D4 100
Cheshire, co., N.H., U.S. ...E2 122
Cheshire Reservoir, res., Ma., U.S. ...A1 114
Chesley, On., Can. ...C3 89
Chesnee, S.C., U.S. ...A4 133
Chester, Eng., U.K. ...D5 12
Chester, Ca., U.S. ...B3 98
Chester, Ct., U.S. ...D6 100
Chester, Ga., U.S. ...D3 103
Chester, Il., U.S. ...F4 106
Chester, Md., U.S. ...C5 113
Chester, stm., Md., U.S. ...B5 113
Chester, Mt., U.S. ...B6 119
Chester, N.H., U.S. ...E4 122
Chester, N.Y., U.S. ...D6 125
Chester, Pa., U.S. ...G11 131
Chester, co., Pa., U.S. ...G10 131
Chester, S.C., U.S. ...B5 133
Chester, co., S.C., U.S. ...B5 133
Chester, co., Tn., U.S. ...B3 135
Chester, Va., U.S. ...C5 139
Chester, Vt., U.S. ...E3 138
Chester, W.V., U.S. ...A4 141
Chester Basin, N.S., Can. ...E5 87
Chester Depot, Vt., U.S. ...E3 138
Chesterfield, In., U.S. ...D6 107
Chesterfield, S.C., U.S. ...B7 133
Chesterfield, co., S.C., U.S. ...B7 133
Chesterfield, co., Va., U.S. ...C5 139
Chesterton, In., U.S. ...A3 107
Chestertown, Md., U.S. ...B5 113
Chesterville, On., Can. ...B9 89
Chesuncook Lake, l., Me., U.S. ...C3 112
Cheswick, Pa., U.S. ...h14 131
Cheswold, De., U.S. ...D3 101
Cheta see Heta, stm., Russia ...B11 26
Chetac, Lake, l., Wi., U.S. ...C2 142
Chetco, stm., Or., U.S. ...E2 130
Chetek, Wi., U.S. ...C2 142
Chetek, Lake, l., Wi., U.S. ...C2 142
Chetopa, Ks., U.S. ...E8 109
Chetumal, Mex. ...D7 78
Chetumal, Bahía, b., N.A. ...B2 80
Chetwynd, B.C., Can. ...B7 85
Chevak, Ak., U.S. ...C6 95
Chevreuil, Point, c., La., U.S. ...E4 111
Chevy Chase, Md., U.S. ...C3 113
Chewack, stm., Wa., U.S. ...A5 140
Chewelah, Wa., U.S. ...A8 140
Cheyenne, co., Co., U.S. ...C8 99
Cheyenne, co., Ks., U.S. ...C2 109
Cheyenne, co., Ne., U.S. ...C2 120
Cheyenne, Ok., U.S. ...B2 129
Cheyenne, Wy., U.S. ...E8 143
Cheyenne, stm., U.S. ...C7 92
Cheyenne, stm., U.S. ...C4 134
Cheyenne, Dry Fork, stm., Wy., U.S. ...C7 143
Cheyenne River Indian Reservation, S.D., U.S. ...B4 134
Cheyenne Wells, Co., U.S. ...C8 99
Chhapra, India ...D4 40
Chhatarpur, India ...E3 40
Chhatrapur, India ...F5 40
Chhattisgarh, state, India ...E4 40
Chhindwāra, India ...E3 40
Chi, stm., Thai. ...C4 34
Chiai, Tai. ...E5 30
Chiange, Ang. ...B1 56
Chiang Kham, Thai. ...C4 34
Chiang Khan, Thai. ...C4 34
Chiang Mai, Thai. ...C4 34
Chiang Rai, Thai. ...C3 34
Chiapas, state, Mex. ...D6 78
Chiba, Japan ...C4 31
Chiblow Lake, l., On., Can. ...A1 89
Chibougamau, P.Q., Can. ...k12 90
Chibuto, Moz. ...C5 56
Chicago, Il., U.S. ...B6 106

Chicago Heights, Il., U.S. ...B6 106
Chicago Sanitary and Ship Canal, Il., U.S. ...k8 106
Chicamacomico, stm., Md., U.S. ...D6 113
Chicapa, stm., Afr. ...E4 54
Chichagof Island, i., Ak., U.S. ...m22 95
Chichén Itzá, hist., Mex. ...C7 78
Chickahominy, stm., Va., U.S. ...C5 139
Chickamauga, Ga., U.S. ...B1 103
Chickamauga and Chattanooga National Military Park, U.S. ...k11 135
Chickamauga Dam, Tn., U.S. ...h11 135
Chickamauga Lake, res., Tn., U.S. ...D8 135
Chickasaw, Al., U.S. ...E1 94
Chickasaw, co., Ia., U.S. ...A5 108
Chickasaw, co., Ms., U.S. ...B5 117
Chickasawhay, stm., Ms., U.S. ...D5 117
Chickasaw National Recreation Area, Ok., U.S. ...C5 129
Chickasha, Ok., U.S. ...B4 129
Chickasha, Lake, res., Ok., U.S. ...B3 129
Chickwolnepy Stream, stm., N.H., U.S. ...A4 122
Chiclayo, Peru ...E4 70
Chico, Ca., U.S. ...C3 98
Chico, stm., Arg. ...F3 69
Chicomba, Ang. ...A1 56
Chicopee, Ga., U.S. ...B3 103
Chicopee, Ma., U.S. ...B2 114
Chicora, Pa., U.S. ...E2 131
Chicot, Lake, l., Ar., U.S. ...D4 97
Chicot Island, i., La., U.S. ...E6 111
Chicoutimi, P.Q., Can. ...A6 90
Chicoutimi, stm., P.Q., Can. ...A6 90
Chidambaram, India ...G3 40
Chiefland, Fl., U.S. ...C4 102
Chieti, Italy ...C5 18
Chifeng, China ...C11 28
Chignecto, Cape, c., N.S., Can. ...D5 87
Chignecto Bay, b., Can. ...D5 87
Chigubo, Moz. ...C5 56
Chihli, Gulf of see Bo Hai, b., China ...D11 28
Chihuahua, Mex. ...B3 78
Chihuahua, state, Mex. ...B3 78
Chihuahuan Desert, des., N.A. ...A3 78
Chikaskia, stm., U.S. ...A4 129
Chik Ballāpur, India ...G3 40
Chikmagalūr, India ...G3 40
Chilās, Pak. ...C10 42
Childersburg, Al., U.S. ...B3 94
Childress, Tx., U.S. ...B2 136
Childress, co., Tx., U.S. ...B2 136
Chile, ctry., S.A. ...D2 69
Chilecito, Arg. ...D4 72
Chile Rise ...L29 64
Chilhowie, Va., U.S. ...f10 139
Chilko, stm., B.C., Can. ...D6 85
Chilko Lake, l., B.C., Can. ...D5 85
Chillán, Chile ...E2 69
Chillicothe, Il., U.S. ...C4 106
Chillicothe, Mo., U.S. ...B4 118
Chillicothe, Oh., U.S. ...C3 128
Chilliwack, B.C., Can. ...E7 85
Chillum, Md., U.S. ...f9 113
Chiloé, Isla Grande de, i., Chile ...F2 69
Chiloquin, Or., U.S. ...E5 130
Chilpancingo de los Bravo, Mex. ...D5 78
Chilton, co., Al., U.S. ...C3 94
Chilton, Wi., U.S. ...D5 142
Chiluage, Ang. ...E4 54
Chilung, Tai. ...D5 30
Chimacum, Wa., U.S. ...A3 140
Chimayo, N.M., U.S. ...A4 124
Chimborazo, vol., Ec. ...D4 70
Chimbote, Peru ...E4 70
Chimney Rock, mtn., Ne., U.S. ...C2 120
Chimoio, Moz. ...B5 56
China, ctry., Asia ...D8 28
China Grove, N.C., U.S. ...B2 126
China Lake, l., Me., U.S. ...D3 112
Chinandega, Nic. ...C2 80
Chincha Alta, Peru ...F4 70
Chinchilla, Austl. ...F5 62
Chincoteague, Va., U.S. ...C7 139
Chincoteague Bay, b., U.S. ...D7 113
Chinde, Moz. ...B6 56
Chindwin, stm., Mya. ...A3 34
Chingola, Zam. ...A4 56
Chin Hills, Mya. ...B4 34
Chinhoyi, Zimb. ...B5 56
Chinitna Point, c., Ak., U.S. ...h15 95
Chinju, S. Kor. ...D13 28
Chinle, Az., U.S. ...A6 96
Chino, Ca., U.S. ...F5 98
Chinook, Mt., U.S. ...B7 119
Chinook, Wa., U.S. ...C2 140
Chinook, Lake, res., Or., U.S. ...C5 130
Chino Valley, Az., U.S. ...C3 96

Chinsali, Zam. ...A5 56
Chinvali, Geor. ...A10 44
Chioco, Moz. ...B5 56
Chioggia, Italy ...B4 18
Chios see Khíos, Grc. ...E11 18
Chipata, Zam. ...A5 56
Chipita Park, Co., U.S. ...C6 99
Chipley, Fl., U.S. ...u16 102
Chipman, N.B., Can. ...C4 87
Chipola, stm., Fl., U.S. ...B1 102
Chippewa, co., Mi., U.S. ...B6 115
Chippewa, co., Mn., U.S. ...E3 116
Chippewa, stm., Mn., U.S. ...E3 116
Chippewa, stm., Wi., U.S. ...D2 142
Chippewa, co., Wi., U.S. ...C2 142
Chippewa, Lake, l., Wi., U.S. ...C2 142
Chippewa Falls, Wi., U.S. ...D2 142
Chipuxet, stm., R.I., U.S. ...F3 132
Chiquimula, Guat. ...C2 80
Chiquinquirá, Col. ...B5 70
Chīrāla, India ...F4 40
Chirfa, Niger ...B7 50
Chiricahua Mountains, mts., Az., U.S. ...E6 96
Chiricahua National Monument, Az., U.S. ...F6 96
Chiricahua Peak, mtn., Az., U.S. ...F6 96
Chirikof Island, i., Ak., U.S. ...D8 95
Chiriquí, Golfo de, b., Pan. ...D3 80
Chiriquí, Laguna de, b., Pan. ...D3 80
Chiromo, Mwi. ...B6 56
Chirripó, Cerro, mtn., C.R. ...D3 80
Chisago, co., Mn., U.S. ...E6 116
Chisago City, Mn., U.S. ...E6 116
Chisholm, Me., U.S. ...D2 112
Chisholm, Mn., U.S. ...C6 116
Chishui, stm., China ...D2 30
Chişinău, Mol. ...F10 20
Chisos Mountains, mts., Tx., U.S. ...E1 136
Chita see Čita, Russia ...D13 26
Chitado, Ang. ...E4 54
Chitato, Ang. ...F3 54
Chitembo, Ang. ...F3 54
Chitina, stm., Ak., U.S. ...g19 95
Chitose, Japan ...B4 31
Chitradurga, India ...G3 40
Chitrāl, Pak. ...C10 42
Chitré, Pan. ...D3 80
Chittagong, Bngl. ...E6 40
Chittaurgarh, India ...E2 40
Chittenango, N.Y., U.S. ...B5 125
Chittenden, co., Vt., U.S. ...C2 138
Chittenden Reservoir, res., Vt., U.S. ...D3 138
Chittoor, India ...G3 40
Chitungwiza, Zimb. ...B5 56
Chiumbe (Tshumbe), stm., Afr. ...E4 54
Chiume, Ang. ...B3 56
Chivacoa, Ven. ...C6 80
Chivilcoy, Arg. ...E5 72
Chŏâm Khsant, Camb. ...D4 34
Chocolate Mountains, mts., U.S. ...F6 96
Chocope, Peru ...E4 70
Choctaw, co., Al., U.S. ...C1 94
Choctaw, co., Ms., U.S. ...B4 117
Choctaw, co., Ok., U.S. ...B4 129
Choctaw, co., Ok., U.S. ...C6 129
Choctawhatchee Bay, b., Fl., U.S. ...u15 102
Choctaw Indian Reservation, Ms., U.S. ...C4 117
Choele Choel, Arg. ...E3 69
Chojnice, Pol. ...C4 20
Chŏkwe, Moz. ...C5 56
Cholet, Fr. ...D6 16
Choluteca, Hond. ...C2 80
Choluteca, stm., Hond. ...C2 80
Choma, Zam. ...B4 56
Chomutov, Czech Rep. ...D2 20
Chon Buri, Thai. ...D4 34
Chone, Ec. ...D3 70
Chong'an, China ...D4 30
Ch'ŏngju, N. Kor. ...C13 28
Chongqing, China ...F9 28
Chongqing, prov., China ...E9 28
Chongxin, China ...B2 30
Chongzuo, China ...G9 28
Chŏnju, S. Kor. ...D13 28
Chonos, Archipiélago de los, is., Chile ...G2 69
Choptank, stm., Md., U.S. ...C6 113
Chornomors'ke, Ukr. ...G12 20
Chortkiv, Ukr. ...E8 20
Chōshi, Japan ...C4 31
Chos Malal, Arg. ...F3 72
Choteau, Mt., U.S. ...C4 119
Chouteau, co., Mt., U.S. ...B7 119
Chouteau, Ok., U.S. ...A6 129
Chowan, stm., N.C., U.S. ...A6 126
Chowan, co., N.C., U.S. ...A6 126
Chowchilla, Ca., U.S. ...D3 98
Choybalsan, Mong. ...B10 28
Choyr, Mong. ...B9 28
Chrisman, Il., U.S. ...D6 106
Christchurch, N.Z. ...p13 63c
Christian, co., Il., U.S. ...D4 106
Christian, co., Ky., U.S. ...D2 110

Christian, co., Mo., U.S. ...E4 118
Christiana, De., U.S. ...B3 101
Christiana, Pa., U.S. ...G9 131
Christiansburg, Va., U.S. ...C2 139
Christian Sound, strt., Ak., U.S. ...n22 95
Christina, stm., Ab., Can. ...A5 84
Christina, stm., De., U.S. ...B3 101
Christina Lake, l., Mn., U.S. ...D3 116
Christina Peak, mtn., Nv., U.S. ...D6 121
Christmas, Fl., U.S. ...D5 102
Christmas Island, i., Christ. I. ...F4 58
Christmas Island see Kiritimati, atoll, Kir. ...D14 58
Christmas Island, dep., Oc. ...I4 32
Christmas Lake, l., Or., U.S. ...D6 130
Christmas Ridge ...G22 64
Christopher, Il., U.S. ...F4 106
Chubbuck, Id., U.S. ...G6 105
Chubut, stm., Arg. ...F3 69
Chugach Islands, is., Ak., U.S. ...h16 95
Chugach Mountains, mts., Ak., U.S. ...g18 95
Chugwater, Wy., U.S. ...E8 143
Chugwater Creek, stm., Wy., U.S. ...E8 143
Chuhuïv, Ukr. ...E14 20
Chukchi Sea ...E5 82
Chukotsk Peninsula see Čukotskij poluostrov, pen., Russia ...C20 26
Chula Vista, Ca., U.S. ...F5 98
Chulucanas, Peru ...E3 70
Chumbicha, Arg. ...D4 72
Chumphon, Thai. ...D3 34
Chum Saeng, Thai. ...C4 34
Chunchula, Al., U.S. ...E1 94
Chungking see Chongqing, China ...F9 28
Chuntuquí, Guat. ...B1 80
Chupadera Mesa, mtn., N.M., U.S. ...D3 124
Chuquibamba, Peru ...B3 72
Chuquicamata, Chile ...B3 69
Chur, Switz. ...A2 18
Church Hill, Tn., U.S. ...C11 135
Churchill, Mb., Can. ...f9 86
Churchill, stm., Nf., Can. ...h9 88
Churchill, stm., Can. ...G21 82
Churchill, co., Nv., U.S. ...D3 121
Churchill, Cape, c., Mb., Can. ...f9 86
Churchill, Mount, mtn., B.C., Can. ...E6 85
Churchill Falls, wtfl., Nf., Can. ...h8 88
Churchill Lake, l., Sk., Can. ...m7 91
Churchill Lake, l., Me., U.S. ...B3 112
Church Point, La., U.S. ...D3 111
Church Rock, N.M., U.S. ...B1 124
Churchton, Md., U.S. ...C4 113
Churchville, N.Y., U.S. ...B3 125
Chūru, India ...D2 40
Churubusco, In., U.S. ...B7 107
Chuska Mountains, mts., Az., U.S. ...A6 96
Chuuk Islands, is., Micron. ...D9 58
Chuvashia see Čuvašija, state, Russia ...D6 26
Chuxian, China ...C4 30
Chuxiong, China ...F8 28
Cianjur, Indon. ...E3 36
Cianorte, Braz. ...C7 72
Ciatura, Geor. ...A10 44
Cibecue, Az., U.S. ...C5 96
Cibola, co., N.M., U.S. ...C1 124
Cibolo Creek, stm., Tx., U.S. ...h7 136
Cicero, Il., U.S. ...B6 106
Cicero, In., U.S. ...D5 107
Cide, Tur. ...B5 44
Ciechanów, Pol. ...C6 20
Ciego de Ávila, Cuba ...A4 80
Cienfuegos, Cuba ...A3 80
Cieza, Spain ...H6 16
Çifteler, Tur. ...C4 44
Çiganak, Kaz. ...E9 26
Cihanbeyli, Tur. ...C5 44
Čiili, Kaz. ...B9 42
Čikoj, stm., Asia ...D12 26
Cilacap, Indon. ...E3 36
Çıldır Gölü, l., Tur. ...B10 44
Çilik, Kaz. ...B11 42
Cimarron, Ks., U.S. ...E3 109
Cimarron, N.M., U.S. ...A5 124
Cimarron, co., Ok., U.S. ...e8 129
Cimarron, stm., U.S. ...D8 92
Čimbaj, Uzb. ...B7 42
Cimljanskoe vodohranilišče, res., Russia ...E7 22
Čina, Tanjung, c., Indon. ...E2 36
Çınar, Tur. ...D9 44
Cincinnati, Oh., U.S. ...C1 128
Çine, Tur. ...D3 44
Cinnaminson, N.J., U.S. ...D3 123
Cinto, Monte, mtn., Fr. ...C2 18

Name	Map Ref.	Page

Cintra, Golfe de, b., W. Sah. .B1 50
Cipolletti, Arg. E3 69
Čirčik, Uzb. E8 26
Circle, Ak., U.S. B11 95
Circle, Mt., U.S. C11 119
Circle Pines, Mn., U.S. m12 116
Circleville, Oh., U.S. C3 128
Cirebon, Indon. E3 36
Cirò Marina, Italy E6 18
Cisco, Tx., U.S. C3 136
Ciskei, hist. reg., S. Afr. E4 56
Cisnădie, Rom. G8 20
Cispus, stm., Wa., U.S. C4 140
Cissna Park, Il., U.S. C6 106
Čistopol', Russia C9 22
Čita, Russia D13 26
Citlaltépetl, Volcán see Pico
   de Orizaba, Volcán,
   vol., Mex. D5 78
Citra, Fl., U.S. C4 102
Citronelle, Al., U.S. D1 94
Citrus, co., Fl., U.S. D4 102
City of Refuge National
   Historical Park, Hi., U.S. .D5 104
City View, S.C., U.S. B3 133
Ciudad Acuña, Mex. B4 78
Ciudad Anáhuac, Mex. B4 78
Ciudad Bolívar, Ven. B7 70
Ciudad Camargo, Mex. B5 78
Ciudad Camargo, Mex. B3 78
Ciudad Constitución, Mex. . .C2 78
Ciudad del Carmen, Mex. . . .D6 78
Ciudad del Este, Para. D7 72
Ciudad de Libertador General
   San Martín, Arg. C5 72
Ciudad de México (Mexico
   City), Mex. D5 78
Ciudad de Nutrias, Ven. D6 80
Ciudad Guayana, Ven. B7 70
Ciudad Juárez, Mex. A3 78
Ciudad Madero, Mex. C5 78
Ciudad Mante, Mex. C5 78
Ciudad Miguel Alemán,
   Mex. B5 78
Ciudad Netzahualcóyotl,
   Mex. D5 78
Ciudad Obregón, Mex. B3 78
Ciudad Ojeda, Ven. C5 80
Ciudad Real, Spain H5 16
Ciudad Rodrigo, Spain G3 16
Ciudad Valles, Mex. C5 78
Ciudad Victoria, Mex. C5 78
Ciutadella, Spain G8 16
Civitanova Marche, Italy C4 18
Civitavecchia, Italy C3 18
Çivril, Tur. C3 44
Cizre, Tur. D10 44
C.J. Strike Reservoir, res., Id.,
   U.S. G3 105
Clackamas, Or., U.S. h12 130
Clackamas, co., Or., U.S. . . .B4 130
Clacton-on-Sea, Eng., U.K. . .E7 12
Claflin, Ks., U.S. D5 109
Claiborne, Al., U.S. B2 111
Claiborne, co., Ms., U.S. D3 117
Claiborne, co., Tn., U.S. C10 135
Claiborne, Lake, res., La.,
   U.S. B3 111
Clair, N.B., Can. B1 87
Claire, Lake, l., Ab., Can. . . .f8 84
Clair Engle Lake, res., Ca.,
   U.S. B2 98
Clairton, Pa., U.S. F2 131
Clallam, co., Wa., U.S. B1 140
Clallam Bay, Wa., U.S. A1 140
Clam Lake, l., Wi., U.S. C1 142
Clan Alpine Mountains, mts.,
   Nv., U.S. D4 121
Clanton, Al., U.S. C3 94
Clanwilliam, S. Afr. E2 56
Clara City, Mn., U.S. F3 116
Clara Peak, mtn., Az., U.S. . .C2 96
Clare, Mi., U.S. E6 115
Clare, co., Mi., U.S. E6 115
Claremont, Ca., U.S. m13 98
Claremont, mtn., Ca., U.S. . .C3 98
Claremont, N.C., U.S. B1 126
Claremont, N.H., U.S. D2 122
Claremore, Ok., U.S. A6 129
Clarence, Ia., U.S. C6 108
Clarence, Mo., U.S. B5 118
Clarence Strait, strt., Austl. . .C5 60
Clarence Strait, strt., Ak.,
   U.S. n23 95
Clarendon, Ar., U.S. C4 97
Clarendon, co., S.C., U.S. . . .D7 133
Clarendon, Tx., U.S. B2 136
Clarendon, stm., Vt., U.S. . . .E2 138
Clarendon Hills, Il., U.S. k9 106
Clarenville, Nf., Can. D4 88
Claresholm, Ab., Can. D4 84
Claridge, Pa., U.S. F2 131
Clarinda, Ia., U.S. D2 108
Clarion, Ia., U.S. B4 108
Clarion, Pa., U.S. D3 131
Clarion, stm., Pa., U.S. D3 131
Clarion, co., Pa., U.S. D3 131
Clarión, Isla, i., Mex. D2 78
Clarion Fracture Zone G25 64
Clarissa, Mn., U.S. D4 116
Clark, co., Ar., U.S. C2 97
Clark, co., Id., U.S. E6 105
Clark, co., Il., U.S. D6 106
Clark, co., In., U.S. H6 107
Clark, co., Ks., U.S. E4 109

Clark, co., Ky., U.S. C5 110
Clark, co., Mo., U.S. A6 118
Clark, N.J., U.S. B4 123
Clark, co., Nv., U.S. G6 121
Clark, co., Oh., U.S. C2 128
Clark, S.D., U.S. C8 134
Clark, co., S.D., U.S. C8 134
Clark, co., Wa., U.S. D3 140
Clark, co., Wi., U.S. D3 142
Clark, Lake, l., Ak., U.S. C9 95
Clark, Point, c., On., Can. . . .C3 89
Clarkdale, Az., U.S. C3 96
Clarkdale, Ga., U.S. h7 103
Clarke, co., Al., U.S. D2 94
Clarke, co., Ga., U.S. C3 103
Clarke, co., Ia., U.S. C4 108
Clarke, co., Ms., U.S. C5 117
Clarke, co., Va., U.S. A4 139
Clarke Island, i., Austl. I4 62
Clarkesville, Ga., U.S. B3 103
Clarkfield, Mn., U.S. F3 116
Clark Fork, stm., U.S. C1 119
Clarks, La., U.S. B3 111
Clarksburg, Md., U.S. B3 113
Clarksburg, W.V., U.S. B4 141
Clarksdale, Ms., U.S. A3 117
Clarks Grove, Mn., U.S. G5 116
Clark's Harbour, N.S., Can. . .F4 87
Clarks Hill, In., U.S. D4 107
Clarks Hill Lake, res., U.S. . .E11 92
Clarkson, Ky., U.S. C3 110
Clarkson, Ne., U.S. C8 120
Clarks Summit, Pa., U.S. m18 131
Clarkston, Ga., U.S. h8 103
Clarkston, Mi., U.S. F7 115
Clarkston, Ut., U.S. B3 137
Clarkston, Wa., U.S. C8 140
Clarksville, Ar., U.S. B2 97
Clarksville, De., U.S. F5 101
Clarksville, Ia., U.S. B5 108
Clarksville, In., U.S. H6 107
Clarksville, Tn., U.S. A4 135
Clarksville, Tx., U.S. C5 136
Clarksville, Va., U.S. D4 139
Clarkton, Mo., U.S. E8 118
Clarkton, N.C., U.S. C4 126
Clatskanie, Or., U.S. A3 130
Clatsop, co., Or., U.S. A3 130
Claude, Tx., U.S. B2 136
Clawson, Mi., U.S. o15 115
Claxton, Ga., U.S. D5 103
Clay, co., Al., U.S. B4 94
Clay, co., Ar., U.S. A5 97
Clay, co., Fl., U.S. B5 102
Clay, co., Ga., U.S. E2 103
Clay, co., Ia., U.S. A2 108
Clay, co., Il., U.S. E5 106
Clay, co., In., U.S. F3 107
Clay, co., Ks., U.S. C6 109
Clay, co., Ky., U.S. C6 110
Clay, co., Mn., U.S. D2 116
Clay, co., Mo., U.S. B3 118
Clay, co., Ms., U.S. B5 117
Clay, co., N.C., U.S. f9 126
Clay, co., Ne., U.S. D7 120
Clay, co., S.D., U.S. E8 134
Clay, co., Tn., U.S. C8 135
Clay, co., Tx., U.S. C3 136
Clay, co., W.V., U.S. C3 141
Clay Center, Ks., U.S. C6 109
Clay Center, Ne., U.S. D7 120
Clay City, Il., U.S. E5 106
Clay City, In., U.S. F3 107
Clay City, Ky., U.S. C6 110
Clay Creek, stm., S.D., U.S. . .D8 134
Claymont, De., U.S. A4 101
Clayoquot Sound, strt., B.C.,
   Can. E4 85
Claypool, Az., U.S. D5 96
Claysburg, Pa., U.S. F5 131
Claysville, Pa., U.S. F1 131
Clayton, Al., U.S. D4 94
Clayton, De., U.S. C3 101
Clayton, Ga., U.S. B3 103
Clayton, co., Ga., U.S. C2 103
Clayton, co., Ia., U.S. B6 108
Clayton, In., U.S. E4 107
Clayton, La., U.S. C4 111
Clayton, Mo., U.S. f13 118
Clayton, N.C., U.S. B4 126
Clayton, N.J., U.S. D2 123
Clayton, N.M., U.S. A6 124
Clayton, N.Y., U.S. A4 125
Clayton, Ok., U.S. C6 129
Claytor Lake, res., Va., U.S. . .C2 139
Clear, stm., R.I., U.S. B2 132
Clear Boggy Creek, stm., Ok.,
   U.S. C5 129
Clear Creek, co., Co., U.S. . . .B5 99
Clear Creek, stm., Tn., U.S. . .C9 135
Clear Creek, stm., Wy., U.S. . .B6 143
Cleare, Cape, c., Ak., U.S. . . .D10 95
Clearfield, Ky., U.S. B6 110
Clearfield, Pa., U.S. D5 131
Clearfield, co., Pa., U.S. D5 131
Clearfield, Ut., U.S. B3 137
Clear Fork, stm., W.V., U.S. . .D3 141
Clear Fork, stm., W.V., U.S. . .n13 141
Clearlake, Ca., U.S. C2 98
Clear Lake, res., Ca., U.S. C2 98
Clear Lake, Ia., U.S. A4 108
Clear Lake, l., Ia., U.S. A4 108
Clear Lake, S.D., U.S. C9 134

Clear Lake, l., Ut., U.S. D3 137
Clearlake, Wa., U.S. A3 140
Clear Lake, Wi., U.S. C1 142
Clear Lake Reservoir, res., Ca.,
   U.S. B3 98
Clear Lake Shores, Tx., U.S. . .r15 136
Clear Stream, stm., N.H.,
   U.S. g7 122
Clearwater, B.C., Can. D7 85
Clearwater, stm., Can. A5 84
Clearwater, Fl., U.S. E4 102
Clearwater, stm., Id., U.S. . . .C2 105
Clearwater, co., Id., U.S. C3 105
Clearwater, Ks., U.S. E6 109
Clearwater, co., Mn., U.S. . . .C3 116
Clearwater, stm., Mn., U.S. . .C6 116
Clearwater, S.C., U.S. E4 133
Clearwater Lake, res., Mo.,
   U.S. D7 118
Clearwater Mountains, mts.,
   Id., U.S. C2 105
Cleburne, co., Al., U.S. B4 94
Cleburne, co., Ar., U.S. B3 97
Cleburne, Tx., U.S. C4 136
Cle Elum, Wa., U.S. B4 140
Cle Elum, stm., Wa., U.S. . . .B4 140
Cle Elum Lake, res., Wa.,
   U.S. B4 140
Clementon, N.J., U.S. D3 123
Clemmons, N.C., U.S. A2 126
Clemson, S.C., U.S. B2 133
Clendenin, W.V., U.S. C3 141
Clendening Lake, res., Oh.,
   U.S. B4 128
Cleona, Pa., U.S. F9 131
Clermont, Austl. E4 62
Clermont, P.Q., Can. B7 90
Clermont, Fl., U.S. D5 102
Clermont, co., Oh., U.S. C1 128
Clermont-Ferrand, Fr. E8 16
Cnossus see Knossós, hist.,
   Grc. G10 18
Coachella, Ca., U.S. F5 98
Coachella Canal, Ca.,
   U.S. F6 98
Coahoma, co., Ms., U.S. A3 117
Coahoma, Tx., U.S. C2 136
Coahuila, state, Mex. B4 78
Coal, co., Ok., U.S. C5 129
Coal, stm., W.V., U.S. C3 141
Coal Branch, N.B., Can. C4 87
Coal City, Il., U.S. B5 106
Coal Creek, stm., Ok., U.S. . .B6 129
Coaldale, Ab., Can. E4 84
Coal Fork, W.V., U.S. C3 141
Coal Fork, stm., W.V., U.S. . .m13 141
Coalgate, Ok., U.S. C5 129
Coal Grove, Oh., U.S. D3 128
Coal Hill, Ar., U.S. B2 97
Coalhurst, Ab., Can. E4 84
Coalinga, Ca., U.S. D3 98
Coalmont, Tn., U.S. D8 135
Coalville, Ut., U.S. C4 137
Coalwood, W.V., U.S. D3 141
Coaraci, Braz. D4 74
Coari, Braz. D7 70
Coasters Harbor Island, i., R.I.,
   U.S. E5 132
Coast Mountains, mts., N.A. .G13 82
Coast Ranges, mts., U.S. C3 92
Coatesville, Pa., U.S. G10 131
Coaticook, P.Q., Can. D6 90
Coats, N.C., U.S. B4 126
Coats Land, reg., Ant. D2 67
Coatzacoalcos, Mex. D6 78
Cobalt, On., Can. p19 89
Cobán, Guat. B1 80
Cobar, Austl. G4 62
Cobb, co., Ga., U.S. C2 103
Cobb, stm., Mn., U.S. G5 116
Cobble Mountain Reservoir,
   res., Ma., U.S. B2 114
Cobbosseecontee Lake, l., Me.,
   U.S. D3 112
Cobden, On., Can. B8 89
Cobden, Il., U.S. F4 106
Cobequid Mountains, mts., N.S.,
   Can. D5 87
Cobham, stm., Can. C4 86
Cobija, Bol. F6 70
Cobleskill, N.Y., U.S. C6 125
Cobourg, On., Can. D6 89
Cobourg Peninsula, pen.,
   Austl. C5 60
Cóbuè, Moz. A5 56
Cobun Creek, stm., W.V.,
   U.S. h11 141
Coburg, Ger. E12 12
Coburg, Or., U.S. C3 130
Cocachacra, Peru B3 72
Cochabamba, Bol. B4 72
Cocheco, stm., N.H., U.S. . . .D5 122
Cochin see Kochi, India H3 40
Cochise, co., Az., U.S. F5 96
Cochise Head, mtn., Az.,
   U.S. E6 96
Cochiti Indian Reservation,
   N.M., U.S. h8 124
Cochiti Reservoir, res., N.M.,
   U.S. B3 124
Cochituate, Ma., U.S. g10 114
Cochituate, Lake, l., Ma.,
   U.S. g10 114
Cochran, Ga., U.S. D3 103
Cochran, co., Tx., U.S. C1 136
Cochrane, Ab., Can. D3 84
Cochrane, On., Can. o19 89

Clinton Reservoir, res., N.J.,
   U.S. A4 123
Clintonville, Wi., U.S. D5 142
Clintwood, Va., U.S. e9 139
Clio, Al., U.S. D4 94
Clio, Mi., U.S. E7 115
Clio, S.C., U.S. B8 133
Clipperton, Île, atoll, Oc. . . .G28 64
Clipperton Fracture Zone . . .H25 64
Clive, Ia., U.S. e8 108
Clodomira, Arg. D5 72
Cloncurry, Austl. E3 62
Clonmel, Ire. D3 12
Cloquet, Mn., U.S. D6 116
Cloquet, stm., Mn., U.S. C6 116
Clorinda, Arg. D6 72
Closter, N.J., U.S. B5 123
Clothier, W.V., U.S. n12 141
Cloud, co., Ks., U.S. C6 109
Cloudcroft, N.M., U.S. E4 124
Cloud Peak, mtn., Wy., U.S. .B5 143
Clover, S.C., U.S. A5 133
Cloverdale, Al., U.S. A2 94
Cloverdale, Ca., U.S. C2 98
Cloverdale, In., U.S. E4 107
Cloverport, Ky., U.S. C3 110
Clovis, Ca., U.S. D4 98
Clovis, N.M., U.S. C6 124
Clute, Tx., U.S. r14 136
Clyde, Ks., U.S. C6 109
Clyde, N.C., U.S. f10 126
Clyde, N.Y., U.S. B4 125
Clyde, Oh., U.S. A3 128
Clyde, Tx., U.S. C3 136
Clyde, Firth of, b., Scot.,
   U.K. C4 12
Clymer, Pa., U.S. E3 131
Cnossus see Knossós, hist.,
   Grc. G10 18
Coachella, Ca., U.S. F5 98
Coachella Canal, Ca.,
   U.S. F6 98

Cochranton, Pa., U.S. C1 131
Cocke, co., Tn., U.S. D10 135
Cockeysville, Md., U.S. B4 113
Cockrell Hill, Tx., U.S. n10 136
Coco, stm., N.A. F8 76
Coco, Cayo, i., Cuba A4 80
Coco, Isla del, i., C.R. D2 80
Cocoa, Fl., U.S. D6 102
Cocoa Beach, Fl., U.S. D6 102
Coco Channel, strt., Asia D2 34
Coco Islands, is., Mya. D2 34
Coconino, co., Az., U.S. B3 96
Cocopah Indian Reservation,
   Az., U.S. E1 96
Cocos Islands, dep., Oc. F3 58
Cocos Ridge H5 66
Cod, Cape, c., Ma., U.S. C7 114
Codajás, Braz. D7 70
Coden, Al., U.S. E1 94
Codington, co., S.D., U.S. . . .C8 134
Codó, Braz. B3 74
Cody, Wy., U.S. B3 143
Coeburn, Va., U.S. f9 139
Coen, Austl. C3 62
Coeroeni (Corentyne), stm.,
   S.A. C8 70
Coëtivy, i., Sey. i13 57b
Coeur d'Alene, Id., U.S. B2 105
Coeur d'Alene, stm., Id.,
   U.S. B2 105
Coeur d'Alene Indian
   Reservation, Id., U.S. B2 105
Coeur d'Alene Lake, res., Id.,
   U.S. B2 105
Coeur d'Alene Mountains,
   mts., Id., U.S. B2 105
Coffee, co., Al., U.S. D3 94
Coffee, co., Ga., U.S. E4 103
Coffee, co., Tn., U.S. B5 135
Coffeeville, Ms., U.S. B4 117
Coffey, co., Ks., U.S. D8 109
Coffeyville, Ks., U.S. E8 109
Coffs Harbour, Austl. G5 62
Coggon, Ia., U.S. B6 108
Cognac, Fr. E6 16
Cohansey, stm., N.J., U.S. . . .E2 123
Cohasset, Ma., U.S. B6 114
Cohasset, Mn., U.S. C5 116
Cohocton, stm., N.Y., U.S. . . .C3 125
Cohoes, N.Y., U.S. C7 125
Cohoon, Lake, res., Va.,
   U.S. k14 139
Cohutta Mountain, mtn., Ga.,
   U.S. B2 103
Coiba, Isla de, i., Pan. D3 80
Coihaique, Chile G2 69
Coimbatore, India G3 40
Coimbra, Port. G2 16
Coipasa, Lago, l., Bol. B4 72
Cojutepeque, El Sal. C2 80
Cokato, Mn., U.S. E4 116
Coke, co., Tx., U.S. D2 136
Cokeville, Wy., U.S. D2 143
Čokurdah, Russia B16 26
Colac, Austl. H3 62
Colatina, Braz. E3 74
Colbeck, Cape, c., Ant. D25 67
Colbert, co., Al., U.S. A2 94
Colbert, Ok., U.S. D5 129
Colborne, On., Can. C7 89
Colby, Ks., U.S. C2 109
Colby, Wi., U.S. D3 142
Colchester, Eng., U.K. E7 12
Colchester, Ct., U.S. C6 100
Colchester, Il., U.S. C3 106
Colcord, Ok., U.S. A7 129
Cold, stm., N.H., U.S. C4 122
Cold, stm., N.H., U.S. D2 122
Cold Bay, Ak., U.S. E7 95
Cold Lake, Ab., Can. B5 84
Cold Spring, Ky., U.S. A5 110
Cold Spring, Mn., U.S. E4 116
Coldwater, On., Can. C5 89
Coldwater, Ks., U.S. E4 109
Coldwater, Mi., U.S. G5 115
Coldwater, stm., Ms., U.S. . . .A3 117
Coldwater, Ms., U.S. A4 117
Coldwater, Oh., U.S. B1 128
Coldwater Creek, stm., U.S. . .e9 129
Cole, co., Mo., U.S. C5 118
Colebrook, N.H., U.S. g7 122
Colebrook River Lake, res.,
   Ct., U.S. A3 100
Cole Camp, Mo., U.S. C4 118
Coleen, stm., Ak., U.S. B11 95
Coleman, Mi., U.S. E6 115
Coleman, Tx., U.S. D3 136
Coleman, co., Tx., U.S. D3 136
Coleman, Wi., U.S. C5 142
Coleraine, N. Ire., U.K. C5 12
Coleraine, Mn., U.S. C5 116
Coles, co., Il., U.S. D5 106
Colesberg, S. Afr. E4 56
Colfax, Ca., U.S. C3 98
Colfax, Ia., U.S. C4 108
Colfax, Il., U.S. C5 106
Colfax, In., U.S. D4 107
Colfax, La., U.S. C3 111
Colfax, co., Ne., U.S. C8 120
Colfax, co., N.M., U.S. A5 124
Colfax, Wa., U.S. C8 140
Colfax, Wi., U.S. D2 142
Colhué Huapi, Lago, l.,
   Arg. G3 69
Colima, Mex. D4 78

Name	Map Ref.	Page

Colima, state, Mex. D4 78
Colinas, Braz. C3 74
Coll, i., Scot., U.K. B3 12
College, Ak., U.S. B10 95
Collegedale, Tn., U.S. . . .h11 135
College Park, Ga., U.S. C2 103
College Park, Md., U.S. C4 113
College Place, Wa., U.S. . . .C7 140
College Station, Ar., U.S. . .C3 97
College Station, Tx., U.S. . .D4 136
Collegeville, In., U.S. C3 107
Collegeville, Pa., U.S. F11 131
Colleton, co., S.C., U.S. . . .F6 133
Collie, Austl. G2 60
Collier, co., Fl., U.S. F5 102
Colliers, W.V., U.S. f8 141
Collierville, Tn., U.S. B2 135
Collin, co., Tx., U.S. C4 136
Collingdale, Pa., U.S. p20 131
Collingswood, N.J., U.S. . . .D2 123
Collingsworth, co., Tx., U.S. .B2 136
Collingwood, On., Can. C4 89
Collins, Ms., U.S. D4 117
Collins Park, De., U.S. B3 101
Collinsville, Al., U.S. A4 94
Collinsville, Ct., U.S. B4 100
Collinsville, Il., U.S. E4 106
Collinsville, Ms., U.S. C5 117
Collinsville, Ok., U.S. A6 129
Collinwood, Tn., U.S. B4 135
Collipulli, Chile D2 69
Colmar, Fr. C10 16
Colmar Manor, Md., U.S. . . .f9 113
Colo, Ia., U.S. B4 108
Cologne see Köln, Ger. . . .E10 12
Coloma, Mi., U.S. F4 115
Colombia, ctry., S.A. C5 70
Colombo, Braz. D8 72
Colombo, Sri L. H3 40
Colón, Arg. E5 72
Colón, Cuba A3 80
Colón, Pan. D3 80
Colon, Mi., U.S. G5 115
Colón, Archipiélago de
  (Galapagos Islands), is.,
  Ec. C2 70
Colonial Beach, Va., U.S. . .B6 139
Colonial Heights, Tn., U.S. .C11 135
Colonial Heights, Va., U.S. . .C5 139
Colonial National Historical
  Park, Va., U.S. C6 139
Colonie, N.Y., U.S. C7 125
Colorado, stm., Arg. E4 69
Colorado, stm., N.A. E5 92
Colorado, stm., Tx., U.S. . . .D3 136
Colorado, co., Tx., U.S. E4 136
Colorado, state, U.S. B5 99
Colorado City, Az., U.S. A3 96
Colorado City, Co., U.S. . . .D6 99
Colorado City, Tx., U.S. C2 136
Colorado City, Lake, res., Tx.,
  U.S. C2 136
Colorado National Monument,
  Co., U.S. B2 99
Colorado River Aqueduct,
  aq., Ca., U.S. F6 98
Colorado River Indian
  Reservation, U.S. D1 96
Colorado Springs, Co., U.S. . .C6 99
Colquitt, Ga., U.S. E2 103
Colquitt, co., Ga., U.S. E3 103
Colstrip, Mt., U.S. E10 119
Colton, S.D., U.S. D9 134
Coltons Point, Md., U.S. . . .D4 113
Columbia, stm., N.A. B3 92
Columbia, Al., U.S. D4 94
Columbia, co., Ar., U.S. D2 97
Columbia, co., Fl., U.S. B4 102
Columbia, co., Ga., U.S. C4 103
Columbia, Il., U.S. E3 106
Columbia, Ky., U.S. C4 110
Columbia, Md., U.S. B4 113
Columbia, Mo., U.S. C5 118
Columbia, Ms., U.S. D4 117
Columbia, N.C., U.S. B6 126
Columbia, co., N.Y., U.S. . . .C7 125
Columbia, co., Or., U.S. B3 130
Columbia, Pa., U.S. F9 131
Columbia, co., Pa., U.S. D9 131
Columbia, S.C., U.S. C5 133
Columbia, Tn., U.S. B4 135
Columbia, co., Wa., U.S. . . .C7 140
Columbia, co., Wi., U.S. E4 142
Columbia, Mount, mtn.,
  Can. C2 84
Columbia City, In., U.S. B7 107
Columbia City, Or., U.S. B4 130
Columbia Falls, Mt., U.S. . . .B2 119
Columbia Heights, Mn.,
  U.S. m12 116
Columbia Lake, res., Ct.,
  U.S. C6 100
Columbia Mountains, mts.,
  B.C., Can. C7 85
Columbia Mountains, mts.,
  N.A. H15 82
Columbiana, Al., U.S. B3 94
Columbiana, Oh., U.S. B5 128
Columbiana, co., Oh., U.S. . .B5 128
Columbiaville, Mi., U.S. E7 115
Columbus, Ga., U.S. D2 103
Columbus, In., U.S. F6 107
Columbus, Ks., U.S. E9 109
Columbus, Ms., U.S. B5 117
Columbus, Mt., U.S. E7 119

Columbus, N.C., U.S. f10 126
Columbus, co., N.C., U.S. . . .C4 126
Columbus, Ne., U.S. C8 120
Columbus, N.M., U.S. F2 124
Columbus, Oh., U.S. C2 128
Columbus, Tx., U.S. E4 136
Columbus, Wi., U.S. E4 142
Columbus Air Force Base, mil.,
  Ms., U.S. B5 117
Columbus Grove, Oh., U.S. . .B1 128
Columbus Junction, Ia., U.S. .C6 108
Columbus Lake, res., Ms.,
  U.S. B5 117
Colusa, Ca., U.S. C2 98
Colusa, co., Ca., U.S. C2 98
Colver, Pa., U.S. E4 131
Colville, stm., Ak., U.S. B9 95
Colville, Wa., U.S. A8 140
Colville, stm., Wa., U.S. A8 140
Colville Indian Reservation,
  Wa., U.S. A6 140
Colvos Passage, strt., Wa.,
  U.S. f10 140
Colwich, Ks., U.S. E6 109
Colwood, B.C., Can. h12 85
Comacchio, Italy B4 18
Comacchio, Valli di, l.,
  Italy B4 18
Comal, co., Tx., U.S. E3 136
Comalcalco, Mex. D6 78
Coman, Mount, mtn., Ant. . .D34 67
Comanche, co., Ks., U.S. . . .E4 109
Comanche, Ok., U.S. C4 129
Comanche, co., Ok., U.S. . . .C3 129
Comanche, Tx., U.S. D3 136
Comanche, co., Tx., U.S. . . .D3 136
Comandante Fontana, Arg. . .D6 72
Comayagua, Hond. C2 80
Combahee, stm., S.C., U.S. . .F6 133
Combarbalá, Chile D2 69
Comber, On., Can. E2 89
Combermere Bay, b., Mya. . .C2 34
Combined Locks, Wi., U.S. . .h9 142
Combs, Ky., U.S. C6 110
Comer, Ga., U.S. B3 103
Comfort, Tx., U.S. E3 136
Comilla, Bngl. E6 40
Comitán, Mex. D6 78
Comite, stm., La., U.S. D4 111
Commerce, Ga., U.S. B3 103
Commerce, Ok., U.S. A7 129
Commerce, Tx., U.S. C5 136
Commerce City, Co., U.S. . . .B6 99
Committee Bay, b., N.T.,
  Can. E22 82
Common Fence Point, R.I.,
  U.S. D6 132
Communism Peak see Ismail
  Samani, pik, mtn., Taj. . . .J9 26
Como, Italy B2 18
Como, Ms., U.S. A4 117
Como, Lago di, l., Italy B2 18
Comodoro Rivadavia, Arg. . .G3 69
Comores, Archipel des, is.,
  Afr. A7 56
Comorin, Cape, c., India . . .H3 40
Comoros, ctry., Afr. A7 56
Comox, B.C., Can. E5 85
Compiègne, Fr. C8 16
Compostela, Mex. C4 78
Compton, P.Q., Can. D6 90
Compton, Ca., U.S. n12 98
Comrat, Mol. F10 20
Comstock, Mi., U.S. F5 115
Conanicut Island, i., R.I.,
  U.S. E5 132
Conanicut Point, c., R.I.,
  U.S. E5 132
Concarneau, Fr. D5 16
Conceição da Barra, Braz. . . .E4 74
Conceição do Araguaia,
  Braz. C2 74
Concepción, Arg. D4 72
Concepción, Chile D2 69
Concepción, Para. C6 72
Concepción del Oro, Mex. . . .C4 78
Concepción del Uruguay,
  Arg. E6 72
Conception, Point, c., Ca.,
  U.S. E3 98
Conception Bay, b., Nf.,
  Can. E5 88
Conception Bay South, Nf.,
  Can. E5 88
Conchas Lake, res., N.M.,
  U.S. B5 124
Concho, stm., Tx., U.S. D2 136
Concho, co., Tx., U.S. D3 136
Conchos, stm., Mex. B3 78
Concord, Ca., U.S. h8 98
Concord, Ma., U.S. B5 114
Concord, stm., Ma., U.S. . . .A5 114
Concord, Mi., U.S. F6 115
Concord, Mo., U.S. g13 118
Concord, N.C., U.S. B2 126
Concord, N.H., U.S. D3 122
Concordia, Arg. E6 72
Concórdia, Braz. D7 72
Concordia, Ks., U.S. C6 109
Concordia, co., La., U.S. C4 111
Concordia, Mo., U.S. C4 118
Concrete, Wa., U.S. A4 140
Conda, Ang. F2 54
Condobolin, Austl. G4 62

Condon, Or., U.S. B6 130
Condoto, Col. D4 80
Conecuh, co., Al., U.S. D2 94
Conecuh, stm., U.S. D3 94
Conejos, stm., Co., U.S. D4 99
Conejos, co., Co., U.S. D4 99
Conejos Peak, mtn., Co.,
  U.S. D4 99
Conemaugh, Pa., U.S. F4 131
Conemaugh River Lake, res.,
  Pa., U.S. F3 131
Congamond Lakes, l., U.S. . .A4 100
Congaree, stm., S.C., U.S. . . .D6 133
Congaree Swamp National
  Monument, S.C., U.S. . . .D6 133
Congo, ctry., Afr. C3 54
Congo (Zaïre), stm., Afr. D2 54
Congo, Democratic Republic
  of the, ctry., Afr. D4 54
Congress, Az., U.S. C3 96
Conimicut Point, c., R.I.,
  U.S. D5 132
Conklin, N.Y., U.S. C5 125
Connaught, hist. reg., Ire. . . .D2 12
Conneaut, Oh., U.S. A5 128
Conneaut Creek, stm., Oh.,
  U.S. A5 128
Conneaut Lake, l., Pa., U.S. . .C1 131
Connecticut, stm., U.S. C5 100
Connecticut, state, U.S. C5 100
Connell, Wa., U.S. C7 140
Connellsville, Pa., U.S. F2 131
Connersville, In., U.S. E7 107
Conover, N.C., U.S. B1 126
Conowingo, Md., U.S. A5 113
Conrad, Ia., U.S. B5 108
Conrad, Mt., U.S. B5 119
Conroe, Tx., U.S. D5 136
Conselheiro Lafaiete, Braz. . .F3 74
Conselheiro Pena, Braz. E3 74
Conshohocken, Pa., U.S. . . .F11 131
Consolación del Sur, Cuba . .A3 80
Con Son, is., Viet. E5 34
Consort, Ab., Can. C5 84
Constance see Konstanz,
  Ger. G11 12
Constance, Lake, l., Eur. A2 18
Constanţa, Rom. G10 20
Constantina, Spain I4 16
Constantine see Qacentina,
  Alg. C6 48
Constantine, Mi., U.S. G5 115
Constantine, Cape, c., Ak.,
  U.S. D8 95
Constantinople see Istanbul,
  Tur. B3 44
Constitución, Chile E2 69
Contas, stm., Braz. D3 74
Content Keys, is., Fl., U.S. . . .H5 102
Continental, Oh., U.S. A1 128
Continental Peak, mtn., Wy.,
  U.S. D4 143
Continental Reservoir, res., Co.,
  U.S. D3 99
Contoocook, N.H., U.S. D3 122
Contoocook, stm., N.H.,
  U.S. D3 122
Contra Costa, co., Ca., U.S. . .D3 98
Contrecoeur, P.Q., Can. D4 90
Converse, In., U.S. C6 107
Converse, S.C., U.S. B4 133
Converse, co., Wy., U.S. C7 143
Convoy, Oh., U.S. B1 128
Conway, Ar., U.S. B3 97
Conway, co., Ar., U.S. B3 97
Conway, Fl., U.S. D5 102
Conway, Mo., U.S. D5 118
Conway, N.C., U.S. A5 126
Conway, N.H., U.S. C4 122
Conway, Pa., U.S. E1 131
Conway, S.C., U.S. D9 133
Conway, Lake, res., Ar.,
  U.S. B3 97
Conway Lake, l., N.H.,
  U.S. C4 122
Conway Springs, Ks., U.S. . . .E6 109
Conyers, Ga., U.S. C2 103
Coober Pedy, Austl. F5 60
Cook, co., Ga., U.S. E3 103
Cook, co., Il., U.S. B6 106
Cook, Mn., U.S. C6 116
Cook, co., Mn., U.S. k9 116
Cook, Cape, c., B.C., Can. . .D4 85
Cook, Mount, mtn., N.Z. . . .p12 63c
Cooke, co., Tx., U.S. C4 136
Cookes Peak, mtn., N.M.,
  U.S. E2 124
Cookeville, Tn., U.S. C8 135
Cook Inlet, b., Ak., U.S. D9 95
Cook Islands, dep., Oc. F13 58
Cook Point, c., Md., U.S. . . .C5 113
Cookshire, P.Q., Can. D6 90
Cookson, Ok., U.S. B7 129
Cooktown, Austl. D4 62
Cooleemee, N.C., U.S. B2 126
Coolgardie, Austl. G3 60
Coolidge, Az., U.S. E4 96
Coolidge, Ga., U.S. E3 103
Cooma, Austl. H4 62
Coonabarabran, Austl. G4 62
Coonamble, Austl. G4 62
Coonoor, India G3 40
Coon Rapids, Ia., U.S. C3 108
Coon Rapids, Mn., U.S. E5 116

Coon Valley, Wi., U.S. E2 142
Cooper, co., Mo., U.S. C5 118
Cooper, stm., S.C., U.S. F8 133
Cooper, Tx., U.S. C5 136
Cooper Creek, stm., Austl. . .F2 62
Cooper Mountain, mtn., Ak.,
  U.S. g17 95
Coopersburg, Pa., U.S. F11 131
Cooperstown, N.D., U.S. . . .B7 127
Cooperstown, N.Y., U.S. . . .C6 125
Coopersville, Mi., U.S. E5 115
Coorow, Austl. F2 60
Coos, co., N.H., U.S. A4 122
Coos, co., Or., U.S. D2 130
Coos, stm., Or., U.S. D2 130
Coosa, co., Al., U.S. C3 94
Coosa, stm., U.S. C3 94
Coosada, Al., U.S. C3 94
Coosawhatchie, stm., S.C.,
  U.S. F5 133
Coos Bay, Or., U.S. D2 130
Cootamundra, Austl. G4 62
Copalis Beach, Wa., U.S. . . .B1 140
Copan, Ok., U.S. A6 129
Copan Reservoir, res., Ok.,
  U.S. A6 129
Copenhagen see København,
  Den. I5 10
Copiah, co., Ms., U.S. D3 117
Copiapó, Chile C2 69
Coplay, Pa., U.S. E10 131
Copper, stm., Ak., U.S. C11 95
Copperas Cove, Tx., U.S. . . .D4 136
Copper Butte, mtn., Wa.,
  U.S. A7 140
Copper Mountain, mtn., Wy.,
  U.S. C5 143
Copper Mountains, mts., Az.,
  U.S. E2 96
Coquille, Or., U.S. D2 130
Coquimbo, Chile C2 69
Corabia, Rom. H8 20
Coral Gables, Fl., U.S. G6 102
Coral Sea, Oc. F9 58
Coral Sea Basin J18 64
Coralville, Ia., U.S. C6 108
Coralville Lake, res., Ia.,
  U.S. C5 108
Coraopolis, Pa., U.S. E1 131
Corbeil-Essonnes, Fr. C8 16
Corbin, Ky., U.S. D5 110
Corcoran, Ca., U.S. D4 98
Corcoran, Mn., U.S. m11 116
Corcovado, Golfo, b., Chile . .F2 69
Corcovado, Volcán, vol.,
  Chile F2 69
Cordele, Ga., U.S. E3 103
Cordell, Ok., U.S. B3 129
Cordell Hull Lake, res., Tn.,
  U.S. C8 135
Córdoba, Arg. E5 72
Córdoba, Mex. D5 78
Córdoba, Spain I4 16
Córdova, Peru A2 72
Cordova see Córdoba,
  Spain I4 16
Cordova, Ak., U.S. C10 95
Cordova, Al., U.S. B2 94
Cordova, N.C., U.S. C3 126
Cordova, N.M., U.S. A4 124
Cordova Peak, mtn., Ak.,
  U.S. C10 95
Corentyne (Coeroeni), stm.,
  S.A. C8 70
Corfu see Kérkira, i., Grc. . . .E7 18
Corfu see Kérkira, Grc. E7 18
Coria, Spain H3 16
Corinna, Me., U.S. D3 112
Corinne, Ut., U.S. B3 137
Corinne Key, i., Fl., U.S. G6 102
Corinth see Kórinthos, Grc. . .F9 18
Corinth, Ms., U.S. A5 117
Corinth, N.Y., U.S. B7 125
Corinth, Gulf of see
  Korinthiakós Kólpos,
  b., Grc. E9 18
Corinto, Braz. E3 74
Corisco, Isla de i., Eq. Gui. . .C1 54
Cork, Ire. E2 12
Çorlu, Tur. B2 44
Cormorant Lake, l., Mb.,
  Can. B1 86
Cornelia, Ga., U.S. B3 103
Cornélio Procópio, Braz. F1 74
Cornelius, N.C., U.S. B2 126
Cornelius, Or., U.S. g11 130
Cornell, Wi., U.S. C2 142
Corner Brook, Nf., Can. D3 88
Cornersville, Tn., U.S. B5 135
Cornfield Point, c., Ct.,
  U.S. D6 100
Cornie Bayou, stm., U.S. D3 97
Corning, Ar., U.S. A5 97
Corning, Ca., U.S. C2 98
Corning, Ia., U.S. D3 108
Corning, N.Y., U.S. C3 125
Cornish, Me., U.S. E2 112
Corno Grande, mtn., Italy . . .C4 18
Cornville, Az., U.S. C4 96
Cornwall, On., Can. B10 89
Cornwall, hist. reg., Eng.,
  U.K. E4 12
Cornwall, Pa., U.S. F9 131
Cornwall on Hudson, N.Y.,
  U.S. D6 125

Coro, Ven. A6 70
Coroatá, Braz. B3 74
Corocoro Island, i., S.A. D7 80
Čoroh, stm., Asia B9 44
Coroico, Bol. B4 72
Coromandel Coast, India . . .G4 40
Corona, Ca., U.S. F5 98
Coronado, Ca., U.S. F5 98
Coronado, Bahía de, b.,
  C.R. D3 80
Coronado National Memorial,
  Az., U.S. F5 96
Coronation, Ab., Can. C5 84
Coronation Gulf, b., N.T.,
  Can. E17 82
Coronation Island, i., Ant. . .B36 67
Coronation Island, i., Ak.,
  U.S. n22 95
Coronel Murta, Braz. B9 72
Coronel Oviedo, Para. D6 72
Coronel Suárez, Arg. F5 72
Coronel Vivida, Braz. D7 72
Coropuna, Nevado, vol.,
  Peru G5 70
Corozal, Belize B2 80
Corozal, Col. D4 80
Corpus Christi, Tx., U.S. F4 136
Corpus Christi Naval Air
  Station, mil., Tx., U.S. . . .F4 136
Correctionville, Ia., U.S. B2 108
Correntina, Braz. A9 72
Corrib, Lough, l., Ire. D2 12
Corrientes, Arg. D6 72
Corrientes, Cabo, c., Col. . . .B4 70
Corrientes, Cabo, c., Mex. . .C3 78
Corrigan, Tx., U.S. D5 136
Corriganville, Md., U.S. k13 113
Corrigin, Austl. G2 60
Corriverton, Guy. B8 70
Corry, Pa., U.S. C2 131
Corse (Corsica), i., Fr. C2 18
Corse, Cap, c., Fr. C2 18
Corsica see Corse, i., Fr. C2 18
Corsica, S.D., U.S. D7 134
Corsicana, Tx., U.S. C4 136
Corson, co., S.D., U.S. B4 134
Corson Inlet, b., N.J., U.S. . .E3 123
Cort Adelaer, Kap, c.,
  Grnld. F31 82
Corte, Fr. C2 18
Cortés, Mar de see California,
  Golfo de, b., Mex. B2 78
Cortez, Co., U.S. D2 99
Cortez, Fl., U.S. q10 102
Cortez, Sea of see California,
  Golfo de, b., Mex. B2 78
Cortez Mountains, mts., Nv.,
  U.S. C5 121
Cortland, Il., U.S. B5 106
Cortland, N.Y., U.S. C4 125
Cortland, co., N.Y., U.S. C4 125
Cortland, Oh., U.S. A5 128
Çorum, Tur. B6 44
Corumbá, Braz. G8 70
Corunna see A Coruña,
  Spain F2 16
Corunna, Mi., U.S. F6 115
Coruripe, Braz. D4 74
Corvallis, Or., U.S. C3 130
Corydon, Ia., U.S. D4 108
Corydon, In., U.S. H5 107
Corydon, Ky., U.S. C2 110
Coryell, co., Tx., U.S. D4 136
Cos, i., Grc. F11 18
Cos see Kos, i., Grc. F11 18
Cosenza, Italy E6 18
Coshocton, Oh., U.S. B4 128
Coshocton, co., Oh., U.S. . . .B4 128
Cosmoledo, Atoll de, i.,
  Sey. i11 57b
Cosmopolis, Wa., U.S. C2 140
Cosmos, Mn., U.S. F4 116
Cosne-sur-Loire, Fr. D8 16
Cossatot, stm., Ar., U.S. C1 97
Costa Mesa, Ca., U.S. n13 98
Costa Rica, Mex. C3 78
Costa Rica, ctry., N.A. F8 76
Costilla, co., Co., U.S. D5 99
Coswig, Ger. E13 12
Cotabato, Phil. E8 34
Coteau-Landing, P.Q., Can. . .D3 90
Cote d'Ivoire, ctry., C. Iv. . . .E5 50
Cotonou, Benin E5 50
Cotopaxi, vol., Ec. D4 70
Cottage Grove, Mn., U.S. . .n13 116
Cottage Grove, Or., U.S. D3 130
Cottage Grove Reservoir, res.,
  Or., U.S. D3 130
Cottam, On., Can. E2 89
Cottbus, Ger. E14 12
Cotter, Ar., U.S. A3 97
Cottle, co., Tx., U.S. B2 136
Cottleville, Mo., U.S. f12 118
Cotton, co., Ok., U.S. C3 129
Cottondale, Al., U.S. B2 94
Cotton Plant, Ar., U.S. B4 97
Cottonport, La., U.S. C3 111
Cotton Valley, La., U.S. B2 111
Cottonwood, Al., U.S. D4 94
Cottonwood, Az., U.S. C3 96
Cottonwood, Ca., U.S. B2 98
Cottonwood, Id., U.S. C2 105
Cottonwood, stm., Ks., U.S. .D7 109

Name	Map Ref.	Page
Cottonwood, Mn., U.S.	F3	116
Cottonwood, co., Mn., U.S.	F3	116
Cottonwood, stm., Mn., U.S.	F3	116
Cottonwood Creek, stm., Wy., U.S.	C4	143
Cottonwood Falls, Ks., U.S.	D7	109
Cotuit, Ma., U.S.	C7	114
Cotulla, Tx., U.S.	E3	136
Coudersport, Pa., U.S.	C5	131
Cougar Reservoir, res., Or., U.S.	C4	130
Coulee Creek, stm., Wa., U.S.	g13	140
Coulee Dam, Wa., U.S.	B7	140
Coulee Dam National Recreation Area, Wa., U.S.	A7	140
Coulterville, Il., U.S.	E4	106
Counce, Tn., U.S.	B3	135
Council, Id., U.S.	E2	105
Council Bluffs, Ia., U.S.	C2	108
Council Grove, Ks., U.S.	D7	109
Council Grove Lake, res., Ks., U.S.	D7	109
Council Mountain, mtn., Id., U.S.	E2	105
Country Homes, Wa., U.S.	B8	140
Coupeville, Wa., U.S.	A3	140
Courland Lagoon, b., Eur.	B6	20
Courtenay, B.C., Can.	E5	85
Courte Oreilles, Lac, l., Wi., U.S.	C2	142
Courtland, On., Can.	E4	89
Courtland, Al., U.S.	A2	94
Courtland, Va., U.S.	D5	139
Coushatta, La., U.S.	B2	111
Cove Creek, stm., Ut., U.S.	E3	137
Covedale, Oh., U.S.	o12	128
Coventry, Eng., U.K.	D6	12
Coventry, Ct., U.S.	B6	100
Coventry, R.I., U.S.	D3	132
Cove Point, c., Md., U.S.	D5	113
Covilhã, Port.	G3	16
Covina, Ca., U.S.	m13	98
Covington, co., Al., U.S.	D3	94
Covington, Ga., U.S.	C3	103
Covington, In., U.S.	D3	107
Covington, Ky., U.S.	A5	110
Covington, La., U.S.	D5	111
Covington, co., Ms., U.S.	D4	117
Covington, Oh., U.S.	B1	128
Covington, Tn., U.S.	B2	135
Covington, Va., U.S.	C3	139
Cowan, Tn., U.S.	B5	135
Cowansville, P.Q., Can.	D5	90
Cowarts, Al., U.S.	D4	94
Cow Creek, stm., Wa., U.S.	C7	140
Cowee Mountains, mts., N.C., U.S.	f9	126
Cowell, Austl.	G2	62
Cowen, Mount, mtn., Mt., U.S.	E6	119
Coweta, co., Ga., U.S.	C2	103
Coweta, Ok., U.S.	B6	129
Cow Head, Nf., Can.	D3	88
Cowichan Bay, B.C., Can.	g12	85
Cow Lakes, l., Or., U.S.	D9	130
Cowley, co., Ks., U.S.	E7	109
Cowley, Wy., U.S.	B4	143
Cowlington, Ok., U.S.	B7	129
Cowlitz, co., Wa., U.S.	C2	140
Cowlitz, stm., Wa., U.S.	C3	140
Cowpasture, stm., Va., U.S.	B3	139
Cowpen Mountain, mtn., Ga., U.S.	B2	103
Cowpens, S.C., U.S.	A4	133
Cowra, Austl.	G4	62
Coxim, Braz.	G9	70
Coxsackie, N.Y., U.S.	C7	125
Cox's Bāzār, Bngl.	E6	40
Cox's Cove, Nf., Can.	D2	88
Coyuca de Catalán, Mex.	D4	78
Cozad, Ne., U.S.	D6	120
Cozumel, Mex.	C7	78
Cozumel, Isla, i., Mex.	C7	78
Crab Creek, stm., Wa., U.S.	C6	140
Crab Creek, stm., Wa., U.S.	B7	140
Crab Orchard, Ky., U.S.	C5	110
Crab Orchard, Tn., U.S.	D9	135
Crab Orchard, W.V., U.S.	n13	141
Crab Orchard Lake, res., Il., U.S.	F4	106
Crabtree, Pa., U.S.	F3	131
Crabtree Mills, P.Q., Can.	D4	90
Cracow see Kraków, Pol.	D5	20
Cradock, S. Afr.	E4	56
Crafton, Pa., U.S.	k13	131
Craig, Ak., U.S.	D13	95
Craig, Co., U.S.	A3	99
Craig, co., Ok., U.S.	A6	129
Craig, co., Va., U.S.	C2	139
Craig Air Force Base, mil., Al., U.S.	C3	94
Craig Creek, stm., Va., U.S.	C2	139
Craighead, co., Ar., U.S.	B5	97
Craigsville, Va., U.S.	B3	139
Craigsville, W.V., U.S.	C4	141
Craiova, Rom.	G7	20
Cramerton, N.C., U.S.	B1	126
Cranberry Lake, l., N.Y., U.S.	A6	125
Cranberry Portage, Mb., Can.	B1	86
Cranbrook, Austl.	G2	60
Cranbrook, B.C., Can.	E10	85
Crandall, Tx., U.S.	n10	136
Crandon, Wi., U.S.	C5	142
Crane, Mo., U.S.	E4	118
Crane, co., Tx., U.S.	D1	136
Crane, Tx., U.S.	D1	136
Crane Creek, stm., Oh., U.S.	e7	128
Crane Creek Reservoir, res., Id., U.S.	E2	105
Crane Lake, l., Il., U.S.	C3	106
Crane Lake, l., Mn., U.S.	B6	116
Crane Mountain, mtn., Or., U.S.	E6	130
Crane Prairie Reservoir, res., Or., U.S.	D5	130
Cranford, N.J., U.S.	B4	123
Cranston, R.I., U.S.	C4	132
Crater Lake, l., Or., U.S.	E4	130
Crater Lake National Park, Or., U.S.	E4	130
Craters of the Moon National Monument, Id., U.S.	F5	105
Crateús, Braz.	C3	74
Crato, Braz.	C4	74
Craven, co., N.C., U.S.	B5	126
Crawford, co., Ar., U.S.	B1	97
Crawford, Ga., U.S.	C3	103
Crawford, co., Ga., U.S.	D3	103
Crawford, co., Ia., U.S.	B2	108
Crawford, co., Il., U.S.	D6	106
Crawford, co., In., U.S.	H4	107
Crawford, co., Ks., U.S.	E9	109
Crawford, co., Mi., U.S.	D6	115
Crawford, co., Mo., U.S.	D6	118
Crawford, Ms., U.S.	B5	117
Crawford, Ne., U.S.	B2	120
Crawford, co., Oh., U.S.	B3	128
Crawford, co., Pa., U.S.	C1	131
Crawford, co., Wi., U.S.	E3	142
Crawford Lake, l., Me., U.S.	C5	112
Crawford Notch State Park, N.H., U.S.	B4	122
Crawfordsville, Ar., U.S.	B5	97
Crawfordsville, In., U.S.	D4	107
Crawfordville, Fl., U.S.	B2	102
Crawley, Eng., U.K.	E6	12
Crazy Mountains, mts., Mt., U.S.	D6	119
Crazy Peak, mtn., Mt., U.S.	D6	119
Crazy Woman Creek, stm., Wy., U.S.	B6	143
Creal Springs, Il., U.S.	F5	106
Creedmoor, N.C., U.S.	A4	126
Creek, co., Ok., U.S.	B5	129
Cree Lake, l., Sk., Can.	m7	91
Creemore, On., Can.	C4	89
Creighton, Ne., U.S.	B8	120
Creighton, Pa., U.S.	h14	131
Creil, Fr.	C8	16
Crema, Italy	B2	18
Cremona, Italy	B3	18
Crenshaw, co., Al., U.S.	D3	94
Crenshaw, Ms., U.S.	A3	117
Creola, Al., U.S.	E1	94
Cres, Otok, i., Cro.	B5	18
Cresaptown, Md., U.S.	k13	113
Crescent, Ok., U.S.	B4	129
Crescent, Or., U.S.	D5	130
Crescent, Lake, l., Wa., U.S.	A2	140
Crescent City, Ca., U.S.	B1	98
Crescent City, Fl., U.S.	C5	102
Crescent Lake, l., Fl., U.S.	C5	102
Crescent Lake, l., Or., U.S.	D5	130
Crescent Springs, Ky., U.S.	h13	110
Cresco, Ia., U.S.	A5	108
Cresskill, N.J., U.S.	h9	123
Cresson, Pa., U.S.	F4	131
Cressona, Pa., U.S.	E9	131
Crested Butte, Co., U.S.	C4	99
Crest Hill, Il., U.S.	k8	106
Crestline, Oh., U.S.	B3	128
Creston, B.C., Can.	E9	85
Creston, Ia., U.S.	C3	108
Creston, Oh., U.S.	B4	128
Crestone Peak, mtn., Co., U.S.	D5	99
Crestview, Fl., U.S.	u15	102
Crestview, Hi., U.S.	g10	104
Crestwood, Ky., U.S.	B4	110
Crestwood Village, N.J., U.S.	D4	123
Creswell, Or., U.S.	D3	130
Crete see Kríti, i., Grc.	G10	18
Crete, Il., U.S.	B6	106
Crete, Ne., U.S.	D9	120
Crete, Sea of see Kritikón Pélagos, Grc.	G10	18
Creve Coeur, Il., U.S.	C4	106
Crewe, Va., U.S.	C4	139
Criciúma, Braz.	D8	72
Cricket, N.C., U.S.	A1	126
Cridersville, Oh., U.S.	B1	128
Crimean Mountains see Kryms'ki hory, mts., Ukr.	G13	20
Crimean Peninsula see Kryms'kyi pivostriv, pen., Ukr.	G12	20
Crisfield, Md., U.S.	E6	113
Crisp, co., Ga., U.S.	E3	103
Cristalândia, Braz.	F10	70
Cristalina, Braz.	C2	74
Cristóbal Colón, Pico, mtn., Col.	A5	70
Crittenden, co., Ar., U.S.	B5	97
Crittenden, Ky., U.S.	B5	110
Crittenden, co., Ky., U.S.	e9	110
Crivitz, Wi., U.S.	C6	142
Crna Gora (Montenegro), state, Yugo.	C7	18
Croatia, ctry., Eur.	B5	18
Crocker, Mo., U.S.	D5	118
Crockett, Ca., U.S.	g8	98
Crockett, co., Tn., U.S.	B2	135
Crockett, Tx., U.S.	D5	136
Crockett, co., Tx., U.S.	D2	136
Crofton, Ky., U.S.	C2	110
Crofton, Md., U.S.	B4	113
Crofton, Ne., U.S.	B8	120
Croix, Lac la, l., Mn., U.S.	B6	116
Croker, Cape, c., Austl.	C5	60
Croker, Cape, c., On., Can.	C4	89
Croker Island, i., Austl.	C5	60
Cromona, Ky., U.S.	C7	110
Cromwell, Ct., U.S.	C5	100
Crook, co., Or., U.S.	C6	130
Crook, co., Wy., U.S.	B8	143
Crooked, stm., Or., U.S.	C6	130
Crooked Creek, stm., Pa., U.S.	C7	131
Crooked Creek, stm., U.S.	E3	109
Crooked Creek Lake, res., Pa., U.S.	E3	131
Crooked Island, i., Bah.	D10	76
Crooked Island Passage, strt., Bah.	A5	80
Crooked Lake, l., Fl., U.S.	E5	102
Crooked Lake, l., Mn., U.S.	B7	116
Crooks, S.D., U.S.	D9	134
Crooks, co., Nv., U.S.	B2	121
Crookston, Mn., U.S.	C2	116
Crooksville, Oh., U.S.	C3	128
Crosby, Mn., U.S.	D5	116
Crosby, N.D., U.S.	A2	127
Crosby, Tx., U.S.	r14	136
Crosby, co., Tx., U.S.	C2	136
Crosby, Mount, mtn., Wy., U.S.	C3	143
Crosbyton, Tx., U.S.	C2	136
Cross, co., Ar., U.S.	B5	97
Cross Bay, b., Mb., Can.	C2	86
Cross City, Fl., U.S.	C3	102
Cross Creek, stm., W.V., U.S.	f8	141
Crossett, Ar., U.S.	D4	97
Crossfield, Ab., Can.	D3	84
Cross Island, i., Me., U.S.	D5	112
Cross Lake, l., Me., U.S.	A4	112
Cross Lake, res., La., U.S.	B2	111
Crosslake, Mn., U.S.	D4	116
Cross Lanes, W.V., U.S.	C3	141
Crossman Peak, mtn., Az., U.S.	C1	96
Cross Plains, Tn., U.S.	A5	135
Cross Plains, Tx., U.S.	C3	136
Cross Plains, Wi., U.S.	E4	142
Cross Sound, strt., Ak., U.S.	k21	95
Crossville, Al., U.S.	A4	94
Crossville, Il., U.S.	E5	106
Crossville, Tn., U.S.	D8	135
Croswell, Mi., U.S.	E8	115
Crothersville, In., U.S.	G6	107
Croton-on-Hudson, N.Y., U.S.	D7	125
Crouse, N.C., U.S.	B1	126
Crow, stm., Mn., U.S.	F4	116
Crow Agency, Mt., U.S.	E9	119
Crow Creek, stm., U.S.	A6	99
Crow Creek Indian Reservation, S.D., U.S.	C6	134
Crowder, Ms., U.S.	A3	117
Crowell, Tx., U.S.	C3	136
Crow Indian Reservation, Mt., U.S.	E9	119
Crowley, co., Co., U.S.	C7	99
Crowley, La., U.S.	D3	111
Crowley, Tx., U.S.	n9	136
Crowley, Lake, res., Ca., U.S.	D4	98
Crowleys Ridge, mtn., U.S.	B5	97
Crown Point, In., U.S.	B3	107
Crown Point, La., U.S.	k11	111
Crownpoint, N.M., U.S.	B1	124
Crow Peak, mtn., Mt., U.S.	D5	119
Crowsnest Pass, Ab., Can.	E3	84
Crowsnest Pass, Can.	E3	84
Crow Wing, stm., Mn., U.S.	D4	116
Crow Wing, co., Mn., U.S.	D4	116
Crozet, Va., U.S.	B4	139
Crozet, Archipel, is., Afr.	N15	46
Crozet Basin	L9	64
Cruces, Cuba	A3	80
Crump Lake, l., Or., U.S.	E7	130
Cruz, Cabo, c., Cuba	B4	80
Cruz Alta, Braz.	D7	72
Cruz del Eje, Arg.	E5	72
Cruzeiro, Braz.	F2	74
Cruzeiro do Sul, Braz.	E5	70
Crystal, stm., Co., U.S.	B3	99
Crystal, Mn., U.S.	m12	116
Crystal Bay, b., Fl., U.S.	D4	102
Crystal Bay, Nv., U.S.	D1	121
Crystal Beach, Fl., U.S.	D4	102
Crystal City, Mb., Can.	E2	86
Crystal City, Mo., U.S.	C7	118
Crystal City, Tx., U.S.	E3	136
Crystal Falls, Mi., U.S.	B2	115
Crystal Lake, Ct., U.S.	B6	100
Crystal Lake, l., Ct., U.S.	B6	100
Crystal Lake, Il., U.S.	A5	106
Crystal Lake, l., Il., U.S.	u16	102
Crystal Lake, l., Mi., U.S.	D4	115
Crystal Lake, l., N.H., U.S.	D4	122
Crystal Lake, l., Vt., U.S.	B4	138
Crystal Lawns, Il., U.S.	k8	106
Crystal Pond, res., Ct., U.S.	B7	100
Crystal River, Fl., U.S.	D4	102
Crystal Springs, Ms., U.S.	D3	117
Ču, stm., Asia	B10	42
Cúa, Ven.	C6	80
Cuamba, Moz.	A6	56
Cuando (Kwando), stm., Afr.	B3	56
Cuangar, Ang.	B2	56
Cuango (Kwango), stm., Afr.	E3	54
Cuango, Ang.	E3	54
Cuango, Ang.	E3	54
Cuanza, stm., Ang.	E3	52
Cuauhtémoc, Mex.	C7	78
Cuba, ctry., N.A.	D9	76
Cuba, Il., U.S.	C3	106
Cuba, Mo., U.S.	C6	118
Cuba, N.M., U.S.	A3	124
Cuba, N.Y., U.S.	C2	125
Cuba City, Wi., U.S.	F3	142
Cubal, Ang.	F2	54
Cubango (Okavango), stm., Afr.	B2	56
Cubero, N.M., U.S.	B2	124
Çubuk, Tur.	B5	44
Cucharas, stm., Co., U.S.	D6	99
Cúcuta, Col.	B5	70
Cudahy, Wi., U.S.	F6	142
Cuddalore, India	G3	40
Cuddapah, India	G3	40
Cuddy Mountain, mtn., Id., U.S.	E2	105
Cue, Austl.	E2	60
Cuenca, Ec.	D4	70
Cuenca, Spain	G5	16
Cuencamé de Cenicéros, Mex.	C4	78
Cuernavaca, Mex.	D5	78
Cuero, Tx., U.S.	E4	136
Cuiabá, Braz.	G8	70
Cuilo (Kwilu), stm., Afr.	E3	54
Cuima, Ang.	A2	56
Cuíto, stm., Ang.	B2	56
Cuito Cuanavale, Ang.	B2	56
Cuitzeo, Lago de, l., Mex.	D4	78
Cuivre, West Fork, stm., Mo., U.S.	B6	118
Cukai, Malay.	C2	36
Čukotskij poluostrov, pen., Russia	C20	26
Çulakkurgan, Kaz.	B9	42
Culberson, co., Tx., U.S.	o12	136
Culbertson, Mt., U.S.	B12	119
Culbertson, Ne., U.S.	D5	120
Culebra Peak, mtn., Co., U.S.	D5	99
Culfa, Azer.	C11	44
Culiacán, Mex.	C3	78
Cullen, La., U.S.	B2	111
Cullera, Spain	H6	16
Cullman, co., Al., U.S.	A3	94
Cullman, Al., U.S.	A3	94
Culloden, W.V., U.S.	C2	141
Cullowhee, N.C., U.S.	f9	126
Čul'man, Russia	D14	26
Culpeper, Va., U.S.	B4	139
Culpeper, co., Va., U.S.	B5	139
Culver, In., U.S.	B5	107
Culver City, Ca., U.S.	m12	98
Culvers Lake, l., N.J., U.S.	A3	123
Čulym, Russia	D10	26
Čulym, stm., Russia	D10	26
Cumaná, Ven.	A7	70
Cumberland, B.C., Can.	E5	85
Cumberland, co., Il., U.S.	D5	106
Cumberland, Ky., U.S.	D7	110
Cumberland, co., Ky., U.S.	D4	110
Cumberland, Md., U.S.	k13	113
Cumberland, co., Me., U.S.	E2	112
Cumberland, co., N.C., U.S.	C4	126
Cumberland, co., N.J., U.S.	E2	123
Cumberland, co., Pa., U.S.	F7	131
Cumberland, co., Tn., U.S.	D8	135
Cumberland, stm., U.S.	D4	110
Cumberland, Wi., U.S.	C2	142
Cumberland, stm., U.S.	D4	110
Cumberland, Lake, res., Ky., U.S.	D5	110
Cumberland Center, Me., U.S.	g7	112
Cumberland Foreside, Me., U.S.	E2	112
Cumberland Gap, U.S.	D6	110
Cumberland Gap National Historical Park, U.S.	D6	110
Cumberland Island National Seashore, Ga., U.S.	F5	103
Cumberland Lake, l., Sk., Can.	C4	91
Cumbres Pass, Co., U.S.	D4	99
Čumikan, Russia	D15	26
Cuming, co., Ne., U.S.	C9	120
Cumming, Ga., U.S.	B2	103
Çumra, Tur.	D5	44
Cunani, Braz.	C9	70
Čundža, Kaz.	B11	42
Cunene (Kunene), stm., Afr.	B1	56
Cuneo, Italy	B1	18
Čunja, stm., Russia	C11	26
Cunnamulla, Austl.	F4	62
Cupar, Sk., Can.	G3	91
Cupira, Braz.	C9	70
Curaçao, i., Neth. Ant.	C6	80
Curanilahue, Chile	E2	69
Curecanti National Recreation Area, Co., U.S.	C3	99
Curepipe, Mrts.	g10	57a
Curicó, Chile	D2	69
Curitiba, Braz.	D8	72
Curitibanos, Braz.	D7	72
Curlew Creek, stm., Wa., U.S.	A7	140
Curlew Lake, l., Wa., U.S.	A7	140
Currais Novos, Braz.	C4	74
Currant Mountain, mtn., Nv., U.S.	E6	121
Current, stm., U.S.	A5	97
Currituck, co., N.C., U.S.	A6	126
Curry, co., N.M., U.S.	C6	124
Curry, co., Or., U.S.	E2	130
Curtea de Argeş, Rom.	G8	20
Curtin Springs, Austl.	F5	60
Curtis, Ne., U.S.	D5	120
Curtis Island, i., Austl.	E5	62
Curtisville, Pa., U.S.	E2	131
Cururupu, Braz.	B3	74
Curuzú Cuatiá, Arg.	D6	72
Curvelo, Braz.	E3	74
Curwensville, Pa., U.S.	E4	131
Curwensville Lake, res., Pa., U.S.	E4	131
Curwood, Mount, mtn., Mi., U.S.	B2	115
Cusco, Peru	F5	70
Cushing, Ok., U.S.	B5	129
Cushman, Lake, res., Wa., U.S.	B2	140
Cusseta, Ga., U.S.	D2	103
Custer, co., Co., U.S.	C5	99
Custer, co., Id., U.S.	E4	105
Custer, co., Mt., U.S.	D11	119
Custer, co., Ne., U.S.	C6	120
Custer, co., Ok., U.S.	B2	129
Custer, S.D., U.S.	D2	134
Custer, co., S.D., U.S.	D2	134
Custer Battlefield National Monument, Mt., U.S.	E9	119
Cut, Nuhu, i., Indon.	E8	36
Cut Bank, Mt., U.S.	B4	119
Cut Bank Creek, stm., N.D., U.S.	A4	127
Cutchogue, N.Y., U.S.	m16	125
Cuthbert, Ga., U.S.	E2	103
Cutler Ridge, Fl., U.S.	s13	102
Cut Off, La., U.S.	E5	111
Cuttack, India	E5	40
Cuttyhunk Island, i., Ma., U.S.	D6	114
Čuvašija, state, Russia	D6	26
Cuvier, Cape, c., Austl.	E1	60
Cuxhaven, Ger.	D11	12
Cuyahoga, stm., Oh., U.S.	A4	128
Cuyahoga, co., Oh., U.S.	A4	128
Cuyahoga Falls, Oh., U.S.	A4	128
Cuyama, stm., Ca., U.S.	E4	98
Cuyamaca Peak, mtn., Ca., U.S.	F5	98
Cuyo Islands, is., Phil.	D8	34
Cuyuni, stm., S.A.	D7	80
C.W. McConaughy, Lake, res., Ne., U.S.	C4	120
Cyclades see Kikládhes, is., Grc.	F10	18
Cynthiana, In., U.S.	H2	107
Cynthiana, Ky., U.S.	B5	110
Cypress Creek, stm., Tx., U.S.	r14	136
Cypress Hills Provincial Park, Sk., Can.	H1	91
Cypress Lake, l., Fl., U.S.	D5	102
Cypress Quarters, Fl., U.S.	E6	102
Cypress Swamp, sw., U.S.	F4	101
Cyprus, ctry., Asia	E5	44
Cyprus, North see North Cyprus, ctry., Asia	E5	44
Cyrenaica see Barqah, hist. reg., Libya	E8	14
Cyril, Ok., U.S.	C3	129
Cythera see Kíthira, i., Grc.	F9	18
Cythnos see Kíthnos, i., Grc.	F10	18
Czech Republic, ctry., Eur.	E3	20
Częstochowa, Pol.	D5	20

D

Dabajuro, Ven.	C5	80
Dabeiba, Col.	D4	80
Dabhoi, India	E2	40
Dabie Shan, mts., China	E11	28
Dabola, Gui.	D2	50
Dabou, C. Iv.	E4	50
Daboya, Ghana	E4	50
Dacca see Dhaka, Bngl.	E6	40
Dac Glei, Viet.	C5	34
Dachau, Ger.	F12	12
Dacono, Co., U.S.	A6	99
Dacula, Ga., U.S.	C3	103
Dade, co., Fl., U.S.	G6	102
Dade, co., Ga., U.S.	B1	103
Dade, co., Mo., U.S.	D3	118
Dade City, Fl., U.S.	D4	102
Dadeville, Al., U.S.	C4	94
Dādra and Nagar Haveli, ter., India	E2	40
Dādu, Pak.	D2	40
Daet, Phil.	D8	34
Dafang, China	D2	30
Dafeng, China	C5	30
Daga Medo, Eth.	B8	54
Dagana, Sen.	C1	50

Name	Map Ref.	Page
Dagestan, state, Russia	E6	26
Dagestan see Altaj, state, Russia	A5	28
Daggett, co., Ut., U.S.	C6	137
Dagsboro, De., U.S.	F5	101
Dagu, China	B4	30
Daguan, China	D1	30
Dagupan, Phil.	C8	34
Da Hinggan Ling, mts., China	B12	28
Dahlak Archipelago, is., Erit.	G4	38
Dahlonega, Ga., U.S.	B3	103
Dāhod, India	E2	40
Dahomey see Benin, ctry., Afr.	D5	50
Dahra, Libya	E8	48
Dahūk, Iraq	D10	44
Dailing, China	A1	31
Daingerfield, Tx., U.S.	C5	136
Dairen see Dalian, China	D12	28
Dakar, Sen.	D1	50
Dakhla, W. Sah.	B1	50
Dākoānk, India	H6	40
Dakoro, Niger	D6	50
Dakota, co., Mn., U.S.	F5	116
Dakota, co., Ne., U.S.	B9	120
Dakota City, Ia., U.S.	B3	108
Dakota City, Ne., U.S.	B9	120
Đakovica, Yugo.	C8	18
Đakovo, Cro.	B7	18
Dalaba, Gui.	D2	50
Dalälven, stm., Swe.	F7	10
Dalandzadgad, Mong.	C8	28
Dalarna, hist. reg., Swe.	F6	10
Da Lat, Viet.	D5	34
Dālbandin, Pak.	E8	42
Dalby, Austl.	F5	62
Dale, co., Al., U.S.	D4	94
Dale, In., U.S.	H4	107
Dale City, Va., U.S.	B5	139
Dale Hollow Lake, res., U.S.	C8	135
Daleville, Al., U.S.	D4	94
Daleville, In., U.S.	D6	107
Dalhart, Tx., U.S.	A1	136
Dalhousie, N.B., Can.	A3	87
Dalhousie, India	C3	40
Dali, China	F8	28
Dali, China	C2	30
Dalian, China	D12	28
Dall, Mount, mtn., Ak., U.S.	f15	95
Dallam, co., Tx., U.S.	A1	136
Dallas, co., Al., U.S.	C2	94
Dallas, co., Ar., U.S.	D3	97
Dallas, Ga., U.S.	C2	103
Dallas (part of Melcher), Ia., U.S.	C4	108
Dallas, co., Ia., U.S.	C3	108
Dallas, co., Mo., U.S.	D4	118
Dallas, N.C., U.S.	B1	126
Dallas, Or., U.S.	C3	130
Dallas, Pa., U.S.	D10	131
Dallas, Tx., U.S.	C4	136
Dallas, co., Tx., U.S.	C4	136
Dallas Center, Ia., U.S.	C4	108
Dallas City, Il., U.S.	C2	106
Dallas Naval Air Station, mil., Tx., U.S.	n9	136
Dallastown, Pa., U.S.	G8	131
Dalli Rājhara, India	E4	40
Dall Island, i., Ak., U.S.	n23	95
Dalmacija, hist. reg., Eur.	C6	18
Dalmatia see Dalmacija, hist. reg., Eur.	C6	18
Dal'negorsk, Russia	E15	26
Dal'nerečensk, Russia	B14	28
Daloa, C. Iv.	E3	50
Dalqū, Sudan	F11	48
Dāltenganj, India	E4	40
Dalton, Ga., U.S.	B2	103
Dalton, Ma., U.S.	B1	114
Dalton, Oh., U.S.	B4	128
Dalton, Pa., U.S.	C10	131
Dalton Gardens, Id., U.S.	B2	105
Dalupiri Island, i., Phil.	C8	34
Dalvík, Ice.	l19	10a
Dalwallinu, Austl.	G2	60
Daly, stm., Austl.	C5	60
Daly City, Ca., U.S.	h8	98
Daly Waters, Austl.	D5	60
Damān, India	E2	40
Damanhūr, Egypt	E10	14
Damar, Pulau, i., Indon.	E7	36
Damaraland, hist. reg., Nmb.	C2	56
Damariscotta, Me., U.S.	D3	112
Damariscotta Lake, l., Me., U.S.	D3	112
Damascus see Dimashq, Syria	F7	44
Damascus, Md., U.S.	B3	113
Damascus, Va., U.S.	f10	139
Damaturu, Nig.	D7	50
Damāvand, Qolleh-ye, vol., Iran	C6	42
Damba, Ang.	C3	54
Dambarta, Nig.	D6	50
Dāmghān, Iran	C6	42
Damietta, Egypt	E10	14
Damoh, India	E3	40
Damongo, Ghana	E4	50
Dampier, Austl.	E2	60
Dampier, Selat, strt., Indon.	D8	36
Dan, stm., U.S.	D3	139
Dana, In., U.S.	E3	107
Danakil, reg., Afr.	H13	48
Danané, C. Iv.	E3	50
Da Nang, Viet.	C5	34
Danbury, Ct., U.S.	D2	100
Danbury, Tx., U.S.	r14	136
Dandeli, India	F2	40
Dandong, China	C12	28
Dandridge, Tn., U.S.	C10	135
Dane, co., Wi., U.S.	E4	142
Danfeng, China	C3	30
Dangchang, China	C1	30
Dangriga, Belize	B2	80
Dangshan, China	C4	30
Dania, Fl., U.S.	F6	102
Daniels, co., Mt., U.S.	B11	119
Danielson, Ct., U.S.	B8	100
Daniels Pass, Ut., U.S.	C4	137
Danilov, Russia	C7	22
Danlí, Hond.	C2	80
Dannemora, N.Y., U.S.	f11	125
Dannevirke, N.Z.	p14	63c
Dansville, N.Y., U.S.	C3	125
Dante, Va., U.S.	f9	139
Danube, stm., Eur.	C9	14
Danube, Mouths of the, mth., Eur.	G10	20
Danvers, Il., U.S.	C4	106
Danvers, Ma., U.S.	A6	114
Danville, P.Q., Can.	D5	90
Danville, Ar., U.S.	B2	97
Danville, Ca., U.S.	h9	98
Danville, Ia., U.S.	D6	108
Danville, Il., U.S.	C6	106
Danville, In., U.S.	E4	107
Danville, Ky., U.S.	C5	110
Danville, Oh., U.S.	B3	128
Danville, Pa., U.S.	E8	131
Danville, Va., U.S.	D3	139
Danxian, China	F2	30
Danzig see Gdańsk, Pol.	B5	20
Daocheng, China	F8	28
Daoukro, C. Iv.	E4	50
Daoxian, China	D3	30
Dapaong, Togo	D5	50
Dapchi, Nig.	D7	50
Daphne, Al., U.S.	E2	94
Da Qaidam, China	D7	28
Dar'ā, Syria	F7	44
Dārāb, Iran	E6	42
Darabani, Rom.	E9	20
Dārayyā, Syria	F7	44
Darbhanga, India	D5	40
Darby, Mt., U.S.	D2	119
Darby, Pa., U.S.	G11	131
Dardanelle, Ar., U.S.	B2	97
Dardanelle Lake, res., Ar., U.S.	B2	97
Dardanelles see Çanakkale Boğazı, strt., Tur.	C1	44
Dare, co., N.C., U.S.	B7	126
Darende, Tur.	C7	44
Dar es Salaam, Tan.	E7	54
Dargan-Ata, Turk.	B8	42
Dargaville, N.Z.	o13	63c
Darhan, Mong.	B9	28
Darien, Ct., U.S.	E2	100
Darien, Ga., U.S.	E5	103
Darien, Wi., U.S.	F5	142
Dārjiling, India	D5	40
Darke, co., Oh., U.S.	B1	128
Darlag, China	E7	28
Darley Woods, De., U.S.	h8	101
Darling, stm., Austl.	G3	62
Darling, Lake, res., N.D., U.S.	A4	127
Darling Range, mts., Austl.	G2	60
Darlington, Eng., U.K.	C6	12
Darlington, In., U.S.	D4	107
Darlington, Md., U.S.	A5	113
Darlington, S.C., U.S.	C8	133
Darlington, co., S.C., U.S.	C8	133
Darlington, Wi., U.S.	F3	142
Darłowo, Pol.	B4	20
Darmstadt, Ger.	F11	12
Darnah, Libya	D9	48
Darnley, Cape, c., Ant.	C12	67
Darrah, Mount, mtn., Can.	E3	84
Darreh Gaz, Iran	C7	42
Darrington, Wa., U.S.	A4	140
Dart, Cape, c., Ant.	D27	67
Daru, Pap. N. Gui.	H11	32
Darvaza, Turk.	E7	26
Darwin, Austl.	C5	60
Dašhovuz, Turk.	E7	26
Dassel, Mn., U.S.	E4	116
Dastgardān, Iran	D7	42
Date, Japan	B4	31
Datia, India	D3	40
Datil Mountains, mts., N.M., U.S.	C2	124
Datong, China	B1	30
Datong, China	C10	28
Datu, Tanjung, c., Asia	C3	36
Daufuskie Island, i., S.C., U.S.	G6	133
Daung Kyun, i., Mya.	D3	34
Dauphin, Mb., Can.	D1	86
Dauphin, co., Pa., U.S.	F8	131
Dauphin Island, i., Al., U.S.	E1	94
Dauphin Island, i., Al., U.S.	E1	94
Dauphin Lake, l., Mb., Can.	D2	86
Dāvangere, India	G3	40
Davao, Phil.	E9	34
Davao Gulf, b., Phil.	E9	34
Dāvarzan, Iran	C7	42
Daveluyville, P.Q., Can.	C5	90
Davenport, Fl., U.S.	D5	102
Davenport, Ia., U.S.	C7	108
Davenport, Ok., U.S.	B5	129
Davenport, Wa., U.S.	B7	140
David, Pan.	D3	80
David City, Ne., U.S.	C8	120
Davidson, N.C., U.S.	B2	126
Davidson, co., N.C., U.S.	B2	126
Davidson, co., Tn., U.S.	A5	135
Davidsville, Pa., U.S.	F4	131
Davie, Fl., U.S.	F6	102
Davie, co., N.C., U.S.	B2	126
Daviess, co., In., U.S.	G3	107
Daviess, co., Ky., U.S.	C2	110
Daviess, co., Mo., U.S.	B3	118
Davis, Ca., U.S.	C3	98
Davis, co., Ia., U.S.	D5	108
Davis, Ok., U.S.	C4	129
Davis, co., Ut., U.S.	C3	137
Davis, W.V., U.S.	B5	141
Davis, Mount, mtn., Pa., U.S.	G3	131
Davis Creek, stm., W.V., U.S.	m12	141
Davis Dam, U.S.	H7	121
Davis Islands, is., Fl., U.S.	p11	102
Davis Lake, l., Or., U.S.	E5	130
Davis-Monthan Air Force Base, mil., Az., U.S.	E5	96
Davison, Mi., U.S.	E7	115
Davison, co., S.D., U.S.	D7	134
Davis Sea, Ant.	C13	67
Davisstrædet see Davis Strait, strt., N.A.	E28	82
Davis Strait, strt., N.A.	E28	82
Davisville, R.I., U.S.	E4	132
Dawa, stm., Afr.	C7	54
Dawei, Mya.	D3	34
Dawes, co., Ne., U.S.	B2	120
Dawna Range, mts., Mya.	C3	34
Daws Island, i., S.C., U.S.	G6	133
Dawson, Ga., U.S.	E2	103
Dawson, co., Ga., U.S.	B2	103
Dawson, Mn., U.S.	F2	116
Dawson, co., Mt., U.S.	C11	119
Dawson, co., Ne., U.S.	D6	120
Dawson, co., Tx., U.S.	C1	136
Dawson, Isla, i., Chile	H2	69
Dawson, Mount, mtn., B.C., Can.	D9	85
Dawson Creek, B.C., Can.	B5	85
Dawson Springs, Ky., U.S.	C2	110
Dax, Fr.	F6	16
Daxian, China	E9	28
Daxing, China	B4	30
Daxue Shan, mts., China	E8	28
Day, co., S.D., U.S.	B8	134
Dayao, China	A4	30
Dayong, China	D3	30
Dayr az-Zawr, Syria	E9	44
Daysland, Ab., Can.	C4	84
Dayton, Ia., U.S.	B3	108
Dayton, In., U.S.	D4	107
Dayton, Ky., U.S.	h14	110
Dayton, Md., U.S.	B4	113
Dayton, Mn., U.S.	m12	116
Dayton, Nv., U.S.	D2	121
Dayton, Oh., U.S.	C1	128
Dayton, Or., U.S.	B3	130
Dayton, Tn., U.S.	D8	135
Dayton, Tx., U.S.	D5	136
Dayton, Va., U.S.	B4	139
Dayton, Wa., U.S.	C8	140
Dayton, Wy., U.S.	B5	143
Daytona Beach, Fl., U.S.	C5	102
Dayu, China	F10	28
Da Yunhe (Grand Canal), China	D11	28
Dayville, Ct., U.S.	B8	100
Dazhu, China	C2	30
De Aar, S. Afr.	E3	56
Dead, North Branch, stm., Me., U.S.	C2	112
Dead, South Branch, stm., Me., U.S.	C2	112
Dead Creek, stm., Vt., U.S.	C2	138
Dead Diamond, stm., N.H., U.S.	g7	122
Dead Indian Peak, mtn., Wy., U.S.	B3	143
Dead Lake, l., Me., U.S.	D3	116
Dead Lakes, l., Fl., U.S.	B1	102
Deadman Bay, b., Fl., U.S.	C3	102
Deadman Creek, stm., Wa., U.S.	g14	140
Dead Sea, l., Asia	G6	44
Deadwood, S.D., U.S.	C2	134
Deadwood Reservoir, res., Id., U.S.	E3	105
Deaf Smith, co., Tx., U.S.	B1	136
Deakin, Austl.	G4	60
Deale, Md., U.S.	C4	113
Deal Island, Md., U.S.	D6	113
Deal Island, i., Md., U.S.	D6	113
Dean, stm., B.C., Can.	C4	85
Dean Channel, strt., B.C., Can.	C4	85
Deán Funes, Arg.	E5	72
Dearborn, co., In., U.S.	F7	107
Dearborn, Mi., U.S.	F7	115
Dearborn Heights, Mi., U.S.	p15	115
Death Valley, val., Ca., U.S.	D5	98
Death Valley National Park, U.S.	D5	98
Deba, Nig.	D7	50
De Baca, co., N.M., U.S.	C5	124
Debao, China	E2	30
Debar, Fl., U.S.	D5	102
Debauch Mountain, mtn., Ak., U.S.	C8	95
Dęblin, Pol.	D6	20
Debre Birhan, Eth.	B7	54
Debrecen, Hung.	F6	20
Debre Mark'os, Eth.	A7	54
Debre Tabor, Eth.	H3	38
Debre Zeyit, Eth.	B7	54
De Cade, Lake, l., La., U.S.	E5	111
Decatur, Al., U.S.	A3	94
Decatur, Ar., U.S.	A1	97
Decatur, Ga., U.S.	C2	103
Decatur, co., Ga., U.S.	F2	103
Decatur, co., Ia., U.S.	D4	108
Decatur, Il., U.S.	D5	106
Decatur, In., U.S.	C8	107
Decatur, co., In., U.S.	F6	107
Decatur, co., Ks., U.S.	C3	109
Decatur, Mi., U.S.	F5	115
Decatur, Ms., U.S.	C4	117
Decatur, Ne., U.S.	B9	120
Decatur, co., Tn., U.S.	D9	135
Decatur, Tn., U.S.	B3	135
Decatur, Tx., U.S.	C4	136
Decatur, Lake, res., Il., U.S.	D5	106
Decaturville, Tn., U.S.	B3	135
Decazeville, Fr.	E8	16
Deccan, plat., India	G3	40
Deception, Mount, mtn., Wa., U.S.	B2	140
Decherd, Tn., U.S.	B5	135
Děčín, Czech Rep.	D3	20
Deckerville, Mi., U.S.	E8	115
Decorah, Ia., U.S.	A6	108
Dedham, Ma., U.S.	B5	114
Dedoplis Ckaro, Geor.	B12	44
Dédougou, Burkina	D4	50
Deep, stm., N.C., U.S.	B3	126
Deep Creek, stm., Ut., U.S.	C2	137
Deep Creek, stm., Ut., U.S.	F3	137
Deep Creek, stm., Ut., U.S.	B3	137
Deep Creek, stm., Wa., U.S.	g13	140
Deep Creek Lake, res., Md., U.S.	K12	113
Deep Creek Mountains, mts., Id., U.S.	G6	105
Deep Fork, stm., Ok., U.S.	B5	129
Deep Inlet, b., Nf., Can.	g10	88
Deep Red Creek, stm., Ok., U.S.	C3	129
Deep River, On., Can.	A7	89
Deep River, Ct., U.S.	D6	100
Deer Creek, stm., Oh., U.S.	C2	128
Deer Creek Indian Reservation, Mn., U.S.	C5	116
Deerfield, Il., U.S.	h9	106
Deerfield, Ks., U.S.	E2	109
Deerfield, Ma., U.S.	A2	114
Deerfield, Mi., U.S.	G7	115
Deerfield, Wi., U.S.	E4	142
Deerfield, stm., U.S.	A2	114
Deerfield Beach, Fl., U.S.	F6	102
Deer Island, pen., Ma., U.S.	g12	114
Deer Island, i., Ms., U.S.	f8	117
Deer Isle, i., Me., U.S.	D4	112
Deer Lake, l., Nf., Can.	D3	88
Deer Lake, Nf., Can.	D3	88
Deer Lake, l., Mn., U.S.	C5	116
Deer Lodge, Mt., U.S.	D4	119
Deer Lodge, co., Mt., U.S.	E3	119
Deer Park, N.Y., U.S.	n15	125
Deer Park, Oh., U.S.	o13	128
Deer Park, Wa., U.S.	B8	140
Deer Peak, mtn., Co., U.S.	C5	99
Deer River, Mn., U.S.	C5	116
Defiance, Oh., U.S.	A1	128
Defiance, co., Oh., U.S.	A1	128
Defiance, Mount, mtn., Or., U.S.	B5	130
De Forest, Wi., U.S.	E4	142
De Funiak Springs, Fl., U.S.	u15	102
Dêgê, China	E7	28
Degeh Bur, Eth.	B8	54
Dégelis, P.Q., Can.	B9	90
Degerfors, Swe.	G6	10
De Graff, Oh., U.S.	B2	128
De Gray Lake, res., Ar., U.S.	C2	97
Dehiwala-Mount Lavinia, Sri L.	H3	40
Dehlorān, Iran	F12	44
Dehra Dūn, India	C3	40
Dehui, China	C13	28
Dej, Rom.	F7	20
Dejnau, Turk.	C8	42
De Kalb, co., Al., U.S.	A4	94
De Kalb, co., Ga., U.S.	C2	103
De Kalb, Il., U.S.	B5	106
De Kalb, co., Il., U.S.	B5	106
De Kalb, co., In., U.S.	B7	107
De Kalb, co., Mo., U.S.	B3	118
De Kalb, Ms., U.S.	C5	117
De Kalb, co., Tn., U.S.	D8	135
De Kalb, Tx., U.S.	C5	136
Dekese, D.R.C.	D4	54
Delafield, Wi., U.S.	m11	142
Delanco, N.J., U.S.	C3	123
De Land, Fl., U.S.	C5	102
Delano, Ca., U.S.	E4	98
Delano, Mn., U.S.	E5	116
Delano Peak, mtn., Ut., U.S.	E3	137
Delārām, Afg.	D8	42
Delaronde Lake, l., Sk., Can.	C2	91
Delavan, Il., U.S.	C4	106
Delavan, Wi., U.S.	F5	142
Delaware, co., Ia., U.S.	B6	108
Delaware, co., In., U.S.	D7	107
Delaware, stm., Ks., U.S.	C8	109
Delaware, co., N.Y., U.S.	C5	125
Delaware, Oh., U.S.	B2	128
Delaware, co., Oh., U.S.	B2	128
Delaware, co., Ok., U.S.	A7	129
Delaware, co., Pa., U.S.	G11	131
Delaware, stm., U.S.	G11	131
Delaware, state, U.S.	D3	101
Delaware, East Branch, stm., N.Y., U.S.	C5	125
Delaware Bay, b., U.S.	D13	92
Delaware City, De., U.S.	B3	101
Delaware Lake, res., Oh., U.S.	B3	128
Delaware Water Gap, N.J., U.S.	B2	123
Delaware Water Gap National Recreation Area, U.S.	B2	123
Delbarton, W.V., U.S.	D2	141
Delcambre, La., U.S.	E4	111
Del City, Ok., U.S.	B4	129
De Leon, Tx., U.S.	C3	136
De Leon Springs, Fl., U.S.	C5	102
Delfzijl, Neth.	D10	12
Delgado, Cabo, c., Moz.	A7	56
Delhi, India	D3	40
Delhi, La., U.S.	B4	111
Delhi, N.Y., U.S.	C6	125
Delice, stm., Tur.	B6	44
Delicias, Mex.	B3	78
Delingde, Russia	B13	26
Delingha, China	D7	28
De Lisle, Ms., U.S.	E4	117
Dellenbaugh, Mount, mtn., Az., U.S.	A2	96
Dell Rapids, S.D., U.S.	D9	134
Dellys, Alg.	I8	16
Del Mar, Ca., U.S.	o15	98
Delmar, De., U.S.	G3	101
Delmar, Md., U.S.	D6	113
Delmar, N.Y., U.S.	C7	125
Delmenhorst, Ger.	D11	12
Del Norte, co., Ca., U.S.	B2	98
Del Norte, Co., U.S.	D4	99
Deloraine, Mb., Can.	E1	86
Delos see Dhílos, hist., Grc.	F10	18
Del Park Manor, De., U.S.	i7	101
Delphi see Dhelfoí, hist., Grc.	E9	18
Delphi, In., U.S.	C4	107
Delphos, Oh., U.S.	B1	128
Delran, N.J., U.S.	C3	123
Delray Beach, Fl., U.S.	F6	102
Del Rio, Tx., U.S.	E2	136
Delson, P.Q., Can.	q19	90
Delta, Co., U.S.	C2	99
Delta, co., Co., U.S.	C3	99
Delta, co., Mi., U.S.	C3	115
Delta, reg., Ms., U.S.	B3	117
Delta, Oh., U.S.	A2	128
Delta, co., Tx., U.S.	C5	136
Delta, Ut., U.S.	D3	137
Delta Junction, Ak., U.S.	C10	95
Delta Peak, mtn., B.C., Can.	A3	85
Delta Reservoir, res., N.Y., U.S.	B5	125
Deltaville, Va., U.S.	C6	139
Deltona, Fl., U.S.	D5	102
Del Verme Falls, wtfl., Eth.	B8	54
Demarest, N.J., U.S.	h9	123
Demba, D.R.C.	D4	54
Dembia, C.A.R.	B4	54
Dembi Dolo, Eth.	B6	54
Demidov, Russia	B11	20
Deming, N.M., U.S.	E2	124
Demirci, Tur.	C3	44
Demjanskoe, Russia	D8	26
Demmin, Ger.	D13	12
Democratic Republic of the Congo see Congo, Democratic Republic of the, ctry., Afr.	D4	52
Demopolis, Al., U.S.	C2	94
Demorest, Ga., U.S.	B3	103
Demotte, In., U.S.	B3	107
Dempo, Gunung, vol., Indon.	D2	36
Demta, Indon.	G11	32
Denakil see Danakil, reg., Afr.	H13	48
Denali National Park, Ak., U.S.	C9	95
Denan, Eth.	B8	54
Denare Beach, Sk., Can.	C4	91

Name	Map Ref.	Page
Denau, Uzb.	F8	26
Dengas, Niger	D6	50
Dengkou, China	A2	30
Dêngqên, China	E7	28
Dengxian, China	C3	30
Denham, Austl.	F1	60
Denham, Mount, mtn., Jam.	B4	80
Denham Springs, La., U.S.	D5	111
Den Helder, Neth.	D9	12
Dénia, Spain	H7	16
Deniliquin, Austl.	H4	62
Denison, Ia., U.S.	B2	108
Denison, Tx., U.S.	C4	136
Denison Dam, U.S.	D5	129
Denizli, Tur.	D3	44
Denmark, Austl.	G2	60
Denmark, S.C., U.S.	E5	133
Denmark, Wi., U.S.	D6	142
Denmark, ctry., Eur.	I4	10
Denmark Strait, strt.	E34	82
Dennehotso, Az., U.S.	A6	96
Dennis, Ma., U.S.	C7	114
Dennison, Oh., U.S.	B4	128
Dennis Port, Ma., U.S.	C7	114
Denny Terrace, S.C., U.S.	C5	133
Denpasar, Indon.	E5	36
Dent, co., Mo., U.S.	D6	118
Denton, Md., U.S.	C6	113
Denton, N.C., U.S.	B2	126
Denton, Tn., U.S.	C4	136
Denton, co., Tx., U.S.	C4	136
D'Entrecasteaux, Point, c., Austl.	G2	60
D'Entrecasteaux Islands, is., Pap. N. Gui.	H13	32
Dentsville, S.C., U.S.	C6	133
Denver, Co., U.S.	B6	99
Denver, Ia., U.S.	B5	108
Denver, Pa., U.S.	F9	131
Denver, co., Co., U.S.	B6	99
Denver City, Tx., U.S.	C1	136
Denville, N.J., U.S.	B4	123
Deoghar, India	E5	40
Deolāli, India	F2	40
De Pere, Wi., U.S.	D5	142
Depew, N.Y., U.S.	C2	125
Depoe Bay, Or., U.S.	C2	130
Deposit, N.Y., U.S.	C5	125
Depue, Il., U.S.	B4	106
Dêqên, China	F7	28
Deqing, China	E3	30
De Queen, Ar., U.S.	C1	97
De Queen Reservoir, res., Ar., U.S.	C1	97
De Quincy, La., U.S.	D2	111
Dera Ghāzi Khān, Pak.	E10	42
Dera Ismāīl Khān, Pak.	D10	42
Derbent, Russia	E6	26
Derby, Austl.	D3	60
Derby, Eng., U.K.	D6	12
Derby, Ct., U.S.	D3	100
Derby, Ks., U.S.	E6	109
Derby, Vt., U.S.	B4	138
Derby Line, Vt., U.S.	A4	138
Derg, Lough, l., Ire.	D2	12
Dergači, Russia	D8	22
De Ridder, La., U.S.	D2	111
Derik, Tur.	D9	44
Derma, Ms., U.S.	B4	117
Dermott, Ar., U.S.	D4	97
Dernieres, Isles, is., La., U.S.	E5	111
Derry see Londonderry, N. Ire., U.K.	C3	12
Derry, N.H., U.S.	E4	122
Derry, Pa., U.S.	F3	131
Derventa, Bos.	B6	18
Derwood, Md., U.S.	B3	113
Des Allemands, La., U.S.	E5	111
Désappointement, Îles du, is., Fr. Poly.	F15	58
Des Arc, Ar., U.S.	C4	97
Desbiens, P.Q., Can.	A6	90
Descanso, Mex.	A1	78
Deschaillons [-sur-Saint-Laurent], P.Q., Can.	C5	90
Deschambault, P.Q., Can.	C6	90
Deschambault Lake, l., Sk., Can.	C4	91
Deschutes, co., Or., U.S.	D5	130
Deschutes, stm., Or., U.S.	B6	130
Desē, Eth.	H12	48
Deseado, stm., Arg.	G3	69
Desengaño, Punta, c., Arg.	G3	69
Deseret Peak, mtn., Ut., U.S.	C3	137
Deseronto, On., Can.	C7	89
Desert Creek Peak, mtn., Nv., U.S.	E2	121
Desert Hot Springs, Ca., U.S.	F5	98
Desert Peak, mtn., Ut., U.S.	B3	137
Desert Valley, val., Nv., U.S.	B3	121
Desha, Ar., U.S.	B4	97
Desha, co., Ar., U.S.	D4	97
Deshler, Ne., U.S.	D8	120
Deshler, Oh., U.S.	A2	128
Des Lacs, stm., N.D., U.S.	A4	127
Desloge, Mo., U.S.	D7	118
De Smet, S.D., U.S.	C8	134
Des Moines, Ia., U.S.	C4	108
Des Moines, Wa., U.S.	B3	140
Des Moines, co., Ia., U.S.	D6	108
Des Moines, stm., U.S.	D5	108
Desna, stm., Eur.	D11	20
De Soto, Ia., U.S.	C3	108
De Soto, Il., U.S.	F4	106
De Soto, Ks., U.S.	D9	109
De Soto, Mo., U.S.	C7	118
De Soto, co., Fl., U.S.	E5	102
De Soto, co., La., U.S.	B2	111
De Soto, co., Ms., U.S.	A3	117
Despard, W.V., U.S.	k10	141
Des Peres, Mo., U.S.	f13	118
Des Plaines, Il., U.S.	A6	106
Des Plaines, stm., U.S.	k8	106
Desroches, i., Sey.	i12	57b
Dessau, Ger.	E13	12
Destin, Fl., U.S.	u15	102
Destrehan, La., U.S.	E5	111
Detour, Point, c., Mi., U.S.	C4	115
Detroit, Mi., U.S.	F7	115
Detroit Lake, res., Or., U.S.	C4	130
Detroit Lakes, Mn., U.S.	D3	116
Dettifoss, wtfl, Ice.	l20	10a
Deuel, co., Ne., U.S.	C3	120
Deuel, co., S.D., U.S.	C9	134
Deutsche Bucht, b., Ger.	C10	12
Deux-Montagnes, P.Q., Can.	p19	90
Deux Montagnes, Lac des, l., P.Q., Can.	q19	90
Deva, Rom.	G7	20
De Valls Bluff, Ar., U.S.	C4	97
Develi, Tur.	C6	44
Deventer, Neth.	D10	12
DeView, Bayou, stm., Ar., U.S.	B4	97
Devils Island see Diable, Île du, i., Fr. Gu.	B9	70
Devils Lake, N.D., U.S.	A7	127
Devils Lake, l., N.D., U.S.	A6	127
Devils Paw, mtn., Ak., U.S.	k23	95
Devils Postpile National Monument, Ca., U.S.	D4	98
Devils Tower National Monument, Wy., U.S.	B8	143
Devil Track Lake, l., Mn., U.S.	k9	116
Devine, Tx., U.S.	E3	136
DeVola, Oh., U.S.	C4	128
Devon, Ab., Can.	C4	84
Devonport, Austl.	I4	62
Devonshire, De., U.S.	h7	101
Devrek, Tur.	B4	44
Dewar, Ok., U.S.	B6	129
Dewās, India	E3	40
Dewees Inlet, b., S.C., U.S.	k12	133
Dewees Island, i., S.C., U.S.	F8	133
Dewey, Az., U.S.	C3	96
Dewey, Ok., U.S.	A6	129
Dewey, co., Ok., U.S.	B2	129
Dewey, co., S.D., U.S.	B4	134
Dewey Beach, De., U.S.	F5	101
Dewey Lake, res., Ky., U.S.	C7	110
Deweyville, Tx., U.S.	D6	136
De Witt, Ar., U.S.	C4	97
De Witt, Ia., U.S.	C7	108
De Witt, Mi., U.S.	F6	115
De Witt, N.Y., U.S.	B4	125
De Witt, co., Il., U.S.	C4	106
De Witt, co., Tx., U.S.	E4	136
Dexing, China	D4	30
Dexter, Ia., U.S.	C3	108
Dexter, Me., U.S.	C3	112
Dexter, Mi., U.S.	F7	115
Dexter, Mo., U.S.	E8	118
Dexter, N.M., U.S.	D5	124
Dexter, Lake, l., Fl., U.S.	C5	102
Dezfūl, Iran	D5	42
Dezhou, China	D11	28
Dežneva, mys, c., Russia	C21	26
Dhahran see Aẓ-Ẓahrān, Sau. Ar.	E5	42
Dhaka, Bngl.	E6	40
Dhamtari, India	E4	40
Dhanbād, India	E5	40
Dhār, India	E3	40
Dharān, Nepal	D5	40
Dharmapuri, India	G3	40
Dhawalāgiri, mtn., Nepal	D4	40
Dhelfoí, hist., Grc.	E9	18
Dhenkānāl, India	E5	40
Dhílos, hist., Grc.	F10	18
Dhodhekánisos, is., Grc.	F11	18
Dhone, India	F3	40
Dhoomadheere, Som.	C8	54
Dhorāji, India	E2	40
Dhuburi, India	D5	40
Dhule, India	E2	40
Diable, Île du, i., Fr. Gu.	B9	70
Diablo, Canyon, val., Az., U.S.	C4	96
Diablo, Mount, mtn., Ca., U.S.	h9	98
Diablo, Pico del, mtn., Mex.	A1	78
Diablo Dam, Wa., U.S.	A4	140
Diablo Lake, res., Wa., U.S.	A4	140
Diablo Range, mts., Ca., U.S.	D3	98
Diablotins, Morne, vol., Dom.	B7	80
Diaca, Moz.	A6	56
Dialakoto, Sen.	D2	50
Diamante, Arg.	F4	72
Diamantina, Braz.	E3	74
Diamantina, stm., Austl.	E3	62
Diamantino, Braz.	F8	70
Diamond Harbour, India	E5	40
Diamond Head, crat., Hi., U.S.	B4	104
Diamond Hill, R.I., U.S.	B4	132
Diamond Hill Reservoir, res., R.I., U.S.	A4	132
Diamond Lake, Il., U.S.	h9	106
Diamond Lake, l., Or., U.S.	D4	130
Diamond Mountains, mts., Nv., U.S.	D6	121
Diamond Peak, mtn., Co., U.S.	A2	99
Diamond Peak, mtn., Id., U.S.	E5	105
Diamond Peak, mtn., Or., U.S.	D4	130
Diamond Peak, mtn., Wa., U.S.	C8	140
Diamondville, Wy., U.S.	E2	143
Dianbai, China	E3	30
Dianjiang, China	C2	30
Dianópolis, Braz.	F10	70
Diapaga, Burkina	D5	50
Diaz, Ar., U.S.	B4	97
Dibaya, D.R.C.	C4	54
D'Iberville, Ms., U.S.	E5	117
Diboll, Tx., U.S.	D5	136
Dibrugarh, India	D6	40
Dickens, co., Tx., U.S.	C2	136
Dickenson, co., Va., U.S.	e9	139
Dickerson, Md., U.S.	B3	113
Dickey, co., N.D., U.S.	C7	127
Dickeyville, Wi., U.S.	F3	142
Dickinson, N.D., U.S.	C3	127
Dickinson, co., Ia., U.S.	A2	108
Dickinson, co., Ks., U.S.	D6	109
Dickinson, co., Mi., U.S.	B3	115
Dickinson Dam, N.D., U.S.	C3	127
Dickson, Ok., U.S.	C5	129
Dickson, Tn., U.S.	A4	135
Dickson, co., Tn., U.S.	A4	135
Dickson City, Pa., U.S.	D10	131
Dicle see Tigris, stm., Asia	D5	42
Didao, China	A2	31
Didbiran, Russia	D15	26
Didsbury, Ab., Can.	D3	84
Dīdwāna, India	D2	40
Diefenbaker, Lake, res., Sk., Can.	F2	91
Diego de Almagro, Isla, i., Chile	H1	69
Diégo-Suarez see Antsirañana, Madag.	A8	56
Diéma, Mali	D3	50
Dien Bien, Viet.	B4	34
Diepholz, Ger.	D11	12
Dieppe, N.B., Can.	C5	87
Dieppe, Fr.	C7	16
Dierks, Ar., U.S.	C1	97
Di'er Songhua see Songhua, stm., China	B14	28
Dif, Kenya	C8	54
Diffa, Niger	D7	50
Dighton, Ks., U.S.	D3	109
Digne, Fr.	E10	16
Digos, Phil.	E9	34
Digul, stm., Indon.	H10	32
Diinsor, Som.	C8	54
Dijlah see Tigris, stm., Asia	D5	42
Dijon, Fr.	D9	16
Dike, Ia., U.S.	B5	108
Dikhil, Dji.	H13	48
Dikili, Tur.	C2	44
Dikson, Russia	B10	26
Dikwa, Nig.	D7	50
Dīla, Eth.	B7	54
Dili, E. Timor	E7	36
Dillard, Or., U.S.	D3	130
Dill City, Ok., U.S.	B2	129
Dilley, Tx., U.S.	E3	136
Dillingham, Ak., U.S.	D8	95
Dillon, Mt., U.S.	E4	119
Dillon, S.C., U.S.	C9	133
Dillon, co., S.C., U.S.	C9	133
Dillon Lake, res., Oh., U.S.	B3	128
Dillon Reservoir, res., Co., U.S.	B4	99
Dillonvale, Oh., U.S.	B5	128
Dillsboro, In., U.S.	F7	107
Dillsburg, Pa., U.S.	F7	131
Dilolo, D.R.C.	F4	54
Dilworth, Mn., U.S.	D2	116
Dimāpur, India	D6	40
Dimashq (Damascus), Syria	F7	44
Dimbokro, C. Iv.	E4	50
Dimitrovgrad, Bul.	C10	18
Dimitrovgrad, Russia	D6	26
Dimlang, mtn., Nig.	E7	50
Dimmit, co., Tx., U.S.	E3	136
Dimmitt, Tx., U.S.	B1	136
Dimondale, Mi., U.S.	F6	115
Dinagat Island, i., Phil.	D9	34
Dinajpur, Bngl.	D5	40
Dinan, Fr.	C5	16
Dinar, Tur.	C4	44
Dinaric Alps, mts., Eur.	G4	20
Dindigul, India	G3	40
Dinghai, China	E12	28
Dingle Bay, b., Ire.	D1	12
Dingmans Ferry, Pa., U.S.	D12	131
Dingolfing, Ger.	F13	12
Dingtao, China	B4	30
Dinguiraye, Gui.	D2	50
Dingxiang, China	B3	30
Dingxing, China	B4	30
Dinner Point, c., Fl., U.S.	D4	102
Dinokwe, Bots.	C4	56
Dinosaur National Monument, U.S.	C6	137
Dinuba, Ca., U.S.	D4	98
Dinwiddie, co., Va., U.S.	C5	139
Dioura, Mali	D3	50
Diourbel, Sen.	D1	50
Dipolog, Phil.	E8	34
Dīr, Pak.	C10	42
Diré, Mali	C4	50
Dirē Dawa, Eth.	B8	54
Dirico, Ang.	B3	56
Dirj, Libya	E6	14
Dirk Hartog Island, i., Austl.	F1	60
Dirkou, Niger	C7	50
Dirty Devil, stm., Ut., U.S.	E5	137
Disappointment, Cape, c., S. Geor.	H9	69
Disappointment, Cape, c., Wa., U.S.	C1	140
Disappointment, Lake, l., Austl.	E3	60
Dishman, Wa., U.S.	g14	140
Disko, i., Grnld.	E28	82
Dismal, stm., Ne., U.S.	C5	120
Dispur, India	D6	40
Disraëli, P.Q., Can.	D6	90
District of Columbia, dept., U.S.	f8	113
Distrito Federal, state, Braz.	E3	74
Distrito Federal, state, Mex.	D5	78
Diu, India	E2	40
Dīvāndarreh, Iran	E12	44
Divernon, Il., U.S.	D4	106
Divide, co., N.D., U.S.	A2	127
Divide Peak, mtn., Wy., U.S.	E5	143
Divinópolis, Braz.	F7	74
Divisor, Serra do, plat., S.A.	E5	70
Divnoe, Russia	A4	42
Divo, C. Iv.	E3	50
Divriği, Tur.	C8	44
Dix, stm., Ky., U.S.	C5	110
Dixfield, Me., U.S.	D2	112
Dixie, co., Fl., U.S.	C3	102
Dixie Valley, val., Nv., U.S.	D4	121
Dixon, Ca., U.S.	C3	98
Dixon, Il., U.S.	B4	106
Dixon, Mo., U.S.	D5	118
Dixon, N.M., U.S.	A4	124
Dixon, co., Ne., U.S.	B9	120
Dixon Entrance, strt., N.A.	H13	82
Dixonville, Pa., U.S.	E3	131
Diyarbakır, Tur.	D9	44
Djado, Plateau du, plat., Niger	B7	50
Djamâa, Alg.	E5	14
Djambala, Congo	D2	54
Djanet, Alg.	B6	50
Djat'kovo, Russia	C13	20
Djelfa, Alg.	E5	14
Djemila, hist., Alg.	I9	16
Djenné, Mali	D4	50
Djibo, Burkina	D4	50
Djibouti, Dji.	H13	48
Djibouti, ctry., Afr.	H13	48
Djoku-Punda, D.R.C.	E4	54
Djougou, Benin	E5	50
Djoum, Cam.	C2	54
Djugu, D.R.C.	C6	54
Djurtjuli, Russia	C9	22
Dmitrija Lapteva, proliv, strt., Russia	B16	26
Dmitrijev-L'govskij, Russia	C13	20
Dmitrovsk see Dnipropetrovs'k, Ukr.	E13	20
Dnepr see Dniester, stm., Eur.	F11	20
Dnieper (Dnepr) (Dnipro), stm., Eur.	F12	20
Dniester (Nistru) (Dnister), stm., Eur.	F11	20
Dniprodzerzhyns'k, Ukr.	E13	20
Dniprodzerzhyns'ke vodoskhovyshche, res., Ukr.	E13	20
Dnipropetrovs'k, Ukr.	E13	20
Dnister see Dniester, stm., Eur.	F11	20
Dno, Russia	C5	22
Dôa, Moz.	B5	56
Doaktown, N.B., Can.	C3	87
Doba, Chad	E8	50
Dobbs Ferry, N.Y., U.S.	g13	125
Dobele, Lat.	H10	10
Doberai, Jazirah, pen., Indon.	D8	36
Dobo, Indon.	H9	32
Doboj, Bos.	B7	18
Dobrič, Bul.	C11	18
Dobrjanka, Russia	C10	22
Dobruja, hist. reg., Eur.	H9	20
Dobson, N.C., U.S.	A2	126
Doce, stm., Braz.	E3	74
Docena, Al., U.S.	f7	94
Doctors Lake, l., Fl., U.S.	m8	102
Doddridge, co., W.V., U.S.	B4	141
Dodecanese see Dhodhekánisos, is., Grc.	F11	18
Dodge, Ne., U.S.	C9	120
Dodge, co., Ga., U.S.	D3	103
Dodge, co., Mn., U.S.	G6	116
Dodge, co., Ne., U.S.	C9	120
Dodge, co., Wi., U.S.	E5	142
Dodge Center, Mn., U.S.	F6	116
Dodge City, Ks., U.S.	E3	109
Dodgeville, Wi., U.S.	F3	142
Dodoma, Tan.	E7	54
Doerun, Ga., U.S.	E3	103
Doe Run, Mo., U.S.	D7	118
Dog, stm., Vt., U.S.	C3	138
Dogai Coring, l., China	E5	28
Dog Island, i., Fl., U.S.	C2	102
Dog Keys Pass, strt., Ms., U.S.	g8	117
Dog Lake, l., Mb., Can.	D2	86
Do Gonbadān, Iran	D6	42
Dogondoutchi, Niger	D5	50
Doğubayazıt, Tur.	C11	44
Doğu Karadeniz Dağları, mts., Tur.	B8	44
Doha see Ad-Dawhah, Qatar	E6	42
Dokka, Nor.	F4	10
Dokuchaievs'k, Ukr.	F14	20
Dolbeau, P.Q., Can.	k12	90
Dole, Fr.	D9	16
Dolgeville, N.Y., U.S.	B6	125
Dolinsk, Russia	B16	28
Dollar Bay, Mi., U.S.	A2	115
Dolomite, Al., U.S.	B3	94
Dolomites see Dolomiti, mts., Italy	A3	18
Dolomiti, mts., Italy	A3	18
Dolores, Arg.	E6	72
Dolores, Col.	D2	99
Dolores, Ur.	F6	72
Dolores, co., Co., U.S.	D2	99
Dolores, stm., U.S.	E7	137
Dolphin Island, i., Ut., U.S.	B3	137
Dolton, Il., U.S.	k9	106
Dolyns'ka, Ukr.	E12	20
Dombås, Nor.	E3	10
Dome Mountain, mtn., Az., U.S.	k9	96
Dome Peak, mtn., Co., U.S.	B3	99
Domeyko, Chile	C2	69
Dominica, ctry., N.A.	E12	76
Dominican Republic, ctry., N.A.	H12	75
Dominique, Canal de la see Martinique Passage, strt., N.A.	B7	80
Domo, Eth.	I14	48
Dom Pedrito, Braz.	E7	72
Don, stm., Russia	E6	26
Dona Ana, N.M., U.S.	E3	124
Dona Ana, co., N.M., U.S.	E2	124
Donaldsonville, La., U.S.	D4	111
Donalsonville, Ga., U.S.	E2	103
Donau see Danube, stm., Eur.	C9	14
Donauwörth, Ger.	F12	12
Don Benito, Spain	H4	16
Dondo, Ang.	E2	54
Dondo, Moz.	B5	56
Dondra Head, c., Sri L.	H4	40
Donegal, Ire.	C2	12
Donegal Bay, b., Ire.	C2	12
Doneraile, S.C., U.S.	C8	133
Donets'k, Ukr.	F14	20
Dong, stm., China	B7	34
Dong'an, China	D3	30
Dongara, Austl.	F1	60
Dongchuan, China	D1	30
Dongfang, China	H9	28
Donggala, Indon.	D5	36
Donghai Dao, i., China	G10	28
Dong Hoi, Viet.	C5	34
Dongjingcheng, China	B1	31
Dongo, Ang.	A2	56
Dongping, China	B4	30
Dongsheng, China	B3	30
Dongtai, China	C5	30
Dongting Hu, l., China	F10	28
Dongzhi, China	C4	30
Doniphan, Mo., U.S.	E7	118
Doniphan, co., Ks., U.S.	C8	109
Donkey Creek, stm., Wy., U.S.	B7	143
Donkin, N.S., Can.	C10	87
Donley, co., Tx., U.S.	B2	136
Dønna, Nor.	C5	10
Donna, Tx., U.S.	F3	136
Donnacona, P.Q., Can.	C6	90
Donnellson, Ia., U.S.	D6	108
Donner Pass, Ca., U.S.	C3	98
Donnybrook, Austl.	G2	60
Donora, Pa., U.S.	F2	131
Donostia (San Sebastián), Spain	F6	16
Donskaja grjada, hills, Eur.	E7	22
Don Upland see Donskaja grjada, hills, Eur.	E7	22
Doolow, Som.	J13	48
Dooly, co., Ga., U.S.	D3	103
Doonerak, Mount, mtn., Ak., U.S.	B9	95
Door, co., Wi., U.S.	D6	142
Dora, Al., U.S.	B2	94
Doraville, Ga., U.S.	h8	103
Dorcheat, Bayou, stm., U.S.	B2	111
Dorchester, N.B., Can.	D5	87
Dorchester, Eng., U.K.	E5	12
Dorchester, Ne., U.S.	D8	120
Dorchester, co., Md., U.S.	D5	113
Dorchester, co., S.C., U.S.	E7	133
Dordogne, stm., Fr.	E7	16
Dordrecht, Neth.	E9	12
Doré Lake, l., Sk., Can.	C2	91

Name	Map Ref.	Page

Dorena Lake, res., Or., U.S. . . **D3** 130
Dori, Burkina **D4** 50
Dorion-Vaudreuil, P.Q.,
Can. **q18** 90
Dormont, Pa., U.S. **k13** 131
Dornbirn, Aus. **G11** 12
Dorogobuž, Russia **B12** 20
Dorohoi, Rom. **F9** 20
Dorothy Pond, Ma., U.S. . . . **B4** 114
Dorr, Mi., U.S. **F5** 115
Dorre Island, i., Austl. **F1** 60
Dorset, Vt., U.S. **E2** 138
Dorsey, Md., U.S. **B4** 113
Dortmund, Ger. **E10** 12
Dorton, Ky., U.S. **C7** 110
Dörtyol, Tur. **D7** 44
Do Rūd, Iran **D5** 42
Doruma, D.R.C. **C5** 54
Dorval, P.Q., Can. **q19** 90
Dosatuj, Russia **D13** 26
Dos Bahías, Cabo, c., Arg. . . **G3** 69
Dosso, Niger **D5** 50
Dossor, Kaz. **E9** 22
Dothan, Al., U.S. **D4** 94
Douala, Cam. **C1** 54
Douarnenez, Fr. **C4** 16
Double Beach, Ct., U.S. . . . **D4** 100
Double Island Point, c.,
Austl. **F5** 62
Doublespring Pass, Id., U.S. **E5** 105
Double Springs, Al., U.S. . . **A2** 94
Doubletop Peak, mtn., Wy.,
U.S. **C2** 143
Doubs, stm., Eur. **D9** 16
Douentza, Mali **C4** 50
Dougherty, co., Ga., U.S. . . **E2** 103
Douglas, I. of Man **C4** 12
Douglas, S. Afr. **D3** 56
Douglas, Az., U.S. **F6** 96
Douglas, Ga., U.S. **E4** 103
Douglas, Mi., U.S. **F4** 115
Douglas, Wy., U.S. **D7** 143
Douglas, co., Co., U.S. . . . **B6** 99
Douglas, co., Ga., U.S. . . . **C2** 103
Douglas, co., Il., U.S. **D5** 106
Douglas, co., Ks., U.S. . . . **D8** 109
Douglas, co., Mn., U.S. . . . **E3** 116
Douglas, co., Mo., U.S. . . . **E5** 118
Douglas, co., Ne., U.S. . . . **C9** 120
Douglas, co., Nv., U.S. . . . **E2** 121
Douglas, co., Or., U.S. . . . **D3** 130
Douglas, co., S.D., U.S. . . . **D7** 134
Douglas, co., Wa., U.S. . . . **B6** 140
Douglas, co., Wi., U.S. . . . **B2** 142
Douglas, Mount, mtn., Ak.,
U.S. **D9** 95
Douglas Channel, strt., B.C.,
Can. **C3** 85
Douglas Lake, l., Mi., U.S. . **C6** 115
Douglas Lake, res., Tn., U.S. **D10** 135
Douglass, Ks., U.S. **E7** 109
Douglastown, N.B., Can. . . **B4** 87
Douglasville, Ga., U.S. . . . **C2** 103
Dourados, Braz. **H9** 70
Dourbali, Chad **D8** 50
Douro (Duero), stm., Eur. . . **G2** 16
Dousman, Wi., U.S. **E5** 142
Dove Creek, Co., U.S. **D2** 99
Dover, Eng., U.K. **E7** 12
Dover, Ar., U.S. **B2** 97
Dover, De., U.S. **D3** 101
Dover, Fl., U.S. **D4** 102
Dover, Ma., U.S. **h10** 114
Dover, N.H., U.S. **D5** 122
Dover, N.J., U.S. **B3** 123
Dover, Oh., U.S. **B4** 128
Dover, Pa., U.S. **F8** 131
Dover, Tn., U.S. **A4** 135
Dover, Strait of, strt., Eur. . **B7** 16
Dover Air Force Base, mil.,
De., U.S. **D4** 101
Dover-Foxcroft, Me., U.S. . . **C3** 112
Dover Plains, N.Y., U.S. . . . **D7** 125
Dowagiac, Mi., U.S. **G4** 115
Dowlatābād, Iran **E7** 42
Downers Grove, Il., U.S. . . **B5** 106
Downey, Ca., U.S. **n12** 98
Downey, Id., U.S. **G6** 105
Downingtown, Pa., U.S. . . **F10** 131
Downpatrick, N. Ire., U.K. . . **C4** 12
Downs, Ks., U.S. **C5** 109
Downs Mountain, mtn.,
Wy., U.S. **C3** 143
Downton, Mount, mtn.,
B.C., Can. **C5** 85
Dows, Ia., U.S. **B4** 108
Doylestown, Oh., U.S. . . . **B4** 128
Doylestown, Pa., U.S. . . . **F11** 131
Doyline, La., U.S. **B2** 111
Dra'a, Hamada du, des.,
Alg. **E3** 48
Dracena, Braz. **F1** 74
Dracut, Ma., U.S. **A5** 114
Drăgăşani, Rom. **G8** 20
Dragør, Den. **I5** 10
Drain, Or., U.S. **D3** 130
Drakensberg, mts., Afr. . . . **D4** 56
Drake Passage, strt. **B33** 67
Drake Peak, mtn., Or., U.S. **E6** 130
Dráma, Grc. **D10** 18
Drammen, Nor. **G4** 10
Draper, Ut., U.S. **C4** 137
Drau (Dráva), stm., Eur. . . . **F2** 20
Dráva (Drau), stm., Eur. . . . **G4** 20
Drayton, On., Can. **D4** 89

Drayton, N.D., U.S. **A8** 127
Drayton, S.C., U.S. **B4** 133
Drayton Plains, Mi., U.S. . . **F7** 115
Drayton Valley, Ab., Can. . . **C3** 84
Dresden, On., Can. **E2** 89
Dresden, Ger. **E13** 12
Dresden, Oh., U.S. **B3** 128
Dresden, Tn., U.S. **A3** 135
Dresslerville, Nv., U.S. . . . **E2** 121
Dreux, Fr. **C7** 16
Drew, Ms., U.S. **B3** 117
Drew, co., Ar., U.S. **D4** 97
Drews Reservoir, res., Or.,
U.S. **E6** 130
Drexel, Mo., U.S. **C3** 118
Drexel, N.C., U.S. **B1** 126
Drexel, Oh., U.S. **C1** 128
Drift, Ky., U.S. **C7** 110
Drinit, Gjiri i b., Alb. **D7** 18
Driskill Mountain, hill, La.,
U.S. **B3** 111
Drobeta-Turnu Severin,
Rom. **G7** 20
Drogheda, Ire. **D3** 12
Drohobych, Ukr. **E7** 20
Drumheller, Ab., Can. **D4** 84
Drum Island, i., S.C., U.S. . **k12** 133
Drummond, Lake, l., Va.,
U.S. **D6** 139
Drummond Island, i., Mi.,
U.S. **C7** 115
Drummondville, P.Q., Can. . **D5** 90
Drumright, Ok., U.S. **B5** 129
Druskininkai, Lith. **I11** 10
Družba, Kaz. **B4** 28
Družina, Russia **C16** 26
Drybranch, W.V., U.S. . . . **m13** 141
Dry Cimarron, stm., U.S. . . **A6** 124
Dry Creek Mountain, mtn.,
Nv., U.S. **B5** 121
Dryden, On., Can. **o16** 89
Dryden, N.Y., U.S. **C4** 125
Dry Fork, stm., Mo., U.S. . . **D6** 118
Dry Fork, stm., W.V., U.S. . . **D3** 141
Dry Fork, stm., W.V., U.S. . . **B5** 141
Dry Ridge, Ky., U.S. **B5** 110
Dry Tortugas, is., Fl., U.S. . **H5** 102
Dschang, Cam. **B1** 54
Duarte, Pico, mtn., Dom.
Rep. **B5** 80
Dubach, La., U.S. **B3** 111
Dubai see Dubayy, U.A.E. . . **E7** 42
Dubăsari, Mol. **F10** 20
Du Bay, Lake, res., Wi.,
U.S. **D4** 142
Dubayy (Dubai), U.A.E. . . . **E7** 42
Dubbo, Austl. **G4** 62
Dublin (Baile Átha Cliath),
Ire. **D3** 12
Dublin, Ga., U.S. **D4** 103
Dublin, In., U.S. **E7** 107
Dublin, N.H., U.S. **E2** 122
Dublin, Oh., U.S. **k10** 128
Dublin, Pa., U.S. **F11** 131
Dublin, Tx., U.S. **C3** 136
Dublin, Va., U.S. **C2** 139
Dubno, Ukr. **D8** 20
Dubois, In., U.S. **H4** 107
Du Bois, Pa., U.S. **D4** 131
Dubois, Wy., U.S. **C3** 143
Dubois, co., In., U.S. **H4** 107
Duboistown, Pa., U.S. . . . **D7** 131
Dubovka, Russia **E7** 22
Dubréka, Gui. **E2** 50
Dubrovnik, Cro. **C7** 18
Dubrovytsia, Ukr. **D9** 20
Dubuque, Ia., U.S. **B7** 108
Dubuque, co., Ia., U.S. . . . **B7** 108
Duchesne, Ut., U.S. **C5** 137
Duchesne, co., Ut., U.S. . . **C5** 137
Duchesne, stm., Ut., U.S. . . **C5** 137
Duck, stm., Tn., U.S. **B4** 135
Duck Bay, Mb., Can. **C1** 86
Duck Creek, stm., Oh., U.S. **C4** 128
Duck Creek, stm., Wi., U.S. **h9** 142
Duck Lake, Sk., Can. **E2** 91
Duck Lake, l., Me., U.S. . . . **C4** 112
Duck Mountain Provincial
Park, Sk., Can. **F5** 91
Duck Valley Indian
Reservation, U.S. **B5** 121
Duckwater Indian
Reservation, Nv., U.S. . . **E6** 121
Duckwater Peak, mtn., Nv.,
U.S. **E6** 121
Du Couedic, Cape, c.,
Austl. **H2** 62
Dudinka, Russia **C10** 26
Dudley, Eng., U.K. **D5** 12
Dudley, Ma., U.S. **B4** 114
Duenweg, Mo., U.S. **D3** 118
Duero (Douro), stm., Eur. . . **G4** 16
Due West, S.C., U.S. **C3** 133
Duffer Peak, mtn., Nv., U.S. **B3** 121
Dufourspitze, mtn., Eur. . . **B1** 18
Dugger, In., U.S. **F3** 107
Dugi Otok, i., Cro. **C5** 18
Duifken Point, c., Austl. . . **C3** 62
Duisburg, Ger. **E10** 12
Duitama, Col. **B5** 70
Duke Island, i., Ak., U.S. . **n24** 95
Dukes, co., Ma., U.S. **D6** 114
Duk Fadiat, Sudan **I11** 48

Dukhān, Qatar **E6** 42
Dukku, Nig. **D7** 50
Dukou, China **F8** 28
Dulan, China **D7** 28
Dulce, N.M., U.S. **A2** 124
Dulce, stm., Arg. **E5** 72
Dul'durga, Russia **D13** 26
Duluth, Ga., U.S. **B2** 103
Duluth, Mn., U.S. **D6** 116
Dūmā, Syria **F7** 44
Dumaguete, Phil. **E8** 34
Dumaran Island, i., Phil. . . **D7** 34
Dumas, Ar., U.S. **D4** 97
Dumas, Tx., U.S. **B2** 136
Dumfries, Scot., U.K. **C5** 12
Dumfries, Va., U.S. **B5** 139
Dumont, Ia., U.S. **B5** 108
Dumont, N.J., U.S. **B5** 123
Dumraon, India **D4** 40
Duna see Danube, stm.,
Eur. **C9** 14
Dunai see Danube, stm.,
Eur. **C9** 14
Dunaïvtsi, Ukr. **E9** 20
Dunaj see Danube, stm.,
Eur. **C9** 14
Dunărea see Danube, stm.,
Eur. **C9** 14
Dunaújváros, Hung. **F5** 20
Dunav see Danube, stm.,
Eur. **C9** 14
Dunay see Danube, stm.,
Eur. **C9** 14
Dunbar, Pa., U.S. **G2** 131
Dunbar, W.V., U.S. **C3** 141
Duncan, B.C., Can. **E6** 85
Duncan, Az., U.S. **E6** 96
Duncan, Ok., U.S. **C4** 129
Duncan, S.C., U.S. **B3** 133
Duncan Falls, Oh., U.S. . . **C4** 128
Duncan Lake, res., B.C.,
Can. **D9** 85
Duncannon, Pa., U.S. **F7** 131
Duncan Passage, strt., India **G6** 40
Duncansville, Pa., U.S. . . . **F5** 131
Duncanville, Tx., U.S. . . . **n10** 136
Dundalk, On., Can. **C4** 89
Dundalk, Ire. **C3** 12
Dundalk, Md., U.S. **B4** 113
Dundalk Bay, b., Ire. **D3** 12
Dundas, On., Can. **D5** 89
Dundee, S. Afr. **D5** 56
Dundee, Scot., U.K. **B5** 12
Dundee, Fl., U.S. **D5** 102
Dundee, Il., U.S. **A5** 106
Dundee, Mi., U.S. **G7** 115
Dundee, N.Y., U.S. **C4** 125
Dundee, Or., U.S. **h11** 130
Dundy, co., Ne., U.S. **D4** 120
Dunedin, N.Z. **q13** 63c
Dunedin, Fl., U.S. **D4** 102
Dunellen, N.J., U.S. **B4** 123
Dunfermline, Scot., U.K. . . **B5** 12
Dūngarpur, India **E2** 40
Dungarvan, Ire. **D3** 12
Dungeness, stm., Wa., U.S. **A2** 140
Dungu, D.R.C. **C5** 54
Dunham, P.Q., Can. **D5** 90
Dunhuang, China **C6** 28
Dunkard Creek, stm., U.S. . **B4** 141
Dunkerque, Fr. **B8** 16
Dunkerton, Ia., U.S. **B5** 108
Dunkirk see Dunkerque, Fr. **B8** 16
Dunkirk, In., U.S. **D7** 107
Dunkirk, N.Y., U.S. **C1** 125
Dunkirk, Oh., U.S. **B2** 128
Dunklin, co., Mo., U.S. . . . **E7** 118
Dunkwa, Ghana **E4** 50
Dún Laoghaire, Ire. **D3** 12
Dunlap, Ia., U.S. **C2** 108
Dunlap, Il., U.S. **C4** 106
Dunlap, In., U.S. **A6** 107
Dunlap, Tn., U.S. **D8** 135
Dunleary see Dún
Laoghaire, Ire. **D3** 12
Dunleith, De., U.S. **i7** 101
Dunloup Creek, stm., W.V.,
U.S. **n13** 141
Dunmore, Pa., U.S. **D10** 131
Dunmore, Lake, l., Vt., U.S. **D2** 138
Dunn, N.C., U.S. **B4** 126
Dunn, co., N.D., U.S. **B3** 127
Dunn, co., Wi., U.S. **D2** 142
Dunnellon, Fl., U.S. **C4** 102
Dunnville, On., Can. **E5** 89
Dunqulah, Sudan **G11** 48
Dunseith, N.D., U.S. **A5** 127
Dunsmuir, Ca., U.S. **B2** 98
Dunville, Nf., Can. **E5** 88
Dunwoody, Ga., U.S. **h8** 103
Duolun, China **C11** 28
Duomula, China **E4** 28
Du Page, co., Il., U.S. . . . **B5** 106
Du Page, stm., Il., U.S. . . . **k8** 106
Duplin, co., N.C., U.S. . . . **C5** 126
Dupont, In., U.S. **G6** 107
Dupont, Pa., U.S. **n18** 131
Dupont City, W.V., U.S. . . **m12** 141
Dupont Manor, De., U.S. . . **D3** 101
Duque de York, Isla, i.,
Chile **H1** 69
Duquesne, Pa., U.S. **F2** 131
Du Quoin, Il., U.S. **E4** 106

Durand, Il., U.S. **A4** 106
Durand, Mi., U.S. **F6** 115
Durand, Wi., U.S. **D2** 142
Durango, Mex. **E8** 78
Durango, Co., U.S. **D3** 99
Durango, state, Mex. **E8** 78
Durant, Ia., U.S. **C7** 108
Durant, Ms., U.S. **B4** 117
Durant, Ok., U.S. **D5** 129
Durazno, Ur. **E6** 72
Durban, S. Afr. **D5** 56
Durg, India **E4** 40
Durgāpur, India **E5** 40
Durham, On., Can. **C4** 89
Durham, Eng., U.K. **C6** 12
Durham, Ca., U.S. **C3** 98
Durham, Ct., U.S. **D5** 100
Durham, N.C., U.S. **B4** 126
Durham, N.H., U.S. **D5** 122
Durham, co., N.C., U.S. . . . **A4** 126
Durmitor, mtn., Yugo. **C7** 18
Durrell, Nf., Can. **D4** 88
Durrës, Alb. **D7** 18
Dursunbey, Tur. **C3** 44
D'Urville Island, i., N.Z. . . **p13** 63c
Duryea, Pa., U.S. **D10** 131
Dušanbe, Taj. **F8** 26
Dušekan, Russia **C12** 26
Dushan, China **F9** 28
Dushanbe see Dušanbe,
Taj. **F8** 26
Dushanzi, China **C4** 28
Duson, La., U.S. **D3** 111
Düsseldorf, Ger. **E10** 12
Dutchess, co., N.Y., U.S. . **D7** 125
Dutch Island, i., R.I., U.S. . **F4** 132
Dutton, On., Can. **E3** 89
Dutton, Mount, mtn., Ut.,
U.S. **E3** 137
Duval, co., Fl., U.S. **B5** 102
Duval, co., Tx., U.S. **F3** 136
Duxbury, Ma., U.S. **B6** 114
Duyun, China **F9** 28
Düzce, Tur. **B4** 44
Dvina Bay see Dvinskaja
guba, b., Russia **A6** 22
Dvinskaja guba, b., Russia **A6** 22
Dwārka, India **E1** 40
Dwight, Il., U.S. **B5** 106
Dwight D. Eisenhower
Lock, N.Y., U.S. **f9** 125
Dworshak Reservoir, res.,
Id., U.S. **C3** 105
Dyer, In., U.S. **A2** 107
Dyer, Tn., U.S. **A3** 135
Dyer, co., Tn., U.S. **A2** 135
Dyersburg, Tn., U.S. **A2** 135
Dyersville, Ia., U.S. **B6** 108
Dyess Air Force Base, mil.,
U.S. **C3** 136
Dysart, Ia., U.S. **B5** 108
Džalinda, Russia **A12** 28
Džambejty, Kaz. **D9** 22
Džanybek, Kaz. **E8** 22
Džardžan, Russia **C14** 26
Dzaudžikau see
Vladikavkaz, Russia . . . **E6** 26
Dzerzhinsk see Dzjaržynsk,
Bela. **C9** 20
Dzerzhinsk see Dzeržinsk,
Russia **C7** 22
Dzeržinsk, Russia **C7** 22
Džetygara, Kaz. **D8** 26
Dzhambul see Žambyl, Kaz. **E9** 26
Dzhankoi, Ukr. **G13** 20
Dzhezkazgan see
Žezkazgan, Kaz. **E10** 22
Dzierżoniów, Pol. **D4** 20
Džizak, Uzb. **E8** 26
Dzjaržynsk, Bela. **C9** 20
Džugba, Russia **G15** 20
Džugdžur, hrebet, mts.,
Russia **D15** 26
Dzüünharaa, Mong. **B9** 28
Dzuunmod, Mong. **B9** 28

E

Eads, Co., U.S. **C8** 99
Eagan, Mn., U.S. **n12** 116
Eagar, Az., U.S. **C6** 96
Eagle, Co., U.S. **B4** 99
Eagle, Id., U.S. **F2** 105
Eagle, Ne., U.S. **h12** 120
Eagle, Wi., U.S. **F5** 142
Eagle, co., Co., U.S. **B4** 99
Eagle, stm., Nf., Can. . . . **B2** 88
Eagle Creek Reservoir, res.,
In., U.S. **E5** 107
Eagle Grove, Ia., U.S. . . . **B4** 108
Eagle Key, i., Fl., U.S. . . **G6** 102
Eagle Lake, Me., U.S. . . . **A4** 112
Eagle Lake, Mn., U.S. . . . **F5** 116
Eagle Lake, Tx., U.S. **E4** 136
Eagle Lake, l., Ca., U.S. . . **B3** 98
Eagle Lake, l., Me., U.S. . . **A4** 112
Eagle Lake, l., Me., U.S. . . **A4** 112
Eagle Lake, l., Ms., U.S. . . **C3** 117
Eagle Lake, l., Wi., U.S. . . **C4** 142
Eagle Mountain, mtn., Mn.,
U.S. **k9** 116
Eagle Mountain Lake, res.,
Tx., U.S. **m9** 136

Eagle Nest Lake, l., N.M.,
U.S. **A4** 124
Eagle Pass, Tx., U.S. . . . **E2** 136
Eagle Peak, mtn., Ca., U.S. **B3** 98
Eagle Point, Or., U.S. . . . **E4** 130
Eagle River, Wi., U.S. . . . **C4** 142
Eagletail Mountains, mts.,
Az., U.S. **D2** 96
Eagletail Peak, mtn., Az.,
U.S. **D2** 96
Eagleton, Ok., U.S. **C7** 129
Earle, Ar., U.S. **B5** 97
Earlham, Ia., U.S. **C3** 108
Earlimart, Ca., U.S. **E4** 98
Earlington, Ky., U.S. **C2** 110
Earlville, Ia., U.S. **B6** 108
Earlville, Il., U.S. **B5** 106
Early, Ia., U.S. **B2** 108
Early, co., Ga., U.S. **E2** 103
Earth, Tx., U.S. **B1** 136
Easley, S.C., U.S. **B2** 133
East, stm., Ct., U.S. **D5** 100
East, stm., N.Y., U.S. . . . **k13** 125
East, stm., Wi., U.S. **h9** 142
East Alton, Il., U.S. **E3** 106
East Angus, P.Q., Can. . . **D6** 90
East Arlington, Vt., U.S. . . **E2** 138
East Aurora, N.Y., U.S. . . **C2** 125
East Bangor, Pa., U.S. . . **E11** 131
East Bank, W.V., U.S. . . **m13** 141
East Barre, Vt., U.S. **C4** 138
East Baton Rouge, co., La.,
U.S. **D4** 111
East Bay, b., Fl., U.S. . . . **u16** 102
East Bay, b., Tx., U.S. . . **R15** 136
East Beckwith Mountain,
mtn., Co., U.S. **C3** 99
East Berlin, Ct., U.S. **C5** 100
East Berlin, Pa., U.S. **G8** 131
East Bernard, Tx., U.S. . . **E4** 136
East Bernstadt, Ky., U.S. . **C5** 110
East Bethel, Mn., U.S. . . . **E5** 116
East Billerica, Ma., U.S. . . **f11** 114
Eastborough, Ks., U.S. . . **g12** 109
Eastbourne, Eng., U.K. . . **E7** 12
East Brady, Pa., U.S. **E2** 131
East Branch Clarion River
Lake, res., Pa., U.S. . . . **C4** 131
East Brewton, Al., U.S. . . **D2** 94
East Bridgewater, Ma., U.S. **B6** 114
East Brimfield Lake, res.,
Ma., U.S. **B3** 114
East Brooklyn, Ct., U.S. . . **B8** 100
East Broughton, P.Q., Can. **C6** 90
East Brunswick, N.J., U.S. **C4** 123
East Butte, mtn., Mt., U.S. **B5** 119
East Cache Creek, stm.,
Ok., U.S. **C3** 129
East Caicos, i., T./C. Is. . . **A5** 80
East Cape, c., N.Z. **o14** 63c
East Cape, c., Fl., U.S. . . **G5** 102
East Carbon, Ut., U.S. . . . **D5** 137
East Caroline Basin **H17** 64
East Carroll, co., La., U.S. . **B4** 111
East Chicago, In., U.S. . . **A3** 107
East Chop, c., Ma., U.S. . . **D6** 114
East China Sea, Asia . . . **F12** 28
East Cleveland, Oh., U.S. . **g9** 128
East Cote Blanche Bay, b.,
La., U.S. **E4** 111
East Dennis, Ma., U.S. . . . **C7** 114
East Derry, N.H., U.S. . . . **E4** 122
East Detroit, Mi., U.S. . . **p16** 115
East Douglas, Ma., U.S. . . **B4** 114
East Dubuque, Il., U.S. . . **A3** 106
Eastend, Sk., Can. **H1** 91
Easter Island see Pascua,
Isla de, i., Chile **K28** 64
Eastern Bay, b., Md., U.S. . **C5** 113
Eastern Desert, des., Egypt **E11** 48
Eastern Ghāts, mts., India . **G3** 40
Eastern Neck Island, i., Md.,
U.S. **B5** 113
Eastern Point, c., Ma., U.S. **f13** 114
Eastern Sayans see
Vostočnyj Sajan, mts.,
Russia **D11** 26
Easterville, Mb., Can. . . . **C2** 86
East Falkland, i., Falk. Is. . **H5** 69
East Falmouth, Ma., U.S. . **C6** 114
East Feliciana, co., La., U.S. **D4** 111
East Flat Rock, N.C., U.S. . **f10** 126
East Fork, stm., Wy., U.S. . **D3** 143
East Fork Lake, res., Oh.,
U.S. **C1** 128
East Frisian Islands see
Ostfriesische Inseln, is.,
Ger. **D10** 12
East Gaffney, S.C., U.S. . . **A4** 133
East Galesburg, Il., U.S. . . **C3** 106
East Granby, Ct., U.S. . . . **B5** 100
East Grand Forks, Mn., U.S. **C2** 116
East Grand Rapids, Mi., U.S. **F5** 115
East Greenville, Pa., U.S. . **F10** 131
East Greenwich, R.I., U.S. . **D4** 132
East Gwillimbury, On., Can. **C5** 89
East Hampstead, N.H., U.S. **E4** 122
East Hampton, Ct., U.S. . . **C5** 100
Easthampton, Ma., U.S. . . **B2** 114
East Hartford, Ct., U.S. . . **B5** 100
East Hartland, Ct., U.S. . . **B4** 100
East Haven, Ct., U.S. . . . **D4** 100
East Helena, Mt., U.S. . . . **D5** 119
East Jordan, Mi., U.S. . . . **C5** 115
Eastlake, Oh., U.S. **A4** 128

Name	Map Ref.	Page
East Lake Tohopekaliga, l., Fl., U.S.	D5	102
Eastland, Tx., U.S.	C3	136
Eastland, co., Tx., U.S.	C3	136
East Lansing, Mi., U.S.	F6	115
East Las Vegas, Nv., U.S.	G6	121
East Liverpool, Oh., U.S.	B5	128
East London (Oos-Londen), S. Afr.	E4	56
East Longmeadow, Ma., U.S.	B2	114
East Los Angeles, Ca., U.S.	m12	98
East Lyme, Ct., U.S.	D7	100
East Lynn Lake, res., W.V., U.S.	C2	141
Eastmain-Opinaca, Réservoir, res., P.Q., Can.	h11	90
Eastman, P.Q., Can.	D5	90
Eastman, Ga., U.S.	D3	103
East Mariana Basin	G18	64
East Matunuck, R.I., U.S.	F3	132
East Middlebury, Vt., U.S.	D2	138
East Millinocket, Me., U.S.	C4	112
East Moline, Il., U.S.	B3	106
East Montpelier, Vt., U.S.	C4	138
East Naples, Fl., U.S.	F5	102
East Newnan, Ga., U.S.	C2	103
East Nishnabotna, stm., Ia., U.S.	C2	108
East Norriton, Pa., U.S.	o20	131
East Olympia, Wa., U.S.	C3	140
Easton, Md., U.S.	C5	113
Easton, Pa., U.S.	E11	131
Easton Reservoir, res., Ct., U.S.	E2	100
East Orange, N.J., U.S.	B4	123
East Orleans, Ma., U.S.	C8	114
Eastover, S.C., U.S.	D6	133
East Pacific Rise	M27	64
East Pakistan see Bangladesh, ctry., Asia	B2	34
East Palatka, Fl., U.S.	C5	102
East Palestine, Oh., U.S.	B5	128
East Pass, strt., Fl., U.S.	C2	102
East Pea Ridge, W.V., U.S.	C2	141
East Peoria, Il., U.S.	C4	106
East Pepperell, Ma., U.S.	A4	114
East Petersburg, Pa., U.S.	F9	131
East Pittsburgh, Pa., U.S.	k14	131
East Point, c., P.E., Can.	C8	87
Eastpoint, Fl., U.S.	C2	102
East Point, Ga., U.S.	C2	103
East Point, c., Ma., U.S.	B6	114
East Point, c., N.J., U.S.	E2	123
Eastport, Nf., Can.	D5	88
Eastport, Me., U.S.	D6	112
East Prairie, Mo., U.S.	E8	118
East Providence, R.I., U.S.	C4	132
East Pryor Mountain, mtn., Mt., U.S.	E8	119
East Quogue, N.Y., U.S.	n16	125
East Range, mts., Nv., U.S.	C4	121
East Ridge, Tn., U.S.	h11	135
East River, Ct., U.S.	D5	100
East Rochester, N.Y., U.S.	B3	125
East Rockingham, N.C., U.S.	C3	126
East Rutherford, N.J., U.S.	h8	123
East Saint Louis, Il., U.S.	E3	106
East Sea see Japan, Sea of, Asia	C14	28
East Selkirk, Mb., Can.	D3	86
East Siberian Sea see Vostočno-Sibirskoe more, Russia	B17	26
Eastsound, Wa., U.S.	A3	140
East Spencer, N.C., U.S.	B2	126
East Stroudsburg, Pa., U.S.	D11	131
East Tawas, Mi., U.S.	D7	115
East Timor, ctry., Asia	E7	36
East Troy, Wi., U.S.	F5	142
East Vestal, N.Y., U.S.	C4	125
East View, W.V., U.S.	k10	141
East Walker, stm., U.S.	E2	121
East Walpole, Ma., U.S.	h11	114
East Wareham, Ma., U.S.	C6	114
East Washington, Pa., U.S.	F1	131
East Wenatchee, Wa., U.S.	B5	140
East Windsor, N.J., U.S.	C3	123
East York, On., Can.	D5	89
Eaton, Co., U.S.	A6	99
Eaton, In., U.S.	D7	107
Eaton, co., Mi., U.S.	F6	115
Eaton, Oh., U.S.	C1	128
Eaton Rapids, Mi., U.S.	F6	115
Eatonton, Ga., U.S.	C3	103
Eatontown, N.J., U.S.	C4	123
Eatonville, Wa., U.S.	C3	140
Eau Claire, Wi., U.S.	D2	142
Eau Claire, co., Wi., U.S.	D2	142
Eau Claire, stm., Wi., U.S.	D2	142
Eau Claire, Lac à l', l., P.Q., Can.	g11	90
Eauripik Rise	H17	64
Ebano, Mex.	C5	78
Ebebiyín, Eq. Gui.	C2	54
Ebensburg, Pa., U.S.	F4	131
Eber Gölü, l., Tur.	C4	44
Eberswalde-Finow, Ger.	D13	12
Ebetsu, Japan	B4	31
Ebinur Hu, l., China	B4	28
Ebolowa, Cam.	C2	54
Ebre see Ebro, stm., Spain	G7	16
Ebre, Delta de l', Spain	G7	16
Ebro, stm., Spain	G7	16
Eccles, W.V., U.S.	n13	141
Ech Cheliff, Alg.	C5	48
Echeng, China	C3	30
Echo Bay, Nv., U.S.	G7	121
Echo Lake, l., Me., U.S.	D3	112
Echo Lake, l, Vt., U.S.	B5	138
Echols, co., Ga., U.S.	F4	103
Echuca, Austl.	H3	62
Eckerö, i., Fin.	F8	10
Eckhart Mines, Md., U.S.	k13	113
Eckville, Ab., Can.	C3	84
Eclectic, Al., U.S.	C3	94
Econfina, stm., Fl., U.S.	B3	102
Écorces, Rivière aux, stm., P.Q., Can.	A6	90
Ecorse, Mi., U.S.	p15	115
Ecru, Ms., U.S.	A4	117
Ector, co., Tx., U.S.	D1	136
Ecuador, ctry., S.A.	D4	70
Edcouch, Tx., U.S.	F4	136
Eddy, co., N.D., U.S.	B7	127
Eddy, co., N.M., U.S.	E5	124
Eddystone, Pa., U.S.	p20	131
Eddyville, Ia., U.S.	C5	108
Eddyville, Ky., U.S.	e9	110
Ede, Nig.	E5	50
Edéa, Cam.	C2	54
Eden, Ga., U.S.	D5	103
Eden, Md., U.S.	D6	113
Eden, N.C., U.S.	A3	126
Eden, N.Y., U.S.	C2	125
Eden, Tx., U.S.	D3	136
Edenburg, S. Afr.	D4	56
Eden Prairie, Mn., U.S.	n12	116
Edenton, N.C., U.S.	A6	126
Eden Valley, Mn., U.S.	E4	116
Edfu, Egypt	F11	48
Edgar, co., Il., U.S.	D6	106
Edgar, Ne., U.S.	D8	120
Edgar, Wi., U.S.	D4	142
Edgard, La., U.S.	D5	111
Edgartown, Ma., U.S.	D6	114
Edgecombe, co., N.C., U.S.	B5	126
Edgecumbe, Cape, c., Ak., U.S.	m21	95
Edgefield, S.C., U.S.	D4	133
Edgefield, co., S.C., U.S.	D4	133
Edgeley, N.D., U.S.	C7	127
Edgemere, Md., U.S.	B5	113
Edgemont, S.D., U.S.	D2	134
Edgemoor, De., U.S.	A3	101
Edgeøya, i., Nor.	B4	26
Edgerton, Ks., U.S.	D8	109
Edgerton, Mn., U.S.	G2	116
Edgerton, Oh., U.S.	A1	128
Edgerton, Wi., U.S.	F4	142
Edgerton, Wy., U.S.	C6	143
Edgewater, Al., U.S.	f7	94
Edgewater, Fl., U.S.	D6	102
Edgewater, Md., U.S.	C4	113
Edgewater, N.J., U.S.	h9	123
Edgewater Park, N.J., U.S.	C3	123
Edgewood, Ia., U.S.	B6	108
Edgewood, In., U.S.	D6	107
Edgewood, Ky., U.S.	h13	110
Edgewood, Md., U.S.	B5	113
Edgewood, N.M., U.S.	B3	124
Edgewood, Oh., U.S.	A5	128
Edgewood, Pa., U.S.	k14	131
Edgewood, Wa., U.S.	f11	140
Edgeworth, Pa., U.S.	h13	131
Édhessa, Grc.	D9	18
Edina, Mn., U.S.	F5	116
Edina, Mo., U.S.	A5	118
Edinboro, Pa., U.S.	C1	131
Edinburg, Il., U.S.	D4	106
Edinburg, Tx., U.S.	F3	136
Edinburg, Va., U.S.	B4	139
Edinburgh, Scot., U.K.	C5	12
Edinburgh, In., U.S.	F6	107
Edinet, Mol.	E9	20
Edirne, Tur.	B2	44
Edison, Ga., U.S.	E2	103
Edison, N.J., U.S.	B4	123
Edisto, stm., S.C., U.S.	E6	133
Edisto Island, i., S.C., U.S.	F7	133
Edith, Mount, mtn., Mt., U.S.	D5	119
Edjeleh, Alg.	E6	48
Edmond, Ok., U.S.	B4	129
Edmonds, Wa., U.S.	B3	140
Edmonson, co., Ky., U.S.	C3	110
Edmonton, Ab., Can.	C4	84
Edmonton, Ky., U.S.	D4	110
Edmore, Mi., U.S.	E5	115
Edmunds, co., S.D., U.S.	B6	134
Edmundston, N.B., Can.	B1	87
Edna, Tx., U.S.	E4	136
Edon, Oh., U.S.	A1	128
Édouard, Lac, l., P.Q., Can.	B5	90
Edremit, Tur.	C2	44
Edremit Körfezi, b., Tur.	C2	44
Edson, Ab., Can.	C2	84
Edson Butte, mtn., Or., U.S.	E2	130
Eduardo Castex, Arg.	F5	72
Edward, Lake, l., Afr.	D5	54
Edwards, co., Il., U.S.	E5	106
Edwards, co., Ks., U.S.	E4	109
Edwards, Ms., U.S.	C3	117
Edwards, co., Tx., U.S.	E2	136
Edwards Air Force Base, mil., Ca., U.S.	E5	98
Edwardsburg, Mi., U.S.	G4	115
Edwards Butte, mtn., Or., U.S.	B3	130
Edwardsville, Il., U.S.	E4	106
Edwardsville, Ks., U.S.	k16	109
Edwardsville, Pa., U.S.	n17	131
Edward VII Peninsula, pen., Ant.	D25	67
Eel, stm., Ca., U.S.	B2	98
Eel, stm., In., U.S.	E5	107
Eel, stm., In., U.S.	C6	107
Éfaté, i., Vanuatu	k9	62a
Efes (Ephesus), hist., Tur.	D2	44
Effigy Mounds National Monument, Ia., U.S.	A6	108
Effingham, co., Ga., U.S.	D5	103
Effingham, Il., U.S.	D5	106
Effingham, co., Il., U.S.	D5	106
Efland, N.C., U.S.	A3	126
Efremov, Russia	C15	20
Egadi, Isole, is., Italy	E4	18
Egan Range, mts., Nv., U.S.	E7	121
Eganville, On., Can.	B7	89
Egedesminde, Grnld.	E29	82
Eger, Hung.	F6	20
Eggenfelden, Ger.	F13	12
Egg Harbor City, N.J., U.S.	D3	123
Egg Island Point, c., N.J., U.S.	E2	123
Egijn, stm., Mong.	A8	28
Eglin Air Force Base, mil., Fl., U.S.	u15	102
Egmont, Cape, c., N.Z.	o13	63c
Egmont, Mount see Taranaki, Mount, vol., N.Z.	o13	63c
Egmont Bay, b., P.E., Can.	C5	87
Egmont Channel, strt., Fl., U.S.	p10	102
Egmont Key, i., Fl., U.S.	p10	102
Eğridir, Tur.	D4	44
Eğridir Gölü, l., Tur.	C4	44
Egvekinot, Russia	C20	26
Egypt, ctry., Afr.	E10	48
Egypt, Lake of, res., Il., U.S.	F5	106
Eha-Amufu, Nig.	E6	50
Ehrenberg, Az., U.S.	D1	96
Eibar, Spain	F5	16
Eielson Air Force Base, mil., Ak., U.S.	C10	95
Eigersund, Nor.	G2	10
Eight Degree Channel, strt., Asia	H2	40
Eights Coast, Ant.	D31	67
Eighty Mile Beach, Austl.	D3	60
Eindhoven, Neth.	E9	12
Eirunepé, Braz.	E6	70
Eisenach, Ger.	E12	12
Eisenerz, Aus.	G14	12
Eisenhower, Mount, mtn., N.H., U.S.	B4	122
Eisenhüttenstadt, Ger.	D14	12
Eisenstadt, Aus.	G15	12
Eivissa, Spain	H7	16
Eivissa (Ibiza), i., Spain	H7	16
Ejin Qi, China	C8	28
Ejsk, Russia	F15	22
Ejura, Ghana	E4	50
Ekaterinburg, Russia	D8	26
Ekibastuz, Kaz.	D9	26
Ekimčan, Russia	G20	26
Ekonda, Russia	C12	26
Ela, Mya.	C3	34
El Aaiún, W. Sah.	A2	50
Elaine, Ar., U.S.	C5	97
El-Alamein, Egypt	E9	14
Elan', Russia	D7	22
Elancy, Russia	D12	26
El-Arish, Egypt	E10	14
Elat, Isr.	E2	42
Elat, Gulf of see Aqaba, Gulf of, b.	E2	42
Elath see Elat, Isr.	E2	42
Elazığ, Tur.	C8	44
Elba, Al., U.S.	D3	94
Elba, Isola d', i., Italy	C3	18
El Banco, Col.	D5	80
Elbasan, Alb.	D7	18
Elbe see Labe, stm., Eur.	E14	12
Elberfeld, In., U.S.	H3	107
Elbert, co., Co., U.S.	B6	99
Elbert, co., Ga., U.S.	B4	103
Elbert, Mount, mtn., Co., U.S.	B4	99
Elberta, Ga., U.S.	D3	103
Elberton, Ga., U.S.	B4	103
El Beyyadh, Alg.	E4	14
Elbistan, Tur.	C7	44
Elblag, Pol.	B5	20
El Boulaïda, Alg.	C5	48
Elbow, stm., Ab., Can.	D3	84
Elbow Lake, Mn., U.S.	E3	116
El'brus, gora, mtn., Russia	E6	26
Elbrus, Mount see El'brus, gora, mtn., Russia	E6	26
Elburn, Il., U.S.	B5	106
Elburz Mountains see Alborz, Reshteh-ye Kūhhā-ye, mts., Iran	C6	42
El Cajon, Ca., U.S.	F5	98
El Calafate, Arg.	H2	69
El Callao, Ven.	D7	80
El Campo, Tx., U.S.	E4	136
El Capitan, mtn., Mt., U.S.	D2	119
El Capitan Reservoir, res., Ca., U.S.	o16	98
El Carmen de Bolívar, Col.	B4	70
El Centro, Ca., U.S.	F6	98
El Cerrito, Ca., U.S.	h8	98
Elcho Island, i., Austl.	C6	60
El Cuervo Butte, mtn., N.M., U.S.	k9	124
Elda, Spain	H6	16
El-Dab'a, Egypt	G3	44
El Djazaïr (Algiers), Alg.	C5	48
El Djelfa, Alg.	E4	14
Eldon, Ia., U.S.	D5	108
Eldon, Mo., U.S.	C5	118
Eldora, Ia., U.S.	B4	108
Eldorado, Arg.	D7	72
El Dorado, Ar., U.S.	D3	97
El Dorado, co., Ca., U.S.	C3	98
Eldorado, Il., U.S.	F5	106
El Dorado, Ks., U.S.	E7	109
Eldorado, Tx., U.S.	D2	136
El Dorado, Ven.	D7	80
Eldorado Peak, mtn., Wa., U.S.	A4	140
Eldorado Springs, Co., U.S.	B5	99
El Dorado Springs, Mo., U.S.	D3	118
Eldoret, Kenya	C7	54
Eldridge, Ia., U.S.	C7	108
Eleanor, W.V., U.S.	C3	141
Elec, Russia	D5	26
Electra, Tx., U.S.	C3	136
Electra Lake, res., Co., U.S.	D3	99
Electric Peak, mtn., Co., U.S.	C5	99
Electric Peak, mtn., Mt., U.S.	E6	119
Elefantes (Olifants), stm., Afr.	C5	56
El Encanto, Col.	D5	70
Elephant Butte Reservoir, res., N.M., U.S.	D2	124
Eleuthera, i., Bah.	C9	76
Eleven Mile Canyon Reservoir, res., Co., U.S.	C5	99
Eleven Point, stm., U.S.	A4	97
El-Fayoum, Egypt	E11	48
Elgin, Scot., U.K.	B5	12
Elgin, Ia., U.S.	B6	108
Elgin, Il., U.S.	A5	106
Elgin, Mn., U.S.	F6	116
Elgin, N.D., U.S.	C4	127
Elgin, Ne., U.S.	C7	120
Elgin, Ok., U.S.	C3	129
Elgin, Or., U.S.	B9	130
Elgin, S.C., U.S.	B6	133
Elgin, Tx., U.S.	D4	136
El-Gîza, Egypt	E11	48
Elgon, Mount, mtn., Afr.	C6	54
El Grara, Alg.	E4	14
El Ḥammâmi, reg., Maur.	B2	50
El Ḥank, clf., Afr.	B3	50
El Hierro, i., Spain	A1	50
Elhovo, Blg.	C11	18
Eliase, Indon.	E8	36
Elida, Oh., U.S.	B1	128
El-Iskandarîya, Egypt	D10	48
Elista, Russia	E6	26
Elizabeth, Austl.	G2	62
Elizabeth, Co., U.S.	B6	99
Elizabeth, N.J., U.S.	B4	123
Elizabeth, W.V., U.S.	B3	141
Elizabeth, Cape, c., Wa., U.S.	B1	140
Elizabeth City, N.C., U.S.	A6	126
Elizabeth Islands, is., Ma., U.S.	D6	114
Elizabethton, Tn., U.S.	C11	135
Elizabethtown, Ky., U.S.	C4	110
Elizabethtown, N.C., U.S.	C4	126
Elizabethtown, Pa., U.S.	F8	131
Elizabethville, Pa., U.S.	E8	131
Elizavety, mys, c., Russia	D16	26
El-Jadida, Mor.	D3	48
El Jebel, Co., U.S.	B3	99
Ełk, Pol.	C7	20
Elk, stm., Co., U.S.	A4	99
Elk, stm., Ks., U.S.	E7	109
Elk, co., Ks., U.S.	E7	109
Elk, co., Pa., U.S.	D5	131
Elk, stm., Wi., U.S.	C3	142
Elk, stm., W.V., U.S.	C3	141
Elk, stm., U.S.	A2	94
Elkader, Ia., U.S.	B6	108
Elk City, Id., U.S.	D3	105
Elk City, Ok., U.S.	B2	129
Elk City Lake, res., Ks., U.S.	E7	109
Elk Creek, stm., Ok., U.S.	B2	129
Elk Creek, stm., S.D., U.S.	C3	134
El Kef, Tun.	C6	48
El Kerě, Eth.	B8	54
Elkford, B.C., Can.	D10	85
Elk Grove, Ca., U.S.	C3	98
Elk Grove Village, Il., U.S.	h9	106
El-Khârga, Egypt	E11	48
Elkhart, stm., In., U.S.	B6	107
Elkhart, co., In., U.S.	A6	107
Elkhart, Ks., U.S.	E2	109
Elkhart, Tx., U.S.	D5	136
Elkhart Lake, Wi., U.S.	E5	142
Elkhead Mountains, mts., Co., U.S.	A3	99
Elkhorn, Mb., Can.	E1	86
Elk Horn, Ia., U.S.	C2	108
Elkhorn, stm., Ne., U.S.	B7	120
Elkhorn, Ne., U.S.	g12	120
Elkhorn, Wi., U.S.	F5	142
Elkhorn City, Ky., U.S.	C7	110
Elkhorn Peaks, mts., Id., U.S.	F7	105
Elkin, N.C., U.S.	A2	126
Elkins, Ar., U.S.	A1	97
Elkins, W.V., U.S.	C5	141
Elkland, Pa., U.S.	C7	131
Elk Mills, Md., U.S.	A6	113
Elk Mound, Wi., U.S.	D2	142
Elk Mountain, mtn., N.M., U.S.	D1	124
Elk Mountain, mtn., Wy., U.S.	E6	143
Elk Mountain, mtn., Wy., U.S.	E6	143
Elk Mountains, mts., Co., U.S.	B3	99
Elk Mountains, mts., U.S.	D1	134
Elko, Nv., U.S.	C6	121
Elko, co., Nv., U.S.	B6	121
Elk Peak, mtn., Mt., U.S.	D6	119
Elk Point, Ab., Can.	C5	84
Elk Point, S.D., U.S.	E9	134
Elk Rapids, Mi., U.S.	D5	115
Elkridge, Md., U.S.	B4	113
Elk River, Mn., U.S.	E5	116
Elkton, Ky., U.S.	D2	110
Elkton, Md., U.S.	A6	113
Elkton, Mi., U.S.	E7	115
Elkton, S.D., U.S.	C9	134
Elkton, Va., U.S.	B4	139
Elkview, W.V., U.S.	m13	141
Elkville, Il., U.S.	F4	106
Ellaville, Ga., U.S.	D2	103
Ellen, Mount, mtn., Ut., U.S.	E5	137
Ellendale, De., U.S.	E4	101
Ellendale, N.D., U.S.	C7	127
Ellensburg, Wa., U.S.	C5	140
Ellenton, Fl., U.S.	E4	102
Ellenville, N.Y., U.S.	D6	125
Ellerbe, N.C., U.S.	B3	126
Ellerslie, Md., U.S.	k13	113
Ellesmere Island, i., Can.	B24	82
Ellettsville, In., U.S.	F4	107
Ellice Islands see Tuvalu, ctry., Oc.	E11	58
Ellicott City, Md., U.S.	B4	113
Ellijay, Ga., U.S.	B2	103
Ellington, Ct., U.S.	B6	100
Ellington, Mo., U.S.	D7	118
Ellinwood, Ks., U.S.	D5	109
Elliot, S. Afr.	E4	56
Elliot Lake, On., Can.	A2	89
Elliott, co., Ky., U.S.	B6	110
Elliott, Ms., U.S.	B4	117
Elliott Bay, b., Wa., U.S.	e11	140
Elliott Key, i., Fl., U.S.	G6	102
Ellis, Ks., U.S.	D4	109
Ellis, co., Ks., U.S.	D4	109
Ellis, stm., N.H., U.S.	B4	122
Ellis, co., Ok., U.S.	A2	129
Ellis, co., Tx., U.S.	C4	136
Elliston, Va., U.S.	C2	139
Ellisville, Mo., U.S.	f12	118
Ellisville, Ms., U.S.	D4	117
Ellore see Elūru, India	F4	40
Elloree, S.C., U.S.	D6	133
Ellport, Pa., U.S.	E1	131
Ellsworth, Ks., U.S.	D5	109
Ellsworth, co., Ks., U.S.	D5	109
Ellsworth, Me., U.S.	D4	112
Ellsworth, Pa., U.S.	F1	131
Ellsworth, Wi., U.S.	D1	142
Ellsworth Air Force Base, mil., S.D., U.S.	C2	134
Ellsworth Land, reg., Ant.	D32	67
Ellsworth Mountains, mts., Ant.	D32	67
Ellwood City, Pa., U.S.	E1	131
Elm, stm., N.D., U.S.	B8	127
Elma, Ia., U.S.	A5	108
Elma, Wa., U.S.	C2	140
Elmadağ, Tur.	C5	44
El-Mahalla el-Kubra, Egypt	G4	44
Emalı, Tur.	D3	44
El-Mansûra, Egypt	E10	14
Elm City, N.C., U.S.	B5	126
Elm Creek, Ne., U.S.	D6	120
Elmendorf Air Force Base, mil., Ak., U.S.	C10	95
El Menia, Alg.	D5	48
Elm Grove, W.V., U.S.	m11	142
Elmhurst, Il., U.S.	B6	106
Elmhurst, Pa., U.S.	D10	131
El-Minya, Egypt	E11	48
Elmira, N.Y., U.S.	C4	125
El Mirage, Az., U.S.	k8	96
Elmira Heights, N.Y., U.S.	C4	125
Elmont, N.Y., U.S.	k13	125
Elmora, Pa., U.S.	E4	131
Elmore, co., Al., U.S.	C3	94
Elmore, co., Id., U.S.	F3	105
Elmore, Mn., U.S.	G4	116
Elmore, Oh., U.S.	A2	128
El Morro National Monument, N.M., U.S.	B1	124
El Mreyyé, reg., Maur.	C3	50
Elmsdale, N.S., Can.	E6	87
Elmshorn, Ger.	D11	12
Elm Springs, Ar., U.S.	A1	97
Elmvale, On., Can.	C5	89
Elmwood, Il., U.S.	C3	106
Elmwood, Wi., U.S.	D1	142
Elmwood Park, Il., U.S.	k9	106
Elmwood Park, N.J., U.S.	h8	123
Elmwood Place, Oh., U.S.	o13	128
Elnora, In., U.S.	G3	107
Eloise, Fl., U.S.	E5	102

Name	Map Ref.	Page
Elon College, N.C., U.S.	A3	126
Elora, On., Can.	D4	89
Elorza, Ven.	D6	80
Ēloten, Turk.	C8	42
Eloy, Az., U.S.	E4	96
El Paso, co., Co., U.S.	C6	99
El Paso, Il., U.S.	C4	106
El Paso, Tx., U.S.	o11	136
El Paso, co., Tx., U.S.	o11	136
El Pital, Cerro, mtn., N.A.	C2	80
El Portal, Fl., U.S.	s13	102
El Prado, N.M., U.S.	A4	124
El Progreso, Hond.	B2	80
El Puerto de Santa María, Spain	I3	16
El-Qâhira (Cairo), Egypt	D10	48
El-Qasr, Egypt	E10	48
El Reno, Ok., U.S.	B4	129
Elrose, Sk., Can.	F1	91
Elroy, Wi., U.S.	E3	142
Elsa, Tx., U.S.	F3	136
Elsah, Il., U.S.	E3	106
El Salto, Mex.	C3	78
El Salvador, ctry., N.A.	C2	80
El Sauzal, Mex.	A1	78
Elsberry, Mo., U.S.	B7	118
Elsie, Mi., U.S.	E6	115
Elsinore, Ut., U.S.	E3	137
El'sk, Bela.	D10	20
Elsmere, De., U.S.	B3	101
Elsmere, Ky., U.S.	B5	110
El Sueco, Mex.	B3	78
El-Suweis, Egypt	E11	48
Eltham, N.Z.	o13	63c
El Tigre, Ven.	B7	70
El Toco, Chile	C4	72
Elton, La., U.S.	D3	111
El Toro Marine Corps Air Station, mil., Ca., U.S.	n13	98
El Turbio, Arg.	H2	69
El-Uqsor, Egypt	E11	48
Elūru, India	F4	40
El Vado Reservoir, res., N.M., U.S.	A3	124
Elvas, Port.	H3	16
Elvins, Mo., U.S.	D7	118
Elwha, stm., Wa., U.S.	A2	140
Elwell, Lake, res., Mt., U.S.	B5	119
Elwood, In., U.S.	D6	107
Elwood, Ks., U.S.	C9	109
Elwood, Ne., U.S.	D6	120
Elx, Spain	H6	16
Ely, Eng., U.K.	D7	12
Ely, Mn., U.S.	C7	116
Ely, Nv., U.S.	D7	121
Elyria, Oh., U.S.	A3	128
Elysburg, Pa., U.S.	E8	131
Emämshahr, Iran	C7	42
Emanuel, co., Ga., U.S.	D4	103
Emba, stm., Kaz.	E7	26
Emba, Kaz.	E10	22
Embarras, stm., Il., U.S.	E6	106
Embarrass, stm., Wi., U.S.	D5	142
Embro, On., Can.	D4	89
Embu, Kenya	D7	54
Emden, Ger.	D10	12
Emerald, Austl.	E4	62
Emerson, Mb., Can.	E3	86
Emerson, Ga., U.S.	B2	103
Emerson, Ne., U.S.	B9	120
Emerson, N.J., U.S.	h8	123
Emery, co., Ut., U.S.	E5	137
Emet, Tur.	C3	44
Emiliano Zapata, Mex.	D6	78
Emily, Mn., U.S.	D5	116
Emily, Lake, l., Mn., U.S.	E3	116
Eminence, Ky., U.S.	B4	110
Emirdağ, Tur.	C4	44
Emmaus, Pa., U.S.	E11	131
Emmen, Neth.	D10	12
Emmet, co., Ia., U.S.	A3	108
Emmet, co., Mi., U.S.	C6	115
Emmetsburg, Ia., U.S.	A3	108
Emmett, Id., U.S.	F2	105
Emmitsburg, Md., U.S.	A3	113
Emmonak, Ak., U.S.	C7	95
Emmons, co., N.D., U.S.	C5	127
Emory Peak, mtn., Tx., U.S.	E1	136
Empalme, Mex.	B2	78
Empangeni, S. Afr.	D5	56
Empedrado, Arg.	D6	72
Emperor Seamounts	D19	64
Empire, La., U.S.	E6	111
Empire, Nv., U.S.	C2	121
Empoli, Italy	C3	18
Emporia, Ks., U.S.	D7	109
Emporia, Va., U.S.	D5	139
Emporium, Pa., U.S.	D5	131
Empty Quarter see Ar-Rub' al-Khālī, des., Asia	G6	38
Emsworth, Pa., U.S.	h13	131
Encampment, Wy., U.S.	E6	143
Encarnación, Para.	D6	72
Enchilayas, Mex.	A2	78
Encinitas, Ca., U.S.	F5	98
Encontrados, Ven.	D5	80
Encounter Bay, b., Austl.	F2	62
Ende, Indon.	E6	36
Enderby, B.C., Can.	D8	85
Enderby Land, reg., Ant.	D9	67
Enderlin, N.D., U.S.	C8	127
Enders Reservoir, res., Ne., U.S.	D4	120
Endicott, N.Y., U.S.	C4	125
Endicott Mountains, mts., Ak., U.S.	B9	95
Endless Lake, l., Me., U.S.	C4	112
Endwell, N.Y., U.S.	C4	125
Enewetak, atoll, Marsh. Is.	C10	58
Enfield (Thompsonville), Ct., U.S.	B5	100
Enfield, N.C., U.S.	A5	126
Enfield, N.H., U.S.	C2	122
Engel's, Russia	D6	26
Enggano, Pulau, i., Indon.	E2	36
England, state, U.K.	D6	12
England, Ar., U.S.	C4	97
Englee, Nf., Can.	C3	88
Engleside, Va., U.S.	g12	139
Englewood, Co., U.S.	B6	99
Englewood, Fl., U.S.	F4	102
Englewood, N.J., U.S.	B5	123
Englewood, Oh., U.S.	C1	128
Englewood, Tn., U.S.	D9	135
Englewood Cliffs, N.J., U.S.	h9	123
English, In., U.S.	H5	107
English Băzăr see Ingrāj Bāzār, India	E5	40
English Channel, strt., Eur.	C5	16
English Coast, Ant.	D33	67
Enid, Ok., U.S.	A4	129
Enid Lake, res., Ms., U.S.	A4	117
Enigma, Ga., U.S.	E3	103
Enisej (Yenisey), stm., Russia	C10	26
eNjesuthi, mtn., Afr.	D4	56
Enka, N.C., U.S.	f10	126
Enköping, Swe.	G7	10
Enna, Italy	F5	18
Ennedi, plat., Chad	G9	48
Ennis, Mt., U.S.	E5	119
Ennis, Tx., U.S.	C4	136
Enoch, Ut., U.S.	F2	137
Enola, Pa., U.S.	F8	131
Enontekiö, Fin.	B10	10
Enoree, stm., S.C., U.S.	B3	133
Enoree, S.C., U.S.	B4	133
Enosburg Falls, Vt., U.S.	B3	138
Enriquillo, Lago, l., Dom. Rep.	B5	80
Enschede, Neth.	D10	12
Ensenada, Mex.	A1	78
Enshi, China	E9	28
Enshu Bay see Enshū-nada, Japan	D3	31
Enshū-nada, Japan	D3	31
Ensley, Fl., U.S.	u14	102
Entebbe, Ug.	C6	54
Enterprise, Al., U.S.	D4	94
Enterprise, Ks., U.S.	D6	109
Enterprise, Or., U.S.	B9	130
Enterprise, Ut., U.S.	F2	137
Enterprise, W.V., U.S.	B4	141
Entiat, stm., Wa., U.S.	B5	140
Entiat, Lake, l., Wa., U.S.	B5	140
Entiat Mountains, mts., Wa., U.S.	B5	140
Entroncamento, Port.	H2	16
Enugu, Nig.	E6	50
Enumclaw, Wa., U.S.	B4	140
Enurmino, Russia	C20	26
Enyamba, D.R.C.	D5	54
Eola Hills, Or., U.S.	h11	130
Epena, Congo	C3	54
Épernay, Fr.	C8	16
Ephesus see Efes, hist., Tur.	D2	44
Ephraim, Ut., U.S.	D4	137
Ephrata, Pa., U.S.	F9	131
Ephrata, Wa., U.S.	B6	140
Épi, i., Vanuatu	I9	62a
Epinal, Fr.	C10	16
Epirus see Ípeiros, hist. reg., Grc.	E8	18
Epping, N.H., U.S.	D4	122
Epukiro, Nmb.	C2	56
Epworth, Ia., U.S.	B7	108
Eqlīd, Iran	D6	42
Equatorial Guinea, ctry., Eq. Gui.	C1	54
Erath, La., U.S.	E3	111
Erath, co., Tx., U.S.	C3	136
Erbaa, Tur.	B7	44
Erciş, Tur.	C10	44
Erciyes Dağı, vol., Tur.	C6	44
Érd, Hung.	F5	20
Erdek, Tur.	B2	44
Erdemli, Tur.	D6	44
Erdene see Ulaan-Uul, Mong.	C10	28
Erebus, Mount, mtn., Ant.	D21	67
Erechim, Braz.	D7	72
Ereğli, Tur.	B4	44
Ereğli, Tur.	D5	44
Erenhot, China	C10	28
Erfoud, Mor.	E3	14
Erfurt, Ger.	E12	12
Ergani, Tur.	C8	44
Ergel, Mong.	C9	28
Ergene, stm., Tur.	B2	44
Ergeni, Russia	E6	26
Ergun see Argun', stm., Asia	D14	26
Erick, Ok., U.S.	B2	129
Erickson, Mb., Can.	D2	86
Erie, Co., U.S.	A5	99
Erie, Il., U.S.	B3	106
Erie, Ks., U.S.	E8	109
Erie, Mi., U.S.	G7	115
Erie, co., N.Y., U.S.	C2	125
Erie, co., Oh., U.S.	A3	128
Erie, Pa., U.S.	B1	131
Erie, co., Pa., U.S.	C1	131
Erie, Lake, l., N.A.	C11	92
Erie Canal, N.Y., U.S.	B5	125
Erimo-misaki, c., Japan	C16	28
Erin, On., Can.	D4	89
Erin, Tn., U.S.	A4	135
Eritrea, ctry., Afr.	G12	48
Erlangen, Ger.	F12	12
Erlanger, Ky., U.S.	A5	110
Erling, Lake, res., Ar., U.S.	D2	97
Ermelo, S. Afr.	D4	56
Ermenek, Tur.	D5	44
Ermolaevo, Russia	D10	22
Ermoúpolis, Grc.	F10	18
Erne, Lower Lough, l., N. Ire., U.K.	C3	12
Erne, Upper Lough, l., Eur.	C3	12
Erode, India	G3	40
Erofej Pavlovič, Russia	D14	26
Eropol, Russia	C18	26
Er-Rachidia, Mor.	E3	14
Errego, Moz.	B6	56
Erromango, i., Vanuatu	I9	62a
Eršov, Russia	D8	22
Ertai, China	B6	28
Ertil', Russia	D16	22
Ertis see Irtysh, stm., Asia	D8	26
Ertix see Irtysh, stm., Asia	D8	26
Erwin, N.C., U.S.	B4	126
Erwin, Tn., U.S.	C11	135
Eryuan, China	A3	34
Erzgebirge, mts., Eur.	E9	8
Erzin, Russia	D11	26
Erzincan, Tur.	C8	44
Erzurum, Tur.	C9	44
Esa'ala, Pap. N. Gui.	H13	32
Esbjerg, Den.	I3	10
Escalante, Ut., U.S.	F4	137
Escalante, stm., Ut., U.S.	F4	137
Escalon, Ca., U.S.	D3	98
Escambia, co., Al., U.S.	D2	94
Escambia, stm., Fl., U.S.	u14	102
Escambia, co., Fl., U.S.	u14	102
Escanaba, Mi., U.S.	C3	115
Escanaba, stm., Mi., U.S.	B3	115
Escárcega, Mex.	D6	78
Escarpada Point, c., Phil.	C8	34
Escatawpa, Ms., U.S.	E5	117
Escatawpa, stm., U.S.	D5	117
Escondido, stm., Nic.	C3	80
Escondido, Ca., U.S.	F5	98
Escoumins, Rivière des, stm., P.Q., Can.	A8	90
Escuinapa de Hidalgo, Mex.	C3	78
Escuintla, Guat.	C1	80
Escuminac, Point, c., N.B., Can.	B5	87
Eséka, Cam.	C2	54
Eşfahān, Iran	D6	42
Esil', Kaz.	D8	26
Ëškar-Ola, Russia	D6	26
Eskilstuna, Swe.	G7	10
Eskimo Lakes, l., N.T., Can.	E13	82
Eskişehir, Tur.	C4	44
Esla, stm., Spain	G4	16
Eslāmābād, Iran	E12	44
Eslāmshahr, Iran	C6	42
Eşme, Tur.	C3	44
Esmeralda, co., Nv., U.S.	F4	121
Esmeraldas, Ec.	C4	70
Esmond, R.I., U.S.	B4	132
Espanola, On., Can.	A3	89
Espanola, N.M., U.S.	B3	124
Esparto, Ca., U.S.	C2	98
Esperança, Braz.	D6	70
Esperance, Austl.	G3	60
Esperance Bay, b., Austl.	G3	60
Esperanza, Arg.	E5	72
Esperanza, Mex.	B3	78
Espinhaço, Serra do, mts., Braz.	E3	74
Espinho, Port.	G2	16
Espírito Santo, state, Braz.	E3	74
Espíritu Santo, i., Vanuatu	j9	62a
Espíritu Santo, Isla del, i., Mex.	C2	78
Esplanada, Braz.	D4	74
Espoo, Fin.	F11	10
Espungabera, Moz.	C5	56
Espy, Pa., U.S.	D9	131
Esquel, Arg.	F2	69
Esquimalt, B.C., Can.	E6	85
Esquina, Arg.	D6	72
Essaouira, Mor.	D3	48
Essej, Russia	C12	26
Essen, Ger.	E10	12
Essendon, Mount, mtn., Austl.	E3	60
Essequibo, stm., Guy.	C8	70
Essex, On., Can.	E2	89
Essex, Ct., U.S.	D6	100
Essex, Ia., U.S.	D2	108
Essex, Ma., U.S.	A6	114
Essex, co., Ma., U.S.	A5	114
Essex, Md., U.S.	B5	113
Essex, co., N.J., U.S.	B4	123
Essex, co., N.Y., U.S.	B7	125
Essex, co., Va., U.S.	C6	139
Essex, Vt., U.S.	B2	138
Essex, co., Vt., U.S.	B5	138
Essex Junction, Vt., U.S.	C2	138
Essexville, Mi., U.S.	E7	115
Esslingen am Neckar, Ger.	F11	12
Estacada, Or., U.S.	B4	130
Estacado, Llano, pl., U.S.	C1	136
Estacado, Llano, pl., U.S.	E7	92
Estados, Isla de los, i., Arg.	H4	69
Eştahbān, Iran	E6	42
Estância, Braz.	D4	74
Estancia, N.M., U.S.	C3	124
Estcourt, S. Afr.	D4	56
Estelí, Nic.	C2	80
Estella, Spain	F5	16
Estelline, S.D., U.S.	C9	134
Estepona, Spain	I4	16
Estero Bay, b., Ca., U.S.	E3	98
Estero Bay, b., Fl., U.S.	F5	102
Estero Island, i., Fl., U.S.	F5	102
Estes Park, Co., U.S.	A5	99
Estherville, Ia., U.S.	A3	108
Estherwood, La., U.S.	D3	111
Estill, co., Ky., U.S.	C6	110
Estill, S.C., U.S.	F5	133
Estill Springs, Tn., U.S.	B5	135
Estonia, ctry., Eur.	G11	10
Estremadura, hist. reg., Port.	H2	16
Esztergom, Hung.	F5	20
Etah, Grnld.	C25	82
Étampes, Fr.	C8	16
Étang-du-Nord, P.Q., Can.	B8	87
Etāwah, India	D3	40
Ethel, W.V., U.S.	n12	141
Ethel Creek, Austl.	E3	60
Ethiopia, ctry., Afr.	I12	48
Etna, Pa., U.S.	k14	131
Etna, Monte, vol., Italy	F5	18
Etobicoke, On., Can.	D5	89
Etolin Island, i., Ak., U.S.	m23	95
Etolin Strait, strt., Ak., U.S.	C6	95
Etosha Pan, pl., Nmb.	B2	56
Etowah, co., Al., U.S.	A3	94
Etowah, stm., Ga., U.S.	B2	103
Etowah, Tn., U.S.	D9	135
Et Tīdra, i., Maur.	C1	50
Ettrick, Va., U.S.	C5	139
Eua, i., Tonga	G12	58
Euboea see Évvoia, i., Grc.	E9	18
Euboea, Gulf of see Vórios Evvoïkós Kólpos, b., Grc.	E9	18
Eucla, Austl.	G4	60
Euclid, Oh., U.S.	A4	128
Eudora, Ar., U.S.	D4	97
Eudora, Ks., U.S.	D8	109
Eufaula, Al., U.S.	D4	94
Eufaula, Ok., U.S.	B6	129
Eufaula Lake, res., Ok., U.S.	B6	129
Eugene, Or., U.S.	C3	130
Eugenia, Punta, c., Mex.	B1	78
Eugmo, i., Fin.	E10	10
Eunice, La., U.S.	D3	111
Eunice, N.M., U.S.	E6	124
Euphrates (Al-Furāt), stm., Asia	D4	42
Eupora, Ms., U.S.	B4	117
Eureka, Ca., U.S.	B1	98
Eureka, Ks., U.S.	E7	109
Eureka, Mo., U.S.	f12	118
Eureka, Mt., U.S.	B1	119
Eureka, Nv., U.S.	D5	121
Eureka, co., Nv., U.S.	D5	121
Eureka, S.C., U.S.	B5	133
Eureka, S.D., U.S.	B6	134
Eureka Springs, Ar., U.S.	A2	97
Euroa, Austl.	H4	62
Europe, cont.	C13	4
Eustis, Fl., U.S.	D5	102
Eutaw, Al., U.S.	C2	94
Eutsuk Lake, l., B.C., Can.	C4	85
Evangeline, co., La., U.S.	D3	111
Evans, Co., U.S.	A6	99
Evans, Ga., U.S.	C4	103
Evans, co., Ga., U.S.	D5	103
Evans, W.V., U.S.	C3	141
Evans, Mount, mtn., Co., U.S.	B5	99
Evansburg, Ab., Can.	C3	84
Evans City, Pa., U.S.	E1	131
Evansdale, Ia., U.S.	B5	108
Evanston, Il., U.S.	A6	106
Evanston, Wy., U.S.	E2	143
Evansville, Il., U.S.	E4	106
Evansville, In., U.S.	I2	107
Evansville, Wi., U.S.	F4	142
Evansville, Wy., U.S.	D6	143
Eva Perón see La Plata, Arg.	F6	72
Evart, Mi., U.S.	E5	115
Evarts, Ky., U.S.	D6	110
Eveleth, Mn., U.S.	C6	116
Evensk, Russia	C17	26
Everest, Mount, mtn., Asia	D5	40
Everett, Ma., U.S.	g11	114
Everett, Pa., U.S.	F5	131
Everett, Wa., U.S.	B3	140
Everett Lake, res., N.H., U.S.	D3	122
Everglades National Park, Fl., U.S.	G5	102
Evergreen, Al., U.S.	D3	94
Evergreen, Co., U.S.	B5	99
Evergreen Park, Il., U.S.	k9	106
Everly, Ia., U.S.	A2	108
Everson, Wa., U.S.	A3	140
Evje, Nor.	G2	10
Évora, Port.	H3	16
Évreux, Fr.	C7	16
Évros (Marica) (Meriç), stm., Eur.	D11	18
E.V. Spence Reservoir, res., Tx., U.S.	D2	136
Évvoia, i., Grc.	E9	18
Ewa, Hi., U.S.	B3	104
Ewa Beach, Hi., U.S.	B3	104
Ewa Beach, Hi., U.S.	g9	104
Ewing Township, N.J., U.S.	C3	123
Ewo, Congo	D2	54
Excelsior Mountain, mtn., Ca., U.S.	C4	98
Excelsior Mountains, mts., Nv., U.S.	E3	121
Excelsior Springs, Mo., U.S.	B3	118
Exeter, On., Can.	D3	89
Exeter, Eng., U.K.	E5	12
Exeter, Ca., U.S.	D4	98
Exeter, Ne., U.S.	D8	120
Exeter, N.H., U.S.	E5	122
Exeter, stm., N.H., U.S.	E5	122
Exeter, Pa., U.S.	D10	131
Exira, Ia., U.S.	C3	108
Exmore, Va., U.S.	C7	139
Exmouth, Austl.	E1	60
Exmouth Gulf, b., Austl.	E1	60
Experiment, Ga., U.S.	C2	103
Exploits, stm., Nf., Can.	D3	88
Exploits, Bay of, b., Nf., Can.	D4	88
Export, Pa., U.S.	F2	131
Extremadura, hist. reg., Spain	H3	16
Exuma Cays, is., Bah.	A4	80
Exuma Sound, strt., Bah.	D9	76
Eyasi, Lake, l., Tan.	D7	54
Eyl, Som.	I14	48
Eylar Mountain, mtn., Ca., U.S.	D3	98
Eyota, Mn., U.S.	G6	116
Eyre, Austl.	G4	60
Eyre North, Lake, l., Austl.	F2	62
Eyre Peninsula, pen., Austl.	G2	62
Ezequiel Ramos Mexía, Embalse, res., Arg.	E3	69
Ezine, Tur.	C2	44

F

Name	Map Ref.	Page
Fabens, Tx., U.S.	o11	136
Fabius, stm., Mo., U.S.	A6	118
Fabriano, Italy	C4	18
Fachi, Niger	C7	50
Factoryville, Pa., U.S.	C10	131
Fada, Chad	G9	48
Fada-Ngourma, Burkina	D5	50
Faenza, Italy	B3	18
Faeroe Islands see Faroe Islands, is., Far. Is.	B12	4
Făgăraş, Rom.	G8	20
Fagernes, Nor.	F3	10
Fagersta, Swe.	G6	10
Fairacres, N.M., U.S.	E3	124
Fairbank, Ia., U.S.	B5	108
Fairbanks, Ak., U.S.	C10	95
Fair Bluff, N.C., U.S.	C3	126
Fairborn, Oh., U.S.	C1	128
Fairburn, Ga., U.S.	C2	103
Fairbury, Il., U.S.	C5	106
Fairbury, Ne., U.S.	D8	120
Fairchance, Pa., U.S.	G2	131
Fairchild Air Force Base, mil., Wa., U.S.	g13	140
Fairdale, Ky., U.S.	B4	110
Fairfax, Ca., U.S.	C2	98
Fairfax, De., U.S.	A3	101
Fairfax, Ia., U.S.	C6	108
Fairfax, Mn., U.S.	F4	116
Fairfax, Mo., U.S.	A2	118
Fairfax, Ok., U.S.	A5	129
Fairfax, S.C., U.S.	F5	133
Fairfax, Va., U.S.	B5	139
Fairfax, co., Va., U.S.	B5	139
Fairfield, Al., U.S.	B3	94
Fairfield, Ca., U.S.	C2	98
Fairfield, Ct., U.S.	E2	100
Fairfield, co., Ct., U.S.	D2	100
Fairfield, Ia., U.S.	C6	108
Fairfield, Il., U.S.	E5	106
Fairfield, Me., U.S.	D3	112
Fairfield, Mt., U.S.	C5	119
Fairfield, Oh., U.S.	n12	128
Fairfield, co., Oh., U.S.	C3	128
Fairfield, co., S.C., U.S.	C5	133
Fairfield, Tx., U.S.	D4	136
Fairfield Bay, Ar., U.S.	B3	97
Fairfield Pond, l., Vt., U.S.	B3	138
Fair Grove, Mo., U.S.	D4	118
Fair Grove, N.C., U.S.	B2	126
Fairhaven, Ma., U.S.	C6	114
Fair Haven, Mi., U.S.	F8	115
Fair Haven, N.J., U.S.	C4	123
Fair Haven, Vt., U.S.	D2	138
Fairhope, Al., U.S.	E2	94
Fair Isle, i., Scot., U.K.	i19	12
Fairland, In., U.S.	E6	107
Fairland, Ok., U.S.	A7	129
Fair Lawn, N.J., U.S.	h8	123
Fairlawn, Va., U.S.	C2	139
Fairlea, W.V., U.S.	D4	141
Fairmont, Il., U.S.	C6	106
Fairmont, Mn., U.S.	G4	116
Fairmont, N.C., U.S.	C3	126
Fairmont, Ne., U.S.	D8	120
Fairmont, W.V., U.S.	B4	141

Name	Map Ref.	Page
Fairmount, Ga., U.S.	B2	103
Fairmount, In., U.S.	D6	107
Fairmount Heights, Md., U.S.	f9	113
Fair Oaks, Ga., U.S.	h7	103
Fairoaks, Pa., U.S.	h13	131
Fair Plain, Mi., U.S.	F4	115
Fairport, N.Y., U.S.	B3	125
Fairport Harbor, Oh., U.S.	A4	128
Fairvale, N.B., Can.	D4	87
Fairview, Ab., Can.	A1	84
Fairview, Mt., U.S.	C12	119
Fairview, N.J., U.S.	h8	123
Fairview, Ok., U.S.	A3	129
Fairview, Pa., U.S.	B1	131
Fairview, Tn., U.S.	B4	135
Fairview, Ut., U.S.	D4	137
Fairview Heights, Il., U.S.	E3	106
Fairview Park, In., U.S.	E3	107
Fairview Park, Oh., U.S.	g9	128
Fairview Peak, mtn., Nv., U.S.	D3	121
Fairview Peak, mtn., Or., U.S.	D4	130
Fairway, Ks., U.S.	k16	109
Fairweather Mountain, mtn., N.A.	G12	82
Fais, i., Micron.	E11	32
Faisalabad, Pak.	D10	42
Faison, N.C., U.S.	B4	126
Faizābād, India	D4	40
Fakfak, Indon.	D8	36
Fakse Bugt, b., Den.	I5	10
Faku, China	C12	28
Falaba, S.L.	E2	50
Falam, Mya.	B2	34
Falconer, N.Y., U.S.	C1	125
Falcon Heights, Mn., U.S.	n12	116
Falcon Heights, Or., U.S.	E5	130
Fălești, Mol.	F9	20
Falfurrias, Tx., U.S.	F3	136
Falher, Ab., Can.	B2	84
Falkenberg, Swe.	H5	10
Falkland Islands, is., Falk. Is.	H4	69
Falkland Sound, strt., Falk. Is.	H4	69
Falköping, Swe.	G5	10
Falkville, Al., U.S.	A3	94
Fall, stm., Ks., U.S.	E7	109
Fall Branch, Tn., U.S.	C11	135
Fallbrook, Ca., U.S.	F5	98
Fall City, Wa., U.S.	B4	140
Fall Creek, Wi., U.S.	D2	142
Falling Creek, stm., Va., U.S.	n17	139
Falling Rock Creek, stm., W.V., U.S.	m13	141
Fall Mountain Lake, Ct., U.S.	C4	100
Fallon, co., Mt., U.S.	D12	119
Fallon, Nv., U.S.	D3	121
Fallon Indian Reservation, Nv., U.S.	D3	121
Fallon Naval Air Station, mil., Nv., U.S.	D3	121
Fall River, Ma., U.S.	C5	114
Fall River, co., S.D., U.S.	D2	134
Fall River, Wi., U.S.	E4	142
Fall River Lake, res., Ks., U.S.	E7	109
Falls, co., Tx., U.S.	D4	136
Falls Church, Va., U.S.	g12	139
Falls City, Ne., U.S.	D10	120
Falls City, Or., U.S.	C3	130
Falls Creek, Pa., U.S.	D4	131
Fallston, Md., U.S.	A5	113
Falmouth, N.S., Can.	E5	87
Falmouth, Eng., U.K.	E4	12
Falmouth, Ky., U.S.	B5	110
Falmouth, Ma., U.S.	C6	114
Falmouth, Me., U.S.	E2	112
Falmouth, Va., U.S.	B5	139
False Bay see Valsbaai, b., S. Afr.	E2	56
False Cape, c., Va., U.S.	D6	102
False Cape, c., Va., U.S.	D7	139
Falster, i., Den.	I5	10
Fălticeni, Rom.	F9	20
Falun, Swe.	F6	10
Fanchang, China	C4	30
Fancy Farm, Ky., U.S.	f9	110
Fangak, Sudan	B6	54
Fangcheng, China	C3	30
Fangcheng, China	E2	30
Fangxian, China	C3	30
Fangzheng, China	A1	31
Fannin, co., Ga., U.S.	B2	103
Fannin, co., Tx., U.S.	C4	136
Fanny, Mount, mtn., Or., U.S.	B9	130
Fano, Italy	C4	18
Fan Si Pan, mtn., Viet.	B4	34
Faradje, D.R.C.	C5	54
Faradofay see Tôlañaro, Madag.	D8	56
Farafangana, Madag.	C8	56
Farāh, Afg.	D8	42
Farallon de Medinilla, i., N. Mar. Is.	C12	32
Farallon de Pajaros, i., N. Mar. Is.	B12	32
Faranah, Gui.	F3	50
Farasān, Jazā'ir, is., Sau. Ar.	G4	38
Farewell, Cape, c., N.Z.	p13	63c
Fargo, Ga., U.S.	F4	103
Fargo, N.D., U.S.	C9	127
Faribault, Mn., U.S.	F5	116
Faribault, co., Mn., U.S.	G4	116
Farīdābād, India	D3	40
Farley, Ia., U.S.	B6	108
Farmer City, Il., U.S.	C5	106
Farmers Branch, Tx., U.S.	n10	136
Farmersburg, In., U.S.	F3	107
Farmerville, La., U.S.	B3	111
Farmingdale, Me., U.S.	D3	112
Farmington, Ar., U.S.	A1	97
Farmington, stm., Ct., U.S.	B4	100
Farmington, Ia., U.S.	D6	108
Farmington, Il., U.S.	C3	106
Farmington, Me., U.S.	D2	112
Farmington, Mi., U.S.	p15	115
Farmington, Mn., U.S.	F5	116
Farmington, Mo., U.S.	D7	118
Farmington, N.H., U.S.	D4	122
Farmington, N.M., U.S.	A1	124
Farmington, Ut., U.S.	C4	137
Farmington Hills, Mi., U.S.	o15	115
Farmland, In., U.S.	D7	107
Farmville, N.C., U.S.	B5	126
Farmville, Va., U.S.	C4	139
Farnham, P.Q., Can.	D5	90
Faro, Braz.	D8	70
Faro, Port.	I3	16
Faroe Islands, dep., Eur.	o23	10b
Faroe Islands, is., Far. Is.	B12	4
Fårön, i., Swe.	H8	10
Fårösund, Swe.	H8	10
Farquhar, Atoll de, is., Sey.	j12	57b
Farrell, Pa., U.S.	D1	131
Farrukhābād, India	D3	40
Fartak, Ra's, c., Yemen	G6	38
Farvel, Kap, c., Grnld.	G31	82
Farwell, Mi., U.S.	E6	115
Farwell, Tx., U.S.	B1	136
Fasā, Iran	E6	42
Fastiv, Ukr.	D10	20
Fatick, Sen.	D1	50
Fatsa, Tur.	B7	44
Faulk, co., S.D., U.S.	B6	134
Faulkland Heights, De., U.S.	i7	101
Faulkner, co., Ar., U.S.	B3	97
Faulkton, S.D., U.S.	B6	134
Fauquier, co., Va., U.S.	B5	139
Fauske, Nor.	C6	10
Fawnie Nose, mtn., B.C., Can.	C5	85
Faxaflói, b., Ice.	l17	10a
Faya-Largeau, Chad	C8	50
Fayd, Sau. Ar.	E4	42
Fayette, Al., U.S.	B2	94
Fayette, co., Al., U.S.	B3	94
Fayette, co., Ga., U.S.	C2	103
Fayette, Ia., U.S.	B6	108
Fayette, co., Ia., U.S.	B6	108
Fayette, co., Il., U.S.	D5	106
Fayette, co., In., U.S.	E7	107
Fayette, co., Ky., U.S.	B5	110
Fayette, Mo., U.S.	B5	118
Fayette, Ms., U.S.	D2	117
Fayette, co., Oh., U.S.	C2	128
Fayette, co., Pa., U.S.	G2	131
Fayette, co., Tn., U.S.	B2	135
Fayette, co., Tx., U.S.	E4	136
Fayetteville, Ar., U.S.	A1	97
Fayetteville, Ga., U.S.	C2	103
Fayetteville, N.C., U.S.	B4	126
Fayetteville, Pa., U.S.	G6	131
Fayetteville, Tn., U.S.	B5	135
Fayetteville, W.V., U.S.	C3	141
Fāzilka, India	C2	40
Fazzān, hist. reg., Libya	A7	50
Fdérik, Maur.	B2	50
Fear, Cape, c., N.C., U.S.	D5	126
Feather, stm., Ca., U.S.	C3	98
Fécamp, Fr.	C7	16
Federal, Arg.	E6	72
Federalsburg, Md., U.S.	C6	113
Federated States of Micronesia see Micronesia, Federated States of, ctry., Oc.	D8	58
Feeding Hills, Ma., U.S.	B2	114
Fehmarn, i., Ger.	C12	12
Feijó, Braz.	E5	70
Feira de Santana, Braz.	D4	74
Felipe Carrillo Puerto, Mex.	D7	78
Fellsmere, Fl., U.S.	E6	102
Felton, Ca., U.S.	D2	98
Felton, De., U.S.	D3	101
Femunden, l., Nor.	E4	10
Fence, stm., Mi., U.S.	B2	115
Fence Lake, l., Wi., U.S.	C4	142
Fenelon Falls, On., Can.	C6	89
Fengcheng, China	F11	28
Fengdu, China	F9	28
Fengfeng, China	B3	30
Fenghuang, China	D2	30
Fengning, China	A4	30
Fengqing, China	B3	34
Fengqiu, China	B3	30
Fengrun, China	B4	30
Fengtai, China	C4	30
Fengzhen, China	A3	30
Fenimore Pass, strt., Ak., U.S.	E4	95
Fennimore, Wi., U.S.	F3	142
Fennville, Mi., U.S.	F4	115
Fenoarivo Atsinanana, Madag.	B8	56
Fenton, Mi., U.S.	F7	115
Fentress, co., Tn., U.S.	C9	135
Fenwick Island, i., S.C., U.S.	k11	133
Fenyang, China	D10	28
Fenyi, China	D3	30
Feodosiia, Ukr.	G13	20
Fer, Point au, c., La., U.S.	E4	111
Ferdinand, In., U.S.	H4	107
Ferdows, Iran	D7	42
Fergana, Uzb.	E9	26
Fergana Mountains see Ferganskij hrebet, mts., Kyrg.	A2	40
Ferganskij hrebet, mts., Kyrg.	A2	40
Fergus, On., Can.	D4	89
Fergus, co., Mt., U.S.	C7	119
Fergus Falls, Mn., U.S.	D2	116
Ferguson, Ky., U.S.	C5	110
Ferguson, Mo., U.S.	C7	118
Ferkéssédougou, C. Iv.	E3	50
Ferlo, reg., Sen.	C2	50
Ferme-Neuve, P.Q., Can.	C2	90
Fermo, Italy	C4	18
Fermont, P.Q., Can.	h13	90
Fernandina Beach, Fl., U.S.	B5	102
Fernandópolis, Braz.	F1	74
Fernando Póo see Bioko, i., Eq. Gui.	C1	54
Fernán-Núñez, Spain	I4	16
Fern Creek, Ky., U.S.	g11	110
Ferndale, Ca., U.S.	B1	98
Ferndale, Md., U.S.	B4	113
Ferndale, Mi., U.S.	p15	115
Ferndale, Pa., U.S.	F4	131
Ferndale, Wa., U.S.	A3	140
Fernie, B.C., Can.	E10	85
Fernley, Nv., U.S.	D2	121
Fern Ridge Lake, res., Or., U.S.	C3	130
Fernwood, Id., U.S.	B2	105
Fernwood, Ms., U.S.	D3	117
Feroe Islands see Faroe Islands, dep., Far. Is.	C5	8
Ferrara, Italy	B3	18
Ferrelo, Cape, c., Or., U.S.	E2	130
Ferriday, La., U.S.	C4	111
Ferris, Tx., U.S.	C4	136
Ferris Mountains, mts., Wy., U.S.	D5	143
Ferro see El Hierro, i., Spain	A1	50
Ferrol, Spain	F2	16
Ferron, Ut., U.S.	D4	137
Ferrum, Va., U.S.	D2	139
Ferry, co., Wa., U.S.	A7	140
Ferry Farms, Va., U.S.	B5	139
Ferryland, Nf., Can.	E5	88
Ferry Point, c., N.J., U.S.	k7	123
Fertile, Mn., U.S.	C2	116
Fès, Mor.	D4	48
Feshi, D.R.C.	E3	54
Fessenden, N.D., U.S.	B6	127
Festus, Mo., U.S.	C7	118
Fetești, Rom.	G9	20
Fethiye, Tur.	D3	44
Fetisovo, Kaz.	B6	42
Feuilles, Rivière aux, stm., P.Q., Can.	g12	90
Feyzābād, Afg.	C10	42
Fianarantsoa, Madag.	C8	56
Fianga, Chad	E8	50
Fichė, Eth.	B7	54
Ficksburg, S. Afr.	D4	56
Fidalgo Island, i., Wa., U.S.	A3	140
Fieldale, Va., U.S.	D3	139
Fields, Lake, l., Fl., U.S.	B3	102
Fields, Lake, l., La., U.S.	k10	111
Fier, Alb.	D7	18
Fifteenmile Creek, stm., Wy., U.S.	B4	143
Fifteen Mile Falls Reservoir, res., U.S.	C5	138
Fifth Cataract, wtfl., Sudan	G11	48
Figtree, Zimb.	C4	56
Figueira da Foz, Port.	E2	16
Figueres, Spain	F8	16
Figuig, Mor.	C4	48
Fiji, ctry., Oc.	m10	63b
Filchner Ice Shelf, ice, Ant.	D1	67
Filer, Id., U.S.	G4	105
Filingué, Niger	D5	50
Fílippoi, hist., Grc.	D10	18
Fillmore, Ca., U.S.	E4	98
Fillmore, co., Mn., U.S.	G6	116
Fillmore, co., Ne., U.S.	D8	120
Fillmore, Ut., U.S.	E3	137
Fimi, D.R.C.	C3	54
Findlay, Il., U.S.	D5	106
Findlay, Oh., U.S.	A2	128
Fingoè, Moz.	B5	56
Finike, Tur.	D4	44
Finke, Austl.	D6	60
Finland, ctry., Eur.	E12	10
Finland, Gulf of, b., Eur.	G10	10
Finley, N.D., U.S.	B8	127
Finley, Tn., U.S.	A2	135
Finney, co., Ks., U.S.	D3	109
Flin Flon, Mb., Can.	B1	86
Finnmark, state, Nor.	B11	10
Finn Mountain, mtn., Ak., U.S.	C8	95
Fins, Oman	F7	42
Finspång, Swe.	G6	10
Fircrest, Wa., U.S.	f10	140
Firebaugh, Ca., U.S.	D3	98
Firenze (Florence), Italy	C4	18
Firestone, Co., U.S.	A6	99
Fīrozābād, India	D3	40
Fīrozpur, India	C2	40
First Cataract, wtfl., Egypt	F11	48
First Connecticut Lake, l., N.H., U.S.	f7	122
Fīrūzābād, Iran	E6	42
Fish, stm., Al., U.S.	E2	94
Fish Creek, stm., W.V., U.S.	g8	141
Fisher, Il., U.S.	C5	106
Fisher, co., Tx., U.S.	C2	136
Fisher Bay, b., Mb., Can.	D3	86
Fishermans Island, i., Va., U.S.	h15	139
Fishers, In., U.S.	E5	107
Fishers Island, i., N.Y., U.S.	m16	125
Fishers Peak, mtn., Co., U.S.	D6	99
Fishersville, Va., U.S.	B4	139
Fishing Bay, b., Md., U.S.	D5	113
Fishing Creek, Md., U.S.	D5	113
Fishing Creek, stm., N.C., U.S.	A5	126
Fishing Creek, stm., S.C., U.S.	B5	133
Fishing Creek, stm., W.V., U.S.	B4	141
Fishing Creek Reservoir, res., S.C., U.S.	B6	133
Fishkill, N.Y., U.S.	D7	125
Fish Lake, l., Ut., U.S.	E4	137
Fish River Lake, l., Me., U.S.	B4	112
Fishtrap Lake, res., Ky., U.S.	C7	110
Fiskdale, Ma., U.S.	B3	114
Fisterra, Cabo de, c., Spain	F2	16
Fitchburg, Ma., U.S.	A4	114
Fitzgerald, Ga., U.S.	E3	103
Fitz Roy, Arg.	G3	69
Fitzroy, stm., Austl.	D3	60
Fitzroy Crossing, Austl.	D4	60
Fitzwilliam, N.H., U.S.	E2	122
Fitzwilliam Island, i., On., Can.	B3	89
Fiume see Rijeka, Cro.	B5	18
Five Island Lake, l., Ia., U.S.	A3	108
Fivemile Creek, stm., Wy., U.S.	C4	143
Five Points, N.M., U.S.	B3	124
Fizi, D.R.C.	D5	54
Flagler, co., Fl., U.S.	C5	102
Flagler Beach, Fl., U.S.	C5	102
Flagstaff, Az., U.S.	B4	96
Flagstaff Lake, l., Or., U.S.	E7	130
Flambeau, stm., Wi., U.S.	C3	142
Flaming Gorge Dam, Ut., U.S.	C6	137
Flaming Gorge National Recreation Area, U.S.	E3	143
Flaming Gorge Reservoir, res., U.S.	E3	143
Flaming Gorge Reservoir, res., U.S.	C6	92
Flanagan, Il., U.S.	C5	106
Flandreau, S.D., U.S.	C9	134
Flandreau Indian Reservation, S.D., U.S.	C9	134
Flat, stm., Mi., U.S.	E5	115
Flat, stm., N.C., U.S.	A4	126
Flat, stm., R.I., U.S.	E2	132
Flat Brook, stm., N.J., U.S.	A3	123
Flathead, co., Mt., U.S.	B2	119
Flathead, South Fork, stm., Mt., U.S.	C3	119
Flathead Indian Reservation, Mt., U.S.	C2	119
Flathead Lake, l., Mt., U.S.	C2	119
Flathead Valley, val., Mt., U.S.	C2	119
Flat Lake, l., La., U.S.	k9	111
Flat Lick, Ky., U.S.	D6	110
Flatonia, Tx., U.S.	E4	136
Flat River, Mo., U.S.	D7	118
Flat River Reservoir, res., R.I., U.S.	D3	132
Flatrock, stm., In., U.S.	F6	107
Flat Rock, Mi., U.S.	F7	115
Flat Rock, N.C., U.S.	f10	126
Flattery, Cape, c., Austl.	C4	62
Flattery, Cape, c., Wa., U.S.	A1	140
Flatwoods, Ky., U.S.	B7	110
Fleetwood, Pa., U.S.	F10	131
Fleming, co., Ky., U.S.	B6	110
Fleming-Neon, Ky., U.S.	C7	110
Flemingsburg, Ky., U.S.	B6	110
Flemington, N.J., U.S.	B3	123
Flemington, Pa., U.S.	D7	131
Flen, Swe.	G7	10
Flensburg, Ger.	C11	12
Fletcher, N.C., U.S.	f10	126
Fletcher, Ok., U.S.	C3	129
Flinders, stm., Austl.	D3	62
Flinders Bay, b., Austl.	G2	60
Flinders Island, i., Austl.	H4	62
Flinders Reefs, rf., Austl.	D4	62
Flin Flon, Mb., Can.	B1	86
Flint, stm., Ga., U.S.	E2	103
Flint, Mi., U.S.	E7	115
Flint, i., Kir.	F14	58
Flint City, Al., U.S.	A3	94
Flint Creek Range, mts., Mt., U.S.	D3	119
Flint Run, stm., W.V., U.S.	k9	141
Flippin, Ar., U.S.	A3	97
Flisa, Nor.	F5	10
Flomaton, Al., U.S.	D2	94
Flora, Il., U.S.	E5	106
Flora, In., U.S.	C4	107
Flora, Ms., U.S.	C3	117
Florala, Al., U.S.	D3	94
Floral City, Fl., U.S.	D4	102
Florence see Firenze, Italy	C3	18
Florence, Al., U.S.	A2	94
Florence, Az., U.S.	D4	96
Florence, Co., U.S.	C5	99
Florence, Ks., U.S.	D7	109
Florence, Ky., U.S.	A5	110
Florence, Ms., U.S.	C3	117
Florence, N.J., U.S.	C3	123
Florence, Or., U.S.	D2	130
Florence, co., S.C., U.S.	C8	133
Florence, S.C., U.S.	C8	133
Florence, co., Wi., U.S.	C5	142
Florenceville, N.B., Can.	C2	87
Florencia, Col.	C4	70
Flores, i., Indon.	E6	36
Flores, Laut (Flores Sea), Indon.	E6	36
Flores Sea see Flores, Laut, Indon.	E6	36
Florești, Mol.	F10	20
Floresville, Tx., U.S.	E3	136
Florham Park, N.J., U.S.	B4	123
Floriano, Braz.	C3	74
Florianópolis, Braz.	D8	72
Florida, Cuba	A4	80
Florida, N.Y., U.S.	D6	125
Florida, Ur.	E6	72
Florida, state, U.S.	E5	102
Florida, Cape, c., Fl., U.S.	G6	102
Florida, Straits of, strt., N.A.	G11	92
Florida Bay, b., Fl., U.S.	H6	102
Floridablanca, Col.	D5	80
Florida City, Fl., U.S.	G6	102
Florida Keys, is., Fl., U.S.	H6	102
Florida Mountains, mts., N.M., U.S.	E2	124
Florida State Indian Reservation, Fl., U.S.	F5	102
Florien, La., U.S.	C2	111
Flórina, Grc.	D8	18
Florissant, Mo., U.S.	f13	118
Florissant Fossil Beds National Monument, Co., U.S.	C5	99
Florø, Nor.	F1	10
Flossmoor, Il., U.S.	k9	106
Flovilla, Ga., U.S.	C3	103
Flower Brook, stm., Vt., U.S.	E2	138
Flowery Branch, Ga., U.S.	B3	103
Flowood, Ms., U.S.	C3	117
Floyd, co., Ga., U.S.	B1	103
Floyd, stm., Ia., U.S.	B1	108
Floyd, co., Ia., U.S.	A5	108
Floyd, co., In., U.S.	H6	107
Floyd, co., Ky., U.S.	C7	110
Floyd, co., Tx., U.S.	B2	136
Floyd, co., Va., U.S.	D2	139
Floydada, Tx., U.S.	C2	136
Floyds Fork, stm., Ky., U.S.	B4	110
Floyds Knobs, In., U.S.	H6	107
Flushing see Vlissingen, Neth.	E8	12
Flushing, Mi., U.S.	E7	115
Flushing, Oh., U.S.	B4	128
Fluvanna, co., Va., U.S.	C4	139
Foard, co., Tx., U.S.	B3	136
Foča, Bos.	C7	18
Focșani, Rom.	G9	20
Foggia, Italy	D5	18
Fogland Point, c., R.I., U.S.	E6	132
Fogo, Nf., Can.	D4	88
Fogo, i., C.V.	g10	50a
Fogo, Cape, c., Nf., Can.	D5	88
Fogo Island, i., Nf., Can.	D4	88
Foix, Fr.	F7	16
Fokku, Nig.	D5	50
Folādī, Koh-e, mtn., Afg.	D9	42
Folda, i., Nor.	C6	10
Foley, Al., U.S.	E2	94
Foley, Mn., U.S.	E5	116
Foligno, Italy	C4	18
Folkestone, Eng., U.K.	E7	12
Folkston, Ga., U.S.	F4	103
Follansbee, W.V., U.S.	A4	141
Folly Beach, S.C., U.S.	F8	133
Folly Island, i., S.C., U.S.	F8	133
Folsom, Ca., U.S.	C3	98
Fomboni, Com.	A7	56
Fonda, Ia., U.S.	B3	108
Fond du Lac, Wi., U.S.	E5	142
Fond du Lac, co., Wi., U.S.	E5	142
Fond du Lac Indian Reservation, Mn., U.S.	D6	116
Fonseca, Golfo de, b., N.A.	C2	80
Fontainebleau, Fr.	C8	16
Fontana, Ca., U.S.	m14	98
Fontana, Wi., U.S.	F5	142
Fontana Lake, res., N.C., U.S.	f9	126
Fontanelle, Ia., U.S.	C3	108
Fonte Boa, Braz.	D6	70
Fontenay-le-Comte, Fr.	D6	16
Fontenelle Reservoir, res., Wy., U.S.	D2	143
Fontur, c., Ice.	k21	10a
Foochow see Fuzhou, China	F11	28
Footville, Wi., U.S.	F4	142
Foraker, Mount, mtn., Ak., U.S.	f16	95
Forbes, Austl.	G4	62
Forbes, Mount, mtn., Ab., Can.	D2	84

Name	Map Ref.	Page

Forcados, Nig. E6 50
Forchheim, Ger. F12 12
Ford, co., Il., U.S. C5 106
Ford, co., Ks., U.S. E4 109
Ford, stm., Mi., U.S. C3 115
Ford City, Ca., U.S. E4 98
Ford City, Pa., U.S. E2 131
Fordoche, La., U.S. D4 111
Fords Prairie, Wa., U.S. C2 140
Fordyce, Ar., U.S. D3 97
Forécariah, Gui. E2 50
Forel, Mont, mtn.,
    Grnld. E32 82
Foreman, Ar., U.S. D1 97
Forest, On., Can. D2 89
Forest, Ms., U.S. C4 117
Forest, stm., N.D., U.S. A8 127
Forest, Oh., U.S. B2 128
Forest, co., Pa., U.S. C3 131
Forest, co., Wi., U.S. C5 142
Forest Acres, S.C., U.S. C6 133
Forestburg, Ab., Can. C4 84
Forest City, Ia., U.S. A4 108
Forest City, N.C., U.S. B1 126
Forest City, Pa., U.S. C11 131
Forestdale, R.I., U.S. B3 132
Forest Dale, Vt., U.S. D2 138
Forest Glen, La., U.S. h12 111
Forest Grove, Or., U.S. B3 130
Forest Hill, Md., U.S. A5 113
Forest Hills, Pa., U.S. k14 131
Forest Knolls, Ca., U.S. g7 98
Forest Lake, Mn., U.S. E6 116
Forest Park, Ga., U.S. h8 103
Forest Park, Il., U.S. k9 106
Forillon, Parc National de,
    P.Q., Can. k14 90
Fork Creek, stm., W.V.,
    U.S. m12 141
Forked Deer, stm., Tn.,
    U.S. B2 135
Forkland, Al., U.S. C2 94
Forks, Wa., U.S. B1 140
Forlì, Italy B4 18
Formentera, i., Spain H7 16
Formia, Italy D4 18
Formiga, Braz. F2 74
Formosa, Arg. D6 72
Formosa see Taiwan, ctry.,
    Asia B8 34
Formosa, Braz. E2 74
Formosa, Serra, plat., Braz. . .F9 70
Formosa Strait see Taiwan
    Strait, strt., Asia E4 30
Forney, Tx., U.S. C4 136
Forrest, Austl. G4 60
Forrest, Il., U.S. C5 106
Forrest, co., Ms., U.S. D4 117
Forrest City, Ar., U.S. B5 97
Forrester Island, i., Ak.,
    U.S. n23 95
Forreston, Il., U.S. A4 106
Forsayth, Austl. D3 62
Forst, Ger. E14 12
Forsyth, Ga., U.S. C3 103
Forsyth, co., Ga., U.S. B2 103
Forsyth, co., Ga., U.S. D5 106
Forsyth, Il., U.S. 106
Forsyth, Mo., U.S. E4 118
Forsyth, Mt., U.S. D10 119
Forsyth, co., N.C., U.S. A2 126
Fortaleza, Braz. B4 74
Fort Apache Indian
    Reservation, Az., U.S. . . .D5 96
Fort-Archambault see Sarh,
    Chad B3 54
Fort Ashby, W.V., U.S. B6 141
Fort Atkinson, Wi., U.S. F5 142
Fort Beaufort, S. Afr. E4 56
Fort Belknap Indian
    Reservation, Mt., U.S. . . .B8 119
Fort Belvoir, mil., Va., U.S. . .g12 139
Fort Bend, co., Tx., U.S. E5 136
Fort Benjamin Harrison, mil.,
    In., U.S. k10 107
Fort Benning, mil., Ga.,
    U.S. D2 103
Fort Benton, Mt., U.S. C6 119
Fort Berthold Indian
    Reservation, N.D., U.S. . .B3 127
Fort Bidwell Indian
    Reservation, Ca., U.S. . . .B3 98
Fort Bliss, mil., Tx., U.S. o11 136
Fort Bragg, Ca., U.S. C2 98
Fort Bragg, mil., N.C., U.S. . .B3 126
Fort Branch, In., U.S. H2 107
Fort Calhoun, Ne., U.S. C9 120
Fort Campbell, mil., U.S. A4 135
Fort Carson, mil., Co., U.S. . .C6 99
Fort Chipewyan, Ab., Can. . . .f8 84
Fort Clatsop National
    Memorial, hist., Or., U.S. .A3 130
Fort Cobb, Ok., U.S. B3 129
Fort Cobb Reservoir, res., Ok.,
    U.S. B3 129
Fort Collins, Co., U.S. A5 99
Fort Coulonge, P.Q., Can. . . .B8 89
Fort-Dauphin see Tôlañaro,
    Madag. D8 56
Fort Davis, Tx., U.S. o13 136
Fort Davis National Historic
    Site, hist., Tx., U.S. o13 136
Fort Defiance, Az., U.S. B6 96
Fort-de-France, Mart. C7 80
Fort Deposit, Al., U.S. D3 94
Fort Detrick, mil., Md., U.S. . .B3 113
Fort Dix, mil., N.J., U.S. C3 123
Fort Dodge, Ia., U.S. B3 108

Fort Donelson National
    Battlefield, Tn., U.S. A4 135
Fort Edward, N.Y., U.S. B7 125
Fort Erie, On., Can. E6 89
Fort Eustis, mil., Va., U.S. . . .h14 139
Fort Fairfield, Me., U.S. B5 112
Fort Frances, On., Can. o16 89
Fort Gaines, Ga., U.S. E1 103
Fort Gay, W.V., U.S. C2 141
Fort Gibson, Ok., U.S. B6 129
Fort Gibson Lake, res., Ok.,
    U.S. A6 129
Fort Gordon, mil., Ga., U.S. . .C4 103
Fort Greely, mil., Ak., U.S. . . .C10 95
Forth, Firth of, b., Scot.,
    U.K. B5 12
Fort Hall, Id., U.S. F6 105
Fort Hall Indian Reservation,
    Id., U.S. F6 105
Fort Hood, mil., Tx., U.S. D4 136
Fort Howard, Md., U.S. B5 113
Fort Huachuca, mil., Az.,
    U.S. F5 96
Fort Jackson, mil., S.C.,
    U.S. C6 133
Fort Jefferson National
    Monument, Fl., U.S. H4 102
Fort Kent, Me., U.S. A4 112
Fort Knox, mil., Ky., U.S. B4 110
Fort-Lamy see N'Djamena,
    Chad D8 50
Fort Laramie, Wy., U.S. D8 143
Fort Laramie National Historic
    Site, hist., Wy., U.S. D8 143
Fort Lauderdale, Fl., U.S. F6 102
Fort Lawn, S.C., U.S. B6 133
Fort Leavenworth, mil., Ks.,
    U.S. C9 109
Fort Lee, N.J., U.S. B5 123
Fort Lee, mil., Va., U.S. C5 139
Fort Leonard Wood, mil., Mo.,
    U.S. D5 118
Fort Lewis, mil., Wa., U.S. . . .B3 140
Fort Loramie, Oh., U.S. B1 128
Fort Loudon, Pa., U.S. G6 131
Fort Loudoun Lake, res., Tn.,
    U.S. D9 135
Fort Lupton, Co., U.S. A6 99
Fort MacArthur, mil., Ca.,
    U.S. n12 98
Fort Macleod, Ab., Can. E4 84
Fort Madison, Ia., U.S. D6 108
Fort Matanzas National
    Monument, Fl., U.S. C5 102
Fort McClellan, mil., Al.,
    U.S. B4 94
Fort McDermitt Indian
    Reservation, U.S. B4 121
Fort McDowell Indian
    Reservation, Az., U.S. . . .D4 96
Fort McHenry National
    Monument and Historic
    Shrine, Md., U.S. g11 113
Fort McMurray, Ab., Can. A5 84
Fort Meade, Fl., U.S. E5 102
Fort Meade, mil., Md., U.S. . .B4 113
Fort Meadow Reservoir, res.,
    Ma., U.S. g9 114
Fort Mill, S.C., U.S. A6 133
Fort Mitchell, Al., U.S. C4 94
Fort Mitchell, Ky., U.S. h13 110
Fort Mojave Indian
    Reservation, U.S. C1 96
Fort Monmouth, mil., N.J.,
    U.S. C4 123
Fort Monroe, mil., Va.,
    U.S. h15 139
Fort Morgan, Co., U.S. A7 99
Fort Myer, mil., Va., U.S. g12 139
Fort Myers, Fl., U.S. F5 102
Fort Myers Beach, Fl., U.S. . .F5 102
Fort Nelson, B.C., Can. m18 85
Fort Oglethorpe, Ga., U.S. . . .B1 103
Fort Payne, Al., U.S. A4 94
Fort Peck Indian Reservation,
    Mt., U.S. B11 119
Fort Peck Lake, res., Mt.,
    U.S. C9 119
Fort Pierce, Fl., U.S. E6 102
Fort Pierce Inlet, b., Fl.,
    U.S. E6 102
Fort Pierre, S.D., U.S. C5 134
Fort Plain, N.Y., U.S. C6 125
Fort Polk, mil., La., U.S. C2 111
Fort Portal, Ug. C6 54
Fort Randall Dam, S.D.,
    U.S. D7 134
Fort Recovery, Oh., U.S. B1 128
Fortress Mountain, mtn., Wy.,
    U.S. B3 143
Fort Richardson, mil., Ak.,
    U.S. C10 95
Fort Riley, mil., Ks., U.S. C7 109
Fort Ritchie, mil., Md., U.S. . .A3 113
Fort Rucker, mil., Al., U.S. . . .D4 94
Fort Saint James, B.C., Can. . .B5 85
Fort Saint John, B.C., Can. . . .A7 85
Fort Sam Houston, mil., Tx.,
    U.S. k7 136
Fort Saskatchewan, Ab., Can. .C4 84
Fort Scott, Ks., U.S. E9 109
Fort-Ševčenko, Kaz. E7 26
Fort Shafter, mil., Hi., U.S. . . .g10 104
Fort Shawnee, Oh., U.S. B1 128
Fort Sill, mil., Ok., U.S. C3 129
Fort Smith, Ar., U.S. B1 97
Fort Stewart, mil., Ga., U.S. . .D5 103

Fort Stockton, Tx., U.S. D1 136
Fort Sumner, N.M., U.S. C5 124
Fort Sumter National
    Monument, S.C., U.S. . . .k12 133
Fort Supply Lake, res., Ok.,
    U.S. A2 129
Fort Thomas, Ky., U.S. h14 110
Fort Totten, N.D., U.S. B7 127
Fort Totten Indian Reservation,
    N.D., U.S. B7 127
Fortuna, Ca., U.S. B1 98
Fortune, Nf., Can. E4 88
Fortune Bay, b., Nf., Can. E4 88
Fort Union National
    Monument, N.M., U.S. . .B5 124
Fort Valley, Ga., U.S. D3 103
Fort Vermilion, Ab., Can. f7 84
Fortville, In., U.S. E6 107
Fort Wainwright, mil., Ak.,
    U.S. C10 95
Fort Walton Beach, Fl.,
    U.S. u15 102
Fort Washington Forest, Md.,
    U.S. C4 113
Fort Wayne, In., U.S. B7 107
Fort William, Scot., U.K. B4 12
Fort Wingate, N.M., U.S. B1 124
Fort Worth, Tx., U.S. C4 136
Fort Wright, Ky., U.S. h13 110
Forty Fort, Pa., U.S. D10 131
Fort Yukon, Ak., U.S. B10 95
Fort Yuma Indian Reservation,
    Ca., U.S. F6 98
Foshan, China G10 28
Foso, Ghana E4 50
Fossano, Italy B1 18
Fossil Butte National
    Monument, Wy., U.S. . . .E2 143
Fossil Lake, l., Or., U.S. D6 130
Foss Reservoir, res., Ok.,
    U.S. B2 129
Fosston, Mn., U.S. C3 116
Foster, co., N.D., U.S. B6 127
Foster, Or., U.S. C4 130
Foster Village, Hi., U.S. g10 104
Fostoria, Oh., U.S. A2 128
Fougamou, Gabon D2 54
Fougères, Fr. C6 16
Fouke, Ar., U.S. D2 97
Foulamôri, Gui. D2 50
Foumban, Cam. B2 54
Foundiougne, Sen. D1 50
Fountain, Co., U.S. C6 99
Fountain, co., In., U.S. D3 107
Fountain City, In., U.S. E8 107
Fountain City, Wi., U.S. D2 142
Fountain Hill, Pa., U.S. E11 131
Fountain Inn, S.C., U.S. B3 133
Fountain Peak, mtn., Ca.,
    U.S. E6 98
Fourche LaFave, stm., Ar.,
    U.S. C2 97
Fourche Maline, stm., Ok.,
    U.S. C6 129
Four Mountains, Islands of,
    is., Ak., U.S. E6 95
Four Oaks, N.C., U.S. B4 126
Fourth Cataract, wtfl.,
    Sudan G11 48
Fouta Djalon, reg., Gui. D2 50
Foveaux Strait, strt., N.Z. q12 63c
Fowler, Ca., U.S. D4 98
Fowler, Co., U.S. C6 99
Fowler, In., U.S. C3 107
Fowler, Mi., U.S. E6 115
Fowlerville, Mi., U.S. F6 115
Fowman, Iran D13 44
Fox, stm., Mb., Can. B4 86
Fox, stm., Mi., U.S. B4 115
Fox, stm., Wi., U.S. D5 142
Fox, stm., Wi., U.S. B5 106
Fox, stm., U.S. A6 118
Foxboro, On., Can. C7 89
Foxboro, Ma., U.S. B5 114
Fox Creek, Ab., Can. B2 84
Foxe Basin, b., N.T.,
    Can. E24 82
Fox Island, i., R.I., U.S. E4 132
Fox Island, i., Wa., U.S. f10 140
Fox Islands, is., Ak., U.S. E6 95
Fox Lake, Il., U.S. A5 106
Fox Lake, l., Il., U.S. h8 106
Fox Lake, Wi., U.S. E5 142
Fox Mountain, mtn., Nv.,
    U.S. B2 121
Fox Point, Wi., U.S. E6 142
Fox River Grove, Il., U.S. h8 106
Foxworth, Ms., U.S. D4 117
Foz do Cunene, Ang. B1 56
Foz do Iguaçu, Braz. D7 72
Frackville, Pa., U.S. E9 131
Fraga, Spain G7 16
Fram Basin E22 144
Framingham, Ma., U.S. B5 114
Franca, Braz. F2 74
France, ctry., Eur. D8 16
Francesville, In., U.S. C4 107
Franceville, Gabon D2 54
Francis, Lake, l., N.H., U.S. . . .f7 122
Francis Case, Lake, res., S.D.,
    U.S. D6 134
Francistown, Bots. C4 56
Franconia, N.H., U.S. B3 122
Franconia Notch, N.H.,
    U.S. B3 122

Francs Peak, mtn., Wy., U.S. . .C3 143
Franken, hist. reg., Ger. E11 12
Frankenmuth, Mi., U.S. E7 115
Frankford, On., Can. C7 89
Frankford, De., U.S. F5 101
Frankfort, Il., U.S. m9 106
Frankfort, In., U.S. D4 107
Frankfort, Ks., U.S. C7 109
Frankfort, Ky., U.S. B5 110
Frankfort, Mi., U.S. D4 115
Frankfort, N.Y., U.S. B5 125
Frankfort, Oh., U.S. C2 128
Frankfurt, Ger. D14 12
Frankfurt am Main, Ger. E11 12
Franklin, co., Al., U.S. A2 94
Franklin, co., Ar., U.S. B2 97
Franklin, co., Fl., U.S. C2 102
Franklin, Ga., U.S. C1 103
Franklin, co., Ga., U.S. B3 103
Franklin, co., Ia., U.S. B4 108
Franklin, co., Id., U.S. G7 105
Franklin, co., Il., U.S. E4 106
Franklin, In., U.S. F5 107
Franklin, co., In., U.S. F7 107
Franklin, co., Ks., U.S. D8 109
Franklin, Ky., U.S. D3 110
Franklin, co., Ky., U.S. B5 110
Franklin, La., U.S. E4 111
Franklin, co., La., U.S. B4 111
Franklin, Ma., U.S. B5 114
Franklin, co., Ma., U.S. A2 114
Franklin, Me., U.S. C2 112
Franklin, co., Me., U.S. C2 112
Franklin, co., Mo., U.S. C6 118
Franklin, co., Ms., U.S. D3 117
Franklin, N.C., U.S. f9 126
Franklin, co., N.C., U.S. A4 126
Franklin, Ne., U.S. D7 120
Franklin, co., Ne., U.S. D7 120
Franklin, N.H., U.S. D3 122
Franklin, N.J., U.S. A3 123
Franklin, co., N.Y., U.S. f10 125
Franklin, Oh., U.S. C1 128
Franklin, co., Oh., U.S. B2 128
Franklin, Pa., U.S. D2 131
Franklin, co., Pa., U.S. G6 131
Franklin, Tn., U.S. B5 135
Franklin, Tx., U.S. D4 136
Franklin, co., Tx., U.S. C5 136
Franklin, Va., U.S. D6 139
Franklin, co., Va., U.S. D3 139
Franklin, co., Vt., U.S. B2 138
Franklin, co., Wa., U.S. C6 140
Franklin, Wi., U.S. n11 142
Franklin, W.V., U.S. C5 141
Franklin, Point, c., Ak.,
    U.S. A8 95
Franklin D. Roosevelt Lake,
    res., Wa., U.S. B7 140
Franklin Falls Reservoir, res.,
    N.H., U.S. C3 122
Franklin Grove, Il., U.S. B4 106
Franklin Lake, l., Nv., U.S. . . .C6 121
Franklin Park, Il., U.S. k9 106
Franklinton, La., U.S. D5 111
Franklinton, N.C., U.S. A4 126
Franklinville, N.Y., U.S. C2 125
Frankston, Tx., U.S. C5 136
Frankton, In., U.S. D6 107
Fransfontein, Nmb. C2 56
Franz Josef Land see Franca-
    losifá, Zemlja, is., Russia . .B7 26
Fraser, stm., B.C., Can. E7 85
Fraser, stm., Nf., Can. g9 88
Fraser, Mount, mtn., Can. C8 85
Fraserburg, S. Afr. E3 56
Fraserburgh, Scot., U.K. B5 12
Fraser Island, i., Austl. F5 62
Fraser Lake, B.C., Can. B5 85
Fraser Plateau, plat., B.C.,
    Can. D6 85
Frazee, Mn., U.S. D3 116
Frazeysburg, Oh., U.S. B3 128
Frazier Park, Ca., U.S. E4 98
Frederic, Wi., U.S. C1 142
Frederica, De., U.S. D4 101
Fredericia, Den. I3 10
Frederick, Co., U.S. A6 99
Frederick, Md., U.S. B3 113
Frederick, co., Md., U.S. B3 113
Frederick, Ok., U.S. C2 129
Frederick, co., Va., U.S. A4 139
Fredericksburg, Ia., U.S. B5 108
Fredericksburg, Tx., U.S. D3 136
Fredericksburg, Va., U.S. B5 139
Frederick Sound, strt., Ak.,
    U.S. m23 95
Fredericktown, Mo., U.S. D7 118
Fredericktown, Oh., U.S. B3 128
Fredericktown, Pa., U.S. F1 131
Fredericton, N.B., Can. D3 87
Fredericton Junction, N.B.,
    Can. D3 87
Frederikshåb, Grnld. F29 82
Frederikshavn, Den. H4 10
Fredonia, Az., U.S. A3 96
Fredonia, Ks., U.S. E8 109
Fredonia, N.Y., U.S. C1 125
Fredonia, Wi., U.S. E6 142
Fredrikstad, Nor. G4 10
Freeborn, co., Mn., U.S. G5 116
Freeburg, Il., U.S. E4 106
Freedom, Pa., U.S. E1 131
Freedom, Wy., U.S. D2 143
Freehold, N.J., U.S. C4 123
Freeland, Mi., U.S. E6 115
Freeland, Pa., U.S. D10 131

Freelandville, In., U.S. G3 107
Freel Peak, mtn., Ca., U.S. . . .C4 98
Freels, Cape, c., Nf., Can. D5 88
Freels, Cape, c., Nf., Can. E5 88
Freeman, S.D., U.S. D8 134
Freeman, Lake, l., In., U.S. . . .C4 107
Freemansburg, Pa., U.S. E11 131
Freemason Island, i., La.,
    U.S. E7 111
Freeport, Bah. C9 76
Freeport, Il., U.S. A4 106
Freeport, Me., U.S. E2 112
Freeport, N.Y., U.S. n15 125
Freeport, Pa., U.S. E2 131
Freeport, Tx., U.S. E5 136
Freer, Tx., U.S. F3 136
Freestone, co., Tx., U.S. D4 136
Freetown, S.L. E2 50
Freetown, In., U.S. G5 107
Freezeout Mountains, mts.,
    Wy., U.S. D6 143
Fregenal de la Sierra, Spain . .H3 16
Freiburg, Ger. G10 12
Freising, Ger. F12 12
Freistadt, Aus. F14 12
Fréjus, Fr. F10 16
Fremantle, Austl. G2 60
Fremont, Ca., U.S. D2 98
Fremont, co., Co., U.S. C5 99
Fremont, Ia., U.S. C5 108
Fremont, co., Ia., U.S. D2 108
Fremont, co., Id., U.S. E7 105
Fremont, In., U.S. A8 107
Fremont, Mi., U.S. E5 115
Fremont, N.C., U.S. B5 126
Fremont, Ne., U.S. C9 120
Fremont, Oh., U.S. A2 128
Fremont, stm., Ut., U.S. E4 137
Fremont, co., Wy., U.S. C4 143
Fremont Island, i., Ut., U.S. . . .B3 137
Fremont Lake, l., Wy., U.S. . . .D3 143
Fremont Peak, mtn., Wy.,
    U.S. C3 143
French Broad, stm., U.S. D10 135
Frenchburg, Ky., U.S. C6 110
French Creek, stm., Pa.,
    U.S. C2 131
French Frigate Shoals, rf., Hi.,
    U.S. m14 104
French Guiana, dep., S.A. C9 70
French Lick, In., U.S. G4 107
Frenchman Bay, b., Me.,
    U.S. D4 112
Frenchman Creek, stm.,
    U.S. D4 120
Frenchman Hills, Wa.,
    U.S. C6 140
Frenchman Lake, l., Nv.,
    U.S. G6 121
French Polynesia, dep.,
    Oc. F15 58
French Settlement, La.,
    U.S. D5 111
French Somaliland see
    Djibouti, ctry., Afr. H13 48
Frenda, Alg. J7 16
Freshfield, Mount, mtn.,
    Can. D2 84
Fresnillo, Mex. F9 78
Fresno, Ca., U.S. D4 98
Fresno, co., Ca., U.S. D4 98
Fresno Reservoir, res., Mt.,
    U.S. B6 119
Frewsburg, N.Y., U.S. C1 125
Freycinet Peninsula, pen.,
    Austl. I4 62
Fria, Gui. D2 50
Fria, Cape, c., Nmb. B1 56
Friars Point, Ms., U.S. A3 117
Frías, Arg. D4 72
Fribourg, Switz. A1 18
Friday Harbor, Wa., U.S. A2 140
Fridley, Mn., U.S. m12 116
Fridtjof Nansen, Mount, mtn.,
    Ant. E25 67
Friedrichshafen, Ger. G11 12
Friend, Ne., U.S. D8 120
Friendsville, Tn., U.S. D9 135
Fries, Va., U.S. D2 139
Frio, co., Tx., U.S. E3 136
Frio, stm., Tx., U.S. E3 136
Frio, Cabo, c., Braz. F3 74
Friona, Tx., U.S. B1 136
Frisco, Co., U.S. B4 99
Frisco City, Al., U.S. D2 94
Frisco Peak, mtn., Ut.,
    U.S. E2 137
Frisian Islands, is., Eur. D9 12
Frissell, Mount, mtn., U.S. . . .A2 100
Fritch, Tx., U.S. B2 136
Friza, proliv, strt., Russia B17 28
Frobisher Bay, b., N.T.,
    Can. F26 82
Frobisher Lake, l., Sk.,
    Can. m7 91
Frolovo, Russia E7 22
Frome, Lake, l., Austl. G3 62
Frontenac, Ks., U.S. E9 109
Frontera, Mex. B4 78
Frontera, Mex. D6 78
Frontier, co., Ne., U.S. D5 120
Front Range, mts., Co.,
    U.S. A5 99
Front Royal, Va., U.S. B4 139
Frosinone, Italy D4 18

Name	Map Ref.	Page
Frostburg, Md., U.S.	k13	113
Frostproof, Fl., U.S.	E5	102
Frøya, i., Nor.	E3	10
Fruita, Co., U.S.	B2	99
Fruit Heights, Ut., U.S.	B4	137
Fruitland, Id., U.S.	F2	105
Fruitland, Md., U.S.	D6	113
Fruitland, N.M., U.S.	A1	124
Fruitland Park, Fl., U.S.	D5	102
Fruitport, Mi., U.S.	E4	115
Fruitvale, B.C., Can.	E9	85
Fruitvale, Co., U.S.	B2	99
Fruitvale, Wa., U.S.	C5	140
Fruitville, Fl., U.S.	E4	102
Frunze see Bishkek, Kyrg.	E9	26
Frutal, Braz.	E2	74
Fryeburg, Me., U.S.	D2	112
Fu'an, China	D4	30
Fuding, China	D5	30
Fuerte, stm., Mex.	B3	78
Fuerte Olimpo, Para.	C6	72
Fuerteventura, i., Spain	A2	50
Fuga Island, i., Phil.	C8	34
Fuji, Japan	C3	31
Fuji, Mount see Fuji-san, vol., Japan	D15	28
Fujian, prov., China	F11	28
Fujin, China	B14	28
Fuji-san, vol., Japan	D15	28
Fujiyama see Fuji-san, vol., Japan	D15	28
Fukui, Japan	D15	28
Fukuoka, Japan	E14	28
Fukushima, Japan	C4	31
Fukuyama, Japan	D2	31
Fulaga Passage, i., Fiji	m11	63b
Fulda, Ger.	E11	12
Fulda, Mn., U.S.	G3	116
Fuling, China	D2	30
Fullerton, Ca., U.S.	n13	98
Fullerton, Ne., U.S.	C8	120
Fulton, co., Ar., U.S.	A4	97
Fulton, co., Ga., U.S.	C2	103
Fulton, co., Il., U.S.	C3	106
Fulton, Il., U.S.	B3	106
Fulton, co., In., U.S.	B5	107
Fulton, Ky., U.S.	f9	110
Fulton, co., Ky., U.S.	f8	110
Fulton, Md., U.S.	B4	113
Fulton, Mo., U.S.	C6	118
Fulton, Ms., U.S.	A5	117
Fulton, N.Y., U.S.	B4	125
Fulton, co., N.Y., U.S.	B6	125
Fulton, co., Oh., U.S.	A1	128
Fulton, co., Pa., U.S.	G5	131
Fultondale, Al., U.S.	f7	94
Funafuti, i., Tuvalu	E11	58
Funchal, Port.	D1	48
Fundy, Bay of, b., Can.	D4	87
Fundy National Park, N.B., Can.	D4	87
Funhalouro, Moz.	C5	56
Funing, China	C4	30
Funing, China	B4	30
Funkstown, Md., U.S.	A2	113
Funsi, Ghana	D4	50
Funtua, Nig.	D6	50
Fuping, China	C2	30
Fuqing, China	D4	30
Fuquay-Varina, N.C., U.S.	B4	126
Furnace Brook, stm., Vt., U.S.	D3	138
Furnas, co., Ne., U.S.	D6	120
Furnas, Represa de, res., Braz.	F2	74
Furneaux Group, is., Austl.	I4	62
Fürstenwalde, Ger.	D14	12
Furudal, Swe.	F6	10
Fushun, China	C12	28
Fusui, China	G9	28
Futuna, Île, i., Wal./F.	F12	58
Fuxin, China	A5	30
Fuyang, China	E11	28
Fuyu, China	B12	28
Fuyuan, China	D1	30
Fuzhou, China	F11	28
Fuzhou, China	F11	28
Füzuli, Azer.	C12	44
Fyffe, Al., U.S.	A4	94
Fyn, i., Den.	I4	10

G

Gaalkacyo, Som.	I14	48
Gabbs, Nv., U.S.	E4	121
Gabela, Ang.	F2	54
Gaberones see Gaborone, Bots.	C4	56
Gabès, Tun.	D7	48
Gabon, ctry., Afr.	D2	54
Gaborone, Bots.	C4	56
Gabriola, B.C., Can.	f12	85
Gabrovo, Blg.	C10	18
Gabú, Gui.-B.	D2	50
Gachsārān, Iran	D6	42
Gadag, India	F3	40
Gäddede, Swe.	D6	10
Gadsden, Al., U.S.	A3	94
Gadsden, co., Fl., U.S.	B2	102
Gadwāl, India	F3	40
Gaeta, Italy	D4	18
Gaeta, Golfo di, b., Italy	D4	18
Gaffney, S.C., U.S.	A4	133
Gafsa, Tun.	D6	48
Gag, Pulau, i., Indon.	D7	36
Gagarin, Russia	B13	20

Gage, co., Ne., U.S.	D9	120
Gagetown, N.B., Can.	D3	87
Gagnoa, C. Iv.	E3	50
Gagra, Geor.	A9	44
Gahanna, Oh., U.S.	k11	128
Gaillard, Lake, l., Ct., U.S.	D5	100
Gaines, co., Tx., U.S.	C1	136
Gainesboro, Tn., U.S.	C8	135
Gaines Creek, stm., Ok., U.S.	C6	129
Gainesville, Fl., U.S.	C4	102
Gainesville, Ga., U.S.	B3	103
Gainesville, Mo., U.S.	E5	118
Gainesville, Tx., U.S.	C4	136
Gainesville, Va., U.S.	g11	139
Gairdner, Lake, l., Austl.	G2	62
Gaithersburg, Md., U.S.	B3	113
Gaixian, China	C12	28
Gaizina Kalns, Lat.	H11	10
Gajny, Russia	B9	22
Galán, Cerro, mtn., Arg.	D4	72
Galapagos Islands see Colón, Archipiélago de, is., Ec.	C2	70
Galashiels, Scot., U.K.	C5	12
Galați, Rom.	G9	20
Galatia, Il., U.S.	F5	106
Galax, Va., U.S.	D2	139
Galdhøpiggen, mtn., Nor.	F3	10
Galela, Indon.	C7	36
Galena, Ak., U.S.	C8	95
Galena, Il., U.S.	A3	106
Galena, Ks., U.S.	E9	109
Galesburg, Il., U.S.	C3	106
Galesburg, Mi., U.S.	F5	115
Gales Ferry, Ct., U.S.	D7	100
Galesville, Md., U.S.	C4	113
Galesville, Wi., U.S.	D2	142
Galeton, Pa., U.S.	C6	131
Gali, Geor.	A9	44
Galič, Russia	C7	22
Galicia, hist. reg., Eur.	E7	20
Galilee, Sea of, l., Isr.	F6	44
Galion, Oh., U.S.	B3	128
Galisteo Creek, stm., N.M., U.S.	k8	124
Galiuro Mountains, mts., Az., U.S.	E5	96
Gallant, Al., U.S.	B3	94
Gallatin, co., Il., U.S.	F5	106
Gallatin, co., Ky., U.S.	B5	110
Gallatin, Mo., U.S.	B4	118
Gallatin, co., Mt., U.S.	E5	119
Gallatin, stm., Mt., U.S.	E5	119
Gallatin, Tn., U.S.	A5	135
Gallatin Range, mts., Mt., U.S.	E5	119
Gallaway, Tn., U.S.	B2	135
Galle, Sri L.	H4	40
Gallia, co., Oh., U.S.	D3	128
Galliano, La., U.S.	E5	111
Gallinas, Punta, c., Col.	A5	70
Gallinas Mountains, mts., N.M., U.S.	C2	124
Gallipoli, Italy	D6	18
Gallipoli see Gelibolu, Tur.	B2	44
Gallipolis, Oh., U.S.	D3	128
Gallitzin, Pa., U.S.	F4	131
Gällivare, Swe.	C9	10
Gallo Mountains, mts., N.M., U.S.	C1	124
Galloo Island, i., N.Y., U.S.	B4	125
Gallup, N.M., U.S.	B1	124
Galt, Ca., U.S.	C3	98
Galtat Zemmour, W. Sah.	A2	50
Galva, Il., U.S.	B3	106
Galva, Ks., U.S.	D6	109
Galveston, In., U.S.	C5	107
Galveston, Tx., U.S.	E5	136
Galveston, co., Tx., U.S.	E5	136
Galveston Bay, b., Tx., U.S.	E5	136
Galveston Island, i., Tx., U.S.	E5	136
Galway, Ire.	D2	12
Galway Bay, b., Ire.	D2	12
Gamarra, Col.	B5	70
Gambēla, Eth.	B6	54
Gambell, Ak., U.S.	C5	95
Gambia, stm., Afr.	D2	50
Gambia, The, ctry., Afr.	D1	50
Gambier, Oh., U.S.	B3	128
Gambier, Îles, is., Fr. Poly.	G16	58
Gambo, Nf., Can.	D4	88
Gamboma, Congo	D3	54
Gamboula, C.A.R.	C3	54
Gambrills, Md., U.S.	B4	113
Gan, stm., China	D4	30
Ganado, Az., U.S.	B6	96
Ganado, Tx., U.S.	E4	136
Gananoque, On., Can.	C8	89
Gäncä, Azer.	B12	44
Gand see Gent, Bel.	E8	12
Ganda, Ang.	F2	54
Gandajika, D.R.C.	E4	54
Gandak, stm., Asia	D4	40
Gander, Nf., Can.	D4	88
Gander, stm., Nf., Can.	D4	88
Gander Lake, l., Nf., Can.	D4	88
Gandesa, Spain	G7	16
Gāndhinagar, India	E2	40
Gandhi Reservoir see Gāndhi Sāgar, res., India	E3	40
Gāndhi Sāgar, res., India	E3	40
Gandia, Spain	H6	16

Gandu, Braz.	D4	74
Ganga see Ganges, stm., Asia	D5	40
Gangānagar, India	D2	40
Gangaw, Mya.	B2	34
Gangdisê Shan, mts., China	E4	28
Ganges (Ganga), stm., Asia	D5	40
Ganges, B.C., Can.	g12	85
Ganges, Mouths of the, mth., Asia	B1	34
Gang Mills, N.Y., U.S.	C3	125
Gangotri, India	C3	40
Gangtok, India	D5	40
Gangu, China	E9	28
Gannett Peak, mtn., Wy., U.S.	C3	143
Ganquan, China	B2	30
Gansu, prov., China	D8	28
Gantt, S.C., U.S.	B3	133
Gantt Lake, res., Al., U.S.	D3	94
Ganzê, China	E8	28
Ganzhou, China	F10	28
Gao, Mali	C4	50
Gao'an, China	D4	30
Gaolan, China	B1	30
Gaomi, China	B4	30
Gaoping, China	B3	30
Gaoua, Burkina	D4	50
Gaoual, Gui.	D2	50
Gaoxian, China	D1	30
Gaoyi, China	B3	30
Gaoyou, China	C4	30
Gaoyou Hu, l., China	C4	30
Gaozhou, China	E3	30
Gap, Fr.	E10	16
Gap, Pa., U.S.	G9	131
Gapan, Phil.	C8	34
Garagumskij kanal imeni Prezidenta Turkmenistana S.A. Nijazova (Kara-Kum Canal), Turk.	C8	42
Garagumy, des., Turk.	F7	26
Garanhuns, Braz.	C4	74
Garber, Ok., U.S.	A4	129
Garberville, Ca., U.S.	B2	98
Garda, Lago di, l., Italy	B3	18
Garden, co., Ne., U.S.	C3	120
Gardena, Ca., U.S.	n12	98
Garden City, Ga., U.S.	D5	103
Garden City, Id., U.S.	F2	105
Garden City, Ks., U.S.	E3	109
Garden City, Mi., U.S.	p15	115
Garden City, Mo., U.S.	C3	118
Gardendale, Al., U.S.	B3	94
Garden Grove, Ca., U.S.	n13	98
Garden Island, i., Mi., U.S.	C5	115
Garden Plain, Ks., U.S.	E6	109
Gardeyz, Afg.	D9	42
Gardiner, Me., U.S.	D3	112
Gardiner, Mt., U.S.	E6	119
Gardiner, Or., U.S.	D2	130
Gardiners Island, i., N.Y., U.S.	m16	125
Gardner, Il., U.S.	B5	106
Gardner, Ks., U.S.	D9	109
Gardner, Ma., U.S.	A4	114
Gardner Canal, strt., B.C., Can.	C3	85
Gardner Lake, l., Ct., U.S.	C6	100
Gardner Lake, l., Me., U.S.	D5	112
Gardner Pinnacles, Hi., U.S.	k14	104
Gardnerville, Nv., U.S.	E2	121
Garfield, co., Co., U.S.	B2	99
Garfield, co., Mt., U.S.	C9	119
Garfield, co., Ne., U.S.	C6	120
Garfield, N.J., U.S.	h8	123
Garfield, co., Ok., U.S.	A4	129
Garfield, co., Ut., U.S.	F4	137
Garfield, co., Wa., U.S.	C8	140
Garfield Heights, Oh., U.S.	h9	128
Garfield Mountain, mtn., Mt., U.S.	F4	119
Garfield Peak, mtn., Wy., U.S.	D5	143
Garibaldi, Or., U.S.	B3	130
Garibaldi, Mount, mtn., B.C., Can.	E6	85
Garies, S. Afr.	E2	56
Garissa, Kenya	D7	54
Garland, co., Ar., U.S.	C2	97
Garland, N.C., U.S.	C4	126
Garland, Tx., U.S.	n10	136
Garland, Ut., U.S.	B3	137
Garm, Taj.	C10	42
Garmī, Iran	C13	44
Garmisch-Partenkirchen, Ger.	G12	12
Garmsār, Iran	C6	42
Garnavillo, Ia., U.S.	B6	108
Garner, Ia., U.S.	A4	108
Garner, N.C., U.S.	B4	126
Garnet Range, mts., Mt., U.S.	D3	119
Garnett, Ks., U.S.	D8	109
Garnish, Nf., Can.	E4	88
Garonne, stm., Eur.	E6	16
Garoua, Cam.	B2	54
Garoua Boulaï, Cam.	B2	54
Garrard, co., Ky., U.S.	C5	110
Garretson, S.D., U.S.	D9	134
Garrett, In., U.S.	B7	107
Garrett, co., Md., U.S.	k12	113
Garrett Park, Md., U.S.	B3	113

Garrettsville, Oh., U.S.	A4	128
Garrison, Ky., U.S.	B6	110
Garrison, Md., U.S.	B4	113
Garrison, N.D., U.S.	B4	127
Garrison Dam, N.D., U.S.	B4	127
Garsen, Kenya	D8	54
Garut, Indon.	E3	36
Garvin, co., Ok., U.S.	C4	129
Garwolin, Pol.	D6	20
Gary, In., U.S.	A3	107
Gary, W.V., U.S.	D3	141
Garyarsa, China	E4	28
Garysburg, N.C., U.S.	A5	126
Garyville, La., U.S.	D5	111
Garza, co., Tx., U.S.	C2	136
Garza-Little Elm Reservoir, res., Tx., U.S.	C4	136
Gasan-Kuli, Turk.	C6	42
Gas City, In., U.S.	D6	107
Gascogne, hist. reg., Fr.	F7	16
Gasconade, stm., Mo., U.S.	C6	118
Gasconade, co., Mo., U.S.	C6	118
Gascony see Gascogne, hist. reg., Fr.	F7	16
Gascoyne, stm., Austl.	E1	60
Gascoyne Junction, Austl.	F2	60
Gashaka, Nig.	E7	50
Gashua, Nig.	D7	50
Gasparilla Island, i., Fl., U.S.	F4	102
Gaspé, P.Q., Can.	k14	90
Gaspésie, Péninsule de la, pen., P.Q., Can.	k13	90
Gassaway, W.V., U.S.	C4	141
Gassville, Ar., U.S.	A3	97
Gasteiz, Spain	F5	16
Gaston, In., U.S.	D7	107
Gaston, N.C., U.S.	A5	126
Gaston, co., N.C., U.S.	B1	126
Gaston, S.C., U.S.	D5	133
Gaston, Lake, res., U.S.	A5	126
Gastonia, N.C., U.S.	B1	126
Gaston Dam, N.C., U.S.	A5	126
Gastre, Arg.	F3	69
Gatčina, Russia	C5	22
Gate City, Va., U.S.	f9	139
Gates, co., N.C., U.S.	A6	126
Gates, Tn., U.S.	B2	135
Gates of the Arctic National Park, Ak., U.S.	B9	95
Gatesville, Tx., U.S.	D4	136
Gatineau, P.Q., Can.	D2	90
Gatineau, stm., P.Q., Can.	D2	90
Gatineau, Parc de la, P.Q., Can.	D2	90
Gatlinburg, Tn., U.S.	D10	135
Gatton, Austl.	F5	62
Gauley, stm., W.V., U.S.	C3	141
Gauley Bridge, W.V., U.S.	C3	141
Gaustatoppen, mtn., Nor.	G3	10
Gautier, Ms., U.S.	f8	117
Gávdhos, i., Grc.	G10	18
Gavins Point Dam, U.S.	B8	120
Gävle, Swe.	F7	10
Gawler Ranges, mts., Austl.	G2	62
Gaya, India	E5	40
Gaya, Nig.	D6	50
Gaya, Niger	D5	50
Gay Head, c., Ma., U.S.	D6	114
Gaylord, Mi., U.S.	C6	115
Gaylord, Mn., U.S.	F4	116
Gayndah, Austl.	F5	62
Gaza see Ghazzah, Gaza	G6	44
Gazandzyk, Turk.	C7	42
Gazaoua, Niger	D6	50
Gaza Strip, Asia	G6	44
Gaziantep, Tur.	D7	44
Gazimağusa (Famagusta), N. Cyp.	E5	44
Gazimağusa Körfezi, b., N. Cyp.	E6	44
Gazipaşa, Tur.	D5	44
Gbanga, Lib.	E3	50
Gboko, Nig.	E6	50
Gdańsk, Pol.	B5	20
Gdov, Russia	G12	10
Gdynia, Pol.	B5	20
Gearhart, Or., U.S.	A3	130
Gearhart Mountain, mtn., Or., U.S.	E6	130
Geary, N.B., Can.	D3	87
Geary, co., Ks., U.S.	D7	109
Geary, Ok., U.S.	B3	129
Geauga, co., Oh., U.S.	A4	128
Gebe, Pulau, i., Indon.	D7	36
Gebze, Tur.	B3	44
Gediz, Tur.	C3	44
Geelong, Austl.	H3	62
Geesthacht, Ger.	D12	12
Geilo, Nor.	F3	10
Geist Reservoir, res., In., U.S.	E6	107
Geita, Tan.	D6	54
Gejiu, China	G8	28
Gela, Italy	F5	18
Gelasa, Selat, strt., Indon.	D3	36
Gelendžik, Russia	G15	20
Gelibolu, Tur.	B2	44
Gelsenkirchen, Ger.	E10	12
Gem, co., Id., U.S.	E2	105
Gemena, D.R.C.	C3	54
Gemlik, Tur.	B3	44

Gemlik Körfezi, b., Tur.	B3	44
Genalē (Jubba), stm., Afr.	B8	54
Genç, Tur.	C9	44
General Acha, Arg.	F5	72
General Alvear, Arg.	F4	72
General Carneiro, Braz.	B7	72
General Carrera, Lago, l., S.A.	G2	69
General Conesa, Arg.	F4	69
General Eugenio A. Garay, Para.	C5	72
General Juan José Ríos, Mex.	B3	78
General Juan Madariaga, Arg.	F6	72
General La Madrid, Arg.	F5	72
General Pico, Arg.	F5	72
General Pinedo, Arg.	D5	72
General Roca, Arg.	E3	69
General Villegas, Arg.	F5	72
Genesee, Id., U.S.	C2	105
Genesee, co., Mi., U.S.	E7	115
Genesee, Mi., U.S.	E7	115
Genesee, co., N.Y., U.S.	B2	125
Genesee, stm., N.Y., U.S.	C2	125
Geneseo, Il., U.S.	B3	106
Geneseo, N.Y., U.S.	C3	125
Geneva see Genève, Switz.	A1	18
Geneva, Al., U.S.	D4	94
Geneva, co., Al., U.S.	D4	94
Geneva, Il., U.S.	B5	106
Geneva, In., U.S.	C8	107
Geneva, Ne., U.S.	D8	120
Geneva, N.Y., U.S.	C4	125
Geneva, Oh., U.S.	A5	128
Geneva, Lake, l., Eur.	A1	18
Geneva, Lake, l., Wi., U.S.	F5	142
Geneva-on-the-Lake, Oh., U.S.	A5	128
Genève (Geneva), Switz.	A1	18
Gengma, China	B3	34
Genoa see Genova, Italy	B2	18
Genoa, Il., U.S.	A5	106
Genoa, Ne., U.S.	C8	120
Genoa, Nv., U.S.	D2	121
Genoa, Oh., U.S.	A2	128
Genoa, Gulf of see Genova, Golfo di, b., Italy	B2	18
Genoa City, Wi., U.S.	F5	142
Genola, Ut., U.S.	D4	137
Genova, Italy	B2	18
Genova, Golfo di, b., Italy	B2	18
Gent, Bel.	E8	12
Gentry, Ar., U.S.	A1	97
Gentry, co., Mo., U.S.	A3	118
Geographe Bay, b., Austl.	G2	60
George, stm., P.Q., Can.	g13	90
George, S. Afr.	E3	56
George, Ia., U.S.	A2	108
George, co., Ms., U.S.	E5	117
George, Cape, c., N.S., Can.	D8	87
George, Lake, l., Fl., U.S.	C5	102
George, Lake, l., N.Y., U.S.	B7	125
George B. Stevenson Reservoir, res., Pa., U.S.	D6	131
George Peak, mtn., Ut., U.S.	B2	137
George Town, Austl.	I4	62
Georgetown, Austl.	D3	62
Georgetown, P.E., Can.	C7	87
George Town, Cay. Is.	B3	80
Georgetown, Gam.	D2	50
Georgetown, Guy.	B8	70
George Town (Penang), Malay.	B2	36
Georgetown, Ca., U.S.	C3	98
Georgetown, Co., U.S.	B5	99
Georgetown, Ct., U.S.	D2	100
Georgetown, De., U.S.	F4	101
Georgetown, Ga., U.S.	E1	103
Georgetown, Il., U.S.	D6	106
Georgetown, In., U.S.	H6	107
Georgetown, Ky., U.S.	B5	110
Georgetown, Ma., U.S.	A6	114
Georgetown, Oh., U.S.	D2	128
Georgetown, S.C., U.S.	E9	133
Georgetown, co., S.C., U.S.	E9	133
Georgetown, Tx., U.S.	D4	136
George V Coast, Ant.	C20	67
George Washington Birthplace National Monument, Va., U.S.	B6	139
George Washington Carver National Monument, Mo., U.S.	E3	118
George West, Tx., U.S.	E3	136
Georgia, ctry., Asia	A10	44
Georgia, state, U.S.	D3	103
Georgiana, Al., U.S.	D3	94
Georgian Bay, b., On., Can.	B3	89
Georgina, stm., Austl.	E2	62
Gera, Ger.	E13	12
Gerald, Mo., U.S.	C6	118
Geraldine, Al., U.S.	A4	94
Geraldton, Austl.	F1	60
Geraldton, On., Can.	o18	89
Gerber Reservoir, res., Or., U.S.	E5	130
Gerdine, Mount, mtn., Ak., U.S.	C9	95
Gerede, Tur.	B5	44
Gereshk, Afg.	D8	42
Gering, Ne., U.S.	C2	120
Gerlach, Nv., U.S.	C2	121

Name	Map Ref.	Page
Gerlachovský štít, mtn., Slvk.	E6	20
Germantown, Il., U.S.	E4	106
Germantown, Md., U.S.	B3	113
Germantown, Oh., U.S.	C1	128
Germantown, Tn., U.S.	B2	135
Germantown, Wi., U.S.	E5	142
Germany, ctry., Eur.	E12	12
Germiston, S. Afr.	D4	56
Gerona see Girona, Spain	G8	16
Geronimo, Ok., U.S.	C3	129
Gervais, Or., U.S.	B4	130
Gêrzê, China	C4	40
Geser, Indon.	D8	36
Getafe, Spain	G5	16
Gettysburg, Pa., U.S.	G7	131
Gettysburg, S.D., U.S.	C6	134
Geyve, Tur.	B4	44
Ghadāmis, Libya	E6	48
Ghāghara, stm., Asia	D4	40
Ghana, ctry., Afr.	E4	50
Ghanzi, Bots.	C3	56
Ghardaïa, Alg.	D5	48
Gharyān, Libya	D7	48
Ghāt, Libya	F7	48
Ghawdex, i., Malta	F5	18
Ghazāl, Bahr al-, stm., Sudan	B5	54
Ghāziābād, India	D3	40
Ghāzipur, India	D4	40
Ghaznī, Afg.	D9	42
Ghazzah, Gaza	G6	44
Gheen, Mn., U.S.	C6	116
Gheorgheni, Rom.	F8	20
Gherla, Rom.	F7	20
Ghilizane, Alg.	J7	16
Ghorīān, Afg.	D8	42
Gianitsá, Grc.	D9	18
Giant's Causeway, N. Ire., U.K.	C3	12
Giants Neck, Ct., U.S.	D7	100
Gibara, Cuba	A4	80
Gibbon, Mn., U.S.	F4	116
Gibbon, Ne., U.S.	D7	120
Gibbons, Ab., Can.	C4	84
Gibb River, Austl.	D4	60
Gibbstown, N.J., U.S.	D2	123
Gibeon, Nmb.	D2	56
Gibraltar, dep., Eur.	I4	16
Gibraltar, Strait of, strt.	J4	16
Gibsland, La., U.S.	B2	111
Gibson, Ga., U.S.	C4	103
Gibson, co., In., U.S.	H2	107
Gibson, co., Tn., U.S.	A3	135
Gibsonburg, Oh., U.S.	A2	128
Gibson City, Il., U.S.	C5	106
Gibson Desert, des., Austl.	E3	60
Gibsonia, Pa., U.S.	h14	131
Gibson Island, i., Md., U.S.	B5	113
Gibsons, B.C., Can.	E6	85
Gibsonton, Fl., U.S.	p11	102
Gibsonville, N.C., U.S.	A3	126
Giddings, Tx., U.S.	D4	136
Gideon, Mo., U.S.	E8	118
Gien, Fr.	D8	16
Giessen, Ger.	E11	12
Gifford, Fl., U.S.	E6	102
Gifford, Il., U.S.	C5	106
Gifford Creek, Austl.	E2	60
Gifu, Japan	D15	28
Gig Harbor, Wa., U.S.	B3	140
Giglio, Isola del, i., Italy	C3	18
Gihon, stm., Vt., U.S.	B3	138
Gijón, Spain	F4	16
Gila, co., Az., U.S.	D5	96
Gila, stm., U.S.	E5	92
Gila Bend, Az., U.S.	E3	96
Gila Bend Indian Reservation, Az., U.S.	D3	96
Gila Bend Mountains, mts., Az., U.S.	D2	96
Gila Cliff Dwellings National Monument, N.M., U.S.	D1	124
Gila Mountains, mts., Az., U.S.	D6	96
Gila Peak, mtn., Az., U.S.	D6	96
Gila River Indian Reservation, Az., U.S.	D4	96
Gilbert, Az., U.S.	D4	96
Gilbert, Ia., U.S.	B4	108
Gilbert, La., U.S.	B4	111
Gilbert, Mn., U.S.	C6	116
Gilbert Islands see Kiribati, is., Kir.	D11	58
Gilbert Peak, mtn., Wa., U.S.	C4	140
Gilbert Plains, Mb., Can.	D1	86
Gilbertsville, Ky., U.S.	f9	110
Gilbertsville, Pa., U.S.	F10	131
Gilbertville, Ia., U.S.	B5	108
Gilbués, Braz.	E10	70
Gilchrist, co., Fl., U.S.	C4	102
Gilchrist, Or., U.S.	D5	130
Gilcrest, Co., U.S.	A6	99
Giles, Tn., U.S.	B4	135
Giles, co., Va., U.S.	C2	139
Gilford Island, i., B.C., Can.	D4	85
Gilgandra, Austl.	G4	62
Gilgil, Kenya		
Gilgit, Pak.	C10	42
Gillam, Mb., Can.	A4	86
Gillespie, Il., U.S.	D4	106
Gillespie, co., Tx., U.S.	D3	136
Gillespie Dam, Az., U.S.	D3	96
Gillett, Ar., U.S.	C4	97
Gillett, Wi., U.S.	D5	142
Gillette, Wy., U.S.	B7	143
Gilliam, co., Or., U.S.	B6	130
Gilman, Il., U.S.	C5	106
Gilman, Vt., U.S.	C5	138
Gilmanton, N.H., U.S.	D4	122
Gilmer, co., Ga., U.S.	B2	103
Gilmer, Tx., U.S.	C5	136
Gilmer, co., W.V., U.S.	C4	141
Gilpin, co., Co., U.S.	B5	99
Gilroy, Ca., U.S.	D3	98
Gīmbī, Eth.	B7	54
Gimie, Mount, vol., St. Luc.	C7	80
Gimli, Mb., Can.	D3	86
Gingoog, Phil.	E9	34
Gīnīr, Eth.	B8	54
Giralia, Austl.	E1	60
Girard, Il., U.S.	D4	106
Girard, Ks., U.S.	E9	109
Girard, Oh., U.S.	A5	128
Girard, Pa., U.S.	B1	131
Girardot, Col.	E5	80
Girardville, Pa., U.S.	E9	131
Giresun, Tur.	B8	44
Girona, Spain	G8	16
Gironde, est., Fr.	E6	16
Girvan, Scot., U.K.	C4	12
Gisborne, N.Z.	o14	63c
Gitarama, Rw.	D5	54
Gitega, Bdi.	D5	54
Giurgiu, Rom.	H8	20
Giyon, Eth.	B7	54
Giza see El-Gîza, Egypt	E11	48
Giza, Pyramids of, Egypt	F10	14
Giẕduvan, Uzb.	B8	42
Giẕiga, Russia	C18	26
Giẕycko, Pol.	B6	20
Gjirokastër, Alb.	D8	18
Gjøvik, Nor.	F4	10
Gjumri, Arm.	B10	44
Glacier, co., Mt., U.S.	B3	119
Glacier Bay, b., Ak., U.S.	k21	95
Glacier Bay National Park, Ak., U.S.	D12	95
Glacier National Park, B.C., Can.	D9	85
Glacier National Park, Mt., U.S.	B2	119
Glacier Peak, mtn., Wa., U.S.	A4	140
Gladbrook, Ia., U.S.	B5	108
Glade Creek, stm., Wa., U.S.	C6	140
Glade Creek, stm., W.V., U.S.	n14	141
Glade Creek, stm., W.V., U.S.	n13	141
Glades, co., Fl., U.S.	F5	102
Glade Spring, Va., U.S.	f10	139
Gladewater, Tx., U.S.	C5	136
Gladstone, Austl.	E5	62
Gladstone, Mb., Can.	D2	86
Gladstone, Mi., U.S.	C4	115
Gladstone, Mo., U.S.	h10	118
Gladstone, Or., U.S.	B4	130
Gladwin, Mi., U.S.	E6	115
Gladwin, co., Mi., U.S.	D6	115
Glåma, stm., Nor.	F4	10
Glascock, co., Ga., U.S.	C4	103
Glasford, Il., U.S.	C4	106
Glasgow, Scot., U.K.	C4	12
Glasgow, Ky., U.S.	C4	110
Glasgow, Mo., U.S.	B5	118
Glasgow, Mt., U.S.	B10	119
Glasgow, Va., U.S.	C3	139
Glasgow, W.V., U.S.	m13	141
Glassboro, N.J., U.S.	D2	123
Glasscock, co., Tx., U.S.	D2	136
Glassport, Pa., U.S.	F2	131
Glastonbury, Ct., U.S.	C5	100
Glazier Lake, l., Me., U.S.	A3	112
Glazov, Russia	D7	26
Gleason, Tn., U.S.	A3	135
Glen Allan, Ms., U.S.	B2	117
Glen Allen, Va., U.S.	C5	139
Glenboro, Mb., Can.	E2	86
Glenbrook, Nv., U.S.	D2	121
Glen Burnie, Md., U.S.	B4	113
Glen Canyon Dam, Az., U.S.	A4	96
Glen Canyon National Recreation Area, U.S.	F5	137
Glencoe, On., Can.	E3	89
Glencoe, Al., U.S.	B4	94
Glencoe, Il., U.S.	A6	106
Glencoe, Mn., U.S.	F4	116
Glen Cove, N.Y., U.S.	h13	125
Glendale, Az., U.S.	D3	96
Glendale, Ca., U.S.	m12	98
Glendale, Ms., U.S.	D4	117
Glendale, Oh., U.S.	C1	128
Glendale, Or., U.S.	E3	130
Glendale, R.I., U.S.	B2	132
Glendale, S.C., U.S.	B4	133
Glendale, Wi., U.S.	m12	142
Glen Dale, W.V., U.S.	B4	141
Glendale Heights, W.V., U.S.	g8	141
Glendive, Mt., U.S.	C12	119
Glendo, Wy., U.S.	D7	143
Glendora, Ca., U.S.	m13	98
Glendo Reservoir, res., Wy., U.S.	D8	143
Glenelg, Md., U.S.	B4	113
Glen Ellis Falls, wtfl., N.H., U.S.	B4	122
Glen Ellyn, Il., U.S.	k8	106
Glenham, N.Y., U.S.	D7	125
Glen Innes, Austl.	F5	62
Glen Jean, W.V., U.S.	D3	141
Glen Lake, l., Mi., U.S.	D5	115
Glen Lyon, Pa., U.S.	D9	131
Glenmora, La., U.S.	D3	111
Glenn, co., Ca., U.S.	C2	98
Glennallen, Ak., U.S.	f19	95
Glenns Ferry, Id., U.S.	G3	105
Glennville, Ga., U.S.	E5	103
Glenolden, Pa., U.S.	p20	131
Glenpool, Ok., U.S.	B5	129
Glen Raven, N.C., U.S.	A3	126
Glen Ridge, N.J., U.S.	h8	123
Glen Rock, N.J., U.S.	h8	123
Glen Rock, Pa., U.S.	G8	131
Glenrock, Wy., U.S.	D7	143
Glen Rose, Tx., U.S.	C4	136
Glenrothes, Scot., U.K.	B5	12
Glenroy, Austl.	E1	60
Glens Falls, N.Y., U.S.	B7	125
Glen Ullin, N.D., U.S.	C4	127
Glenview, Il., U.S.	h9	106
Glenville, Mn., U.S.	G5	116
Glenville, W.V., U.S.	C4	141
Glenwood, Nf., Can.	D4	88
Glenwood, Ar., U.S.	C2	97
Glenwood, Ga., U.S.	D4	103
Glenwood, Ia., U.S.	C2	108
Glenwood, Mn., U.S.	E3	116
Glenwood, Va., U.S.	D3	139
Glenwood City, Wi., U.S.	C1	142
Glenwood Springs, Co., U.S.	B3	99
Glidden, Ia., U.S.	B3	108
Glide, Or., U.S.	D3	130
Glittertinden, mtn., Nor.	F3	10
Gliwice, Pol.	D5	20
Globe, Az., U.S.	D5	96
Głogów, Pol.	D4	20
Gloster, Ms., U.S.	D2	117
Gloucester, On., Can.	h12	89
Gloucester, Eng., U.K.	E5	12
Gloucester, Ma., U.S.	A6	114
Gloucester, co., N.J., U.S.	D2	123
Gloucester, co., Va., U.S.	C6	139
Gloucester City, N.J., U.S.	D2	123
Gloucester Point, Va., U.S.	C6	139
Glouster, Oh., U.S.	C3	128
Glover Island, i., Nf., Can.	D3	88
Gloversville, N.Y., U.S.	B6	125
Glovertown, Nf., Can.	D4	88
Gloverville, S.C., U.S.	E4	133
Głubokij, Russia	E7	22
Głuchołazy, Pol.	D4	20
Gluck, S.C., U.S.	C2	133
Glyndon, Md., U.S.	B4	113
Glyndon, Mn., U.S.	D2	116
Glynn, co., Ga., U.S.	E5	103
Gmünd, Aus.	F14	12
Gmunden, Aus.	G13	12
Gnadenhutten, Oh., U.S.	B4	128
Gnarp, Swe.	E7	10
Gniezno, Pol.	C4	20
Gnowangerup, Austl.	G2	60
Goa, state, India	F2	40
Goālpāra, India	D6	40
Goat Island, i., R.I., U.S.	F5	132
Goat Mountain, mtn., Mt., U.S.	C3	119
Goat Rock Dam, U.S.	C4	94
Goba, Eth.	B7	54
Gobabis, Nmb.	C2	56
Gobernador Gregores, Arg.	G2	69
Gobi, des., Asia	C7	28
Gobles, Mi., U.S.	F5	115
Gobō, Japan	D3	31
Goðafoss, wtfl., Ice.	l20	10a
Godāvari, stm., India	F3	40
Goddard, Ks., U.S.	E6	109
Goderich, On., Can.	D3	89
Godfrey, Il., U.S.	E3	106
Godhavn, Grnld.	E29	82
Godhra, India	I2	40
Gödöllő, Hung.	F5	20
Gods, stm., Mb., Can.	A5	86
Gods Lake, l., Mb., Can.	B4	86
Godthåb (Nuuk), Grnld.	F29	82
Goff Creek, stm., Ok., U.S.	e9	129
Goffstown, N.H., U.S.	D3	122
Gogebic, co., Mi., U.S.	n12	115
Gogebic, Lake, l., Mi., U.S.	m12	115
Goiana, Braz.	C5	74
Goianésia, Braz.	E2	74
Goiânia, Braz.	E2	74
Goiás, state, Braz.	F10	70
Goiás, Braz.	E1	74
Gojra, Pak.	D10	42
Gök, stm., Tur.	B6	44
Gökçeada, i., Tur.	B1	44
Gökova Körfezi, b., Tur.	D2	44
Göksun, Tur.	C7	44
Gokwe, Zimb.	B4	56
Golāghāt, India	D6	40
Golconda, Il., U.S.	F5	106
Golconda, Nv., U.S.	C4	121
Gölcük, Tur.	B3	44
Gold Bar, Wa., U.S.	B4	140
Gold Beach, Or., U.S.	E2	130
Gold Coast see Southport, Austl.	F5	62
Golden, B.C., Can.	D9	85
Golden, Co., U.S.	B5	99
Golden City, Mo., U.S.	D3	118
Goldendale, Wa., U.S.	D5	140
Golden Gate Bridge, Ca., U.S.	h7	98
Golden Gate National Recreation Area, Ca., U.S.	h7	98
Golden Hinde, mtn., B.C., Can.	E5	85
Golden Meadow, La., U.S.	E5	111
Golden Spike National Historic Site, hist., Ut., U.S.	B3	137
Golden Valley, Mn., U.S.	n12	116
Golden Valley, co., Mt., U.S.	D7	119
Golden Valley, co., N.D., U.S.	B2	127
Goldfield, Ia., U.S.	B4	108
Goldfield, Nv., U.S.	F4	121
Gold Hill, Or., U.S.	E3	130
Goldsboro, N.C., U.S.	B5	126
Goldsby, Ok., U.S.	B4	129
Goldsworthy, Austl.	E2	60
Goldthwaite, Tx., U.S.	D3	136
Goleniów, Pol.	C3	20
Goleta, Ca., U.S.	E4	98
Golfito, C.R.	D3	80
Golf Manor, Oh., U.S.	o13	128
Gölhisar, Tur.	D3	44
Goliad, Tx., U.S.	E4	136
Goliad, co., Tx., U.S.	E4	136
Gölköy, Tur.	B7	44
Golmud, China	B6	40
Golpāyegān, Iran	D6	42
Goma, D.R.C.	D5	54
Gomati, stm., India	D4	40
Gombe, Nig.	D7	50
Gombi, Nig.	D7	50
Gomel see Homel', Bela.	C11	20
Gómez Palacio, Mex.	B4	78
Gonaïves, Haiti	B5	80
Gonam, Russia	D15	26
Gonâve, Golfe de la, b., Haiti	B5	80
Gonâve, Île de la, i., Haiti	B5	80
Gonbad-e Qābūs, Iran	C7	42
Gonda, India	D4	40
Gondal, India	I2	40
Gonder, Eth.	H12	48
Gondia, India	I4	40
Gönen, Tur.	B2	44
Gongbo'gyamda, China	E6	28
Gongcheng, China	E3	30
Gongga Shan, mtn., China	F8	28
Gongxian, China	C3	30
Gongzhuling, China	C12	28
Gonzales, Ca., U.S.	D3	98
Gonzales, La., U.S.	D5	111
Gonzales, co., Tx., U.S.	E4	136
Gonzales, Tx., U.S.	E4	136
González, Mex.	C5	78
Gonzalez, Fl., U.S.	u14	102
Goochland, co., Va., U.S.	C5	139
Goode, Mount, mtn., Ak., U.S.	g18	95
Goodfellow Air Force Base, mil., Tx., U.S.	D2	136
Good Hope, Cape of, c., S. Afr.	E2	56
Good Hope Mountain, mtn., B.C., Can.	D5	85
Goodhue, co., Mn., U.S.	F6	116
Gooding, Id., U.S.	G4	105
Gooding, co., Id., U.S.	F4	105
Goodland, In., U.S.	C3	107
Goodland, Ks., U.S.	C2	109
Goodlettsville, Tn., U.S.	g10	135
Goodman, Mo., U.S.	E3	118
Goodman, Ms., U.S.	C4	117
Good Pine, La., U.S.	C3	111
Goodsprings, Nv., U.S.	H6	121
Goodview, Mn., U.S.	F7	116
Goodwater, Al., U.S.	B3	94
Goodwell, Ok., U.S.	e9	129
Goodyear, Az., U.S.	D3	96
Goondiwindi, Austl.	F5	62
Goose, stm., N.D., U.S.	B8	127
Goose Bay, b., Nf., Can.	B1	88
Gooseberry Creek, stm., Wy., U.S.	B4	143
Goose Creek, S.C., U.S.	F7	133
Goose Creek, stm., Va., U.S.	A5	139
Goose Creek, stm., U.S.	G5	105
Goose Creek Reservoir, res., S.C., U.S.	k11	133
Goose Lake, l., U.S.	B3	98
Goose Pond, l., N.H., U.S.	C2	122
Goqên, China	F7	28
Gorakhpur, India	D4	40
Gorda, Punta, c., Cuba	A3	80
Gordion, hist., Tur.	C4	44
Gordo, Al., U.S.	B2	94
Gordon, Ga., U.S.	D3	103
Gordon, co., Ga., U.S.	B2	103
Gordon, Ne., U.S.	B3	120
Gordon Downs, Austl.	D4	60
Gordonsville, Tn., U.S.	C8	135
Gordonsville, Va., U.S.	B4	139
Goré, Chad	E8	50
Gorē, Eth.	B7	54
Gore, N.Z.	q12	63c
Gore, Ok., U.S.	B6	129
Gore Bay, On., Can.	B2	89
Gore Point, c., Ak., U.S.	h16	95
Gore Range, mts., Co., U.S.	B4	99
Goreville, Il., U.S.	F5	106
Gorgān, Iran	C6	42
Gorge High Dam, Wa., U.S.	A4	140
Gorham, Me., U.S.	E2	112
Gorham, N.H., U.S.	B4	122
Gori, Geor.	A11	44
Gorizia, Italy	B4	18
Gorjačij Ključ, Russia	G15	20
Gor'kij see Nižnij Novgorod, Russia	D6	26
Gorkiy Reservoir see Gor'kovskoe vodohranilišče, res., Russia	C7	22
Gor'kovskoe vodohranilišče, res. Russia	C7	22
Görlitz, Ger.	E14	12
Gorlovka see Horlivka, Ukr.	E15	20
Gorman, Tx., U.S.	C3	136
Gorna Orjahovica, Blg.	C10	18
Gornjackij, Russia	A11	22
Gorno-Altajsk, Russia	D10	26
Gornozavodsk, Russia	B16	28
Gorodec, Russia	C7	22
Goroka, Pap. N. Gui.	H12	32
Gorong, Pulau, i., Indon.	D8	36
Gorontalo, Indon.	C6	36
Gorzów Wielkopolski, Pol.	C3	20
Gosford, Austl.	G5	62
Goshen, In., U.S.	A6	107
Goshen, N.Y., U.S.	D6	125
Goshen, Oh., U.S.	C1	128
Goshen, co., Wy., U.S.	D8	143
Goshute Indian Reservation, U.S.	D7	121
Goshute Lake, l., Nv., U.S.	C7	121
Goshute Mountains, mts., Nv., U.S.	C7	121
Goslar, Ger.	E12	12
Gosnells, Austl.	G2	60
Gosper, co., Ne., U.S.	D6	120
Gosport, In., U.S.	F4	107
Gossinga, Sudan	B5	54
Gostivar, Mac.	D8	18
Gostyń, Pol.	D4	20
Gostynin, Pol.	C5	20
Göteborg (Gothenburg), Swe.	H4	10
Gothenburg see Göteborg, Swe.	H4	10
Gothenburg, Ne., U.S.	D5	120
Gotland, i., Swe.	H8	10
Gotō-rettō, is., Japan	E13	28
Gotska Sandön, i., Swe.	G8	10
Göttingen, Ger.	E11	12
Goubone, Chad	B8	50
Goudoumaria, Niger	D7	50
Gough Island, i., St. Hel.	N9	46
Gouin, Réservoir, res., P.Q., Can.	I25	82
Goulburn, Austl.	G4	62
Goulburn Islands, is., Austl.	C5	60
Gould, Ar., U.S.	D4	97
Goulding, Fl., U.S.	u14	102
Gould Island, i., R.I., U.S.	E5	132
Goulds, Fl., U.S.	s13	102
Goundam, Mali	C4	50
Goundi, Chad	E8	50
Gouré, Niger	D7	50
Gouverneur, N.Y., U.S.	f9	125
Gove, co., Ks., U.S.	D3	109
Governador Valadares, Braz.	E3	74
Govind Ballabh Pant Reservoir see Govind Ballabh Pant Sāgar, res., India	E4	40
Govind Ballabh Pant Sāgar, res., India	E4	40
Gowanda, N.Y., U.S.	C2	125
Gower, Mo., U.S.	B3	118
Gowrie, Ia., U.S.	B3	108
Goya, Arg.	D6	72
Göyçay, Azer.	B12	44
Gozo see Ghawdex, i., Malta	F5	18
Graaff-Reinet, S. Afr.	E3	56
Grabill, In., U.S.	B8	107
Grabo, C. Iv.	F3	50
Grace, Id., U.S.	G7	105
Graceville, Fl., U.S.	u16	102
Graceville, Mn., U.S.	E2	116
Gracewood, Ga., U.S.	C4	103
Gracias a Dios, Cabo, c., N.A.	F8	76
Gradaús, Braz.	E9	70
Grady, co., Ga., U.S.	F2	103
Grady, co., Ok., U.S.	C4	129
Graettinger, Ia., U.S.	A3	108
Grafton, Austl.	F5	62
Grafton, Ma., U.S.	B4	114
Grafton, N.D., U.S.	A8	127
Grafton, co., N.H., U.S.	C3	122
Grafton, Oh., U.S.	A3	128
Grafton, Va., U.S.	h15	139
Grafton, W.V., U.S.	B4	141
Grafton, Wi., U.S.	E6	142
Graham, co., Az., U.S.	E5	96
Graham, co., Ks., U.S.	C4	109
Graham, N.C., U.S.	A3	126
Graham, co., N.C., U.S.	f9	126

Name	Map Ref.	Page

Graham, Tx., U.S. C3 136
Graham, Lake, res., Tx., U.S. C3 136
Graham, Mount, mtn., Az., U.S. E6 96
Graham Island, i., B.C., Can. C1 85
Graham Lake, l., Me., U.S. . .D4 112
Graham Land, reg., Ant. . . .C34 67
Grahamstown, S. Afr. E4 56
Grahn, Ky., U.S. B6 110
Grainger, co., Tn., U.S. . . .C10 135
Grain Valley, Mo., U.S. B3 118
Grajaú, Braz. C2 74
Grajewo, Pol. C7 20
Grambling, La., U.S. B3 111
Gramercy, La., U.S. h10 111
Granada, Col. E5 80
Granada, Nic. C2 80
Granada, Spain I5 16
Granbury, Tx., U.S. C4 136
Granby, P.Q., Can. D5 90
Granby, Co., U.S. A5 99
Granby, Ct., U.S. B4 100
Granby, Mo., U.S. E3 118
Granby, Lake, res., Co., U.S. A5 99
Gran Canaria, i., Spain A1 50
Gran Chaco, reg., S.A. C5 72
Grand, stm., On., Can. D4 89
Grand, co., Co., U.S. A4 99
Grand, stm., Mi., U.S. E5 115
Grand, stm., Mo., U.S. A3 118
Grand, stm., Oh., U.S. A4 128
Grand, stm., S.D., U.S. B4 134
Grand, co., Ut., U.S. E6 137
Grand Bahama, i., Bah. C9 76
Grand Bank, Nf., Can. E4 88
Grand-Bassam, C. Iv. E4 50
Grand Bay, N.B., Can. D3 87
Grand Bay, Al., U.S. E1 94
Grand Bend, On., Can. D3 89
Grand Blanc, Mi., U.S. F7 115
Grand Caillou, La., U.S. E5 111
Grand Canal see Da Yunhe, China D11 28
Grand Canyon, Az., U.S. . . .A3 96
Grand Canyon, Az., U.S. . . .A3 96
Grand Canyon National Park, Az., U.S. B3 96
Grand Cayman, i., Cay. Is. . .B3 80
Grand Centre, Ab., Can. B5 84
Grand Cess, stm. F3 50
Grand Coteau, La., U.S. D3 111
Grand Coulee, Wa., U.S. . . .B6 140
Grand Coulee Dam, Wa., U.S. B6 140
Grande, stm., Bol. G7 70
Grande, stm., Braz. F1 74
Grande, stm., Ven. D7 80
Grande, Bahía, b., Arg. H3 69
Grande, Boca, mth., Ven. . . .D7 80
Grande, Ilha, i., Braz. F3 74
Grande, Rio see Rio Grande, stm., N.A. B5 78
Grande-Anse, N.B., Can. . . .B4 87
Grande Cache, Ab., Can. . . .C1 84
Grande Comore see Njazidja, i., Com. A7 56
Grande de Matagalpa, stm., Nic. C3 80
Grande de Santiago, stm., Mex. C4 78
Grande do Gurupá, Ilha, i., Braz. B1 74
Grand-Entrée, P.Q., Can. . . .B8 87
Grande Prairie, Ab., Can. . . .B1 84
Grand Erg de Bilma, des., Niger C7 50
Grand Erg Occidental, des., Alg. D5 48
Grand Erg Oriental, des., Alg. D6 48
Grande rivière de la Baleine, stm., P.Q., Can. g11 90
Grande Ronde, stm., U.S. . . .C8 140
Grandes, Salinas, pl., Arg. . .E4 72
Grandes-Bergeronnes, P.Q., Can. A8 90
Grande-Terre, i., Guad. B7 80
Grand Falls (Grand-Sault), N.B., Can. B2 87
Grand Falls, wtfl., Me., U.S. .C5 112
Grand Falls [-Windsor], Nf., Can. D4 88
Grandfather Mountain, mtn., N.C., U.S. A1 126
Grandfield, Ok., U.S. C3 129
Grand Forks, B.C., Can. E8 85
Grand Forks, N.D., U.S. B8 127
Grand Forks, co., N.D., U.S. .B8 127
Grand Forks Air Force Base, mil., N.D., U.S. B8 127
Grand Harbour, N.B., Can. . .E3 87
Grand Haven, Mi., U.S. E4 115
Grand Island, i., La., U.S. . . .D6 111
Grand Island, i., Mi., U.S. . . .B4 115
Grand Island, Ne., U.S. D7 120
Grand Isle, La., U.S. E6 111
Grand Isle, co., Vt., U.S. B2 138
Grand Junction, Co., U.S. . . .B2 99
Grand Junction, Tn., U.S. . . .B3 108
Grand Lake, l., N.B., Can. . . .D3 87
Grand Lake, l., Nf., Can. D3 88
Grand Lake, l., La., U.S. E6 111

Grand Lake, l., La., U.S. E3 111
Grand Lake, l., Mi., U.S. C7 115
Grand Lake, l., Oh., U.S. B1 128
Grand Lake Matagamon, l., Me., U.S. B4 112
Grand Lake Seboeis, l., Me., U.S. B4 112
Grand Ledge, Mi., U.S. F6 115
Grand Manan Island, i., N.B., Can. E3 87
Grand Marais, Mn., U.S. k9 116
Grand Meadow, Mn., U.S. . . .G6 116
Grand-Mère, P.Q., Can. C5 90
Grand Mound, Ia., U.S. C7 108
Grand Portage Indian Reservation, Mn., U.S. . .k10 116
Grand Portage National Monument, Mn., U.S. . .h10 116
Grand Prairie, Tx., U.S. n10 136
Grand Rapids, Mi., U.S. F5 115
Grand Rapids, Mn., U.S. C5 116
Grand Rapids, Oh., U.S. f6 128
Grand Saline, Tx., U.S. C5 136
Grand Terre Islands, is., La., U.S. E6 111
Grand Teton, mtn., Wy., U.S. C2 143
Grand Teton National Park, Wy., U.S. C2 143
Grand Tower, Il., U.S. F4 106
Grand Traverse, co., Mi., U.S. D5 115
Grand Traverse Bay, b., Mi., U.S. C5 115
Grand Turk, T./C. Is. A5 76
Grand Valley, On., Can. D4 89
Grandview, Mb., Can. D1 86
Grandview, In., U.S. I4 107
Grandview, Mo., U.S. C3 118
Grandview, Wa., U.S. C6 140
Grandview Heights, Oh., U.S. m10 128
Grandville, Mi., U.S. F5 115
Grandy, N.C., U.S. A7 126
Granger, Ia., U.S. C4 108
Granger, In., U.S. A5 107
Granger, Tx., U.S. D4 136
Granger, Wa., U.S. C5 140
Grängesberg, Swe. F6 10
Grangeville, Id., U.S. D2 105
Gran Guardia, Arg. D6 72
Granisle, B.C., Can. B4 85
Granite, co., Mt., U.S. D3 119
Granite, Ok., U.S. C2 129
Granite City, Il., U.S. E3 106
Granite Falls, Mn., U.S. F3 116
Granite Falls, N.C., U.S. B1 126
Granite Falls, Wa., U.S. A4 140
Granite Lake, res., Nf., Can. .D3 88
Granite Mountain, mtn., Ak., U.S. B7 95
Granite Mountains, mts., Az., U.S. E2 96
Granite Mountains, mts., Wy., U.S. D5 143
Granite Pass, Wy., U.S. B5 143
Granite Peak, mtn., Mt., U.S. E7 119
Granite Peak, mtn., Nv., U.S. C2 121
Granite Peak, mtn., Nv., U.S. B4 121
Granite Peak, mtn., Ut., U.S. C2 137
Granite Peak, mtn., Ut., U.S. E3 137
Granite Peak, mtn., Wy., U.S. D4 143
Granite Quarry, N.C., U.S. . .B2 126
Granite Range, mts., Nv., U.S. C2 121
Graniteville, S.C., U.S. D4 133
Graniteville, Vt., U.S. C4 138
Granja, Braz. B3 74
Grant, Al., U.S. A3 94
Grant, co., Ar., U.S. C3 97
Grant, co., In., U.S. D6 107
Grant, co., Ks., U.S. E2 109
Grant, co., Ky., U.S. B5 110
Grant, co., La., U.S. C3 111
Grant, Mi., U.S. E5 115
Grant, co., Mn., U.S. E2 116
Grant, co., N.D., U.S. C4 127
Grant, co., Ne., U.S. C4 120
Grant, co., N.M., U.S. E1 124
Grant, co., Ok., U.S. A4 129
Grant, co., Or., U.S. C7 130
Grant, co., S.D., U.S. B8 134
Grant, co., Wa., U.S. B6 140
Grant, co., Wi., U.S. F3 142
Grant, co., W.V., U.S. B5 141
Grant, Mount, mtn., Nv., U.S. E3 121
Grant City, Mo., U.S. A3 118
Grant Park, Il., U.S. B6 106
Grant Range, mts., Nv., U.S. E6 121
Grants, N.M., U.S. B2 124
Grantsburg, Wi., U.S. C1 142
Grants Pass, Or., U.S. E3 130
Grantsville, Ut., U.S. C3 137
Grantsville, W.V., U.S. C3 141
Grant Town, W.V., U.S. B4 141
Grantville, Ga., U.S. C2 103
Granville, Fr. C6 16

Granville, Il., U.S. B4 106
Granville, co., N.C., U.S. A4 126
Granville, N.Y., U.S. B7 125
Granville, Oh., U.S. B3 128
Granville, W.V., U.S. h11 141
Granville Lake, l., Mb., Can. A1 86
Grapeland, Tx., U.S. D5 136
Grapeview, Wa., U.S. B3 140
Grapevine, Tx., U.S. C4 136
Grapevine Lake, res., Tx., U.S. n9 136
Grapevine Peak, mtn., Nv., U.S. G4 121
Gräsö, i., Swe. F8 10
Grasonville, Md., U.S. C5 113
Grass, stm., Mb., Can. B2 86
Grass, stm., N.Y., U.S. f9 125
Grasse, Fr. F10 16
Grass Lake, l., Il., U.S. h8 106
Grass Lake, Il., U.S. h8 106
Grass Lake, Mi., U.S. F6 115
Grass Valley, Ca., U.S. C3 98
Grassy Brook, stm., Vt., U.S. .E3 138
Grassy Lake, l., La., U.S. k9 111
Grates Point, c., Nf., Can. D5 88
Gratiot, co., Mi., U.S. E6 115
Gratis, Oh., U.S. C1 128
Grave Creek, stm., W.V., U.S. g8 141
Gravelly Branch, stm., De., U.S. F4 101
Gravelly Range, mts., Mt., U.S. E4 119
Gravenhage, 's- see 's-Gravenhage, Neth. D8 12
Gravenhurst, On., Can. C5 89
Grave Peak, mtn., Id., U.S. . . .C4 105
Graves, co., Ky., U.S. f9 110
Gravette, Ar., U.S. A1 97
Gray, Fr. D9 16
Gray, Ga., U.S. C3 103
Gray, co., Ks., U.S. E3 109
Gray, Ky., U.S. D5 110
Gray, La., U.S. k10 111
Gray, Me., U.S. g7 112
Gray, co., Tx., U.S. B2 136
Grayback Mountain, mtn., Or., U.S. E3 130
Gray Court, S.C., U.S. B3 133
Grayland, Wa., U.S. C1 140
Grayling, Mi., U.S. D6 115
Graylyn Crest, De., U.S. A3 101
Grays Harbor, b., Wa., U.S. . . .C1 140
Grays Harbor, co., Wa., U.S. B2 140
Grays Lake, sw., Id., U.S. F7 105
Grayslake, Il., U.S. A5 106
Grayson, Ky., U.S. B7 110
Grayson, co., Ky., U.S. C3 110
Grayson, co., Tx., U.S. C4 136
Grayson, co., Va., U.S. D1 139
Grayson Lake, res., Ky., U.S. B7 110
Grays Peak, mtn., Co., U.S. B5 99
Gray Summit, Mo., U.S. g12 118
Graysville, Al., U.S. f7 94
Graysville, Tn., U.S. D8 135
Grayville, Il., U.S. E5 106
Graz, Aus. G14 12
Great Alfold see Alföld, pl., Hung. F6 20
Great Artesian Basin, bas., Austl. F3 62
Great Australian Bight, b., Austl. G4 60
Great Averill Pond, l., Vt., U.S. B5 138
Great Barrier Island, i., N.Z. o14 63c
Great Barrier Reef, rf., Austl. D4 62
Great Barrington, Ma., U.S. . .B1 114
Great Basin, bas., U.S. C4 92
Great Basin National Park, Nv., U.S. E7 121
Great Bay, b., N.H., U.S. D5 122
Great Bay, b., N.J., U.S. D4 123
Great Bear Lake, l., N.T., Can. E15 82
Great Belt see Storebælt, strt., Den. I4 10
Great Bend, Ks., U.S. D5 109
Great Britain see United Kingdom, ctry., Eur. C6 12
Great Captain Island, i., Ct., U.S. E1 100
Great Channel, strt., Asia E2 34
Great Dismal Swamp, sw., U.S. D6 139
Great Divide Basin, bas., Wy., U.S. E4 143
Great Dividing Range, mts., Austl. H4 62
Great East Lake, l., U.S. C5 122
Great Egg Harbor, stm., N.J., U.S. D3 123
Greater Antilles, is., N.A. E9 76
Greater Khingan Range see Da Hinggan Ling, mts., China B12 28
Greater Sunda Islands, is., Asia D3 36
Great Exuma, i., Bah. D9 76
Great Falls, wtfl., Md., U.S. . . .B3 113

Great Falls, Mt., U.S. C5 119
Great Falls, S.C., U.S. B6 133
Great Falls Dam, Tn., U.S. D6 135
Greathouse Peak, mtn., Mt., U.S. D7 119
Great Inagua, i., Bah. D10 76
Great Indian Desert (Thar Desert), des., Asia D2 40
Great Island, spit, Ma., U.S. . .C7 114
Great Island, i., N.C., U.S. B6 126
Great Karroo, plat., S. Afr. . . .E3 56
Great Lakes Naval Training Center, mil., Il., U.S. h9 106
Great Miami, stm., U.S. C1 128
Great Misery Island, i., Ma., U.S. f12 114
Great Moose Lake, l., Me., U.S. D3 112
Great Namaqualand, hist. reg., Nmb. D2 56
Great Neck, N.Y., U.S. h13 125
Great Nicobar, i., India H6 40
Great Ouse, stm., Eng., U.K. . .D7 12
Great Pee Dee, stm., U.S. D9 133
Great Plains, pl., N.A. E9 75
Great Point, c., Ma., U.S. D7 114
Great Ruaha, stm., Tan. E7 54
Great Sacandaga Lake, l., N.Y., U.S. C6 125
Great Salt Lake, l., Ut., U.S. B3 137
Great Salt Lake Desert, des., Ut., U.S. C2 137
Great Salt Plains Lake, res., Ok., U.S. A3 129
Great Salt Pond, b., R.I., U.S. h7 132
Great Sand Dunes National Monument, Co., U.S. D5 99
Great Sandy Desert, des., Austl. E3 60
Great Slave Lake, l., N.T., Can. F17 82
Great Smoky Mountains, mts., U.S. B8 135
Great Smoky Mountains National Park, U.S. B8 135
Great Swamp, sw., R.I., U.S. . .F3 132
Great Victoria Desert, des., Austl. F4 60
Great Village, N.S., Can. D6 87
Great Wall see Chang Cheng, hist., China B2 30
Great Wass Island, i., Me., U.S. D5 112
Great Yarmouth, Eng., U.K. . .D7 12
Great Zab, stm., Asia D10 44
Gréboun, mtn., Niger C6 50
Greece, ctry., Eur. E8 18
Greece, N.Y., U.S. B3 125
Greeley, Co., U.S. A6 99
Greeley, co., Ks., U.S. D2 109
Greeley, co., Ne., U.S. C7 120
Greeley, Pa., U.S. D12 131
Green, stm., Il., U.S. B4 106
Green, stm., Ky., U.S. C2 110
Green, co., Ky., U.S. C4 110
Green, Or., U.S. D3 130
Green, stm., Wa., U.S. B3 140
Green, co., Wi., U.S. F4 142
Green, stm., U.S. A1 99
Green, stm., U.S. D6 92
Green Acres, De., U.S. h8 101
Greenacres, Wa., U.S. B8 140
Greenacres City, Fl., U.S. F6 102
Greenback, Tn., U.S. D9 135
Green Bay, Wi., U.S. D6 142
Green Bay, b., Mi., U.S. D3 115
Green Bay, b., U.S. B10 92
Greenbelt, Md., U.S. C4 113
Greenbriar, Va., U.S. g12 139
Greenbrier, Ar., U.S. B3 97
Green Brier, Tn., U.S. A5 135
Greenbrier, stm., W.V., U.S. . .D4 141
Greenbrier, co., W.V., U.S. . . .D4 141
Greenbush, Mn., U.S. B2 116
Greencastle, In., U.S. E4 107
Greencastle, Pa., U.S. G6 131
Green City, Mo., U.S. A5 118
Green Cove Springs, Fl., U.S. C5 102
Greendale, In., U.S. F8 107
Greendale, Wi., U.S. F6 142
Greene, co., Al., U.S. C1 94
Greene, co., Ar., U.S. A5 97
Greene, co., Ga., U.S. C3 103
Greene, Ia., U.S. B5 108
Greene, co., Il., U.S. D3 106
Greene, co., In., U.S. F4 107
Greene, co., Mo., U.S. D4 118
Greene, co., Ms., U.S. D5 117
Greene, N.Y., U.S. C5 125
Greene, co., N.Y., U.S. C6 125
Greene, co., N.C., U.S. B5 126
Greene, co., Oh., U.S. C2 128
Greene, co., Pa., U.S. G1 131
Greene, co., Tn., U.S. C11 135
Greene, co., Va., U.S. B4 139
Greeneville, Tn., U.S. C11 135
Green Fall, stm., U.S. F1 132
Greenfield, Ca., U.S. D3 98
Greenfield, Il., U.S. D3 106
Greenfield, In., U.S. E6 107
Greenfield, Ma., U.S. A2 114

Greenfield, Mo., U.S. D4 118
Greenfield, N.H., U.S. E3 122
Greenfield, Oh., U.S. C2 128
Greenfield, Tn., U.S. A3 135
Greenfield, Wi., U.S. n12 142
Greenfield Plaza, Ia., U.S. e8 108
Green Forest, Ar., U.S. A2 97
Green Harbor, Ma., U.S. B6 114
Green Hill Pond, l., R.I., U.S. G3 132
Greenhills, Oh., U.S. n12 128
Green Lake, l., Me., U.S. D4 112
Green Lake, l., Wi., U.S. E5 142
Green Lake, l., Wi., U.S. E5 142
Green Lake, co., Wi., U.S. E4 142
Greenland, dep., N.A. D30 82
Greenland, Ar., U.S. B1 97
Greenland, N.H., U.S. D5 122
Greenland Basin D23 144
Greenland Sea B9 46
Greenlee, co., Az., U.S. D6 96
Green Lookout Mountain, mtn., Wa., U.S. D3 140
Green Mountain, mtn., Wy., U.S. D5 143
Green Mountain Reservoir, res., Co., U.S. B4 99
Green Mountains, mts., Vt., U.S. F2 138
Greenock, Scot., U.K. C4 12
Greenock, Pa., U.S. F2 131
Green Peter Lake, res., Or., U.S. C4 130
Green Pond, Al., U.S. B2 94
Green Pond, l., N.J., U.S. A4 123
Greenport, N.Y., U.S. m16 125
Green River, Ut., U.S. E5 137
Green River, Wy., U.S. E3 143
Green River Lake, res., Ky., U.S. C4 110
Green River Lock and Dam, U.S. I2 107
Green River Reservoir, res., Vt., U.S. B3 138
Green Rock, Il., U.S. B3 106
Greensboro, Al., U.S. C2 94
Greensboro, Ga., U.S. C3 103
Greensboro, Md., U.S. C6 113
Greensboro, N.C., U.S. A3 126
Greensburg, In., U.S. F7 107
Greensburg, Ks., U.S. E4 109
Greensburg, Ky., U.S. C4 110
Greensburg, Pa., U.S. F2 131
Greens Peak, mtn., Az., U.S. C6 96
Green Springs, Oh., U.S. A2 128
Greensville, co., Va., U.S. D5 139
Green Swamp, sw., N.C., U.S. C4 126
Greentown, In., U.S. D6 107
Greenup, Il., U.S. D5 106
Greenup, Ky., U.S. B7 110
Greenup, co., Ky., U.S. B7 110
Green Valley, Az., U.S. F5 96
Greenview, Il., U.S. C4 106
Greenville, Lib. E3 50
Greenville, Al., U.S. D3 94
Greenville, Ca., U.S. B3 98
Greenville, De., U.S. A3 101
Greenville, Ga., U.S. C2 103
Greenville, Il., U.S. E4 106
Greenville, Ky., U.S. C2 110
Greenville, Me., U.S. C3 112
Greenville, Mi., U.S. E5 115
Greenville, Ms., U.S. B2 117
Greenville, N.C., U.S. B5 126
Greenville, N.H., U.S. E3 122
Greenville, Oh., U.S. B1 128
Greenville, Pa., U.S. D1 131
Greenville, R.I., U.S. C3 132
Greenville, S.C., U.S. B3 133
Greenville, co., S.C., U.S. B3 133
Greenville, Tx., U.S. C4 136
Greenville Creek, stm., Oh., U.S. B1 128
Greenville Junction, Me., U.S. C3 112
Greenwich, Ct., U.S. E1 100
Greenwich, N.Y., U.S. B7 125
Greenwich, Oh., U.S. A3 128
Greenwich Bay, b., R.I., U.S. . .D4 132
Greenwich Point, c., Ct., U.S. E1 100
Greenwood, B.C., Can. E8 85
Greenwood, Ar., U.S. B1 97
Greenwood, De., U.S. E3 101
Greenwood, In., U.S. E5 107
Greenwood, co., Ks., U.S. E7 109
Greenwood, La., U.S. B2 111
Greenwood, Mo., U.S. k11 118
Greenwood, Ms., U.S. B3 117
Greenwood, Pa., U.S. E5 131
Greenwood, S.C., U.S. C3 133
Greenwood, co., S.C., U.S. . . .C3 133
Greenwood, Wi., U.S. D3 142
Greenwood, Lake, res., In., U.S. G4 107
Greenwood, Lake, res., S.C., U.S. C4 133
Greenwood Lake, l., Mn., U.S. C7 116
Greenwood Lake, N.Y., U.S. . .D6 125
Greenwood Lake, l., U.S. A4 123
Greer, co., Ok., U.S. C2 129
Greer, S.C., U.S. B3 133
Greers Ferry Lake, res., Ar., U.S. B3 97

Name	Map Ref.	Page
Greeson, Lake, res., Ar., U.S.	C2	97
Gregg, co., Tx., U.S.	C5	136
Gregory, S.D., U.S.	D6	134
Gregory, co., S.D., U.S.	D6	134
Gregory Range, mts., Austl.	D3	62
Greifswald, Ger.	C13	12
Greilickville, Mi., U.S.	D5	115
Gremiha, Russia	C5	26
Grenada, ctry., N.A.	F12	76
Grenada, Ms., U.S.	B4	117
Grenada, co., Ms., U.S.	B4	117
Grenada Lake, res., Ms., U.S.	B4	117
Grenadines, is., N.A.	F12	76
Grenen, c., Den.	H4	10
Grenoble, Fr.	E9	16
Grenville, P.Q., Can.	D3	90
Grenville, Cape, c., Austl.	C3	62
Grenville, Point, c., Wa., U.S.	B1	140
Gresham, Or., U.S.	B4	130
Gresik, Indon.	D2	36
Gresik, Indon.	E4	36
Gretna, Mb., Can.	E3	86
Gretna, Fl., U.S.	B2	102
Gretna, La., U.S.	E5	111
Gretna, Ne., U.S.	C9	120
Gretna, Va., U.S.	D3	139
Grevená, Grc.	D8	18
Grey, stm., Nf., Can.	E3	88
Greybull, Wy., U.S.	B4	143
Greybull, stm., Wy., U.S.	B4	143
Greylock, Mount, mtn., Ma., U.S.	A1	114
Greymouth, N.Z.	p13	63c
Grey Range, mts., Austl.	F3	62
Greys, stm., Wy., U.S.	C2	143
Greytown, S. Afr.	D5	56
Gridley, Ca., U.S.	C3	98
Gridley, Il., U.S.	C5	106
Griffin, Ga., U.S.	C2	103
Griffiss Air Force Base, mil., N.Y., U.S.	B5	125
Griffith, Austl.	G4	62
Griffith, In., U.S.	A3	107
Grifton, N.C., U.S.	B5	126
Griggs, co., N.D., U.S.	B7	127
Griggsville, Il., U.S.	D3	106
Grim, Cape, c., Austl.	I3	62
Grimes, Ia., U.S.	C4	108
Grimes, co., Tx., U.S.	D4	136
Grimsby, On., Can.	D5	89
Grimsby, Eng., U.K.	I2	12
Grímsey, i., Ice.	k20	10a
Grimshaw, Ab., Can.	A2	84
Grimsley, Tn., U.S.	C9	135
Grímsstaðir, Ice.	l20	10a
Grindall Creek, Va., U.S.	n18	139
Grinnell, Ia., U.S.	C5	108
Griswold, Ia., U.S.	C2	108
Grizzly Mountain, mtn., Id., U.S.	B2	105
Grizzly Mountain, mtn., Or., U.S.	C6	130
Grizzly Mountain, mtn., Wa., U.S.	A7	140
Grjazi, Russia	C15	20
Grjazovec, Russia	C7	22
Groais Island, i., Nf., Can.	C4	88
Groblersdal, S. Afr.	D4	56
Grodno see Hrodna, Bela.	C7	20
Groesbeck, Tx., U.S.	D4	136
Groningen, Neth.	D10	12
Groom Lake, l., Nv., U.S.	F6	121
Groom Range, mts., Nv., U.S.	F6	121
Groote Eylandt, i., Austl.	C6	60
Grootfontein, Nmb.	B2	56
Gros Morne National Park, Nf., Can.	D3	88
Grosse Isle Naval Air Station, mil., Mi., U.S.	p15	115
Grosse Pointe Park, Mi., U.S.	p16	115
Grosse Pointe Woods, Mi., U.S.	p16	115
Grosseto, Italy	C3	18
Grossglockner, mtn., Aus.	G13	12
Grossmont, Ca., U.S.	o16	98
Gros Ventre, stm., Wy., U.S.	C2	143
Gros Ventre Range, mts., Wy., U.S.	C2	143
Groswater Bay, b., Nf., Can.	H28	82
Groton, Ct., U.S.	D7	100
Groton, N.Y., U.S.	C4	125
Groton, S.D., U.S.	B7	134
Groton Long Point, Ct., U.S.	D7	100
Grottoes, Va., U.S.	B4	139
Grouse Creek, stm., Ut., U.S.	B2	137
Grouse Creek Mountain, mtn., Id., U.S.	E5	105
Grove, Ok., U.S.	A7	129
Grove City, Fl., U.S.	F4	102
Grove City, Oh., U.S.	C2	128
Grove City, Pa., U.S.	D1	131
Grove Hill, Al., U.S.	D2	94
Groveland, Fl., U.S.	D5	102
Groveland, Ma., U.S.	A5	114
Grove Mountains, mts., Ant.	D12	67
Grove Point, c., Md., U.S.	B5	113
Groveport, Oh., U.S.	C3	128
Grover City, Ca., U.S.	E3	98
Groves, Tx., U.S.	E6	136
Groveton, N.H., U.S.	A3	122
Groveton, Tx., U.S.	D5	136
Groveton, Va., U.S.	g12	139
Grovetown, Ga., U.S.	C4	103
Groveville, N.J., U.S.	C3	123
Growa Point, c., Lib.	F3	50
Growler Peak, mtn., Az., U.S.	E2	96
Groznyj, Russia	E6	26
Grudziądz, Pol.	C5	20
Gruetli-Laager, Tn., U.S.	D8	135
Grulla, Tx., U.S.	F3	136
Grünau, Nmb.	D2	56
Grundy, co., Ia., U.S.	B5	108
Grundy, co., Il., U.S.	B5	106
Grundy, co., Mo., U.S.	A4	118
Grundy, co., Tn., U.S.	D8	135
Grundy, Va., U.S.	e9	139
Grundy Center, Ia., U.S.	B5	108
Grunthal, Mb., Can.	E3	86
Gruver, Tx., U.S.	A2	136
Guacanayabo, Golfo de, b., Cuba	A4	80
Guadalajara, Mex.	C4	78
Guadalajara, Spain	G5	16
Guadalcanal, i., Sol. Is.	B7	62
Guadalquivir, stm., Spain	I4	16
Guadalquivir, Marismas del, sw., Spain	I3	16
Guadalupe, Mex.	C4	78
Guadalupe, Mex.	B4	78
Guadalupe, Az., U.S.	m9	96
Guadalupe, Ca., U.S.	E3	98
Guadalupe, co., N.M., U.S.	C5	124
Guadalupe, co., Tx., U.S.	E4	136
Guadalupe, Isla, i., Mex.	B1	78
Guadalupe Mountains, mts., U.S.	E5	124
Guadalupe Mountains National Park, Tx., U.S.	o12	136
Guadalupe Peak, mtn., Tx., U.S.	o12	136
Guadeloupe, dep., N.A.	E12	76
Guadeloupe Passage, strt., N.A.	B7	80
Guadiana, stm., Eur.	I3	16
Guadix, Spain	I5	16
Guaíra, Braz.	C7	72
Guajará-Mirim, Braz.	F6	70
Guaje, Laguna del, l., Mex.	B4	78
Gualeguay, Arg.	E6	72
Gualeguaychú, Arg.	E6	72
Guam, dep., Oc.	D12	32
Guaminí, Arg.	F5	72
Guamúchil, Mex.	B3	78
Guanaja, Isla de, i., Hond.	B2	80
Guanajuato, Mex.	C4	78
Guanajuato, state, Mex.	C4	78
Guanambi, Braz.	D3	74
Guanare, Ven.	B6	70
Guane, Cuba	A3	80
Guang'an, China	E9	28
Guangde, China	C4	30
Guangdong, prov., China	G10	28
Guangji, China	D4	30
Guangling, China	B3	30
Guangnan, China	G8	28
Guangxi Zhuangzu Zizhiqu, prov., China	G9	28
Guangyuan, China	E9	28
Guangzhou (Canton), China	E3	30
Guano Lake, l., Or., U.S.	E7	130
Guantánamo, Cuba	A4	80
Guantao, China	B4	30
Guanxian, China	E8	28
Guanyun, China	C4	30
Guapí, Col.	C4	70
Guápiles, C.R.	C3	80
Guaporé, stm., S.A.	F7	70
Guarabira, Braz.	C4	74
Guarapari, Braz.	F3	74
Guarapuava, Braz.	D7	72
Guaratuba, Braz.	D8	72
Guarda, Port.	G3	16
Guardafui, Cape see Gwardafuy, Gees, c., Som.	H15	48
Guardo, Spain	F4	16
Guarenas, Ven.	C6	80
Guárico, stm., Ven.	D6	80
Guasave, Mex.	B3	78
Guasdualito, Ven.	B5	70
Guasipati, Ven.	B7	70
Guatemala, Guat.	C1	80
Guatemala, ctry., N.A.	D6	78
Guatemala Basin	G29	64
Guaviare, stm., Col.	C6	70
Guaxupé, Braz.	F2	74
Guayana see Guayana, ctry., S.A.	B8	70
Guayana see Ciudad Guayana, Ven.	B7	70
Guayape, stm., Hond.	C2	80
Guayaquil, Ec.	D3	70
Guayaquil, Golfo de, b., S.A.	D3	70
Guaymallén, Arg.	E4	72
Guaymas, Mex.	B2	78
Gubaha, Russia	C10	22
Gubbio, Italy	C4	18
Guben, Ger.	E14	12
Guben (Guben), Pol.	D3	20
Gubin (Guben), Pol.	D3	20
Gubkin, Russia	D14	20
Gudauta, Geor.	A9	44
Gudermes, Russia	B5	42
Gudivāda, India	F4	40
Gudiyāttam, India	G3	40
Gūdūr, India	G3	40
Guékédou, Gui.	E2	50
Guélengdeng, Chad	D8	50
Guelma, Alg.	D5	14
Guelph, On., Can.	D4	89
Guercif, Mor.	E3	14
Güere, stm., Ven.	D7	80
Guéret, Fr.	D7	16
Guernsey, dep., Eur.	F5	12
Guernsey, co., Oh., U.S.	B4	128
Guernsey, Wy., U.S.	D8	143
Guerrero, Mex.	B3	78
Guerrero, state, Mex.	D4	78
Guerrero Negro, Mex.	B2	78
Gueydan, La., U.S.	D3	111
Guga, Russia	D15	26
Gugē, mtn., Eth.	B7	54
Guguan, i., N. Mar. Is.	C12	32
Guiana Basin	G9	64
Guide, China	D8	28
Guiding, China	D2	30
Guildford, Eng., U.K.	E6	12
Guilford, Ct., U.S.	D5	100
Guilford, Me., U.S.	C3	112
Guilford, co., N.C., U.S.	A3	126
Guilin, China	F10	28
Guimarães, Port.	G2	16
Guimaras Island, i., Phil.	D8	34
Guin, Al., U.S.	B2	94
Guinea, ctry., Afr.	D2	50
Guinea, Gulf of, b., Afr.	I10	46
Guinea Basin	H13	64
Guinea-Bissau, ctry., Afr.	D1	50
Güines, Cuba	A3	80
Guingamp, Fr.	C5	16
Guiping, China	E3	30
Güira de Melena, Cuba	A3	80
Guiratinga, Braz.	B7	72
Güiria, Ven.	A7	70
Guitry, C. Iv.	E3	50
Guiuan, Phil.	D9	34
Guixi, China	D4	30
Guixian, China	G9	28
Guiyang, China	F9	28
Guizhou, prov., China	F9	28
Gujarāt, state, India	E2	40
Gujrānwāla, Pak.	D10	42
Gujrāt, Pak.	D10	42
Gulbarga, India	F3	40
Gulbene, Lat.	H12	10
Gulf, co., Fl., U.S.	C1	102
Gulf, The see Persian Gulf, b., Asia	E6	42
Gulf Gate Estates, Fl., U.S.	E4	102
Gulf Islands National Seashore, U.S.	E5	117
Gulf of Alaska Seamount Province	B1	144
Gulfport, Fl., U.S.	E4	102
Gulfport, Ms., U.S.	E4	117
Gulf Shores, Al., U.S.	E2	94
Gulgong, Austl.	G4	62
Gulian, China	A12	28
Gulistan, Uzb.	B9	42
Gullfoss, wtfl., Ice.	l19	10a
Gull Island, l., N.C., U.S.	B7	126
Gullivan Bay, b., Fl., U.S.	G5	102
Gull Lake, l., Ab., Can.	C4	84
Gull Lake, l., Mn., U.S.	D4	116
Güllük Körfezi, b., Tur.	D2	44
Gulu, Ug.	C6	54
Gumboro, De., U.S.	G4	101
Gumdag, Turk.	C6	42
Gumel, Nig.	D6	50
Gümüşhane, Tur.	B8	44
Guna, India	E3	40
Gundagai, Austl.	H4	62
Gundji, D.R.C.	A4	54
Gungu, D.R.C.	C3	54
Gunisao, stm., Mb., Can.	C3	86
Gunmi, Nig.	D6	50
Gunnbjørn Fjeld, mtn., Grnld.	E34	82
Gunnedah, Austl.	G5	62
Gunnison, Co., U.S.	C4	99
Gunnison, co., Co., U.S.	C3	99
Gunnison, stm., Co., U.S.	C2	99
Gunnison, Ms., U.S.	B3	117
Gunnison, Ut., U.S.	D4	137
Gunnison, Mount, mtn., Co., U.S.	C3	99
Gunpowder Neck, c., Md., U.S.	B5	113
Gunpowder River, b., Md., U.S.	B5	113
Guntakal, India	F3	40
Gunter Air Force Base, mil., Al., U.S.	C3	94
Guntersville, Al., U.S.	A3	94
Guntersville Lake, res., Al., U.S.	A3	94
Guntown, Ms., U.S.	A5	117
Guntūr, India	F4	40
Gunungsitoli, Indon.	C1	36
Guoyang, China	C4	30
Gupis, Pak.	C10	42
Gurdon, Ar., U.S.	D2	97
Gurdžaani, Geor.	B11	44
Guri, Embalse de, res., Ven.	B7	70
Gurley, Al., U.S.	A3	94
Gurnee, Il., U.S.	h9	106
Gurnet Point, c., Ma., U.S.	B6	114
Gurskøya, i., Nor.	E1	10
Gürün, Tur.	C7	44
Gurupi, stm., Braz.	B2	74
Gurupi, Braz.	D2	74
Gusau, Nig.	D6	50
Gusev, Russia	B7	20
Gushi, China	C4	30
Gušgy, Turk.	F8	26
Gusinoozersk, Russia	A9	28
Guspini, Italy	E2	18
Gustav Holm, Kap, c., Grnld.	E33	82
Gustine, Ca., U.S.	D3	98
Güstrow, Ger.	D13	12
Guthrie, co., Ia., U.S.	C3	108
Guthrie, Ky., U.S.	D2	110
Guthrie, Ok., U.S.	B4	129
Guthrie, W.V., U.S.	m12	141
Guthrie Center, Ia., U.S.	C3	108
Guttenberg, Ia., U.S.	B6	108
Guttenberg, N.J., U.S.	h8	123
Guwāhāti, India	D6	40
Guyana, ctry., S.A.	B8	70
Guyandotte, stm., W.V., U.S.	C2	141
Guyang, China	A3	30
Guymon, Ok., U.S.	e9	129
Guysborough, N.S., Can.	D8	87
Guyton, Ga., U.S.	D5	103
Guyuan, China	D9	28
Guzar, Uzb.	C9	42
Güzelyurt Körfezi, b., N. Cyp.	E5	44
Guzmán, Mex.	D4	78
Gwaai, Zimb.	B4	56
Gwādar, Pak.	E8	42
Gwalia, Austl.	F3	60
Gwalior, India	D3	40
Gwanda, Zimb.	C4	56
Gwardafuy, Gees, c., Som.	H15	48
Gwayi, stm., Zimb.	B4	56
Gweru, Zimb.	B4	56
Gweta, Bots.	C4	56
Gwinhurst, De., U.S.	h8	101
Gwinn, Mi., U.S.	B3	115
Gwinner, N.D., U.S.	C8	127
Gwinnett, co., Ga., U.S.	C2	103
Gwydyr Bay, b., Ak., U.S.	A10	95
Gwynns Falls, stm., Md., U.S.	g10	113
Gyangzê, China	F5	28
Gyaring Co, l., China	E5	28
Gyaring Hu, l., China	E7	28
Gyda, Russia	B9	26
Gydanskij poluostrov, pen., Russia	B9	26
Gyldenløves Fjord, b., Grnld.	F31	82
Gympie, Austl.	F5	62
Gyöngyös, Hung.	F5	20
Győr, Hung.	F4	20
Gypsum, Co., U.S.	B4	99
Gyzylarbat, Turk.	F7	26

H

Name	Map Ref.	Page
Haakon, co., S.D., U.S.	C4	134
Haapsalu, Est.	G10	10
Haarlem, Neth.	D9	12
Haast, N.Z.	p12	63c
Habarovo, Russia	A11	22
Habarovsk, Russia	E15	26
Ḥabbānīyah, Buḥayrat al-, res., Iraq	F10	44
Habersham, co., Ga., U.S.	B3	103
Hachijō-jima, i., Japan	E15	28
Hachinohe, Japan	C16	28
Hachiōji, Japan	C3	31
Hackberry, La., U.S.	E2	111
Hackensack, N.J., U.S.	B4	123
Hackensack, stm., N.J., U.S.	h8	123
Hackettstown, N.J., U.S.	B3	123
Hackleburg, Al., U.S.	A2	94
Haddam, Ct., U.S.	D5	100
Haddock, Ga., U.S.	C3	103
Haddonfield, N.J., U.S.	D2	123
Haddon Heights, N.J., U.S.	D2	123
Hadejia, stm., Nig.	D6	50
Hadejia, Nig.	D7	50
Hadera, Isr.	F6	44
Haderslev, Den.	I3	10
Hadībū, Yemen	H6	38
Ḥadīthah, Iraq	D4	42
Hadjout, Alg.	I8	16
Hadley Lake, l., Me., U.S.	D5	112
Hadrian's Wall, Eng., U.K.	C5	12
Haeju, N. Kor.	D13	28
Hafik, Tur.	C7	44
Hafnarfjörður, Ice.	I17	10a
Haft Gel, Iran	D5	42
Hagan, Ga., U.S.	D5	103
Hagåtña (Agana), Guam	D11	32
Hagemeister Island, i., Ak., U.S.	D7	95
Hagerman, Id., U.S.	G4	105
Hagerman, N.M., U.S.	D5	124
Hagerstown, In., U.S.	E7	107
Hagerstown, Md., U.S.	A2	113
Hagfors, Swe.	F5	10
Haggin, Mount, mtn., Mt., U.S.	D3	119
Hagi, Japan	D2	31
Ha Giang, Viet.	B5	34
Hague, Sk., Can.	E2	91
Haguenau, Fr.	C10	16
Hagues Peak, mtn., Co., U.S.	A5	99
Ha! Ha!, Baie des, b., P.Q., Can.	C2	88
Hahira, Ga., U.S.	F3	103
Hahnville, La., U.S.	E5	111
Haicheng, China	A5	30
Hai Duong, Viet.	B5	34
Haifa see Ḥefa, Isr.	D2	42
Haig, Austl.	G4	60
Haikang, China	E3	30
Haikou, China	G10	28
Haiku, Hi., U.S.	C5	104
Ḥā'il, Sau. Ar.	E4	38
Hailar, China	B11	28
Hailey, Id., U.S.	F4	105
Haileybury, On., Can.	p20	89
Haileyville, Ok., U.S.	C6	129
Hailin, China	B1	31
Hailun, China	B13	28
Haimen, China	E4	30
Haimen, China	F12	28
Hainan, prov., China	H9	28
Hainan Dao, i., China	H9	28
Hainan Island see Hainan Dao, i., China	H9	28
Haines, Ak., U.S.	D12	95
Haines City, Fl., U.S.	D5	102
Haining, China	C5	30
Hai Ninh, Viet.	B5	34
Hai Phong, Viet.	B5	34
Haisyn, Ukr.	E10	20
Haiti, ctry., N.A.	H12	75
Haitun, China	B7	40
Haiyuan, China	B2	30
Haizhou, China	E11	28
Haizhou Wan, b., China	B4	30
Hajdúböszörmény, Hung.	F6	20
Hajnówka, Pol.	C7	20
Hakkâri, Tur.	D10	44
Hakodate, Japan	C16	28
Ḥalab (Aleppo), Syria	D7	44
Halachó, Mex.	C6	78
Ḥalā'ib, Sudan	F12	48
Halawa, Cape, c., Hi., U.S.	B5	104
Halawa Heights, Hi., U.S.	g10	104
Halberstadt, Ger.	E12	12
Halden, Nor.	G4	10
Haldimand, On., Can.	E5	89
Haldwāni, India	D3	40
Hale, co., Al., U.S.	C2	94
Hale, co., Tx., U.S.	B2	136
Haleakala Crater, crat., Hi., U.S.	C5	104
Haleakala National Park, Hi., U.S.	C6	104
Hale Center, Tx., U.S.	B2	136
Haleiwa, Hi., U.S.	B3	104
Hales Corners, Wi., U.S.	n11	142
Halethorpe, Md., U.S.	B4	113
Haleyville, Al., U.S.	A2	94
Half Moon Bay, Ca., U.S.	k8	98
Halfway, Md., U.S.	A2	113
Haliburton, On., Can.	B6	89
Halibut Point, c., Ma., U.S.	A6	114
Halicarnassus, hist., Tur.	D2	44
Halifax, N.S., Can.	E6	87
Halifax, co., N.C., U.S.	A5	126
Halifax, Va., U.S.	D4	139
Halifax, co., Va., U.S.	D4	139
Haliimaile, Hi., U.S.	C5	104
Hall, co., Ga., U.S.	B3	103
Hall, co., Ne., U.S.	D7	120
Hall, co., Tx., U.S.	B2	136
Halla, Mount see Halla-san, mtn., S. Kor.	E13	28
Hallam Peak, mtn., B.C., Can.	C8	85
Hallandale, Fl., U.S.	G6	102
Ḥallāniyah, Juzur al-, is., Oman	G7	38
Halla-san, mtn., S. Kor.	E13	28
Halle, Ger.	E12	12
Hällefors, Swe.	G6	10
Hallein, Aus.	G13	12
Hallettsville, Tx., U.S.	E4	136
Hallie, Wi., U.S.	D2	142
Hall Island, i., Ak., U.S.	C5	95
Hall Meadow Brook Reservoir, res., Ct., U.S.	B3	100
Hall Mountain, mtn., Wa., U.S.	A8	140
Hallock, Mn., U.S.	B2	116
Hallowell, Me., U.S.	D3	112
Halls, Tn., U.S.	B2	135
Hallsberg, Swe.	G6	10
Halls Creek, Austl.	C4	60
Halls Creek, stm., Ut., U.S.	F5	137
Halls Crossroads, Tn., U.S.	m14	135
Halls Stream, stm., N.H., U.S.	f7	122
Hallstahammar, Swe.	G7	10
Hallstead, Pa., U.S.	C10	131
Hallsville, Mo., U.S.	B5	118
Hallsville, Tx., U.S.	C5	136
Halmahera, i., Indon.	C7	36
Halmahera, Laut (Halmahera Sea), Indon.	D7	36
Halmahera Sea see Halmahera, Laut, Indon.	D7	36
Hal'mer-Ju, Russia	A11	22
Halmstad, Swe.	H5	10
Halsey, Or., U.S.	C3	130
Hälsingland, hist. reg., Swe.	F7	10
Halstad, Mn., U.S.	C2	116
Halstead, Ks., U.S.	E6	109

Name	Map Ref.	Page

Haltiatunturi, mtn., Eur. . . . **B9** 10
Halton Hills, On., Can. . . . **D5** 89
Hamada, Japan **D2** 31
Hamadān, Iran **D5** 42
Ḥamāh, Syria **E7** 44
Ḥamāh, state, Syria **E7** 44
Hamamatsu, Japan **E15** 28
Hamar, Nor. **F4** 10
Hamarøya, Nor. **B6** 10
Hambantota, Sri L. **H4** 40
Hamblen, co., Tn., U.S. . . . **C10** 135
Hamburg, Ger. **D12** 12
Hamburg, Ar., U.S. **D4** 97
Hamburg, Ia., U.S. **D2** 108
Hamburg, N.Y., U.S. **C2** 125
Hamburg, Pa., U.S. **E10** 131
Hamden, Ct., U.S. **D4** 100
Hamden, Oh., U.S. **C3** 128
Hämeenlinna, Fin. **F11** 10
Hamel, Mn., U.S. **m11** 116
Hameln, Ger. **D11** 12
Hamersley Range, mts.,
    Austl. **E2** 60
Hami, China **C6** 28
Hamilton, Austl. **H3** 62
Hamilton, Ber. **B12** 76
Hamilton, On., Can. **D5** 89
Hamilton, N.Z. **o14** 63c
Hamilton, Al., U.S. **A2** 94
Hamilton, Il., U.S. **C2** 106
Hamilton, In., U.S. **A8** 107
Hamilton, Mi., U.S. **F4** 115
Hamilton, Mo., U.S. **B3** 118
Hamilton, Ms., U.S. **B5** 117
Hamilton, Mt., U.S. **D2** 119
Hamilton, N.Y., U.S. **C5** 125
Hamilton, Oh., U.S. **C1** 128
Hamilton, Tx., U.S. **D3** 136
Hamilton, Va., U.S. **A5** 139
Hamilton, co., Fl., U.S. . . . **B3** 102
Hamilton, co., Ia., U.S. . . . **B4** 108
Hamilton, co., Il., U.S. . . . **E5** 106
Hamilton, co., In., U.S. . . . **D5** 107
Hamilton, co., Ks., U.S. . . . **E2** 109
Hamilton, co., Ne., U.S. . . . **D7** 120
Hamilton, co., N.Y., U.S. . . **B6** 125
Hamilton, co., Oh., U.S. . . . **C1** 128
Hamilton, co., Tn., U.S. . . . **D8** 135
Hamilton, co., Tx., U.S. . . . **D3** 136
Hamilton, Lake, res., Ar.,
    U.S. **C2** 97
Hamilton, Mount, mtn., Ak.,
    U.S. **C8** 95
Hamilton, Mount, mtn., Ca.,
    U.S. **k9** 98
Hamilton, Mount, mtn., Nv.,
    U.S. **D6** 121
Hamilton Inlet, b., Nf., Can. **A2** 88
Hamilton Reservoir, res.,
    Ma., U.S. **B3** 114
Hamilton Sound, strt., Nf.,
    Can. **D4** 88
Hamilton Square, N.J., U.S. **C3** 123
Hamina, Fin. **F12** 10
Hamiota, Mb., Can. **D1** 86
Hamīrpur, India **D4** 40
Hamlet, In., U.S. **B4** 107
Hamlet, N.C., U.S. **C3** 126
Hamlet, Mount, mtn., Ak.,
    U.S. **B6** 95
Hamlin, Pa., U.S. **D11** 131
Hamlin, Tx., U.S. **C2** 136
Hamlin, W.V., U.S. **C2** 141
Hamlin, co., S.D., U.S. . . . **C8** 134
Hamlin Lake, l., Mi., U.S. . . **D4** 115
Hamm, Ger. **E10** 12
Hammamet, Tun. **F3** 18
Hammamet, Golfe de, b.,
    Tun. **F3** 18
Hammam Lif, Tun. **F3** 18
Ḥammār, Hawr al, l., Iraq . **G12** 44
Hammerfest, Nor. **A10** 10
Hammon, Ok., U.S. **B2** 129
Hammonasset, stm., Ct.,
    U.S. **D5** 100
Hammonasset Point, c., Ct.,
    U.S. **E5** 100
Hammond, In., U.S. **A2** 107
Hammond, La., U.S. **D5** 111
Hammond, Wi., U.S. **D1** 142
Hammond Bay, b., Mi., U.S. **C6** 115
Hammonton, N.J., U.S. . . . **D3** 123
Hamningberg, Nor. **A14** 10
Hampden, Nf., Can. **D3** 88
Hampden, Me., U.S. **D4** 112
Hampden, co., Ma., U.S. . . **B2** 114
Hampden Highlands, Me.,
    U.S. **D4** 112
Hampshire, Il., U.S. **A5** 106
Hampshire, co., Ma., U.S. . **B2** 114
Hampshire, co., W.V., U.S. . **B6** 141
Hampstead, Md., U.S. **A4** 113
Hampstead, N.C., U.S. . . . **C5** 126
Hampton, N.B., Can. **D4** 87
Hampton, Ar., U.S. **D3** 97
Hampton, Ga., U.S. **C2** 103
Hampton, Ia., U.S. **B4** 108
Hampton, N.H., U.S. **E5** 122
Hampton, S.C., U.S. **F5** 133
Hampton, Tn., U.S. **C11** 135
Hampton, Va., U.S. **C6** 139
Hampton, co., S.C., U.S. . . **F5** 133
Hampton Bays, N.Y., U.S. . **n16** 125
Hampton Beach, N.H., U.S. **E5** 122

Hampton Butte, mtn., Or.,
    U.S. **D6** 130
Hampton Roads, Va., U.S. . **k15** 139
Hampton Roads Bridge-
    Tunnel, Va., U.S. **k15** 139
Ḥamrā', Al-Ḥamādah al-,
    des., Libya **F6** 14
Hamra, As Saquia al, stm.,
    W. Sah. **A2** 50
Hams Fork, stm., Wy., U.S. **E2** 143
Hamtramck, Mi., U.S. **p15** 115
Ḥāmūn, Daryācheh-ye, l.,
    Iran **D8** 42
Han, stm., China **E9** 28
Hana, Hi., U.S. **C6** 104
Hanahan, S.C., U.S. **F7** 133
Hanalei Bay, b., Hi., U.S. . . **A2** 104
Hanamaki, Japan **D16** 28
Hanamaulu, Hi., U.S. **B2** 104
Hanapepe, Hi., U.S. **B2** 104
Hânceşti, Mol. **F10** 20
Hanceville, Al., U.S. **A3** 94
Hancheng, China **D10** 28
Hancock, Md., U.S. **A1** 113
Hancock, Mi., U.S. **A2** 115
Hancock, Mn., U.S. **E3** 116
Hancock, co., Ga., U.S. . . . **C3** 103
Hancock, co., Ia., U.S. . . . **A4** 108
Hancock, co., Il., U.S. . . . **C2** 106
Hancock, co., In., U.S. . . . **E6** 107
Hancock, co., Ky., U.S. . . . **C3** 110
Hancock, co., Me., U.S. . . . **D4** 112
Hancock, co., Ms., U.S. . . . **E4** 117
Hancock, co., Oh., U.S. . . . **A2** 128
Hancock, co., Tn., U.S. . . . **C10** 135
Hancock, co., W.V., U.S. . . **A4** 141
Hand, co., S.D., U.S. **C6** 134
Handan, China **D10** 28
Handyga, Russia **C15** 26
Hanford, Ca., U.S. **D4** 98
Hangayn nuruu, mts.,
    Mong. **B7** 28
Hangchow see Hangzhou,
    China **E12** 28
Hanggin Houqi, China . . . **C9** 28
Hanggin Qi, China **D9** 28
Hangman Creek, stm., Wa.,
    U.S. **B8** 140
Hangokurt, Russia **B11** 22
Hangu, China **B4** 30
Hangzhou, China **E12** 28
Hangzhou Wan, b., China . **C5** 30
Hanjiang, China **F11** 28
Hankinson, N.D., U.S. **C9** 127
Hanko, Fin. **G10** 10
Hanna, Ab., Can. **D5** 84
Hanna, Wy., U.S. **E6** 143
Hanna City, Il., U.S. **C4** 106
Hannahville Indian
    Reservation, Mi., U.S. . **C3** 115
Hannibal, Mo., U.S. **B6** 118
Hannover, Ger. **D11** 12
Hanöbukten, b., Swe. **I6** 10
Ha Noi, Viet. **B5** 34
Hanover, On., Can. **C3** 89
Hanover see Hannover,
    Ger. **D11** 12
Hanover, Il., U.S. **A3** 106
Hanover, In., U.S. **G7** 107
Hanover, Ks., U.S. **C7** 109
Hanover, Ma., U.S. **B6** 114
Hanover, Mn., U.S. **m11** 116
Hanover, N.H., U.S. **C2** 122
Hanover, Pa., U.S. **G8** 131
Hanover, co., Va., U.S. . . . **C5** 139
Hanover Park, Il., U.S. . . . **k8** 106
Hansen, Id., U.S. **G4** 105
Hansford, co., Tx., U.S. . . . **A2** 136
Hanson, Ma., U.S. **B6** 114
Hanson, co., S.D., U.S. . . . **D8** 134
Hanstholm, Den. **H3** 10
Hantsport, N.S., Can. **D5** 87
Hanty-Mansijsk, Russia . . . **C8** 26
Hanyin, China **C2** 30
Hanzhong, China **E9** 28
Hāora, India **E5** 40
Haparanda, Swe. **D11** 10
Hapčeranga, Russia **E13** 26
Hapeville, Ga., U.S. **C2** 103
Happy Valley, N.M., U.S. . . **E5** 124
Happy Valley-Goose Bay,
    Nf., Can. **B1** 88
Hāpur, India **D3** 40
Ḥaraḍ, Sau. Ar. **F5** 38
Harahan, La., U.S. **k11** 111
Haralson, co., Ga., U.S. . . . **C1** 103
Harare, Zimb. **B5** 56
Harazé Mangueigne, Chad **B4** 54
Harbala, Russia **C14** 26
Harbeson, De., U.S. **F4** 101
Harbin, China **B13** 28
Harbor, Or., U.S. **E2** 130
Harbor Beach, Mi., U.S. . . **E8** 115
Harborcreek, Pa., U.S. . . . **B2** 131
Harbor Springs, Mi., U.S. . **C6** 115
Harbour Breton, Nf., Can. . **E4** 88
Harbour Grace, Nf., Can. . . **E5** 88
Harcuvar Mountains, mts.,
    Az., U.S. **D2** 96
Hardangerfjorden, b., Nor. **F2** 10
Hardee, co., Fl., U.S. **E5** 102
Hardeeville, S.C., U.S. . . . **G5** 133
Hardeman, co., Tn., U.S. . . **B2** 135
Hardeman, co., Tx., U.S. . . **B3** 136
Hardin, Il., U.S. **D3** 106

Hardin, Mt., U.S. **E9** 119
Hardin, co., Ia., U.S. **B4** 108
Hardin, co., Il., U.S. **F5** 106
Hardin, co., Ky., U.S. **C4** 110
Hardin, co., Oh., U.S. **B2** 128
Hardin, co., Tn., U.S. **B3** 135
Hardin, co., Tx., U.S. **D5** 136
Harding, S. Afr. **E4** 56
Harding, co., N.M., U.S. . . **B5** 124
Harding, co., S.D., U.S. . . . **B2** 134
Harding, Lake, res., U.S. . . **C4** 94
Hardinsburg, Ky., U.S. . . . **C3** 110
Hardisty, Ab., Can. **C5** 84
Hardoi, India **D4** 40
Hardwick, Ga., U.S. **C3** 103
Hardwick, Vt., U.S. **B4** 138
Hardwood Ridge, mtn., Pa.,
    U.S. **D11** 131
Hardy, co., W.V., U.S. **B6** 141
Hardy Lake, res., In., U.S. . **G6** 107
Hare Bay, Nf., Can. **D4** 88
Hare Bay, b., Nf., Can. . . . **C4** 88
Hārer, Eth. **B8** 54
Hargeysa, Som. **I13** 48
Har Hu, l., China **D7** 28
Hari, stm., Indon. **D2** 36
Haridwār, India **D3** 40
Harīrūd, stm., Asia **D8** 42
Harkers Island, N.C., U.S. . **C6** 126
Harlan, Ia., U.S. **C2** 108
Harlan, In., U.S. **B8** 107
Harlan, Ky., U.S. **D6** 110
Harlan, co., Ky., U.S. **D6** 110
Harlan, co., Ne., U.S. **D6** 120
Harlan County Lake, res.,
    Ne., U.S. **E6** 120
Harlem, Fl., U.S. **F6** 102
Harlem, Ga., U.S. **C4** 103
Harlem, Mt., U.S. **B8** 119
Harleyville, S.C., U.S. **E7** 133
Harlingen, Tx., U.S. **F4** 136
Harlow, Eng., U.K. **E7** 12
Harlowton, Mt., U.S. **D7** 119
Harmânli, Bul. **D10** 18
Harmon, co., Ok., U.S. . . . **C2** 129
Harmon Creek, stm., W.V.,
    U.S. **f8** 141
Harmony, In., U.S. **E3** 107
Harmony, Mn., U.S. **G6** 116
Harmony, Pa., U.S. **E1** 131
Harmony, R.I., U.S. **B3** 132
Harnett, co., N.C., U.S. . . . **B4** 126
Harney, co., Or., U.S. **D7** 130
Harney, Lake, l., Fl., U.S. . . **D5** 102
Harney Lake, l., Or., U.S. . . **D7** 130
Harney Peak, mtn., S.D.,
    U.S. **D2** 134
Härnösand, Swe. **E7** 10
Haro Strait, strt., Wa., U.S. . **A2** 140
Harper, Lib. **F3** 50
Harper, Ks., U.S. **E5** 109
Harper, co., Ks., U.S. **E5** 109
Harper, co., Ok., U.S. **A2** 129
Harper, Mount, mtn., Ak.,
    U.S. **C11** 95
Harpers Ferry, W.V., U.S. . . **B7** 141
Harpers Ferry National
    Historical Park, W.V.,
    U.S. **B7** 141
Harpersville, Al., U.S. **B3** 94
Harpeth, stm., Tn., U.S. . . . **A5** 135
Harqin Qi, China **A4** 30
Harquahala Mountain, mtn.,
    Az., U.S. **D2** 96
Harquahala Mountains,
    mts., Az., U.S. **D2** 96
Harrah, Ok., U.S. **B4** 129
Harricana, stm., Can. **H24** 82
Harriman, Tn., U.S. **D9** 135
Harriman Reservoir, res.,
    Vt., U.S. **F3** 138
Harrington, De., U.S. **E3** 101
Harrington Park, N.J., U.S. . **h9** 123
Harris, Mn., U.S. **E6** 116
Harris, co., Ga., U.S. **D2** 103
Harris, co., Tx., U.S. **E5** 136
Harris, Lake, l., Fl., U.S. . . **D5** 102
Harrisburg, Ar., U.S. **B5** 97
Harrisburg, Il., U.S. **F5** 106
Harrisburg, Or., U.S. **C3** 130
Harrisburg, Pa., U.S. **F8** 131
Harrisburg, S.D., U.S. **D9** 134
Harrismith, S. Afr. **E5** 56
Harrison, Ar., U.S. **A2** 97
Harrison, Mi., U.S. **D6** 115
Harrison, N.J., U.S. **k8** 123
Harrison, N.Y., U.S. **h13** 125
Harrison, Oh., U.S. **C1** 128
Harrison, Tn., U.S. **h11** 135
Harrison, co., Ia., U.S. . . . **C2** 108
Harrison, co., In., U.S. . . . **H5** 107
Harrison, co., Ky., U.S. . . . **B5** 110
Harrison, co., Mo., U.S. . . **A3** 118
Harrison, co., Ms., U.S. . . . **E4** 117
Harrison, co., Oh., U.S. . . . **B4** 128
Harrison, co., Tx., U.S. . . . **C5** 136
Harrison, co., W.V., U.S. . . **B4** 141
Harrison, Cape, c., Nf., Can.**g10** 88
Harrison Bay, b., Ak., U.S. . **A9** 95
Harrisonburg, Va., U.S. . . . **B4** 139
Harrison Hot Springs, B.C.,
    Can. **f14** 85

Harrison Lake, l., B.C., Can. **E7** 85
Harrisonville, Mo., U.S. . . **C3** 118
Harriston, On., Can. **D4** 89
Harristown, Il., U.S. **D4** 106
Harrisville, R.I., U.S. **B2** 132
Harrisville, Ut., U.S. **B3** 137
Harrisville, W.V., U.S. **B3** 141
Harrodsburg, Ky., U.S. . . . **C5** 110
Harrow, On., Can. **E2** 89
Harry S. Truman Reservoir,
    res., Mo., U.S. **C4** 118
Harry Strunk Lake, res., Ne.,
    U.S. **D5** 120
Harsīn, Iran **E12** 44
Harstad, Nor. **B7** 10
Hart, Mi., U.S. **E4** 115
Hart, Tx., U.S. **B1** 136
Hart, co., Ga., U.S. **B4** 103
Hart, co., Ky., U.S. **C4** 110
Hart, Lake, l., Fl., U.S. . . . **D5** 102
Hartford, Al., U.S. **D4** 94
Hartford, Ar., U.S. **B1** 97
Hartford, Ct., U.S. **B5** 100
Hartford, Ia., U.S. **C4** 108
Hartford, Il., U.S. **E3** 106
Hartford, Ky., U.S. **C3** 110
Hartford, Mi., U.S. **F4** 115
Hartford, S.D., U.S. **D9** 134
Hartford, Vt., U.S. **D4** 138
Hartford, Wi., U.S. **E5** 142
Hartford, co., Ct., U.S. . . . **B4** 100
Hartford City, In., U.S. . . . **D7** 107
Hartington, Ne., U.S. **B8** 120
Hartland, N.B., Can. **C2** 87
Hartland, Me., U.S. **D3** 112
Hartland, Wi., U.S. **E5** 142
Hartlepool, Eng., U.K. . . . **C6** 12
Hartley, Ia., U.S. **A2** 108
Hartley, co., Tx., U.S. **B1** 136
Hartney, Mb., Can. **E1** 86
Hartselle, Al., U.S. **A3** 94
Hartshorne, Ok., U.S. **C6** 129
Hartsville, S.C., U.S. **C7** 133
Hartsville, Tn., U.S. **A5** 135
Hartville, Oh., U.S. **B4** 128
Hartwell, Ga., U.S. **B4** 103
Hartwell Lake, res., U.S. . . **B1** 133
Harvard, Il., U.S. **A5** 106
Harvard, Ne., U.S. **D7** 120
Harvard, Mount, mtn., Co.,
    U.S. **C4** 99
Harvey, Il., U.S. **B6** 106
Harvey, La., U.S. **E5** 111
Harvey, Mi., U.S. **B3** 115
Harvey, N.D., U.S. **B6** 127
Harvey, co., Ks., U.S. **D6** 109
Harvey Lake, res., Pa., U.S. **m16** 131
Harveys Creek, stm., Pa.,
    U.S. **n16** 131
Harwich, Eng., U.K. **E7** 12
Harwich Port, Ma., U.S. . . **C7** 114
Harwinton, Ct., U.S. **B3** 100
Haryāna, prov., India **D3** 40
Hasalbag, China **B3** 40
Hasbrouck Heights, N.J.,
    U.S. **h8** 123
Haskell, Ar., U.S. **C3** 97
Haskell, Ok., U.S. **B6** 129
Haskell, Tx., U.S. **C3** 136
Haskell, co., Ks., U.S. **E3** 109
Haskell, co., Ok., U.S. . . . **B6** 129
Haskell, co., Tx., U.S. **C3** 136
Haskovo, Bul. **D10** 18
Hassan, India **G3** 40
Hassayampa, stm., Az., U.S. **D3** 96
Hasselt, Bel. **E9** 12
Hassi Messaoud, Alg. **D6** 48
Hässleholm, Swe. **H5** 10
Hastings, On., Can. **C7** 89
Hastings, N.Z. **o14** 63c
Hastings, Eng., U.K. **E7** 12
Hastings, Mi., U.S. **F5** 115
Hastings, Mn., U.S. **F6** 116
Hastings, Ne., U.S. **D7** 120
Hastings, Pa., U.S. **E4** 131
Hastings-on-Hudson, N.Y.,
    U.S. **h13** 125
Hat Creek, stm., S.D., U.S. **D2** 134
Hatfield, In., U.S. **I3** 107
Hatfield, Pa., U.S. **F11** 131
Hatgal, Mong. **A8** 28
Hāthras, India **D3** 40
Ha Tinh, Viet. **C5** 34
Hat Mountain, mtn., Az.,
    U.S. **E3** 96
Hatteras, N.C., U.S. **B7** 126
Hatteras, Cape, c., N.C.,
    U.S. **B7** 126
Hatteras Inlet, b., N.C., U.S. **B7** 126
Hattiesburg, Ms., U.S. . . . **D4** 117
Hatton, N.D., U.S. **B8** 127
Hat Yai, Thai. **E4** 34
Hatyrka, Russia **C19** 26
Haubstadt, In., U.S. **H2** 107

Haugesund, Nor. **G1** 10
Haughton, La., U.S. **B2** 111
Haukeligrend, Nor. **G2** 10
Haukivesi, l., Fin. **E13** 10
Hauraki Gulf, b., N.Z. **o13** 63c
Hauser, Or., U.S. **D2** 130
Haut, Isle au, i., Me., U.S. . **D4** 112
Haut Atlas, mts., Mor. **E2** 14
Hauula, Hi., U.S. **B4** 104
Havana see La Habana,
    Cuba **A3** 80
Havana, Fl., U.S. **B2** 102
Havana, Il., U.S. **C3** 106
Havasu, Lake, res., U.S. . . . **C1** 96
Havasupai Indian
    Reservation, Az., U.S. . . **A3** 96
Havelock, On., Can. **C7** 89
Havelock, N.C., U.S. **C6** 126
Havelock Island, i., India . . **G6** 40
Haven, Ks., U.S. **E6** 109
Haverford [Township], Pa.,
    U.S. **o20** 131
Haverhill, Ma., U.S. **A5** 114
Haverstraw, N.Y., U.S. . . . **D7** 125
Haviland, Ks., U.S. **E4** 109
Havre see Le Havre, Fr. . . . **C7** 16
Havre, Mt., U.S. **B7** 119
Havre de Grace, Md., U.S. . **A5** 113
Havre North, Mt., U.S. . . . **B7** 119
Havza, Tur. **B6** 44
Haw, stm., N.C., U.S. **B3** 126
Hawaii, co., Hi., U.S. **D6** 104
Hawaii, state, U.S. **C5** 104
Hawaii, i., Hi., U.S. **D6** 104
Hawaii, i., Hi., U.S. **i17** 92a
Hawaiian Islands, is., Hi.,
    U.S. **m14** 104
Hawaiian Ridge **F22** 64
Hawaii Volcanoes National
    Park, Hi., U.S. **D6** 104
Hawarden, Ia., U.S. **A1** 108
Hawera, N.Z. **o13** 63c
Hawesville, Ky., U.S. **C3** 110
Hawi, Hi., U.S. **C6** 104
Hawke Bay, b., N.Z. **o14** 63c
Hawker, Austl. **G2** 62
Hawkes, Mount, mtn., Ant. **E34** 87
Hawkesbury, On., Can. . . . **B10** 89
Hawkesbury Island, i., B.C.,
    Can. **C3** 85
Hawkins, co., Tn., U.S. . . . **C11** 135
Hawkinsville, Ga., U.S. . . . **D3** 103
Hawley, Mn., U.S. **D2** 116
Hawley, Pa., U.S. **D11** 131
Haworth, N.J., U.S. **h9** 123
Haw River, N.C., U.S. **A3** 126
Hawthorne, Ca., U.S. **n12** 98
Hawthorne, Fl., U.S. **C4** 102
Hawthorne, N.J., U.S. **B4** 123
Hawthorne, Nv., U.S. **E3** 121
Hawthorne, N.Y., U.S. . . . **g13** 125
Hawza, W. Sah. **A2** 50
Haxtun, Co., U.S. **A8** 99
Hay, Austl. **G3** 62
Hayden, Az., U.S. **E5** 96
Hayden, Co., U.S. **A3** 99
Hayden Lake, l., Id., U.S. . . **B2** 105
Hayes, La., U.S. **D3** 111
Hayes, co., Ne., U.S. **D4** 120
Hayes, stm., Mb., Can. . . . **B5** 86
Hayes, Mount, mtn., Ak.,
    U.S. **C10** 95
Hayfield, Mn., U.S. **G6** 116
Hayford Peak, mtn., Nv.,
    U.S. **G6** 121
Haymock Lake, l., Me., U.S. **B3** 112
Haynesville, La., U.S. **B2** 111
Hayneville, Al., U.S. **C3** 94
Hayrabolu, Tur. **B2** 44
Hays, Ks., U.S. **D4** 109
Hays, N.C., U.S. **A1** 126
Hays, co., Tx., U.S. **D3** 136
Hays Canyon Peak, mtn.,
    Nv., U.S. **B2** 121
Hay Springs, Ne., U.S. . . . **B3** 120
Haystack Mountain, mtn.,
    Nv., U.S. **B6** 121
Haysville, Ks., U.S. **g12** 109
Hayti, Mo., U.S. **E8** 118
Hayti Heights, Mo., U.S. . . **E8** 118
Hayward, Ca., U.S. **h8** 98
Hayward, Wi., U.S. **B2** 142
Haywood, co., N.C., U.S. . **f9** 126
Haywood, co., Tn., U.S. . . **B2** 135
Hazard, Ky., U.S. **C6** 110
Hazardville, Ct., U.S. **B6** 100
Hazārībāg, India **E5** 40
Hazel Crest, Il., U.S. **k9** 106
Hazel Dell, Wa., U.S. **D3** 140
Hazel Green, Al., U.S. . . . **A3** 94
Hazel Park, Mi., U.S. **p15** 115
Hazelton Pyramid, mtn.,
    Wy., U.S. **B5** 143
Hazelwood, N.C., U.S. . . . **f10** 126
Hazen, Ar., U.S. **C4** 97
Hazen, N.D., U.S. **B4** 127
Hazen Bay, b., Ak., U.S. . . **C6** 95
Hazlehurst, Ms., U.S. **D3** 117
Hazlet, N.J., U.S. **C4** 123
Hazleton, Ia., U.S. **B6** 108
Hazleton, Pa., U.S. **E10** 131
Head Harbor Island, i., Me.,
    U.S. **D5** 112

Name	Map Ref.	Page

Headland, Al., U.S. **D4** 94
Headley, Mount, mtn., Mt.,
　U.S. **C1** 119
Healdsburg, Ca., U.S. **C2** 98
Healdton, Ok., U.S. **C4** 129
Healesville, Austl. **H4** 62
Healy, Ak., U.S. **C10** 95
Heard, co., Ga., U.S. **C1** 103
Hearne, Tx., U.S. **D4** 136
Hearst, On., Can. **o19** 89
Heart, stm., N.D., U.S. . . . **C3** 127
Heart Butte Dam, N.D.,
　U.S. **C4** 127
Heart Lake, l., Wy., U.S. . . **B2** 143
Heart's Content, Nf., Can. . **E5** 88
Heath, Oh., U.S. **B3** 128
Heath Springs, S.C., U.S. . . **B6** 133
Heavener, Ok., U.S. **C7** 129
Hebbronville, Tx., U.S. . . . **F3** 136
Hebei, state, China **D11** 28
Heber, Az., U.S. **C5** 96
Heber City, Ut., U.S. **C4** 137
Heber Springs, Ar., U.S. . . . **B3** 97
Hébertville, P.Q., Can. . . . **A6** 90
Hebgen Lake, res., Mt., U.S. **F5** 119
Hebi, China **D10** 28
Hebrides, is., Scot., U.K. . . **D4** 6
Hebrides, Sea of the, Scot.,
　U.K. **B3** 12
Hebron, N.S., Can. **F3** 87
Hebron, Il., U.S. **A5** 106
Hebron, In., U.S. **B3** 107
Hebron, Ky., U.S. **h13** 110
Hebron, Md., U.S. **D6** 113
Hebron, N.D., U.S. **C3** 127
Hebron, Ne., U.S. **D8** 120
Hebron, Oh., U.S. **C3** 128
Hebron see Al-Khalīl, W.B. . **G6** 44
Hecate Strait, strt., B.C.,
　Can. **C2** 85
Hecelchakán, Mex. **C6** 78
Heceta Island, i., Ak., U.S. . **n23** 95
Hechi, China **G9** 28
Hechuan, China **D2** 30
Hecla Island, i., Mb., Can. . **D3** 86
Hector, Mn., U.S. **F4** 116
Hedemora, Swe. **F6** 10
He Devil, mtn., Id., U.S. . . **D2** 105
Hedrick, Ia., U.S. **C5** 108
Ḥefa (Haifa), Isr. **D2** 42
Hefei, China **E11** 28
Heflin, Al., U.S. **B4** 94
Hefner, Lake, res., Ok., U.S. **B4** 129
Hegang, China **B14** 28
Hegins, Pa., U.S. **E9** 131
Heide, Ger. **C11** 12
Heidelberg, Ger. **F11** 12
Heidelberg, Ms., U.S. **D5** 117
Heidrick, Ky., U.S. **D6** 110
Heilbron, S. Afr. **D4** 56
Heilbronn, Ger. **F11** 12
Heilong (Amur), stm., Asia . **D14** 26
Heilongjiang, state, China . . **B13** 28
Heilongjiang see Heilong,
　stm., Asia **D16** 26
Heilongjiang see Amur,
　stm., Asia **D16** 26
Heinävesi, Fin. **E13** 10
Hejaz see Al-Ḥijāz, reg.,
　Sau. Ar. **E3** 38
Hejian, China **B4** 30
Hejiang, China **D2** 30
Hekimhan, Tur. **C7** 44
Hekla, vol., Ice. **l19** 10a
Hekou, China **G8** 28
Helagsfjället, mtn., Swe. . . **E5** 10
Helena, Al., U.S. **B3** 94
Helena, Ar., U.S. **C5** 97
Helena, Ga., U.S. **D4** 103
Helena, Mt., U.S. **D4** 119
Helena, Ok., U.S. **A3** 129
Helensville, N.Z. **o13** 63c
Helgoländer Bucht, b., Ger. **C11** 12
Heli, China **A2** 31
Hellam, Pa., U.S. **G8** 131
Hellertown, Pa., U.S. **E11** 131
Hellín, Spain **H6** 16
Hells Canyon, val., U.S. . . **B10** 130
Hells Canyon National
　Recreation Area, U.S. . **B10** 130
Hell-Ville see Andoany,
　Madag. **A8** 56
Helmand, stm., Asia **D8** 42
Helmeringhausen, Nmb. . . **D2** 56
Helmstedt, Ger. **D12** 12
Helotes, Tx., U.S. **h7** 136
Helper, Ut., U.S. **D5** 137
Helsingborg, Swe. **H5** 10
Helsingfors see Helsinki,
　Fin. **F11** 10
Helsingør, Den. **H5** 10
Helsinki (Helsingfors), Fin. . **F11** 10
Hematite, Mo., U.S. **C7** 118
Hemet, Ca., U.S. **F5** 98
Hemingford, Ne., U.S. **B2** 120
Hemingway, S.C., U.S. . . . **D9** 133
Hemlock, Mi., U.S. **E6** 115
Hemlock Reservoir, res.,
　Ct., U.S. **E2** 100
Hemmingford, P.Q., Can. . . **D4** 90
Hemphill, Tx., U.S. **D6** 136
Hemphill, co., Tx., U.S. . . **B2** 136
Hempstead, N.Y., U.S. . . . **n15** 125
Hempstead, Tx., U.S. **D4** 136
Hempstead, co., Ar., U.S. . **D2** 97

Hemsön, i., Swe. **E8** 10
Henagar, Al., U.S. **A4** 94
Henan, state, China **E10** 28
Hendek, Tur. **B4** 44
Henderson, Ky., U.S. **C2** 110
Henderson, La., U.S. **D4** 111
Henderson, Mn., U.S. **F5** 116
Henderson, N.C., U.S. . . . **A4** 126
Henderson, Ne., U.S. **D8** 120
Henderson, Nv., U.S. **G7** 121
Henderson, Tn., U.S. **B3** 135
Henderson, Tx., U.S. **C5** 136
Henderson, co., Il., U.S. . . **C3** 106
Henderson, co., Ky., U.S. . . **C2** 110
Henderson, co., N.C., U.S. . **f10** 126
Henderson, co., Tn., U.S. . . **B3** 135
Henderson, co., Tx., U.S. . . **C5** 136
Henderson Island, i., Pit. . . **G17** 58
Henderson's Point, Ms.,
　U.S. **g7** 117
Hendersonville, N.C., U.S. . **f10** 126
Hendersonville, Tn., U.S. . . **A5** 135
Hendricks, Mn., U.S. **F2** 116
Hendricks, co., In., U.S. . . **E4** 107
Hendry, co., Fl., U.S. **F5** 102
Hengshan, China **D9** 28
Hengshan, China **D3** 30
Hengxian, China **E2** 30
Hengyang, China **F10** 28
Heniches'k, Ukr. **F13** 20
Henlawson, W.V., U.S. . . . **n12** 141
Henlopen, Cape, c., De.,
　U.S. **E5** 101
Hennebont, Fr. **D5** 16
Hennepin, co., Mn., U.S. . . **E5** 116
Hennessey, Ok., U.S. **A4** 129
Henniker, N.H., U.S. **D3** 122
Henning, Mn., U.S. **D3** 116
Henning, Tn., U.S. **B2** 135
Henrico, co., Va., U.S. . . . **C5** 139
Henrietta, N.C., U.S. **B1** 126
Henrietta, Tx., U.S. **C3** 136
Henrietta Maria, Cape, c.,
　On., Can. **n19** 89
Henry, Il., U.S. **B4** 106
Henry, co., Al., U.S. **D4** 94
Henry, co., Ga., U.S. **C2** 103
Henry, co., Ia., U.S. **C6** 108
Henry, co., Il., U.S. **B3** 106
Henry, co., In., U.S. **E7** 107
Henry, co., Ky., U.S. **B4** 110
Henry, co., Mo., U.S. **C4** 118
Henry, co., Oh., U.S. **A1** 128
Henry, co., Tn., U.S. **A3** 135
Henry, co., Va., U.S. **D3** 139
Henry, Mount, mtn., Mt.,
　U.S. **B1** 119
Henryetta, Ok., U.S. **B6** 129
Henrys Fork, stm., U.S. . . . **E2** 143
Henryville, P.Q., Can. **D4** 90
Henryville, In., U.S. **G6** 107
Hensall, On., Can. **D3** 89
Hentiesbaai, Nmb. **C1** 56
Henzada, Myan. **C3** 34
Hephzibah, Ga., U.S. **C4** 103
Heppner, Or., U.S. **B7** 130
Hepu, China **G9** 28
Hequ, China **B3** 30
Herāt, Afg. **D8** 42
Herbert G. West, Lake, res.,
　Wa., U.S. **C7** 140
Herbes, Isle aux, i., Al., U.S. **E1** 94
Herculaneum, Mo., U.S. . . **C7** 118
Hereford, Eng., U.K. **D5** 12
Hereford, Md., U.S. **A4** 113
Hereford, Tx., U.S. **B1** 136
Hereford Inlet, b., N.J., U.S. **E3** 123
Herford, Ger. **D11** 12
Herington, Ks., U.S. **D7** 109
Herkimer, N.Y., U.S. **B6** 125
Herkimer, co., N.Y., U.S. . . **B5** 125
Hermann, Mo., U.S. **C6** 118
Hermano Peak, mtn., Co.,
　U.S. **D2** 99
Hermantown, Mn., U.S. . . **D6** 116
Hermanus, S. Afr. **E2** 56
Herminie, Pa., U.S. **F2** 131
Hermiston, Or., U.S. **B7** 130
Hermitage, Nf., Can. **E4** 88
Hermitage, Ar., U.S. **D3** 97
Hermitage Bay, b., Nf., Can. **E3** 88
Hermit Islands, is., Pap. N.
　Gui. **G12** 32
Hermon, Mount, mtn., Asia **F6** 44
Hermosillo, Mex. **B2** 78
Hernando, Fl., U.S. **D4** 102
Hernando, Ms., U.S. **A4** 117
Hernando, co., Fl., U.S. . . **D4** 102
Herndon, Va., U.S. **B5** 139
Herning, Den. **H3** 10
Heron Lake, Mn., U.S. . . . **G3** 116
Herrera, Arg. **D5** 72
Herrin, Il., U.S. **F4** 106
Herring Bay, b., Md., U.S. . **C4** 113
Herring Cove, N.S., Can. . . **E6** 87
Herrington Lake, res., Ky.,
　U.S. **C5** 110
Herscher, Il., U.S. **B5** 106
Hershey, Pa., U.S. **F8** 131
Hertford, N.C., U.S. **A6** 126
Hertford, co., N.C., U.S. . . **A5** 126
Hervey Bay, b., Austl. **E5** 62
Heshan, China **E2** 30
Heshun, China **B3** 30
Hesperia, Ca., U.S. **E5** 98

Hesperia, Mi., U.S. **E4** 115
Hesperus Mountain, mtn.,
　Co., U.S. **D2** 99
Hesston, Ks., U.S. **D6** 109
Heta, stm., Russia **B11** 26
Hettinger, N.D., U.S. **D3** 127
Hettinger, co., N.D., U.S. . . **C3** 127
Hexian, China **G10** 28
Heyburn, Id., U.S. **G5** 105
Heyuan, China **E3** 30
Heyworth, Il., U.S. **C5** 106
Heze, China **B4** 30
Hialeah, Fl., U.S. **G6** 102
Hiawatha, Ia., U.S. **B6** 108
Hiawatha, Ks., U.S. **C8** 109
Hibbing, Mn., U.S. **C6** 116
Hickam Air Force Base, mil.,
　Hi., U.S. **g10** 104
Hickman, Ky., U.S. **f8** 110
Hickman, Ne., U.S. **D9** 120
Hickman, co., Ky., U.S. . . . **f8** 110
Hickman, co., Tn., U.S. . . . **B4** 135
Hickory, N.C., U.S. **B1** 126
Hickory, co., Mo., U.S. . . . **D4** 118
Hicksville, N.Y., U.S. **E7** 125
Hicksville, Oh., U.S. **A1** 128
Hico, Tx., U.S. **D3** 136
Hico, W.V., U.S. **C3** 141
Hidalgo, Mex. **C5** 78
Hidalgo, Tx., U.S. **F3** 136
Hidalgo, state, Mex. **C5** 78
Hidalgo, co., N.M., U.S. . . **F1** 124
Hidalgo, co., Tx., U.S. . . . **F3** 136
Hidalgo del Parral, Mex. . . **B3** 78
Hidden Lake, res., Md.,
　U.S. **C6** 113
Hiddenite, N.C., U.S. **B1** 126
Hieroglyphic Mountains,
　mts., Az., U.S. **k8** 96
Higbee, Mo., U.S. **B5** 118
Higganum, Ct., U.S. **D5** 100
Higgins Lake, l., Mi., U.S. . **D6** 115
Higgins Millpond, res., Md.,
　U.S. **C6** 113
Higginsville, Mo., U.S. . . . **B4** 118
High Bridge, N.J., U.S. . . . **B3** 123
High Falls Reservoir, res.,
　Wi., U.S. **C5** 142
High Island, i., Mi., U.S. . . **C5** 115
Highland, Il., U.S. **E4** 106
Highland, In., U.S. **A3** 107
Highland, Ks., U.S. **C8** 109
Highland, Mi., U.S. **o14** 115
Highland, N.Y., U.S. **D7** 125
Highland, Wi., U.S. **E3** 142
Highland, co., Oh., U.S. . . **C2** 128
Highland, co., Va., U.S. . . **B3** 139
Highland Lake, l., Me., U.S. **g7** 112
Highland Lakes, N.J., U.S. . **A4** 123
Highland Park, Il., U.S. . . . **A6** 106
Highland Park, Mi., U.S. . . **p15** 115
Highland Park, Tx., U.S. . . **n10** 136
Highland Peak, mtn., Ca.,
　U.S. **C4** 98
Highland Point, c., Fl., U.S. **G5** 102
Highlands, N.C., U.S. **f9** 126
Highlands, N.J., U.S. **C5** 123
Highlands, Tx., U.S. **r14** 136
Highlands, co., Fl., U.S. . . **E5** 102
Highland Springs, Va., U.S. **C5** 139
High Level, Ab., Can. **f7** 84
Highmore, S.D., U.S. **C6** 134
High Point, N.C., U.S. . . . **B2** 126
High Prairie, Ab., Can. . . . **B2** 84
High Ridge, Mo., U.S. . . . **g12** 118
High River, Ab., Can. **D4** 84
Highrock Lake, l., Mb., Can. **B1** 86
High Rock Lake, res., N.C.,
　U.S. **B2** 126
High Spire, Pa., U.S. **F8** 131
High Springs, Fl., U.S. . . . **C4** 102
Hightstown, N.J., U.S. . . . **C3** 123
Highwood, Il., U.S. **A6** 106
Highwood Baldy, mtn., Mt.,
　U.S. **C6** 119
Highwood Mountains, mts.,
　Mt., U.S. **C6** 119
Higuera de Abuya, Mex. . . **C3** 78
Higüey, Dom. Rep. **B6** 80
Hiiumaa, i., Est. **G10** 10
Hiko Range, mts., Nv., U.S. **F6** 121
Hilbert, Wi., U.S. **D5** 142
Hildale, Ut., U.S. **F3** 137
Hilden, N.S., Can. **D6** 87
Hildesheim, Ger. **D11** 12
Hill, co., Mt., U.S. **B6** 119
Hill, co., Tx., U.S. **D4** 136
Hillaby, Mount, mtn., Barb. **80** 80
Hill City, Ks., U.S. **C4** 109
Hill City, S.D., U.S. **D2** 134
Hillcrest, Il., U.S. **B4** 106
Hillcrest Heights, Md., U.S. **C4** 113
Hilliard, Fl., U.S. **B5** 102
Hilliard, Oh., U.S. **k10** 128
Hill Lake, l., Ar., U.S. **h10** 97
Hills, Ia., U.S. **C6** 108
Hills, Mn., U.S. **G2** 116
Hillsboro, Il., U.S. **D4** 106
Hillsboro, Ks., U.S. **D6** 109
Hillsboro, Mo., U.S. **C7** 118
Hillsboro, N.D., U.S. **B8** 127
Hillsboro, N.H., U.S. **D3** 122
Hillsboro, Oh., U.S. **C2** 128
Hillsboro, Or., U.S. **B4** 130
Hillsboro, Tx., U.S. **C4** 136
Hillsboro, Wi., U.S. **E3** 142

Hillsboro Canal, Fl., U.S. . . **F6** 102
Hillsborough, N.B., Can. . . **D5** 87
Hillsborough, N.C., U.S. . . **A3** 126
Hillsborough, co., Fl., U.S. . **E4** 102
Hillsborough, co., N.H.,
　U.S. **E3** 122
Hillsborough Bay, b., P.E.I.,
　Can. **C6** 87
Hillsburgh, On., Can. **D4** 89
Hills Creek Lake, res., Or.,
　U.S. **D4** 130
Hillsdale, Mi., U.S. **G6** 115
Hillsdale, N.J., U.S. **g8** 123
Hillsdale, co., Mi., U.S. . . **G6** 115
Hillside, N.J., U.S. **k8** 123
Hillsville, Pa., U.S. **D1** 131
Hillsville, Va., U.S. **D2** 139
Hilo, Hi., U.S. **D6** 104
Hilo Bay, b., Hi., U.S. . . . **D6** 104
Hilok, Russia **D13** 26
Hilton, N.Y., U.S. **B3** 125
Hilton Head Island, S.C.,
　U.S. **G6** 133
Hilton Head Island, i., S.C.,
　U.S. **G6** 133
Hilvan, Tur. **D8** 44
Himāchal Pradesh, prov.,
　India **C3** 40
Himalayas, mts., Asia **C3** 40
Himatnagar, India **E2** 40
Himeji, Japan **D2** 31
Ḥimṣ, Syria **E7** 44
Hinchinbrook Island, i.,
　Austl. **D4** 62
Hinchinbrook Island, i., Ak.,
　U.S. **g18** 95
Hinckley, Il., U.S. **B5** 106
Hinckley, Mn., U.S. **D6** 116
Hinckley, Ut., U.S. **D3** 137
Hinckley Reservoir, res.,
　N.Y., U.S. **B5** 125
Hindman, Ky., U.S. **C7** 110
Hinds, co., Ms., U.S. **C3** 117
Hindu Kush, mts., Asia . . . **C1** 40
Hindupur, India **G3** 40
Hines, Or., U.S. **D7** 130
Hinesville, Ga., U.S. **E5** 103
Hinganghāt, India **E3** 40
Hingham, Ma., U.S. **B6** 114
Hingham Bay, b., Ma., U.S. **g12** 114
Hingol, stm., Pak. **E9** 42
Hingoli, India **F3** 40
Hinis, Tur. **C9** 44
Hinnøya, i., Nor. **B6** 10
Hinsdale, Il., U.S. **k9** 106
Hinsdale, N.H., U.S. **E2** 122
Hinsdale, co., Co., U.S. . . **D3** 99
Hinton, Ab., Can. **C2** 84
Hinton, Ia., U.S. **B1** 108
Hinton, Ok., U.S. **B3** 129
Hinton, W.V., U.S. **D4** 141
Hīrākud Reservoir, res.,
　India **E4** 40
Hiram, Ga., U.S. **C2** 103
Hiram, Oh., U.S. **A4** 128
Hirara, Japan **B9** 34
Hirfanlı Barajı, res., Tur. . . **C5** 44
Hiriyūr, India **G3** 40
Hirosaki, Japan **C16** 28
Hiroshima, Japan **E14** 28
Hirson, Fr. **C9** 16
Hirtshals, Den. **H3** 10
Hisār, India **D3** 40
Hispaniola, i., N.A. **A5** 80
Hita, Japan **D2** 31
Hitachi, Japan **D16** 28
Hitchcock, Tx., U.S. **r14** 136
Hitchcock, co., Ne., U.S. . . **D4** 120
Hitchcock Lake, Ct., U.S. . **C4** 100
Hitoyoshi, Japan **D2** 31
Hiva, Uzb. **B8** 42
Hiwassee, stm., Tn., U.S. . **D9** 135
Hiwassee Lake, res., N.C.,
　U.S. **f8** 126
Hjälmaren, l., Swe. **G6** 10
Hjelmelandsvågen, Nor. . . . **G2** 10
Hjørring, Den. **H3** 10
Hkakabo Razi, mtn., Myan. **A3** 34
Hlukhiv, Ukr. **D12** 20
Hlusk, Bela. **C10** 20
Hlybokae, Bela. **B9** 20
Ho, Ghana **E5** 50
Hoa Binh, Viet. **B5** 34
Hoagland, In., U.S. **C8** 107
Hoback, stm., Wy., U.S. . . **C2** 143
Hobart, Austl. **I4** 62
Hobart, In., U.S. **A3** 107
Hobart, Ok., U.S. **B2** 129
Hobbs, N.M., U.S. **E6** 124
Hobbs Coast, Ant. **D28** 67
Hobe Sound, Fl., U.S. . . . **E6** 102
Hoboken, N.J., U.S. **k8** 123
Hobyo, Som. **I14** 48
Ho Chi Minh City see
　Thanh Pho Ho Chi
　Minh, Viet. **D5** 34
Hockessin, De., U.S. **A3** 101
Hocking, co., Oh., U.S. . . **C3** 128
Hocking, stm., Oh., U.S. . . **C3** 128
Hockley, co., Tx., U.S. . . . **C1** 136
Hôd, reg., Maur. **C3** 50
Hodeida see Al-Hudaydah,
　Yemen **H4** 38
Hodgeman, co., Ks., U.S. . **D4** 109

Hodgenville, Ky., U.S. . . . **C4** 110
Hodges Village Reservoir,
　res., Ma., U.S. **B4** 114
Hódmezővásárhely, Hung. . **F6** 20
Hodna, Chott el, l., Alg. . . **C5** 48
Hodonín, Czech Rep. **E4** 20
Hodžejli, Uzb. **B7** 42
Hoeryŏng-ŭp, N. Kor. . . . **B1** 31
Hof, Ger. **E12** 12
Höfðakaupstaður, Ice. . . . **l18** 10a
Hoffman Estates, Il., U.S. . **h8** 106
Hofors, Swe. **F7** 10
Hofsjökull, Ice. **l19** 10a
Hōfu, Japan **D2** 31
Höganäs, Swe. **H5** 10
Hogansville, Ga., U.S. . . . **C2** 103
Hogback Mountain, mtn.,
　Mt., U.S. **F4** 119
Hoggar see Ahaggar, mts.,
　Alg. **F6** 48
Hog Island, i., Fl., U.S. . . . **C3** 102
Hog Island, i., Mi., U.S. . . **C5** 115
Hog Island, i., N.C., U.S. . . **B6** 126
Hog Island, i., R.I., U.S. . . **D5** 132
Hog Island, i., Va., U.S. . . **C7** 139
Hoh, stm., Wa., U.S. **B1** 140
Hohenwald, Tn., U.S. **B4** 135
Hoh Head, c., Wa., U.S. . . **B1** 140
Hohhot, China **C10** 28
Hohoe, Ghana **E5** 50
Ho-Ho-Kus, N.J., U.S. . . . **h8** 123
Hoh Xil Shan, mts., China . **D5** 28
Hoi An, Viet. **C5** 34
Hoima, Ug. **C6** 54
Hoisington, Ks., U.S. **D5** 109
Hojniki, Bela. **D10** 20
Hokah, Mn., U.S. **G7** 116
Hoke, co., N.C., U.S. **B3** 126
Hokes Bluff, Al., U.S. **B4** 94
Hokitika, N.Z. **p13** 63c
Hokkaidō, i., Japan **C16** 28
Hoktemberjan, Arm. **B11** 44
Hola Prystan', Ukr. **F12** 20
Holbrook, Az., U.S. **C5** 96
Holbrook, Ma., U.S. **B5** 114
Holcomb, Ks., U.S. **E3** 109
Holden, Ma., U.S. **B4** 114
Holden, Mo., U.S. **C4** 118
Holden, W.V., U.S. **D2** 141
Holdenville, Ok., U.S. . . . **B5** 129
Holdrege, Ne., U.S. **D6** 120
Hole in the Mountain Peak,
　mtn., Nv., U.S. **C6** 121
Holgate, Oh., U.S. **A1** 128
Holguín, Cuba **A4** 80
Holladay, Ut., U.S. **C4** 137
Holland, In., U.S. **H3** 107
Holland, Mi., U.S. **F4** 115
Holland, Oh., U.S. **A2** 128
Holland, Tx., U.S. **D4** 136
Hollandale, Ms., U.S. **B3** 117
Hollandia see Jayapura,
　Indon. **G11** 32
Holland Island, i., Md., U.S. **D5** 113
Holland Point, c., Md., U.S. **C4** 113
Holland Straits, strt., Md.,
　U.S. **D5** 113
Holley, N.Y., U.S. **B2** 125
Holliday, Tx., U.S. **C3** 136
Hollidaysburg, Pa., U.S. . . **F5** 131
Hollins, Va., U.S. **C3** 139
Hollis, Ok., U.S. **C2** 129
Hollister, Ca., U.S. **D3** 98
Hollister, Mo., U.S. **E4** 118
Holliston, Ma., U.S. **B5** 114
Holloman Air Force Base,
　mil., N.M., U.S. **E3** 124
Hollow Rock, Tn., U.S. . . . **A3** 135
Hollowtop Mountain, mtn.,
　Mt., U.S. **E4** 119
Holly, Co., U.S. **C8** 99
Holly, Mi., U.S. **F7** 115
Holly Grove, Ar., U.S. . . . **C4** 97
Holly Hill, Fl., U.S. **C5** 102
Holly Hill, S.C., U.S. **E7** 133
Holly Pond, Al., U.S. **A3** 94
Holly Ridge, N.C., U.S. . . **C5** 126
Holly Shelter Swamp, sw.,
　N.C., U.S. **C5** 126
Holly Springs, Ga., U.S. . . **B2** 103
Holly Springs, Ms., U.S. . . **A4** 117
Holly Springs, N.C., U.S. . . **B4** 126
Hollywood, Al., U.S. **A4** 94
Hollywood, Fl., U.S. **F6** 102
Hollywood, Md., U.S. . . . **D4** 113
Hollywood, S.C., U.S. . . . **k11** 133
Hollywood Indian
　Reservation, Fl., U.S. . . **r3** 102
Holmen, Wi., U.S. **E2** 142
Holmes, co., Fl., U.S. **u16** 102
Holmes, co., Ms., U.S. . . . **B3** 117
Holmes, co., Oh., U.S. . . . **B4** 128
Holmes, Mount, mtn., Wy.,
　U.S. **B2** 143
Holmsk, Russia **E16** 26
Holoby, Ukr. **D8** 20
Holstebro, Den. **H3** 10
Holstein, Ia., U.S. **B2** 108
Holsteinsborg, Grnld. **E29** 82
Holston, stm., Tn., U.S. . . **C11** 135
Holston, Middle Fork, stm.,
　Va., U.S. **f10** 139
Holston High Knob, mtn.,
　Tn., U.S. **C11** 135
Holt, Al., U.S. **B2** 94

Name	Map Ref.	Page
Holt, Mi., U.S.	F6	115
Holt, co., Mo., U.S.	A2	118
Holt, co., Ne., U.S.	B7	120
Holt Lake, res., Al., U.S.	B2	94
Holton, Ks., U.S.	C8	109
Holtville, Ca., U.S.	F6	98
Holualoa, Hi., U.S.	D6	104
Holy Cross, Mountain of the, mtn., Co., U.S.	B4	99
Holyhead, Wales, U.K.	D4	12
Holyoke, Co., U.S.	A8	99
Holyoke, Ma., U.S.	B2	114
Holyoke Range, hills, Ma., U.S.	B2	114
Homalin, Myan.	B2	34
Hombori Tondo, mtn., Mali	C4	50
Hombre Muerto, Salar del, pl., Arg.	D4	72
Homecroft, In., U.S.	m10	107
Homedale, Id., U.S.	F2	105
Home Hill, Austl.	D4	62
Homel', Bela.	C11	20
Homeland, Ga., U.S.	F4	103
Home Place, In., U.S.	E5	107
Homer, Ak., U.S.	D9	95
Homer, Ga., U.S.	B3	103
Homer, Il., U.S.	C6	106
Homer, La., U.S.	B2	111
Homer, Mi., U.S.	F6	115
Homer, N.Y., U.S.	C4	125
Homer City, Pa., U.S.	E3	131
Homerville, Ga., U.S.	E4	103
Homer Youngs Peak, mtn., Mt., U.S.	E3	119
Homestead, Fl., U.S.	G6	102
Homestead, Pa., U.S.	k14	131
Homestead National Monument of America, Ne., U.S.	D9	120
Homewood, Al., U.S.	g7	94
Homewood, Il., U.S.	B6	106
Homewood, Oh., U.S.	C1	128
Hominy, Ok., U.S.	A5	129
Hominy Creek, stm., Ok., U.S.	A5	129
Homme Dam, N.D., U.S.	A8	127
Homochitto, stm., Ms., U.S.	D2	117
Homosassa, Fl., U.S.	D4	102
Homs see Al-Khums, Libya	E6	14
Homs see Ḥimṣ, Syria	E7	44
Honaker, Va., U.S.	e10	139
Honan see Henan, state, China	E10	28
Honaunau, Hi., U.S.	D6	104
Honda, Col.	B5	70
Hondo, Tx., U.S.	E3	136
Hondo, stm., N.A.	B2	80
Hondo, Rio, stm., N.M., U.S.	D4	124
Honduras, ctry., N.A.	C2	80
Honduras, Gulf of, b., N.A.	B2	80
Honea Path, S.C., U.S.	C3	133
Honefoss, Nor.	F4	10
Honeoye Falls, N.Y., U.S.	C3	125
Honesdale, Pa., U.S.	C11	131
Honey Brook, Pa., U.S.	F10	131
Honey Grove, Tx., U.S.	C5	136
Honey Lake, l., Ca., U.S.	B3	98
Honeypot Glen, Ct., U.S.	C4	100
Honeyville, Ut., U.S.	B3	137
Hong, Song see Red, stm., Asia	B4	34
Hon Gai, Viet.	B5	34
Honga River, b., Md., U.S.	D5	113
Hongjiang, China	F9	28
Hong Kong see Xianggang, China	E3	30
Hongliuyuan, China	C7	28
Hongshui, stm., China	G9	28
Hongtong, China	B3	30
Hongze, China	C4	30
Hongze Hu, l., China	E11	28
Honiara, Sol. Is.	B6	62
Honjō, Japan	C3	31
Honokaa, Hi., U.S.	C6	104
Honolulu, Hi., U.S.	B4	104
Honolulu, co., Hi., U.S.	B3	104
Honolulu International Airport, Hi., U.S.	g10	104
Honomu, Hi., U.S.	D6	104
Honouliuli, Hi., U.S.	g9	104
Honshū, i., Japan	D16	28
Honuapo Bay, b., Hi., U.S.	D6	104
Honuu, Russia	C16	26
Hood, co., Tx., U.S.	C4	136
Hood, Mount, mtn., Or., U.S.	B5	130
Hood Canal, b., Wa., U.S.	B2	140
Hoodoo Peak, mtn., Wa., U.S.	A5	140
Hood Point, c., Austl.	G2	60
Hood River, Or., U.S.	B5	130
Hood River, co., Or., U.S.	B5	130
Hoodsport, Wa., U.S.	B2	140
Hoogeveen, Neth.	D10	12
Hooker, Ok., U.S.	e9	129
Hooker, co., Ne., U.S.	C5	120
Hooker Creek, Austl.	D5	60
Hooksett, N.H., U.S.	D4	122
Hoonah, Ak., U.S.	D12	95
Hoopa Valley Indian Reservation, Ca., U.S.	B2	98
Hooper, Ne., U.S.	C9	120
Hooper Bay, Ak., U.S.	C6	95
Hooper Islands, is., Md., U.S.	D5	113
Hooper Strait, strt., Md., U.S.	D5	113
Hoopes Reservoir, res., De., U.S.	A3	101
Hoopeston, Il., U.S.	C6	106
Hoorn, Neth.	D9	12
Hoosac Range, mts., U.S.	A1	114
Hoosic, stm., U.S.	C7	125
Hoosick Falls, N.Y., U.S.	C7	125
Hoover Dam, U.S.	G7	121
Hoover Reservoir, res., Oh., U.S.	B3	128
Hooverson Heights, W.V., U.S.	f8	141
Hopa, Tur.	B9	44
Hopatcong, N.J., U.S.	B3	123
Hopatcong, Lake, l., N.J., U.S.	A3	123
Hope, B.C., Can.	E7	85
Hope, Ar., U.S.	D2	97
Hope, In., U.S.	F6	107
Hope, R.I., U.S.	D3	132
Hope, Point, c., Ak., U.S.	B6	95
Hopedale, Il., U.S.	C4	106
Hopedale, Ma., U.S.	B4	114
Hope Island, i., R.I., U.S.	E5	132
Hopelchén, Mex.	D7	78
Hope Mills, N.C., U.S.	C4	126
Hopër, stm., Russia	D7	22
Hopes Advance, Cap, c., P.Q., Can.	f13	90
Hopetoun, Austl.	G3	60
Hopetown, S. Afr.	D3	56
Hope Valley, R.I., U.S.	E2	132
Hopewell, Va., U.S.	C5	139
Hopewell Junction, N.Y., U.S.	D7	125
Hopi Indian Reservation, Az., U.S.	A5	96
Hopkins, Mn., U.S.	n12	116
Hopkins, S.C., U.S.	D6	133
Hopkins, co., Ky., U.S.	C2	110
Hopkins, co., Tx., U.S.	C5	136
Hopkinsville, Ky., U.S.	D2	110
Hopkinton, Ia., U.S.	B6	108
Hopkinton, Ma., U.S.	B4	114
Hopkinton, R.I., U.S.	F1	132
Hopkinton Lake, res., N.H., U.S.	D3	122
Hopwood, Pa., U.S.	G2	131
Hoquiam, Wa., U.S.	C2	140
Hor, Russia	A2	31
Horace, N.D., U.S.	C9	127
Horace Mountain, mtn., Ak., U.S.	B10	95
Horasan, Tur.	B10	44
Horatio, Ar., U.S.	D1	97
Horicon, Wi., U.S.	E5	142
Horine, Mo., U.S.	C7	118
Horlick Mountains, mts., Ant.	E29	67
Horlivka, Ukr.	E15	20
Hormuz, Strait of, strt., Asia	E7	42
Horn, c., Ice.	k17	10a
Horn, Cape see Hornos, Cabo de, c., Chile	I3	69
Hornavan, l., Swe.	C7	10
Hornell, N.Y., U.S.	C3	125
Hornersville, Mo., U.S.	E7	118
Horn Island, i., Ms., U.S.	E5	117
Horn Island Pass, strt., Ms., U.S.	g8	117
Horn Lake, Ms., U.S.	A3	117
Hornos, Cabo de (Horn, Cape), c., Chile	I3	69
Horodenka, Ukr.	E8	20
Horodnia, Ukr.	D11	20
Horodok, Ukr.	E7	20
Horqin Youyi Qianqi, China	B12	28
Horry, co., S.C., U.S.	D10	133
Horse, stm., Ct., U.S.	C6	100
Horse Cave, Ky., U.S.	C4	110
Horse Creek, stm., U.S.	E8	143
Horse Creek Reservoir, res., Co., U.S.	C7	99
Horsehead Lake, l., N.D., U.S.	B6	127
Horseheads, N.Y., U.S.	C4	125
Horse Heaven Hills, hills, Wa., U.S.	C6	140
Horsens, Den.	I3	10
Horse Peak, mtn., N.M., U.S.	D1	124
Horseshoe Bend, Id., U.S.	F2	105
Horseshoe Bend National Military Park, Al., U.S.	C4	94
Horseshoe Cove, b., Fl., U.S.	C3	102
Horseshoe Point, c., Fl., U.S.	C3	102
Horseshoe Reservoir, res., Az., U.S.	C4	96
Horsham, Austl.	H3	62
Horten, Nor.	G4	10
Horton, Ks., U.S.	C8	109
Horton, stm., N.T., Can.	E15	82
Hortonia, Lake, l., Vt., U.S.	D2	138
Hortonville, Wi., U.S.	D5	142
Horyn', stm., Eur.	D9	20
Hosa'ina, Eth.	B7	54
Hoschton, Ga., U.S.	B3	103
Hosedahard, Russia	A10	22
Hoshāb, Pak.	E8	42
Hoshangābād, India	E3	40
Hoshiārpur, India	C3	40
Hospers, Ia., U.S.	A2	108
Hospet, India	F3	40
Hosta Butte, mtn., N.M., U.S.	B1	124
Hotan, China	D3	28
Hotan, stm., China	A4	40
Hotazel, S. Afr.	D3	56
Hotchkiss, Co., U.S.	C3	99
Hot Creek Range, mts., Nv., U.S.	E5	121
Hot Creek Valley, val., Nv., U.S.	E5	121
Hot Spring, co., Ar., U.S.	C2	97
Hot Springs, S.D., U.S.	D2	134
Hot Springs, co., Wy., U.S.	C4	143
Hot Springs National Park, Ar., U.S.	C2	97
Hot Springs National Park, Ar., U.S.	C2	97
Hot Springs Peak, mtn., Ca., U.S.	B3	98
Hot Springs Peak, mtn., Nv., U.S.	B4	121
Houaïlou, N. Cal.	l9	62a
Houghton, Mi., U.S.	A2	115
Houghton, N.Y., U.S.	C2	125
Houghton, co., Mi., U.S.	B2	115
Houghton Lake, Mi., U.S.	D6	115
Houghton Lake, l., Mi., U.S.	D6	115
Houghton Lake Heights, Mi., U.S.	D6	115
Houlton, Me., U.S.	B5	112
Houma, China	D10	28
Houma, La., U.S.	E5	111
Housatonic, stm., U.S.	D3	100
House Springs, Mo., U.S.	g12	118
Houston, De., U.S.	E3	101
Houston, Mn., U.S.	G7	116
Houston, Mo., U.S.	D6	118
Houston, Ms., U.S.	B4	117
Houston, Pa., U.S.	F1	131
Houston, Tx., U.S.	E5	136
Houston, co., Al., U.S.	D4	94
Houston, co., Ga., U.S.	D3	103
Houston, co., Mn., U.S.	G7	116
Houston, co., Tn., U.S.	A4	135
Houston, co., Tx., U.S.	D5	136
Houston, stm., La., U.S.	D2	111
Houston, Lake, res., Tx., U.S.	r14	136
Houston Intercontinental Airport, Tx., U.S.	r14	136
Houtman Abrolhos, is., Austl.	F1	60
Houtzdale, Pa., U.S.	E5	131
Hovd, Mong.	B6	28
Hovd, stm., Mong.	B6	28
Hovenweep National Monument, Ut., U.S.	F6	137
Hoverla, hora, mtn., Ukr.	E8	20
Hovmantorp, Swe.	H6	10
Hövsgöl nuur, l., Mong.	A8	28
Howard, Ks., U.S.	E7	109
Howard, S.D., U.S.	C8	134
Howard, Wi., U.S.	D5	142
Howard, co., Ar., U.S.	C2	97
Howard, co., Ia., U.S.	A5	108
Howard, co., In., U.S.	C5	107
Howard, co., Md., U.S.	B4	113
Howard, co., Mo., U.S.	B5	118
Howard, co., Ne., U.S.	C7	120
Howard, co., Tx., U.S.	C2	136
Howard City, Mi., U.S.	E5	115
Howard Hanson Reservoir, res., Wa., U.S.	B4	140
Howard Lake, Mn., U.S.	E4	116
Howard Prairie Lake, res., Or., U.S.	E4	130
Howards Grove-Millersville, Wi., U.S.	E6	142
Howe, Cape, c., Austl.	H5	62
Howell, Mi., U.S.	F7	115
Howell, co., Mo., U.S.	E6	118
Howells, Ne., U.S.	C8	120
Howe Sound, strt., B.C., Can.	E6	85
Howick, P.Q., Can.	D4	90
Howland, Me., U.S.	C4	112
Howland Island, i., Oc.	H21	64
Hoxie, Ar., U.S.	A5	97
Hoxie, Ks., U.S.	C3	109
Hoyerswerda, Ger.	E14	12
Hoyt Lakes, Mn., U.S.	C6	116
Hradec Králové, Czech Rep.	D3	20
Hrodno, Bela.	C7	20
Hron, stm., Slvk.	E5	20
Hsilo, Tai.	E5	30
Hsinchu, Tai.	E5	30
Hsipaw, Myan.	B3	34
Huacho, Peru	F4	70
Huachuca City, Az., U.S.	F5	96
Hua Hin, Thai.	D3	34
Huai'an, China	E11	28
Huai'an, China	A3	30
Huaibin, China	E3	30
Huaiji, China	E3	30
Huailai, China	A4	30
Huainan, China	E11	28
Huairou, China	A4	30
Huaiyang, China	E11	28
Huajuapan de León, Mex.	D5	78
Hualahuises, Mex.	D5	78
Hualalai, vol., Hi., U.S.	D6	104
Hualapai Indian Reservation, Az., U.S.	B2	96
Hualapai Mountains, mts., Az., U.S.	C2	96
Hualapai Peak, mtn., Az., U.S.	B2	96
Hualien, Tai.	E5	30
Huallaga, stm., Peru	E4	70
Huambo, Ang.	F3	54
Huanan, China	A2	31
Huancavelica, Peru	F4	70
Huancayo, Peru	F4	70
Huang (Yellow), stm., China	D11	28
Huangchuan, China	E11	28
Huangho see Huang, stm., China	D11	28
Huanghua, China	B4	30
Huanglong, China	B2	30
Huangshi, China	E11	28
Huangxian, China	B5	30
Huangyan, China	D5	30
Huangyuan, China	D8	28
Huanta, Peru	A3	72
Huánuco, Peru	E4	70
Huanxian, China	B2	30
Huaral, Peru	F4	70
Huarocondo, Peru	A3	72
Huascarán, Nevado, mtn., Peru	E4	70
Huasco, Chile	C2	69
Huatabampo, Mex.	B3	78
Huauchinango, Mex.	C5	78
Huaxian, China	E3	30
Huaxian, China	B3	30
Huazhou, China	E3	30
Hubbard, Ia., U.S.	B4	108
Hubbard, Oh., U.S.	A5	128
Hubbard, Or., U.S.	B4	130
Hubbard, Tx., U.S.	D4	136
Hubbard, co., Mn., U.S.	C4	116
Hubbard Creek Lake, res., Tx., U.S.	C3	136
Hubbard Lake, l., Mi., U.S.	D7	115
Hubbardton, stm., Vt., U.S.	D2	138
Hubbell, Mi., U.S.	A2	115
Hubei, state, China	E10	28
Hubli-Dhārwār, India	F3	40
Huckleberry Mountain, mtn., Or., U.S.	D4	130
Huddersfield, Eng., U.K.	D6	12
Hudiksvall, Swe.	F7	10
Hudson, P.Q., Can.	D3	90
Hudson, Co., U.S.	A6	99
Hudson, Fl., U.S.	D4	102
Hudson, Ia., U.S.	B5	108
Hudson, Il., U.S.	C5	106
Hudson, Ma., U.S.	B4	114
Hudson, Mi., U.S.	G6	115
Hudson, N.C., U.S.	B1	126
Hudson, N.H., U.S.	E4	122
Hudson, N.Y., U.S.	C7	125
Hudson, Oh., U.S.	A4	128
Hudson, Wi., U.S.	D1	142
Hudson, Wy., U.S.	D4	143
Hudson, co., N.J., U.S.	B4	123
Hudson, stm., U.S.	E7	125
Hudson, Lake, res., Ok., U.S.	A6	129
Hudson Bay, b., Can.	G24	82
Hudson Falls, N.Y., U.S.	B7	125
Hudson Hope, B.C., Can.	A6	85
Hudson Lake, In., U.S.	A4	107
Hudson Strait, strt., Can.	F25	82
Hudsonville, Mi., U.S.	F5	115
Hudspeth, co., Tx., U.S.	o12	136
Hudžand, Taj.	E8	26
Hue, Viet.	C5	34
Huehuetenango, Guat.	B1	80
Huelva, Spain	I3	16
Huércal-Overa, Spain	I6	16
Huerfano, co., Co., U.S.	D5	99
Huerfano, stm., Co., U.S.	D6	99
Huerfano Mountain, mtn., N.M., U.S.	A2	124
Huesca, Spain	F6	16
Huéscar, Spain	I5	16
Huetamo de Núñez, Mex.	D4	78
Hueytown, Al., U.S.	g6	94
Huffakers, Nv., U.S.	D2	121
Hufrat an-Naḥās, Sudan	B4	54
Hughenden, Austl.	E3	62
Hughes, Ar., U.S.	C5	97
Hughes, co., Ok., U.S.	B5	129
Hughes, co., S.D., U.S.	C5	134
Hughes, North Fork, stm., W.V., U.S.	B3	141
Hughes, South Fork, stm., W.V., U.S.	B3	141
Hughesville, Md., U.S.	C4	113
Hughesville, Pa., U.S.	D8	131
Hugli, stm., India	E5	40
Hugo, Co., U.S.	B7	99
Hugo, Mn., U.S.	m13	116
Hugo, Ok., U.S.	C6	129
Hugo Lake, res., Ok., U.S.	C6	129
Hugoton, Ks., U.S.	E2	109
Hūich'ŏn, N. Kor.	C13	28
Huilai, China	E4	30
Huili, China	F8	28
Huimin, China	B4	30
Huinca Renancó, Arg.	E5	72
Huishui, China	D2	30
Huitong, China	D2	30
Huixian, China	C2	30
Huixtla, Mex.	D6	78
Huize, China	F8	28
Huizhou, China	E3	30
Hujirt, Mong.	B8	28
Hulah Lake, res., Ok., U.S.	A5	129
Hulett, Wy., U.S.	B8	143
Hulin, China	B14	28
Hull, P.Q., Can.	D2	90
Hull, Ia., U.S.	A1	108
Hull, Ma., U.S.	B6	114
Huma, China	A13	28
Humaitá, Braz.	E7	70
Humaitá, Para.	D6	72
Humansdorp, S. Afr.	E3	56
Humansville, Mo., U.S.	D4	118
Humbe, Ang.	B1	56
Humble, Tx., U.S.	E5	136
Humboldt, Ia., U.S.	B3	108
Humboldt, Ks., U.S.	E8	109
Humboldt, Ne., U.S.	D10	120
Humboldt, Tn., U.S.	B3	135
Humboldt, co., Ca., U.S.	B2	98
Humboldt, co., Ia., U.S.	B3	108
Humboldt, co., Nv., U.S.	B3	121
Humboldt Range, mts., Nv., U.S.	C3	121
Humenné, Slvk.	E6	20
Hummels Wharf, Pa., U.S.	E8	131
Humphrey, Ar., U.S.	C4	97
Humphrey, Ne., U.S.	C8	120
Humphreys, co., Ms., U.S.	B3	117
Humphreys, co., Tn., U.S.	A4	135
Humphreys, Mount, mtn., Ca., U.S.	D4	98
Humphreys Peak, mtn., Az., U.S.	B4	96
Humpty Doo, Austl.	C5	60
Hūn, Libya	F7	14
Hun, stm., China	A5	30
Húnaflói, b., Ice.	k18	10a
Hunan, state, China	F10	28
Hunchun, China	B2	31
Hundred Acre Pond, l., R.I., U.S.	E3	132
Hunedoara, Rom.	G7	20
Hungary, ctry., Eur.	F5	20
Hŭngdŏki-dong, N. Kor.	D13	28
Hungry Horse, Mt., U.S.	B2	119
Hungry Horse Reservoir, res., Mt., U.S.	B3	119
Hunjiang, China	C13	28
Hunsberge, mts., Nmb.	D2	56
Hunt, co., Tx., U.S.	C4	136
Hunt, stm., R.I., U.S.	D4	132
Hunterdon, co., N.J., U.S.	B3	123
Hunter Island, i., Austl.	I3	62
Hunter Island, i., B.C., Can.	D3	85
Huntertown, In., U.S.	B7	107
Huntingburg, In., U.S.	H4	107
Huntingdon, P.Q., Can.	D3	90
Huntingdon, Pa., U.S.	F6	131
Huntingdon, Tn., U.S.	A3	135
Huntingdon, co., Pa., U.S.	F5	131
Hunting Island, i., S.C., U.S.	G7	133
Huntington, Ar., U.S.	B1	97
Huntington, In., U.S.	C7	107
Huntington, N.Y., U.S.	E7	125
Huntington, Tx., U.S.	D5	136
Huntington, Ut., U.S.	D5	137
Huntington, W.V., U.S.	C2	141
Huntington, co., In., U.S.	C6	107
Huntington Beach, Ca., U.S.	F4	98
Huntington Lake, res., In., U.S.	C7	107
Huntington Woods, Mi., U.S.	p15	115
Huntingtown, Md., U.S.	C4	113
Huntland, Tn., U.S.	B5	135
Huntley, Il., U.S.	A5	106
Hunt Mountain, mtn., Wy., U.S.	B5	143
Huntsville, On., Can.	B5	89
Huntsville, Al., U.S.	A3	94
Huntsville, Ar., U.S.	A2	97
Huntsville, Mo., U.S.	B5	118
Huntsville, Tn., U.S.	C9	135
Huntsville, Tx., U.S.	D5	136
Hunucmá, Mex.	C7	78
Hunyuan, China	D10	28
Huon Gulf, b., Pap. N. Gui.	H12	62
Huoxian, China	B3	30
Hurd, Cape, c., On., Can.	B3	89
Hurghada, Egypt	E11	48
Hurley, Ms., U.S.	E5	117
Hurley, N.M., U.S.	E1	124
Hurley, N.Y., U.S.	D6	125
Hurley, Wi., U.S.	B3	142
Hurlock, Md., U.S.	C6	113
Huron, Oh., U.S.	A3	128
Huron, S.D., U.S.	C7	134
Huron, co., Mi., U.S.	E7	115
Huron, co., Oh., U.S.	A3	128
Huron, stm., Mi., U.S.	p14	115
Huron, Lake, l., N.A.	C11	92
Huron Mountains, hills, Mi., U.S.	B3	115
Hurricane, Ut., U.S.	F2	137
Hurricane, W.V., U.S.	C2	141
Hurst, Il., U.S.	F4	106
Hurst, Tx., U.S.	C3	139
Hurtsboro, Al., U.S.	C4	94
Húsavík, Ice.	k20	10a

Name	Map Ref.	Page
Huși, Rom.	F10	20
Hustisford, Wi., U.S.	E5	142
Husum, Ger.	C11	12
Hutag, Mong.	B8	28
Hutchins, Tx., U.S.	n10	136
Hutchinson, Ks., U.S.	D6	109
Hutchinson, Mn., U.S.	F4	116
Hutchinson, co., S.D., U.S.	D8	134
Hutchinson, co., Tx., U.S.	B2	136
Hutchinson Island, i., Fl., U.S.	E6	102
Hutchinson Island, i., S.C., U.S.	k11	133
Hutch Mountain, mtn., Az., U.S.	C4	96
Huttig, Ar., U.S.	D3	97
Huwei, Tai.	E5	30
Huxian, China	C2	30
Huxley, Ia., U.S.	C4	108
Hūzgān, Iran	G13	44
Huzhou, China	E12	28
Hužir, Russia	A9	28
Hvannadalshnúkur, mtn., Ice.	m20	10a
Hwange, Zimb.	B4	56
Hwang Ho see Huang, stm., China	D11	28
Hyannis, Ma., U.S.	C7	114
Hyannis Port, Ma., U.S.	C7	114
Hyargas nuur, l., Mong.	B6	28
Hyattsville, Md., U.S.	C4	113
Hybla Valley, Va., U.S.	g12	139
Hyco, stm., Va., U.S.	D3	139
Hyco Lake, res., N.C., U.S.	A3	126
Hydaburg, Ak., U.S.	D13	95
Hyde, Pa., U.S.	D5	131
Hyde, co., N.C., U.S.	B6	126
Hyde, co., S.D., U.S.	C6	134
Hyden, Austl.	G2	60
Hyde Park, N.Y., U.S.	D7	125
Hyde Park, Ut., U.S.	B4	137
Hyder, Ak., U.S.	D13	95
Hyderābād, India	F3	40
Hyderābād, Pak.	E9	42
Hydeville, Vt., U.S.	D2	138
Hydra see Ídhra, i., Grc.	F9	18
Hydro, Ok., U.S.	B3	129
Hyères, Fr.	F10	16
Hyesan, N. Kor.	C13	28
Hymera, In., U.S.	F3	107
Hyndman, Pa., U.S.	G4	131
Hyndman Peak, mtn., Id., U.S.	F4	105
Hyrum, Ut., U.S.	B4	137
Hythe, Ab., Can.	B1	84
Hyvinkää, Fin.	F11	10

I

Name	Map Ref.	Page
Iaçu, Braz.	D3	74
Ialomiţa, stm., Rom.	G9	20
Iamonia, Lake, l., Fl., U.S.	B2	102
Iași, Rom.	F9	20
Iatt, Lake, res., La., U.S.	C3	111
Iba, Phil.	C7	34
Ibadan, Nig.	E5	50
Ibagué, Col.	C4	70
Ibaiti, Braz.	F1	74
Ibapah Peak, mtn., Ut., U.S.	D2	137
Ibarra, Ec.	C4	70
Ibembo, D.R.C.	C4	54
Iberia, Mo., U.S.	C5	118
Iberia, co., La., U.S.	E4	111
Iberian Mountains see Ibérico, Sistema, mts., Spain	G5	16
Ibérico, Sistema, mts., Spain	G5	16
Iberville, P.Q., Can.	D4	90
Iberville, co., La., U.S.	D4	111
Iberville, Mont d' (Caubvick, Mount), mtn., Can.	g14	90
Ibiá, Braz.	E2	74
Ibicaraí, Braz.	D4	74
Ibiza see Eivissa, i., Spain	H7	16
Ibonma, Indon.	D8	36
Ibotirama, Braz.	D3	74
'Ibrī, Oman	F7	42
Ica, Peru	F4	70
Içá (Putumayo), stm., S.A.	D6	70
Içana, Braz.	C6	70
Içana (Isana), stm., S.A.	C6	70
Ice Harbor Dam, Wa., U.S.	C7	140
İçel, Tur.	D6	44
Iceland, ctry., Eur.	l18	10a
Iceland Basin	B25	144
Ichaikaronji, India	F2	40
Ichchāpuram, India	F4	40
Ichnia, Ukr.	D12	20
Icicle Creek, stm., Wa., U.S.	B5	140
Ičinskaja Sopka, vulkan, vol., Russia	D17	26
Icó, Braz.	C4	74
Icy Cape, c., Ak., U.S.	A7	95
Icy Strait, strt., Ak., U.S.	k22	95
Ida, Mi., U.S.	G7	115
Ida, co., Ia., U.S.	B2	108
Ida, Lake, l., Mn., U.S.	D3	116
Idabel, Mo., U.S.	D7	129
Ida Grove, Ia., U.S.	B2	108
Idah, Nig.	E6	50
Idaho, co., Id., U.S.	D3	105
Idaho, state, U.S.	E3	105
Idaho Falls, Id., U.S.	F6	105
Idaho Springs, Co., U.S.	B5	99
Idalou, Tx., U.S.	C2	136
Idamay, W.V., U.S.	k10	141
Idaville, In., U.S.	C4	107
Ider, Al., U.S.	A4	94
Ídhi Óros, mtn., Grc.	G10	18
Ídhra, i., Grc.	F9	18
İdil, Tur.	D9	44
Idiofa, D.R.C.	D3	54
Idlib, state, Syria	E7	44
Idoûkâl-en-Taghès, mtn., Niger	C6	50
Idutywa, S. Afr.	E4	56
Ifakara, Tan.	E7	54
Ife, Nig.	E5	50
Iferouâne, Niger	C6	50
Ifôghas, Adrar des, mts., Afr.	C5	50
Iganga, Ug.	C6	54
Igarapé-Açu, Braz.	B2	74
Igarka, Russia	C10	26
Igboho, Nig.	E5	50
Iğdır, Tur.	C11	44
Iglesias, Italy	E2	18
Ignacio, Co., U.S.	D3	99
Iguaçu, stm., S.A.	D7	72
Iguala, Mex.	D5	78
Igualada, Spain	G7	16
Iguassu Falls see Iguaçu, Cataratas do, wtfl, Braz.	D7	72
Iguatu, Braz.	C4	74
Iguazú see Iguaçu, stm., S.A.	D7	72
Iguéla, Gabon	D1	54
Iguîdi, 'Erg, dunes, Afr.	A3	50
Iharaña, Madag.	A8	56
Iheya-shima, i., Japan	g6	31a
Ihosy, Madag.	C8	56
Iisalmi, Fin.	E12	10
Iizuka, Japan	D2	31
Ijâfene, des., Maur.	B3	50
Ijebu-Ode, Nig.	E5	50
IJsselmeer, l., Neth.	D9	12
Ijuí, Braz.	D7	72
Ika, Russia	D12	26
Ikaría, i., Grc.	F11	18
Ikeja, Nig.	E5	50
Ikela, D.R.C.	D4	54
Ikerre, Nig.	E6	50
Ikom, Nig.	E6	50
Ikot-Ekpene, Nig.	E6	50
Ila, Nig.	E5	50
Ilagan, Phil.	C8	34
Īlām, Iran	D5	42
Ilan, Tai.	E5	30
Ilaro, Nig.	E5	50
Iława, Pol.	C5	20
Ilbenge, Russia	C14	26
Île-à-la-Crosse, Lac, l., Sk., Can.	B2	91
Ilebo, D.R.C.	D4	54
Île-de-France, hist. reg., Fr.	C8	16
Île-Perrot, P.Q., Can.	q19	90
Ilesha, Nig.	E5	50
Ilha de Moçambique, Moz.	B7	56
Ilhéus, Braz.	D4	74
Iliamna Lake, l., Ak., U.S.	D8	95
Iliamna Volcano, vol., Ak., U.S.	C9	95
Iligan, Phil.	E8	34
Iligan Bay, b., Phil.	E8	34
Ilion, N.Y., U.S.	B5	125
Ilio Point, c., Hi., U.S.	B4	104
Ilizi, Alg.	E6	48
Iljinskij, Russia	E16	26
Illampu, Nevado, mtn., Bol.	G6	70
Illana Bay, b., Phil.	E8	34
Illapel, Chile	D2	69
Illéla, Niger	D6	50
Illichivs'k, Ukr.	F11	20
Illimani, Nevado, mtn., Bol.	B4	72
Illinois, state, U.S.	C4	106
Illinois, stm., Il., U.S.	B5	106
Illinois, stm., Or., U.S.	E3	130
Illinois, stm., U.S.	A7	129
Illinois Peak, mtn., Id., U.S.	B3	105
Illiopolis, Il., U.S.	D4	106
Illmo, Mo., U.S.	D8	118
Il'men', ozero, l., Russia	C5	22
Ilo, Peru	G5	70
Iloilo, Phil.	D8	34
Ilorin, Nig.	E5	50
Ilovlja, Russia	F15	8
Ilwaco, Wa., U.S.	C1	140
Ilwaki, Indon.	E7	36
Imabari, Japan	D2	31
Imandra, ozero, l., Russia	C15	10
Imatra, Fin.	F13	10
Imboden, Ar., U.S.	A4	97
Īmī, Eth.	B8	54
İmişli, Azer.	C13	44
Imlay, Nv., U.S.	C3	121
Imlay City, Mi., U.S.	E7	115
Immokalee, Fl., U.S.	F5	102
Imnaha, stm., Or., U.S.	B10	130
Imola, Italy	B3	18
Imperatriz, Braz.	C2	74
Imperia, Italy	C2	18
Imperial, Ca., U.S.	F6	98
Imperial, Mo., U.S.	C7	118
Imperial, Ne., U.S.	D4	120
Imperial, Pa., U.S.	k13	131
Imperial, co., Ca., U.S.	F6	98
Imperial Beach, Ca., U.S.	o15	98
Imperial Dam, U.S.	E1	96
Imperial Reservoir, res., U.S.	E1	96
Imperial Valley, val., Ca., U.S.	F6	98
Impfondo, Congo	C3	54
Imphāl, India	E6	40
I-n-Amenas, Alg.	E6	48
Inanwatan, Indon.	D8	36
Inari, Fin.	B12	10
Inarijärvi, l., Fin.	B12	10
In Belbel, Alg.	E4	14
Inca, Spain	H8	16
Inca de Oro, Chile	C3	69
İnce Burun, c., Tur.	A6	44
Inch'ŏn, S. Kor.	D13	28
Incline Village, Nv., U.S.	D2	121
Indé, Mex.	B3	78
Independence, Ia., U.S.	B6	108
Independence, Ks., U.S.	E8	109
Independence, Ky., U.S.	B5	110
Independence, La., U.S.	D5	111
Independence, Mo., U.S.	B3	118
Independence, Or., U.S.	C3	130
Independence, Va., U.S.	D1	139
Independence, Wi., U.S.	D2	142
Independence, co., Ar., U.S.	B4	97
Independence, stm., N.Y., U.S.	B5	125
Independence Mountains, mts., Nv., U.S.	C5	121
Independence National Historical Park, Pa., U.S.	p21	131
Independence Rock, mtn., Wy., U.S.	D5	143
Inderborskij, Kaz.	E7	26
India, ctry., Asia	E3	40
Indian, stm., On., Can.	B7	89
Indian, stm., De., U.S.	F4	101
Indian, stm., Mi., U.S.	B4	115
Indian, stm., N.Y., U.S.	A5	125
Indiana, Pa., U.S.	E3	131
Indiana, co., Pa., U.S.	E3	131
Indiana, state, U.S.	E5	107
Indiana Dunes National Lakeshore, In., U.S.	A3	107
Indianapolis, In., U.S.	E5	107
Indian Bay, b., Fl., U.S.	D4	102
Indian Cedar Swamp, sw., R.I., U.S.	F2	132
Indian Creek, stm., Oh., U.S.	C1	128
Indian Creek, stm., S.D., U.S.	B2	134
Indian Creek, stm., Tn., U.S.	B3	135
Indian Creek, stm., W.V., U.S.	D4	141
Indian Creek, stm., W.V., U.S.	k9	141
Indian Head, Md., U.S.	C3	113
Indian Island, i., N.C., U.S.	B6	126
Indian Lake, l., Mi., U.S.	C4	115
Indian Lake, l., N.Y., U.S.	B6	125
Indian Lake, l., Oh., U.S.	B2	128
Indian Lake, l., R.I., U.S.	F4	132
Indian Neck, Ct., U.S.	D4	100
Indian Ocean	J11	64
Indianola, Ia., U.S.	C4	108
Indianola, Ms., U.S.	B3	117
Indianola, Ne., U.S.	D5	120
Indian Peak, mtn., Ut., U.S.	E2	137
Indian Peak, mtn., Wy., U.S.	B3	143
Indian Prairie Canal, Fl., U.S.	E5	102
Indian River, Mi., U.S.	C6	115
Indian River, b., Fl., U.S.	E6	102
Indian River, b., De., U.S.	D6	102
Indian River Bay, b., De., U.S.	F5	101
Indian Rock, mtn., Wa., U.S.	D5	140
Indian Rocks Beach, Fl., U.S.	p10	102
Indian Springs, Nv., U.S.	G6	121
Indian Stream, stm., N.H., U.S.	f7	122
Indiantown, Fl., U.S.	E6	102
Indian Trail, N.C., U.S.	B2	126
Indiga, Russia	A8	22
Indigirka, stm., Russia	C16	26
Indio, Ca., U.S.	F5	98
Indochina, reg., Asia	C4	34
Indonesia, ctry., Asia	D4	36
Indore, India	E3	40
Indramayu, Indon.	E3	36
Indrāvati, stm., India	F4	40
Indus, stm., Asia	D1	40
İnegöl, Tur.	B3	44
Infiernillo, Presa del, res., Mex.	D4	78
Ingal, Niger	C6	50
Ingalls, In., U.S.	E6	107
Ingalls Park, Il., U.S.	B5	106
Ingende, D.R.C.	D3	54
Ingersoll, On., Can.	D4	89
Ingham, Austl.	D4	62
Ingham, co., Mi., U.S.	F6	115
Ingleside, Tx., U.S.	F4	136
Inglewood, Ca., U.S.	n12	98
Ingolstadt, Ger.	F12	12c
Ingraham, Lake, l., Fl., U.S.	G5	102
Ingrāj Bāzār, India	E5	40
Ingram, Pa., U.S.	k13	131
Ingrid Christensen Coast, Ant.	D12	67
In Guezzam, Alg.	G6	48
Ingušetija, state, Russia	E6	26
Ingushetia see Ingušetija, state, Russia	E6	26
Inhaca, Ilha da, i., Moz.	D5	56
Inhambane, Moz.	C6	56
Inhambupe, Braz.	F12	70
Inhaminga, Moz.	B6	56
Inharrime, Moz.	C6	56
Inhassoro, Moz.	C6	56
Inhulets', Ukr.	F12	20
Inhumas, Braz.	E2	74
Inírida, stm., Col.	C6	70
Inkerman, N.B., Can.	B5	87
Inkom, Id., U.S.	G6	105
Inkster, Mi., U.S.	p15	115
Inland Sea see Seto-naikai, Japan	E14	28
Inman, Ks., U.S.	D6	109
Inman, S.C., U.S.	A3	133
Inn, stm., Eur.	G12	12
Inner Channel, strt., Belize	B2	80
Inner Hebrides, is., Scot., U.K.	B3	12
Inner Mongolia see Nei Monggol Zizhiqu, prov., China	C10	28
Innisfail, Austl.	D4	62
Innisfail, Ab., Can.	C4	84
Innsbruck, Aus.	G12	12
Inola, Ok., U.S.	A6	129
Inongo, D.R.C.	D3	54
Inowrocław, Pol.	C5	20
In Salah, Alg.	E5	48
Inscription House Ruin, hist., Az., U.S.	A5	96
Institute, W.V., U.S.	m12	141
Inta, Russia	C8	26
Interlachen, Fl., U.S.	C5	102
International Falls, Mn., U.S.	B5	116
Inthanon, Doi, mtn., Thai.	C3	34
Intracoastal Waterway, U.S.	E4	111
Inukjuak, P.Q., Can.	g11	90
Invercargill, N.Z.	q12	63c
Inverell, Austl.	F5	62
Inver Grove Heights, Mn., U.S.	n12	116
Invermere, B.C., Can.	D9	85
Inverness, Scot., U.K.	B4	12
Inverness, Ca., U.S.	C2	98
Inverness, Fl., U.S.	D4	102
Inverness, Ms., U.S.	B3	117
Inverway, Austl.	D4	60
Investigator Strait, strt., Austl.	H2	62
Invisible Mountain, mtn., Id., U.S.	F5	105
Inwood, Ia., U.S.	A1	108
Inwood, N.Y., U.S.	k13	125
Inwood, W.V., U.S.	B6	141
Inyangani, mtn., Zimb.	B5	56
Inyan Kara Creek, stm., Wy., U.S.	B8	143
Inyan Kara Mountain, mtn., Wy., U.S.	B8	143
Inyo, co., Ca., U.S.	D5	98
Inyo, Mount, mtn., Ca., U.S.	D5	98
Inyo Mountains, mts., Ca., U.S.	D4	98
Ioánnina, Grc.	E8	18
Iola, Ks., U.S.	E8	109
Iola, Wi., U.S.	D4	142
Iona, Id., U.S.	F7	105
Ione, Ca., U.S.	C3	98
longo, Ang.	E3	54
Ionia, Mi., U.S.	F5	115
Ionia, co., Mi., U.S.	F5	115
Ionian Islands see Iónioi Nísoi, is., Grc.	E7	18
Ionian Sea, Eur.	E7	18
Iónioi Nísoi (Ionian Islands), is., Grc.	E7	18
Iony, ostrov, i., Russia	D16	26
Íos, i., Grc.	F10	18
Iosco, co., Mi., U.S.	D7	115
Iota, La., U.S.	D3	111
Iowa, La., U.S.	D2	111
Iowa, co., Ia., U.S.	C5	108
Iowa, co., Wi., U.S.	E3	142
Iowa, state, U.S.	C4	108
Iowa, stm., Ia., U.S.	C6	108
Iowa, West Branch, stm., Ia., U.S.	B4	108
Iowa City, Ia., U.S.	C6	108
Iowa Falls, Ia., U.S.	B4	108
Iowa Indian Reservation, U.S.	C8	109
Iowa Lake, l., U.S.	A3	108
Iowa Park, Tx., U.S.	C3	136
Ipameri, Braz.	E2	74
Ipatinga, Braz.	E3	74
Ipatovo, Russia	A4	42
Ipeiros, hist. reg., Grc.	E8	18
Iphigenia Bay, b., Ak., U.S.	n22	95
Ipiales, Col.	C4	70
Ipiaú, Braz.	D4	74
Ipoh, Malay.	C2	36
Iporá, Braz.	E1	74
Ippy, C.A.R.	B4	54
Ipswich, Austl.	F5	62
Ipswich, Eng., U.K.	D7	12
Ipswich, Ma., U.S.	A6	114
Ipswich, S.D., U.S.	B6	134
Ipswich, stm., Ma., U.S.	A5	114
Ipu, Braz.	B3	74
Iqaluit, Nu., Can.	F26	82
Iquique, Chile	B2	69
Iquitos, Peru	D5	70
Iraan, Tx., U.S.	D2	136
Iráklion, Grc.	G10	18
Iran, ctry., Asia	D6	42
Iran Mountains, mts., Asia	C5	36
Īrānshahr, Iran	E8	42
Irapuato, Mex.	C4	78
Iraq, ctry., Asia	D4	42
Irati, Braz.	D7	72
Irazú, Volcán, vol., C.R.	C3	80
Irbid, Jord.	D3	42
Irbīl, Iraq	C4	42
Irbit, Russia	C11	22
Irecê, Braz.	D3	74
Iredell, co., N.C., U.S.	B2	126
Ireland, ctry., Eur.	D2	12
Irgiz, Kaz.	E8	26
Irígui, reg., Afr.	C3	50
Iriklinskij, Russia	D10	22
Iringa, Tan.	E7	54
Iriomote-jima, i., Japan	B8	34
Irion, co., Tx., U.S.	D2	136
Iriri, stm., Braz.	D9	70
Irish, Mount, mtn., Nv., U.S.	F6	121
Irish Sea, Eur.	D4	12
Irkutsk, Russia	D12	26
Irminger Basin	C26	144
Irmo, S.C., U.S.	C5	133
Iroise, b., Fr.	C4	16
Iron, co., Mi., U.S.	B2	115
Iron, co., Mo., U.S.	D7	118
Iron, co., Ut., U.S.	F2	137
Iron, co., Wi., U.S.	B3	142
Irondale, Al., U.S.	f7	94
Irondequoit, N.Y., U.S.	B3	125
Iron Gate, val., Eur.	G7	20
Iron Gate Reservoir, res., Ca., U.S.	B2	98
Iron Knob, Austl.	G2	62
Iron Mountain, Mi., U.S.	C2	115
Iron Mountain, mtn., Az., U.S.	D4	96
Iron Mountains, mts., U.S.	D1	139
Iron Ridge, Wi., U.S.	E5	142
Iron River, Mi., U.S.	B2	115
Iron River, Wi., U.S.	B2	142
Ironton, Mo., U.S.	D7	118
Ironton, Oh., U.S.	D3	128
Ironwood, Mi., U.S.	n11	115
Iroquois, On., Can.	C9	89
Iroquois, co., Il., U.S.	C6	106
Iroquois, stm., U.S.	C6	106
Iroquois, Lake, l., Vt., U.S.	B2	138
Iroquois Falls, On., Can.	o19	89
Irosin, Phil.	D8	34
Irpin', Ukr.	D11	20
Irrawaddy see Ayeyarwady, stm., Myan.	C3	34
Irricana, Ab., Can.	D4	84
Irrigon, Or., U.S.	B7	130
Irtyš see Irtysh, stm., Asia	D8	26
Irtysh, stm., Asia	D8	26
Irtysj see Irtysh, stm., Asia	D8	26
Irtyšsk, Kaz.	D9	26
Irumu, D.R.C.	C5	54
Irún, Spain	F6	16
Iruña see Pamplona, Spain	F6	16
Irvine, Ca., U.S.	n13	98
Irvine, Ky., U.S.	C6	110
Irving, Tx., U.S.	n10	136
Irvington, Al., U.S.	E1	94
Irvington, Il., U.S.	E4	106
Irvington, Ky., U.S.	C3	110
Irvington, N.J., U.S.	k8	123
Irvington, N.Y., U.S.	g13	125
Irwin, Pa., U.S.	F2	131
Irwin, co., Ga., U.S.	E3	103
Irwinton, Ga., U.S.	D3	103
Isa, Nig.	D6	50
Isabel, Mount, mtn., Wy., U.S.	D2	143
Isabela, Isla, i., Ec.	D1	70
Isabella, co., Mi., U.S.	E6	115
Isabella Indian Reservation, Mi., U.S.	E6	115
Isabella Lake, l., Mn., U.S.	C7	116
Ísafjardardjúp, Ice.	k17	10a
Ísafjörður, Ice.	k17	10a
Isana (Içana), stm., S.A.	C5	70
Isanga, D.R.C.	D4	54
Isangel, Vanuatu	k9	62a
Isanti, Mn., U.S.	E5	116
Isanti, co., Mn., U.S.	E5	116
Isar, stm., Eur.	F13	12
Ischia, Isola d', i., Italy	D4	18
Ise, Japan	D3	31
Isernia, Italy	D5	18
Iset', stm., Russia	D8	26
Iseyin, Nig.	E5	50
Isfahan see Eşfahān, Iran	D6	42
Ishigaki, Japan	B8	34
Ishikari, stm., Japan	B4	31
Ishikawa, Japan	A9	34
Ishinomaki, Japan	D16	28
Ishpeming, Mi., U.S.	B3	115
Išim, Russia	D8	26
Išim, stm., Asia	D9	26
Isinglass, stm., N.H., U.S.	D4	122
Isiolo, Kenya	C7	54
Isiro, D.R.C.	C5	54
İskår, stm., Bul.	C10	18
İskenderun, Tur.	D7	44
İskenderun Körfezi, b., Tur.	D6	44
İskilip, Tur.	B6	44
Islāmābād, Pak.	D10	42

Name	Map Ref.	Page

Islamorada, Fl., U.S. H6 102
Island, co., Wa., U.S. A3 140
Island Beach, N.J., U.S. D4 123
Island City, Or., U.S. B8 130
Island Falls, Me., U.S. B4 112
Island Lake, I., Mb., Can. C3 86
Island Park, R.I., U.S. E6 132
Island Park Reservoir, res., Id.,
 U.S. E7 105
Island Pond, I., N.H., U.S. ...E4 122
Island Pond, Vt., U.S. B5 138
Islands, Bay of, b., Nf., Can. .D2 88
Isla Vista, Ca., U.S. E4 98
Islay, i., Scot., U.K. C3 12
Isle-aux-Morts, Nf., Can. E2 88
Isle of Man, dep., Eur. C4 12
Isle of Palms, S.C., U.S. k12 133
Isle of Wight, co., Va., U.S. .D6 139
Isle of Wight Bay, b., Md.,
 U.S. D7 113
Isle Royale National Park, Mi.,
 U.S. h9 115
Islesboro Island, i., Me., U.S. D4 112
Isleta, N.M., U.S. C3 124
Isleta Indian Reservation, N.M.,
 U.S. C3 124
Islington, Ma., U.S. h11 114
Ismailia, Egypt D11 48
Ismail Samani, pik
 (Kommunizma, pik),
 mtn., Taj. F9 26
İsmayıllı, Azer. B13 44
Isoka, Zam. A5 56
Isola, Ms., U.S. B3 117
Isparta, Tur. D4 44
İspir, Tur. B9 44
Israel, ctry., Asia D2 42
Israel, stm., N.H., U.S. B3 122
Issaquah, Wa., U.S. B3 140
Issaquena, co., Ms., U.S. C2 117
Issia, C. Iv. E3 50
Issoire, Fr. E8 16
Issoudun, Fr. D8 16
Issyk-Kul', Kyrg. E9 26
Issyk-Kul', ozero, l., Kyrg. ..E9 26
İstanbul, Tur. B3 44
İstanbul Boğazı (Bosporus),
 strt., Tur. B3 44
Isto, Mount, mtn., Ak., U.S. ..B11 95
Istokpoga, Lake, l., Fl., U.S. .E5 102
Itabaiana, Braz. D4 74
Itabaiana, Braz. C4 74
Itaberaba, Braz. D3 74
Itaberaí, Braz. E2 74
Itabira, Braz. E3 74
Itabuna, Braz. D4 74
Itacoatiara, Braz. D8 70
Itaguí, Col. B4 70
Itaipu Reservoir, res., S.A. ..C7 72
Itaituba, Braz. D8 70
Itajaí, Braz. D8 72
Itajubá, Braz. F2 74
Itajuípe, Braz. D4 74
Italy, ctry., Eur. C4 18
Italy, Tx., U.S. C4 136
Itamaraju, Braz. E4 74
Itambé, Braz. E3 74
Itānagar, India D6 40
Itaobim, Braz. E3 74
Itapecuru-Mirim, Braz. B3 74
Itaperuna, Braz. F3 74
Itapetinga, Braz. E3 74
Itapetininga, Braz. F2 74
Itapipoca, Braz. B4 74
Itapiranga, Braz. D7 72
Itaporanga, Braz. C4 74
Itaquari, Braz. F3 74
Itaqui, Braz. D6 72
Itārsi, India E3 40
Itasca, Il., U.S. k8 106
Itasca, co., Mn., U.S. C5 116
Itasca, Tx., U.S. C4 136
Itasca, Lake, l., Mn., U.S. ...C3 116
Itaúna, Braz. F3 74
Itawamba, co., Ms., U.S. A5 117
Itenes see Guaporé, stm.,
 S.A. F7 70
Iténez see Guaporé, stm.,
 S.A. F7 70
Ithaca see Itháki, i., Grc. ...E8 18
Ithaca, Mi., U.S. E6 115
Ithaca, N.Y., U.S. C4 125
Itháki, i., Grc. E8 18
Itimbiri, stm., D.R.C. C4 54
Itoigawa, Japan C3 31
Itoko, D.R.C. D4 54
Itta Bena, Ms., U.S. B3 117
Ituango, Col. D4 80
Ituberá, Braz. D4 74
Ituiutaba, Braz. E2 74
Itumbiara, Braz. E2 74
Iturama, Braz. E1 74
Iturup, ostrov, i., Russia E16 26
Ituverava, Braz. F2 74
Itzehoe, Ger. D11 12
Iuka, Ms., U.S. A5 117
Iul'tin, Russia C20 26
Iva, S.C., U.S. C2 133
Ivanava, Bela. C8 20
Ivangorod, Russia G13 10
Ivanhoe, Mn., U.S. F2 116
Ivanhoe, Va., U.S. D10 20
Ivano-Frankivs'k, Ukr. E8 20
Ivanovo, Russia D6 26
Ivdel', Russia C8 26

Ivigtut, Grnld. F30 82
Ivins, Ut., U.S. F2 137
Ivohibe, Madag. C8 56
Ivory Coast see Cote d'Ivoire,
 ctry., Afr. E3 50
Ivoryton, Ct., U.S. D6 100
Ivrea, Italy B1 18
Iwaki, Japan D16 28
Iwo, Nig. E5 50
Ixmiquilpan, Mex. C5 78
Ixtapa, Mex. D4 78
Ixtepec, Mex. D5 78
Izabal, Lago de, l., Guat. B2 80
Izamal, Mex. C7 78
Izard, co., Ar., U.S. A4 97
Izberbaš, Russia A12 44
Iževsk, Russia D7 26
Iziaslav, Ukr. D9 20
Izium, Ukr. E14 20
Ižma, stm., Russia A9 22
Izmaïl, Ukr. G10 20
İzmir, Tur. C2 44
İzmir Körfezi, b., Tur. C2 44
İzmit, Tur. B3 44
İzmit Körfezi, b., Tur. B3 44
İznik, Tur. B3 44
İznik Gölü, l., Tur. B3 44
Izucar de Matamoros, Mex. D5 78
Izu-shotō, is., Japan E15 28
Izu Trench F17 64

J

Jabal, Baḥr al- (Mountain Nile),
 stm., Sudan I11 48
Jabalpur, India E3 40
Jabiru, Austl. C5 60
Jablah, Syria E6 44
Jablonec nad Nisou,
 Czech Rep. D3 20
Jablonovyj hrebet, mts.,
 Russia D13 26
Jaboatão, Braz. C4 74
Jaboticabal, Braz. F2 74
Jacareí, Braz. F2 74
Jacarezinho, Braz. F2 74
Jaciara, Braz. B7 72
Jacinto City, Tx., U.S. r14 136
Jack, co., Tx., U.S. C3 136
Jackfish Lake, l., Sk., Can. ..D1 91
Jackman, Me., U.S. C2 112
Jackman Station, Me., U.S. C2 112
Jack Mountain, mtn., Mt.,
 U.S. D4 119
Jack Mountain, mtn., Wa.,
 U.S. A5 140
Jackpot, Nv., U.S. B7 121
Jacksboro, Tn., U.S. C9 135
Jacksboro, Tx., U.S. C3 136
Jacks Mountain, mtn., Pa.,
 U.S. E6 131
Jackson, Al., U.S. D2 94
Jackson, co., Al., U.S. A3 94
Jackson, co., Ar., U.S. B4 97
Jackson, Ca., U.S. C3 98
Jackson, co., Co., U.S. A4 99
Jackson, co., Fl., U.S. B1 102
Jackson, Ga., U.S. C3 103
Jackson, co., Ga., U.S. B3 103
Jackson, co., Ia., U.S. B7 108
Jackson, co., Il., U.S. F4 106
Jackson, co., In., U.S. G5 107
Jackson, co., Ks., U.S. C8 109
Jackson, Ky., U.S. C6 110
Jackson, co., Ky., U.S. C5 110
Jackson, La., U.S. D4 111
Jackson, co., La., U.S. B3 111
Jackson, Mi., U.S. F6 115
Jackson, co., Mi., U.S. F6 115
Jackson, co., Mn., U.S. G3 116
Jackson, Mn., U.S. G4 116
Jackson, Mo., U.S. D8 118
Jackson, co., Mo., U.S. B3 118
Jackson, Ms., U.S. C3 117
Jackson, co., Ms., U.S. E5 117
Jackson, co., N.C., U.S. f9 126
Jackson, Oh., U.S. C3 128
Jackson, co., Oh., U.S. C3 128
Jackson, co., Ok., U.S. C2 129
Jackson, co., Or., U.S. E4 130
Jackson, S.C., U.S. E4 133
Jackson, co., S.D., U.S. D4 134
Jackson, Tn., U.S. B3 135
Jackson, co., Tn., U.S. C8 135
Jackson, co., Tx., U.S. E4 136
Jackson, stm., Va., U.S. C3 139
Jackson, Wi., U.S. E5 142
Jackson, co., Wi., U.S. D3 142
Jackson, co., W.V., U.S. C3 141
Jackson, Wy., U.S. C2 143
Jackson, Lake, l., Fl., U.S. ..B2 102
Jackson, Lake, l., Fl., U.S. ..E5 102
Jackson, Mount, mtn., Ant. D34 67
Jackson, Mount, mtn., N.H.,
 U.S. B4 122
Jackson Center, Oh., U.S. B1 128
Jackson Lake, res., Wy.,
 U.S. C2 143
Jackson Mountains, mts., Nv.,
 U.S. B3 121
Jackson's Arm, Nf., Can. D3 88
Jacksons Gap, Al., U.S. C4 94
Jacksonville, Al., U.S. B4 94
Jacksonville, Ar., U.S. C3 97
Jacksonville, Fl., U.S. B5 102

Jacksonville, Il., U.S. D3 106
Jacksonville, N.C., U.S. C5 126
Jacksonville, Or., U.S. E4 130
Jacksonville, Tx., U.S. D5 136
Jacksonville Beach, Fl., U.S. .B5 102
Jacksonville Naval Air Station,
 mil., Fl., U.S. B5 102
Jacks Peak, mtn., Ut., U.S. ...E3 137
Jacmel, Haiti B5 80
Jacobābād, Pak. E9 42
Jacobina, Braz. D3 74
Jacques-Cartier, stm., P.Q.,
 Can. B6 90
Jacques-Cartier, Détroit de,
 strt., P.Q., Can. I27 82
Jacquet River, N.B., Can. B4 87
Jacundá, Braz. B2 74
Jada, Nig. E7 50
Jaén, Peru E4 70
Jaén, Spain I5 16
Jaffa, Cape, c., Austl. H2 62
Jaffna, Sri L. H4 40
Jaffrey, N.H., U.S. E2 122
Jagādhri, India C3 40
Jagdalpur, India F4 40
Jagersfontein, S. Afr. D4 56
Jagodnoe, Russia C16 26
Jagtiāl, India F3 40
Jaguaquara, Braz. D4 74
Jaguarão, Braz. E7 72
Jaguaribe, Braz. C4 74
Jahrom, Iran E6 42
Jailolo, Indon. C7 36
Jaipur, India D3 40
Jaisalmer, India D2 40
Jājapur, India E5 40
Jakarta, Indon. E3 36
Jakobshavn, Grnld. E29 82
Jakša, Russia B10 22
Jakutija, state, Russia C14 26
Jakutsk, Russia C14 26
Jal, N.M., U.S. E6 124
Jalālābād, Afg. D10 42
Jalandhar, India C3 40
Jalapa see Xalapa, Mex. D5 78
Jālaun, India D3 40
Jālgaon, India E3 40
Jalingo, Nig. E7 50
Jalisco, state, Mex. C4 78
Jālna, India F3 40
Jālor, India D2 40
Jalostotitlán, Mex. C4 78
Jalpāiguri, India D5 40
Jalūlā', Iraq E11 42
Jamaica, ctry., N.A. E9 76
Jamaica Bay, b., N.Y., U.S. ...k13 125
Jamaica Channel, strt., N.A. ..B4 80
Jamal, poluostrov, pen.,
 Russia B8 26
Jamantau, gora, mtn.,
 Russia D7 26
Jambi, Indon. D2 36
Jambol, Blg. C11 18
Jambusar, India E2 40
James, stm., Mo., U.S. E4 118
James, stm., Va., U.S. C5 139
James, stm., U.S. C8 92
James, Lake, l., In., U.S. A7 107
James, Lake, res., N.C.,
 U.S. B1 126
James Bay, b., Can. H23 82
James Branch, stm., De.,
 U.S. F3 101
Jamesburg, N.J., U.S. C4 123
James City, N.C., U.S. B5 126
James City, co., Va., U.S. C6 139
James Island, i., Md., U.S. ...C5 113
James Island, i., S.C., U.S. ..k12 133
James Island, i., S.C., U.S. ..F8 133
James River Bridge, Va.,
 U.S. k15 139
Jamestown, Austl. G2 62
Jamestown, In., U.S. E4 107
Jamestown, Ky., U.S. D4 110
Jamestown, N.C., U.S. B3 126
Jamestown, N.D., U.S. C7 127
Jamestown, N.Y., U.S. C1 125
Jamestown, Oh., U.S. C2 128
Jamestown, R.I., U.S. F5 132
Jamestown, Tn., U.S. C9 135
James Town, Wy., U.S. E3 143
Jamestown Dam, N.D., U.S. C7 127
Jamestown Reservoir, res.,
 N.D., U.S. C7 127
Jamkhandi, India F3 40
Jammerbugten, b., Den. H3 10
Jammu, India C2 40
Jammu and Kashmir, hist.
 reg., Asia C10 38
Jamnagar, India E2 40
Jämsä, Fin. F11 10
Jamshedpur, India E5 40
Jamsk, Russia D17 26
Jämtland, hist. reg., Swe. E6 10
Jamuna, stm., Bngl. D5 40
Jana, stm., Russia C15 26
Janaúba, Braz. E3 74
Janaucu, Ilha, i., Braz. C10 70
Janesville, Ca., U.S. B3 98
Janesville, Ia., U.S. B5 108
Janesville, Mn., U.S. F5 116
Janesville, Wi., U.S. F4 142
Jan Mayen, i., Nor. D23 144
Jan Mayen Ridge D24 144
Jansenville, S. Afr. E3 56

Janskij, Russia C15 26
Janskij zaliv, b., Russia B15 26
Januária, Braz. E3 74
Jaora, India E3 40
Japan, ctry., Asia D15 28
Japan, Sea of (East Sea), Asia C14 28
Japan Basin D16 64
Japan Trench E17 64
Japurá (Caquetá), stm., S.A. ..D6 70
Jaraguá, Braz. E2 74
Jaransk, Russia C8 22
Jarānwāla, Pak. D10 42
Jarcevo, Russia B12 20
Jardim, Braz. C6 72
Jardín América, Arg. D6 72
Jari, stm., Braz. C9 70
Jarocin, Pol. D4 20
Jarosław, Pol. D7 20
Jaroslavl', Russia D6 26
Jarrettsville, Md., U.S. A5 113
Jar-Sale, Russia A13 22
Järva-Jaani, Est. G11 10
Järvenpää, Fin. F11 10
Jarvis Island, i., Oc. E13 58
Jašikan, Ghana E5 50
Jāsk, Iran E7 42
Jaškul', Russia A5 44
Jasło, Pol. E6 20
Jasmine Estates, Fl., U.S. D4 102
Jasnogorsk, Russia B14 20
Jason Islands, is., Falk. Is. .H4 69
Jasonville, In., U.S. F3 107
Jasper, Al., U.S. B2 94
Jasper, Fl., U.S. B4 102
Jasper, Ga., U.S. B2 103
Jasper, co., Ga., U.S. C3 103
Jasper, co., Ia., U.S. C4 108
Jasper, co., Il., U.S. D5 106
Jasper, In., U.S. H4 107
Jasper, co., In., U.S. B3 107
Jasper, Mo., U.S. D3 118
Jasper, co., Mo., U.S. D3 118
Jasper, co., Ms., U.S. C4 117
Jasper, co., S.C., U.S. G5 133
Jasper, Tn., U.S. D8 135
Jasper, co., Tx., U.S. D5 136
Jasper, Tx., U.S. D6 136
Jasper National Park, Ab.,
 Can. C1 84
Jataí, Braz. E1 74
Jatni, India E5 40
Jaú, Braz. F2 74
Jaunpur, India D4 40
Java (Jawa), i., Indon. E3 36
Java Sea see Jawa, Laut,
 Indon. D3 36
Java Trench I13 64
Jawa (Java), i., Indon. E3 36
Jawa, Laut (Java Sea), Indon. .D3 36
Jawhar, Som. J14 48
Jay, co., In., U.S. D7 107
Jay, Ok., U.S. A7 129
Jaya, Puncak, mtn., Indon. G10 32
Jayapura, Indon. G11 32
Jaypur, India F4 40
Jaz Mūrīān, Hāmūn-e, l.,
 Iran E7 42
J. B. Thomas, Lake, res., Tx.,
 U.S. C2 136
Jean, Nv., U.S. H6 121
Jeanerette, La., U.S. E4 111
Jean Lafitte National Historical
 Park, La., U.S. k12 111
Jeannette, Pa., U.S. F2 131
Jebba, Nig. E5 50
Jeddore Lake, res., Nf., Can. .D3 88
Jeff Davis, co., Ga., U.S. E4 103
Jeff Davis, co., Tx., U.S. o12 136
Jefferson, co., Al., U.S. B3 94
Jefferson, co., Ar., U.S. C3 97
Jefferson, co., Co., U.S. B5 99
Jefferson, co., Fl., U.S. B3 102
Jefferson, Ga., U.S. B3 103
Jefferson, co., Ga., U.S. C4 103
Jefferson, co., Ia., U.S. C5 108
Jefferson, Ia., U.S. B3 108
Jefferson, co., Id., U.S. F6 105
Jefferson, co., Il., U.S. E5 106
Jefferson, co., In., U.S. G6 107
Jefferson, co., Ks., U.S. C8 109
Jefferson, co., Ky., U.S. B4 110
Jefferson, La., U.S. k11 111
Jefferson, co., Mo., U.S. C7 118
Jefferson, co., Ms., U.S. D2 117
Jefferson, co., Mt., U.S. D4 119
Jefferson, stm., Mt., U.S. E5 119
Jefferson, N.C., U.S. A1 126
Jefferson, co., Ne., U.S. D8 120
Jefferson, co., N.Y., U.S. A5 125
Jefferson, Oh., U.S. A5 128
Jefferson, co., Oh., U.S. B5 128
Jefferson, co., Ok., U.S. C4 129
Jefferson, co., Or., U.S. C5 130
Jefferson, Or., U.S. C3 130
Jefferson, S.C., U.S. B7 133
Jefferson, co., Tn., U.S. C10 135
Jefferson, Tx., U.S. C5 136
Jefferson, co., Tx., U.S. E5 136
Jefferson, co., Wa., U.S. B1 140
Jefferson, Wi., U.S. E5 142
Jefferson, co., Wi., U.S. E5 142

Jefferson, co., W.V., U.S. B7 141
Jefferson, Mount, mtn., Id.,
 U.S. E7 105
Jefferson, Mount, mtn., Nv.,
 U.S. E5 121
Jefferson, Mount, mtn., Or.,
 U.S. C5 130
Jefferson City, Mo., U.S. C5 118
Jefferson City, Tn., U.S. C10 135
Jefferson Davis, co., La.,
 U.S. D3 111
Jefferson Davis, co., Ms.,
 U.S. D4 117
Jefferson Farms, De., U.S. i7 101
Jefferson Proving Ground,
 mil., In., U.S. G7 107
Jeffersontown, Ky., U.S. B4 110
Jeffersonville, Ga., U.S. D3 103
Jeffersonville, In., U.S. H6 107
Jeffersonville, Ky., U.S. C6 110
Jeffersonville, Oh., U.S. C2 128
Jeffrey, W.V., U.S. D3 141
Jeffrey City, Wy., U.S. D5 143
Jeffreys Creek, stm., S.C.,
 U.S. C8 133
Jega, Nig. D5 50
Jehossee Island, i., S.C.,
 U.S. k11 133
Jēkabpils, Lat. H11 10
Jekyll Island, i., Ga., U.S. ..E5 103
Jelenia Góra, Pol. D3 20
Jelgava, Lat. H10 10
Jellico, Tn., U.S. C9 135
Jelm Mountain, mtn., Wy.,
 U.S. E7 143
Jemaja, Pulau, i., Indon. C3 36
Jember, Indon. E4 36
Jemez, stm., N.M., U.S. k7 124
Jemez Canyon Dam, N.M.,
 U.S. k7 124
Jemez Indian Reservation,
 N.M., U.S. h7 124
Jemez Pueblo, N.M., U.S. B3 124
Jemison, Al., U.S. C3 94
Jena, Ger. E12 12
Jena, La., U.S. C3 111
Jeneponto, Indon. E5 36
Jenkins, co., Ga., U.S. D5 103
Jenkins, Ky., U.S. C7 110
Jenkintown, Pa., U.S. o21 131
Jenks, Ok., U.S. A6 129
Jennings, co., In., U.S. G6 107
Jennings, La., U.S. D3 111
Jennings, Mo., U.S. f13 118
Jensen Beach, Fl., U.S. E6 102
Jens Munks Ø, i., Grnld. F32 82
Jequié, Braz. D3 74
Jequitinhonha, Braz. E3 74
Jequitinhonha, stm., Braz. E3 74
Jerada, Mor. D4 48
Jerauld, co., S.D., U.S. C7 134
Jérémie, Haiti B5 80
Jeremoabo, Braz. D4 74
Jerez de García Salinas,
 Mex. C4 78
Jerez de la Frontera, Spain ...I3 16
Jerez de los Caballeros,
 Spain H3 16
Jericho see Arīḥā, Gaza G6 44
Jericho, Vt., U.S. B3 138
Jerid, Chott, l., Tun. D6 48
Jerimoth Hill, R.I., U.S. C1 132
Jermyn, Pa., U.S. C10 131
Jerome, Id., U.S. G4 105
Jerome, co., Id., U.S. G4 105
Jerome, Pa., U.S. F4 131
Jersey, dep., Eur. F5 12
Jersey, co., Il., U.S. D3 106
Jersey City, N.J., U.S. B4 123
Jersey Mountain, mtn., Id.,
 U.S. E3 105
Jersey Shore, Pa., U.S. D7 131
Jerseyville, Il., U.S. D3 106
Jerusalem see Yerushalayim,
 Isr. G6 42
Jervis Inlet, b., B.C., Can. ..D6 85
Jesi, Italy C5 18
Jessamine, co., Ky., U.S. C5 110
Jesselton see Kota Kinabalu,
 Malay. B5 36
Jessore, Bngl. E5 40
Jessup, Md., U.S. B4 113
Jessup, Pa., U.S. m18 131
Jesup, Ga., U.S. E5 103
Jesup, Ia., U.S. B5 108
Jesup, Lake, l., Fl., U.S. D5 102
Jésus, Île, i., P.Q., Can. p19 90
Jesús Carranza, Mex. I13 78
Jesús María, Arg. E5 72
Jetmore, Ks., U.S. D4 109
Jewel Cave National
 Monument, S.D., U.S. D2 134
Jewell, Ia., U.S. B4 108
Jewell, co., Ks., U.S. C5 109
Jewett City, Ct., U.S. C8 100
Jhālāwār, India E3 40
Jhang Sadar, Pak. D10 42
Jhānsi, India D3 40
Jharkhand, state, India E4 40
Jhelum, Pak. D10 42
Jhunjhunūn, India D3 40
Jiahe, China D3 30
Jiali, China C6 40
Jialing, stm., China E8 28
Jiamusi, China B14 28

Name	Map Ref.	Page
Ji'an, China	D3	30
Jianchang, China	A4	30
Jianchuan, China	F8	28
Jiande, China	D4	30
Jiang'an, China	D2	30
Jiangcheng, China	B4	34
Jiangjin, China	F9	28
Jiangle, China	D4	30
Jiangling, China	C3	30
Jiangmen, China	G10	28
Jiangsu, prov., China	E11	28
Jiangxi, prov., China	F11	28
Jianli, China	D3	30
Jian'ou, China	F11	28
Jianping, China	A4	30
Jianshui, China	G8	28
Jianyang, China	D4	30
Jianyang, China	C1	30
Jiaocheng, China	B3	30
Jiaonan, China	B4	30
Jiaoxian, China	D12	28
Jiaozuo, China	D10	28
Jiashan, China	C4	30
Jibiya, Nig.	D6	50
Jicarilla Apache Indian Reservation, N.M., U.S.	A2	124
Jičín, Czech Rep.	D3	20
Jiddah, Sau. Ar.	F3	38
Jiexiu, China	B3	30
Jieyang, China	G11	28
Jihlava, Czech Rep.	E3	20
Jijel, Alg.	I9	16
Jijiga, Eth.	B8	54
Jilib, Som.	J13	48
Jilin, prov., China	C13	28
Jilin, China	C13	28
Jill, Kediet ej, mtn., Maur.	B2	50
Jīma, Eth.	B7	54
Jimbolia, Rom.	G6	20
Jiménez (Ciudad Jiménez), Mex.	B4	78
Jimeta, Nig.	E7	50
Jim Hogg, co., Tx., U.S.	F3	136
Jim Lake, res., N.D., U.S.	B7	127
Jimo, China	B5	30
Jim Thorpe, Pa., U.S.	E10	131
Jim Wells, co., Tx., U.S.	F3	136
Jinan, China	D11	28
Jincheng, China	B3	30
Jīnd, India	D3	40
Jingdezhen, China	F11	28
Jinggangshan, China	F10	28
Jinghai, China	B4	30
Jinghong, China	G8	28
Jingning, China	B2	30
Jingxi, China	E2	30
Jingxian, China	D2	30
Jinhua, China	F11	28
Jining, China	D11	28
Jining, China	C10	28
Jinja, Ug.	C6	54
Jinning, China	E1	30
Jinsha, China	D2	30
Jinshi, China	F10	28
Jinzhai, China	C4	30
Jinzhou, China	C12	28
Jinzhou, China	D12	28
Ji-Paraná, Braz.	F7	70
Jishou, China	D2	30
Jisr ash-Shughūr, Syria	E7	44
Jiu, stm., Rom.	G7	20
Jiujiang, China	F11	28
Jiulong (Kowloon), China	E3	30
Jiuquan, China	D7	28
Jiutai, China	C13	28
Jixi, China	B14	28
Jixian, China	C11	28
Jīzān, Sau. Ar.	G4	38
Joanna, S.C., U.S.	C4	133
João Pessoa, Braz.	C5	74
João Pinheiro, Braz.	E2	74
Job Peak, mtn., Nv., U.S.	D3	121
Jocassee, Lake, res., U.S.	B1	133
Jódar, Spain	I5	16
Jo Daviess, co., Il., U.S.	A3	106
Jodhpur, India	D2	40
Joe Batt's Arm [-Barr'd Islands-Shoal Bay], Nf., Can.	D4	88
Joensuu, Fin.	E13	10
Joes Brook, stm., Vt., U.S.	C4	138
Joes Creek, stm., W.V., U.S.	m12	141
Joetsu, Japan	D15	28
Joffre, Mount, mtn., Can.	D3	84
Johannesburg, S. Afr.	D4	56
John, Cape, c., N.S., Can.	D6	87
John Day, Or., U.S.	C8	130
John Day, stm., Or., U.S.	B6	130
John Day Dam, U.S.	D5	140
John Day Fossil Beds National Monument, Or.,	C6	130
John F. Kennedy Space Center, hist., Fl., U.S.	D6	102
John H. Kerr Dam, Va., U.S.	D4	139
John H. Kerr Reservoir, res., U.S.	D4	139
John Martin Reservoir, res., Co., U.S.	C7	99
John Muir National Historical Site, hist., Ca., U.S.	h8	98
John Redmond Reservoir, res., Ks., U.S.	D8	109
John Sevier, Tn., U.S.	m14	135
Johns Island, i., S.C., U.S.	F7	133
Johnson, co., Ar., U.S.	B2	97
Johnson, co., Ga., U.S.	D4	103
Johnson, co., Ia., U.S.	C6	108
Johnson, co., Il., U.S.	F5	106
Johnson, co., In., U.S.	F5	107
Johnson, Ks., U.S.	E2	109
Johnson, co., Ks., U.S.	D9	109
Johnson, co., Ky., U.S.	C7	110
Johnson, co., Mo., U.S.	C4	118
Johnson, co., Ne., U.S.	D9	120
Johnson, co., Tn., U.S.	C12	135
Johnson, co., Tx., U.S.	C4	136
Johnson, Vt., U.S.	B3	138
Johnson, co., Wy., U.S.	B6	143
Johnsonburg, Pa., U.S.	D4	131
Johnson City, N.Y., U.S.	C5	125
Johnson City, Tn., U.S.	C11	135
Johnson City, Tx., U.S.	D3	136
Johnson Creek, Wi., U.S.	E5	142
Johnsonville, S.C., U.S.	D9	133
Johns Pass, strt., Fl., U.S.	p10	102
Johnston, Ia., U.S.	e8	108
Johnston, co., N.C., U.S.	B4	126
Johnston, co., Ok., U.S.	C5	129
Johnston, R.I., U.S.	C4	132
Johnston, S.C., U.S.	D4	133
Johnston Atoll, atoll, Oc.	G22	64
Johnston City, Il., U.S.	F5	106
Johnston Key, i., Fl., U.S.	H5	102
Johnstown, Co., U.S.	A6	99
Johnstown, N.Y., U.S.	B6	125
Johnstown, Oh., U.S.	B3	128
Johnstown, Pa., U.S.	F4	131
John W. Flannagan Reservoir, res., Va., U.S.	e9	139
Johor Bahru, Malay.	C2	36
Joigny, Fr.	C8	16
Joiner, Ar., U.S.	B5	97
Joinville, Braz.	D8	72
Jokkmokk, Swe.	C8	10
Jolfā, Iran	C11	44
Joliet, Il., U.S.	B5	106
Joliette, P.Q., Can.	C4	90
Jolo, Phil.	E8	34
Jolo Island, i., Phil.	E8	34
Jomda, China	E7	28
Jones, co., Ga., U.S.	C3	103
Jones, co., Ia., U.S.	B6	108
Jones, co., Ms., U.S.	D4	117
Jones, co., N.C., U.S.	B5	126
Jones, Ok., U.S.	B4	129
Jones, co., S.D., U.S.	D5	134
Jones, co., Tx., U.S.	C3	136
Jonesboro, Ar., U.S.	B5	97
Jonesboro, Ga., U.S.	C2	103
Jonesboro, Il., U.S.	F4	106
Jonesboro, In., U.S.	D6	107
Jonesboro, La., U.S.	B3	111
Jonesborough, Tn., U.S.	C11	135
Jonesburg, Mo., U.S.	C6	118
Jones Creek, Tx., U.S.	s14	136
Jones Mill, Ar., U.S.	C3	97
Jonesport, Me., U.S.	D5	112
Jonestown, Ms., U.S.	A3	117
Jonesville, La., U.S.	C4	111
Jonesville, Mi., U.S.	G6	115
Jonesville, N.C., U.S.	A2	126
Jonesville, S.C., U.S.	B4	133
Jonesville, Va., U.S.	f8	139
Joniškis, Lith.	H10	10
Jonquière, P.Q., Can.	A6	90
Jonuta, Mex.	D6	78
Joplin, Mo., U.S.	D3	118
Joppatowne, Md., U.S.	B5	113
Jordan, ctry., Asia	D3	42
Jordan, stm., Asia	F6	44
Jordan, Mn., U.S.	F5	116
Jordan, stm., Ut., U.S.	C4	137
Jordan Creek, stm., U.S.	E9	130
Jordan Lake, res., Al., U.S.	C3	94
Jorhāt, India	D6	40
Jornado del Muerto, des., N.M., U.S.	D3	124
Joroinen, Fin.	E12	10
Jos, Nig.	E6	50
José de San Martín, Arg.	F2	69
Joseph, Or., U.S.	B9	130
Joseph, Lac, l., P.Q., Can.	h8	88
Joseph Bonaparte Gulf, b., Austl.	C4	60
Joseph City, Az., U.S.	C5	96
Josephine, co., Or., U.S.	E3	130
Joshua, Tx., U.S.	n9	136
Joshua Tree, Ca., U.S.	E5	98
Joshua Tree National Monument, Ca., U.S.	F6	98
Jostedalsbreen, ice, Nor.	F2	10
Jourdanton, Tx., U.S.	E3	136
Jovellanos, Cuba	A3	80
J. Percy Priest Lake, res., Tn., U.S.	A5	135
Juab, co., Ut., U.S.	D2	137
Juan Aldama, Mex.	C4	78
Juan de Fuca, Strait of, strt., N.A.	B3	92
Juan Fernandez, Archipiélago, is., Chile	E1	72
Juanjuí, Peru	E4	70
Juazeiro, Braz.	C3	74
Juazeiro do Norte, Braz.	C4	74
Juba, Sudan	J11	48
Jubba (Genalē), stm., Afr.	C8	54
Juby, Cap, c., Mor.	A2	50
Júcar, stm., Spain	H6	16
Juchitán de Zaragoza, Mex.	D5	78
Judenburg, Aus.	G14	12
Judith, stm., Mt., U.S.	C7	119
Judith, Point, c., R.I., U.S.	G4	101
Judith Basin, co., Mt., U.S.	C6	119
Judith Island, i., N.C., U.S.	B6	126
Judith Mountains, mts., Mt., U.S.	C7	119
Judith Peak, mtn., Mt., U.S.	C7	119
Judsonia, Ar., U.S.	B4	97
Juhnov, Russia	B13	22
Juidongshan, China	E4	30
Juiz de Fora, Braz.	F3	74
Jukta, Russia	C12	26
Julesburg, Co., U.S.	A8	99
Juliaca, Peru	G5	70
Julia Creek, Austl.	E3	62
Julian, Ca., U.S.	F5	98
Julian, W.V., U.S.	C3	141
Julian Alps, mts., Eur.	A4	18
Juliana Top, mtn., Sur.	C8	70
Julianehåb, Grnld.	F30	82
Jumba, Som.	D8	54
Jumbo Peak, mtn., Nv., U.S.	G7	121
Jumilla, Spain	H6	16
Jump, stm., Wi., U.S.	C3	142
Jūnāgadh, India	E2	40
Junction, Tx., U.S.	D3	136
Junction City, Ar., U.S.	D3	97
Junction City, Ks., U.S.	C7	109
Junction City, Ky., U.S.	C5	110
Junction City, La., U.S.	A3	111
Junction City, Or., U.S.	C3	130
Jundiaí, Braz.	F2	74
Juneau, Ak., U.S.	D13	95
Juneau, Wi., U.S.	E5	142
Juneau, co., Wi., U.S.	E3	142
Junee, Austl.	G4	62
June in Winter, Lake, l., Fl., U.S.	E5	102
Jungar Qi, China	D10	28
Junggar Pendi, bas., China	B5	28
Juniata, Ne., U.S.	D7	120
Juniata, co., Pa., U.S.	F7	131
Juniata, stm., Pa., U.S.	F7	131
Junín, Arg.	E5	72
Junior Lake, l., Me., U.S.	C4	112
Juniper Mountains, mts., Az., U.S.	B2	96
Junipero Serra Peak, mtn., Ca., U.S.	D3	98
Jūniyah, Leb.	F6	44
Junlian, China	D1	30
Junxian, China	E10	28
Jupiter, Fl., U.S.	F6	102
Jupiter Inlet, b., Fl., U.S.	F6	102
Jupiter Island, i., Fl., U.S.	E6	102
Jur, Russia	D15	26
Jura, i., Scot., U.K.	C4	12
Jurga, Russia	D10	26
Jūrmala, Lat.	H10	10
Juruá, stm., S.A.	E6	70
Juruena, stm., Braz.	F8	70
Jurumirim, Represa, res., Braz.	C8	72
Juškozero, Russia	B5	22
Jussara, Braz.	B7	72
Justin, Tx., U.S.	C4	136
Jutaí, stm., Braz.	D6	70
Jutiapa, Guat.	C1	80
Juticalpa, Hond.	C2	80
Jutland see Jylland, reg., Den.	I3	10
Juventud, Isla de la, i., Cuba	A3	80
Juxian, China	B4	30
Južno-Sahalinsk, Russia	E16	26
Južno-Ural'sk, Russia	D11	22
Jylland, reg., Den.	I3	10
Jyväskylä, Fin.	E11	10

K

Name	Map Ref.	Page
K2 (Qogir Feng), mtn., Asia	B3	40
Kaaawa, Hi., U.S.	f10	104
Kaahka, Turk.	C7	42
Kaala, mtn., Hi., U.S.	f9	104
Kaalualu Bay, b., Hi., U.S.	E6	104
Kaaumakua, Puu, mtn., Hi., U.S.	f10	104
Kabaena, Pulau, i., Indon.	E6	36
Kabala, S.L.	E2	50
Kabale, Ug.	D5	54
Kabalega Falls, wtfl., Ug.	C6	54
Kabalo, D.R.C.	E5	54
Kabambare, D.R.C.	D5	54
Kabardino-Balkarija, state, Russia	E6	26
Kabba, Nig.	E6	50
Kabetogama Lake, l., Mn., U.S.	B5	116
Kabinda, D.R.C.	E4	54
Kabīr Kūh, mts., Iran	F12	44
Kābol, Afg.	D9	42
Kabompo, stm., Zam.	A3	56
Kabongo, D.R.C.	E5	54
Kabūdarāhang, Iran	E13	44
Kābūd see Kābol, Afg.	D9	42
Kabwe, Zam.	A4	56
Kabylie, reg., Alg.	I9	16
Kachchh, Gulf of, b., India	E1	40
Kachess Lake, res., Wa., U.S.	B4	140
Kačkanar, Russia	C10	22
Kadan Kyun, i., Mya.	D3	34
Kade, Ghana	E4	50
Kadınhanı, Tur.	C5	44
Kadiolo, Mali	D3	50
Kadirli, Tur.	D7	44
Kadoka, S.D., U.S.	D4	134
Kadoma, Zimb.	B4	56
Kaduna, stm., Nig.	D6	50
Kaduna, Nig.	D6	50
Kāduqlī, Sudan	H10	48
Kadykčan, Russia	C16	26
Kadžerom, Russia	B10	22
Kaédi, Maur.	C2	50
Kaélé, Cam.	A2	54
Kaena Point, c., Hi., U.S.	B3	104
Kafanchan, Nig.	E6	50
Kaffrine, Sen.	D1	50
Kafia Kingi, Sudan	I9	48
Kafue, Zam.	B4	56
Kafue, stm., Zam.	A4	56
Kaga, Japan	C3	31
Kaga Bandoro, C.A.R.	B3	54
Kagan, Uzb.	C8	42
Kagera, stm., Afr.	D6	54
Kağızman, Tur.	B10	44
Kagoshima, Japan	E14	28
Kagul see Cahul, Mol.	G10	20
Kahaluu, Hi., U.S.	g10	104
Kahaluu, Hi., U.S.	D6	104
Kahama, Tan.	D6	54
Kahana Bay, b., Hi., U.S.	f10	104
Kahemba, D.R.C.	E3	54
Kahoka, Mo., U.S.	A6	118
Kahoolawe, i., Hi., U.S.	C5	104
Kahramanmaraş, Tur.	D7	44
Kahuku, Hi., U.S.	B4	104
Kahuku Point, c., Hi., U.S.	B4	104
Kahului, Hi., U.S.	C5	104
Kahului Bay, b., Hi., U.S.	C5	104
Kai, Kepulauan, is., Indon.	E8	36
Kaibab Indian Reservation, Az., U.S.	A3	96
Kaifeng, China	E10	28
Kaikoura, N.Z.	p13	63c
Kailahun, S.L.	E2	50
Kailas see Kangrinboqê Feng, mtn., China	E4	28
Kailas Range see Gangdisê Shan, mts., China	E4	28
Kaili, China	D2	30
Kailu, China	C12	28
Kailua, Hi., U.S.	B4	104
Kailua Bay, b., Hi., U.S.	g11	104
Kailua Kona, Hi., U.S.	D6	104
Kainji Lake, res., Nig.	D5	50
Kaiping, China	E3	30
Kairouan, Tun.	C7	48
Kaiserslautern, Ger.	F10	12
Kaitaia, N.Z.	o13	63c
Kaixian, China	C2	30
Kaiyuan, China	E1	30
Kaiyuan, China	C12	28
Kajaani, Fin.	D12	10
Kajakī, Band-e, res., Afg.	D9	42
Kajang, Malay.	C2	36
Kajiado, Kenya	D7	54
Kajnar, Kaz.	E9	26
Kaka, Sudan	A6	54
Kakamas, S. Afr.	D3	56
Kakamega, Kenya	C6	54
Kaka Point, c., Hi., U.S.	C5	104
Kakata, Lib.	E2	50
Kake, Ak., U.S.	D13	95
Kakhovka Reservoir see Kakhovs'ke vodoskhovyshche, res., Ukr.	F13	20
Kakhovs'ke vodoskhovyshche, res., Ukr.	F13	20
Kākināda, India	F4	40
Kalaa Kebira, Tun.	G3	18
Kalaallit Nunaat see Greenland, dep., N.A.	D30	82
Kalabahi, Indon.	E6	36
Kalabo, Zam.	A3	56
Kalač, Russia	D7	22
Kalač-na-Donu, Russia	E7	22
Kaladan, stm., Asia	B2	34
Kalahari Desert, des., Afr.	C3	56
Kalajoki, Fin.	D10	10
Kalakan, Russia	D13	26
Kalama, Wa., U.S.	C3	140
Kalámai, Grc.	F8	18
Kalamazoo, Mi., U.S.	F5	115
Kalamazoo, stm., Mi., U.S.	F5	115
Kalamazoo, co., Mi., U.S.	F5	115
Kalamits'ka zatoka, b., Ukr.	G12	20
Kalanchak, Ukr.	F12	20
Kalao, Pulau, i., Indon.	E6	36
Kalaotoa, Pulau, i., Indon.	E6	36
Kalasin, Thai.	B3	34
Kalāt, Pak.	E9	42
Kalaupapa Peninsula, pen., Hi., U.S.	B5	104
Kalawao, co., Hi., U.S.	B5	104
Kalbarri, Austl.	F1	60
Kale, Tur.	D3	44
Kalecik, Tur.	B5	44
Kaleden, B.C., Can.	E8	85
Kalemie, D.R.C.	E5	54
Kalemyo, Mya.	B2	34
Kalena, Puu, mtn., Hi., U.S.	g9	104
Kalene Hill, Zam.	A3	56
Kalevala, Russia	D14	10
Kalewa, Mya.	B2	34
Kalgin Island, i., Ak., U.S.	g16	95
Kalgoorlie-Boulder, Austl.	G3	60
Kalibo, Phil.	D8	34
Kalima, D.R.C.	D5	54
Kalimantan see Borneo, i., Asia	D4	36
Kálimnos, Grc.	F11	18
Kálimnos, i., Grc.	F11	18
Kālimpang, India	D5	40
Kalinin see Tver', Russia	D5	26
Kaliningrad, Russia	Z4	26
Kalinkavičy, Bela.	C10	20
Kalispel Indian Reservation, Wa., U.S.	A8	140
Kalispell, Mt., U.S.	B2	119
Kalisz, Pol.	D5	20
Kalixälven, stm., Swe.	C9	10
Kalmar, Swe.	H7	10
Kalmarsund, strt., Swe.	H7	10
Kalmykija, state, Russia	E6	26
Kalohi Channel, strt., Hi., U.S.	C4	104
Kaloli Point, c., Hi., U.S.	D7	104
Kalomo, Zam.	B4	56
Kalona, Ia., U.S.	C6	108
Kalone Peak, mtn., B.C., Can.	C4	85
Kalpin, China	A3	40
Kalsūbai, mtn., India	F2	40
Kaluga, Russia	D5	26
Kalundborg, Den.	I4	10
Kalush, Ukr.	E8	20
Kalutara, Sri L.	H4	40
Kalyān, India	F2	40
Kama, D.R.C.	D5	54
Kama, stm., Russia	D7	26
Kamaishi, Japan	D16	28
Kamakou, mtn., Hi., U.S.	B5	104
Kamālia, Pak.	D10	42
Kaman, Tur.	C5	44
Kamarān, i., Yemen	G4	38
Kama Reservoir see Kamskoe vodohranilišče, res., Russia	C10	22
Kamas, Ut., U.S.	C4	137
Kambalda, Austl.	G3	60
Kambove, D.R.C.	F5	54
Kamčatka, poluostrov, pen., Russia	D17	26
Kamchatka Peninsula see Kamčatka, poluostrov, pen., Russia	D17	26
Kamen', gora, mtn., Russia	C11	26
Kamenka, Russia	D15	26
Kamenka, Russia	D7	22
Kamen'-na-Obi, Russia	D10	26
Kamenskoe, Russia	C18	26
Kamensk-Ural'skij, Russia	C11	22
Kāmet, mtn., Asia	C3	40
Kamiah, Id., U.S.	C2	105
Kamiak Butte, mtn., Wa., U.S.	C8	140
Kam'ianets'-Podil's'kyi, Ukr.	E9	20
Kamina, D.R.C.	E5	54
Kamloops, B.C., Can.	D7	85
Kamo, Arm.	B11	44
Kampala, Ug.	C6	54
Kampar, Malay.	C2	36
Kampen, Neth.	D9	12
Kampeska, Lake, l., S.D., U.S.	C8	134
Kamphaeng Phet, Thai.	C3	34
Kâmpóng Cham, Camb.	D5	34
Kâmpóng Chhnãng, Camb.	D4	34
Kâmpóng Saôm, Camb.	D4	34
Kâmpóng Thum, Camb.	D4	34
Kâmpôt, Camb.	D4	34
Kampti, Burkina	E4	50
Kampuchea see Cambodia, ctry., Asia	D4	34
Kamskoe vodohranilišče, res., Russia	C10	22
Kamuela (Waimea), Hi., U.S.	C6	104
Kamyšin, Russia	D6	26
Kamyšlov, Russia	C11	22
Kanab, Ut., U.S.	F3	137
Kanab Creek, stm., U.S.	A3	96
Kanabec, co., Mn., U.S.	E5	116
Kanaga Island, i., Ak., U.S.	E4	95
Kanairiktok, stm., Nf., Can.	g9	88
Kananga, D.R.C.	E4	54
Kanapou Bay, b., Hi., U.S.	C5	104
Kanaš, Russia	C8	22
Kanata, On., Can.	B9	89
Kanawha, Ia., U.S.	B4	108
Kanawha, stm., W.V., U.S.	C3	141
Kanawha, co., W.V., U.S.	C3	141
Kanazawa, Japan	D15	28
Kānchenjunga, mtn., Asia	D5	40
Kānchipuram, India	G3	40
Kandahār, Afg.	D9	42
Kandalakša, Russia	C15	10
Kandalaksha Bay see Kandalakskaja guba, b., Russia	A5	22

Name	Map Ref.	Page

Kandalakškaja guba, b., Russia A5 22
Kandale, D.R.C. E3 54
Kandangan, Indon. D5 36
Kandi, Benin D5 50
Kandıra, Tur. B4 44
Kandiyohi, co., Mn., U.S. . . E3 116
Kandy, Sri L. H4 40
Kane, Pa., U.S. C4 131
Kane, co., Il., U.S. B5 106
Kane, co., Ut., U.S. F3 137
Kanem, prov., Chad D8 50
Kaneohe, Hi., U.S. B4 104
Kaneohe Bay, b., Hi., U.S. . g10 104
Kaneohe Bay Marine Corps Air Station, mil., Hi., U.S. g10 104
Kangaba, Mali D3 50
Kangal, Tur. C7 44
Kangān, Iran E6 42
Kangar, Malay. B2 36
Kangaroo Island, i., Austl. . . H2 62
Kangāvar, Iran E12 44
Kangbao, China A3 30
Kangean, Pulau, i., Indon. . E5 36
Kanggye, N. Kor. C13 28
Kango, Gabon C2 54
Kangpu, China A3 34
Kangrinboqê Feng, mtn., China E4 28
Kangshan, Tai. E5 30
Kangto, mtn., Asia A2 34
Kaniama, D.R.C. E4 54
Kaniet Islands, is., Pap. N. Gui. G12 32
Kanin, poluostrov, pen., Russia C6 26
Kaningo, Kenya D7 54
Kanin Nos, Russia A7 22
Kanin Nos, mys, c., Russia . C6 26
Kanjiža, Yugo. A8 18
Kankakee, Il., U.S. B6 106
Kankakee, co., Il., U.S. B6 106
Kankakee, stm., U.S. B5 106
Kankan, Gui. D3 50
Kānker, India E4 40
Kanmaw Kyun, i., Myan. . . D3 34
Kannapolis, N.C., U.S. B2 126
Kannonkoski, Fin. E11 10
Kano, Nig. D6 50
Kanopolis, Ks., U.S. D5 109
Kanopolis Lake, res., Ks., U.S. D5 109
Kanoya, Japan D2 31
Kānpur, India D4 40
Kansas, Il., U.S. D6 106
Kansas, state, U.S. D5 109
Kansas, stm., Ks., U.S. C7 109
Kansas City, Ks., U.S. C9 109
Kansas City, Mo., U.S. B3 118
Kansk, Russia D11 26
Kantang, Thai. E3 34
Kantchari, Burkina D5 50
Kantemirovka, Russia E15 20
Kanye, Bots. D4 56
Kaohsiung, Tai. E5 30
Kaoko Veld, plat., Nmb. . . . B1 56
Kaolack, Sen. D1 50
Kaoma, Zam. A3 56
Kaouar, reg., Niger C7 50
Kapaa, Hi., U.S. A2 104
Kapaau, Hi., U.S. C6 104
Kapan, Arm. C12 44
Kapanga, D.R.C. E4 54
Kapapa Island, i., Hi., U.S. . g10 104
Kapčagaj, Kaz. B11 42
Kapčagajskoe vodohranilišče, res., Kaz. B11 42
Kapchagay Reservoir see Kapčagajskoe vodohranilišče, res., Kaz. B11 42
Kapfenberg, Aus. G14 12
Kapiri Mposhi, Zam. A4 56
Kaplan, La., U.S. D3 111
Kapoeta, Sudan C6 54
Kaposvár, Hung. F4 20
Kaptai Lake see Karnaphuli Reservoir, res., Bngl. . . E6 40
Kapuas, stm., Indon. D3 36
Kapuas, stm., Indon. D4 36
Kapuas Hulu, Pegunungan (Kapuas Hulu, Pergunungan), mts., Asia C4 36
Kapuas Hulu, Pergunungan (Kapuas Hulu, Pegunungan), mts., Asia C4 36
Kapuskasing, On., Can. . . . o19 89
Kapuvár, Hung. F4 20
Kapyl', Bela. C9 20
Kara, Russia C8 26
Kara-Balta, Kyrg. A2 40
Karabaš, Russia C11 22
Kara-Bogaz-Gol, zaliv, b., Turk. E7 26
Kara-Bogaz-Gol Gulf see Kara-Bogaz-Gol, zaliv, b., Turk. E7 26
Karabük, Tur. B5 44
Karabula, Russia D11 26
Karaburun, Tur. C2 44
Karabutak, Kaz. E11 22
Karacabey, Tur. B3 44

Karačaevo-Čerkesija, state, Russia E6 26
Karačev, Russia C13 20
Karāchi, Pak. F9 42
Karād, India F2 40
Karaganda, Kaz. E9 26
Karaginskij, ostrov, i., Russia D18 26
Karaginskij zaliv, b., Russia . D18 26
Kāraikkudi, India G3 40
Karaj, Iran C6 42
Karakaya Baraji, res., Tur. . . C8 44
Karakelong, Pulau, i., Indon. F8 32
Karakol, Kyrg. E9 26
Karakoram Pass, Asia B3 40
Karakoram Range, mts., Asia B3 40
Karakul', Uzb. C8 42
Kara-Kum Canal see Garagumskij kanal imeni Prezidenta Turkmenistana S.A. Nijazova, Turk. C8 42
Karaman, Tur. D5 44
Karamay, China B4 28
Karamea Bight, b., N.Z. . . . p13 63c
Karapınar, Tur. D5 44
Karasay, China B4 40
Karasburg, Nmb. D2 56
Kara Sea see Karskoe more, Russia B8 26
Karasu, Tur. B4 44
Karasu, stm., Tur. C9 44
Karasuk, Russia D9 26
Karatau, Kaz. B10 42
Karatau, hrebet, mts., Kaz. . E8 26
Karatobe, Kaz. E9 22
Karaton, Kaz. A6 42
Karatsu, Japan D1 31
Karaul, Kaz. B3 28
Karaul, Russia B10 26
Karawang, Indon. E3 36
Karažal, Kaz. B2 28
Karbalā', Iraq D4 42
Karbalā', state, Iraq F10 42
Kårböle, Swe. F6 10
Karcag, Hung. F6 20
Kardeljevo, Cro. C6 18
Kardhítsa, Grc. E8 18
Kärdžali, Bul. D10 18
Karelia see Karelija, state, Russia C5 26
Karelia, hist. reg., Eur. C12 6
Karelija, state, Russia C5 26
Karema, Tan. E6 54
Karesuando, Swe. B10 10
Kargopol', Russia C5 26
Kariba, Zimb. B4 56
Kariba, Lake, res., Afr. B4 56
Karibib, Nmb. C2 56
Karigasniemi, Fin. B11 10
Karimata, Selat (Karimata Strait), strt., Indon. . . . D3 36
Karimata Strait see Karimata, Selat, strt., Indon. D3 36
Karīmganj, India E6 40
Karīmnagar, India F3 40
Karimunjawa, Pulau, i., Indon. E4 36
Karisimbi, Volcan, vol., Afr. . D5 54
Karkaralinsk, Kaz. B3 28
Karkar Island, i., Pap. N. Gui. G12 32
Karkheh, stm., Iran G12 44
Karkinits'ka zatoka, b., Ukr. G12 20
Karkūk, Iraq C4 42
Karlivka, Ukr. E13 20
Karl-Marx-Stadt see Chemnitz, Ger. E13 12
Karlovac, Cro. B5 18
Karlovy Vary, Czech Rep. . . D2 20
Karlshamn, Swe. H6 10
Karlskoga, Swe. G6 10
Karlskrona, Swe. H6 10
Karlsruhe, Ger. F11 12
Karlstad, Swe. G5 10
Karlstad, Mn., U.S. B2 116
Karma, Niger D5 50
Karnāl, India D3 40
Karnaphuli Reservoir, res., Bngl. E6 40
Karnātaka, prov., India G3 40
Karnes, co., Tx., U.S. E4 136
Karnes City, Tx., U.S. E4 136
Karns, Tn., U.S. n13 135
Kárpathos, i., Grc. G11 18
Karpogory, Russia B7 22
Karratha, Austl. E2 60
Kars, Tur. B10 44
Karsakpaj, Kaz. B1 28
Karši, Uzb. F8 26
Karskie Vorota, proliv, strt., Russia B7 26
Karskoe more, Russia B8 26
Kartaly, Russia D8 26
Karufa, Indon. D8 36
Kārūn, stm., Iran G13 44
Karūr, India G3 40
Karviná, Czech Rep. E5 20
Kārwār, India G2 40
Karymskoe, Russia A10 28
Kasai (Cassai), stm., Afr. . . D3 54
Kasaji, D.R.C. F4 54
Kasama, Zam. A5 56
Kasane, Bots. B4 56
Kasanga, Tan. E6 54

Kasangulu, D.R.C. D3 54
Kāsaragod, India G3 40
Kasempa, Zam. A4 56
Kasenga, D.R.C. F5 54
Kasenye, D.R.C. C6 54
Kasese, D.R.C. D5 54
Kasese, Ug. C6 54
Kāshān, Iran D6 42
Kashgar see Kashi, China . . D3 28
Kashi, China D3 28
Kāshmar, Iran C7 42
Kasimov, Russia B16 20
Kasiruta, Pulau, i., Indon. . . D7 36
Kaskaskia, stm., Il., U.S. . . . D5 106
Kaslo, B.C., Can. E9 85
Kasongo, D.R.C. D5 54
Kasongo-Lunda, D.R.C. . . . E3 54
Kásos, i., Grc. G11 18
Kasota, Mn., U.S. F5 116
Kaspi, Geor. B11 44
Kaspijsk, Russia A12 44
Kaspijskij, Russia E6 26
Kassalā, Sudan G12 48
Kassandra, Gulf of see Kassándras, Kólpos, b., Grc. D9 18
Kassándras, Kólpos, b., Grc. D9 18
Kassel, Ger. E11 12
Kasserine, Tun. C6 48
Kasson, Mn., U.S. F6 116
Kastamonu, Tur. B5 44
Kastoría, Grc. D8 18
Kasulu, Tan. D6 54
Kasūr, Pak. D10 42
Kataba, Zam. B4 56
Katahdin, Mount, mtn., Me., U.S. C4 112
Katako-Kombe, D.R.C. D4 54
Katanga, hist. reg., D.R.C. . E4 54
Katangli, Russia D16 26
Katanning, Austl. G2 60
Katchall Island, i., India . . . H6 40
Katerîni, Grc. E8 18
Kates Needle, mtn., Ak., U.S. m24 95
Katha, Myan. B3 34
Katherîna, Gebel, mtn., Egypt E11 48
Katherine, Austl. C5 60
Kāthiāwār Peninsula, pen., India E2 40
Kathleen, Fl., U.S. D4 102
Kāthmāndau, Nepal D5 40
Kati, Mali D3 50
Katihār, India D5 40
Katiola, C. Iv. E3 50
Katmai, Mount, mtn., Ak., U.S. D9 95
Katmai National Park, Ak., U.S. D9 95
Kātmāndu see Kāthmāndau, Nepal D5 40
Katompi, D.R.C. D5 54
Katoomba, Austl. G5 62
Katowice, Pol. D5 20
Katrineholm, Swe. G7 10
Katsina, Nig. D6 50
Kattakurgan, Uzb. C9 42
Kattegat, strt., Eur. B12 12
Katy, Tx., U.S. r14 136
Kauai, co., Hi., U.S. B1 104
Kauai, i., Hi., U.S. A2 104
Kauai Channel, strt., Hi., U.S. h17 92a
Kauai Channel, strt., Hi., U.S. B3 104
Kau Desert, des., Hi., U.S. . D6 104
Kaufbeuren, Ger. G12 12
Kaufman, Tx., U.S. C4 136
Kaufman, co., Tx., U.S. C4 136
Kauira Head, c., Hi., U.S. . . C6 104
Kaukauna, Wi., U.S. D5 142
Kaula Island, i., Hi., U.S. . . m15 104
Kaulakahi Channel, strt., Hi., U.S. A2 104
Kaumakani, Hi., U.S. B2 104
Kaunakakai, Hi., U.S. B4 104
Kauna Point, c., Hi., U.S. . . D6 104
Kaura-Namoda, Nig. D6 50
Kavača, Russia C19 26
Kavadarci, Mac. D8 18
Kavála, Grc. D10 18
Kavali, India G4 40
Kavaratti, India G2 40
Kāveri, stm., India G3 40
Kavieng, Pap. N. Gui. G13 32
Kavīr, Dasht-e, des., Iran . . D6 42
Kawaihoa Point, c., Hi., U.S. B1 104
Kawaikini, mtn., Hi., U.S. . . A2 104
Kawambwa, Zam. A4 56
Kawasaki, Japan D15 28
Kawerau, N.Z. o14 63c
Kawich Peak, mtn., Nv., U.S. F5 121
Kawich Range, mts., Nv., U.S. F5 121
Kaw Lake, res., Ok., U.S. . . A5 129
Kaxgar, stm., China D3 28
Kay, co., Ok., U.S. A4 129
Kaya, Burkina D4 50
Kaycee, Wy., U.S. C6 143
Kayenta, Az., U.S. A5 96
Kayes, Mali D2 50
Kayseri, Tur. C6 44

Kaysville, Ut., U.S. B4 137
Kayuagung, Indon. D2 36
Kazače, Russia B15 26
Kazahskij melkosopočnik, hills, Kaz. D9 26
Kazakh Hills see Kazahskij melkosopočnik, hills, Kaz. D9 26
Kazakhstan, ctry., Asia E8 26
Kazalinsk, Kaz. A8 42
Kazan', Russia D6 26
Kazanka, Ukr. F12 20
Kazanlăk, Bul. C10 18
Kazan-rettō, is., Japan F17 64
Kāzerūn, Iran E6 42
Kazincbarcika, Hung. E6 20
Kaztalovka, Kaz. E8 22
Kazym, Russia B12 22
Kéa, i., Grc. F10 18
Keaau, Hi., U.S. D6 104
Keahiakahoe, Puu, mtn., Hi., U.S. g10 104
Keahole Point, c., Hi., U.S. . D5 104
Kealaikahiki Channel, strt., Hi., U.S. C5 104
Kealaikahiki Point, c., Hi., U.S. C5 104
Kealakekua, Hi., U.S. D6 104
Kealia, Hi., U.S. A2 104
Keams Canyon, Az., U.S. . . B5 96
Keanapapa Point, c., Hi., U.S. C4 104
Keansburg, N.J., U.S. C4 123
Kearney, Mo., U.S. B3 118
Kearney, Ne., U.S. D6 120
Kearney, co., Ne., U.S. D7 120
Kearns, Ut., U.S. C4 137
Kearny, Az., U.S. D5 96
Kearny, N.J., U.S. h8 123
Kearny, co., Ks., U.S. D2 109
Keban Barajı, res., Tur. C8 44
Keban Reservoir see Keban Barajı, res., Tur. C8 44
Kébèmer, Sen. C1 50
Kebnekaise, mtn., Swe. . . . C8 10
K'ebrī Dehar, Eth. B8 54
Kecskemét, Hung. F5 20
Kedges Straits, strt., Md., U.S. D5 113
Kedgwick, N.B., Can. B2 87
Kediri, Indon. E4 36
Kedon, Russia C17 26
Kédougou, Sen. D2 50
Keego Harbor, Mi., U.S. . . . o15 115
Keene, N.H., U.S. E2 122
Keene, Tx., U.S. n9 136
Keer-Weer, Cape, c., Austl. . C3 62
Keeseville, N.Y., U.S. f11 125
Keesler Air Force Base, mil., Ms., U.S. E5 117
Keetmanshoop, Nmb. D2 56
Keet Seel Ruin, hist., Az., U.S. A5 96
Keewatin, On., Can. E4 86
Keewatin, Mn., U.S. C6 116
Kefallinía, i., Grc. E8 18
Kefamenanu, Indon. E6 36
Keffi, Nig. E6 50
Keflavík, Ice. m17 10a
Kegonsa, Lake, l., Wi., U.S. F4 142
Kehra, Est. G11 10
Ke-hsi Mānsām, Myan. B3 34
Keila, Est. G11 10
Keiser, Ar., U.S. B5 97
Keith, co., Ne., U.S. C4 120
Keizer, Or., U.S. C3 130
Kejimkujik National Park, N.S., Can. E4 87
Kekaha, Hi., U.S. B2 104
Kékes, mtn., Hung. F5 20
K'elafo, Eth. B8 54
Kelan, China B3 30
Kelantan, stm., Malay. B2 36
Kelibia, Tun. F3 18
Kelkit, Tur. B8 44
Kelkit, stm., Tur. B7 44
Keller, Tx., U.S. n9 136
Kellerberrin, Austl. G2 60
Kelleys Island, i., Oh., U.S. . A3 128
Kellogg, Ia., U.S. C5 108
Kellogg, Id., U.S. B2 105
Kelloselkä, Fin. C13 10
Kelly Air Force Base, mil., Tx., U.S. k7 136
Kelly Island, i., De., U.S. . . . D4 101
Kellyville, Ok., U.S. B5 129
Kélo, Chad E8 50
Kelowna, B.C., Can. E8 85
Kelso, Wa., U.S. C3 140
Keluang, Malay. C2 36
Kem', Russia C5 26
Kembé, C.A.R. C4 54
Kemerovo, Russia D10 26
Kemi, Fin. D11 10
Kemijärvi, Fin. C12 10
Kemijoki, stm., Fin. C11 10
Kemmerer, Wy., U.S. E2 143
Kemp, Tx., U.S. C4 136
Kemp, Lake, res., Tx., U.S. . C3 136
Kemper, co., Ms., U.S. C5 117
Kempsey, Austl. G10 62
Kempten, Ger. G12 12
Kemptville, On., Can. B9 89
Kemul, Kong, mtn., Indon. . C5 36

Kenai, Ak., U.S. C9 95
Kenai Fjords National Park, Ak., U.S. D10 95
Kenai Mountains, mts., Ak., U.S. h16 95
Kenai Peninsula, pen., Ak., U.S. h16 95
Kenansville, N.C., U.S. C5 126
Kenbridge, Va., U.S. D4 139
Kendal, Eng., U.K. C5 12
Kendall, Fl., U.S. s13 102
Kendall, co., Il., U.S. B5 106
Kendall, co., Tx., U.S. E3 136
Kendall Park, N.J., U.S. C3 123
Kendallville, In., U.S. B7 107
Kendari, Indon. D6 36
Kendawangan, Indon. D4 36
Kenedy, Tx., U.S. E4 136
Kenedy, co., Tx., U.S. F4 136
Kenema, S.L. E2 50
Kenge, D.R.C. D3 54
Kēng Tung, Myan. B3 34
Kenhardt, S. Afr. D3 56
Kenilworth, Il., U.S. h9 106
Kénitra, Mor. D3 48
Kenly, N.C., U.S. B4 126
Kenmare, N.D., U.S. A3 127
Kenmore, N.Y., U.S. C2 125
Kennaday Peak, mtn., Wy., U.S. E6 143
Kennebago Lake, l., Me., U.S. C2 112
Kennebec, co., Me., U.S. . . D3 112
Kennebec, stm., Me., U.S. . D3 112
Kennebunk, Me., U.S. E2 112
Kennebunkport, Me., U.S. . E2 112
Kennedy, Cape see Canaveral, Cape, c., Fl., U.S. D6 102
Kennedy Entrance, strt., Ak., U.S. D9 95
Kenner, La., U.S. E5 111
Kennesaw, Ga., U.S. B2 103
Kennesaw Mountain, mtn., Ga., U.S. C2 103
Kennett, Mo., U.S. E7 118
Kennett Square, Pa., U.S. . . G10 131
Kennewick, Wa., U.S. C6 140
Keno, Or., U.S. E5 130
Kenosha, Wi., U.S. F6 142
Kenosha, co., Wi., U.S. F5 142
Kenova, W.V., U.S. C2 141
Kensett, Ar., U.S. B4 97
Kensico Reservoir, res., N.Y., U.S. g13 125
Kensington, P.E., Can. C6 87
Kensington, Ct., U.S. C4 100
Kensington, Md., U.S. B3 113
Kent, Oh., U.S. A4 128
Kent, Wa., U.S. B3 140
Kent, co., De., U.S. D3 101
Kent, co., Md., U.S. B5 113
Kent, co., Mi., U.S. E5 115
Kent, co., R.I., U.S. D2 132
Kent, co., Tx., U.S. C2 136
Kentau, Kaz. B9 42
Kent City, Mi., U.S. E5 115
Kent Island, i., De., U.S. . . . D4 101
Kent Island, i., Md., U.S. . . . C5 113
Kentland, In., U.S. C3 107
Kenton, De., U.S. D3 101
Kenton, Oh., U.S. B2 128
Kenton, Tn., U.S. A2 135
Kenton, co., Ky., U.S. B5 110
Kent Point, c., Md., U.S. . . . C5 113
Kentucky, state, U.S. C4 110
Kentucky, stm., Ky., U.S. . . B5 110
Kentucky Lake, res., U.S. . . D10 92
Kentwood, La., U.S. D5 111
Kentwood, Mi., U.S. F5 115
Kenvil, N.J., U.S. B3 123
Kenvir, Ky., U.S. D6 110
Kenya, ctry., Afr. C7 54
Kenya, Mount see Kirinyaga, mtn., Kenya . D7 54
Kenyon, Mn., U.S. F6 116
Kenyon, R.I., U.S. F2 132
Keokea, Hi., U.S. C5 104
Keokuk, Ia., U.S. D6 108
Keokuk, co., Ia., U.S. C5 108
Keokuk Lock and Dam, U.S. D6 108
Keosauqua, Ia., U.S. D6 108
Keota, Ia., U.S. C6 108
Keota, Ok., U.S. B7 129
Keowee, Lake, res., S.C., U.S. B2 133
Kepno, Pol. D4 20
Kerala, prov., India G3 40
Kerang, Austl. H3 62
Keratéa, Grc. F11 10
Kerava, Fin. F11 10
Kerch, Ukr. G14 20
Kerch Strait, strt., Eur. G14 20
Keremeos, B.C., Can. E8 85
Keren, Erit. G12 48
Kerguélen, Îles, is., Afr. . . . M10 64
Kerguelen Plateau N10 64
Kerhonkson, N.Y., U.S. D6 125
Kericho, Kenya D7 54
Kerinci, Gunung, vol., Indon. D2 36

Name	Map Ref.	Page
Kerkhoven, Mn., U.S.	E3	116
Kerki, Turk.	C9	42
Kerkiči, Turk.	F8	26
Kérkira, Grc.	E7	18
Kérkira (Corfu), i., Grc.	E7	18
Kermadec Islands, is., N.Z.	G12	58
Kermadec Ridge	L20	64
Kermadec Trench	L21	64
Kermān, Iran	D7	42
Kermānshāh (Bākhtarān), Iran	D5	42
Kermit, Tx., U.S.	D1	136
Kermode, Mount, mtn., B.C., Can.	C2	85
Kern, co., Ca., U.S.	E4	98
Kern, stm., Ca., U.S.	E4	98
Kernersville, N.C., U.S.	A2	126
Kernville, Ca., U.S.	E4	98
Kérouané, Gui.	E3	50
Kerr, co., Tx., U.S.	D3	136
Kerr, Lake, l., Fl., U.S.	C5	102
Kerrville, Tx., U.S.	D3	136
Kersey, Co., U.S.	A6	99
Kershaw, S.C., U.S.	B6	133
Kershaw, co., S.C., U.S.	C6	133
Kerulen, stm., Asia	B10	28
Keşan, Tur.	B2	44
Kesennuma, Japan	D16	28
Keshena, Wi., U.S.	D5	142
Keskin, Tur.	C5	44
Kesten'ga, Russia	D14	10
Keszthely, Hung.	F4	20
Ket', stm., Russia	D10	26
Keta, Ghana	E5	50
Ketapang, Indon.	D3	36
Ketchikan, Ak., U.S.	D13	95
Ketchum, Id., U.S.	F4	105
Kete-Krachi, Ghana	E4	50
Kętrzyn, Pol.	B6	20
Kettering, Oh., U.S.	C1	128
Kettle, stm., Mn., U.S.	D6	116
Kettle Creek, stm., Pa., U.S.	D6	131
Kettle Creek Lake, res., Pa., U.S.	D6	131
Kettle Falls, Wa., U.S.	A7	140
Keuka Lake, l., N.Y., U.S.	C3	125
Kewanee, Il., U.S.	B4	106
Kewaskum, Wi., U.S.	E5	142
Kewaunee, Wi., U.S.	D6	142
Kewaunee, co., Wi., U.S.	D6	142
Keweenaw, co., Mi., U.S.	A2	115
Keweenaw Bay, b., Mi., U.S.	B2	115
Keweenaw Peninsula, pen., Mi., U.S.	A3	115
Keweenaw Point, c., Mi., U.S.	A3	115
Keya Paha, co., Ne., U.S.	B6	120
Keya Paha, stm., U.S.	A5	120
Keyhole Reservoir, res., Wy., U.S.	B8	143
Key Largo, Fl., U.S.	G6	102
Keyport, N.J., U.S.	C4	123
Keyser, W.V., U.S.	B6	141
Keystone, Wa., U.S.	D3	141
Keystone Heights, Fl., U.S.	C4	102
Keystone Lake, res., Ok., U.S.	A5	129
Keystone Peak, mtn., Az., U.S.	F4	96
Keysville, Va., U.S.	C4	139
Key West, Fl., U.S.	H5	102
Key West Naval Air Station, mil., Fl., U.S.	H5	102
Kezar Falls, Me., U.S.	E2	112
Kezar Lake, l., Me., U.S.	D2	112
Kezi, Zimb.	C4	56
Kežma, Russia	D12	26
Khābūr, Nahr al-, stm., Asia	E9	44
Khadki, India	F2	40
Khairpur, Pak.	E9	42
Khajrāho, India	E4	40
Khakhea, Bots.	C3	56
Khalkhāl, Iran	D13	44
Khalkidhikí, hist. reg., Grc.	D9	18
Khalkís, Grc.	E9	18
Khambhāt, India	E2	40
Khambhāt, Gulf of, b., India	E2	40
Khāmgaon, India	E3	40
Khammam, India	F4	40
Khānābād, Afg.	C9	42
Khān al-Baghdādī, Iraq	F10	44
Khānaqīn, Iraq	E11	44
Khandwa, India	E3	40
Khānewāl, Pak.	D10	42
Khaniá, Grc.	G9	18
Khaníon, Kólpos, b., Grc.	G9	18
Khanka, Lake, l., Asia	C14	28
Khānpur, Pak.	E10	42
Kharagpur, India	E5	40
Khargon, India	E3	40
Kharkiv, Ukr.	E14	20
Khartoum see Al-Kharṭūm, Sudan	G11	48
Khāsh, Afg.	D8	42
Khāsh, Iran	E8	42
Khashm al-Qirbah, Sudan	H12	48
Khemis Melyana, Alg.	I8	14
Khenchla, Alg.	D5	14
Khenifra, Mor.	E2	14
Kherson, Ukr.	F12	20
Khíos, Grc.	E11	18
Khíos, i., Grc.	E10	18
Khmel'nyts'kyi, Ukr.	E9	20
Khmil'nyk, Ukr.	E9	20
Kholm, Afg.	C9	42
Khomeynīshahr, Iran	D6	42
Khong see Mekong, stm., Asia	C4	34
Khon Kaen, Thai.	C4	34
Khorramābād, Iran	D5	42
Khorramshahr, Iran	D5	42
Khotyn, Ukr.	E9	20
Khouribga, Mor.	D3	48
Khrystynivka, Ukr.	E10	20
Khulna, Bngl.	E5	40
Khust, Ukr.	E7	20
Khuzdār, Pak.	E9	42
Khvoy, Iran	C4	42
Khyber Pass, Asia	C2	40
Kiama, D.R.C.	E3	54
Kiamba, Phil.	E8	34
Kiamichi, stm., Ok., U.S.	C6	129
Kiamika, stm., P.Q., Can.	C2	90
Kiana, Ak., U.S.	B7	95
Kiangarow, Mount, mtn., Austl.	F5	62
Kiawah Island, i., S.C., U.S.	F7	133
Kibangou, Congo	D2	54
Kibombo, D.R.C.	D5	54
Kibondo, Tan.	D6	54
Kibre Mengist, Eth.	B7	54
Kičevo, Mac.	D8	18
Kickamuit, stm., R.I., U.S.	D5	132
Kickapoo, stm., Wi., U.S.	E3	142
Kickapoo, Lake, res., Tx., U.S.	C3	136
Kickapoo Indian Reservation, Ks., U.S.	C8	109
Kicking Horse Pass, Can.	D2	84
Kidal, Mali	C5	50
Kidatu, Tan.	E7	54
Kidder, co., N.D., U.S.	C6	127
Kidira, Sen.	D2	50
Kiefer, Ok., U.S.	B5	129
Kiel, Ger.	C12	12
Kiel, Wi., U.S.	E5	142
Kiel Bay see Kieler Bucht, b., Ger.	C12	12
Kiel Canal see Nord-Ostsee-Kanal, Ger.	C11	12
Kielce, Pol.	D6	20
Kieler Bucht, b., Ger.	C12	12
Kiester, Mn., U.S.	G5	116
Kiev see Kyïv, Ukr.	D11	20
Kiev Reservoir see Kyïvs'ke vodoskhovyshche, res., Ukr.	D11	20
Kiffa, Maur.	C2	50
Kigali, Rw.	D6	54
Kigoma, Tan.	D5	54
Kihčik, Russia	D17	26
Kihei, Hi., U.S.	C5	104
Kiholo Bay, b., Hi., U.S.	D5	104
Kii Strait see Kii-suidō, strt., Japan	E15	28
Kii-suidō, strt., Japan	E15	28
Kikinda, Yugo.	B8	18
Kikládhes, is., Grc.	F10	18
Kikori, Pap. N. Gui.	H11	32
Kikwit, D.R.C.	E3	54
Kil, Swe.	G5	10
Kilauea, Hi., U.S.	A2	104
Kilauea Crater, crat., Hi., U.S.	D6	104
Kilauea Point, c., Hi., U.S.	A2	104
Kilchu-ŭp, N. Kor.	B1	31
Kildurk, Austl.	D4	60
Kilgore, Tx., U.S.	C5	136
Kilibo, Benin	E5	50
Kiliia, Ukr.	G10	20
Kilimanjaro, mtn., Tan.	D7	54
Kilimli, Tur.	B4	44
Kilindoni, Tan.	E7	54
Kilis, Tur.	D7	44
Kilkenny, Ire.	D3	12
Kilkís, Grc.	D9	18
Killaloe Station, On., Can.	B7	89
Killam, Ab., Can.	C5	84
Killarney, Mb., Can.	E2	86
Killarney Provincial Park, On., Can.	A3	89
Killdeer, N.D., U.S.	B3	127
Killeen, Tx., U.S.	D4	136
Killen, Al., U.S.	A2	94
Killian, La., U.S.	h10	111
Killona, La., U.S.	h11	111
Kilmarnock, Scot., U.K.	C4	12
Kilmarnock, Va., U.S.	C6	139
Kilmichael, Ms., U.S.	B4	117
Kiln, Ms., U.S.	E4	117
Kilomines, D.R.C.	C6	54
Kilosa, Tan.	E7	54
Kilttān Island, i., India	G2	40
Kilwa, D.R.C.	E5	54
Kilwa Kivinje, Tan.	E7	54
Kimba, Austl.	G2	62
Kimball, Mn., U.S.	E4	116
Kimball, Ne., U.S.	C2	120
Kimball, S.D., U.S.	D7	134
Kimball, co., Ne., U.S.	C2	120
Kimball, Mount, mtn., Ak., U.S.	C11	95
Kimberley, B.C., Can.	E9	85
Kimberley, S. Afr.	D3	56
Kimberley Plateau, plat., Austl.	D4	60
Kimberlin Heights, Tn., U.S.	n14	135
Kimberly, Al., U.S.	B3	94
Kimberly, Id., U.S.	G4	105
Kimberly, W.V., U.S.	m13	141
Kimberly, Wi., U.S.	h9	142
Kimble, co., Tx., U.S.	D3	136
Kimch'aek, N. Kor.	C13	28
Kimito, i., Fin.	G10	10
Kimry, Russia	C6	22
Kinabalu, Gunong, mtn., Malay.	B5	36
Kinabatangan, stm., Malay.	B5	36
Kinbasket Lake, res., B.C., Can.	D8	85
Kincaid, Il., U.S.	D4	106
Kincaid, W.V., U.S.	m13	141
Kincaid, Lake, res., Il., U.S.	D4	106
Kincardine, On., Can.	C3	89
Kincheloe Air Force Base, mil., Mi., U.S.	B6	115
Kinda, D.R.C.	E5	54
Kinder, La., U.S.	D3	111
Kindia, Gui.	D2	50
Kindu, D.R.C.	D5	54
Kine, N.C., U.S.	A2	126
Kineṧma, Russia	C7	22
King, N.C., U.S.	A2	126
King, Wi., U.S.	D4	142
King, co., Tx., U.S.	C2	136
King, co., Wa., U.S.	B3	140
King and Queen, co., Va., U.S.	C6	139
Kingaroy, Austl.	F5	62
King City, Ca., U.S.	D3	98
King City, Mo., U.S.	A3	118
King Cove, Ak., U.S.	E7	95
Kingfield, Me., U.S.	D2	112
Kingfisher, Ok., U.S.	B4	129
Kingfisher, co., Ok., U.S.	B3	129
King George, co., Va., U.S.	B5	139
Kingisepp, Russia	G13	10
King Island, i., Austl.	H3	62
King Island, i., B.C., Can.	C4	85
King Lear Peak, mtn., Nv., U.S.	B3	121
King Leopold Ranges, mts., Austl.	D3	60
Kingman, Az., U.S.	B1	96
Kingman, Ks., U.S.	E5	109
Kingman, co., Ks., U.S.	E5	109
King Mountain, mtn., Or., U.S.	D8	130
King Mountain, mtn., Or., U.S.	E3	130
Kingombe, D.R.C.	D5	54
King Peak, mtn., Ca., U.S.	B1	98
Kings, Ms., U.S.	C3	117
Kings, co., Ca., U.S.	D4	98
Kings, co., N.Y., U.S.	E7	125
Kings, stm., Ar., U.S.	A2	97
Kings, stm., Ca., U.S.	D4	98
Kings, stm., Nv., U.S.	B3	121
King Salmon, Ak., U.S.	D8	95
Kingsburg, Ca., U.S.	D4	98
Kingsbury, co., S.D., U.S.	C8	134
Kings Canyon National Park, Ca., U.S.	D4	98
Kingsey-Falls, P.Q., Can.	D5	90
Kingsford, Mi., U.S.	C2	115
Kingsland, Ga., U.S.	F5	103
Kingsland, Tx., U.S.	D3	136
Kingsley, Ia., U.S.	B2	108
Kingsley, Mi., U.S.	D5	115
King's Lynn, Eng., U.K.	D7	12
Kings Mountain, N.C., U.S.	B1	126
King Sound, strt., Austl.	D3	60
Kings Peak, mtn., Ut., U.S.	C5	137
King's Point, Nf., Can.	D3	88
Kingsport, Tn., U.S.	C11	135
Kingston, On., Can.	C8	89
Kingston, Jam.	B4	80
Kingston, Ga., U.S.	B2	103
Kingston, Id., U.S.	B2	105
Kingston, Ma., U.S.	C6	114
Kingston, N.H., U.S.	E4	122
Kingston, N.Y., U.S.	D6	125
Kingston, Oh., U.S.	C3	128
Kingston, Ok., U.S.	D5	129
Kingston, Pa., U.S.	D10	131
Kingston, R.I., U.S.	F3	132
Kingston, Tn., U.S.	D9	135
Kingston Springs, Tn., U.S.	A4	135
Kingston upon Hull, Eng., U.K.	D6	12
Kingstown see Dún Laoghaire, Ire.	D3	12
Kingstown, St. Vin.	C7	80
Kingstree, S.C., U.S.	D8	133
Kingsville, On., Can.	E2	89
Kingsville, Md., U.S.	B5	113
Kingsville (North Kingsville), Oh., U.S.	A5	128
Kingsville, Tx., U.S.	F4	136
Kingsville Naval Air Station, mil., Tx., U.S.	F4	136
King William, co., Va., U.S.	B5	139
King William's Town, S. Afr.	E4	56
Kingwood, W.V., U.S.	B5	141
Kinistino, Sk., Can.	E3	91
Kinkaid Lake, res., Il., U.S.	F4	106
Kinkala, Congo	D2	54
Kinloch, Mo., U.S.	f13	118
Kinmundy, Il., U.S.	E5	106
Kinnaird Head, c., Scot., U.K.	B6	12
Kinnelon, N.J., U.S.	B4	123
Kinney, co., Tx., U.S.	E2	136
Kinsey, Al., U.S.	D4	94
Kinshasa, D.R.C.	D3	54
Kinsley, Ks., U.S.	E4	109
Kinston, N.C., U.S.	B5	126
Kintampo, Ghana	E4	50
Kintyre, pen., Scot., U.K.	C4	12
Kinyeti, mtn., Sudan	J11	48
Kinzia, D.R.C.	D3	54
Kiowa, Ks., U.S.	E5	109
Kiowa, Ok., U.S.	C6	129
Kiowa, co., Co., U.S.	C8	99
Kiowa, co., Ks., U.S.	E4	109
Kiowa, co., Ok., U.S.	C2	129
Kiowa Creek, stm., Ok., U.S.	A1	129
Kiparissiakós Kólpos, b., Grc.	F8	18
Kipembawe, Tan.	E6	54
Kipengere Range, mts., Tan.	E6	54
Kipili, Tan.	E6	54
Kipini, Kenya	D8	54
Kipnuk, Ak., U.S.	C7	95
Kipushi, D.R.C.	F5	54
Kirbyville, Tx., U.S.	D6	136
Kirensk, Russia	D12	26
Kirgiz Range, mts., Asia	A2	40
Kiri, D.R.C.	D3	54
Kiribati, ctry., Oc.	E12	58
Kiribati, is., Kir.	D11	58
Kırıkhan, Tur.	D7	44
Kırıkkale, Tur.	C5	44
Kirinyaga (Kenya, Mount), mtn., Kenya	D7	54
Kiriši, Russia	C5	22
Kiritimati (Christmas Island), atoll, Kir.	D14	58
Kırkağaç, Tur.	C2	44
Kirkcaldy, Scot., U.K.	B5	12
Kirkenes, Nor.	B14	10
Kirkjubæjarklaustur, Ice.	m19	10a
Kirkland, Il., U.S.	A5	106
Kirkland, Wa., U.S.	B3	140
Kirkland Lake, On., Can.	o19	89
Kırklareli, Tur.	B2	44
Kirklin, In., U.S.	D5	107
Kirkpatrick, Mount, mtn., Ant.	E22	67
Kirksville, Mo., U.S.	A5	118
Kirkwall, Scot., U.K.	A5	12
Kirkwood, S. Afr.	E4	56
Kirkwood, De., U.S.	B3	101
Kirkwood, Il., U.S.	C3	106
Kirkwood, Mo., U.S.	f13	118
Kirov, Russia	B13	20
Kirov, Russia	D6	26
Kirovabad see Gäncä, Azer.	B12	44
Kirovakan see Vanadzor, Arm.	B11	44
Kirovohrad, Ukr.	E12	20
Kirovsk, Russia	A5	22
Kirovsk, Turk.	C8	42
Kirovskij, Russia	D17	26
Kirovskij, Russia	A2	31
Kirs, Russia	C9	22
Kirsanov, Russia	D7	22
Kırşehir, Tur.	C6	44
Kīrthar Range, mts., Pak.	E9	42
Kirtland, N.M., U.S.	A1	124
Kirtland Air Force Base, mil., N.M., U.S.	k7	124
Kiruna, Swe.	C9	10
Kirwin Reservoir, res., Ks., U.S.	C4	109
Kisangani, D.R.C.	C5	54
Kisar, Pulau, i., Indon.	E7	36
Kisaran, Indon.	C1	36
Kishangarh Bās, India	D2	40
Kishi, Nig.	E5	50
Kishinev see Chişinău, Mol.	F10	20
Kishiwada, Japan	D3	31
Kishwaukee, stm., Il., U.S.	A5	106
Kisii, Kenya	D6	54
Kisiju, Tan.	E7	54
Kiska Island, i., Ak., U.S.	E3	95
Kiskunfélegyháza, Hung.	F5	20
Kiskunhalas, Hung.	F5	20
Kislovodsk, Russia	B4	42
Kismaayo, Som.	D8	54
Kissidougou, Gui.	E2	50
Kissimmee, Fl., U.S.	D5	102
Kissimmee, stm., Fl., U.S.	E5	102
Kissimmee, Lake, l., Fl., U.S.	E5	102
Kississing Lake, l., Mb., Can.	B1	86
Kistler, W.V., U.S.	D3	141
Kisumu, Kenya	D6	54
Kisvárda, Hung.	E7	20
Kita, Mali	D3	50
Kitaibaraki, Japan	C4	31
Kitakyūshū, Japan	E14	28
Kitale, Kenya	C7	54
Kitami, Japan	E7	28
Kit Carson, co., Co., U.S.	B8	99
Kitchener, On., Can.	D4	89
Kíthira, i., Grc.	F9	18
Kíthnos, i., Grc.	F10	18
Kitimat, B.C., Can.	B3	85
Kitsap, co., Wa., U.S.	B3	140
Kitscoty, Ab., Can.	C5	84
Kittanning, Pa., U.S.	E2	131
Kittatinny Mountain, mtn., U.S.	B2	123
Kittery, Me., U.S.	E2	112
Kittery Point, Me., U.S.	E2	112
Kittitas, Wa., U.S.	C5	140
Kittitas, co., Wa., U.S.	B4	140
Kitts, Ky., U.S.	D6	110
Kittson, co., Mn., U.S.	B2	116
Kitty Hawk, N.C., U.S.	A7	126
Kitty Hawk Bay, b., N.C., U.S.	A7	126
Kitui, Kenya	D7	54
Kitwe, Zam.	A4	56
Kiunga, Kenya	D8	54
Kiviõli, Est.	G12	10
Kivu, Lac, l., Afr.	D5	54
Kizëma, Russia	B7	22
Kızılcahamam, Tur.	B5	44
Kızılırmak, stm., Tur.	B6	44
Kızıltepe, Tur.	D9	44
Kizljar, Russia	B5	42
Kizyl-Atrek, Turk.	C6	42
Kjusjur, Russia	B14	26
Kjustendil, Bul.	C9	18
Klabat, Gunung, vol., Indon.	C7	36
Kladno, Czech Rep.	D3	20
Klagenfurt, Aus.	G14	12
Klaipėda, Lith.	I9	10
Klamath, co., Or., U.S.	E5	130
Klamath, stm., U.S.	B2	98
Klamath Falls, Or., U.S.	E5	130
Klamath Mountains, mts., U.S.	E2	130
Klang, Malay.	C2	36
Klatovy, Czech Rep.	E2	20
Klawer, S. Afr.	E2	56
Klawock, Ak., U.S.	D13	95
Kleberg, co., Tx., U.S.	F4	136
Klerksdorp, S. Afr.	D4	56
Kletna, Russia	C12	20
Klickitat, Wa., U.S.	D4	140
Klickitat, co., Wa., U.S.	D4	140
Klickitat, stm., Wa., U.S.	C4	140
Klimpfjäll, Swe.	D6	10
Klin, Russia	C6	22
Klincy, Russia	C12	20
Klipplaat, S. Afr.	E3	56
Ključevskaja Sopka, vulkan, vol., Russia	D18	26
Kłobuck, Pol.	D5	20
Kłodzko, Pol.	D4	20
Klondike, hist. reg., Yk., Can.	F12	82
Klondike Gold Rush National Historical Park, Ak., U.S.	k22	95
Kluczbork, Pol.	D5	20
Klutina Lake, l., Ak., U.S.	g19	95
Knapp Creek, stm., W.V., U.S.	C5	141
Knee Lake, l., Mb., Can.	B4	86
Kneža, Bul.	C10	18
Knife, stm., N.D., U.S.	B3	127
Knightdale, N.C., U.S.	B4	126
Knight Inlet, b., B.C., Can.	D5	85
Knight Island, i., Ak., U.S.	g18	95
Knightstown, In., U.S.	E6	107
Knightsville, In., U.S.	E3	107
Knightville Reservoir, res., Ma., U.S.	B2	114
Knittelfeld, Aus.	G14	12
Knob Noster, Mo., U.S.	C4	118
Knollwood, W.V., U.S.	m12	141
Knossós, hist., Grc.	G10	18
Knott, co., Ky., U.S.	C6	110
Knox, In., U.S.	B4	107
Knox, Pa., U.S.	D2	131
Knox, co., Il., U.S.	B3	106
Knox, co., In., U.S.	G3	107
Knox, co., Ky., U.S.	D6	110
Knox, co., Me., U.S.	D4	112
Knox, co., Mo., U.S.	A5	118
Knox, co., Ne., U.S.	B8	120
Knox, co., Oh., U.S.	B3	128
Knox, co., Tn., U.S.	C10	135
Knox, co., Tx., U.S.	C3	136
Knox, Cape, c., B.C., Can.	B1	85
Knox City, Tx., U.S.	C3	136
Knox Coast, Ant.	C15	67
Knoxville, Ia., U.S.	C4	108
Knoxville, Il., U.S.	C3	106
Knoxville, Tn., U.S.	D10	135
Knysna, S. Afr.	E3	56
Kōbe, Japan	E15	28
København (Copenhagen), Den.	I6	10
Koblenz, Ger.	E10	12
Kobroor, Pulau, i., Indon.	H9	32
Kobryn, Bela.	C8	20
Kobuk, stm., Ak., U.S.	B8	95
Kobuk Valley National Park, Ak., U.S.	B8	95
Kočani, Mac.	D9	18
Kočevo, Russia	C9	22
Kochi (Cochin), India	H3	40
Kōchi, Japan	E14	28
Koch Peak, mtn., Mt., U.S.	E5	119
Kodaikānal, India	G3	40
Kodiak, Ak., U.S.	D9	95
Kodiak Island, i., Ak., U.S.	D9	95
Kodok, Sudan	B6	54
Koës, Nmb.	D2	56
Kofa Mountains, mts., Az., U.S.	D2	96
Köflach, Aus.	G14	12
Koforidua, Ghana	E4	50
Kōfu, Japan	D15	28
Kogaluk, stm., Nf., Can.	g9	88
Køge, Den.	I5	10

Name	Map Ref.	Page

Kohala Mountains, mts., Hi., U.S. ...C6 104
Kohāt, Pak. ...D10 42
Kohīma, India ...D6 40
Kohler, Wi., U.S. ...E6 142
Kohtla-Järve, Est. ...G12 10
Koihoa, India ...H6 40
Koindu, S.L. ...E2 50
Kojgorodok, Russia ...B9 22
Kojonup, Austl. ...G2 60
Kokand, Uzb. ...E9 26
Kokanee Glacier Provincial Park, B.C., Can. ...E9 85
Kokčetav, Kaz. ...D8 26
Kokemäki, Fin. ...F10 10
Kokenau, Indon. ...G10 32
Kokkola, Fin. ...E10 10
Kokoda, Pap. N. Gui. ...H12 32
Koko Head, c., Hi., U.S. ...B4 104
Kokolik, stm., Ak., U.S. ...B7 95
Kokomo, In., U.S. ...D5 107
Koko Nor see Qinghai Hu, l., China ...D8 28
Kokosing, stm., Oh., U.S. ...B3 128
Kokstad, S. Afr. ...E4 56
Kola, Russia ...B15 10
Kolaka, Indon. ...D6 36
Kola Peninsula see Kol'skij poluostrov, pen., Russia .C5 26
Kolār Gold Fields, India ...G3 40
Kolbio, Kenya ...D8 54
Kolda, Sen. ...D2 50
Kolding, Den. ...I3 10
Kole, D.R.C. ...D4 54
Kolea, Alg. ...I8 16
Kolguev, ostrov, i., Russia ..C6 26
Kolhāpur, India ...F2 40
Kolka, Lat. ...H10 10
Kolkata (Calcutta), India ...E5 40
Kolmogorovo, Russia ...D11 26
Köln (Cologne), Ger. ...E10 12
Koło, Pol. ...C5 20
Koloa, Hi., U.S. ...B2 104
Kołobrzeg, Pol. ...B3 20
Kolokani, Mali ...D3 50
Kolomna, Russia ...D5 26
Kolonia see Palikir, Micron. .D9 58
Kolonodale, Indon. ...D6 36
Kolpaševo, Russia ...D10 26
Kolpino, Russia ...C5 22
Kol'skij poluostrov, pen., Russia ...C5 26
Kolwezi, D.R.C. ...F5 54
Kolyma, stm., Russia ...C17 26
Kolymskaja, Russia ...C17 26
Komandorskie ostrova, is., Russia ...D18 26
Komandorski Islands see Komandorskie ostrova, is., Russia ...D18 26
Komárno, Slvk. ...F5 20
Komatipoort, S. Afr. ...D5 56
Kome Island, i., Ug. ...D6 54
Komi, state, Russia ...C7 26
Komló, Hung. ...F5 20
Kommunarsk see Alchevs'k, Ukr. ...E15 20
Kommunizma, pik see Ismail Samani, pik, Taj. ..F9 26
Komodo, Pulau, i., Indon. ..E5 36
Komoé, stm., Afr. ...E4 50
Komotiní, Grc. ...D10 18
Komsomolec, Kaz. ...D11 22
Komsomolec, ostrov, i., Russia ...A11 26
Komsomol'sk-na-Amure, Russia ...D15 26
Konahuanui, Puu, mtn., Hi., U.S. ...g10 104
Konārak, hist., India ...F5 40
Konawa, Ok., U.S. ...C5 129
Kondagaon, India ...F4 40
Kondinin, Austl. ...G2 60
Kondoa, Tan. ...D7 54
Kondopoga, Russia ...C5 26
Kondoz, Afg. ...C9 42
Koné, N. Cal. ...I8 62a
Kong, stm., Asia ...C5 34
Kongolo, D.R.C. ...E5 54
Kongor, Sudan ...B6 54
Kongsvinger, Nor. ...F5 10
Kongur Shan, China ...D3 28
Königsberg see Kaliningrad, Russia ...D4 20
Konin, Pol. ...C5 20
Konna, Mali ...D4 50
Konomoc, Lake, res., Ct., U.S. ...D7 100
Konoša, Russia ...C6 26
Konotop, Ukr. ...D12 20
Konstanz, Ger. ...G11 12
Kontagora, Nig. ...D6 50
Kontcha, Cam. ...B2 54
Kon Tum, Viet. ...D5 34
Konya, Tur. ...D5 44
Konza, Kenya ...D7 54
Konžakovskij Kamen', gora, mtn., Russia ...C10 22
Koochiching, co., Mn., U.S. .B4 116
Kookynie, Austl. ...F3 60
Koolau Range, mts., Hi., U.S. ...f10 104
Koontz Lake, In., U.S. ...B5 107
Kooskia, Id., U.S. ...C3 105
Kootenai, co., Id., U.S. ...B2 105

Kootenay Lake, l., B.C., Can. ...E9 85
Kootenay National Park, B.C., Can. ...D9 85
Kópasker, Ice. ...k20 10a
Kópavogur, Ice. ...I18 10a
Kopejsk, Russia ...C11 22
Kopet Mountains, mts., Asia ...C7 42
Köping, Swe. ...G6 10
Koppang, Nor. ...F4 10
Koppel, Pa., U.S. ...E1 131
Koprivnica, Cro. ...A6 18
Korab (Korabit, Maja e), mtn., Eur. ...D8 18
Korabit, Maja e (Korab), mtn., Eur. ...D8 18
Korāput, India ...F4 40
Korba, India ...E4 40
Korbol, Chad ...D8 50
Korçë, Alb. ...D8 18
Korea, North, ctry., Asia ...C13 28
Korea, South, ctry., Asia ...D10 28
Korea Bay, b., Asia ...D12 28
Korea Strait, strt., Asia ...E13 28
Korenovsk, Russia ...A3 42
Korf, Russia ...C18 26
Korfovskij, Russia ...A3 31
Korhogo, C. Iv. ...E3 50
Korinthiakós Kólpos, b., Grc. ...E9 18
Kórinthos, Grc. ...F9 18
Kōriyama, Japan ...C4 31
Korjakskaja Sopka, vulkan, vol., Russia ...D17 26
Korjakskoe nagor'e, mts., Russia ...C18 26
Korjažma, Russia ...B8 22
Korkino, Russia ...D11 22
Korkuteli, Tur. ...D4 44
Korla, China ...C5 28
Korliki, Russia ...C10 26
Kornat, Otok, i., Cro. ...C5 18
Korogwe, Tan. ...E7 54
Koronadal, Phil. ...E8 34
Koronis, Lake, l., Mn., U.S. .E4 116
Koror, Palau ...E9 32
Koro Sea, Fiji ...F12 58
Korosten', Ukr. ...D10 20
Korostyshiv, Ukr. ...D10 20
Korovin Volcano, vol., Ak., U.S. ...E5 95
Korsakov, Russia ...E16 26
Korsnäs, Fin. ...E9 10
Kos, i., Grc. ...F11 18
Koš-Agač, Russia ...D10 26
Koščagyl, Kaz. ...A6 42
Kościan, Pol. ...C4 20
Kościerzyna, Pol. ...B4 20
Kosciusko, co., In., U.S. ...B6 107
Kosciusko, Ms., U.S. ...B4 117
Kosciusko, Mount, mtn., Austl. ...H4 62
Koshkonong, Lake, l., Wi., U.S. ...F5 142
Košice, Slvk. ...E6 20
Kosju, Russia ...A10 22
Koslan, Russia ...B8 22
Kosovska Mitrovica, Yugo. ..C8 18
Kossou, Lac de, res., C. Iv. ..E3 50
Kossuth, co., Ia., U.S. ...A3 108
Kostiantynivka, Ukr. ...E14 20
Kostopil', Ukr. ...D9 20
Kostroma, Russia ...C7 22
Kostrzyn, Pol. ...C3 20
Koszalin, Pol. ...B4 20
Kőszeg, Hung. ...F4 20
Kota, India ...D3 40
Kotaagung, Indon. ...E2 36
Kotabaru, Indon. ...G6 32
Kotabaru see Jayapura, Indon. ...G11 32
Kota Belud, Malay. ...B5 36
Kota Bharu, Malay. ...B2 36
Kotabumi, Indon. ...D2 36
Kota Kinabalu, Malay. ...B5 36
Kotamobagu, Indon. ...C6 36
Kotel'nič, Russia ...C8 22
Kotel'nikovo, Russia ...E7 22
Kotel'nyj, ostrov, i., Russia .B15 26
Kotido, Ug. ...C6 54
Kotka, Fin. ...F12 10
Kot Kapūra, India ...C2 40
Kotlas, Russia ...C6 26
Kotlik, Ak., U.S. ...C7 95
Kotovs'k, Ukr. ...F10 20
Kotri, Pak. ...E9 42
Kottagüdem, India ...F4 40
Kottayam, India ...H3 40
Kotte see Sri Jayewardenepura Kotte, Sri L. ...H4 40
Kotto, stm., C.A.R. ...B4 54
Kotuj, stm., Russia ...C12 26
Kotzebue, Ak., U.S. ...B7 95
Kotzebue Sound, strt., Ak., U.S. ...B7 95
Kouchibouguac National Park, N.B., Can. ...C5 87
Koudougou, Burkina ...D4 50
Kouki, C.A.R. ...B3 54
Koulamoutou, Gabon ...D2 54
Koulikoro, Mali ...D3 50
Koumac, N. Cal. ...I8 62a
Koumbia, Gui. ...D2 50
Koumra, Chad ...E8 50

Koundâra, Gui. ...D2 50
Kounradskij, Kaz. ...B2 28
Kountze, Tx., U.S. ...D5 136
Kourou, Fr. Gu. ...B9 70
Kouroussa, Gui. ...D3 50
Kousséri, Cam. ...D8 50
Koussi, Emi, mtn., Chad ...C8 50
Koutiala, Mali ...D3 50
Kouts, In., U.S. ...B3 107
Kouvola, Fin. ...F12 10
Kovdozero, ozero, res., Russia ...C15 10
Kovel', Ukr. ...D8 20
Kovrov, Russia ...C7 22
Kowloon see Jiulong, China ...E3 30
Koyukuk, stm., Ak., U.S. ...B8 95
Kozan, Tur. ...D6 44
Kozáni, Grc. ...D8 18
Kozel'sk, Russia ...B13 20
Kozhikode (Calicut), India .G3 40
Koziatyn, Ukr. ...E10 20
Kozlu, Tur. ...B4 44
Kpalimé, Togo ...E5 50
Kra, Isthmus of, isth., Asia ..D3 34
Krâchéh, Camb. ...D5 34
Kragerø, Nor. ...G3 10
Kragujevac, Yugo. ...B8 18
Kraków, Pol. ...D5 20
Kralendijk, Neth. Ant. ...C6 80
Kraljevo, Yugo. ...C8 18
Kramators'k, Ukr. ...E14 20
Kramfors, Swe. ...E7 10
Kranj, Slvn. ...A5 18
Krasnik, Pol. ...D7 20
Krasnoarmiis'k, Ukr. ...E14 20
Krasnodar, Russia ...E5 26
Krasnogorsk, Russia ...B16 28
Krasnohrad, Ukr. ...E13 20
Krasnojarsk, Russia ...D11 26
Krasnoperekops'k, Ukr. ...G12 20
Krasnosel'kup, Russia ...C10 26
Krasnoturjinsk, Russia ...C11 22
Krasnoufimsk, Russia ...C10 22
Krasnoural'sk, Russia ...D8 26
Krasnoviršersk, Russia ...B10 22
Krasnovodsk see Turkmenbaši, Turk. ...E7 26
Krasnoyarsk see Krasnojarsk, Russia ...D11 26
Krasnoznamenskoje, Kaz. ...D8 26
Krasnyi Luch, Ukr. ...E15 20
Krasnystaw, Pol. ...D7 20
Krasyliv, Ukr. ...E9 20
Krebs, Ok., U.S. ...C6 129
Kremenchug Reservoir see Kremenchuts'ke vodoskhovyshche, res., Ukr. ...E12 20
Kremenchuk, Ukr. ...E12 20
Kremenchuts'ke vodoskhovyshche, res., Ukr. ...E12 20
Kremenets', Ukr. ...D8 20
Kremmling, Co., U.S. ...A4 99
Kretinga, Lith. ...I9 10
Kreuztal, Ger. ...E11 12
Kribi, Cam. ...C1 54
Krishna, stm., India ...F3 40
Krishnanagar, India ...E5 40
Kristiansand, Nor. ...G3 10
Kristianstad, Swe. ...I6 10
Kristiansund, Nor. ...E2 10
Kristiinankaupunki, Fin. ...E9 10
Kristineberg, Swe. ...D8 10
Kristinehamn, Swe. ...G6 10
Kríti (Crete), i., Grc. ...G10 18
Kritikón Pélagos, Grc. ...G10 18
Krjukovo, Russia ...C17 26
Krk, Otok, i., Cro. ...B5 18
Krnov, Czech Rep. ...D4 20
Kroměříž, Czech Rep. ...E4 20
Krŏng Kaôh Kŏng, Camb. ..D4 34
Kronštadt, Russia ...B4 22
Kroonstad, S. Afr. ...D4 56
Kropotkin, Russia ...A4 42
Krosno, Pol. ...E6 20
Krotoszyn, Pol. ...C4 20
Krotz Springs, La., U.S. ...D4 111
Krugersdorp, S. Afr. ...D4 56
Krui, Indon. ...E2 36
Krung Thep (Bangkok), Thai. ...D4 34
Kruševac, Yugo. ...C8 18
Kruzof Island, i., Ak., U.S. ..m21 95
Kryčaŭ, Bela. ...C11 20
Krymsk, Russia ...G14 20
Kryms'ki hory, mts., Ukr. ..G13 20
Kryms'kyi pivostriv (Crimean Peninsula), pen., Ukr. ...G12 20
Kryvyi Rih, Ukr. ...F12 20
Ksar-el-Kebir, Mor. ...J4 16
Ksenevka, Russia ...A11 26
Kšenskij, Russia ...D14 20
Kuala Kangsar, Malay. ...C2 36
Kualakapuas, Indon. ...D4 36
Kuala Krai, Malay. ...B2 36
Kuala Lipis, Malay. ...C2 36
Kuala Lumpur, Malay. ...C2 36
Kuala Pilah, Malay. ...C2 36
Kuala Terengganu, Malay. ..B2 36
Kuantan, Malay. ...C2 36
Kuban', stm., Russia ...E6 26
Kuching, Malay. ...C4 36
Kuçovë, Alb. ...D8 18

Kudat, Malay. ...B5 36
Kudus, Indon. ...E4 36
Kudymkar, Russia ...C9 22
Kuee Ruins, hist., Hi., U.S. .D6 104
Kufstein, Aus. ...G13 12
Kūhdasht, Iran ...F12 44
Kuito, Ang. ...F3 54
Kuiu Island, i., Ak., U.S. ...m23 95
Kujawy, reg., Pol. ...C5 20
Kujbyšev see Samara, Russia .D7 26
Kujbyševo, Russia ...D9 26
Kujbyševskoe vodohranilišče, res., Russia ...D8 22
Kujgan, Kaz. ...A10 42
Kujū-san, vol., Japan ...D2 31
Kukawa, Nig. ...D7 50
Kula, Tur. ...C3 44
Kula, Hi., U.S. ...C5 104
Kula Kangri, mtn., Bhu. ...D6 40
Kuldiga, Lat. ...H9 10
Kule, Bots. ...C3 56
Kulebaki, Russia ...C7 22
Kuljab, Taj. ...F8 26
Kulmbach, Ger. ...E12 12
Kuloj, Russia ...B7 22
Kulpmont, Pa., U.S. ...E9 131
Kul'sary, Kaz. ...E7 26
Kulu, Tur. ...C5 44
Kulumadau, Pap. N. Gui. ..H13 32
Kumagaya, Japan ...C3 31
Kumai, Indon. ...D4 36
Kumai, Teluk, b., Indon. ...D4 36
Kumamoto, Japan ...E14 28
Kumanovo, Mac. ...C8 18
Kumba, Cam. ...C1 54
Kumbakonam, India ...G3 40
Kumasi, Ghana ...E4 50
Kume-jima, i., Japan ...A9 34
Kuminskij, Russia ...C12 22
Kumluca, Tur. ...D4 44
Kumo, Nig. ...E7 50
Kumta, India ...G2 40
Kumukahi, Cape, c., Hi., U.S. ...D7 104
Kuna, Id., U.S. ...F2 105
Kunašir, ostrov, i., Russia ..E16 26
Kundāpura, India ...G2 40
Kundur, Pulau, i., Indon. ...C2 36
Kunene (Cunene), stm., Afr. .B1 56
Kunghit Island, i., B.C., Can. .C2 85
Kungrad, Uzb. ...B7 42
Kungur, Russia ...C10 22
Kunhing, Mya. ...B3 34
Kunlun Shan, mts., China ..D5 28
Kunming, China ...F8 28
Kununurra, Austl. ...D4 60
Kunya, Nig. ...D6 50
Kuopio, Fin. ...E12 10
Kupang, Indon. ...F6 36
Kup'ians'k, Ukr. ...E14 20
Kupreanof Island, i., Ak., U.S. ...m23 95
Kuqa, China ...C4 28
Kuqa, China ...C4 28
Kür, stm., Asia ...C13 44
Kuraymah, Sudan ...G11 48
Kurčatov, Russia ...D13 20
Kürdämir, Azer. ...B13 44
Kurdistan, hist. reg., Asia ..D10 44
Kure, Japan ...D3 31
Kure Island, i., Hi., U.S. ...k12 104
Kurejka, stm., Russia ...C10 26
Kuresaare, Est. ...G10 10
Kurgan, Russia ...D8 26
Kurgan-Tjube, Taj. ...C9 42
Kuril Islands see Kuril'skie ostrova, is., Russia ...E16 26
Kuril'sk, Russia ...B17 28
Kuril'skie ostrova (Kuril Islands), is., Russia ...E16 26
Kuril Trench ...A7 144
Kurmuk, Sudan ...H11 48
Kurnool, India ...F3 40
Kursk, Russia ...D5 26
Kurtalan, Tur. ...D9 44
Kurtamyš, Russia ...D11 22
Kurtistown, Hi., U.S. ...D6 104
Kuruman, stm., S. Afr. ...D3 56
Kuruman, S. Afr. ...D3 56
Kurume, Japan ...E14 28
Kurumkan, Russia ...D13 26
Kurunegala, Sri L. ...H4 40
Kuşadası, Tur. ...D2 44
Kuşadası Körfezi, b., Tur. ...D2 44
Kuščevskaja, Russia ...F15 20
Kuş Gölü, l., Tur. ...B2 44
Kushiro, Japan ...C16 28
Kushui, China ...D8 26
Kuskokwim, stm., Ak., U.S. .C8 95
Kuskokwim Bay, b., Ak., U.S. D7 95
Kuskokwim Mountains, mts., Ak., U.S. ...C8 95
Kūstī, Sudan ...H11 48
Kut, Ko, i., Thai. ...D4 34
Kütahya, Tur. ...C3 44
Kutch, Gulf of see Kachchh, Gulf of, b., India ...E1 40
Kutch, Rann of, reg., Asia ..E1 40
Kutina, Cro. ...B6 18

Kutno, Pol. ...C5 20
Kutu, D.R.C. ...D3 54
Kutztown, Pa., U.S. ...E10 131
Kuujjuaq, P.Q., Can. ...g13 90
Kuusamo, Fin. ...D13 10
Kuusankoski, Fin. ...F12 10
Kuvango, Ang. ...A2 56
Kuwait, ctry., Asia ...E5 42
Kuwait see Al-Kuwayt, Kuw. .E5 42
Kuybyshev see Samara, Russia ...D7 26
Kuybyshev see Kujbyšev, Russia ...D9 26
Kuybyshev Reservoir see Kujbyševskoe vodohranilišče, res., Russia ...D8 22
Kuytun, Mount, mtn., Asia ..E10 26
Kuz'movka, Russia ...C11 26
Kuzneck, Russia ...D6 26
Kuzomen', Russia ...A6 22
Kvænangen, b., Nor. ...A9 10
Kvaløya, i., Nor. ...B8 10
Kvareli, Geor. ...B11 44
Kwa, stm., D.R.C. ...D3 54
Kwakoegron, Sur. ...B8 70
Kwamouth, D.R.C. ...D3 54
Kwando (Cuando), stm., Afr. .B3 56
Kwangju, S. Kor. ...D13 28
Kwango (Cuango), stm., Afr. .D3 54
Kwangsi Chuang see Guangxi Zhuangzu Zizhiqu, state, China ...G9 28
Kwekwe, Zimb. ...B4 56
Kwenge, stm., Afr. ...E3 54
Kwethluk, Ak., U.S. ...C7 95
Kwidzyn, Pol. ...C5 20
Kwilu (Cuilo), stm., Afr. ...D3 54
Kyaikto, Mya. ...C3 34
Kyaukkyi, Mya. ...B3 34
Kyaukme, Mya. ...B3 34
Kyaukpyu, Mya. ...C2 34
Kyaukse, Mya. ...B3 34
Kyauktaw, Mya. ...B2 34
Kyaunggon, Mya. ...C3 34
Kyïv (Kiev), Ukr. ...D11 20
Kyïv's'ke vodoskhovyshche, res., Ukr. ...D11 20
Kyle, Tx., U.S. ...E4 136
Kyoga, Lake, l., Ug. ...C6 54
Kyōngju, S. Kor. ...C1 31
Kyŏngsŏng-ŭp, N. Kor. ...B1 31
Kyōto, Japan ...D15 28
Kyrgyzstan, ctry., Asia ...A2 40
Kyštovka, Russia ...D9 26
Kyštym, Russia ...C11 22
Kyuquot Sound, strt., B.C., Can. ...E4 85
Kyūshū, i., Japan ...E14 28
Kyushu-Palau Ridge ...G16 64
Kyyiv see Kyïv, Ukr. ...D11 20
Kyyjärvi, Fin. ...E11 10
Kyzyl, Russia ...D11 26
Kyzylkum, des., Asia ...B8 42
Kzyl-Orda, Kaz. ...E8 26
Kzyltu, Kaz. ...D9 26

L

Laascaanood, Som. ...I14 48
La Asunción, Ven. ...C7 80
Laau Point, c., Hi., U.S. ...B4 104
Laayoune see El Aaiún, W. Sah. ...A2 50
Labadieville, La., U.S. ...E5 111
La Bañeza, Spain ...F4 16
La Barca, Mex. ...C4 78
La Barge, Wy., U.S. ...D2 143
La Barge Creek, stm., Wy., U.S. ...D2 143
La Baule-Escoublac, Fr. ...D5 16
Labe, stm., Eur. ...E14 12
Labé, Gui. ...D2 50
La Belle, Fl., U.S. ...F5 102
La Belle, Mo., U.S. ...A6 118
Labette, co., Ks., U.S. ...E8 109
Labinsk, Russia ...B4 42
Labis, Malay. ...C2 36
Laboulaye, Arg. ...E5 72
Labrador, reg., Nf., Can. ...g9 88
Labrador Basin ...B28 144
Labrador City, Nf., Can. ...h8 88
Labrador Sea, N.A. ...F29 82
Lábrea, Braz. ...E7 70
Labuan, Malay. ...B5 36
Labuan, Pulau, i., Malay. ...B5 36
Labuha, Indon. ...G8 32
Labuhanbajo, Indon. ...E5 36
Labytnangi, Russia ...A12 26
Laç, Alb. ...D7 18
La Canada Flintridge, Ca., U.S. ...m12 98
La Carlota, Arg. ...E5 72
La Carlota, Phil. ...D8 34
La Carolina, Spain ...H5 16
Lac-Bouchette, P.Q., Can. ..A5 90
Lac-Brome, P.Q., Can. ...D5 90
Laccadive, Minicoy and Amīndivi Islands see Lakshadweep, ter., India ...G2 40
Laccadive Islands see Lakshadweep, is., India .G2 40
Lac-Carré, P.Q., Can. ...C3 90

Name	Map Ref.	Page
Lac Courte Oreilles Indian Reservation, Wi., U.S.	C2	142
Lac du Bonnet, Mb., Can.	D3	86
Lac du Flambeau, Wi., U.S.	B4	142
Lac du Flambeau Indian Reservation, Wi., U.S.	C3	142
La Ceiba, Hond.	B2	80
La Center, Ky., U.S.	e9	110
Lac-Etchemin, P.Q., Can.	C7	90
Lacey, Wa., U.S.	B3	140
La Chaux-de-Fonds, Switz.	A1	18
Lachine, P.Q., Can.	D4	90
La Chorrera, Col.	D5	70
La Chorrera, Pan.	D3	80
Lachute, P.Q., Can.	D3	90
La Citadelle, hist., Haiti	B5	80
Lackawanna, N.Y., U.S.	C2	125
Lackawanna, co., Pa., U.S.	D10	131
Lackland Air Force Base, mil., Tx., U.S.	k7	136
Lac La Biche, Ab., Can.	B5	84
Lac la Hache, B.C., Can.	D7	85
Laclede, co., Mo., U.S.	D5	118
Lac-Mégantic, P.Q., Can.	D7	90
Lacolle, P.Q., Can.	D4	90
La Columna see Bolívar, Pico, mtn., Ven.	B5	70
Lacombe, Ab., Can.	C4	84
Lacombe, La., U.S.	D6	111
Lacon, Il., U.S.	B4	106
La Concepción, Pan.	D3	80
La Concepción, Ven.	C5	80
Laconia, N.H., U.S.	C4	122
Laconia, Gulf of see Lakonikós Kólpos, b., Grc.	F9	18
La Conner, Wa., U.S.	A3	140
Lacoochee, Fl., U.S.	D4	102
La Coruña see A Coruña, Spain	F2	16
Lac qui Parle, stm., Mn., U.S.	F2	116
Lac qui Parle, co., Mn., U.S.	F2	116
La Creek Lake, l., S.D., U.S.	D4	134
La Crescent, Mn., U.S.	G7	116
La Crete, Ab., Can.	f7	84
La Crosse, In., U.S.	B4	107
La Crosse, Ks., U.S.	D4	109
La Crosse, Wi., U.S.	E2	142
La Crosse, co., Wi., U.S.	E2	142
La Crosse, stm., Wi., U.S.	E3	142
La Cygne, Ks., U.S.	D9	109
Ladākh Range, mts., Asia	C3	40
Ladd, Il., U.S.	B4	106
Ladies Island, i., S.C., U.S.	G6	133
La Dique, i., Sey.	h13	57b
Lādīz, Iran	E8	42
Ladoga, In., U.S.	E4	107
Ladoga, Lake see Ladožskoe ozero, l., Russia	C5	26
La Dorada, Col.	D5	80
Ladožskoe ozero, l., Russia	C5	26
Ladson, S.C., U.S.	F7	133
Ladybrand, S. Afr.	D4	56
Lady Lake, Fl., U.S.	D5	102
Lady Laurier, Mount, mtn., B.C., Can.	A6	85
Ladysmith, B.C., Can.	E6	85
Ladysmith, S. Afr.	D4	56
Ladysmith, Wi., U.S.	C2	142
Lae, Pap. N. Gui.	H12	32
La Encantada, Mex.	B4	78
Læsø, i., Den.	H4	10
La Esperanza, Hond.	C2	80
La Estrada see A Estrada, Spain	F2	16
La Farge, Wi., U.S.	E3	142
Lafayette, co., Ar., U.S.	D2	97
Lafayette, co., Fl., U.S.	B5	99
Lafayette, co., Fl., U.S.	C3	102
Lafayette, Ga., U.S.	B1	103
Lafayette, In., U.S.	D4	107
Lafayette, La., U.S.	D3	111
Lafayette, co., La., U.S.	D3	111
Lafayette, co., Mo., U.S.	B4	118
Lafayette, co., Ms., U.S.	A4	117
Lafayette, N.C., U.S.	B3	126
Lafayette, Or., U.S.	B3	130
La Fayette, R.I., U.S.	E4	132
Lafayette, Tn., U.S.	A5	135
Lafayette, co., Wi., U.S.	F3	142
Lafayette, Mount, mtn., N.H., U.S.	B3	122
La Feria, Tx., U.S.	F4	136
Lafia, Nig.	E6	50
Lafiagi, Nig.	E6	50
Lafitte, La., U.S.	k11	111
La Flèche, Fr.	D6	16
La Follette, Tn., U.S.	C9	135
La Fontaine, In., U.S.	C6	107
Lafourche, La., U.S.	E5	111
Lafourche, co., La., U.S.	E5	111
La France, S.C., U.S.	B2	133
La Galite, i., Tun.	F2	18
Lagarto, Braz.	D4	74
Lagawe, Phil.	C8	34
Lågen, stm., Nor.	F3	10
Lages, Braz.	D7	72
Laghouat, Alg.	D5	48
Lago, Mount, mtn., Wa., U.S.	A5	140
Lagoa da Prata, Braz.	F2	74
Lago da Pedra, Braz.	B2	74
La Gomera, i., Spain	A1	50
Lagonoy Gulf, b., Phil.	D8	34
Lagos, Nig.	E5	50
Lagos, Port.	I2	16
Lagos de Moreno, Mex.	C4	78
La Gouèra, W. Sah.	B1	50
La Grande, stm., P.Q., Can.	h11	90
La Grande, Or., U.S.	B8	130
La Grande Deux, Réservoir, res., P.Q., Can.	h11	90
Lagrange, Austl.	D3	60
La Grange, Ga., U.S.	C1	103
La Grange, Il., U.S.	B6	106
Lagrange, co., In., U.S.	A7	107
Lagrange, In., U.S.	A7	107
La Grange, Ky., U.S.	B4	110
La Grange, Mo., U.S.	A6	118
La Grange, N.C., U.S.	B5	126
Lagrange, Oh., U.S.	A3	128
La Grange, Tx., U.S.	E4	136
La Grange Park, Il., U.S.	k9	106
La Gran Sabana, pl., Ven.	B7	70
La Guadeloupe (Saint-Evariste), P.Q., Can.	D7	90
La Guajira, Península de, pen., S.A.	A5	70
La Guardia, Bol.	B5	72
La Guardia see A Guardia, Spain	G2	16
Laguna, Braz.	D8	72
Laguna, N.M., U.S.	B2	124
Laguna Beach, Ca., U.S.	F5	98
Laguna Dam, U.S.	E1	96
Laguna Indian Reservation, N.M., U.S.	C2	124
La Habana (Havana), Cuba	A3	80
La Habra, Ca., U.S.	n13	98
Lahad Datu, Malay.	C5	36
Lahad Datu, Telukan, b., Malay.	C5	36
Lahaina, Hi., U.S.	C5	104
La Harpe, Il., U.S.	C3	106
La Harpe, Ks., U.S.	E8	109
Lahat, Indon.	D2	36
La Have, stm., N.S., Can.	E5	87
Lahdenpohja, Russia	F14	10
Lāhījān, Iran	C6	42
Lahoma, Ok., U.S.	A3	129
Lahore, Pak.	D10	42
Lahti, Fin.	F11	10
Laï, Chad	E8	50
Lai Chau, Viet.	B4	34
Laie, Hi., U.S.	B4	104
Lai-hka, Mya.	B3	34
Laingsburg, S. Afr.	E3	56
Laingsburg, Mi., U.S.	F6	115
Lainioälven, stm., Swe.	B9	10
Lais, Indon.	D2	36
Laisamis, Kenya	C7	54
Laiwu, China	B4	30
Laiwui, Indon.	G8	32
Laiyang, China	B5	30
Laizhou Wan, b., China	D11	28
La Jara, Co., U.S.	D5	99
La Jolla, Point, c., Ca., U.S.	o15	98
La Junta, Co., U.S.	D7	99
Lake, co., Ca., U.S.	C2	98
Lake, co., Co., U.S.	B4	99
Lake, co., Fl., U.S.	D5	102
Lake, co., Il., U.S.	A6	106
Lake, co., In., U.S.	B3	107
Lake, co., Mi., U.S.	E5	115
Lake, co., Mn., U.S.	C7	116
Lake, co., Mt., U.S.	C2	119
Lake, co., Oh., U.S.	A4	128
Lake, co., Or., U.S.	E6	130
Lake, co., S.D., U.S.	C8	134
Lake, co., Tn., U.S.	A2	135
Lake Alfred, Fl., U.S.	D5	102
Lake Andes, S.D., U.S.	D7	134
Lake Ariel, Pa., U.S.	D11	131
Lake Arrowhead, Ca., U.S.	E5	98
Lake Arthur, La., U.S.	D3	111
Lakeba, i., Fiji	m11	63b
Lake Benton, Mn., U.S.	F2	116
Lake Bluff, Il., U.S.	A6	106
Lake Butler, Fl., U.S.	B4	102
Lake Cargelligo, Austl.	G4	62
Lake Charles, La., U.S.	D2	111
Lake Chelan National Recreation Area, Wa., U.S.	A5	140
Lake City, Ar., U.S.	B5	97
Lake City, Fl., U.S.	B4	102
Lake City, Ia., U.S.	B3	108
Lake City, Mi., U.S.	D5	115
Lake City, Mn., U.S.	F6	116
Lake City, Pa., U.S.	B1	131
Lake City, S.C., U.S.	D8	133
Lake City, Tn., U.S.	C9	135
Lake Clark National Park, Ak., U.S.	C9	95
Lake Cowichan, B.C., Can.	g11	85
Lake Creek, stm., Wa., U.S.	B7	140
Lake Crystal, Mn., U.S.	F4	116
Lake Delta, N.Y., U.S.	B5	125
Lake Delton, Wi., U.S.	E4	142
Lake District, reg., Eng., U.K.	G5	12
Lake Elsinore, Ca., U.S.	F5	98
Lake Erie Beach, N.Y., U.S.	C1	125
Lakefield, On., Can.	C6	89
Lakefield, Mn., U.S.	G3	116
Lake Forest, Il., U.S.	A6	106
Lake Fork, stm., Ut., U.S.	C5	137
Lake Geneva, Wi., U.S.	F5	142
Lake Hamilton, Ar., U.S.	g7	97
Lake Havasu City, Az., U.S.	C1	96
Lake Helen, Fl., U.S.	D5	102
Lakehurst, N.J., U.S.	C4	123
Lakehurst Naval Air Station, mil., N.J., U.S.	C4	123
Lake in the Hills, Il., U.S.	h8	106
Lake Jackson, Tx., U.S.	r14	136
Lake Katrine, N.Y., U.S.	D7	125
Lake King, Austl.	G2	60
Lakeland, Fl., U.S.	D5	102
Lakeland, Ga., U.S.	E3	103
Lake Linden, Mi., U.S.	A2	115
Lake Louise, Ab., Can.	D2	84
Lake Magdalene, Fl., U.S.	o11	102
Lake Mary, Fl., U.S.	D5	102
Lake Mead National Recreation Area, U.S.	H7	121
Lake Meredith National Recreation Area, Tx., U.S.	B2	136
Lake Mills, Ia., U.S.	A4	108
Lake Mills, Wi., U.S.	E5	142
Lakemore, Oh., U.S.	A4	128
Lake Mountain, mtn., Wy., U.S.	E6	143
Lake Nebagamon, Wi., U.S.	B2	142
Lake Odessa, Mi., U.S.	F5	115
Lake of the Woods, co., Mn., U.S.	B4	116
Lake Orion, Mi., U.S.	F7	115
Lake Oswego, Or., U.S.	B4	130
Lake Ozark, Mo., U.S.	C5	118
Lake Park, Fl., U.S.	F6	102
Lake Park, Ia., U.S.	A2	108
Lake Park, Mn., U.S.	D2	116
Lake Placid, Fl., U.S.	E5	102
Lake Placid, N.Y., U.S.	A7	125
Lake Pontchartrain Causeway, La., U.S.	h11	111
Lakeport, Ca., U.S.	C2	98
Lake Preston, S.D., U.S.	C8	134
Lake Providence, La., U.S.	B4	111
Lake Range, mts., Nv., U.S.	C2	121
Lakes Entrance, Austl.	H4	62
Lake Shore, Md., U.S.	B5	113
Lakeshore, Ms., U.S.	E4	117
Lakeside, Az., U.S.	C6	96
Lakeside, Ca., U.S.	F5	98
Lakeside, Ct., U.S.	D3	100
Lakeside, Mt., U.S.	B2	119
Lakeside, Oh., U.S.	A3	128
Lakeside, Or., U.S.	D2	130
Lakeside, Wa., U.S.	A3	140
Lakeside Park, Ky., U.S.	h13	110
Lake Station, In., U.S.	A3	107
Lake Station, Ok., U.S.	A5	129
Lake Stevens, Wa., U.S.	A3	140
Lake Superior Provincial Park, On., Can.	p18	89
Lake Swamp, stm., S.C., U.S.	C8	133
Lake Tansi Village, Tn., U.S.	D8	135
Lake Valley, val., Nv., U.S.	E7	121
Lake View, Ia., U.S.	B2	108
Lakeview, Mi., U.S.	E5	115
Lakeview, Oh., U.S.	B2	128
Lakeview, Or., U.S.	E6	130
Lake View, S.C., U.S.	C9	133
Lake Villa, Il., U.S.	h8	106
Lake Village, Ar., U.S.	D4	97
Lake Village, In., U.S.	B3	107
Lakeville, Ct., U.S.	B2	100
Lakeville, In., U.S.	A5	107
Lakeville, Ma., U.S.	C6	114
Lakeville, Mn., U.S.	F5	116
Lake Waccamaw, N.C., U.S.	C4	126
Lake Wales, Fl., U.S.	E5	102
Lakewood, Ca., U.S.	n12	98
Lakewood, Co., U.S.	B5	99
Lakewood, Ia., U.S.	f8	108
Lakewood, Il., U.S.	D5	106
Lakewood, N.J., U.S.	C4	123
Lakewood, N.Y., U.S.	C1	125
Lakewood, Oh., U.S.	A4	128
Lakewood, Wa., U.S.	B3	140
Lake Worth, Fl., U.S.	F6	102
Lake Worth Inlet, b., Fl., U.S.	F7	102
Lake Zurich, Il., U.S.	h8	106
Lakhdaria, Alg.	I8	16
Lakhīmpur, India	D4	40
Lakin, Ks., U.S.	E2	109
Lakonikós Kólpos, b., Grc.	F9	18
Lakota, N.D., U.S.	A7	127
Laksefjorden, b., Nor.	A12	10
Lakshadweep, ter., India	G2	40
Lakshadweep, is., India	G2	40
Lakshadweep Sea, Asia	G2	40
Lalara, Gabon	C2	54
Lalībela, Eth.	H12	48
La Libertad, Guat.	B1	80
La Línea de la Concepción, Spain	I4	16
Lalitpur, India	E3	40
La Loche see Churchill, stm., Sk., Can.	G21	82
La Luz, N.M., U.S.	E4	124
La Malbaie, P.Q., Can.	B7	90
La Mancha, reg., Spain	H5	16
La Manche see English Channel, strt., Eur.	C5	16
Lamap, Vanuatu	k9	62a
Lamar, co., Al., U.S.	B1	94
Lamar, Ar., U.S.	B2	97
Lamar, Co., U.S.	C8	99
Lamar, co., Ga., U.S.	C2	103
Lamar, Mo., U.S.	D3	118
Lamar, co., Ms., U.S.	D4	117
Lamar, Pa., U.S.	D7	131
Lamar, S.C., U.S.	C7	133
Lamar, co., Tx., U.S.	C5	136
Lamar, stm., Wy., U.S.	B2	143
La Mauricie, Parc National de, P.Q., Can.	C5	90
Lamb, co., Tx., U.S.	B1	136
Lambaréné, Gabon	D2	54
Lambayeque, Peru	E4	70
Lambert, Ms., U.S.	A3	117
Lambert Glacier, ice, Ant.	D11	67
Lamberton, Mn., U.S.	F3	116
Lambertville, Mi., U.S.	G7	115
Lambertville, N.J., U.S.	C3	123
Lame Deer, Mt., U.S.	E10	119
Lamèque, N.B., Can.	B5	87
Lamèque, Île, i., N.B., Can.	B5	87
La Mesa, Ca., U.S.	F5	98
La Mesa, N.M., U.S.	E3	124
Lamesa, Tx., U.S.	C2	136
Lamía, Grc.	E9	18
Lamoille, Nv., U.S.	C6	121
Lamoille, stm., Vt., U.S.	B3	138
Lamoille, co., Vt., U.S.	B3	138
La Moine, stm., Il., U.S.	C3	106
Lamon Bay, b., Phil.	D8	34
Lamoni, Ia., U.S.	D4	108
Lamont, Ab., Can.	C4	84
Lamont, Ca., U.S.	E4	98
La Monte, Mo., U.S.	C4	118
La Motte, Isle, i., Vt., U.S.	B2	138
La Moure, co., N.D., U.S.	C7	127
La Moure, N.D., U.S.	C7	127
Lampang, Thai.	C3	34
Lampasas, Tx., U.S.	D3	136
Lampasas, co., Tx., U.S.	D3	136
Lampazos de Naranjo, Mex.	B4	78
Lamphun, Thai.	C3	34
Lampman, Sk., Can.	H4	91
Lamprey, stm., N.H., U.S.	D4	122
Lamu, Kenya	D8	54
Lanai, i., Hi., U.S.	C4	104
Lanai City, Hi., U.S.	C5	104
Lanaihale, mtn., Hi., U.S.	C5	104
Lanark, On., Can.	C8	89
Lanark, Il., U.S.	A4	106
Lanark, W.V., U.S.	D3	141
Lanbi Kyun, i., Mya.	D3	34
Lancang see Mekong, stm., Asia	A3	34
Lancaster, On., Can.	B10	89
Lancaster, Eng., U.K.	C5	12
Lancaster, Ca., U.S.	E4	98
Lancaster, Ky., U.S.	C5	110
Lancaster, Mo., U.S.	A5	118
Lancaster, co., Ne., U.S.	D9	120
Lancaster, N.H., U.S.	B3	122
Lancaster, N.Y., U.S.	C2	125
Lancaster, Oh., U.S.	C3	128
Lancaster, Pa., U.S.	F9	131
Lancaster, co., Pa., U.S.	G9	131
Lancaster, S.C., U.S.	B6	133
Lancaster, co., S.C., U.S.	B6	133
Lancaster, Tx., U.S.	n10	136
Lancaster, co., Va., U.S.	C6	139
Lancaster, Wi., U.S.	F3	142
Lance Creek, stm., Wy., U.S.	C8	143
Lanchow see Lanzhou, China	D8	28
Lanciano, Italy	C5	18
Lancun, China	B5	30
Lândana, Ang.	E2	54
Land Between the Lakes, U.S.	f9	110
Landeck, Aus.	G12	12
Landegode, Nor.	C6	10
Lander, co., Nv., U.S.	C4	121
Lander, Wy., U.S.	D4	143
Landerneau, Fr.	C4	16
Landes, reg., Fr.	E6	16
Landess, In., U.S.	C6	107
Landis, N.C., U.S.	B2	126
Lando, S.C., U.S.	B5	133
Landrum, S.C., U.S.	A3	133
Land's End, c., Eng., U.K.	E4	12
Lands End, c., R.I., U.S.	F5	132
Landshut, Ger.	F13	12
Landskrona, Swe.	I5	10
Lane, co., Or., U.S.	D3	109
Lane, co., Or., U.S.	C4	130
La Negra, Chile	A2	72
Lanesboro, Mn., U.S.	G7	116
Lanett, Al., U.S.	C4	94
Langdon, N.D., U.S.	A7	127
Langeland, i., Den.	I4	10
Langeloth, Pa., U.S.	F1	131
Langfang, China	B4	30
Langford, S.D., U.S.	B8	134
Langford, S.C., U.S.	B4	133
Langjökull, ice, Ice.	l20	10a
Langkawi, Pulau, i., Malay.	B1	36
Langlade, Wi., U.S.	C4	142
Langley, B.C., Can.	f13	85
Langley, S.C., U.S.	E4	133
Langley, Wa., U.S.	A3	140
Langley Air Force Base, mil., Va., U.S.	h15	139
Langley Park, Md., U.S.	f9	113
Langøya, i., Nor.	B6	10
Langres, Fr.	D9	16
Langsa, Indon.	C1	36
Lang Son, Viet.	B5	34
Langston, Ok., U.S.	B4	129
Languedoc, hist. reg., Fr.	F8	16
L'Anguille, stm., Ar., U.S.	B5	97
Langzhong, China	E9	28
Lanham, Md., U.S.	C4	113
Lanier, co., Ga., U.S.	E3	103
Länkäran, Azer.	C13	44
Lannion, Fr.	C5	16
Lannon, Wi., U.S.	m11	142
L'Annonciation, P.Q., Can.	C3	90
Lanping, China	A4	34
Lansdale, Pa., U.S.	F11	131
Lansdowne, Md., U.S.	B4	113
L'Anse, Mi., U.S.	B2	115
L'Anse-au-Loup, Nf., Can.	C3	88
L'Anse Indian Reservation, Mi., U.S.	B2	115
Lansford, Pa., U.S.	E10	131
Lanshan, China	D3	30
Lansing, Ia., U.S.	A6	108
Lansing, Il., U.S.	B6	106
Lansing, Ks., U.S.	C9	109
Lansing, Mi., U.S.	F6	115
Lantana, Fl., U.S.	F6	102
Lanxi, China	F11	28
Lanzarote, i., Spain	A2	50
Lanzhou, China	D8	28
Laoag, Phil.	C8	34
Laoang, Phil.	D9	34
Lao Cai, Viet.	B4	34
Laoha, stm., China	C12	28
Laohekou, China	E10	28
Laon, Fr.	C8	16
La Orchila, Isla, i., Ven.	C6	80
La Oroya, Peru	F4	70
Laos, ctry., Asia	B3	32
La Palma, Pan.	D4	80
La Palma, i., Spain	A1	50
La Paragua, Ven.	B7	70
La Paz, Arg.	E6	72
La Paz, Bol.	B4	72
La Paz, Mex.	C2	78
La Paz, co., Az., U.S.	D2	96
La Perouse Strait, strt., Asia	B16	29
La Pine, Or., U.S.	D5	130
Lapinlahti, Fin.	E12	10
La Place, La., U.S.	h11	111
Lapland (Lappland), hist. reg., Eur.	B8	10
La Plata, Arg.	F6	72
La Plata, co., Co., U.S.	D3	99
La Plata, Md., U.S.	C4	113
La Plata, Mo., U.S.	A5	118
La Plata Mountains, mts., Co., U.S.	D3	99
La Plata Peak, mtn., Co., U.S.	B4	99
La Platte, stm., Vt., U.S.	C2	138
La Pocatière, P.Q., Can.	B7	90
Laporte, Co., U.S.	A5	99
La Porte, In., U.S.	A4	107
La Porte, co., In., U.S.	A4	107
La Porte, Tx., U.S.	r14	136
La Porte City, Ia., U.S.	B5	108
Lappeenranta, Fin.	F13	10
Lappland (Lapland), hist. reg., Eur.	B8	10
La Prairie, P.Q., Can.	D4	90
La Pryor, Tx., U.S.	E3	136
Laptev Sea see Laptevyh, more, Russia	B14	26
Laptevyh, more, Russia	B14	26
La Push, Wa., U.S.	B1	140
Lapwai, Id., U.S.	C2	105
La Quiaca, Arg.	A3	72
L'Áquila, Italy	C4	18
Lār, Iran	E6	42
Larache, Mor.	C3	48
Laramie, co., Wy., U.S.	E8	143
Laramie, Wy., U.S.	E7	143
Laramie, stm., U.S.	E7	143
Laramie Mountains, mts., Wy., U.S.	D7	143
Laramie Peak, mtn., Wy., U.S.	D7	143
Larantuka, Indon.	E6	36
Lärbro, Swe.	H8	10
Larchmont, N.Y., U.S.	h13	125
Larchwood, Ia., U.S.	A1	108
Laredo, Spain	F5	16
Laredo, Tx., U.S.	F3	136
Largo, Fl., U.S.	E4	102
Largo, Cañon, N.M., U.S.	A2	124
Largo, Key, i., Fl., U.S.	G6	102
Larimer, co., Co., U.S.	A5	99
Larimore, N.D., U.S.	B8	127
La Rioja, Arg.	B3	72
La Rioja, reg., Spain	F5	16
Lárisa, Grc.	E9	18
Lārkāna, Pak.	E2	42
Lark Harbour, Nf., Can.	D2	88
Larkspur, Ca., U.S.	h7	98
Larksville, Pa., U.S.	n17	131
Larnaca see Lárnax, Cyp.	E5	44
Lárnax, Cyp.	E5	44
Larne, N. Ire., U.K.	C4	12
Larned, Ks., U.S.	D4	109

Name	Map Ref.	Page

La Rochelle, Fr. — D6 — 16
La Roche-sur-Yon, Fr. — D6 — 16
La Roda, Spain — H5 — 16
La Romana, Dom. Rep. — B6 — 80
Larose, La., U.S. — E5 — 111
Larrimah, Austl. — D5 — 60
Larsen Ice Shelf, Ant. — C34 — 67
Larue, co., Ky., U.S. — C4 — 110
Larvik, Nor. — G4 — 10
LaSalle, P.Q., Can. — q19 — 90
La Salle, Co., U.S. — A6 — 99
La Salle, Il., U.S. — B4 — 106
La Salle, co., Il., U.S. — B4 — 106
La Salle, co., Il., U.S. — C3 — 111
La Salle, co., Tx., U.S. — E3 — 136
Las Animas, Co., U.S. — C7 — 99
Las Animas, co., Co., U.S. — D6 — 99
La Sarre, P.Q., Can. — k11 — 90
Las Casitas, mtn., Mex. — C3 — 78
Las Choapas, Mex. — D6 — 78
La Scie, Nf., Can. — D4 — 88
Las Cruces, N.M., U.S. — E3 — 124
La Selle, Morne, mtn., Haiti — B5 — 80
La Serena, Chile — C2 — 69
La Serena, reg., Spain — H4 — 16
La Seyne-sur-Mer, Fr. — F9 — 16
Las Flores, Arg. — F6 — 72
Lāsh-e Joveyn, Afg. — D8 — 42
Las Heras, Arg. — G3 — 69
Lashio, Myan. — B3 — 34
Lashkar Gāh, Afg. — D8 — 42
Las Margaritas, Mex. — D6 — 78
Las Minas, Cerro, mtn., Hond. — C2 — 80
La Solana, Spain — H5 — 16
Las Palmas de Gran Canaria, Spain — A1 — 50
La Spezia, Italy — B2 — 18
Las Piedras, Ur. — E6 — 72
Las Plumas, Arg. — F3 — 69
Las Rosas, Mex. — D6 — 78
Lassen, co., Ca., U.S. — B3 — 98
Lassen Peak, vol., Ca., U.S. — B3 — 98
Lassen Volcanic National Park, Ca., U.S. — B3 — 98
L'Assomption, P.Q., Can. — D4 — 90
Las Tablas, Pan. — D3 — 80
Last Mountain Lake, l., Sk., Can. — F3 — 91
Lastoursville, Gabon — D2 — 54
Las Tunas, Cuba — A4 — 80
Las Varas, Mex. — B3 — 78
Las Varas, Mex. — C3 — 78
Las Vegas, N.M., U.S. — B4 — 124
Las Vegas, Nv., U.S. — G6 — 121
Latah, co., Id., U.S. — C2 — 105
Latakia see Al-Lādhiqīyah, Syria — E6 — 44
Lathrop, Mo., U.S. — B3 — 118
Latimer, co., Ok., U.S. — C6 — 129
Latina, Italy — D4 — 18
Laton, Ca., U.S. — D4 — 98
La Tortuga, Isla, i., Ven. — C6 — 80
Latouche Treville, Cape, c., Austl. — D3 — 60
Latour Peak, mtn., Id., U.S. — B2 — 105
Latrobe, Pa., U.S. — F3 — 131
Latta, S.C., U.S. — C9 — 133
La Tuque, P.Q., Can. — B5 — 90
Lātūr, India — F3 — 40
Latvia, ctry., Eur. — H11 — 10
Lauderdale, Ms., U.S. — C5 — 117
Lauderdale, co., Al., U.S. — A2 — 94
Lauderdale, co., Ms., U.S. — C5 — 117
Lauderdale, co., Tn., U.S. — B2 — 135
Lauderdale Lakes, Fl., U.S. — r13 — 102
Laughlin, Nv., U.S. — H7 — 121
Laughlin Air Force Base, mil., Tx., U.S. — E2 — 136
Laughlin Peak, mtn., N.M., U.S. — A5 — 124
Laughlintown, Pa., U.S. — F3 — 131
Launceston, Austl. — I4 — 62
Launching Point, c., P.E., Can. — S7 — 87
La Unión, Chile — F2 — 69
La Unión, El Sal. — C2 — 80
La Unión, Spain — I6 — 16
Laurel, De., U.S. — F3 — 101
Laurel, Fl., U.S. — E4 — 102
Laurel, Md., U.S. — B4 — 113
Laurel, Ms., U.S. — D4 — 117
Laurel, Mt., U.S. — E7 — 119
Laurel, Ne., U.S. — B8 — 120
Laurel, Va., U.S. — C5 — 139
Laurel, co., Ky., U.S. — C5 — 110
Laurel, stm., Ky., U.S. — D5 — 110
Laurel Bay, S.C., U.S. — G6 — 133
Laurel Creek, stm., W.V., U.S. — n14 — 141
Laurel Creek, stm., W.V., U.S. — m12 — 141
Laureldale, Pa., U.S. — F10 — 131
Laurel Fork, stm., W.V., U.S. — C5 — 141
Laurel Hill, N.C., U.S. — C3 — 126
Laurel River Lake, res., Ky., U.S. — D5 — 110
Laurence G. Hanscom Air Force Base, mil., Ma., U.S. — g10 — 114
Laurence Harbor, N.J., U.S. — C4 — 123
Laurens, Ia., U.S. — B3 — 108
Laurens, S.C., U.S. — C3 — 133
Laurens, co., Ga., U.S. — D4 — 103

Laurens, co., S.C., U.S. — C4 — 133
Laurentides, P.Q., Can. — D4 — 90
Laurentides, Parc Provincial des, P.Q., Can. — B6 — 90
Lau Ridge — K21 — 64
Laurier, P.Q., Can. — C6 — 90
Laurierville, P.Q., Can. — C6 — 90
Laurinburg, N.C., U.S. — C3 — 126
Laurium, Mi., U.S. — A2 — 115
Lausanne, Switz. — A1 — 18
Laut, Pulau, i., Indon. — C3 — 36
Laut, Pulau, i., Indon. — D5 — 36
Laut, Selat, strt., Indon. — D5 — 36
Lautaro, Chile — E2 — 69
Lauzon (part of Lévis-Lauzon), P.Q., Can. — C6 — 90
Lava Beds National Monument, Ca., U.S. — B3 — 98
Lavaca, Ar., U.S. — B1 — 97
Lavaca, co., Tx., U.S. — E4 — 136
Laval, P.Q., Can. — D4 — 90
Laval, Fr. — C6 — 16
La Vale, Md., U.S. — k13 — 113
La Vall d'Uixó, Spain — H6 — 16
Lavaltrie, P.Q., Can. — D4 — 90
Laveen, Az., U.S. — m8 — 96
La Vega, Dom. Rep. — B5 — 80
L'Avenir, P.Q., Can. — D5 — 90
La Vergne, Tn., U.S. — A5 — 135
La Verkin, Ut., U.S. — F2 — 137
La Verne, Ca., U.S. — m13 — 98
Laverne, Ok., U.S. — A2 — 129
Laverton, Austl. — F3 — 60
La Veta, Co., U.S. — D5 — 99
La Victoria, Ven. — C6 — 80
La Vila Joiosa, Spain — H6 — 16
La Vista, Ne., U.S. — g12 — 120
Lavonia, Ga., U.S. — B3 — 103
Lavon Lake, res., Tx., U.S. — m10 — 136
Lavras, Braz. — F2 — 74
Lavumisa, Swaz. — D5 — 56
Lawai, Hi., U.S. — B2 — 104
Lawn, Nf., Can. — E4 — 88
Lawra, Ghana — D4 — 50
Lawrence, In., U.S. — E5 — 107
Lawrence, Ks., U.S. — D8 — 109
Lawrence, Ma., U.S. — A5 — 114
Lawrence, N.Y., U.S. — k13 — 125
Lawrence, co., Al., U.S. — A2 — 94
Lawrence, co., Ar., U.S. — A4 — 97
Lawrence, co., Il., U.S. — E6 — 106
Lawrence, co., In., U.S. — G4 — 107
Lawrence, co., Ky., U.S. — B7 — 110
Lawrence, co., Mo., U.S. — D4 — 118
Lawrence, co., Ms., U.S. — D3 — 117
Lawrence, co., Oh., U.S. — D3 — 128
Lawrence, co., Pa., U.S. — E1 — 131
Lawrence, co., Tn., U.S. — B4 — 135
Lawrenceburg, In., U.S. — F8 — 107
Lawrenceburg, Ky., U.S. — B5 — 110
Lawrenceburg, Tn., U.S. — B4 — 135
Lawrence Park, Pa., U.S. — B1 — 131
Lawrenceville, Ga., U.S. — C3 — 103
Lawrenceville, Il., U.S. — E6 — 106
Lawrenceville, Va., U.S. — D5 — 139
Lawson, Mo., U.S. — B3 — 118
Lawsonia, Md., U.S. — E6 — 113
Lawtell, La., U.S. — D3 — 111
Lawton, Mi., U.S. — F5 — 115
Lawton, Ok., U.S. — C3 — 129
Lawz, Jabal al-, mtn., Sau. Ar. — E3 — 42
Laxå, Swe. — G6 — 10
Lay Lake, res., Al., U.S. — B3 — 94
Laysan Island, i., Hi., U.S. — k13 — 104
Layton, Ut., U.S. — B4 — 137
Lazarev, Russia — D16 — 26
Lázaro Cárdenas, Mex. — D4 — 78
Lazo, Russia — B2 — 31
Leachville, Ar., U.S. — B5 — 97
Lead, S.D., U.S. — C2 — 134
Leadbetter Point, c., Wa., U.S. — C1 — 140
Leadville, Co., U.S. — B4 — 99
Leadwood, Mo., U.S. — D7 — 118
Leaf, stm., Ms., U.S. — D5 — 117
Leake, co., Ms., U.S. — C4 — 117
Leakesville, Ms., U.S. — D5 — 117
Lealman, Fl., U.S. — p10 — 102
Leamington, On., Can. — E2 — 89
Leary, Ga., U.S. — E2 — 103
Leatherman Peak, mtn., Id., U.S. — E5 — 105
Leavenworth, Ks., U.S. — C9 — 109
Leavenworth, Wa., U.S. — B5 — 140
Leavenworth, co., Ks., U.S. — C8 — 109
Leavittsburg, Oh., U.S. — A5 — 128
Leawood, Ks., U.S. — D9 — 109
Lebanon, De., U.S. — D4 — 101
Lebanon, Il., U.S. — E4 — 106
Lebanon, In., U.S. — D5 — 107
Lebanon, Ky., U.S. — C4 — 110
Lebanon, Mo., U.S. — D5 — 118
Lebanon, N.H., U.S. — C2 — 122
Lebanon, Oh., U.S. — C1 — 128
Lebanon, Or., U.S. — C4 — 130
Lebanon, Pa., U.S. — F9 — 131
Lebanon, Tn., U.S. — A5 — 135
Lebanon, Va., U.S. — f9 — 139
Lebanon, co., Pa., U.S. — F8 — 131
Lebanon, ctry., Asia — E6 — 44
Lebanon Junction, Ky., U.S. — C4 — 110

Lebanon Mountains see Lubnān, Jabal, mts., Leb. — F6 — 44
Lebedjan', Russia — C15 — 20
Lebedyn, Ukr. — D13 — 20
Lebesby, Nor. — A12 — 10
Lebjaže, Kaz. — D9 — 26
Lebo, Ks., U.S. — D8 — 109
Łębork, Pol. — B4 — 20
Lebu, Chile — E2 — 69
Lecce, Italy — D7 — 18
Lecco, Italy — B2 — 18
Le Center, Mn., U.S. — F5 — 116
Lecompte, La., U.S. — C3 — 111
Lecompton, Ks., U.S. — C8 — 109
Le Creusot, Fr. — D9 — 16
Le Claire, Ia., U.S. — C7 — 108
Lechang, China — D3 — 30
Ledo, India — D7 — 40
Ledu, China — B1 — 30
Leduc, Ab., Can. — C4 — 84
Lee, Ma., U.S. — B1 — 114
Lee, co., Al., U.S. — C4 — 94
Lee, co., Ar., U.S. — C5 — 97
Lee, co., Fl., U.S. — F5 — 102
Lee, co., Ga., U.S. — E2 — 103
Lee, co., Ia., U.S. — D6 — 108
Lee, co., Il., U.S. — B4 — 106
Lee, co., Ky., U.S. — C6 — 110
Lee, co., Ms., U.S. — A5 — 117
Lee, co., N.C., U.S. — B3 — 126
Lee, co., S.C., U.S. — C7 — 133
Lee, co., Tx., U.S. — D4 — 136
Lee, co., Va., U.S. — f8 — 139
Lee Lake, l., Ms., U.S. — B3 — 117
Leechburg, Pa., U.S. — E2 — 131
Leech Lake, l., Mn., U.S. — C4 — 116
Leech Lake Indian Reservation, Mn., U.S. — C4 — 116
Lee Creek, stm., U.S. — B1 — 97
Leeds, Eng., U.K. — D6 — 12
Leeds, Al., U.S. — B3 — 94
Leelanau, co., Mi., U.S. — D5 — 115
Leelanau, Lake, l., Mi., U.S. — C5 — 115
Lee Park, Pa., U.S. — n17 — 131
Leer, Ger. — D10 — 12
Leesburg, Fl., U.S. — D5 — 102
Leesburg, Ga., U.S. — E2 — 103
Leesburg, Oh., U.S. — C2 — 128
Leesburg, Va., U.S. — A5 — 139
Lees Summit, Mo., U.S. — C3 — 118
Leesville, La., U.S. — C2 — 111
Leesville, S.C., U.S. — D4 — 133
Leesville Lake, res., Va., U.S. — C3 — 139
Leeton, Austl. — G4 — 62
Leeton, Mo., U.S. — C4 — 118
Leetonia, Oh., U.S. — B5 — 128
Leetsdale, Pa., U.S. — h13 — 131
Leeuwarden, Neth. — D9 — 12
Leeuwin, Cape, c., Austl. — G1 — 60
Leeward Islands, is., N.A. — E12 — 76
Leflore, co., Ms., U.S. — B3 — 117
Le Flore, co., Ok., U.S. — C7 — 129
Lega Hida, Eth. — B8 — 54
Legal, Ab., Can. — C4 — 84
Leganés, Spain — G5 — 16
Legaspi, Phil. — D8 — 34
Leghorn see Livorno, Italy — C3 — 18
Legnica, Pol. — D4 — 20
Le Grand, Ca., U.S. — D3 — 98
Le Grand, Ia., U.S. — B5 — 108
Leh, India — C3 — 40
Le Havre, Fr. — C7 — 16
Lehi, Ut., U.S. — C4 — 137
Lehigh, co., Pa., U.S. — E10 — 131
Lehigh, stm., Pa., U.S. — E10 — 131
Lehigh Acres, Fl., U.S. — F5 — 102
Lehighton, Pa., U.S. — E10 — 131
Lehua Island, i., Hi., U.S. — A1 — 104
Lehututu, Bots. — C3 — 56
Leicester, Eng., U.K. — D6 — 12
Leicester, Ma., U.S. — B4 — 114
Leiden, Neth. — D9 — 12
Leighton, Al., U.S. — A2 — 94
Leinster, hist. reg., Ire. — D3 — 12
Leipsic, De., U.S. — D3 — 101
Leipsic, Oh., U.S. — A2 — 128
Leipsic, stm., De., U.S. — C3 — 101
Leipzig, Ger. — E13 — 12
Leiria, Port. — F2 — 16
Leisler, Mount, mtn., Austl. — E4 — 60
Leisure City, Fl., U.S. — s13 — 102
Leitchfield, Ky., U.S. — C3 — 110
Leiyang, China — D3 — 30
Leizhou Bandao, pen., China — E3 — 30
Leka, Nor. — D4 — 10
Leland, Il., U.S. — B5 — 106
Leland, Ms., U.S. — B3 — 117
Leleiwi Point, c., Hi., U.S. — D7 — 104
Leleque, Arg. — F2 — 69
Leling, China — B4 — 30
Leli Shan, mtn., China — A4 — 28
Le Mans, Fr. — C7 — 16
Le Mars, Ia., U.S. — B1 — 108
Lema Shilindi, Eth. — C8 — 54
Lemesós, Cyp. — E5 — 44
Lemhi, co., Id., U.S. — E4 — 105
Lemhi, stm., Id., U.S. — E5 — 105
Lemhi Pass, Id., U.S. — E5 — 105
Lemhi Range, mts., Id., U.S. — E5 — 105
Lemmon, S.D., U.S. — B3 — 134

Lemmon, Mount, mtn., Az., U.S. — E5 — 96
Lemmon Valley, Nv., U.S. — D2 — 121
Lemnos see Límnos, i., Grc. — E10 — 18
Lemon, Lake, l., In., U.S. — F5 — 107
Lemon Fair, stm., Vt., U.S. — C2 — 138
Lemon Grove, Ca., U.S. — o15 — 98
Lemon Island, i., S.C., U.S. — G6 — 133
Lemont, Il., U.S. — B5 — 106
Lemont, Pa., U.S. — E6 — 131
Lemonweir, stm., Wi., U.S. — D3 — 142
Lemoore, Ca., U.S. — D4 — 98
Lemoore Naval Air Station, mil., Ca., U.S. — D4 — 98
Lempa, stm., N.A. — C2 — 80
Lem Peak, mtn., Id., U.S. — E5 — 105
Lena, Il., U.S. — A4 — 106
Lena, stm., Russia — B14 — 26
Lenakan see Gjumri, Arm. — B10 — 44
Leningrad see Sankt-Peterburg, Russia — D5 — 26
Leninogorsk, Kaz. — A4 — 28
Lenin Peak, mtn., Asia — B2 — 40
Leninsk, Kaz. — E8 — 26
Leninsk-Kuzneckij, Russia — D10 — 26
Leninskoe, Russia — E15 — 26
Lenoir, N.C., U.S. — B1 — 126
Lenoir, co., N.C., U.S. — B5 — 126
Lenoir City, Tn., U.S. — D9 — 135
Lenore Lake, l., Sk., Can. — E3 — 91
Lenore Lake, l., Wa., U.S. — B6 — 140
Lenox, Ga., U.S. — E3 — 103
Lenox, Ia., U.S. — D3 — 108
Lenox, Ma., U.S. — B1 — 114
Lens, Fr. — B8 — 16
Lensk, Russia — C13 — 26
Lentini, Italy — F5 — 18
Léo, Burkina — D4 — 50
Leo, In., U.S. — B7 — 107
Leoben, Aus. — G14 — 12
Leola, S.D., U.S. — B7 — 134
Leominster, Ma., U.S. — A4 — 114
León, Mex. — C4 — 78
León, Nic. — C2 — 80
León, Spain — F4 — 16
Leon, Ia., U.S. — D4 — 108
Leon, Ks., U.S. — E7 — 109
Leon, co., Fl., U.S. — B2 — 102
Leon, co., Tx., U.S. — D4 — 136
Leonard, Tx., U.S. — C4 — 136
Leonardo, N.J., U.S. — C4 — 123
Leonardtown, Md., U.S. — D4 — 113
Leonia, N.J., U.S. — h9 — 123
Leonora, Austl. — F3 — 60
Leonville, La., U.S. — D4 — 111
Leopold and Astrid Coast, Ant. — C13 — 67
Léopoldville see Kinshasa, D.R.C. — D3 — 54
Leoti, Ks., U.S. — D2 — 109
Lepanto, Ar., U.S. — B5 — 97
Lepar, Pulau, i., Indon. — D3 — 36
Lepe, Spain — I3 — 16
Leping, China — D4 — 30
Lepel', Bela. — B10 — 20
L'Épiphanie, P.Q., Can. — D4 — 90
Lepsy, Kaz. — B3 — 28
Le Puy, Fr. — E8 — 16
Le Roy, Il., U.S. — C5 — 106
Le Roy, Mn., U.S. — G6 — 116
Le Roy, N.Y., U.S. — C3 — 125
Lerwick, Scot., U.K. — h19 — 12a
Léry, P.Q., Can. — q19 — 90
Lery, Lake, l., La., U.S. — k12 — 111
Lesbos see Lésvos, i., Grc. — E10 — 18
Les Cayes, Haiti — E5 — 80
Leskovac, Yugo. — C8 — 18
Leslie, Mi., U.S. — F6 — 115
Leslie, S.C., U.S. — B6 — 133
Leslie, co., Ky., U.S. — C6 — 110
Lesosibirsk, Russia — D11 — 26
Lesotho, ctry., Afr. — D4 — 56
Lesozavodsk, Russia — B14 — 26
Les Sables-d'Olonne, Fr. — D6 — 16
Lesser Antilles, is. — F12 — 76
Lesser Caucasus, mts., Asia — B11 — 44
Lesser Khingan Range see Xiao Hinggan Ling, mts., China — A1 — 31
Lesser Slave Lake, l., Ab., Can. — B3 — 84
Lesser Sunda Islands see Tenggara, Nusa, is., Indon. — E5 — 36
Lester Prairie, Mn., U.S. — F4 — 116
Le Sueur, Mn., U.S. — F5 — 116
Le Sueur, co., Mn., U.S. — F5 — 116
Lešukonskoe, Russia — B8 — 22
Lésvos, i., Grc. — E10 — 18
Leszno, Pol. — D4 — 20
Letcher, co., Ky., U.S. — C7 — 110
Leteri, China — B4 — 30
Lethbridge, Ab., Can. — E4 — 84
Lethbridge, Nf., Can. — D5 — 88
Lethem, Guy. — C8 — 70
Leti, Kepulauan, is., Indon. — E7 — 36
Leticia, Col. — D6 — 70
Leting, China — B4 — 30
Letlhakane, Bots. — C3 — 56
Letsôk-aw Kyun, i., Myan. — D3 — 34
Levádhia, Grc. — E9 — 18

Levanger, Nor. — E4 — 10
Levelland, Tx., U.S. — C1 — 136
Leveque, Cape, c., Austl. — D3 — 60
Levice, Slvk. — E5 — 20
Levin, N.Z. — p14 — 63c
Levisa Fork, stm., U.S. — C7 — 110
Lévis [-Lauzon], P.Q., Can. — C6 — 90
Levittown, N.Y., U.S. — E7 — 125
Levittown, Pa., U.S. — F12 — 131
Levkás, i., Grc. — E8 — 18
Levy, co., Fl., U.S. — C4 — 102
Levy Lake, l., Fl., U.S. — C4 — 102
Lewes, De., U.S. — E5 — 101
Lewes and Rehoboth Canal, De., U.S. — F5 — 101
Lewis, co., Id., U.S. — C2 — 105
Lewis, co., Ky., U.S. — B6 — 110
Lewis, co., Mo., U.S. — A6 — 118
Lewis, co., N.Y., U.S. — B5 — 125
Lewis, co., Tn., U.S. — B4 — 135
Lewis, co., W.V., U.S. — C4 — 141
Lewis, co., Wa., U.S. — C3 — 140
Lewis, stm., Wa., U.S. — C4 — 140
Lewis, stm., Wy., U.S. — B2 — 143
Lewis, Isle of, i., Scot., U.K. — A3 — 12
Lewis, Mount, mtn., Nv., U.S. — C5 — 121
Lewis and Clark, co., Mt., U.S. — C4 — 119
Lewis and Clark Cavern, Mt., U.S. — D5 — 119
Lewis and Clark Lake, res., U.S. — E8 — 134
Lewisburg, Ky., U.S. — D3 — 110
Lewisburg, Oh., U.S. — C1 — 128
Lewisburg, Pa., U.S. — E8 — 131
Lewisburg, Tn., U.S. — B5 — 135
Lewisburg, W.V., U.S. — D4 — 141
Lewis Creek, stm., Vt., U.S. — C2 — 138
Lewis Lake, l., Wy., U.S. — B2 — 143
Lewisport, Ky., U.S. — C3 — 110
Lewisporte, Nf., Can. — D4 — 88
Lewis Smith Lake, res., Al., U.S. — B2 — 94
Lewiston, Id., U.S. — C1 — 105
Lewiston, Me., U.S. — D2 — 112
Lewiston, Mn., U.S. — G7 — 116
Lewiston, N.Y., U.S. — B1 — 125
Lewiston, Ut., U.S. — B4 — 137
Lewiston Peak, mtn., Ut., U.S. — C3 — 137
Lewiston Woodville, N.C., U.S. — A5 — 126
Lewistown, Il., U.S. — C3 — 106
Lewistown, Mt., U.S. — C7 — 119
Lewistown, Pa., U.S. — E6 — 131
Lewisville, Ar., U.S. — D2 — 97
Lewisville, Tx., U.S. — C4 — 136
Lewisville Lake, res., Tx., U.S. — C4 — 136
Lexington, Al., U.S. — A2 — 94
Lexington, Il., U.S. — C5 — 106
Lexington, Ky., U.S. — B5 — 110
Lexington, Ma., U.S. — B5 — 114
Lexington, Mi., U.S. — E8 — 115
Lexington, Mo., U.S. — B4 — 118
Lexington, Ms., U.S. — B3 — 117
Lexington, N.C., U.S. — B2 — 126
Lexington, Ne., U.S. — D6 — 120
Lexington, Oh., U.S. — B3 — 128
Lexington, Ok., U.S. — B4 — 129
Lexington, S.C., U.S. — D5 — 133
Lexington, Tn., U.S. — B3 — 135
Lexington, Va., U.S. — C3 — 139
Lexington, co., S.C., U.S. — D5 — 133
Lexington Park, Md., U.S. — D5 — 113
Leye, China — E2 — 30
Leyte, i., Phil. — D9 — 34
Lezhë, Alb. — D7 — 18
L'gov, Russia — D13 — 20
Lhasa, China — D5 — 40
Lhazê, China — D5 — 40
Lhokseumawe, Indon. — B1 — 36
Lhorong, China — E7 — 28
L'Hospitalet de Llobregat, Spain — G8 — 16
Lhünzê, China — D6 — 40
Liancheng, China — A7 — 30
Lianga, Phil. — E9 — 34
Lianjiang, China — E3 — 30
Lianxian, China — G10 — 28
Lianyungang, China — E11 — 28
Liao, stm., China — C12 — 28
Liaocheng, China — B4 — 30
Liaodong Bandao, pen., China — D12 — 28
Liaodong Bay see Liaodong Wan, b., China — C12 — 28
Liaodong Wan, b., China — C12 — 28
Liaoning, state, China — C12 — 28
Liaotung, Gulf of see Liaodong Wan, b., China — C12 — 28
Liaotung Bay see Liaodong Wan, b., China — C12 — 28
Liaoyang, China — A5 — 30
Liaoyuan, China — C13 — 28
Liard, stm., Can. — F15 — 82
Libagon, Phil. — D9 — 34
Libby, Mt., U.S. — B1 — 119
Libenge, D.R.C. — C3 — 54
Liberal, Ks., U.S. — E3 — 109
Liberal, Mo., U.S. — D3 — 118
Liberec, Czech Rep. — D3 — 20
Liberia, C.R. — C2 — 80

Name	Map Ref.	Page

Liberia, ctry., Afr. E3 50
Liberty, In., U.S. E8 107
Liberty, Ky., U.S. C5 110
Liberty, Mo., U.S. B3 118
Liberty, Ms., U.S. D3 117
Liberty, N.C., U.S. B3 126
Liberty, N.Y., U.S. D6 125
Liberty, S.C., U.S. B2 133
Liberty, Tx., U.S. D5 136
Liberty, co., Fl., U.S. B2 102
Liberty, co., Ga., U.S. E5 103
Liberty, co., Mt., U.S. B5 119
Liberty, co., Tx., U.S. D5 136
Liberty Center, Oh., U.S. A1 128
Liberty Lake, Wa., U.S. g14 140
Liberty Lake, res., Md., U.S. B4 113
Libertyville, Il., U.S. A6 106
Lībīyah, Aṣ-Ṣaḥrā' al-
  (Libyan Desert), des.,
  Afr. E9 48
Libo, China D2 30
Libourne, Fr. E6 16
Libreville, Gabon C1 54
Libuse, La., U.S. C3 111
Libya, ctry., Afr. E8 48
Libyan Desert see Lībīyah,
  Aṣ-Ṣaḥrā' al-, des., Afr. E9 48
Licancábur, Cerro, vol., S.A. C4 72
Licata, Italy F4 18
Lice, Tur. C9 44
Lichinga, Moz. A6 56
Lichuan, China C2 30
Lichuan, China D4 30
Lick Creek, stm., Tn., U.S. . C11 135
Licking, Mo., U.S. D6 118
Licking, co., Oh., U.S. B3 128
Licking, stm., Ky., U.S. B6 110
Lida, Bela. C8 20
Lida, Lake, l., Mn., U.S. ... D3 116
Liden, Swe. E7 10
Lidgerwood, N.D., U.S. C8 127
Lidköping, Swe. G5 10
Lido di Ostia, Italy D4 18
Lidzbark Warmiński, Pol. .. B6 20
Liebig, Mount, mtn., Austl. .E5 60
Liechtenstein, ctry., Eur. ... A2 18
Liège, Bel. E9 12
Lienz, Aus. G13 12
Liepāja, Lat. H9 10
Lièvre, Rivière du, stm.,
  P.Q., Can. D2 90
Lifou, i., N. Cal. l9 62a
Lighthouse Inlet, b., S.C.,
  U.S. k12 133
Lighthouse Point, c., Fl.,
  U.S. C2 102
Lighthouse Point, c., La.,
  U.S. E3 111
Lighthouse Point, c., Mi.,
  U.S. C5 115
Lightning Creek, stm., Wy.,
  U.S. C8 143
Ligonier, In., U.S. B6 107
Ligonier, Pa., U.S. F3 131
Ligurian Apennines see
  Appennino Ligure, mts.,
  Italy B2 18
Ligurian Sea, Eur. C2 18
Lihue, Hi., U.S. B2 104
Lijiang, China F8 28
Likasi, D.R.C. F5 54
Likati, D.R.C. C4 54
Lilbourn, Mo., U.S. E8 118
Lilburn, Ga., U.S. h8 103
Lille, Fr. B8 16
Lillebælt, strt., Den. I3 10
Lillehammer, Nor. F4 10
Lillesand, Nor. G3 10
Lillestrøm, Nor. G4 10
Lillian, Al., U.S. E2 94
Lillington, N.C., U.S. B4 126
Lillinonah, Lake, l., Ct., U.S. C2 100
Lillooet, B.C., Can. D7 85
Lillooet, stm., B.C., Can. .. D6 85
Lilly, Pa., U.S. F4 131
Lilly Fork, stm., W.V., U.S. . m13 141
Lilly Grove, W.V., U.S. ... D3 141
Lilongwe, Mwi. A5 56
Liloy, Phil. E8 34
Lily, Ky., U.S. C5 110
Lima, Peru F4 70
Lima, N.Y., U.S. C3 125
Lima, Oh., U.S. B1 128
Lima Reservoir, res., Mt.,
  U.S. F4 119
Limay Mahuida, Arg. F4 72
Limbe, Cam. C1 54
Limbé, Haiti B5 80
Limeira, Braz. F2 74
Limerick, Ire. D2 12
Limestone, Me., U.S. A5 112
Limestone, co., Al., U.S. ... A2 94
Limestone, co., Tx., U.S. .. D4 136
Limestone Point, pen., Mb.,
  Can. C2 86
Limfjorden, l., Den. H3 10
Limingen, l., Nor. D5 10
Limmen Bight, b., Austl. ... C6 60
Límnos, i., Grc. E10 18
Limoges, On., Can. B9 89
Limoges, Fr. E7 16
Limón, Hond. B2 80
Limon, Co., U.S. B7 99
Limoux, Fr. F8 16
Limpopo, stm., Afr. C5 56

Lin'an, China C4 30
Linapacan Strait, strt., Phil. .D7 34
Linares, Chile E2 69
Linares, Mex. C5 78
Linares, Spain H5 16
Lincoln, Arg. E5 72
Lincoln, On., Can. D5 89
Lincoln, Eng., U.K. D6 12
Lincoln, Al., U.S. B3 94
Lincoln, Ar., U.S. B1 97
Lincoln, Ca., U.S. C3 98
Lincoln, De., U.S. E4 101
Lincoln, Id., U.S. F6 105
Lincoln, Il., U.S. C4 106
Lincoln, Ks., U.S. C5 109
Lincoln, Ma., U.S. g10 114
Lincoln, Me., U.S. C4 112
Lincoln, Mo., U.S. C4 118
Lincoln, Ne., U.S. D9 120
Lincoln, N.H., U.S. B3 122
Lincoln, co., Ar., U.S. D4 97
Lincoln, co., Co., U.S. C7 99
Lincoln, co., Ga., U.S. C4 103
Lincoln, co., Id., U.S. G4 105
Lincoln, co., Ks., U.S. C5 109
Lincoln, co., Ky., U.S. C5 110
Lincoln, co., La., U.S. B3 111
Lincoln, co., Me., U.S. D3 112
Lincoln, co., Mn., U.S. F2 116
Lincoln, co., Mo., U.S. B7 118
Lincoln, co., Ms., U.S. D3 117
Lincoln, co., Mt., U.S. B1 119
Lincoln, co., N.C., U.S. B1 126
Lincoln, co., Ne., U.S. D5 120
Lincoln, co., N.M., U.S. D4 124
Lincoln, co., Nv., U.S. F6 121
Lincoln, co., Ok., U.S. B5 129
Lincoln, co., Or., U.S. C3 130
Lincoln, co., S.D., U.S. D9 134
Lincoln, co., Tn., U.S. B5 135
Lincoln, co., W.V., U.S. C2 141
Lincoln, co., Wa., U.S. B7 140
Lincoln, co., Wi., U.S. C4 142
Lincoln, co., Wy., U.S. D2 143
Lincoln, Mount, mtn., Co.,
  U.S. B4 99
Lincoln Acres, Ca., U.S. .. o15 98
Lincoln City, Or., U.S. C2 130
Lincoln Hav see Lincoln
  Sea, N.A. B28 82
Lincoln Heights, Oh., U.S. . o13 128
Lincoln Park, Co., U.S. C5 99
Lincoln Park, Mi., U.S. ... p15 115
Lincoln Park, N.J., U.S. B4 123
Lincoln Sea, N.A. B28 82
Lincolnshire, Il., U.S. h9 106
Lincoln Tomb State
  Memorial, hist., Il., U.S. D4 106
Lincolnton, Ga., U.S. C4 103
Lincolnton, N.C., U.S. B1 126
Lincolnville, S.C., U.S. h11 133
Lincolnwood, Il., U.S. h9 106
Lincroft, N.J., U.S. C4 123
Lindale, Ga., U.S. B1 103
Lindale, Tx., U.S. C5 136
Linden, Guy. B8 70
Linden, Al., U.S. C2 94
Linden, In., U.S. D4 107
Linden, Mi., U.S. F7 115
Linden, N.J., U.S. k8 123
Linden, Tn., U.S. B4 135
Linden, Tx., U.S. C5 136
Lindenhurst, Il., U.S. h8 106
Lindenhurst, N.Y., U.S. ... n15 125
Lindenwold, N.J., U.S. D3 123
Lindesberg, Swe. G6 10
Lindesnes, c., Nor. H2 10
Lindi, Tan. E7 54
Lindon, Ut., U.S. C4 137
Lindsay, On., Can. C6 89
Lindsay, Ca., U.S. D4 98
Lindsay, Ok., U.S. C4 129
Lindsborg, Ks., U.S. D6 109
Lindstrom, Mn., U.S. E6 116
Line Islands, is., Oc. E14 58
Linesville, Pa., U.S. C1 131
Lineville, Al., U.S. B4 94
Linfen, China D10 28
Lingao, China F2 30
Lingayen, Phil. C8 34
Lingayen Gulf, b., Phil. C8 34
Lingen, Ger. D10 12
Lingga, Kepulauan, is.,
  Indon. D3 36
Lingga, Pulau, i., Indon. ... D2 36
Lingle, Wy., U.S. D8 143
Linglestown, Pa., U.S. F8 131
Lingqiu, China B3 30
Lingshan, China E2 30
Lingshui, China F3 30
Linguère, Sen. C1 50
Lingyuan, China A4 30
Linhai, China F12 28
Linhares, Braz. E3 74
Linhe, China C9 28
Linière, P.Q., Can. C7 90
Linköping, Swe. G6 10
Linkou, China B14 28
Linn, Mo., U.S. C6 118
Linn, co., Ia., U.S. B6 108
Linn, co., Ks., U.S. D9 109
Linn, co., Mo., U.S. B4 118
Linn, co., Or., U.S. C4 130
Lino Lakes, Mn., U.S. ... m12 116

Linqing, China B4 30
Linquan, China C4 30
Linru, China E10 28
Lins, Braz. F2 74
Lintan, China C1 30
Linthicum Heights, Md.,
  U.S. B4 113
Linton, In., U.S. F3 107
Linton, N.D., U.S. C5 127
Linwood, N.J., U.S. E3 123
Linxi, China C11 28
Linxia, China D8 28
Linyi, China D11 28
Linyi, China B4 30
Linz, Aus. F14 12
Lion, Golfe du, b., Fr. F9 16
Lion, Gulf of see Lion,
  Golfe du, b., Fr. F9 16
Lipa, Phil. D8 34
Lipeck, Russia D5 26
Lipova, Rom. F6 20
Lipscomb, Al., U.S. B3 94
Lipscomb, co., Tx., U.S. ... A2 136
Lipu, China E3 30
Lira, Ug. C6 54
Lisala, D.R.C. C4 54
Lisboa (Lisbon), Port. H2 16
Lisbon see Lisboa, Port. ... H2 16
Lisbon, Ia., U.S. C6 108
Lisbon, Md., U.S. B3 113
Lisbon, Me., U.S. D2 112
Lisbon, N.D., U.S. C8 127
Lisbon, N.H., U.S. B3 122
Lisbon, Oh., U.S. B5 128
Lisbon Center, Me., U.S. ... f7 112
Lisbon Falls, Me., U.S. E2 112
Lisburne, Cape, c., Ak., U.S. B6 95
Lishui, China F11 28
Lisianski Island, i., Hi., U.S. k13 104
Lisieux, Fr. C7 16
Liski, Russia D5 26
Lisle, Il., U.S. k8 106
L'Islet-sur-Mer, P.Q., Can. . B7 90
L'Isle-Verte, P.Q., Can. A8 90
Lismore, Austl. F5 62
Listowel, On., Can. D4 89
Litang, China E8 28
Litang, China G9 28
Litchfield, Ct., U.S. C3 100
Litchfield, Il., U.S. D4 106
Litchfield, Mi., U.S. F6 115
Litchfield, Mn., U.S. E4 116
Litchfield, co., Ct., U.S. B2 100
Litchfield Park, Az., U.S. ... m8 96
Lithgow, Austl. G5 62
Lithia Springs, Ga., U.S. ... h7 103
Lithonia, Ga., U.S. C2 103
Lithuania, ctry., Eur. B3 20
Lititz, Pa., U.S. F9 131
Litovko, Russia B15 28
Little, stm., Ct., U.S. C7 100
Little, stm., Ky., U.S. D2 110
Little, stm., La., U.S. C3 111
Little, stm., N.C., U.S. B3 126
Little, stm., Ok., U.S. B5 129
Little, stm., S.C., U.S. C2 133
Little, stm., Tn., U.S. n14 135
Little, stm., Va., U.S. D7 129
Little, stm., Va., U.S. D2 139
Little, stm., Vt., U.S. C3 138
Little, stm., U.S. B5 97
Little Acres, Az., U.S. D5 96
Little Andaman, i., India ... G6 40
Little Arkansas, stm., Ks.,
  U.S. C6 109
Little Belt see Lillebælt, strt.,
  Den. I3 10
Little Belt Mountains, mts.,
  Mt., U.S. D6 119
Little Bighorn, stm., U.S. ... E9 119
Little Black, stm., Me., U.S. A3 112
Little Blue, stm., In., U.S. .. H5 107
Little Blue, stm., U.S. C6 109
Little Bow, stm., Ab., Can. . D4 84
Little Cacapon, stm., W.V.,
  U.S. B6 141
Little Catalina, Nf., Can. ... D5 88
Little Cayman, i., Cay. Is. .. B3 80
Little Cedar, stm., U.S. A5 108
Little Churchill, stm., Mb.,
  Can. A4 86
Little Chute, Wi., U.S. D5 142
Little Coal, stm., W.V., U.S. C3 141
Little Colorado, stm., Az.,
  U.S. B4 96
Little Compton, R.I., U.S. .. E6 132
Little Creek, De., U.S. D4 101
Little Creek Naval
  Amphibious Base, mil.,
  Va., U.S. k15 139
Little Creek Peak, mtn., Ut.,
  U.S. F3 137
Little Current, On., Can. ... B3 89
Little Diomede Island, i.,
  Ak., U.S. B6 95
Little Egg Harbor, b., N.J.,
  U.S. D4 123
Little Egg Inlet, b., N.J., U.S. E4 123
Little Falls, Mn., U.S. E4 116
Little Falls, N.J., U.S. B4 123
Little Falls, N.Y., U.S. B6 125
Little Ferry, N.J., U.S. h8 123
Littlefield, Tx., U.S. C1 136
Little Fishing Creek, stm.,
  W.V., U.S. h9 141

Littlefork, Mn., U.S. B5 116
Little Fork, stm., Mn., U.S. . B5 116
Little Goose Creek, stm.,
  Wy., U.S. B6 143
Little Gunpowder Falls,
  stm., Md., U.S. A4 113
Little Humboldt, stm., Nv.,
  U.S. B4 121
Little Inagua, i., Bah. D10 76
Little Kanawha, stm., W.V.,
  U.S. C4 141
Little Karroo, plat., S. Afr. .. E3 56
Little Lake, Mi., U.S. B3 115
Little Lake, l., La., U.S. E5 111
Little Lynches, stm., S.C.,
  U.S. C7 133
Little Manatee, stm., Fl.,
  U.S. p11 102
Little Mecatina, stm., Can. . h9 88
Little Miami, stm., Oh., U.S. C1 128
Little Minch, The, strt.,
  Scot., U.K. B3 12
Little Missouri, stm., Ar.,
  U.S. D2 97
Little Missouri, stm., U.S. .. B7 92
Little Muddy, stm., Il., U.S. E4 106
Little Muddy, stm., N.D.,
  U.S. A2 127
Little Namaqualand, hist.
  reg., S. Afr. D2 56
Little Nicobar, i., India H6 40
Little Osage, stm., U.S. E9 109
Little Otter Creek, stm., Vt.,
  U.S. C2 138
Little Owyhee, stm., U.S. ... B5 121
Little Pee Dee, stm., S.C.,
  U.S. C9 133
Little Powder, stm., U.S. .. F11 119
Little Red, stm., Ar., U.S. .. B4 97
Little River, co., Ar., U.S. .. D1 97
Little River Inlet, b., S.C.,
  U.S. D10 133
Little Rock, Ar., U.S. C3 97
Little Rock, stm., U.S. A1 108
Little Rock Air Force Base,
  mil., Ar., U.S. C3 97
Little Sable Point, c., Mi.,
  U.S. E4 115
Little Salt Lake, l., Ut., U.S. F3 137
Little Sandy, stm., Ky., U.S. B6 110
Little Sandy Creek, stm.,
  Wy., U.S. D3 143
Little Sebago Lake, l., Me.,
  U.S. g7 112
Little Silver, N.J., U.S. C4 123
Little Sioux, stm., U.S. B2 108
Little Sioux, West Fork,
  stm., Ia., U.S. B2 108
Little Smoky, stm., Ab., Can. B2 84
Little Snake, stm., U.S. A2 99
Little Spokane, stm., Wa.,
  U.S. B8 140
Littlestown, Pa., U.S. G7 131
Little Tallapoosa, stm., U.S. B4 94
Little Tenmile Creek, stm.,
  W.V., U.S. k10 141
Little Tennessee, stm., U.S. D9 135
Littleton, Co., U.S. B6 99
Littleton, Ma., U.S. f10 114
Littleton, N.C., U.S. A5 126
Littleton, N.H., U.S. B3 122
Littleville, Al., U.S. A2 94
Little Wabash, stm., Il., U.S. E5 106
Little Walnut, stm., Ks., U.S. g13 109
Little White, stm., S.D., U.S. D5 134
Little Wolf, stm., Wi., U.S. . D4 142
Little Wood, stm., Id., U.S. . F4 105
Little Zab, stm., Asia E10 44
Liucheng, China G9 28
Liuzhou, China G9 28
Live Oak, Ca., U.S. C3 98
Live Oak, Fl., U.S. B4 102
Live Oak, co., Tx., U.S. E3 136
Livermore, Ca., U.S. h9 98
Livermore, Ky., U.S. C2 110
Livermore, Mount, mtn.,
  Tx., U.S. o12 136
Livermore Falls, Me., U.S. . D2 112
Liverpool, Eng., U.K. D5 12
Livingston, Guat. B2 80
Livingston, Al., U.S. C1 94
Livingston, Ca., U.S. D3 98
Livingston, Il., U.S. E4 106
Livingston, La., U.S. D5 111
Livingston, N.J., U.S. B4 123
Livingston, Tn., U.S. C8 135
Livingston, Tx., U.S. D5 136
Livingston, co., Il., U.S. C5 106
Livingston, co., Ky., U.S. ... e9 110
Livingston, co., La., U.S. ... D5 111
Livingston, co., Mi., U.S. ... F7 115
Livingston, co., Mo., U.S. .. B4 118
Livingston, co., N.Y., U.S. . C3 125
Livingston, Lake, res., Tx.,
  U.S. D5 136
Livingstone, Zam. B4 56
Livingstone Falls, wtfl., Afr. E2 54
Livingstonia, Mwi. A5 56
Livny, Russia C14 20
Livonia, La., U.S. D4 111
Livonia, Mi., U.S. F7 115
Livorno, Italy C3 18
Liwale, Tan. E7 54

Liwonde, Mwi. B6 56
Lixi, China F10 28
Lixian, China D3 30
Lizard Head Pass, Co., U.S. D3 99
Lizard Head Peak, mtn.,
  Wy., U.S. D3 143
Lizella, Ga., U.S. D3 103
Ljahovskie ostrova, is.,
  Russia B15 26
Ljubercy, Russia C6 22
Ljubljana, Slvn. A5 18
Ljudinovo, Russia C13 20
Ljungby, Swe. H5 10
Ljusdal, Swe. F7 10
Ljusnan, stm., Swe. E6 10
Ljusterö, i., Swe. G8 10
Llancanelo, Laguna, l., Arg. F4 72
Llano, Tx., U.S. D3 136
Llano, co., Tx., U.S. D3 136
Llano, stm., Tx., U.S. D3 136
Llano Estacado see
  Estacado, Llano, pl.,
  U.S. C1 136
Llanos, pl., S.A. B6 70
Lleida, Spain G7 16
Llera de Canales, Mex. C5 78
Lloyd, Ky., U.S. B7 110
Lloydminster, Ab., Can. C5 84
Lloyds, stm., Nf., Can. D3 88
Llucmajor, Spain H8 16
Llullaillaco, Volcán, vol.,
  S.A. C4 72
Loami, Il., U.S. D4 106
Loange, stm., Afr. E3 54
Lobamba, Swaz. D5 56
Lobatse, Bots. D4 56
Lobelville, Tn., U.S. B4 135
Lobería, Arg. F6 72
Lobito, Ang. F2 54
Lobos, Cay i., Bah. A4 80
Lobster Lake, l., Me., U.S. . C3 112
Lobva, Russia C11 22
Locarno, Switz. A2 18
Loch Raven Reservoir, res.,
  Md., U.S. B4 113
Lochsa, stm., Id., U.S. C3 105
Lockeport, N.S., Can. F4 87
Lockesburg, Ar., U.S. D1 97
Lockhart, Tx., U.S. E4 136
Lock Haven, Pa., U.S. D7 131
Lockland, Oh., U.S. o13 128
Lockney, Tx., U.S. B2 136
Lockport, Il., U.S. B5 106
Lockport, La., U.S. E5 111
Lockport, N.Y., U.S. B2 125
Lockwood, Mo., U.S. D4 118
Lockwood, Mt., U.S. E8 119
Loc Ninh, Viet. D5 34
Locust, N.C., U.S. B2 126
Locust Fork, stm., Al., U.S. . B3 94
Locust Grove, Ga., U.S. C2 103
Locust Grove, Ok., U.S. A6 129
Lodejnoe Pole, Russia B5 22
Lodgepole Creek, stm., U.S. C3 120
Lodi, Italy B2 18
Lodi, Ca., U.S. C3 98
Lodi, N.J., U.S. h8 123
Lodi, Oh., U.S. A3 128
Lodi, Wi., U.S. E4 142
Lodja, D.R.C. D4 54
Lodwar, Kenya C7 54
Łódź, Pol. D5 20
Loei, Thai. C4 34
Lofoten, is., Nor. B5 10
Lofoten Basin D21 144
Loga, Niger D5 50
Logan, Ia., U.S. C2 108
Logan, Ks., U.S. C4 109
Logan, N.M., U.S. B6 124
Logan, Oh., U.S. C3 128
Logan, Ut., U.S. B4 137
Logan, W.V., U.S. D3 141
Logan, co., Ar., U.S. B2 97
Logan, co., Co., U.S. A7 99
Logan, co., Il., U.S. C4 106
Logan, co., Ks., U.S. D2 109
Logan, co., Ky., U.S. D3 110
Logan, co., N.D., U.S. C6 127
Logan, co., Ne., U.S. C5 120
Logan, co., Oh., U.S. B2 128
Logan, co., Ok., U.S. B4 129
Logan, co., W.V., U.S. D3 141
Logan, Mount, mtn., Yk.,
  Can. F11 82
Logan, Mount, mtn., Wa.,
  U.S. A5 140
Logandale, Nv., U.S. G7 121
Logan Lake, B.C., Can. D7 85
Logan Martin Lake, res., Al.,
  U.S. B3 94
Logan Pass, Mt., U.S. B2 119
Logansport, In., U.S. C5 107
Logansport, La., U.S. C2 111
Loganville, Ga., U.S. C3 103
Loganville, Pa., U.S. G8 131
Loggieville, N.B., Can. B4 87
Log Lane Village, Co., U.S. . A7 99
Logone, stm., Afr. B3 54
Logroño, Spain F5 16
Løgstør, Den. H3 10
Loi-kaw, Myan. C3 34
Loimaa, Fin. F10 10
Loire, stm., Fr. D6 16

Name	Map Ref.	Page
Loja, Ec.	D4	70
Loja, Spain	I4	16
Lokandu, D.R.C.	D5	54
Lokan tekojärvi, res., Fin.	C12	10
Lokichokio, Kenya	C6	54
Lokoja, Nig.	E6	50
Lokolama, D.R.C.	D3	54
Lola, Gui.	E3	50
Lola, Mount, mtn., Ca., U.S.	C3	98
Loliondo, Tan.	D7	54
Lolland, i., Den.	I4	10
Lolo, Mt., U.S.	D2	119
Lolo Pass, U.S.	C4	105
Lom, Bul.	C9	18
Lomami, stm., D.R.C.	C4	54
Lomas de Zamora, Arg.	E6	72
Lombard, Il., U.S.	k8	106
Lomblen, Pulau, i., Indon.	E6	36
Lombok, i., Indon.	E5	36
Lombok, Selat, strt., Indon.	E5	36
Lomé, Togo	E5	50
Lomela, D.R.C.	D4	54
Lomié, Cam.	C2	54
Lomira, Wi., U.S.	E5	142
Lomonosov, Russia	G13	10
Lomonosov Ridge	E8	144
Lompoc, Ca., U.S.	E3	98
Lom Sak, Thai.	C4	34
Łomża, Pol.	C7	20
Lonaconing, Md., U.S.	k13	113
Loncoche, Chile	E2	69
London, On., Can.	E3	89
London, Eng., U.K.	E6	12
London, Ar., U.S.	B2	97
London, Ky., U.S.	C5	110
London, Oh., U.S.	C2	128
Londonderry, N. Ire., U.K.	C3	12
Londonderry, N.H., U.S.	E4	122
Londonderry, Cape, c., Austl.	C4	60
Londonderry, Isla, i., Chile	I2	69
Londontown, Md., U.S.	C4	113
Londrina, Braz.	F1	74
Lone Grove, Ok., U.S.	C4	129
Lone Mountain, mtn., Nv., U.S.	E4	121
Lone Pine, Ca., U.S.	D4	98
Lone Tree, Ia., U.S.	C6	108
Long, co., Ga., U.S.	E5	103
Longa, proliv, strt., Russia	B19	26
Long Bar Harbor, Md., U.S.	B5	113
Long Beach, Ca., U.S.	F4	98
Long Beach, In., U.S.	A4	107
Long Beach, Md., U.S.	D5	113
Long Beach, Ms., U.S.	g7	117
Long Beach, N.Y., U.S.	E7	125
Long Beach, Wa., U.S.	C1	140
Longboat Key, Fl., U.S.	q10	102
Longboat Key, i., Fl., U.S.	E4	102
Longboat Pass, strt., Fl., U.S.	q10	102
Long Branch, N.J., U.S.	C5	123
Longbranch, Wa., U.S.	B3	140
Long Creek Mountain, mtn., Wy., U.S.	D5	143
Longde, China	B2	30
Longford, Ire.	D3	12
Long Grove, Ia., U.S.	C7	108
Long Harbour [-Mount Arlington Heights], Nf., Can.	E5	88
Longhua, China	A4	30
Longiram, Indon.	D5	36
Long Island, i., Bah.	D10	76
Long Island, i., N.S., Can.	E3	87
Long Island, i., Ma., U.S.	g12	114
Long Island, i., Me., U.S.	g7	112
Long Island, i., N.Y., U.S.	E7	125
Long Island Sound, strt., U.S.	E7	125
Longjiang, China	B12	28
Long Key, i., Fl., U.S.	H6	102
Long Lake, Il., U.S.	h8	106
Long Lake, l., Me., U.S.	A4	112
Long Lake, l., Me., U.S.	D2	112
Long Lake, l., Mi., U.S.	D5	115
Long Lake, l., Mi., U.S.	C7	115
Long Lake, l., Mn., U.S.	D4	116
Long Lake, l., N.D., U.S.	C6	127
Long Lake, l., N.Y., U.S.	B6	125
Long Lake, l., Wa., U.S.	f10	140
Long Lake, l., Wi., U.S.	C2	142
Longli, China	F9	28
Longling, China	B3	34
Longmeadow, Ma., U.S.	B2	114
Longmen, China	B6	34
Longmont, Co., U.S.	A5	99
Longnan, China	E3	30
Long Point, c., Mb., Can.	C2	86
Long Point, pen., On., Can.	E4	89
Long Pond, res., Fl., U.S.	C4	102
Long Prairie, Mn., U.S.	E4	116
Longquan, China	D4	30
Long Range Mountains, mts., Nf., Can.	D3	88
Longreach, Austl.	E3	62
Longshan, China	D2	30
Longs Peak, mtn., Co., U.S.	A5	99
Long Strait see Longa, proliv, strt., Russia	B19	26
Longueuil, P.Q., Can.	D4	90
Long View, N.C., U.S.	B1	126
Longview, Tx., U.S.	C5	136
Longview, Wa., U.S.	C3	140
Longxi, China	E8	28
Longxian, China	C2	30
Long Xuyen, Viet.	D5	34
Longyan, China	D4	30
Longzhou, China	G9	28
Lonoke, Ar., U.S.	C4	97
Lonoke, co., Ar., U.S.	C4	97
Lonsdale, Mn., U.S.	F5	116
Lonsdale, R.I., U.S.	B4	132
Lons-le-Saunier, Fr.	D9	16
Lõogootee, In., U.S.	G4	107
Lookout, Ky., U.S.	C7	110
Lookout, Cape, c., N.C., U.S.	C6	126
Lookout, Point, c., Mi., U.S.	d7	115
Lookout Mountain, Tn., U.S.	h11	135
Lookout Mountain, mtn., Or., U.S.	C6	130
Lookout Mountain, mtn., U.S.	D8	135
Lookout Pass, U.S.	B3	105
Lookout Point Lake, res., Or., U.S.	D4	130
Loongana, Austl.	G4	60
Loon Lake, Wa., U.S.	A8	140
Loon Lake, l., Me., U.S.	B3	112
Loop Creek, stm., W.V., U.S.	m13	141
Loosahatchie, stm., Tn., U.S.	B2	135
Lop, China	B4	40
Lopatka, mys, c., Russia	D17	26
Lop Buri, Thai.	D4	34
Lopez, Cap, c., Gabon	D1	54
Lopez Island, i., Wa., U.S.	A3	140
Lop Nor (Lop Nur), l., China	C6	28
Lop Nor (Lop Nur), l., China	C6	28
Lopphavet, Nor.	A9	10
Lora, Hāmūn-i-, l., Asia	E8	42
Lorain, Oh., U.S.	A3	128
Lorain, co., Oh., U.S.	A3	128
Loramie, Lake, res., Oh., U.S.	B1	128
Lorca, Spain	I6	16
Lord Howe Rise	K19	64
Lordsburg, N.M., U.S.	E1	124
Loreauville, La., U.S.	D4	111
Lorenzo, Tx., U.S.	C2	136
Loreto, Braz.	E10	70
Loreto, Mex.	B2	78
Lorette, Mb., Can.	E3	86
Loretteville, P.Q., Can.	C6	90
Loretto, Ky., U.S.	C4	110
Loretto, Pa., U.S.	F4	131
Loretto, Tn., U.S.	B4	135
Lorica, Col.	B4	70
Lorient, Fr.	D5	16
Loris, S.C., U.S.	C10	133
Lorn, Firth of, b., Scot., U.K.	B4	12
Lorne, Austl.	H3	62
Lorne, N.B., Can.	B3	87
Lorraine, hist. reg., Fr.	C9	16
Los, Îles de, is., Gui.	E2	50
Los Alamos, N.M., U.S.	B3	124
Los Alamos, co., N.M., U.S.	B3	124
Los Altos, Ca., U.S.	k8	98
Los Angeles, Ca., U.S.	E4	98
Los Angeles, co., Ca., U.S.	E4	98
Los Angeles Aqueduct, Ca., U.S.	E4	98
Los Banos, Ca., U.S.	D3	98
Los Blancos, Arg.	C5	72
Los Fresnos, Tx., U.S.	F4	136
Los Gatos, Ca., U.S.	D2	98
Los Lunas, N.M., U.S.	C3	124
Los Mochis, Mex.	B3	78
Los Pinos, stm., Co., U.S.	D3	99
Los Ranchos de Albuquerque, N.M., U.S.	B3	124
Los Roques, Islas, is., Ven.	C6	80
Lost, stm., In., U.S.	G4	107
Lost, stm., W.V., U.S.	B6	141
Lost, stm., Wa., U.S.	A5	140
Lost Creek, stm., Wy., U.S.	D4	143
Lost Peak, mtn., Ut., U.S.	F2	137
Lost Ranger Peak, mtn., Co., U.S.	A4	99
Lost River Glacial Caverns, N.H., U.S.	B3	122
Lost River Range, mts., Id., U.S.	E5	105
Lost Trail Pass, U.S.	D5	105
Losuia, Pap. N. Gui.	H13	32
Los Vilos, Chile	D2	69
Lot, stm., Fr.	E7	16
Lota, Chile	F3	72
Lotawana, Lake, res., Mo., U.S.	k11	118
Lotbinière, P.Q., Can.	C6	90
Loto, D.R.C.	D4	54
Lotung, Tai.	E5	30
Louang Namtha, Laos	B4	34
Louangphrabang, Laos	C4	34
Loubomo, Congo	D2	54
Loudon, Tn., U.S.	D9	135
Loudon, co., Tn., U.S.	D9	135
Loudonville, Oh., U.S.	B3	128
Loudoun, co., Va., U.S.	A5	139
Louga, Sen.	C1	50
Louhi, Russia	A5	22
Louisa, Va., U.S.	B4	139
Louisa, co., Ia., U.S.	C6	108
Louisa, co., Va., U.S.	C5	139
Louisa, Lake, l., Fl., U.S.	D5	102
Louisbourg, N.S., Can.	D10	87
Louisburg, Ks., U.S.	D9	109
Louisburg, N.C., U.S.	A4	126
Louisdale, N.S., Can.	D8	87
Louise, Lake, l., Ak., U.S.	f18	95
Louise Island, i., B.C., Can.	C2	85
Louiseville, P.Q., Can.	C5	90
Louisiana, Mo., U.S.	B6	118
Louisiana, state, U.S.	C3	111
Louisiana Point, c., La., U.S.	E2	111
Louis Trichardt, S. Afr.	C4	56
Louisville, Al., U.S.	D4	94
Louisville, Co., U.S.	B5	99
Louisville, Ga., U.S.	C4	103
Louisville, Il., U.S.	E5	106
Louisville, Ky., U.S.	B4	110
Louisville, Ms., U.S.	B4	117
Louisville, Ne., U.S.	D9	120
Louisville, Oh., U.S.	B4	128
Louisville Ridge	L22	64
Louis-XIV, Pointe, c., P.Q., Can.	h11	90
Loum, Cam.	C1	54
Loup, co., Ne., U.S.	C6	120
Loup, stm., Ne., U.S.	C8	120
Loup City, Ne., U.S.	C7	120
Lourdes, Nf., Can.	D2	88
Lourdes, Fr.	F6	16
Lourenço Marques see Maputo, Moz.	D5	56
Louviers, Co., U.S.	B6	99
Love, co., Ok., U.S.	D4	129
Loveč, Bul.	C10	18
Loveland, Co., U.S.	A5	99
Loveland, Oh., U.S.	n13	128
Loveland Park, Oh., U.S.	C1	128
Loveland Pass, Co., U.S.	B5	99
Lovell, Wy., U.S.	B4	143
Lovelock, Nv., U.S.	C3	121
Lovely, Ky., U.S.	C7	110
Lovenia, Mount, mtn., Ut., U.S.	C5	137
Love Point, c., Md., U.S.	B5	113
Loves Park, Il., U.S.	A4	106
Lovettsville, Va., U.S.	A5	139
Loving, N.M., U.S.	E5	124
Loving, co., Tx., U.S.	D1	136
Lovington, Ia., U.S.	e8	108
Lovington, Il., U.S.	D5	106
Lovington, N.M., U.S.	E6	124
Lóvua, Ang.	E4	54
Lowden, Ia., U.S.	C7	108
Lowell, Ar., U.S.	A1	97
Lowell, In., U.S.	B3	107
Lowell, Ma., U.S.	A5	114
Lowell, Mi., U.S.	F5	115
Lowell, N.C., U.S.	B1	126
Lowell, Or., U.S.	D4	130
Lowell, Vt., U.S.	B3	138
Lowell, Lake, res., Id., U.S.	F2	105
Lowellville, Oh., U.S.	A5	128
Lower Arrow Lake, res., B.C., Can.	E8	85
Lower Brule Indian Reservation, S.D., U.S.	C6	134
Lower California see Baja California, pen., Mex.	B2	78
Lower Hutt, N.Z.	p14	63c
Lower Klamath Lake, l., Ca., U.S.	B3	98
Lower Matecumbe Key, i., Fl., U.S.	H6	102
Lower New York Bay, b., N.J., U.S.	B4	123
Lower Otay Lake, res., Ca., U.S.	o16	98
Lower Paia, Hi., U.S.	C5	104
Lower Red Lake, l., Mn., U.S.	C3	116
Lower Rice Lake, l., Mn., U.S.	C3	116
Lower Salmon Dam, Id., U.S.	G4	105
Lower Trajan's Wall, hist., Eur.	G10	20
Lower West Pubnico, N.S., Can.	F4	87
Lowestoft, Eng., U.K.	D7	12
Lowndes, co., Al., U.S.	C3	94
Lowndes, co., Ga., U.S.	F3	103
Lowndes, co., Ms., U.S.	B5	117
Lowry City, Mo., U.S.	C4	118
Lowville, N.Y., U.S.	B5	125
Loxley, Al., U.S.	E2	94
Loxton, Austl.	G4	62
Loyal, Wi., U.S.	D3	142
Loyall, Ky., U.S.	D6	110
Loyalsock Creek, stm., Pa., U.S.	D8	131
Loyalty Islands see Loyauté, Îles, is., N. Cal.	I9	62a
Loyauté, Îles, is., N. Cal.	I9	62a
Loznica, Yugo.	B7	18
Lozova, Ukr.	E14	20
Lualaba, stm., Afr.	D5	54
Lua Makika, crat., Hi., U.S.	C5	104
Lu'an, China	C4	30
Luan, stm., China	C11	28
Luanda, Ang.	E2	54
Luang, Thale, l., Thai.	E4	34
Luanginga, stm., Afr.	A3	56
Luangwa, stm., Afr.	A5	56
Luanping, China	A4	30
Luanshya, Zam.	A4	56
Luan Toro, Arg.	F4	72
Luapula, stm., Afr.	A4	56
Luau, Ang.	F4	54
Luba, Eq. Gui.	C1	54
Lubang Islands, is., Phil.	D8	34
Lubango, Ang.	A1	56
Lubbock, Tx., U.S.	C2	136
Lubbock, co., Tx., U.S.	C2	136
Lubec, Me., U.S.	D6	112
Lübeck, Ger.	D12	12
Lubefu, D.R.C.	D4	54
Lubin, Pol.	D4	20
Lublin, Pol.	D7	20
Lubny, Ukr.	D12	20
Lubudi, D.R.C.	F5	54
Lubuklinggau, Indon.	D2	36
Lubumbashi, D.R.C.	F5	54
Lubutu, D.R.C.	D5	54
Lucama, N.C., U.S.	B4	126
Lucan, On., Can.	D3	89
Lucapa, Ang.	E4	54
Lucas, co., Ia., U.S.	C4	108
Lucas, co., Oh., U.S.	A2	128
Lucasville, Oh., U.S.	D3	128
Lucca, Italy	C3	18
Luce, co., Mi., U.S.	B5	115
Lucedale, Ms., U.S.	E5	117
Lucena, Phil.	D8	34
Lucena, Spain	I4	16
Lučenec, Slvk.	E5	20
Lucera, Italy	D5	18
Lucerne see Luzern, Switz.	A2	18
Lucerne, Ca., U.S.	C2	98
Lucerne, Lake see Vierwaldstätter See, l., Switz.	A2	18
Lucernemines, Pa., U.S.	E3	131
Lucerne Valley, Ca., U.S.	E5	98
Luceville, P.Q., Can.	A9	90
Lucira, Ang.	A1	56
Luck, Wi., U.S.	C1	142
Luckenwalde, Ger.	E13	12
Lucknow, On., Can.	D3	89
Lucknow, India	D4	40
Lucky Peak Lake, res., Id., U.S.	F3	105
Luçon, Fr.	D6	16
Lucusse, Ang.	A3	56
Lüda see Dalian, China	D12	28
Lüderitz, Nmb.	D2	56
Ludhiāna, India	C3	40
Ludington, Mi., U.S.	E4	115
Ludlow, Ky., U.S.	h13	110
Ludlow, Ma., U.S.	B3	114
Ludlow, Vt., U.S.	E3	138
Ludogorie, reg., Bul.	C11	18
Ludowici, Ga., U.S.	E5	103
Ludvika, Swe.	F6	10
Ludwigsburg, Ger.	F11	12
Ludwigslust, Ger.	D12	12
Luebo, D.R.C.	E4	54
Luena, Ang.	F3	54
Luena, D.R.C.	E5	54
Lueyang, China	C2	30
Lufeng, China	E4	30
Lufkin, Tx., U.S.	D5	136
Luga, Russia	C4	22
Lugano, Switz.	A2	18
Luganville, Vanuatu	k9	62a
Lugards Falls, wtfl, Kenya	D7	54
Lugela, Moz.	B6	56
Lugo, Italy	B3	18
Lugo, Spain	F3	16
Lugoff, S.C., U.S.	C6	133
Lugoj, Rom.	G6	20
Lugovoj, Kaz.	B10	42
Luhans'k, Ukr.	E15	20
Luishia, D.R.C.	F5	54
Luiza, D.R.C.	E4	54
Lukachukai, Az., U.S.	A6	96
Luke Air Force Base, mil., Az., U.S.	D3	96
Lukenie, stm., D.R.C.	D3	54
Lukojanov, Russia	D7	22
Lukolela, D.R.C.	D3	54
Lukolela, D.R.C.	E4	54
Lukula, D.R.C.	E2	54
Lukulu, Zam.	A3	56
Lumana, D.R.C.	D5	54
Lumber, stm., U.S.	C9	133
Lumber City, Ga., U.S.	E4	103
Lumberport, W.V., U.S.	B4	141
Lumberton, Ms., U.S.	D4	117
Lumberton, N.C., U.S.	C3	126
Lumbo, Moz.	B7	56
Lumby, B.C., Can.	D8	85
Lumding, India	D6	40
Lumbala N'guimbo, Ang.	A3	56
Lumpkin, Ga., U.S.	D2	103
Lumpkin, co., Ga., U.S.	B2	103
Lumsden, Nf., Can.	D5	88
Lumut, Tanjung, c., Indon.	D3	36
Luna, co., N.M., U.S.	E2	124
Luna Pier, Mi., U.S.	G7	115
Lund, Swe.	I5	10
Lund, Nv., U.S.	E6	121
Lundar, Mb., Can.	D2	86
Lundazi, Zam.	A5	56
Lüneburg, Ger.	D12	12
Lunenburg, Ma., U.S.	A4	114
Lunenburg, co., Va., U.S.	D4	139
Lunéville, Fr.	C10	16
Lungué-Bungo (Lungwebungu), stm., Afr.	A2	56
Lungwebungu (Lungué-Bungo), stm., Afr.	A3	56
Luninec, Bela.	C9	20
Luobei, China	A2	31
Luochuan, China	B2	30
Luoding, China	E3	30
Luohe, China	E10	28
Luotian, China	C4	30
Luoyang, China	E10	28
Luoyuan, China	D4	30
Luozi, D.R.C.	E2	54
Lupanshui, China	D1	30
Lupeni, Rom.	G7	20
Luputa, D.R.C.	E4	54
Luqu, China	E8	28
Luray, Va., U.S.	B4	139
Lure, Lake, res., N.C., U.S.	f10	126
Luremo, Ang.	E3	54
Lúrio, Moz.	A7	56
Lúrio, stm., Moz.	A6	56
Lusaka, Zam.	B4	56
Lusambo, D.R.C.	D4	54
Lusanga, D.R.C.	D3	54
Lusangi, D.R.C.	D5	54
Lusby, Md., U.S.	D5	113
Luseland, Sk., Can.	E1	91
Lushnjë, Alb.	D7	18
Lushoto, Tan.	D7	54
Lüshun, China	D12	28
Lusk, Wy., U.S.	D8	143
Lūt, dasht-e, des., Iran	D7	42
Lutcher, La., U.S.	D5	111
Luther, Ok., U.S.	B4	129
Lutherstadt Eisleben, Ger.	E12	12
Lutherstadt Wittenberg, Ger.	E13	12
Luthersville, Ga., U.S.	C2	103
Lutherville-Timonium, Md., U.S.	B4	113
Luton, Eng., U.K.	E6	12
Łutselk'e, N.T., Can.	F17	82
Luts'k, Ukr.	D8	20
Luttrell, Tn., U.S.	C10	135
Lutz, Fl., U.S.	D4	102
Lützow-Holm Bay, b., Ant.	C8	67
Luuq, Som.	J13	48
Luverne, Al., U.S.	D3	94
Luverne, Mn., U.S.	G2	116
Luwingu, Zam.	A4	56
Luwuk, Indon.	D6	36
Luxapallila Creek, stm., U.S.	B5	117
Luxembourg, Lux.	F9	12
Luxembourg, ctry., Eur.	C10	16
Luxemburg, Wi., U.S.	D6	142
Luxi, China	D7	28
Luxomni, Ga., U.S.	h8	103
Luxor see El-Uqsor, Egypt	E11	48
Luza, Russia	B8	22
Luzern, Switz.	A2	18
Luzerne, Pa., U.S.	n17	131
Luzerne, co., Pa., U.S.	D9	131
Luzhai, China	E2	30
Luzhou, China	F9	28
Luziânia, Braz.	E2	74
Luzilândia, Braz.	B3	74
Luzon, i., Phil.	C8	34
Luzon Strait, strt., Asia	B8	34
L'viv, Ukr.	E8	20
L'vov see L'viv, Ukr.	E8	20
Lyallpur see Faisalabad, Pak.	D10	42
Lycksele, Swe.	D8	10
Lycoming, co., Pa., U.S.	D7	131
Lycoming Creek, stm., Pa., U.S.	D7	131
Lydenburg, S. Afr.	D5	56
Lyell, Mount, mtn., Can.	D2	84
Lyford, Tx., U.S.	F4	136
Lykens, Pa., U.S.	E8	131
Lyle, Wa., U.S.	D4	140
Lyman, S.C., U.S.	B3	133
Lyman, Wy., U.S.	E2	143
Lyman, co., S.D., U.S.	D6	134
Lyman Lake, res., Az., U.S.	C6	96
Lyme Bay, b., Eng., U.K.	E5	12
Lynch, Ky., U.S.	D7	110
Lynchburg, Oh., U.S.	C2	128
Lynchburg, Tn., U.S.	B5	135
Lynchburg, Va., U.S.	C3	139
Lynches, stm., S.C., U.S.	D8	133
Lynden, Wa., U.S.	A3	140
Lynde Point, c., Ct., U.S.	D6	100
Lyndhurst, N.J., U.S.	h8	123
Lyndhurst, Oh., U.S.	g9	128
Lyndon, Ks., U.S.	D8	109
Lyndon B. Johnson National Historical Site, hist., Tx., U.S.	D3	136
Lyndon B. Johnson Space Center, sci., Tx., U.S.	r14	136
Lyndonville, Vt., U.S.	B4	138
Lyndora, Pa., U.S.	E2	131
Lyngen, b., Nor.	B9	10

Name	Map Ref.	Page
Lynn, Al., U.S.	A2	94
Lynn, In., U.S.	D8	107
Lynn, Ma., U.S.	B6	114
Lynn, co., Tx., U.S.	C2	136
Lynn, Lake, res., W.V., U.S.	B5	141
Lynn Canal, b., Ak., U.S.	k22	95
Lynnfield, Ma., U.S.	f11	114
Lynn Garden, Tn., U.S.	C11	135
Lynn Haven, Fl., U.S.	u16	102
Lynnhaven Roads, b., Va., U.S.	k15	139
Lynnville, In., U.S.	H3	107
Lynnwood, Wa., U.S.	B3	140
Lynwood, Ca., U.S.	n12	98
Lyon, Fr.	E9	16
Lyon, co., Ia., U.S.	A1	108
Lyon, co., Ks., U.S.	D7	109
Lyon, co., Ky., U.S.	C1	110
Lyon, co., Mn., U.S.	F3	116
Lyon, co., Nv., U.S.	D2	121
Lyons, Co., U.S.	A5	99
Lyons, Ga., U.S.	D4	103
Lyons, Il., U.S.	k9	106
Lyons, In., U.S.	G3	107
Lyons, Ks., U.S.	D5	109
Lyons, Mi., U.S.	F6	115
Lyons, Ne., U.S.	C9	120
Lyons, N.Y., U.S.	B3	125
Lyons, Or., U.S.	C4	130
Lysekil, Swe.	G4	10
Lyster Station, P.Q., Can.	C6	90
Lys'va, Russia	D7	26
Lysychans'k, Ukr.	E15	20
Lytle, Tx., U.S.	E3	136
Lyubotyn, Ukr.	E13	20
M		
Maalaea Bay, b., Hi., U.S.	C5	104
Ma'an, Jord.	D3	42
Ma'anshan, China	C4	30
Maarianhamina, Fin.	F8	10
Ma'arrat an-Nu'mān, Syria	E7	44
Maas (Meuse), stm., Eur.	B9	16
Maastricht, Neth.	E9	12
Mabank, Tx., U.S.	C4	136
Mabel, Mn., U.S.	G7	116
Maben, Ms., U.S.	B4	117
Mableton, Ga., U.S.	h7	103
Mabote, Moz.	C5	56
Mabscott, W.V., U.S.	D3	141
Mabton, Wa., U.S.	C5	140
Mača, Russia	D13	26
Macaé, Braz.	F3	74
Macaíba, Braz.	C4	74
Macapá, Braz.	A1	74
Macará, Ec.	D4	70
Macau, Braz.	C4	74
Macau see Aomen, China	B6	34
MacClenny, Fl., U.S.	B4	102
MacDill Air Force Base, mil., Fl., U.S.	E4	102
MacDonnell Ranges, mts., Austl.	E5	60
MacDowell Reservoir, res., N.H., U.S.	E2	122
Macedonia, Oh., U.S.	A4	128
Macedonia, hist. reg., Eur.	D9	18
Macedonia, ctry., Eur.	D8	18
Maceió, Braz.	C4	74
Macenta, Gui.	E3	50
Macerata, Italy	C4	18
Maces Bay, b., N.B., Can.	D3	87
MacGregor, Mb., Can.	E2	86
Machado, stm., Braz.	E7	70
Machakos, Kenya	D7	54
Machala, Ec.	D4	70
Macheke, Zimb.	B5	56
Macheng, China	C3	30
Machias, Me., U.S.	D5	112
Machias, stm., Me., U.S.	D5	112
Machias, stm., Me., U.S.	B4	112
Machias Bay, b., Me., U.S.	D5	112
Machias Lakes, l., Me., U.S.	C5	112
Machilīpatnam, India	F4	40
Machiques, Ven.	A5	70
Macho, Arroyo del, val., N.M., U.S.	C4	124
Machupicchu, Peru	F5	70
Machupicchu, hist., Peru	A3	72
Mackay, Austl.	D4	62
Mackay, Lake, l., Austl.	E4	60
MacKenzie, B.C., Can.	B6	85
Mackenzie, stm., N.T., Can.	E13	82
Mackenzie Bay, b., Can.	E12	82
Mackenzie Mountains, mts., Can.	F14	82
Mackinac, co., Mi., U.S.	B5	115
Mackinac, Straits of, strt., Mi., U.S.	C6	115
Mackinac Bridge, Mi., U.S.	C6	115
Mackinac Island, i., Mi., U.S.	C6	115
Mackinaw, Il., U.S.	C4	106
Mackinaw, stm., Il., U.S.	C4	106
Mackinaw City, Mi., U.S.	C6	115
Mackinnon Road, Kenya	D7	54
Maclean, Austl.	F5	62
Maclear, S. Afr.	E4	56
Macleod, Lake, l., Austl.	E1	60
Maclovio Herrera, Mex.	B3	78
Macomb, Il., U.S.	C3	106
Macomb, co., Mi., U.S.	F8	115
Macomer, Italy	D2	18
Mâcon, Fr.	D9	16
Macon, Ga., U.S.	D3	103
Macon, Il., U.S.	D5	106
Macon, Mo., U.S.	B5	118
Macon, Ms., U.S.	B5	117
Macon, co., Al., U.S.	C4	94
Macon, co., Ga., U.S.	D2	103
Macon, co., Il., U.S.	D4	106
Macon, co., Mo., U.S.	B5	118
Macon, co., N.C., U.S.	f9	126
Macon, co., Tn., U.S.	A5	135
Macon, Bayou, stm., U.S.	B4	111
Macoupin, co., Il., U.S.	D4	106
Macquarie Island, i., Austl.	J23	4
Macquarie Ridge	N18	64
MacTier, On., Can.	B5	89
Macungie, Pa., U.S.	E10	131
Macuspana, Mex.	D6	78
Mad, stm., Ca., U.S.	B2	98
Mad, stm., Ct., U.S.	B3	100
Mad, stm., N.H., U.S.	C3	122
Mad, stm., Oh., U.S.	C2	128
Mad, stm., Vt., U.S.	C3	138
Madagascar, ctry., Afr.	B8	56
Madagascar Basin	K8	64
Madagascar Plateau	L7	64
Madame, Isle, i., N.S., Can.	D9	87
Madang, Pap. N. Gui.	H12	32
Madaoua, Niger	D6	50
Madawaska, Me., U.S.	A4	112
Madawaska, stm., Can.	B4	90
Madawaska, stm., On., Can.	B7	89
Madawaska Lake, l., Me., U.S.	A4	112
Madaya, Myan.	B3	34
Madeira, Oh., U.S.	o13	128
Madeira, stm., S.A.	E7	70
Madeira, Arquipélago da, is., Port.	D1	48
Madeira Islands see Madeira, Arquipélago da, is., Port.	D1	48
Madeleine, Îles de la, is., P.Q., Can.	B8	87
Madelia, Mn., U.S.	F4	116
Madeline Island, i., Wi., U.S.	B3	142
Maden, Tur.	C8	44
Madera, Mex.	B3	78
Madera, Ca., U.S.	D3	98
Madera, co., Ca., U.S.	D4	98
Madera see Madeira, stm., S.A.	E7	70
Madhya Pradesh, prov., India	E3	40
Madill, Ok., U.S.	C5	129
Madimba, D.R.C.	D3	54
Madingo-Kayes, Congo	D2	54
Madingou, Congo	D2	54
Madirovalo, Madag.	B8	56
Madison, Al., U.S.	A3	94
Madison, Ar., U.S.	B5	97
Madison, Ct., U.S.	D5	100
Madison, Fl., U.S.	B3	102
Madison, Ga., U.S.	C3	103
Madison, Il., U.S.	E3	106
Madison, In., U.S.	G7	107
Madison, Ks., U.S.	D7	109
Madison, Me., U.S.	D3	112
Madison, Mn., U.S.	E2	116
Madison, Ms., U.S.	C3	117
Madison, N.C., U.S.	A3	126
Madison, Ne., U.S.	C8	120
Madison, N.J., U.S.	B4	123
Madison, Oh., U.S.	A4	128
Madison, S.D., U.S.	D8	134
Madison, W.V., U.S.	C3	141
Madison, Wi., U.S.	E4	142
Madison, co., Al., U.S.	A3	94
Madison, co., Ar., U.S.	B2	97
Madison, co., Fl., U.S.	B3	102
Madison, co., Ga., U.S.	B3	103
Madison, co., Ia., U.S.	C3	108
Madison, co., Id., U.S.	F7	105
Madison, co., Il., U.S.	E4	106
Madison, co., In., U.S.	D6	107
Madison, co., Ky., U.S.	C5	110
Madison, co., La., U.S.	B4	111
Madison, co., Mo., U.S.	D7	118
Madison, co., Ms., U.S.	C4	117
Madison, co., Mt., U.S.	E5	119
Madison, co., N.C., U.S.	f10	126
Madison, co., Ne., U.S.	C8	120
Madison, co., N.Y., U.S.	C5	125
Madison, co., Oh., U.S.	C2	128
Madison, co., Tn., U.S.	B3	135
Madison, co., Tx., U.S.	D5	136
Madison, co., Va., U.S.	B4	139
Madison Heights, Mi., U.S.	o15	115
Madison Heights, Va., U.S.	C3	139
Madison Lake, Mn., U.S.	F5	116
Madison Range, mts., Mt., U.S.	E5	119
Madisonville, Ky., U.S.	C2	110
Madisonville, La., U.S.	D5	111
Madisonville, Tn., U.S.	D9	135
Madisonville, Tx., U.S.	D5	136
Madoc, On., Can.	C7	89
Mado Gashi, Kenya	C7	54
Madoi, China	E7	28
Madona, Lat.	H12	10
Madrakah, Ra's al-, c., Oman	G7	38
Madras see Chennai, India	G4	40
Madras, Or., U.S.	C5	130
Madras see Tamil Nādu, prov., India	G3	40
Madre, Laguna, b., Tx., U.S.	F4	136
Madre, Laguna, l., Mex.	B5	78
Madre, Sierra, mts., Phil.	C8	34
Madre de Dios, stm., S.A.	F6	70
Madre de Dios, Isla, i., Chile	H1	69
Madre del Sur, Sierra, mts., Mex.	D5	78
Madre Occidental, Sierra, mts., Mex.	B3	78
Madre Oriental, Sierra, mts., Mex.	C4	78
Madrid, Spain	G5	16
Madrid, Ia., U.S.	C4	108
Madura, i., Indon.	E4	36
Madura, Selat, strt., Indon.	E4	36
Madurai, India	H3	40
Maebashi, Japan	D15	28
Mae Hong Son, Thai.	C3	34
Mae Sariang, Thai.	C3	34
Maeser, Ut., U.S.	C6	137
Mae Sot, Thai.	C3	34
Maestra, Sierra, mts., Cuba	B4	80
Maevatanana, Madag.	B8	56
Maéwo, i., Vanuatu	k9	62a
Mafeteng, Leso.	C4	56
Mafia Island, i., Tan.	D7	54
Magadan, Russia	D17	26
Magadi, Kenya	D7	54
Magallanes, Estrecho de (Magellan, Strait of), strt., S.A.	H2	69
Magangué, Col.	B5	70
Magaria, Niger	D6	50
Magazine, Ar., U.S.	B2	97
Magazine Mountain, mtn., Ar., U.S.	B2	97
Magdagači, Russia	D14	26
Magdalena, Bol.	F7	70
Magdalena, N.M., U.S.	C2	124
Magdalena, stm., Col.	D5	80
Magdalena, stm., Mex.	A2	78
Magdalena, Isla, i., Chile	F2	69
Magdalena de Kino, Mex.	A2	78
Magdalena Mountains, mts., N.M., U.S.	D2	124
Magdeburg, Ger.	D12	12
Magee, Ms., U.S.	D4	117
Magelang, Indon.	E4	36
Magellan, Strait of see Magallanes, Estrecho de, strt., S.A.	H2	69
Maggie Creek, stm., Nv., U.S.	C5	121
Maggiore, Lago, l., Eur.	B2	18
Maghâgha, Egypt	F10	14
Maghama, Maur.	C2	50
Magic Reservoir, res., Id., U.S.	F4	105
Maglie, Italy	D7	18
Magna, Ut., U.S.	C3	137
Magnetawan, stm., On., Can.	B4	89
Magnitogorsk, Russia	D7	26
Magnolia, Ar., U.S.	D2	97
Magnolia, Ky., U.S.	C4	110
Magnolia, Ms., U.S.	D3	117
Magnolia, N.C., U.S.	C4	126
Magnolia, Oh., U.S.	B4	128
Magoffin, co., Ky., U.S.	C6	110
Magog, P.Q., Can.	D5	90
Magothy River, b., Md., U.S.	B4	113
Magrath, Ab., Can.	E4	84
Magruder Mountain, mtn., Nv., U.S.	F4	121
Magway, Mya.	B2	34
Mahābād, Iran	C5	42
Mahābaleshwar, India	F2	40
Mahabe, Madag.	B8	56
Mahābhārat Lek, mts., Nepal	D4	40
Mahabo, Madag.	C7	56
Mahačkala, Russia	E6	26
Mahagi, D.R.C.	C6	54
Mahajanga, Madag.	B8	56
Mahakam, stm., Indon.	C5	36
Mahalapye, Bots.	C4	56
Mahānadi, stm., India	E4	40
Mahanoro, Madag.	B8	56
Mahanoy City, Pa., U.S.	E9	131
Mahārāshtra, prov., India	E3	40
Maha Sarakham, Thai.	C4	34
Mahaska, co., Ia., U.S.	C5	108
Mahbūbnagar, India	F3	40
Mahd adh-Dhahab, Sau. Ar.	F4	38
Mahdia, Tun.	G3	18
Mahe, India	G3	40
Mahé, i., Sey.	h13	57b
Mahébourg, Mrts.	g10	57a
Mahenge, Tan.	E7	54
Mahesāna, India	E2	40
Mahi, stm., India	E2	40
Mahilëu, Bela.	C11	20
Mahnomen, Mn., U.S.	C3	116
Mahnomen, co., Mn., U.S.	C3	116
Mahogany Mountain, mtn., Or., U.S.	D9	130
Mahomet, Il., U.S.	C5	106
Mahón see Maó, Spain	H9	16
Mahone Bay, N.S., Can.	E5	87
Mahoning, co., Oh., U.S.	B5	128
Mahoning, stm., U.S.	A5	128
Mahopac, N.Y., U.S.	D7	125
Mahuva, India	E2	40
Mahwah, N.J., U.S.	A4	123
Maicao, Col.	C5	80
Maiden, N.C., U.S.	B1	126
Maidstone Lake, l., Vt., U.S.	B5	138
Maiduguri, Nig.	D7	50
Maili, Hi., U.S.	g9	104
Maili Point, c., Hi., U.S.	g9	104
Main, stm., Ger.	F11	12
Main Channel, strt., On., Can.	B3	89
Mai-Ndombe, Lac, l., D.R.C.	D3	54
Maine, hist. reg., Fr.	C6	16
Maine, state, U.S.	C3	112
Maine, Gulf of, b., N.A.	C14	92
Mainland, i., Scot., U.K.	A5	12
Mainland, i., Scot., U.K.	h19	12a
Main Pass, strt., La., U.S.	E6	111
Mainz, Ger.	E11	12
Maio, i., C.V.	g10	50a
Maipú, Arg.	F6	72
Maiquetía, Ven.	A6	70
Maisonnette, N.B., Can.	B4	87
Maitland, Austl.	G5	62
Maitland, On., Can.	C9	89
Maíz, Islas del, is., Nic.	C3	80
Maize, Ks., U.S.	g12	109
Maizuru, Japan	C3	31
Maja, stm., Russia	C15	26
Majene, Indon.	D5	36
Majī, Eth.	B7	54
Majkop, Russia	E6	26
Major, co., Ok., U.S.	A3	129
Majorca see Mallorca, i., Spain	H8	16
Majuro, atoll, Marsh. Is.	D11	58
Maka, Sen.	D2	50
Makabana, Congo	D2	54
Makaha, Hi., U.S.	g9	104
Makaha Point, c., Hi., U.S.	A2	104
Makah Indian Reservation, Wa., U.S.	A1	140
Makahuena Point, c., Hi., U.S.	B2	104
Makakilo City, Hi., U.S.	g9	104
Makapuu Head, c., Hi., U.S.	B4	104
Makarakomburu, Mount, mtn., Sol. Is.	B6	62
Makarov, Russia	B16	28
Makarov Basin	E34	144
Makasar see Ujungpandang, Indon.	E5	36
Makasar, Selat (Makassar Strait), strt., Indon.	D5	36
Makassar Strait see Makasar, Selat, strt., Indon.	D5	36
Makat, Kaz.	E7	26
Makawao, Hi., U.S.	C5	104
Makaweli, Hi., U.S.	B2	104
Makeni, S.L.	E2	50
Makgadikgadi, pl., Bots.	C4	56
Makiïvka, Ukr.	E14	20
Makindu, Kenya	D7	54
Makkah, Sau. Ar.	F3	38
Makó, Hung.	F6	20
Makokou, Gabon	C2	54
Makoua, Congo	D3	54
Makrān Coast, Asia	E7	42
Mākū, Iran	C11	44
Makumbi, D.R.C.	E4	54
Makurdi, Nig.	E6	50
Makushin Volcano, vol., Ak., U.S.	E6	95
Mala, Peru	A2	72
Malabar, Fl., U.S.	D6	102
Malabar Coast, India	G2	40
Malabo, Eq. Gui.	C1	54
Malacca see Melaka, Malay.	C2	36
Malacca, Strait of, strt., Asia	C1	36
Malad City, Id., U.S.	G6	105
Maladzečna, Bela.	B9	20
Málaga, Col.	D5	80
Málaga, Spain	I4	16
Malagarasi, Tan.	E6	54
Malaimbandy, Madag.	C8	56
Malaja Kuril'skaja Grjada, is., Russia	B5	31
Malajaroslavec, Russia	B14	20
Malaja Višera, Russia	C5	22
Malakāl, Sudan	I11	48
Malakoff, Tx., U.S.	C4	136
Malakula, i., Vanuatu	I9	62a
Malambo, Col.	C5	80
Malang, Indon.	E4	36
Malanje, Ang.	D3	54
Malanville, Benin	D5	50
Mälaren, l., Swe.	G7	10
Malartic, P.Q., Can.	k11	90
Malaspina Glacier, Ak., U.S.	D11	95
Malatya, Tur.	C8	44
Mala Vyska, Ukr.	E11	20
Malawi, ctry., Afr.	A5	56
Malaŵi, Lake see Nyasa, Lake, l., Afr.	F6	54
Malaya see Semenanjung Malaysia, hist. reg., Malay.	C2	36
Malaybalay, Phil.	E9	34
Malāyer, Iran	C5	42
Malay Peninsula, pen., Asia	B2	36
Malaysia, ctry., Asia	C4	36
Malazgirt, Tur.	C10	44
Malbaie, stm., P.Q., Can.	B7	90
Malbork, Pol.	C5	20
Malbrán, Arg.	D5	72
Malcolm, Austl.	F3	60
Malden, Ma., U.S.	B5	114
Malden, Mo., U.S.	E8	118
Malden, W.V., U.S.	m12	141
Malden, i., Kir.	E14	58
Maldives, ctry., Asia	I10	24
Maldonado, Ur.	E7	72
Mālegaon, India	E2	40
Malek Kandī, Iran	D12	44
Malema, Moz.	A6	56
Malha Wells, Sudan	G10	48
Malheur, co., Or., U.S.	D9	130
Malheur, stm., Or., U.S.	D9	130
Malheur Lake, l., Or., U.S.	D8	130
Mali, Gui.	D2	50
Mali, ctry., Afr.	C4	50
Malibu, Ca., U.S.	m11	98
Malin, Or., U.S.	E5	130
Malindi, Kenya	D8	54
Malinga, Congo	D2	54
Malka, Russia	D17	26
Malkara, Tur.	B2	44
Mallawi, Egypt	F10	14
Malletts Bay, b., Vt., U.S.	B2	138
Mallorca (Majorca), i., Spain	H8	16
Malmberget, Swe.	C9	10
Malmesbury, S. Afr.	E2	56
Malmö, Swe.	I5	10
Malmstrom Air Force Base, mil., Mt., U.S.	C5	119
Maloelap, atoll, Marsh. Is.	D11	58
Malolos, Phil.	D8	34
Malone, N.Y., U.S.	f10	125
Maloney Reservoir, res., Ne., U.S.	C5	120
Malonga, D.R.C.	F4	54
Malošujka, Russia	B6	22
Måløy, Nor.	F1	10
Malpelo, Isla de, i., Col.	C3	70
Malpeque Bay, b., P.E.I., Can.	C6	87
Malta, Il., U.S.	B5	106
Malta, Mt., U.S.	B9	119
Malta, ctry., Eur.	G5	18
Maltahöhe, Nmb.	C2	56
Maluku (Moluccas), is., Indon.	D7	36
Maluku, Laut (Molucca Sea), Indon.	C7	36
Malumfashi, Nig.	D6	50
Mālvan, India	F2	40
Malvern, Ar., U.S.	C3	97
Malvern, Ia., U.S.	D2	108
Malvern, Oh., U.S.	B4	128
Malvern, Pa., U.S.	o19	131
Malverne, N.Y., U.S.	k13	125
Malyj Enisej, stm., Russia	A7	28
Malyn, Ukr.	D10	20
Mama, Russia	D13	26
Mamala Bay, b., Hi., U.S.	g10	104
Mamallapuram, hist., India	G4	40
Mamaroneck, N.Y., U.S.	h13	125
Mamburao, Phil.	D8	34
Mamfe, Cam.	B1	54
Mammoth, Az., U.S.	E5	96
Mammoth Cave National Park, Ky., U.S.	C4	110
Mammoth Lakes, Ca., U.S.	D4	98
Mammoth Spring, Ar., U.S.	A4	97
Mamoré, stm., S.A.	F6	70
Mamou, Gui.	D2	50
Mamou, La., U.S.	D3	111
Mamoudzou, May.	A8	56
Mampikony, Madag.	B8	56
Mamuju, Indon.	D5	36
Man, C. Iv.	E3	50
Man, W.V., U.S.	D3	141
Manacapuru, Braz.	D7	70
Manacor, Spain	H8	16
Manado, Indon.	C6	36
Managua, Nic.	C2	80
Managua, Lago de, l., Nic.	C2	80
Manakara, Madag.	C8	56
Manāli, India	C3	40
Manama see Al-Manāmah, Bahr.	E6	42
Manam Island, i., Pap. N. Gui.	G12	32
Manana Island, i., Hi., U.S.	g11	104
Mananara Avaratra, Madag.	B8	56
Mananjary, Madag.	C8	56
Manankoro, Mali	D3	50
Manantico Creek, stm., N.J., U.S.	E3	123
Mana Point, c., Hi., U.S.	A2	104
Manas, China	C4	28
Manas Hu, l., China	B5	28
Manasquan, N.J., U.S.	C4	123
Manasquan, stm., N.J., U.S.	C4	123
Manassa, Co., U.S.	D5	99
Manassas, Va., U.S.	B5	139
Manassas National Battlefield Park, Va., U.S.	g11	139
Manassas Park, Va., U.S.	B5	139
Manatee, co., Fl., U.S.	E4	102
Manatee, stm., Fl., U.S.	E4	102
Manatuto, E. Timor	E7	36
Manaus, Braz.	D7	70
Manavgat, Tur.	D4	44

Name	Map Ref.	Page
Manawa, Wi., U.S.	D5	142
Manbij, Syria	D7	44
Mancelona, Mi., U.S.	D5	115
Manchester, Eng., U.K.	D5	12
Manchester, Ct., U.S.	B5	100
Manchester, Ga., U.S.	D2	103
Manchester, Ia., U.S.	B6	108
Manchester, Ky., U.S.	C6	110
Manchester, Ma., U.S.	A6	114
Manchester, Md., U.S.	A4	113
Manchester, Me., U.S.	D3	112
Manchester, Mi., U.S.	F6	115
Manchester, Mo., U.S.	f12	118
Manchester, N.H., U.S.	E4	122
Manchester, N.Y., U.S.	C3	125
Manchester, Oh., U.S.	D2	128
Manchester, Pa., U.S.	F8	131
Manchester, Tn., U.S.	B5	135
Manchester, Vt., U.S.	E2	138
Manchester Center, Vt., U.S.	E2	138
Manchuria, hist. reg., China	B13	28
Mancos, Co., U.S.	D2	99
Mancos, stm., U.S.	D2	99
Manda, Tan.	F6	54
Mandabe, Madag.	C7	56
Manda Island, i., Kenya	D8	54
Mandal, Nor.	G2	10
Mandalay, Mya.	B3	34
Mandalgovĭ, Mong.	B9	28
Mandalī, Iraq	D5	42
Mandalya, Gulf of see Güllük Körfezi, b., Tur.	D2	44
Mandan, N.D., U.S.	C5	127
Mandar, Teluk, b., Indon.	D5	36
Mandara Mountains, mts., Afr.	A2	54
Mandeb, Bab el, strt.	H4	38
Mandera, Kenya	C8	54
Mandeville, Jam.	B4	80
Mandeville, Ar., U.S.	D2	97
Mandeville, La., U.S.	D5	111
Mandimba, Moz.	A6	56
Mandioli, Pulau, i., Indon.	D7	36
Mandla, India	E4	40
Mandritsara, Madag.	B8	56
Mandsaur, India	E3	40
Manduria, Italy	D6	18
Mändvi, India	E1	40
Mandya, India	G3	40
Manendragarh, India	E4	40
Manfalût, Egypt	E11	48
Manfredonia, Italy	D5	18
Manfredonia, Golfo di, b., Italy	D6	18
Manga, Braz.	D3	74
Manga, reg., Niger	D7	50
Mangabeiras, Chapada das, Braz.	C2	74
Mangai, D.R.C.	D3	54
Mangalia, Rom.	H10	20
Mangalore, India	G2	40
Mangchang, China	F9	28
Mange, China	C4	40
Manggar, Indon.	D3	36
Mangkalihat, Tanjung, c., Indon.	C5	36
Mangnai, China	D6	28
Mangochi, Mwi.	A6	56
Mangoky, stm., Madag.	C7	56
Mangole, Pulau, i., Indon.	D7	36
Mangum, Ok., U.S.	C2	129
Manhattan, Ks., U.S.	C7	109
Manhattan, Mt., U.S.	E5	119
Manhattan Beach, Ca., U.S.	n12	98
Manhattan Island, i., N.Y., U.S.	h13	125
Manheim, Pa., U.S.	F9	131
Manhuaçu, Braz.	F3	74
Manica, Moz.	B5	56
Manicoré, Braz.	E7	70
Manicouagan, Réservoir, res., P.Q., Can.	h13	90
Manignan, C. Iv.	D3	50
Manila, Phil.	D8	34
Manila, Ar., U.S.	B5	97
Manila, Ia., U.S.	C2	108
Manipur, state, India	D6	40
Manisa, Tur.	C2	44
Manistee, Mi., U.S.	D4	115
Manistee, co., Mi., U.S.	D4	115
Manistee, stm., Mi., U.S.	D5	115
Manistique, Mi., U.S.	C4	115
Manistique, stm., Mi., U.S.	B4	115
Manistique Lake, l., Mi., U.S.	B5	115
Manito, Il., U.S.	C4	106
Manitoba, prov., Can.	C3	86
Manitoba, Lake, l., Mb., Can.	D2	86
Manitou, Mb., Can.	E2	86
Manitou, Lake, l., On., Can.	B3	89
Manitou Island, i., Mi., U.S.	A3	115
Manitou Lake, l., Sk., Can.	E1	91
Manitoulin Island, i., On., Can.	B2	89
Manitou Springs, Co., U.S.	C6	99
Manitowoc, Wi., U.S.	D6	142
Manitowoc, co., Wi., U.S.	D6	142
Manitowoc, stm., Wi., U.S.	h10	142
Maniwaki, P.Q., Can.	C2	90
Manizales, Col.	B4	70
Manja, Madag.	C7	56
Manjakandriana, Madag.	B8	56
Manjimup, Austl.	G2	60
Mänjra, stm., India	F3	40
Mankanza, D.R.C.	C3	54
Mankato, Ks., U.S.	C5	109
Mankato, Mn., U.S.	F5	116
Manlius, N.Y., U.S.	C5	125
Manly, Ia., U.S.	A4	108
Manmäd, India	E2	40
Manna, Indon.	D2	36
Mannar, Gulf of, b., Asia	H3	40
Mannford, Ok., U.S.	A5	129
Mannheim, Ger.	F11	12
Manning, Ab., Can.	A2	84
Manning, Ia., U.S.	C2	108
Manning, S.C., U.S.	D7	133
Mannington, W.V., U.S.	B4	141
Manns Creek, stm., W.V., U.S.	n14	141
Mannville, Ab., Can.	C5	84
Manokin, stm., Md., U.S.	D6	113
Manokotak, Ak., U.S.	D8	95
Manokwari, Indon.	D8	36
Manomet, Ma., U.S.	C6	114
Manomet Point, c., Ma., U.S.	C6	114
Manono, D.R.C.	E5	54
Manor, Tx., U.S.	D4	136
Manouane, Lac, l., P.Q., Can.	h12	90
Manresa, Spain	G7	16
Mansa, Zam.	A4	56
Manseau, P.Q., Can.	C5	90
Mansfield, Eng., U.K.	D6	12
Mansfield, Ar., U.S.	B1	97
Mansfield, Il., U.S.	C5	106
Mansfield, La., U.S.	B2	111
Mansfield, Ma., U.S.	B5	114
Mansfield, Mo., U.S.	D5	118
Mansfield, Oh., U.S.	B3	128
Mansfield, Pa., U.S.	C7	131
Mansfield, Tx., U.S.	n9	136
Mansfield, Mount, mtn., Vt., U.S.	B3	138
Mansfield Center, Ct., U.S.	B7	100
Mansfield Hollow Lake, res., Ct., U.S.	B7	100
Mansôa, Gui.-B.	D1	50
Manson, Ia., U.S.	B3	108
Manson, Wa., U.S.	B5	140
Mansonville, P.Q., Can.	D5	90
Mansura, La., U.S.	C3	111
Manta, Ec.	D3	70
Mantachie, Ms., U.S.	A5	117
Manteca, Ca., U.S.	D3	98
Manteno, Il., U.S.	B6	106
Manteo, N.C., U.S.	B7	126
Manti, Ut., U.S.	D4	137
Mantiqueira, Serra da, mts., Braz.	F2	74
Manton, Mi., U.S.	D5	115
Mantorville, Mn., U.S.	F6	116
Mántova, Italy	B3	18
Mantua, Oh., U.S.	A4	128
Mantua, Ut., U.S.	B4	137
Manturovo, Russia	C7	22
Mäntyluoto, Fin.	F9	10
Manuae, atoll, Cook Is.	F14	58
Manui, Pulau, i., Indon.	D6	36
Manukau, N.Z.	o13	63c
Manumuskin, stm., N.J., U.S.	E3	123
Manus Island, i., Pap. N. Gui.	G12	32
Manvel, Tx., U.S.	r14	136
Manville, N.J., U.S.	B3	123
Manville, R.I., U.S.	B4	132
Many, La., U.S.	C2	111
Manyara, Lake, l., Tan.	D7	54
Many Farms, Az., U.S.	A6	96
Manyoni, Tan.	E6	54
Manzanillo, Cuba	D4	80
Manzanillo, Mex.	D4	78
Manzanillo Bay, b., N.A.	A5	80
Manzano Mountains, mts., N.M., U.S.	C3	124
Manzano Peak, mtn., N.M., U.S.	C3	124
Manzhouli, China	B11	28
Manzini, Swaz.	D5	56
Mao, Chad	D8	50
Mao, Dom. Rep.	B5	80
Maó, Spain	H9	16
Maoke, Pegunungan, mts., Indon.	G10	32
Maoming, China	G10	28
Mapastepec, Mex.	D6	78
Mapi, Indon.	H10	32
Mapinhane, Moz.	C6	56
Maple, stm., Ia., U.S.	B2	108
Maple, stm., N.D., U.S.	C8	127
Maple, stm., U.S.	D4	130
Maple Bluff, Wi., U.S.	E4	142
Maple Grove, Mn., U.S.	m12	116
Maple Heights, Oh., U.S.	h9	128
Maple Lake, Mn., U.S.	E5	116
Maple Plain, Mn., U.S.	m11	116
Maple Shade, N.J., U.S.	D2	123
Maplesville, Al., U.S.	C3	94
Mapleton, Ia., U.S.	B2	108
Mapleton, Mn., U.S.	G5	116
Mapleton, N.D., U.S.	C8	127
Mapleton, Or., U.S.	C3	130
Mapleton, Ut., U.S.	C4	137
Maple Valley, Wa., U.S.	f11	140
Mapleville, R.I., U.S.	B2	132
Maplewood, Mn., U.S.	n12	116
Maplewood, Mo., U.S.	f13	118
Maplewood, N.J., U.S.	B4	123
Maputo, Moz.	D5	56
Maqteïr, reg., Maur.	B2	50
Maquela do Zombo, Ang.	E3	54
Maquinchao, Arg.	F3	69
Maquoketa, Ia., U.S.	B7	108
Maquoketa, stm., Ia., U.S.	B6	108
Maquoketa, Nortn Fork, stm., Ia., U.S.	B7	108
Marabá, Braz.	C2	74
Maracá, Ilha de, i., Braz.	C9	70
Maracaibo, Ven.	A5	70
Maracaibo, Lago de, l., Ven.	B5	70
Maracaju, Braz.	C6	72
Maracás, Braz.	D3	74
Maracay, Ven.	A6	70
Marādah, Libya	E8	48
Maradi, Niger	D6	50
Marāgheh, Iran	C5	42
Marahuaca, Cerro, mtn., Ven.	C6	70
Marais des Cygnes, stm., U.S.	D8	109
Marajó, Baía de, b., Braz.	B2	74
Marajó, Ilha de, i., Braz.	B2	74
Maralal, Kenya	C7	54
Marampa, S.L.	E2	50
Marana, Az., U.S.	E4	96
Marand, Iran	C5	42
Maranguape, Braz.	B4	74
Maranhão, stm., Braz.	A8	72
Maranhão, state, Braz.	B2	74
Marañón, stm., Peru	D5	70
Marathon, Fl., U.S.	H5	102
Marathon, Wi., U.S.	D4	142
Marathon, co., Wi., U.S.	D4	142
Marawi, Phil.	E8	34
Marbella, Spain	I4	16
Marble, Mn., U.S.	C5	116
Marble, N.C., U.S.	f9	126
Marble Bar, Austl.	E2	60
Marble Canyon, Az., U.S.	A4	96
Marble Falls, Tx., U.S.	D3	136
Marble Hall, S. Afr.	C4	56
Marblehead, Ma., U.S.	B6	114
Marble Hill, Mo., U.S.	D8	118
Marbleton, Wy., U.S.	D2	143
Marburg, Ger.	E11	12
Marbury, Md., U.S.	C3	113
Marceline, Mo., U.S.	B5	118
Marcellus, Mi., U.S.	F5	115
March Air Force Base, mil., Ca., U.S.	F5	98
Marche, hist. reg., Fr.	D7	16
Mar Chiquita, Laguna, l., Arg.	E5	72
Marco, Fl., U.S.	G5	102
Marcus, Ia., U.S.	B2	108
Marcus Baker, Mount, mtn., Ak., U.S.	g18	95
Marcus Hook, Pa., U.S.	G11	131
Marcus Island see Minami-Tori-shima, i., Japan	F18	64
Marcy, Mount, mtn., N.Y., U.S.	A7	125
Mardān, Pak.	D10	42
Mar del Plata, Arg.	F6	72
Mardin, Tur.	D5	44
Maré, i., N. Cal.	l9	62a
Mareeba, Austl.	D4	62
Marengo, co., Al., U.S.	C2	94
Marengo, Ia., U.S.	C5	108
Marengo, Il., U.S.	A5	106
Marengo, In., U.S.	H5	107
Marfa, Tx., U.S.	o12	136
Margaret, Al., U.S.	B3	94
Margaret River, Austl.	G1	60
Margarita, Isla de, i., Ven.	A7	70
Margate, Fl., U.S.	F6	102
Margate City, N.J., U.S.	E3	123
Margherita Peak, mtn., Afr.	C5	54
Margilan, Uzb.	B10	42
Margrethe, Lake, l., Mi., U.S.	D6	115
Marha, Russia	C14	26
Marhanets', Ukr.	F13	20
Maria, Îles, is., Fr. Poly.	G14	58
María Elena, Chile	B3	69
Maria Island, i., Austl.	C6	60
Mariakani, Kenya	D7	54
Marian, Lake, l., Fl., U.S.	E5	102
Mariana Islands, is., Oc.	C11	32
Mariana Ridge	G17	64
Mariana Trench	G17	64
Marianna, Ar., U.S.	C5	97
Marianna, Fl., U.S.	B1	102
Marias, stm., Mt., U.S.	B4	119
Marias Pass, Mt., U.S.	B3	119
Mariato, Punta, c., Pan.	D3	80
Marica, Slvn.	A5	18
Marica (Évros) (Meriç), stm., Eur.	C10	18
Maricopa, Az., U.S.	E3	96
Maricopa, co., Az., U.S.	D3	96
Maricopa, co., Ca., U.S.	E4	98
Maricopa Mountains, mts., Az., U.S.	m7	96
Marie Byrd Land, reg., Ant.	D29	67
Marie-Galante, i., Guad.	B7	80
Mariemont, Oh., U.S.	o13	128
Mariental, Nmb.	C2	56
Marienville, Pa., U.S.	D3	131
Maries, co., Mo., U.S.	C6	118
Mariestad, Swe.	G5	10
Marietta, Ga., U.S.	C2	103
Marietta, Oh., U.S.	C4	128
Marietta, Ok., U.S.	D4	129
Marietta, S.C., U.S.	A2	133
Marieville, P.Q., Can.	D4	90
Marijampolė, Lith.	I10	10
Marij El, state, Russia	D6	26
Marília, Braz.	F2	74
Marimba, Ang.	E3	54
Marin, co., Ca., U.S.	C2	98
Mar''ina Horka, Bela.	C10	20
Marinduque, i., Phil.	D8	34
Marine, Il., U.S.	E4	106
Marine City, Mi., U.S.	F8	115
Marine On St. Croix, Mn., U.S.	E6	116
Marinette, Wi., U.S.	C6	142
Marinette, co., Wi., U.S.	C5	142
Maringá, Braz.	F1	74
Maringouin, La., U.S.	D4	111
Marion, Al., U.S.	C2	94
Marion, co., Al., U.S.	A2	94
Marion, Ar., U.S.	B5	97
Marion, co., Ar., U.S.	A3	97
Marion, co., Fl., U.S.	C4	102
Marion, co., Ga., U.S.	D2	103
Marion, Ia., U.S.	B6	108
Marion, co., Ia., U.S.	C4	108
Marion, Il., U.S.	F5	106
Marion, co., Il., U.S.	E4	106
Marion, In., U.S.	C6	107
Marion, co., In., U.S.	E5	107
Marion, Ks., U.S.	D6	109
Marion, co., Ks., U.S.	D6	109
Marion, Ky., U.S.	e9	110
Marion, co., Ky., U.S.	C4	110
Marion, La., U.S.	B3	111
Marion, Mi., U.S.	D5	115
Marion, co., Mo., U.S.	B6	118
Marion, Ms., U.S.	C5	117
Marion, co., Ms., U.S.	D4	117
Marion, N.C., U.S.	B1	126
Marion, Oh., U.S.	B2	128
Marion, co., Oh., U.S.	B2	128
Marion, co., Or., U.S.	C4	130
Marion, Pa., U.S.	G6	131
Marion, S.C., U.S.	C9	133
Marion, co., S.C., U.S.	C9	133
Marion, S.D., U.S.	D8	134
Marion, co., Tn., U.S.	D8	135
Marion, co., Tx., U.S.	C5	136
Marion, Va., U.S.	f10	139
Marion, Wi., U.S.	D5	142
Marion, co., W.V., U.S.	B4	141
Marion, Lake, res., S.C., U.S.	E7	133
Marion Reef, rf., Austl.	D5	62
Marion Station, Md., U.S.	D6	113
Marionville, Mo., U.S.	D4	118
Mariposa, Ca., U.S.	D3	98
Mariposa, co., Ca., U.S.	D3	98
Mariscal Estigarribia, Para.	C5	72
Marissa, Il., U.S.	E4	106
Maritime Alps, mts., Eur.	B1	18
Maritime Atlas see Atlas Tellien, mts., Alg.	D4	14
Mariupol', Ukr.	F14	20
Märjamaa, Est.	G11	10
Marka, Som.	J13	48
Märkāpur, India	F3	40
Markdale, On., Can.	C4	89
Marked Tree, Ar., U.S.	B5	97
Markesan, Wi., U.S.	E5	142
Markham, On., Can.	D5	89
Markham, Il., U.S.	k9	106
Markham, Tx., U.S.	E4	136
Markit, China	B3	40
Markland Lock and Dam, U.S.	B5	110
Markle, In., U.S.	C7	107
Markovo, Russia	C19	26
Marks, Russia	D8	22
Marks, Ms., U.S.	A3	117
Marksville, La., U.S.	C3	111
Mark Twain Lake, res., Mo., U.S.	B6	118
Marlboro, N.Y., U.S.	D6	125
Marlboro, co., S.C., U.S.	B8	133
Marlboro, Va., U.S.	n17	139
Marlborough, Ct., U.S.	C6	100
Marlborough, Ma., U.S.	B4	114
Marlborough, N.H., U.S.	E2	122
Marlette, Mi., U.S.	E7	115
Marley, Md., U.S.	B4	113
Marlin, Tx., U.S.	D4	136
Marlinton, W.V., U.S.	C4	141
Marlow, Ok., U.S.	C4	129
Marlowe, W.V., U.S.	B7	141
Marlton, N.J., U.S.	D3	123
Marmaduke, Ar., U.S.	A5	97
Marmande, Fr.	E7	16
Marmara, Sea of see Marmara Denizi, Tur.	B3	44
Marmara Denizi, Tur.	B3	44
Marmaris, Tur.	D3	44
Marmora, On., Can.	C7	89
Marne, stm., Fr.	C8	16
Maroa, Il., U.S.	C5	106
Maroa, Ven.	C6	70
Maroantsetra, Madag.	B8	56
Maromandia, Madag.	A8	56
Maromokotro, mtn., Madag.	A8	56
Marondera, Zimb.	B5	56
Maroni, stm., S.A.	C9	70
Maros, Indon.	E5	36
Maroua, Cam.	A2	54
Marovoay, Madag.	B8	56
Marowijne see Maroni, stm., S.A.	C9	70
Marquesas Islands see Marquises, Îles, is., Fr. Poly.	E16	58
Marquesas Keys, is., Fl., U.S.	H4	102
Marquette, Mi., U.S.	B3	115
Marquette, co., Mi., U.S.	B3	115
Marquette, co., Wi., U.S.	E4	142
Marquette Heights, Il., U.S.	C4	106
Marquises, Îles, is., Fr. Poly.	E16	58
Marrah, Jabal, Sudan	H9	48
Marrakech, Mor.	D3	48
Marrero, La., U.S.	E5	111
Marromeu, Moz.	B6	56
Mars, Pa., U.S.	E1	131
Marsá al-Burayqah, Libya	D8	48
Marsabit, Kenya	C7	54
Marsala, Italy	F4	18
Marseille, Fr.	F9	16
Marseilles, Il., U.S.	B5	106
Marshall, Sk., Can.	D1	91
Marshall, Lib.	E2	50
Marshall, co., Al., U.S.	A3	94
Marshall, Ar., U.S.	B3	97
Marshall, co., Ia., U.S.	C4	108
Marshall, Il., U.S.	D6	106
Marshall, co., Il., U.S.	B4	106
Marshall, co., In., U.S.	B5	107
Marshall, co., Ks., U.S.	C7	109
Marshall, co., Ky., U.S.	f9	110
Marshall, Mi., U.S.	F6	115
Marshall, co., Mn., U.S.	B2	116
Marshall, Mo., U.S.	B4	118
Marshall, co., Ms., U.S.	A4	117
Marshall, N.C., U.S.	f10	126
Marshall, co., Ok., U.S.	C5	129
Marshall, co., S.D., U.S.	B8	134
Marshall, co., Tn., U.S.	B5	135
Marshall, Tx., U.S.	C5	136
Marshall, Va., U.S.	B5	139
Marshall, Wi., U.S.	E4	142
Marshall, co., W.V., U.S.	B4	141
Marshall Islands, is., Marsh. Is.	F24	4
Marshall Islands, ctry., Oc.	C10	58
Marshallton, De., U.S.	B3	101
Marshalltown, Ia., U.S.	B5	108
Marshallville, Ga., U.S.	D3	103
Marshes Siding, Ky., U.S.	D5	110
Marshfield, Ma., U.S.	B6	114
Marshfield, Mo., U.S.	D5	118
Marshfield, Wi., U.S.	D3	142
Marshfield Hills, Ma., U.S.	B6	114
Marsh Fork, stm., W.V., U.S.	n13	141
Mars Hill, Me., U.S.	B5	112
Mars Hill, N.C., U.S.	f10	126
Marsh Island, i., La., U.S.	E4	111
Marsh Lake, res., Mn., U.S.	E2	116
Marsh Peak, mtn., Ut., U.S.	C6	137
Marshville, N.C., U.S.	C2	126
Marsing, Id., U.S.	F2	105
Märsta, Swe.	G7	10
Marston, Mo., U.S.	E8	118
Mart, Tx., U.S.	D4	136
Martaban, Gulf of, b., Mya.	C3	34
Martapura, Indon.	D4	36
Martapura, Indon.	D2	36
Marthasville, Mo., U.S.	C6	118
Martha's Vineyard, i., Ma., U.S.	D6	114
Martí, Cuba	A4	80
Martigny, Switz.	A1	18
Martigues, Fr.	F9	16
Martin, Slvk.	E5	20
Martin, co., Fl., U.S.	E6	102
Martin, co., In., U.S.	G4	107
Martin, co., Ky., U.S.	C7	110
Martin, Ky., U.S.	C7	110
Martin, co., Mn., U.S.	G4	116
Martin, co., N.C., U.S.	B5	126
Martin, S.D., U.S.	D4	134
Martin, Tn., U.S.	A3	135
Martin, co., Tx., U.S.	C2	136
Martinez, Ca., U.S.	C2	98
Martinez, Ga., U.S.	C4	103
Martínez de la Torre, Mex.	C5	78
Martinique, dep., N.A.	F12	76
Martinique Passage, strt., N.A.	B7	80
Martin Lake, res., Al., U.S.	C4	94
Martin Point, c., Ak., U.S.	A11	95
Martinsburg, Pa., U.S.	F5	131
Martinsburg, W.V., U.S.	B7	141
Martins Ferry, Oh., U.S.	B5	128
Martinsville, Il., U.S.	D6	106
Martinsville, In., U.S.	F5	107
Martinsville, Va., U.S.	D3	139
Marton, N.Z.	p14	63c
Martos, Spain	I5	16
Martti, Fin.	C13	10
Martuni, Arm.	B11	44
Marutea, atoll, Fr. Poly.	F15	58
Marv Dasht, Iran	D6	42
Marvell, Ar., U.S.	C5	97
Marvine, Mount, mtn., Ut., U.S.	E4	137
Mary, Turk.	F8	26
Mary, Lake, l., Mn., U.S.	E3	116
Mary, Lake, l., Ms., U.S.	D2	117
Maryborough, Austl.	H3	62
Maryborough, Austl.	F5	62
Maryland, state, U.S.	B4	113

Name	Map Ref.	Page
Maryland City, Md., U.S.	B4	113
Maryland Heights, Mo., U.S.	f13	118
Maryland Point, c., Md., U.S.	D3	113
Marys, stm., Nv., U.S.	B6	121
Marys Peak, mtn., Or., U.S.	C3	130
Marystown, Nf., Can.	E4	88
Marysville, Ca., U.S.	C3	98
Marysville, Ks., U.S.	C7	109
Marysville, Mi., U.S.	F8	115
Marysville, Oh., U.S.	B2	128
Marysville, Pa., U.S.	F8	131
Marysville, Wa., U.S.	A3	140
Maryville, Mo., U.S.	A3	118
Maryville, Tn., U.S.	D10	135
Masai Steppe, plat., Tan.	D7	54
Masaka, Ug.	D6	54
Masalembu Besar, Pulau, i., Indon.	E4	36
Masallı, Azer.	C13	44
Masan, S. Kor.	D13	28
Masasi, Tan.	F7	54
Masaya, Nic.	C2	80
Masbate, Phil.	D8	34
Masbate, i., Phil.	D8	34
Mascarene Basin	J8	64
Mascarene Islands, is., Afr.	g10	57a
Mascarene Plateau	I8	64
Mascasín, Arg.	E4	72
Mascoma, stm., N.H., U.S.	C2	122
Mascoma Lake, l., N.H., U.S.	C2	122
Mascot, Tn., U.S.	C10	135
Mascouche, P.Q., Can.	D4	90
Mascoutah, Il., U.S.	E4	106
Maseru, Leso.	D4	56
Mashapaug Pond, l., Ct., U.S.	A7	100
Mashava, Zimb.	B5	56
Mashhad, Iran	C7	42
Mashra'ar Raqq, Sudan	I10	48
Masi-Manimba, D.R.C.	D3	54
Masindi, Ug.	C6	54
Maṣīrah, i., Oman	F7	38
Maṣīrah, Khalīj, b., Oman	G7	38
Masjed-e Soleymān, Iran	D5	42
Maskinongé, P.Q., Can.	C4	90
Mason, co., Il., U.S.	C4	106
Mason, co., Ky., U.S.	B6	110
Mason, Mi., U.S.	F6	115
Mason, co., Mi., U.S.	D4	115
Mason, Nv., U.S.	E2	121
Mason, Oh., U.S.	C1	128
Mason, Tx., U.S.	D3	136
Mason, co., Tx., U.S.	D3	136
Mason, co., Wa., U.S.	B2	140
Mason, W.V., U.S.	B2	141
Mason, co., W.V., U.S.	C3	141
Mason City, Ia., U.S.	A4	108
Mason City, Il., U.S.	C4	106
Masontown, Pa., U.S.	G2	131
Masontown, W.V., U.S.	B5	141
Masqaṭ, Oman	F7	38
Massa, Italy	B2	18
Massabesic Lake, l., N.H., U.S.	E4	122
Massac, co., Il., U.S.	F5	106
Massachusetts, state, U.S.	B4	114
Massachusetts Bay, b., Ma., U.S.	B6	114
Massacre Lake, l., Nv., U.S.	B2	121
Massangena, Moz.	C5	56
Massapoag Lake, l., Ma., U.S.	h11	114
Massasecum, Lake, l., N.H., U.S.	D3	122
Massawa, Erit.	G12	48
Massena, N.Y., U.S.	f10	125
Massenya, Chad	D8	50
Masset, B.C., Can.	C1	85
Massey, On., Can.	A2	89
Massillon, Oh., U.S.	B4	128
Massina, reg., Mali	D4	50
Massinga, Moz.	C6	56
Massive, Mount, mtn., Co., U.S.	B4	99
Maştağa, Azer.	B14	44
Masterton, N.Z.	p14	63c
Mastic Beach, N.Y., U.S.	n16	125
Mastung, Pak.	E9	42
Masuda, Japan	D2	31
Masuria see Mazury, reg., Pol.	C6	20
Masury, Oh., U.S.	A5	128
Masvingo, Zimb.	C5	56
Matadi, D.R.C.	E2	54
Matagalpa, Nic.	C2	80
Matagorda, co., Tx., U.S.	E5	136
Matagorda Bay, b., Tx., U.S.	E4	136
Matagorda Island, i., Tx., U.S.	E4	136
Matagorda Peninsula, pen., Tx., U.S.	E5	136
Matala, Ang.	A2	56
Matale, Sri L.	H4	40
Matam, Sen.	C2	50
Matamoras, Pa., U.S.	D12	131
Matamoros, Mex.	B5	78
Matamoros, Mex.	B4	78
Matane, P.Q., Can.	k13	90
Matanuska, stm., Ak., U.S.	g18	95
Matanzas, Cuba	A3	80
Matanzas Inlet, b., Fl., U.S.	C5	102
Matapan, Cape see Taínaron, Ákra, c., Grc.	F9	18
Matara, Sri L.	H4	40
Mataram, Indon.	E5	36
Mataranka, Austl.	C5	60
Mataró, Spain	G8	16
Mātātīla Dam, India	D3	40
Matawan, N.J., U.S.	C4	123
Matehuala, Mex.	A4	78
Matera, Italy	D6	18
Matewan, W.V., U.S.	D2	141
Mather, Pa., U.S.	G1	131
Mather Peaks, mts., Wy., U.S.	B5	143
Mathews, La., U.S.	E5	111
Mathews, Va., U.S.	C6	139
Mathews, co., Va., U.S.	C6	139
Mathews, Lake, l., Ca., U.S.	n14	98
Mathis, Tx., U.S.	E4	136
Mathiston, Ms., U.S.	B4	117
Mathura, India	D3	40
Mati, Phil.	E9	34
Matinicus Island, i., Me., U.S.	E3	112
Mato, Cerro, mtn., Ven.	B6	70
Matoaca, Va., U.S.	n18	139
Mato Grosso, Braz.	E5	68
Mato Grosso, state, Braz.	F8	70
Mato Grosso, Planalto do, plat., Braz.	F8	70
Mato Grosso do Sul, state, Braz.	B6	72
Matosinhos, Port.	G2	16
Maṭraḥ, Oman	F7	42
Matsqui, B.C., Can.	f13	85
Matsue, Japan	D14	28
Matsumoto, Japan	C3	31
Matsuyama, Japan	E14	28
Mattamiscontis Lake, l., Me., U.S.	C4	112
Mattamuskeet, Lake, l., N.C., U.S.	B6	126
Mattapoisett, Ma., U.S.	C6	114
Mattaponi, stm., Va., U.S.	C5	139
Mattawa, On., Can.	A6	89
Mattawamkeag, Me., U.S.	C4	112
Mattawamkeag, stm., Me., U.S.	C4	112
Mattawamkeag Lake, l., Me., U.S.	C4	112
Matterhorn (Cervino), mtn., Eur.	A1	18
Matterhorn, mtn., Nv., U.S.	B6	121
Matteson, Il., U.S.	k9	106
Matthews, Mo., U.S.	E8	118
Matthews, N.C., U.S.	B2	126
Matthew Town, Bah.	A5	80
Mattituck, N.Y., U.S.	n16	125
Mattoon, Il., U.S.	D5	106
Mattoon, Lake, res., Il., U.S.	D5	106
Mattydale, N.Y., U.S.	B4	125
Matunuck, R.I., U.S.	G3	132
Maturín, Ven.	B7	70
Matveev Kurgan, Russia	F15	20
Maúa, Moz.	A6	56
Maubeuge, Fr.	B8	16
Maud, Ok., U.S.	B5	129
Maués, Braz.	D8	70
Mauganj, India	E4	40
Maugansville, Md., U.S.	A2	113
Maug Islands, is., N. Mar. Is.	C12	32
Maui, i., Hi., U.S.	C6	104
Maui, co., Hi., U.S.	B5	104
Mauldin, S.C., U.S.	B3	133
Maumee, Oh., U.S.	A2	128
Maumee, stm., U.S.	A2	128
Maumee Bay, b., U.S.	G7	115
Maumelle, Lake, res., Ar., U.S.	C3	97
Maumere, Indon.	E6	36
Maun, Bots.	B3	56
Mauna Kea, vol., Hi., U.S.	D6	104
Maunaloa, Hi., U.S.	B4	104
Mauna Loa, vol., Hi., U.S.	D6	104
Maunalua Bay, b., Hi., U.S.	g10	104
Maunawili, Hi., U.S.	g10	104
Maupihaa, atoll, Fr. Poly.	F14	58
Maurepas, Lake, l., La., U.S.	D5	111
Maurice, Ia., U.S.	B1	108
Maurice, stm., N.J., U.S.	E2	123
Mauritania, ctry., Afr.	C2	50
Mauritius, ctry., Afr.	f10	57a
Mauritius, i., Mrts.	G11	52
Maury, co., Tn., U.S.	B4	135
Maury City, Tn., U.S.	B2	135
Maury Island, i., Wa., U.S.	f11	140
Mauston, Wi., U.S.	E3	142
Maverick, co., Tx., U.S.	E2	136
Mavinga, Ang.	B3	56
Mawlaik, Mya.	B2	34
Mawlamyine, Mya.	C3	34
Maxinkuckee, Lake, l., In., U.S.	B5	107
Maxixe, Moz.	C6	56
Max Meadows, Va., U.S.	D2	139
Maxton, N.C., U.S.	C3	126
Maxville, On., Can.	B10	89
Maxwell, Ia., U.S.	C4	108
Maxwell Acres, W.V., U.S.	g8	141
Maxwell Air Force Base, mil., Al., U.S.	C3	94
Mayaguana, i., Bah.	D10	76
Mayaguana Passage, strt., Bah.	A5	80
Mayagüez, P.R.	B6	80
Mayang, China	D2	30
Mayenne, Fr.	C6	16
Mayer, Az., U.S.	C3	96
Mayerthorpe, Ab., Can.	C3	84
Mayes, co., Ok., U.S.	A6	129
Mayesville, S.C., U.S.	D7	133
Mayfield, Ky., U.S.	f9	110
Mayfield, Pa., U.S.	C10	131
Mayfield Heights, Oh., U.S.	A4	128
Mayfield Lake, res., Wa., U.S.	C3	140
Mayflower, Ar., U.S.	C3	97
Mayking, Ky., U.S.	C7	110
Maymyo, Mya.	B3	34
Maynard, Ma., U.S.	B5	114
Maynardville, Tn., U.S.	C10	135
Mayne, B.C., Can.	g12	85
Mayo, stm., Mex.	B3	78
Mayo, Md., U.S.	C4	113
Mayo, S.C., U.S.	A4	133
Mayodan, N.C., U.S.	A3	126
Mayo Ndaga, Nig.	E7	50
Mayon Volcano, vol., Phil.	D8	34
Mayotte, dep., Afr.	A8	56
May Park, Or., U.S.	B8	130
Mayport Naval Station, mil., Fl., U.S.	B5	102
Maysville, Ga., U.S.	B3	103
Maysville, Ky., U.S.	B6	110
Maysville, Mo., U.S.	B3	118
Maysville, N.C., U.S.	C5	126
Maysville, Ok., U.S.	C4	129
Mayumba, Gabon	D2	54
Māyūram, India	G3	40
Mayville, Mi., U.S.	E7	115
Mayville, N.D., U.S.	B8	127
Mayville, N.Y., U.S.	C1	125
Mayville, Wi., U.S.	E5	142
Maywood, Il., U.S.	k9	106
Maywood, N.J., U.S.	h8	123
Mazabuka, Zam.	B4	56
Mazamet, Fr.	F8	16
Mazara del Vallo, Italy	F4	18
Mazār-e Sharīf, Afg.	C9	42
Mazaruni, stm., Guy.	D7	80
Mazatlán, Mex.	C3	78
Mazatzal Mountains, mts., Az., U.S.	C4	96
Mazatzal Peak, mtn., Az., U.S.	C4	96
Mažeikiai, Lith.	H10	10
Mazeppa, Mn., U.S.	F6	116
Mazomanie, Wi., U.S.	E4	142
Mazon, Il., U.S.	B5	106
Mazury, reg., Pol.	C6	20
Mazyr, Bela.	C10	20
Mbabane, Swaz.	D5	56
M'bahiakro, C. Iv.	E4	50
Mbaïki, C.A.R.	C3	54
Mbaké, Sen.	D1	50
Mbala, Zam.	E6	54
Mbale, Ug.	C6	54
Mbalmayo, Cam.	C2	54
Mbamba Bay, Tan.	F6	54
Mbandaka, D.R.C.	C3	54
Mbanga, Cam.	C1	54
Mbanza-Ngungu (Thysville), D.R.C.	E2	54
Mbarara, Ug.	D6	54
Mbeya, Tan.	E6	54
Mbigou, Gabon	D2	54
Mbinda, Congo	D2	54
Mbini, Eq. Gui.	C1	54
Mboi, D.R.C.	E4	54
Mboki, C.A.R.	B5	54
Mbouda, Cam.	B2	54
Mbour, Sen.	D1	50
Mbout, Maur.	C2	50
Mbuji-Mayi, D.R.C.	E4	54
McAdam, N.B., Can.	D2	87
McAdoo, Pa., U.S.	E9	131
McAfee Peak, mtn., Nv., U.S.	B6	121
McAlester, Ok., U.S.	C6	129
McAlester, Lake, res., Ok., U.S.	B6	129
McAllen, Tx., U.S.	F3	136
McAlmont, Ar., U.S.	h10	97
McAlpine, Md., U.S.	B4	113
McAlpine Lock and Dam, U.S.	H6	107
McArthur, Oh., U.S.	C3	128
McBee, S.C., U.S.	C7	133
McCall, Id., U.S.	E2	105
McCalla, Al., U.S.	g6	94
McCamey, Tx., U.S.	D1	136
McCammon, Id., U.S.	G6	105
McCandless, Pa., U.S.	h13	131
McCartney Mountain, mtn., Mt., U.S.	E4	119
McCaysville, Ga., U.S.	B2	103
McChord Air Force Base, mil., Wa., U.S.	f11	140
McClain, co., Ok., U.S.	C4	129
McCleary, Wa., U.S.	B2	140
McClintock, Mount, mtn., Ant.	D20	67
McCloud, Ca., U.S.	B2	98
McClure, Pa., U.S.	E7	131
McColl, S.C., U.S.	B8	133
McComas, W.V., U.S.	D3	141
McComb, Ms., U.S.	D3	117
McComb, Oh., U.S.	A2	128
McCone, co., Mt., U.S.	C11	119
McConnell Air Force Base, mil., Ks., U.S.	g12	109
McConnellsburg, Pa., U.S.	G6	131
McConnelsville, Oh., U.S.	C4	128
McCook, Ne., U.S.	D5	120
McCook, co., S.D., U.S.	D8	134
McCordsville, In., U.S.	E6	107
McCormick, S.C., U.S.	D3	133
McCormick, co., S.C., U.S.	D3	133
McCracken, co., Ky., U.S.	e9	110
McCreary, Mb., Can.	D2	86
McCreary, co., Ky., U.S.	D5	110
McCrory, Ar., U.S.	B4	97
McCulloch, co., Tx., U.S.	D3	136
McCullough Mountain, mtn., Nv., U.S.	H6	121
McCurtain, co., Ok., U.S.	C7	129
McDermitt, Nv., U.S.	B4	121
McDonald, co., Mo., U.S.	E3	118
McDonough, Ga., U.S.	C2	103
McDonough, co., Il., U.S.	C3	106
McDougall, Mount, mtn., Wy., U.S.	D2	143
McDowell, Ky., U.S.	C7	110
McDowell, co., N.C., U.S.	f10	126
McDowell, co., W.V., U.S.	D3	141
McDowell Mountains, mts., Az., U.S.	k9	96
McDowell Peak, mtn., Az., U.S.	k9	96
McDuffie, co., Ga., U.S.	C4	103
McElroy Creek, stm., W.V., U.S.	k9	141
Mcensk, Russia	C14	20
McEwen, Tn., U.S.	A4	135
McFarland, Ca., U.S.	E4	98
McFarland, Wi., U.S.	E4	142
McGehee, Ar., U.S.	D4	97
McGill, Nv., U.S.	D7	121
McGrath, Ak., U.S.	C8	95
McGregor, stm., B.C., Can.	B7	85
McGregor, Ia., U.S.	A6	108
McGregor, Tx., U.S.	D4	136
McGregor Lake, l., Ab., Can.	D4	84
McGuire, Mount, mtn., Id., U.S.	D4	105
McGuire Air Force Base, mil., N.J., U.S.	C3	123
McHenry, Il., U.S.	A5	106
McHenry, co., Il., U.S.	A5	106
McHenry, Md., U.S.	k12	113
McHenry, co., N.D., U.S.	A5	127
Mchinji, Mwi.	A5	56
McIntosh, co., Ga., U.S.	E5	103
McIntosh, Mn., U.S.	C3	116
McIntosh, co., N.D., U.S.	C6	127
McIntosh, co., Ok., U.S.	B6	129
McKean, co., Pa., U.S.	C4	131
McKee, Ky., U.S.	C6	110
McKeesport, Pa., U.S.	F2	131
McKees Rocks, Pa., U.S.	F1	131
McKenzie, co., N.D., U.S.	B2	127
McKenzie, stm., Or., U.S.	C4	130
McKenzie, Tn., U.S.	A3	135
McKinley, co., N.M., U.S.	B1	124
McKinley, Mount, mtn., Ak., U.S.	C9	95
McKinleyville, Ca., U.S.	B1	98
McKinney, Tx., U.S.	C4	136
McKinney, Lake, l., Ks., U.S.	E2	109
McKittrick Summit, mtn., Ca., U.S.	E4	98
McLaughlin, S.D., U.S.	B5	134
McLean, co., Il., U.S.	C4	106
McLean, Il., U.S.	C4	106
McLean, co., Ky., U.S.	C2	110
McLean, co., N.D., U.S.	B4	127
McLean, Va., U.S.	g12	139
McLeansboro, Il., U.S.	E5	106
McLennan, Ab., Can.	B2	84
McLennan, co., Tx., U.S.	D4	136
McLeod, co., Mn., U.S.	F4	116
M'Clintock Channel, strt., N.T., Can.	D19	82
McLoud, Ok., U.S.	B4	129
McLoughlin, Mount, mtn., Or., U.S.	D4	130
McLouth, Ks., U.S.	C8	109
McMechen, W.V., U.S.	B4	141
McMillan, Lake, res., N.M., U.S.	E5	124
McMinn, co., Tn., U.S.	D9	135
McMinnville, Or., U.S.	B3	130
McMinnville, Tn., U.S.	D8	135
McMullen, co., Tx., U.S.	E3	136
McMurdo Sound, strt., Ant.	D21	67
McNairy, co., Tn., U.S.	B3	135
McNary, co., Ky., U.S.	C6	96
McNary Dam, U.S.	B7	130
McNeil, Ar., U.S.	D2	97
McNeil Island, i., Wa., U.S.	f10	140
McNeill, Ms., U.S.	E4	117
McPherson, Ks., U.S.	D6	109
McPherson, co., Ks., U.S.	D6	109
McPherson, co., Ne., U.S.	C4	120
McPherson, co., S.D., U.S.	B6	134
McQueeney, Tx., U.S.	h7	136
McRae, Ar., U.S.	B4	97
McRae, Ga., U.S.	D4	103
McRoberts, Ky., U.S.	C7	110
McSherrystown, Pa., U.S.	G7	131
Mdandu, Tan.	E6	54
Mead, Wa., U.S.	B8	140
Mead, Lake, res., U.S.	A1	96
Meade, stm., Ak., U.S.	B8	95
Meade, Ks., U.S.	E3	109
Meade, co., Ks., U.S.	E3	109
Meade, co., Ky., U.S.	C3	110
Meade, co., S.D., U.S.	C3	134
Meaden Peak, mtn., Co., U.S.	A3	99
Meade Peak, mtn., Id., U.S.	G7	105
Meadow, stm., W.V., U.S.	C4	141
Meadow Creek, stm., W.V., U.S.	n14	141
Meadow Lands, Pa., U.S.	F1	131
Meadow Valley Wash, val., Nv., U.S.	F7	121
Meadowview, Va., U.S.	f10	139
Meadville, Pa., U.S.	C1	131
Meaford, On., Can.	C4	89
Meagher, co., Mt., U.S.	D6	119
Meander Creek Reservoir, res., Oh., U.S.	A5	128
Meaux, Fr.	C8	16
Mebane, N.C., U.S.	A3	126
Mecca see Makkah, Sau. Ar.	F3	38
Mecca, Ca., U.S.	F5	98
Mechanic Falls, Me., U.S.	D2	112
Mechanicsburg, Oh., U.S.	B2	128
Mechanicsburg, Pa., U.S.	F7	131
Mechanicsville, Ia., U.S.	C6	108
Mechanicsville, Md., U.S.	D4	113
Mechanicsville, Va., U.S.	C5	139
Mechanicville, N.Y., U.S.	C7	125
Mechant, Lake, l., La., U.S.	E4	111
Mecklenburg, hist. reg., Ger.	D12	12
Mecklenburg, co., N.C., U.S.	B2	126
Mecklenburg, co., Va., U.S.	D4	139
Mecklenburg Bay see Mecklenburger Bucht, b., Ger.	C12	12
Mecklenburger Bucht, b., Ger.	C12	12
Mecosta, co., Mi., U.S.	E5	115
Mecúfi, Moz.	A7	56
Medan, Indon.	C1	36
Medanosa, Punta, c., Arg.	G3	69
Medaryville, In., U.S.	B4	107
Meddybumps Lake, l., Me., U.S.	C5	112
Medellín, Col.	B4	70
Médenine, Tun.	D7	48
Mederdra, Maur.	C1	50
Medfield, Ma., U.S.	h10	114
Medford, Ma., U.S.	B5	114
Medford, Mn., U.S.	F5	116
Medford, Ok., U.S.	A4	129
Medford, Or., U.S.	E4	130
Medford, Wi., U.S.	C3	142
Medford Lakes, N.J., U.S.	D3	123
Medgidia, Rom.	G10	20
Media, Pa., U.S.	G11	131
Mediapolis, Ia., U.S.	C6	108
Mediaş, Rom.	F8	20
Medical Lake, Wa., U.S.	B8	140
Medicine Bow, Wy., U.S.	E6	143
Medicine Bow, stm., Wy., U.S.	E6	143
Medicine Bow Mountains, mts., U.S.	E6	143
Medicine Bow Peak, mtn., Wy., U.S.	E6	143
Medicine Hat, Ab., Can.	D5	84
Medicine Lodge, Ks., U.S.	E5	109
Medicine Lodge, stm., U.S.	E4	109
Medina see Al-Madīnah, Sau. Ar.	F3	38
Medina, N.Y., U.S.	B2	125
Medina, Oh., U.S.	A4	128
Medina, co., Oh., U.S.	A4	128
Medina, Tn., U.S.	B3	135
Medina, stm., Tx., U.S.	k7	136
Medina, co., Tx., U.S.	E3	136
Medina, Wa., U.S.	e11	140
Medina del Campo, Spain	G4	16
Medinīpur, India	E4	40
Mediterranean Sea	D5	14
Mediterranean, Mar see Mediterranean Sea	D5	14
Mednogorsk, Russia	D10	22
Mednyj, ostrov, i., Russia	D18	26
Medora, In., U.S.	G5	107
Médouneu, Gabon	C2	54
Medveževorsk, Russia	B5	22
Medvežji ostrova, is., Russia	B18	26
Medway, stm., N.S., Can.	E5	87
Medway, Ma., U.S.	B5	114
Medway, Me., U.S.	C4	112
Meekatharra, Austl.	F2	60
Meeker, Co., U.S.	A3	99
Meeker, co., Mn., U.S.	E4	116
Meeker, co., Ok., U.S.	B5	129
Meelpaeg Lake, res., Nf., Can.	D3	88
Meerut, India	D3	40
Meeteetse, Wy., U.S.	B4	143
Méga, Eth.	C7	54
Mégantic, Lac, l., P.Q., Can.	D7	90
Mégantic, Mont, mtn., P.Q., Can.	D6	90
Meggett, S.C., U.S.	F7	133

Name	Map Ref.	Page
Meghālaya, state, India	D6	40
Meghri, Arm.	C12	44
Meharry, Mount, mtn., Austl.	H20	4
Meherrin, stm., U.S.	A4	126
Mehlville, Mo., U.S.	f13	118
Mehtar Lām, Afg.	D10	42
Meia Meia, Tan.	E7	54
Meiganga, Cam.	B2	54
Meigs, Ga., U.S.	E2	103
Meigs, co., Oh., U.S.	C3	128
Meigs, co., Tn., U.S.	D9	135
Meiktila, Mya.	B3	34
Meiningen, Ger.	E12	12
Meishan, China	C1	30
Meitan, China	D2	30
Meizhou, China	G11	28
Mejillones, Chile	B2	69
Mékambo, Gabon	C2	54
Mek'elē, Eth.	H12	48
Mékhé, Sen.	C1	50
Meknès, Mor.	D3	48
Mekong, stm., Asia	D5	34
Mékôngk see Mekong, stm., Asia	D5	34
Melaka, Malay.	C2	36
Melanesia, is., Oc.	E10	58
Melbourne, Austl.	H4	62
Melbourne, Ar., U.S.	A4	97
Melbourne, Fl., U.S.	D6	102
Melbourne, Ia., U.S.	C4	108
Melbourne, Ky., U.S.	h14	110
Melbourne Beach, Fl., U.S.	D6	102
Melcher, Ia., U.S.	C4	108
Melchor Múzquiz, Mex.	B4	78
Melenki, Russia	C7	22
Meleuz, Russia	D10	22
Mélèzes, Rivière aux, stm., P.Q., Can.	g12	90
Melfi, Chad	D8	50
Melilla, Sp. N. Afr.	J5	16
Melipilla, Chile	E3	72
Melita, Mb., Can.	E1	86
Melitopol', Ukr.	F13	20
Mellen, Wi., U.S.	B3	142
Mellette, co., S.D., U.S.	D5	134
Melo, Ur.	E7	72
Melocheville, P.Q., Can.	q19	90
Melos see Mílos, i., Grc.	L8	18
Melrhir, Chott, l., Alg.	D6	48
Melrose, Austl.	F3	60
Melrose, Fl., U.S.	C4	102
Melrose, Ma., U.S.	B5	114
Melrose, Mn., U.S.	E4	116
Melrose, N.M., U.S.	C6	124
Melton Hill Lake, res., Tn., U.S.	D9	135
Meluco, Moz.	A6	56
Melun, Fr.	C8	16
Melvern Lake, res., Ks., U.S.	D8	109
Melville, La., U.S.	D4	111
Melville, Cape, c., Austl.	C3	62
Melville, Lake, l., Nf., Can.	B2	88
Melville Island, i., Austl.	C5	60
Melville Sound, strt., N.T., Can.	B14	82
Melvin, Ky., U.S.	C7	110
Memboro, Indon.	E5	36
Memel see Klaipėda, Lith.	I9	10
Memmingen, Ger.	G11	12
Mempawah, Indon.	C3	36
Memphis, Fl., U.S.	p10	102
Memphis, Mi., U.S.	F8	115
Memphis, Mo., U.S.	A5	118
Memphis, Tn., U.S.	B1	135
Memphis, Tx., U.S.	B2	136
Memphis Naval Air Station, mil., Tn., U.S.	B2	135
Mena, Ukr.	D12	20
Mena, Ar., U.S.	C1	97
Menahga, Mn., U.S.	D3	116
Ménaka, Mali	C5	50
Menan, Id., U.S.	F7	105
Menands, N.Y., U.S.	C7	125
Menard, co., Il., U.S.	C4	106
Menard, Tx., U.S.	D3	136
Menard, co., Tx., U.S.	D3	136
Menasha, Wi., U.S.	D5	142
Mende, Fr.	E8	16
Mendeleyev Ridge	E4	144
Mendenhall, Ms., U.S.	D4	117
Mendham, N.J., U.S.	B3	123
Mendī, Eth.	B7	54
Mendi, Pap. N. Gui.	H11	32
Mendocino, co., Ca., U.S.	C2	98
Mendocino Fracture Zone	E23	64
Mendon, Il., U.S.	C2	106
Mendon, Mi., U.S.	F5	115
Mendon, Ut., U.S.	B4	137
Mendota, Ca., U.S.	D3	98
Mendota, Il., U.S.	B4	106
Mendota, Lake, l., Wi., U.S.	E4	142
Mendoza, Arg.	E4	72
Mene Grande, Ven.	D5	80
Menemen, Tur.	C2	44
Mengcheng, China	C4	30
Menggala, Indon.	D3	36
Menghai, China	B4	34
Mengjiawan, China	B2	30
Mengzi, China	G8	28
Menifee, co., Ky., U.S.	C6	110
Menindee, Austl.	G3	62
Menlo Park, Ca., U.S.	k8	98
Menno, S.D., U.S.	D8	134
Menominee, Mi., U.S.	C3	115
Menominee, co., Mi., U.S.	C3	115
Menominee, co., Wi., U.S.	C5	142
Menominee, stm., U.S.	C6	142
Menominee Indian Reservation, Wi., U.S.	C5	142
Menomonee, stm., Wi., U.S.	m11	142
Menomonee Falls, Wi., U.S.	E5	142
Menomonie, Wi., U.S.	D2	142
Menongue, Ang.	A2	56
Menor, Mar, b., Spain	I6	16
Menorca (Minorca), i., Spain	G9	16
Mentawai, Kepulauan, is., Indon.	D1	36
Mentawai, Selat, strt., Indon.	D1	36
Mentone, In., U.S.	B5	107
Mentor, Oh., U.S.	A4	128
Mentor-on-the-Lake, Oh., U.S.	A4	128
Menzel Bourguiba, Tun.	F2	18
Menzies, Austl.	F3	60
Meoqui, Mex.	B3	78
Meppen, Ger.	D10	12
Mequinenza, Embalse de, res., Spain	G6	16
Mequon, Wi., U.S.	E6	142
Merambéllou, Kólpos, b., Grc.	G10	18
Meramec, stm., Mo., U.S.	C7	118
Merano, Italy	A3	18
Merasheen Island, i., Nf., Can.	E4	88
Merauke, Indon.	H11	32
Meraux, La., U.S.	k12	111
Mercāra, India	G3	40
Merced, Ca., U.S.	D3	98
Merced, co., Ca., U.S.	D3	98
Merced, stm., Ca., U.S.	D3	98
Mercedes, Arg.	D6	72
Mercedes, Ur.	E6	72
Mercedes, Tx., U.S.	F4	136
Mercer, co., Il., U.S.	B3	106
Mercer, co., Ky., U.S.	C5	110
Mercer, co., Mo., U.S.	A4	118
Mercer, co., N.D., U.S.	B4	127
Mercer, co., N.J., U.S.	C3	123
Mercer, co., Oh., U.S.	B1	128
Mercer, Pa., U.S.	D1	131
Mercer, co., Pa., U.S.	D1	131
Mercer, Wi., U.S.	B3	142
Mercer, co., W.V., U.S.	D3	141
Mercer Island, Wa., U.S.	B3	140
Mercer Island, i., Wa., U.S.	e11	140
Mercersburg, Pa., U.S.	G6	131
Mercerville, N.J., U.S.	C3	123
Mercier, P.Q., Can.	D4	90
Meredith, N.H., U.S.	C3	122
Meredith, Lake, l., Co., U.S.	C7	99
Meredith, Lake, res., Tx., U.S.	B2	136
Meredosia, Il., U.S.	D3	106
Meredosia Lake, l., Il., U.S.	D3	106
Mereeg, Som.	J14	48
Merefa, Ukr.	E14	20
Merenkurkku (Norra Kvarken), strt., Eur.	E9	10
Mergui, Mya.	I5	34
Mergui Archipelago, is., Mya.	D3	34
Meriç (Évros) (Marica), stm., Eur.	D11	18
Mérida, Mex.	C7	78
Mérida, Spain	H3	16
Mérida, Ven.	B5	70
Mérida, Cordillera de, mts., Ven.	B5	70
Meriden, Ct., U.S.	C4	100
Meriden, Ks., U.S.	C8	109
Meridian, Id., U.S.	F2	105
Meridian, Ms., U.S.	C5	117
Meridian, Pa., U.S.	E2	131
Meridian, Tx., U.S.	D4	136
Meridian Hills, In., U.S.	k10	107
Meridian Naval Air Station, mil., Ms., U.S.	C5	117
Meridianville, Al., U.S.	A3	94
Merikarvia, Fin.	F9	10
Merín, Laguna see Mirim, Lagoa, b., S.A.	E7	72
Meriwether, co., Ga., U.S.	C2	103
Merkel, Tx., U.S.	C2	136
Merlin, On., Can.	E2	89
Mermentau, stm., La., U.S.	E3	111
Mermentau, La., U.S.	D3	111
Meron, Har, mtn., Isr.	F6	44
Meron, Mount see Meron, Har, mtn., Isr.	F6	44
Merredin, Austl.	G2	60
Merriam, Ks., U.S.	k16	109
Merrick, co., Ne., U.S.	C7	120
Merrickville, On., Can.	C9	89
Merrill, Ia., U.S.	B1	108
Merrill, Mi., U.S.	E6	115
Merrill, Or., U.S.	E5	130
Merrill, Wi., U.S.	C4	142
Merrillville, In., U.S.	B3	107
Merrimac, Ma., U.S.	A5	114
Merrimack, N.H., U.S.	E4	122
Merrimack, co., N.H., U.S.	D3	122
Merrimack, stm., U.S.	A5	114
Merritt, B.C., Can.	D7	85
Merritt Island, Fl., U.S.	D6	102
Merritt Reservoir, res., Ne., U.S.	B5	120
Merrymeeting Lake, l., N.H., U.S.	D4	122
Merryville, La., U.S.	D2	111
Mersa Matruh, Egypt	D10	48
Mersing, Malay.	C2	36
Merthyr Tydfil, Wales, U.K.	E5	12
Merton, Wi., U.S.	m11	142
Meru, Kenya	C7	54
Merwin, Lake, res., Wa., U.S.	C3	140
Merzifon, Tur.	B6	44
Mesa, Az., U.S.	D4	96
Mesa, co., Co., U.S.	C2	99
Mesabi Range, Mn., U.S.	C6	116
Mesa Mountain, mtn., Co., U.S.	D4	99
Mesa Verde National Park, Co., U.S.	D2	99
Mescalero, N.M., U.S.	D4	124
Mescalero Indian Reservation, N.M., U.S.	D4	124
Meschede, Ger.	E11	12
Meshgīn Shahr, Iran	C12	44
Mesilla, N.M., U.S.	E3	124
Mesolóngion, Grc.	E8	18
Mesopotamia, hist. reg., Asia	D4	42
Mesquite, N.M., U.S.	E3	124
Mesquite, Nv., U.S.	G7	121
Mesquite, Tx., U.S.	n10	136
Messalonskee Lake, l., Me., U.S.	D3	112
Messina, Italy	E5	18
Messina, S. Afr.	C5	56
Messina, Stretto di, strt., Italy	E5	18
Messiniakós Kólpos, b., Grc.	F9	18
Mestghanem, Alg.	C4	48
Mestre, Italy	B4	18
Meta, stm., S.A.	B5	70
Métabetchouan, P.Q., Can.	A6	90
Métabetchouane, stm., P.Q., Can.	A5	90
Metairie, La., U.S.	k11	111
Metamora, Il., U.S.	C4	106
Metán, Arg.	D5	72
Metapán, El Sal.	C2	80
Metapontum, hist., Italy	D6	18
Metcalfe, On., Can.	B9	89
Metcalfe, co., Ky., U.S.	C4	110
Metcalfe, Ms., U.S.	B2	117
Metedeconk, North Branch, stm., N.J., U.S.	C4	123
Metedeconk, South Branch, stm., N.J., U.S.	C3	123
Meteghan, N.S., Can.	E3	87
Meteghan River, N.S., Can.	E3	87
Metéora, rel., Grc.	E8	18
Meteor Crater, crat., Az., U.S.	C4	96
Methow, stm., Wa., U.S.	A5	140
Methuen, Ma., U.S.	A5	114
Metlakatla, Ak., U.S.	D13	95
Metonga, Lake, l., Wi., U.S.	C5	142
Metro, Indon.	E3	36
Metropolis, Il., U.S.	F5	106
Mettawee, stm., U.S.	E2	138
Metter, Ga., U.S.	D4	103
Metuchen, N.J., U.S.	B4	123
Metz, Fr.	C13	16
Metzger, Or., U.S.	h12	130
Meulaboh, Indon.	C1	36
Meuse (Maas), stm., Eur.	C9	16
Mexia, Tx., U.S.	D4	136
Mexia, Lake, res., Tx., U.S.	D4	136
Mexiana, Ilha, i., Braz.	A2	74
Mexicali, Mex.	A1	78
México, state, Mex.	D4	78
Mexico, ctry., N.A.	C4	78
Mexico, In., U.S.	C5	107
Mexico, Me., U.S.	D2	112
Mexico, Mo., U.S.	B6	118
Mexico, Gulf of, b., N.A.	F10	92
Mexico Basin	F4	66
Mexico City see Ciudad de México, Mex.	D5	78
Meyersdale, Pa., U.S.	G3	131
Meyísti, i., Grc.	F12	18
Meymaneh, Afg.	C8	42
Mezcala, Mex.	D5	78
Mežđurečenskij, Russia	C12	22
Mezen', Russia	C6	26
Mezen', stm., Russia	C6	26
Mezenskaja guba, b., Russia	A7	22
Mezőtúr, Hung.	F6	20
Mfangano Island, i., Kenya	D6	54
Mgeta, Tan.	E7	54
M'Goun, Irhil, mtn., Mor.	E2	48
Mhow, India	I6	40
Miahuatlán de Porfírio Díaz, Mex.	D5	78
Miajadas, Spain	H4	16
Miaméré, C.A.R.	B3	54
Miami, Az., U.S.	D5	96
Miami, Fl., U.S.	G6	102
Miami, co., In., U.S.	C5	107
Miami, co., Ks., U.S.	D9	109
Miami, co., Oh., U.S.	B1	128
Miami, Ok., U.S.	A7	129
Miami Beach, Fl., U.S.	s13	102
Miami Canal, Fl., U.S.	F6	102
Miami International Airport, Fl., U.S.	s13	102
Miamisburg, Oh., U.S.	C1	128
Miami Shores, Fl., U.S.	s13	102
Miami Springs, Fl., U.S.	s13	102
Mianchi, China	C3	30
Miāndoāb, Iran	D12	44
Miandrivazo, Madag.	B8	56
Miāneh, Iran	C5	42
Mianning, China	A4	34
Mianus Reservoir, res., U.S.	E1	100
Mianwāli, Pak.	D10	42
Mianyang, China	E8	28
Mianzhu, China	C1	30
Miass, Russia	D8	26
Mica Mountain, mtn., Az., U.S.	E5	96
Micco, Fl., U.S.	E6	102
Miccosukee, Lake, res., Fl., U.S.	B2	102
Michalovce, Slvk.	E6	20
Michelson, Mount, mtn., Ak., U.S.	B11	95
Michie, Tn., U.S.	B3	135
Michigamme, Lake, l., Mi., U.S.	B2	115
Michigamme Reservoir, res., Mi., U.S.	B2	115
Michigan, stm., Co., U.S.	A4	99
Michigan, state, U.S.	E6	115
Michigan, Lake, l., U.S.	C10	92
Michigan Center, Mi., U.S.	F6	115
Michigan City, In., U.S.	A4	107
Michigan Island, i., Wi., U.S.	B3	142
Michoacán, state, Mex.	D4	78
Micronesia, is., Oc.	C9	58
Micronesia, Federated States of, ctry., Oc.	D8	58
Mičurinsk, Russia	C16	20
Mid-Atlantic Ridge	F9	66
Middelburg, S. Afr.	D4	56
Middelburg, S. Afr.	E3	56
Middelfart, Den.	I3	10
Middle, stm., Ia., U.S.	C3	108
Middle, stm., Mn., U.S.	B2	116
Middle America Trench	G28	64
Middle Andaman, i., India	G6	40
Middleboro (Middleborough Center), Ma., U.S.	C6	114
Middlebourne, W.V., U.S.	B4	141
Middleburg, Fl., U.S.	B5	102
Middleburg, Pa., U.S.	E7	131
Middleburg Heights, Oh., U.S.	h9	128
Middlebury, Ct., U.S.	C3	100
Middlebury, In., U.S.	A6	107
Middlebury, Vt., U.S.	C2	138
Middle Caicos, i., T./C. Is.	A5	80
Middlefield, Ct., U.S.	C5	100
Middlefield, Oh., U.S.	A4	128
Middle Island Creek, stm., W.V., U.S.	B3	141
Middle Nodaway, stm., Ia., U.S.	C3	108
Middle Park, val., Co., U.S.	A4	99
Middle Patuxent, stm., Md., U.S.	B4	113
Middleport, N.Y., U.S.	B2	125
Middleport, Oh., U.S.	C3	128
Middle Raccoon, stm., Ia., U.S.	C3	108
Middle River, Md., U.S.	B5	113
Middlesboro, Ky., U.S.	D6	110
Middlesbrough, Eng., U.K.	C6	12
Middlesex, co., Ct., U.S.	D5	100
Middlesex, co., Ma., U.S.	A5	114
Middlesex, N.C., U.S.	B4	126
Middlesex, N.J., U.S.	B4	123
Middlesex, co., N.J., U.S.	C4	123
Middlesex, co., Va., U.S.	C6	139
Middlesex Fells Reservation, Ma., U.S.	g11	114
Middleton, N.S., Can.	E4	87
Middleton, Id., U.S.	F2	105
Middleton, Ma., U.S.	A5	114
Middleton, Wi., U.S.	E4	142
Middletown, Ca., U.S.	C2	98
Middletown, Ct., U.S.	C5	100
Middletown, De., U.S.	C3	101
Middletown, In., U.S.	D6	107
Middletown, Ky., U.S.	g11	110
Middletown, Md., U.S.	B2	113
Middletown, N.J., U.S.	C4	123
Middletown, N.Y., U.S.	D6	125
Middletown, Oh., U.S.	C1	128
Middletown, Pa., U.S.	F8	131
Middletown, R.I., U.S.	E5	132
Middletown, Va., U.S.	A4	139
Midfield, Al., U.S.	g7	94
Mid-Indian Basin	I10	64
Mid-Indian Ridge	I9	64
Midland, On., Can.	C5	89
Midland, Mi., U.S.	E6	115
Midland, co., Mi., U.S.	E6	115
Midland, N.C., U.S.	B2	126
Midland, Pa., U.S.	E1	131
Midland, Tx., U.S.	D1	136
Midland, co., Tx., U.S.	D1	136
Midland City, Al., U.S.	D4	94
Midland Park, Ks., U.S.	g12	109
Midland Park, N.J., U.S.	B4	123
Midland Park, S.C., U.S.	k11	133
Midlothian, Il., U.S.	k9	106
Midlothian, Tx., U.S.	C4	136
Midongy Atsimo, Madag.	C8	56
Mid-Pacific Mountains	F18	64
Midvale, Ut., U.S.	C4	137
Midville, Ga., U.S.	D4	103
Midway, De., U.S.	F5	101
Midway, Ky., U.S.	B5	110
Midway, Pa., U.S.	G7	131
Midway, Ut., U.S.	C4	137
Midway Islands, dep., Oc.	B12	58
Midwest, Wy., U.S.	C6	143
Midwest City, Ok., U.S.	B4	129
Midyat, Tur.	D9	44
Międzyrzecz, Pol.	C3	20
Miekojärvi, l., Fin.	C11	10
Mielec, Pol.	D6	20
Mieres, Spain	F4	16
Mifflin, co., Pa., U.S.	E6	131
Mifflinburg, Pa., U.S.	E7	131
Mifflinville, Pa., U.S.	D9	131
Miguel Alemán, Presa, res., Mex.	D5	78
Miguel Auza, Mex.	C4	78
Mihajlov, Russia	B15	20
Mihajlovka, Russia	D6	26
Mikasa, Japan	C16	28
Mikínai, hist., Grc.	F9	18
Mikindani, Tan.	F8	54
Mikkeli, Fin.	F12	10
Míkonos, i., Grc.	F10	18
Mikumi, Tan.	E7	54
Mikun', Russia	B9	22
Milaca, Mn., U.S.	E5	116
Milagro, Ec.	D4	70
Milam, co., Tx., U.S.	D4	136
Milan see Milano, Italy	B2	18
Milan, Ga., U.S.	D3	103
Milan, Il., U.S.	B3	106
Milan, In., U.S.	F7	107
Milan, Mi., U.S.	F7	115
Milan, Mo., U.S.	A4	118
Milan, N.M., U.S.	B2	124
Milan, Oh., U.S.	A3	128
Milan, Tn., U.S.	B3	135
Milange, Moz.	B6	56
Milano (Milan), Italy	B2	18
Milâs, Tur.	D2	44
Milazzo, Italy	E5	18
Milbank, S.D., U.S.	B9	134
Mildmay, On., Can.	C3	89
Mildura, Austl.	G3	62
Mile, China	G8	28
Milesburg, Pa., U.S.	E6	131
Miles City, Mt., U.S.	D11	119
Milestone, Sk., Can.	G3	91
Milet (Miletus), hist., Tur.	D2	44
Miletus see Milet, hist., Tur.	D2	44
Milford, Ct., U.S.	E3	100
Milford, De., U.S.	E4	101
Milford, Ia., U.S.	A2	108
Milford, Il., U.S.	C6	106
Milford, In., U.S.	B6	107
Milford, Ma., U.S.	B4	114
Milford, Me., U.S.	D4	112
Milford, Mi., U.S.	F7	115
Milford, Ne., U.S.	D8	120
Milford, N.H., U.S.	E3	122
Milford, Oh., U.S.	C1	128
Milford, Pa., U.S.	D12	131
Milford, Ut., U.S.	E2	137
Milford Haven, Wales, U.K.	E4	12
Milford Lake, res., Ks., U.S.	C6	109
Milford Station, N.S., Can.	D6	87
Milḩ, Baḥr al-, res., Iraq	F10	44
Mililani Town, Hi., U.S.	g9	104
Milk, stm., N.A.	B6	92
Mil'kovo, Russia	D17	26
Milk River, Ab., Can.	E4	84
Mill, stm., Ma., U.S.	h9	114
Millard, co., Ut., U.S.	D2	137
Millau, Fr.	E8	16
Millbrae, Ca., U.S.	h8	98
Millbrook, On., Can.	C6	89
Millbrook, Al., U.S.	C3	94
Mill Brook, stm., Vt., U.S.	B5	138
Millburn, N.J., U.S.	B4	123
Millbury, Ma., U.S.	B4	114
Millbury, Oh., U.S.	e7	128
Mill City, Or., U.S.	C4	130
Mill Creek, stm., N.J., U.S.	D4	123
Mill Creek, stm., Oh., U.S.	B2	128
Mill Creek, stm., Tn., U.S.	g10	135
Millcreek, Ut., U.S.	C4	137
Mill Creek, stm., W.V., U.S.	C3	141
Mill Creek, W.V., U.S.	C5	141
Mill Creek, stm., W.V., U.S.	m13	141
Millcreek Township, Pa., U.S.	B1	131
Milledgeville, Ga., U.S.	C3	103
Milledgeville, Il., U.S.	B4	106
Millen, Ga., U.S.	D5	103
Miller, co., Ar., U.S.	D2	97
Miller, co., Mo., U.S.	C5	118
Miller, S.D., U.S.	C7	134
Miller, Mount, mtn., Ak., U.S.	C11	95
Millerovo, Russia	E7	22
Miller Peak, mtn., Az., U.S.	F5	96
Miller Run, stm., Vt., U.S.	B4	138
Millers, stm., Ma., U.S.	A3	114
Millersburg, In., U.S.	A6	107
Millersburg, Ky., U.S.	B5	110
Millersburg, Oh., U.S.	B4	128
Millersburg, Pa., U.S.	E8	131
Millersport, Oh., U.S.	C3	128

Name	Map Ref.	Page
Millersville, Pa., U.S.	F9	131
Millet, Ab., Can.	C4	84
Mill Hall, Pa., U.S.	D7	131
Millicent, Austl.	H3	62
Milliken, Co., U.S.	A6	99
Millington, Mi., U.S.	E7	115
Millington, Tn., U.S.	B2	135
Millinocket, Me., U.S.	C4	112
Millinocket Lake, l., Me., U.S.	B4	112
Millinocket Lake, l., Me., U.S.	C4	112
Millis, Ma., U.S.	B5	114
Millport, Al., U.S.	B1	94
Millry, Al., U.S.	D1	94
Mills, co., Ia., U.S.	C2	108
Mills, co., Tx., U.S.	D3	136
Mills, Wy., U.S.	D6	143
Millsboro, De., U.S.	F4	101
Millsboro, Pa., U.S.	G1	131
Millstadt, Il., U.S.	E3	106
Millstone, stm., N.J., U.S.	C4	123
Milltown, In., U.S.	H5	107
Milltown, N.J., U.S.	C4	123
Milltown, Wi., U.S.	C1	142
Milltown [-Head of Bay d'Espoir], Nf., Can.	E4	88
Millvale, Pa., U.S.	k14	131
Mill Valley, Ca., U.S.	D2	98
Millville, Ma., U.S.	B4	114
Millville, N.J., U.S.	E2	123
Millville, Pa., U.S.	D9	131
Millville, Ut., U.S.	B4	137
Millville Lake, N.H., U.S.	E4	122
Millwood, Wa., U.S.	g14	140
Millwood Lake, res., Ar., U.S.	D1	97
Milner Dam, Id., U.S.	G5	105
Milnor, N.D., U.S.	C8	127
Milo, Ia., U.S.	C4	108
Milo, Me., U.S.	C4	112
Mílos, Grc.	F10	18
Mílos, i., Grc.	F10	18
Milparinka, Austl.	F3	62
Milroy, In., U.S.	F7	107
Milroy, Pa., U.S.	E6	131
Milstead, Ga., U.S.	C3	103
Milton, On., Can.	D5	89
Milton, De., U.S.	E4	101
Milton, Fl., U.S.	u14	102
Milton, Il., U.S.	E7	107
Milton, Ma., U.S.	B5	114
Milton, N.H., U.S.	D5	122
Milton, Pa., U.S.	D8	131
Milton, Vt., U.S.	B2	138
Milton, Wa., U.S.	f11	140
Milton, Wi., U.S.	F5	142
Milton, W.V., U.S.	C2	141
Milton, Lake, l., Oh., U.S.	A4	128
Miltona, Lake, l., Mn., U.S.	D3	116
Milton-Freewater, Or., U.S.	B8	130
Milton Keynes, Eng., U.K.	D6	12
Milton Reservoir, res., Co., U.S.	A6	99
Milverton, On., Can.	D4	89
Milwaukee, Wi., U.S.	E6	142
Milwaukee, stm., Wi., U.S.	m12	142
Milwaukee, co., Wi., U.S.	E6	142
Milwaukie, Or., U.S.	B4	130
Mims, Fl., U.S.	D6	102
Min, stm., China	F8	28
Min, stm., China	D4	30
Mina, Nv., U.S.	E3	121
Mīnā' al-Aḥmadī, Kuw.	E5	42
Mīnāb, Iran	E7	42
Minahasa, pen., Indon.	C6	36
Minami-Tori-shima, i., Japan	F18	64
Minas, Ur.	E6	72
Minas Basin, b., N.S., Can.	D5	87
Minas Channel, strt., N.S., Can.	D5	87
Minas Gerais, state, Braz.	E2	74
Minatare, Ne., U.S.	C2	120
Minatitlán, Mex.	D6	78
Minbya, Mya.	B2	34
Minco, Ok., U.S.	B4	129
Mindanao, i., Phil.	E8	34
Mindanao Sea see Bohol Sea, Phil.	E8	34
Mindelo, C.V.	g10	50a
Minden, Ger.	D11	12
Minden, La., U.S.	B2	111
Minden, Ne., U.S.	D7	120
Minden, Nv., U.S.	E2	121
Minden, W.V., U.S.	D3	141
Mindoro, i., Phil.	D8	34
Mindoro Strait, strt., Phil.	D8	34
Mine Hill, N.J., U.S.	B3	123
Mineiros, Braz.	B7	72
Mineola, N.Y., U.S.	E7	125
Mineola, Tx., U.S.	C5	136
Miner, Mo., U.S.	E8	118
Miner, co., S.D., U.S.	D8	134
Mineral, co., Co., U.S.	D4	99
Mineral, co., Mt., U.S.	C1	119
Mineral, co., Nv., U.S.	E3	121
Mineral, co., W.V., U.S.	B6	141
Mineral Point, Wi., U.S.	F3	142
Mineral Springs, Ar., U.S.	D2	97
Mineral Wells, Tx., U.S.	C3	136
Minersville, Pa., U.S.	E9	131
Minersville, Ut., U.S.	E3	137
Minerva, Oh., U.S.	B4	128
Minetto, N.Y., U.S.	B4	125
Minfeng, China	D4	28
Mingãçevir, Azer.	B12	44
Mingãçevir su anbarı, res., Azer.	B12	44
Mingechaur Reservoir see Mingãçevir su anbarı, res., Azer.	B12	44
Mingenew, Austl.	F2	60
Mingo, co., W.V., U.S.	D2	141
Mingo Junction, Oh., U.S.	B5	128
Minho (Miño), stm., Eur.	G2	16
Minicoy Island, i., India	H2	40
Minidoka, co., Id., U.S.	G5	105
Minidoka Dam, Id., U.S.	G5	105
Minier, Il., U.S.	C4	106
Minisink Island, i., N.J., U.S.	A3	123
Minitonas, Mb., Can.	C1	86
Minle, China	D8	28
Minna, Nig.	E6	50
Minneapolis, Ks., U.S.	C6	109
Minneapolis, Mn., U.S.	F5	116
Minnedosa, Mb., Can.	D2	86
Minnedosa, stm., Mb., Can.	D1	86
Minnehaha, co., S.D., U.S.	D9	134
Minneola, Ks., U.S.	E3	109
Minneota, Mn., U.S.	F3	116
Minnesota, stm., Mn., U.S.	F2	116
Minnesota, state, U.S.	E4	116
Minnesota Lake, Mn., U.S.	G5	116
Minnetonka, Mn., U.S.	n12	116
Minnetonka, Lake, l., Mn., U.S.	n11	116
Minnewaska, Lake, l., Mn., U.S.	E3	116
Miño (Minho), stm., Eur.	F3	16
Minocqua, Wi., U.S.	C4	142
Minonk, Il., U.S.	C4	106
Minooka, Il., U.S.	B5	106
Minot, N.D., U.S.	A4	127
Minot Air Force Base, mil., N.D., U.S.	A4	127
Minqin, China	B1	30
Minqing, China	D4	30
Minquadale, De., U.S.	i7	101
Minsk, Bela.	B9	20
Minster, Oh., U.S.	B1	128
Mint Hill, N.C., U.S.	B2	126
Minto, N.B., Can.	C3	87
Minturn, Co., U.S.	B4	99
Minusinsk, Russia	D11	26
Minute Man National Historical Park, Ma., U.S.	g10	114
Minvoul, Gabon	C2	54
Minxian, China	E8	28
Minya see El-Minya, Egypt	E11	48
Mio, Mi., U.S.	D6	115
Mīrābād, Afg.	D8	42
Mirabel, P.Q., Can.	D3	90
Mirabella, Gulf of see Merambéllou, Kólpos, b., Grc.	G10	18
Mirador, Braz.	E11	70
Miraflores, Col.	B5	70
Miraj, India	F2	40
Miramar, Fl., U.S.	s13	102
Miramar Naval Air Station, mil., Ca., U.S.	F5	98
Miramichi Bay, b., N.B., Can.	B5	87
Miranda, stm., Braz.	B6	72
Miranda de Ebro, Spain	F5	16
Mirbāt, Oman	G6	38
Miri, Malay.	C4	36
Miria, Niger	D6	50
Mirim, Lagoa (Merín, Laguna), b., S.A.	E7	72
Mirnyj, Russia	C13	26
Mīrpur, Pak.	D10	42
Mīrpur Khās, Pak.	E9	42
Mirror Lake, l., N.H., U.S.	C4	122
Mirtóön Pélagos, Grc.	F9	18
Mirzāpur, India	D4	40
Miscouche, P.E., Can.	C6	87
Miscou Island, i., N.B., Can.	B5	87
Miscou Point, c., N.B., Can.	A5	87
Misenheimer, N.C., U.S.	B2	126
Mishan, China	B14	28
Mishawaka, In., U.S.	A5	107
Misheguk Mountain, mtn., Ak., U.S.	B7	95
Mishicot, Wi., U.S.	D6	142
Miskitos, Cayos, is., Nic.	C3	80
Miskolc, Hung.	E6	20
Misool, Pulau, i., Indon.	D8	36
Mispillion, stm., De., U.S.	E4	101
Miṣrātah, Libya	D8	48
Missaukee, co., Mi., U.S.	D5	115
Missaukee, Lake, l., Mi., U.S.	D5	115
Mission, Ks., U.S.	m16	109
Mission, S.D., U.S.	D5	134
Mission, Tx., U.S.	F3	136
Mission Range, mts., Mt., U.S.	C3	119
Mission Viejo, Ca., U.S.	n13	98
Missisquoi, stm., Vt., U.S.	B3	138
Missisquoi Bay, b., Vt., U.S.	A2	138
Mississauga, On., Can.	D5	89
Mississinewa, stm., U.S.	D7	107
Mississinewa Lake, res., In., U.S.	C6	107
Mississippi, co., Ar., U.S.	B5	97
Mississippi, co., Mo., U.S.	E8	118
Mississippi, state, U.S.	C4	117
Mississippi, stm., U.S.	E9	92
Mississippi Delta, La., U.S.	E6	111
Mississippi Sound, strt., U.S.	E5	117
Mississippi State, Ms., U.S.	B5	117
Missoula, Mt., U.S.	D2	119
Missoula, co., Mt., U.S.	D2	119
Missouri, state, U.S.	C5	118
Missouri, stm., U.S.	D9	92
Missouri City, Tx., U.S.	r14	136
Missouri Valley, Ia., U.S.	C2	108
Mistassini, P.Q., Can.	h12	90
Mistassini, Lac, l., P.Q., Can.	h12	90
Misti, Volcán, vol., Peru	G5	70
Mita, Punta de, c., Mex.	C3	78
Mitchell, stm., Austl.	D3	62
Mitchell, Austl.	F4	62
Mitchell, On., Can.	D3	89
Mitchell, co., Ga., U.S.	E2	103
Mitchell, co., Ia., U.S.	A5	108
Mitchell, Il., U.S.	E3	106
Mitchell, In., U.S.	G5	107
Mitchell, co., Ks., U.S.	C5	109
Mitchell, co., N.C., U.S.	e10	126
Mitchell, Ne., U.S.	C2	120
Mitchell, S.D., U.S.	D7	134
Mitchell, co., Tx., U.S.	C2	136
Mitchell, Lake, res., Al., U.S.	C3	94
Mitchell, Lake, l., Mi., U.S.	D5	115
Mitchell, Mount, mtn., N.C., U.S.	f10	126
Mitchell Island, i., La., U.S.	E6	111
Mitchellville, Ia., U.S.	C4	108
Mitilíni, Grc.	E11	18
Mitkof Island, i., Ak., U.S.	m23	95
Mito, Japan	C4	31
Mitsiwa see Massawa, Erit.	G12	48
Mitú, Col.	C5	70
Mitumba, Monts, mts., D.R.C.	E5	54
Mitwaba, D.R.C.	E5	54
Mitzic, Gabon	C2	54
Miyake-jima, i., Japan	E15	28
Miyako, Japan	D16	28
Miyako-jima, i., Japan	B9	34
Miyakonojō, Japan	E14	28
Miyazaki, Japan	E14	28
Miyazu, Japan	D15	28
Miyoshi, Japan	D2	31
Miyun, China	A4	30
Mizan Teferī, Eth.	B7	54
Mizdah, Libya	D7	48
Mizen Head, c., Ire.	E2	12
Mizhi, China	B3	30
Mizoram, state, India	E6	40
Mizusawa, Japan	C4	31
Mjakit, Russia	C17	26
Mjölby, Swe.	G6	10
Mjøsa, l., Nor.	F4	10
Mkalama, Tan.	D6	54
Mkokotoni, Tan.	D7	54
Mladá Boleslav, Czech Rep.	D3	20
Mlanje Peak see Sapitwa, mtn., Mwi.	B6	56
Mława, Pol.	C6	20
Mmabatho, S. Afr.	D4	56
Moab, Ut., U.S.	E6	137
Moala, i., Fiji	m10	63b
Moamba, Moz.	D5	56
Moanda, Gabon	D2	54
Moapa River Indian Reservation, Nv., U.S.	G7	121
Moba, D.R.C.	E5	54
Mobaye, C.A.R.	C4	54
Moberly, Mo., U.S.	B5	118
Mobile, Al., U.S.	E1	94
Mobile, stm., Al., U.S.	E1	94
Mobile, co., Al., U.S.	E1	94
Mobile Bay, b., Al., U.S.	E1	99
Mobridge, S.D., U.S.	B5	134
Mobutu Sese Seko, Lac see Albert, Lake, l., Afr.	C6	54
Moca, Dom. Rep.	B5	80
Mocanaqua, Pa., U.S.	D9	131
Moc Chau, Viet.	B4	34
Mocha see Al-Mukhā, Yemen	H4	38
Mochudi, Bots.	C4	56
Mocímboa da Praia, Moz.	A7	56
Mocksville, N.C., U.S.	B2	126
Moclips, Wa., U.S.	B1	140
Môco, Morro de, mtn., Ang.	F3	54
Mococa, Braz.	F4	74
Moctezuma, Mex.	B3	78
Mocuba, Moz.	B6	56
Model Reservoir, res., Co., U.S.	D6	99
Módena, Italy	B3	18
Modesto, Ca., U.S.	D3	98
Modoc, Ca., U.S.	B3	98
Modoc, co., Ca., U.S.	B3	98
Modowi, Indon.	G9	32
Moe, Austl.	H4	62
Moen-jo-Daro, hist., Pak.	E9	42
Moenkopi, Az., U.S.	A4	96
Moffat, co., Co., U.S.	A2	99
Moffat Tunnel, Co., U.S.	B5	99
Mogadishu see Muqdisho, Som.	J14	48
Mogadore, Oh., U.S.	A4	128
Mogaung, Mya.	A3	34
Mogincual, Moz.	B7	56
Mogoča, Russia	D13	26
Mogogh, Sudan	B6	54
Mogok, Mya.	B3	34
Mogollon Mountains, mts., N.M., U.S.	D1	124
Mogollon Rim, clf., Az., U.S.	C5	96
Mogotón, mtn., N.A.	F7	76
Mogzon, Russia	A10	28
Mohall, N.D., U.S.	A4	127
Mohammed, Râs, c., Egypt	F10	14
Mohave, co., Az., U.S.	B1	96
Mohave, Lake, res., U.S.	H7	121
Mohave Mountains, mts., Az., U.S.	C1	96
Mohave Valley, Az., U.S.	C1	96
Mohawk, stm., N.H., U.S.	g7	122
Mohawk, N.Y., U.S.	C5	125
Mohawk, stm., N.Y., U.S.	C6	125
Mohawk Lake, l., N.J., U.S.	A3	123
Mohawk Mountains, mts., Az., U.S.	E2	96
Mohe, China	A12	28
Mohican, stm., Oh., U.S.	B3	128
Mohns Ridge	D23	144
Mohnton, Pa., U.S.	F10	131
Mohnyin, Mya.	B3	34
Mohyliv-Podil's'kyi, Ukr.	E9	20
Mo i Rana, Nor.	C6	10
Moisie, P.Q., Can.	h8	88
Mojave, Ca., U.S.	E4	98
Mojave, stm., Ca., U.S.	E5	98
Mojave Desert, des., Ca., U.S.	E5	98
Mojo, Eth.	B7	54
Mojynty, Kaz.	E9	26
Mokapu Peninsula, pen., Hi., U.S.	g10	104
Mokapu Point, c., Hi., U.S.	g11	104
Mokelumne, stm., Ca., U.S.	C3	98
Mokena, Il., U.S.	k9	106
Mokhotlong, Leso.	D4	56
Moknine, Tun.	G3	18
Mokolo, Cam.	A2	54
Mokp'o, S. Kor.	E13	28
Moku Manu, i., Hi., U.S.	g11	104
Mola di Bari, Italy	D6	18
Molalla, Or., U.S.	B4	130
Moldavia see Moldova, ctry., Eur.	F10	20
Moldavia, hist. reg., Rom.	F9	20
Molde, Nor.	E2	10
Moldova, ctry., Eur.	F10	20
Moldoveanu, Vârful, mtn., Rom.	G8	20
Molepolole, Bots.	C4	56
Molfetta, Italy	D6	18
Moline, Il., U.S.	B3	106
Moline, Ks., U.S.	E7	109
Molino, Fl., U.S.	u14	102
Mollendo, Peru	G5	70
Molokai, i., Hi., U.S.	B5	104
Molokai Fracture Zone	F24	64
Molokini, i., Hi., U.S.	C5	104
Molopo, stm., Afr.	D3	56
Molotov see Perm', Russia	D7	26
Moloundou, Cam.	C3	54
Molson Lake, l., Mb., Can.	B3	86
Moluccas see Maluku, is., Indon.	D7	36
Molucca Sea see Maluku, Laut, Indon.	C7	36
Moma, Moz.	B6	56
Mombasa, Kenya	D7	54
Mombetsu, Japan	C16	28
Momence, Il., U.S.	B6	106
Mompós, Col.	D5	80
Momskij hrebet, mts., Russia	C16	26
Møn, i., Den.	I5	10
Monaca, Pa., U.S.	E1	131
Monaco, ctry., Eur.	C1	18
Monadnock, Mount, mtn., N.H., U.S.	E2	122
Monadnock Mountain, mtn., Vt., U.S.	B5	138
Monahans, Tx., U.S.	D1	136
Mona Passage, strt., N.A.	B6	80
Mona Quimbundo, Ang.	E3	54
Monarch Mills, S.C., U.S.	B4	133
Monarch Pass, Co., U.S.	C4	99
Monashee Mountains, mts., B.C., Can.	D8	85
Monastir, Tun.	G3	18
Monção, Braz.	D10	70
Mončegorsk, Russia	C15	10
Mönchengladbach, Ger.	E10	12
Moncks Corner, S.C., U.S.	E7	133
Monclova, Mex.	B4	78
Moncton, N.B., Can.	C5	87
Mondjamboli, D.R.C.	C4	54
Mondovi, Wi., U.S.	D2	142
Monee, Il., U.S.	B6	106
Monessen, Pa., U.S.	F2	131
Monett, Mo., U.S.	E4	118
Monette, Ar., U.S.	B5	97
Monfalcone, Italy	B4	18
Monforte de Lemos, Spain	F3	16
Mongalla, Sudan	B6	54
Möng Hpãyak, Mya.	B3	34
Möng Hsat, Mya.	B3	34
Mongo, Chad	D8	50
Mongol Altayn nuruu, mts., Asia	B6	28
Mongolia, ctry., Asia	B8	28
Mongonu, Nig.	D7	50
Mongu, Zam.	B3	56
Monhegan Island, i., Me., U.S.	E3	112
Monida Pass, U.S.	E6	105
Moniteau, co., Mo., U.S.	C5	118
Monitor Range, mts., Nv., U.S.	E5	121
Monitor Valley, val., Nv., U.S.	D5	121
Monmouth, Il., U.S.	C3	106
Monmouth, co., N.J., U.S.	C4	123
Monmouth, Or., U.S.	C3	130
Monmouth Beach, N.J., U.S.	C5	123
Monmouth Mountain, mtn., B.C., Can.	D6	85
Mono, co., Ca., U.S.	D4	98
Monocacy, stm., Md., U.S.	B3	113
Mono Lake, l., Ca., U.S.	D4	98
Monomonac, Lake, l., U.S.	E3	122
Monomoy Island, i., Ma., U.S.	C7	114
Monomoy Point, c., Ma., U.S.	C7	114
Monon, In., U.S.	C4	107
Monona, Ia., U.S.	A6	108
Monona, co., Ia., U.S.	B1	108
Monona, Wi., U.S.	E4	142
Monona, Lake, l., Wi., U.S.	E4	142
Monongah, W.V., U.S.	B4	141
Monongahela, Pa., U.S.	F2	131
Monongahela, stm., U.S.	G2	131
Monongalia, co., W.V., U.S.	B4	141
Monopoli, Italy	D6	18
Monor, Hung.	F5	20
Monroe, co., Al., U.S.	D2	94
Monroe, co., Ar., U.S.	C4	97
Monroe, co., Fl., U.S.	G5	102
Monroe, Ga., U.S.	C3	103
Monroe, co., Ga., U.S.	D3	103
Monroe, Ia., U.S.	C4	108
Monroe, co., Ia., U.S.	C5	108
Monroe, co., Il., U.S.	E3	106
Monroe, In., U.S.	C8	107
Monroe, co., In., U.S.	F4	107
Monroe, co., Ky., U.S.	D4	110
Monroe, La., U.S.	B3	111
Monroe, Mi., U.S.	G7	115
Monroe, co., Mi., U.S.	G7	115
Monroe, co., Mo., U.S.	B5	118
Monroe, co., Ms., U.S.	B5	117
Monroe, N.C., U.S.	C2	126
Monroe, N.Y., U.S.	D6	125
Monroe, co., N.Y., U.S.	B3	125
Monroe, Oh., U.S.	C1	128
Monroe, co., Oh., U.S.	C4	128
Monroe, co., Pa., U.S.	D11	131
Monroe, Ut., U.S.	E3	137
Monroe, Wa., U.S.	B4	140
Monroe, Wi., U.S.	F4	142
Monroe, co., Wi., U.S.	E3	142
Monroe, co., W.V., U.S.	D4	141
Monroe Center, Ct., U.S.	D3	100
Monroe City, Mo., U.S.	B6	118
Monroe Lake, res., In., U.S.	F5	107
Monroe Park, De., U.S.	h7	101
Monroeville, Al., U.S.	D2	94
Monroeville, In., U.S.	C8	107
Monroeville, Oh., U.S.	A3	128
Monroeville, Pa., U.S.	k14	131
Monrovia, Lib.	E2	50
Monrovia, Ca., U.S.	m13	98
Monrovia, In., U.S.	E5	107
Monson, Ma., U.S.	B3	114
Mönsterås, Swe.	H7	10
Montague, Mi., U.S.	E4	115
Montague, co., Tx., U.S.	C4	136
Montague Island, i., Ak., U.S.	D10	95
Montague Peak, mtn., Ak., U.S.	g18	95
Montague Strait, strt., Ak., U.S.	h18	95
Mont Alto, Pa., U.S.	G6	131
Montana, Blg.	C9	18
Montana, state, U.S.	D7	119
Montargis, Fr.	C8	16
Montauban, Fr.	E7	16
Montauk, N.Y., U.S.	m17	125
Montbard, Fr.	D9	16
Montbéliard, Fr.	D10	16
Montblanc, Spain	G7	16
Montcalm, co., Mi., U.S.	E5	115
Montceau-les-Mines, Fr.	D9	16
Montchanin, De., U.S.	h7	101
Montclair, Ca., U.S.	m13	98
Montclair, N.J., U.S.	B4	123
Mont Clare, Pa., U.S.	o19	131
Mont-de-Marsan, Fr.	E6	16
Monteagle, Tn., U.S.	D8	135
Monte Alegre, Braz.	D8	70
Monte Azul, Braz.	E3	74
Montebello, P.Q., Can.	D3	90
Montebello, Ca., U.S.	m12	98
Montecarlo, Arg.	D7	72
Monte Caseros, Arg.	E6	72
Monte Comán, Arg.	E4	72
Montecristo, Isola di, i., Italy	C3	18
Montego Bay, Jam.	B4	80
Montegut, La., U.S.	E5	111

Name	Map Ref.	Page
Montélimar, Fr.	E9	16
Montello, Nv., U.S.	B7	121
Montello, Wi., U.S.	E4	142
Montemorelos, Mex.	B5	78
Montenegro see Crna Gora, state, Yugo.	C7	18
Monte Patria, Chile	E3	72
Montepuez, Moz.	A6	56
Montepulciano, Italy	C3	18
Monte Quemado, Arg.	D5	72
Monterey, Ca., U.S.	D3	98
Monterey, Tn., U.S.	C8	135
Monterey, co., Ca., U.S.	D3	98
Monterey Bay, b., Ca., U.S.	D2	98
Monterey Park, Ca., U.S.	m12	98
Montería, Col.	B4	70
Montero, Bol.	B5	72
Monterrey, Mex.	B4	78
Montesano, Wa., U.S.	C2	140
Montes Claros, Braz.	E3	74
Montevallo, Al., U.S.	B3	94
Montevideo, Mn., U.S.	F3	116
Montevideo, Ur.	E6	72
Monte Vista, Co., U.S.	D4	99
Montezuma, Ga., U.S.	D2	103
Montezuma, Ia., U.S.	C5	108
Montezuma, In., U.S.	E3	107
Montezuma, Ks., U.S.	E3	109
Montezuma, co., Co., U.S.	D2	99
Montezuma Castle National Monument, Az., U.S.	C4	96
Montezuma Peak, mtn., Az., U.S.	D3	96
Montgomery see Sāhīwāl, Pak.	D10	42
Montgomery, Al., U.S.	C3	94
Montgomery, Il., U.S.	B5	106
Montgomery, La., U.S.	C3	111
Montgomery, Mn., U.S.	F5	116
Montgomery, N.Y., U.S.	D6	125
Montgomery, Oh., U.S.	o13	128
Montgomery, Pa., U.S.	D8	131
Montgomery, W.V., U.S.	C3	141
Montgomery, co., Al., U.S.	C3	94
Montgomery, co., Ar., U.S.	C2	97
Montgomery, co., Ga., U.S.	D4	103
Montgomery, co., Ia., U.S.	C2	108
Montgomery, co., Il., U.S.	D4	106
Montgomery, co., In., U.S.	D4	107
Montgomery, co., Ks., U.S.	E8	109
Montgomery, co., Ky., U.S.	B6	110
Montgomery, co., Md., U.S.	B3	113
Montgomery, co., Mo., U.S.	C6	118
Montgomery, co., Ms., U.S.	B4	117
Montgomery, co., N.C., U.S.	B3	126
Montgomery, co., N.Y., U.S.	C6	125
Montgomery, co., Oh., U.S.	C1	128
Montgomery, co., Pa., U.S.	F11	131
Montgomery, co., Tn., U.S.	A4	135
Montgomery, co., Tx., U.S.	D5	136
Montgomery, co., Va., U.S.	C2	139
Montgomery City, Mo., U.S.	C6	118
Monticello, Ar., U.S.	D4	97
Monticello, Fl., U.S.	B3	102
Monticello, Ga., U.S.	C3	103
Monticello, Ia., U.S.	B6	108
Monticello, Il., U.S.	C5	106
Monticello, In., U.S.	C4	107
Monticello, Ky., U.S.	D5	110
Monticello, Mn., U.S.	E5	116
Monticello, Ms., U.S.	D3	117
Monticello, N.Y., U.S.	D6	125
Monticello, Ut., U.S.	F6	137
Monticello, Wi., U.S.	F4	142
Mont-Joli, P.Q., Can.	A9	90
Mont-Laurier, P.Q., Can.	C2	90
Montmagny, P.Q., Can.	C7	90
Montmorenci, S.C., U.S.	D4	133
Montmorency, co., Mi., U.S.	C6	115
Monto, Austl.	E5	62
Montoro, Spain	H4	16
Montour, co., Pa., U.S.	D8	131
Montour Falls, N.Y., U.S.	C4	125
Montoursville, Pa., U.S.	D8	131
Montpelier, Id., U.S.	G7	105
Montpelier, In., U.S.	C7	107
Montpelier, Oh., U.S.	A1	128
Montpelier, Vt., U.S.	C3	138
Montpellier, Fr.	F8	16
Montréal, P.Q., Can.	D4	90
Montreal, Wi., U.S.	B3	142
Montréal, Île de, i., P.Q., Can.	q19	90
Montreal Lake, l., Sk., Can.	C3	91
Montréal-Nord, P.Q., Can.	p19	90
Montreat, N.C., U.S.	f10	126
Montreux, Switz.	A1	18
Mont-Rolland, P.Q., Can.	D3	90
Montrose, B.C., Can.	E9	85
Montrose, Scot., U.K.	B5	12
Montrose, Al., U.S.	E2	94
Montrose, Co., U.S.	C3	99
Montrose, Ia., U.S.	D6	108
Montrose, Mi., U.S.	E7	115
Montrose, Pa., U.S.	C10	131
Montrose, Va., U.S.	m18	139
Montrose, co., Co., U.S.	C2	99
Mont-Royal, P.Q., Can.	p19	90
Mont-Saint-Michel, Le, Fr.	C6	16
Montserrat, dep., N.A.	E12	76
Montserrat, Monasterio de, Spain	G7	16
Mont-Tremblant, Parc Provincial du, P.Q., Can.	C3	90
Montvale, N.J., U.S.	A4	123
Montville, Ct., U.S.	D7	100
Monument, Co., U.S.	B6	99
Monument Beach, Ma., U.S.	C6	114
Monument Peak, mtn., Co., U.S.	B3	99
Monument Peak, mtn., Id., U.S.	G4	105
Monument Valley, val., Az., U.S.	A5	96
Monywa, Myan.	B2	34
Monza, Italy	B2	18
Monze, Zam.	B4	56
Monzón, Spain	G7	16
Moodus, Ct., U.S.	D6	100
Moodus Reservoir, res., Ct., U.S.	C6	100
Moody, Tx., U.S.	D4	136
Moody, co., S.D., U.S.	C9	134
Moon Lake, l., Ms., U.S.	A3	117
Moora, Austl.	G2	60
Moorcroft, Wy., U.S.	B8	143
Moore, Ok., U.S.	B4	129
Moore, co., N.C., U.S.	B3	126
Moore, co., Tn., U.S.	B5	135
Moore, co., Tx., U.S.	B2	136
Moore, Lake, l., Austl.	F2	60
Moore Dam, U.S.	B3	122
Moorefield, W.V., U.S.	B6	141
Moore Haven, Fl., U.S.	F5	102
Mooreland, Ok., U.S.	A2	129
Moore Reservoir, res., U.S.	B3	122
Moores Creek National Military Park, N.C., U.S.	C4	126
Moores Hill, In., U.S.	F7	107
Moorestown, N.J., U.S.	D3	123
Mooresville, In., U.S.	E5	107
Mooresville, N.C., U.S.	B2	126
Moorhead, Mn., U.S.	D2	116
Moorhead, Ms., U.S.	B3	117
Mooringsport, La., U.S.	B2	111
Moorreesburg, S. Afr.	E2	56
Moose, stm., N.H., U.S.	B4	122
Moose, stm., N.Y., U.S.	B5	125
Moose, stm., Vt., U.S.	B5	138
Moosehead Lake, l., Me., U.S.	C3	112
Moose Jaw, Sk., Can.	G3	91
Moose Lake, Mb., Can.	C1	86
Moose Lake, Mn., U.S.	D6	116
Moose Lake, l., Wi., U.S.	B2	142
Mooseleuk Stream, stm., Me., U.S.	B4	112
Mooselookmeguntic Lake, l., Me., U.S.	D2	112
Moose Mountain Creek, stm., Sk., Can.	H4	91
Moose Mountain Provincial Park, Sk., Can.	H4	91
Moosic, Pa., U.S.	m18	131
Moosup, Ct., U.S.	C8	100
Moosup, stm., U.S.	C1	132
Mopang Lake, l., Me., U.S.	D5	112
Mopti, Mali	D4	50
Moquegua, Peru	G5	70
Mora, Cam.	D7	50
Mora, Spain	H5	16
Mora, Swe.	F6	10
Mora, Mn., U.S.	E5	116
Mora, N.M., U.S.	A4	124
Mora, co., N.M., U.S.	A5	124
Mora, stm., N.M., U.S.	B5	124
Morādābād, India	D3	40
Morafenobe, Madag.	B7	56
Moramanga, Madag.	B8	56
Morant Cays, is., Jam.	B4	80
Moratuwa, Sri L.	H3	40
Morava, hist. reg., Czech Rep.	E4	20
Moravia, Ia., U.S.	D5	108
Morawa, Austl.	F2	60
Morawhanna, Guy.	B8	70
Moray Firth, b., Scot., U.K.	B5	12
Morbi, India	I2	40
Morden, Mb., Can.	E2	86
Mordovia see Mordovija, state, Russia	D6	26
Mordovija, state, Russia	D6	26
Mordvinia see Mordovija, state, Russia	D6	26
Moreau, stm., S.D., U.S.	B3	134
Moreauville, La., U.S.	C4	111
Morecambe Bay, b., Eng., U.K.	D5	12
Moree, Austl.	F4	62
Morehead, Ky., U.S.	B6	110
Morehead City, N.C., U.S.	C6	126
Morehouse, Mo., U.S.	E8	118
Morehouse, co., La., U.S.	B4	111
Morelia, Mex.	D4	78
Morelos, state, Mex.	D5	78
Morena, Sierra, mts., Spain	H4	16
Morenci, Az., U.S.	D6	96
Morenci, Mi., U.S.	G6	115
Moresby Island, i., B.C., Can.	C2	85
Moreton Island, i., Austl.	F5	62
Morey, Lake, l., Vt., U.S.	D4	138
Morey Peak, mtn., Nv., U.S.	E5	121
Morgan, Mn., U.S.	F4	116
Morgan, Ut., U.S.	B4	137
Morgan, co., Al., U.S.	A3	94
Morgan, co., Co., U.S.	A7	99
Morgan, co., Ga., U.S.	C3	103
Morgan, co., Il., U.S.	D3	106
Morgan, co., In., U.S.	F5	107
Morgan, co., Ky., U.S.	C6	110
Morgan, co., Mo., U.S.	C5	118
Morgan, co., Oh., U.S.	C4	128
Morgan, co., Tn., U.S.	C9	135
Morgan, co., Ut., U.S.	B4	137
Morgan, co., W.V., U.S.	B6	141
Morgan City, La., U.S.	E4	111
Morganfield, Ky., U.S.	C2	110
Morgan Hill, Ca., U.S.	D3	98
Morgan Island, i., S.C., U.S.	G6	133
Morgan Point, c., Ct., U.S.	E4	100
Morganton, N.C., U.S.	B1	126
Morgantown, In., U.S.	F5	107
Morgantown, Ky., U.S.	C3	110
Morgantown, Ms., U.S.	D2	117
Morgantown, Tn., U.S.	D8	135
Morgantown, W.V., U.S.	B5	141
Morganza, La., U.S.	D4	111
Morghāb (Murgab), stm., Asia	C8	42
Moriah, Mount, mtn., Nv., U.S.	D7	121
Moriarty, N.M., U.S.	C3	124
Moriki, Nig.	D6	50
Morinville, Ab., Can.	C4	84
Morioka, Japan	D16	28
Morlaix, Fr.	C5	16
Morley, Mo., U.S.	D8	118
Mormon Peak, mtn., Nv., U.S.	G7	121
Morning Sun, Ia., U.S.	C6	108
Mornington Island, i., Austl.	D2	62
Morobe, Pap. N. Gui.	H12	32
Morocco, In., U.S.	C3	107
Morocco, ctry., Afr.	D3	48
Morogoro, Tan.	E7	54
Moro Gulf, b., Phil.	E8	34
Morombe, Madag.	C7	56
Morón, Arg.	E6	72
Morón, Cuba	A4	80
Mörön, Mong.	B8	28
Morondava, Madag.	C7	56
Morón de la Frontera, Spain	I4	16
Moroni, Com.	A7	56
Moroni, Ut., U.S.	D4	137
Morotai, i., Indon.	C7	36
Moroto, Ug.	C6	54
Morozovsk, Russia	E7	22
Morrill, Ne., U.S.	C2	120
Morrill, co., Ne., U.S.	C2	120
Morrilton, Ar., U.S.	B3	97
Morrinhos, Braz.	E2	74
Morris, Mb., Can.	E3	86
Morris, Al., U.S.	B3	94
Morris, Il., U.S.	B5	106
Morris, Mn., U.S.	E3	116
Morris, Ok., U.S.	B6	129
Morris, co., Ks., U.S.	D7	109
Morris, co., N.J., U.S.	B3	123
Morris, co., Tx., U.S.	C5	136
Morrisburg, On., Can.	C9	89
Morris Island, i., S.C., U.S.	F8	133
Morris Jesup, Kap, c., Grnld.	B33	82
Morrison, Il., U.S.	B4	106
Morrison, Ok., U.S.	A4	129
Morrison, co., Mn., U.S.	D4	116
Morrison City, Tn., U.S.	C11	135
Morrisonville, Il., U.S.	D4	106
Morrisonville, N.Y., U.S.	f11	125
Morris Plains, N.J., U.S.	B4	123
Morristown, In., U.S.	E6	107
Morristown, Mn., U.S.	F5	116
Morristown, N.J., U.S.	B4	123
Morristown, Tn., U.S.	C10	135
Morristown National Historical Park, N.J., U.S.	B3	123
Morrisville, N.Y., U.S.	C5	125
Morrisville, Pa., U.S.	F12	131
Morrisville, Vt., U.S.	B3	138
Morro Bay, Ca., U.S.	E3	98
Morro do Chapéu, Braz.	D3	74
Morrow, Oh., U.S.	C1	128
Morrow, co., Oh., U.S.	B3	128
Morrow, co., Or., U.S.	B7	130
Morrumbala, Moz.	B6	56
Morrumbene, Moz.	C6	56
Moršansk, Russia	D7	22
Morse Reservoir, res., In., U.S.	D5	107
Morses Creek, stm., N.J., U.S.	k8	123
Mortes, stm., Braz.	F9	70
Morton, Il., U.S.	C4	106
Morton, Ms., U.S.	C4	117
Morton, Tx., U.S.	C1	136
Morton, Wa., U.S.	C3	140
Morton, co., Ks., U.S.	E2	109
Morton, co., N.D., U.S.	C4	127
Morton Grove, Il., U.S.	h9	106
Morton Pass, Wy., U.S.	E7	143
Mortons Gap, Ky., U.S.	C2	110
Morwell, Austl.	H4	62
Moscow see Moskva, Russia	D5	26
Moscow, Id., U.S.	C2	105
Moscow, Pa., U.S.	m18	131
Moscow Mills, Mo., U.S.	C7	118
Mosel (Moselle), stm., Eur.	B10	16
Moselle, Ms., U.S.	D4	117
Moselle (Mosel), stm., Eur.	C10	16
Moses Coulee, val., Wa., U.S.	B6	140
Moses Lake, Wa., U.S.	B6	140
Moses Lake, l., Wa., U.S.	B6	140
Mosheim, Tn., U.S.	C11	135
Moshi, Tan.	D7	54
Mosinee, Wi., U.S.	D4	142
Mosjøen, Nor.	D5	10
Moskva (Moscow), Russia	D5	26
Mosqueiro, Braz.	B2	74
Mosquera, Col.	C4	70
Mosquito Creek Lake, res., Oh., U.S.	A5	128
Mosquito Lagoon, b., Fl., U.S.	D6	102
Mosquitos, Golfo de los, b., Pan.	D3	80
Moss, Nor.	G4	10
Mossaka, Congo	D3	54
Moss Bluff, La., U.S.	D2	111
Mosselbaai, S. Afr.	E3	56
Mossman, Austl.	D4	62
Mossoró, Braz.	C4	74
Moss Point, Ms., U.S.	E5	117
Most, Czech Rep.	D2	20
Mostar, Bos.	C6	18
Møsting, Kap, c., Grnld.	F32	82
Mosul see Al-Mawṣil, Iraq	C4	42
Møsvatnet, l., Nor.	G3	10
Moswansicut Pond, l., R.I., U.S.	C3	132
Mot'a, Eth.	A7	54
Motagua, stm., N.A.	B2	80
Motala, Swe.	G6	10
Motherwell, Scot., U.K.	C5	12
Motley, co., Tx., U.S.	B2	136
Motril, Spain	I5	16
Mott, N.D., U.S.	C3	127
Motueka, N.Z.	p13	63c
Motyklejka, Russia	D16	26
Mouaskar, Alg.	D4	14
Moudjéria, Maur.	C2	50
Mouila, Gabon	D2	54
Moulins, Fr.	D8	16
Moulouya, Oued, stm., Mor.	D4	48
Moulton, Al., U.S.	A2	94
Moulton, Ia., U.S.	D5	108
Moultrie, Ga., U.S.	E3	103
Moultrie, co., Il., U.S.	D5	106
Moultrie, Lake, res., S.C., U.S.	E7	133
Mounana, Gabon	D2	54
Mound, Mn., U.S.	n11	116
Mound Bayou, Ms., U.S.	B3	117
Mound City, Il., U.S.	F4	106
Mound City, Ks., U.S.	D9	109
Mound City, Mo., U.S.	A2	118
Mound City Group National Monument, Oh., U.S.	C2	128
Moundou, Chad	E8	50
Moundridge, Ks., U.S.	D6	109
Mounds, Il., U.S.	F4	106
Mounds, Ok., U.S.	B5	129
Mounds View, Mn., U.S.	m12	116
Moundsville, W.V., U.S.	B4	141
Moundville, Al., U.S.	C2	94
Mountainair, N.M., U.S.	C3	124
Mountainaire, Az., U.S.	B4	96
Mountain Brook, Al., U.S.	g7	94
Mountain City, Ga., U.S.	B3	103
Mountain City, Nv., U.S.	B6	121
Mountain City, Tn., U.S.	C12	135
Mountain Fork, stm., U.S.	C7	129
Mountain Grove, Mo., U.S.	D5	118
Mountain Home, Ar., U.S.	A3	97
Mountain Home, Id., U.S.	F3	105
Mountain Home Air Force Base, mil., Id., U.S.	F3	105
Mountain Iron, Mn., U.S.	C6	116
Mountain Lake, Mn., U.S.	G4	116
Mountain Lake Park, Md., U.S.	m12	113
Mountain Nile see Jabal, Baḥr al-, stm., Sudan	I11	48
Mountain Pine, Ar., U.S.	C2	97
Mountainside, N.J., U.S.	B4	123
Mountain View, Ar., U.S.	B3	97
Mountain View, Ca., U.S.	k8	98
Mountain View, Mo., U.S.	D6	118
Mountain View, N.M., U.S.	C3	124
Mountain View, Ok., U.S.	B3	129
Mountain Village, Ak., U.S.	C7	95
Mount Airy, Md., U.S.	B3	113
Mount Airy, N.C., U.S.	A2	126
Mount Albert, On., Can.	C5	89
Mount Angel, Or., U.S.	B4	130
Mount Arlington, N.J., U.S.	B3	123
Mount Augustus, Austl.	E2	60
Mount Ayr, Ia., U.S.	D3	108
Mount Barker, Austl.	G2	60
Mount Carmel, Il., U.S.	E6	106
Mount Carmel, Oh., U.S.	o13	128
Mount Carmel [-Mitchell's Brook-Saint Catherine's], Nf., Can.	E5	88
Mount Carroll, Il., U.S.	A4	106
Mount Clare, W.V., U.S.	B4	141
Mount Clemens, Mi., U.S.	F8	115
Mount Desert Island, i., Me., U.S.	D4	112
Mount Dora, Fl., U.S.	D5	102
Mount Forest, On., Can.	D4	89
Mount Gambier, Austl.	H3	62
Mount Gay, W.V., U.S.	D2	141
Mount Gilead, N.C., U.S.	B3	126
Mount Gilead, Oh., U.S.	B3	128
Mount Hagen, Pap. N. Gui.	H11	32
Mount Healthy, Oh., U.S.	o12	128
Mount Holly, N.C., U.S.	B1	126
Mount Holly, N.J., U.S.	D3	123
Mount Holly Springs, Pa., U.S.	F7	131
Mount Hope, Ks., U.S.	E6	109
Mount Hope, W.V., U.S.	D3	141
Mount Hope, stm., Ct., U.S.	B7	100
Mount Hope Bay, b., U.S.	D6	132
Mount Horeb, Wi., U.S.	E4	142
Mount Ida, Ar., U.S.	C2	97
Mount Isa, Austl.	E2	62
Mount Jackson, Va., U.S.	B4	139
Mount Jewett, Pa., U.S.	C4	131
Mount Joy, Pa., U.S.	F9	131
Mount Juliet, Tn., U.S.	A5	135
Mount Kisco, N.Y., U.S.	D7	125
Mount Lebanon, Pa., U.S.	F1	131
Mount Magnet, Austl.	F2	60
Mount Morris, Il., U.S.	A4	106
Mount Morris, Mi., U.S.	E7	115
Mount Morris, N.Y., U.S.	C3	125
Mount Olive, Al., U.S.	B3	94
Mount Olive, Il., U.S.	D4	106
Mount Olive, Ms., U.S.	D4	117
Mount Olive, N.C., U.S.	B4	126
Mount Olive, Tn., U.S.	n14	135
Mount Orab, Oh., U.S.	C2	128
Mount Pearl, Nf., Can.	E5	88
Mount Penn, Pa., U.S.	F10	131
Mount Pleasant, Ia., U.S.	D6	108
Mount Pleasant, Mi., U.S.	E6	115
Mount Pleasant, N.C., U.S.	B2	126
Mount Pleasant, Pa., U.S.	F2	131
Mount Pleasant, S.C., U.S.	F8	133
Mount Pleasant, Tn., U.S.	B4	135
Mount Pleasant, Tx., U.S.	C5	136
Mount Pleasant, Ut., U.S.	D4	137
Mount Pocono, Pa., U.S.	D11	131
Mount Prospect, Il., U.S.	A6	106
Mount Pulaski, Il., U.S.	C4	106
Mountrail, co., N.D., U.S.	A3	127
Mount Rainier, Md., U.S.	f9	113
Mount Rainier National Park, Wa., U.S.	C4	140
Mount Revelstoke National Park, B.C., Can.	D8	85
Mount Riddock, Austl.	E5	60
Mount Rogers National Recreation Area, Va., U.S.	D1	139
Mount Roskill, N.Z.	o13	63c
Mount Rushmore National Memorial, hist., S.D., U.S.	D2	134
Mount Savage, Md., U.S.	k13	113
Mount Shasta, Ca., U.S.	B2	98
Mount Sterling, Il., U.S.	D3	106
Mount Sterling, Ky., U.S.	B6	110
Mount Sterling, Oh., U.S.	C2	128
Mount Uniacke, N.S., Can.	E6	87
Mount Union, Pa., U.S.	F6	131
Mount Vernon, Austl.	E2	60
Mount Vernon, Al., U.S.	D1	94
Mount Vernon, Ga., U.S.	D4	103
Mount Vernon, Ia., U.S.	C6	108
Mount Vernon, Il., U.S.	E5	106
Mount Vernon, In., U.S.	I2	107
Mount Vernon, Ky., U.S.	C5	110
Mount Vernon, Mo., U.S.	D4	118
Mount Vernon, N.Y., U.S.	h13	125
Mount Vernon, Oh., U.S.	B3	128
Mount Vernon, Tx., U.S.	C5	136
Mount Vernon, Wa., U.S.	A3	140
Mount View, R.I., U.S.	D4	132
Mount Washington, Ky., U.S.	B4	110
Mount Wolf, Pa., U.S.	F8	131
Mount Zion, Il., U.S.	D5	106
Moura, Braz.	D7	70
Moussa 'Ali, mtn., Afr.	H4	38
Moussoro, Chad	D8	50
Moutong, Indon.	C6	36
Moville, Ia., U.S.	B1	108
Moweaqua, Il., U.S.	D4	106
Mower, co., Mn., U.S.	G6	116
Moxee City, Wa., U.S.	C5	140
Moyale, Kenya	C7	54
Moyamba, S.L.	E2	50
Moyen Atlas, mts., Mor.	E3	14
Moyo, Pulau, i., Indon.	E5	36
Moyobamba, Peru	E4	70
Moyock, N.C., U.S.	A6	126
Moyu, China	B3	40
Mozambique, ctry., Afr.	B5	56
Mozambique Channel, strt., Afr.	B7	56
Mozambique Plateau	L6	64
Mozdok, Russia	B4	42
Mpala, D.R.C.	E5	54
Mpanda, Tan.	E6	54
Mpika, Zam.	A5	56
Mporokoso, Zam.	E6	54
Mpulungu, Zam.	E6	54
Mpwapwa, Tan.	E7	54
M'Sila, Alg.	J9	16
Mtubatuba, S. Afr.	D5	56
Mtwara, Tan.	F8	54

Name	Map Ref.	Page
Muanda, D.R.C.	E2	54
Muang Hôngsa, Laos	C4	34
Muang Khammouan, Laos	C4	34
Muang Khôngxédôn, Laos	C5	34
Muang Không, Laos	D5	34
Muang Ngoy, Laos	B4	34
Muang Pak-Lay, Laos	C4	34
Muang Pakxan, Laos	C4	34
Muang Phalan, Laos	C5	34
Muang Sing, Laos	B4	34
Muang Thadua, Laos	C4	34
Muang Vangviang, Laos	C4	34
Muang Xaignabouri, Laos	C4	34
Muar, Malay.	C2	36
Muaraenim, Indon.	D2	36
Muarasiberut, Indon.	G2	32
Mubende, Ug.	C6	54
Mubi, Nig.	D7	50
Muchinga Mountains, mts., Zam.	A5	56
Muckleshoot Indian Reservation, Wa., U.S.	f11	140
Mucojo, Moz.	A7	56
Muconda, Ang.	F4	54
Mucujê, Braz.	F11	70
Mud, stm., Ky., U.S.	C3	110
Mud, stm., Mn., U.S.	B3	116
Mud, stm., W.V., U.S.	C2	141
Mudanjiang, China	C13	28
Mud Creek, stm., Ok., U.S.	C4	129
Muddy Boggy Creek, stm., Ok., U.S.	C6	129
Muddy Creek, stm., Ut., U.S.	E4	137
Muddy Creek, stm., Wy., U.S.	C4	143
Muddy Creek, stm., Wy., U.S.	E5	143
Muddy Creek, stm., Wy., U.S.	E2	143
Muddy Creek, stm., Wy., U.S.	D6	143
Muddy Mountains, mts., Nv., U.S.	G7	121
Muddy Peak, mtn., Nv., U.S.	G7	121
Mudgee, Austl.	G4	62
Mud Lake, l., Me., U.S.	A4	112
Mud Lake, l., Nv., U.S.	F4	121
Mueda, Moz.	A6	56
Muenster, Tx., U.S.	C4	136
Mufulira, Zam.	A4	56
Muğla, Tur.	D3	44
Muhlenberg, co., Ky., U.S.	C2	110
Mühlhausen, Ger.	E12	12
Muhu, i., Est.	G10	10
Muié, Ang.	A3	56
Muirkirk, Md., U.S.	B4	113
Muir Woods National Monument, Ca., U.S.	h7	98
Muja, Russia	D13	26
Mujnak, Uzb.	B7	42
Mukacheve, Ukr.	E7	20
Mukah, Malay.	C4	36
Mukden see Shenyang, China	C12	28
Mukilteo, Wa., U.S.	B3	140
Mukinbudin, Austl.	G2	60
Mukomuk, Indon.	D2	36
Mukry, Turk.	C9	42
Mukwonago, Wi., U.S.	F5	142
Mula, Spain	H6	16
Mulberry, Ar., U.S.	B1	97
Mulberry, Fl., U.S.	E4	102
Mulberry, In., U.S.	D4	107
Mulberry, N.C., U.S.	A1	126
Mulberry, stm., Ar., U.S.	B1	97
Mulberry Fork, stm., Al., U.S.	B3	94
Muldraugh, Ky., U.S.	C4	110
Muldrow, Ok., U.S.	B7	129
Muleshoe, Tx., U.S.	B1	136
Mulgrave, N.S., Can.	D8	87
Mulhacén, mtn., Spain	I5	16
Mulhouse, Fr.	D10	16
Mull, Island of, i., Scot., U.K.	B3	12
Mullan, Id., U.S.	B3	105
Mullan Pass, Mt., U.S.	D4	119
Mullens, W.V., U.S.	D3	141
Muller, Pegunungan, mts., Indon.	C4	36
Mullet Key, i., Fl., U.S.	p10	102
Mullett Lake, l., Mi., U.S.	C6	115
Mullewa, Austl.	F2	60
Mullica, stm., N.J., U.S.	D3	123
Mullins, S.C., U.S.	C9	133
Mulongo, D.R.C.	E5	54
Multan, Pak.	D10	42
Multnomah, co., Or., U.S.	B4	130
Mulvane, Ks., U.S.	E6	109
Mumbai (Bombay), India	F2	40
Mumbwa, Zam.	A4	56
Mummy Range, mts., Co., U.S.	A5	99
Mun, stm., Thai.	C4	34
Muna, Mex.	C7	78
Muna, Pulau, i., Indon.	D6	36
München (Munich), Ger.	F12	12
Muncie, In., U.S.	D7	107
Muncy, Pa., U.S.	D8	131
Munday, Tx., U.S.	C3	136
Mundelein, Il., U.S.	A5	106
Münden, Ger.	E11	12
Mundrabilla, Austl.	G4	60
Munford, Al., U.S.	B4	94
Munford, Tn., U.S.	B2	135
Munfordville, Ky., U.S.	C4	110
Mungbere, D.R.C.	C5	54
Munger, India	D5	40
Munhall, Pa., U.S.	k14	131
Munhango, Ang.	F3	54
Munich see München, Ger.	F12	12
Munising, Mi., U.S.	B4	115
Münster, Ger.	E10	12
Munster, In., U.S.	A2	107
Munster, hist. reg., Ire.	D2	12
Munsungan Lake, l., Me., U.S.	B3	112
Muntok, Indon.	D3	36
Munuscong Lake, l., Mi., U.S.	B6	115
Muojärvi, l., Fin.	D13	10
Muonio, Fin.	C10	10
Muqdisho, Som.	J14	48
Mur (Mura), stm., Eur.	F3	20
Mura (Mur), stm., Eur.	F4	20
Muradiye, Tur.	C10	44
Murakami, Japan	C3	31
Murana, Indon.	D8	36
Muraši, Russia	C8	22
Murat, stm., Tur.	C9	44
Murchison, stm., Austl.	F1	60
Murchison Falls see Kabalega Falls, wtfl, Ug.	C6	54
Murcia, Spain	I6	16
Murderkill, stm., De., U.S.	D4	101
Murdo, S.D., U.S.	D5	134
Mureş, stm., Eur.	G7	20
Muret, Fr.	F7	16
Murewa, Zimb.	B5	56
Murfreesboro, Ar., U.S.	C2	97
Murfreesboro, N.C., U.S.	A5	126
Murfreesboro, Tn., U.S.	B5	135
Murgab, Taj.	F9	26
Murgab (Morghāb), stm., Asia	C8	42
Muriaé, Braz.	F3	74
Müritz, l., Ger.	D13	12
Murmansk, Russia	C5	26
Murom, Russia	D6	26
Muroran, Japan	C16	28
Muroto, Japan	D2	31
Murphy, Mo., U.S.	g13	118
Murphy, N.C., U.S.	f8	126
Murphy Island, i., S.C., U.S.	E9	133
Murphysboro, Il., U.S.	F4	106
Murray, Ia., U.S.	C4	108
Murray, Ky., U.S.	f9	110
Murray, Ut., U.S.	C4	137
Murray, co., Ga., U.S.	B2	103
Murray, co., Mn., U.S.	F3	116
Murray, co., Ok., U.S.	C4	129
Murray, stm., Austl.	H3	62
Murray, Lake, l., Pap. N. Gui.	H11	32
Murray, Lake, res., Ok., U.S.	C4	129
Murray, Lake, res., S.C., U.S.	C5	133
Murray Bridge, Austl.	H2	62
Murray Fracture Zone	E24	64
Murray Head, c., P.E., Can.	C7	87
Murraysburg, S. Afr.	E3	56
Murrayville, Ga., U.S.	B3	103
Murree, Pak.	C2	40
Murrells Inlet, S.C., U.S.	D9	133
Murrells Inlet, b., S.C., U.S.	D10	133
Murrumbidgee, stm., Austl.	G4	62
Murrupula, Moz.	B6	56
Mursala, Pulau, i., Indon.	C1	36
Murua Island, i., Pap. N. Gui.	H13	32
Murud, Gunong, mtn., Malay.	C5	36
Murukta, Russia	C12	26
Murwāra, India	E4	40
Murwillumbah, Austl.	F5	62
Murzuq, Libya	E7	48
Murzūq, Idhān, des., Libya.	B7	48
Muş, Tur.	C9	44
Musa Ālī Terara see Moussa 'Ali, mtn., Afr.	H4	38
Musa'id, Libya	E9	14
Musala, Bul.	C9	18
Musan-ŭp, N. Kor.	B1	31
Musay'īd, Qatar	F6	42
Muscat see Masqaṭ, Oman	F7	38
Muscat and Oman see Oman, ctry., Asia	G7	38
Muscatatuck, stm., In., U.S.	G5	107
Muscatine, Ia., U.S.	C6	108
Muscatine, co., Ia., U.S.	C6	108
Muscle Shoals, Al., U.S.	A2	94
Musclow, Mount, mtn., B.C., Can.	C4	85
Muscoda, Wi., U.S.	E3	142
Muscogee, co., Ga., U.S.	D2	103
Musconetcong, stm., N.J., U.S.	B4	123
Muscooten Bay, l., Il., U.S.	C3	106
Muse, Pa., U.S.	F1	131
Musgrave Harbour, Nf., Can.	D5	88
Musgravetown, Nf., Can.	D5	88
Mushie, D.R.C.	D3	54
Mushin, Nig.	E5	50
Musi, stm., Indon.	D2	36
Musicians Seamounts	E22	64
Muskeg Bay, b., Mn., U.S.	B3	116
Muskeget Island, i., Ma., U.S.	D7	114
Muskego, Wi., U.S.	F5	142
Muskego Lake, l., Wi., U.S.	n11	142
Muskegon, Mi., U.S.	E4	115
Muskegon, co., Mi., U.S.	E4	115
Muskegon, stm., Mi., U.S.	E4	115
Muskegon Heights, Mi., U.S.	E4	115
Muskegon Lake, l., Mi., U.S.	E4	115
Muskingum, co., Oh., U.S.	B4	128
Muskingum, stm., Oh., U.S.	C4	128
Muskogee, Ok., U.S.	B6	129
Muskogee, co., Ok., U.S.	B6	129
Musoma, Tan.	D6	54
Musquacook Lakes, l., Me., U.S.	B3	112
Musquodoboit Harbour, N.S., Can.	E6	87
Mussau Island, i., Pap. N. Gui.	G12	32
Musselshell, co., Mt., U.S.	D8	119
Musselshell, stm., Mt., U.S.	D9	119
Mussende, Ang.	F3	54
Mussuma, Ang.	A3	56
Mustafakemalpaşa, Tur.	C3	44
Mustahīl, Eth.	B8	54
Mustang, Ok., U.S.	B4	129
Mustinka, stm., Mn., U.S.	E2	116
Muswellbrook, Austl.	G5	62
Mut, Tur.	D5	44
Mutare, Zimb.	B5	56
Mutoraj, Russia	C12	26
Mutsamudu, Com.	A7	56
Mutshatsha, D.R.C.	F4	54
Mutsu, Japan	C16	28
Mutsu-wan, b., Japan	A16	31
Mutton Mountains, mts., Or., U.S.	C5	130
Muxima, Ang.	E2	54
Muyinga, Bdi.	D6	54
Muyumba, D.R.C.	E5	54
Muzaffarābād, Pak.	D10	42
Muzaffargarh, Pak.	D10	42
Muzaffarnagar, India	D3	40
Muzaffarpur, India	D5	40
Muži, Russia	C8	26
Muzon, Cape, c., Ak., U.S.	n23	95
Muztag, mtn., China	D5	28
Mvuma, Zimb.	B5	56
Mvumba, Zimb.	C5	56
Mweka, D.R.C.	D4	54
Mwene-Ditu, D.R.C.	E4	54
Mwenezi, Zimb.	C5	56
Mweru, Lake, l., Afr.	E5	54
Mwinilunga, Zam.	A3	56
Myakka, stm., Fl., U.S.	E4	102
Myanaung, Myan.	C3	34
Myanmar (Burma), ctry., Asia	B3	34
Myaungmya, Myan.	C2	34
Myerstown, Pa., U.S.	F9	131
Myingyan, Myan.	B3	34
Myitkyinā, Myan.	A3	34
Myittha, Myan.	B3	34
Mykolaïv, Ukr.	F11	20
Mymensingh, Bngl.	E6	40
Mynaral, Kaz.	A10	42
Mýrdalsjökull, Ice.	m19	10a
Myrhorod, Ukr.	E12	20
Myrtle Beach, S.C., U.S.	D10	133
Myrtle Grove, Fl., U.S.	u14	102
Myrtle Point, Or., U.S.	D2	130
Mysore, India	G3	40
Mysore see Karnātaka, prov., India	G3	40
Mystic, Ct., U.S.	D8	100
Mystic Lakes, l., Ma., U.S.	g11	114
Mys Vhodnoj, Russia	B10	26
Mys Želanija, Russia	B8	26
Myszków, Pol.	D5	20
My Tho, Viet.	D5	34
Mzimba, Mwi.	A5	56
Mzuzu, Mwi.	A5	56

N

Name	Map Ref.	Page
Naalehu, Hi., U.S.	D6	104
Naberežnye Čelny, Russia	D7	26
Nabeul, Tun.	C7	48
Nabire, Indon.	G10	32
Nabī Shu'ayb, Jabal an-, mtn., Yemen	G4	38
Nabnasset, Ma., U.S.	A5	114
Nābulus, W.B.	F6	44
Nacala-a-Velha, Moz.	A7	56
Naches, stm., Wa., U.S.	C5	140
Nachingwea, Tan.	F7	54
Náchod, Czech Rep.	D4	20
Nachuge, India	G6	40
Nacimiento, Lake, res., Ca., U.S.	E3	98
Naco, Az., U.S.	F6	96
Nacogdoches, Tx., U.S.	D5	136
Nacogdoches, co., Tx., U.S.	D5	136
Nacozari de García, Mex.	A3	78
Nadiād, India	I4	40
Nador, Mor.	J5	16
Nadvirna, Ukr.	E8	20
Nadym, Russia	C9	26
Næstved, Den.	I4	10
Nafada, Nig.	D7	50
Nafī, Sau. Ar.	E4	42
Naga, Phil.	D8	34
Nāgāland, prov., India	D6	40
Nagano, Japan	D15	28
Nagaoka, Japan	D15	28
Nagaon, India	D6	40
Nāgappattinam, India	G3	40
Nagasaki, Japan	E13	28
Nāgaur, India	D2	40
Nagda, India	E3	40
Nāgercoil, India	H3	40
Nago, Japan	A9	34
Nagoya, Japan	D15	28
Nāgpur, India	E3	40
Nagqu, China	E6	28
Nags Head, N.C., U.S.	B7	126
Nagykanizsa, Hung.	F4	20
Nahant, Ma., U.S.	g12	114
Nahāvand, Iran	E13	44
Nahe, China	B12	28
Nahmakanta Lake, l., Me., U.S.	C3	112
Nahodka, Russia	E15	26
Nahunta, Ga., U.S.	E5	103
Nain, Nf., Can.	g9	88
Nairobi, Kenya	D7	54
Naivasha, Kenya	D7	54
Najafābād, Iran	D6	42
Najd, hist. reg., Sau. Ar.	E4	38
Nájera, Spain	F5	16
Najin, N. Kor.	C14	28
Nakano-shima, i., Japan	E1	31
Nakhichevan see Naxçıvan, Azer.	C11	44
Nakhon Pathom, Thai.	D4	34
Nakhon Phanom, Thai.	C4	34
Nakhon Ratchasima, Thai.	D4	34
Nakhon Sawan, Thai.	C4	34
Nakhon Si Thammarat, Thai.	E3	34
Nakina, On., Can.	o18	89
Nakło nad Notecią, Pol.	C4	20
Naknek, Ak., U.S.	D8	95
Naknek Lake, l., Ak., U.S.	D8	95
Nakonde, Zam.	E6	54
Nakskov, Den.	I4	10
Nakuru, Kenya	D7	54
Nakusp, B.C., Can.	D9	85
Nal'čik, Russia	E6	26
Nalgonda, India	F3	40
Nallıhan, Tur.	B4	44
Nālūt, Libya	D7	48
Namak, daryācheh-ye, l., Iran	D6	42
Namanga, Kenya	D7	54
Namangan, Uzb.	E9	26
Namanock Island, i., N.J., U.S.	A3	123
Namapa, Moz.	A6	56
Namarrói, Moz.	B6	56
Namatanai, Pap. N. Gui.	E9	58
Nambour, Austl.	F5	62
Namekagon, stm., Wi., U.S.	B2	142
Namekagon Lake, l., Wi., U.S.	B2	142
Namen see Namur, Bel.	E9	12
Nametil, Moz.	B6	56
Namhkam, Myan.	B3	34
Namib Desert, des., Nmb.	B1	56
Namibe, Ang.	B1	56
Namibia, ctry., Afr.	C2	56
Namin, Iran	C13	44
Namjagbarwa Feng, mtn., China	F7	28
Namlea, Indon.	D7	36
Nam Ngum Reservoir, res., Laos	C4	34
Nampa, Id., U.S.	F2	105
Nampula, Moz.	B6	56
Namsang, Myan.	B3	34
Namsos, Nor.	D4	10
Namtu, Myan.	B3	34
Namur, Bel.	E9	12
Namutoni, Nmb.	B2	56
Namwala, Zam.	A4	56
Nan, Thai.	C4	34
Nanaimo, B.C., Can.	E5	85
Nanakuli, Hi., U.S.	B3	104
Nanao, Japan	D15	28
Nance, co., Ne., U.S.	C7	120
Nancha, China	A1	31
Nancheng, China	D4	30
Nanchang, China	D4	30
Nanchong, China	E9	28
Nancy, Fr.	C10	16
Nanda Devi, mtn., India	C3	40
Nānded, India	F3	40
Nandurbār, India	E2	40
Nandyāl, India	F3	40
Nanfeng, China	D4	30
Nanga-Eboko, Cam.	C2	54
Nanga Parbat, mtn., Pak.	C10	42
Nangatayap, Indon.	D4	36
Nangong, China	B4	30
Nanjing, China	E11	28
Nankang, China	D3	30
Nanking see Nanjing China	E11	28
Nanle, China	B4	30
Nannine, Austl.	F2	60
Nanning, China	G9	28
Nannup, Austl.	G2	60
Nanping, China	F11	28
Nansei-shotō (Ryukyu Islands), is., Japan	A9	34
Nansemond, stm., Va., U.S.	k14	139
Nansen Basin	E21	144
Nansen Cordillera	E22	144
Nan Shan see Qilian Shan, mts., China	D7	28
Nantes, Fr.	D6	16
Nanticoke, On., Can.	E4	89
Nanticoke, Pa., U.S.	D10	131
Nanticoke, stm., U.S.	D6	113
Nanton, Ab., Can.	D4	84
Nantong, China	E12	28
Nantucket, Ma., U.S.	D7	114
Nantucket, co., Ma., U.S.	D7	114
Nantucket Island, i., Ma., U.S.	D7	114
Nantucket Sound, strt., Ma., U.S.	C7	114
Nantulo, Moz.	A6	56
Nantuxent Point, c., N.J., U.S.	E2	123
Nanty Glo, Pa., U.S.	F4	131
Nanuet, N.Y., U.S.	g12	125
Nanuque, Braz.	E3	74
Nanusa, Kepulauan, is., Indon.	C7	36
Nanxiong, China	F10	28
Nanyang, China	E10	28
Nanyuki, Kenya	C7	54
Nanzhao, China	C3	30
Naoma, W.V., U.S.	n13	141
Naomi Peak, mtn., Ut., U.S.	B4	137
Napa, Ca., U.S.	C2	98
Napa, co., Ca., U.S.	C2	98
Napanee, On., Can.	C8	89
Napatree Point, c., R.I., U.S.	G1	132
Napavine, Wa., U.S.	C3	140
Napè, Laos	C5	34
Naperville, Il., U.S.	B5	106
Napier, N.Z.	o14	63c
Napier Mountains, mts., Ant.	C10	67
Napierville, P.Q., Can.	D4	90
Naples see Napoli, Italy	D5	18
Naples, Fl., U.S.	F5	102
Naples, Tx., U.S.	C5	136
Naples, Ut., U.S.	C6	137
Napo, stm., S.A.	D5	70
Napoleon, N.D., U.S.	C6	127
Napoleon, Oh., U.S.	A1	128
Napoleonville, La., U.S.	E4	111
Napoli (Naples), Italy	D5	18
Napoli, Golfo di, b., Italy	D5	18
Nappanee, In., U.S.	B5	107
Naqādeh, Iran	D11	44
Nara, Japan	E15	28
Nara, Mali	C3	50
Naracoorte, Austl.	H3	62
Naramata, B.C., Can.	E8	85
Naranja, Fl., U.S.	G6	102
Narasapur, India	F4	40
Narathiwat, Thai.	E4	34
Nārāyanganj, Bngl.	E6	40
Narberth, Pa., U.S.	p20	131
Narbonne, Fr.	F8	16
Nar'jan-Mar, Russia	C7	26
Narmada, stm., India	E2	40
Nārnaul, India	D3	40
Narodnaja, gora, hills, Russia	C8	26
Naro-Fominsk, Russia	B14	20
Narooma, Austl.	H5	62
Narragansett, R.I., U.S.	F4	132
Narragansett Bay, b., R.I., U.S.	E5	132
Narraguagus, stm., Me., U.S.	D5	112
Narrandera, Austl.	G4	62
Narrogin, Austl.	G2	60
Narromine, Austl.	G4	62
Narrows, Va., U.S.	C2	139
Narsaq, Grnld.	F30	82
Narva, Est.	G13	10
Narvik, Nor.	B7	10
Naryn, Kyrg.	E9	26
Naryn, stm., Asia	A3	40
Narynkol, Kaz.	C4	28
Näsåker, Swe.	E7	10
Nasca, Peru	F5	70
Naselle, Wa., U.S.	C2	140
Nash, Tx., U.S.	C5	136
Nash, co., N.C., U.S.	A4	126
Nashawena Island, i., Ma., U.S.		
Nāshik, India	E2	40
Nash Stream, stm., N.H., U.S.	A4	122
Nashua, Ia., U.S.	B5	108
Nashua, N.H., U.S.	E3	122
Nashua, stm., U.S.	E3	122
Nashville, Ar., U.S.	D2	97
Nashville, Ga., U.S.	E3	103
Nashville, Il., U.S.	E4	106
Nashville, In., U.S.	F5	107
Nashville, Mi., U.S.	F5	115
Nashville, N.C., U.S.	B5	126
Nashville, Tn., U.S.	A5	135
Nashwauk, Mn., U.S.	C5	116
Nāsir, Sudan	I11	48
Nasīrābād, India	D2	40
Nasīrābād, Pak.	E9	42
Naskaupi, stm., Nf., Can.	g9	88
Nassau, Bah.	D9	76
Nassau, co., Fl., U.S.	B5	102
Nassau, co., N.Y., U.S.	E7	125
Nassau, stm., Fl., U.S.	k8	102

Name	Map Ref.	Page

Nassau Island, i., Cook Is. . . .F13 58
Nassau Sound, b., Fl., U.S. . .B5 102
Nasser, Lake, res., Afr. F11 48
Nässjö, Swe. H6 10
Nasukoin Mountain, mtn., Mt., U.S. B2 119
Nata, Bots. C4 56
Natal, Braz. C4 74
Natalbany, La., U.S. D5 111
Natalia, Tx., U.S. E3 136
Natashquan, stm., Can. h9 88
Natchaug, stm., Ct., U.S. B7 100
Natchez, Ms., U.S. D2 117
Natchitoches, La., U.S. C2 111
Natchitoches, co., La., U.S. . .C2 111
Natick, Ma., U.S. B5 114
National City, Ca., U.S. F5 98
Natitingou, Benin D5 50
Natividade, Braz. F10 70
Natron, Lake, l., Afr. D7 54
Natrona, co., Wy., U.S. D5 143
Natrona Heights, Pa., U.S. . . .E2 131
Natuna Besar, i., Indon. C3 36
Natuna Besar, Kepulauan, is., Indon. C3 36
Natuna Selatan, Kepulauan, is., Indon. C3 36
Natural Bridge, Ut., U.S. F3 137
Natural Bridge, Va., U.S. C3 139
Natural Bridges National Monument, Ut., U.S. F6 137
Naturaliste, Cape, c., Austl. . .G1 60
Nau, Cap de la, c., Spain . . .H7 16
Naugatuck, Ct., U.S. D3 100
Naugatuck, stm., Ct., U.S. . . .D3 100
Nauru, ctry., Oc. E10 58
Naushon Island, i., Ma., U.S. D6 114
Nautilus Park, Ct., U.S. D7 100
Nautla, Mex. C5 78
Nauvoo, Il., U.S. C2 106
Navadwip, India E5 40
Navahrudak, Bela. C8 20
Navajo, co., Az., U.S. B5 96
Navajo Dam, N.M., U.S. A2 124
Navajo Indian Reservation, U.S. A4 96
Navajo Mountain, mtn., Ut., U.S. F5 137
Navajo National Monument, Az., U.S. A5 96
Navajo Reservoir, res., U.S. .A2 124
Navan, On., Can. B9 89
Navapolack, Bela. B10 20
Navarin, mys, c., Russia C19 26
Navarino, Isla, i., Chile I3 69
Navarra, hist. reg., Spain . . .F6 16
Navarre, Oh., U.S. B4 128
Navarro, co., Tx., U.S. D4 136
Navasota, Tx., U.S. D4 136
Navassa Island, i., N.A. B4 80
Navlja, Russia C13 20
Navoi, Uzb. E8 26
Navojoa, Mex. B3 78
Navsāri, India E2 40
Nawābshāh, Pak. E9 42
Nawiliwili Bay, b., Hi., U.S. . .B2 104
Naxçıvan, Azer. C11 44
Naxi, China D2 30
Náxos, Grc. F10 18
Náxos, i., Grc. F10 18
Nayarit, state, Mex. C4 78
Naylor, Mo., U.S. E7 118
Nayoro, Japan C16 28
Nazaré, Braz. D4 74
Nazaré, Port. H2 16
Nazareth see Nazerat, Isr. . . .D3 42
Nazareth, Pa., U.S. E11 131
Nazas, stm., Mex. B4 78
Nazas, Mex. B4 78
Nazca Ridge K5 66
Naze, Japan F13 28
Naze, The see Lindesnes, c., Nor. H2 10
Nazerat, Isr. D3 42
Nazilli, Tur. D3 44
Nazko, stm., B.C., Can. C6 85
Nazran', Russia A11 44
Nazrēt, Eth. B7 54
Nazwá, Oman F7 42
N'dalatando, Ang. E2 54
Ndélé, C.A.R. B4 54
Ndendé, Gabon D2 54
N'Djamena, Chad D8 50
Ndjolé, Gabon D2 54
Ndola, Zam. A4 56
Neagh, Lough, l., N. Ire., U.K. C3 12
Neah Bay, Wa., U.S. A1 140
Néa Páfos, Cyp. E5 44
Neápolis, Grc. F9 18
Near Islands, is., Ak., U.S. . . .E2 95
Nebitdag, Turk. F7 26
Neblina, Pico da, mtn., S.A. . .C6 70
Nebo, Mount, mtn., Ut., U.S. D4 137
Nebraska, state, U.S. C6 120
Nebraska City, Ne., U.S. D10 120
Nechako, stm., B.C., Can. . . .C5 85
Neches, stm., Tx., U.S. D5 136
Necker Island, i., Hi., U.S. . . .m15 104
Necochea, Arg. F6 72
Nederland, Co., U.S. B5 99
Nederland, Tx., U.S. E6 136
Nêdong, China F6 28
Nédroma, Alg. J6 16

Nedrow, N.Y., U.S. C4 125
Needham, Ma., U.S. g11 114
Needle Mountain, mtn., Wy., U.S. B3 143
Needles, Ca., U.S. E6 98
Needville, Tx., U.S. r14 136
Neenah, Wi., U.S. D5 142
Neepawa, Mb., Can. D2 86
Neffs, Oh., U.S. B5 128
Neffsville, Pa., U.S. F9 131
Neftçala, Azer. C13 44
Negage, Ang. E3 54
Negaunee, Mi., U.S. B3 115
Negēlē, Eth. B7 54
Negley, Oh., U.S. B5 128
Negombo, Sri L. H3 40
Negritos, Peru D3 70
Negro, stm., Arg. F4 69
Negro, stm., S.A. D7 70
Negros, i., Phil. E8 34
Neguac, N.B., Can. B4 87
Nehalem, stm., Or., U.S. A3 130
Nehbandān, Iran D7 42
Neiges, Piton des, mtn., Reu. g10 57a
Neijiang, China D2 30
Neill Point, c., Wa., U.S. f11 140
Neillsville, Wi., U.S. D3 142
Nei Monggol Zizhiqu (Inner Mongolia), prov., China .C10 28
Neisse see Nysa, Pol. D4 20
Neiva, Col. C4 70
Nejd see Najd, hist. reg., Sau. Ar. E4 38
Nek'emtē, Eth. B7 54
Nekoosa, Wi., U.S. D4 142
Nelidovo, Russia C5 22
Neligh, Ne., U.S. B7 120
Nel'kan, Russia D15 26
Nellis Air Force Base, mil., Nv., U.S. G6 121
Nellore, India G4 40
Nel'ma, Russia E15 26
Nelson, B.C., Can. E9 85
Nelson, stm., Mb., Can. A4 86
Nelson, N.Z. p13 63c
Nelson, co., Ky., U.S. C4 110
Nelson, co., N.D., U.S. B7 127
Nelson, Ne., U.S. D7 120
Nelson, co., Va., U.S. C4 139
Nelson, Cape, c., Austl. H3 62
Nelsonville, Oh., U.S. C3 128
Nelspruit, S. Afr. D5 56
Néma, Maur. C3 50
Nemacolin, Pa., U.S. G2 131
Nemadji, stm., U.S. B1 142
Nemaha, stm., Ks., U.S. C7 109
Nemaha, co., Ne., U.S. D10 120
Neman (Nemunas), stm., Eur. B7 20
Nembe, Nig. F6 50
Nemunas (Neman), stm., Eur. B7 20
Nemuro, Japan C17 28
Nenana, Ak., U.S. C10 95
Nendo, i., Sol. Is. F10 58
Neodesha, Ks., U.S. E8 109
Neoga, Il., U.S. D5 106
Neola, Ia., U.S. C2 108
Neola, Ut., U.S. C5 137
Neopit, Wi., U.S. D5 142
Neosho, co., Ks., U.S. E8 109
Neosho, Mo., U.S. E3 118
Neosho, stm., Ok., U.S. A6 129
Nepal, ctry., Asia D4 40
Nepālgañj, Nepal D4 40
Nepaug Reservoir, res., Ct., U.S. B3 100
Nepean, On., Can. h12 89
Nepewassi Lake, l., On., Can. A4 89
Nephi, Ut., U.S. D4 137
Nepisiguit, stm., N.B., Can. . .B3 87
Nepisiguit Bay, b., N.B., Can. B4 87
Neponset, stm., Ma., U.S. . . .h11 114
Neptune, N.J., U.S. C4 123
Neptune Beach, Fl., U.S. B5 102
Neptune City, N.J., U.S. C4 123
Nerčinsk, Russia A11 28
Nerčinskij Zavod, Russia D13 26
Nerehta, Russia C7 22
Neriquinha, Ang. B3 56
Nescopeck, Pa., U.S. D9 131
Neshanic, stm., N.J., U.S. C3 123
Neshoba, co., Ms., U.S. C4 117
Neskaupstadur, Ice. l22 10a
Nesna, Nor. C5 10
Nesowadnehunk, l., Me., U.S. B3 112
Nesquehoning, Pa., U.S. E10 131
Ness, co., Ks., U.S. D4 109
Ness, Loch, l., Scot., U.K. B4 12
Ness City, Ks., U.S. D4 109
Néstos, stm., Eur. D10 18
Netanya, Isr. D2 42
Netcong, N.J., U.S. B3 123
Netherlands, ctry., Eur. D9 12
Netherlands Antilles, dep., N.A. F11 76
Netherlands Guiana see Suriname, ctry., S.A. C8 70
Nettie, W.V., U.S. C4 141
Nett Lake, l., Mn., U.S. B5 116
Nett Lake Indian Reservation, Mn., U.S. B6 116

Nettleton, Ms., U.S. A5 117
Neubrandenburg, Ger. D13 12
Neuchâtel, Switz. A1 18
Neuchâtel, Lac de, l., Switz. .A1 18
Neufchâtel-en-Bray, Fr. C7 16
Neumarkt in der Oberpfalz, Ger. F12 12
Neumünster, Ger. C12 12
Neuquén, Arg. E3 69
Neuruppin, Ger. D13 12
Neuse, stm., N.C., U.S. B6 126
Neustrelitz, Ger. D13 12
Neuville, P.Q., Can. C6 90
Nevada, co., Ar., U.S. D2 97
Nevada, co., Ca., U.S. C3 98
Nevada, Ia., U.S. B4 108
Nevada, Mo., U.S. D3 118
Nevada, state, U.S. D5 121
Nevada, Sierra, mts., Ca., U.S. D4 98
Nevada City, Ca., U.S. C3 98
Nevado, Cerro, mtn., Arg. . . .F4 72
Nevado, Cerro, mtn., Col. C5 70
Nevel', Russia A10 22
Nevel'sk, Russia E16 26
Never, Russia D14 26
Nevers, Fr. D8 16
Neversink, stm., N.Y., U.S. . . .D6 125
Nevinnomyssk, Russia B4 42
Nevis, i., St. K./N. B7 80
Nevis, Ben, mtn., Scot., U.K. B4 12
Nevjansk, Russia C11 22
Nevşehir, Tur. C6 44
New, stm., Az., U.S. k8 96
New, stm., N.C., U.S. C5 126
New, stm., U.S. C3 141
Newala, Tan. F7 54
New Albany, In., U.S. H6 107
New Albany, Ms., U.S. A4 117
New Albany, Oh., U.S. k11 128
New Amsterdam, Guy. B8 70
Newark, Ar., U.S. B4 97
Newark, Ca., U.S. h8 98
Newark, De., U.S. B3 101
Newark, Il., U.S. B5 106
Newark, N.J., U.S. B4 123
Newark, N.Y., U.S. B3 125
Newark, Oh., U.S. B3 128
Newark Bay, b., N.J., U.S. . . .k8 123
Newark Lake, l., Nv., U.S. . . .D6 121
New Athens, Il., U.S. E4 106
New Augusta, Ms., U.S. D4 117
Newaygo, Mi., U.S. E5 115
Newaygo, co., Mi., U.S. E5 115
New Baden, Il., U.S. E4 106
New Baltimore, Mi., U.S. F8 115
New Bedford, Ma., U.S. C6 114
New Bedford, Pa., U.S. D1 131
Newberg, Or., U.S. B4 130
New Berlin, Il., U.S. D4 106
New Berlin, Wi., U.S. n11 142
New Bern, N.C., U.S. B5 126
Newbern, Tn., U.S. A2 135
Newberry, Fl., U.S. C4 102
Newberry, Mi., U.S. B5 115
Newberry, S.C., U.S. C4 133
Newberry, co., S.C., U.S. C4 133
New Bethlehem, Pa., U.S. . . .D3 131
New Bloomfield, Pa., U.S. . . .F7 131
New Boston, Mi., U.S. p15 115
New Boston, Oh., U.S. D3 128
New Boston, Tx., U.S. C5 136
New Braunfels, Tx., U.S. E3 136
New Brighton, Mn., U.S. m12 116
New Brighton, Pa., U.S. E1 131
New Britain, i., Pap. N. Gui. .H13 32
New Britain, Ct., U.S. C4 100
New Brockton, Al., U.S. D4 94
New Brunswick, prov., Can. . .C3 87
New Brunswick, N.J., U.S. C4 123
New Buffalo, Mi., U.S. G4 115
Newburg, Wi., U.S. E5 142
Newburgh, On., Can. C8 89
Newburgh, In., U.S. I3 107
Newburgh, N.Y., U.S. D6 125
Newburgh Heights, Oh., U.S. h9 128
Newburyport, Ma., U.S. A6 114
New Caledonia, dep., Oc. . . .I9 62a
New Caledonia Basin K19 64
New Canaan, Ct., U.S. E2 100
New Carlisle, In., U.S. A4 107
New Carlisle, Oh., U.S. C1 128
Newcastle, Austl. F9 62
Newcastle, N.B., Can. C4 87
Newcastle, On., Can. D6 89
Newcastle, S. Afr. D5 56
New Castle, Al., U.S. B3 94
New Castle, co., De., U.S. B3 101
New Castle, De., U.S. B3 101
New Castle, In., U.S. E7 107
New Castle, Ky., U.S. B4 110
New Castle, Ok., U.S. B4 129
New Castle, Pa., U.S. D1 131
New Castle, Wy., U.S. C8 143
Newcastle Waters, Austl. D5 60
Newcastle upon Tyne, Eng., U.K. C6 12
New City, N.Y., U.S. D6 125
Newcomerstown, Oh., U.S. . .B4 128
New Concord, Oh., U.S. C4 128
New Cumberland, Pa., U.S. F8 131

New Cumberland, W.V., U.S. A4 141
Newdegate, Austl. G2 60
New Delhi, India D3 40
Newell, Ia., U.S. B2 108
Newell, S.D., U.S. C2 134
Newell, W.V., U.S. A4 141
New Ellenton, S.C., U.S. E4 133
Newellton, La., U.S. B4 111
New England, N.D., U.S. C3 127
Newenham, Cape, c., Ak., U.S. D7 95
New Fairfield, Ct., U.S. D2 100
Newfane, N.Y., U.S. B2 125
Newfields, N.H., U.S. D5 122
New Florence, Mo., U.S. C6 118
Newfound Gap, U.S. f9 126
Newfound Lake, l., N.H., U.S. C3 122
Newfoundland, i., Nf., Can. .D3 88
Newfoundland and Labrador, prov., Can. D4 88
Newfoundland Basin D9 66
New Franklin, Mo., U.S. B5 118
New Freedom, Pa., U.S. G8 131
New Georgia Sound, strt., Sol. Is. B6 62
New Germany, N.S., Can. E5 87
New Glarus, Wi., U.S. F4 142
New Guinea, i. G11 32
New Hampshire, state, U.S. . .C3 122
New Hampton, Ia., U.S. A5 108
New Hanover, i., Pap. N. Gui. G13 32
New Hanover, co., N.C., U.S. C5 126
New Harbour, Nf., Can. E5 88
New Harmony, In., U.S. H2 107
New Hartford, Ct., U.S. B4 100
New Hartford, Ia., U.S. B5 108
New Haven, Ct., U.S. D4 100
New Haven, co., Ct., U.S. D4 100
New Haven, In., U.S. B7 107
New Haven, Ky., U.S. C4 110
New Haven, Mi., U.S. F8 115
New Haven, Mo., U.S. C6 118
New Haven, stm., Vt., U.S. . . .C2 138
New Haven, W.V., U.S. C3 141
New Haven Harbor, b., Ct., U.S. E4 100
New Hazelton, B.C., Can. B4 85
New Hebrides, ctry., Oc. F10 58
New Hebrides, is., Vanuatu .F10 58
New Hebrides Trench K19 64
New Holland, Ga., U.S. B3 103
New Holland, Pa., U.S. F9 131
New Holstein, Wi., U.S. E5 142
New Hope, Al., U.S. A3 94
New Hope, Ky., U.S. C4 110
New Hope, Mn., U.S. m12 116
New Hope, Pa., U.S. F12 131
New Hudson, Mi., U.S. o14 115
New Iberia, La., U.S. D4 111
Newington, Ct., U.S. C5 100
New Inlet, b., N.C., U.S. D5 126
New Ireland, i., Pap. N. Gui. G13 32
New Jersey, state, U.S. C4 123
New Johnsonville, Tn., U.S. . .A4 135
New Kensington, Pa., U.S. . . .E2 131
New Kent, co., Va., U.S. C5 139
Newkirk, Ok., U.S. A4 129
New Kowloon see Xinjiulong, China E3 30
New Laguna, N.M., U.S. B2 124
New Lake, l., N.C., U.S. B6 126
New Lenox, Il., U.S. B6 106
New Lexington, Oh., U.S. C3 128
New Liskeard, On., Can. p20 89
Newllano, La., U.S. C2 111
New London, Ct., U.S. D7 100
New London, co., Ct., U.S. . . .C7 100
New London, Ia., U.S. D6 108
New London, Mn., U.S. E4 116
New London, Mo., U.S. B6 118
New London, N.H., U.S. D3 122
New London, Oh., U.S. A3 128
New London, Wi., U.S. D5 142
New London Submarine Base, mil., Ct., U.S. D7 100
New Madison, Oh., U.S. C1 128
New Madrid, Mo., U.S. E8 118
New Madrid, co., Mo., U.S. . . .E8 118
Newman, Austl. E2 60
Newman, Ca., U.S. D3 98
Newman, Il., U.S. D6 106
New Manchester, W.V., U.S. e8 141
Newman Grove, Ne., U.S. . . .C8 120
Newman Lake, l., Wa., U.S. . .B8 140
Newmanstown, Pa., U.S. F9 131
Newmarket, On., Can. C5 89
New Market, Al., U.S. A3 94
New Market, In., U.S. E4 107
Newmarket, N.H., U.S. D5 122
New Market, Tn., U.S. C10 135
New Martinsville, W.V., U.S. B4 141
New Matamoras, Oh., U.S. . . .C4 128
New Mexico, state, U.S. C3 124
New Miami, Oh., U.S. C1 128
New Milford, Ct., U.S. C2 100
New Milford, N.J., U.S. h8 123

New Milford, Pa., U.S. C10 131
Newnan, Ga., U.S. C2 103
Newnans Lake, l., Fl., U.S. . . .C4 102
New Norfolk, Austl. I4 62
New Orleans, La., U.S. E5 111
New Orleans Naval Air Station, mil., La., U.S. . . .k11 111
New Oxford, Pa., U.S. G7 131
New Palestine, In., U.S. E6 107
New Paltz, N.Y., U.S. D6 125
New Paris, In., U.S. B6 107
New Paris, Oh., U.S. C1 128
New Philadelphia, Oh., U.S. B4 128
New Philadelphia, Pa., U.S. . .E9 131
New Plymouth, N.Z. o13 63c
New Plymouth, Id., U.S. F2 105
New Point Comfort, c., Va., U.S. C6 139
Newport, Wales, U.K. E5 12
Newport, Ar., U.S. B4 97
Newport, De., U.S. B3 101
Newport, In., U.S. E3 107
Newport, Ky., U.S. A5 110
Newport, Me., U.S. D3 112
Newport, Mi., U.S. G7 115
Newport, Mn., U.S. n13 116
Newport, N.C., U.S. C6 126
Newport, N.H., U.S. D2 122
Newport, Oh., U.S. C4 128
Newport, Or., U.S. C2 130
Newport, Pa., U.S. F7 131
Newport, R.I., U.S. F5 132
Newport, co., R.I., U.S. E5 132
Newport, Tn., U.S. D10 135
Newport, Vt., U.S. B4 138
Newport, Wa., U.S. A8 140
Newport Beach, Ca., U.S. n13 98
Newport News, Va., U.S. C6 139
New Port Richey, Fl., U.S. D4 102
New Prague, Mn., U.S. F5 116
New Preston, Ct., U.S. C2 100
New Providence, i., Bah. C9 76
New Providence, N.J., U.S. . . .B4 123
New Richland, Mn., U.S. G5 116
New Richmond, P.Q., Can. . . .A4 87
New Richmond, Oh., U.S. D1 128
New Richmond, Wi., U.S. C1 142
New River Inlet, b., N.C., U.S. C5 126
New Roads, La., U.S. D4 111
New Rochelle, N.Y., U.S. E7 125
New Rockford, N.D., U.S. B6 127
Newry, N. Ire., U.K. C3 12
New Salem, N.D., U.S. C4 127
New Sarpy, La., U.S. k11 111
New Schwabenland, reg., Ant. D5 67
New Sharon, Ia., U.S. C5 108
New Siberian Islands see Novosibirskie ostrova, is., Russia B16 26
New Site, Al., U.S. B4 94
New Smyrna Beach, Fl., U.S. C6 102
New South Wales, state, Austl. G4 62
New Straitsville, Oh., U.S. C3 128
New Tazewell, Tn., U.S. C10 135
Newton, Al., U.S. D4 94
Newton, co., Ar., U.S. B2 97
Newton, Ga., U.S. E2 103
Newton, co., Ga., U.S. C3 103
Newton, Ia., U.S. C4 108
Newton, Il., U.S. E5 106
Newton, co., In., U.S. B3 107
Newton, Ks., U.S. D6 109
Newton, Ma., U.S. B5 114
Newton, co., Mo., U.S. E3 118
Newton, Ms., U.S. C4 117
Newton, co., Ms., U.S. C4 117
Newton, N.C., U.S. B1 126
Newton, N.J., U.S. A3 123
Newton, Tx., U.S. D6 136
Newton, co., Tx., U.S. D6 136
Newton, Ut., U.S. B4 137
Newton Falls, Oh., U.S. A5 128
Newton Lake, res., Il., U.S. . . .E5 106
Newtown, Ct., U.S. D2 100
New Town, N.D., U.S. B3 127
Newtown, Oh., U.S. C1 128
Newtown Square, Pa., U.S. . .p20 131
New Ulm, Mn., U.S. F4 116
New Vienna, Oh., U.S. C2 128
Newville, Pa., U.S. F7 131
New Washington, In., U.S. . . .G6 107
New Washington, Oh., U.S. B3 128
New Waterford, Oh., U.S. B5 128
New Westminster, B.C., Can. E6 85
New Whiteland, In., U.S. E5 107
New Wilmington, Pa., U.S. . . .D1 131
New Windsor, Il., U.S. B3 106
New Windsor, Md., U.S. A3 113
New Windsor, N.Y., U.S. D6 125
New World Island, i., Nf., Can. D4 88
New York, N.Y., U.S. E7 125
New York, co., N.Y., U.S. k13 125
New York, state, U.S. C5 125
New York Mills, Mn., U.S. D3 116
New Zealand, ctry., Oc. H10 58
Neyrīz, Iran E6 42
Neyshābūr, Iran C7 42

Name	Map Ref.	Page

Nezahualcóyotl, Presa, res.,
Mex. D6 78
Nez Perce, co., Id., U.S. C2 105
Nez Perce Indian Reservation,
Id., U.S. C2 105
Ngabé, Congo D3 54
Ngangala, Sudan C6 54
Ngangla Ringco, l., China . . .E4 28
Ngaoundéré, Cam. B2 54
Ngeaur, i., Palau E9 32
Ngidinga, D.R.C. E3 54
Ngoring Hu, l., China E7 28
Ngouri, Chad D8 50
Nguigmi, Niger D7 50
Nguru, Nig. D7 50
Nha Trang, Viet. D5 34
Nhill, Austl. H3 62
Nhoma, stm., Afr. B2 56
Niafounké, Mali C4 50
Niagara, co., N.Y., U.S. B2 125
Niagara, Wi., U.S. C6 142
Niagara Falls, On., Can. D5 89
Niagara Falls, N.Y., U.S. B1 125
Niagara-on-the-Lake, On.,
Can. D5 89
Niah, Malay. E5 36
Niakaramandougou, C. Iv. . .E3 50
Niamey, Niger D5 50
Niangara, D.R.C. C5 54
Niangua, stm., Mo., U.S. . . .D5 118
Nia-Nia, D.R.C. C5 54
Niantic, Ct., U.S. D7 100
Nias, Pulau, i., Indon. C1 36
Niatupo, Pan. D4 80
Nibley, Ut., U.S. B4 137
Nicaragua, ctry., N.A. 76
Nicaragua, Lago de, l., Nic. . .C2 80
Nicatous Lake, l., Me., U.S. . .C4 112
Nice, Fr. F10 16
Niceville, Fl., U.S. u15 102
Nichinan, Japan E14 28
Nicholas, co., Ky., U.S. B6 110
Nicholas, co., W.V., U.S. C4 141
Nicholas Channel, strt.,
N.A. A3 80
Nicholasville, Ky., U.S. C5 110
Nicholls, Ga., U.S. E4 103
Nichols Hills, Ok., U.S. B4 129
Nicholson, Ms., U.S. E4 117
Nickajack Lake, res., Tn.,
U.S. D8 135
Nickel Centre, On., Can. . . .p19 89
Nickerson, Ks., U.S. D5 109
Nicobar Islands, is., India . .H6 40
Nicolet, P.Q., Can. C5 90
Nicolet, stm., P.Q., Can. C5 90
Nicolet, Lake, l., Mi., U.S. . . .B6 115
Nicollet, co., Mn., U.S. F4 116
Nicollet, Mn., U.S. F4 116
Nicoma Park, Ok., U.S. B4 129
Nicosia, Cyp. E5 44
Nicoya, Golfo de, b., C.R. . . .D2 80
Nicoya, Península de, pen.,
C.R. D2 80
Nidzica, Pol. C6 20
Niellé, C. Iv. D3 50
Nienburg, Ger. D11 12
Nieuw Amsterdam, Sur. B8 70
Nieuw Nickerie, Sur. B8 70
Nigadoo, N.B., Can. B4 87
Niğde, Tur. D6 44
Niger, stm., Afr. E6 50
Niger, ctry., Afr. C6 50
Nigeria, ctry., Afr. E6 50
Nihoa, i., Hi., U.S. m15 104
Niigata, Japan D15 28
Niihama, Japan D2 31
Niihau, i., Hi., U.S. B1 104
Nijmegen, Neth. E10 12
Nikel', Russia B14 10
Nikishka, Ak., U.S. g16 95
Nikkō, Japan D15 28
Nikol'sk, Russia D6 26
Nikol'sk, Russia D8 22
Nikopol', Ukr. F13 20
Niksar, Tur. B7 44
Nikshahr, Iran E8 42
Nikšić, Yugo. C7 18
Nila, Pulau, i., Indon. E7 36
Niland, Ca., U.S. F6 98
Nile, stm., Afr. E11 48
Niles, Il., U.S. h9 106
Niles, Mi., U.S. G4 115
Niles, Oh., U.S. A5 128
Nimach, India E2 40
Nimba, Mount, mtn., Afr. . . .E3 50
Nîmes, Fr. F9 16
Nimrod Lake, res., Ar., U.S. . .C2 97
Nimule, Sudan J11 48
Ninawá, hist., Iraq C4 42
Ninda, Ang. A3 56
Nine Degree Channel, strt.,
India H2 40
Nine Mile Creek, stm., Ut.,
U.S. D5 137
Ninemile Point, c., Mi.,
U.S. C6 115
Ninetyeast Ridge J11 64
Ninety Mile Beach, Austl. . . .H4 62
Ninety Six, S.C., U.S. C3 133
Nineveh see Nīnawá, hist.,
Iraq C4 42
Ning'an, China B1 31
Ningbo, China F12 28
Ningcheng, China C11 28
Ningde, China D4 30

Ningdu, China F11 28
Ninghai, China D5 30
Ninghua, China D4 30
Ningi, Nig. D6 50
Ningming, China E2 30
Ningnan, China A4 34
Ningshan, China C2 30
Ningsia Hui Autonomous
Region see Ningxia Huiza
Zizhiqu, prov., China . . .D9 28
Ningxia Huiza Zizhiqu, prov.,
China D9 28
Ningxiang, China D3 30
Ninh Binh, Viet. B5 34
Ninigo Group, is., Pap. N.
Gui. G11 32
Ninigret Pond, l., R.I., U.S. . .G2 132
Ninilchik, Ak., U.S. C9 95
Ninnescah, stm., Ks., U.S. . . .E6 109
Ninohe, Japan B4 31
Niobrara, co., Wy., U.S. C8 143
Niobrara, stm., U.S. B7 120
Nioki, D.R.C. D3 54
Niono, Mali D3 50
Nioro du Sahel, Mali C3 50
Niort, Fr. D6 16
Niota, Tn., U.S. D9 135
Nipigon, Lake, l., On., Can. . .o17 89
Nipissing, Lake, l., On.,
Can. A5 89
Nipomo, Ca., U.S. E3 98
Nipple Mountain, mtn., Co.,
U.S. D2 99
Niquero, Cuba A4 80
Nirmal, India F3 40
Niscemi, Italy F5 18
Niskayuna, N.Y., U.S. C7 125
Nisqually, stm., Wa., U.S. . . .C3 140
Nisswa, Mn., U.S. D4 116
Nistru (Dniester) (Dnister),
stm., Eur. F10 20
Niterói, Braz. F3 74
Nitra, Slvk. E5 20
Nitro, W.V., U.S. C3 141
Niue, dep., Oc. F13 58
Niuke, China C4 40
Niulakita, i., Tuvalu E11 58
Niverville, Mb., U.S. E3 86
Niwot, Co., U.S. A5 99
Nixa, Mo., U.S. D4 118
Nixon, Nv., U.S. D2 121
Nixon, Tx., U.S. E4 136
Nizāmābād, India F3 40
Nizhyn, Ukr. D11 20
Nizip, Tur. D7 44
Nižneangarsk, Russia D12 26
Nižnee Kujto, ozero, l.,
Russia D14 10
Nižnekamsk, Russia C9 22
Nižneudinsk, Russia D11 26
Nižnevartovsk, Russia C9 26
Nižnij Novgorod (Gor'kij),
Russia D6 26
Nižnij Tagil, Russia D8 26
Nižnjaja Peša, Russia A8 22
Nižnjaja Tunguska, stm.,
Russia C11 26
Njandoma, Russia C6 26
Njazidja, i., Com. A7 56
Njinjo, Tan. E7 54
Njombe, Tan. E6 54
Njuhča, Russia B8 22
Njurba, Russia C13 26
Njuvčim, Russia B9 22
Nkambe, Cam. B2 54
Nkawkaw, Ghana E4 50
Nkhata Bay, Mwi. A5 56
Nkhotakota, Mwi. A5 56
Nkongsamba, Cam. C1 54
Noākhāli, Bngl. E6 40
Noank, Ct., U.S. D8 100
Noatak, Ak., U.S. B7 95
Noatak, stm., Ak., U.S. B7 95
Nobel, On., Can. B4 89
Nobeoka, Japan D2 31
Noble, co., In., U.S. B7 107
Noble, co., Oh., U.S. C4 128
Noble, Ok., U.S. B4 129
Noble, co., Ok., U.S. A4 129
Nobles, co., Mn., U.S. G3 116
Noblesville, In., U.S. D6 107
Nocatee, Fl., U.S. E5 102
Nocona, Tx., U.S. C4 136
Nodaway, co., Mo., U.S. . . .A3 118
Nodaway, stm., U.S. A2 118
Noel, Mo., U.S. E3 118
Nogales, Mex. A2 78
Nogales, Az., U.S. F5 96
Nogent-le-Rotrou, Fr. C7 16
Noginsk, Russia C6 22
Nohar, India D2 40
Noirmoutier, Île de, i., Fr. . . .D5 16
Nokaneng, Bots. B3 56
Nokia, Fin. F10 10
Nokomis, Fl., U.S. E4 102
Nokomis, Il., U.S. D4 106
Nokomis, Lake, res., Wi.,
U.S. C4 142
Nokuku, Vanuatu j9 62a
Nola, C.A.R. C3 54
Nolan, co., Tx., U.S. C2 136
Nolichucky, stm., Tn., U.S. . .C10 135
Nolin, stm., Ky., U.S. C3 110
Nolin Lake, res., Ky., U.S. . . .C3 110
Nolinsk, Russia C9 22

Nomans Land, i., Ma., U.S. . .D6 114
Nome, Ak., U.S. C6 95
Nomininque, P.Q., Can. C2 90
Nonesuch, stm., Me., U.S. . . .g7 112
Nong'an, China C13 28
Nong Khai, Thai. C4 34
Nonquit Pond, l., R.I., U.S. . . .E6 132
Nooksack, North Fork, stm.,
Wa., U.S. A4 140
Nooksack, South Fork, stm.,
Wa., U.S. A3 140
Noonkanbah, Austl. D3 60
Noorvik, Ak., U.S. B7 95
Nootka Sound, strt., B.C.,
Can. E4 85
No Point, Point, c., Md.,
U.S. D5 113
Noquebay, Lake, l., Wi.,
U.S. C6 142
Nóqui, Ang. E2 54
Noranda (part of Rouyn
[-Noranda]), P.Q., Can. . .k11 90
Nora Springs, Ia., U.S. A5 108
Norborne, Mo., U.S. B4 118
Norco, La., U.S. E5 111
Norcross, Ga., U.S. C2 103
Nordaustlandet, i., Nor. A4 26
Norden, Ger. D10 12
Nordenham, Ger. D11 12
Nordenšel'da, arhipelag, is.,
Russia B11 26
Nordfjordeid, Nor. F2 10
Nordhausen, Ger. E12 12
Nordkapp, c., Nor. A11 10
Nord-Ostsee-Kanal, Ger. . . .C11 12
Nordre Strømfjord, b.,
Grnld. E29 82
Nordvik, Russia B13 26
Norfolk, Ct., U.S. B3 100
Norfolk, co., Ma., U.S. B5 114
Norfolk, Ne., U.S. B8 120
Norfolk, N.Y., U.S. f9 125
Norfolk, Va., U.S. D6 139
Norfolk Island, dep., Oc. . . .G10 58
Norfolk Naval Base, mil., Va.,
U.S. k15 139
Norfolk Naval Shipyard, mil.,
Va., U.S. k15 139
Norfolk Ridge K19 64
Norfork Dam, Ar., U.S. A3 97
Norfork Lake, res., U.S. A3 97
Noril'sk, Russia C10 26
Norland, Fl., U.S. s13 102
Norlina, N.C., U.S. A4 126
Normal, Il., U.S. C5 106
Norman, co., Mn., U.S. C2 116
Norman, Ok., U.S. B4 129
Norman, Lake, res., N.C.,
U.S. B2 126
Normandie, hist. reg., Fr. . . .C6 16
Normandie, Collines de, Fr. . .C6 16
Normandy see Normandie,
hist. reg., Fr. C6 16
Normandy, Mo., U.S. f13 118
Normandy, Hills of see
Normandie, Collines de,
Fr. C6 16
Norman Park, Ga., U.S. E3 103
Normanton, Austl. D3 62
Norphlet, Ar., U.S. D3 97
Norquinco, Arg. F2 69
Norra Kvarken (Merenkurkku),
strt., Eur. E9 10
Norrbotten, hist. reg., Swe. .C10 10
Nørresundby, Den. H3 10
Norridge, Il., U.S. k9 106
Norridgewock, Me., U.S. D3 112
Norris, S.C., U.S. B2 133
Norris, Tn., U.S. C9 135
Norris Arm, Nf., Can. D4 88
Norris City, Il., U.S. F5 106
Norris Lake, res., Tn., U.S. . .C10 135
Norris Point, Nf., Can. D3 88
Norristown, Pa., U.S. F11 131
Norrköping, Swe. G7 10
Norrtälje, Swe. G8 10
Norseman, Austl. G3 60
Norsjö, Swe. D8 10
Norsk, Russia D15 26
North, stm., Al., U.S. B2 94
North, stm., Ia., U.S. f8 108
North, stm., Ma., U.S. h12 114
North, S.C., U.S. D5 133
North, stm., W.V., U.S. B6 141
North, Cape, c., N.S.,
Can. B9 87
North Adams, Ma., U.S. A1 114
North Albany, Or., U.S. k11 130
Northam, Austl. G2 60
North America, cont. 4
North American Basin E7 66
North Amherst, Ma., U.S. . . .B2 114
Northampton, Austl. F1 60
Northampton, Eng., U.K. D6 12
Northampton, Ma., U.S. B2 114
Northampton, N.H., U.S. D5 122
Northampton, co., N.C.,
U.S. A5 126
Northampton, Pa., U.S. E11 131
Northampton, co., Pa.,
U.S. E11 131
Northampton, co., Va.,
U.S. C7 139
North Andaman, i.,
India G6 40
North Andover, Ma., U.S. . . .A5 114

North Anna, stm., Va., U.S. . .B5 139
North Anson, Me., U.S. D3 112
North Apollo, Pa., U.S. E2 131
North Arapaho Peak, mtn.,
Co., U.S. A5 99
North Arlington, N.J., U.S. . . .h8 123
North Atlanta, Ga., U.S. h8 103
North Attleboro, Ma., U.S. . .C5 114
North Augusta, S.C., U.S. . . .D4 133
North Aurora, Il., U.S. k8 106
North Australian Basin J14 64
North Baltimore, Oh., U.S. . .A2 128
North Bay, On., Can. A5 89
North Beach, Md., U.S. C4 113
North Belmont, N.C., U.S. . . .B1 126
North Bend, Ne., U.S. C9 120
North Bend, Or., U.S. D2 130
North Bend, Wa., U.S. B4 140
North Bennington, Vt., U.S. . .F2 138
North Bergen, N.J., U.S. h8 123
North Berwick, Me., U.S. E2 112
North Billerica, Ma., U.S. A5 114
Northborough, Ma., U.S. B4 114
North Branch, Mi., U.S. E7 115
North Branch, Mn., U.S. E6 116
North Branch, N.H., U.S. D3 122
North Branch, N.J., U.S. B3 123
North Branford, Ct., U.S. D4 100
Northbridge, Ma., U.S. B4 114
Northbrook, Il., U.S. h9 106
North Brookfield, Ma., U.S. . .B3 114
North Brunswick, N.J., U.S. . .C4 123
North Caicos, i., T./C. Is. A5 80
North Caldwell, N.J., U.S. . . .B4 123
North Canadian, stm., Ok.,
U.S. A5 129
North Canton, Ga., U.S. B2 103
North Canton, Oh., U.S. B4 128
North Cape, c., P.E., Can. . . .B6 87
North Cape see Nordkapp, c.,
Nor. A11 10
North Cape, c., N.Z. n13 63c
North Cape May, N.J., U.S. . .F3 123
North Carolina, state, U.S. . .B3 126
North Cascades National Park,
Wa., U.S. A4 140
North Channel, strt., On.,
Can. A2 89
North Channel, strt., U.K. . . .C4 12
North Charleston, S.C.,
U.S. F8 133
North Chicago, Il., U.S. A6 106
North Clarendon, Vt., U.S. . . .D3 138
Northcliffe, Austl. G2 60
North College Hill, Oh.,
U.S. o12 128
North Conway, N.H., U.S. . . .B4 122
North Corbin, Ky., U.S. D5 110
North Crossett, Ar., U.S. D4 97
North Cyprus, ctry.,
Asia E5 44
North Dakota, state,
U.S. B5 127
North Dartmouth, Ma.,
U.S. C6 114
North Eagle Butte, S.D.,
U.S. B4 134
Northeast, stm., Md.,
U.S. A6 113
North East, Md., U.S. A6 113
North East, Pa., U.S. B2 131
Northeast Cape, c., Ak.,
U.S. C6 95
Northeast Cape Fear, stm.,
N.C., U.S. C5 126
Northeast Harbor, Me.,
U.S. D4 112
North Easton, Ma., U.S. B5 114
Northeast Pond, l., N.H.,
U.S. D5 122
North Edisto, stm., S.C.,
U.S. k11 133
North English, Ia., U.S. C5 108
North English, stm., Ia.,
U.S. C5 108
North Enid, Ok., U.S. A4 129
Northern Cheyenne Indian
Reservation, Mt., U.S. . .E10 119
Northern Cook Islands, is.,
Cook Is. F13 58
Northern Dvina see Severnaja
Dvina, stm., Russia C6 26
Northern Indian Lake, l., Mb.,
Can. A3 86
Northern Ireland, state,
N. Ire., U.K. C3 12
Northern Mariana Islands,
dep., Oc. C9 58
Northern Sporades see Vórioi
Sporádhes, is., Grc. E10 18
Northern Territory, state,
Austl. D5 60
Northfield, Mn., U.S. F5 116
Northfield, N.H., U.S. D3 122
Northfield, N.J., U.S. E3 123
Northfield, Oh., U.S. h9 128
Northfield, Vt., U.S. C3 138
Northfield Falls, Vt., U.S. C3 138
North Fiji Basin J20 64
North Flinders Range, mts.,
Austl. G2 62
North Fond du Lac, Wi.,
U.S. E5 142

North Fork Reservoir, res.,
Or., U.S. B4 130
North Fort Myers, Fl., U.S. . . .F5 102
North Fox Island, i., Mi.,
U.S. C5 115
Northglenn, Co., U.S. B6 99
North Gower, On., Can. B9 89
North Grafton, Ma., U.S. B4 114
North Grosvenordale, Ct.,
U.S. B8 100
North Gulfport, Ms., U.S. . . .E4 117
North Haledon, N.J., U.S. . . .B4 123
North Hampton, N.H., U.S. . .E5 122
North Hartland Reservoir,
res., Vt., U.S. D4 138
North Hatley, P.Q., Can. D6 90
North Haven, Ct., U.S. D4 100
North Head, N.B., Can. E3 87
North Hero Island, i., Vt.,
U.S. B2 138
North Horn Lake, l., Tn.,
U.S. e8 135
North Industry, Oh., U.S. B4 128
North Inlet, b., S.C., U.S. E9 133
North Island, i., N.Z. o14 63c
North Island, i., S.C., U.S. . . .E9 133
North Island Naval Air Station,
mil., Ca., U.S. o15 98
North Islands, is., La., U.S. . . .E7 111
North Judson, In., U.S. B4 107
North Kansas City, Mo.,
U.S. h10 118
North Kingstown, R.I., U.S. . .E4 132
North Kingsville, Oh., U.S. . . .A5 128
North La Junta, Co., U.S. C7 99
Northlake, Il., U.S. k9 106
North Lakhimpur, India D6 40
North Laramie, stm., Wy.,
U.S. D7 143
North Las Vegas, Nv., U.S. . .G6 121
North La Veta Pass, Co.,
U.S. D5 99
North Lewisburg, Oh., U.S. . .B2 128
North Liberty, Ia., U.S. C6 108
North Liberty, In., U.S. A5 107
North Lima, Oh., U.S. B5 128
North Little Rock, Ar.,
U.S. C3 97
North Logan, Ut., U.S. B4 137
North Loon Mountain, mtn.,
Id., U.S. D3 105
North Magnetic Pole D33 144
North Mamm Peak, mtn., Co.,
U.S. B3 99
North Manchester, In., U.S. .C6 107
North Manitou Island, i., Mi.,
U.S. C4 115
North Mankato, Mn., U.S. . . .F4 116
North Miami, Fl., U.S. G6 102
North Miami Beach, Fl.,
U.S. s13 102
North Middletown, Ky., U.S. .B5 110
North Moose Lake, l., Mb.,
Can. B1 86
North Mountain, mtn., Pa.,
U.S. D9 131
North Muskegon, Mi., U.S. . .E4 115
North Myrtle Beach, S.C.,
U.S. D10 133
North Naples, Fl., U.S. F5 102
North New River Canal, Fl.,
U.S. F6 102
North Ogden, Ut., U.S. B4 137
North Olmsted, Oh., U.S. . . .h9 128
North Ossetia see Severnaja
Osetija, state, Russia E6 26
North Palisade, mtn., Ca.,
U.S. D4 98
North Park, val., Co., U.S. . . .A4 99
North Park, Il., U.S. A4 106
North Pass, strt., La., U.S. . . .E7 111
North Pembroke, Ma., U.S. . .B6 114
North Plainfield, N.J., U.S. . . .B4 123
North Plains, pl., N.M., U.S. . .C1 124
North Plains, Or., U.S. B4 130
North Platte, Ne., U.S. C5 120
North Platte, stm., U.S. C7 92
North Point, c., Md., U.S. B5 113
North Point, c., Mi., U.S. C7 115
North Pole E12 144
Northport, Al., U.S. B2 94
North Prairie, Wi., U.S. F5 142
North Providence, R.I., U.S. . .C4 132
North Raccoon, stm., Ia.,
U.S. C3 108
North Reading, Ma., U.S. . . .f11 114
North Richland Hills, Tx.,
U.S. n9 136
Northridge, Oh., U.S. C2 128
North Ridgeville, Oh., U.S. . .A3 128
North Royalton, Oh., U.S. . . .h9 128
North Rustico, P.E., Can. C6 87
North St. Paul, Mn., U.S. . . .m13 116
North Salem, N.H., U.S. E4 122
North Salt Lake, Ut., U.S. . . .C4 137
North Santee, stm., S.C.,
U.S. E9 133
North Saskatchewan, stm.,
Can. H18 82
North Schell Peak, mtn., Nv.,
U.S. D7 121
North Scituate, Ma., U.S. . .h12 114
North Sea, Eur. D6 6
North Shore City, N.Z. o13 63c
North Shoshone Peak, mtn.,
Nv., U.S. D4 121

Name	Map Ref.	Page

North Siberian Lowland see Severo-Sibirskaja nizmennost', pl., Russia . B11 26
North Sioux City, S.D., U.S. . E9 134
North Skunk, stm., Ia., U.S. . C5 108
North Springfield, Vt., U.S. . E3 138
North Springfield Reservoir, res., Vt., U.S. . E4 138
North Star, De., U.S. . A3 101
North Stradbroke Island, i., Austl. . F5 62
North Stratford, N.H., U.S. . A3 122
North Sudbury, Ma., U.S. . g10 114
North Swanzey, N.H., U.S. . E2 122
North Syracuse, N.Y., U.S. . B4 125
North Taranaki Bight, b., N.Z. . o13 63c
North Tarrytown, N.Y., U.S. . D7 125
North Terre Haute, In., U.S. . E3 107
North Thompson, stm., B.C., Can. . D8 85
North Tonawanda, N.Y., U.S. . B2 125
North Troy, Vt., U.S. . B4 138
North Tunica, Ms., U.S. . A3 117
North Twin Lake, l., Wi., U.S. . B4 142
Northumberland, co., Pa., U.S. . D8 131
Northumberland, Pa., U.S. . E8 131
Northumberland, co., Va., U.S. . C6 139
Northumberland Strait, strt., Can. . C6 87
North Umpqua, stm., Or., U.S. . D3 130
North Uxbridge, Ma., U.S. . B4 114
Northvale, N.J., U.S. . g9 123
North Vancouver, B.C., Can. . E6 85
North Vassalboro, Me., U.S. . D3 112
North Vernon, In., U.S. . F6 107
Northville, Mi., U.S. . p15 115
North Wales, Pa., U.S. . F11 131
North Walpole, N.H., U.S. . D2 122
North Warren, Pa., U.S. . C3 131
North Webster, In., U.S. . B6 107
North West Cape, c., Austl. . E1 60
Northwest Miramichi, N.B., Can. . B3 87
Northwest Pacific Basin . E18 64
Northwest Territories, ter., Can. . E15 82
North Wildwood, N.J., U.S. . E3 123
North Wilkesboro, N.C., U.S. . A1 126
North Windham, Ct., U.S. . C7 100
North Windham, Me., U.S. . E2 112
Northwood, Ia., U.S. . A4 108
Northwood, N.D., U.S. . B8 127
North Woodstock, N.H., U.S. B3 122
North York, On., Can. . D5 89
North York, Pa., U.S. . G8 131
Norton, N.B., Can. . D4 87
Norton, Ks., U.S. . C4 109
Norton, co., Ks., U.S. . C4 109
Norton, Ma., U.S. . C5 114
Norton, Oh., U.S. . A4 128
Norton, Va., U.S. . f9 139
Norton Bay, b., Ak., U.S. . C7 95
Norton Pond, l., Vt., U.S. . B5 138
Norton Reservoir, res., Ks., U.S. . C3 109
Norton Shores, Mi., U.S. . E4 115
Norton Sound, strt., Ak., U.S. . C6 95
Nortonville, Ks., U.S. . C8 109
Nortonville, Ky., U.S. . C2 110
Norvegia, Cape, c., Ant. . D3 67
Norwalk, Ca., U.S. . n12 98
Norwalk, Ct., U.S. . E2 100
Norwalk, stm., Ct., U.S. . E2 100
Norwalk, Ia., U.S. . C4 108
Norwalk, Oh., U.S. . A3 128
Norwalk Islands, is., Ct., U.S. . E2 100
Norway, ctry., Eur. . B9 8
Norway, Me., U.S. . D2 112
Norway, Mi., U.S. . C3 115
Norway House, Mb., Can. . C3 86
Norway Lake, l., Mn., U.S. . E3 116
Norwegian Basin . C23 144
Norwegian Sea, Eur. . I22 10a
Norwich, Eng., U.K. . D7 12
Norwich, Ct., U.S. . C7 100
Norwich, N.Y., U.S. . C5 125
Norwich, Vt., U.S. . D4 138
Norwood, On., Can. . C7 89
Norwood, Ma., U.S. . B5 114
Norwood, Mn., U.S. . F5 116
Norwood, N.C., U.S. . B2 126
Norwood, N.J., U.S. . h9 123
Norwood, N.Y., U.S. . f10 125
Norwood, Oh., U.S. . o13 128
Norwood, Pa., U.S. . p20 131
Norwoodville, Ia., U.S. . e8 108
Noshiro, Japan . C16 28
Nosivka, Ukr. . D11 20
Nossob, stm., Afr. . C2 56
Nosy-Varika, Madag. . C8 56
Notasulga, Al., U.S. . C4 94
Notch Peak, mtn., Ut., U.S. . D2 137
Noteć, stm., Pol. . C4 20
Notodden, Nor. . G3 10
Noto-hantō, pen., Japan . C3 31
Notre Dame, Monts, mts., P.Q., Can. . k13 90
Notre Dame Bay, b., Nf., Can. . D4 88
Notre Dame de Lourdes, Mb., Can. . E2 86
Notre-Dame-du-Lac, P.Q., Can. . B9 90
Nottawasaga Bay, b., On., Can. . C4 89
Nottaway, stm., P.Q., Can. . h11 90
Nottingham, Eng., U.K. . D6 12
Nottoway, stm., Va., U.S. . D5 139
Nottoway, co., Va., U.S. . C4 139
Nouâdhibou, Maur. . B1 50
Nouâdhibou, Râs, c., Afr. . B1 50
Nouakchott, Maur. . C1 50
Nouâmghâr, Maur. . C1 50
Nouméa, N. Cal. . I9 62a
Noupoort, S. Afr. . E3 56
Nouveau-Brunswick see New Brunswick, prov., Can. . I26 82
Nouvelle-Calédonie, i., N. Cal. . I9 62a
Nova Caipemba, Ang. . E2 54
Nova Friburgo, Braz. . F3 74
Nova Iguaçu, Braz. . F3 74
Novaja Kazanka, Kaz. . E8 22
Novaja Sibir', ostrov, i., Russia . B17 26
Novaja Zemlja, is., Russia . B7 26
Nova Kakhovka, Ukr. . F12 20
Nova Lima, Braz. . F3 74
Nova Lisboa see Huambo, Ang. . C2 54
Nova Mambone, Moz. . C6 56
Novara, Italy . B2 18
Nova Scotia, prov., Can. . D6 87
Novato, Ca., U.S. . C2 98
Nova Venécia, Braz. . E3 74
Novaya Zemlya see Novaja Zemlja, is., Russia . B7 26
Nova Zagora, Blg. . C11 18
Nové Zámky, Slvk. . E5 20
Novgorod, Russia . D5 26
Novhorod-Sivers'kyi, Ukr. . D12 20
Novi, Mi., U.S. . p15 115
Novikovo, Russia . A4 31
Novi Ligure, Italy . B2 18
Novi Pazar, Blg. . C11 18
Novi Pazar, Yugo. . C8 18
Novi Sad, Yugo. . B7 18
Novo Aripuanã, Braz. . E7 70
Novoazovs'k, Ukr. . F15 20
Novočerkassk, Russia . E7 22
Novodvinsk, Russia . B7 22
Novo Hamburgo, Braz. . D7 72
Novohrad-Volyns'kyi, Ukr. . D9 20
Novokazalinsk, Kaz. . E8 26
Novokujbyševsk, Russia . D8 22
Novokuzneck, Russia . D10 26
Novomihajlovskij, Russia . G15 20
Novomoskovsk, Russia . D5 26
Novomoskovs'k, Ukr. . E13 20
Novomyrhorod, Ukr. . E11 20
Novorossijsk, Russia . E5 26
Novošahtinsk, Russia . F15 20
Novosergievka, Russia . D9 22
Novosibirsk, Russia . D10 26
Novosibirskie ostrova, is., Russia . B16 26
Novotroick, Russia . D10 22
Novotroickoe, Kaz. . B10 42
Novotroïts'ke, Ukr. . F13 20
Novoukraïnka, Ukr. . E11 20
Novouzensk, Russia . D8 22
Novovjatsk, Russia . C8 22
Novovolyns'k, Ukr. . D8 20
Novozybkov, Russia . C11 20
Novyi Buh, Ukr. . F12 20
Novyj Oskol, Russia . D14 20
Novyj Port, Russia . C9 26
Novyj Uzen', Kaz. . E7 26
Nowata, Ok., U.S. . A6 129
Nowata, co., Ok., U.S. . A6 129
Nowood, stm., Wy., U.S. . B5 143
Nowra, Austl. . G5 62
Nowshāk, mtn., Asia . B2 40
Nowy Dwór Mazowiecki, Pol. . C6 20
Nowy Sącz, Pol. . E6 20
Noxon Reservoir, res., Mt., U.S. . C1 119
Noxontown Lake, res., De., U.S. . C3 101
Noxubee, co., Ms., U.S. . B5 117
Noxubee, stm., Ms., U.S. . B5 117
Noyes Island, i., Ak., U.S. . n22 95
Noyo, stm., Ca., U.S. . C2 98
Nsanje, Mwi. . B6 56
Nsawam, Ghana . E4 50
Nsukka, Nig. . E6 50
Nsuta, Ghana . E4 50
Ntomba, Lac, l., D.R.C. . D3 54
Nūbah, Jibāl an-, mts., Sudan . A6 54
Nubanusit Lake, l., N.H., U.S. . E2 122
Nubian Desert, des., Sudan . F11 48
Nuckolls, co., Ne., U.S. . D7 120
Nucla, Co., U.S. . C2 99
Nueces, stm., Tx., U.S. . E3 136
Nueces, co., Tx., U.S. . F4 136
Nueltin Lake, l., Can. . F20 82
Nueva Antioquia, Col. . D6 80
Nueva Gerona, Cuba . A3 80

Nueva Imperial, Chile . E2 69
Nueva Italia de Ruiz, Mex. . D4 78
Nueva Rosita, Mex. . B4 78
Nueve de Julio, Arg. . F5 72
Nuevitas, Cuba . A4 80
Nuevo, Cayo, i., Mex. . C6 78
Nuevo, Golfo, b., Arg. . F4 69
Nuevo Casas Grandes, Mex. . A3 78
Nuevo Laredo, Mex. . B5 78
Nuevo León, state, Mex. . B5 78
Nui, atoll, Tuvalu . E11 58
Nukuʻalofa, Tonga . G12 58
Nukus, Uzb. . E7 26
Nulato, Ak., U.S. . C8 95
Nulhegan, stm., Vt., U.S. . B5 138
Nullagine, Austl. . E3 60
Nullarbor, Austl. . G5 60
Nullarbor Plain, pl., Austl. . G4 60
Numan, Nig. . E7 50
Numancia, hist., Spain . G5 16
Numazu, Japan . D3 31
Nunavut, ter., Can. . E18 82
Nunivak Island, i., Ak., U.S. . D6 95
Nunjiang, China . B13 28
Nuoro, Italy . D2 18
Nuremberg, Pa., U.S. . E9 131
Nurmes, Fin. . E13 10
Nürnberg, Ger. . F12 12
Nusaybin, Tur. . D9 44
Nu Shan, mts., China . F7 28
Nushki, Pak. . E4 42
Nutley, N.J., U.S. . B4 123
Nutter Fort, W.V., U.S. . k10 141
Nutting Lake, Ma., U.S. . f10 114
Nuuanu Pali, Hi., U.S. . g10 104
Nuuk see Godthåb, Grnld. . F29 82
Nyabing, Austl. . G2 60
Nyack, N.Y., U.S. . D7 125
Nyainqêntanglha Shan, mts., China . E6 28
Nyakanazi, Tan. . D6 54
Nyala, Sudan . H10 54
Nyamlell, Sudan . B5 54
Nyanza-Lac, Bdi. . D5 54
Nyasa, Lake (Malaŵi, Lake), l., Afr. . F6 54
Nyasaland see Malaŵi, ctry., Afr. . A5 56
Nyaunglebin, Mya. . C3 34
Nyborg, Den. . I4 10
Nybro, Swe. . H6 10
Nyda, Russia . C9 26
Nye, co., Nv., U.S. . E5 121
Nyeri, Kenya . D7 54
Nyimba, Zam. . A5 56
Nyingchi, China . D6 40
Nyíregyháza, Hung. . F6 20
Nykøbing, Den. . I4 10
Nyköping, Swe. . G7 10
Nylstroom, S. Afr. . C4 56
Nynäshamn, Swe. . G7 10
Nyngan, Austl. . G4 62
Nyš, Russia . D16 26
Nysa, Pol. . D4 20
Nyssa, Or., U.S. . D9 130
Nyunzu, D.R.C. . E5 54
Nzébéla, Gui. . E3 50
Nzérékoré, Gui. . E3 50
N'zeto, Ang. . C2 54
Nzwani, i., Com. . A7 56

O

Oahe, Lake, res., U.S. . B7 92
Oahe Dam, S.D., U.S. . C5 134
Oahu, i., Hi., U.S. . B4 104
Oak Bay, B.C., Can. . h12 85
Oak Bluffs, Ma., U.S. . D6 114
Oak Creek, Co., U.S. . A4 99
Oak Creek, Wi., U.S. . n12 142
Oakdale, Ca., U.S. . D3 98
Oakdale, Ga., U.S. . h8 103
Oakdale, La., U.S. . D3 111
Oakdale, Pa., U.S. . k13 131
Oakes, N.D., U.S. . C7 127
Oakfield, N.Y., U.S. . B2 125
Oakfield, Wi., U.S. . E5 142
Oak Forest, Il., U.S. . k9 106
Oak Grove, Ky., U.S. . D2 110
Oak Grove, La., U.S. . B4 111
Oak Grove, Or., U.S. . B4 130
Oak Harbor, Oh., U.S. . A2 128
Oak Harbor, Wa., U.S. . A3 140
Oak Hill, mtn., Ma., U.S. . f9 114
Oak Hill, Mi., U.S. . o15 115
Oak Hill, Oh., U.S. . D3 128
Oak Hill, W.V., U.S. . D3 141
Oakhurst, Ok., U.S. . A5 129
Oak Island, i., Wi., U.S. . B3 142
Oak Lake, l., Mb., Can. . E1 86
Oakland, Ca., U.S. . D2 98
Oakland, Ia., U.S. . C2 108
Oakland, Il., U.S. . D5 106
Oakland, Md., U.S. . m12 113
Oakland, Me., U.S. . D3 112
Oakland, co., Mi., U.S. . F7 115
Oakland, N.J., U.S. . A4 123
Oakland, Ne., U.S. . C9 120
Oakland, Ok., U.S. . C5 129
Oakland, R.I., U.S. . B2 132
Oakland City, In., U.S. . H3 107
Oakland Park, Fl., U.S. . r13 102
Oak Lawn, Il., U.S. . B6 106
Oaklawn, Ks., U.S. . g12 109

Oakley, Id., U.S. . G5 105
Oakley, Ks., U.S. . C3 109
Oakman, Al., U.S. . B2 94
Oakmont, Pa., U.S. . E2 131
Oak Mountain, mtn., Ga., U.S. . D2 103
Oak Orchard, De., U.S. . F5 101
Oak Park, Il., U.S. . B6 106
Oak Park, Mi., U.S. . p15 115
Oak Ridge, N.C., U.S. . A3 126
Oakridge, Or., U.S. . D4 130
Oak Ridge, Tn., U.S. . C9 135
Oak Ridge Reservoir, res., N.J., U.S. . A3 123
Oakton, Va., U.S. . g12 139
Oaktown, In., U.S. . G3 107
Oak Valley, N.J., U.S. . D2 123
Oakville, On., Can. . D5 89
Oakville, Ct., U.S. . C3 100
Oakville, Mo., U.S. . g13 118
Oakwood, Ga., U.S. . B3 103
Oakwood, Il., U.S. . C6 106
Oakwood, Oh., U.S. . C1 128
Oamaru, N.Z. . q13 63c
Oaxaca, state, Mex. . D5 78
Oaxaca de Juárez, Mex. . D5 78
Ob', stm., Russia . B9 26
Ob Bay see Obskaja guba, b., Russia . C9 26
Obed, stm., Tn., U.S. . C9 135
Oberlin, La., U.S. . D3 111
Oberlin, Oh., U.S. . A3 128
Obetz, Oh., U.S. . C3 128
Obi, Pulau, i., Indon. . D7 36
Obi, Selat, strt., Indon. . D7 36
Óbidos, Braz. . D8 70
Obihiro, Japan . C16 28
Obion, Tn., U.S. . A2 135
Obion, co., Tn., U.S. . A2 135
Obion, stm., Tn., U.S. . A2 135
Oblong, Il., U.S. . D6 106
Obluče, Russia . B14 28
Obninsk, Russia . B14 20
Obo, C.A.R. . B5 54
Obojan', Russia . D14 20
O'Brien, co., Ia., U.S. . A2 108
Obščij syrt, mts., Eur. . D9 22
Observation Peak, mtn., Ca., U.S. . B3 98
Obskaja guba, b., Russia . C9 26
Obuasi, Ghana . E4 50
Obudu, Nig. . E6 50
Ocala, Fl., U.S. . C4 102
Ocaña, Col. . B5 70
Ocaña, Spain . H5 16
Occidental, Cordillera, mts., Col. . E4 80
Occidental, Cordillera, mts., Peru . E4 70
Ocean, co., N.J., U.S. . D4 123
Oceana, co., Mi., U.S. . E4 115
Oceana, W.V., U.S. . D3 141
Oceana Naval Air Station, mil., Va., U.S. . k15 139
Ocean Bluff, Ma., U.S. . B6 114
Ocean City, Fl., U.S. . u15 102
Ocean City, Md., U.S. . D7 113
Ocean City, N.J., U.S. . E3 123
Ocean Grove, Ma., U.S. . C5 114
Ocean Island see Banaba, i., Kir. . E10 58
Ocean Park, Wa., U.S. . C1 140
Oceanport, N.J., U.S. . C4 123
Oceanside, Ca., U.S. . F5 98
Ocean Springs, Ms., U.S. . E5 117
Ocean [Township], N.J., U.S. . C4 123
Ocean View, De., U.S. . F5 101
Ocheda Lake, l., Mn., U.S. . G3 116
Ocheyedan, stm., Ia., U.S. . A2 108
Ochiltree, co., Tx., U.S. . A2 136
Ochlockonee, stm., Fl., U.S. . B2 102
Ochoco Lake, res., Or., U.S. . C6 130
Ocilla, Ga., U.S. . E3 103
Ockelbo, Swe. . F7 10
Ocmulgee, stm., Ga., U.S. . D3 103
Ocoa, Bahía de, b., Dom. Rep. . B5 80
Ocoee, Fl., U.S. . D5 102
Ocoee, Lake, res., Tn., U.S. . D9 135
Oconee, stm., Ga., U.S. . C3 103
Oconee, co., Ga., U.S. . C3 103
Oconee, co., S.C., U.S. . B1 133
Oconee, Lake, res., Ga., U.S. . C3 103
Oconomowoc, Wi., U.S. . E5 142
Oconto, Wi., U.S. . D6 142
Oconto, co., Wi., U.S. . D5 142
Oconto, stm., Wi., U.S. . D5 142
Oconto Falls, Wi., U.S. . D5 142
Ocosingo, Mex. . D6 78
Ocotal, Nic. . C2 80
Ocotlán, Mex. . C4 78
Ocracoke Inlet, b., N.C., U.S. . B6 126
Ocracoke Island, i., N.C., U.S. . B7 126
October Revolution Island see Oktjabr'skoj Revoljucii, ostrov, i., Russia . B11 26
Octoraro Creek, stm., U.S. . A5 113

Ocumare del Tuy, Ven. . C6 80
Oda, Ghana . E4 50
Oda, Jabal, mtn., Sudan . F12 48
Odebolt, Ia., U.S. . B2 108
Odell, Il., U.S. . B5 106
Odell, Or., U.S. . B5 130
Odell Lake, l., Or., U.S. . E5 130
Odem, Tx., U.S. . F4 136
Odemira, Port. . I2 16
Ödemiş, Tur. . C2 44
Odendaalsrus, S. Afr. . D4 56
Odense, Den. . I4 10
Odenton, Md., U.S. . B4 113
Odenville, Al., U.S. . B3 94
Oder, stm., Eur. . C3 20
Odesa, Ukr. . F11 20
Odessa, On., Can. . C8 89
Odessa see Odesa, Ukr. . F11 20
Odessa, De., U.S. . C3 101
Odessa, Mo., U.S. . C4 118
Odessa, Tx., U.S. . D1 136
Odessa, Wa., U.S. . B7 140
Odienné, C. Iv. . E3 50
Odin, Il., U.S. . E4 106
Odon, In., U.S. . G4 107
O'Donnell, Tx., U.S. . C2 136
Odorheiu Secuiesc, Rom. . F8 20
Oeiras, Braz. . C3 74
Oelwein, Ia., U.S. . B6 108
Oenpelli, Austl. . C5 60
Of, Tur. . B9 44
O'Fallon, Il., U.S. . E4 106
O'Fallon, Mo., U.S. . f12 118
Ofanto, stm., Italy . D5 18
Offa, Nig. . E5 50
Offenburg, Ger. . F10 12
Offutt Air Force Base, mil., Ne., U.S. . g3 120
Ofotfjorden, b., Nor. . B7 10
Ogaden, reg., Afr. . I14 48
Ogallala, Ne., U.S. . C4 120
Ogasawara-guntō, is., Japan . F16 64
Ogbomosho, Nig. . E5 50
Ogden, Ia., U.S. . B3 108
Ogden, Ks., U.S. . C7 109
Ogden, Ut., U.S. . B4 137
Ogden, Mount, mtn., N.A. . k23 95
Ogdensburg, N.J., U.S. . A3 123
Ogdensburg, N.Y., U.S. . f9 125
Ogeechee, stm., Ga., U.S. . D5 103
Ogemaw, co., Mi., U.S. . D6 115
Ogle, co., Il., U.S. . A4 106
Oglesby, Il., U.S. . B4 106
Oglethorpe, Ga., U.S. . D2 103
Oglethorpe, co., Ga., U.S. . C3 103
Oglethorpe, Mount, mtn., Ga., U.S. . B2 103
Ogoja, Nig. . E6 50
Ogooué, stm., Afr. . D2 54
Ogre, Lat. . H11 10
Ogunquit, Me., U.S. . E2 112
Ogurdžaly, ostrov, i., Turk. . C6 42
Oha, Russia . D16 26
Ohanet, Alg. . E6 48
Ohatchee, Al., U.S. . B3 94
Ohio, co., In., U.S. . G7 107
Ohio, co., Ky., U.S. . C3 110
Ohio, co., W.V., U.S. . A4 141
Ohio, state, U.S. . B3 128
Ohio, stm., U.S. . D10 92
Ohio Brush Creek, stm., Oh., U.S. . D2 128
Ohio City, Oh., U.S. . B1 128
Ohio Peak, mtn., Co., U.S. . C3 99
Ohioville, Pa., U.S. . E1 131
Ohoopee, stm., Ga., U.S. . D4 103
Ohotsk, Russia . D16 26
Ohrid, Mac. . D8 18
Ohrid, Lake, l., Eur. . C8 14
Oiapoque, Braz. . C9 70
Oiapoque (Oyapok), stm., S.A. . C9 70
Oil City, La., U.S. . B2 111
Oil City, Pa., U.S. . D2 131
Oil Creek, stm., Pa., U.S. . C2 131
Oildale, Ca., U.S. . E4 98
Oil Springs, On., Can. . E2 89
Oilton, Ok., U.S. . A5 129
Oise, stm., Eur. . C8 16
Ōita, Japan . E14 29
Ojai, Ca., U.S. . E4 98
Ojinaga, Mex. . B4 78
Ojmjakon, Russia . C16 26
Ojocaliente, Mex. . C4 78
Ojos del Salado, Cerro see Ojos del Salado, Nevado, mtn., S.A. . D4 72
Ojos del Salado, Nevado, mtn., S.A. . D4 72
Oka, stm., Russia . D6 26
Okaba, Indon. . H10 32
Okahandja, Nmb. . C2 56
Okaloosa, co., Fl., U.S. . u15 102
Okamanpeedan Lake, l., U.S. . A3 108
Okanagan Lake, l., B.C., Can. . D8 85
Okanagan Landing, B.C., Can. . D8 85
Okanogan, Wa., U.S. . A6 140
Okanogan, co., Wa., U.S. . A5 140
Ōkāra, Pak. . D10 42
Okarche, Ok., U.S. . B4 129

Name	Map Ref.	Page
Okatibee Reservoir, res., Ms., U.S.	C5	117
Okaukuejo, Nmb.	B2	56
Okavango (Cubango), stm., Afr.	B3	56
Okavango Delta, Bots.	B3	56
Okawville, Il., U.S.	E4	106
Okaya, Japan	C3	31
Okayama, Japan	E14	28
Okazaki, Japan	D3	31
Okeechobee, co., Fl., U.S.	E6	102
Okeechobee, Fl., U.S.	E6	102
Okeechobee, Lake, l., Fl., U.S.	F6	102
Okeene, Ok., U.S.	A3	129
Okefenokee Swamp, sw., U.S.	F4	103
Okemah, Ok., U.S.	B5	129
Okene, Nig.	E6	50
Okfuskee, co., Ok., U.S.	B5	129
Okhotsk see Ohotsk, Russia	D16	26
Okhotsk, Sea of, Asia	D16	26
Okhotsk Basin	B7	144
Okhtyrka, Ukr.	D13	20
Okinawa, Japan	g6	31a
Okinawa-jima, i., Japan	A9	34
Okinawa-shotō, is., Japan	g6	31a
Okino-Erabu-shima, i., Japan	A9	34
Okino-Tori-shima, i., Japan	G15	34
Oki-shotō, is., Japan	D14	28
Okitipupa, Nig.	E5	50
Oklahoma, co., Ok., U.S.	B4	129
Oklahoma, state, U.S.	B4	129
Oklahoma City, Ok., U.S.	B4	129
Oklawaha, Fl., U.S.	C5	102
Oklawaha, stm., Fl., U.S.	C5	102
Oklawaha, Lake, res., Fl., U.S.	C5	102
Okmulgee, Ok., U.S.	B6	129
Okmulgee, co., Ok., U.S.	B5	129
Okoboji, Ia., U.S.	A2	108
Okobojo Creek, stm., S.D., U.S.	C5	134
Okolona, Ky., U.S.	g11	110
Okolona, Ms., U.S.	B5	117
Okondja, Gabon	D2	54
Okotoks, Ab., Can.	D4	84
Oktibbeha, co., Ms., U.S.	B5	117
Oktjabr'sk, Kaz.	E7	26
Oktjabr'skij, Russia	D9	22
Oktjabr'skoe, Russia	B12	22
Oktjabr'skoj Revoljucii, ostrov, i., Russia	B11	26
Oktwin, Mya.	C3	34
Okushiri-tō, i., Japan	C15	28
Ola, Ar., U.S.	B2	97
Ólafsfjörður, Ice.	k19	10a
Olancha Peak, mtn., Ca., U.S.	D4	98
Olanchito, Hond.	B2	80
Öland, i., Swe.	H7	10
Olanta, S.C., U.S.	D8	133
Olathe, Co., U.S.	C3	99
Olathe, Ks., U.S.	D9	109
Olavarría, Arg.	F5	72
Olbia, Italy	D2	18
Olcott, N.Y., U.S.	B2	125
Old Bahama Channel, strt., N.A.	A4	80
Old Bridge, N.J., U.S.	C4	123
Old Castile see Castilla la Vieja, hist. reg., Spain	G5	16
Oldenburg, Ger.	D11	12
Oldenburg, In., U.S.	F7	107
Oldenburg in Holstein, Ger.	C12	12
Old Faithful Geyser, Wy., U.S.	B2	143
Old Forge, Pa., U.S.	D10	131
Old Fort, N.C., U.S.	f10	126
Oldham, co., Ky., U.S.	B4	110
Oldham, co., Tx., U.S.	B1	136
Old Harbor, Ak., U.S.	D9	95
Old Hickory Lake, res., Tn., U.S.	A5	135
Oldman, stm., Ab., Can.	E4	84
Old Man of the Mountain, N.H., U.S.	B3	122
Oldmans Creek, stm., N.J., U.S.	D2	123
Old Orchard Beach, Me., U.S.	E2	112
Old Perlican, Nf., Can.	D5	88
Old Point Comfort, c., Va., U.S.	h15	139
Old Rhodes Key, i., Fl., U.S.	G6	102
Old River Lake, l., Ar., U.S.	k10	97
Olds, Ab., Can.	D3	84
Old Saybrook, Ct., U.S.	D6	100
Oldsmar, Fl., U.S.	o10	102
Old Tampa Bay, b., Fl., U.S.	p10	102
Old Tappan, N.J., U.S.	g9	123
Old Tate, Bots.	C4	56
Old Topsail Inlet, b., N.C., U.S.	C5	126
Old Town, Me., U.S.	D4	112
Old Wives Lake, l., Sk., Can.	G2	91
Olean, N.Y., U.S.	C2	125
O'Leary, P.E., Can.	C5	87
Olëkma, stm., Russia	C14	26
Olekminsk, Russia	C14	26
Oleksandriia, Ukr.	E12	20
Olenegorsk, Russia	B15	10
Olenëk, stm., Russia	B13	26
Olenëk, Russia	C13	26
Olenëkskij zaliv, b., Russia	B14	26
Olentangy, stm., Oh., U.S.	B3	128
Oléron, Île d', i., Fr.	E6	16
Olevsk, Ukr.	D9	20
Ol'ga, Russia	E15	26
Olga, Mount, mtn., Austl.	F5	60
Ölgiy, Mong.	B6	28
Olhão, Port.	I3	16
Olifants (Elefantes), stm., Afr.	C4	56
Olifants, stm., Nmb.	C2	56
Olifantshoek, S. Afr.	D3	56
Ólimbos, mtn., Cyp.	E5	44
Ólimbos, Óros, mtn., Grc.	D9	18
Olin, Ia., U.S.	B6	108
Olinda, Braz.	C5	74
Olive Branch, Ms., U.S.	A4	117
Olive Hill, Ky., U.S.	B6	110
Olivehurst, Ca., U.S.	C3	98
Oliveira, Braz.	F3	74
Oliver, B.C., Can.	E8	85
Oliver, co., N.D., U.S.	B4	127
Oliver, Pa., U.S.	G2	131
Oliver Dam, U.S.	C5	94
Oliver Springs, Tn., U.S.	C9	135
Olivet, Mi., U.S.	F6	115
Olivia, Mn., U.S.	F4	116
Oljutorskij, mys, c., Russia	D19	26
Olla, La., U.S.	C3	111
Ollagüe, Chile	B3	69
Olmito, Tx., U.S.	F4	136
Olmos, Peru	E4	70
Olmos Park, Tx., U.S.	k7	136
Olmsted, co., Mn., U.S.	G6	116
Olmsted Falls, Oh., U.S.	h9	128
Olney, Il., U.S.	E5	106
Olney, Md., U.S.	B3	113
Olney, Tx., U.S.	C3	136
Olomouc, Czech Rep.	E4	20
Olonec, Russia	B5	22
Olongapo, Phil.	D8	34
Oloron-Sainte-Marie, Fr.	F6	16
Olot, Spain	F8	16
Olovjannaja, Russia	A11	28
Olsztyn, Pol.	C6	20
Olteniţa, Rom.	G9	20
Olton, Tx., U.S.	B1	136
Olustee, Ok., U.S.	C2	129
Olympia, Wa., U.S.	B3	140
Olympic Mountains, mts., Wa., U.S.	B2	140
Olympic National Park, Wa., U.S.	B2	140
Olympus see Ólimbos, mtn., Cyp.	E5	44
Olympus, Mount see Ólimbos, Óros, mtn., Grc.	D9	18
Olympus, Mount, mtn., Wa., U.S.	B2	140
Olyphant, Pa., U.S.	D10	131
Omagh, N. Ire., U.K.	C3	12
Omaha, Ne., U.S.	C10	120
Omaha Indian Reservation, Ne., U.S.	B9	120
Omak, Wa., U.S.	A6	140
Omak Lake, l., Wa., U.S.	A6	140
Oman, ctry., Asia	G7	38
Oman, Gulf of, b., Asia	F7	42
Omar, W.V., U.S.	D3	141
Omarama, N.Z.	p12	63c
Omaruru, Nmb.	C2	56
Omatako, stm., Nmb.	B2	56
Ombai, Selat, strt., Asia	E7	36
Omboué, Gabon	D1	54
Omčak, Russia	C16	26
Omdurman see Umm Durmān, Sudan	G11	48
Omega, Ga., U.S.	E3	103
Omemee, On., Can.	C6	89
Omerville, P.Q., Can.	D5	90
Ometepe, Isla de, i., Nic.	C2	80
Ometepec, Mex.	D5	78
Omineca, stm., B.C., Can.	B5	85
Omineca Mountains, mts., B.C., Can.	A4	85
Ōmiya, Japan	C3	31
Ommaney, Cape, c., Ak., U.S.	D12	95
Omolon, stm., Russia	C17	26
Ompompanoosuc, stm., Vt., U.S.	D4	138
Omro, Wi., U.S.	D5	142
Omsk, Russia	D9	26
Omsukčan, Russia	C17	26
Ōmuda (Ōmuta), Japan	E14	28
Ōmura, Japan	D1	31
Ōmuta (Ōmuda), Japan	E14	28
Omutninsk, Russia	C9	22
Onaga, Ks., U.S.	C7	109
Onalaska, Wa., U.S.	C3	140
Onalaska, Wi., U.S.	E2	142
Onamia, Mn., U.S.	D5	116
Onancock, Va., U.S.	C7	139
Onarga, Il., U.S.	C6	106
Onawa, Ia., U.S.	B1	108
Onawa, Lake, l., Me., U.S.	C3	112
Onaway, Mi., U.S.	C6	115
Ondangwa, Nmb.	B2	56
Ondjiva, Ang.	B2	56
Ondo, Nig.	E5	50
Öndörhaan, Mong.	B10	28
Oneco, Fl., U.S.	E4	102
Onega, stm., Russia	B6	22
Onega, Russia	C5	26
Onega, Lake see Onežskoe ozero, l., Russia	C5	26
Onega Bay see Onežskaja guba, b., Russia	B6	22
One Hundred Fifty Mile House, B.C., Can.	C7	85
One Hundred Mile House, B.C., Can.	D7	85
Oneida, co., Id., U.S.	G6	105
Oneida, co., N.Y., U.S.	C6	110
Oneida, N.Y., U.S.	B5	125
Oneida, co., N.Y., U.S.	B5	125
Oneida, Oh., U.S.	C1	128
Oneida, Tn., U.S.	C9	135
Oneida, co., Wi., U.S.	C4	142
Oneida Lake, l., N.Y., U.S.	B5	125
O'Neill, Ne., U.S.	B7	120
Onekotan, ostrov, i., Russia	E17	26
Oneonta, Al., U.S.	B3	94
Oneonta, N.Y., U.S.	C5	125
Oneşti, Rom.	F9	20
Onežskaja guba, b., Russia	B6	22
Onežskoe ozero, l., Russia	C5	26
Ongole, India	F4	40
Onitsha, Nig.	E6	50
Onida, S.D., U.S.	C5	134
Onondaga, co., N.Y., U.S.	C4	125
Onondaga Indian Reservation, N.Y., U.S.	C4	125
Onota Lake, l., Ma., U.S.	B1	114
Onoway, Ab., Can.	C3	84
Onseepkans, S. Afr.	D2	56
Onset, Ma., U.S.	C6	114
Onslow, Austl.	E1	60
Onslow, co., N.C., U.S.	C5	126
Onslow Bay, b., N.C., U.S.	C5	126
Onsted, Mi., U.S.	F6	115
Ontario, prov., Can.	C6	89
Ontario, Ca., U.S.	E5	98
Ontario, co., N.Y., U.S.	C3	125
Ontario, Oh., U.S.	B3	128
Ontario, Or., U.S.	C10	130
Ontario, Lake, l., N.A.	C12	92
Ontinyent, Spain	H6	16
Ontonagon, Mi., U.S.	m12	115
Ontonagon, co., Mi., U.S.	m12	115
Ontonagon Indian Reservation, Mi., U.S.	B1	115
Oodnadatta, Austl.	F2	62
Ooldea, Austl.	G5	60
Oolitic, In., U.S.	G4	107
Oologah, Ok., U.S.	A6	129
Oologah Lake, res., Ok., U.S.	A6	129
Ooltewah, Tn., U.S.	D8	135
Oostburg, Wi., U.S.	E6	142
Oostende, Bel.	E8	12
Ootsa Lake, l., B.C., Can.	C4	85
Opala, D.R.C.	D4	54
Opa-Locka, Fl., U.S.	s13	102
Opava, Czech Rep.	E4	20
Opelika, Al., U.S.	C4	94
Opelousas, La., U.S.	D3	111
Opequon Creek, stm., W.V., U.S.	B6	141
Opobo, Nig.	F6	50
Opočka, Russia	H13	10
Opole, Pol.	D4	20
Oporto see Porto, Port.	—	—
Opotiki, N.Z.	o14	63c
Opp, Al., U.S.	D3	94
Oppdal, Nor.	E3	10
Oppelo, Ar., U.S.	B3	97
Opportunity, Wa., U.S.	B8	140
Optima Reservoir, res., Ok., U.S.	e9	129
Opuwo, Nmb.	B1	56
Oquawka, Il., U.S.	C3	106
Oracle, Az., U.S.	E5	96
Oradea, Rom.	F6	20
Oradell, N.J., U.S.	h8	123
Oradell Reservoir, res., N.J., U.S.	h9	123
Öræfajökull, ice, Ice.	l20	10a
Orai, India	D3	40
Oraibi, Az., U.S.	B5	96
Oran see Wahran, Alg.	C4	48
Oran, Mo., U.S.	D8	118
Oran, Sebkha d', l., Alg.	J6	16
Orange, Austl.	G4	62
Orange, Fr.	E9	16
Orange, Ca., U.S.	n13	98
Orange, co., Ca., U.S.	F5	98
Orange, Ct., U.S.	D3	100
Orange, co., Fl., U.S.	D5	102
Orange, co., In., U.S.	G4	107
Orange, Ma., U.S.	A3	114
Orange, co., N.C., U.S.	A3	126
Orange, N.J., U.S.	B4	123
Orange, co., N.Y., U.S.	D6	125
Orange, Tx., U.S.	D6	136
Orange, co., Tx., U.S.	D6	136
Orange, Va., U.S.	B4	139
Orange, co., Va., U.S.	B4	139
Orange, Cabo, c., Braz.	C9	70
Orange Beach, Al., U.S.	E2	94
Orangeburg, co., S.C., U.S.	E6	133
Orangeburg, S.C., U.S.	E6	133
Orange City, Fl., U.S.	D5	102
Orange City, Ia., U.S.	B1	108
Orange Grove, Ms., U.S.	E5	117
Orange Grove, Tx., U.S.	F4	136
Orange Lake, l., Fl., U.S.	C4	102
Orange Park, Fl., U.S.	B5	102
Orangeville, On., Can.	D4	89
Orangeville, Ut., U.S.	D4	137
Orange Walk, Belize	B2	80
Oranienburg, Ger.	D13	12
Oranje see Orange, stm., Afr.	D2	56
Oranjemund, Nmb.	D2	56
Oranjestad, Aruba	C6	80
Orbetello, Italy	C3	18
Orbost, Austl.	H4	62
Orcas Island, i., Wa., U.S.	A3	140
Orchard City, Co., U.S.	C3	99
Orchard Homes, Mt., U.S.	D2	119
Orchard Park, N.Y., U.S.	C2	125
Orchards, Wa., U.S.	D3	140
Orchard Valley, Wy., U.S.	E8	143
Orcutt, Ca., U.S.	E3	98
Ord, Ne., U.S.	C7	120
Ord, Mount, mtn., Austl.	D4	60
Ordu, Tur.	B7	44
Ordway, Co., U.S.	C7	99
Ordzhonikidze see Vladikavkaz, Russia	E6	26
Ordzhonikidze, Ukr.	F13	20
Ordzhonikidze see Yenakiieve, Ukr.	E15	20
Ordžonikidzeabad, Taj.	C9	42
Oreana, Il., U.S.	D5	106
Örebro, Swe.	G6	10
Oregon, Il., U.S.	A4	106
Oregon, Mo., U.S.	B2	118
Oregon, co., Mo., U.S.	E6	118
Oregon, Oh., U.S.	A2	128
Oregon, Wi., U.S.	F4	142
Oregon, state, U.S.	C6	130
Oregon Caves National Monument, Or., U.S.	E2	130
Oregon City, Or., U.S.	B4	130
Oregon Inlet, b., N.C., U.S.	B7	126
Orehovo-Zuevo, Russia	C6	22
Orel, Russia	D5	26
Orem, Ut., U.S.	C4	137
Ore Mountains see Erzgebirge, mts., Eur.	E9	8
Orenburg, Russia	D7	26
Orense, Arg.	F6	72
Orestiás, Grc.	D11	18
Orfanoú, Kólpos, b., Grc.	D9	18
Orfordville, Wi., U.S.	F4	142
Organ Mountains, mts., N.M., U.S.	E3	124
Organ Pipe Cactus National Monument, Az., U.S.	E3	96
Orgun, Afg.	D9	42
Orhei, Mol.	F10	20
Orhon, stm., Mong.	A9	28
Oriental, N.C., U.S.	B6	126
Oriental, Cordillera, mts., Col.	D5	80
Oriental, Cordillera, mts., Peru	F5	70
Orikhiv, Ukr.	F13	20
Orillia, On., Can.	C5	89
Orinoco, stm., S.A.	B6	70
Oriola, Spain	H6	16
Orion, Il., U.S.	B3	106
Orissa, state, India	E4	40
Oristano, Italy	E2	18
Oristano, Golfo di, b., Italy	E2	18
Orivesi, Fin.	F11	10
Oriximiná, Braz.	D8	70
Orizaba, Mex.	D5	78
Orkney, S. Afr.	D4	56
Orkney Islands, is., U.K.	A5	12
Orland, Ca., U.S.	C2	98
Orlando, Fl., U.S.	D5	102
Orland Park, Il., U.S.	k9	106
Orléanais, hist. reg., Fr.	C7	16
Orléans, Fr.	D7	16
Orleans, co., La., U.S.	E6	111
Orleans, Ma., U.S.	C7	114
Orleans, co., N.Y., U.S.	B2	125
Orleans, Vt., U.S.	B4	138
Orleans, co., Vt., U.S.	B4	138
Orléans, Île d', i., P.Q., Can.	C6	90
Orlik, Russia	A7	28
Orman Dam, S.D., U.S.	C2	134
Ormāra, Pak.	E8	42
Ormoc, Phil.	D8	34
Ormond Beach, Fl., U.S.	C5	102
Ormstown, P.Q., Can.	D3	90
Örnsköldsvik, Swe.	E8	10
Orocué, Col.	C5	70
Orofino, Id., U.S.	C2	105
Oroluk, atoll, Micron.	D9	58
Oromocto, N.B., Can.	D3	87
Oromocto Lake, l., N.B., Can.	D2	87
Oron, Nig.	F6	50
Orono, Me., U.S.	D4	112
Oronoco, Mn., U.S.	F6	116
Oroquieta, Phil.	E8	34
Orosei, Golfo di, b., Italy	D2	18
Oroville, Ca., U.S.	C3	98
Oroville, Wa., U.S.	A6	140
Oroville, Lake, res., Ca., U.S.	C3	98
Orrick, Mo., U.S.	B3	118
Orrville, Oh., U.S.	B4	128
Orša, Bela.	B11	20
Orsk, Russia	D7	26
Ortaca, Tur.	D3	44
Ortegal, Cabo, c., Spain	F3	16
Orting, Wa., U.S.	B3	140
Ortiz, Mex.	B2	78
Ortonville, Mi., U.S.	F7	115
Ortonville, Mn., U.S.	E2	116
Orto-Tokoj, Kyrg.	A3	40
Orūmīyeh, Iran	C5	42
Orūmīyeh, Daryācheh-ye, l., Iran	C5	42
Oruro, Bol.	B4	72
Orwell, Oh., U.S.	A5	128
Orwigsburg, Pa., U.S.	E9	131
Oš, Kyrg.	E9	26
Osa, Península de, pen., C.R.	D3	80
Osage, Ia., U.S.	A5	108
Osage, co., Ks., U.S.	D8	109
Osage, co., Mo., U.S.	C6	118
Osage, stm., Mo., U.S.	C3	118
Osage, co., Ok., U.S.	A5	129
Osage, Wy., U.S.	C8	143
Osage Beach, Mo., U.S.	C5	118
Osage City, Ks., U.S.	D8	109
Ōsaka, Japan	E15	28
Osakis, Mn., U.S.	E3	116
Osakis, Lake, l., Mn., U.S.	E3	116
Osawatomie, Ks., U.S.	D9	109
Osborne, Ks., U.S.	C5	109
Osborne, co., Ks., U.S.	C5	109
Osburn, Id., U.S.	B3	105
Osceola, Ar., U.S.	B6	97
Osceola, co., Fl., U.S.	E5	102
Osceola, Ia., U.S.	C4	108
Osceola, co., Ia., U.S.	A2	108
Osceola, In., U.S.	A5	107
Osceola, co., Mi., U.S.	E5	115
Osceola, Mo., U.S.	C4	118
Osceola, Ne., U.S.	C8	120
Osceola, Wi., U.S.	C1	142
Osceola Mills, Pa., U.S.	E5	131
Oscoda, Mi., U.S.	D7	115
Oscoda, co., Mi., U.S.	D6	115
Oscura Mountains, mts., N.M., U.S.	D3	124
Osgood, In., U.S.	F7	107
Oshawa, On., Can.	D6	89
Ō-shima, i., Japan	D3	31
Oshkosh, Ne., U.S.	C3	120
Oshkosh, Wi., U.S.	D5	142
Ōshnovīyeh, Iran	D11	44
Oshogbo, Nig.	E5	50
Oshtorīnān, Iran	E13	44
Oshwe, D.R.C.	D3	54
Osijek, Cro.	B7	18
Oskaloosa, Ia., U.S.	C5	108
Oskaloosa, Ks., U.S.	C8	109
Oskarshamn, Swe.	H7	10
Oskū, Iran	D12	44
Oslo, Nor.	G4	10
Oslofjorden, b., Nor.	G4	10
Osmānābād, India	F3	40
Osmancık, Tur.	B6	44
Osmaniye, Tur.	D7	44
Osmond, Ne., U.S.	B8	120
Osnabrück, Ger.	D11	12
Osorno, Chile	F2	69
Osoyoos, B.C., Can.	E8	85
Osoyoos Lake, l., Wa., U.S.	A6	140
Osprey, Fl., U.S.	E4	102
Ossa, Mount, mtn., Austl.	I4	62
Ossabaw Island, i., Ga., U.S.	E5	103
Osseo, Mn., U.S.	m12	116
Osseo, Wi., U.S.	D2	142
Ossian, Ia., U.S.	A6	108
Ossian, In., U.S.	C7	107
Ossining, N.Y., U.S.	D7	125
Ossipee, stm., U.S.	C5	122
Ossipee Lake, l., N.H., U.S.	C4	122
Ossora, Russia	D18	26
Ostaškov, Russia	C5	22
Östersund, Swe.	E6	10
Osterville, Ma., U.S.	C7	114
Ostfriesische Inseln, is., Ger.	D10	12
Ostrava, Czech Rep.	E5	20
Ostróda, Pol.	C5	20
Ostrogožsk, Russia	D15	20
Ostroh, Ukr.	D9	20
Ostrołęka, Pol.	C6	20
Ostrov, Russia	H13	10
Ostrowiec Świętokrzyski, Pol.	D6	20
Ostrów Mazowiecka, Pol.	C6	20
Ostrów Wielkopolski, Pol.	D4	20
Ostuni, Italy	D6	18
Ōsumi-shotō, is., Japan	E14	28
Osuna, Spain	I4	16
Oswegatchie, stm., N.Y., U.S.	f9	125
Oswego, Il., U.S.	B5	106
Oswego, Ks., U.S.	E8	109
Oswego, stm., N.J., U.S.	D4	123
Oswego, N.Y., U.S.	B4	125
Oswego, stm., N.Y., U.S.	B4	125
Oswego, co., N.Y., U.S.	B4	125
Otanmäki, Fin.	D12	10
Otaru, Japan	C16	28
Otava, Fin.	F12	10
Otavi, Nmb.	B2	56
Oteen, N.C., U.S.	f10	126
Otero, co., Co., U.S.	D7	99

Name	Map Ref.	Page
Otero, co., N.M., U.S.	E3	124
Othello, Wa., U.S.	C6	140
Otis Orchards, Wa., U.S.	g14	140
Otis Reservoir, res., Ma., U.S.	B1	114
Otisville, Mi., U.S.	E7	115
Otjikondo, Nmb.	B2	56
Otjiwarongo, Nmb.	C2	56
Otoe, co., Ne., U.S.	D9	120
Otra, stm., Nor.	G2	10
Otradnyj, Russia	D9	22
Ótranto, Italy	D7	18
Otranto, Strait of, strt., Eur.	C7	14
Otsego, Mi., U.S.	F5	115
Otsego, co., Mi., U.S.	C6	115
Otsego, co., N.Y., U.S.	C5	125
Otsego Lake, l., N.Y., U.S.	C6	125
Ōtsu, Japan	C3	31
Ottauquechee, stm., Vt., U.S.	D4	138
Ottawa, On., Can.	B9	89
Ottawa, stm., Can.	I24	82
Ottawa, Il., U.S.	B5	106
Ottawa, Ks., U.S.	D8	109
Ottawa, co., Ks., U.S.	C6	109
Ottawa, co., Mi., U.S.	F4	115
Ottawa, Oh., U.S.	A1	128
Ottawa, stm., Oh., U.S.	e6	128
Ottawa, co., Oh., U.S.	A2	128
Ottawa, co., Ok., U.S.	A7	129
Ottawa Hills, Oh., U.S.	e6	128
Ottenby, Swe.	H7	10
Otterbein, In., U.S.	D3	107
Otter Brook, stm., N.H., U.S.	E2	122
Otter Brook Lake, res., N.H., U.S.	E2	122
Otter Creek, stm., Ut., U.S.	E4	137
Otter Creek, stm., Vt., U.S.	C2	138
Otter Creek Reservoir, res., Ut., U.S.	E4	137
Otter Islands, is., S.C., U.S.	m11	133
Otter Tail, co., Mn., U.S.	D3	116
Otter Tail, stm., Mn., U.S.	D2	116
Otter Tail Lake, l., Mn., U.S.	D3	116
Otterville, On., Can.	E4	89
Ottumwa, Ia., U.S.	C5	108
Otway, Cape, c., Austl.	H3	62
Otwock, Pol.	C6	20
Ouachita, co., Ar., U.S.	D3	97
Ouachita, co., La., U.S.	B3	111
Ouachita, Lake, res., Ar., U.S.	C2	97
Ouachita Mountains, mts., U.S.	E9	92
Ouadda, C.A.R.	B4	54
Ouagadougou, Burkina	D4	50
Ouahigouya, Burkina	D4	50
Ouahran see Wahran, Alg.	C4	48
Oualâta, Maur.	C3	50
Ouallam, Niger	D5	50
Ouallene, Alg.	F5	48
Ouanda Djallé, C.A.R.	B4	54
Ouangolodougou, C. Iv.	E3	50
Ouarâne, reg., Maur.	B2	50
Ouarzazate, Mor.	D3	48
Oubangui (Ubangi), stm., Afr.	D3	54
Oudtshoorn, S. Afr.	E3	56
Oued Rhiou, Alg.	J7	16
Oued-Zem, Mor.	E2	14
Ouellé, C. Iv.	E4	50
Ouémé, stm., Benin	E5	50
Ouessant, Île d', i., Fr.	C4	16
Ouesso, Congo	C3	54
Ouezzane, Mor.	D3	48
Ouham, stm., Afr.	B3	54
Ouidah, Benin	E5	50
Oujda, Mor.	D4	48
Oulu, Fin.	D11	10
Oulujärvi, l., Fin.	D12	10
Oulujoki, stm., Fin.	D12	10
Oum-Chalouba, Chad	G9	48
Oumé, C. Iv.	E3	50
Ounianga Kébir, Chad	G9	48
Ouray, Co., U.S.	C3	99
Ouray, co., Co., U.S.	C3	99
Ouray, Mount, mtn., Co., U.S.	C4	99
Ourense, Spain	F3	16
Ouricuri, Braz.	C3	74
Ourinhos, Braz.	F2	74
Ouro Preto, Braz.	F3	74
Outagamie, co., Wi., U.S.	D5	142
Outardes Quatre, Réservoir, res., P.Q., Can.	h13	90
Outer Hebrides, is., Scot., U.K.	B3	12
Outer Island, i., Wi., U.S.	A3	142
Outer Santa Barbara Passage, strt., Ca., U.S.	F4	98
Outjo, Nmb.	C2	56
Outpost Mountain, mtn., Ak., U.S.	B9	95
Outremont, P.Q., Can.	p19	90
Ouvéa, i., N. Cal.	I9	62a
Ouyen, Austl.	H3	62
Ovalle, Chile	D2	69
Overbrook, Ks., U.S.	D8	109
Overgaard, Az., U.S.	C5	96
Overland, Mo., U.S.	f13	118
Overland Park, Ks., U.S.	m16	109
Overlea, Md., U.S.	B4	113
Overton, Nv., U.S.	G7	121
Overton, co., Tn., U.S.	C8	135
Overton, Tx., U.S.	C5	136
Ovett, Ms., U.S.	D4	117
Ovid, Mo., U.S.	E6	115
Oviedo, Spain	F4	16
Ovoot, Mong.	B10	28
Ovruch, Ukr.	D10	20
Owando, Congo	D3	54
Owasco Lake, l., N.Y., U.S.	C4	125
Owasso, Ok., U.S.	A6	129
Owatonna, Mn., U.S.	F5	116
Owego, N.Y., U.S.	C4	125
Owen, co., In., U.S.	F4	107
Owen, co., Ky., U.S.	B5	110
Owen, Wi., U.S.	D3	142
Owen, Lake, l., Wi., U.S.	B2	142
Owen, Mount, mtn., Co., U.S.	C3	99
Owendo, Gabon	C1	54
Owens, stm., Ca., U.S.	D4	98
Owensboro, Ky., U.S.	C2	110
Owens Cross Roads, Al., U.S.	A3	94
Owens Lake, l., Ca., U.S.	D5	98
Owen Sound, On., Can.	C4	89
Owen Sound, b., On., Can.	C4	89
Owen Stanley Range, mts., Pap. N. Gui.	H12	32
Owensville, In., U.S.	H2	107
Owensville, Mo., U.S.	C6	118
Owensville, Oh., U.S.	C1	128
Owenton, Ky., U.S.	B5	110
Owerri, Nig.	E6	50
Owings Mills, Md., U.S.	B4	113
Owingsville, Ky., U.S.	B6	110
Owl Creek, stm., Wy., U.S.	C4	143
Owl Creek Mountains, mts., Wy., U.S.	C4	143
Owo, Nig.	E6	50
Owosso, Mi., U.S.	E6	115
Owsley, co., Ky., U.S.	C6	110
Owyhee, Nv., U.S.	B5	121
Owyhee, co., Id., U.S.	G2	105
Owyhee, stm., U.S.	E9	130
Owyhee, Lake, res., Or., U.S.	D9	130
Owyhee Dam, Or., U.S.	D9	130
Owyhee Mountains, mts., U.S.	G2	105
Oxbow Dam, U.S.	E2	105
Oxelösund, Swe.	G7	10
Oxford, N.S., Can.	D6	87
Oxford, Eng., U.K.	E6	12
Oxford, Al., U.S.	B4	94
Oxford, Ct., U.S.	D3	100
Oxford, Ga., U.S.	C3	103
Oxford, Ia., U.S.	C6	108
Oxford, In., U.S.	C3	107
Oxford, Ks., U.S.	E6	109
Oxford, Ma., U.S.	B4	114
Oxford, Md., U.S.	C5	113
Oxford, Me., U.S.	D2	112
Oxford, co., Me., U.S.	D2	112
Oxford, Mi., U.S.	F7	115
Oxford, Ms., U.S.	A4	117
Oxford, N.C., U.S.	A4	126
Oxford, Ne., U.S.	D6	120
Oxford, N.Y., U.S.	C5	125
Oxford, Oh., U.S.	C1	128
Oxford, Pa., U.S.	G10	131
Oxford Lake, l., Mb., Can.	B4	86
Oxford Peak, mtn., Id., U.S.	G6	105
Oxnard, Ca., U.S.	E4	98
Oxon Hill, Md., U.S.	f9	113
Oxus see Amu Darya, stm., Asia	B8	42
Oyama, B.C., Can.	D8	85
Oyapok (Oiapoque), stm., S.A.	C9	70
Oyem, Gabon	C2	54
Oyen, Ab., Can.	D5	84
Oyo, Nig.	E5	50
Oyster Bay, N.Y., U.S.	E7	125
Oyster Keys, is., Fl., U.S.	G6	102
Ozamis, Phil.	E8	34
Ozark, Al., U.S.	D4	94
Ozark, Ar., U.S.	B2	97
Ozark, Mo., U.S.	D4	118
Ozark, co., Mo., U.S.	E5	118
Ozark Plateau, plat., U.S.	D9	92
Ozark Reservoir, res., Ar., U.S.	B1	97
Ozarks, Lake of the, res., Mo., U.S.	C5	118
Ozaukee, co., Wi., U.S.	E6	142
Ózd, Hung.	E6	20
Ozernovskij, Russia	D17	26
Ozërnyj, Russia	D11	22
Ozette Lake, l., Wa., U.S.	A1	140
Ozieri, Italy	D2	18
Ozinki, Russia	D8	22
Ozona, Fl., U.S.	o10	102
Ozona, Tx., U.S.	D2	136
Ozurgeti, Geor.	B10	44

P

Name	Map Ref.	Page
Paarl, S. Afr.	E2	56
Paauilo, Hi., U.S.	C6	104
Pabianice, Pol.	D5	20
Pābna, Bngl.	E5	40
Pacajus, Braz.	B4	74
Pacasmayo, Peru	E4	70
Pace, Fl., U.S.	u14	102
Pachacamac, hist., Peru	A2	72
Pachaug Pond, l., Ct., U.S.	C8	100
Pachino, Italy	F5	18
Pachuca de Soto, Mex.	C5	78
Pacific, Mo., U.S.	C7	118
Pacific, Wa., U.S.	f11	140
Pacific, co., Wa., U.S.	C2	140
Pacifica, Ca., U.S.	h8	98
Pacific-Antarctic Ridge	O22	64
Pacific Beach, Wa., U.S.	B1	140
Pacific City, Or., U.S.	B3	130
Pacific Creek, stm., Wy., U.S.	D3	143
Pacific Grove, Ca., U.S.	D3	98
Pacific Ocean	E20	64
Pacific Palisades, Hi., U.S.	g10	104
Pacific Ranges, mts., B.C., Can.	D4	85
Pacific Rim National Park, B.C., Can.	E5	85
Pack Monadnock Mountain, mtn., N.H., U.S.	E3	122
Packwood, Wa., U.S.	C4	140
Pacolet, stm., S.C., U.S.	A4	133
Pacolet, S.C., U.S.	B4	133
Pacolet Mills, S.C., U.S.	B4	133
Pactola Reservoir, res., S.D., U.S.	C2	134
Padang, Indon.	D2	36
Padangpanjang, Indon.	D2	36
Padangsidempuan, Indon.	C1	36
Paddock Lake, Wi., U.S.	n11	142
Paden City, W.V., U.S.	B4	141
Paderborn, Ger.	E11	12
Padma see Ganges, stm., Asia	D5	40
Pádova, Italy	B3	18
Padrauna, India	D4	40
Padre Island, i., Tx., U.S.	F4	136
Padre Island National Seashore, Tx., U.S.	F4	136
Padua see Pádova, Italy	B3	18
Paducah, Ky., U.S.	e9	110
Paducah, Tx., U.S.	B2	136
Paektu, Mount, mtn., Asia	C13	28
Paektu-san see Paektu, Mount, mtn., Asia	C13	28
Paestum, hist., Italy	D5	18
Pafúri, Moz.	C5	56
Pag, Otok, i., Cro.	B5	18
Pagadian, Phil.	E8	34
Pagai Selatan, Pulau, i., Indon.	D2	36
Pagai Utara, Pulau, i., Indon.	D2	36
Pagalu see Annobón, i., Eq. Gui.	C1	52
Pagan, i., N. Mar. Is.	C12	32
Pagasitikós Kólpos, b., Grc.	E9	18
Page, Az., U.S.	A4	96
Page, co., Ia., U.S.	D2	108
Page, co., Va., U.S.	B4	139
Page, W.V., U.S.	C3	141
Pageland, S.C., U.S.	B7	133
Pagoda Peak, mtn., Co., U.S.	A3	99
Pago Pago, Am. Sam.	F12	58
Pagosa Springs, Co., U.S.	D3	99
Paguate, N.M., U.S.	B2	124
Pahala, Hi., U.S.	D6	104
Pahang, stm., Malay.	C2	36
Pahoa, Hi., U.S.	D7	104
Pahokee, Fl., U.S.	F6	102
Pahrump, Nv., U.S.	G6	121
Pahute Mesa, mtn., Nv., U.S.	F5	121
Paia, Hi., U.S.	C5	104
Paide, Est.	G11	10
Päijänne, l., Fin.	F11	10
Pailolo Channel, strt., Hi., U.S.	B5	104
Painan, Indon.	D2	36
Paincourtville, La., U.S.	k9	111
Painesville, Oh., U.S.	A4	128
Paint, stm., Mi., U.S.	B2	115
Paint Creek, stm., Oh., U.S.	C2	128
Paint Creek, stm., W.V., U.S.	m13	141
Paint Creek, North Fork, stm., Oh., U.S.	C2	128
Paint Creek Lake, res., Oh., U.S.	C2	128
Painted Desert, des., Az., U.S.	B4	96
Painted Post, N.Y., U.S.	C3	125
Painted Rock Reservoir, res., Az., U.S.	D3	96
Paintsville, Ky., U.S.	C7	110
Paisley, On., Can.	C3	89
Pajala, Swe.	C10	10
Pakaraima Mountains, mts., S.A.	E7	80
Pakistan, ctry., Asia	E9	42
Pakistan, East see Bangladesh, ctry., Asia	B2	34
Pakokku, Mya.	B3	34
Pakowki Lake, l., Ab., Can.	E5	84
Pak Phanang, Thai.	C2	34
Paks, Hung.	F5	20
Pakxé, Laos	C5	34
Pala, Chad	E7	50
Palacios, Tx., U.S.	E4	136
Palana, Russia	D17	26
Palangkaraya, Indon.	D4	36
Palani, India	G3	40
Palanpur, India	E2	40
Palaoa Point, c., Hi., U.S.	C4	104
Palapye, Bots.	C4	56
Palatine, Il., U.S.	A5	106
Palatka, Fl., U.S.	C5	102
Palau, ctry., Oc.	F10	32
Palau Islands, is., Palau	E9	32
Palaw, Mya.	D3	34
Palawan, i., Phil.	E7	34
Palawan Passage, strt., Phil.	E7	34
Pālayankottai, India	H3	40
Paldiski, Est.	G11	10
Palembang, Indon.	D2	36
Palencia, Spain	F4	16
Palenque, hist., Mex.	D6	78
Palermo, Italy	E4	18
Palestine, hist. reg., Asia	G6	44
Palestine, Ar., U.S.	C5	97
Palestine, Il., U.S.	D6	106
Palestine, Tx., U.S.	D5	136
Palestine, Lake, res., Tx., U.S.	C5	136
Paletwa, Mya.	B2	34
Pālghāt, India	G3	40
Pāli, India	D2	40
Palikea, mtn., Hi., U.S.	g9	104
Palikir, Micron.	D9	58
Palisade, Co., U.S.	B2	99
Palisades Park, N.J., U.S.	h8	123
Palisades Reservoir, res., U.S.	F7	105
Pālitāna, India	E2	40
Palk Strait, strt., Asia	H3	40
Palma, Moz.	A7	56
Palma del Río, Spain	I4	16
Palma de Mallorca, Spain	H8	16
Palmares, Braz.	C4	74
Palmas, Braz.	F10	70
Palma Soriano, Cuba	A4	80
Palm Bay, Fl., U.S.	D6	102
Palm Beach, Fl., U.S.	F6	102
Palm Beach, co., Fl., U.S.	F6	102
Palmdale, Ca., U.S.	E4	98
Palmeira das Missões, Braz.	D7	74
Palmeira dos Índios, Braz.	C4	74
Palmer, Ak., U.S.	C10	95
Palmer, Ma., U.S.	B3	114
Palmer, Mi., U.S.	B3	115
Palmer, Ms., U.S.	D4	117
Palmer, Ne., U.S.	C7	120
Palmer, Tn., U.S.	D8	135
Palmer, Tx., U.S.	n10	136
Palmer Lake, Co., U.S.	B6	99
Palmer Land, reg., Ant.	D34	67
Palmerston, On., Can.	D4	89
Palmerston, atoll, Cook Is.	F13	58
Palmerston North, N.Z.	p14	63c
Palmerton, Pa., U.S.	E10	131
Palmetto, Fl., U.S.	E4	102
Palmetto, Ga., U.S.	C2	103
Palm Harbor, Fl., U.S.	o10	102
Palmi, Italy	E5	18
Palmira, Col.	C4	70
Palms, Isle of, i., S.C., U.S.	F8	133
Palm Springs, Ca., U.S.	F5	98
Palmyra, In., U.S.	H5	107
Palmyra, Mo., U.S.	B6	118
Palmyra, N.J., U.S.	C2	123
Palmyra, N.Y., U.S.	B3	125
Palmyra, Pa., U.S.	F8	131
Palmyra, Wi., U.S.	F5	142
Palmyra see Tudmur, Syria	E8	44
Palo Alto, Ca., U.S.	D2	98
Palo Alto, co., Ia., U.S.	A3	108
Paloich, Sudan	H11	48
Palomar Mountain, mtn., Ca., U.S.	F5	98
Palomas Mountains, mts., Az., U.S.	D2	96
Palo Pinto, co., Tx., U.S.	C3	136
Palopo, Indon.	D6	36
Palo Santo, Arg.	D6	72
Palos Park, Il., U.S.	k9	106
Palos Verdes Estates, Ca., U.S.	n12	98
Palourde, Lake, l., La., U.S.	k9	111
Palouse, Wa., U.S.	C8	140
Palouse, stm., Wa., U.S.	C7	140
Palu, Indon.	D5	36
Palu, Tur.	B4	44
Pamekasan, Indon.	E4	36
Pamiers, Fr.	F7	16
Pamir, mts., Asia	B2	40
Pamlico, stm., N.C., U.S.	B6	126
Pamlico, co., N.C., U.S.	B6	126
Pamlico Sound, strt., N.C., U.S.	B6	126
Pampa, reg., Arg.	F5	72
Pampa, Tx., U.S.	B2	136
Pampa del Infierno, Arg.	D5	72
Pampas, Peru	A3	72
Pamplico, S.C., U.S.	D8	133
Pamplona, Col.	B5	70
Pamplona, Spain	F6	16
Pamunkey, stm., Va., U.S.	C5	139
Pana, Il., U.S.	D4	106
Panaca, Nv., U.S.	F7	121
Panache, Lake, l., On., Can.	A3	89
Panaji, India	F2	40
Panama, ctry., N.A.	I11	75
Panamá, Pan.	D4	80
Panama, Ok., U.S.	B7	129
Panamá, Bahía de, b., Pan.	D4	80
Panamá, Canal de, Pan.	D4	80
Panamá, Golfo de, b., Pan.	D4	80
Panama, Gulf of see Panamá, Golfo de, b., Pan.	D4	80
Panamá, Istmo de, isth., Pan.	D4	80
Panama Basin	H30	64
Panama Canal see Panamá, Canal de, Pan.	D4	80
Panama City see Panamá, Pan.	D4	80
Panama City, Fl., U.S.	u16	102
Panama City Beach, Fl., U.S.	u16	102
Panamint Range, mts., Ca., U.S.	D5	98
Panay, i., Phil.	D8	34
Pancake Range, mts., Nv., U.S.	E6	121
Pančevo, Yugo.	B8	18
Pandharpur, India	F3	40
Pandora, Oh., U.S.	B2	128
Panfilov, Kaz.	E9	26
Pangala, Congo	D2	54
Pangani, Tan.	E7	54
Pangburn, Ar., U.S.	B4	97
Pangi, D.R.C.	D5	54
Pangkajene, Indon.	D5	36
Pangkalanbuun, Indon.	D4	36
Pangkalpinang, Indon.	D3	36
Pango Aluquem, Ang.	E2	54
Panguitch, Ut., U.S.	F3	137
Pangutaran Group, is., Phil.	E7	34
Panhandle, Tx., U.S.	B2	136
Paniau, mtn., Hi., U.S.	B1	104
Panié, Mont, mtn., N. Cal.	I8	62a
Panīpat, India	D3	40
Panj see Amu Darya, stm., Asia	B8	42
Panjang, Indon.	D3	36
Panjgūr, Pak.	E8	42
Pankshin, Nig.	E6	50
Panna, India	E4	40
Pannawonica, Austl.	E2	60
Panola, co., Ms., U.S.	A3	117
Panola, co., Tx., U.S.	C5	136
Panora, Ia., U.S.	C3	108
Pantar, Pulau, i., Indon.	E6	36
Pantelleria, Isola di, i., Italy	F3	18
Pánuco, stm., Mex.	C5	78
Pánuco, Mex.	C5	78
Panxian, China	F8	28
Panyam, Nig.	E6	50
Panyu, China	B6	34
Paola, Italy	E5	18
Paola, Ks., U.S.	D9	109
Paoli, In., U.S.	G5	107
Paoli, Pa., U.S.	o20	131
Paonia, Co., U.S.	C3	99
Pápa, Hung.	F4	20
Papagayo, Golfo de, b., C.R.	C2	80
Papago Indian Reservation, Az., U.S.	E3	96
Papaikou, Hi., U.S.	D6	104
Papantla de Olarte, Mex.	C5	78
Papawai Point, c., Hi., U.S.	C5	104
Papeete, Fr. Poly.	F15	58
Papenburg, Ger.	D10	12
Paphos see Néa Páfos, Cyp.	E5	44
Papigochic, stm., Mex.	B3	78
Papillion, Ne., U.S.	C9	120
Papineauville, P.Q., Can.	D2	90
Paposo, Chile	C3	72
Papua, Gulf of, b., Pap. N. Gui.	H11	32
Papua New Guinea, ctry., Oc.	H11	32
Papun, Mya.	C3	34
Pará see Belém, Braz.	B2	74
Pará, state, Braz.	E9	70
Parabel', Russia	D10	26
Paraburdoo, Austl.	E2	60
Paracatu, Braz.	E2	74
Paracel Islands (Xisha Qundao), is., China	C6	34
Parachute, Co., U.S.	B2	99
Paraćin, Yugo.	C8	18
Paracuru, Braz.	B4	74
Paradis, La., U.S.	k11	111
Paradise, stm., Nf., Can.	B3	88
Paradise, Ca., U.S.	C3	98
Paradise, Nv., U.S.	G6	121
Paradise Hills, N.M., U.S.	B3	124
Paradise Valley, Az., U.S.	k9	96
Paradise Valley, Nv., U.S.	B4	121
Pāradwīp, India	E5	40
Paragould, Ar., U.S.	A5	97
Paraguai (Paraguay), stm., S.A.	B6	72
Paraguaná, Península de, pen., Ven.	C6	80
Paraguay, ctry., S.A.	C6	72
Paraguay (Paraguai), stm., S.A.	C6	72
Paraíba, state, Braz.	C4	74
Paraíba do Sul, stm., Braz.	F3	74
Parakou, Benin	E5	50
Paramaribo, Sur.	B8	70
Paramirim, Braz.	F11	70
Paramount, Md., U.S.	A2	113
Paramus, N.J., U.S.	h8	123
Paramušir, ostrov, i., Russia	D17	26
Paraná, Arg.	E5	72

Name	Map Ref.	Page
Paranã, Braz.	F10	70
Paraná, state, Braz.	C7	72
Paraná, stm., Braz.	F5	68
Paraná, stm., S.A.	E6	72
Paranaguá, Braz.	D8	72
Paranaíba, Braz.	E2	74
Paranapanema, stm., Braz.	C7	72
Paranavaí, Braz.	C7	72
Parang, Phil.	E8	34
Parangaba, Braz.	B4	74
Paranhos, Braz.	C6	72
Paray-le-Monial, Fr.	D9	16
Pārbati, stm., India	D3	40
Parbhani, India	F3	40
Parchment, Mi., U.S.	F5	115
Pardeeville, Wi., U.S.	E4	142
Pardo, stm., Braz.	F2	74
Pardubice, Czech Rep.	E3	20
Parecis, Braz.	A6	72
Parecis, Chapada dos, mts., Braz.	A6	72
Paren', Russia	C18	26
Parepare, Indon.	D5	36
Paria, stm., U.S.	A4	96
Paria, Gulf of, b.	C7	80
Pariaman, Indon.	D2	36
Parigi, Indon.	D6	36
Parika, Guy.	B8	70
Paris, On., Can.	D4	89
Paris, Fr.	C8	16
Paris, Ar., U.S.	B2	97
Paris, Il., U.S.	D6	106
Paris, Ky., U.S.	B5	110
Paris, Mo., U.S.	B5	118
Paris, Tn., U.S.	A3	135
Paris, Tx., U.S.	C5	136
Paris Peak, mtn., Id., U.S.	G7	105
Parita, Bahía de, b., Pan.	D3	80
Park, co., Co., U.S.	B5	99
Park, co., Mt., U.S.	E6	119
Park, stm., N.D., U.S.	A8	127
Park, co., Wy., U.S.	B3	143
Park City, Ks., U.S.	g12	109
Park City, Ut., U.S.	C4	137
Parkdale, P.E., Can.	C6	87
Parke, co., In., U.S.	E3	107
Parker, Az., U.S.	C1	96
Parker, Co., U.S.	B6	99
Parker, Fl., U.S.	u16	102
Parker, S.D., U.S.	D8	134
Parker, co., Tx., U.S.	C4	136
Parker City, In., U.S.	D7	107
Parker Dam, Ca., U.S.	C1	96
Parkersburg, Ia., U.S.	B5	108
Parkersburg, W.V., U.S.	B3	141
Parkers Prairie, Mn., U.S.	D3	116
Parkes, Austl.	G4	62
Parkesburg, Pa., U.S.	G10	131
Park Falls, Wi., U.S.	C3	142
Park Forest, Il., U.S.	B6	106
Park Hall, Md., U.S.	D5	113
Parkhill, On., Can.	D3	89
Park Hills, Ky., U.S.	h13	110
Parkin, Ar., U.S.	B5	97
Parkland, Wa., U.S.	f11	140
Park Layne, Oh., U.S.	C1	128
Park Range, mts., Co., U.S.	A4	99
Park Rapids, Mn., U.S.	D3	116
Park Ridge, Il., U.S.	B6	106
Park Ridge, N.J., U.S.	g8	123
Park River, N.D., U.S.	A8	127
Parkrose, Or., U.S.	B4	130
Parksley, Va., U.S.	C7	139
Parkston, S.D., U.S.	D8	134
Parksville, B.C., Can.	E5	85
Parkville, Md., U.S.	B4	113
Parkville, Mo., U.S.	B3	118
Parkwater, Wa., U.S.	g14	140
Parkwood, N.C., U.S.	B4	126
Parlākimidi, India	F4	40
Parle, Lac qui, l., Mn., U.S.	E3	116
Parlier, Ca., U.S.	D4	98
Parma, Italy	B3	18
Parma, Id., U.S.	F2	105
Parma, Mi., U.S.	F6	115
Parma, Mo., U.S.	E8	118
Parma, Oh., U.S.	A4	128
Parmachenee Lake, l., Me., U.S.	C2	112
Parma Heights, Oh., U.S.	h9	128
Parmer, co., Tx., U.S.	B1	136
Parnaguá, Braz.	F11	70
Parnaíba, stm., Braz.	B3	74
Parnaíba, Braz.	B3	74
Parnassós, mtn., Grc.	E9	18
Pärnu, Est.	G11	10
Paro, Bhu.	D5	40
Paromaj, Russia	D16	26
Parowan, Ut., U.S.	F3	137
Par Pond, res., S.C., U.S.	D5	133
Parral, Chile	F3	72
Parramatta, Austl.	G5	62
Parramore Island, i., Va., U.S.	C7	139
Parras de la Fuente, Mex.	D6	78
Parrish, Al., U.S.	B2	94
Parrsboro, N.S., Can.	D5	87
Parry, Mount, mtn., B.C., Can.	C3	85
Parry Sound, On., Can.	B4	89
Parshall, N.D., U.S.	B3	127
Parsons, Ks., U.S.	E8	109
Parsons, Tn., U.S.	B3	135
Parsons, W.V., U.S.	B5	141
Parsonsburg, Md., U.S.	D7	113
Parthenay, Fr.	D6	16
Partille, Swe.	H5	10
Partizansk, Russia	B2	31
Partridge Point, c., Nf., Can.	C3	88
Paru, stm., Braz.	D9	70
Paru de Oeste, stm., Braz.	C8	70
Pārvatīpuram, India	F4	40
Paryang, China	C4	40
Parys, S. Afr.	D4	56
Pasadena, Nf., Can.	D3	88
Pasadena, Ca., U.S.	E4	98
Pasadena, Md., U.S.	B4	113
Pasadena, Tx., U.S.	r14	136
Pascagoula, Ms., U.S.	E5	117
Pascagoula, stm., Ms., U.S.	E5	117
Pascagoula Bay, b., Ms., U.S.	f8	117
Paşcani, Rom.	F9	20
Pasco, co., Fl., U.S.	D4	102
Pasco, Wa., U.S.	C6	140
Pascoag, R.I., U.S.	B2	132
Pascoag Reservoir, res., R.I., U.S.	B2	132
Pascua, Isla de (Easter Island), i., Chile	K28	64
Pasinler, Tur.	B9	44
Pasir Mas, Malay.	B2	36
Pasni, Pak.	E8	42
Paso de los Libres, Arg.	D6	72
Paso de los Toros, Ur.	E6	72
Paso Robles, Ca., U.S.	E3	98
Pasque Island, i., Ma., U.S.	D6	114
Pasquotank, co., N.C., U.S.	A6	126
Passaic, N.J., U.S.	B4	123
Passaic, co., N.J., U.S.	A4	123
Passaic, stm., N.J., U.S.	h8	123
Passamaquoddy Bay, b., Me., U.S.	C6	112
Passau, Ger.	F13	14
Pass Christian, Ms., U.S.	E4	117
Passero, Capo, c., Italy	F5	18
Passo Fundo, Braz.	D7	72
Passos, Braz.	F2	74
Passumpsic, stm., Vt., U.S.	C4	138
Pastavy, Bela.	B9	20
Pastaza, stm., S.A.	D4	70
Pasto, Col.	C4	70
Pastora Peak, mtn., Az., U.S.	A6	96
Pasuruan, Indon.	E4	36
Pasvalys, Lith.	H11	10
Patadkal, hist., India	F3	40
Patagonia, reg., Arg.	F3	69
Patagonia, Az., U.S.	F5	96
Pātan, India	E2	40
Patapsco, stm., Md., U.S.	B4	113
Pataskala, Oh., U.S.	C3	128
Patchet Brook Reservoir, res., R.I., U.S.	E6	132
Patchogue, N.Y., U.S.	n15	125
Pategi, Nig.	E6	50
Pate Island, i., Kenya	D8	54
Paterna, Spain	H6	16
Paternò, Italy	F5	18
Paterson, N.J., U.S.	B4	123
Pathānkot, India	C3	40
Pathein, Mya.	C2	34
Pathfinder Reservoir, res., Wy., U.S.	D6	143
Patiāla, India	C3	40
Patience Island, i., R.I., U.S.	D5	132
Patman, Lake, res., Tx., U.S.	C5	136
Patna, India	D5	40
Patnos, Tur.	C10	44
Pato Branco, Braz.	D7	72
Patoka, stm., In., U.S.	H2	107
Patoka, In., U.S.	H2	107
Patoka Lake, res., In., U.S.	H4	107
Patos, Braz.	C4	74
Patos, Lagoa dos, b., Braz.	E7	72
Patos de Minas, Braz.	E2	74
Patquía, Arg.	D4	72
Pátrai, Grc.	E8	18
Patraïkós Kólpos, b., Grc.	E8	18
Patrick, co., Va., U.S.	D2	139
Patrick Air Force Base, mil., Fl., U.S.	D6	102
Patrocínio, Braz.	E2	74
Pattani, Thai.	E4	34
Patten, Me., U.S.	C4	112
Patterson, Ga., U.S.	E4	103
Patterson, La., U.S.	E4	111
Patterson Creek, stm., W.V., U.S.	B5	141
Patton, Pa., U.S.	E4	131
Patuākhāli, Bngl.	E6	40
Patuca, stm., Hond.	B3	80
Patuxent, stm., Md., U.S.	D4	113
Patuxent Naval Air Test Center, mil., Md., U.S.	D5	113
Pátzcuaro, Mex.	D4	78
Pau, Fr.	B3	16
Paul, Id., U.S.	G5	105
Paulding, co., Ga., U.S.	C2	103
Paulding, Oh., U.S.	A1	128
Paulding, co., Oh., U.S.	A1	128
Paulina, La., U.S.	h10	111
Paulina Mountains, mts., Or., U.S.	D5	130
Paulina Peak, mtn., Or., U.S.	E5	130
Paulins Kill, stm., N.J., U.S.	A3	123
Paulistana, Braz.	E11	70
Paullina, Ia., U.S.	B2	108
Paulo Afonso, Braz.	C4	74
Paulsboro, N.J., U.S.	D2	123
Paul Stream, stm., Vt., U.S.	B5	138
Pauls Valley, Ok., U.S.	C4	129
Paungde, Mya.	C3	34
Pāveh, Iran	E12	44
Pavia, Italy	B2	18
Pavilion Key, i., Fl., U.S.	G5	102
Pāvilosta, Lat.	H9	10
Pavlof Volcano, vol., Ak., U.S.	D7	95
Pavlohrad, Ukr.	E13	20
Pavlovo, Russia	C7	22
Pavo, Ga., U.S.	F3	103
Pawcatuck, Ct., U.S.	D8	100
Pawcatuck, stm., R.I., U.S.	G1	132
Paw Creek, N.C., U.S.	B2	126
Pawhuska, Ok., U.S.	A5	129
Pawling, N.Y., U.S.	D7	125
Pawnee, Il., U.S.	D4	106
Pawnee, stm., Ks., U.S.	D3	109
Pawnee, co., Ks., U.S.	D4	109
Pawnee, co., Ne., U.S.	D9	120
Pawnee, Ok., U.S.	A5	129
Pawnee, co., Ok., U.S.	A5	129
Pawnee City, Ne., U.S.	D9	120
Pawpaw, Il., U.S.	B5	106
Paw Paw, Mi., U.S.	F5	115
Paw Paw, stm., Mi., U.S.	F4	115
Pawpaw Creek, stm., W.V., U.S.	h10	141
Pawtuckaway Pond, l., N.H., U.S.	D4	122
Pawtucket, R.I., U.S.	C4	132
Pawtuxet, stm., R.I., U.S.	C4	132
Paxton, Il., U.S.	C5	106
Paxton, Ma., U.S.	B4	114
Payakumbuh, Indon.	D2	36
Payette, Id., U.S.	E2	105
Payette, co., Id., U.S.	E2	105
Payette, North Fork, stm., Id., U.S.	E2	105
Payette, South Fork, stm., Id., U.S.	E3	105
Payette Lake, res., Id., U.S.	E3	105
Payne, Oh., U.S.	A1	128
Payne, co., Ok., U.S.	A4	129
Payne, Lac, l., Can.	G25	82
Paynes Find, Austl.	F2	60
Paynesville, Mn., U.S.	E4	116
Paysandú, Ur.	E6	72
Payson, Az., U.S.	C4	96
Payson, Il., U.S.	D2	106
Payson, Ut., U.S.	C4	137
Pazar, Tur.	B9	44
Pazarcık, Tur.	D7	44
Pazardžik, Blg.	C10	18
Paz de Río, Col.	D5	80
Pea, stm., Al., U.S.	D3	94
Peabody, Ks., U.S.	D6	109
Peabody, Ma., U.S.	A6	114
Peabody, stm., N.H., U.S.	B4	122
Peace, stm., Fl., U.S.	E5	102
Peace Dale, R.I., U.S.	F3	132
Peace River, Ab., Can.	A2	84
Peach, co., Ga., U.S.	D3	103
Peacham Pond, res., Vt., U.S.	C4	138
Peach Point, c., Ma., U.S.	f12	114
Peach Springs, Az., U.S.	B2	96
Peak Hill, Austl.	F2	60
Peaks Island, i., Me., U.S.	g7	112
Peale, Mount, mtn., Ut., U.S.	E6	137
Pea Patch Island, i., De., U.S.	B3	101
Pea Ridge, Ar., U.S.	A1	97
Pea Ridge National Military Park, Ar., U.S.	A1	97
Pearisburg, Va., U.S.	C2	139
Pearl, Ms., U.S.	C3	117
Pearl, stm., U.S.	D3	117
Pearland, Tx., U.S.	r14	136
Pearl and Hermes Reef, rf., Hi., U.S.	k12	104
Pearl City, Hi., U.S.	B4	104
Pearl Harbor, b., Hi., U.S.	B3	104
Pearl Harbor Naval Station, mil., Hi., U.S.	g10	104
Pearlington, Ms., U.S.	E4	117
Pearl River, La., U.S.	D6	111
Pearl River, co., Ms., U.S.	E4	117
Pearl River, N.Y., U.S.	g12	125
Pearsall, Tx., U.S.	E3	136
Pearsoll Peak, mtn., Or., U.S.	E3	130
Pearson, Ga., U.S.	E4	103
Peary Land, reg., Grnld.	B32	82
Pease, stm., Tx., U.S.	B3	136
Pebane, Moz.	B6	56
Peć, Yugo.	C8	18
Pecatonica, Il., U.S.	A4	106
Pecatonica, stm., U.S.	A4	106
Pecatonica, East Branch, stm., Wi., U.S.	F4	142
Pečenga, Russia	C5	26
Pechora see Pečora, Russia	C7	26
Pechora see Pečora, stm., Russia	C7	26
Pechora Bay see Pečorskaja guba, b., Russia	A9	22
Peckerwood Lake, res., Ar., U.S.	C4	97
Pečora, Russia	C7	26
Pečora, stm., Russia	C7	26
Pečorskaja guba, b., Russia	A9	22
Pečorskoe more, Russia	C7	26
Pecos, N.M., U.S.	B4	124
Pecos, Tx., U.S.	D1	136
Pecos, co., Tx., U.S.	D1	136
Pecos, stm., U.S.	E7	92
Pecos National Monument, N.M., U.S.	B4	124
Pécs, Hung.	F5	20
Peculiar, Mo., U.S.	C3	118
Peddocks Island, i., Ma., U.S.	g12	114
Pedernales, Ven.	D7	80
Pedra Azul, Braz.	E3	74
Pedreiras, Braz.	B3	74
Pedro Afonso, Braz.	E10	70
Pedro II, Braz.	B3	74
Pedro Juan Caballero, Para.	C6	72
Peebles, Oh., U.S.	D2	128
Peekskill, N.Y., U.S.	D7	125
Peel, stm., Can.	E13	82
Pegasus Bay, b., N.Z.	p13	63c
Pegram, Tn., U.S.	A5	135
Pehuajó, Arg.	F5	72
Peikang, Tai.	E5	30
Peixian, China	C4	30
Pekalongan, Indon.	E3	36
Pekanbaru, Indon.	C2	36
Pekin, Il., U.S.	C4	106
Pekin, In., U.S.	G5	107
Peking see Beijing, China	D11	28
Pelagie, Isole, is., Italy	G4	18
Pelahatchie, Ms., U.S.	C4	117
Pelee Island, i., On., Can.	F2	89
Peleng, Pulau, i., Indon.	D6	36
Pelham, On., Can.	D5	89
Pelham, Al., U.S.	B3	94
Pelham, Ga., U.S.	E2	103
Pelham, N.H., U.S.	E4	122
Pelham Manor, N.Y., U.S.	h13	125
Pelican Bay, b., Mb., Can.	C1	86
Pelican Lake, l., Mb., Can.	C1	86
Pelican Lake, l., Mn., U.S.	D3	116
Pelican Lake, l., Mn., U.S.	B6	116
Pelican Lake, l., Mn., U.S.	E5	116
Pelican Lake, l., Mn., U.S.	D4	116
Pelican Lake, l., Wi., U.S.	C4	142
Pelican Mountain, mtn., Ab., Can.	B4	84
Pelican Rapids, Mn., U.S.	D2	116
Pella, Ia., U.S.	C5	108
Pell City, Al., U.S.	B3	94
Pell Lake, Wi., U.S.	n11	142
Pello, Fin.	C11	10
Peloponnesus see Pelopónnisos, pen., Grc.	F8	18
Pelopónnisos, pen., Grc.	F8	18
Pelotas, Braz.	E7	72
Pelton, Lake, l., La., U.S.	E5	111
Pemadumcook Lake, l., Me., U.S.	C3	112
Pematangsiantar, Indon.	C1	36
Pemba, Moz.	A7	56
Pemba, i., Tan.	E7	54
Pemberton, Austl.	G2	60
Pemberton, Ab., Can.	C3	84
Pemberville, Oh., U.S.	A2	128
Pembina, stm., Ab., Can.	B4	84
Pembina, N.D., U.S.	A8	127
Pembina, co., N.D., U.S.	A8	127
Pembroke, On., Can.	B7	89
Pembroke, Wales, U.K.	E4	12
Pembroke, Ga., U.S.	D5	103
Pembroke, Ky., U.S.	D2	110
Pembroke, Ma., U.S.	B6	114
Pembroke, N.C., U.S.	C3	126
Pembroke, Va., U.S.	C2	139
Pembroke Pines, Fl., U.S.	r13	102
Pemigewasset, stm., N.H., U.S.	C3	122
Pemiscot, co., Mo., U.S.	E8	118
Penang see George Town, Malay.	B2	36
Peñaranda de Bracamonte, Spain	G4	16
Pen Argyl, Pa., U.S.	E11	131
Peñarroya-Pueblonuevo, Spain	H4	16
Penas, Golfo de, b., Chile	G1	69
Peñasco, N.M., U.S.	A4	124
Peñasco, Rio, stm., N.M., U.S.	E4	124
Penbrook, Pa., U.S.	F8	131
Pendembu, S.L.	E2	50
Pendembu, S.L.	E2	50
Pender, co., N.C., U.S.	C4	126
Pender, Ne., U.S.	B9	120
Pendleton, In., U.S.	E6	107
Pendleton, co., Ky., U.S.	B5	110
Pendleton, Or., U.S.	B8	130
Pendleton, S.C., U.S.	B2	133
Pendleton, co., W.V., U.S.	C5	141
Pend Oreille, co., Wa., U.S.	A8	140
Pend Oreille, Lake, l., Id., U.S.	A2	105
Pend Oreille, Mount, mtn., Id., U.S.	A2	105
Penedo, Braz.	D4	74
Penetanguishene, On., Can.	C5	89
Penglai, China	D12	28
Pengshui, China	F9	28
Pengxian, China	C1	30
Penhold, Ab., Can.	C4	84
Peniche, Port.	H2	16
Penida, Nusa, i., Indon.	E5	36
Pennant Point, c., N.S., Can.	E6	87
Pennask Mountain, mtn., B.C., Can.	E7	85
Pennell, Mount, mtn., Ut., U.S.	F5	137
Penneru, stm., India	G3	40
Penn Hills, Pa., U.S.	k14	131
Pennington, co., Mn., U.S.	B2	116
Pennington, co., S.D., U.S.	D2	134
Pennington Gap, Va., U.S.	f8	139
Pennsauken, N.J., U.S.	D2	123
Pennsboro, W.V., U.S.	B4	141
Pennsburg, Pa., U.S.	F11	131
Penns Grove, N.J., U.S.	D2	123
Pennsville, N.J., U.S.	D1	123
Pennsylvania, state, U.S.	E7	131
Pennville, In., U.S.	D7	107
Penn Yan, N.Y., U.S.	C3	125
Penobscot, stm., Me., U.S.	C4	112
Penobscot, co., Me., U.S.	C4	112
Penobscot Bay, b., Me., U.S.	D3	112
Penobscot Lake, l., Me., U.S.	C2	112
Penong, Austl.	G5	60
Penonomé, Pan.	D3	80
Penrhyn, atoll, Cook Is.	E14	58
Penrith, Austl.	G5	62
Penrith, Eng., U.K.	C5	12
Pensacola, Fl., U.S.	u14	102
Pensacola Bay, b., Fl., U.S.	u14	102
Pensacola Dam, Ok., U.S.	A6	129
Pensacola Mountains, mts., Ant.	E36	67
Pentagon Mountain, mtn., Mt., U.S.	C3	119
Pentecost Island see Pentecôte, i., Vanuatu	k9	62a
Pentecôte, i., Vanuatu	k9	62a
Penticton, B.C., Can.	E8	85
Pentland Firth, strt., Scot., U.K.	A5	12
Pentwater, Mi., U.S.	E4	115
Penza, Russia	D6	26
Penzance, Eng., U.K.	E4	12
Penžinskaja guba, b., Russia	C18	26
Peonan Point, c., Mb., Can.	D2	86
Peoria, Az., U.S.	D3	96
Peoria, Il., U.S.	C4	106
Peoria, co., Il., U.S.	C4	106
Peoria Heights, Il., U.S.	C4	106
Peotone, Il., U.S.	B6	106
Pepacton Reservoir, res., N.Y., U.S.	C6	125
Pepeekeo, Hi., U.S.	D6	104
Pepin, Wi., U.S.	D1	142
Pepin, co., Wi., U.S.	D2	142
Pepin, Lake, l., U.S.	D1	142
Pepperell, Ma., U.S.	A4	114
Pequannock, N.J., U.S.	B4	123
Pequest, stm., N.J., U.S.	B2	123
Pequop Mountains, mts., Nv., U.S.	C7	121
Pequot Lakes, Mn., U.S.	D4	116
Perabumulih, Indon.	D2	36
Percival Lakes, l., Austl.	E3	60
Percy, Il., U.S.	E4	106
Perdido, Al., U.S.	D2	94
Perdido, stm., U.S.	E2	94
Perdido Bay, b., Al., U.S.	E2	94
Pereira, Col.	C4	70
Pereislav-Khmel'nyts'kyi, Ukr.	D11	20
Pere Marquette, stm., Mi., U.S.	E4	115
Pereslavl'-Zalesskij, Russia	C6	22
Pergamino, Arg.	E5	72
Pergamum, hist., Tur.	C2	44
Perham, Mn., U.S.	D3	116
Perico, Arg.	C4	72
Pericos, Mex.	B3	78
Peridot, Az., U.S.	D5	96
Périgueux, Fr.	E7	16
Perijá, Serranía de, mts., S.A.	G10	76
Perkasie, Pa., U.S.	F11	131
Perkins, co., Ne., U.S.	D4	120
Perkins, Ok., U.S.	B4	129
Perkins, co., S.D., U.S.	B3	134
Perkinston, Ms., U.S.	E4	117
Perlas, Archipiélago de las, is., Pan.	D4	80
Perlas, Laguna de, b., Nic.	D5	80
Perm', Russia	D7	26
Pernambuco, state, Braz.	C4	74
Pernik, Blg.	C9	18
Perpignan, Fr.	F8	16
Perquimans, co., N.C., U.S.	A6	126
Perrine, Fl., U.S.	G6	102
Perro, Laguna del, l., N.M., U.S.	C4	124
Perrot, Île, i., P.Q., Can.	q19	90
Perry, co., Al., U.S.	C2	94
Perry, co., Ar., U.S.	C3	97
Perry, Fl., U.S.	B3	102
Perry, Ga., U.S.	D3	103
Perry, Ia., U.S.	C3	108
Perry, co., Il., U.S.	E4	106

Name	Map Ref.	Page
Perry, co., In., U.S.	H4	107
Perry, co., Ky., U.S.	C6	110
Perry, co., Mo., U.S.	D8	118
Perry, co., Ms., U.S.	D4	117
Perry, co., Oh., U.S.	C3	128
Perry, co., Pa., U.S.	F7	131
Perry, co., Tn., U.S.	B4	135
Perry Hall, Md., U.S.	B5	113
Perry Lake, res., Ks., U.S.	C8	109
Perryman, Md., U.S.	B5	113
Perrysburg, Oh., U.S.	A2	128
Perry Stream, stm., N.H., U.S.	f7	122
Perry's Victory and International Peace Memorial, hist., Oh., U.S.	A2	128
Perryton, Tx., U.S.	A2	136
Perryville, Ar., U.S.	B3	97
Perryville, Ky., U.S.	C5	110
Perryville, Md., U.S.	A5	113
Perryville, Mo., U.S.	D8	118
Pershing, co., Nv., U.S.	C3	121
Persia see Iran, ctry., Asia	D6	42
Persian Gulf (The Gulf), b., Asia	E6	42
Person, co., N.C., U.S.	A3	126
Perth, Austl.	G2	60
Perth, On., Can.	C8	89
Perth, Scot., U.K.	B5	12
Perth Amboy, N.J., U.S.	B4	123
Perth-Andover, N.B., Can.	D10	87
Perth Basin	K13	64
Peru, Il., U.S.	B4	106
Peru, In., U.S.	C5	107
Peru, Ne., U.S.	D10	120
Peru, ctry., S.A.	E4	70
Peru Basin	J5	66
Peru-Chile Trench	J6	66
Perugia, Italy	C4	18
Peruíbe, Braz.	C8	72
Pervari, Tur.	D10	44
Pervomais'k, Ukr.	E11	20
Pervoural'sk, Russia	D7	26
Pesaro, Italy	C4	18
Pescara, Italy	C5	18
Peshastin, Wa., U.S.	B5	140
Peshāwar, Pak.	D10	42
Peshtigo, Wi., U.S.	C6	142
Peshtigo, stm., Wi., U.S.	C5	142
Pesqueira, Braz.	C4	74
Pessac, Fr.	E6	16
Pëstraja Dresva, Russia	C17	26
Petaḥ Tiqwa, Isr.	F6	44
Petal, Ms., U.S.	D4	117
Petaluma, Ca., U.S.	C2	98
Petatlán, Mex.	D4	78
Petawawa, On., Can.	B7	89
Petawawa, stm., On., Can.	A6	89
Petenwell Lake, res., Wi., U.S.	D4	142
Peterborough, Austl.	G2	62
Peterborough, On., Can.	C6	89
Peterborough, Eng., U.K.	D6	12
Peterborough, N.H., U.S.	E3	122
Peterhead, Scot., U.K.	B6	12
Peter I Island, i., Ant.	C31	67
Peter Pond Lake, l., Sk., Can.	m7	91
Petersburg, Ak., U.S.	D13	95
Petersburg, Il., U.S.	C4	106
Petersburg, In., U.S.	H3	107
Petersburg, Mi., U.S.	G7	115
Petersburg, Oh., U.S.	B5	128
Petersburg, Tx., U.S.	C2	136
Petersburg, Va., U.S.	C5	139
Petersburg, W.V., U.S.	B5	141
Peters Creek, stm., W.V., U.S.	m14	141
Peterson, Al., U.S.	B2	94
Peterson Field, mil., Co., U.S.	C6	99
Petersville, Al., U.S.	A2	94
Peter the Great Bay see Petra Velikogo, zaliv, b., Russia	C14	28
Pétion-Ville, Haiti	B5	80
Petit Bois Island, i., Ms., U.S.	E5	117
Petitcodiac, N.B., Can.	D4	87
Petitcodiac, stm., N.B., Can.	C5	87
Petite Amite, stm., La., U.S.	h10	111
Petite Rivière Noire, Piton de la, mtn., Mrts.	g10	57a
Petit Jean, stm., Ar., U.S.	B2	97
Petit Lac Des Allemands, l., La., U.S.	k11	111
Petit Lake, l., La., U.S.	k12	111
Petit-Rocher, N.B., Can.	B4	87
Petitsikapau Lake, l., Nf., Can.	g8	88
Peto, Mex.	C7	78
Petoskey, Mi., U.S.	C6	115
Petra see Al-Batrā', hist., Jord.	D3	42
Petra Velikogo, zaliv, b., Russia	C14	28
Petrić, Bul.	D9	18
Petrified Forest National Park, Az., U.S.	B6	96
Petrila, Rom.	G7	20
Petrodvorec, Russia	G13	10
Petrograd see Sankt-Peterburg, Russia	D5	26
Petrolândia, Braz.	C4	74
Petroleum, co., Mt., U.S.	C8	119
Petrolia, On., Can.	E2	89
Petrolina, Braz.	C3	74
Petropavlovsk, Kaz.	D8	26
Petropavlovsk-Kamčatskij, Russia	D17	26
Petrópolis, Braz.	F3	74
Petros, Tn., U.S.	C9	135
Petroșani, Rom.	G7	20
Petrovsk, Russia	D8	22
Petrozavodsk, Russia	C5	26
Pettaquamscutt Lake Shores, R.I., U.S.	F4	132
Pettingell Peak, mtn., Co., U.S.	B5	99
Pettis, co., Mo., U.S.	C4	118
Pevek, Russia	C19	26
Pevely, Mo., U.S.	g13	118
Pewaukee, Wi., U.S.	E5	142
Pewaukee Lake, l., Wi., U.S.	m11	142
Pewee Valley, Ky., U.S.	B4	110
Pha-an, Myan.	C3	34
Phalaborwa, S. Afr.	C5	56
Phalodi, India	D2	40
Phangan, Ko, i., Thai.	E4	34
Phangnga, Thai.	E3	34
Phanom Dongrak Range, mts., Asia	D4	34
Phan Rang, Viet.	D5	34
Phan Si Pan see Fan Si Pan, mtn., Viet.	B4	34
Phan Thiet, Viet.	D5	34
Pharr, Tx., U.S.	F3	136
Phatthalung, Thai.	E4	34
Phayao, Thai.	C3	34
Phelps, Ky., U.S.	C7	110
Phelps, N.Y., U.S.	C3	125
Phelps, Wi., U.S.	B4	142
Phelps, co., Mo., U.S.	D6	118
Phelps, co., Ne., U.S.	D6	120
Phelps Lake, l., N.C., U.S.	B6	126
Phenix City, Al., U.S.	C4	94
Phetchabun, Thai.	C4	34
Phetchaburi, Thai.	D3	34
Phibun Mangsahan, Thai.	C5	34
Phichit, Thai.	C4	34
Philadelphia, Ms., U.S.	C4	117
Philadelphia, Pa., U.S.	G11	131
Philadelphia, co., Pa., U.S.	G12	131
Philadelphia Naval Shipyard, mil., Pa., U.S.	P21	131
Phil Campbell, Al., U.S.	A2	94
Philip, S.D., U.S.	C4	134
Philippeville see Skikda, Alg.	C6	48
Philippi, W.V., U.S.	B4	141
Philippi see Filippoi, hist., Grc.	D10	18
Philippine Basin	G15	64
Philippines, ctry., Asia	C8	34
Philippine Sea	H16	24
Philippine Trench	H15	64
Philippopolis see Plovdiv, Bul.	C10	18
Philipsburg, Mt., U.S.	D3	119
Philipsburg, Pa., U.S.	E5	131
Philleo Lake, l., Wa., U.S.	h14	140
Phillips, Me., U.S.	D2	112
Phillips, Tx., U.S.	B2	136
Phillips, Wi., U.S.	C3	142
Phillips, co., Ar., U.S.	C5	97
Phillips, co., Co., U.S.	A8	99
Phillips, co., Ks., U.S.	C4	109
Phillips, co., Mt., U.S.	B8	119
Phillips Brook, stm., N.H., U.S.	A4	122
Phillipsburg, Ks., U.S.	C4	109
Phillipsburg, N.J., U.S.	B2	123
Philmont, N.Y., U.S.	C7	125
Philo, Il., U.S.	C5	106
Philomath, Or., U.S.	C3	130
Philpott Reservoir, res., Va., U.S.	D2	139
Phitsanulok, Thai.	C4	34
Phnom Penh see Phnum Pénh, Camb.	D4	34
Phnum Pénh (Phnom Penh), Camb.	D4	34
Phoenix, Az., U.S.	D3	96
Phoenix, Il., U.S.	k9	106
Phoenix, N.Y., U.S.	B4	125
Phoenix, Or., U.S.	E4	130
Phoenix Islands, is., Kir.	E12	58
Phoenixville, Pa., U.S.	F10	131
Phon, Thai.	C4	34
Phôngsali, Laos	B4	34
Phrae, Thai.	C4	34
Phra Nakhon Si Ayutthaya, Thai.	D4	34
Phuket, Thai.	E3	34
Phuket, Ko, i., Thai.	E3	34
Phumi Chhuk, Camb.	D4	34
Phumi Kâmpóng Srâlau, Camb.	D5	34
Phumi Kaôh Kŏng, Camb.	D4	34
Phu Quoc, Dao, i., Viet.	D4	34
Piacenza, Italy	B2	18
Pianosa, Isola, i., Italy	C3	18
Piatra-Neamţ, Rom.	F9	20
Piatt, co., Il., U.S.	D5	106
Piauí, state, Braz.	C3	74
Piave, stm., Italy	A4	18
Pibor Post, Sudan	I11	48
Picacho, Az., U.S.	E4	96
Picardie, hist. reg., Fr.	C8	16
Picardy see Picardie, hist. reg., Fr.	C8	16
Picayune, Ms., U.S.	E4	117
Piccadilly, Nf., Can.	D2	88
Pichanal, Arg.	C5	72
Picher, Ok., U.S.	A7	129
Pichilemu, Chile	E3	72
Pickaway, co., Oh., U.S.	C2	128
Pickens, Ms., U.S.	C4	117
Pickens, S.C., U.S.	B2	133
Pickens, co., Al., U.S.	B1	94
Pickens, co., Ga., U.S.	B2	103
Pickens, co., S.C., U.S.	B2	133
Pickerel Lake, l., Wi., U.S.	C5	142
Pickering, On., Can.	D5	89
Pickerington, Oh., U.S.	C3	128
Pickett, co., Tn., U.S.	C8	135
Pickwick Lake, res., U.S.	A6	117
Pickworth Point, c., Ma., U.S.	f12	114
Pico de Orizaba, Volcán, vol., Mex.	D5	78
Pico Rivera, Ca., U.S.	n12	98
Picos, Braz.	C3	74
Picton, On., Can.	D7	89
Pictou Island, i., N.S., Can.	D7	87
Picture Butte, Ab., Can.	E4	84
Pictured Rocks National Lakeshore, Mi., U.S.	B4	115
Piedecuesta, Col.	D5	80
Piedmont, Al., U.S.	B4	94
Piedmont, Ca., U.S.	h8	98
Piedmont, Mo., U.S.	D7	118
Piedmont, Ok., U.S.	B4	129
Piedmont, S.C., U.S.	B3	133
Piedmont, W.V., U.S.	B5	141
Piedmont Lake, res., Oh., U.S.	B4	128
Piedra, stm., Co., U.S.	D3	99
Piedras Blancas, Point, c., Ca., U.S.	E3	98
Piedras Negras, Guat.	B1	80
Piedras Negras, Mex.	B4	78
Pieksämäki, Fin.	E12	10
Pielinen, l., Fin.	E13	10
Pierce, Co., U.S.	A6	99
Pierce, Id., U.S.	C3	105
Pierce, Ne., U.S.	B8	120
Pierce, co., Ga., U.S.	E4	103
Pierce, co., N.D., U.S.	A5	127
Pierce, co., Ne., U.S.	B8	120
Pierce, co., Wa., U.S.	C3	140
Pierce, co., Wi., U.S.	D1	142
Pierce, Lake, l., Fl., U.S.	E5	102
Pierce City, Mo., U.S.	E3	118
Pierceton, In., U.S.	B6	107
Pierre, S.D., U.S.	C5	134
Pierrefonds, P.Q., Can.	q19	90
Pierre Part, La., U.S.	k9	111
Pierreville, P.Q., Can.	C5	90
Pierson, Fl., U.S.	C5	102
Pierz, Mn., U.S.	E4	116
Piešťany, Slvk.	E4	20
Pietarsaari, Fin.	E10	10
Pietermaritzburg, S. Afr.	D5	56
Pietersburg, S. Afr.	C4	56
Piet Retief, S. Afr.	D5	56
Pigeon, Mi., U.S.	E7	115
Pigeon, stm., In., U.S.	A6	107
Pigeon, stm., Mn., U.S.	h10	116
Pigeon, stm., Wi., U.S.	k10	142
Pigeon, stm., U.S.	f9	126
Pigeon Cove, Ma., U.S.	A6	114
Pigeon Forge, Tn., U.S.	D10	135
Pigeon Point, c., Mn., U.S.	h10	116
Pigg, stm., Va., U.S.	D3	139
Piggott, Ar., U.S.	A5	97
Pigüé, Arg.	F5	72
Pihlajavesi, l., Fin.	F13	10
Pihtipudas, Fin.	E11	10
Pijijiapan, Mex.	D6	78
Pike, co., Al., U.S.	D4	94
Pike, co., Ar., U.S.	C2	97
Pike, co., Ga., U.S.	C2	103
Pike, co., Il., U.S.	D2	106
Pike, co., In., U.S.	H3	107
Pike, co., Ky., U.S.	C7	110
Pike, co., Mo., U.S.	B6	118
Pike, co., Ms., U.S.	D3	117
Pike, co., Oh., U.S.	C2	128
Pike, co., Pa., U.S.	D11	131
Pike, stm., Wi., U.S.	C5	142
Pike Island Dam, U.S.	f8	141
Pike Lake, Mn., U.S.	D6	116
Pikes Peak, mtn., Co., U.S.	C5	99
Pikesville, Md., U.S.	B4	113
Piketberg, S. Afr.	E3	56
Piketon, Oh., U.S.	C2	128
Pikeville, Ky., U.S.	C7	110
Pikeville, Tn., U.S.	D8	135
Piła, Pol.	C4	20
Pilcomayo, stm., S.A.	A5	72
Pīlibhīt, India	D3	40
Pílos, Grc.	F8	18
Pilot Grove, Mo., U.S.	C5	118
Pilot Knob, Mo., U.S.	D7	118
Pilot Mound, Mb., Can.	E2	86
Pilot Mountain, N.C., U.S.	A2	126
Pilot Peak, mtn., Id., U.S.	D3	105
Pilot Peak, mtn., Nv., U.S.	B7	121
Pilot Peak, mtn., Nv., U.S.	E4	121
Pilot Peak, mtn., Wy., U.S.	B3	143
Pilot Point, Tx., U.S.	C4	136
Pilot Range, mts., Nv., U.S.	B7	121
Pilot Rock, Or., U.S.	B8	130
Pilot Station, Ak., U.S.	C7	95
Pilsen see Plzeň, Czech Rep.	E2	20
Pima, Az., U.S.	E6	96
Pima, co., Az., U.S.	E3	96
Pimmit Hills, Va., U.S.	g12	139
Pinal, co., Az., U.S.	E4	96
Pinaleno Mountains, mts., Az., U.S.	E5	96
Pinal Mountains, mts., Az., U.S.	D5	96
Pinang see George Town, Malay.	B2	36
Pınarbaşı, Tur.	C7	44
Pinar del Río, Cuba	A3	80
Pinardville, N.H., U.S.	E3	122
Pincher Creek, Ab., Can.	E4	84
Pinckard, Al., U.S.	D4	94
Pinckney, Mi., U.S.	F7	115
Pinckney Island, i., S.C., U.S.	G6	133
Pinckneyville, Il., U.S.	E4	106
Pinconning, Mi., U.S.	E7	115
Pindaré-Mirim, Braz.	B2	74
Píndhos Óros, mts., Grc.	E8	18
Pindus Mountains see Píndhos Óros, mts., Grc.	E8	18
Pine, Az., U.S.	C4	96
Pine, co., Mn., U.S.	D6	116
Pine, stm., Mi., U.S.	D7	115
Pine, stm., Mi., U.S.	D5	115
Pine, stm., N.H., U.S.	C4	122
Pine, stm., Wi., U.S.	C5	142
Pine, stm., Wi., U.S.	C4	142
Pine Barrens, reg., N.J., U.S.	D3	123
Pine Bluff, Ar., U.S.	C3	97
Pinebluff, N.C., U.S.	B3	126
Pine Bluffs, Wy., U.S.	E8	143
Pine Bridge, Ct., U.S.	D3	100
Pine Castle, Fl., U.S.	D5	102
Pine City, Mn., U.S.	E6	116
Pine Creek, Austl.	C5	60
Pine Creek, stm., Nv., U.S.	C5	121
Pine Creek, stm., Pa., U.S.	C6	131
Pine Creek, stm., Wa., U.S.	B8	140
Pine Creek Lake, res., Ok., U.S.	C6	129
Pinedale, Wy., U.S.	D3	143
Pine Falls, Mb., Can.	D3	86
Pine Forest Range, mts., Nv., U.S.	B3	121
Pine Grove, Pa., U.S.	E9	131
Pine Grove Mills, Pa., U.S.	E6	131
Pine Hill, N.J., U.S.	D3	123
Pine Hills, Fl., U.S.	D5	102
Pinehouse Lake, l., Sk., Can.	B2	91
Pinehurst, Ma., U.S.	f11	114
Pinehurst, N.C., U.S.	B3	126
Pine Island, Mn., U.S.	F6	116
Pine Island, i., Fl., U.S.	F4	102
Pine Island Sound, strt., Fl., U.S.	F4	102
Pine Key, i., Fl., U.S.	p10	102
Pine Knot, Ky., U.S.	D5	110
Pine Lake, Ga., U.S.	h8	103
Pine Lake, l., In., U.S.	A4	107
Pine Lake, l., Wi., U.S.	C5	142
Pine Lawn, Mo., U.S.	f13	118
Pine Level, N.C., U.S.	B4	126
Pinellas, co., Fl., U.S.	D4	102
Pinellas, Point, c., Fl., U.S.	p10	102
Pinellas Park, Fl., U.S.	E4	102
Pine Mountain, Ga., U.S.	D2	103
Pine Mountain, mtn., Or., U.S.	D6	130
Pine Mountain, mtn., Wy., U.S.	E3	143
Pine Point, Me., U.S.	E2	112
Pine Prairie, La., U.S.	D3	111
Pine Ridge, S.D., U.S.	D3	134
Pine Ridge Indian Reservation, S.D., U.S.	D3	134
Pine River, Mn., U.S.	D4	116
Pines, Lake O' the, res., Tx., U.S.	C5	136
Pinesdale, Mt., U.S.	D2	119
Pinetops, N.C., U.S.	B5	126
Pinetown, S. Afr.	D5	56
Pineville, Ky., U.S.	D6	110
Pineville, La., U.S.	C3	111
Pineville, N.C., U.S.	B2	126
Pineville, W.V., U.S.	D3	141
Pinewood, S.C., U.S.	D7	133
Piney Creek, stm., W.V., U.S.	n13	141
Piney Fork, stm., W.V., U.S.	h9	141
Piney Point, Md., U.S.	D4	113
Piney View, W.V., U.S.	n13	141
Pingdu, China	D10	30
Pingelly, Austl.	G2	60
Pingjiang, China	F10	28
Pingle, China	D2	30
Pingliang, China	D9	28
Pingluo, China	B2	30
Pingquan, China	C11	28
Pingtan, China	D4	30
P'ingtung, Tai.	E5	30
Pingwu, China	E8	28
Pingxiang, China	G9	28
Pingxiang, China	F10	28
Pingyang, China	D5	30
Pingyao, China	B3	30
Pingyin, China	B4	30
Pinheiro, Braz.	B2	74
Pini, Pulau, i., Indon.	C1	36
Pinjarra, Austl.	G2	60
Pinjug, Russia	B8	22
Pinnacles National Monument, Ca., U.S.	D3	98
Pinole, Ca., U.S.	h8	98
Pinopolis Dam, S.C., U.S.	E8	133
Pinos, Mount, mtn., Ca., U.S.	E4	98
Pinrang, Indon.	D5	36
Pins, Île des, i., N. Cal.	l9	62a
Pins, Pointe aux, c., On., Can.	E3	89
Pinsk, Bela.	C9	20
Pinsk Marshes see Polesye, reg., Eur.	D8	20
Pinson, Al., U.S.	f7	94
Pinta, Isla, i., Ec.	C1	70
Pinta, Sierra, mts., Az., U.S.	E2	96
Pintados, Chile	C4	72
Pintwater Range, mts., Nv., U.S.	G6	121
Pioche, Nv., U.S.	F7	121
Piombino, Italy	C3	18
Pioneer, Oh., U.S.	A1	128
Pioneer Mountains, mts., Id., U.S.	F5	105
Pioneer Mountains, mts., Mt., U.S.	E3	119
Pioner, ostrov, i., Russia	B10	26
Piotrków Trybunalski, Pol.	D5	20
Pīpār, India	D2	40
Pipe Spring National Monument, Az., U.S.	A3	96
Pipestem Creek, stm., N.D., U.S.	B6	127
Pipestone, Mn., U.S.	G2	116
Pipestone, co., Mn., U.S.	F2	116
Pipestone National Monument, Mn., U.S.	G2	116
Pipestone Pass, Mt., U.S.	E4	119
Pipmuacan, Réservoir, res., P.Q., Can.	k12	90
Piqua, Oh., U.S.	B1	128
Piracicaba, Braz.	F2	74
Piracuruca, Braz.	B3	74
Piraeus see Piraiévs, Grc.	E9	18
Piraiévs, Grc.	E9	18
Piranhas, Braz.	E1	74
Pīrān Shahr, Iran	D11	44
Pirapora, Braz.	E3	74
Pires do Rio, Braz.	E2	74
Pírgos, Grc.	F8	18
Piripiri, Braz.	B3	74
Pirot, Yugo.	C9	18
Pīr Panjāl Range, mts., Asia	E2	28
Pirtleville, Az., U.S.	F6	96
Piru, Indon.	D7	36
Pisa, Italy	C3	18
Pisagua, Chile	A2	69
Piscataqua, stm., N.H., U.S.	D5	122
Piscataquis, co., Me., U.S.	C3	112
Piscataquis, stm., Me., U.S.	C3	112
Piscataquog, stm., N.H., U.S.	D3	122
Piscataway, N.J., U.S.	B4	123
Pisco, Peru	F4	70
Piseco Lake, l., N.Y., U.S.	B6	125
Písek, Czech Rep.	E3	20
Pisgah, Al., U.S.	A4	94
Pisgah, Oh., U.S.	n13	128
Pisgah, Mount, mtn., Wy., U.S.	B8	143
Pisgah Forest, N.C., U.S.	f10	126
Pishan, China	D2	28
Pismo Beach, Ca., U.S.	E3	98
Pisticci, Italy	D6	18
Pistoia, Italy	C3	18
Pistolet Bay, b., Nf., Can.	C4	88
Pit, stm., Ca., U.S.	B3	98
Pita, Gui.	D2	50
Pitcairn, i., Pit.	k14	131
Pitcairn, dep., Oc.	K26	64
Piteå, Swe.	D9	10
Piteålven, stm., Swe.	C8	10
Pitești, Rom.	G8	20
Pithara, Austl.	G2	60
Pitkin, co., Co., U.S.	B4	99
Pitkjaranta, Russia	B5	22
Pitman, N.J., U.S.	D2	123
Pitt, co., N.C., U.S.	B5	126
Pitt Island, i., B.C., Can.	C3	85
Pittsboro, In., U.S.	E5	107
Pittsboro, N.C., U.S.	B3	126
Pittsburg, Ca., U.S.	g9	98
Pittsburg, Ks., U.S.	E9	109
Pittsburg, Tx., U.S.	C5	136
Pittsburg, co., Ok., U.S.	C6	129
Pittsburgh, Pa., U.S.	F1	131
Pittsfield, Il., U.S.	D3	106
Pittsfield, Ma., U.S.	B1	114
Pittsfield, N.H., U.S.	D4	122
Pittsford, Vt., U.S.	D2	138
Pittston, Pa., U.S.	D10	131
Pittsville, Md., U.S.	D7	113
Pittsville, Wi., U.S.	D3	142
Pittsylvania, co., Va., U.S.	D3	139

Name	Map Ref.	Page
Pium, Braz.	F10	70
Piura, Peru	E3	70
Piute, co., Ut., U.S.	E3	137
Piute Peak, mtn., Ca., U.S.	E4	98
Piute Reservoir, res., Ut., U.S.	E3	137
Pivdennyi Buh, stm., Ukr.	F11	20
Pixley, Ca., U.S.	E4	98
Pjandž, stm., Asia	B1	40
Pjaozero, ozero, l., Russia	D14	10
Pjasina, stm., Russia	B10	26
Pjatigorsk, Russia	B4	42
Placentia, Nf., Can.	E5	88
Placentia Bay, b., Nf., Can.	E4	88
Placer, co., Ca., U.S.	C3	98
Placer Mountain, mtn., N.M., U.S.	k8	124
Placerville, Ca., U.S.	C3	98
Placetas, Cuba	A4	80
Placid, Lake, l., Fl., U.S.	E5	102
Placid, Lake, l., N.Y., U.S.	f11	125
Placitas, N.M., U.S.	B3	124
Plain City, Oh., U.S.	B2	128
Plain City, Ut., U.S.	B3	137
Plain Dealing, La., U.S.	B2	111
Plainfield, Ct., U.S.	C8	100
Plainfield, Il., U.S.	B5	106
Plainfield, In., U.S.	E5	107
Plainfield, N.J., U.S.	B4	123
Plainfield, Vt., U.S.	C4	138
Plainfield, Wi., U.S.	D4	142
Plains, Ga., U.S.	D2	103
Plains, Ks., U.S.	E3	109
Plains, Mt., U.S.	C2	119
Plains, Pa., U.S.	n17	131
Plains, Tx., U.S.	C1	136
Plainview, Ar., U.S.	C2	97
Plainview, Mn., U.S.	F6	116
Plainview, Ne., U.S.	B8	120
Plainview, Tx., U.S.	B2	136
Plainville, Ct., U.S.	C4	100
Plainville, Ks., U.S.	C4	109
Plainville, Ma., U.S.	B5	114
Plainwell, Mi., U.S.	F5	115
Plaistow, N.H., U.S.	E4	122
Plampang, Indon.	E5	36
Planeta Rica, Col.	D4	80
Plankinton, S.D., U.S.	D7	134
Plano, Il., U.S.	B5	106
Plano, Tx., U.S.	C4	136
Plantagenet, On., Can.	B9	89
Plantation, Fl., U.S.	r13	102
Plant City, Fl., U.S.	D4	102
Plantersville, Al., U.S.	C3	94
Plantersville, Ms., U.S.	A5	117
Plantsite, Az., U.S.	D6	96
Plantsville, Ct., U.S.	C4	100
Plaquemine, La., U.S.	D4	111
Plaquemines, co., La., U.S.	E6	111
Plasencia, Spain	G3	16
Plaster Rock, N.B., Can.	C2	87
Plata, Río de la, est., S.A.	E6	72
Plate, Île, i., Sey.	i13	57b
Plato, Col.	B5	70
Platte, S.D., U.S.	D7	134
Platte, co., Mo., U.S.	B3	118
Platte, co., Ne., U.S.	C8	120
Platte, co., Wy., U.S.	D7	143
Platte, stm., Mn., U.S.	E4	116
Platte, stm., Ne., U.S.	D6	120
Platte, stm., U.S.	B3	118
Platte City, Mo., U.S.	B3	118
Platteville, Co., U.S.	A6	99
Platteville, Wi., U.S.	F3	142
Plattsburg, Mo., U.S.	B3	118
Plattsburgh, N.Y., U.S.	f11	125
Plattsmouth, Ne., U.S.	D10	120
Plauen, Ger.	E12	12
Plavsk, Russia	C14	20
Playas Lake, l., N.M., U.S.	F2	124
Playgreen Lake, l., Mb., Can.	B2	86
Play Ku, Viet.	D5	34
Pleasant, stm., Me., U.S.	C3	112
Pleasant, Lake, res., Az., U.S.	D3	96
Pleasant Gap, Pa., U.S.	E6	131
Pleasant Garden, N.C., U.S.	B3	126
Pleasant Grove, Al., U.S.	g7	94
Pleasant Grove, Ut., U.S.	C4	137
Pleasant Hill, Ca., U.S.	h8	98
Pleasant Hill, Ia., U.S.	e8	108
Pleasant Hill, Il., U.S.	D3	106
Pleasant Hill, La., U.S.	C2	111
Pleasant Hill, Mo., U.S.	C3	118
Pleasant Hill, Oh., U.S.	B1	128
Pleasant Lake, In., U.S.	A7	107
Pleasant Lake, l., Me., U.S.	C5	112
Pleasant Lake, l., N.H., U.S.	D4	122
Pleasanton, Ca., U.S.	h9	98
Pleasanton, Ks., U.S.	D9	109
Pleasanton, Tx., U.S.	E3	136
Pleasant Prairie, Wi., U.S.	n12	142
Pleasants, co., W.V., U.S.	B3	141
Pleasant Valley, Ia., U.S.	g11	108
Pleasant Valley, Mo., U.S.	h11	118
Pleasant View, Ut., U.S.	B3	137
Pleasantville, Ia., U.S.	C4	108
Pleasantville, N.J., U.S.	E3	123
Pleasantville, N.Y., U.S.	D7	125
Pleasantville, Oh., U.S.	C3	128
Pleasure Beach, Ct., U.S.	D7	100
Pleasure Ridge Park, Ky., U.S.	g11	110
Pleasureville, Ky., U.S.	B4	110
Plenty, Bay of, b., N.Z.	o14	63c
Plentywood, Mt., U.S.	B12	119
Pleseck, Russia	C6	26
Plessisville, P.Q., Can.	C6	90
Pleszew, Pol.	D4	20
Pleven, Bul.	C10	18
Pljussa, Russia	G13	10
Płock, Pol.	C5	20
Ploiești, Rom.	G9	20
Plomosa Mountains, mts., Az., U.S.	D1	96
Plonge, Lac la, l., Sk., Can.	B2	91
Płońsk, Pol.	C6	20
Plovdiv, Bul.	C10	18
Plover, Wi., U.S.	D4	142
Plover, stm., Wi., U.S.	D4	142
Plum, Pa., U.S.	k14	131
Plumas, co., Ca., U.S.	B3	98
Plum Coulee, Mb., Can.	E3	86
Plumerville, Ar., U.S.	B3	97
Plum Island, i., Ma., U.S.	A6	114
Plummer, Id., U.S.	B2	105
Plumsteadville, Pa., U.S.	F11	131
Plumtree, Zimb.	C4	56
Plunge, Lith.	I9	10
Plutarco Elías Calles, Presa, res., Mex.	B3	78
Plymouth, Monts.	B7	80
Plymouth, Eng., U.K.	E4	12
Plymouth, Ct., U.S.	C3	100
Plymouth, Fl., U.S.	D5	102
Plymouth, In., U.S.	B5	107
Plymouth, Ma., U.S.	C6	114
Plymouth, Mi., U.S.	p15	115
Plymouth, Mn., U.S.	m12	116
Plymouth, N.C., U.S.	B6	126
Plymouth, N.H., U.S.	C3	122
Plymouth, Oh., U.S.	A3	128
Plymouth, Pa., U.S.	D10	131
Plymouth, Wi., U.S.	E6	142
Plymouth, co., Ia., U.S.	B1	108
Plymouth, co., Ma., U.S.	C6	114
Plymouth Bay, b., Ma., U.S.	C6	114
Plzeň, Czech Rep.	E2	20
Pô, Burkina	D4	50
Po, stm., Italy	B3	18
Po, stm., Va., U.S.	B5	139
Pobeda, gora, mtn., Russia	C16	26
Pobedy, Peak, mtn., Asia	B11	42
Pobè, Benin	E5	50
Pocahontas, Ar., U.S.	A5	97
Pocahontas, Ia., U.S.	B3	108
Pocahontas, Il., U.S.	E4	106
Pocahontas, co., Ia., U.S.	B3	108
Pocahontas, co., W.V., U.S.	C4	141
Pocasset, Ma., U.S.	C6	114
Pocatalico, W.V., U.S.	C3	141
Pocatalico, stm., W.V., U.S.	C3	141
Pocatello, Id., U.S.	G6	105
Počep, Russia	C12	20
Počinok, Russia	B12	20
Poções, Braz.	D3	74
Pocola, Ok., U.S.	B7	129
Pocomoke, stm., Md., U.S.	D7	113
Pocomoke City, Md., U.S.	D6	113
Pocomoke Sound, strt., Md., U.S.	E6	113
Poconé, Braz.	B6	72
Pocono Mountains, hills, Pa., U.S.	E11	131
Pocono Pines, Pa., U.S.	D11	131
Poços de Caldas, Braz.	F2	74
Pocotopaug Lake, res., Ct., U.S.	C6	100
Podgorica, Yugo.	C7	18
Podkamennaja Tunguska, Russia	C10	26
Podkamennaja Tunguska, stm., Russia	C11	26
Podol'sk, Russia	C6	22
Podor, Sen.	C2	50
Podporože, Russia	B5	22
Pofadder, S. Afr.	D2	56
Poge, Cape, c., Ma., U.S.	D7	114
Pograničnyj, Russia	C14	28
P'ohang, S. Kor.	D13	28
Pohénégamook, P.Q., Can.	B8	90
Pohjanmaa, reg., Fin.	D11	10
Pohnpei, i., Micron.	D9	58
Pohue Bay, b., Hi., U.S.	E6	104
Pohvistnevo, Russia	D9	22
Poinsett, co., Ar., U.S.	B5	97
Poinsett, Cape, c., Ant.	C16	67
Poinsett, Lake, l., Fl., U.S.	D6	102
Poinsett, Lake, l., S.D., U.S.	C8	134
Point Clear, Al., U.S.	E2	94
Pointe a la Hache, La., U.S.	E6	111
Pointe-à-Pitre, Guad.	B7	80
Pointe-au-Pic, P.Q., Can.	B7	90
Pointe-Calumet, P.Q., Can.	p19	90
Pointe-Claire, P.Q., Can.	D4	90
Pointe Coupee, co., La., U.S.	D4	111
Pointe-des-Cascades, P.Q., Can.	q19	90
Point Edward, On., Can.	D2	89
Pointe-Noire, Congo	D2	54
Pointe-Verte, N.B., Can.	B4	87
Point Fortin, Trin.	C7	80
Point Hope, Ak., U.S.	B6	95
Point Imperial, mtn., Az., U.S.	A4	96
Point Judith Pond, l., R.I., U.S.	F4	132
Point Leamington, Nf., Can.	D4	88
Point Marion, Pa., U.S.	G2	131
Point Mugu Naval Air Station, mil., Ca., U.S.	E4	98
Point of Rocks, Md., U.S.	B2	113
Point Pelee National Park, On., Can.	F2	89
Point Pleasant, N.J., U.S.	C4	123
Point Pleasant, W.V., U.S.	C2	141
Point Pleasant Beach, N.J., U.S.	C4	123
Point Reyes National Seashore, Ca., U.S.	C2	98
Point Roberts, Wa., U.S.	A2	140
Poipu, Hi., U.S.	B2	104
Poison Creek, stm., Wy., U.S.	C5	143
Poisson Blanc, Lac du, res., P.Q., Can.	C2	90
Poitiers, Fr.	D7	16
Poitou, hist. reg., Fr.	D6	16
Poivre Atoll, i., Sey.	i12	57b
Pojarkovo, Russia	B13	28
Pokaran, India	D2	40
Pokegama Lake, l., Mn., U.S.	C5	116
Pokegama Lake, l., Wi., U.S.	C2	142
Pokharā, Nepal	D4	40
Polacca, Az., U.S.	B5	96
Polack, Bela.	B10	20
Pola de Lena, Spain	F4	16
Pola de Siero, Spain	F4	16
Poland, ctry., Eur.	C5	20
Polar Bear Provincial Park, On., Can.	n18	89
Polatlı, Tur.	C5	44
Polecat Creek, stm., Ok., U.S.	B5	129
Pol-e Khomrī, Afg.	C9	42
Polesye, reg., Eur.	D8	20
Polewali, Indon.	D5	36
Policastro, Golfo di, b., Italy	E5	18
Pólis, Cyp.	E5	44
Poljarnyj, Russia	B15	10
Polk, Pa., U.S.	D2	131
Polk, co., Ar., U.S.	C1	97
Polk, co., Fl., U.S.	E5	102
Polk, co., Ga., U.S.	C1	103
Polk, co., Ia., U.S.	C4	108
Polk, co., Mn., U.S.	C2	116
Polk, co., Mo., U.S.	D4	118
Polk, co., N.C., U.S.	f10	126
Polk, co., Ne., U.S.	C8	120
Polk, co., Or., U.S.	C3	130
Polk, co., Tn., U.S.	D9	135
Polk, co., Tx., U.S.	D5	136
Polk, co., Wi., U.S.	C1	142
Polk City, Fl., U.S.	D5	102
Polk City, Ia., U.S.	C4	108
Pol'kino, Russia	B11	26
Pollāchi, India	G3	40
Pollença, Spain	H8	16
Polo, Il., U.S.	B4	106
Polohy, Ukr.	F14	20
Polonnaruwa, Sri L.	H4	40
Polonne, Ukr.	D9	20
Polson, Mt., U.S.	C2	119
Poltava, Ukr.	E13	20
Põltsamaa, Est.	G12	10
Polunočnoe, Russia	B11	22
Polynesia, is., Oc.	I23	64
Pombal, Braz.	C4	74
Pomerania, hist. reg., Eur.	C4	20
Pomeroy, Ia., U.S.	B3	108
Pomeroy, Oh., U.S.	C3	128
Pomeroy, Wa., U.S.	C8	140
Pomme de Terre, stm., Mn., U.S.	E3	116
Pomme de Terre, stm., Mo., U.S.	D4	118
Pomme de Terre Lake, res., Mo., U.S.	D4	118
Pomona, Ca., U.S.	E5	98
Pomona, Ks., U.S.	D8	109
Pomona Lake, res., Ks., U.S.	D7	109
Pompano Beach, Fl., U.S.	F6	102
Pompei, Italy	D5	18
Pompéu, Braz.	E2	74
Pompton Lakes, N.J., U.S.	A4	123
Ponaganset, stm., R.I., U.S.	C2	132
Ponaganset Reservoir, res., R.I., U.S.	B2	132
Ponape see Pohnpei, i., Micron.	D9	58
Ponca, Ne., U.S.	B9	120
Ponca City, Ok., U.S.	A4	129
Ponca Creek, stm., U.S.	A6	120
Ponca Indian Reservation, Ne., U.S.	B7	120
Ponce, P.R.	B6	80
Ponce de Leon Bay, b., Fl., U.S.	G5	102
Ponce de Leon Inlet, b., Fl., U.S.	C6	102
Poncha Pass, Co., U.S.	C4	99
Ponchatoula, La., U.S.	D5	111
Pond, stm., Ky., U.S.	C2	110
Pond Creek, Ok., U.S.	A3	129
Pondera, co., Mt., U.S.	B4	119
Pond Fork, stm., W.V., U.S.	D3	141
Pondicherry, India	G3	40
Pone Island, i., Md., U.S.	D5	113
Ponferrada, Spain	F3	16
Ponoj, Russia	C6	26
Ponoka, Ab., Can.	C4	84
Ponta Delgada, Port.	F7	46
Ponta Grossa, Braz.	D8	72
Pontalina, Braz.	E2	74
Ponta Porã, Braz.	H8	70
Pontarlier, Fr.	D10	16
Pontchartrain, Lake, l., La., U.S.	D5	111
Ponteix, Sk., Can.	H2	91
Ponte Nova, Braz.	F3	74
Pontevedra, Spain	F2	16
Ponte Vedra Beach, Fl., U.S.	B5	102
Pontiac, Il., U.S.	C5	106
Pontiac, Mi., U.S.	F7	115
Pontianak, Indon.	C3	36
Pontine Islands see Ponziane, Isole, is., Italy	D4	18
Pontoosuc Lake, l., Ma., U.S.	B1	114
Pontotoc, Ms., U.S.	A4	117
Pontotoc, co., Ms., U.S.	A4	117
Pontotoc, co., Ok., U.S.	C5	129
Pont-Rouge, P.Q., Can.	C6	90
Pontypool, On., Can.	C6	89
Pontypridd, Wales, U.K.	E5	12
Poole, Eng., U.K.	E5	12
Pooler, Ga., U.S.	D5	103
Pooles Island, i., Md., U.S.	B5	113
Poolesville, Md., U.S.	B3	113
Poopó, Bol.	B4	72
Poopó, Lago, l., Bol.	B4	72
Popayán, Col.	C4	70
Pope, co., Ar., U.S.	B2	97
Pope, co., Il., U.S.	F5	106
Pope, co., Mn., U.S.	E3	116
Pope Air Force Base, mil., N.C., U.S.	B3	126
Poplar, Mt., U.S.	B11	119
Poplar, stm., Can.	C3	86
Poplar, stm., Mn., U.S.	C2	116
Poplar Bluff, Mo., U.S.	E7	118
Poplar Island, i., Md., U.S.	C5	113
Poplarville, Ms., U.S.	E4	117
Popocatépetl, Volcán, vol., Mex.	D5	78
Popokabaka, D.R.C.	E3	54
Popondetta, Pap. N. Gui.	H12	32
Popovo, Bul.	C11	18
Popple, stm., Wi., U.S.	C5	142
Poprad, Slvk.	E6	20
Poquonock, Ct., U.S.	B5	100
Poquonock Bridge, Ct., U.S.	D7	100
Poquoson, Va., U.S.	C6	139
Porangatu, Braz.	D2	74
Porbandar, India	E1	40
Porcher Island, i., B.C., Can.	C2	85
Porcupine, stm., N.A.	E11	82
Porcupine Mountains, mts., Mi., U.S.	m12	115
Pordenone, Italy	B4	18
Pori, Fin.	F9	10
Porirua, N.Z.	p13	63c
Porlamar, Ven.	A7	70
Poronajsk, Russia	E16	26
Porpoise Bay, b., Ant.	C17	67
Porsangen, b., Nor.	A11	10
Porsgrunn, Nor.	G2	10
Portachuelo, Bol.	B5	72
Port Adelaide, Austl.	G2	62
Portadown, N. Ire., U.K.	C3	12
Portage, In., U.S.	A3	107
Portage, Mi., U.S.	F5	115
Portage, Wi., U.S.	F4	131
Portage, Wa., U.S.	E4	142
Portage, co., Oh., U.S.	A4	128
Portage, co., Wi., U.S.	D4	142
Portage, stm., Oh., U.S.	B2	128
Portage Bay, b., Mb., Can.	D2	86
Portage Head, c., Wa., U.S.	A1	140
Portage Lake, l., Me., U.S.	B4	112
Portage Lakes, Oh., U.S.	B4	128
Portage la Prairie, Mb., Can.	E2	86
Portageville, Mo., U.S.	E8	118
Port Alberni, B.C., Can.	E5	85
Portalegre, Port.	H3	16
Portales, N.M., U.S.	C6	124
Port Alfred, S. Afr.	E4	56
Port Alice, B.C., Can.	D4	85
Port Allegany, Pa., U.S.	C5	131
Port Allen, La., U.S.	D4	111
Port Angeles, Wa., U.S.	A2	140
Port Antonio, Jam.	B4	80
Port Aransas, Tx., U.S.	F4	136
Port Arthur see Lüshun, China	D12	28
Port Arthur, Tx., U.S.	E6	136
Port Augusta, Austl.	G2	62
Port au Port [West-Aguathuna-Felix Cove], Nf., Can.	D2	88
Port-au-Prince, Haiti	B5	80
Port au Prince Peninsula, pen., Nf., Can.	D2	88
Port Austin, Mi., U.S.	D7	115
Port Barre, La., U.S.	D4	111
Port Blair, India	G6	40
Port Blandford, Nf., Can.	D4	88
Port Bolivar, Tx., U.S.	E5	136
Port Burwell, On., Can.	E4	89
Port Byron, Il., U.S.	B3	106
Port Carbon, Pa., U.S.	E9	131
Port Carling, On., Can.	B5	89
Port-Cartier-Ouest, P.Q., Can.	k13	90
Port Chalmers, N.Z.	q13	63c
Port Charlotte, Fl., U.S.	F4	102
Port Chester, N.Y., U.S.	E7	125
Port Clinton, Oh., U.S.	A3	128
Port Colborne, On., Can.	E5	89
Port Coquitlam, B.C., Can.	E6	85
Port Deposit, Md., U.S.	A5	113
Port Dickinson, N.Y., U.S.	C5	125
Port Edward, B.C., Can.	B2	85
Port Edward, S. Afr.	E5	56
Port Edwards, Wi., U.S.	D4	142
Portel, Braz.	B1	74
Port Elgin, On., Can.	C3	89
Port Elizabeth, S. Afr.	E4	56
Porter, In., U.S.	A3	107
Porter, Tx., U.S.	D5	136
Porter, co., In., U.S.	B3	107
Porter Creek, stm., W.V., U.S.	m13	141
Porterdale, Ga., U.S.	C3	103
Porterville, Ca., U.S.	D4	98
Port Ewen, N.Y., U.S.	D7	125
Port Fairy, Austl.	H3	62
Port Gamble Indian Reservation, Wa., U.S.	B3	140
Port-Gentil, Gabon	D1	54
Port Gibson, Ms., U.S.	D3	117
Port-Harcourt, Nig.	F6	50
Port Hedland, Austl.	E2	60
Port Hood, N.S., Can.	C8	87
Port Hope, On., Can.	D6	89
Port Hope Simpson, Nf., Can.	B3	88
Port Hueneme, Ca., U.S.	E4	98
Port Huron, Mi., U.S.	F8	115
Portimão, Port.	I2	16
Port Isabel, Tx., U.S.	F4	136
Port Jefferson, N.Y., U.S.	n15	125
Port Jervis, N.Y., U.S.	D6	125
Port Lairge see Waterford, Ire.	D3	12
Portland, Austl.	H3	62
Portland, Ct., U.S.	C5	100
Portland, In., U.S.	D8	107
Portland, Me., U.S.	E2	112
Portland, Mi., U.S.	F6	115
Portland, N.D., U.S.	B8	127
Portland, Or., U.S.	B4	130
Portland, Tn., U.S.	A5	135
Portland, Tx., U.S.	F4	136
Portland, Cape, c., Austl.	I4	62
Portland Inlet, b., B.C., Can.	B2	85
Port Laoise, Ire.	D3	12
Port Lavaca, Tx., U.S.	E4	136
Port Lincoln, Austl.	G2	62
Port Loko, S.L.	E2	50
Port Louis, Mrts.	f10	57a
Port Ludlow, Wa., U.S.	B3	140
Port Macquarie, Austl.	G5	62
Port Madison Indian Reservation, Wa., U.S.	B3	140
Port McNeil, B.C., Can.	D4	85
Port McNicoll, On., Can.	C5	89
Port Monmouth, N.J., U.S.	C4	123
Port Moresby, Pap. N. Gui.	H12	32
Port Morien, N.S., Can.	C10	87
Port Neches, Tx., U.S.	E6	136
Portneuf, P.Q., Can.	C6	90
Port Nolloth, S. Afr.	D2	56
Porto, Port.	G2	16
Porto Alegre, Braz.	E7	72
Porto Amboim, Ang.	F2	54
Portobelo, Pan.	D4	80
Porto de Moz, Braz.	D9	70
Porto Esperança, Braz.	G8	70
Porto Esperidião, Braz.	G8	70
Portoferraio, Italy	C3	18
Port of Spain, Trin.	C7	80
Portola, Ca., U.S.	C3	98
Porto Murtinho, Braz.	H8	70
Porto Nacional, Braz.	D2	74
Porto-Novo, Benin	E5	50
Port Orange, Fl., U.S.	C6	102
Port Orchard, Wa., U.S.	B3	140
Port Orford, Or., U.S.	E2	130
Porto Santana, Braz.	B1	74
Porto Santo, i., Port.	D1	48
Porto Seguro, Braz.	E4	74
Porto Torres, Italy	D2	18
Porto-Vecchio, Fr.	D2	18
Porto Velho, Braz.	E7	70
Portoviejo, Ec.	D3	70
Port Penn, De., U.S.	B3	101
Port Phillip Bay, b., Austl.	H3	62
Port Richey, Fl., U.S.	D4	102
Port Rowan, On., Can.	E4	89
Port Royal, S.C., U.S.	G6	133
Port Royal Island, i., S.C., U.S.	G6	133
Port Royal Sound, strt., S.C., U.S.	G6	133
Port Said see Būr Sa'īd, Egypt	E10	48
Port Saint Joe, Fl., U.S.	C1	102
Port Saint Johns, S. Afr.	E4	56
Port Saint Lucie, Fl., U.S.	E6	102
Port Salerno, Fl., U.S.	E6	102
Port Saunders, Nf., Can.	C3	88
Port Shepstone, S. Afr.	E5	56
Portsmouth, Eng., U.K.	E6	12
Portsmouth, N.H., U.S.	D5	122
Portsmouth, Oh., U.S.	D3	128
Portsmouth, R.I., U.S.	E6	132

Name	Map Ref.	Page

Portsmouth, Va., U.S. D6 139
Portsmouth Naval Shipyard, mil., Me., U.S. D5 122
Port Stanley, On., Can. E3 89
Port Stanley see Stanley, Falk. Is. H5 69
Port Sudan see Būr Sūdān, Sudan G12 48
Port Sulphur, La., U.S. E6 111
Port Talbot, Wales, U.K. . . .E5 12
Porttipahdan tekojärvi, l., Fin. B12 10
Port Townsend, Wa., U.S. . .A3 140
Portugal, ctry., Eur. G3 16
Port Union, Nf., Can. D5 88
Port Vila, Vanuatu k9 62a
Port Washington, N.Y., U.S. .h13 125
Port Washington, Wi., U.S. . .E6 142
Port Wentworth, Ga., U.S. . .D5 103
Porum, Ok., U.S. B6 129
Porvenir, Chile H2 69
Porvoo, Fin. F11 10
Posadas, Arg. D6 72
Posen see Poznań, Pol. C4 20
Posen, Il., U.S. k9 106
Poset, Russia E15 26
Posey, co., In., U.S. H2 107
Poseyville, In., U.S. H2 107
Posio, Fin. C13 10
Poso, Indon. D6 36
Posse, Braz. D2 74
Post, Tx., U.S. C2 136
Post Falls, Id., U.S. B2 105
Postmasburg, S. Afr. D3 56
Postville, Ia., U.S. A6 108
Potawatomi Indian Reservation, Ks., U.S. . . .C8 109
Potchefstroom, S. Afr. D4 56
Poteau, Ok., U.S. B7 129
Poteau, stm., U.S. B7 129
Poteet, Tx., U.S. E3 136
Potenza, Italy D5 18
Potgietersrus, S. Afr. C4 56
Poth, Tx., U.S. E3 136
Potholes Reservoir, res., Wa., U.S. B6 140
Poti, Geor. A9 44
Potiskum, Nig. D7 50
Potlatch, Id., U.S. C2 105
Potomac, Md., U.S. B3 113
Potomac, stm., U.S. D4 113
Potomac Heights, Md., U.S. .C3 113
Potomac Park, Md., U.S. . . .k13 113
Potosí, Bol. B4 72
Potosi, Mo., U.S. D7 118
Potsdam, Ger. D13 12
Potsdam, N.Y., U.S. f10 125
Pottawatomie, co., Ks., U.S. .C7 109
Pottawatomie, co., Ok., U.S. B4 129
Pottawattamie, co., Ia., U.S. .C2 108
Potter, co., Pa., U.S. C6 131
Potter, co., S.D., U.S. B6 134
Potter, co., Tx., U.S. B2 136
Potter Valley, Ca., U.S. C2 98
Potts Creek, stm., U.S. C2 139
Pottstown, Pa., U.S. F10 131
Pottsville, Ar., U.S. B2 97
Pottsville, Pa., U.S. E9 131
Pouce Coupe, B.C., Can. . . .B7 85
Pouch Cove, Nf., Can. E5 88
Poughkeepsie, N.Y., U.S. . . .D7 125
Poulan, Ga., U.S. E3 103
Poulsbo, Wa., U.S. B3 140
Poultney, Vt., U.S. D2 138
Poultney, stm., Vt., U.S. D2 138
Pound, Va., U.S. e9 139
Pound Gap, U.S. C7 110
Pouso Alegre, Braz. F2 74
Poûthĭsăt, Camb. D4 34
Póvoa de Varzim, Port. G2 16
Povungnituk, P.Q., Can. f11 90
Powassan, On., Can. A5 89
Poway, Ca., U.S. F5 98
Powder, stm., Or., U.S. C9 130
Powder, stm., U.S. B6 92
Powder, Middle Fork, stm., Wy., U.S. C6 143
Powder, North Fork, stm., Wy., U.S. C6 143
Powder, South Fork, stm., Wy., U.S. C6 143
Powder River, co., Mt., U.S. .E11 119
Powder River Pass, Wy., U.S. B5 143
Powder Springs, Ga., U.S. . .h8 103
Powell, co., Ky., U.S. C6 110
Powell, co., Mt., U.S. D4 119
Powell, Oh., U.S. B2 128
Powell, Tn., U.S. m13 135
Powell, Wy., U.S. B4 143
Powell, Lake, res., U.S. F5 137
Powell, Lake, res., U.S. D5 92
Powell, Mount, mtn., Co., U.S. B4 99
Powell, Mount, mtn., N.M., U.S. B1 124
Powell Butte, Or., U.S. C5 130
Powell Park, reg., Co., U.S. .A2 99
Powell River, B.C., Can. E5 85
Powellton, W.V., U.S. C3 141
Power, co., Id., U.S. G5 105
Powers, Or., U.S. E2 130
Powerview, Mb., Can. D3 86

Poweshiek, co., Ia., U.S. C5 108
Powhatan, Va., U.S. C5 139
Powhatan, co., Va., U.S. C5 139
Powhatan Point, Oh., U.S. . .C5 128
Poxoréu, Braz. G9 70
Poyang Hu, l., China F11 28
Poyang Lake see Poyang Hu, l., China F11 28
Poygan, Lake, l., Wi., U.S. . . .D5 142
Poynette, Wi., U.S. E4 142
Požarevac, Yugo. B8 18
Poza Rica, Mex. C5 78
Požega, Cro. B6 18
Poznań, Pol. C4 20
Pozo Redondo Mountains, mts., Az., U.S. E3 96
Pozuelos, Ven. C7 80
Prachuap Khiri Khan, Thai. . .D3 34
Prado, Braz. G12 74
Prague see Praha, Czech Rep. D3 20
Prague, Ok., U.S. B5 129
Praha (Prague), Czech Rep. .D3 20
Praia, C.V. h10 50a
Prainha Nova, Braz. E7 70
Prairie, co., Ar., U.S. C4 97
Prairie, stm., Mn., U.S. C5 116
Prairie, co., Mt., U.S. D11 119
Prairie, stm., Wi., U.S. C4 142
Prairie City, Ia., U.S. C4 108
Prairie City, Or., U.S. C8 130
Prairie Creek Reservoir, res., In., U.S. D7 107
Prairie Dog Creek, stm., U.S. C3 109
Prairie du Chien, Wi., U.S. . .E2 142
Prairie du Sac, Wi., U.S. E4 142
Prairie Grove, Ar., U.S. B1 97
Prairies, Rivière des, stm., P.Q., Can. p19 90
Prairie View, Tx., U.S. D5 136
Prairie Village, Ks., U.S. . . .m16 109
Praslin, i., Sey. h13 57b
Pratāpgarh, India E2 40
Pratas Island see Tungsha Tao, i., Tai. E4 30
Prater Mountain, mtn., Wy., U.S. C2 143
Prato, Italy C3 18
Pratt, Ks., U.S. E5 109
Pratt, co., Ks., U.S. E5 109
Prattville, Al., U.S. C3 94
Praya, Indon. E5 36
Preble, co., Oh., U.S. C1 128
Prečistoe, Russia B12 20
Premont, Tx., U.S. F3 136
Prentiss, Ms., U.S. D4 117
Prentiss, co., Ms., U.S. A5 117
Prenzlau, Ger. D13 12
Preparis Island, i., Mya. D2 34
Preparis North Channel, strt., Mya. C2 34
Preparis South Channel, strt., Mya. D2 34
Přerov, Czech Rep. F4 20
Prescott, On., Can. C9 89
Prescott, Ar., U.S. D2 97
Prescott, Az., U.S. C3 96
Prescott, Wi., U.S. D1 142
Presho, S.D., U.S. D5 134
Presidencia Roque Sáenz Peña, Arg. C4 69
Presidente Dutra, Braz. C3 74
Presidente Epitácio, Braz. . . .F1 74
Presidente Prudente, Braz. . .F1 74
Presidential Range, mts., N.H., U.S. B4 122
Presidio, Tx., U.S. p12 136
Presidio, co., Tx., U.S. o12 136
Prešov, Slvk. E6 20
Prespa, Lake, l., Eur. D8 18
Presque Isle, Me., U.S. B5 112
Presque Isle, co., Mi., U.S. . .C6 115
Prestea, Ghana E4 50
Prestea, Ghana E4 50
Preston, Eng., U.K. D5 12
Preston, Ia., U.S. B7 108
Preston, Id., U.S. G7 105
Preston, Mn., U.S. G6 116
Preston, co., W.V., U.S. B5 141
Preston Peak, mtn., Ca., U.S. B2 98
Prestonsburg, Ky., U.S. C7 110
Presumpscot, stm., Me., U.S. g7 112
Pretoria, S. Afr. D4 56
Prettyboy Reservoir, res., Md., U.S. A4 113
Pretty Prairie, Ks., U.S. E5 109
Préveza, Grc. E8 18
Prewitt Reservoir, res., Co., U.S. A7 99
Pribilof Islands, is., Ak., U.S. .D5 95
Příbram, Czech Rep. E3 20
Price, Ut., U.S. D5 137
Price, stm., Ut., U.S. D5 137
Price, co., Wi., U.S. C3 142
Price Inlet, b., S.C., U.S. . . .k12 133
Prichard, Al., U.S. E1 94
Prieska, S. Afr. D3 56
Priest Lake, l., Id., U.S. A2 105
Priest Rapids Dam, Wa., U.S. C6 140
Priest Rapids Lake, res., Wa., U.S. C6 140
Priest River, Id., U.S. A2 105
Prievidza, Slvk. E5 20

Prijedor, Bos. B6 18
Prilep, Mac. D8 18
Prim, Point, c., P.E., Can. . . .C6 87
Primghar, Ia., U.S. A2 108
Primorsk, Russia F13 10
Primorsko-Ahtarsk, Russia . .F15 20
Primrose, R.I., U.S. B3 132
Primrose Lake, l., Can. H18 82
Prince, Lake, res., Va., U.S. .k14 139
Prince Albert National Park, Sk., Can. C2 91
Prince Charles Mountains, mts., Ant. D11 67
Prince Edward, co., Va., U.S. C4 139
Prince Edward Island, prov., Can. C6 87
Prince Edward Island National Park, P.E., Can. C6 87
Prince Edward Islands, is., S. Afr. N13 46
Prince Frederick, Md., U.S. . .C4 113
Prince George, B.C., Can. . . .C6 85
Prince George, co., Va., U.S. C5 139
Prince Georges, co., Md., U.S. C4 113
Prince of Wales, Cape, c., Ak., U.S. B6 95
Prince of Wales Island, i., Austl. C3 62
Prince of Wales Island, i., Ak., U.S. n23 95
Prince Olav Coast, is., Ant. . .C9 67
Prince Rupert, B.C., Can. . . .B2 85
Princes Lakes, In., U.S. F5 107
Princess Anne, Md., U.S. . . .D6 113
Princess Astrid Coast, Ant. . .D5 67
Princess Martha Coast, Ant. .D3 67
Princess Ragnhild Coast, Ant. D7 67
Princess Royal Channel, strt., B.C., Can. C3 85
Princess Royal Island, i., B.C., Can. C3 85
Princeton, B.C., Can. E7 85
Princeton, Fl., U.S. G6 102
Princeton, Ia., U.S. C7 108
Princeton, Il., U.S. B4 106
Princeton, In., U.S. H2 107
Princeton, Ky., U.S. C2 110
Princeton, Me., U.S. C5 112
Princeton, Mn., U.S. E5 116
Princeton, Mo., U.S. A4 118
Princeton, N.C., U.S. B4 126
Princeton, N.J., U.S. C3 123
Princeton, Wi., U.S. E4 142
Princeton, W.V., U.S. D3 141
Princeton, Mount, mtn., Co., U.S. C4 99
Princeville, P.Q., Can. C6 90
Princeville, Il., U.S. C4 106
Princeville, N.C., U.S. B5 126
Prince William, co., Va., U.S. B5 139
Prince William Sound, strt., Ak., U.S. g18 95
Príncipe, i., S. Tom./P. C1 54
Principe Channel, strt., B.C., Can. C3 85
Príncipe da Beira, Braz. F7 70
Prineville, Or., U.S. C6 130
Prineville Reservoir, res., Or., U.S. C6 130
Prinzapolka, Nic. C3 80
Prior Lake, Mn., U.S. F5 116
Priozersk, Russia F14 10
Pripet (Pryp'yat') (Pripjat'), stm., Eur. C9 20
Pripet Marshes, reg., Eur. . .C10 20
Pripyat see Pripet, stm., Eur. .C9 20
Priština, Yugo. C8 18
Pritchards Island, i., S.C., U.S. G6 133
Pritzwalk, Ger. D13 12
Privas, Fr. E9 16
Privolžskaja vozvyšennost', plat., Russia D6 26
Prizren, Yugo. C8 18
Probolinggo, Indon. E4 36
Proctor, Mn., U.S. D6 116
Proctor, Vt., U.S. D2 138
Proctor Lake, res., Tx., U.S. . .C3 136
Proctorsville, Vt., U.S. E3 138
Proddatūr, India G3 40
Progreso, Mex. C7 78
Prohladnyj, Russia F7 22
Prokopevsk, Russia D10 26
Prokuplje, Yugo. C8 18
Proletarskij, Russia D13 20
Prome, Mya. C3 34
Promontory Mountains, mts., Ut., U.S. B3 137
Prophetstown, Il., U.S. B4 106
Propriá, Braz. D4 74
Proserpine, Austl. E4 62
Prospect, Ct., U.S. C4 100
Prospect, Ky., U.S. g11 110
Prospect, Oh., U.S. B2 128
Prospect, Or., U.S. E4 130
Prospect, Pa., U.S. E1 131
Prospect Hill, mtn., Or., U.S. k11 130
Prospect Park, N.J., U.S. B4 123
Prospect Park, Pa., U.S. . . .p20 131
Prosperidad, Phil. E9 34
Prosperity, S.C., U.S. C4 133

Prosperity, W.V., U.S. n13 141
Prosser, Wa., U.S. C6 140
Protection, Ks., U.S. E4 109
Provadija, Blg. C11 18
Provence, hist. reg., Fr. F9 16
Providence, Ky., U.S. C2 110
Providence, R.I., U.S. C4 132
Providence, co., R.I., U.S. . . .C2 132
Providence, stm., R.I., U.S. . .C5 132
Providence, Ut., U.S. B4 137
Providence Point, c., R.I., U.S. D5 132
Providencia, Isla de, i., Col. .C3 80
Providenija, Russia C20 26
Province Lake, l., N.H., U.S. .C5 122
Provincetown, Ma., U.S. B7 114
Provins, Fr. C8 16
Provo, Ut., U.S. C4 137
Provo, stm., Ut., U.S. C4 137
Provost, Ab., Can. C5 84
Prowers, co., Co., U.S. D8 99
Prudence Island, i., R.I., U.S. E5 132
Prudenville, Mi., U.S. D6 115
Prudhoe Bay, b., Ak., U.S. . .A10 95
Prudhoe Bay, Ak., U.S. A10 95
Prut, stm., Eur. G10 20
Pružany, Bela. C8 20
Pryluky, Ukr. D12 22
Prymors'k, Ukr. F14 20
Pryor, Mt., U.S. E8 119
Pryor, Ok., U.S. A6 129
Pryor Mountains, mts., Mt., U.S. E8 119
Pryp'yat' (Pripet) (Pripjat'), stm., Eur. D8 20
Psël (Ps'ol), stm., Eur. D13 20
Pskov, Russia D4 26
Pskov, Lake, l., Eur. G13 10
Ps'ol (Psël), stm., Eur. D13 20
Ptolemaís, Grc. D8 18
Pucallpa, Peru E5 70
Pucheng, China F11 28
Puckaway Lake, l., Wi., U.S. .E4 142
Pudož, Russia B6 22
Pudukkottai, India G3 40
Puebla, state, Mex. D5 78
Puebla de Zaragoza, Mex. . .D5 78
Pueblo, Co., U.S. C6 99
Pueblo, co., Co., U.S. C6 99
Pueblo Mountain, mtn., Or., U.S. E8 130
Pueblo Mountains, mts., Or., U.S. E8 130
Pueblo Reservoir, res., Co., U.S. C6 99
Puente Genil, Spain I4 16
Pueo Point, c., Hi., U.S. B1 104
Puerco, stm., U.S. C6 96
Puerco, Rio, stm., N.M., U.S. B2 124
Puerto Acosta, Bol. B4 72
Puerto Ángel, Mex. D5 78
Puerto Armuelles, Pan. D3 80
Puerto Asís, Col. C4 70
Puerto Ayacucho, Ven. B6 70
Puerto Baquerizo Moreno, Ec. D2 70
Puerto Barrios, Guat. B2 80
Puerto Bermúdez, Peru F5 70
Puerto Berrío, Col. B5 70
Puerto Bolívar, Col. C5 80
Puerto Boyacá, Col. D5 80
Puerto Cabello, Ven. A6 70
Puerto Cabezas, Nic. C3 80
Puerto Carreño, Col. B6 70
Puerto Chicama, Peru E4 70
Puerto Cortés, Hond. B2 80
Puerto Cumarebo, Ven. A6 70
Puerto de la Cruz, Spain A1 50
Puerto del Rosario, Spain . . .A2 50
Puerto Deseado, Arg. G3 69
Puerto Esperanza, Arg. D7 72
Puerto Guaraní, Para. C6 72
Puerto Inírida, Col. E6 80
Puerto Juárez, Mex. C7 78
Puerto La Cruz, Ven. A7 70
Puerto Leguízamo, Col. D5 70
Puerto Libertad, Mex. B2 78
Puerto Limón, C.R. C3 80
Puertollano, Spain H4 16
Puerto Lobos, Arg. F3 69
Puerto Madryn, Arg. F3 69
Puerto Maldonado, Peru F6 70
Puerto Montt, Chile F2 69
Puerto Morazán, Nic. C2 80
Puerto Nariño, Col. D6 80
Puerto Natales, Chile H2 69
Puerto Páez, Ven. B6 70
Puerto Peñasco, Mex. A2 78
Puerto Plata, Dom. Rep. B5 80
Puerto Princesa, Phil. E7 34
Puerto Rico, Bol. F6 70
Puerto Rico, dep., N.A. B6 80
Puerto Rico Trench G7 66
Puerto San José, Guat. C1 80
Puerto San Julián, Arg. G3 69
Puerto Santa Cruz, Arg. H3 69
Puerto Sastre, Para. C6 72
Puerto Suárez, Bol. B6 72
Puerto Vallarta, Mex. C3 78
Puerto Villamil, Ec. D1 70
Puerto Wilches, Col. B5 70

Puerto Ybapobó, Para. C6 72
Pugačov, Russia D8 22
Puget Sound, strt., Wa., U.S. .B3 140
Puget Sound Naval Shipyard, mil., Wa., U.S. e10 140
Pugwash, N.S., Can. D6 87
Puhi, Hi., U.S. B2 104
Pukalani, Hi., U.S. C5 104
Pukaskwa National Park, On., Can. o18 89
Pukch'ŏng-ŭp, N. Kor. C13 28
Pukeashun Mountain, mtn., B.C., Can. D8 85
Pukou, China C4 30
Pula, Cro. B4 18
Pulaski, co., Ar., U.S. C3 97
Pulaski, co., Ga., U.S. D3 103
Pulaski, co., Il., U.S. F4 106
Pulaski, co., In., U.S. B4 107
Pulaski, co., Ky., U.S. C5 110
Pulaski, co., Mo., U.S. D5 118
Pulaski, N.Y., U.S. B4 125
Pulaski, Tn., U.S. B4 135
Pulaski, Va., U.S. C2 139
Pulaski, co., Va., U.S. C2 139
Pulaski, Wi., U.S. D5 142
Puławy, Pol. D7 20
Pulicat Lake, l., India G4 40
Pullman, Wa., U.S. C8 140
Pumphrey, Md., U.S. h11 113
Puná, Isla, i., Ec. D3 70
Punakha, Bhu. D5 40
Punata, Bol. B4 72
Pune, India F2 40
Pungo Lake, l., N.C., U.S. . . .B6 126
Punia, D.R.C. D5 54
Punjab, state, India C3 40
Puno, Peru G5 70
Punta, Cerro de, mtn., P.R. . .B6 80
Punta Alta, Arg. F5 72
Punta Arenas, Chile H2 69
Punta de Díaz, Chile D3 72
Punta del Este, Ur. F7 72
Punta Gorda, Bahía de, b., Nic. C3 80
Punta Gorda, Fl., U.S. F4 102
Puntarenas, C.R. C2 80
Punto Fijo, Ven. A5 70
Punxsutawney, Pa., U.S. E4 131
Puolanka, Fin. D12 10
Puqi, China F10 28
Puquio, Peru F5 70
Purcell, Ok., U.S. B4 129
Purcellville, Va., U.S. A5 139
Purdy, Mo., U.S. E4 118
Purgatoire, stm., Co., U.S. . .D7 99
Purgatoire Peak, mtn., Co., U.S. D5 99
Puri, India F5 40
Pūrnia, India D5 40
Purus (Purús), stm., S.A. D7 70
Purvis, Ms., U.S. D4 117
Purwakarta, Indon. E3 36
Purwokerto, Indon. E3 36
Pusan, S. Kor. D13 28
Pushaw Lake, l., Me., U.S. D4 112
Pushkar, India D2 40
Pushmataha, co., Ok., U.S. C6 129
Puškin, Russia G15 10
Putao, Mya. A3 34
Putaruru, N.Z. o14 63c
Putian, China D4 30
Puting, Tanjung, c., Indon. . . .D4 36
Putnam, Ct., U.S. B8 100
Putnam, co., Fl., U.S. C5 102
Putnam, co., Ga., U.S. C3 103
Putnam, co., Il., U.S. B4 106
Putnam, co., In., U.S. E4 107
Putnam, co., Mo., U.S. A4 118
Putnam, co., N.Y., U.S. D7 125
Putnam, co., Oh., U.S. B1 128
Putnam, co., Tn., U.S. C8 135
Putnam, co., W.V., U.S. C3 141
Putney, Ga., U.S. E2 103
Putney, Vt., U.S. F3 138
Putorana, plato, plat., Russia C11 26
Puttalam, Sri L. H3 40
Puttgarden, Ger. C12 12
Putumayo (Içá), stm., S.A. . . .D5 70
Putussibau, Indon. C4 36
Puukohola Heiau National Historic Site, hist., Hi., U.S. D6 104
Puula, l., Fin. F12 10
Puxico, Mo., U.S. E7 118
Puyallup, Wa., U.S. B3 140
Puyallup, stm., Wa., U.S. C3 140
Puyang, China B3 30
Pweto, D.R.C. E5 54
Pyandzh see Amu Darya, stm., Asia B8 42
Pyapon, Mya. C3 34
Pyhäjoki, Fin. D11 10
Pyhäselkä, l., Fin. E13 10
Pyinmana, Mya. C3 34
Pyles Fork, stm., W.V., U.S. h10 141
Pymatuning Reservoir, res., U.S. C1 131
P'yŏngyang, N. Kor. D13 28
Pyramid Lake, l., Nv., U.S. . .C2 121

Name	Map Ref.	Page

Pyramid Lake Indian
  Reservation, Nv., U.S. . . .D2 121
Pyramid Mountains, mts.,
  N.M., U.S. E1 124
Pyramid Peak, mtn., N.M.,
  U.S. E1 124
Pyramid Peak, mtn., Wy.,
  U.S. C2 143
Pyrenees, mts., Eur. F7 16
Pyriatyn, Ukr. D12 20
Pyu, Mya. C3 34

Q

Qaanaaq see Thule, Grnld. . .C26 82
Qacentina, Alg. C6 48
Qā'emshahr, Iran C6 42
Qā'en, Iran D7 42
Qaidam Pendi, bas., China . .D6 28
Qalāt, Afg. D9 42
Qal'at Bīshah, Sau. Ar. G4 38
Qal'at Sukkar, Iraq G12 44
Qal'eh-ye Now, Afg. D8 42
Qallābāt, Sudan H3 38
Qamar, Ghubbat al-, b.,
  Yemen G6 38
Qamar Bay see Qamar,
  Ghubbat al-, b., Yemen . .G6 38
Qamdo, China E7 28
Qandahār see Kandahār,
  Afg. D9 42
Qandala, Som. H5 38
Qardho, Som. I14 48
Qareh Sū, stm., Iran C12 44
Qarhoh, Som. I14 48
Qareh Sū, stm., Iran C12 44
Qasr el-Boukhari, Alg. J8 16
Qasr Farâfra, Egypt E10 48
Qaṭanā, Syria F7 44
Qatar, ctry., Asia E6 42
Qattâra, Munkhafad el-, depr.,
  Egypt E10 48
Qattara Depression see
  Qattâra, Munkhafad el-,
  depr., Egypt E10 48
Qazimämmäd, Azer. B13 44
Qazvīn, Iran C5 42
Qena, Egypt E11 48
Qeydār, Iran D13 44
Qeshan, China C3 30
Qianwei, China D1 30
Qianxi, China D2 30
Qianyang, China D3 30
Qiemo, China D5 28
Qigong, China A4 34
Qijiang, China D2 30
Qilian Shan, mts., China D7 28
Qimen, China D4 30
Qingdao, China D12 28
Qinghai, prov., China D7 28
Qinghai Hu, l., China D8 28
Qingjiang, China E11 28
Qinglong, China A4 30
Qinglong, China D2 30
Qingshen, China D1 30
Qingtang, China G10 28
Qingyang, China D9 28
Qingyuan, China E3 30
Qing Zang Gaoyuan (Tibet,
  Plateau of), plat., China . .E4 28
Qinhuangdao, China D11 28
Qin Ling, mts., China E9 28
Qinxian, China B3 30
Qinzhou, China E2 30
Qionghai, China F3 30
Qionglai, China E8 28
Qiongzhong, China H9 28
Qiongzhou Haixia, strt.,
  China G9 28
Qiqihar, China B12 28
Qiryat Shemona, Isr. F6 44
Qishn, Yemen G6 38
Qitai, China C5 28
Qiyang, China D3 30
Qobustan, Azer. B13 44
Qogir Feng see K2, mtn.,
  Asia B3 40
Qom, Iran D6 42
Qomolangma Feng see Everest,
  Mount, mtn., Asia D5 40
Qomsheh, Iran D6 42
Qorveh, Iran E12 44
Quabbin Reservoir, res., Ma.,
  U.S. B3 114
Quaddick Reservoir, res., Ct.,
  U.S. B8 100
Quail Oaks, Va., U.S. n18 139
Quaker Hill, Ct., U.S. D7 100
Quakertown, Pa., U.S. F11 131
Qualicum Beach, B.C.,
  Can. E5 85
Quanah, Tx., U.S. B3 136
Quang Ngai, Viet. C5 34
Quannapowitt, Lake, l., Ma.,
  U.S. f11 114
Quantico, Va., U.S. B5 139
Quantico Marine Corps Air
  Station, mil., Va., U.S. . . .B5 139
Quanzhou, China G11 28
Quanzhou, China D3 30
Quapaw, Ok., U.S. A7 129
Qu'Appelle, Sk., Can. G4 91
Qu'Appelle, stm., Can. G4 91
Quarryville, Pa., U.S. G9 131
Quartu Sant'Elena, Italy E2 18
Quartz Mountain, mtn., Or.,
  U.S. D4 130
Quartzsite, Az., U.S. D1 96

Quassapaug, Lake, l., Ct.,
  U.S. C3 100
Quatsino Sound, strt., B.C.,
  Can. D3 85
Quay, co., N.M., U.S. C6 124
Quba, Azer. B13 44
Queanbeyan, Austl. H4 62
Québec, P.Q., Can. C6 90
Quebec, prov., Can. C5 90
Quechee, Vt., U.S. D4 138
Queen, stm., R.I., U.S. E3 132
Queen Annes, co., Md.,
  U.S. B5 113
Queen Bess, Mount, mtn.,
  B.C., Can. D5 85
Queen Charlotte, B.C., Can. . .C1 85
Queen Charlotte Islands, is.,
  B.C., Can. C1 85
Queen Charlotte Mountains,
  mts., B.C., Can. C1 85
Queen Charlotte Sound, strt.,
  B.C., Can. H14 82
Queen Charlotte Strait, strt.,
  B.C., Can. D4 85
Queen City, Mo., U.S. A5 118
Queen City, Tx., U.S. C5 136
Queen Creek, Az., U.S. m9 96
Queen Mary Coast, Ant. . . .C14 67
Queen Maud Land, reg.,
  Ant. D4 67
Queen Maud Mountains, mts.,
  Ant. E25 67
Queens, co., N.Y., U.S. E7 125
Queensland, state, Austl. E3 62
Queenstown, Austl. I4 62
Queenstown, S. Afr. E4 56
Quela, Ang. E3 54
Quelimane, Moz. B6 56
Querétaro, Mex. C4 78
Querétaro, state, Mex. C5 78
Queshan, China C3 30
Quesnel, B.C., Can. C6 85
Quesnel, stm., B.C., Can. C6 85
Quesnel Lake, l., B.C.,
  Can. C7 85
Questa, N.M., U.S. A4 124
Quetico Provincial Park, On.,
  Can. o17 89
Quetta, Pak. D9 42
Quevedo, Ec. D4 70
Quezon City, Phil. D8 34
Quibala, Ang. F3 54
Quibdó, Col. B4 70
Quicksand Pond, l., R.I.,
  U.S. E6 132
Quiculungo, Ang. E3 54
Quidnessett, R.I., U.S. E4 132
Quidnick, R.I., U.S. D3 132
Quidnick Reservoir, res., R.I.,
  U.S. D2 132
Quila, Mex. C3 78
Quilcene, Wa., U.S. B3 140
Quileute Indian Reservation,
  Wa., U.S. B1 140
Quillota, Chile D2 69
Quilon, India H3 40
Quimaria, Ang. E2 54
Quimilí, Arg. D5 72
Quimper, Fr. D4 16
Quimperlé, Fr. D5 16
Quinault, stm., Wa., U.S. B1 140
Quinault, Lake, l., Wa.,
  U.S. B2 140
Quinault Indian Reservation,
  Wa., U.S. B1 140
Quince Mil, Peru F5 70
Quincy, Ca., U.S. C3 98
Quincy, Fl., U.S. B2 102
Quincy, Il., U.S. D2 106
Quincy, Ma., U.S. B5 114
Quincy, Mi., U.S. G6 115
Quincy, Wa., U.S. B6 140
Quincy Bay, b., Ma., U.S. . . .g12 114
Quinebaug, Ct., U.S. A8 100
Quinebaug, stm., Ct., U.S. . . .C8 100
Quinhagak, Ak., U.S. D7 95
Quinlan, Tx., U.S. C4 136
Quinn, stm., Nv., U.S. B3 121
Quinn Canyon Range, mts.,
  Nv., U.S. F6 121
Quinnesec, Mi., U.S. C3 115
Quinnipiac, stm., Ct., U.S. . . .D4 100
Quintana Roo, state, Mex. . .D7 78
Quinter, Ks., U.S. C3 109
Quinton, Ok., U.S. B6 129
Quirinópolis, Braz. E1 74
Quissanga, Moz. A7 56
Quiterajo, Moz. A7 56
Quitman, Ar., U.S. B3 97
Quitman, Ga., U.S. F3 103
Quitman, co., Ga., U.S. E1 103
Quitman, Ms., U.S. C5 117
Quitman, co., Ms., U.S. A3 117
Quitman, Tx., U.S. C5 136
Quito, Ec. D4 70
Quixadá, Braz. B4 74
Quixeramobim, Braz. C4 74
Qujing, China F8 28
Qumarlêb, China E7 28
Qunayyin, Sabkhat al-, l.,
  Libya E8 14
Quonnipaug Lake, l., Ct.,
  U.S. D5 100
Quonochontaug, R.I., U.S. . .G2 132

Quonochontaug Pond, l., R.I.,
  U.S. G2 132
Quonset Point, c., R.I., U.S. . .E4 132
Quseir, Egypt E11 48
Qutdligssat, Grnld. D29 82
Quthing, Leso. E4 56
Qüxü, China D6 40
Quy Nhon, Viet. D5 34
Quzhou, China F11 28

R

Raab see Győr, Hung. F4 20
Raahe, Fin. D11 10
Rab, Otok, i., Cro. B5 18
Rába, stm., Eur. F4 20
Raba, Indon. E5 36
Rabat, Mor. D3 48
Rabaul, Pap. N. Gui. G13 32
Rabbit Creek, stm., S.D.,
  U.S. B3 134
Rabbit Ears Pass, Co., U.S. . .A4 99
Rabi, i., Fiji m11 63b
Rābigh, Sau. Ar. F3 38
Râbniţa, Mol. F10 20
Rabun, co., Ga., U.S. B3 103
Rabun Bald, mtn., Ga., U.S. . .B3 103
Rabyānah, Ramlat, des.,
  Libya F8 48
Raccoon Creek, stm., Oh.,
  U.S. D3 128
Raccourci Island, i., La.,
  U.S. D4 111
Race, Cape, c., Nf., Can. E5 88
Raceland, Ky., U.S. B7 110
Raceland, La., U.S. E5 111
Race Point, c., Ma., U.S. B7 114
Rach Gia, Viet. E4 34
Racine, Wi., U.S. F6 142
Racine, co., Wi., U.S. F5 142
Racine, W.V., U.S. C3 141
Racine Dam, U.S. C3 141
Rădăuţi, Rom. F8 20
Radcliff, Ky., U.S. C4 110
Radford, Va., U.S. C2 139
Radom, Pol. D6 20
Radomsko, Pol. D5 20
Radomyshl', Ukr. D10 20
Rāe Bareli, India D4 40
Raeford, N.C., U.S. C3 126
Rafaela, Arg. E5 72
Rafah, Gaza G6 44
Rafhā', Sau. Ar. E4 38
Rafsanjān, Iran D7 42
Raft, stm., Id., U.S. G5 105
Raft River Mountains, mts.,
  Ut., U.S. B2 137
Raga, Sudan I10 48
Ragay Gulf, b., Phil. D8 34
Ragged Island, i., Me., U.S. . .E4 112
Ragged Island Range, is.,
  Bah. D9 76
Ragged Lake, l., Me., U.S. . .C3 112
Ragged Top Mountain, mtn.,
  Wy., U.S. E7 143
Ragland, Al., U.S. B3 94
Ragusa, Italy F5 18
Rahīmyār Khān, Pak. E10 42
Rahway, N.J., U.S. B4 123
Rahway, stm., N.J., U.S. k7 123
Rāichūr, India F3 40
Raiganj, India D5 40
Raigarh, India E4 40
Railroad Valley, val., Nv.,
  U.S. E6 121
Rainbow Bridge National
  Monument, Ut., U.S. F5 137
Rainbow Falls, wtfl., Tn.,
  U.S. D10 135
Rainbow Flowage, res., Wi.,
  U.S. C4 142
Rainbow Lake, l., Me.,
  U.S. C3 112
Rainelle, W.V., U.S. D4 141
Rainier, Or., U.S. A4 130
Rainier, Wa., U.S. C3 140
Rainier, Mount, mtn., Wa.,
  U.S. C4 140
Rains, co., Tx., U.S. C5 136
Rainsville, Al., U.S. A4 94
Rainy Lake, l., Mn., U.S. B5 116
Rainy River, On., U.S. o16 89
Raipur, India E4 40
Rājahmundry, India F4 40
Rajang, stm., Malay. E4 36
Rājapālaiyam, India H3 40
Rājasthān, state, India D2 40
Rajčihinsk, Russia E14 26
Rāj Gangpur, India E4 40
Rājkot, India E2 40
Rāj Nāndgaon, India E4 40
Rājshāhi, Bngl. E5 40
Rakhiv, Ukr. E8 20
Rakvere, Est. G12 10
Raleigh, Ms., U.S. C4 117
Raleigh, N.C., U.S. B4 126
Raleigh, W.V., U.S. n13 141
Raleigh, co., W.V., U.S. D3 141
Raleigh Bay, b., N.C., U.S. . .C6 126
Ralls, co., Mo., U.S. B6 118
Ralls, Tx., U.S. C2 136
Ralston, Ne., U.S. g12 120
Ralston Valley, val., Nv.,
  U.S. E4 121
Ramah, N.M., U.S. B1 124

Ramah Indian Reservation,
  N.M., U.S. C1 124
Ramapo, stm., N.J., U.S. A4 123
Ramblewood, N.J., U.S. D3 123
Rambouillet, Fr. C7 16
Ramea, N.J., Can. E3 88
Rāmeswaram, India H3 40
Rāmhormoz, Iran D5 42
Ramm, Jabal, mtn., Jord. E3 42
Râmnicu Sărat, Rom. G9 20
Râmnicu Vâlcea, Rom. G8 20
Ramona, Ca., U.S. F5 98
Rampart Range, mts., Co.,
  U.S. B5 99
Rāmpur, India D3 40
Ramree Island, i., Mya. C2 34
Ramsay, Mi., U.S. n12 115
Ramsele, Swe. E7 10
Ramseur, N.C., U.S. B3 126
Ramsey, Il., U.S. D4 106
Ramsey, co., Mn., U.S. E5 116
Ramsey, co., N.D., U.S. A7 127
Ramsey, N.J., U.S. A4 123
Ramsgate, Eng., U.K. E7 12
Ramshorn Peak, mtn., Mt.,
  U.S. E5 119
Ramshorn Peak, mtn., Wy.,
  U.S. C3 143
Ramu, Kenya C8 54
Rāna Pratāp Sāgar, res.,
  India D2 40
Rancagua, Chile D2 69
Rancharia, Braz. F1 74
Ranchester, Wy., U.S. B5 143
Rānchi, India E5 40
Ranchos de Taos, N.M.,
  U.S. A4 124
Rancocas Creek, stm., N.J.,
  U.S. k13 113
Rand, W.V., U.S. C3 141
Randall, co., Tx., U.S. B2 136
Randallstown, Md., U.S. B4 113
Randers, Den. H4 10
Randijaure, l., Swe. C8 10
Randle, Wa., U.S. C4 140
Randleman, N.C., U.S. B3 126
Randolph, co., Al., U.S. B4 94
Randolph, co., Ar., U.S. A4 97
Randolph, co., Ga., U.S. E2 103
Randolph, co., Il., U.S. E4 106
Randolph, co., In., U.S. D7 107
Randolph, Ma., U.S. B5 114
Randolph, Me., U.S. D3 112
Randolph, co., Mo., U.S. B5 118
Randolph, co., N.C., U.S. . . .B3 126
Randolph, Ne., U.S. B8 120
Randolph, Vt., U.S. D3 138
Randolph, Wi., U.S. E5 142
Randolph, co., W.V.,
  U.S. C5 141
Randolph Air Force Base, mil.,
  Tx., U.S. h7 136
Randolph Hills, Md., U.S. B3 113
Random Island, i., Nf.,
  Can. D5 88
Random Lake, Wi., U.S. E6 142
Randsfjorden, l., Nor. F4 10
Rāngāmāti, Bngl. E6 40
Rangeley, Me., U.S. D2 112
Rangeley Lake, l., Me.,
  U.S. D2 112
Rangely, Co., U.S. A2 99
Ranger, Tx., U.S. C3 136
Ranger Lake, l., N.M., U.S. . .D6 124
Rangoon see Yangon, Mya. . .C3 34
Rangpur, Bngl. D5 40
Rānibennur, India G3 40
Rankin, co., Ms., U.S. C4 117
Rankin, Pa., U.S. k14 131
Rann of Kutch see Kutch,
  Rann of, reg., Asia E1 40
Ranohira, Madag. C8 56
Ranong, Thai. E3 34
Ransiki, Indon. D8 36
Ransom, co., N.D., U.S. C8 127
Ranson, W.V., U.S. B7 141
Rantauprapat, Indon. C1 36
Rantoul, Il., U.S. C5 106
Raohe, China A2 31
Raoul, Ga., U.S. B3 103
Rapallo, Italy B2 18
Rapid, stm., Mn., U.S. B4 116
Rapid City, S.D., U.S. C2 134
Rapides, co., La., U.S. C3 111
Rapid River, Mi., U.S. C4 115
Rapids City, Il., U.S. B3 106
Rappahannock, stm., Va.,
  U.S. B5 139
Rappahannock, co., Va.,
  U.S. B4 139
Raquette, stm., N.Y., U.S. . .f10 125
Raquette Lake, l., N.Y.,
  U.S. B6 125
Raraka, atoll, Fr. Poly. F15 58
Raritan, N.J., U.S. B3 123
Raritan, stm., N.J., U.S. C4 123
Raritan Bay, b., N.J., U.S. . . .C4 123
Rarotonga, i., Cook Is. G14 58
Ra's al-Khaymah, U.A.E. E7 42
Ras Dashen Terara, mtn.,
  Eth. H12 48
Rashid, Egypt E10 14
Rasht, Iran C5 42

Rasšua, ostrov, i., Russia E17 26
Ratangarh, India D2 40
Rāth, India D3 40
Rathbun Lake, res., Ia., U.S. . .D5 108
Rathdrum, Id., U.S. B2 105
Rat Islands, is., Ak., U.S. E3 95
Ratlām, India E3 40
Ratnāgiri, India F2 40
Ratnapura, Sri L. H4 40
Raton, N.M., U.S. A5 124
Raton Pass, N.M., U.S. A5 124
Rattlesnake Creek, stm., Oh.,
  U.S. C2 128
Rattlesnake Creek, stm., Wa.,
  U.S. C6 140
Rättvik, Swe. F6 10
Raub, Malay. C2 36
Rauch, Arg. F6 72
Rauma, Fin. F9 10
Raurkela, India E5 40
Ravalli, co., Mt., U.S. D2 119
Raven, Va., U.S. e10 139
Ravena, N.Y., U.S. C7 125
Ravenel, S.C., U.S. k11 133
Ravenna, Italy B4 18
Ravenna, Ky., U.S. C6 110
Ravenna, Mi., U.S. E5 115
Ravenna, Ne., U.S. C7 120
Ravenna, Oh., U.S. A4 128
Raven Park, reg., Co., U.S. . .A2 99
Ravensburg, Ger. G11 12
Ravensthorpe, Austl. G3 60
Ravenswood, W.V., U.S. C3 141
Rāvi, stm., Asia C2 40
Ravnina, Turk. C8 42
Rawaki, atoll, Kir. E12 58
Rāwalpindi, Pak. D10 42
Rawdon, P.Q., Can. C4 90
Rawhide Creek, stm., Wy.,
  U.S. D8 143
Rawlings, Md., U.S. k13 113
Rawlinna, Austl. G4 60
Rawlins, co., Ks., U.S. C2 109
Rawlins, Wy., U.S. E5 143
Rawson, Arg. F3 69
Ray, co., Mo., U.S. B3 118
Ray, N.D., U.S. A2 127
Ray, Cape, c., Nf., Can. E2 88
Raya, Bukit, mtn., Indon. . . .C4 36
Rāyachoti, India G3 40
Rāyadurg, India G3 40
Ray City, Ga., U.S. E3 103
Raymond, Ab., Can. E4 84
Raymond, Il., U.S. D4 106
Raymond, Me., U.S. E3 116
Raymond, Mn., U.S. E3 116
Raymond, Ms., U.S. C3 117
Raymond, N.H., U.S. D4 122
Raymond, Wa., U.S. C2 140
Raymondville, Tx., U.S. F4 136
Raymore, Sk., Can. F3 91
Raymore, Mo., U.S. C3 118
Rayne, La., U.S. D3 111
Raynham, Ma., U.S. C5 114
Raynham Center, Ma., U.S. . .C5 114
Rayong, Thai. D4 34
Raytown, Mo., U.S. h11 118
Rayville, La., U.S. B4 111
Razdol'noe, Russia B2 31
Razgrad, Blg. C11 18
Ré, Île de, i., Fr. D6 16
Reader, W.V., U.S. B4 141
Reading, Eng., U.K. E6 12
Reading, Ma., U.S. A5 114
Reading, Mi., U.S. G6 115
Reading, Oh., U.S. C1 128
Reading, Pa., U.S. F10 131
Readlyn, Ia., U.S. B5 108
Reagan, co., Tx., U.S. D2 136
Real, co., Tx., U.S. E3 136
Real, Cordillera, mts., S.A. . .G6 70
Realicó, Arg. E5 72
Reamstown, Pa., U.S. F9 131
Rebiana Sand Sea see
  Rabyānah, Ramlat, des.,
  Libya F8 48
Rebun-tō, i., Japan B16 28
Recherche, Archipelago of
  the, is., Austl. G3 60
Recife, Braz. C5 74
Reconquista, Arg. D6 72
Rector, Ar., U.S. A5 97
Rècyča, Bela. C11 20
Red, stm., Asia B4 34
Red, stm., N.A. B8 92
Red, stm., Ky., U.S. C6 110
Red, stm., Tn., U.S. A4 135
Red, stm., U.S. E9 92
Red Bank, N.J., U.S. C4 123
Red Bank, Tn., U.S. D8 135
Red Bay, Al., U.S. A1 94
Redberry Lake, l., Sk.,
  U.S. E2 91
Red Bird, stm., Ky., U.S. C6 110
Redbird, Oh., U.S. A4 128
Red Bluff, Ca., U.S. B2 98
Red Bluff Lake, res., U.S. . .o12 136
Red Boiling Springs, Tn.,
  U.S. C8 135
Red Bud, Il., U.S. E4 106
Red Butte, mtn., Ut., U.S. . . .B2 137
Red Cedar, stm., Wi., U.S. . .C2 142
Red Cedar Lake, l., Wi.,
  U.S. C2 142
Redcliff, Ab., Can. D5 84
Redcliffe, Austl. F5 62

Name	Map Ref.	Page

Redcliffe, Mount, mtn., Austl. F3   60
Red Cliff Indian Reservation, Wi., U.S. B2   142
Red Cloud, Ne., U.S. D7   120
Redcloud Peak, mtn., Co., U.S. D3   99
Red Deer, Ab., Can. C4   84
Red Deer, stm., Can. E4   91
Red Deer, stm., Can. D4   84
Redding, Ca., U.S. B2   98
Redding, Ct., U.S. D2   100
Redeye, stm., Mn., U.S. D3   116
Redfield, Ar., U.S. C3   97
Redfield, Ia., U.S. C3   108
Redfield, S.D., U.S. C7   134
Redford, Mi., U.S. F7   115
Redgranite, Wi., U.S. D4   142
Red Hook, N.Y., U.S. C7   125
Red Indian Lake, l., Nf., Can. D3   88
Red Jacket, W.V., U.S. D2   141
Redkey, In., U.S. D7   107
Red Lake, l., Az., U.S. B1   96
Redlake, Mn., U.S. C3   116
Red Lake, stm., Mn., U.S. . . .C2   116
Red Lake, co., Mn., U.S. C2   116
Red Lake Falls, Mn., U.S. . . .C2   116
Red Lake Indian Reservation, Mn., U.S. B3   116
Redlands, Ca., U.S. E5   98
Red Lion, Pa., U.S. G8   131
Red Lodge, Mt., U.S. E7   119
Red Mill Pond, l., De., U.S. . .E5   101
Redmond, Or., U.S. C5   130
Redmond, Ut., U.S. E4   137
Redmond, Wa., U.S. e11   140
Red Mountain, mtn., Ca., U.S. B2   98
Red Mountain, mtn., Mt., U.S. C4   119
Red Mountain Pass, Co., U.S. D3   99
Red Oak, Ga., U.S. h7   103
Red Oak, Ia., U.S. D2   108
Red Oak, Ok., U.S. C6   129
Red Oak, Tx., U.S. n10   136
Red Oaks, La., U.S. h9   111
Redon, Fr. D5   16
Redondo, Wa., U.S. f11   140
Redondo Beach, Ca., U.S. . .n12   98
Redoubt Volcano, vol., Ak., U.S. g15   95
Red Peak, mtn., Co., U.S. . . .B4   99
Red River, co., La., U.S. B2   111
Red River, co., Tx., U.S. C5   136
Red Rock, stm., Mt., U.S. F4   119
Red Rock, Lake, res., Ia., U.S. C4   108
Redruth, Eng., U.K. E4   12
Red Sea F3   38
Red Springs, N.C., U.S. C3   126
Red Table Mountain, mts., Co., U.S. B4   99
Redwater, Ab., Can. C4   84
Redwater, stm., Mt., U.S. . . .C11   119
Redwillow, stm., Can. B7   85
Red Willow, co., Ne., U.S. . . .D5   120
Red Wing, Mn., U.S. F6   116
Redwood, stm., Mn., U.S. F3   116
Redwood, co., Mn., U.S. F3   116
Redwood City, Ca., U.S. D2   98
Redwood Falls, Mn., U.S. F3   116
Redwood National Park, Ca., U.S. B2   98
Redwood Valley, Ca., U.S. . . .C2   98
Ree, Lough, l., Ire. D2   12
Reed City, Mi., U.S. E5   115
Reedley, Ca., U.S. D4   98
Reedsburg, Wi., U.S. E3   142
Reeds Peak, mtn., N.M., U.S. D2   124
Reedsport, Or., U.S. D2   130
Reedsville, Pa., U.S. E6   131
Reedsville, Wi., U.S. D6   142
Reedy, stm., S.C., U.S. C3   133
Reedy Lake, l., Fl., U.S. E5   102
Reefton, N.Z. p13   63c
Reelfoot Lake, l., Tn., U.S. . . .A2   135
Reese, Mi., U.S. E7   115
Reese, stm., Nv., U.S. C4   121
Reese Air Force Base, mil., Tx., U.S. C1   136
Reeves, co., Tx., U.S. o13   136
Reform, Al., U.S. B1   94
Refugio, Tx., U.S. E4   136
Refugio, co., Tx., U.S. E4   136
Regensburg, Ger. F12   12
Reggâne, Alg. E4   48
Reggio di Calabria, Italy F5   18
Reggio nell'Emilia, Italy B3   18
Reghin, Rom. F8   20
Regina, Sk., Can. G3   91
Régina, Fr. Gu. C9   70
Regina Beach, Sk., Can. G3   91
Registro, Braz. C8   72
Regozero, Russia D14   22
Rehoboth, Nmb. C2   56
Rehoboth Bay, b., De., U.S. . . .F5   101
Rehoboth Beach, De., U.S. F5   101
Reid, Mount, mtn., Ak., U.S. . .n24   95
Reidland, Ky., U.S. e9   110
Reidsville, Ga., U.S. D4   103
Reidsville, N.C., U.S. A3   126
Reigate, Eng., U.K. E6   12

Reims, Fr. C9   16
Reinbeck, Ia., U.S. B5   108
Reindeer Island, i., Mb., Can. C3   86
Reindeer Lake, l., Can. G19   82
Reisterstown, Md., U.S. B4   113
Reliance, Wy., U.S. E3   143
Remada, Tun. D7   48
Remanso, Braz. C3   74
Rembang, Indon. E4   36
Remington, In., U.S. C3   107
Remiremont, Fr. C10   16
Remmel Dam, Ar., U.S. g8   97
Remsen, Ia., U.S. B2   108
Rena, Nor. F4   10
Rend Lake, res., Il., U.S. E5   106
Rendsburg, Ger. C11   12
Renforth, N.B., Can. D4   87
Renfrew, On., Can. B8   89
Rengat, Indon. O2   36
Rengo, Chile E3   72
Reng Tläng, mtn., Asia B2   34
Rennes, Fr. C6   16
Reno, co., Ks., U.S. E5   109
Reno, Nv., U.S. D2   121
Reno, Lake, l., Mn., U.S. E3   116
Reno Hill, mtn., Wy., U.S. . . .D6   143
Renovo, Pa., U.S. D6   131
Renqiu, China B4   30
Rensselaer, In., U.S. C3   107
Rensselaer, N.Y., U.S. C7   125
Rensselaer, co., N.Y., U.S. . . .C7   125
Renton, Wa., U.S. B3   140
Renville, Mn., U.S. F3   116
Renville, co., Mn., U.S. F4   116
Renville, co., N.D., U.S. A4   127
Reo, Indon. E6   36
Repentigny, P.Q., Can. D4   90
Repetek, Turk. C8   42
Republic, co., Ks., U.S. C6   109
Republic, Mi., U.S. B3   115
Republic, Mo., U.S. D4   118
Republic, Pa., U.S. G2   131
Republic, Wa., U.S. A7   140
Republican, stm., U.S. C6   109
Republican, stm., U.S. C8   92
Republic of Korea see Korea, South, ctry., Asia D10   28
Reşadiye, Tur. B7   44
Reserve, La., U.S. h10   111
Resistencia, Arg. D6   72
Reşiţa, Rom. G6   20
Resolute, N.T., Can. D20   82
Resolution Island, i., N.Z. . . .q12   63c
Reston, Mb., Can. E1   86
Reston, Va., U.S. B5   139
Réthimnon, Grc. G10   18
Réunion, dep., Afr. g10   57a
Reus, Spain G7   16
Reutlingen, Ger. F11   12
Revelo, Ky., U.S. D5   110
Revelstoke, B.C., Can. D8   85
Revelstoke, Lake, res., B.C., Can. D8   85
Reventazón, Peru E3   70
Revere, Ma., U.S. g11   114
Revillagigedo, Islas, is., Mex. D2   78
Revillagigedo Island, i., Ak., U.S. n24   95
Revin, Fr. C9   16
Rewa, India E4   40
Rex, Ga., U.S. h8   103
Rexburg, Id., U.S. F7   105
Rexton, N.B., Can. C5   87
Rey, Isla del, i., Pan. D4   80
Reyes, Point, c., Ca., U.S. . . .C2   98
Reyhanlı, Tur. D7   44
Reykjanes Ridge B26   144
Reykjavík, Ice. I18   10a
Reynolds, Ga., U.S. D2   103
Reynolds, co., Mo., U.S. D6   118
Reynoldsburg, Oh., U.S. C3   128
Reynoldsville, Pa., U.S. D4   131
Reynosa, Mex. B5   78
Rezé, Fr. D6   16
Rēzekne, Lat. H12   10
Rhaetian Alps, mts., Eur. A2   18
Rhea, co., Tn., U.S. D9   135
Rheims see Reims, Fr. C9   16
Rheine, Ger. D10   12
Rhine (Rhein), stm., Eur. A5   14
Rhinebeck, N.Y., U.S. D7   125
Rhinelander, Wi., U.S. C4   142
Rhir, Cap, c., Mor. D2   48
Rho, Italy B2   18
Rhode Island, i., R.I., U.S. E5   132
Rhode Island, state, U.S. D3   132
Rhode Island, state, U.S. C13   92
Rhode Island Sound, strt., U.S. F5   132
Rhodes see Ródhos, i., Grc. . . .G12   18
Rhodesia see Zimbabwe, ctry., Afr. B4   56
Rhodes Peak, mtn., Id., U.S. . .C4   105
Rhodes' Tomb, hist., Zimb. . . .C4   56
Rhodope Mountains, mts., Eur. D10   18
Rhône, stm., Eur. E9   16
Riachão do Jacuípe, Braz. B4   74
Rialto, Ca., U.S. m14   98
Riau, Kepulauan, is., Indon. . .C2   36
Riaza, Spain G5   16
Ribáuè, Moz. A6   56
Ribe, Den. I3   10

Ribeira do Pombal, Braz. . . .D4   74
Ribeira Grande, C.V. g9   50a
Ribeirão, Braz. C4   74
Ribeirão Preto, Braz. F2   74
Riberalta, Bol. F6   70
Rib Lake, Wi., U.S. C3   142
Riccione, Italy B4   18
Rice, co., Ks., U.S. D5   109
Rice, Mn., U.S. E4   116
Rice, co., Mn., U.S. F5   116
Riceboro, Ga., U.S. E5   103
Rice Lake, l., On., Can. C6   89
Rice Lake, l., Mn., U.S. D5   116
Rice Lake, Wi., U.S. C1   142
Riceville, Ia., U.S. A5   108
Rich, co., Ut., U.S. B4   137
Rich, Cape, c., On., Can. C4   89
Richards Bay, S. Afr. D5   56
Richardson, co., Ne., U.S. . . .D10   120
Richardson, Tx., U.S. n10   136
Richardson Lakes, l., Me., U.S. D2   112
Richard Toll, Sen. C1   50
Richardton, N.D., U.S. C3   127
Rich Creek, Va., U.S. C2   139
Riche, Pointe, c., Nf., Can. . . .C3   88
Richfield, Mn., U.S. F5   116
Richfield, Ut., U.S. E3   137
Richford, Vt., U.S. B3   138
Rich Hill, Mo., U.S. C3   118
Richibucto, N.B., Can. C5   87
Richland, Ga., U.S. D2   103
Richland, co., Il., U.S. E5   106
Richland, co., La., U.S. B4   111
Richland, Mo., U.S. D5   118
Richland, co., Mt., U.S. C12   119
Richland, co., N.D., U.S. C8   127
Richland, co., Oh., U.S. B3   128
Richland, co., S.C., U.S. D6   133
Richland, Wa., U.S. C6   140
Richland, co., Wi., U.S. E3   142
Richland Balsam, mtn., N.C., U.S. f10   126
Richland Center, Wi., U.S. . . .E3   142
Richland Creek, stm., Tn., U.S. B5   135
Richlands, N.C., U.S. C5   126
Richlands, Va., U.S. e10   139
Richlandtown, Pa., U.S. F11   131
Richmond, Austl. E3   62
Richmond, B.C., Can. E6   85
Richmond, P.Q., Can. D5   90
Richmond, N.Z. p13   63c
Richmond, Ca., U.S. D2   98
Richmond, co., Ga., U.S. C4   103
Richmond, Il., U.S. A5   106
Richmond, In., U.S. E8   107
Richmond, Ky., U.S. C5   110
Richmond, Me., U.S. D3   112
Richmond, Mi., U.S. F8   115
Richmond, Mn., U.S. E4   116
Richmond, Mo., U.S. B4   118
Richmond, co., N.C., U.S. . . .B3   126
Richmond, co., N.Y., U.S. E6   125
Richmond, Tx., U.S. E5   136
Richmond, Ut., U.S. B4   137
Richmond, Va., U.S. C5   139
Richmond, co., Va., U.S. C6   139
Richmond, Vt., U.S. C3   138
Richmond Heights, Fl., U.S. . .s13   102
Richmond Heights, Mo., U.S. f13   118
Richmond Hill, On., Can. D5   89
Richmond Hill, Ga., U.S. E5   103
Richmond National Battlefield Park, Va., U.S. n18   139
Rich Square, N.C., U.S. A5   126
Richton, Ms., U.S. D5   117
Richwood, Oh., U.S. B2   128
Richwood, W.V., U.S. C4   141
Rickman, Tn., U.S. C8   135
Riddle, Or., U.S. E3   130
Riddle Mountain, mtn., Or., U.S. D8   130
Rideau, stm., On., Can. B9   89
Ridgecrest, Ca., U.S. E5   98
Ridge Farm, Il., U.S. D6   106
Ridgefield, Ct., U.S. D2   100
Ridgefield, N.J., U.S. h8   123
Ridgefield, Wa., U.S. D3   140
Ridgefield Park, N.J., U.S. . . .B4   123
Ridgeland, Ms., U.S. C3   117
Ridgeland, S.C., U.S. G6   133
Ridgeley, W.V., U.S. B6   141
Ridgely, Md., U.S. C6   113
Ridgely, Tn., U.S. A2   135
Ridge Spring, S.C., U.S. D4   133
Ridgetop, Tn., U.S. A5   135
Ridgetown, On., Can. E3   89
Ridgeview, W.V., U.S. C3   141
Ridgeville, In., U.S. D7   107
Ridgeville, S.C., U.S. E7   133
Ridgeway, Va., U.S. D3   139
Ridgewood, N.J., U.S. B4   123
Ridgway, Il., U.S. F5   106
Ridgway, Pa., U.S. D4   131
Riding Mountain National Park, Mb., Can. D1   86
Ridley Park, Pa., U.S. p20   131
Riesa, Ger. E13   12
Rieti, Italy G7   18
Rif, mts., Mor. E3   14
Riffe Lake, res., Wa., U.S. . . .C3   140

Rifle, Co., U.S. B3   99
Rifle, stm., Mi., U.S. D6   115
Rift Valley, val., Afr. C6   54
Rīga, Lat. H11   10
Riga, Gulf of, b., Eur. G10   10
Rigaud, P.Q., Can. D3   90
Rigby, Id., U.S. F7   105
Rīgestān, reg., Afg. D9   42
Rigo, Pap. N. Gui. H12   32
Riihimäki, Fin. F11   10
Riiser-Larsen Peninsula, pen., Ant. C8   67
Rijeka, Cro. B5   18
Riley, Ks., U.S. C7   109
Riley, co., Ks., U.S. C7   109
Riley, Mount, mtn., N.M., U.S. F2   124
Rimbey, Ab., Can. C3   84
Rimersburg, Pa., U.S. D3   131
Rimini, Italy B4   18
Rimouski, P.Q., Can. A9   90
Rimouski, stm., P.Q., Can. . . .A9   90
Rimouski-Est, P.Q., Can. A9   90
Rimrock Lake, res., Wa., U.S. C4   140
Rinca, Pulau, i., Indon. E5   36
Rincon, Ga., U.S. D5   103
Rincón del Bonete, Lago Artificial de, res., Ur. E6   72
Rincón de Romos, Mex. C4   78
Rincon Mountains, mts., Az., U.S. E5   96
Ringdove, Vanuatu k9   62a
Ringgold, Ga., U.S. B1   103
Ringgold, co., Ia., U.S. D3   108
Ringgold, La., U.S. B2   111
Ringim, Nig. D6   50
Ringkøbing, Den. H3   10
Ringkøbing Fjord, b., Den. . . .I3   10
Ringling, Ok., U.S. C4   129
Ringvassøya, i., Nor. B8   10
Ringwood, N.J., U.S. A4   123
Rinjani, Gunung, vol., Indon. E5   36
Rio, Fl., U.S. E6   102
Rio, Wi., U.S. E4   142
Rio Arriba, co., N.M., U.S. . . .A2   124
Rio Blanco, co., Co., U.S. . . .B2   99
Riobamba, Ec. D4   70
Rio Branco, Braz. E6   70
Rio Branco, Braz. E6   70
Río Bravo, Mex. B5   78
Río Claro, Braz. F2   74
Rio Cuarto, Arg. E5   72
Río de Janeiro, Braz. F3   74
Río de Janeiro, state, Braz. . .F3   74
Rio Dell, Ca., U.S. B1   98
Río Gallegos, Arg. H3   69
Río Grande, Arg. H3   69
Rio Grande, Braz. E7   72
Río Grande, Mex. C4   78
Rio Grande (Bravo), stm., N.A. F7   92
Rio Grande, co., Co., U.S. . . .D4   99
Rio Grande, Oh., U.S. D3   128
Rio Grande City, Tx., U.S. . . .F3   136
Rio Grande do Norte, state, Braz. E12   70
Rio Grande do Sul, state, Braz. D7   72
Rio Grande Reservoir, res., Co., U.S. D3   99
Ríohacha, Col. A5   70
Río Hato, Pan. D3   80
Rio Hondo, Tx., U.S. F4   136
Rio Largo, Braz. C4   74
Riom, Fr. E8   16
Río Mayo, Arg. G2   69
Ríonegro, Col. D5   80
Rio Negro, Pantanal do, sw., Braz. G8   70
Rio Rancho, N.M., U.S. B3   124
Rio Real, Braz. D4   74
Ríosucio, Col. D4   80
Río Tercero, Arg. E5   72
Rio Tinto, Braz. C4   74
Rio Verde, Braz. E1   74
Ríoverde, Mex. C5   78
Rio Verde de Mato Grosso, Braz. B7   72
Rio Vista, Ca., U.S. C3   98
Ripley, co., In., U.S. F7   107
Ripley, co., Mo., U.S. E7   118
Ripley, Ms., U.S. A5   117
Ripley, Oh., U.S. D2   128
Ripley, Tn., U.S. B2   135
Ripley, W.V., U.S. C3   141
Ripon, Eng., U.K. G11   12
Ripon, Wi., U.S. E5   142
Rippowam, stm., Ct., U.S. . . .E1   100
Ririe Lake, res., Id., U.S. F7   105
Rishiri-tō, i., Japan B16   28
Rishon LeZiyyon, Isr. G6   44
Rising Sun, De., U.S. D3   101
Rising Sun, In., U.S. G8   107
Rising Sun, Md., U.S. A5   113
Rison, Ar., U.S. D3   97
Ristijärvi, Fin. D13   10
Ritchie, co., W.V., U.S. B3   141
Ritter, Mount, mtn., Ca., U.S. D4   98
Rittman, Oh., U.S. B4   128
Ritzville, Wa., U.S. B7   140
Riva del Garda, Italy B3   18
Rivanna, stm., Va., U.S. C4   139

Rivas, Nic. C2   80
Rivera, Ur. E6   72
Riverbank, Ca., U.S. D3   98
River Bourgeois, N.S., Can. . . .D9   87
River Cess, Lib. E3   50
Riverdale, Ca., U.S. D4   98
Riverdale, Il., U.S. k9   106
Riverdale, Md., U.S. C4   113
River Edge, N.J., U.S. h8   123
River Falls, Al., U.S. D3   94
River Falls, Wi., U.S. D1   142
River Forest, Il., U.S. k9   106
River Grove, Il., U.S. k9   106
Riverhead, N.Y., U.S. n16   125
River Hebert, N.S., Can. D5   87
River Heights, Ut., U.S. B4   137
River Hills, Wi., U.S. m12   142
River Pines, Ma., U.S. f10   114
River Ridge, La., U.S. k11   111
River Road, Or., U.S. C3   130
River Rouge, Mi., U.S. p15   115
Rivers, Mb., Can. D1   86
Riversdale, S. Afr. E3   56
Riverside, Al., U.S. B3   94
Riverside, co., Ca., U.S. F5   98
Riverside, Ca., U.S. F5   98
Riverside, Ia., U.S. C6   108
Riverside, Il., U.S. k9   106
Riverside, N.J., U.S. C3   123
Riverside, Pa., U.S. E8   131
Riverside Reservoir, res., Co., U.S. A6   99
Riverton, Mb., Can. D3   86
Riverton, N.Z. q12   63c
Riverton, Il., U.S. D4   106
Riverton, Ks., U.S. E9   109
Riverton, N.J., U.S. C3   123
Riverton, Ut., U.S. C4   137
Riverton, Vt., U.S. C3   138
Riverton, Wy., U.S. C4   143
Riverton Heights, Wa., U.S. . .f11   140
River Vale, N.J., U.S. h8   123
Riverview, Fl., U.S. p11   102
Riverview, Mi., U.S. p15   115
Rivesville, W.V., U.S. B4   141
Riviera Beach, Fl., U.S. F6   102
Riviera Beach, Md., U.S. B4   113
Rivière-du-Loup, P.Q., Can. . . .B8   90
Rivière-Verte, N.B., Can. B1   87
Rivne, Ukr. D9   20
Rivoli, Italy B1   18
Riyadh see Ar-Riyāḍ, Sau. Ar. F5   38
Rizhao, China D11   28
Rjazan', Russia D6   26
Rjažsk, Russia C16   20
Rjukan, Nor. G3   10
Roachdale, In., U.S. E4   107
Road Town, Br. Vir. Is. B7   80
Roane, co., Tn., U.S. D9   135
Roane, co., W.V., U.S. C3   141
Roan Mountain, Tn., U.S. . . .C11   135
Roanne, Fr. D8   16
Roanoke, Al., U.S. B4   94
Roanoke, Il., U.S. C4   106
Roanoke, In., U.S. C7   107
Roanoke, La., U.S. D3   111
Roanoke, Tx., U.S. m9   136
Roanoke, Va., U.S. C3   139
Roanoke, co., Va., U.S. C2   139
Roanoke, stm., U.S. A5   126
Roanoke see Staunton, stm., U.S. D12   92
Roanoke Island, i., N.C., U.S. B7   126
Roanoke Rapids, N.C., U.S. .A5   126
Roanoke Rapids Lake, res., U.S. A5   126
Roaring Fork, stm., Co., U.S. C4   99
Roaring Spring, Pa., U.S. . . .F5   131
Roatán, Isla de, i., Hond. B2   80
Robbins, Il., U.S. k9   106
Robbins, N.C., U.S. B3   126
Robbinsdale, Mn., U.S. m12   116
Robbinsville, N.C., U.S. f9   126
Robe, Austl. H2   62
Roberta, Ga., U.S. D2   103
Robert Lee, Tx., U.S. D2   136
Roberts, co., S.D., U.S. B8   134
Roberts, co., Tx., U.S. B2   136
Roberts, Wi., U.S. C1   142
Roberts, Point, c., Wa., U.S. A2   140
Robert's Arm, Nf., Can. D4   88
Roberts Creek Mountain, mtn., Nv., U.S. D5   121
Robertsdale, Al., U.S. E2   94
Robert S. Kerr Reservoir, res., Ok., U.S. B6   129
Roberts Mountain, mtn., Ak., U.S. C6   95
Roberts Mountain, mtn., Wy., U.S. D3   143
Robertson, co., Ky., U.S. B5   110
Robertson, co., Tn., U.S. A5   135
Robertsonville, P.Q., Can. . . .C6   90
Roberts Port, Lib. E2   50
Robertville, N.B., Can. B4   87
Roberval, P.Q., Can. A5   90
Robeson, co., N.C., U.S. C3   126
Robins, Ia., U.S. B6   108
Robinson, Il., U.S. D6   106

Name	Map Ref.	Page

Róbinson Crusoe, Isla, i.,
Chile E2   72
Robinson Fork, stm., W.V.,
U.S. m14   141
Robinson Fork, stm., W.V.,
U.S. k9   141
Robinvale, Austl. G3   62
Roblin, Mb., Can. D1   86
Roboré, Bol. B6   72
Robson, Mount, mtn., B.C.,
Can. C8   85
Robstown, Tx., U.S. F4   136
Roca Partida, Isla, i., Mex. . .D2   78
Rocha, Ur. E7   72
Rochefort, Fr. E6   16
Rochelle, Ga., U.S. E3   103
Rochelle, Il., U.S. B4   106
Rochelle Park, N.J., U.S. . . .h8   123
Rochester, Il., U.S. D4   106
Rochester, In., U.S. B5   107
Rochester, Mi., U.S. F7   115
Rochester, Mn., U.S. F6   116
Rochester, N.H., U.S. D5   122
Rochester, N.Y., U.S. B3   125
Rochester, Pa., U.S. E1   131
Rochester, Vt., U.S. D3   138
Rochester, Wa., U.S. C2   140
Rochester, Wi., U.S. n11   142
Rock, co., Mn., U.S. G2   116
Rock, co., Ne., U.S. B6   120
Rock, co., Wi., U.S. F4   142
Rock, stm., U.S. B3   106
Rock, stm., U.S. A1   108
Rockall, i., Scot., U.K. D3   6
Rockall Rise B24   144
Rockaway, N.J., U.S. B3   123
Rockaway, Or., U.S. B3   130
Rockbridge, co., Va., U.S. . .C3   139
Rockcastle, stm., Ky., U.S. . .C5   110
Rockcastle, co., Ky., U.S. . . .C5   110
Rockcliffe Park, On., Can. . .h12   89
Rock Creek, Mn., U.S. E6   116
Rock Creek, stm., Nv., U.S. . .C5   121
Rock Creek, stm., Or., U.S. . .B6   130
Rock Creek, stm., Wa., U.S. . .B8   140
Rock Creek, stm., Wa., U.S. . .D5   140
Rock Creek, stm., Wy., U.S. . .E6   143
Rock Creek, stm., U.S. B3   113
Rock Creek, stm., U.S. h14   140
Rock Creek Butte, mtn., Or.,
U.S. C8   130
Rockdale, co., Ga., U.S. C3   103
Rockdale, Il., U.S. B5   106
Rockdale, Md., U.S. B4   113
Rockdale, Tx., U.S. D4   136
Rockefeller Plateau, plat.,
Ant. E27   67
Rockfall, Ct., U.S. C5   100
Rock Falls, Il., U.S. B4   106
Rockford, Ia., U.S. A5   108
Rockford, Il., U.S. A4   106
Rockford, Mi., U.S. E5   115
Rockford, Mn., U.S. E5   116
Rockford, Oh., U.S. B1   128
Rockford, Tn., U.S. D10   135
Rock Hall, Md., U.S. B5   113
Rockhampton, Austl. E5   62
Rockhampton Downs, Austl. .D6   60
Rock Hill, S.C., U.S. B5   133
Rockingham, Austl. G2   60
Rockingham, N.C., U.S. C3   126
Rockingham, co., N.C., U.S. .A3   126
Rockingham, co., N.H.,
U.S. D4   122
Rockingham, co., Va., U.S. . .B4   139
Rock Island, P.Q., Can. D5   90
Rock Island, i., Fl., U.S. C3   102
Rock Island, Il., U.S. B3   106
Rock Island, i., Wi., U.S. B3   106
Rock Island, i., Wi., U.S. C7   142
Rock Lake, l., Wa., U.S. B8   140
Rockland, On., Can. B9   89
Rockland, Ma., U.S. B6   114
Rockland, Me., U.S. D3   112
Rockland, co., N.Y., U.S. . . .D6   125
Rockledge, Fl., U.S. D6   102
Rockledge, Pa., U.S. o20   131
Rocklin, Ca., U.S. C3   98
Rock Mountain, mtn., Co.,
U.S. D3   99
Rockport, In., U.S. I3   107
Rockport, Ma., U.S. A6   114
Rockport, Me., U.S. D3   112
Rock Port, Mo., U.S. A2   118
Rockport, Tx., U.S. F4   136
Rock Rapids, Ia., U.S. A1   108
Rock River, Wy., U.S. E7   143
Rocksprings, Tx., U.S. D2   136
Rock Springs, Wy., U.S. E3   143
Rockstone, Guy. B8   70
Rockton, Il., U.S. A4   106
Rock Valley, Ia., U.S. A1   108
Rockville, In., U.S. E3   107
Rockville, Md., U.S. B3   113
Rockville Centre, N.Y., U.S. .n15   125
Rockwall, Tx., U.S. C4   136
Rockwall, co., Tx., U.S. C4   136
Rockwell, Ia., U.S. B4   108
Rockwell, N.C., U.S. B2   126
Rockwell City, Ia., U.S. B3   108
Rockwell Park, N.C., U.S. . . .B2   126
Rockwood, Mi., U.S. F7   115
Rockwood, Pa., U.S. G3   131
Rockwood, Tn., U.S. D9   135

Rocky, stm., N.C., U.S. B2   126
Rocky, stm., S.C., U.S. C2   133
Rocky, East Branch, stm., Oh.,
U.S. h9   128
Rocky, West Branch, stm., Oh.,
U.S. h9   128
Rocky Boys Indian Reservation,
Mt., U.S. B7   119
Rocky Ford, Co., U.S. C7   99
Rocky Fork Lake, l., Oh., U.S.C2   128
Rocky Harbour, Nf., Can. . . .D3   88
Rocky Hill, Ct., U.S. C5   100
Rocky Lake, l., Me., U.S. D5   112
Rocky Mount, N.C., U.S. B5   126
Rocky Mount, Va., U.S. D3   139
Rocky Mountain, mtn., Mt.,
U.S. C4   119
Rocky Mountain House, Ab.,
Can. C3   84
Rocky Mountain National
Park, Co., U.S. A5   99
Rocky Mountains, mts.,
N.A. B5   92
Rocky Ripple, In., U.S. k10   107
Rocky River, Oh., U.S. A4   128
Rocky Top, mtn., Or., U.S. . .C4   130
Rodbār, Afg. D8   42
Roddickton, Nf., Can. C3   88
Rodeo, Arg. E4   72
Roderfield, W.V., U.S. D3   141
Rodez, Fr. E8   16
Ródhos, Grc. F12   18
Ródhos (Rhodes), i., Grc. . .G12   18
Rodney, On., Can. E3   89
Rodney, Cape, c., Ak., U.S. .C6   95
Rodney Village, De., U.S. . . .D3   101
Rodrigues, i., Mrts. F12   52
Roebourne, Austl. E2   60
Roebuck, S.C., U.S. B4   133
Roeland Park, Ks., U.S. . . .k16   109
Roeselare, Bel. E8   12
Roff, Ok., U.S. C5   129
Roger Mills, co., Ok., U.S. . .B2   129
Rogers, Ar., U.S. A1   97
Rogers, Mn., U.S. E5   116
Rogers, co., Ok., U.S. A6   129
Rogers, Tx., U.S. D4   136
Rogers, Mount, mtn., Va.,
U.S. f10   139
Rogers City, Mi., U.S. C7   115
Rogers Lake, res., Ct., U.S. . .D6   100
Rogers Pass, Mt., U.S. C4   119
Rogersville, N.B., Can. C4   87
Rogersville, Al., U.S. A2   94
Rogersville, Mo., U.S. D4   118
Rogersville, Tn., U.S. C10   135
Rogue, stm., Or., U.S. E2   130
Rogue River, Or., U.S. E3   130
Rohri, Pak. E9   42
Rohtak, India D3   40
Roi Et, Thai. C4   34
Rokan, stm., Indon. C2   36
Roland, Ia., U.S. B4   108
Roland, Ok., U.S. B7   129
Roland, Lake, res., Md.,
U.S. g11   113
Rolette, N.D., U.S. A6   127
Rolette, co., N.D., U.S. A6   127
Rolfe, Ia., U.S. B3   108
Rolla, Mo., U.S. D6   118
Rolla, N.D., U.S. A6   127
Rollingbay, Wa., U.S. e10   140
Rolling Fork, stm., Ar., U.S. .C1   97
Rolling Fork, stm., Ky., U.S. .C4   110
Rolling Fork, Ms., U.S. C3   117
Rolling Meadows, Il., U.S. . .h8   106
Rollingstone, Mn., U.S. F7   116
Rollinsford, N.H., U.S. D5   122
Rolvsøya, i., Nor. A10   10
Roma, Austl. E4   62
Roma (Rome), Italy D4   18
Roma, Tx., U.S. F3   136
Romain, Cape, c., S.C., U.S. .F9   133
Roman, Rom. F9   20
Romanche Gap I12   66
Romang, Pulau, i., Indon. . . .E7   36
Romania, ctry., Eur. F8   20
Roman Nose Mountain, mtn.,
Or., U.S. D3   99
Romano, Cape, c., Fl., U.S. .G5   102
Romano, Cayo, i., Cuba A4   80
Romans-sur-Isère, Fr. E9   16
Romanzof, Cape, c., Ak.,
U.S. C6   95
Romanzof Mountains, mts.,
Ak., U.S. B11   95
Rome see Roma, Italy D4   18
Rome, Ga., U.S. B1   103
Rome, Il., U.S. C4   106
Rome, N.Y., U.S. B5   125
Rome City, In., U.S. B7   107
Romeo, Mi., U.S. F7   115
Romeoville, Il., U.S. k8   106
Romney, W.V., U.S. B6   141
Romny, Ukr. D12   20
Romulus, Mi., U.S. p15   115
Ronan, Mt., U.S. C2   119
Roncador, Serra do, plat.,
Braz. D1   74
Ronceverte, W.V., U.S. D4   141
Ronda, Spain I4   16
Rondônia, state, Braz. F7   70
Rondonópolis, Braz. G9   70
Rong'an, China D2   30

Rongcheng, China B5   30
Ronge, Lac la, l., Sk., Can. . .B3   91
Rongelap, atoll, Marsh. Is. . .C10   58
Rongjiang, China D2   30
Rongxian, China E3   30
Rønne, Den. I6   10
Ronneby, Swe. H6   10
Ronne Ice Shelf, ice, Ant. . . .D34   67
Roodhouse, Il., U.S. D3   106
Rooks, co., Ks., U.S. C4   109
Roosevelt, stm., Braz. E7   70
Roosevelt, co., Mt., U.S. B11   119
Roosevelt, co., N.M., U.S. . . .D5   124
Roosevelt, Ut., U.S. C5   137
Roosevelt Island, i., Ant. D24   67
Roosevelt Park, Mi., U.S. E4   115
Root, stm., Mn., U.S. G7   116
Root, stm., Wi., U.S. n12   142
Roper, N.C., U.S. B6   126
Roper Valley, Austl. C5   60
Ropi, Fin. B9   10
Roraima, state, Braz. C7   70
Roraima, Mount, mtn., S.A. . .B7   70
Røros, Nor. E4   10
Rosamond, Ca., U.S. E4   98
Rosario, Arg. E5   72
Rosário, Braz. B3   74
Rosario, Mex. C3   78
Rosario, Para. C6   72
Rosario de la Frontera, Arg. .D5   72
Rosário do Sul, Braz. E6   72
Rosário Oeste, Braz. F8   70
Roscoe, Il., U.S. A5   106
Roscoe, Tx., U.S. C2   136
Roscommon, Ire. D2   12
Roscommon, Mi., U.S. D6   115
Roscommon, co., Mi., U.S. . .D6   115
Rose, Mount, mtn., Nv.,
U.S. D2   121
Roseau, Dom. B7   80
Roseau, Mn., U.S. B3   116
Roseau, co., Mn., U.S. B3   116
Roseau, South Fork, stm.,
Mn., U.S. B3   116
Rose-Blanche [-Harbour le
Cou], Nf., Can. E2   88
Roseboro, N.C., U.S. C4   126
Rosebud, co., Mt., U.S. D10   119
Rosebud, S.D., U.S. D5   134
Rosebud, Tx., U.S. D4   136
Rosebud Indian Reservation,
S.D., U.S. D5   134
Roseburg, Or., U.S. D3   130
Rosedale, In., U.S. E3   107
Rosedale, Md., U.S. g11   113
Rosedale, Ms., U.S. B2   117
Rose Hill, Ks., U.S. E6   109
Rose Hill, N.C., U.S. C4   126
Rose Hill, Va., U.S. f8   139
Roseland, Fl., U.S. E6   102
Roseland, In., U.S. A5   107
Roseland, La., U.S. D5   111
Roseland, Oh., U.S. B3   128
Roselle, Il., U.S. k8   106
Roselle, N.J., U.S. k7   123
Roselle Park, N.J., U.S. k7   123
Rosemère, P.Q., Can. p19   90
Rosemount, Mn., U.S. F5   116
Rosenberg, Tx., U.S. E5   136
Rosendale, Wi., U.S. E5   142
Rosenheim, Ger. G13   12
Rose Peak, mtn., Az., U.S. . .D6   96
Rosepine, La., U.S. D2   111
Rose Point, c., B.C., Can. . . .B8   85
Roseto, Pa., U.S. E11   131
Rosetta see Rashid, Egypt . .E10   14
Roseville, Ca., U.S. C3   98
Roseville, Il., U.S. C3   106
Roseville, Mi., U.S. o16   115
Roseville, Mn., U.S. m12   116
Roseville, Oh., U.S. C3   128
Rosewood Heights, Il., U.S. . .E3   106
Rosiclare, Il., U.S. F5   106
Roșiori de Vede, Rom. G8   20
Roskilde, Den. I5   10
Roslavl', Russia C12   20
Roslyn, Wa., U.S. B4   140
Roslyn Heights, N.Y., U.S. . .h13   125
Ross, Oh., U.S. C1   128
Ross, co., Oh., U.S. C2   128
Rossano, Italy E6   18
Ross Barnett Reservoir, res.,
Ms., U.S. C3   117
Rossburn, Mb., Can. D1   86
Ross Dam, Wa., U.S. A4   140
Rossford, Oh., U.S. A2   128
Ross Ice Shelf, ice, Ant. E23   67
Rossignol, Lake, l., N.S.,
Can. E4   87
Ross Island, i., Ant. D22   67
Ross Island, i., Mb., Can. . . .B3   86
Ross Lake National Recreation
Area, Wa., U.S. A5   140
Rossland, B.C., Can. E9   85
Rosso, Maur. C1   50
Rossoš', Russia D15   20
Ross Sea, Ant. D24   67
Røssvatnet, l., Nor. D5   10
Rossville, Ga., U.S. B1   103
Rossville, Il., U.S. C6   106
Rossville, In., U.S. D4   107
Rossville, Ks., U.S. C8   109
Roštkala, Taj. C10   42
Rostock, Ger. D12   12
Rostov, Russia C6   22

Rostov-na-Donu, Russia E6   26
Roswell, Ga., U.S. B2   103
Roswell, N.M., U.S. D5   124
Rota, i., N. Mar. Is. D12   32
Rotan, Tx., U.S. C2   136
Rothesay, N.B., Can. D4   87
Rothschild, Wi., U.S. D4   142
Rothsville, Pa., U.S. F9   131
Roti, Pulau, i., Indon. F6   36
Rotorua, N.Z. o14   63c
Rotterdam, Neth. E9   12
Rotterdam, N.Y., U.S. C6   125
Roubaix, Fr. B8   16
Rouen, Fr. C7   16
Rouge, stm., P.Q., Can. D3   90
Rough, stm., Ky., U.S. C3   110
Rough River Lake, res., Ky.,
U.S. C3   110
Rouiba, Alg. I8   16
Roulette, Pa., U.S. C5   131
Round Island, i., Ms., U.S. . .g8   117
Round Lake, Il., U.S. h8   106
Round Lake Beach, Il., U.S. .h8   106
Round Mountain, Nv., U.S. . .E4   121
Round Rock, Tx., U.S. D4   136
Roundup, Mt., U.S. D8   119
Round Valley Indian
Reservation, Ca., U.S. . . .C2   98
Round Valley Reservoir, res.,
N.J., U.S. B3   123
Rouses Point, N.Y., U.S. . . .f11   125
Routt, co., Co., U.S. A3   99
Rouyn [-Noranda], P.Q.,
Can. k11   90
Rouzerville, Pa., U.S. G6   131
Rovaniemi, Fin. C11   10
Rovereto, Italy B3   18
Rovigo, Italy B3   18
Rovuma (Ruvuma), stm.,
Afr. F8   54
Rowan, co., Ky., U.S. B6   110
Rowan, co., N.C., U.S. B2   126
Rowland, N.C., U.S. C3   126
Rowlesburg, W.V., U.S. B5   141
Roxas, Phil. D8   34
Roxboro, N.C., U.S. A4   126
Roxburgh, N.Z. q12   63c
Roxton Falls, P.Q., Can. D5   90
Roxton Pond, P.Q., Can. D5   90
Roy, Ut., U.S. B3   137
Royal, stm., Me., U.S. g7   112
Royal Center, In., U.S. C4   107
Royale, Isle, i., Mi., U.S. h9   115
Royal Gorge, val., Co.,
U.S. C5   99
Royal Oak, Mi., U.S. F7   115
Royal Pines, N.C., U.S. f10   126
Royalton, Il., U.S. F4   106
Royalton, Mn., U.S. E4   116
Royan, Fr. E6   16
Royersford, Pa., U.S. F10   131
Royerton, In., U.S. D7   107
Royse City, Tx., U.S. C4   136
Royston, B.C., Can. E5   85
Royston, Ga., U.S. B3   103
Rtišcevo, Russia D7   22
Ruacana Falls, wtfl., Afr. B1   56
Ruapehu, Mount, vol., N.Z. .o14   63c
Rubcovsk, Russia D10   26
Rubidoux, Ca., U.S. n14   98
Rubondo Island, i., Tan. D6   54
Ruby Dome, mtn., Nv., U.S. .C6   121
Ruby Lake, l., Nv., U.S. C6   121
Ruby Mountains, mts., Nv.,
U.S. C6   121
Ruby Range, mts., Co., U.S. .C3   99
Ruby Range, mts., Mt., U.S. .E4   119
Rudarpur, Mi., U.S. B6   115
Rudnja, Russia B11   20
Rudnyj, Kaz. D8   26
Rudolf, Lake (Turkana, Lake),
l., Afr. C7   54
Rudyard, Mi., U.S. B6   115
Rufiji, stm., Tan. E7   54
Rufino, Arg. E4   72
Rufisque, Sen. D1   50
Rufus Woods Lake, res., Wa.,
U.S. A6   140
Rugby, N.D., U.S. A6   127
Rügen, i., Ger. C13   12
Ruhengeri, Rw. D5   54
Rui'an, China F12   28
Ruidoso, N.M., U.S. D4   124
Ruidoso Downs, N.M., U.S. .D4   124
Ruijin, China F11   28
Ruiz, Mex. C3   78
Ruki, stm., D.R.C. D3   54
Rukwa, Lake, l., Tan. E6   54
Ruleville, Ms., U.S. B3   117
Rum, stm., Mn., U.S. D5   116
Rum Cay, i., Bah. B7   18
Rum Creek, stm., W.V., U.S. .n12   141
Rumford, Me., U.S. D2   112
Rum Jungle, Austl. C5   60
Rumoi, Japan C16   28
Rumphi, Mwi. A5   56
Rumson, N.J., U.S. C4   123
Rumstick Point, c., R.I.,
U.S. D5   132
Runan, China E10   28
Runge, Tx., U.S. E4   136
Rungwa, Tan. E6   54
Runnels, co., Tx., U.S. D3   136

Runnemede, N.J., U.S. D2   123
Ruoqiang, China D5   28
Rupat, Pulau, i., Indon. C2   36
Rupert, Id., U.S. G5   105
Rupert, W.V., U.S. D4   141
Rupert, Rivière de, stm., P.Q.,
Can. h11   90
Rural Hall, N.C., U.S. A2   126
Rural Retreat, Va., U.S. D1   139
Rurrenabaque, Bol. A4   72
Rusagonis, N.B., Can. D3   87
Rusape, Zimb. B5   56
Ruse, Blg. C11   18
Rush, co., In., U.S. E6   107
Rush, co., Ks., U.S. D4   109
Rush, stm., Mn., U.S. F4   116
Rush, stm., Wi., U.S. D1   142
Rush City, Mn., U.S. E6   116
Rush Creek, stm., Oh., U.S. .B2   128
Rush Creek, stm., Ok., U.S. .C4   129
Rushford, Mn., U.S. G7   116
Rush Lake, l., Mn., U.S. E5   116
Rush Lake, l., Mn., U.S. D3   116
Rush Lake, l., Wi., U.S. E5   142
Rushmere, Va., U.S. h14   139
Rush Springs, Ok., U.S. C4   129
Rushville, Il., U.S. C3   106
Rushville, In., U.S. E7   107
Rushville, Ne., U.S. B3   120
Rusk, Tx., U.S. D5   136
Rusk, co., Tx., U.S. C5   136
Rusk, co., Wi., U.S. C2   142
Ruskin, Fl., U.S. E4   102
Russas, Braz. B4   74
Russell, Mb., Can. D1   86
Russell, On., Can. B9   89
Russell, co., Al., U.S. C4   94
Russell, Ks., U.S. D5   109
Russell, co., Ks., U.S. D5   109
Russell, Ky., U.S. B7   110
Russell, co., Ky., U.S. D4   110
Russell, Pa., U.S. C3   131
Russell, co., Va., U.S. f9   139
Russell, Mount, mtn., Ak.,
U.S. f16   95
Russell Cave National
Monument, Al., U.S. A4   94
Russell Fork, stm., U.S. C7   110
Russell Springs, Ky., U.S. . . .C4   110
Russellville, Al., U.S. A2   94
Russellville, Ar., U.S. B2   97
Russellville, Ky., U.S. D3   110
Russellville, Mo., U.S. C5   118
Russellville, Tn., U.S. C10   135
Russia, ctry., Eur. C11   20
Russian, stm., Ca., U.S. C2   98
Russiaville, In., U.S. D5   107
Russkaja Gavan', Russia B8   26
Rustavi, Geor. B11   44
Rustburg, Va., U.S. C3   139
Rustenburg, S. Afr. D4   56
Ruston, La., U.S. B3   111
Ruston, Wa., U.S. B3   140
Rutana, Bdi. D6   54
Ruteng, Indon. E6   36
Ruth, Nv., U.S. D6   121
Rutherford, co., N.C., U.S. . .B1   126
Rutherford, N.J., U.S. B4   123
Rutherford, Tn., U.S. A3   135
Rutherford, co., Tn., U.S. . . .B5   135
Rutherfordton, N.C., U.S. . . .B1   126
Ruthven, Ia., U.S. A3   108
Rutland, Ma., U.S. B4   114
Rutland, Vt., U.S. D3   138
Rutland, co., Vt., U.S. D2   138
Rutledge, Ga., U.S. C3   103
Rutledge, Tn., U.S. C10   135
Rutog, China C3   40
Rutshuru, D.R.C. D5   54
Ruvuma (Rovuma), stm.,
Afr. F8   54
Ruy Barbosa, Braz. D3   74
Ruzaevka, Russia D7   22
Rwanda, ctry., Afr. D5   54
Ryan, Ok., U.S. C4   129
Ryan Peak, mtn., Id., U.S. . .F4   105
Rybače, Kaz. E10   26
Rybačij, poluostrov, pen.,
Russia B15   10
Rybinsk, Russia D5   22
Rybinskoe vodohranilišče,
res., Russia D5   26
Rybinsk Reservoir see
Rybinskoe vodohranilišče,
res., Russia D5   26
Rybnik, Pol. D5   20
Rycroft, Ab., Can. B1   84
Rye, N.H., U.S. D5   122
Rye, N.Y., U.S. h13   125
Rye Beach, N.H., U.S. E5   122
Rye Patch Dam, Nv., U.S. . . .C3   121
Rye Patch Reservoir, res.,
Nv., U.S. C3   121
Ryl'sk, Russia D13   20
Ryukyu Islands see Nansei-
shotō, is., Japan A9   34
Ryukyu Trench F15   64
Rzeszów, Pol. D7   20
Ržev, Russia D5   26

S

Saarbrücken, Ger. F10   12
Saaremaa, i., Est. G10   10
Saarijärvi, Fin. E11   10

Name	Map Ref.	Page

Saarlouis, Ger. — F10 — 12
Saatlı, Azer. — C13 — 44
Saba, i., Neth. Ant. — B7 — 80
Šabac, Yugo. — B7 — 18
Sabadell, Spain — G8 — 16
Sabah, hist. reg., Malay. — B5 — 36
Sabana, Archipiélago de, is., Cuba — A3 — 80
Sabanalarga, Col. — C5 — 80
Sabattus, Me., U.S. — D2 — 112
Šāberī, Hāmūn-e, l., Asia — D8 — 42
Sabetha, Ks., U.S. — C8 — 109
Sabhā, Libya — E7 — 48
Sabi (Save), stm., Afr. — B5 — 56
Sabillasville, Md., U.S. — A3 — 113
Sabina, Oh., U.S. — C2 — 128
Sabinal, Tx., U.S. — E3 — 136
Sabinal, Cayo, i., Cuba — A4 — 80
Sabinas, Mex. — B4 — 78
Sabinas Hidalgo, Mex. — B4 — 78
Sabine, co., La., U.S. — C2 — 111
Sabine, co., Tx., U.S. — D6 — 136
Sabine, stm., U.S. — E9 — 92
Sabine, stm., U.S. — D6 — 136
Sabine Lake, l., U.S. — E2 — 111
Sabine Pass, strt., U.S. — E2 — 111
Sabirabad, Azer. — B13 — 44
Sable, Cape, c., Fl., U.S. — G5 — 102
Sable Island, i., N.S., Can. — F10 — 87
Sabrina Coast, Ant. — C16 — 67
Sabula, Ia., U.S. — B7 — 108
Şabyā, Sau. Ar. — G4 — 38
Sabzevār, Iran — C7 — 42
Sac, co., Ia., U.S. — B2 — 108
Sac, stm., Mo., U.S. — D4 — 118
Sacajawea, Lake, res., Wa., U.S. — C7 — 140
Sacajawea Peak, mtn., Or., U.S. — B9 — 130
Sacandaga Lake, l., N.Y., U.S. — B6 — 125
Sac and Fox Indian Reservation, Ia., U.S. — C5 — 108
Sacaton, Az., U.S. — D4 — 96
Sac City, Ia., U.S. — B2 — 108
Săcele, Rom. — G8 — 20
Sachse, Tx., U.S. — n10 — 136
Sachsen, hist. reg., Ger. — E13 — 12
Sachuest Point, c., R.I., U.S. — F6 — 132
Sackville, N.B., Can. — D5 — 87
Saco, Me., U.S. — E2 — 112
Saco, stm., U.S. — E2 — 112
Saco, East Branch, stm., N.H., U.S. — B4 — 122
Sacramento, Ca., U.S. — C3 — 98
Sacramento, co., Ca., U.S. — C3 — 98
Sacramento, stm., Ca., U.S. — C3 — 98
Sacramento, stm., N.M., U.S. — E4 — 124
Sacramento Mountains, mts., N.M., U.S. — E4 — 124
Sacramento Valley, val., Ca., U.S. — C2 — 98
Sacré-Coeur-Saguenay, P.Q., Can. — A8 — 90
Sacred Heart, Mn., U.S. — F3 — 116
Ṣa'dah, Yemen — G4 — 38
Saddle, stm., N.J., U.S. — h8 — 123
Saddleback Mountain, mtn., Az., U.S. — k8 — 96
Saddle Brook, N.J., U.S. — h8 — 123
Saddlebunch Keys, is., Fl., U.S. — H5 — 102
Saddle Mountain, mtn., Or., U.S. — B3 — 130
Saddle Mountains, mts., Wa., U.S. — C5 — 140
Saddle River, N.J., U.S. — A4 — 123
Sa Dec, Viet. — D5 — 34
Sado, i., Japan — D15 — 28
Sado-kaikyō, strt., Japan — C3 — 31
Šadrinsk, Russia — D8 — 26
Saegertown, Pa., U.S. — C1 — 131
Safâga, Egypt — E11 — 48
Safety Harbor, Fl., U.S. — E4 — 102
Säffle, Swe. — G5 — 10
Safford, Az., U.S. — E6 — 96
Safi, Mor. — D3 — 48
Safonovo, Russia — B12 — 20
Safonovo, Russia — A8 — 22
Safranbolu, Tur. — B5 — 44
Saga, China — F5 — 28
Saga, Japan — D2 — 31
Sagadahoc, co., Me., U.S. — E3 — 112
Sagaing, Myan. — B3 — 34
Sagamore Hills, Oh., U.S. — h9 — 128
Saganaga Lake, l., Mn., U.S. — B7 — 116
Sāgar, India — E3 — 40
Sagarmāthā see Everest, Mount, mtn., Asia — D5 — 40
Sagay, Phil. — D8 — 34
Sag Harbor, N.Y., U.S. — m16 — 125
Saginaw, Mi., U.S. — E7 — 115
Saginaw, Tx., U.S. — n9 — 136
Saginaw, co., Mi., U.S. — E6 — 115
Saginaw Bay, b., Mi., U.S. — E7 — 115
Sagiz, Kaz. — E10 — 22
Saglek Bay, b., Nf., Can. — f9 — 88
Sagonar, Russia — A6 — 28
Saguache, co., Co., U.S. — C4 — 99
Sagua de Tánamo, Cuba — A4 — 80
Sagua la Grande, Cuba — A3 — 80
Saguaro Lake, res., Az., U.S. — k10 — 96

Saguaro National Monument (Tucson Mountain Section), Az., U.S. — E4 — 96
Saguaro National Monument, Az., U.S. — E5 — 96
Saguenay, stm., P.Q., Can. — A7 — 90
Sagunt, Spain — H6 — 16
Sahagún, Col. — C4 — 80
Sahalin, ostrov, i., Russia — D16 — 26
Sahāranpur, India — D3 — 40
Sahara, des., Afr. — F6 — 48
Sahel see Sudan, reg., Afr. — H8 — 48
Sāhīwāl, Pak. — D10 — 42
Sāhīwāl, Pak. — D10 — 42
Şahnen, Iran — E12 — 44
Šahrisabz, Uzb. — F8 — 26
Sahuaripa, Mex. — B3 — 78
Sahuarita, Az., U.S. — F5 — 96
Šahunja, Russia — C8 — 22
Sa Huynh, Viet. — D5 — 34
Saibai Island, i., Austl. — B3 — 62
Saïda, Alg. — E4 — 14
Saidpur, Bngl. — D5 — 40
Saidu, Pak. — D10 — 42
Saigon see Thanh Pho Ho Chi Minh, Viet. — D5 — 34
Saiki, Japan — D2 — 31
Šaim, Russia — B11 — 22
Saimaa, l., Fin. — F13 — 10
Şā'īn Dezh, Iran — D12 — 44
Saint Adolphe, Mb., Can. — E3 — 86
Sainte-Agathe, P.Q., Can. — C6 — 90
Sainte-Agathe-des-Monts, P.Q., Can. — C3 — 90
Saint-Aimé (Massueville), P.Q., Can. — D5 — 90
Saint-Alban, P.Q., Can. — C5 — 90
Saint Alban's, Nf., Can. — E4 — 88
Saint Albans, Vt., U.S. — B2 — 138
Saint Albans, W.V., U.S. — C3 — 141
Saint Albans Bay, b., Vt., U.S. — B2 — 138
Saint Albert, Ab., Can. — C4 — 84
Saint-Amand-Montrond, Fr. — D8 — 16
Saint-Ambroise, P.Q., Can. — A6 — 90
Saint-André-Avellin, P.Q., Can. — D2 — 90
Saint-André-Est, P.Q., Can. — D3 — 90
Saint Andrew Bay, b., Fl., U.S. — u16 — 102
Saint Andrews, N.B., Can. — D2 — 87
Saint Andrews, Scot., U.K. — B5 — 12
Saint Andrews, S.C., U.S. — C5 — 133
Saint Andrews, S.C., U.S. — F7 — 133
Saint Anne, Il., U.S. — B6 — 106
Sainte-Anne-de-Beaupré, P.Q., Can. — B7 — 90
Sainte-Anne [-de-Bellevue], P.Q., Can. — q19 — 90
Sainte Anne-de-Madawaska, N.B., Can. — B1 — 87
Sainte Anne-des-Chênes, Mb., Can. — E3 — 86
Saint-Anselme, P.Q., Can. — C7 — 90
Saint Ansgar, Ia., U.S. — A5 — 108
Saint Anthony, Nf., Can. — C4 — 88
Saint Anthony, Id., U.S. — F7 — 105
Saint Antoine, N.B., Can. — C5 — 87
Saint-Apollinaire, P.Q., Can. — C6 — 90
Saint Arnaud, Austl. — H3 — 62
Saint Arthur, N.B., Can. — B3 — 87
Saint-Aubert, P.Q., Can. — B7 — 90
Saint Augustin, stm., Can. — C2 — 88
Saint Augustine, Fl., U.S. — C5 — 102
Saint Austell, Eng., U.K. — E4 — 12
Saint-Avold, Fr. — C10 — 16
Saint-Basile [-Sud], P.Q., Can. — C6 — 90
Saint-Bernard, P.Q., Can. — C6 — 90
Saint Bernard, Al., U.S. — A3 — 94
Saint Bernard, La., U.S. — E6 — 111
Saint Bernard, Oh., U.S. — o13 — 128
Saint Bernard, co., La., U.S. — E6 — 111
Saint Bernice, In., U.S. — E2 — 107
Saint Bride, Mount, mtn., Ab., Can. — D3 — 84
Saint Bride's, Nf., Can. — E4 — 88
Saint-Brieuc, Fr. — C5 — 16
Saint-Bruno, P.Q., Can. — A6 — 90
Saint-Casimir, P.Q., Can. — C5 — 90
Saint Catharines, On., Can. — D5 — 89
Saint Catherine, Lake, l., Vt., U.S. — E2 — 138
Saint Catherines Island, i., Ga., U.S. — E5 — 103
Saint-Célestin (Annaville), P.Q., Can. — C5 — 90
Saint-Césaire, P.Q., Can. — D4 — 90
Saint-Chamond, Fr. — E9 — 16
Saint Charles, P.Q., Can. — C7 — 90
Saint Charles, Il., U.S. — B5 — 106
Saint Charles, Mi., U.S. — E6 — 115
Saint Charles, Mn., U.S. — G6 — 116
Saint Charles, Mo., U.S. — C7 — 118
Saint Charles, co., La., U.S. — E5 — 111
Saint Charles, co., Mo., U.S. — C7 — 118
Saint Christopher (Saint Kitts), i., St. K./N. — B7 — 80
Saint Christopher and Nevis see Saint Kitts and Nevis, ctry., N.A. — E12 — 76

Saint-Chrysostome, P.Q., Can. — D4 — 90
Saint Clair, Mi., U.S. — F8 — 115
Saint Clair, Mn., U.S. — F5 — 116
Saint Clair, Mo., U.S. — C6 — 118
Saint Clair, Pa., U.S. — E9 — 131
Saint Clair, co., Al., U.S. — B3 — 94
Saint Clair, co., Il., U.S. — E3 — 106
Saint Clair, co., Mi., U.S. — F8 — 115
Saint Clair, co., Mo., U.S. — C4 — 118
Saint Clair Shores, Mi., U.S. — p16 — 115
Saint Clairsville, Oh., U.S. — B5 — 128
Saint Claude, Mb., Can. — E2 — 86
Saint Cloud, Fl., U.S. — D5 — 102
Saint Cloud, Mn., U.S. — E4 — 116
Saint-Coeur-de-Marie, P.Q., Can. — A6 — 90
Saint-Constant, P.Q., Can. — q19 — 90
Sainte-Croix, P.Q., Can. — C6 — 90
Saint Croix, co., Wi., U.S. — C1 — 142
Saint Croix, i., V.I.U.S. — B7 — 80
Saint Croix, co., Wi., U.S. — C1 — 142
Saint Croix, Lake, l., U.S. — D1 — 142
Saint Croix Falls, Wi., U.S. — C1 — 142
Saint Croix Stream, stm., Me., U.S. — B4 — 112
Saint-Damase, P.Q., Can. — D4 — 90
Saint David, Az., U.S. — F5 — 96
Saint-David-de-l'Auberivière, P.Q., Can. — n17 — 90
Saint-Denis, P.Q., Can. — D4 — 90
Saint-Denis, Reu. — g10 — 57a
Saint-Dié, Fr. — C10 — 16
Saint-Dizier, Fr. — C9 — 16
Saint-Dominique, P.Q., Can. — D5 — 90
Saint Edward, Ne., U.S. — C8 — 120
Saint Eleanor's, P.E., Can. — C6 — 87
Saint Elias, Cape, c., Ak., U.S. — D11 — 95
Saint Elias, Mount, mtn., N.A. — F11 — 82
Saint-Élie, Fr. Gu. — C9 — 70
Saint Elmo, Al., U.S. — E1 — 94
Saint Elmo, Il., U.S. — D5 — 106
Saint-Éphrem [-de-Tring], P.Q., Can. — C7 — 90
Saint-Étienne, Fr. — E9 — 16
Saint-Eustache, P.Q., Can. — D4 — 90
Saint-Félix-de-Valois, P.Q., Can. — A5 — 90
Saint-Félix-de-Valois, P.Q., Can. — C4 — 90
Saint-Ferdinand (Bernierville), P.Q., Can. — C6 — 90
Saint-Ferréol [-les-Neiges], P.Q., Can. — B7 — 90
Saint-Flavien, P.Q., Can. — C6 — 90
Sainte-Foy, P.Q., Can. — n17 — 90
Saint Francis, Ks., U.S. — C2 — 109
Saint Francis, Mn., U.S. — E5 — 116
Saint Francis, S.D., U.S. — D5 — 134
Saint Francis, Wi., U.S. — n12 — 142
Saint Francis, co., Ar., U.S. — B5 — 97
Saint Francis, stm., U.S. — A5 — 97
Saint Francis, Cape, c., Nf., Can. — E5 — 88
Saint Francis, Cape, c., S. Afr. — E3 — 56
Saint Francisville, Il., U.S. — E6 — 106
Saint Francisville, La., U.S. — D4 — 111
Saint Francois, co., Mo., U.S. — D7 — 118
Saint-François, stm., P.Q., Can. — D5 — 90
Saint-François, Lac, l., P.Q., Can. — D6 — 90
Saint Francois Mountains, hills, Mo., U.S. — D7 — 118
Saint Froid Lake, l., Me., U.S. — B4 — 112
Saint-Fulgence, P.Q., Can. — A7 — 90
Saint-Gabriel, P.Q., Can. — C4 — 90
Saint-Gaudens, Fr. — F7 — 16
Saint-Gédéon, P.Q., Can. — D7 — 90
Sainte Genevieve, Mo., U.S. — D7 — 118
Sainte Genevieve, co., Mo., U.S. — D7 — 118
Saint George, Austl. — F4 — 62
Saint George, N.B., Can. — D3 — 87
Saint George, On., Can. — D4 — 89
Saint George, S.C., U.S. — E6 — 133
Saint George, Ut., U.S. — F2 — 137
Saint George, Cape, c., Nf., Can. — D2 — 88
Saint George, Cape, c., Fl., U.S. — C1 — 102
Saint George Island, i., Ak., U.S. — D6 — 95
Saint George Island, i., Fl., U.S. — C2 — 102
Saint George's, Nf., Can. — D2 — 88
Saint-Georges, P.Q., Can. — C5 — 90
Saint-Georges, Fr. Gu. — C9 — 70
Saint George's, Gren. — C7 — 80
Saint George's Bay, b., Nf., Can. — D2 — 88
Saint Georges Bay, b., N.S., Can. — D8 — 87
Saint George's Channel, strt., Eur. — B3 — 16
Saint-Georges-Ouest (part of Ville-Saint-Georges), P.Q., Can. — C7 — 90

Saint-Gervais, P.Q., Can. — C7 — 90
Saint-Gilles, P.Q., Can. — C6 — 90
Saint Gotthard Pass see San Gottardo, Passo del, Switz. — A2 — 18
Saint-Grégoire (Larochelle), P.Q., Can. — C5 — 90
Saint-Guillaume-d'Upton, P.Q., Can. — D5 — 90
Saint Helen, Lake, l., Mi., U.S. — D6 — 115
Saint Helena, Ca., U.S. — C2 — 98
Saint Helena, co., La., U.S. — D5 — 111
Saint Helena, dep., Afr. — K9 — 46
Saint Helena Island, i., S.C., U.S. — G6 — 133
Saint Helena Sound, strt., S.C., U.S. — G7 — 133
Saint Helens, Or., U.S. — B4 — 130
Saint Helens, Mount, vol., Wa., U.S. — C3 — 140
Saint Helier, Jersey — F5 — 12
Saint Henry, Oh., U.S. — B1 — 128
Saint-Honoré, P.Q., Can. — D7 — 90
Saint-Hubert, P.Q., Can. — q20 — 90
Saint-Hubert-de-Témiscouata, P.Q., Can. — B8 — 90
Saint-Hyacinthe, P.Q., Can. — D5 — 90
Saint Ignace, Mi., U.S. — C6 — 115
Saint Ignatius, Mt., U.S. — C2 — 119
Saint Isidore de Prescott, On., Can. — B10 — 89
Saint Jacobs, On., Can. — D4 — 89
Saint Jacques, N.B., Can. — B1 — 87
Saint-Jacques, P.Q., Can. — D4 — 90
Saint James, Mn., U.S. — G4 — 116
Saint James, Mo., U.S. — D6 — 118
Saint James, co., La., U.S. — D5 — 111
Saint James, Cape, c., B.C., Can. — D2 — 85
Saint James City, Fl., U.S. — F4 — 102
Saint-Jean, stm., P.Q., Can. — A7 — 90
Saint-Jean, Lac, l., P.Q., Can. — A5 — 90
Saint Jean Baptiste, Mb., Can. — E3 — 86
Saint-Jean-Chrysostome, P.Q., Can. — o17 — 90
Saint-Jean-d'Angély, Fr. — E6 — 16
Saint-Jean-sur-Richelieu, P.Q., Can. — D4 — 90
Saint-Jérôme, P.Q., Can. — D3 — 90
Saint Jo, Tx., U.S. — C4 — 136
Saint-Joachim, P.Q., Can. — B7 — 90
Saint Joe, stm., Id., U.S. — B3 — 105
Saint John, N.B., Can. — D3 — 87
Saint John, In., U.S. — B3 — 107
Saint John, Ks., U.S. — E5 — 109
Saint John, i., V.I.U.S. — B7 — 80
Saint John, stm., N.A. — B14 — 92
Saint John, Cape, c., Nf., Can. — D4 — 88
Saint John Bay, b., Nf., Can. — C3 — 88
Saint John's, Antig. — B7 — 80
Saint John's, Nf., Can. — E5 — 88
Saint Johns, Az., U.S. — C6 — 96
Saint Johns, Mi., U.S. — F6 — 115
Saint Johns, co., Fl., U.S. — C5 — 102
Saint Johns, stm., Fl., U.S. — B5 — 102
Saint Johnsbury, Vt., U.S. — C4 — 138
Saint Johnsville, N.Y., U.S. — B6 — 125
Saint John the Baptist, co., La., U.S. — D5 — 111
Saint Jones, stm., De., U.S. — D4 — 101
Saint Joseph, Il., U.S. — C5 — 106
Saint Joseph, La., U.S. — C4 — 111
Saint Joseph, Mi., U.S. — F4 — 115
Saint Joseph, Mn., U.S. — E4 — 116
Saint Joseph, Mo., U.S. — B3 — 118
Saint Joseph, Tn., U.S. — B4 — 135
Saint Joseph, co., In., U.S. — A5 — 107
Saint Joseph, co., Mi., U.S. — G5 — 115
Saint Joseph, stm., U.S. — F5 — 115
Saint-Joseph, Lac, l., P.Q., Can. — n16 — 90
Saint Joseph, Lake, l., On., Can. — o17 — 89
Saint Joseph Bay, b., Fl., U.S. — C1 — 102
Saint Joseph Point, c., Fl., U.S. — v16 — 102
Saint Joseph Sound, strt., Fl., U.S. — o10 — 102
Saint-Jovite, P.Q., Can. — C3 — 90
Saint-Junien, Fr. — E7 — 16
Saint Kilda, i., Scot., U.K. — B2 — 12
Saint Kitts see Saint Christopher, i., St. K./N. — B7 — 80
Saint Kitts and Nevis, ctry., N.A. — E12 — 76
Saint-Lambert, P.Q., Can. — p19 — 90
Saint Landry, co., La., U.S. — D3 — 111
Saint-Laurent, P.Q., Can. — p19 — 90
Saint-Laurent du Maroni, Fr. Gu. — B9 — 70
Saint Lawrence, co., N.Y., U.S. — A5 — 125
Saint Lawrence, Nf., Can. — E4 — 88
Saint Lawrence, stm., N.A. — B14 — 92

Saint Lawrence, Cape, c., N.S., Can. — B9 — 87
Saint Lawrence, Gulf of, b., Can. — I27 — 82
Saint Lawrence Island, i., Ak., U.S. — C5 — 95
Saint Lawrence Islands National Park, On., Can. — C9 — 89
Saint Léonard, N.B., Can. — B2 — 87
Saint-Léonard [-d'Aston], P.Q., Can. — C5 — 90
Saint-Liboire, P.Q., Can. — D5 — 90
Saint-Lô, Fr. — C6 — 16
Saint-Louis, Sen. — C1 — 50
Saint Louis, Mi., U.S. — E6 — 115
Saint Louis, Mo., U.S. — C7 — 118
Saint Louis, co., Mn., U.S. — C6 — 116
Saint Louis, co., Mo., U.S. — C7 — 118
Saint-Louis, stm., U.S. — D6 — 116
Saint-Louis, Lac, l., P.Q., Can. — q19 — 90
Saint Louis Bay, b., Ms., U.S. — f7 — 117
Saint-Louis-de-Gonzague, P.Q., Can. — D3 — 90
Saint-Louis-de-Kent, N.B., Can. — C5 — 87
Saint-Louis-du-Ha! Ha!, P.Q., Can. — B8 — 90
Saint Louis Park, Mn., U.S. — n12 — 116
Saint-Luc, P.Q., Can. — D4 — 90
Saint Lucia, ctry., N.A. — F12 — 76
Saint Lucia, Lake, l., S. Afr. — D5 — 56
Saint Lucia Channel, strt., N.A. — C7 — 80
Saint Lucie, co., Fl., U.S. — E6 — 102
Saint Lucie Canal, Fl., U.S. — F6 — 102
Saint Lucie Inlet, b., Fl., U.S. — E6 — 102
Sainte-Madeleine, P.Q., Can. — D4 — 90
Saint Magnus Bay, b., Scot., U.K. — h19 — 12a
Saint-Malo, Mb., Can. — E3 — 86
Saint-Malo, Fr. — C6 — 16
Saint-Malo, Golfe de, b., Fr. — C5 — 16
Saint-Marc, Haiti — B5 — 80
Saint-Marc [-des-Carrières], P.Q., Can. — C5 — 90
Saint Margaret Bay, b., Nf., Can. — C3 — 88
Sainte-Marguerite, stm., P.Q., Can. — A7 — 90
Sainte-Marie, P.Q., Can. — C6 — 90
Sainte Marie, Nosy, i., Madag. — B8 — 56
Saint Maries, Id., U.S. — B2 — 105
Sainte-Marthe, P.Q., Can. — D3 — 90
Saint Martin, co., La., U.S. — D4 — 111
Saint-Martin, i., N.A. — B7 — 80
Saint Martin, Lake, l., Mb., Can. — D2 — 86
Saint Martin Island, i., Mi., U.S. — C4 — 115
Saint Martinville, La., U.S. — D4 — 111
Saint Mary, co., La., U.S. — E4 — 111
Saint Mary-of-the-Woods, In., U.S. — E3 — 107
Saint Mary Peak, mtn., Austl. — G2 — 62
Saint Marys, Austl. — I4 — 62
Saint Mary's, Nf., Can. — E5 — 88
Saint Marys, On., Can. — D3 — 89
Saint Marys, Ak., U.S. — C7 — 95
Saint Marys, Ga., U.S. — F5 — 103
Saint Marys, In., U.S. — A5 — 107
Saint Marys, Ks., U.S. — C7 — 109
Saint Marys, Oh., U.S. — B1 — 128
Saint Marys, Pa., U.S. — D4 — 131
Saint Marys, W.V., U.S. — B3 — 141
Saint Marys, co., Md., U.S. — D4 — 113
Saint Marys, stm., N.S., Can. — D8 — 87
Saint Marys, stm., Md., U.S. — D5 — 113
Saint Marys, stm., U.S. — F5 — 103
Saint Marys, stm., U.S. — C8 — 107
Saint Mary's, Cape, c., Nf., Can. — E4 — 88
Saint Mary's Bay, b., Nf., Can. — E5 — 88
Saint Marys Bay, b., N.S., Can. — E3 — 87
Saint Marys City, Md., U.S. — D5 — 113
Saint Matthew Island, i., Ak., U.S. — C5 — 95
Saint Matthews, Ky., U.S. — B4 — 110
Saint Matthews, S.C., U.S. — D6 — 133
Saint-Maurice, stm., P.Q., Can. — C5 — 90
Saint Michael, Mn., U.S. — E5 — 116
Saint Michaels, Md., U.S. — C5 — 113
Saint-Michel [-de-Bellechasse], P.Q., Can. — C7 — 90
Saint-Nazaire, Fr. — D5 — 16
Saint-Nicolas, P.Q., Can. — o17 — 90
Saint-Odilon, P.Q., Can. — C7 — 90
Saint-Omer, Fr. — B8 — 16
Saint-Ours, P.Q., Can. — D4 — 90
Saint-Pacôme, P.Q., Can. — B8 — 90
Saint-Pamphile, P.Q., Can. — C8 — 90
Saint Paris, Oh., U.S. — B2 — 128
Saint-Pascal, P.Q., Can. — B8 — 90
Saint Paul, Ab., Can. — B5 — 84
Saint-Paul, Reu. — g10 — 57a
Saint Paul, Ak., U.S. — D5 — 95

Name	Map Ref.	Page
Saint Paul, In., U.S.	F6	107
Saint Paul, Ks., U.S.	E8	109
Saint Paul, Mn., U.S.	F5	116
Saint Paul, Mo., U.S.	f12	118
Saint Paul, Ne., U.S.	C7	120
Saint Paul, Va., U.S.	f9	139
Saint Paul Island, i., Ak., U.S.	D5	95
Saint Paul Park, Mn., U.S.	n12	116
Saint Pauls, N.C., U.S.	C4	126
Sainte-Perpétue-de-L'Islet, P.Q., Can.	B8	90
Saint Peter, Mn., U.S.	F5	116
Saint Peter Port, Guernsey	F5	12
Saint Peters, N.S., Can.	D9	87
Saint Peters, Mo., U.S.	C7	118
Saint Petersburg see Sankt-Peterburg, Russia	D5	26
Saint Petersburg, Fl., U.S.	E4	102
Saint Petersburg Beach, Fl., U.S.	p10	102
Saint Phillips Island, i., S.C., U.S.	G6	133
Saint-Pie, P.Q., Can.	D5	90
Saint-Pierre, Reu.	g10	57a
Saint-Pierre, St. P./M.	E3	88
Saint Pierre, i., Sey.	i12	57b
Saint-Pierre, Lac, l., P.Q., Can.	C5	90
Saint Pierre and Miquelon, dep., N.A.	I28	82
Saint Pierre-Jolys, Mb., Can.	E3	86
Saint-Prime, P.Q., Can.	A5	90
Saint Quentin, N.B., Can.	B2	87
Saint-Quentin, Fr.	C8	16
Saint-Raphaël, P.Q., Can.	C7	90
Saint-Raphaël, Fr.	F10	16
Saint-Raymond, P.Q., Can.	C6	90
Saint-Rédempteur, P.Q., Can.	o17	90
Saint Regis, Mt., U.S.	C1	119
Saint Regis, West Branch, stm., N.Y., U.S.	f10	125
Saint-Rémi, P.Q., Can.	D4	90
Saint-Romuald, P.Q., Can.	C6	90
Saint Rose, La., U.S.	k11	111
Sainte Rose du Lac, Mb., Can.	D2	86
Saintes, Fr.	E6	16
Saint Sauveur, In., U.S.	B4	87
Saint-Sauveur-des-Monts, P.Q., Can.	D3	90
Saint-Siméon, P.Q., Can.	B8	90
Saint Simons Island, Ga., U.S.	E5	103
Saint Simons Island, i., Ga., U.S.	E5	103
Saint Stephen, N.B., Can.	D2	87
Saint Stephen, S.C., U.S.	E8	133
Saint Tammany, co., La., U.S.	D5	111
Sainte-Thècle, P.Q., Can.	C5	90
Sainte-Thérèse, P.Q., Can.	D4	90
Saint Thomas, On., Can.	E3	89
Saint Thomas, i., V.I.U.S.	B6	80
Saint Timothée, P.Q., Can.	q18	90
Saint-Tite, P.Q., Can.	C5	90
Saint-Tropez, Fr.	F10	16
Sainte-Véronique, P.Q., Can.	C3	90
Saint-Victor, P.Q., Can.	C7	90
Saint Vincent, i., St. Vin.	C7	80
Saint Vincent and the Grenadines, ctry., N.A.	F12	76
Saint Vincent Island, i., Fl., U.S.	C1	102
Saint Vincent Passage, strt., N.A.	C7	80
Saint Vincent's [Saint Stephens-Peter's River], Nf., Can.	E5	88
Saint Walburg, Sk., Can.	D1	91
Saint-Zacharie, P.Q., Can.	C7	90
Saipan, i., N. Mar. Is.	C12	32
Sajama, Nevado, mtn., Bol.	B4	72
Sakakawea, Lake, res., N.D., U.S.	B3	127
Sakania, D.R.C.	F5	54
Sakarya, Tur.	B4	44
Sakarya, stm., Tur.	B4	44
Sakata, Japan	D15	28
Sakété, Benin	E5	50
Sakha see Jakutija, state, Russia	C14	26
Sakhalin see Sahalin, ostrov, i., Russia	D16	26
Sakon Nakhon, Thai.	C4	34
Sakonnet, stm., R.I., U.S.	E6	132
Sakonnet Point, c., R.I., U.S.	E6	132
Sakrivier, S. Afr.	E3	56
Saky, Ukr.	E4	20
Sal, i., C.V.	g10	50a
Sal, Point, c., Ca., U.S.	E3	98
Sala, Swe.	G7	10
Salaberry-de-Valleyfield, P.Q., Can.	D3	90
Salacgrīva, Lat.	H11	10
Sala Consilina, Italy	D5	18
Salada, Laguna, l., Mex.	A1	78
Saladillo, Arg.	F6	72
Salado, stm., Arg.	F4	72
Salado, stm., Arg.	F6	72
Salado, stm., Arg.	D5	72
Salado, stm., Mex.	B5	78
Salado, Rio, stm., N.M., U.S.	C2	124
Salaga, Ghana	E4	50
Salal, Chad	D8	50
Şalālah, Oman	G6	38
Salamanca, Mex.	C4	78
Salamanca, Spain	G4	16
Salamanca, N.Y., U.S.	C2	125
Salamís, i., Grc.	F9	18
Salamis, hist., N. Cyp.	E5	44
Salamīyah, Syria	E7	44
Salamonie, stm., In., U.S.	C6	107
Salamonie Lake, res., In., U.S.	C6	107
Salavat, Russia	D7	26
Salawati, i., Indon.	D8	36
Sala y Gómez, Isla, i., Chile	K28	64
Sala y Gomez Ridge	K28	64
Saldanha, S. Afr.	E2	56
Saldus, Lat.	H10	10
Sale, Austl.	H4	62
Salé, Mor.	E2	14
Sale Creek, Tn., U.S.	D8	135
Salehard, Russia	C8	26
Salem, India	G3	40
Salem, Ar., U.S.	A4	97
Salem, Il., U.S.	E5	106
Salem, In., U.S.	G5	107
Salem, Ky., U.S.	e9	110
Salem, Ma., U.S.	A6	114
Salem, Mo., U.S.	D6	118
Salem, N.H., U.S.	E4	122
Salem, N.J., U.S.	D2	123
Salem, Oh., U.S.	B5	128
Salem, Or., U.S.	C4	130
Salem, S.D., U.S.	D8	134
Salem, Ut., U.S.	C4	137
Salem, Va., U.S.	C2	139
Salem, W.V., U.S.	B4	141
Salem, Wi., U.S.	n11	142
Salem, co., N.J., U.S.	D2	123
Salem, stm., N.J., U.S.	D2	123
Salem, Lake, l., Vt., U.S.	B4	138
Salerno, Italy	D5	18
Salerno, Golfo di, b., Italy	D5	18
Salgótarján, Hung.	E5	20
Salgueiro, Braz.	C4	74
Salida, Co., U.S.	C5	99
Salihli, Tur.	C3	44
Salihorsk, Bela.	C9	20
Salima, Mwi.	A5	56
Salina, Ks., U.S.	D6	109
Salina, Ok., U.S.	A6	129
Salina, Ut., U.S.	E4	137
Salina Cruz, Mex.	D5	78
Salinas, Braz.	E3	74
Salinas, Ec.	D3	70
Salinas, Ca., U.S.	D3	98
Salinas, stm., N.A.	B1	80
Salinas, stm., Ca., U.S.	D3	98
Salinas de Hidalgo, Mex.	C4	78
Salinas Peak, mtn., N.M., U.S.	D3	124
Salinas Pueblo Missions National Monument, N.M., U.S.	C3	124
Saline, Mi., U.S.	F7	115
Saline, co., Ar., U.S.	C3	97
Saline, co., Il., U.S.	F5	106
Saline, co., Ks., U.S.	D6	109
Saline, co., Mo., U.S.	B4	118
Saline, co., Ne., U.S.	D8	120
Saline, stm., Ar., U.S.	C1	97
Saline, stm., Ar., U.S.	D4	97
Saline, stm., Ks., U.S.	C3	109
Saline, North Fork, stm., Il., U.S.	F5	106
Saline Lake, res., La., U.S.	C3	111
Salineville, Oh., U.S.	B5	128
Salinópolis, Braz.	B2	74
Salisbury, Austl.	G2	62
Salisbury, N.B., Can.	C4	87
Salisbury, Ct., U.S.	B2	100
Salisbury, Ma., U.S.	A6	114
Salisbury, Md., U.S.	D6	113
Salisbury, Mo., U.S.	B5	118
Salisbury, N.C., U.S.	B2	126
Salisbury see Harare, Zimb.	B5	56
Salish Mountains, mts., Mt., U.S.	B2	119
Salkehatchie, stm., S.C., U.S.	E5	133
Salla, Fin.	C13	10
Sallisaw, Ok., U.S.	B7	129
Salluit, P.Q., Can.	f11	90
Salmās, Iran	C11	44
Salmo, B.C., Can.	E9	85
Salmon, Id., U.S.	D5	105
Salmon, stm., N.B., Can.	C4	87
Salmon, stm., Id., U.S.	D3	105
Salmon Creek, Wa., U.S.	D3	140
Salmon Creek Reservoir, res., Id., U.S.	G4	105
Salmon Falls, stm., U.S.	D5	122
Salmon Falls Creek, stm., U.S.	G4	105
Salmon Mountains, mts., Ca., U.S.	B2	98
Salmon Point, c., On., Can.	D7	89
Salmon River Mountains, mts., Id., U.S.	E3	105
Salmon River Reservoir, res., N.Y., U.S.	B5	125
Salo, Fin.	F10	10
Salò, Italy	B3	18
Salome, Az., U.S.	D2	96
Salon-de-Provence, Fr.	F9	16
Salonika see Thessaloníki, Grc.	D9	18
Salonika, Gulf of see Thermaïkós Kólpos, b., Grc.	D9	18
Salonta, Rom.	F6	20
Sal'sk, Russia	E7	22
Salt, stm., Az., U.S.	D4	96
Salt, stm., Ky., U.S.	C4	110
Salt, stm., Mo., U.S.	B6	118
Salta, Arg.	C4	72
Salt Creek, stm., N.M., U.S.	D5	124
Salt Creek, stm., Oh., U.S.	C3	128
Salt Creek, stm., Wy., U.S.	C6	143
Salter Path, N.C., U.S.	C6	126
Salt Fork Lake, res., Oh., U.S.	B4	128
Saltillo, Mex.	B4	78
Saltillo, Ms., U.S.	A5	117
Salt Lake, co., Ut., U.S.	C3	137
Salt Lake, l., Hi., U.S.	g10	104
Salt Lake, l., N.M., U.S.	E6	124
Salt Lake City, Ut., U.S.	C4	137
Salto, Ur.	E6	72
Salton Sea, l., Ca., U.S.	F5	98
Saltonstall, Lake, l., Ct., U.S.	D4	100
Salt Point, c., Ca., U.S.	C2	98
Salt River Indian Reservation, Az., U.S.	k9	96
Salt River Range, mts., Wy., U.S.	D2	143
Saltsburg, Pa., U.S.	F3	131
Salt Springs, Fl., U.S.	C5	102
Saltville, Va., U.S.	f10	139
Salt Wells Creek, stm., Wy., U.S.	E4	143
Saluda, S.C., U.S.	C4	133
Saluda, co., S.C., U.S.	C4	133
Saluda, stm., S.C., U.S.	C4	133
Saluda Dam, S.C., U.S.	C5	133
Salūm, Egypt	D10	48
Sālūr, India	F4	40
Salvador, Braz.	D4	74
Salvador, El see El Salvador, ctry., N.A.	C2	80
Salvador, Lake, l., La., U.S.	E5	111
Salween, stm., Asia	G7	38
Salyan, Azer.	C13	44
Salyān, Nepal	D4	40
Salyersville, Ky., U.S.	C6	110
Salzburg, Aus.	G13	12
Salzgitter, Ger.	D12	12
Samah, Libya	F7	14
Samalūt, Egypt	F10	14
Samana Cay, i., Bah.	A5	80
Samandağı, Tur.	D6	44
Samar, i., Phil.	D9	34
Samara (Kujbyšev), Russia	D7	26
Samarai, Pap. N. Gui.	I13	32
Samarinda, Indon.	D5	36
Samarkand, Uzb.	F8	26
Sāmarrā', Iraq	D4	42
Samar Sea, Phil.	D8	34
Şamaxi, Azer.	B13	44
Samba Caju, Ang.	E3	54
Sambalpur, India	E4	40
Sambas, Indon.	C3	36
Sambava, Madag.	A9	56
Sambhal, India	D3	40
Sāmbhar, India	D3	40
Sambir, Ukr.	E7	20
Samboja, Indon.	D5	36
Samborombón, Bahía, b., Arg.	F6	72
Samch'ŏk, S. Kor.	D13	28
Same, Tan.	D7	54
Samfya, Zam.	A4	56
Sämkir, Azer.	B11	44
Sammamish, Lake, l., Wa., U.S.	e11	140
Samoa, ctry., Oc.	F12	58
Samoa Islands, is., Oc.	F12	58
Samoded, Russia	B7	22
Sámos, i., Grc.	F11	18
Samoset, Fl., U.S.	q10	102
Samothrace see Samothráki, i., Grc.	D10	18
Samothráki, i., Grc.	D10	18
Sampit, Indon.	D4	36
Sampit, stm., S.C., U.S.	E9	133
Sampit, Teluk, b., Indon.	D4	36
Sampson, co., N.C., U.S.	B4	126
Sam Rayburn Reservoir, res., Tx., U.S.	D5	136
Samsang, China	C4	40
Samson, Al., U.S.	D3	94
Sam Son, Viet.	C5	34
Samsun, Tur.	B7	44
Samtredia, Geor.	A10	44
Samuels, Id., U.S.	A2	105
Samui, Ko, i., Thai.	E4	34
Samur, stm., Asia	B13	44
Samut Prakan, Thai.	D4	34
Samut Songkhram, Thai.	D4	34
San, Mali	D4	50
Şan'ā', Yemen	G3	38
Sanaba, Burkina	D4	50
Sanaga, stm., Cam.	C2	54
San Agustin, Cape, c., Phil.	E9	34
San Agustin, Plains of, pl., N.M., U.S.	C2	124
Sanak Islands, is., Ak., U.S.	E7	95
San Ambrosio, Isla, i., Chile	H7	2
Sanana, Pulau, i., Indon.	D7	36
Sanandaj, Iran	C5	42
San Andreas, Ca., U.S.	C3	98
San Andrés, Col.	A3	70
San Andres, Isla de, i., Col.	A3	70
San Andres Mountains, mts., N.M., U.S.	E3	124
San Andres Peak, mtn., N.M., U.S.	E3	124
San Andrés Tuxtla, Mex.	D5	78
San Angelo, Tx., U.S.	D2	136
San Anselmo, Ca., U.S.	h7	98
San Antonio, Chile	E3	72
San Antonio, Tx., U.S.	E3	136
San Antonio, Cabo, c., Arg.	F6	72
San Antonio, Cabo de, c., Cuba	A2	80
San Antonio Bay, b., Tx., U.S.	E4	136
San Antonio de los Baños, Cuba	A3	80
San Antonio Mountain, mtn., N.M., U.S.	A3	124
San Antonio Oeste, Arg.	F4	69
San Augustine, Tx., U.S.	D5	136
San Augustine, co., Tx., U.S.	D5	136
San Benedetto del Tronto, Italy	C4	18
San Benedicto, Isla, i., Mex.	D2	78
San Benito, Guat.	B2	80
San Benito, Tx., U.S.	F4	136
San Benito, co., Ca., U.S.	D3	98
San Benito Mountain, mtn., Ca., U.S.	D3	98
San Bernardino, Ca., U.S.	E5	98
San Bernardino, co., Ca., U.S.	E5	98
San Blas, Cape, c., Fl., U.S.	v16	102
San Borja, Bol.	A4	72
Sanborn, Ia., U.S.	A2	108
Sanborn, co., S.D., U.S.	D7	134
Sanbornville, N.H., U.S.	C4	122
San Bruno, Ca., U.S.	D2	98
San Carlos, Arg.	D4	72
San Carlos, Chile	E2	69
San Carlos, Phil.	D8	34
San Carlos, Phil.	C8	34
San Carlos, Az., U.S.	D5	96
San Carlos, Ca., U.S.	k8	98
San Carlos, Ven.	D6	80
San Carlos de Bariloche, Arg.	F2	69
San Carlos de Bolívar, Arg.	F5	72
San Carlos del Zulia, Ven.	B5	70
San Carlos de Río Negro, Ven.	C6	70
San Carlos Indian Reservation, Az., U.S.	D5	96
San Carlos Lake, res., Az., U.S.	D5	96
Sánchez, Dom. Rep.	B6	80
San Clemente, Ca., U.S.	F5	98
San Clemente Island, i., Ca., U.S.	F4	98
San Cristóbal, Arg.	E5	72
San Cristóbal, Dom. Rep.	B5	80
San Cristóbal, Ven.	B5	70
San Cristóbal, Isla, i., Ec.	D2	70
San Cristóbal de las Casas, Mex.	D6	78
Sancti Spíritus, Cuba	A4	80
Sancy, Puy de, mtn., Fr.	E8	16
Sandakan, Malay.	B5	36
Sandaré, Mali	D2	50
Sand Creek, stm., Wy., U.S.	C7	143
Sandefjord, Nor.	G4	10
Sanders, Az., U.S.	B6	96
Sanders, co., Mt., U.S.	C1	119
Sanderson, Tx., U.S.	D1	136
Sandersville, Ga., U.S.	D4	103
Sandersville, Ms., U.S.	D4	117
Sand Hill, Ma., U.S.	h13	114
Sand Hill, stm., Mn., U.S.	C2	116
Sandia Crest, mtn., N.M., U.S.	k8	124
Sandia Indian Reservation, N.M., U.S.	k7	124
Sandia Mountains, mts., N.M., U.S.	k8	124
San Diego, Ca., U.S.	F5	98
San Diego, Tx., U.S.	F3	136
San Diego, co., Ca., U.S.	F5	98
San Diego, Cabo, c., Arg.	o15	69
San Diego, Cabo, c., Arg.	H3	69
San Diego Naval Station, mil., Ca., U.S.	o15	98
San Diego Naval Training Center, mil., Ca., U.S.	o15	98
Sand Island, i., Hi., U.S.	g10	104
Sand Island, i., Wi., U.S.	A3	142
Sand Key, i., Fl., U.S.	E4	102
Sandlick Creek, stm., W.V., U.S.	n13	141
Sandnes, Nor.	G1	10
Sandoa, D.R.C.	E4	54
Sandoval, Il., U.S.	E4	106
Sandoval, co., N.M., U.S.	B2	124
Sandoway, Myan.	C2	34
Sand Point, Ak., U.S.	D7	95
Sandpoint, Id., U.S.	A2	105
Sands Key, i., Fl., U.S.	s3	102
Sand Springs, Ok., U.S.	A5	129
Sandston, Va., U.S.	m18	139
Sandstone, Austl.	F2	60
Sandstone, Mn., U.S.	D6	116
Sandusky, Mi., U.S.	E8	115
Sandusky, Oh., U.S.	A3	128
Sandusky, co., Oh., U.S.	A2	128
Sandusky, stm., Oh., U.S.	B2	128
Sandvika, Nor.	G4	10
Sandviken, Swe.	F7	10
Sandwich, Il., U.S.	B5	106
Sandwich, Ma., U.S.	C7	114
Sandwich Bay, b., Nf., Can.	B3	88
Sandy, Or., U.S.	B4	130
Sandy, Ut., U.S.	C4	137
Sandy, stm., Me., U.S.	D2	112
Sandy Cape, c., Austl.	E5	62
Sandy Creek, stm., Oh., U.S.	B4	128
Sandy Creek, stm., Ok., U.S.	C2	129
Sandy Hook, Ct., U.S.	D2	100
Sandy Hook, spit, N.J., U.S.	C5	123
Sandy Island, i., S.C., U.S.	D9	133
Sandykači, Turk.	F8	26
Sandy Lake, l., Nf., Can.	D3	88
Sandy Lake, l., On., Can.	n16	89
Sandy Neck, pen., Ma., U.S.	C7	114
Sandy Point, c., R.I., U.S.	h7	132
Sandy Springs, Ga., U.S.	h8	103
Sandy Springs, S.C., U.S.	B2	133
Sandyville, Md., U.S.	A4	113
San Felipe, Chile	E3	72
San Felipe, Col.	C6	70
San Felipe, Mex.	A2	78
San Felipe, Ven.	A6	70
San Felipe Indian Reservation, N.M., U.S.	k8	124
San Felipe Pueblo, N.M., U.S.	B3	124
San Fernando, Chile	D2	69
San Fernando, Mex.	C5	78
San Fernando, Phil.	C8	34
San Fernando, Phil.	C8	34
San Fernando, Spain	I3	16
San Fernando, Trin.	C7	80
San Fernando, Ca., U.S.	m12	98
San Fernando de Apure, Ven.	B6	70
San Fernando de Atabapo, Ven.	C6	70
San Fernando del Valle de Catamarca, Arg.	D4	72
Sanford, Fl., U.S.	D5	102
Sanford, Me., U.S.	E2	112
Sanford, Mi., U.S.	E6	115
Sanford, N.C., U.S.	B3	126
Sanford, Mount, mtn., Ak., U.S.	C11	95
San Francisco, Arg.	E5	72
San Francisco, Ca., U.S.	D2	98
San Francisco, co., Ca., U.S.	D2	98
San Francisco Bay, b., Ca., U.S.	h8	98
San Francisco del Oro, Mex.	B3	78
San Francisco del Rincón, Mex.	C4	78
San Francisco de Macorís, Dom. Rep.	B5	80
San Gabriel Mountains, mts., Ca., U.S.	m12	98
Sangamner, India	F2	40
Sangamon, co., Il., U.S.	D4	106
Sangamon, stm., Il., U.S.	C5	106
Sangar, Russia	C14	26
Sange, D.R.C.	E5	54
Sanger, Ca., U.S.	D4	98
Sanger, Tx., U.S.	C4	136
Sanggau, Indon.	C4	36
Sangha, stm., Afr.	D3	54
Sangihe, Kepulauan, is., Indon.	C7	36
Sangihe, Pulau, i., Indon.	C7	36
San Gil, Col.	C5	80
San Giovanni in Fiore, Italy	E6	18
Sangiyn Dalay, Mong.	C9	28
Sāngli, India	F2	40
Sangmélima, Cam.	C2	54
San Gorgonio Mountain, mtn., Ca., U.S.	E5	98
San Gottardo, Passo del, Switz.	A2	18
Sanibel, Fl., U.S.	F4	102
Sanibel Island, i., Fl., U.S.	F4	102
San Ignacio, Mex.	B2	78
San Ignacio, Para.	D6	72
San Ignacio de Moxo, Bol.	A4	72
San Ignacio de Velasco, Bol.	G7	70
Sanilac, co., Mi., U.S.	E8	115
San Isidro, Arg.	C5	80
San Jacinto, Col.	D4	80
San Jacinto, Ca., U.S.	F5	98
San Jacinto, co., Tx., U.S.	D5	136
San Jacinto, stm., Tx., U.S.	r14	136
San Javier, Bol.	B5	72
San Joaquín, Bol.	F7	70
San Joaquin, co., Ca., U.S.	D3	98
San Joaquin, stm., Ca., U.S.	D3	98
San Joaquin Valley, val., Ca., U.S.	D3	98
San Jorge, Arg.	E5	72
San Jorge, Golfo, b., Arg.	G3	69
San Jose, C.R.	D3	80
San Jose, Ca., U.S.	D3	98
San José, i., Mex.	C3	78
San José de Chiquitos, Bol.	B5	72
San José de Guanipa, Ven.	D7	80
San José de Jáchal, Arg.	C4	72
San José de las Lajas, Cuba	A3	80

Name	Map Ref.	Page
San José del Cabo, Mex.	C3	78
San José del Guaviare, Col.	C5	70
San Jose Island, i., Tx., U.S.	E4	136
San Juan, Arg.	E4	72
San Juan, P.R.	B6	80
San Juan, Tx., U.S.	F3	136
San Juan, co., Co., U.S.	D3	99
San Juan, co., N.M., U.S.	A1	124
San Juan, co., Ut., U.S.	F5	137
San Juan, co., Wa., U.S.	A2	140
San Juan, stm., N.A.	F8	76
San Juan Bautista, Para.	D6	72
San Juan Capistrano, Ca., U.S.	F5	98
San Juan de Colón, Ven.	D5	80
San Juan de la Maguana, Dom. Rep.	B5	80
San Juan del Norte, Nic.	C3	80
San Juan de los Morros, Ven.	D6	80
San Juan del Sur, Nic.	C2	80
San Juan Island, i., Wa., U.S.	A2	140
San Juan Mountains, mts., Co., U.S.	D3	99
San Justo, Arg.	E5	72
Sankt Gallen, Switz.	A2	18
Sankt-Peterburg (Saint Petersburg), Russia	D5	26
Sankt Pölten, Aus.	F14	12
Sankuru, stm., D.R.C.	D4	54
San Lázaro, Cabo, c., Mex.	D3	78
San Leandro, Ca., U.S.	h8	98
Şanlıurfa, Tur.	D8	44
San Lorenzo, Arg.	E5	72
San Lorenzo, Bol.	C5	72
San Lorenzo, Ec.	C4	70
San Lorenzo, Cabo, c., Ec.	D3	70
Sanlúcar de Barrameda, Spain	I3	16
San Lucas, Bol.	C4	72
San Lucas, Mex.	C3	78
San Lucas, Cabo, c., Mex.	C3	78
San Luis, Arg.	E4	72
San Luis, Guat.	B2	80
San Luis, Az., U.S.	E1	96
San Luis, Co., U.S.	D5	99
San Luis, Point, c., Ca., U.S.	E3	98
San Luis Obispo, Ca., U.S.	E3	98
San Luis Obispo, co., Ca., U.S.	E3	98
San Luis Pass, strt., Tx., U.S.	r14	136
San Luis Peak, mtn., Co., U.S.	D4	99
San Luis Potosí, Mex.	C4	78
San Luis Potosí, state, Mex.	C4	78
San Luis Río Colorado, Mex.	A2	78
San Luis Valley, val., Co., U.S.	D4	99
San Manuel, Az., U.S.	E5	96
San Marcos, Tx., U.S.	E4	136
San Marcos, stm., Tx., U.S.	h8	136
San Marino, As., U.S.	m12	98
San Marino, ctry., Eur.	C4	18
San Martín, Arg.	E4	72
San Martín, Col.	E5	80
San Martín, Lago, l., S.A.	G2	69
San Martín de los Andes, Arg.	F2	69
San Mateo, Ca., U.S.	D2	98
San Mateo, co., Ca., U.S.	D2	98
San Mateo Mountains, mts., N.M., U.S.	B2	124
San Mateo Mountains, mts., N.M., U.S.	D2	124
San Matías, Golfo, b., Arg.	F4	69
Sanmenxia, China	E10	28
San Miguel, El Sal.	C2	80
San Miguel, co., Co., U.S.	D2	99
San Miguel, co., N.M., U.S.	B5	124
San Miguel, stm., Co., U.S.	C2	99
San Miguel, Golfo de, b., Pan.	D4	80
San Miguel de Tucumán, Arg.	D4	72
San Miguel Island, i., Ca., U.S.	E3	98
San Miguel Mountains, mts., Co., U.S.	D2	99
Sanming, China	D4	30
Sannâr, Sudan	H11	48
San Nicolás, Peru	B2	72
San Nicolás de los Arroyos, Arg.	E5	72
San Nicolás de los Garza, Mex.	B4	78
San Nicolas Island, i., Ca., U.S.	F4	98
Sânnicolau Mare, Rom.	F6	20
Sannikova, proliv, strt., Russia	B15	26
Sanok, Pol.	E7	20
San Pablo, Phil.	D8	34
San Pablo Bay, b., Ca., U.S.	g8	98
San Patricio, co., Tx., U.S.	E4	136
San Pedro, Arg.	C5	72
San Pedro, Arg.	E6	72
San-Pédro, C. Iv.	F3	50
San Pedro, stm., N.A.	A2	78
San Pedro, stm., Az., U.S.	E5	96
San Pedro Bay, b., Ca., U.S.	n12	98
San Pedro de las Colonias, Mex.	B4	78
San Pedro de Macorís, Dom. Rep.	B6	80
San Pedro de Ycuamandiyú, Para.	C6	72
San Pedro Peaks, mts., N.M., U.S.	A3	124
San Pedro Sula, Hond.	B2	80
Sanpete, co., Ut., U.S.	D4	137
San Pietro, Isola di, i., Italy	E2	18
Sanpoil, stm., Wa., U.S.	A7	140
San Quintín, Cabo, c., Mex.	A1	78
San Rafael, Arg.	E4	72
San Rafael, Ca., U.S.	D2	98
San Rafael, N.M., U.S.	B2	124
San Rafael, Ven.	C5	80
San Rafael, stm., Ut., U.S.	D5	137
San Rafael Knob, mtn., Ut., U.S.	E5	137
San Rafael Mountains, mts., Ca., U.S.	E4	98
San Ramon, Ca., U.S.	h9	98
San Ramón de la Nueva Orán, Arg.	C5	72
San Remo, Italy	C1	18
San Roque, Punta, c., Mex.	B2	78
San Saba, Tx., U.S.	D3	136
San Saba, co., Tx., U.S.	D3	136
San Salvador, El Sal.	C2	80
San Salvador, i., Bah.	D10	76
San Salvador de Jujuy, Arg.	C4	72
Sansanné-Mango, Togo	D5	50
San Sebastián see Donostia, Spain	F6	16
San Severo, Italy	D5	18
San Simon, stm., Az., U.S.	E6	96
Santa Ana, Bol.	A4	72
Santa Ana, El Sal.	C1	80
Santa Ana, Mex.	A2	78
Santa Ana, Ca., U.S.	F5	98
Santa Ana, stm., Ca., U.S.	n13	98
Santa Ana Indian Reservation, N.M., U.S.	h7	124
Santa Ana Mountains, mts., Ca., U.S.	n13	98
Santa Anna, Tx., U.S.	D3	136
Santa Bárbara, Hond.	B2	80
Santa Bárbara, Mex.	B3	78
Santa Barbara, Ca., U.S.	E4	98
Santa Bárbara, Ven.	D5	80
Santa Barbara, co., Ca., U.S.	E3	98
Santa Barbara Channel, strt., Ca., U.S.	E3	98
Santa Barbara Island, i., Ca., U.S.	F4	98
Santa Catalina, Gulf of, b., Ca., U.S.	F5	98
Santa Catalina Island, i., Ca., U.S.	F4	98
Santa Catalina Mountains, mts., Az., U.S.	E5	96
Santa Catarina, state, Braz.	D7	72
Santa Catarina, Ilha de, i., Braz.	D8	72
Santa Clara, Cuba	A3	80
Santa Clara, Ca., U.S.	D2	98
Santa Clara, Ut., U.S.	F2	137
Santa Clara, co., Ca., U.S.	D3	98
Santa Clara, stm., Ca., U.S.	E4	98
Santa Claus, In., U.S.	H4	107
Santa Cruz, Phil.	D8	34
Santa Cruz, Ca., U.S.	D2	98
Santa Cruz, N.M., U.S.	B3	124
Santa Cruz, co., Az., U.S.	F5	96
Santa Cruz, co., Ca., U.S.	D2	98
Santa Cruz, stm., Az., U.S.	E4	96
Santa Cruz, Isla, i., Ec.	D1	70
Santa Cruz de la Palma, Spain	A1	50
Santa Cruz de la Sierra, Bol.	B5	72
Santa Cruz del Quiché, Guat.	B1	80
Santa Cruz del Sur, Cuba	A4	80
Santa Cruz de Tenerife, Spain	A1	50
Santa Cruz do Sul, Braz.	D7	72
Santa Cruz Island, i., Ca., U.S.	F4	98
Santa Cruz Islands, is., Sol. Is.	F10	58
Santa Elena, Arg.	E6	72
Santa Fe, Arg.	E5	72
Santa Fe, N.M., U.S.	B4	124
Santa Fe, Tx., U.S.	r14	136
Santa Fe, co., N.M., U.S.	B3	124
Santa Fe, stm., N.M., U.S.	h8	124
Santa Fe Baldy, mtn., N.M., U.S.	B4	124
Santa Fé do Sul, Braz.	F1	74
Santa Filomena, Braz.	E10	70
Santa Helena, Braz.	B2	74
Santa Helena de Goiás, Braz.	E1	74
Santai, China	E9	28
Santa Inés, Isla, i., Chile	H2	69
Santa Isabel, Arg.	F4	72
Santa Isabel, i., Sol. Is.	B6	62
Santa Isabel see Malabo, Eq. Gui.	C1	54
Santa Lucia Range, mts., Ca., U.S.	E3	98
Santa Magdalena, Isla, i., Mex.	B2	78
Santa Margarita, Isla, i., Mex.	C2	78
Santa Maria, Braz.	D7	72
Santa Maria, Ca., U.S.	E3	98
Santa Maria, i., Vanuatu	j9	62a
Santa Maria, stm., Az., U.S.	C2	96
Santa Maria, Cabo de, c., Ang.	A1	56
Santa María, Isla, i., Ec.	D1	70
Santa Maria Mountains, mts., Az., U.S.	C3	96
Santa Marta, Col.	A5	70
Santa Monica, Ca., U.S.	m12	98
Santana, Braz.	D3	74
Santana do Livramento, Braz.	E6	72
Santander, Phil.	E8	34
Santander, Spain	F5	16
Santanilla, Islas, is., Hond.	B3	80
Sant'Antioco, Italy	E2	18
Sant'Antioco, Isola di, i., Italy	E2	18
Sant Antoni de Portmany, Spain	H7	16
Santa Paula, Ca., U.S.	E4	98
Santaquin, Ut., U.S.	D4	137
Santarém, Braz.	D9	70
Santarém, Port.	F2	16
Santa Rita, Hond.	B2	80
Santa Rita, Ven.	C5	80
Santa Rosa, Arg.	F5	72
Santa Rosa, Braz.	D7	72
Santa Rosa, Ec.	D4	70
Santa Rosa, Ca., U.S.	C2	98
Santa Rosa, N.M., U.S.	C5	124
Santa Rosa, Ven.	D6	80
Santa Rosa, co., Fl., U.S.	u14	102
Santa Rosa de Copán, Hond.	C2	80
Santa Rosa Island, i., Ca., U.S.	F3	98
Santa Rosa Island, i., Fl., U.S.	u14	102
Santa Rosalía, Mex.	B2	78
Santa Rosa Range, mts., Nv., U.S.	B4	121
Šantarskie ostrova, is., Russia	D15	26
Santa Sylvina, Arg.	D5	72
Santa Vitória do Palmar, Braz.	E7	72
Santa Ynez, Ca., U.S.	E3	98
Santee, Ca., U.S.	o16	98
Santee, S.C., U.S.	E8	133
Santee Dam, S.C., U.S.	E7	133
Santee Indian Reservation, Ne., U.S.	B8	120
Sant Feliu de Guíxols, Spain	G8	16
Santiago, Braz.	D7	72
Santiago, Chile	D2	69
Santiago, Mex.	C3	78
Santiago, Pan.	D3	80
Santiago, i., C.V.	h10	50a
Santiago, Isla, i., Ec.	D1	70
Santiago de Compostela, Spain	F2	16
Santiago de Cuba, Cuba	B4	80
Santiago del Estero, Arg.	D5	72
Santiago de los Caballeros, Dom. Rep.	B5	80
Santiago Ixcuintla, Mex.	C3	78
Santiago Jamiltepec, Mex.	D5	78
Santiago Papasquiaro, Mex.	B3	78
Santiago Peak, mtn., Ca., U.S.	n13	98
Santiago Reservoir, res., Ca., U.S.	n13	98
Santiam Pass, Or., U.S.	C4	130
Sant Jordi, Golf de, b., Spain	G7	16
Santo Amaro, Braz.	D4	74
Santo André, Braz.	F2	74
Santo Ângelo, Braz.	D7	72
Santo Antão, i., C.V.	g10	50a
Santo Antônio, S. Tom./P.	C1	54
Santo Antônio de Jesus, Braz.	D4	74
Santo Antônio do Içá, Braz.	D6	70
Santo Domingo, Dom. Rep.	B6	80
Santo Domingo see Hispaniola, i., N.A.	A5	80
Santo Domingo Indian Reservation, N.M., U.S.	h8	124
Santo Domingo Pueblo, N.M., U.S.	B3	124
Santorini see Thíra, i., Grc.	F10	18
Santos, Braz.	F2	74
Santos Dumont, Braz.	F3	74
Santo Tomé de Guayana see Ciudad Guayana, Ven.	B7	70
San Valentín, Monte, mtn., Chile	G2	69
San Vicente, El Sal.	C2	80
San Vicente de Cañete, Peru	F4	70
San Vicente del Caguán, Col.	C5	70
San Vicente Reservoir, res., Ca., U.S.	o16	98
San Xavier Indian Reservation, Az., U.S.	E4	96
Sanya, China	H9	28
Sanyuan, China	E9	28
Sanza Pombo, Ang.	E3	54
São Bento, Braz.	B3	74
São Borja, Braz.	D6	72
São Carlos, Braz.	F2	74
São Domingos, Braz.	A8	72
São Domingos, Gui.-B.	D1	50
São Francisco, Braz.	E3	74
São Francisco, stm., Braz.	C4	74
São Francisco do Sul, Braz.	D8	72
São Gabriel, Braz.	E7	72
Sao Hill, Tan.	E7	54
São João da Barra, Braz.	F3	74
São João da Boa Vista, Braz.	F2	74
São João da Madeira, Port.	G2	16
São João Del Rei, Braz.	F3	74
São João do Araguaia, Braz.	E10	70
São Jorge, i., Port.	F7	46
São José, Braz.	D8	72
São José do Rio Preto, Braz.	F2	74
São José dos Campos, Braz.	F2	74
São Leopoldo, Braz.	D7	72
São Lourenço, Pantanal de, sw., Braz.	G8	70
São Lourenço do Sul, Braz.	E7	72
São Luís, Braz.	B3	74
São Luís Gonzaga, Braz.	D7	72
São Manuel, stm., Braz.	E8	70
São Mateus, Braz.	E4	74
São Miguel, i., Port.	F7	46
São Miguel do Araguaia, Braz.	D1	74
Saona, Isla, i., Dom. Rep.	B6	80
Saône, stm., Fr.	D9	16
São Nicolau, i., C.V.	g10	50a
São Paulo, Braz.	F2	74
São Paulo, state, Braz.	C7	72
São Paulo de Olivença, Braz.	D6	70
São Raimundo Nonato, Braz.	C3	74
São Roque, Cabo de, c., Braz.	C4	74
São Sebastião, Braz.	F2	74
São Sebastião, Ilha de, i., Braz.	F2	74
São Sebastião do Paraíso, Braz.	F2	74
São Simão, Represa de, res., Braz.	B7	72
São Tomé, S. Tom./P.	C1	54
São Tomé, i., S. Tom./P.	C1	54
São Tomé, Cabo de, c., Braz.	F3	74
Sao Tome and Principe, ctry., Afr.	C1	54
São Vicente, Braz.	F2	74
São Vicente, i., C.V.	g9	50a
São Vicente, Cabo de, c., Port.	I2	16
Sapé, Braz.	C4	74
Sapele, Nig.	E6	50
Sapelo Island, i., Ga., U.S.	E5	103
Sapitwa, mtn., Mwi.	B6	56
Sapp Creek, stm., Ne., U.S.	E5	120
Sapphire Mountains, mts., Mt., U.S.	D3	119
Sappington, Mo., U.S.	f13	118
Sapporo, Japan	C16	28
Sapulpa, Ok., U.S.	B5	129
Sapwe, D.R.C.	F5	54
Saqqez, Iran	C5	42
Sarāb, Iran	C5	42
Saraburi, Thai.	D4	34
Saragossa see Zaragoza, Spain	G6	16
Sarajevo, Bos.	C7	18
Sarakhs, Iran	C8	42
Saraktaš, Russia	D10	22
Saraland, Al., U.S.	E1	94
Saranac, Mi., U.S.	F5	115
Saranac, stm., N.Y., U.S.	F11	125
Saranac Lake, N.Y., U.S.	f10	125
Saranac Lakes, l., N.Y., U.S.	f10	125
Sarandë, Alb.	E8	18
Saranpaul', Russia	B11	22
Saransk, Russia	D6	26
Sarapul, Russia	D7	26
Sarasota, Fl., U.S.	E4	102
Sarasota, co., Fl., U.S.	E4	102
Sarasota Bay, b., Fl., U.S.	E4	102
Saratoga, Ca., U.S.	k8	98
Saratoga, Tx., U.S.	D5	136
Saratoga, Wy., U.S.	E6	143
Saratoga, co., N.Y., U.S.	B7	125
Saratoga Lake, l., N.Y., U.S.	C7	125
Saratoga National Historical Park, N.Y., U.S.	B7	125
Saratoga Springs, N.Y., U.S.	B7	125
Saratov, Russia	D6	26
Saratov Reservoir see Saratovskoe vodohranilišče, res., Russia	D8	22
Saratovskoe vodohranilišče, res., Russia	D8	22
Saravan, Laos	C5	34
Sarawak, hist. reg., Malay.	C4	36
Saray, Tur.	B2	44
Saraya, Gui.	D2	50
Sarayköy, Tur.	D3	44
Sarek, mtn., Swe.	C7	10
Sar-e Pol, Afg.	C9	42
Sarepta, La., U.S.	B2	111
Sargent, Ga., U.S.	C2	103
Sargent, Ne., U.S.	C6	120
Sargent, co., N.D., U.S.	C8	127
Sargodha, Pak.	D10	42
Sarh, Chad	B3	54
Sārī, Iran	C6	42
Sarigan, i., N. Mar. Is.	C12	32
Sarıkamış, Tur.	B10	44
Sarıkaya, Tur.	C6	44
Sarikei, Malay.	C4	36
Sarīr, Libya	F8	14
Sariwŏn, N. Kor.	D13	28
Sarıyar Baraji, res., Tur.	C4	44
Šarja, Russia	D6	26
Şarkikaraağaç, Tur.	C4	44
Şarkışla, Tur.	C7	44
Şarköy, Tur.	B2	44
Sarmi, Indon.	G10	32
Särna, Swe.	F5	10
Sarnia, On., Can.	E2	89
Sarny, Ukr.	D9	20
Saronic Gulf see Saronikós Kólpos, b., Grc.	F9	18
Saronikós Kólpos, b., Grc.	F9	18
Saros Körfezi, b., Tur.	B2	44
Sarpy, co., Ne., U.S.	C9	120
Sarreguemines, Fr.	C10	16
Sartell, Mn., U.S.	E4	116
Sartène, Fr.	D2	18
Şārūr, Azer.	C11	44
Sarus see Seyhan, stm., Tur.	D6	44
Saryg-Sep, Russia	D11	26
Sarykamyšskoe ozero, l., Asia	B7	42
Saryozek, Kaz.	E9	26
Sarysu, stm., Kaz.	E8	26
Sary-Taš, Kyrg.	B2	40
Sasabeneh, Eth.	B8	54
Sāsarām, India	E4	40
Sasebo, Japan	D1	31
Saskatchewan, prov., Can.	E3	91
Saskatchewan, stm., Can.	H19	82
Saskylah, Russia	B13	26
Sasovo, Russia	B16	20
Sassafras, stm., Md., U.S.	B5	113
Sassafras Mountain, mtn., U.S.	A2	133
Sassandra, C. Iv.	E3	50
Sassandra, stm., C. Iv.	E3	50
Sassari, Italy	D2	18
Sassnitz, Ger.	C13	12
Satah Mountain, mtn., B.C., Can.	C5	85
Sata-misaki, c., Japan	D2	31
Satanta, Ks., U.S.	E3	109
Sātāra, India	F2	40
Säter, Swe.	F6	10
Satilla, stm., Ga., U.S.	E5	103
Satka, Russia	D10	22
Satluj see Sutlej, stm., Asia	D2	40
Satna, India	E4	40
Sátoraljaújhely, Hung.	E6	20
Sātpura Range, mts., India	E3	40
Satsuma, Al., U.S.	E1	94
Satu Mare, Rom.	F7	20
Satun, Thai.	E3	34
Satus Creek, stm., Wa., U.S.	C5	140
Sauceda Mountains, mts., Az., U.S.	E3	96
Sauðárkrókur, Ice.	I19	10a
Saudi Arabia, ctry., Asia	F4	38
Saufley Field Naval Air Station, mil., Fl., U.S.	u14	102
Saugatuck, Mi., U.S.	F4	115
Saugatuck, stm., Ct., U.S.	D2	100
Saugatucket, stm., R.I., U.S.	F4	132
Saugatuck Reservoir, res., Ct., U.S.	D2	100
Saugerties, N.Y., U.S.	C7	125
Saugus, Ma., U.S.	B5	114
Saugus, stm., Ma., U.S.	g11	114
Sauk, co., Wi., U.S.	E4	142
Sauk, stm., Mn., U.S.	E4	116
Sauk, stm., Wa., U.S.	A4	140
Sauk Centre, Mn., U.S.	E4	116
Sauk City, Wi., U.S.	E4	142
Sauk Rapids, Mn., U.S.	E4	116
Saukville, Wi., U.S.	E6	142
Saül, Fr. Gu.	C9	70
Saulnierville, N.S., Can.	E3	87
Sault-au-Mouton, P.Q., Can.	A8	90
Sault Sainte Marie, On., Can.	p18	89
Sault Sainte Marie, Mi., U.S.	B6	115
Saumarez Reef, rf., Austl.	E5	62
Saumlaki, Indon.	E8	36
Saumur, Fr.	D6	16
Saunders, co., Ne., U.S.	C9	120
Saunderstown, R.I., U.S.	E4	132
Saurimo, Ang.	E4	54
Sausalito, Ca., U.S.	D2	98
Sava, stm., Eur.	G5	20
Savage, Md., U.S.	B4	113
Savage, stm., Md., U.S.	k12	113
Savage River Reservoir, res., Md., U.S.	k12	113
Savai'i, i., Samoa	F12	58
Savalou, Benin	E5	50
Savanna, Il., U.S.	A3	106
Savanna, Ok., U.S.	C6	129
Savannah, Ga., U.S.	D5	103
Savannah, Mo., U.S.	B3	118

Name	Map Ref.	Page

Savannah, Tn., U.S. B3 135
Savannah, stm., U.S. E11 92
Savannah, stm., U.S. F5 133
Savannah River Plant, sci.,
  S.C., U.S. E4 133
Savannakhét, Laos C4 34
Savanna Lake, l., Md., U.S. . D6 113
Savanna-la-Mar, Jam. B4 80
Savaştepe, Tur. C2 44
Savè, Benin E5 50
Save (Sabi), stm., Afr. C5 56
Sāveh, Iran C6 42
Savelugu, Ghana E4 50
Saverne, Fr. C10 16
Savitaipale, Fin. F12 10
Savona, Italy B2 18
Savonlinna, Fin. F13 10
Savoonga, Ak., U.S. C5 95
Savoy, Il., U.S. C5 106
Savu Sea see Sawu, Laut,
  Indon. E6 36
Sawāi Mādhopur, India . . . D3 40
Sawākin, Sudan G12 48
Sawankhalok, Thai. C3 34
Sawatch Range, mts., Co.,
  U.S. B4 99
Sawdā', Jabal as-, hills,
  Libya F7 14
Sawdā', Qurnat as-, mtn.,
  Leb. E7 44
Sawnee Mountain, mtn.,
  Ga., U.S. B2 103
Sawtooth Mountains, mts.,
  Id., U.S. F4 105
Sawtooth National
  Recreation Area, Id.,
  U.S. E3 105
Sawu, Laut (Savu Sea),
  Indon. E6 36
Sawu, Pulau, i., Indon. . . . F6 36
Sawyer, co., Wi., U.S. C2 142
Sawyerville, P.Q., Can. . . . D6 90
Saxonburg, Pa., U.S. E2 131
Saxtons, stm., Vt., U.S. . . . E3 138
Saxtons River, Vt., U.S. . . . E3 138
Sayan Mountains, mts., Asia D11 26
Saybrook, Il., U.S. C5 106
Saybrook Manor, Ct., U.S. . D6 100
Saydā, Leb. F6 44
Saydel, Ia., U.S. e8 108
Sayhūt, Yemen G6 38
Saylac, Som. H4 38
Saylesville, R.I., U.S. B4 132
Saylorsburg, Pa., U.S. E11 131
Saylorville, Ia., U.S. e8 108
Saylorville Lake, res., Ia.,
  U.S. C4 108
Saynshand, Mong. C10 28
Sayre, Al., U.S. B3 94
Sayre, Ok., U.S. B2 129
Sayre, Pa., U.S. C8 131
Sayreville, N.J., U.S. C4 123
Sayula, Mex. D4 78
Sayville, N.Y., U.S. n15 125
Saywūn, Yemen G5 38
Sba, Alg. F3 14
Scalp Level, Pa., U.S. F4 131
Scanlon, Mn., U.S. D6 116
Scapegoat Mountain, mtn.,
  Mt., U.S. C3 119
Scappoose, Or., U.S. B4 130
Scarborough, On., Can. . . . m15 89
Scarborough, Trin. C7 80
Scarborough, Eng., U.K. . . . C6 12
Scarborough, Me., U.S. . . . E2 112
Scarbro, W.V., U.S. n13 141
Scarsdale, N.Y., U.S. h13 125
Ščekino, Russia C14 20
Ščerbakovo, Russia C18 26
Schaefferstown, Pa., U.S. . . F9 131
Schaller, Ia., U.S. B2 108
Schaumburg, Il., U.S. h8 106
Schell Creek Range, mts.,
  Nv., U.S. D7 121
Schenectady, N.Y., U.S. . . . C7 125
Schenectady, co., N.Y., U.S. C6 125
Schererville, In., U.S. B3 107
Schertz, Tx., U.S. h7 136
Schiller Park, Il., U.S. k9 106
Schio, Italy D6 18
Schleicher, co., Tx., U.S. . . D2 136
Schleswig, Ger. C11 12
Schleswig, Ia., U.S. B2 108
Schley, co., Ga., U.S. D2 103
Schofield, Wi., U.S. D4 142
Schofield Barracks, mil., Hi.,
  U.S. g9 104
Schoharie, co., N.Y., U.S. . . C6 125
Schoharie Creek, stm., N.Y.,
  U.S. C6 125
Schoodic Lake, l., Me., U.S. C4 112
Schoolcraft, Mi., U.S. F5 115
Schoolcraft, co., Mi., U.S. . B4 115
Schroon Lake, l., N.Y., U.S. B7 125
Schulenburg, Tx., U.S. E4 136
Schulter, Ok., U.S. B6 129
Schurz, Nv., U.S. E3 121
Schuyler, Ne., U.S. C8 120
Schuyler, co., Il., U.S. C3 106
Schuyler, co., Mo., U.S. . . . A5 118
Schuyler, co., N.Y., U.S. . . C4 125
Schuylkill, co., Pa., U.S. . . . E9 131
Schuylkill, stm., Pa., U.S. . . F10 131
Schuylkill Haven, Pa., U.S. . E9 131

Schwaben, hist. reg., Ger. . F11 12
Schwarzwald (Black Forest),
  mts., Ger. F11 12
Schwedt, Ger. D14 12
Schwerin, Ger. D12 12
Schwyz, Switz. A2 18
Sciacca, Italy F4 18
Science Hill, Ky., U.S. C5 110
Scilly, Isles of, is., Eng., U.K. F3 12
Scio, Or., U.S. C4 130
Scioto, co., Oh., U.S. D3 128
Scioto, stm., Oh., U.S. B2 128
Scituate, Ma., U.S. B6 114
Scituate Reservoir, res., R.I.,
  U.S. C3 132
Scobey, Mt., U.S. B11 119
Scofield Reservoir, res., Ut.,
  U.S. D4 137
Scotch Plains, N.J., U.S. . . . B4 123
Scotia, Ca., U.S. B1 98
Scotia, N.Y., U.S. C7 125
Scotia Ridge N8 66
Scotia Sea B36 67
Scotland, On., Can. D4 89
Scotland, S.D., U.S. D8 134
Scotland, prov., U.K. B5 12
Scotland, co., Mo., U.S. . . . A5 118
Scotland, co., N.C., U.S. . . C3 126
Scotland Neck, N.C., U.S. . A5 126
Scotlandville, La., U.S. . . . D4 111
Scotrun, Pa., U.S. D11 131
Scotstown, P.Q., Can. D6 90
Scott, La., U.S. D3 111
Scott, co., Ar., U.S. C1 97
Scott, co., Ia., U.S. C7 108
Scott, co., Il., U.S. D3 106
Scott, co., In., U.S. G6 107
Scott, co., Ks., U.S. D3 109
Scott, co., Ky., U.S. B5 110
Scott, co., Mn., U.S. F5 116
Scott, co., Mo., U.S. D8 118
Scott, co., Ms., U.S. C4 117
Scott, co., Tn., U.S. C9 135
Scott, co., Va., U.S. f9 139
Scott, Cape, c., B.C., Can. . D3 85
Scott, Mount, mtn., Or.,
  U.S. E4 130
Scott Air Force Base, mil.,
  Il., U.S. E4 106
Scott City, Ks., U.S. D3 109
Scott City, Mo., U.S. D8 118
Scottdale, Ga., U.S. h8 103
Scottdale, Pa., U.S. F2 131
Scott Mountain, mtn., Id.,
  U.S. E3 105
Scott Peak, mtn., Id., U.S. . E6 105
Scott Reef, rf., Austl. C3 60
Scott Reservoir, res., N.C.,
  U.S. A1 126
Scottsbluff, Ne., U.S. C2 120
Scotts Bluff, co., Ne., U.S. . C2 120
Scotts Bluff National
  Monument, Ne., U.S. . . C2 120
Scottsboro, Al., U.S. A3 94
Scottsburg, In., U.S. G6 107
Scottsdale, Az., U.S. D4 96
Scottsville, Ky., U.S. D3 110
Scottsville, N.Y., U.S. B3 125
Scottville, Mi., U.S. E4 115
Scraggly Lake, l., Me., U.S. B4 112
Scranton, Ks., U.S. D8 109
Scranton, Pa., U.S. D10 131
Scranton, S.C., U.S. D8 133
Screven, Ga., U.S. E4 103
Screven, co., Ga., U.S. . . . D5 103
Scribner, Ne., U.S. C9 120
Ščučinsk, Kaz. D8 26
Scugog, Lake, l., On., Can. . C6 89
Scurry, co., Tx., U.S. C2 136
Scutari see Shkodër, Alb. . . C7 18
Scutari, Lake, l., Eur. C7 18
Scyros see Skíros, i., Grc. . . E10 18
Seaboard, N.C., U.S. A5 126
Seabreeze, De., U.S. F5 101
Seabrook, N.H., U.S. E5 122
Seabrook, Tx., U.S. r14 136
Seabrook Island, i., S.C.,
  U.S. F7 133
Seadrift, Tx., U.S. E4 136
Seaford, De., U.S. F3 101
Seaford, Va., U.S. h15 139
Seaforth, On., Can. D3 89
Seagoville, Tx., U.S. n10 136
Seagraves, Tx., U.S. C1 136
Sea Islands, is., U.S. E11 92
Sea Isle City, N.J., U.S. . . . E3 123
Seal Cove, Nf., Can. D3 88
Seal Point, c., P.E., Can. . . C5 87
Seal Rock, Or., U.S. C2 130
Sealy, Tx., U.S. E4 136
Seaman, Oh., U.S. D2 128
Seaman Range, mts., Nv.,
  U.S. F6 121
Searchlight, Nv., U.S. H7 121
Searcy, Ar., U.S. B4 97
Searcy, co., Ar., U.S. B3 97
Searles Lake, l., Ca., U.S. . . E5 98
Searsport, Me., U.S. D4 112
Seaside, Or., U.S. B3 130
Seat Pleasant, Md., U.S. . . C4 113
Seattle, Wa., U.S. B3 140
Seattle-Tacoma International
  Airport, Wa., U.S. f11 140
Seaview, Wa., U.S. C1 140

Sebago Lake, l., Me., U.S. . E2 112
Šebalino, Russia D10 26
Sebangka, Pulau, i., Indon. . C2 36
Sebastian, Fl., U.S. E6 102
Sebastian, co., Ar., U.S. . . . B1 97
Sebastian, Cape, c., Or.,
  U.S. E2 130
Sebastian Inlet, b., Fl., U.S. E6 102
Sebastián Vizcaíno, Bahía,
  b., Mex. B2 78
Sebasticook Lake, l., Me.,
  U.S. D3 112
Sebec Lake, l., Me., U.S. . . C3 112
Sebeka, Mn., U.S. D3 116
Šebekino, Russia D14 20
Sebeş, Rom. C7 20
Sebewaing, Mi., U.S. E7 115
Şebinkarahisar, Tur. B8 44
Seboeis, stm., Me., U.S. . . . B4 112
Seboeis Lake, l., Me., U.S. . C4 112
Seboomook Lake, l., Me.,
  U.S. C3 112
Sebree, Ky., U.S. C2 110
Sebring, Fl., U.S. E5 102
Sebring, Oh., U.S. B4 128
Secaucus, N.J., U.S. h8 123
Sechelt, B.C., Can. E6 85
Sechura, Bahía de, b., Peru E3 70
Second Lake, l., N.H., U.S. . f7 122
Second Mesa, Az., U.S. . . . B5 96
Secret Lake, l., R.I., U.S. . . E4 132
Section, Al., U.S. A4 94
Security, Co., U.S. C6 99
Seda, China E8 28
Sedalia, Mo., U.S. C4 118
Sedan, Fr. C9 16
Sedan, Ks., U.S. E7 109
Sedgewick, Ab., Can. C5 84
Sedgewick, Mount, mtn.,
  N.M., U.S. B1 124
Sedgwick, Ks., U.S. E6 109
Sedgwick, co., Co., U.S. . . A8 99
Sedgwick, co., Ks., U.S. . . E6 109
Sédhiou, Sen. D1 50
Sedley, Va., U.S. D6 139
Sedona, Az., U.S. C4 96
Sedro Woolley, Wa., U.S. . . A3 140
Seekonk, Ma., U.S. C5 114
Seekonk, stm., R.I., U.S. . . C4 132
Seeley, Ca., U.S. F6 98
Seeley Lake, Mt., U.S. C3 119
Seelyville, In., U.S. F3 107
Şefaatli, Tur. C6 44
Sefadu, S.L. E2 50
Seferihisar, Tur. C2 44
Segamat, Malay. C2 36
Segesta, hist., Italy F4 18
Segezha, Russia C5 26
Ségou, Mali D3 50
Segovia, Spain G4 16
Seguam Island, i., Ak., U.S. E5 95
Seguam Pass, strt., Ak., U.S. E5 95
Séguédine, Niger B7 50
Séguéla, C. Iv. E3 50
Seguin, Tx., U.S. E4 136
Segura, stm., Spain I6 16
Seiling, Ok., U.S. A3 129
Seinäjoki, Fin. E10 10
Seine, stm., Fr. C7 16
Seine, Baie de la, b., Fr. . . C6 16
Sejm, stm., Eur. D12 20
Sejmčan, Russia C17 26
Şeki, Azer. B12 44
Sekiu, Wa., U.S. A1 140
Sekondi-Takoradi, Ghana . . F4 50
Selah, Wa., U.S. C5 140
Selaru, Pulau, i., Indon. . . . E8 36
Selatan, Tanjung, c., Indon. D4 36
Selawik, Ak., U.S. B7 95
Selawik Lake, l., Ak., U.S. . B7 95
Selayar, Pulau, i., Indon. . . E6 36
Selby, S.D., U.S. B5 134
Selbyville, De., U.S. G5 101
Selçuk, Tur. D2 44
Seldovia, Ak., U.S. D9 95
Selebi-Phikwe, Bots. C4 56
Selenge, D.R.C. D3 54
Selenge, stm., Asia E12 26
Sélibabi, Maur. C2 50
Seligman, Az., U.S. B3 96
Šelihova, zaliv, b., Russia . . D17 26
Selinsgrove, Pa., U.S. E8 131
Seljord, Nor. G10 10
Selkirk, Mb., Can. D3 86
Sellersburg, In., U.S. H6 107
Sellersville, Pa., U.S. F11 131
Sells, Az., U.S. F4 96
Selma, Al., U.S. C2 94
Selma, Ca., U.S. D4 98
Selma, In., U.S. D7 107
Selma, N.C., U.S. B4 126
Selmer, Tn., U.S. B3 135
Selvagens, Ilhas, is., Port. . . D1 48
Selvas, for., Braz. E6 70
Selway, stm., Id., U.S. C3 105
Selwyn Lake, l., Can. G15 82
Selwyn Mountains, mts.,
  Can. F13 82
Selwyn Range, mts., Austl. . B3 62
Semara, W. Sah. A2 50
Semarang, Indon. E4 36
Semenanjung Malaysia, hist.
  reg., Malay. C2 36
Semenivka, Ukr. C12 20
Semenov, Russia C7 22

Semey see Semipalatinsk,
  Kaz. D10 26
Semiluki, Russia D15 20
Seminoe Mountains, mts.,
  Wy., U.S. D6 143
Seminoe Reservoir, res.,
  Wy., U.S. D6 143
Seminole, Ok., U.S. B5 129
Seminole, Tx., U.S. C1 136
Seminole, co., Fl., U.S. . . . D5 102
Seminole, co., Ga., U.S. . . . F2 103
Seminole, co., Ok., U.S. . . . B5 129
Seminole, Lake, res., U.S. . F2 103
Semipalatinsk, Kaz. D10 26
Semisopochnoi Island, i.,
  Ak., U.S. E3 95
Semitau, Indon. C4 36
Semmes, Al., U.S. E1 94
Semnān, Iran C6 42
Senachwine Lake, l., Il., U.S. B4 106
Senador Pompeu, Braz. . . . C4 74
Senaki, Geor. A10 44
Sena Madureira, Braz. E6 70
Senanga, Zam. B3 56
Senath, Mo., U.S. E7 118
Senatobia, Ms., U.S. A4 117
Sendai, Japan D16 28
Sendelingsdrif, Nmb. D2 56
Seneca, Il., U.S. B5 106
Seneca, Ks., U.S. C7 109
Seneca, Mo., U.S. E3 118
Seneca, Pa., U.S. D2 131
Seneca, S.C., U.S. B2 133
Seneca, co., N.Y., U.S. . . . C4 125
Seneca, co., Oh., U.S. A2 128
Seneca Falls, N.Y., U.S. . . . C4 125
Seneca Lake, l., N.Y., U.S. . C4 125
Senecaville Lake, res., Oh.,
  U.S. C4 128
Séneégal, stm., Afr. C2 50
Senegal, ctry., Afr. D1 50
Senekal, S. Afr. D4 56
Senftenberg, Ger. E13 12
Senhor do Bonfim, Braz. . . D3 74
Senica, Slvk. E4 20
Senigallia, Italy C4 18
Senja, i., Nor. B7 10
Šenkursk, Russia B7 22
Senneterre, P.Q., Can. k11 90
Senoia, Ga., U.S. C2 103
Senqu see Orange, stm.,
  Afr. D2 56
Sens, Fr. C6 16
Senta, Yugo. B8 18
Sentinel, Ok., U.S. B2 129
Seoni, India E3 40
Seoul see Sŏul, S. Kor. D13 28
Sepanjang, Pulau, i., Indon. E5 36
Sepik, stm., Pap. N. Gui. . . G11 32
Sept-Îles (Seven Islands),
  P.Q., Can. h13 90
Sepulga, stm., Al., U.S. . . . D3 94
Sequatchie, co., Tn., U.S. . . D8 135
Sequatchie, stm., Tn., U.S. . D8 135
Sequim, Wa., U.S. A2 140
Sequoia National Park, Ca.,
  U.S. D4 98
Sequoyah, co., Ok., U.S. . . B7 129
Šerabad, Uzb. C9 42
Serafimovič, Russia E7 22
Seram (Ceram), i., Indon. . D7 36
Seram, Laut (Ceram Sea),
  Indon. D7 36
Serang, Indon. E3 36
Serasan, Pulau, i., Indon. . . C3 36
Serasan, Selat, strt., Indon. . C3 36
Serbia see Srbija, prov.,
  Yugo. B8 18
Serdobsk, Russia D7 22
Sered', Slvk. E4 20
Serengeti Plain, pl., Tan. . . D6 54
Serenje, Zam. A5 56
Sergač, Russia C8 22
Sergeant Bluff, Ia., U.S. . . . B1 108
Sergeevka, Russia B2 31
Sergeja Kirova, ostrova, is.,
  Russia B10 26
Sergiev Posad, Russia D5 26
Serginskij, Russia C8 26
Sergipe, state, Braz. D4 74
Sérifos, i., Grc. F10 18
Serik, Tur. D4 44
Serlovaja Gora, Russia A11 28
Serov, Russia D8 26
Serowe, Bots. C4 56
Serpa, Port. I3 16
Serpiente, Boca de la, strt. . D7 80
Serpuhov, Russia B14 20
Serra do Navio, Braz. C9 70
Sérrai, Grc. D9 18
Serra Talhada, Braz. C4 74
Serrezuela, Arg. E4 72
Serrinha, Braz. D4 74
Sertânia, Braz. C4 74
Sêrxü, China E7 28
Sese Islands, is., Ug. D6 54
Sesfontein, Nmb. B1 56
Sesheke, Zam. B3 56
Sesser, Il., U.S. E4 106
Sestroreck, Russia F13 10
Sète, Fr. F8 16

Sete Lagoas, Braz. E3 74
Seth, W.V., U.S. C3 141
Sétif, Alg. C6 48
Seto-naikai, Japan E14 28
Setté Cama, Gabon D1 54
Setúbal, Port. H2 16
Setúbal, Baía de, b., Port. . H2 16
Seul, Lac, l., On., Can. o16 89
Seul Choix Point, c., Mi.,
  U.S. C5 115
Sevan, Arm. B11 44
Sevana Lich, l., Arm. B11 44
Sevastopol', Ukr. G12 20
Seven Devils Lake, res., Ar.,
  U.S. D4 97
Seven Devils Mountains,
  mts., Id., U.S. D2 105
Seven Hills, Oh., U.S. h9 128
Seven Mile Beach, N.J., U.S.E3 123
Severn, stm., On., Can. . . . n17 89
Severn, stm., On., Can. . . . D5 12
Severnaja Dvina, stm.,
  Russia C6 26
Severnaja Osetija, state,
  Russia E6 26
Severnaja Sos'va, stm.,
  Russia B11 22
Severnaja Zemlja, is., Russia B12 26
Severna Park, Md., U.S. . . . B4 113
Severn River, b., Md., U.S. . B4 113
Severnyje uvaly, hills, Russia D6 26
Severodvinsk, Russia C5 26
Severo-Enisejskij, Russia . . C11 26
Severomorsk, Russia B15 10
Severo-Sibirskaja
  nizmennost', pl., Russia B11 26
Severoural'sk, Russia B11 22
Sevier, co., Ar., U.S. D1 97
Sevier, co., Tn., U.S. D10 135
Sevier, co., Ut., U.S. E4 137
Sevier, stm., Ut., U.S. D3 137
Sevier Bridge Reservoir,
  res., Ut., U.S. D4 137
Sevier Lake, l., Ut., U.S. . . E2 137
Sevierville, Tn., U.S. D10 135
Sevilla, Col. E4 80
Sevilla (Seville), Spain I4 16
Seville see Sevilla, Spain . . I4 16
Seville, Oh., U.S. A4 128
Sewanee, Tn., U.S. D8 135
Seward, Ak., U.S. C10 95
Seward, Ne., U.S. D8 120
Seward, co., Ks., U.S. E3 109
Seward, co., Ne., U.S. D8 120
Seward Peninsula, pen., Ak.,
  U.S. B7 95
Sewickley, Pa., U.S. E1 131
Sexsmith, Ab., Can. B1 84
Seychelles, ctry., Afr. i12 57b
Seychelles, is., Afr. h13 57b
Seydişehir, Tur. D4 44
Seydisfjördur, Ice. l21 10a
Seyhan, stm., Tur. D6 44
Seyhan Baraji, res., Tur. . . D6 44
Seymour, Austl. H4 62
Seymour, Ct., U.S. D3 100
Seymour, Ia., U.S. D4 108
Seymour, In., U.S. G6 107
Seymour, Mo., U.S. D5 118
Seymour, Tx., U.S. C3 136
Seymour, Wi., U.S. D5 142
Seymour Inlet, b., B.C.,
  Can. D4 85
Seymour Johnson Air Force
  Base, mil., N.C., U.S. . . B5 126
Seymour Lake, l., Vt., U.S. . B4 138
Seymourville, La., U.S. . . . h9 111
Sfântu Gheorghe, Rom. . . . G8 20
Sfax, Tun. D7 48
's-Gravenhage (The Hague),
  Neth. D8 12
Shaanxi, state, China D9 28
Shabbona, Il., U.S. B5 106
Shabeelle (Shebelē Wenz,
  Wabē), stm., Afr. C8 54
Shabunda, D.R.C. D5 54
Shache, China D3 28
Shackelford, co., Tx., U.S. . C3 136
Shackleton Ice Shelf, Ant. . C14 67
Shackleton Range, mts.,
  Ant. E2 67
Shadehill Dam, S.D., U.S. . B3 134
Shadehill Reservoir, res.,
  S.D., U.S. B3 134
Shadow Mountain National
  Recreation Area, Co.,
  U.S. A4 99
Shady Cove, Or., U.S. E4 130
Shady Side, Md., U.S. C4 113
Shadyside, Oh., U.S. C5 128
Shady Spring, W.V., U.S. . . D3 141
Shafer, Lake, l., In., U.S. . . C4 107
Shafer Butte, mtn., Id., U.S. F2 105
Shafter, Ca., U.S. E4 98
Shaftsbury, Vt., U.S. E2 138
Shag Rocks, rock, S. Geor. . H8 69
Shah Alam, Malay. C2 36
Shahdol, India E4 40
Shāhjahānpur, India D3 40
Shāhpura, India D2 40
Shahr-e Kord, Iran D6 42
Shahr-e Rey, Iran C6 42
Shājāpur, India E3 40
Shakawe, Bots. B3 56

Name	Map Ref.	Page
Shaker Heights, Oh., U.S.	A4	128
Shaki, Nig.	E5	50
Shakopee, Mn., U.S.	F5	116
Shala Hāyk', l., Eth.	B7	54
Shallotte, N.C., U.S.	D4	126
Shallotte Inlet, b., N.C., U.S.	D4	126
Shallowater, Tx., U.S.	C2	136
Shām, Jabal ash-, mtn., Oman	F7	38
Shambe, Sudan	B6	54
Shambu, Eth.	B7	54
Shamokin, Pa., U.S.	E8	131
Shamokin Dam, Pa., U.S.	E8	131
Shamrock, Tx., U.S.	B2	136
Shamva, Zimb.	B5	56
Shandī, Sudan	G11	48
Shandong, state, China	D11	28
Shandong Bandao, pen., China	D12	28
Shangcai, China	C3	30
Shangcheng, China	C4	30
Shangchuan Dao, i., China	E3	30
Shangdu, China	A3	30
Shanghai, China	E12	28
Shanghang, China	D4	30
Shangqiu, China	E11	28
Shangrao, China	F11	28
Shangxian, China	E10	28
Shangzhi, China	B13	28
Shanhaiguan, China	A4	30
Shannock, R.I., U.S.	F2	132
Shannon, Ga., U.S.	B1	103
Shannon, Il., U.S.	A4	106
Shannon, Ms., U.S.	A5	117
Shannon, co., Mo., U.S.	D6	118
Shannon, co., S.D., U.S.	D3	134
Shannon, stm., Ire.	D2	12
Shannon, Lake, l., Wa., U.S.	A4	140
Shannontown, S.C., U.S.	D7	133
Shantou, China	G11	28
Shantung Peninsula see Shandong Bandao, pen., China	D12	28
Shanxi, state, China	D10	28
Shanxian, China	C4	30
Shanyin, China	B3	30
Shaoguan, China	G10	28
Shaowu, China	F11	28
Shaoxing, China	E12	28
Shaoyang, China	F10	28
Shaqrā', Sau. Ar.	E5	38
Shaqrā', Yemen	H5	38
Shara, gora, mtn., Asia	A10	44
Shark Bay, b., Austl.	F1	60
Sharkey, co., Ms., U.S.	C3	117
Shark Point, c., Fl., U.S.	H5	102
Sharm El Sheikh, Egypt	E11	48
Sharon, Ct., U.S.	B2	100
Sharon, Ma., U.S.	B5	114
Sharon, Pa., U.S.	D1	131
Sharon, Tn., U.S.	A3	135
Sharon, Wi., U.S.	F5	142
Sharon Hill, Pa., U.S.	p20	131
Sharon Park, Oh., U.S.	n12	128
Sharon Springs, Ks., U.S.	D2	109
Sharonville, Oh., U.S.	n13	128
Sharp, co., Ar., U.S.	A4	97
Sharpe, Lake, res., S.D., U.S.	C6	134
Sharpes, Fl., U.S.	D6	102
Sharpley, De., U.S.	h7	101
Sharpsburg, Md., U.S.	B2	113
Sharpsburg, N.C., U.S.	B5	126
Sharpsburg, Pa., U.S.	k14	131
Sharpsville, In., U.S.	D5	107
Sharpsville, Pa., U.S.	D1	131
Sharptown, Md., U.S.	C6	113
Shashe, stm., Afr.	C4	56
Shashemenē, Eth.	B7	54
Shashi, China	E10	28
Shasta, co., Ca., U.S.	B3	98
Shasta, Mount, vol., Ca., U.S.	B2	98
Shasta Lake, res., Ca., U.S.	B2	98
Shattuck, Ok., U.S.	A2	129
Shaw, Ms., U.S.	B3	117
Shaw Air Force Base, mil., S.C., U.S.	D7	133
Shawano, Wi., U.S.	D5	142
Shawano, co., Wi., U.S.	D5	142
Shawano Lake, l., Wi., U.S.	D5	142
Shawinigan, P.Q., Can.	C5	90
Shawinigan-Sud, P.Q., Can.	C5	90
Shawnee, Ks., U.S.	k16	109
Shawnee, Ok., U.S.	B5	129
Shawnee, co., Ks., U.S.	D8	109
Shawneetown, Il., U.S.	F5	106
Shawsheen, stm., Ma., U.S.	f11	114
Shay Gap, Austl.	E3	60
Shaykh, Jabal ash- see Hermon, Mount, mtn., Asia	F6	44
Shaykh Sa'd, Iraq	F12	44
Shaykh 'Uthmān, Yemen	H5	38
Shebelē Wenz, Wabē (Shabeelle), stm., Afr.	B8	54
Sheberghān, Afg.	C9	42
Sheboygan, Wi., U.S.	E6	142
Sheboygan, co., Wi., U.S.	E6	142
Sheboygan, stm., Wi., U.S.	k10	142
Sheboygan Falls, Wi., U.S.	E6	142
Shediac, N.B., Can.	C5	87
Sheenjek, stm., Ak., U.S.	B11	95
Sheep Mountain, mtn., Az., U.S.	E1	96
Sheep Mountain, mtn., Wy., U.S.	B5	143
Sheep Mountain, mtn., Wy., U.S.	C2	143
Sheep Peak, mtn., Nv., U.S.	G6	121
Sheep Range, mts., Nv., U.S.	G6	121
Sheet Harbour, N.S., Can.	E7	87
Sheffield, Eng., U.K.	D6	12
Sheffield, Al., U.S.	A2	94
Sheffield, Ia., U.S.	B4	108
Sheffield, Il., U.S.	B4	106
Sheffield, Pa., U.S.	C3	131
Sheffield Lake, Oh., U.S.	A3	128
Shehong, China	C2	30
Sheila, N.B., Can.	B5	87
Shekhūpura, Pak.	D10	42
Shelagyote Peak, mtn., B.C., Can.	B4	85
Shelbiana, Ky., U.S.	C7	110
Shelbina, Mo., U.S.	B5	118
Shelburn, In., U.S.	F3	107
Shelburne, On., Can.	C4	89
Shelburne Falls, Ma., U.S.	A2	114
Shelburne Pond, l., Vt., U.S.	C2	138
Shelby, Al., U.S.	B3	94
Shelby, Ia., U.S.	C2	108
Shelby, In., U.S.	B3	107
Shelby, Mi., U.S.	E4	115
Shelby, Ms., U.S.	B3	117
Shelby, Mt., U.S.	B5	119
Shelby, N.C., U.S.	B1	126
Shelby, Oh., U.S.	B3	128
Shelby, co., Al., U.S.	B3	94
Shelby, co., Ia., U.S.	C2	108
Shelby, co., Il., U.S.	D5	106
Shelby, co., In., U.S.	E6	107
Shelby, co., Ky., U.S.	B4	110
Shelby, co., Mo., U.S.	B5	118
Shelby, co., Oh., U.S.	B1	128
Shelby, co., Tn., U.S.	B2	135
Shelby, co., Tx., U.S.	D5	136
Shelbyville, Il., U.S.	D5	106
Shelbyville, In., U.S.	F6	107
Shelbyville, Ky., U.S.	B4	110
Shelbyville, Tn., U.S.	B5	135
Shelbyville, Lake, res., Il., U.S.	D5	106
Sheldon, Ia., U.S.	A2	108
Sheldon, Il., U.S.	C6	106
Sheldon, Tx., U.S.	r14	136
Shelekhov, Gulf of see Šelihova, zaliv, b., Russia	C17	26
Shelikof Strait, strt., Ak., U.S.	D9	95
Shell Creek, stm., Wy., U.S.	B5	143
Shell Creek, stm., U.S.	A2	99
Shelley, Id., U.S.	F6	105
Shellharbour, Austl.	G5	62
Shell Lake, Wi., U.S.	C2	142
Shell Lake, l., Mn., U.S.	D3	116
Shell Lake, l., Wi., U.S.	C2	142
Shellman, Ga., U.S.	E2	103
Shell Rock, Ia., U.S.	B5	108
Shell Rock, stm., Ia., U.S.	B5	108
Shellsburg, Ia., U.S.	B6	108
Shelly Mountain, mtn., Id., U.S.	F5	105
Shelter Island, N.Y., U.S.	m16	125
Shelton, Ct., U.S.	D3	100
Shelton, Ne., U.S.	D7	120
Shelton, Wa., U.S.	B2	140
Shemya Air Force Base, mil., Ak., U.S.	E2	95
Shenandoah, Ia., U.S.	D2	108
Shenandoah, Pa., U.S.	E9	131
Shenandoah, Va., U.S.	B4	139
Shenandoah, co., Va., U.S.	B4	139
Shenandoah, stm., U.S.	A5	139
Shenandoah, North Fork, stm., Va., U.S.	B4	139
Shenandoah, South Fork, stm., Va., U.S.	B4	139
Shenandoah Mountain, mtn., U.S.	B3	139
Shenandoah National Park, Va., U.S.	B4	139
Shenango River Lake, res., U.S.	D1	131
Shendam, Nig.	E6	50
Shenipsit Lake, l., Ct., U.S.	B6	100
Shenmu, China	B3	30
Shenqiu, China	C4	30
Shenxian, China	B4	30
Shenyang, China	C12	28
Shenzhen, China	E3	30
Shepaug, stm., Ct., U.S.	C2	100
Shepaug Dam, Ct., U.S.	D2	100
Shepaug Reservoir, res., Ct., U.S.	C2	100
Shepetivka, Ukr.	D9	20
Shepherd, Mi., U.S.	E6	115
Shepherd, Tx., U.S.	D5	136
Shepherdstown, W.V., U.S.	B7	141
Shepherdsville, Ky., U.S.	C4	110
Sheppard Air Force Base, mil., Tx., U.S.	C3	136
Shepparton, Austl.	H4	62
Sherborn, Ma., U.S.	h10	114
Sherbro Island, i., S.L.	E2	50
Sherbrooke, P.Q., Can.	D6	90
Sherburn, Mn., U.S.	G4	116
Sherburne, co., Mn., U.S.	E5	116
Sheridan, Ar., U.S.	C3	97
Sheridan, Il., U.S.	B5	106
Sheridan, In., U.S.	D5	107
Sheridan, Mi., U.S.	E5	115
Sheridan, Mt., U.S.	E4	119
Sheridan, Or., U.S.	B3	130
Sheridan, Wy., U.S.	B6	143
Sheridan, co., Ks., U.S.	C3	109
Sheridan, co., Mt., U.S.	B12	119
Sheridan, co., N.D., U.S.	B5	127
Sheridan, co., Ne., U.S.	B3	120
Sheridan, co., Wy., U.S.	B5	143
Sheridan, Mount, mtn., Wy., U.S.	B2	143
Sherman, Tx., U.S.	C4	136
Sherman, co., Ks., U.S.	C2	109
Sherman, co., Ne., U.S.	C6	120
Sherman, co., Or., U.S.	B6	130
Sherman, co., Tx., U.S.	A2	136
Sherman Reservoir, res., Ne., U.S.	C7	120
Sherpur, Bngl.	D6	40
Sherrill, N.Y., U.S.	B5	125
Sherwood, P.E., Can.	C6	87
Sherwood, Ar., U.S.	C3	97
Sherwood, Or., U.S.	h12	130
Sherwood, Wi., U.S.	h9	142
Sherwood Manor, Ct., U.S.	A5	100
Sherwood Park, De., U.S.	i7	101
Shetek, Lake, l., Mn., U.S.	G3	116
Shetland Islands, is., Scot., U.K.	h19	12a
Shetucket, stm., Ct., U.S.	C7	100
Sheyenne, stm., N.D., U.S.	C8	127
Sheyenne Lake, res., N.D., U.S.	B5	127
Shiawassee, co., Mi., U.S.	F6	115
Shibām, Yemen	G5	38
Shicheng, China	A7	34
Shickshinny, Pa., U.S.	D9	131
Shidao, China	D12	28
Shiguaigou, China	A3	30
Shijiazhuang, China	D10	28
Shikārpur, Pak.	E9	42
Shikoku, i., Japan	E14	28
Shilabo, Eth.	B8	54
Shiliguri, India	D5	40
Shillington, Pa., U.S.	F10	131
Shillong, India	D6	40
Shiloh National Military Park, Tn., U.S.	B3	135
Shimla, India	C3	40
Shimoga, India	G3	40
Shimonoseki, Japan	E14	28
Shīndand, Afg.	D8	42
Shiner, Tx., U.S.	E4	136
Shinglehouse, Pa., U.S.	C5	131
Shingū, Japan	E15	28
Shinnston, W.V., U.S.	B4	141
Shinyanga, Tan.	D6	54
Shiocton, Wi., U.S.	D5	142
Shiono-misaki, c., Japan	D3	31
Shiping, China	B4	34
Ship Island, i., Ms., U.S.	E5	117
Ship Island Pass, strt., Ms., U.S.	g7	117
Shippegan, N.B., Can.	B5	87
Shippensburg, Pa., U.S.	F6	131
Shiprock, N.M., U.S.	A1	124
Ship Rock, mtn., N.M., U.S.	A1	124
Shīrāz, Iran	E6	42
Shiretoko-misaki, c., Japan	B5	31
Shirley, In., U.S.	E6	107
Shirley, Ma., U.S.	A4	114
Shirley Mountains, mts., Wy., U.S.	D6	143
Shīrvān, Iran	C7	42
Shishaldin Volcano, vol., Ak., U.S.	E7	95
Shishmaref, Ak., U.S.	B6	95
Shithāthah, Iraq	F10	44
Shively, Ky., U.S.	B4	110
Shivpuri, India	D3	40
Shizuoka, Japan	C3	31
Shkodër, Alb.	C7	18
Shoal Creek, stm., U.S.	B4	135
Shoal Harbour, Nf., Can.	D4	88
Shoal Lake, Mb., Can.	D1	86
Shoals, In., U.S.	G4	107
Shoals, Isles of, is., Me., U.S.	E2	112
Shoalwater, Cape, c., Wa., U.S.	C1	140
Shoemakersville, Pa., U.S.	F10	131
Shongopovi, Az., U.S.	B5	96
Shonto, Az., U.S.	A5	96
Shoreham, Mi., U.S.	F4	115
Shores Acres, R.I., U.S.	E4	132
Shoreview, Mn., U.S.	m12	116
Shorewood, Il., U.S.	k8	106
Shorewood, Mn., U.S.	n11	116
Shorewood, Wi., U.S.	E6	142
Short Beach, Ct., U.S.	D4	100
Shoshone, Id., U.S.	G4	105
Shoshone, co., Id., U.S.	B3	105
Shoshone, stm., Wy., U.S.	B4	143
Shoshone Falls, wtfl, Id., U.S.	G4	105
Shoshone Lake, l., Wy., U.S.	B2	143
Shoshone Mountains, mts., Nv., U.S.	E4	121
Shoshone Peak, mtn., Nv., U.S.	G5	121
Shoshone Range, mts., Nv., U.S.	C5	121
Shoshong, Bots.	C4	56
Shoshoni, Wy., U.S.	C4	143
Shostka, Ukr.	D12	20
Shouchang, China	D4	30
Shouguang, China	B4	30
Shouxian, China	C4	30
Shreve, Oh., U.S.	B3	128
Shreveport, La., U.S.	B2	111
Shrewsbury, Eng., U.K.	D5	12
Shrewsbury, Ma., U.S.	B4	114
Shrewsbury, N.J., U.S.	C4	123
Shrewsbury, Pa., U.S.	G8	131
Shuangcheng, China	B13	28
Shuangjiang, China	B3	34
Shuangliao, China	C12	28
Shuangyashan, China	B14	28
Shubenacadie, N.S., Can.	D6	87
Shubrâ El-Kheima, Egypt	E10	14
Shuksan, Mount, mtn., Wa., U.S.	A4	140
Shule, China	B3	40
Shullsburg, Wi., U.S.	F3	142
Shumagin Islands, is., Ak., U.S.	E7	95
Shunde, China	B6	34
Shungnak, Ak., U.S.	B8	95
Shurugwi, Zimb.	B5	56
Shuyang, China	C4	30
Shwebo, Myan.	B3	34
Shwenyaung, Myan.	B3	34
Shyok, stm., Asia	C3	40
Siālkot, Pak.	D10	42
Siam see Thailand, ctry., Asia	C4	34
Siam, Gulf of see Thailand, Gulf of, b., Asia	D4	34
Sian see Xi'an, China	E9	28
Siargao Island, i., Phil.	E9	34
Šiaškotan, ostrov, i., Russia	E17	26
Siau, Pulau, i., Indon.	C7	36
Šibaj, Russia	D10	22
Šibenik, Cro.	C5	18
Siberia see Sibir', reg., Russia	C12	26
Siberut, Pulau, i., Indon.	D1	36
Sibi, Pak.	E9	42
Sibircevo, Russia	B2	31
Sibirjakova, ostrov, i., Russia	B9	26
Sibiti, Congo	D2	54
Sibiu, Rom.	G8	20
Sibley, Ia., U.S.	A2	108
Sibley, La., U.S.	B2	111
Sibley, co., Mn., U.S.	F4	116
Sibolga, Indon.	C1	36
Sibsāgar, India	D6	40
Sibu, Malay.	C4	36
Sibuguey Bay, b., Phil.	E8	34
Sibut, C.A.R.	B3	54
Sibutu Island, i., Phil.	F7	34
Sibuyan Island, i., Phil.	D8	34
Sibuyan Sea, Phil.	D8	34
Sicamous, B.C., Can.	D8	85
Sichuan, prov., China	E8	28
Sicilia (Sicily), i., Italy	F4	18
Sicily see Sicilia, i., Italy	F4	18
Sicily, Strait of, strt.	F3	18
Sico Tinto, stm., Hond.	B2	80
Sicuani, Peru	F5	70
Siddipet, India	F3	40
Sidéradougou, Burkina	D4	50
Siderno, Italy	E6	18
Sidhi, India	E4	40
Sîdi Barrâni, Egypt	D10	48
Sidi bel Abbès, Alg.	C4	48
Sidi-Ifni, Mor.	C2	48
Sidley, Mount, mtn., Ant.	D28	67
Sidney, B.C., Can.	E6	85
Sidney, Ia., U.S.	D2	108
Sidney, Il., U.S.	C5	106
Sidney, Mt., U.S.	C12	119
Sidney, Ne., U.S.	C3	120
Sidney, N.Y., U.S.	C5	125
Sidney, Oh., U.S.	B1	128
Sidney Lanier, Lake, res., Ga., U.S.	B2	103
Sidon see Şaydā, Leb.	F6	44
Sidra, Gulf of see Surt, Khalīj, b., Libya	D8	48
Sidrolândia, Braz.	C6	72
Siedlce, Pol.	C7	20
Siegen, Ger.	E11	12
Siena, Italy	C3	18
Sieradz, Pol.	D5	20
Sierpc, Pol.	C5	20
Sierra, co., Ca., U.S.	C3	98
Sierra, co., N.M., U.S.	D2	124
Sierra Blanca Peak, mtn., N.M., U.S.	D4	124
Sierra Estrella, mts., Az., U.S.	m8	96
Sierra Gorda, Chile	C4	72
Sierra Leone, ctry., Afr.	E2	50
Sierra Madre, Ca., U.S.	m12	98
Sierra Nevada see Nevada, Sierra, mts., Ca., U.S.	D4	98
Sierra Vista, Az., U.S.	F5	96
Siesta Key, i., Fl., U.S.	E4	102
Sieverodonets'k, Ukr.	E15	20
Sífnos, i., Grc.	F10	18
Sig, Alg.	J6	16
Sighetu Marmaţiei, Rom.	F7	20
Sighişoara, Rom.	F8	20
Siglan, Russia	D17	26
Siglufjörður, Ice.	k19	10a
Signal Mountain, Tn., U.S.	D8	135
Signal Peak, mtn., Az., U.S.	D1	96
Signal Peak, mtn., Ut., U.S.	F2	137
Sigourney, Ia., U.S.	C5	108
Siguatepeque, Hond.	C2	80
Siguiri, Gui.	D3	50
Sigulda, Lat.	H11	10
Siguri Falls, wtfl, Tan.	E7	54
Sihanoukville see Kâmpóng Saôm, Camb.	D4	34
Sihote-Alin', mts., Russia	E15	26
Siirt, Tur.	D9	44
Sīkar, India	D3	40
Sikasso, Mali	D3	50
Sikeston, Mo., U.S.	E8	118
Sikiá, Grc.	D9	18
Sikiang see Xi, stm., China	G10	28
Sikkim, prov., India	D5	40
Šikotan, ostrov, i., Russia	E16	26
Siktjah, Russia	B14	26
Silao, Mex.	C4	78
Silchar, India	E6	40
Şile, Tur.	B3	44
Siler City, N.C., U.S.	B3	126
Silesia, hist. reg., Eur.	D4	20
Siletz, Or., U.S.	C3	130
Silghāt, India	D6	40
Silhouette, i., Sey.	h13	57b
Siling Co, l., China	E5	28
Silistra, Bul.	B11	18
Silivri, Tur.	B3	44
Šiljan, l., Swe.	F6	10
Silka, Russia	D13	26
Šilka, stm., Russia	D13	26
Silkeborg, Den.	H3	10
Sillery, P.Q., Can.	n17	90
Sillustani, hist., Peru	B3	72
Silly, Russia	B16	26
Silsbee, Tx., U.S.	D5	136
Silt, Co., U.S.	B3	99
Šilutė, Lith.	I9	10
Silvan, Tur.	C9	44
Silvassa, India	E2	40
Silver Bay, Mn., U.S.	C7	116
Silver Bow, co., Mt., U.S.	E4	119
Silver City, N.M., U.S.	E1	124
Silver City, Nv., U.S.	D2	121
Silver Creek, Ne., U.S.	C8	120
Silver Creek, N.Y., U.S.	C1	125
Silver Creek, stm., Or., U.S.	D7	130
Silverdale, Wa., U.S.	B3	140
Silver Grove, Ky., U.S.	h14	110
Silver Hill, Md., U.S.	f9	113
Silver Lake, Ks., U.S.	C8	109
Silver Lake, Ma., U.S.	f11	114
Silver Lake, Mn., U.S.	F4	116
Silver Lake, Wi., U.S.	F5	142
Silver Lake, l., De., U.S.	D3	101
Silver Lake, l., Ia., U.S.	A3	108
Silver Lake, l., Me., U.S.	C3	112
Silver Lake, l., N.H., U.S.	C4	122
Silver Lake, l., N.H., U.S.	E2	122
Silver Lake, l., Or., U.S.	D7	130
Silver Lake, l., Wa., U.S.	g13	140
Silverpeak, Nv., U.S.	F4	121
Silver Peak Range, mts., Nv., U.S.	F4	121
Silver Spring, Md., U.S.	C3	113
Silver Springs, Nv., U.S.	D2	121
Silver Star Mountain, mtn., Wa., U.S.	A5	140
Silverthrone Mountain, mtn., B.C., Can.	D4	85
Silvertip Mountain, mtn., U.S.	C3	119
Silverton, Co., U.S.	D3	99
Silverton, Id., U.S.	B3	105
Silverton, N.J., U.S.	C4	123
Silverton, Oh., U.S.	o13	128
Silverton, Or., U.S.	C4	130
Silvies, stm., Or., U.S.	D7	130
Silview, De., U.S.	B3	101
Silvis, Il., U.S.	B3	106
Šimanovsk, Russia	D14	26
Simao, China	G8	28
Simav, stm., Tur.	C3	44
Simba, D.R.C.	A4	54
Simcoe, On., Can.	E4	89
Simcoe, Lake, l., On., Can.	C5	89
Simeulue, Palau, i., Indon.	C1	36
Simferopol', Ukr.	G13	20
Simití, Col.	B5	70
Simi Valley, Ca., U.S.	E4	98
Simmesport, La., U.S.	D4	111
Simms Stream, stm., N.H., U.S.	g7	122
Simonette, stm., Ab., Can.	B1	84
Simon's Town, S. Afr.	E2	56
Simpson, Pa., U.S.	C11	131
Simpson, co., Ky., U.S.	D3	110
Simpson, co., Ms., U.S.	D4	117
Simpson Creek, stm., W.V., U.S.	k10	141
Simpson Desert, des., Austl.	E6	60
Simpsonville, Ky., U.S.	B4	110
Simpsonville, S.C., U.S.	B3	133

Name	Map Ref.	Page
Simsboro, La., U.S.	B3	111
Simsbury, Ct., U.S.	B4	100
Simušir, ostrov, i., Russia	E17	26
Sinabang, Indon.	C1	36
Sinai, pen., Egypt	E11	48
Sinai Peninsula see Sinai, pen., Egypt	E11	48
Sinaloa, state, Mex.	B3	78
Sīnāwin, Libya	D7	48
Sincelejo, Col.	B4	70
Sinclair, Wy., U.S.	E5	143
Sindangbarang, Indon.	E3	36
Sindara, Gabon	D2	54
Sindor, Russia	B9	22
Sinfra, C. Iv.	E3	50
Singalamwe, Nmb.	B3	56
Singapore, Sing.	C2	36
Singapore, ctry., Asia	C2	36
Singaraja, Indon.	H6	32
Singen, Ger.	G11	12
Singida, Tan.	D6	54
Singkaling Hkāmti, Myan.	A3	34
Singkang, Indon.	D6	36
Singkawang, Indon.	C3	36
Singkep, Pulau, i., Indon.	D2	36
Singleton, Austl.	G5	62
Sinjai, Indon.	E6	36
Sinjār, Iraq	D9	44
Sinkāt, Sudan	G12	48
Sinkiang see Xinjiang Uygur Zizhiqu, prov., China	C5	28
Sinnemahoning Creek, stm., Pa., U.S.	D5	131
Sinop, Tur.	A6	44
Sinskoe, Russia	C14	26
Sintang, Indon.	C4	36
Sint Helenabaai, b., S. Afr.	E2	56
Sinton, Tx., U.S.	E4	136
Siocon, Phil.	E8	34
Siófok, Hung.	F5	20
Sion, Switz.	A1	18
Sioux, co., Ia., U.S.	A1	108
Sioux, co., N.D., U.S.	C4	127
Sioux, co., Ne., U.S.	B2	120
Sioux Center, Ia., U.S.	A1	108
Sioux City, Ia., U.S.	B1	108
Sioux Falls, S.D., U.S.	D9	134
Sioux Lookout, On., Can.	o17	89
Sioux Rapids, Ia., U.S.	B2	108
Sipalay, Phil.	E8	34
Siping, China	C12	28
Sipiwesk Lake, l., Mb., Can.	B3	86
Siple, Mount, mtn., Ant.	D28	67
Sipsey, stm., Al., U.S.	B2	94
Sipsey Fork, stm., Al., U.S.	A2	94
Sipura, Pulau, i., Indon.	D1	36
Siquijor Island, i., Phil.	E8	34
Si Racha, Thai.	D4	34
Siracusa, Italy	F5	18
Sirājganj, Bngl.	E5	40
Sir Douglas, Mount, mtn., Can.	D3	84
Sir Edward Pellew Group, is., Austl.	D6	60
Siren, Wi., U.S.	C1	142
Siret, stm., Eur.	G9	20
Sīrjān, Iran	E7	42
Şırnak, Tur.	D10	44
Sirohi, India	E2	40
Sironj, India	E3	40
Síros, i., Grc.	F10	18
Sirsa, India	D3	40
Sir Sandford, Mount, mtn., B.C., Can.	D9	85
Sirte, Gulf of see Surt, Khalīj, b., Libya	D8	48
Sir Wilfrid Laurier, Mount, mtn., B.C., Can.	C8	85
Sisaba, mtn., Tan.	E5	54
Sisak, Cro.	B6	18
Si Sa Ket, Thai.	C4	34
Sishen, S. Afr.	D3	56
Sisian, Arm.	C12	44
Siskiyou, co., Ca., U.S.	B2	98
Siskiyou Mountains, mts., U.S.	F3	130
Siskiyou Pass, Or., U.S.	E4	130
Sisŏphŏn, Camb.	D4	34
Sisseton, S.D.	B8	134
Sisseton Indian Reservation, U.S.	B8	134
Sissiboo, stm., N.S., Can.	E4	87
Sisson Branch Reservoir, res., N.B., Can.	B2	87
Sissonville, W.V., U.S.	C3	141
Sisters, Or., U.S.	C5	130
Sistersville, W.V., U.S.	B4	141
Sītāpur, India	D4	40
Sitasjaure, l., Eur.	C7	10
Sitka, Ak., U.S.	D12	95
Sitka National Historical Park, Ak., U.S.	m22	95
Sitka Sound, strt., Ak., U.S.	m22	95
Sittoung, stm., Myan.	C3	34
Sittwe, Myan.	B2	34
Sivas, Tur.	C7	44
Sivers'kyi Donets' see Northern Donets, stm., Eur.	E14	20
Sivrihisar, Tur.	C4	44
Siwa, Egypt	E10	48
Sixian, China	C4	30
Sixth Cataract, wtfl, Sudan	G11	48
Siyäzän, Azer.	B13	44
Siziwang Qi, China	A3	30
Sjælland, i., Den.	I4	10
Skadovs'k, Ukr.	F12	20
Skærbæk, Den.	I3	10
Skagen, Den.	H4	10
Skagerrak, strt., Eur.	B11	12
Skagit, co., Wa., U.S.	A4	140
Skagway, Ak., U.S.	D12	95
Skamania, co., Wa., U.S.	D3	140
Skanderborg, Den.	H3	10
Skaneateles, N.Y., U.S.	C4	125
Skaneateles Lake, l., N.Y., U.S.	C4	125
Skārdu, Pak.	C11	42
Skarżysko-Kamienna, Pol.	D6	20
Skaudvilė, Lith.	I10	10
Skaw, The see Grenen, c., Den.	H4	10
Skegness, Eng., U.K.	D7	12
Skeleton Lake, l., On., Can.	B5	89
Skellefteå, Swe.	D9	10
Skellefteälven, stm., Swe.	D8	10
Ski, Nor.	G4	10
Skiatook, Ok., U.S.	A5	129
Skiatook Reservoir, res., Ok., U.S.	A5	129
Skien, Nor.	G3	10
Skierniewice, Pol.	D6	20
Skihist Mountain, mtn., B.C., Can.	D7	85
Skikda, Alg.	C6	48
Skillet Fork, stm., Il., U.S.	E5	106
Skive, Den.	H3	10
Sklad, Russia	B14	26
Skokie, Il., U.S.	A6	106
Skokomish Indian Reservation, Wa., U.S.	B2	140
Skópelos, i., Grc.	E9	18
Skopin, Russia	C15	20
Skopje, Mac.	C8	18
Skövde, Swe.	G5	10
Skowhegan, Me., U.S.	D3	112
Skull Valley, val., Ut., U.S.	C3	137
Skull Valley Indian Reservation, Ut., U.S.	C3	137
Skuna, stm., Ms., U.S.	B4	117
Skunk, stm., Ia., U.S.	D6	108
Skvyra, Ukr.	E10	20
Skwentna, stm., Ak., U.S.	g15	95
Skye, Island of, i., Scot., U.K.	B3	12
Skykomish, stm., Wa., U.S.	B4	140
Skyland, N.C., U.S.	f10	126
Skyland, Nv., U.S.	D2	121
Skyline, Al., U.S.	A3	94
Slagnäs, Swe.	D8	10
Slamet, Gunung, vol., Indon.	E3	36
Slancy, Russia	G13	10
Slater, Ia., U.S.	C4	108
Slater, Mo., U.S.	B4	118
Slater, S.C., U.S.	A3	133
Slatersville, R.I., U.S.	A3	132
Slatersville Reservoir, res., R.I., U.S.	B3	132
Slatina, Rom.	G8	20
Slatington, Pa., U.S.	E10	131
Slaton, Tx., U.S.	C2	136
Slaughter, La., U.S.	D4	111
Slautnoe, Russia	C18	26
Slave, stm., Can.	F17	82
Slave Lake, Ab., Can.	B3	84
Slavgorod, Russia	D9	26
Slavjanka, Russia	B2	31
Slavjansk-na-Kubani, Russia	G15	20
Slavonia see Slavonija, hist. reg., Cro.	B6	18
Slavonija, hist. reg., Cro.	B6	18
Slavonski Brod, Cro.	B6	18
Slavuta, Ukr.	D9	20
Sławno, Pol.	B4	20
Slayton, Mn., U.S.	G3	116
Sleeping Bear Dunes National Lakeshore, Mi., U.S.	D4	115
Sleeping Bear Point, c., Mi., U.S.	D4	115
Sleepy Eye, Mn., U.S.	F4	116
Slickville, Pa., U.S.	F2	131
Slidell, La., U.S.	D6	111
Sliderock Mountain, mtn., Mt., U.S.	D3	119
Sligo, Ire.	C2	12
Slinger, Wi., U.S.	E5	142
Slippery Rock, Pa., U.S.	D1	131
Sliven, Bul.	C11	18
Sljudjanka, Russia	D12	26
Sloan, Il., U.S.	B1	108
Sloan, N.Y., U.S.	C2	125
Slobodskoj, Russia	D7	26
Slobozia, Mol.	F10	20
Slobozia, Rom.	G9	20
Slocomb, Al., U.S.	D4	94
Slonim, Bela.	C8	20
Slope, co., N.D., U.S.	C2	127
Slough, Eng., U.K.	E6	12
Slovakia, ctry., Eur.	E6	20
Slovenia, ctry., Eur.	A5	18
Slov'jans'k, Ukr.	E14	20
Sluch, stm., Ukr.	D9	20
Sluck, Bela.	C9	20
Słupsk, Pol.	B4	20
Smackover, Ar., U.S.	D3	97
Småland, hist. reg., Swe.	H6	10
Small Point, c., Me., U.S.	g8	112
Smallwood Reservoir, res., Nf., Can.	g8	88
Smarhon', Bela.	B9	20
Smederevo, Yugo.	B8	18
Smethport, Pa., U.S.	C5	131
Smidovič, Russia	B14	28
Šmidta, ostrov, i., Russia	A9	26
Smila, Ukr.	E11	20
Smith, co., Ks., U.S.	C5	109
Smith, co., Ms., U.S.	C4	117
Smith, co., Tn., U.S.	A5	135
Smith, co., Tx., U.S.	C5	136
Smith, stm., Mt., U.S.	D5	119
Smith, stm., U.S.	D3	139
Smith and Sayles Reservoir, res., R.I., U.S.	B2	132
Smith Bay, b., Ak., U.S.	A9	95
Smith Canyon, val., Co., U.S.	D7	99
Smith Center, Ks., U.S.	C5	109
Smithers, B.C., Can.	B4	85
Smithers, W.V., U.S.	C3	141
Smithfield, N.C., U.S.	B4	126
Smithfield, Pa., U.S.	G2	131
Smithfield, Ut., U.S.	B4	137
Smithfield, Va., U.S.	D6	139
Smith Island, i., Va., U.S.	C7	139
Smith Island, i., U.S.	D5	113
Smith Mountain Lake, res., Va., U.S.	C3	139
Smith Peak, mtn., Id., U.S.	A2	105
Smith Point, c., Ma., U.S.	D7	114
Smith Point, c., U.S.	C6	139
Smiths, Al., U.S.	C4	94
Smithsburg, Md., U.S.	A2	113
Smiths Falls, On., Can.	C8	89
Smiths Grove, Ky., U.S.	C3	110
Smithton, Austl.	I4	62
Smithton, Il., U.S.	E4	106
Smithtown, N.Y., U.S.	n15	125
Smithville, Ga., U.S.	E2	103
Smithville, Mo., U.S.	B3	118
Smithville, Ms., U.S.	A5	117
Smithville, Oh., U.S.	B4	128
Smithville, Tn., U.S.	D8	135
Smithville, Tx., U.S.	D4	136
Smithville Lake, res., Mo., U.S.	B3	118
Smoke Creek Desert, des., Nv., U.S.	C2	121
Smokey, Cape, c., N.S., Can.	C9	87
Smokey Dome, mtn., Id., U.S.	F4	105
Smoky, stm., Ab., Can.	B1	84
Smoky Hill, stm., U.S.	D5	109
Smoky Lake, Ab., Can.	B4	84
Smoky Mountains, mts., Id., U.S.	F4	105
Smøla, i., Nor.	E3	10
Smolensk, Russia	D5	26
Smoljan, Bul.	D10	18
Smooth Rock Falls, On., Can.	o19	89
Smoothstone Lake, l., Sk., Can.	C2	91
Smyrna see İzmir, Tur.	C2	44
Smyrna, De., U.S.	C3	101
Smyrna, Ga., U.S.	C2	103
Smyrna, Tn., U.S.	B5	135
Smyrna, stm., De., U.S.	C3	101
Smyth, co., Va., U.S.	f10	139
Snake, stm., Mn., U.S.	B1	116
Snake, stm., Ne., U.S.	B4	120
Snake, stm., U.S.	C2	90
Snake, stm., U.S.	D5	116
Snake Range, mts., Nv., U.S.	E7	121
Snake River Plain, pl., Id., U.S.	F2	105
Snake River Range, mts., U.S.	C2	143
Sneads, Fl., U.S.	B2	102
Sneedville, Tn., U.S.	C10	135
Snihurivka, Ukr.	F12	20
Snipe Keys, is., Fl., U.S.	H5	102
Snøhetta, mtn., Nor.	E3	10
Snohomish, Wa., U.S.	B3	140
Snohomish, co., Wa., U.S.	A4	140
Snoqualmie, Wa., U.S.	B4	140
Snoqualmie, stm., Wa., U.S.	B4	140
Snoqualmie Pass, Wa., U.S.	B4	140
Snøtinden, mtn., Nor.	C5	10
Snowbank Lake, l., Mn., U.S.	B7	116
Snowdon, mtn., Wales, U.K.	D4	12
Snowdrift see Łutselk'e, N.T., Can.	F17	82
Snowflake, Az., U.S.	C5	96
Snow Hill, Md., U.S.	D7	113
Snow Hill, N.C., U.S.	B5	126
Snowking Mountain, mtn., Wa., U.S.	A4	140
Snow Lake, Mb., Can.	B1	86
Snowmass Mountain, mtn., Co., U.S.	B3	99
Snow Peak, mtn., Wa., U.S.	A7	140
Snowshoe Lake, l., Me., U.S.	B4	112
Snowshoe Peak, mtn., Mt., U.S.	B1	119
Snow Water Lake, l., Nv., U.S.	C7	121
Snowy Mountains, mts., Austl.	H4	62
Snowyside Peak, mtn., Id., U.S.	F4	105
Snyder, Ok., U.S.	C3	129
Snyder, Tx., U.S.	C2	136
Snyder, co., Pa., U.S.	E7	131
Soacha, Col.	E5	80
Soalala, Madag.	B8	56
Soap Lake, Wa., U.S.	B6	140
Sobradinho, Represa de, res., Braz.	D3	74
Sobral, Braz.	B3	74
Socastee, S.C., U.S.	D9	133
Soči, Russia	E5	26
Social Circle, Ga., U.S.	C3	103
Société, Archipel de la (Society Islands), is., Fr. Poly.	F14	58
Society Hill, S.C., U.S.	B8	133
Society Islands see Société, Archipel de la, Fr. Poly.	F14	58
Socorro, Col.	B5	70
Socorro, N.M., U.S.	C3	124
Socorro, co., N.M., U.S.	D2	124
Socorro, Isla, i., Mex.	D2	78
Socotra see Suquṭrā, i., Yemen	H6	38
Soc Trang, Viet.	E5	34
Sodankylä, Fin.	C12	10
Soda Springs, Id., U.S.	G7	105
Soddy-Daisy, Tn., U.S.	D8	135
Söderhamn, Swe.	F7	10
Södertälje, Swe.	G7	10
Sodo, Eth.	B7	54
Sodus, N.Y., U.S.	B3	125
Soe, Indon.	E6	36
Sofala, Moz.	C5	56
Sofia see Sofija, Bul.	C9	18
Sofija, Bul.	C9	18
Sogamoso, Col.	D5	80
Sognefjorden, b., Nor.	F1	10
Sog Xian, China	E6	28
Sointula, B.C., Can.	D4	85
Soissons, Fr.	C8	16
Sojat, India	D2	40
Šojna, Russia	A7	22
Söke, Tur.	D2	44
Sokodé, Togo	E5	50
Sokol, Russia	C7	22
Sokol, Russia	B14	26
Sokółka, Pol.	C7	20
Sokolo, Mali	D3	50
Sokoto, Nig.	D6	50
Sokoto, stm., Nig.	D5	50
Solai, Kenya	C7	54
Solana, Fl., U.S.	F5	102
Solano, Phil.	C8	34
Solano, co., Ca., U.S.	C3	98
Solāpur, India	F3	40
Soldier, stm., Ia., U.S.	C2	108
Soldier Key, i., Fl., U.S.	s13	102
Soldotna, Ak., U.S.	g16	95
Soledad, Col.	A5	70
Soledad, Ca., U.S.	D3	98
Soledad Díez Gutiérrez, Mex.	C4	78
Solikamsk, Russia	D7	26
Sol'-Ileck, Russia	D10	22
Solimões see Amazon, stm., S.A.	D6	70
Sollefteå, Swe.	E7	10
Sóller, Spain	H8	16
Šologoncy, Russia	C13	26
Solomon, Ks., U.S.	D6	109
Solomon, stm., Ks., U.S.	C6	109
Solomon Basin	I18	64
Solomon Islands, ctry., Oc.	B6	62
Solomons, Md., U.S.	D5	113
Solomon Sea, Oc.	B5	62
Solon, China	B12	28
Solon, Ia., U.S.	C6	108
Solon, Oh., U.S.	A4	128
Solothurn, Switz.	A1	18
Solov'evsk, Russia	A11	28
Solvay, N.Y., U.S.	B4	125
Solway Firth, b., U.K.	C5	12
Solwezi, Zam.	A4	56
Soma, Tur.	C2	44
Somabhula, Zimb.	B4	56
Somalia, ctry., Afr.	I14	46
Somali Basin	H8	64
Sombor, Yugo.	B7	18
Sombrerete, Mex.	C4	78
Sombrero Channel, strt., India	H6	40
Somerdale, N.J., U.S.	D2	123
Somers, Ct., U.S.	B6	100
Somers, Mt., U.S.	B2	119
Somerset, Mb., Can.	E2	86
Somerset, Ky., U.S.	C5	110
Somerset, Ma., U.S.	C5	114
Somerset, N.J., U.S.	B3	123
Somerset, Oh., U.S.	C3	128
Somerset, Pa., U.S.	F3	131
Somerset, Tx., U.S.	k7	136
Somerset, Wi., U.S.	C1	142
Somerset, co., Md., U.S.	D6	113
Somerset, co., Me., U.S.	C2	112
Somerset, co., N.J., U.S.	B3	123
Somerset, co., Pa., U.S.	G3	131
Somerset, East, S. Afr.	E4	56
Somerset Reservoir, res., Vt., U.S.	E3	138
Somers Point, N.J., U.S.	E3	123
Somersville, Ct., U.S.	B6	100
Somersworth, N.H., U.S.	D5	122
Somerton, Az., U.S.	E1	96
Somervell, co., Tx., U.S.	C4	136
Somerville, Ma., U.S.	B5	114
Somerville, N.J., U.S.	B3	123
Somerville, Tn., U.S.	B2	135
Somerville, Tx., U.S.	D4	136
Somerville Lake, res., Tx., U.S.	D4	136
Somonauk, Il., U.S.	B5	106
Son, stm., India	E4	40
Sønderborg, Den.	I3	10
Søndre Strømfjord, Grnld.	E29	82
Søndre Strømfjord, b., Grnld.	E29	82
Sondrio, Italy	A3	18
Sonepur, India	E4	40
Song, Nig.	E7	50
Song Cau, Viet.	D5	34
Songea, Tan.	F7	54
Songhua, stm., China	B14	28
Songhua Hu, res., China	C13	28
Songkhla, Thai.	E4	34
Songnim, N. Kor.	D13	28
Songololo, D.R.C.	E2	54
Songpan, China	C1	30
Sonid Youqi, China	C10	28
Sonīpat, India	D3	40
Sonkël', ozero, l., Kyrg.	A3	40
Son La, Viet.	B4	34
Sonmiāni Bay, b., Pak.	E9	42
Sonneberg, Ger.	E12	12
Sonoma, Ca., U.S.	C2	98
Sonoma, co., Ca., U.S.	C2	98
Sonoma Peak, mtn., Nv., U.S.	C4	121
Sonoma Range, mts., Nv., U.S.	C4	121
Sonora, Ca., U.S.	D3	98
Sonora, Tx., U.S.	D2	136
Sonora, state, Mex.	B2	78
Sonora, stm., Mex.	B2	78
Sonoran Desert, des., N.A.	E5	92
Sonoyta, Mex.	A2	78
Sonqor, Iran	E12	44
Sonsón, Col.	D4	80
Sonsonate, El Sal.	C1	80
Sonsorol Islands, is., Palau	E9	32
Son Tay, Viet.	B5	34
Sonthofen, Ger.	G12	12
Soochow see Suzhou, China	E12	28
Soperton, Ga., U.S.	D4	103
Sophia, W.V., U.S.	D3	141
Sopot, Pol.	B5	20
Sopron, Hung.	F4	20
Sopur, India	C2	40
Sorel, P.Q., Can.	C4	90
Sorgun, Tur.	C6	44
Soria, Spain	C5	16
Soroca, Mol.	E10	20
Sorocaba, Braz.	F2	74
Soročinsk, Russia	D9	22
Sorong, Indon.	D8	36
Soroti, Ug.	C6	54
Sørøya, i., Nor.	A10	10
Sorrento, La., U.S.	D5	111
Sør Rondane Mountains, mts., Ant.	D7	67
Sorsele, Swe.	D7	10
Sorsogon, Phil.	D8	34
Sort, Spain	F7	16
Sortavala, Russia	F14	10
Sosnogorsk, Russia	B9	22
Sosnovka, Russia	A7	22
Sosnovo-Ozërskoe, Russia	A10	28
Sosnowiec, Pol.	D5	20
Sos'va, Russia	B11	22
Sotouboua, Togo	E5	50
Soucook, stm., N.H., U.S.	D4	122
Soudan, Mn., U.S.	C6	116
Souderton, Pa., U.S.	F11	131
Souhegan, stm., N.H., U.S.	E3	122
Sŏul (Seoul), S. Kor.	D13	28
Souq Ahras, Alg.	F1	18
Sources, Mont-aux-, mtn., Afr.	D4	56
Soure, Braz.	B2	74
Souris, Mb., Can.	E1	86
Souris, P.E., Can.	C7	87
Souris, stm., N.A.	B7	92
Sousa, Braz.	C4	74
Sousse, Tun.	C7	48
South, stm., Ia., U.S.	C4	108
South, stm., N.C., U.S.	C4	126
South Acton, Ma., U.S.	g10	114
South Africa, ctry., Afr.	E3	56
South Amboy, N.J., U.S.	C4	123
South America	G9	4
South Amherst, Ma., U.S.	B2	114
South Amherst, Oh., U.S.	A3	128
Southampton, On., Can.	C3	89
Southampton, Eng., U.K.	E6	12
Southampton, N.Y., U.S.	n16	125
Southampton, co., Va., U.S.	D5	139
South Andaman, i., India	G6	40
South Anna, stm., Va., U.S.	C5	139
South Australia, state, Austl.	F5	60
South Australian Basin	L16	64
Southaven, Ms., U.S.	A3	117
South Bald Mountain, mtn., Co., U.S.	A5	99
South Baldy, mtn., N.M., U.S.	D2	124

Name	Map Ref.	Page

South Barre, Vt., U.S. **C3** 138
South Bay, Fl., U.S. **F6** 102
South Beloit, Il., U.S. **A4** 106
South Bend, In., U.S. **A5** 107
South Bend, Wa., U.S. **C2** 140
South Berwick, Me., U.S. . . .**E2** 112
South Bloomfield, Oh., U.S. .**C3** 128
South Boston, Va., U.S. **D4** 139
South Bound Brook, N.J.,
 U.S. **B3** 123
South Branch Lake, l., Me.,
 U.S. **C4** 112
Southbridge, Ma., U.S. **B3** 114
South Bristol, Me., U.S. **E3** 112
South Britain, Ct., U.S. **D3** 100
South Broadway, Wa., U.S. . .**C5** 140
South Burlington, Vt., U.S. . .**C2** 138
Southbury, Ct., U.S. **D3** 100
South Carolina, state, U.S. . .**D6** 133
South Charleston, Oh., U.S. .**C2** 128
South Charleston, W.V., U.S. .**C3** 141
South Chicago Heights, Il.,
 U.S. **m9** 106
South China Basin **G14** 64
South China Sea, Asia **D5** 32
South Coffeyville, Ok., U.S. . .**A6** 129
South Congaree, S.C., U.S. . .**D5** 133
South Connellsville, Pa.,
 U.S. **G2** 131
South Dakota, state, U.S. . . .**C5** 134
South Dartmouth, Ma., U.S. .**C6** 114
South Daytona, Fl., U.S. **C5** 102
South Deerfield, Ma., U.S. . .**B2** 114
South Dennis, Ma., U.S. **C7** 114
South Duxbury, Ma., U.S. . . .**B6** 114
South East Cape, c., Austl. . .**I4** 62
Southeast Cape, c., Ak.,
 U.S. **C6** 95
Southeast Indian Ridge **M13** 64
South Easton, Ma., U.S. **B5** 114
Southeast Pacific Basin **O25** 64
Southeast Pass, strt., La.,
 U.S. **E7** 111
South East Point, c., Austl. . .**H4** 62
Southeast Point, c., R.I., U.S. .**h7** 132
South Elgin, Il., U.S. **B5** 106
Southend-on-Sea, Eng., U.K. .**E7** 12
Southern Alps, mts., N.Z. . . .**p13** 63c
Southern Cook Islands, is.,
 Cook Is. **F13** 58
Southern Cross, Austl. **G2** 60
Southern Indian Lake, l., Mb.,
 Can. **f8** 86
Southern Ocean **J19** 4
Southern Pines, N.C., U.S. . .**B3** 126
Southern Ute Indian
 Reservation, Co., U.S. . . .**D2** 99
South Euclid, Oh., U.S. **g9** 128
Southey, Sk., Can. **G3** 91
South Fabius, stm., Mo.,
 U.S. **A5** 118
South Fallsburg, N.Y., U.S. . .**D6** 125
Southfield, Mi., U.S. **o15** 115
South Fiji Basin **K20** 64
South Fork, Pa., U.S. **F4** 131
South Fox Island, i., Mi.,
 U.S. **C5** 115
South Fulton, Tn., U.S. **A3** 135
South Gastonia, N.C., U.S. . .**B1** 126
South Gate, Ca., U.S. **n12** 98
Southgate, Ky., U.S. **h14** 110
Southgate, Mi., U.S. **p15** 115
South Georgia, i., S. Geor. . .**H9** 69
South Glastonbury, Ct., U.S. .**C5** 100
South Glens Falls, N.Y.,
 U.S. **B7** 125
South Grafton, Ma., U.S. . . .**B4** 114
South Grand, stm., Mo.,
 U.S. **C3** 118
South Hadley, Ma., U.S. **B2** 114
South Hadley Falls, Ma.,
 U.S. **B2** 114
South Hamilton, Ma., U.S. . .**A6** 114
South Haven, In., U.S. **A3** 107
South Haven, Mi., U.S. **F4** 115
South Hero Island, i., Vt.,
 U.S. **B2** 138
South Hill, Va., U.S. **D4** 139
South Hingham, Ma., U.S. . .**h12** 114
South Holland, Il., U.S. **k9** 106
South Holston Lake, res.,
 U.S. **A9** 135
South Hooksett, N.H., U.S. . .**D4** 122
South Hopkinton, R.I., U.S. . .**F1** 132
South Houston, Tx., U.S. . . .**r14** 136
South Hutchinson, Ks., U.S. .**f11** 109
South Indian Basin **N12** 64
South Indian Lake, Mb.,
 Can. **A2** 86
Southington, Ct., U.S. **C4** 100
South International Falls, Mn.,
 U.S. **B5** 116
South Island, i., N.Z. **I10** 58
South Island, i., S.C., U.S. . .**E9** 133
South Jacksonville, Il., U.S. . .**D3** 106
South Jordan, Ut., U.S. **C3** 137
South Kenosha, Wi., U.S. . . .**F6** 142
South Korea see Korea, South,
 ctry., Asia **D10** 28
South Lake Tahoe, Ca.,
 U.S. **C4** 98
South Lancaster, Ma., U.S. . .**B4** 114
South Lebanon, Oh., U.S. . . .**C1** 128
South Lyon, Mi., U.S. **F7** 115

South Manitou Island, i., Mi.,
 U.S. **C4** 115
South Marsh Island, i., Md.,
 U.S. **D5** 113
South Miami, Fl., U.S. **G6** 102
South Miami Heights, Fl.,
 U.S. **s13** 102
South Mills, N.C., U.S. **A6** 126
South Milwaukee, Wi., U.S. . .**F6** 142
Southmont, N.C., U.S. **B2** 126
South Moose Lake, l., Mb.,
 Can. **C1** 86
South Mountain, mtn., Id.,
 U.S. **G2** 105
South Mountain, mtn., N.M.,
 U.S. **k8** 124
South Mountains, mts., Az.,
 U.S. **m8** 96
South Mountains, mts., N.C.,
 U.S. **B1** 126
South New River Canal, Fl.,
 U.S. **r3** 102
South Ogden, Ut., U.S. **B4** 137
Southold, N.Y., U.S. **m16** 125
South Orange, N.J., U.S. . . .**B4** 123
South Orkney Islands, is.,
 Ant. **C36** 67
South Paris, Me., U.S. **D2** 112
South Park, val., Co., U.S. . .**B5** 99
South Pass, strt., La., U.S. . .**F6** 111
South Pass, Wy., U.S. **D4** 143
South Patrick Shores, Fl.,
 U.S. **D6** 102
South Pekin, Il., U.S. **C4** 106
South Pittsburg, Tn., U.S. . . .**D8** 135
South Plainfield, N.J., U.S. . .**B4** 123
South Platte, stm., U.S. **C7** 92
South Point, c., Mi., U.S. . . .**D7** 115
Southport (Gold Coast),
 Austl. **F5** 62
Southport, Fl., U.S. **u16** 102
Southport, In., U.S. **E5** 107
Southport, N.C., U.S. **D4** 126
Southport, N.Y., U.S. **C4** 125
South Portland, Me., U.S. . . .**E2** 112
South Portsmouth, Ky., U.S. .**B6** 110
South Range, Mi., U.S. **A2** 115
South River, On., Can. **B5** 89
South River, b., Md., U.S. . . .**C4** 113
South River, N.J., U.S. **C4** 123
South Royalton, Vt., U.S. . . .**D3** 138
South Saint Paul, Mn., U.S. . .**n12** 116
South Sandwich Islands, is.,
 S. Geor. **B2** 67
South Sandwich Trench **N11** 66
South San Francisco, Ca.,
 U.S. **h8** 98
South Shetland Islands, is.,
 Ant. **B35** 67
Southside, Al., U.S. **B3** 94
Southside Place, Tx., U.S. . . .**r14** 136
South Sioux City, Ne., U.S. . .**B9** 120
South Skunk, stm., Ia.,
 U.S. **C4** 108
South Streator, Il., U.S. **B5** 106
South Taranaki Bight, b.,
 N.Z. **o13** 63c
South Tasman Rise **M17** 64
South Toms River, N.J.,
 U.S. **D4** 123
South Torrington, Wy.,
 U.S. **D8** 143
South Tucson, Az., U.S. **E5** 96
South Venice, Fl., U.S. **E4** 102
South Ventana Cone, vol.,
 Ca., U.S. **D3** 98
South Waverly, Pa., U.S. **C8** 131
South Wellfleet, Ma.,
 U.S. **C8** 114
South Wellington, B.C.,
 Can. **f12** 85
South Wenatchee, Wa.,
 U.S. **B5** 140
South West Africa see
 Namibia, ctry., Afr. **C2** 56
South West Cape, c., N.Z. . .**q12** 63c
Southwest Channel, strt., Fl.,
 U.S. **E4** 102
South West City, Mo.,
 U.S. **E3** 118
Southwest Harbor, Me.,
 U.S. **D4** 112
Southwest Head, c., N.B.,
 Can. **E3** 87
Southwest Indian Ridge **L8** 64
Southwest Miramichi, stm.,
 N.B., Can. **C3** 87
Southwest Pacific Basin **L23** 64
Southwest Pass, strt., La.,
 U.S. **E3** 111
Southwest Pass, strt., La.,
 U.S. **F6** 111
Southwest Point, c., R.I.,
 U.S. **h7** 132
South Weymouth Naval Air
 Station, mil., Ma., U.S. . .**h12** 114
South Whitley, In., U.S. **B6** 107
South Williamson, Ky., U.S. .**C7** 110
South Williamsport, Pa.,
 U.S. **D7** 131
South Windham, Ct., U.S. . . .**C7** 100
South Windham, Me.,
 U.S. **E2** 112
South Windsor, Ct., U.S. **B5** 100
Southwood Acres, Ct., U.S. . .**A5** 100
South Woodstock, Ct., U.S. . .**B8** 100

South Yarmouth, Ma., U.S. . .**C7** 114
South Zanesville, Oh., U.S. . .**C3** 128
Sovetsk, Russia **C8** 22
Sovetsk, Russia **I9** 10
Sovetskaja Gavan', Russia . .**E16** 26
Sovlets'kyi, Ukr. **G13** 20
Soyo, Ang. **E2** 54
Sozh, stm., Eur. **C11** 20
Spain, ctry., Eur. **H5** 16
Spalding, co., Ga., U.S. **C2** 103
Spanaway, Wa., U.S. **B3** 140
Spangler, Pa., U.S. **E4** 131
Spaniard's Bay, Nf., Can. . . .**E5** 88
Spanish Fork, Ut., U.S. **C4** 137
Spanish Fort, Al., U.S. **E2** 94
Spanish Lake, Mo., U.S. **f13** 118
Spanish Peak, mtn., Or.,
 U.S. **C7** 130
Spanish Sahara see Western
 Sahara, dep., Afr. **B2** 50
Spanish Town, Jam. **B4** 80
Sparks, Ga., U.S. **E3** 103
Sparks, Nv., U.S. **D2** 121
Sparta, Ga., U.S. **C4** 103
Sparta, Il., U.S. **E4** 106
Sparta, Mi., U.S. **E5** 115
Sparta, Mo., U.S. **D4** 118
Sparta, N.C., U.S. **A1** 126
Sparta (Lake Mohawk), N.J.,
 U.S. **A3** 123
Sparta, Tn., U.S. **D8** 135
Sparta, Wi., U.S. **E3** 142
Spartanburg, S.C., U.S. **B4** 133
Spartanburg, co., S.C., U.S. .**B3** 133
Spárti, Grc. **F9** 18
Spartivento, Capo, c., Italy . .**E7** 18
Sparwood, B.C., Can. **E10** 85
Spassk-Dal'nij, Russia **E15** 26
Spavinaw Creek, stm., Ok.,
 U.S. **A7** 129
Spear, Cape, c., Nf., Can. . . .**E5** 88
Spearfish, S.D., U.S. **C2** 134
Spearman, Tx., U.S. **A2** 136
Spearville, Ks., U.S. **E4** 109
Speed, In., U.S. **H6** 107
Speedway, In., U.S. **E5** 107
Speke Gulf, b., Tan. **D6** 54
Spence Bay see Taloyoak,
 N.T., Can. **E21** 82
Spencer, Ia., U.S. **A2** 108
Spencer, In., U.S. **F4** 107
Spencer, co., In., U.S. **H4** 107
Spencer, co., Ky., U.S. **B4** 110
Spencer, Ma., U.S. **B4** 114
Spencer, N.C., U.S. **B2** 126
Spencer, Tn., U.S. **D8** 135
Spencer, W.V., U.S. **C3** 141
Spencer, Wi., U.S. **D3** 142
Spencer, Cape, c., Austl. **H2** 62
Spencer, Cape, c., Ak., U.S. .**k21** 95
Spencer Gulf, b., Austl. **G2** 62
Spencer Lake, l., Me., U.S. . .**C2** 112
Spencerport, N.Y., U.S. **B3** 125
Spencerville, Md., U.S. **B4** 113
Spencerville, Oh., U.S. **B1** 128
Sperry, Ok., U.S. **A6** 129
Spesutie Island, i., Md., U.S. .**B5** 113
Speyer, Ger. **F11** 12
Spezia see La Spezia, Italy . .**B2** 18
Spiceland, In., U.S. **E7** 107
Spicer, Mn., U.S. **E4** 116
Spider Lake, l., Wi., U.S. **B2** 142
Spindale, N.C., U.S. **B1** 126
Spink, co., S.D., U.S. **C7** 134
Spirit Lake, Ia., U.S. **A2** 108
Spirit Lake, l., Ia., U.S. **A2** 108
Spirit Lake, Id., U.S. **B2** 105
Spirit Lake, l., Wa., U.S. **C3** 140
Spirit River, Ab., Can. **B1** 84
Spirit River Flowage, res.,
 Wi., U.S. **C4** 142
Spiro, Ok., U.S. **B7** 129
Spišská Nová Ves, Slvk. **E6** 20
Spitsbergen, i., Nor. **B3** 26
Spittal an der Drau, Aus. . . .**G13** 12
Split, Cro. **C6** 18
Split, Cape, c., N.S., Can. . . .**D5** 87
Split Lake, l., Mb., Can. **A4** 86
Split Rock Creek, stm., U.S. .**G2** 116
Spofford Lake, l., N.H., U.S. .**E2** 122
Spokane, Wa., U.S. **B8** 140
Spokane, co., Wa., U.S. **B8** 140
Spokane, stm., U.S. **B8** 140
Spokane, Mount, mtn., Wa.,
 U.S. **B8** 140
Spokane Indian Reservation,
 Wa., U.S. **B8** 140
Spoleto, Italy **C4** 18
Spoon, stm., Il., U.S. **C3** 106
Spooner, Wi., U.S. **C2** 142
Spooner Lake, l., Wi., U.S. . .**C2** 142
Sredinnyj hrebet, mts.,
 Russia **D17** 26
Spornoe, Russia **C17** 26
Spotswood, N.J., U.S. **C4** 123
Spotsylvania, co., Va., U.S. . .**B5** 139
Sprague, stm., Or., U.S. **E5** 130
Sprague, W.V., U.S. **n13** 141
Sprague Lake, l., Wa., U.S. . .**B7** 140
Spratly Islands, is., Asia **E6** 34
Spring, stm., Ar., U.S. **A4** 97
Spring Arbor, Mi., U.S. **F6** 115
Spring Bay, b., Ut., U.S. **B3** 137
Springbok, S. Afr. **D2** 56
Springboro, Oh., U.S. **C1** 128
Spring Brook, stm., Pa., U.S. .**n18** 131
Spring City, Pa., U.S. **F10** 131
Spring City, Tn., U.S. **D9** 135

Spring City, Ut., U.S. **D4** 137
Spring Creek, stm., N.D.,
 U.S. **B3** 127
Spring Creek, stm., Nv.,
 U.S. **C4** 121
Spring Creek, stm., N.C., U.S. **D4** 120
Springdale, Nf., Can. **D3** 88
Springdale, Ar., U.S. **A1** 97
Springdale, Oh., U.S. **n13** 128
Springdale, Pa., U.S. **E2** 131
Springdale, S.C., U.S. **D5** 133
Springer, N.M., U.S. **A5** 124
Springerville, Az., U.S. **C6** 96
Springfield, Co., U.S. **D8** 99
Springfield, Fl., U.S. **u16** 102
Springfield, Il., U.S. **D4** 106
Springfield, Ky., U.S. **C4** 110
Springfield, Ma., U.S. **B2** 114
Springfield, Mn., U.S. **F4** 116
Springfield, Mo., U.S. **D4** 118
Springfield, Ne., U.S. **C9** 120
Springfield, N.J., U.S. **B4** 123
Springfield, Oh., U.S. **C2** 128
Springfield, Or., U.S. **C4** 130
Springfield, Pa., U.S. **p20** 131
Springfield, S.D., U.S. **E8** 134
Springfield, Tn., U.S. **A5** 135
Springfield, Va., U.S. **g12** 139
Springfield, Vt., U.S. **E4** 138
Springfield, Lake, res., Il.,
 U.S. **D4** 106
Springfontein, S. Afr. **E4** 56
Spring Garden, Guy. **B8** 70
Spring Glen, Ut., U.S. **D5** 137
Spring Green, Wi., U.S. **E3** 142
Spring Grove, Il., U.S. **h8** 106
Spring Grove, Mn., U.S. **G7** 116
Spring Grove, Pa., U.S. **G8** 131
Spring Hill, Fl., U.S. **D4** 102
Spring Hill, Ks., U.S. **D9** 109
Springhill, La., U.S. **A2** 111
Spring Hill, Tn., U.S. **B5** 135
Spring Hope, N.C., U.S. **B4** 126
Spring Island, i., S.C., U.S. . .**G6** 133
Spring Lake, l., Me., U.S. . . .**C2** 112
Spring Lake, Mi., U.S. **E4** 115
Spring Lake, N.C., U.S. **B4** 126
Spring Lake, N.J., U.S. **C4** 123
Spring Lake, res., U.S. **B3** 106
Spring Lake Heights, N.J.,
 U.S. **C4** 123
Spring Mountains, mts., Nv.,
 U.S. **G6** 121
Springport, Mi., U.S. **F6** 115
Springs, S. Afr. **D4** 56
Springside, Sk., Can. **F4** 91
Springsure, Austl. **E4** 62
Springvale, Me., U.S. **E2** 112
Spring Valley, Ca., U.S. **o16** 98
Spring Valley, Il., U.S. **B4** 106
Spring Valley, Mn., U.S. **G6** 116
Spring Valley, N.Y., U.S. **g12** 125
Spring Valley, Wi., U.S. **D1** 142
Springville, Al., U.S. **B3** 94
Springville, Ia., U.S. **B6** 108
Springville, N.Y., U.S. **C2** 125
Springville, Ut., U.S. **C4** 137
Spruce Fork, stm., W.V.,
 U.S. **m12** 141
Spruce Grove, Ab., Can. **C4** 84
Spruce Knob, mtn., W.V.,
 U.S. **C6** 141
Spruce Knob-Seneca Rocks
 National Recreation Area,
 W.V., U.S. **C5** 141
Spruce Mountain, mtn., Az.,
 U.S. **C3** 96
Spruce Mountain, mtn., Nv.,
 U.S. **C7** 121
Spruce Pine, N.C., U.S. **f10** 126
Spruce Run Reservoir, res.,
 N.J., U.S. **B3** 123
Spur, Tx., U.S. **C2** 136
Spurr, Mount, mtn., Ak.,
 U.S. **g15** 95
Squam Lake, l., N.H., U.S. . .**C4** 122
Squapan Lake, l., Me., U.S. .**B4** 112
Square Lake, l., Me., U.S. . . .**A4** 112
Squatec, P.Q., Can. **B9** 90
Squaw Cap Mountain, mtn.,
 N.B., Can. **B3** 87
Squaw Hill, mtn., Wy., U.S. . .**E7** 143
Squaw Peak, mtn., Mt., U.S. .**C2** 119
Squibnocket Point, c., Ma.,
 U.S. **D6** 114
Squillace, Golfo di, b., Italy . .**E6** 18
Squire, W.V., U.S. **D3** 141
Srbija (Serbia), state, Yugo. . .**B8** 18
Srbobran, Yugo. **B7** 18
Srednee Kujto, ozero, l.,
 Russia **D14** 10
Srednekolymsk, Russia **C17** 26
Srednerusskaja vozvyšennost',
 plat., Russia **D5** 26
Srednesibirskoe ploskogor'e,
 plat., Russia **C12** 26
Śrem, Pol. **C4** 20
Sremska Mitrovica, Yugo. . . .**B7** 18
Sretensk, Russia **D13** 26
Sri Jayewardenepura Kotte,
 Sri L. **H4** 40
Śrīkākulam, India **F4** 40
Sri Kālahasti, India **G3** 40

Sri Lanka, ctry., Asia **H4** 40
Srīnagar, India **C2** 40
Stack Reservoir, res., R.I.,
 U.S. **C3** 132
Stade, Ger. **D11** 12
Stafford, Eng., U.K. **D5** 12
Stafford, Ks., U.S. **E5** 109
Stafford, co., Ks., U.S. **D5** 109
Stafford, Va., U.S. **B5** 139
Stafford, co., Va., U.S. **B5** 139
Stafford Pond, l., R.I., U.S. . .**D6** 132
Stafford Springs, Ct., U.S. . . .**B6** 100
Staked Plain see Estacado,
 Llano, pl., U.S. **E7** 92
Stakhanov, Ukr. **E15** 20
Stalin see Varna, Blg. **C11** 18
Stalingrad see Volgograd,
 Russia **E6** 26
Stalinogorsk see
 Novomoskovsk, Russia . .**D5** 26
Stalinsk see Novokuzneck,
 Russia **D10** 26
Stalowa Wola, Pol. **D7** 20
Stambaugh, Mi., U.S. **B2** 115
Stamford, Ct., U.S. **E1** 100
Stamford, Tx., U.S. **C3** 136
Stamford, Vt., U.S. **F2** 138
Stamford, Lake, res., Tx.,
 U.S. **C3** 136
Stamping Ground, Ky., U.S. .**B5** 110
Stampriet, Nmb. **C2** 56
Stamps, Ar., U.S. **D2** 97
Stanaford, W.V., U.S. **D3** 141
Stanberry, Mo., U.S. **A3** 118
Standerton, S. Afr. **D4** 56
Standing Rock Indian
 Reservation, U.S. **B4** 134
Standish, Mi., U.S. **E7** 115
Stanfield, Az., U.S. **E3** 96
Stanfield, Or., U.S. **B7** 130
Stanford, Ky., U.S. **C5** 110
Stanislaus, co., Ca., U.S. **D3** 98
Stanley, Falk. Is. **H5** 69
Stanley, N.C., U.S. **B1** 126
Stanley, N.D., U.S. **A3** 127
Stanley, co., S.D., U.S. **C5** 134
Stanley, Va., U.S. **B4** 139
Stanley, Wi., U.S. **D3** 142
Stanley Falls, wtfl., D.R.C. . . .**C5** 54
Stanley Reservoir, res., India .**G3** 40
Stanleytown, Va., U.S. **D3** 139
Stanleyville, N.C., U.S. **A2** 126
Stanly, co., N.C., U.S. **B2** 126
Stanovoe nagor'e, mts.,
 Russia **D13** 26
Stanovoj hrebet, mts.,
 Russia **D14** 26
Stanovoy Mountains see
 Stanovoe nagor'e, mts.,
 Russia **D13** 26
Stanstead, P.Q., Can. **D5** 90
Stanthorpe, Austl. **F5** 62
Stanton, Ia., U.S. **D2** 108
Stanton, co., Ks., U.S. **E2** 109
Stanton, Ky., U.S. **C6** 110
Stanton, Mi., U.S. **E5** 115
Stanton, Ne., U.S. **C8** 120
Stanton, co., Ne., U.S. **C8** 120
Stanton, Tx., U.S. **C2** 136
Stantonsburg, N.C., U.S. **B5** 126
Stanwood, Ia., U.S. **C6** 108
Stanwood, Wa., U.S. **A3** 140
Staples, Mn., U.S. **D4** 116
Stapleton, Al., U.S. **E2** 94
Star, Id., U.S. **F2** 105
Star, N.C., U.S. **B3** 126
Staraja Russa, Russia **C5** 22
Stara Planina (Balkan
 Mountains), mts., Eur. . . .**C9** 18
Stara Zagora, Blg. **C10** 18
Starbuck, i., Kir. **E14** 58
Starbuck, Mn., U.S. **E3** 116
Star City, Ar., U.S. **D4** 97
Star City, W.V., U.S. **B5** 141
Stargard Szczeciński, Pol. . . .**C3** 20
Stargo, Az., U.S. **D6** 96
Stark, co., Il., U.S. **B4** 106
Stark, co., N.D., U.S. **C3** 127
Stark, co., Oh., U.S. **B4** 128
Starke, Fl., U.S. **C4** 102
Starke, co., In., U.S. **B4** 107
Starks, La., U.S. **D2** 111
Starkville, Ms., U.S. **B5** 117
Star Lake, l., Mn., U.S. **D3** 116
Starobil's'k, Ukr. **E15** 20
Starodub, Russia **C12** 20
Starogard Gdański, Pol. **C5** 20
Star Peak, mtn., Nv., U.S. . . .**C3** 121
Starr, co., Tx., U.S. **F3** 136
Startex, S.C., U.S. **B3** 133
Staryj Oskol, Russia **D5** 26
State Center, Ia., U.S. **B4** 108
State College, Pa., U.S. **E6** 131
Stateline, Nv., U.S. **E2** 121
State Line, Pa., U.S. **G6** 131
Staten Island see Estados, Isla
 de los, i., Arg. **H4** 69
Staten Island, i., N.Y., U.S. . .**k12** 123
Statenville, Ga., U.S. **F4** 103
Statesboro, Ga., U.S. **D5** 103
Statesville, N.C., U.S. **B2** 126
Statham, Ga., U.S. **C3** 103
Statue of Liberty National
 Monument, N.J., U.S. . . .**k8** 123
Staunton, Il., U.S. **D4** 106

Name	Map Ref.	Page

Staunton, Va., U.S. B3 139
Staunton, stm., U.S. D12 92
Stavanger, Nor. G1 10
Stavropol see Toljatti,
  Russia D6 26
Stavropol', Russia E6 26
Stawell, Austl. H3 62
Stayner, On., Can. C4 89
Stayton, Or., U.S. C4 130
Steamboat, Nv., U.S. D2 121
Steamboat Mountain, mtn.,
  Mt., U.S. C4 119
Steamboat Mountain, mtn.,
  Wy., U.S. E4 143
Steamboat Springs, Co., U.S. A4 99
Stearns, Ky., U.S. D5 110
Stearns, co., Mn., U.S. E4 116
Stearns Brook, stm., N.H.,
  U.S. A4 122
Stebbins, Ak., U.S. C7 95
Steele, Mo., U.S. B3 94
Steele, co., Mn., U.S. F5 116
Steele, Mo., U.S. E8 118
Steele, N.D., U.S. C6 127
Steele, co., N.D., U.S. B8 127
Steele, Mount, mtn., Wy.,
  U.S. E6 143
Steeleville, Il., U.S. E4 106
Steelton, Pa., U.S. F8 131
Steelville, Mo., U.S. D6 118
Steens Mountain, mts., Or.,
  U.S. E8 130
Stefanie, Lake, l., Afr. C7 54
Steger, Il., U.S. B6 106
Steilacoom, Wa., U.S. f10 140
Steinbach, Mb., Can. E3 86
Steinhatchee, stm., Fl., U.S. .C3 102
Steinkjer, Nor. E4 10
Steinkopf, S. Afr. D2 56
Stellenbosch, S. Afr. E2 56
Stendal, Ger. D12 12
Stepanakert see Xankändi,
  Azer. C12 44
Stephen, Mn., U.S. B2 116
Stephens, Ar., U.S. D2 97
Stephens, co., Ga., U.S. B3 103
Stephens, co., Ok., U.S. C4 129
Stephens, co., Tx., U.S. C3 136
Stephens City, Va., U.S. A4 139
Stephens Lake, res., Mb.,
  Can. A4 86
Stephenson, co., Il., U.S. . . .A4 106
Stephenson, Mi., U.S. C3 115
Stephens Passage, strt., Ak.,
  U.S. m23 95
Stephenville, Nf., Can. D2 88
Stephenville, Tx., U.S. C3 136
Stephenville Crossing, Nf.,
  Can. D2 88
Sterkstroom, S. Afr. E4 56
Sterling, Ak., U.S. g16 95
Sterling, Co., U.S. A7 99
Sterling, Il., U.S. B4 106
Sterling, Ks., U.S. D5 109
Sterling, Ok., U.S. C3 129
Sterling, co., Tx., U.S. D2 136
Sterling, Va., U.S. A5 139
Sterling City, Tx., U.S. D2 136
Sterling Heights, Mi., U.S. . .o15 115
Sterling Reservoir, res., Co.,
  U.S. A7 99
Sterlington, La., U.S. B3 111
Sterlitamak, Russia D7 26
Stettler, Ab., Can. C4 84
Steuben, co., In., U.S. A7 107
Steuben, co., N.Y., U.S. C3 125
Steubenville, Oh., U.S. B5 128
Stevens, co., Ks., U.S. E2 109
Stevens, co., Mn., U.S. E3 116
Stevens, co., Wa., U.S. A7 140
Stevens Creek Dam, U.S. . . .C4 103
Stevenson, Al., U.S. A4 94
Stevenson, Ct., U.S. D3 100
Stevenson, Wa., U.S. D4 140
Stevenson Lake, l., Mb.,
  Can. C4 86
Stevens Pass, Wa., U.S. B4 140
Stevens Peak, mtn., Id., U.S. .B3 105
Stevens Point, Wi., U.S. D4 142
Stevensville, Md., U.S. C5 113
Stevensville, Mi., U.S. F4 115
Stevensville, Mt., U.S. D2 119
Stewart, co., Ga., U.S. D2 103
Stewart, co., Tn., U.S. A4 135
Stewart Island, i., N.Z. q12 63c
Stewart Mountain, mtn., Az.,
  U.S. k9 96
Stewartstown, Pa., U.S. G8 131
Stewartsville, Mo., U.S. B3 118
Stewartville, Mn., U.S. G6 116
Stewiacke, N.S., Can. D6 87
Steyr, Aus. F14 12
Stigler, Ok., U.S. B6 129
Stikine, stm., Ak., U.S. D13 95
Still, stm., Ct., U.S. B3 100
Stillaguamish, North Fork, stm.,
  Wa., U.S. A4 140
Stillaguamish, South Fork, stm.,
  Wa., U.S. A4 140
Stillhouse Hollow Lake, res.,
  Tx., U.S. D4 136
Stillman Valley, Il., U.S. A4 106
Stillmore, Ga., U.S. D4 103
Stillwater, Mn., U.S. E6 116
Stillwater, co., Mt., U.S. E7 119
Stillwater, Ok., U.S. A4 129

Stillwater Range, mts., Nv.,
  U.S. D3 121
Stillwater Reservoir, res., N.Y.,
  U.S. B5 125
Stillwater Reservoir, res., R.I.,
  U.S. B3 132
Stilwell, Ok., U.S. B7 129
Stimson, Mount, mtn., Mt.,
  U.S. B3 119
Stine Mountain, mtn., Mt.,
  U.S. E3 119
Stinking Lake, l., N.M., U.S. .A3 124
Stinnett, Tx., U.S. B2 136
Štip, Mac. D9 18
Stirling, Austl. E5 60
Stirling, Austl. G2 60
Stirling, Ab., Can. E4 84
Stirling, On., Can. C7 89
Stockbridge, Ga., U.S. C2 103
Stockbridge, Mi., U.S. F6 115
Stockbridge-Munsee Indian
  Reservation, Wi., U.S. . . .D5 142
Stockdale, Tx., U.S. E4 136
Stockholm, Swe. G8 10
Stockton, Ca., U.S. D3 98
Stockton, Il., U.S. A3 106
Stockton, Ks., U.S. C4 109
Stockton, Md., U.S. D7 113
Stockton, Mo., U.S. D4 118
Stockton Island, i., Wi., U.S. .B3 142
Stockton Lake, res., Mo.,
  U.S. D4 118
Stoddard, co., Mo., U.S. E8 118
Stoddard, Wi., U.S. E2 142
Stœng Trèng, Camb. D5 34
Stoke-on-Trent, Eng., U.K. . .D5 12
Stokes, co., N.C., U.S. A2 126
Stokesdale, N.C., U.S. A3 126
Stolbovoj, ostrov, i., Russia . .B15 26
Stolin, Bela. D9 20
Stollings, W.V., U.S. n12 141
Stone, co., Ar., U.S. B3 97
Stone, co., Mo., U.S. E4 118
Stone, co., Ms., U.S. E4 117
Stoneboro, Pa., U.S. D1 131
Stone Corral Lake, l., Or.,
  U.S. E7 130
Stoneham, Ma., U.S. g11 114
Stonehaven, Scot., U.K. B5 12
Stonehenge, hist., Eng., U.K. .E6 12
Stone Mountain, Ga., U.S. . .C2 103
Stone Mountain, mtn., Ga.,
  U.S. C2 103
Stones River National
  Battlefield, hist., Tn.,
  U.S. B4 135
Stoneville, N.C., U.S. A3 126
Stonewall, Mb., Can. D3 86
Stonewall, La., U.S. B2 111
Stonewall, Ms., U.S. C5 117
Stonewall, co., Tx., U.S. C2 136
Stonewood, W.V., U.S. k10 141
Stoney Creek, On., Can. D5 89
Stonington, Ct., U.S. D8 100
Stonington, Il., U.S. D4 106
Stonington, Me., U.S. D4 112
Stono, stm., S.C., U.S. k11 133
Stono Inlet, b., S.C., U.S. . . .F8 133
Stony Brook, stm., N.J.,
  U.S. C3 123
Stony Brook, N.Y., U.S. n15 125
Stony Creek, stm., Va.,
  U.S. C5 139
Stony Island, i., N.Y., U.S. . .B4 125
Stony Plain, Ab., Can. C3 84
Stony Point, N.C., U.S. B1 126
Storavan, l., Swe. D8 10
Storebælt, strt., Den. I4 10
Storey, co., Nv., U.S. D2 121
Storlien, Swe. E5 10
Storm Bay, b., Austl. I4 64
Storm Lake, Ia., U.S. B2 108
Storm Lake, l., Ia., U.S. B2 108
Storm Mountain, mtn., Ak.,
  U.S. h16 95
Stornoway, Scot., U.K. A3 12
Storrs, Ct., U.S. B7 100
Storsjön, l., Swe. E6 10
Storslett, Nor. B9 10
Storuman, Swe. D7 10
Storuman, l., Swe. D7 10
Story, co., Ia., U.S. B4 108
Story, Wy., U.S. B6 143
Story City, Ia., U.S. B4 108
Stoŭbcy, Bela. C9 20
Stoughton, Sk., Can. H4 91
Stoughton, Ma., U.S. B5 114
Stoughton, Wi., U.S. F4 142
Stover, Mo., U.S. C5 118
Stow, Oh., U.S. A4 128
Stow Creek, stm., N.J.,
  U.S. E2 123
Stowe, Pa., U.S. F10 131
Stowe, Vt., U.S. C3 138
Stoyoma Mountain, mtn., B.C.,
  Can. E7 85
Strabane, Pa., U.S. F1 131
Strafford, Mo., U.S. D4 118
Strafford, co., N.H., U.S. . . .D4 122
Straffordville, On., Can. E4 89
Strakonice, Czech Rep. F9 20
Stralsund, Ger. C13 12
Strand, S. Afr. E2 56
Stranraer, Scot., U.K. C4 12
Strasbourg, Fr. C10 16
Strasburg, Co., U.S. B6 99

Strasburg, Oh., U.S. B4 128
Strasburg, Pa., U.S. G9 131
Strasburg, Va., U.S. B4 139
Stratford, On., Can. D3 89
Stratford, N.Z. o13 63c
Stratford, Ct., U.S. E3 100
Stratford, N.J., U.S. B4 108
Stratford, N.J., U.S. D2 123
Stratford, Ok., U.S. C5 129
Stratford, Tx., U.S. A1 136
Stratford, Wi., U.S. D3 142
Stratford Point, c., Ct., U.S. . .E3 100
Stratham, N.H., U.S. D5 122
Strathmore, Ab., Can. D4 84
Strathmore, Ca., U.S. D4 98
Strathroy, On., Can. E3 89
Stratton, Co., U.S. B8 99
Straubing, Ger. F13 12
Strawberry, stm., Ar., U.S. . .A4 97
Strawberry, stm., Ut., U.S. . .C5 137
Strawberry Mountain, mtn.,
  Or., U.S. C8 130
Strawberry Point, Ia., U.S. . .B6 108
Strawberry Point, c., Ma.,
  U.S. B6 114
Strawberry Range, mts., Or.,
  U.S. C8 130
Strawberry Reservoir, res., Ut.,
  U.S. C4 137
Streaky Bay, b., Austl. G5 60
Streator, Il., U.S. B5 106
Strelka-Čunja, Russia C12 26
Strimón (Struma), stm., Eur. . .D9 18
Strimon, Gulf of see Orfanoú,
  Kólpos, b., Grc. D9 18
Stromsburg, Ne., U.S. C8 120
Strömsund, Swe. E6 10
Strong, Ar., U.S. D3 97
Strong, Me., U.S. D2 112
Strong, stm., Ms., U.S. C4 117
Strong City, Ks., U.S. D7 109
Stronghurst, Il., U.S. C3 106
Strongsville, Oh., U.S. A4 128
Stroud, Ok., U.S. B5 129
Stroudsburg, Pa., U.S. E11 131
Stroudwater, stm., Me., U.S. .g7 112
Strum, Wi., U.S. D2 142
Struma (Strimón), stm., Eur. .D9 18
Strumica, Mac. D9 18
Struthers, Oh., U.S. A5 128
Strydenburg, S. Afr. D3 56
Stryi, Ukr. E7 20
Stryker, Oh., U.S. A1 128
Stuart, Fl., U.S. E6 102
Stuart, Ia., U.S. C3 108
Stuart, Ne., U.S. B6 120
Stuart, Va., U.S. D2 139
Stuart, Mount, mtn., Wa.,
  U.S. B5 140
Stuart Lake, l., B.C., Can. . . .B5 85
Stuarts Draft, Va., U.S. B3 139
Stull, stm., Can. B5 86
Stump Lake, l., N.D., U.S. . . .B7 127
Stump Pond, res., R.I., U.S. . .D2 132
Stupino, Russia B15 20
Sturbridge, Ma., U.S. B3 114
Sturgeon, stm., Mi., U.S. B4 115
Sturgeon, Mo., U.S. B5 118
Sturgeon Bay, b., Mb., Can. .C3 86
Sturgeon Bay, Wi., U.S. D6 142
Sturgeon Falls, On., Can. . . .A5 89
Sturgeon Lake, l., On., Can. .C6 89
Sturgis, Sk., Can. F4 91
Sturgis, Ky., U.S. e10 110
Sturgis, Mi., U.S. G5 115
Sturgis, S.D., U.S. C2 134
Sturtevant, Wi., U.S. F6 142
Sturt Stony Desert, des.,
  Austl. F3 62
Stutsman, co., N.D., U.S. . . .B6 127
Stutterheim, S. Afr. E4 56
Stuttgart, Ger. F11 12
Stuttgart, Ar., U.S. C4 97
Styr, stm., Eur. D8 20
Suaita, Col. D5 80
Šubarkuduk, Kaz. E10 22
Sübät, stm., Sudan Il1 48
Subei, China B7 40
Sublette, Ks., U.S. E3 109
Sublette, co., Wy., U.S. D2 143
Sublett Range, mts., Id.,
  U.S. G6 105
Sublimity, Or., U.S. C4 130
Subotica, Yugo. A7 18
Sucarnoochee, stm., Al.,
  U.S. C1 94
Succasunna, N.J., U.S. B3 123
Suceava, Rom. F9 20
Sucre, Bol. B4 72
Sud, Canal du, strt., Haiti . . .B5 80
Sudan, ctry., Afr. H10 48
Sudan, reg., Afr. H8 48
Sudbury, On., Can. A4 89
Sudbury, Ma., U.S. B5 114
Sudbury, stm., Ma., U.S. B5 114
Sudbury Center, Ma., U.S. . .g10 114
Sudbury Reservoir, res., Ma.,
  U.S. g10 114
Suez see El-Suweis, Egypt . .E11 48
Suez, Gulf of see Suweis,
  Khalîg el-, b., Egypt F10 14
Suez Canal see Suweis, Qanâ
  el-, Egypt E10 14
Suffern, N.Y., U.S. D6 125
Suffield, Ct., U.S. B5 100

Suffolk, co., Ma., U.S. B5 114
Suffolk, co., N.Y., U.S. n15 125
Suffolk, Va., U.S. D6 139
Sugar, stm., N.H., U.S. D2 122
Sugar, stm., U.S. F4 142
Sugar City, Id., U.S. F7 105
Sugar Creek, Mo., U.S. h11 118
Sugar Creek, stm., Oh.,
  U.S. C2 128
Sugar Creek, stm., Pa.,
  U.S. C8 131
Sugarcreek, Pa., U.S. D2 131
Sugar Grove, Va., U.S. D1 139
Sugar Hill, Ga., U.S. B2 103
Sugar Island, i., Mi., U.S. . . .B6 115
Sugar Land, Tx., U.S. E5 136
Sugar Loaf, Va., U.S. C3 139
Sugarloaf Mountain, mtn.,
  Mt., U.S. C4 119
Sugar Notch, Pa., U.S. n17 131
Suggi Lake, l., Sk., Can. C4 91
Suğla Gölü, l., Tur. D5 44
Suhag, Egypt E11 48
Suhana, Russia C13 26
Suhar, Oman F7 38
Sühbaatar, Mong. A9 28
Suhl, Ger. E12 12
Suhona, stm., Russia C6 26
Suhumi, Geor. A9 44
Suiattle, stm., Wa., U.S. A4 140
Suichang, China D4 30
Suichuan, China D3 30
Suide, China D10 28
Suijiang, China D1 30
Suining, China C4 30
Suining, China E9 28
Suitland, Md., U.S. C4 113
Suixi, China C4 30
Suiyang, China B2 31
Suizhong, China C12 28
Suizhou, China E10 28
Sukabumi, Indon. E3 36
Sukadana, Indon. D3 36
Sukaraja, Indon. D4 36
Sukarnapura see Jayapura,
  Indon. G11 32
Sukhothai, Thai. C3 34
Sukkertoppen, Grnld. E29 82
Sukkozero, Russia B5 22
Sukkur, Pak. E9 42
Sukses, Nmb. C2 56
Sukumo, Japan D2 31
Sula, Kepulauan, is., Indon. . .D7 36
Sulaiman Range, mts., Pak. . .E9 42
Sulawesi (Celebes), i.,
  Indon. D6 36
Sulawesi, Laut see Celebes
  Sea, Asia C6 36
Sulechów, Pol. C3 20
Sulligent, Al., U.S. B1 94
Sullana, Peru D3 70
Sullivan, Il., U.S. D5 106
Sullivan, In., U.S. F3 107
Sullivan, co., In., U.S. F3 107
Sullivan, Mo., U.S. C6 118
Sullivan, co., Mo., U.S. A4 118
Sullivan, co., N.H., U.S. D2 122
Sullivan, co., N.Y., U.S. D6 125
Sullivan, co., Pa., U.S. D9 131
Sullivan, co., Tn., U.S. C11 135
Sullivan Lake, l., Ab., Can. . . .D5 84
Sullivans Island, S.C., U.S. . .k12 133
Sully, Ia., U.S. C5 108
Sully, co., S.D., U.S. C5 134
Sulmona, Italy C4 18
Sulphur, La., U.S. D2 111
Sulphur, Ok., U.S. C5 129
Sulphur, stm., U.S. D2 97
Sulphur Spring Range, mts.,
  Nv., U.S. C5 121
Sulphur Springs, Tx., U.S. . . .C5 136
Sultan, Wa., U.S. B4 140
Sultänpur, India D4 40
Sulu Archipelago, is., Phil. . . .F7 34
Sulüq, Libya D9 48
Sulu Sea, Asia E7 34
Sumas, Wa., U.S. A3 140
Sumatera (Sumatra), i.,
  Indon. C2 36
Sumatra see Sumatera, i.,
  Indon. C2 36
Sumba, i., Indon. F5 36
Sumba, Selat, strt., Indon. . . .E6 36
Sumbawa, i., Indon. E5 36
Sumbawa Besar, Indon. E5 36
Sumbawanga, Tan. C6 54
Sumbe, Ang. F2 54
Sumedang, Indon. m13 36
Šumen, Blg. C11 18
Sumenep, Indon. E4 36
Sumgait, Russia C8 22
Sumiha, Russia C11 22
Sumisu-jima, i., Japan E16 28
Sumiton, Al., U.S. B2 94
Summerford, Nf., Can. D4 88
Summer Island, i., Mi.,
  U.S. C4 115
Summer Lake, l., Or., U.S. . . .E6 130
Summerland, B.C., Can. E8 85
Summers, co., W.V., U.S. . . .D4 141
Summerside, P.E., Can. C6 87
Summersville, W.V., U.S. C4 141
Summersville Lake, res., W.V.,
  U.S. C4 141
Summerton, S.C., U.S. D7 133

Summertown, Tn., U.S. B4 135
Summerville, Ga., U.S. B1 103
Summerville, S.C., U.S. E7 133
Summit, co., Co., U.S. B4 99
Summit, Il., U.S. k9 106
Summit, Ms., U.S. D3 117
Summit, N.J., U.S. B4 123
Summit, co., Oh., U.S. A4 128
Summit, Tn., U.S. h11 135
Summit, co., Ut., U.S. C5 137
Summit Hill, Pa., U.S. E10 131
Summit Lake, l., Ia., U.S. C3 108
Summit Lake Indian
  Reservation, Nv., U.S. . . .B2 121
Summit Mountain, mtn., Nv.,
  U.S. D5 121
Summit Peak, mtn., Co.,
  U.S. D4 99
Summitville, In., U.S. D6 107
Sumner, Ia., U.S. B5 108
Sumner, Il., U.S. E6 106
Sumner, co., Ks., U.S. E6 109
Sumner, co., Tn., U.S. A5 135
Sumner, Wa., U.S. B3 140
Sumner, Lake, res., N.M.,
  U.S. C5 124
Sumner Dam, N.M., U.S. . . .C5 124
Sumner Strait, strt., Ak.,
  U.S. m23 95
Šumperk, Czech Rep. E4 20
Sumqayıt, Azer. B13 44
Sumrall, Ms., U.S. D4 117
Šumšu, ostrov, i., Russia . . .D17 26
Sumter, co., Al., U.S. C1 94
Sumter, co., Fl., U.S. D4 102
Sumter, co., Ga., U.S. D2 103
Sumter, S.C., U.S. D7 133
Sumter, co., S.C., U.S. D7 133
Sumy, Ukr. D13 20
Sumzom, China D7 40
Sun, stm., Mt., U.S. C4 119
Sunapee, N.H., U.S. D2 122
Sunapee Lake, l., N.H., U.S. .D2 122
Sunbright, Tn., U.S. C9 135
Sunbury, Oh., U.S. B3 128
Sunbury, Pa., U.S. E8 131
Sunchales, Arg. E5 72
Suncho Corral, Arg. D5 72
Sun City, Az., U.S. k8 96
Suncook, N.H., U.S. D4 122
Suncook, stm., N.H., U.S. . . .D4 122
Suncook Lakes, l., N.H.,
  U.S. D4 122
Sunda, Selat, strt., Indon. . . .E3 36
Sundance, Wy., U.S. B8 143
Sundance Mountain, mtn.,
  Wy., U.S. B8 143
Sundarbans, reg., Asia B1 34
Sunda Shelf H13 64
Sunda Strait see Sunda, Selat,
  strt., Indon. E3 36
Sunderland, On., Can. C5 89
Sunderland, Eng., U.K. C6 12
Sundown, Austl. F5 60
Sundown, Tx., U.S. C1 136
Sundre, Ab., Can. D3 84
Sundridge, On., Can. B5 89
Sundsvall, Swe. E7 10
Sunflower, Ms., U.S. B3 117
Sunflower, co., Ms., U.S. B3 117
Sunflower, Mount, mtn., Ks.,
  U.S. C2 109
Sungaidareh, Indon. D2 36
Sungai Kolok, Thai. E4 34
Sungai Petani, Malay. B2 36
Sungari see Songhua, stm.,
  China B14 28
Sungari Reservoir see Songhua
  Hu, res., China C13 28
Sungurlu, Tur. B6 44
Sunland Park, N.M., U.S. . . .F3 124
Sunlight Creek, stm., Wy.,
  U.S. B3 143
Sunman, In., U.S. F7 107
Sunne, Swe. G5 10
Sunnyside, Nf., Can. E5 88
Sunnyside, Wa., U.S. C5 140
Sunnyvale, Ca., U.S. k8 98
Sun Prairie, Wi., U.S. E4 142
Sunray, Tx., U.S. A2 136
Sunset, La., U.S. D3 111
Sunset, Ut., U.S. B4 137
Sunset Beach, N.C., U.S. f9 104
Sunset Crater National
  Monument, Az., U.S. B4 96
Sunset Lake, l., Vt., U.S. D2 138
Sunshine, Austl. H3 62
Suntar, Russia C13 26
Suntar-Hajata, hrebet, mts.,
  Russia C16 26
Suntaug Lake, l., Ma.,
  U.S. f11 114
Sun Valley, Id., U.S. F4 105
Sun Valley, Nv., U.S. D2 121
Sunyani, Ghana E4 50
Suojärvi, Russia B5 22
Suomussalmi, Fin. D13 10
Superior, Az., U.S. D4 96
Superior, Mt., U.S. C2 119
Superior, Ne., U.S. D7 120
Superior, Wi., U.S. B1 142
Superior, Wy., U.S. E4 143
Superior, Lake, l., N.A. B10 92
Superstition Mountains, mts.,
  Az., U.S. m10 96
Suphan Buri, Thai. D4 34

Name	Map Ref.	Page

Suquamish, Wa., U.S. B3 140
Suquṭrā, i., Yemen H6 38
Şür, Leb. F6 44
Şür, Oman F7 38
Sur, Point, c., Ca., U.S. . . .D3 98
Sura, stm., Russia E15 6
Surakarta, Indon. E4 36
Sürat, India E2 40
Süratgarh, India D2 40
Surat Thani, Thai. E3 34
Surendranagar, India E2 40
Surfside, Fl., U.S. s13 102
Surfside Beach, S.C., U.S. . .D10 133
Surgoinsville, Tn., U.S. C11 135
Surgut, Russia C9 26
Surigao, Phil. E9 34
Surigao Strait, strt., Phil. . .E9 34
Surin, Thai. D4 34
Suriname, ctry., S.A. C8 70
Surprise, Az., U.S. k8 96
Surrey, N.D., U.S. A4 127
Surry, co., N.C., U.S. A2 126
Surry, co., Va., U.S. C6 139
Surry Mountain Lake, res.,
  N.H., U.S. D2 122
Surt, Libya D8 48
Surt, Khalīj, b., Libya D8 48
Sürüç, Tur. D8 44
Surulangun, Indon. D2 36
Šuryškary, Russia A12 22
Süsangerd, Iran G13 44
Susanville, Ca., U.S. B3 98
Suşehri, Tur. B8 44
Susitna, stm., Ak., U.S. C10 95
Susquehanna, Pa., U.S. C10 131
Susquehanna, co., Pa., U.S. .C10 131
Susquehanna, stm., U.S. A5 113
Susquehanna, West Branch,
  stm., Pa., U.S. D5 131
Sussex, N.B., Can. D4 87
Sussex, co., De., U.S. F4 101
Sussex, N.J., U.S. A3 123
Sussex, co., N.J., U.S. A3 123
Sussex, co., Va., U.S. D5 139
Sussex, Wi., U.S. m11 142
Susuman, Russia C16 26
Susurluk, Tur. C3 44
Sutherland, S. Afr. E3 56
Sutherland, Ia., U.S. B2 108
Sutherland, Ne., U.S. C4 120
Sutherland, Or., U.S. D3 130
Sutherlin, Or., U.S. D3 130
Sutlej (Satluj), stm., Asia . .D2 40
Sutter, co., Ca., U.S. C3 98
Sutter Creek, Ca., U.S. C3 98
Sutton, P.Q., Can. D5 90
Sutton, Ne., U.S. D8 120
Sutton, co., Tx., U.S. D2 136
Sutton, W.V., U.S. C4 141
Sutton Lake, res., W.V., U.S. .C4 141
Sutwik Island, i., Ak., U.S. . .D8 95
Süüj, Mong. B8 28
Suur Munamägi, Est. H12 10
Suva, Fiji F11 58
Suwałki, Pol. B7 20
Suwanee, Ga., U.S. B2 103
Suwannee, co., Fl., U.S. B3 102
Suwannee, stm., U.S. C4 102
Suwannee Sound, strt., Fl.,
  U.S. C3 102
Suwanose-jima, i., Japan . . .F14 28
Suwarrow, atoll, Cook Is. . . .F13 58
Suweis, Khalîg el- (Suez, Gulf
  of), b., Egypt F10 14
Suweis, Qanâ el- (Suez Canal),
  Egypt E10 14
Suwŏn, S. Kor. D13 28
Suzak, Kaz. B9 42
Suzhou, China E11 28
Suzhou, China E12 28
Svalbard, dep., Nor. D20 144
Svaliava, Ukr. E7 20
Svappavaara, Swe. C9 10
Svatove, Ukr. E15 20
Svay Riĕng, Camb. D5 34
Sveg, Swe. E6 10
Švenčionėliai, Lith. I11 10
Svendborg, Den. I4 10
Svensen, Or., U.S. A3 130
Sverdlovsk see Ekaterinburg,
  Russia D8 26
Sverdrup, ostrov, i., Russia .B9 26
Svetlahorsk, Bela. C10 20
Svetlaja, Russia E15 26
Svetlograd, Russia A4 42
Svetlyj, Russia D13 26
Svetlyj, Russia D11 22
Svetogorsk, Russia F13 10
Svirsk, Russia A8 28
Svištov, Blg. C10 18
Svitavy, Czech Rep. E4 20
Svjatoj Nos, mys, c., Russia .A7 22
Svjatoj Nos, mys, c., Russia .B15 26
Svobodnyj, Russia D14 26
Svolvær, Nor. B6 10
Swabia see Schwaben, hist.
  reg., Ger. F11 12
Swain, co., N.C., U.S. f9 126
Swain Reefs, rf., Austl. E5 62
Swainsboro, Ga., U.S. D4 103
Swakopmund, Nmb. C1 56
Swampscott, Ma., U.S. B6 114
Swan, stm., Can. C1 86
Swan Creek, stm., Oh., U.S. .e6 128
Swan Falls, wtfl., Id., U.S. . .F2 105

Swan Hill, Austl. H3 62
Swan Hills, Ab., Can. B3 84
Swan Islands see Santanilla,
  Islas, is., Hond. B3 80
Swan Lake, l., Mb., Can. . . .C1 86
Swan Lake, l., Me., U.S. D4 112
Swan Lake, l., Ne., U.S. C3 120
Swannanoa, N.C., U.S. f10 126
Swan Peak, mtn., Mt., U.S. . .C3 119
Swan Range, mts., Mt., U.S. .C3 119
Swan River, Mb., Can. C1 86
Swansboro, N.C., U.S. C5 126
Swansea, Wales, U.K. E4 12
Swansea, Il., U.S. E4 106
Swanson Lake, res., Ne.,
  U.S. D4 120
Swanton, Oh., U.S. A2 128
Swanton, Vt., U.S. B2 138
Swanzey Center, N.H., U.S. . .E2 122
Swarthmore, Pa., U.S. p20 131
Swartswood Lake, l., N.J.,
  U.S. A3 123
Swartz Creek, Mi., U.S. F7 115
Swayzee, In., U.S. C6 107
Swaziland, ctry., Afr. D5 56
Swea City, Ia., U.S. A3 108
Sweden, ctry., Eur. E7 10
Swedru, Ghana E4 50
Sweeny, Tx., U.S. r14 136
Sweet Grass, co., Mt., U.S. . .E7 119
Sweet Home, Or., U.S. C4 130
Sweetser, In., U.S. C6 107
Sweet Springs, Mo., U.S. . . .C4 118
Sweetwater, Tn., U.S. D9 135
Sweetwater, Tx., U.S. C2 136
Sweetwater, stm., Wy., U.S. . .D4 143
Sweetwater, co., Wy., U.S. . . .E3 143
Sweetwater Creek, Fl., U.S. . .p10 102
Sweetwater Creek, stm., Ok.,
  U.S. B1 129
Swellendam, S. Afr. E3 56
Swepsonville, N.C., U.S. A3 126
Świdwin, Pol. C3 20
Świebodzin, Pol. C3 20
Świecie, Pol. C5 20
Swift, co., Mn., U.S. E3 116
Swift, stm., N.H., U.S. B4 122
Swift Creek, stm., N.C.,
  U.S. B5 126
Swift Creek, stm., Va., U.S. . .n17 139
Swift Diamond, stm., N.H.,
  U.S. g7 122
Swifton, Ar., U.S. B4 97
Swift Reservoir, res., Wa.,
  U.S. C3 140
Swindon, Eng., U.K. E6 12
Swinomish Indian
  Reservation, Wa., U.S. . .A3 140
Świnoujście, Pol. C3 20
Swisher, Ia., U.S. C6 108
Swisher, co., Tx., U.S. B2 136
Swissvale, Pa., U.S. k14 131
Switzer, W.V., U.S. D3 141
Switzerland, ctry., Eur. A2 18
Switzerland, Fl., U.S. m8 102
Switzerland, co., In., U.S. . . .G7 107
Swoyerville, Pa., U.S. D10 131
Syalah, Russia C14 26
Sycamore, Al., U.S. B3 94
Sycamore, Il., U.S. B5 106
Sycamore, Oh., U.S. B2 128
Sycamore Creek, stm., W.V.,
  U.S. m13 141
Sydenham, On., Can. C8 89
Sydney, Austl. G5 62
Sykesville, Md., U.S. B4 113
Sykesville, Pa., U.S. D4 131
Syktyvkar, Russia C7 26
Sylacauga, Al., U.S. B3 94
Sylhet, Bngl. E6 40
Sylt, i., Ger. C11 12
Sylva, N.C., U.S. f9 126
Sylvania, Al., U.S. A4 94
Sylvania, Ga., U.S. D5 103
Sylvania, Oh., U.S. A2 128
Sylvan Lake, Ab., Can. C3 84
Sylvan Lake, l., In., U.S. B7 107
Sylvan Lake, Mi., U.S. o15 115
Sylvan Pass, Wy., U.S. B2 143
Sylvester, Ga., U.S. E3 103
Sym, Russia C10 26
Šymkent, Kaz. E8 26
Symmes Creek, stm., Oh.,
  U.S. D3 128
Symsonia, Ky., U.S. f9 110
Syracuse, In., U.S. B6 107
Syracuse, Ks., U.S. E2 109
Syracuse, Ne., U.S. D9 120
Syracuse, N.Y., U.S. B4 125
Syracuse, Ut., U.S. B3 137
Syrdarja, Uzb. F9 42
Syr Darya (Syrdar'ja), stm.,
  Asia B9 42
Syria, ctry., Asia E8 44
Syriam, Mya. C3 34
Syrian Desert, des., Asia F8 44
Syros see Ermoúpolis, Grc. . .F10 18
Sysladobsis Lake, l., Me.,
  U.S. C4 112
Syvash, zatoka, strt., Ukr. . .F13 20
Syzran', Russia D6 26
Szamotuły, Pol. C4 20
Szczecin, Pol. C3 20
Szczecinek, Pol. C4 20
Szczytno, Pol. C6 20

Szechwan see Sichuan, state,
  China E8 28
Szeged, Hung. F6 20
Székesfehérvár, Hung. F5 20
Szekszárd, Hung. F5 20
Szentes, Hung. F6 20
Szolnok, Hung. F6 20
Szombathely, Hung. . . . . . . .F4 20\

T

Tabar Islands, is., Pap. N.
  Gui. G13 32
Tabarka, Tun. F2 18
Tabasco, state, Mex. D6 78
Tabayin, Mya. B3 34
Tabbys Peak, mtn., Ut., U.S. .C3 137
Tabelbala, Alg. E4 48
Taber, Ab., Can. E4 84
Tablas Island, i., Phil. D8 34
Table Head, c., Nf., Can. B4 88
Table Mountain, mtn., Az.,
  U.S. E5 96
Table Rock Lake, res., U.S. . .E4 118
Table Top, mtn., Az., U.S. . . .E3 96
Tábor, Czech Rep. E3 20
Tabor, Russia B17 26
Tabor, Ia., U.S. D2 108
Tabora, Tan. D6 54
Tabor City, N.C., U.S. C4 126
Tabou, C. Iv. F3 50
Tabrīz, Iran C5 42
Tabūk, Sau. Ar. E3 38
Tabuleiro do Norte, Braz. . . .C4 74
Täby, Swe. G8 10
Tacloban, Phil. D9 34
Tacna, Peru G5 70
Tacoma, Wa., U.S. B3 140
Taconic Range, mts., U.S. . . .A1 114
Tacuarembó, Ur. E6 72
Tacurong, Phil. E8 34
Tademaït, Plateau du, plat.,
  Alg. E5 48
Tadjemout, Alg. A5 50
Tadoussac, P.Q., Can. A8 90
T'aebaek-sanmaek, mts.,
  Asia D13 28
Taegu, S. Kor. D13 28
Taejŏn, S. Kor. D13 28
Tafalla, Spain F6 16
Tafo, Ghana E4 50
Taft, Ca., U.S. E4 98
Taft, Tx., U.S. F4 136
Taganrog, Russia F15 20
Tagant, reg., Maur. C2 50
Tagaytay, Phil. D8 34
Tagbilaran, Phil. E8 34
Taguke, China E4 28
Tagum, Phil. E9 34
Tagus, stm., Eur. H2 16
Tahan, Gunong, mtn.,
  Malay. C2 36
Tahat, mtn., Alg. F6 48
Tahiataš, Uzb. B7 42
Tahifet, Alg. B6 50
Tahiti, i., Fr. Poly. F15 58
Tahlequah, Ok., U.S. B7 129
Tahoe, Lake, l., U.S. E1 121
Tahoe, Lake, l., U.S. D3 92
Tahoe City, Ca., U.S. C3 98
Tahoka, Tx., U.S. C2 136
Taholah, Wa., U.S. B1 140
Tahoua, Niger D6 50
Tahquamenon, stm., Mi.,
  U.S. B5 115
Tahsis, B.C., Can. E4 85
Tahtā, Egypt F10 14
Tahta-Bazar, Turk. C8 42
Tahtakupyr, Uzb. B8 42
Tahtsa Peak, mtn., B.C.,
  Can. C4 85
Tahulandang, Pulau, i.,
  Indon. C7 36
Tahuna, Indon. C7 36
Tai'an, China D11 28
Taibai Shan, mtn., China . . .C2 30
Taibus Qi, China A4 30
T'aichung, Tai. E5 30
Taigu, China B3 30
Taihang Shan, mts., China . .B3 30
Taihape, N.Z. o14 63c
Taihe, China D3 30
Tai Hu, l., China E11 28
Taihu, China C4 30
Taikang, China C4 30
Tailai, China B12 28
Tai Lake see Tai Hu, l.,
  China E11 28
Taimba, Russia C11 26
Tai'nan, Tai. E5 30
Taínaron, Ákra, c., Grc. F9 18
Tainaron, Cape see Taínaron,
  Ákra, c., Grc. F9 18
T'aipei, Tai. D5 30
Taiping, Malay. C2 36
Taisha, Japan C2 31
Taishan, China E3 30
Taishun, China F11 28
Taitao, Península de, pen.,
  Chile G1 69
T'aitung, Tai. E5 30
Taivalkoski, Fin. D13 10
Taiwan, ctry., Asia B8 34
Taiwan Strait, strt., Asia E4 28
Taiyuan, China D10 28

Taizhou, China C4 30
Ta'izz, Yemen H4 38
Tajikistan, ctry., Asia B2 40
Tāj Mahal, hist., India D3 40
Tajmyr, ozero, l., Russia . . .B12 26
Tajmyr, poluostrov, pen.,
  Russia B12 26
Tajo see Tagus, stm., Eur. . . .H5 16
Tajšet, Russia D11 26
Tak, Thai. C3 34
Takāb, Iran D12 44
Takalar, Indon. E5 36
Takamatsu, Japan E14 28
Takaoka, Japan C3 31
Takasaki, Japan C3 31
Takatsuki, Japan D3 31
Takêv, Camb. D4 34
Takhli, Thai. C4 34
Takikawa, Japan B4 31
Takla Lake, l., B.C., Can. B5 85
Taklimakan Shamo, des.,
  China D4 28
Takoma Park, Md., U.S. f8 113
Taku Glacier, ice, Ak., U.S. . .k22 95
Takum, Nig. E7 50
Takutea, i., Cook Is. F14 58
Talak, reg., Niger C6 50
Talara, Peru D3 70
Talas, Kyrg. E9 26
Talasea, Pap. N. Gui. H13 32
Talata Mafara, Nig. D6 50
Talaud, Kepulauan, is.,
  Indon. C7 36
Talavera de la Reina, Spain .H4 16
Talawdī, Sudan A6 54
Talbot, co., Ga., U.S. D2 103
Talbot, co., Md., U.S. C5 113
Talbot Island, i., Fl., U.S. . . .B5 102
Talbot Lake, l., Mb., Can. . . .B2 86
Talbotton, Ga., U.S. D2 103
Talca, Chile E2 69
Talcahuano, Chile E2 69
Taldykorgan, Kaz. E9 26
Talent, Or., U.S. E4 130
Talgar, Kaz. B11 42
Taliabu, Pulau, i., Indon. . . .D6 36
Taliaferro, co., Ga., U.S. C4 103
Talihina, Ok., U.S. C6 129
Talish Mountains see Ṭāvāleš,
  Kühhā-ye, mts., Asia D13 44
Taliwang, Indon. E5 36
Talkeetna, Ak., U.S. C10 95
Talkeetna Mountains, mts.,
  Ak., U.S. f17 95
Tall 'Afar, Iraq D10 44
Tallahassee, Fl., U.S. B2 102
Tallahatchie, stm., Ms., U.S. .B3 117
Tallahatchie, co., Ms., U.S. . .B3 117
Tallangatta, Austl. H4 62
Tallapoosa, co., Al., U.S. C4 94
Tallapoosa, Ga., U.S. C1 103
Tallapoosa, stm., U.S. C3 94
Tallassee, Al., U.S. C4 94
Talleyville, De., U.S. A3 101
Tallinn, Est. G11 10
Tall Kūjik, Syria D9 44
Tallmadge, Oh., U.S. A4 128
Tallulah, La., U.S. B4 111
Tal'ne, Ukr. E11 20
Talok, Indon. C5 36
Taloqān, Afg. C9 42
Taloyoak, N.T., Can. E21 82
Talquin, Lake, res., Fl., U.S. .B2 102
Talsi, Lat. H10 10
Taltal, Chile C2 69
Talu, Indon. C1 36
Taluk, Indon. D2 36
Tama, Ia., U.S. C5 108
Tama, co., Ia., U.S. B5 108
Tamale, Ghana E4 50
Tamalpais, Mount, mtn., Ca.,
  U.S. h7 98
Tamaqua, Pa., U.S. E10 131
Tamaroa, Il., U.S. E4 106
Tamaulipas, state, Mex. C5 78
Tamazulapan del Progreso,
  Mex. D5 78
Tamazunchale, Mex. C5 78
Tambacounda, Sen. D2 50
Tambej, Russia B9 26
Tambelan, Kepulauan, is.,
  Indon. C3 36
Tamberías, Arg. E4 72
Tambohorano, Madag. B7 56
Tambora, Gunung, vol.,
  Indon. E5 36
Tambov, Russia D6 26
Tamburá, Sudan I10 48
Tamchekket, Maur. C2 50
Tame, Col. B5 70
Tamel Aike, Arg. G2 69
Tamenghest, Alg. F6 48
Tamiahua, Mex. C5 78
Tamiahua, Laguna de, l.,
  Mex. C5 78
Tamiami Canal, Fl., U.S. G6 102
Tamil Nādu, state, India G3 40
Tam Ky, Viet. C5 34
Tampa, Fl., U.S. E4 102
Tampa Bay, b., Fl., U.S. E4 102
Tampere, Fin. F10 10
Tampico, Mex. C5 78
Tampico, Il., U.S. B4 106

Tam Quan, Viet. D5 34
Tamsagbulag, Mong. B11 28
Tamu, Mya. B2 34
Tamworth, Austl. G5 62
Tana (Teno), stm., Eur. B12 10
Tana, stm., Kenya D7 54
Tanabe, Japan D3 31
Tanafjorden, b., Nor. A13 10
Tanaga Island, i., Ak., U.S. . .E4 95
Tanahbala, Pulau, i., Indon. .D1 36
Tanahjampea, Pulau, i.,
  Indon. E5 36
Tanahmasa, Pulau, i., Indon. .D1 36
Tanahmerah, Indon. H11 32
Tanami Desert, des., Austl. . .D4 60
Tanana, Ak., U.S. B9 95
Tanana, stm., Ak., U.S. C10 95
Tananarive see Antananarivo,
  Madag. B8 56
Tanch'ŏn-ŭp, N. Kor. C13 28
Tandag, Phil. E9 34
Ţăndărei, Rom. G9 20
Tandil, Arg. F6 72
Tanega-shima, i., Japan E14 28
Taney, co., Mo., U.S. E4 118
Taneycomo, Lake, res., Mo.,
  U.S. E4 118
Tanezrouft, des., Afr. B4 50
Tanga, Tan. E7 54
Tanganyika see Tanzania,
  ctry., Afr. E6 54
Tanganyika, Lake, l., Afr. E5 54
Tanger, Mor. C3 48
Tanggula Shan, mts., China .E5 28
Tanghe, China C3 30
Tangier, Va., U.S. C7 139
Tangier Island, i., Va., U.S. . .C6 139
Tangier Sound, strt., Md.,
  U.S. D6 113
Tangipahoa, co., La., U.S. . . .D5 111
Tangipahoa, stm., La., U.S. . .D5 111
Tangmai, China C7 40
Tangra Yumco, l., China C5 40
Tangshan, China D11 28
Tangyin, China B3 30
Tanguyuan, China A1 31
Tanhoj, Russia A9 28
Tanimbar, Kepulauan, is.,
  Indon. E8 36
Tanjungbalai, Indon. C1 36
Tanjungpandan, Indon. D3 36
Tanjungpinang, Indon. C2 36
Tanjungredep, Indon. C5 36
Tānk, Pak. D10 42
Tanna, i., Vanuatu k9 62a
Tännäs, Swe. E5 10
Tanner, Al., U.S. A3 94
Tannu-Ola Mountains, mts.,
  Asia A6 28
Tanout, Niger C6 50
Tanta, Egypt D11 48
Tan-Tan, Mor. A2 50
Tantoyuca, Mex. C5 78
Tanzania, ctry., Afr. E6 54
Taormina, Italy F5 18
Taos, Mo., U.S. C5 118
Taos, N.M., U.S. A4 124
Taos, co., N.M., U.S. A4 124
Taos Pueblo, N.M., U.S. A4 124
Taoudenni, Mali B4 50
Taounate, Mor. E3 14
Taourirt, Mor. E3 14
Tapa, Est. G11 10
Tapachula, Mex. E6 78
Tapajós, stm., Braz. D8 70
Tapaktuan, Indon. C1 36
Taphan Hin, Thai. C4 34
Tāpi, stm., India E2 40
Tappahannock, Va., U.S. C6 139
Tappan, N.Y., U.S. g13 125
Tappan, Lake, res., N.J.,
  U.S. g9 123
Tappan Lake, res., Oh., U.S. .B4 128
Tapul Group, is., Phil. E8 34
Tapuruquara, Braz. D6 70
Taqäţu' Ḩayyā, Sudan G12 48
Taquari Novo, stm., Braz. . . .G8 70
Tar, stm., N.C., U.S. B5 126
Tara, On., Can. C3 89
Tara, Russia D9 26
Tarabuco, Bol. B5 72
Ţarābulus (Tripoli), Leb. E6 44
Ţarābulus (Tripoli), Libya . . .D7 48
Ţarābulus (Tripolitania), hist.
  reg., Libya E7 14
Tarakan, Indon. C5 36
Taranaki, Mount (Egmont,
  Mount), vol., N.Z. o13 63c
Tarancón, Spain G5 16
Taranto, Italy D6 18
Taranto, Golfo di, b., Italy . .D6 18
Taranto, Gulf of see Taranto,
  Golfo di, b., Italy D6 18
Tarapoto, Peru E4 70
Taraquá, Braz. C6 70
Tarara, Alg. A6 50
Tarata, Bol. B4 72
Taraúacá, Braz. E5 70
Tarawa, atoll, Kir. D11 58
Tarazona, Spain G6 16
Tarbagatay Range, mts.,
  Asia B4 28
Tarbes, Fr. F7 16
Tarboro, N.C., U.S. B5 126

Name	Map Ref.	Page
Tarbū, Libya	E8	48
Tarcoola, Austl.	G5	60
Tardoki-Jani, gora, mtn., Russia	B15	28
Taree, Austl.	G5	62
Tareja, Russia	B11	26
Tarentum, Pa., U.S.	E2	131
Tarfaya, Mor.	E2	48
Targhee Pass, U.S.	E7	105
Târgoviște, Blg.	C11	18
Târgoviște, Rom.	G8	20
Târgu Jiu, Rom.	G7	20
Târgu Mureș, Rom.	F8	20
Târgu-Neamț, Rom.	F9	20
Târgu Ocna, Rom.	F9	20
Tarifa, Spain	I4	16
Tariffville, Ct., U.S.	B4	100
Tarija, Bol.	C5	72
Tarim, stm., China	C4	28
Tarim Pendi, bas., China	D4	28
Tarin Kowt, Afg.	D9	42
Tarkastad, S. Afr.	E4	56
Tarkio, Mo., U.S.	A2	118
Tarko-Sale, Russia	C9	26
Tarkwa, Ghana	E4	50
Tarma, Peru	F4	70
Tarn, stm., Fr.	F7	16
Tärnaby, Swe.	D6	10
Târnăveni, Rom.	F8	20
Tarnobrzeg, Pol.	D6	20
Tarnów, Pol.	E6	20
Tarpey, Ca., U.S.	D4	98
Tarpon, Lake, l., Fl., U.S.	o10	102
Tarpon Springs, Fl., U.S.	D4	102
Tarquinia, Italy	C3	18
Tarragona, Spain	G7	16
Tarrant, Al., U.S.	B3	94
Tarrant, co., Tx., U.S.	C4	136
Tarryall Mountains, mts., Co., U.S.	B5	99
Tarrytown, N.Y., U.S.	D7	125
Tarsus, Tur.	D6	44
Tartagal, Arg.	C5	72
Tärtär, Azer.	B12	44
Tartu, Est.	G12	10
Tarutung, Indon.	C1	36
Tasāwah, Libya	A7	50
Tasbuget, Kaz.	B9	42
Taseko Mountain, mtn., B.C., Can.	D6	85
Ţashk, Daryācheh-ye, l., Iran	E6	42
Tashkent see Taškent, Uzb.	E8	26
Taškent, Uzb.	E8	26
Taškepri, Turk.	C8	42
Taşköprü, Tur.	B6	44
Tasman Basin	M18	64
Tasmania, state, Austl.	I4	62
Tasmania, i., Austl.	I3	62
Tasman Sea, Oc.	L18	64
Taşova, Tur.	B7	44
Tasso, Tn., U.S.	D9	135
Taštagol, Russia	D10	26
Tata, Hung.	F5	20
Tatarbunary, Ukr.	G10	20
Tatarija, state, Russia	D6	26
Tatarsk, Russia	D9	26
Tatarskij proliv, strt., Russia	E16	26
Tatarstan see Tatarija, state, Russia	D6	26
Tatar Strait see Tatarskij proliv, strt., Russia	E16	26
Tate, Ga., U.S.	B2	103
Tate, co., Ms., U.S.	A4	117
Tateville, Ky., U.S.	D5	110
Tatnam, Cape, c., Mb., Can.	f9	86
Tatta, Pak.	F9	42
Tattnall, co., Ga., U.S.	D4	103
Tatum, N.M., U.S.	D6	124
Tatvan, Tur.	C10	44
Tauá, Braz.	C3	74
Taučik, Kaz.	B6	42
Taujskaja guba, b., Russia	D17	26
Taum Sauk Mountain, mtn., Mo., U.S.	D6	118
Taunggyi, Mya.	B3	34
Taungup, Mya.	C2	34
Taunton, Eng., U.K.	E5	12
Taunton, stm., Ma., U.S.	C5	114
Taunton, Ma., U.S.	C5	114
Taupo, N.Z.	o14	63c
Taupo, Lake, l., N.Z.	o14	63c
Tauranga, N.Z.	o14	63c
Taureau, Réservoir, res., P.Q., Can.	C4	90
Taurus Mountains see Toros Dağları, mts., Tur.	D5	44
Ţavālesh, Kūhhā-ye, mts., Asia	D13	44
Tavares, Fl., U.S.	D5	102
Tavas, Tur.	D3	44
Tavda, Russia	D8	26
Tavda, stm., Russia	D8	26
Tavernier, Fl., U.S.	G6	102
Taveuni, i., Fiji	m11	63b
Tavşanlı, Tur.	C3	44
Tawakoni, Lake, res., Tx., U.S.	C4	136
Tawas City, Mi., U.S.	D7	115
Tawas Lake, l., Mi., U.S.	D7	115
Tawau, Malay.	C5	36
Tawitawi Group, is., Phil.	E8	34
Ţawkar, Sudan	G12	48
Ţāwūq, Iraq	E11	44
Taxco de Alarcón, Mex.	D5	78
Taxkorgan Tajik Zizhixian, China	B3	40
Taylor, B.C., Can.	A7	85
Taylor, Ar., U.S.	D2	97
Taylor, Az., U.S.	C5	96
Taylor, stm., Co., U.S.	C4	99
Taylor, co., Fl., U.S.	B3	102
Taylor, co., Ga., U.S.	D2	103
Taylor, co., Ia., U.S.	D3	108
Taylor, co., Ky., U.S.	C4	110
Taylor, Mi., U.S.	p15	115
Taylor, Pa., U.S.	D10	131
Taylor, Tx., U.S.	D4	136
Taylor, co., Tx., U.S.	C3	136
Taylor, co., Wi., U.S.	C3	142
Taylor, co., W.V., U.S.	B4	141
Taylor, Mount, mtn., N.M., U.S.	B2	124
Taylor Mill, Ky., U.S.	k14	110
Taylor Mountain, mtn., Id., U.S.	E4	105
Taylor Park Reservoir, res., Co., U.S.	C4	99
Taylors, S.C., U.S.	B3	133
Taylors Falls, Mn., U.S.	E6	116
Taylors Island, i., Md., U.S.	D5	113
Taylorsville, In., U.S.	F6	107
Taylorsville, Ky., U.S.	B4	110
Taylorsville, Ms., U.S.	D4	117
Taylorsville, N.C., U.S.	B1	126
Taylorville, Il., U.S.	D4	106
Taymā', Sau. Ar.	E3	38
Taymyr Peninsula see Tajmyr, poluostrov, pen., Russia	B12	26
Tay Ninh, Viet.	D5	34
Taytay, Phil.	D7	34
Taz, stm., Russia	D9	26
Taza, Mor.	E3	14
Tazewell, co., Il., U.S.	C4	106
Tazewell, Tn., U.S.	C10	135
Tazewell, Va., U.S.	e10	139
Tazewell, co., Va., U.S.	e10	139
Tazovskij, Russia	C9	26
Tbessa, Alg.	C6	48
Tbilisi, Geor.	B11	44
Tchaourou, Benin	E5	50
Tchefuncta, stm., La., U.S.	D5	111
Tchibanga, Gabon	D2	54
Tchula, Ms., U.S.	B3	117
Tczew, Pol.	B5	20
Tea, S.D., U.S.	D9	134
Teague, Tx., U.S.	D4	136
Teakean Butte, mtn., Id., U.S.	C2	105
Teaneck, N.J., U.S.	h8	123
Teapa, Mex.	D6	78
Teaticket, Ma., U.S.	C6	114
Te Awamutu, N.Z.	o14	63c
Tebingtinggi, Indon.	C1	36
Tebingtinggi, Pulau, i., Indon.	C2	36
Téboursouk, Tun.	F2	18
Techlé, W. Sah.	B2	50
Tecka, Arg.	F2	69
Tecomán, Mex.	D4	78
Tecpan de Galeana, Mex.	D4	78
Tecuala, Mex.	C3	78
Tecuci, Rom.	G9	20
Tecumseh, On., Can.	E2	89
Tecumseh, Ks., U.S.	k14	109
Tecumseh, Mi., U.S.	G7	115
Tecumseh, Ne., U.S.	D9	120
Tecumseh, Ok., U.S.	B5	129
Tedžen, Turk.	F8	26
Teeli, Russia	D10	26
Teeswater, On., Can.	C3	89
Tefé, Braz.	D7	70
Tégama, reg., Niger	C6	50
Tegal, Indon.	E3	36
Tegucigalpa, Hond.	C2	80
Tehachapi, Ca., U.S.	E4	98
Tehachapi Mountains, mts., Ca., U.S.	E4	98
Tehama, co., Ca., U.S.	B2	98
Tehrān, Iran	C6	42
Tehuacán, Mex.	D5	78
Tehuantepec, Golfo de, b., Mex.	D6	78
Tehuantepec, Istmo de, isth., Mex.	I13	78
Teide, Pico del, mtn., Spain	A1	50
Teixeira Pinto, Gui.-B.	D1	50
Tejo see Tagus, stm., Eur.	H3	16
Tekamah, Ne., U.S.	C9	120
Tekax, Mex.	C7	78
Tekeli, Kaz.	E9	26
Tekes, China	A4	40
Tekirdağ, Tur.	B2	44
Tekoa, Wa., U.S.	B8	140
Tekonsha, Mi., U.S.	F5	115
Telavi, Geor.	B11	44
Tel Aviv-Yafo, Isr.	D2	42
Teleckoe, ozero, l., Russia	A5	28
Telêmaco Borba, Braz.	C7	72
Telemark, state, Nor.	G3	10
Telén, Arg.	F4	72
Telescope Peak, mtn., Ca., U.S.	D5	98
Telfair, co., Ga., U.S.	E4	103
Telford, Eng., U.K.	I5	12
Telford, Pa., U.S.	F11	131
Télimélé, Gui.	D2	50
Telkwa, B.C., Can.	B4	85
Tell City, In., U.S.	I4	107
Teller, co., Co., U.S.	C5	99
Tellicherry, India	G3	40
Tellico Plains, Tn., U.S.	D9	135
Telluride, Co., U.S.	D3	99
Telos Lake, l., Me., U.S.	B3	112
Telsen, Arg.	F3	69
Telukbatang, Indon.	D3	36
Teluk Intan, Malay.	C2	36
Tema, Ghana	E5	50
Temax, Mex.	C7	78
Tembilahan, Indon.	D2	36
Temecula, Ca., U.S.	F5	98
Teminaabuan, Indon.	D8	36
Temir, Kaz.	E10	22
Temirtau, Kaz.	E9	26
Témiscouata, Lac, l., P.Q., Can.	B9	90
Te-Moak Indian Reservation, Nv., U.S.	C6	121
Temora, Austl.	G4	62
Temosachic, Mex.	B3	78
Tempe, Az., U.S.	D4	96
Temperance, Mi., U.S.	G7	115
Temperance, stm., Mn., U.S.	C8	116
Temple, Ga., U.S.	C1	103
Temple, Ok., U.S.	C3	129
Temple, Pa., U.S.	F10	131
Temple, Tx., U.S.	D4	136
Temple Terrace, Fl., U.S.	o11	102
Temrjuk, Russia	G14	20
Temuco, Chile	E2	69
Tenafly, N.J., U.S.	B5	123
Tenaha, Tx., U.S.	D5	136
Tena Kourou, mtn., Burkina	D4	50
Tenāli, India	F4	40
Tenasserim, Mya.	D3	34
Tendaho, Eth.	H13	48
Ten Degree Channel, strt., India	H6	40
Ténéré, des., Niger	C6	50
Tenerife, i., Spain	A1	50
Tengchong, China	G7	28
Tenggara, Nusa (Lesser Sunda Islands), is., Indon.	E5	36
Tengiz, ozero, l., Kaz.	D8	26
Tengréla, C. Iv.	D3	50
Tengxian, China	E3	30
Tengxian, China	B4	30
Tenino, Wa., U.S.	C3	140
Tenke, D.R.C.	F5	54
Tenkeli, Russia	C16	26
Tenkiller Ferry Lake, res., Ok., U.S.	B6	129
Tenkodogo, Burkina	D4	50
Tenmile, stm., B.C.	B5	132
Tenmile Creek, stm., W.V., U.S.	k10	141
Tennant Creek, Austl.	D5	60
Tennessee, state, U.S.	B5	135
Tennessee Pass, Co., U.S.	B4	99
Tennessee Ridge, Tn., U.S.	A4	135
Tennille, Ga., U.S.	D4	103
Teno (Tana), stm., Eur.	B12	10
Tenosique, Mex.	D6	78
Tensas, co., La., U.S.	B4	111
Tensas, stm., La., U.S.	B4	111
Tensaw, stm., Al., U.S.	E2	94
Ten Sleep, Wy., U.S.	B5	143
Tenterfield, Austl.	F5	62
Ten Thousand Islands, is., Fl., U.S.	G5	102
Teófilo Otoni, Braz.	E3	74
Tepa, Indon.	E7	36
Tepehuanes, Mex.	B3	78
Tepic, Mex.	C4	78
Téra, Niger	D5	50
Teramo, Italy	C4	18
Terceira, i., Port.	F6	14
Terebovla, Ukr.	E8	20
Terek, Russia	A11	44
Terek, stm., Russia	B5	42
Teresina, Braz.	C3	74
Tergüün Bogd uul, mtn., Mong.	C8	28
Termas de Río Hondo, Arg.	D5	72
Terme, Tur.	B7	44
Termez, Uzb.	C9	42
Términos, Laguna de, b., Mex.	D6	78
Ternej, Russia	A3	31
Terneuzen, Neth.	E8	12
Terni, Italy	C4	18
Ternopil', Ukr.	E8	20
Terpenija, mys, c., Russia	E16	26
Terra Alta, W.V., U.S.	B5	141
Terrace, B.C., Can.	B3	85
Terracina, Italy	D1	18
Terra Nova National Park, Nf., Can.	D4	88
Terrassa, Spain	G8	16
Terrebonne, P.Q., Can.	D4	90
Terrebonne, co., La., U.S.	E5	111
Terrebonne, Or., U.S.	C5	130
Terrebonne Bay, b., La., U.S.	E5	111
Terre Haute, In., U.S.	F3	107
Terre Hill, Pa., U.S.	F9	131
Terrell, co., Ga., U.S.	E2	103
Terrell, Tx., U.S.	C4	136
Terrell, co., Tx., U.S.	D1	136
Terrell Hills, Tx., U.S.	k7	136
Terrenceville, Nf., Can.	E4	88
Terry, Ms., U.S.	C3	117
Terry, Mt., U.S.	D11	119
Terry, co., Tx., U.S.	C1	136
Terrytown, Ne., U.S.	C2	120
Terryville, Ct., U.S.	C3	100
Teruel, Spain	G6	16
Teseney, Erit.	G12	48
Teshekpuk Lake, l., Ak., U.S.	A9	95
Teshio, Japan	B4	31
Tessalit, Mali	B5	50
Tessaoua, Niger	D6	50
Tesuque, N.M., U.S.	B4	124
Tete, Moz.	B5	56
Teteriv, stm., Ukr.	D10	20
Teton, co., Id., U.S.	F7	105
Teton, stm., Mt., U.S.	B5	119
Teton, co., Mt., U.S.	C4	119
Teton, co., Wy., U.S.	C2	143
Teton Pass, Wy., U.S.	C2	143
Teton Range, mts., Wy., U.S.	C2	143
Teton Village, Wy., U.S.	C2	143
Tetouan, Mor.	C3	48
Tetovo, Mac.	C8	18
Teulon, Mb., Can.	D3	86
Teutopolis, Il., U.S.	D5	106
Tevere, stm., Italy	C4	18
Teverya, Isr.	D3	42
Tewksbury, Ma., U.S.	A5	114
Texada Island, i., B.C., Can.	E5	85
Texarkana, Ar., U.S.	D1	97
Texarkana, Tx., U.S.	C5	136
Texas, co., Mo., U.S.	D5	118
Texas, co., Ok., U.S.	e9	129
Texas, state, U.S.	D3	136
Texas City, Tx., U.S.	E5	136
Texhoma, Ok., U.S.	e9	129
Texico, N.M., U.S.	C6	124
Texoma, Lake, res., U.S.	D5	129
Texel, i., Neth.	D9	12
Tezpur, India	D6	40
Teziutlán, Mex.	D5	78
Thabana-Ntlenyana, mtn., Leso.	D4	56
Thabazimbi, S. Afr.	C4	56
Thai Binh, Viet.	B5	34
Thailand, ctry., Asia	C4	34
Thailand, Gulf of, b., Asia	D4	34
Thai Nguyen, Viet.	B5	34
Thames, stm., On., Can.	E3	89
Thames, N.Z.	o14	63c
Thames, stm., Eng., U.K.	E7	12
Thames, stm., Ct., U.S.	D7	100
Thamesville, On., Can.	E3	89
Thāna, India	F2	40
Thanh Hoa, Viet.	C5	34
Thanh Pho Ho Chi Minh (Saigon), Viet.	D5	34
Thanjāvūr, India	G3	40
Tharād, India	E2	40
Thar Desert (Great Indian Desert), des., Asia	D2	40
Tharrawaddy, Mya.	C3	34
Tharros, hist., Italy	E2	18
Tharthār, Buḩayrat ath-, res., Iraq	E10	44
Thásos, i., Grc.	D10	18
Thásos, Grc.	D10	18
Thatcher, Az., U.S.	E6	96
Thaton, Mya.	C3	34
Thayer, Mo., U.S.	E6	118
Thayer, co., Ne., U.S.	D8	120
Thayetmyo, Mya.	C3	34
Thazi, Mya.	B3	34
Thealka, Ky., U.S.	C7	110
Thebes see Thívai, Grc.	E9	18
The Dalles, Or., U.S.	B5	130
The Dells, val., Wi., U.S.	E4	142
Thedford, On., Can.	D3	89
The Everglades, sw., Fl., U.S.	G6	102
The Flat Tops, mts., Co., U.S.	B3	99
The Flume, wtfl., N.H., U.S.	B3	122
The Graves, is., Ma., U.S.	g12	114
The Hague see 's-Gravenhage, Neth.	D8	12
The Heads, c., Or., U.S.	E2	130
The Little Minch see Little Minch, The, strt., Scot., U.K.	B3	12
The Minch, strt., Scot., U.K.	A4	12
The Narrows, strt., Wa., U.S.	f10	140
Theodore, Al., U.S.	E1	94
Theodore Roosevelt Lake, res., Az., U.S.	D4	96
Theodore Roosevelt National Park (South Unit), N.D., U.S.	C2	127
Theodore Roosevelt National Park (North Unit), N.D., U.S.	B2	127
The Pas, Mb., Can.	C1	86
The Plains, Oh., U.S.	C3	128
Theresa, Wi., U.S.	E5	142
Thermaïkós Kólpos, b., Grc.	D9	18
Thermopílai, hist., Grc.	E9	18
Thermopolis, Wy., U.S.	C4	143
Thermopylae see Thermopílai, hist., Grc.	E9	18
The Rockies, mts., Wa., U.S.	C3	140
Thessalía, hist. reg., Grc.	E9	18
Thessalon, On., Can.	p19	89
Thessaloníki (Salonika), Grc.	D9	18
Thessaly see Thessalía, hist. reg., Grc.	E9	18
Thetford Mines, P.Q., Can.	C6	90
The Thimbles, is., Ct., U.S.	E5	100
The Valley, Anguilla	B7	80
The Village, Ok., U.S.	B4	129
The Wash, b., Eng., U.K.	D7	12
Thibodaux, La., U.S.	E5	111
Thief, stm., Mn., U.S.	B2	116
Thief Lake, l., Mn., U.S.	B3	116
Thief River Falls, Mn., U.S.	B2	116
Thielsen, Mount, mtn., Or., U.S.	D4	130
Thiensville, Wi., U.S.	E6	142
Thiès, Sen.	D1	50
Thika, Kenya	D7	54
Thimphu, Bhu.	D6	40
Thingvellir, Ice.	l18	10a
Thio, N. Cal.	l9	62a
Thionville, Fr.	C10	16
Thíra, i., Grc.	F10	18
Third Cataract, wtfl., Sudan	G11	48
Third Lake, l., N.H., U.S.	f7	122
Thiruvananthapuram (Trivandrum), India	H3	40
Thisted, Den.	H3	10
Thistilfjörður, b., Ice.	k21	10a
Thívai, Grc.	E9	18
Thjórsá, stm., Ice.	m18	10a
Thomas, co., Ga., U.S.	F3	103
Thomas, co., Ks., U.S.	C2	109
Thomas, co., Ne., U.S.	C5	120
Thomas, Ok., U.S.	B3	129
Thomasboro, Il., U.S.	C5	106
Thomaston, Ct., U.S.	C3	100
Thomaston, Ga., U.S.	D2	103
Thomaston, Me., U.S.	D3	112
Thomaston Reservoir, res., Ct., U.S.	C3	100
Thomasville, Al., U.S.	D2	94
Thomasville, Ga., U.S.	F3	103
Thomasville, N.C., U.S.	B2	126
Thompson, Mb., Can.	B3	86
Thompson, Ct., U.S.	B8	100
Thompson, N.D., U.S.	B8	127
Thompson, stm., U.S.	A4	118
Thompson Falls, Mt., U.S.	C1	119
Thompson Island, i., Ma., U.S.	g11	114
Thompson Lake, l., U.S.	D2	112
Thompson Peak, mtn., Ca., U.S.	B2	98
Thompson Peak, mtn., N.M., U.S.	h9	124
Thompson Reservoir, res., Or., U.S.	E5	130
Thomson, Ga., U.S.	C4	103
Thongwa, Mya.	C3	34
Thonon-les-Bains, Fr.	D10	16
Thonotosassa, Fl., U.S.	D4	102
Thonze, Mya.	C3	34
Thorburn, N.S., Can.	D7	87
Thoreau, N.M., U.S.	B1	124
Thornbury, On., Can.	C4	89
Thorndale, Tx., U.S.	D4	136
Thornton, Co., U.S.	C5	99
Thorntown, In., U.S.	D4	107
Thorold, On., Can.	D5	89
Thorp, Wi., U.S.	D3	142
Thorsby, Al., U.S.	C3	94
Thorshavn see Tórshavn, Far. Is.	n23	10b
Thórshöfn, Ice.	k21	10a
Thouars, Fr.	D6	16
Thousand Islands, is., N.Y., U.S.	A4	125
Thousand Lake Mountain, mtn., Ut., U.S.	E4	137
Thousand Springs Creek, stm., U.S.	B7	121
Thrace, hist. reg., Eur.	D11	18
Thrakikón Pélagos, Grc.	D10	18
Three Fingered Jack, mtn., Or., U.S.	C5	130
Three Forks, Mt., U.S.	E5	119
Three Hills, Ab., Can.	D4	84
Three Hummock Island, i., Austl.	I4	62
Three Kings Islands, is., N.Z.	n13	63c
Three Lakes, Wi., U.S.	C4	142
Three Mile Plains, N.S., Can.	E5	87
Three Oaks, Mi., U.S.	G4	115
Three Pagodas Pass, Asia	C3	34
Three Points, Cape, c., Ghana	F4	50
Three Rivers, Ma., U.S.	B3	114
Three Rivers, Mi., U.S.	G5	115
Three Rivers, Tx., U.S.	E3	136
Three Sisters, mtn., Or., U.S.	C5	130
Three Springs, Austl.	F2	60
Throckmorton, co., Tx., U.S.	C3	136
Throop, Pa., U.S.	m18	131
Thule (Qaanaaq), Grnld.	C26	82
Thun	A1	14
Thunder Bay, On., Can.	o17	89

Name	Map Ref.	Page
Thunder Bay, stm., Mi., U.S.	D6	115
Thunder Bay, b., Mi., U.S.	D7	115
Thunderbird, Lake, res., Ok., U.S.	B4	129
Thunderbolt, Ga., U.S.	D5	103
Thunder Butte Creek, stm., S.D., U.S.	B3	134
Thurmont, Md., U.S.	A3	113
Thurso, P.Q., Can.	D2	90
Thurso, Scot., U.K.	A5	12
Thurston, co., Ne., U.S.	B9	120
Thurston, co., Wa., U.S.	C2	140
Thy, reg., Den.	H3	10
Thyolo, Mwi.	B6	56
Tianchang, China	C4	30
Tiandong, China	E2	30
Tianguá, Braz.	B3	74
Tianjin, China	D11	28
Tianjun, China	D7	28
Tianlin, China	E2	30
Tianmen, China	E10	28
Tianshui, China	E9	28
Tiantai, China	F12	28
Tianyang, China	E2	30
Tianzhu, China	D8	28
Tiassalé, C. Iv.	E4	50
Tibasti, Sarīr, des., Libya	B8	50
Tibati, Cam.	B2	54
Tiber see Tevere, stm., Italy	C4	18
Tiberias see Teverya, Isr.	D3	42
Tibesti, mts., Afr.	B8	50
Tibet see Xizang Zizhiqu, prov., China	E5	28
Tibet, Plateau of see Qing Zang Gaoyuan, plat., China	E4	28
Tiburón, Isla, i., Mex.	B2	78
Tice, Fl., U.S.	F5	102
Tichît, Maur.	C3	50
Tickfaw, stm., La., U.S.	C5	111
Ticonderoga, N.Y., U.S.	B7	125
Ticul, Mex.	C7	78
Tidaholm, Swe.	G5	10
Tide Head, N.B., Can.	B3	87
Tidjikja, Maur.	C2	50
Tiébissou, C. Iv.	E3	50
Tieli, China	A1	31
Tieling, China	C12	28
Tien Shan, mts., Asia	C3	28
Tientsin see Tianjin, China	D11	28
Tierp, Swe.	F7	10
Tierra Amarilla, N.M., U.S.	A3	124
Tierra Blanca, Mex.	D5	78
Tierra de Campos, reg., Spain	F4	16
Tierra del Fuego, i., S.A.	H3	69
Tietê, stm., Braz.	F1	74
Tieton, Wa., U.S.	C5	140
Tieton, stm., Wa., U.S.	C4	140
Tieton Dam, Wa., U.S.	C4	140
Tiffany Mountain, mtn., Wa., U.S.	A6	140
Tiffin, Oh., U.S.	A2	128
Tiffin, stm., Oh., U.S.	A1	128
Tift, co., Ga., U.S.	E3	103
Tifton, Ga., U.S.	E3	103
Tigard, Or., U.S.	h12	130
Tigerton, Wi., U.S.	D4	142
Tighina, Mol.	F10	20
Tigil', Russia	D17	26
Tignall, Ga., U.S.	C4	103
Tignish, P.E., Can.	C5	87
Tigris (Dicle) (Dijlah), stm., Asia	D5	42
Tiguentourine, Alg.	F5	14
Tihert, Alg.	D4	14
Tihoreck, Russia	E6	26
Tihvin, Russia	C5	22
Tijuana, Mex.	A1	78
Tikal, hist., Guat.	B2	80
Tikamgarh, India	E3	40
Tikrit, Iraq	D4	42
Tikšeozero, ozero, l., Russia	C15	10
Tiksi, Russia	B14	26
Tilburg, Neth.	E9	12
Tilbury, On., Can.	E2	89
Tilden, Il., U.S.	E4	106
Tilden, Ne., U.S.	B8	120
Tilghman, Md., U.S.	C5	113
Tilghman Island, i., Md., U.S.	C5	113
Tilimsen, Alg.	D4	48
Tillabéri, Niger	D5	50
Tillamook, Or., U.S.	B3	130
Tillamook, co., Or., U.S.	B3	130
Tillanchãng Dwïp, i., India	H6	40
Tillery, Lake, res., N.C., U.S.	B2	126
Tillman, co., Ok., U.S.	C2	129
Tillmans Corner, Al., U.S.	E1	94
Tillsonburg, On., Can.	E4	89
Tílos, i., Grc.	F11	18
Tilton, Il., U.S.	C6	106
Tilton, N.H., U.S.	D3	122
Tiltonsville, Oh., U.S.	B5	128
Timanskij krjaž, Russia	C7	26
Timaru, N.Z.	p13	63c
Timaševsk, Russia	G15	20
Timbalier Island, i., La., U.S.	E5	111
Timbaúba, Braz.	C4	74
Timbedgha, Maur.	C3	50
Timberlake, Va., U.S.	C3	139
Timberville, Va., U.S.	B4	139
Timbuktu see Tombouctou, Mali	C4	50
Timimoun, Alg.	E5	48
Timirist, Râs, c., Maur.	C1	50

Name	Map Ref.	Page
Timişoara, Rom.	G6	20
Timmins, On., Can.	o19	89
Timmonsville, S.C., U.S.	C8	133
Timms Hill, Wi., U.S.	C3	142
Timon, Braz.	C3	74
Timor, i., Asia	E7	36
Timor Sea	F6	58
Timošino, Russia	B6	22
Timpanogos Cave National Monument, Ut., U.S.	C4	137
Timšer, Russia	B9	22
Tims Ford Lake, res., Tn., U.S.	B5	135
Tinaca Point, c., Phil.	E9	34
Tinaquillo, Ven.	C6	80
Tindouf, Alg.	E3	48
Tinghert, Ḥamâdat, plat., Afr.	E7	48
Tingmerkpuk Mountain, mtn., Ak., U.S.	B7	95
Tingo María, Peru	E4	70
Tingsryd, Swe.	H6	10
Tinian, i., N. Mar. Is.	D12	32
Tinker Air Force Base, mil., Ok., U.S.	B4	129
Tinley Park, Il., U.S.	k9	106
Tinniswood, Mount, mtn., B.C., Can.	D6	85
Tinogasta, Arg.	D4	72
Tínos, i., Grc.	F10	18
Tinsukia, India	D7	40
Tintina, Arg.	D5	72
Tinton Falls, N.J., U.S.	C4	123
Tioga, La., U.S.	C3	111
Tioga, N.D., U.S.	A3	127
Tioga, co., N.Y., U.S.	C4	125
Tioga, stm., Pa., U.S.	B7	131
Tioga, co., Pa., U.S.	C7	131
Tiogue Lake, res., R.I., U.S.	D3	132
Tioman, Pulau, i., Malay.	C2	36
Tionesta Creek, stm., Pa., U.S.	C3	131
Tionesta Lake, res., Pa., U.S.	D3	131
Tioughnioga, stm., N.Y., U.S.	C4	125
Tipitapa, Nic.	C2	80
Tippah, co., Ms., U.S.	A5	117
Tippah, stm., Ms., U.S.	A4	117
Tipp City, Oh., U.S.	C1	128
Tippecanoe, stm., In., U.S.	C4	107
Tippecanoe, co., In., U.S.	D4	107
Tipperary, Austl.	C5	60
Tipton, Ca., U.S.	D4	98
Tipton, Ia., U.S.	C6	108
Tipton, In., U.S.	D5	107
Tipton, co., In., U.S.	D5	107
Tipton, Mo., U.S.	C5	118
Tipton, Ok., U.S.	C2	129
Tipton, co., Tn., U.S.	B2	135
Tipton, Mount, mtn., Az., U.S.	B1	96
Tiptonville, Tn., U.S.	A2	135
Tirana see Tiranë, Alb.	D7	18
Tiranë, Alb.	D7	18
Tiraspol, Mol.	F10	20
Tire, Tur.	C2	44
Tirebolu, Tur.	B8	44
Tiree, i., Scot., U.K.	B3	12
Tírnavos, Grc.	E9	18
Tiruchchirāppalli, India	G3	40
Tirunelveli, India	H3	40
Tirupati, India	G3	40
Tiruppur, India	G3	40
Tiruvannāmalai, India	G3	40
Tirūvottiyūr, India	G4	40
Tisa (Tisza) (Tysa), stm., Eur.	G6	20
Tishomingo, co., Ms., U.S.	A5	117
Tishomingo, Ok., U.S.	C5	129
Tiskilwa, Il., U.S.	B4	106
Tissemsilt, Alg.	J7	16
Tista, stm., Asia	A1	34
Tisza (Tisa) (Tysa), stm., Eur.	F6	20
Titicaca, Lago, l., S.A.	E4	68
Titilãgarh, India	E4	40
Titograd see Podgorica, Yugo.	G7	18
Titonka, Ia., U.S.	A3	108
Titov Veles, Mac.	D8	18
Titran, Nor.	E3	10
Titule, D.R.C.	C5	54
Titus, co., Tx., U.S.	C5	136
Titusville, Fl., U.S.	D6	102
Titusville, Pa., U.S.	C2	131
Tivaouane, Sen.	C1	50
Tiverton, On., Can.	C3	89
Tiverton, R.I., U.S.	D6	132
Tizimín, Mex.	C7	78
Tizi-Ouzou, Alg.	C5	48
Tjeggelvas, l., Swe.	C7	10
Tjukalinsk, Russia	D9	26
Tjul'gan, Russia	D10	22
Tjumen', Russia	D8	26
Tkibuli, Geor.	A10	44
Tkvarčeli, Geor.	A9	44
Tlahualilo de Zaragoza, Mex.	B4	78
Tlalnepantla, Mex.	D5	78
Tlaquepaque, Mex.	C4	78
Tlaxcala, state, Mex.	D5	78
Tlaxcala de Xicohténcatl, Mex.	D5	78
Tmassah, Libya	A8	50
Toamasina, Madag.	B8	56
Toano, Va., U.S.	C6	139

Name	Map Ref.	Page
Toano Range, mts., Nv., U.S.	C7	121
Toast, N.C., U.S.	A2	126
Toba, Danau, l., Indon.	C1	36
Tobacco Root Mountains, mts., Mt., U.S.	E5	119
Tobago, i., Trin.	C7	80
Toba Inlet, b., B.C., Can.	D5	85
Toba Kākar Range, mts., Pak.	D9	42
Tobejuba, Isla, i., Ven.	D7	80
Tobin, Mount, mtn., Nv., U.S.	C4	121
Tobin Lake, l., Sk., Can.	D4	91
Tobin Range, mts., Nv., U.S.	C4	121
Tobique, stm., N.B., Can.	B2	87
Tobol, stm., Asia	D8	26
Tobol, Kaz.	D11	22
Tobol'sk, Russia	D8	26
Tobyhanna, Pa., U.S.	D11	131
Tocantínia, Braz.	E10	70
Tocantinópolis, Braz.	C2	74
Tocantins, state, Braz.	D2	74
Tocantins, stm., Braz.	B2	74
Toccoa, Ga., U.S.	B3	103
Toccoa, stm., Ga., U.S.	B2	103
Toccoa Falls, Ga., U.S.	B3	103
Tocopilla, Chile	B2	69
Todd, co., Ky., U.S.	D2	110
Todd, co., Mn., U.S.	D4	116
Todd, co., S.D., U.S.	D5	134
Tofield, Ab., U.S.	C4	84
Tofino, B.C., Can.	E5	85
Togiak, Ak., U.S.	D7	95
Togian, Kepulauan, is., Indon.	D6	36
Togo, ctry., Afr.	E5	50
Togtoh, China	A3	30
Togwotee Pass, Wy., U.S.	C2	143
Tohakum Peak, mtn., Nv., U.S.	C2	121
Tohatchi, N.M., U.S.	B1	124
Tohopekaliga, Lake, l., Fl., U.S.	D5	102
Toiyabe Range, mts., Nv., U.S.	D4	121
Tok, Ak., U.S.	C11	95
Tokelau, dep., Oc.	E12	58
Tokat, Tur.	B7	44
Tokmak, Kyrg.	A3	40
Tokmak, Ukr.	F13	20
Tokoroa, N.Z.	o14	63c
Toktogul, Kyrg.	A2	40
Tokuno-shima, i., Japan	A9	34
Tokushima, Japan	D2	31
Tōkyō, Japan	D16	28
Tôlañaro, Madag.	D8	56
Toledo, Braz.	C7	72
Toledo, Spain	H4	16
Toledo, Ia., U.S.	B5	108
Toledo, Il., U.S.	D5	106
Toledo, Oh., U.S.	A2	128
Toledo, Or., U.S.	C3	130
Toledo Bend Reservoir, res., U.S.	C2	111
Toledo Bend Reservoir, res., U.S.	E9	92
Toler, Ky., U.S.	C7	110
Toliara, Madag.	C7	56
Tolima, Nevado del, vol., Col.	C4	70
Tolitoli, Indon.	C6	36
Toljatti, Russia	D6	26
Tol'ka, Russia	C10	26
Tolland, co., Ct., U.S.	B6	100
Tolland, Ct., U.S.	B6	100
Tollesboro, Ky., U.S.	B6	110
Tolleson, Az., U.S.	m8	96
Tolmezzo, Italy	A4	18
Tolo, D.R.C.	D3	54
Tolo, Gulf of see Tolo, Teluk, b., Indon.	D6	36
Tolo, Teluk, b., Indon.	D6	36
Tolono, Il., U.S.	D5	106
Tolstoj, mys, c., Russia	D17	26
Tolt Reservoir, res., Wa., U.S.	B4	140
Tolú, Col.	D4	80
Toluca, Il., U.S.	C4	106
Toluca de Lerdo, Mex.	D5	78
Tomah, Wi., U.S.	E3	142
Tomahawk, Wi., U.S.	C4	142
Tomahawk Lake, l., Wi., U.S.	C4	142
Tomakomai, Japan	C16	28
Tomaszów Lubelski, Pol.	D7	20
Tomaszów Mazowiecki, Pol.	D6	20
Tomball, Tx., U.S.	D5	136
Tombe, Sudan	B6	54
Tombigbee, stm., U.S.	D1	94
Tombouctou, Mali	C4	50
Tombstone, Az., U.S.	F5	96
Tombua, Ang.	B1	56
Tomé, Chile	F3	72
Tomé-Açu, Braz.	B2	74
Tomelloso, Spain	H5	16
Tom Green, co., Tx., U.S.	D2	136
Tomini, Indon.	C6	36
Tomini, Gulf of see Tomini, Teluk, b., Indon.	D6	36
Tomini, Teluk, b., Indon.	D6	36
Tom Nevers Head, c., Ma., U.S.	D8	114

Name	Map Ref.	Page
Tomo, stm., Col.	B6	70
Tompkins, co., N.Y., U.S.	C4	125
Tompkinsville, Ky., U.S.	D4	110
Tom Price, Austl.	E2	60
Tomptokan, Russia	D15	26
Toms, stm., N.J., U.S.	C4	123
Toms River, N.J., U.S.	C4	123
Tomsk, Russia	D10	26
Tonalá, Mex.	D6	78
Tonasket, Wa., U.S.	A6	140
Tonawanda Indian Reservation, N.Y., U.S.	B2	125
Tondano, Indon.	C6	36
Tonekābon, Iran	C6	42
Tonga, ctry., Oc.	F12	58
Tonga Ridge	J21	64
Tongatapu, i., Tonga	G12	58
Tonga Trench	K21	64
Tongcheng, China	E11	28
Tongchuan, China	D9	28
Tongguan, China	E10	28
Tonghai, China	G8	28
Tonghua, China	C13	28
Tongjiang, China	A2	31
Tongjiang, China	F9	28
Tongjosŏn-man, b., N. Kor.	D13	28
Tongliao, China	C12	28
Tongoy, Chile	D2	69
Tongren, China	B1	30
Tongren, China	F9	28
Tongsa Dzong, Bhu.	D6	40
Tongtian, stm., China	E7	28
Tongue, stm., Mt., U.S.	E10	119
Tongue, stm., Tx., U.S.	p13	136
Tongxian, China	D11	28
Tongyu, China	C12	28
Tongzi, China	F9	28
Tonk, India	D3	40
Tonkawa, Ok., U.S.	A4	129
Tonkin, Gulf of, b., Asia	B5	34
Tônlé Sab, Bœng, l., Camb.	D4	34
Tonle Sap see Tônlé Sab, Bœng, l., Camb.	D4	34
Tonopah, Nv., U.S.	E4	121
Tønsberg, Nor.	G4	10
Tonstad, Nor.	G2	10
Tonto National Monument, Az., U.S.	D4	96
Tonto Natural Bridge, Az., U.S.	C4	96
Tooele, Ut., U.S.	C3	137
Tooele, co., Ut., U.S.	C2	137
Toole, co., Mt., U.S.	B5	119
Toombs, co., Ga., U.S.	D4	103
Toomsboro, Ga., U.S.	D3	103
Toora-Hem, Russia	D11	26
Toowoomba, Austl.	F5	62
Topeka, In., U.S.	A6	107
Topeka, Ks., U.S.	C8	109
Topock, Az., U.S.	C1	96
Topol'čany, Slvk.	E5	20
Topolobampo, Mex.	B3	78
Topozero, ozero, l., Russia	D14	10
Toppenish, Wa., U.S.	C5	140
Topsfield, Me., U.S.	A6	114
Topsham, Me., U.S.	E3	112
Top Springs, Austl.	D5	60
Topton, Pa., U.S.	F10	131
Toquima Range, mts., Nv., U.S.	E5	121
Tor, Eth.	B6	54
Torbalı, Tur.	C2	44
Torbat-e Ḥeydarīyeh, Iran	C7	42
Torbat-e Jām, Iran	C8	42
Torbay, Nf., Can.	E5	88
Torbay see Torquay, Eng., U.K.	E5	12
Torbert, Mount, mtn., Ak., U.S.	g15	95
Torch Lake, l., Mi., U.S.	D5	115
Tordesillas, Spain	G4	16
Töre, Swe.	D10	10
Torez, Ukr.	E15	20
Torino (Turin), Italy	B1	18
Torit, Sudan	J11	48
Torneälven (Tornionjoki), stm., Eur.	C9	10
Torneträsk, l., Swe.	B8	10
Torngat Mountains, mts., Can.	f8	88
Tornio, Fin.	D11	10
Tornionjoki (Torneälven), stm., Eur.	C10	10
Tornquist, Arg.	F5	72
Toro, Spain	G4	16
Tororo, Ug.	C6	54
Toros Dağları, Tur.	D5	44
Torrance, Ca., U.S.	n12	98
Torrance, co., N.M., U.S.	C3	124
Torrelavega, Spain	F4	16
Torremolinos, Spain	I4	16
Torrens, Lake, l., Austl.	G2	62
Torrent, Spain	H6	16
Torreón, Mex.	B4	78
Torres, Îles, is., Vanuatu	j9	62a
Torres Strait, strt., Oc.	B3	62
Torres Vedras, Port.	H2	16
Torrington, Ct., U.S.	B3	100
Torrington, Wy., U.S.	D8	143
Tórshavn, Far. Is.	n23	10b

Name	Map Ref.	Page
Tórtolas, Cerro las, mtn., S.A.	D4	72
Tortosa, Spain	G7	16
Tortue, Île de la, i., Haiti	A5	80
Toruń, Pol.	C5	20
Toržok, Russia	C5	22
Tostado, Arg.	D5	72
Tõstamaa, Est.	G10	10
Tosya, Tur.	B5	44
Totagatic, stm., Wi., U.S.	B2	142
Totana, Spain	I6	16
Toteng, Bots.	C3	56
Tot'ma, Russia	B7	22
Totowa, N.J., U.S.	B4	123
Totson Mountain, mtn., Ak., U.S.	C8	95
Tottenham (part of Alliston Beeton Tecumseth and Tottenham), On., Can.	C5	89
Tottori, Japan	C2	31
Touba, C. Iv.	E3	50
Toubkal, Jebel, mtn., Mor.	D3	48
Touchet, stm., Wa., U.S.	C7	140
Toudao see Songhua, stm., China	B14	28
Touggourt, Alg.	D6	48
Touisset, Ma., U.S.	C5	114
Toul, Fr.	C9	16
Touliu, Tai.	E5	30
Toulon, Fr.	F9	16
Toulon, Il., U.S.	B4	106
Toulouse, Fr.	F7	16
Toumodi, C. Iv.	E3	50
Toungoo, Mya.	D4	34
Touraine, hist. reg., Fr.	D7	16
Tournai, Bel.	E8	12
Tours, Fr.	D7	16
Toussaint Creek, stm., Oh., U.S.	f7	128
Toussidé, Pic, vol., Chad	B8	50
Toutle, North Fork, stm., Wa., U.S.	C3	140
Touwsrivier, S. Afr.	E3	56
Tovarkovskij, Russia	C15	20
Tovuz, Azer.	B11	44
Towanda, Il., U.S.	C5	106
Towanda, Ks., U.S.	E7	109
Towanda, Pa., U.S.	C9	131
Towanda Creek, stm., Pa., U.S.	C8	131
Tower City, Pa., U.S.	E8	131
Town Creek, Al., U.S.	A2	94
Towner, N.D., U.S.	A5	127
Towner, co., N.D., U.S.	A6	127
Towns, co., Ga., U.S.	B3	103
Townsend, De., U.S.	C3	101
Townsend, Mt., U.S.	D5	119
Townshend Reservoir, res., Vt., U.S.	E3	138
Townsville, Austl.	D4	62
Towson, Md., U.S.	B4	113
Towuti, Danau, l., Indon.	D6	36
Toyama, Japan	D15	28
Toyohashi, Japan	D3	31
Toyota, Japan	C3	31
Tozeur, Tun.	D6	48
Trabzon, Tur.	B8	44
Tracadie, N.B., Can.	B5	87
Tracie, N.B., Can.	B5	87
Tracy, P.Q., Can.	C4	90
Tracy, Ca., U.S.	D3	98
Tracy, Mn., U.S.	F3	116
Tracy City, Tn., U.S.	D8	135
Tracyton, Wa., U.S.	e10	140
Tradewater, stm., Ky., U.S.	C2	110
Traer, Ia., U.S.	B5	108
Trafford, Pa., U.S.	k14	131
Trafford, Lake, l., Fl., U.S.	F5	102
Trail, B.C., Can.	E9	85
Trail Creek, In., U.S.	A4	107
Traill, co., N.D., U.S.	B8	127
Trail Ridge, mtn., U.S.	F4	103
Tralee, Ire.	D2	12
Tranås, Swe.	G6	10
Trancas, Arg.	D4	72
Trang, Thai.	E3	34
Trangan, Pulau, i., Indon.	E8	36
Trani, Italy	D6	18
Transantarctic Mountains, mts., Ant.	E32	67
Transkei, hist. reg., S. Afr.	E4	56
Transylvania, hist. reg., Rom.	F7	20
Transylvania, co., N.C., U.S.	f10	126
Transylvanian Alps see Carpaţii Meridionali, mts., Rom.	G7	20
Trapani, Italy	E4	18
Trappe, Md., U.S.	C5	113
Trapper Peak, mtn., Mt., U.S.	E2	119
Traralgon, Austl.	H4	62
Trârza, reg., Maur.	C1	50
Trasimeno, Lago, l., Italy	C3	18
Travelers Rest, S.C., U.S.	B3	133
Traverse, co., Mn., U.S.	E2	116
Traverse, Lake, l., U.S.	B9	134
Traverse City, Mi., U.S.	D5	115
Tra Vinh, Viet.	E5	34
Travis, co., Tx., U.S.	D4	136
Travis Air Force Base, mil., Ca., U.S.	C2	98
Travnik, Bos.	B6	18
Tray Mountain, mtn., Ga., U.S.	B3	103

Name	Map Ref.	Page
Trayning, Austl.	G2	60
Treasure, co., Mt., U.S.	D9	119
Treasure Island Naval Station, mil., Ca., U.S.	h8	98
Třebíč, Czech Rep.	E3	20
Trebišov, Slvk.	E6	20
Trego, co., Ks., U.S.	D4	109
Treherne, Mb., Can.	E2	86
Treinta y Tres, Ur.	E7	72
Trelew, Arg.	F3	69
Trelleborg, Swe.	I5	10
Tremblant, Mont, mtn., P.Q., Can.	C3	90
Tremont, Il., U.S.	C4	106
Tremont, Pa., U.S.	E9	131
Tremonton, Ut., U.S.	B3	137
Tremp, Spain	F7	16
Trempealeau, Wi., U.S.	D2	142
Trempealeau, stm., Wi., U.S.	D2	142
Trempealeau, co., Wi., U.S.	D2	142
Trenche, stm., P.Q., Can.	B5	90
Trenčín, Slvk.	E5	20
Trenque Lauquen, Arg.	F5	72
Trent, stm., Eng., U.K.	D6	12
Trent, stm., N.C., U.S.	B5	126
Trente et un Milles, Lac des, l., P.Q., Can.	C2	90
Trento, Italy	A3	18
Trenton, On., Can.	C7	89
Trenton, Fl., U.S.	C4	102
Trenton, Ga., U.S.	B1	103
Trenton, Il., U.S.	E4	106
Trenton, Mi., U.S.	F7	115
Trenton, Mo., U.S.	A4	118
Trenton, Ne., U.S.	D4	120
Trenton, N.J., U.S.	C3	123
Trenton, Oh., U.S.	C1	128
Trenton, Tn., U.S.	B3	135
Trepassey, Nf., Can.	E5	88
Trepassey Bay, b., Nf., Can.	E5	88
Tres Arroyos, Arg.	F5	72
Tresckow, Pa., U.S.	E10	131
Três Corações, Braz.	F2	74
Tres Esquinas, Col.	C4	70
Três Lagoas, Braz.	F1	74
Tres Marías, Islas, is., Mex.	C3	78
Três Marias, Represa de, res., Braz.	E2	74
Tres Puntas, Cabo, c., Arg.	G3	69
Três Rios, Braz.	F3	74
Tres Zapotes, hist., Mex.	D5	78
Treutlen, co., Ga., U.S.	D4	103
Treviso, Italy	B4	18
Trevor, Wi., U.S.	n11	142
Trevorton, Pa., U.S.	E8	131
Treynor, Ia., U.S.	C2	108
Trezevant, Tn., U.S.	A3	135
Triadelphia, W.V., U.S.	A4	141
Triadelphia Reservoir, res., Md., U.S.	B3	113
Triangle, Va., U.S.	B5	139
Tribune, Ks., U.S.	D2	109
Tricase, Italy	E7	18
Trichinopoly see Tiruchchirāppalli, India	G3	40
Trichūr, India	G3	40
Tri City, Or., U.S.	E3	130
Trident Peak, mtn., Nv., U.S.	B3	121
Trier, Ger.	F10	12
Trieste, Italy	B4	18
Trigg, co., Ky., U.S.	D2	110
Triglav, mtn., Slvn.	A4	18
Trigo Mountains, mts., Az., U.S.	D1	96
Tríkala, Grc.	E8	18
Trikora, Puncak, mtn., Indon.	G10	32
Tri Lakes, In., U.S.	B7	107
Trimble, co., Ky., U.S.	B4	110
Trimble, Tn., U.S.	A2	135
Trimont, Mn., U.S.	G4	116
Trincomalee, Sri L.	H4	40
Tring Jonction, P.Q., Can.	C6	90
Trinidad, Bol.	A5	72
Trinidad, Col.	B5	70
Trinidad, Cuba	A3	80
Trinidad, i., Trin.	C7	80
Trinidad, Ur.	E6	72
Trinidad, Co., U.S.	D6	99
Trinidad, Tx., U.S.	C4	136
Trinidad and Tobago, ctry., N.A.	F12	76
Trinidad Head, c., Ca., U.S.	B1	98
Trinity, Al., U.S.	A2	94
Trinity, stm., Ca., U.S.	B2	98
Trinity, co., Ca., U.S.	B2	98
Trinity, Tx., U.S.	D5	136
Trinity, co., Tx., U.S.	D5	136
Trinity, stm., Tx., U.S.	D5	136
Trinity Bay, b., Nf., Can.	D5	88
Trinity Islands, is., Ak., U.S.	D9	95
Trinity Mountain, mtn., Id., U.S.	F3	105
Trinity Mountains, mts., Ca., U.S.	B2	98
Trinity Peak, mtn., Nv., U.S.	C3	121
Trinity Range, mts., Nv., U.S.	C3	121
Trion, Ga., U.S.	B1	103
Tripoli see Ṭarābulus, Leb.	E6	44
Tripoli see Ṭarābulus, Libya	D7	48
Tripoli, Ia., U.S.	B5	108
Trípolis, Grc.	F9	18
Tripolitania see Ṭarābulus, hist. reg., Libya	E7	14
Tripp, S.D., U.S.	D8	134
Tripp, co., S.D., U.S.	D6	134
Tripura, state, India	E6	40
Tristan da Cunha Group, is., St. Hel.	M8	46
Triumph, La., U.S.	E6	111
Trivandrum see Thiruvananthapuram, India	H3	40
Trnava, Slvk.	E4	20
Trochu, Ab., Can.	D4	84
Troick, Russia	D8	26
Troicko-Pečorsk, Russia	B10	22
Trois-Pistoles, P.Q., Can.	A8	90
Trois-Rivières, P.Q., Can.	C5	90
Trois-Rivières-Ouest, P.Q., Can.	C5	90
Troïts'ke, Ukr.	F11	20
Trollhättan, Swe.	G5	10
Tromsø, Nor.	B8	10
Trona, Ca., U.S.	E5	98
Tronador, Monte, mtn., S.A.	F2	69
Trondheim, Nor.	E4	10
Trondheimsfjorden, b., Nor.	E4	10
Trophy Mountain, mtn., B.C., Can.	D8	85
Trotwood, Oh., U.S.	C1	128
Troup, co., Ga., U.S.	C1	103
Trousdale, co., Tn., U.S.	A5	135
Trout, stm., Fl., U.S.	m8	102
Trout, stm., Vt., U.S.	B3	138
Trout Creek, On., Can.	B5	89
Trout Creek Pass, Co., U.S.	C5	99
Trout Lake, l., On., Can.	o16	89
Trout Lake, l., Mn., U.S.	B6	116
Trout Lake, Wa., U.S.	D4	140
Trout Lake, l., Wi., U.S.	B4	142
Troutman, N.C., U.S.	B2	126
Trout Peak, mtn., Wy., U.S.	B3	143
Trout River, Nf., Can.	D2	88
Troy see Truva, hist., Tur.	C2	44
Troy, Al., U.S.	D4	94
Troy, Id., U.S.	C2	105
Troy, Il., U.S.	E4	106
Troy, Ks., U.S.	C8	109
Troy, Mi., U.S.	o15	115
Troy, Mo., U.S.	C7	118
Troy, Mt., U.S.	B1	119
Troy, N.C., U.S.	B3	126
Troy, N.H., U.S.	E2	122
Troy, N.Y., U.S.	C7	125
Troy, Oh., U.S.	B1	128
Troy, Pa., U.S.	C8	131
Troy, Tn., U.S.	A2	135
Troyes, Fr.	C8	16
Troy Peak, mtn., Nv., U.S.	E6	121
Trubč'evsk, Russia	C12	22
Truchas Peak, mtn., N.M., U.S.	B4	124
Trucial States see United Arab Emirates, ctry., Asia	F6	42
Truckee, Ca., U.S.	C3	98
Truckee, stm., U.S.	D2	121
Trujillo, Hond.	B2	80
Trujillo, Peru	E4	70
Trujillo, Spain	H4	16
Trujillo, Ven.	B5	70
Truk Islands see Chuuk Islands, is., Micron.	D9	58
Truman, Mn., U.S.	G4	116
Trumann, Ar., U.S.	B5	97
Trumansburg, N.Y., U.S.	C4	125
Trumbull, Ct., U.S.	E3	100
Trumbull, co., Oh., U.S.	A5	128
Trumbull, Mount, mtn., Az., U.S.	A2	96
Trussville, Al., U.S.	B3	94
Trustom Pond, l., R.I., U.S.	G3	132
Truth or Consequences (Hot Springs), N.M., U.S.	D2	124
Truva (Troy), hist., Tur.	C2	44
Tryon, N.C., U.S.	f10	126
Trzcianka, Pol.	C4	20
Tsaidam Basin see Qaidam Pendi, bas., China	D6	28
Tsala Apopka Lake, l., Fl., U.S.	D4	102
Tsaratanana, mts., Madag.	A8	56
Tsaratanana, Madag.	B8	56
Tsau, Bots.	C3	56
Tsavo, Kenya	D7	54
Tschida, Lake, res., N.D., U.S.	C4	127
Tselinograd see Astana, Kaz.	D9	26
Tses, Nmb.	D2	56
Tsévié, Togo	E5	50
Tshabong, Bots.	D3	56
Tshane, Bots.	C3	56
Tshela, D.R.C.	E2	54
Tshikapa, D.R.C.	E4	54
Tshofa, D.R.C.	E5	54
Tshumbe (Chiumbe), stm., Afr.	E4	54
Tsimlyansk Reservoir see Cimljanskoe vodohranilišče, res., Russia	E7	22
Tsintsabis, Nmb.	B2	56
Tsiombe, Madag.	D8	56
Tsiroanomandidy, Madag.	B8	56
Tsu, Japan	D3	31
Tsugaru-kaikyō, strt., Japan	C16	28
Tsumeb, Nmb.	B2	56
Tsuruoka, Japan	D15	28
Tsushima, is., Japan	D1	31
Tsuyama, Japan	C2	31
Tswaane, Bots.	C3	56
Tual, Indon.	E8	36
Tualatin, stm., Or., U.S.	h11	130
Tuamotu, Îles, is., Fr. Poly.	F15	58
Tuamotu Ridge	J24	64
Tuangku, Pulau, i., Indon.	C1	36
Tuapse, Russia	E5	26
Tuba City, Az., U.S.	A4	96
Tuban, Indon.	E4	36
Tubarão, Braz.	D8	72
Tübingen, Ger.	F11	12
Ṭubruq, Libya	D9	48
Tubuai, i., Fr. Poly.	G15	58
Tucacas, Ven.	A6	70
Tucannon, stm., Wa., U.S.	C8	140
Tucano, Braz.	D4	74
Tuckahoe, stm., N.J., U.S.	E3	123
Tuckahoe, N.Y., U.S.	h13	125
Tuckanarra, Austl.	F2	60
Tucker, Ga., U.S.	h8	103
Tucker, co., W.V., U.S.	B5	141
Tucker Island, i., N.J., U.S.	E4	123
Tuckerman, Ar., U.S.	B4	97
Tuckernuck Island, i., Ma., U.S.	D7	114
Tuckerton, N.J., U.S.	D4	123
Tucson, Az., U.S.	E5	96
Tucumcari, N.M., U.S.	B6	124
Tucumcari Mountain, mtn., N.M., U.S.	B6	124
Tucupita, Ven.	B7	70
Tucuruí, Braz.	B2	74
Tucuruí, Represa de, res., Braz.	B2	74
Tudela, Spain	F6	16
Tudmur, Syria	E8	44
Tugaloo Lake, res., U.S.	B1	133
Tugela, stm., S. Afr.	D5	56
Tug Fork, stm., U.S.	C2	141
Tuguegarao City, Phil.	C8	34
Tugur, Russia	D15	26
Tujmazy, Russia	D9	22
Tukangbesi, Kepulauan, is., Indon.	E6	36
Tûkrah, Libya	E8	14
Tukums, Lat.	H10	10
Tukuyu, Tan.	E6	54
Tukwila, Wa., U.S.	f11	140
Tula, Mex.	C5	78
Tula, Russia	D5	26
Tulalip Indian Reservation, Wa., U.S.	A3	140
Tulancingo, Mex.	C5	78
Tulare, Ca., U.S.	D4	98
Tulare, co., Ca., U.S.	D4	98
Tulare Lake, l., Ca., U.S.	D4	98
Tularosa, N.M., U.S.	D3	124
Tularosa Mountains, mts., N.M., U.S.	D1	124
Tularosa Valley, val., N.M., U.S.	E3	124
Tulbagh, S. Afr.	E2	56
Tulcán, Ec.	C4	70
Tulcea, Rom.	G10	20
Tul'chyn, Ukr.	E10	20
Tule Lake, sw., Ca., U.S.	B3	98
Tule River Indian Reservation, Ca., U.S.	E4	98
Tule Valley, val., Ut., U.S.	D2	137
Tuli, Zimb.	C4	56
Tulia, Tx., U.S.	B2	136
Tullahoma, Tn., U.S.	B5	135
Tulle, Fr.	E7	16
Tully, Austl.	D4	62
Tulsa, Ok., U.S.	A6	129
Tulsa, co., Ok., U.S.	B6	129
Tuluá, Col.	E4	80
Tulun, Russia	D12	26
Tulungagung, Indon.	E4	36
Tumacacori National Monument, Az., U.S.	F4	96
Tumaco, Col.	C4	70
Tuman-gang (Tumen), stm., Asia	B1	31
Tumanovo, Russia	B3	20
Tumbarumba, Austl.	H4	62
Tumbes, Peru	D3	70
Tumble Mountain, mtn., Mt., U.S.	E7	119
Tumbler Ridge, B.C., Can.	B7	85
Tumen (Tuman-gang), stm., Asia	B1	31
Tumen, China	C13	28
Tumeremo, Ven.	B7	70
Tumkūr, India	G3	40
Tumuc-Humac Mountains, mts., S.A.	C8	70
Tumut, Austl.	H4	62
Tumwater, Wa., U.S.	B3	140
Tunceli, Tur.	C7	44
Tunduru, Tan.	E7	54
Tunga, Nig.	E6	50
Tungabhadra, stm., India	F3	40
Tungabhadra Reservoir, res., India	F3	40
Tungkang, Tai.	E5	30
Tungsha Tao (Pratas Island), i., Tai.	G5	30
Tuni, India	F4	40
Tunica, Ms., U.S.	A3	117
Tunica, co., Ms., U.S.	A3	117
Tunis, Tun.	C7	48
Tunis, Golfe de, b., Tun.	F3	18
Tunis, Gulf of see Tunis, Golfe de, b., Tun.	F3	18
Tunisia, ctry., Afr.	D7	48
Tunja, Col.	B5	70
Tunkhannock, Pa., U.S.	C10	131
Tunk Lake, l., Me., U.S.	D4	112
Tunnel Hill, Ga., U.S.	B1	103
Tunp Range, mts., Wy., U.S.	D2	143
Tununak, Ak., U.S.	C6	95
Tunuyán, Arg.	E4	72
Tunxi, China	D4	30
Tuolumne, Ca., U.S.	D3	98
Tuolumne, stm., Ca., U.S.	D3	98
Tuolumne, co., Ca., U.S.	C4	98
Tupã, Braz.	F1	74
Tupaciguara, Braz.	E2	74
Tupelo, Ms., U.S.	A5	117
Tupiza, Bol.	C4	72
Tupper Lake, N.Y., U.S.	A6	125
Tupper Lake, l., N.Y., U.S.	A6	125
Tura, India	D6	40
Tura, Russia	C11	26
Tura, stm., Russia	D18	6
Turan, Russia	A6	28
Turan Lowland, pl., Asia	B7	42
Turayf, Sau. Ar.	G8	44
Turbat, Pak.	E8	42
Turbeville, S.C., U.S.	D7	133
Turbo, Col.	B4	70
Turda, Rom.	F7	20
Turgaj, stm., Kaz.	E8	26
Turgaj, Kaz.	E8	26
Turgajskaja ložbina, reg., Kaz.	D8	26
Turgutlu, Tur.	C2	44
Turhal, Tur.	B7	44
Turia, stm., Spain	H6	16
Turin see Torino, Italy	B1	18
Turinsk, Russia	C11	22
Turkana, Lake see Rudolf, Lake, l., Afr.	C7	54
Turkestan, Kaz.	E8	26
Turkey, ctry., Asia	C3	38
Turkey, stm., Ia., U.S.	B6	108
Turkey Creek, stm., Ok., U.S.	A3	129
Turkey Point, c., Md., U.S.	B5	113
Turkish Republic of Northern Cyprus see North Cyprus, ctry., Asia	C2	44
Turkmenbaši, Turk.	E7	26
Turkmenistan, ctry., Asia	C7	42
Türkoğlu, Tur.	D7	44
Turks and Caicos Islands, dep., N.A.	D10	76
Turks Islands, is., T./C. Is.	A5	80
Turku (Åbo), Fin.	F10	10
Turley, Ok., U.S.	A6	129
Turlock, Ca., U.S.	D3	98
Turnbull, Mount, mtn., Az., U.S.	D5	96
Turner, co., Ga., U.S.	E3	103
Turner, Or., U.S.	C4	130
Turner, co., S.D., U.S.	D8	134
Turner Valley, Ab., Can.	D3	84
Turnor Lake, l., Sk., Can.	m7	91
Turnu Măgurele, Rom.	H8	20
Turpan, China	C5	28
Turpan Pendi, depr., China	C5	28
Turquino, Pico, mtn., Cuba	B4	80
Turrell, Ar., U.S.	B5	97
Turret Peak, mtn., Az., U.S.	C4	96
Turtle Creek, Pa., U.S.	k14	131
Turtle Flambeau Flowage, res., Wi., U.S.	B3	142
Turtle Lake, l., Sk., Can.	D1	91
Turtle Lake, N.D., U.S.	B5	127
Turtle Lake, Wi., U.S.	C1	142
Turtle Mountain Indian Reservation, N.D., U.S.	A6	127
Turuhansk, Russia	C10	26
Tuscaloosa, Al., U.S.	B2	94
Tuscaloosa, co., Al., U.S.	B2	94
Tuscarawas, Oh., U.S.	B4	128
Tuscarawas, co., Oh., U.S.	B4	128
Tuscarora Indian Reservation, N.Y., U.S.	B2	125
Tuscarora Mountain, mtn., Pa., U.S.	F6	131
Tuscarora Mountains, mts., Nv., U.S.	B5	121
Tuscola, Il., U.S.	D5	106
Tuscola, co., Mi., U.S.	E7	115
Tuscumbia, Al., U.S.	A2	94
Tuskegee, Al., U.S.	C4	94
Tusket, stm., N.S., Can.	E4	87
Tustumena Lake, l., Ak., U.S.	g16	95
Tutak, Tur.	C10	44
Tuticorin, India	H3	40
Tutrakan, Blg.	B11	18
Tuttle, Ok., U.S.	B4	129
Tuttle Creek Lake, res., Ks., U.S.	C7	109
Tuttlingen, Ger.	F11	12
Tutuila, i., Am. Sam.	F12	58
Tutupaca, Volcán, vol., Peru	G5	70
Tututalak Mountain, mtn., Ak., U.S.	B7	95
Tutwiler, Ms., U.S.	A3	117
Tuva, state, Russia	D11	26
Tuvalu, ctry., Oc.	E11	58
Ṭuwayq, Jabal, mts., Sau. Ar.	F5	38
Tuxedo, N.C., U.S.	f10	126
Tuxedo Park, De., U.S.	i7	101
Tuxpan, Mex.	C3	78
Tuxpan de Rodríguez Cano, Mex.	C5	78
Tuxtepec, Mex.	D5	78
Tuxtla Gutiérrez, Mex.	D6	78
Tuyen Quang, Viet.	B5	34
Tuy Hoa, Viet.	D5	34
Tūysarkān, Iran	E13	44
Tuz, Iraq	E11	44
Tuz Gölü, l., Tur.	C5	44
Tuzigoot National Monument, Az., U.S.	C4	96
Tuzla, Bos.	B7	18
Tver', Russia	D5	26
Tweed, On., Can.	C7	89
Tweedsmuir Provincial Park, B.C., Can.	C4	85
Tweedy Mountain, mtn., Mt., U.S.	E4	119
Twelvepole Creek, stm., W.V., U.S.	C2	141
Twentymile Creek, stm., W.V., U.S.	C3	141
Twentynine Palms, Ca., U.S.	E5	98
Twentynine Palms Marine Corps Base, mil., Ca., U.S.	E5	98
Twiggs, co., Ga., U.S.	D3	103
Twillingate, Nf., Can.	D4	88
Twin Buttes, mtn., Or., U.S.	C4	130
Twin Buttes Reservoir, res., Tx., U.S.	D2	136
Twin City, Ga., U.S.	D4	103
Twin Creek, stm., Oh., U.S.	C1	128
Twin Falls, Id., U.S.	G4	105
Twin Falls, co., Id., U.S.	G4	105
Twin Knolls, Az., U.S.	m9	96
Twin Lakes, l., Ct., U.S.	A2	100
Twin Lakes, Ga., U.S.	F3	103
Twin Lakes, l., Ia., U.S.	B3	108
Twin Lakes, l., Me., U.S.	C4	112
Twin Lakes, Wi., U.S.	F5	142
Twin Mountains, mtn., Wy., U.S.	E7	143
Twin Peaks, mts., Id., U.S.	E4	105
Twin Rivers, N.J., U.S.	C4	123
Twinsburg, Oh., U.S.	A4	128
Twin Valley, Mn., U.S.	C2	116
Twisp, Wa., U.S.	A5	140
Two Harbors, Mn., U.S.	C7	116
Two Hills, Ab., Can.	C5	84
Two Mile Beach, N.J., U.S.	F3	123
Two Rivers, Wi., U.S.	D6	142
Two Rivers, North Branch, stm., Mn., U.S.	B2	116
Two Rivers, South Branch, stm., Mn., U.S.	B2	116
Tybee Island, Ga., U.S.	D6	103
Tygart Lake, res., W.V., U.S.	B5	141
Tygart River, Falls of the, wtfl., W.V., U.S.	k10	141
Tygart Valley, stm., W.V., U.S.	B4	141
Tyger, stm., S.C., U.S.	B4	133
Tyler, Mn., U.S.	F2	116
Tyler, Tx., U.S.	C5	136
Tyler, co., Tx., U.S.	D5	136
Tyler, co., W.V., U.S.	B4	141
Tyler, Lake, res., Tx., U.S.	C5	136
Tyler Branch, stm., Vt., U.S.	B3	138
Tyler Heights, W.V., U.S.	C3	141
Tylertown, Ms., U.S.	D3	117
Tymochtee Creek, stm., Oh., U.S.	B2	128
Tynda, Russia	D14	26
Tyndall, S.D., U.S.	E8	134
Tyndall Air Force Base, mil., Fl., U.S.	u16	102
Tyne, stm., Eng., U.K.	C5	12
Tyonek, Ak., U.S.	C9	95
Tyre see Ṣūr, Leb.	F6	44
Tyrifjorden, l., Nor.	F3	10
Tyrma, Russia	A14	28
Tyrone, N.M., U.S.	E1	124
Tyrone, Ok., U.S.	e9	129
Tyrone, Pa., U.S.	E5	131
Tyronza, Ar., U.S.	B5	97
Tyrrell, co., N.C., U.S.	B6	126
Tyrrhenian Sea, Eur.	D3	18
Tysa (Tisa) (Tisza), stm., Eur.	E7	20
Tysnesøya, i., Nor.	G1	10
Tzaneen, S. Afr.	C5	56

U

Name	Map Ref.	Page
Uaupés (Vaupés), stm., S.A.	C6	70
Ubá, Braz.	F3	74
Ubangi (Oubangui), stm., Afr.	D3	54
Ubatã, Braz.	D4	74
Ube, Japan	E14	28
Úbeda, Spain	I5	16
Uberaba, Braz.	E2	74
Uberlândia, Braz.	E2	74
Ubly, Mi., U.S.	E8	115
Ubon Ratchathani, Thai.	C4	34
Ubrique, Spain	I4	16
Ubundu, D.R.C.	D5	54
Učaly, Russia	D10	22

Name	Map Ref.	Page
Učami, Russia	C11	26
Ucar, Azer.	B12	44
Ucayali, stm., Peru	E5	70
Uchiura-wan, b., Japan	C16	28
Uchiza, Peru	E4	70
Učkuduk, Uzb.	B8	42
Ucluelet, B.C., Can.	E5	85
Ucon, Id., U.S.	F7	105
Udagamandalam, India	G3	40
Udaipur, India	E2	40
Udall, Ks., U.S.	E6	109
Uddevalla, Swe.	G4	10
Uddjaure, l., Swe.	D7	10
Udgīr, India	F3	40
Udine, Italy	A4	18
Udmurtia see Udmurtija, state, Russia	D7	26
Udmurtija, state, Russia	D7	26
Udon Thani, Thai.	C4	34
Udupi, India	G2	40
Ueda, Japan	C3	31
Uedinenija, ostrov, i., Russia	B10	26
Uele, stm., D.R.C.	C4	54
Uel'kal', Russia	C19	26
Uelzen, Ger.	D12	12
Ufa, Russia	D7	26
Uganda, ctry., Afr.	C6	54
Ugarit, hist., Syria	E6	44
Ugashik Lakes, l., Ak., U.S.	D8	95
Uglegorsk, Russia	E16	26
Uglič, Russia	C6	22
Uherské Hradiště, Czech Rep.	E4	20
Uhrichsville, Oh., U.S.	B4	128
Uhta, Russia	C7	26
Uíge, Ang.	E3	54
Uil, Kaz.	E9	22
Uinta, stm., Ut., U.S.	C5	137
Uinta, co., Wy., U.S.	E2	143
Uintah, co., Ut., U.S.	D6	137
Uintah and Ouray Indian Reservation, Ut., U.S.	C5	137
Uinta Mountains, mts., Ut., U.S.	C5	137
Uitenhage, S. Afr.	E6	56
Uivak, Cape, c., Nf., Can.	f9	88
Ujar, Russia	D11	26
Ujelang, atoll, Marsh. Is.	D10	58
Ujiji, Tan.	D5	54
Ujjain, India	E3	40
Ujungpandang, Indon.	E5	36
Uka, Russia	D18	26
Ukara Island, i., Tan.	D6	54
Ukerewe Island, i., Tan.	D6	54
Ukiah, Ca., U.S.	C2	98
Ukyr, Russia	B9	28
Ulaanbaatar (Ulan Bator), Mong.	B9	28
Ulaangom, Mong.	B6	28
Ulaan-Uul, Mong.	C10	28
Ulak Island, i., Ak., U.S.	E4	95
Ulan Bator see Ulaanbaatar, Mong.	B9	28
Ulan-Ude, Russia	D12	26
Ulan Ul Hu, l., China	C6	40
Ulchin, S. Kor.	C1	31
Ulcinj, Yugo.	D7	18
Ulhāsnagar, India	F2	40
Uliastay, Mong.	B7	28
Ulja, Russia	D16	26
Uljanovsk, Russia	D6	26
Ullŭng-do, i., S. Kor.	C2	31
Ulm, Ger.	F11	12
Ulóngué, Moz.	A5	56
Ulsan, S. Kor.	C1	31
Ulster, hist. reg., Eur.	C3	12
Ulster, co., N.Y., U.S.	D6	125
Ulu, Indon.	C7	36
Ulu, Russia	C14	26
Ulúa, stm., Hond.	B2	80
Ulundi, S. Afr.	D5	56
Ulungur Hu, l., China	B5	28
Uluru (Ayers Rock), mtn., Austl.	F5	60
Ulverstone, Austl.	I4	62
Ulysses, Ks., U.S.	E2	109
Umán, Mex.	C7	78
Uman', Ukr.	E11	20
Umanak, Grnld.	D29	82
Umarkot, Pak.	E9	42
Umatilla, Fl., U.S.	D5	102
Umatilla, Or., U.S.	B7	130
Umatilla, stm., Or., U.S.	B7	130
Umatilla, co., Or., U.S.	B8	130
Umatilla Indian Reservation, Or., U.S.	B8	130
Umba, Russia	A5	22
Umbagog Lake, l., U.S.	A4	122
Umboi Island, i., Pap. N. Gui.	H12	32
Umcolcus Lake, l., Me., U.S.	B4	112
Umeå, Swe.	D9	10
Umeälven, stm., Swe.	D9	10
Umm al-'Abīd, Libya	A8	50
Umm Durmān, Sudan	G11	48
Umm Lajj, Sau. Ar.	E3	42
Umnak Island, i., Ak., U.S.	E6	95
Umpqua, stm., Or., U.S.	D3	130
Umsaskis Lake, l., Me., U.S.	B3	112
Umtata, S. Afr.	E4	56
Umuarama, Braz.	H9	70
Umzinto, S. Afr.	E5	56
Unadilla, Ga., U.S.	D3	103
Unadilla, stm., N.Y., U.S.	C5	125
Unaí, Braz.	E2	74
Unalakleet, Ak., U.S.	C7	95
Unalaska Island, i., Ak., U.S.	E6	95
'Unayzah, Sau. Ar.	E4	38
'Unayzah, Jabal, mtn., Asia	F8	44
Uncasville, Ct., U.S.	D7	100
Uncompahgre, stm., Co., U.S.	C3	99
Uncompahgre Mountains, mts., Co., U.S.	C3	99
Uncompahgre Peak, mtn., Co., U.S.	C3	99
Underwood, Al., U.S.	B3	94
Underwood, N.D., U.S.	B4	127
Uneča, Russia	C12	20
Ungava, Péninsule d', pen., P.Q., Can.	g12	90
Ungava Bay, b., Can.	G26	82
Ungava Peninsula see Ungava, Péninsule d', pen., P.Q., Can.	F25	82
União, Braz.	B3	74
Uniãoda Vitória, Braz.	D7	72
União dos Palmares, Braz.	C4	74
Unicoi, Tn., U.S.	C11	135
Unicoi, co., Tn., U.S.	C11	135
Unicoi Mountains, mts., U.S.	D9	135
Unimak Island, i., Ak., U.S.	D7	95
Unimak Pass, strt., Ak., U.S.	E6	95
Unión, Arg.	F4	72
Union, co., Ar., U.S.	D3	97
Union, co., Fl., U.S.	B4	102
Union, co., Ga., U.S.	B2	103
Union, co., Ia., U.S.	C3	108
Union, co., Il., U.S.	F4	106
Union, co., In., U.S.	E8	107
Union, co., Ky., U.S.	C2	110
Union, Ky., U.S.	k13	110
Union, co., La., U.S.	B3	111
Union, Mo., U.S.	C6	118
Union, co., Ms., U.S.	A4	117
Union, co., N.C., U.S.	B2	126
Union, co., N.J., U.S.	B4	123
Union, co., N.M., U.S.	A6	124
Union, co., Oh., U.S.	B2	128
Union, Or., U.S.	B9	130
Union, co., Or., U.S.	B8	130
Union, co., Pa., U.S.	E7	131
Union, S.C., U.S.	B4	133
Union, co., S.C., U.S.	B4	133
Union, co., S.D., U.S.	E9	134
Union, co., Tn., U.S.	C10	135
Union, Wa., U.S.	B2	140
Union, West Branch, stm., Me., U.S.	D4	112
Union Beach, N.J., U.S.	C4	123
Union Bridge, Md., U.S.	A3	113
Union City, Ca., U.S.	h8	98
Union City, Ga., U.S.	C2	103
Union City, In., U.S.	D8	107
Union City, Mi., U.S.	F5	115
Union City, N.J., U.S.	h8	123
Union City, Oh., U.S.	B1	128
Union City, Ok., U.S.	B4	129
Union City, Pa., U.S.	C2	131
Union City, Tn., U.S.	A2	135
Union Flat Creek, stm., Wa., U.S.	C8	140
Union Gap, Wa., U.S.	C5	140
Union Grove, Wi., U.S.	F5	142
Union Lake, l., N.J., U.S.	E2	123
Union Pier, Mi., U.S.	G4	115
Union Point, Ga., U.S.	C3	103
Union Springs, Al., U.S.	C4	94
Uniontown, Al., U.S.	C2	94
Uniontown, Ky., U.S.	C2	110
Uniontown, Oh., U.S.	B4	128
Uniontown, Pa., U.S.	G2	131
Union Village, R.I., U.S.	B3	132
Union Village Reservoir, res., Vt., U.S.	D4	138
Unionville, Ct., U.S.	B4	100
Unionville, Mo., U.S.	A4	118
United Arab Emirates, ctry., Asia	F6	42
United Arab Republic see Egypt, ctry., Afr.	E10	48
United Kingdom, ctry., Eur.	C6	12
United Nations Headquarters, N.Y., U.S.	h12	125
United States, ctry., N.A.	D6	92
United States Air Force Academy, Co., U.S.	B6	99
United States Military Academy, mil., N.Y., U.S.	C6	125
United States Naval Academy, mil., Md., U.S.	C4	113
Unity Reservoir, res., Or., U.S.	C8	130
University City, Mo., U.S.	C7	118
University Heights, Ia., U.S.	C6	108
University Heights, Oh., U.S.	h9	128
University Park, Ia., U.S.	C5	108
University Park, N.M., U.S.	E3	124
University Park, Tx., U.S.	n10	136
University Place, Wa., U.S.	f10	140
Unnão, India	D4	40
Unuli Horog, China	B6	40
Ünye, Tur.	B7	44
Unža, stm., Russia	C7	22
Upata, Ven.	B7	70
Upernavik, Grnld.	D28	82
Upington, S. Afr.	D3	56
Upland, Ca., U.S.	E5	98
Upland, In., U.S.	D7	107
Upolu, i., Samoa	F12	58
Upolu Point, c., Hi., U.S.	C6	104
Upper Ammonoosuc, stm., N.H., U.S.	A4	122
Upper Arlington, Oh., U.S.	B2	128
Upper Arrow Lake, res., B.C., Can.	D9	85
Upperco, Md., U.S.	A4	113
Upper Darby, Pa., U.S.	G11	131
Upper Greenwood Lake, N.J., U.S.	A4	123
Upper Humber, stm., Nf., Can.	D3	88
Upper Hutt, N.Z.	p14	63c
Upper Iowa, stm., Ia., U.S.	A5	108
Upper Island Cove, Nf., Can.	E5	88
Upper Klamath Lake, l., Or., U.S.	E4	130
Upper Marlboro, Md., U.S.	C4	113
Upper New York Bay, b., U.S.	k8	123
Upper Red Lake, l., Mn., U.S.	B4	116
Upper Saddle River, N.J., U.S.	A4	123
Upper Sandusky, Oh., U.S.	B2	128
Upper Sheila [Haut Sheila], N.B., Can.	B5	87
Upper Volta see Burkina Faso, ctry., Afr.	D4	50
Uppland, hist. reg., Swe.	F7	10
Uppsala, Swe.	G7	10
Upright, Cape, c., Ak., U.S.	C5	95
Upshur, co., Tx., U.S.	C5	136
Upshur, co., W.V., U.S.	C4	141
Upson, co., Ga., U.S.	D2	103
Upton, P.Q., Can.	D5	90
Upton, Ky., U.S.	C4	110
Upton, Ma., U.S.	B4	114
Upton, co., Tx., U.S.	D2	136
Upton, Wy., U.S.	B8	143
Uraj, Russia	B12	22
Urakawa, Japan	B4	31
Ural, stm.	E9	22
Ural Mountains see Ural'skie gory, mts., Russia	D7	26
Ural'sk, Kaz.	D7	26
Ural'skie gory (Ural Mountains), mts., Russia	D7	26
Urania, La., U.S.	C3	111
Ura-Tjube, Taj.	C9	42
Urbana, Il., U.S.	C5	106
Urbana, Oh., U.S.	B2	128
Urbancrest, Oh., U.S.	m10	128
Urbandale, Ia., U.S.	C4	108
Urbino, Italy	C4	18
Ures, Mex.	B2	78
Urfa see Şanliurfa, Tur.	D8	44
Urgenč, Uzb.	E8	26
Ürgüp, Tur.	C6	44
Uribia, Col.	A5	70
Urjung-Haja, Russia	B13	26
Urjupinsk, Russia	D7	22
Urla, Tur.	C2	44
Urmia see Orūmīyeh, Iran	C5	42
Urmia, Lake see Orūmīyeh, Daryācheh-ye, l., Iran	C5	42
Uromi, Nig.	E6	50
Uroševac, Yugo.	C8	18
Urrao, Col.	D4	80
Uruapan del Progreso, Mex.	D4	78
Uruguai (Uruguay), stm., S.A.	E6	72
Uruguaiana, Braz.	D6	72
Uruguay, ctry., S.A.	E6	72
Uruguay (Uruguai), stm., S.A.	D6	72
Ürümqi, China	C5	28
Urundi see Burundi, ctry., Afr.	D5	54
Urup, ostrov, i., Russia	E17	26
Urziceni, Rom.	G9	20
Uržum, Russia	C8	22
Usa, Japan	D2	31
Uşak, Tur.	C3	44
Usakos, Nmb.	C2	56
Usborne, Mount, mtn., Falk. Is.	H5	69
Usedom, i., Eur.	B3	20
Ushuaia, Arg.	H3	69
Usinsk, Russia	C7	26
Usman', Russia	C15	20
Usoke, Tan.	E6	54
Usole-Sibirskoe, Russia	D12	26
Ussuri (Wusuli), stm., Asia	E15	26
Ussurijsk, Russia	E15	26
Ust'-Barguzin, Russia	D12	26
Ust'-Belaja, Russia	C19	26
Ust'-Čaun, Russia	C19	26
Ust'-Cil'ma, Russia	A9	22
Ust'-Ilimsk, Russia	D12	26
Ústí nad Labem, Czech Rep.	E3	20
Ustinov see Iževsk, Russia	D7	26
Ustka, Pol.	B4	20
Ust'-Kamčatsk, Russia	D18	26
Ust'-Kamenogorsk, Kaz.	E10	26
Ust'-Koksa, Russia	A5	28
Ust'-Kujda, Russia	C15	26
Ust'-Kut, Russia	D12	26
Ust'-Lyža, Russia	A10	22
Ust'-Maja, Russia	C15	26
Ust'-Man'ja, Russia	B11	22
Ust'-Nera, Russia	C16	26
Ust'-Njukža, Russia	D14	26
Ust'-Tym, Russia	D10	26
Ust-Urt Plateau, plat., Asia	B7	42
Usu, China	C4	28
Usulután, El Sal.	C2	80
Usumacinta, stm., N.A.	D6	78
Ušumun, Russia	A13	28
Utah, co., Ut., U.S.	C4	137
Utah, state, U.S.	D4	137
Utah Lake, l., Ut., U.S.	C4	137
Ute Creek, stm., N.M., U.S.	A6	124
Ute Mountain Indian Reservation, U.S.	D2	99
Utena, Lith.	I11	10
Ute Reservoir, res., N.M., U.S.	B6	124
Utete, Tan.	E7	54
Uthai Thani, Thai.	C4	34
Utiariti, Braz.	F8	70
Utica, Il., U.S.	B5	106
Utica, Mi., U.S.	F7	115
Utica, Ms., U.S.	C3	117
Utica, Ne., U.S.	D8	120
Utica, N.Y., U.S.	B5	125
Utica, Oh., U.S.	B3	128
Utiel, Spain	H6	16
Utikuma Lake, l., Ab., Can.	B3	84
Utila, Isla de, i., Hond.	B2	80
Utopia, Austl.	E5	60
Utrecht, Neth.	D9	12
Utrecht, S. Afr.	D5	56
Utrera, Spain	I4	16
Utsunomiya, Japan	D16	28
Uttaradit, Thai.	C4	34
Uttaranchal, state, India	D3	40
Uttar Pradesh, state, India	D3	40
Uusikaupunki, Fin.	F9	10
Uvalde, Tx., U.S.	E3	136
Uvalde, co., Tx., U.S.	E3	136
Uvarovo, Russia	D7	22
Uvinza, Tan.	E6	54
Uvira, D.R.C.	D5	54
Uvs Lake, l., Asia	A6	28
Uwajima, Japan	E14	28
Uwayl, Sudan	B5	54
Uwharrie, stm., N.C., U.S.	B3	126
Uxbridge, Ma., U.S.	B4	114
Uyo, Nig.	E6	50
Uyuni, Bol.	C4	72
Uyuni, Salar de, pl., Bol.	C4	72
Uzbekistan, ctry., Asia	C8	42
Uzhhorod, Ukr.	E7	20
Uzlovaja, Russia	C15	20
Uzunköprü, Tur.	B2	44
Užur, Russia	D11	26

V

Vaal, stm., S. Afr.	D4	56
Vaaldam, res., S. Afr.	D4	56
Vaasa, Fin.	E9	10
Vác, Hung.	F5	20
Vaca Key, i., Fl., U.S.	H5	102
Vacaria, Braz.	D7	72
Vacaville, Ca., U.S.	C3	98
Vache, Île à, i., Haiti	B5	80
Vacherie, La., U.S.	h10	111
Vadodara, India	E2	40
Vadsø, Nor.	A13	10
Vaduz, Liech.	G11	12
Vaga, stm., Russia	B7	22
Vah, stm., Russia	C9	26
Váh, stm., Slvk.	E4	20
Vaiden, Ms., U.S.	B4	117
Vail, Co., U.S.	B4	99
Vajgač, ostrov, i., Russia	B7	26
Vākhān, hist. reg., Afg.	C10	42
Valdai Hills see Valdajskaja vozvyšennost', Russia	C5	22
Valdaj, Russia	C5	22
Valdajskaja vozvyšennost', Russia	C5	22
Val-David, P.Q., Can.	C3	90
Valday see Valdaj, Russia	C5	22
Valdemarsvik, Swe.	G7	10
Valders, Wi., U.S.	D6	142
Valdepeñas, Spain	H5	16
Valdés, Península, pen., Arg.	F4	69
Valdese, N.C., U.S.	B1	126
Valdez, Ak., U.S.	C10	95
Val-d'Or, P.Q., Can.	k11	90
Valdosta, Ga., U.S.	F3	103
Vale, Or., U.S.	D9	130
Valemount, B.C., Can.	C8	85
Valença, Braz.	D4	74
Valença do Piauí, Braz.	C3	74
Valence, Fr.	E9	16
València, Spain	H6	16
Valencia, Az., U.S.	m7	96
Valencia, co., N.M., U.S.	C3	124
Valencia, Ven.	B6	70
València, Golf de, b., Spain	H7	16
Valencia de Alcántara, Spain	H3	16
Valencia Heights, S.C., U.S.	D6	133
Valenciennes, Fr.	B8	16
Valentine, Ne., U.S.	B5	120
Valera, Ven.	B5	70
Valga, Est.	H12	10
Valhalla, N.Y., U.S.	D7	125
Valhermoso Springs, Al., U.S.	A3	94
Valjevo, Yugo.	B7	18
Valkeakoski, Fin.	F11	10
Valladolid, Mex.	C7	78
Valladolid, Spain	G4	16
Vallecito Reservoir, res., Co., U.S.	D3	99
Valle de la Pascua, Ven.	B6	70
Valledupar, Col.	A5	70
Vallée-Jonction, P.Q., Can.	C7	90
Vallegrande, Bol.	B5	72
Valle Hermoso, Mex.	B5	78
Vallejo, Ca., U.S.	C2	98
Vallenar, Chile	C2	69
Valletta, Malta	G5	18
Valley, stm., Mb., Can.	D1	86
Valley, co., Id., U.S.	E3	105
Valley, co., Mt., U.S.	B10	119
Valley, Ne., U.S.	C9	120
Valley, co., Ne., U.S.	C6	120
Valley Center, Ks., U.S.	E6	109
Valley City, N.D., U.S.	C8	127
Valley Cottage, N.Y., U.S.	g13	125
Valley East, On., Can.	p19	89
Valley Falls, Ks., U.S.	C8	109
Valley Falls, R.I., U.S.	B4	132
Valley Forge, Pa., U.S.	o20	131
Valley Mills, Tx., U.S.	D4	136
Valley Park, Mo., U.S.	f12	118
Valley Springs, S.D., U.S.	D9	134
Valley Station, Ky., U.S.	g11	110
Valley Stream, N.Y., U.S.	n15	125
Valleyview, Ab., Can.	B2	84
Valley View, Pa., U.S.	E8	131
Valliant, Ok., U.S.	D6	129
Valls, Spain	G7	16
Vallscreek, W.V., U.S.	D3	141
Valmeyer, Il., U.S.	E3	106
Valmiera, Lat.	H11	10
Valona see Vlorë, Alb.	D7	18
Vālpārai, India	G3	40
Valparaíso, Chile	C2	69
Valparaiso, Fl., U.S.	u15	102
Valparaiso, In., U.S.	B3	107
Vals, Tanjung, c., Indon.	H10	32
Valsbaai, b., S. Afr.	E2	56
Valtimo, Fin.	E13	10
Valujki, Russia	D15	20
Val Verde, Ut., U.S.	C4	137
Val Verde, co., Tx., U.S.	E2	136
Valverde del Camino, Spain	I3	16
Van, Tur.	C10	44
Van, Tx., U.S.	C5	136
Van, W.V., U.S.	n12	141
Vanadzor, Arm.	B11	44
Van Alstyne, Tx., U.S.	C4	136
Vanavara, Russia	C12	26
Van Buren, Ar., U.S.	B1	97
Van Buren, co., Ar., U.S.	B3	97
Van Buren, co., Ia., U.S.	D6	108
Van Buren, In., U.S.	C6	107
Van Buren, Me., U.S.	A5	112
Van Buren, co., Mi., U.S.	F4	115
Van Buren, Mo., U.S.	E6	118
Van Buren, co., Tn., U.S.	D8	135
Vanč, Taj.	C10	42
Vance, co., N.C., U.S.	A4	126
Vance Air Force Base, mil., Ok., U.S.	A3	129
Vanceboro, N.C., U.S.	B5	126
Vanceburg, Ky., U.S.	B6	110
Vancleave, Ms., U.S.	E5	117
Vancouver, B.C., Can.	E6	85
Vancouver, Wa., U.S.	D3	140
Vancouver Island, i., B.C., Can.	E4	85
Vancouver Island Ranges, mts., B.C., Can.	D4	85
Vandalia, Il., U.S.	E4	106
Vandalia, Mo., U.S.	B6	118
Vandenberg Air Force Base, mil., Ca., U.S.	E3	98
Vander, N.C., U.S.	B4	126
Vanderbilt Peak, mtn., N.M., U.S.	E1	124
Vanderburgh, co., In., U.S.	H2	107
Vandergrift, Pa., U.S.	E2	131
Vanderhoof, B.C., Can.	C5	85
Vanderlin Island, i., Austl.	D2	62
Van Diemen Gulf, b., Austl.	C5	60
Vänern, l., Swe.	G5	10
Vänersborg, Swe.	G5	10
Vangaindrano, Madag.	F9	56
Van Gölü, l., Tur.	C10	44
Van Horn, Tx., U.S.	o12	136
Van Horne, Ia., U.S.	B5	108
Vanier, On., Can.	h12	89
Vanimo, Pap. N. Gui.	G11	32
Vanino, Russia	B16	28
Vankarem, Russia	C20	26
Vankleek Hill, On., Can.	B10	89
Van Kull, Kill, stm., N.J., U.S.	k8	123
Van Lear, Ky., U.S.	C7	110
Van Meter, Ia., U.S.	C4	108
Vännäs, Swe.	E8	10
Vannes, Fr.	D5	16
Van Rees, Pegunungan, mts., Indon.	G10	32
Vanrhynsdorp, S. Afr.	E2	56

Name	Map Ref.	Page

Vansant, Va., U.S. ...e9 139
Vanua Lava, i., Vanuatu ... j9 62a
Vanua Levu, i., Fiji ...F11 58
Vanuatu, ctry., Oc. ...F10 58
Van Vleck, Tx., U.S. ...r14 136
Van Wert, Oh., U.S. ...B1 128
Van Wert, co., Oh., U.S. ...B1 128
Vanwyksvlei, S. Afr. ...E3 56
Van Zandt, co., Tx., U.S. ...C5 136
Vārānasi (Benares), India ...D4 40
Varangerfjorden, b., Nor. ..A13 10
Varaždin, Cro. ...A6 18
Varberg, Swe. ...H5 10
Vardaman, Ms., U.S. ...B4 117
Vardar (Axiós), stm., Eur. ...D9 18
Varde, Den. ...I3 10
Vardø, Nor. ...A14 10
Varennes, P.Q., Can. ...D4 90
Varese, Italy ...B2 18
Varginha, Braz. ...F2 74
Varina, Va., U.S. ...C5 139
Varkaus, Fin. ...E12 10
Värmland, hist. reg., Swe. ..G5 10
Varna, Blg. ...C11 18
Varna, Russia ...D11 22
Värnamo, Swe. ...H6 10
Varnville, S.C., U.S. ...F5 133
Varto, Tur. ...C9 44
Várzea Grande, Braz. ...B6 72
Vashon, Point, c., Wa., U.S. ...e11 140
Vashon Island, i., Wa., U.S. ...f11 140
Vaslui, Rom. ...F9 20
Vass, N.C., U.S. ...B3 126
Vassar, Mi., U.S. ...E7 115
Vastenjaure, l., Swe. ...C7 10
Västerås, Swe. ...G7 10
Västerbotten, hist. reg., Swe. ...D8 10
Västerdalälven, stm., Swe. ..F5 10
Västervik, Swe. ...H7 10
Vasto, Italy ...C5 18
Vasylivka, Ukr. ...F13 20
Vasyl'kiv, Ukr. ...D11 20
Vatican City, ctry., Eur. ...D4 18
Vatnajökull, ice, Ice. ...I20 10a
Vatomandry, Madag. ...B8 56
Vatra Dornei, Rom. ...F8 20
Vättern, l., Swe. ...G6 10
Vaudreuil, P.Q., Can. ...D3 90
Vaughan, On., Can. ...D5 89
Vaughn, Mt., U.S. ...C5 119
Vaughn, N.M., U.S. ...C4 124
Vaukavysk, Bela. ...C8 20
Vaupés (Uaupés) stm., S.A. ...C5 70
Vauxhall, Ab., Can. ...D4 84
Vava'u, i., Tonga ...F12 58
Vavoua, C. Iv. ...E3 50
Vavuniya, Sri L. ...H4 40
Växjö, Swe. ...H6 10
Vaygach Island see Vajgač, ostrov, i., Russia ...B7 26
Važgort, Russia ...B8 22
Veazie, Me., U.S. ...D4 112
Veedersburg, In., U.S. ...D3 107
Veendam, Neth. ...D10 12
Vega, i., Nor. ...D4 10
Vegreville, Ab., Can. ...C4 84
Veinticinco de Mayo, Arg. ...F5 72
Vejle, Den. ...I3 10
Vélez-Málaga, Spain ...I4 16
Velika Morava, stm., Yugo. ...B8 18
Velikie Luki, Russia ...D5 26
Velikij Ustjug, Russia ...C6 26
Vélingara, Sen. ...D2 50
Velletri, Italy ...D4 18
Vellore, India ...G3 40
Velma, Ok., U.S. ...C4 129
Vel'sk, Russia ...C6 26
Velva, N.D., U.S. ...A5 127
Venado Tuerto, Arg. ...E5 72
Venango, co., Pa., U.S. ...D2 131
Vendôme, Fr. ...D7 16
Veneta, Or., U.S. ...C3 130
Venézia (Venice), Italy ...B4 18
Venezuela, ctry., S.A. ...B6 70
Venezuela, Golfo de, b., S.A. ...A5 70
Venezuela, Gulf of see Venezuela, Golfo de, b., S.A. ...A5 70
Venezuelan Basin ...G7 66
Veniaminof, Mount, mtn., Ak., U.S. ...D8 95
Venice see Venézia, Italy ..B4 18
Venice, Fl., U.S. ...E4 102
Venice, Il., U.S. ...E3 106
Venice, Gulf of, b., Eur. ...B4 18
Venta, stm., Eur. ...H10 10
Ventimiglia, Italy ...C1 18
Ventnor City, N.J., U.S. ...E4 123
Ventspils, Lat. ...H9 10
Ventura (San Buenaventura), Ca., U.S. ...E4 98
Ventura, co., Ca., U.S. ...E4 98
Vera, Arg. ...D5 72
Vera, Spain ...I6 16
Veracruz, state, Mex. ...D5 78
Veracruz, Mex. ...D5 78
Verāval, India ...E2 40
Verbania, Italy ...B2 18
Vercelli, Italy ...B2 18
Verchères, P.Q., Can. ...D4 90

Verda, Ky., U.S. ...D6 110
Verde, stm., Az., U.S. ...C4 96
Verden, Ger. ...D11 12
Verdi, Nv., U.S. ...D2 121
Verdigre, Ne., U.S. ...B7 120
Verdigris, Ok., U.S. ...A6 129
Verdigris, stm., U.S. ...A6 129
Verdi Peak, mtn., Nv., U.S. ..C6 121
Verdun, P.Q., Can. ...q19 90
Verdun-sur-Meuse, Fr. ...C9 16
Vereeniging, S. Afr. ...D4 56
Vereščagino, Russia ...C10 26
Vergennes, Vt., U.S. ...C2 138
Verhneimbatsk, Russia ...C10 26
Verhnemulomskoe vodohranilišče, res., Russia ...B14 10
Verhnetulomskij, Russia ...B14 10
Verhneural'sk, Russia ...D10 22
Verhnij Baskunčak, Russia ..E8 22
Verhnij Ufalej, Russia ...C11 22
Verhnjaja Amga, Russia ...D14 26
Verhnjaja Inta, Russia ...A11 22
Verhnjaja Salda, Russia ...C11 22
Verhojansk, Russia ...C15 26
Verhojanskij hrebet, mts., Russia ...C14 26
Verhoture, Russia ...C11 22
Verkhoyansk see Verhojansk, Russia ...C15 26
Vermilion, Ab., Can. ...C5 84
Vermilion, stm., Ab., Can. ..C5 84
Vermilion, stm., Il., U.S. ...C5 106
Vermilion, co., Il., U.S. ...C6 106
Vermilion, stm., La., U.S. ...E3 111
Vermilion, co., La., U.S. ...E3 111
Vermilion, stm., Mn., U.S. ..B6 116
Vermilion, Oh., U.S. ...A3 128
Vermilion, stm., Oh., U.S. ..A3 128
Vermilion Bay, b., La., U.S. ..E3 111
Vermilion Lake, l., Mn., U.S. ...C6 116
Vermilion Pass, Can. ...D2 84
Vermillion, co., In., U.S. ...E2 107
Vermillion, S.D., U.S. ...E9 134
Vermillion, East Fork, stm., S.D., U.S. ...D8 134
Vermillon, stm., P.Q., Can. ..B4 90
Vermont, Il., U.S. ...C3 106
Vermont, state, U.S. ...D3 138
Vermontville, Mi., U.S. ...F5 115
Vernal, Ut., U.S. ...C6 137
Vernon, B.C., Can. ...D8 85
Vernon, Al., U.S. ...B1 94
Vernon, co., La., U.S. ...C2 111
Vernon, co., Mo., U.S. ...D3 118
Vernon, Tx., U.S. ...B3 136
Vernon, co., Wi., U.S. ...E3 142
Vernon Hills, Il., U.S. ...h9 106
Vernonia, Or., U.S. ...B3 130
Vero Beach, Fl., U.S. ...E6 102
Véroia, Grc. ...D9 18
Verona, On., Can. ...C8 89
Verona, Italy ...B3 18
Verona, Ms., U.S. ...A5 117
Verona, N.J., U.S. ...B4 123
Verona, Pa., U.S. ...k14 131
Verona, Wi., U.S. ...E4 142
Verret, Lake, l., La., U.S. ...E4 111
Versailles, Fr. ...C8 16
Versailles, In., U.S. ...F7 107
Versailles, Ky., U.S. ...B5 110
Versailles, Mo., U.S. ...C5 118
Versailles, Oh., U.S. ...B1 128
Vert, Cap, c., Sen. ...D1 50
Vertientes, Cuba ...A4 80
Vesele, Ukr. ...F13 20
Vešenskaja, Russia ...F15 8
Vesoul, Fr. ...D10 16
Vestal, N.Y., U.S. ...C4 125
Vestavia Hills, Al., U.S. ...g7 94
Vesterålen, is., Nor. ...B6 10
Vestfjorden, b., Nor. ...C5 10
Vestmannaeyjar, Ice. ...m18 10a
Vesuvio, vol., Italy ...D5 18
Vesuvius see Vesuvio, vol., Italy ...D5 18
Veszprém, Hung. ...F4 20
Vetlanda, Swe. ...H6 10
Vetluga, Russia ...C8 22
Vetluga, stm., Russia ...C8 22
Vevay, In., U.S. ...G7 107
Vezirköprü, Tur. ...B6 44
Viacha, Bol. ...B4 72
Vian, Ok., U.S. ...B7 129
Viana, Braz. ...B2 74
Viana do Castelo, Port. ...G2 16
Viangchan (Vientiane), Laos ...C4 34
Viangphoukha, Laos ...B4 34
Viareggio, Italy ...C3 18
Viborg, Den. ...H3 10
Viborg, S.D., U.S. ...D8 134
Vibo Valentia, Italy ...E5 18
Viburnum, Mo., U.S. ...D6 118
Vic, Spain ...G8 16
Vicebsk, Bela. ...B11 20
Vicente, Point, c., Ca., U.S. ...n12 98
Vicente Guerrero, Presa, res., Mex. ...C5 78
Vicenza, Italy ...B3 18
Vichada, stm., Col. ...C5 70
Vichy, Fr. ...D8 16
Vici, Ok., U.S. ...A2 129
Vicksburg, Mi., U.S. ...F5 115
Vicksburg, Ms., U.S. ...C3 117

Vicksburg National Military Park, Ms., U.S. ...C3 117
Victor, Ia., U.S. ...C5 108
Victor, N.Y., U.S. ...C3 125
Victoria, stm., Austl. ...D5 60
Victoria, state, Austl. ...H3 62
Victoria see Limbe, Cam. ...C1 54
Victoria, B.C., Can. ...E6 85
Victoria, Nf., Can. ...E5 88
Victoria, Chile ...E2 69
Victoria see Xianggang, China ...E3 30
Victoria, Gui. ...D2 50
Victoria, Sey. ...h13 57b
Victoria, Ks., U.S. ...D4 109
Victoria, Tx., U.S. ...E4 136
Victoria, co., Tx., U.S. ...E4 136
Victoria, Lake, l., Afr. ...D6 54
Victoria, Mount, mtn., Pap. N. Gui. ...H12 32
Victoria Falls, wtfl., Afr. ...B4 56
Victoria Harbour, On., Can. ...C5 89
Victoria Island, i., Can. ...D18 82
Victoria Lake, res., Nf., Can. ..D3 88
Victoria Land, reg., Ant. ...D21 67
Victoria Nile, stm., Ug. ...C6 54
Victoria Peak, mtn., Belize ..B2 80
Victoria River Downs, Austl. ..D5 60
Victorias, Phil. ...D8 34
Victoriaville, P.Q., Can. ...C6 90
Victoria West, S. Afr. ...E3 56
Victorville, Ca., U.S. ...E5 98
Vicuña Mackenna, Arg. ...E5 72
Vidalia, Ga., U.S. ...D4 103
Vidalia, La., U.S. ...C4 111
Vidin, Blg. ...C9 18
Vidisha, India ...E3 40
Vidor, Tx., U.S. ...D5 136
Viedma, Arg. ...F4 69
Viedma, Lago, l., Arg. ...G2 69
Vienna see Wien, Aus. ...F15 12
Vienna, Ga., U.S. ...D3 103
Vienna, Il., U.S. ...F5 106
Vienna, Mo., U.S. ...C6 118
Vienna, Va., U.S. ...B5 139
Vienna, W.V., U.S. ...B3 141
Vienne, Fr. ...E9 16
Vienne, stm., Fr. ...D7 16
Vientiane see Viangchan, Laos ...C4 34
Vieques, Isla de, i., P.R. ...B6 80
Vierwaldstätter See, l., Switz. ...A2 18
Vierzon, Fr. ...D8 16
Vieste, Italy ...D6 18
Vietnam, ctry., Asia ...C5 34
Viet Tri, Viet. ...B5 34
Vieux Desert, Lac, l., Wi., U.S. ...B4 142
Vigan, Phil. ...C8 34
Vigo, Spain ...F2 16
Vigo, co., In., U.S. ...F3 107
Vijayawāda, India ...F4 40
Vike, Arm. ...C11 44
Viking, Ab., Can. ...C5 84
Vikna, Nor. ...D4 10
Vikna, i., Nor. ...D4 10
Vikramasingapuram, India ..H3 40
Vila de Sena, Moz. ...B6 56
Vila do Ibo, Moz. ...A7 56
Vila Fontes, Moz. ...B6 56
Vila Gamito, Moz. ...B6 56
Vilagarcía de Arousa, Spain .F2 16
Vilanandro, Tanjona, c., Madag. ...B7 56
Vilankulo, Moz. ...C6 56
Vilanova i la Geltrú, Spain .G7 16
Vila Real, Port. ...G3 16
Vilas, co., Wi., U.S. ...B4 142
Vila Velha, Braz. ...F3 74
Vilejka, Bela. ...B9 20
Vilhelmina, Swe. ...D7 10
Vilhena, Braz. ...F7 70
Viljandi, Est. ...G11 10
Viljuj, stm., Russia ...C14 26
Viljujsk, Russia ...C14 26
Vil'kickogo, proliv, strt., Russia ...B11 26
Villa Ángela, Arg. ...D5 72
Villa Bella, Bol. ...F6 70
Villacañas, Spain ...H5 16
Villacarrillo, Spain ...H5 16
Villach, Aus. ...G13 12
Villa Dolores, Arg. ...E4 72
Villa Grove, Il., U.S. ...D5 106
Villaguay, Arg. ...E6 72
Villahermosa, Mex. ...D6 78
Villaldama, Mex. ...D4 78
Villalonga, Arg. ...E4 69
Villa María, Arg. ...E4 72
Villa Mercedes, Arg. ...E4 72
Villa Montes, Bol. ...C5 72
Villanueva de la Serena, Spain ...H4 16
Villa Ocampo, Arg. ...D6 72
Villa Ojo de Agua, Arg. ...D5 72
Villa Park, Il., U.S. ...k8 106
Villa Rica, Ga., U.S. ...C2 103
Villarrica, Chile ...E2 69
Villarrica, Para. ...D6 72
Villarrobledo, Spain ...H5 16
Villas, N.J., U.S. ...C9 134
Villa Unión, Mex. ...C3 78
Villa Valeria, Arg. ...E4 72
Villavicencio, Col. ...C5 70

Villefranche-sur-Saône, Fr. ..E9 16
Villena, Spain ...H6 16
Villeneuve-sur-Lot, Fr. ...E7 16
Ville Platte, La., U.S. ...D3 111
Ville Saint-Georges, P.Q., Can. ...C7 90
Villeurbanne, Fr. ...E9 16
Villisca, Ia., U.S. ...D3 108
Vilnius, Lith. ...I11 10
Vilonia, Ar., U.S. ...B3 97
Vimmerby, Swe. ...H6 10
Viña del Mar, Chile ...D2 69
Vinalhaven, Me., U.S. ...D4 112
Vinalhaven Island, i., Me., U.S. ...D4 112
Vinaròs, Spain ...G7 16
Vincennes, In., U.S. ...G2 107
Vincennes Bay, b., Ant. ...C15 67
Vincent, Al., U.S. ...B3 94
Vindhya Range, mts., India ..E3 40
Vine Brook, stm., Ma., U.S. .g11 114
Vinegar Hill, mtn., Or., U.S. .C8 130
Vine Grove, Ky., U.S. ...C4 110
Vineland, N.J., U.S. ...E2 123
Vineyard Haven, Ma., U.S. ..D6 114
Vineyard Sound, strt., Ma., U.S. ...D6 114
Vinh, Viet. ...C5 34
Vinh Long, Viet. ...D5 34
Vinita, Ok., U.S. ...A6 129
Vinkovci, Cro. ...B7 18
Vinson Massif, mtn., Ant. ...D32 67
Vinton, Ia., U.S. ...B5 108
Vinton, La., U.S. ...D2 111
Vinton, co., Oh., U.S. ...C3 128
Vinton, Va., U.S. ...C3 139
Viola, Il., U.S. ...B3 106
Violet, La., U.S. ...k12 111
Virac, Phil. ...D8 34
Viramgām, India ...E2 40
Virandozero, Russia ...C14 8
Viranşehir, Tur. ...D8 44
Virden, Mb., Can. ...E1 86
Virden, Il., U.S. ...D4 106
Vire, Fr. ...C6 16
Virgin, stm., U.S. ...G8 121
Virginia, S. Afr. ...D4 56
Virginia, Al., U.S. ...g6 94
Virginia, Il., U.S. ...D3 106
Virginia, Mn., U.S. ...C6 116
Virginia, state, U.S. ...C4 139
Virginia Beach, Va., U.S. ...D7 139
Virginia City, Nv., U.S. ...D2 121
Virginia Peak, mtn., Nv., U.S. ...D2 121
Virgin Gorda, i., Br. Vir. Is. ..B7 80
Virgin Islands, dep., N.A. ..B7 80
Virgin Islands, is., N.A. ...E11 76
Viroqua, Wi., U.S. ...E3 142
Virovitica, Cro. ...B6 18
Virrat, Fin. ...E10 10
Virtsu, Est. ...G10 10
Virudunagar, India ...H3 40
Vis, Otok, i., Cro. ...C6 18
Visalia, Ca., U.S. ...D4 98
Visayan Sea, Phil. ...D8 34
Visby, Swe. ...H8 10
Viscount Melville Sound, strt., N.T., Can. ...D17 82
Viseu, Port. ...G3 16
Vishākhapatnam, India ...H4 40
Vista, Ca., U.S. ...F5 98
Vistula see Wisła, stm., Pol. ...C5 20
Vitarte, Peru ...F4 70
Viterbo, Italy ...C3 18
Viti Levu, i., Fiji ...F11 58
Vitim, Russia ...D13 26
Vitim, stm., Russia ...D13 26
Vitória, Braz. ...F3 74
Vitoria see Gasteiz, Spain ..F5 16
Vitória da Conquista, Braz. ..D3 74
Vitré, Fr. ...C6 16
Vitry-le-François, Fr. ...C9 16
Vittoria, Italy ...F5 18
Vittorio Veneto, Italy ...B4 18
Vivian, La., U.S. ...B2 111
Vize, ostrov, i., Russia ...B9 26
Vizianagaram, India ...F4 40
Vizinga, Russia ...B9 22
Vjatka, stm., Russia ...D7 26
Vjatskie Poljany, Russia ...C9 22
Vjazemskij, Russia ...B14 26
Vjaz'ma, Russia ...B13 20
Vladikavkaz, Russia ...E6 26
Vladikavkaz see Ordzhonikidze, Ukr. ...F13 20
Vladimir, Russia ...D6 26
Vladivostok, Russia ...E15 26
Vlissingen, Neth. ...E8 12
Vlorë, Alb. ...D7 18
Vogel Peak see Dimlang, mtn., Nig. ...E7 50
Vohimena, Tanjona, c., Madag. ...D8 56
Voi, Kenya ...D7 54
Voinjama, Lib. ...E3 50
Voj-Vož, Russia ...B9 22
Volcano, Hi., U.S. ...D6 104
Volcano Islands see Kazan-rettō, is., Japan ..F17 64
Volga, stm., Russia ...E6 26
Volga-Baltic Canal see Volgo-Baltijskij kanal, Russia ...B6 22

Volga Plateau see Privolžskaja vozvyšennost', plat., Russia ...D6 26
Volgo-Baltijskij kanal, Russia ...B6 22
Volgodonsk, Russia ...E6 26
Volgograd, Russia ...E6 26
Volgograd Reservoir see Volgogradskoe vodohranilišče, res., Russia ...D8 22
Volgogradskoe vodohranilišče, res., Russia ...D8 22
Volhov, Russia ...D12 6
Volksrust, S. Afr. ...D4 56
Volnovakha, Ukr. ...F14 20
Voločanka, Russia ...B11 26
Volodarskoe, Kaz. ...D8 26
Volodymyr-Volyns'kyi, Ukr. ...D8 20
Vologda, Russia ...D6 26
Vólos, Grc. ...E9 18
Volos, Gulf of see Pagasitikós Kólpos, b., Grc. ...E9 18
Volosovo, Russia ...G13 10
Vol'sk, Russia ...D6 26
Volta, stm., Ghana ...E5 50
Volta Lake, res., Ghana ...E5 50
Volta Redonda, Braz. ...F3 74
Volterra, Italy ...C3 18
Volusia, co., Fl., U.S. ...C5 102
Volžsk, Russia ...C8 22
Volžskij, Russia ...E6 26
Vondrozo, Madag. ...C8 56
Von Frank Mountain, mtn., Ak., U.S. ...C9 95
Vonore, Tn., U.S. ...D9 135
Vordingborg, Den. ...I4 10
Vórioi Sporádhes, is., Grc. ..E10 18
Vórios Evvoïkós Kólpos, b., Grc. ...E9 18
Vorkuta, Russia ...C8 26
Vormsi, i., Est. ...G10 10
Voronež, Russia ...D5 26
Voroshilovsk see Alchevs'k, Ukr. ...E15 20
Vorpommern, hist. reg., Ger. ...D13 12
Võrtsjärv, l., Est. ...G12 10
Võru, Est. ...H12 10
Vosges, mts., Fr. ...C10 16
Voss, Nor. ...F2 10
Vostočno-Sibirskoe more, Russia ...B17 26
Vostočnyj Sajan, mts., Russia ...D11 26
Vostok, i., Kir. ...F14 58
Votkinsk, Russia ...D7 26
Votuporanga, Braz. ...F2 74
Voyageurs National Park, Mn., U.S. ...B5 116
Vožega, Russia ...B7 22
Voznesens'k, Ukr. ...F11 20
Vraca, Blg. ...C9 18
Vrangelja, ostrov, i., Russia ...B20 26
Vranje, Yugo. ...C8 18
Vrede, S. Afr. ...D4 56
Vršac, Yugo. ...B8 18
Vryburg, S. Afr. ...D3 56
Vryheid, S. Afr. ...D5 56
Vsevidof, Mount, mtn., Ak., U.S. ...E6 95
Vukovar, Cro. ...B7 18
Vulcan, Ab., Can. ...D4 84
Vyborg, Russia ...C4 26
Vyčegda, stm., Russia ...C6 26
Vym', stm., Russia ...B9 22
Vyšnij Voločok, Russia ...C5 26
Vytegra, Russia ...B6 22

W

Wa, Ghana ...D4 50
Waajid, Som. ...C8 54
Waal, stm., Eur. ...E9 12
Waawaa, Puu, mtn., Hi., U.S. ...D6 104
Wabag, Pap. N. Gui. ...H11 32
Wabana (Bell Island), Nf., Can. ...E5 88
Wabasca, Ab., Can. ...B4 84
Wabasca, stm., Ab., Can. ...f1 84
Wabash, co., Il., U.S. ...E6 106
Wabash, In., U.S. ...C6 107
Wabash, co., In., U.S. ...C6 107
Wabash, stm., U.S. ...H2 107
Wabash, stm., U.S. ...D10 92
Wabasha, Mn., U.S. ...F6 116
Wabasha, co., Mn., U.S. ...F6 116
Wabasso, Fl., U.S. ...E6 102
Wabasso, Mn., U.S. ...F3 116
Wabaunsee, co., Ks., U.S. ...D7 109
Wabeno, Wi., U.S. ...C5 142
Wabowden, Mb., Can. ...B2 86
Wabush, Nf., Can. ...h8 88
Waccamaw, stm., U.S. ...D9 133
Waccamaw, Lake, l., N.C., U.S. ...C4 126
Waccasassa Bay, b., Fl., U.S. ...C4 102
Wachusett Mountain, mtn., Ma., U.S. ...B4 114
Wachusett Reservoir, res., Ma., U.S. ...B4 114
Waco, Tx., U.S. ...D4 136

Name	Map Ref.	Page

Waco Lake, res., Tx., U.S. . **D4** 136
Waconda Lake, res., Ks.,
  U.S. **C5** 109
Waconia, Mn., U.S. **F5** 116
Waddān, Libya **E8** 48
Waddenzee, strt., Neth. . . . **D9** 12
Waddi Chappal, Afr. **B2** 54
Waddington, Mount, mtn.,
  B.C., Can. **D5** 85
Wadena, Mn., U.S. **D3** 116
Wadena, co., Mn., U.S. . . . **D4** 116
Wadesboro, N.C., U.S. **C2** 126
Wādī Ḥalfā', Sudan **F11** 48
Wading, stm., N.J., U.S. . . . **D3** 123
Wadley, Ga., U.S. **D4** 103
Wad Madanī, Sudan **H11** 48
Wadmalaw Island, i., S.C.,
  U.S. **F7** 133
Wadsworth, Il., U.S. **h9** 106
Wadsworth, Nv., U.S. **D2** 121
Wadsworth, Oh., U.S. **A4** 128
Wafangdian, China **B5** 30
Wagadugu see
  Ouagadougou, Burkina **D4** 50
Wagener, S.C., U.S. **D5** 133
Wagga Wagga, Austl. **H4** 62
Wagin, Austl. **G2** 60
Wagner, S.D., U.S. **D7** 134
Wagoner, Ok., U.S. **B6** 129
Wagoner, co., Ok., U.S. . . . **B6** 129
Wagontire Mountain, mtn.,
  Or., U.S. **D7** 130
Waha, Libya **E9** 48
Wahai, Indon. **D7** 36
Wāh Cantonment, Pak. . . . **D10** 42
Wahiawa, Hi., U.S. **B3** 104
Wahiawa Reservoir, res.,
  Hi., U.S. **g9** 104
Wahkiakum, co., Wa., U.S. **C2** 140
Wahoo, Ne., U.S. **C9** 120
Wahpeton, N.D., U.S. **C9** 127
Wahran, Alg. **C4** 48
Wahweap Creek, stm., Ut.,
  U.S. **F4** 137
Waialua, Hi., U.S. **B3** 104
Waialua Bay, b., Hi., U.S. . **B3** 104
Waianae, Hi., U.S. **B3** 104
Waianae Range, mts., Hi.,
  U.S. **f9** 104
Waidhofen an der Ybbs,
  Aus. **G14** 12
Waigeo, Pulau, i., Indon. . . **C8** 36
Waikabubak, Indon. **E5** 36
Waikapu, Hi., U.S. **C5** 104
Waikato, stm., N.Z. **o14** 63c
Waikiki Beach, Hi., U.S. . . **g10** 104
Wailua, Hi., U.S. **A2** 104
Wailuku, Hi., U.S. **C5** 104
Waimanalo, Hi., U.S. **B4** 104
Waimanalo Bay, b., Hi.,
  U.S. **g11** 104
Waimate, N.Z. **p13** 63c
Waimea, Hi., U.S. **B2** 104
Waimea, Hi., U.S. **f9** 104
Wainganga, stm., India . . . **E3** 40
Waingapu, Indon. **E6** 36
Wainwright, Ab., Can. **C5** 84
Wainwright, Ak., U.S. **A8** 95
Waipahu, Hi., U.S. **B3** 104
Waipara, N.Z. **p13** 63c
Waipio Acres, Hi., U.S. . . . **g9** 104
Waipio Peninsula, pen., Hi.,
  U.S. **g10** 104
Wairoa, N.Z. **o14** 63c
Waitara, N.Z. **o13** 63c
Waitemata, N.Z. **o13** 63c
Waite Park, Mn., U.S. **E4** 116
Waits, stm., Vt., U.S. **C4** 138
Waitsburg, Wa., U.S. **C7** 140
Wajir, Kenya **C8** 54
Waka, D.R.C. **C4** 54
Waka, Eth. **B7** 54
Wakarusa, In., U.S. **A5** 107
Wakarusa, stm., Ks., U.S. . . **D8** 109
Wakasa-wan, b., Japan . . . **C3** 31
Wakatomika Creek, stm.,
  Oh., U.S. **B3** 128
Wakayama, Japan **E15** 28
Wake, co., N.C., U.S. **B4** 126
WaKeeney, Ks., U.S. **C4** 109
Wakefield, P.Q., Can. **D2** 90
Wakefield, Ks., U.S. **C6** 109
Wakefield, Ma., U.S. **B5** 114
Wakefield, Mi., U.S. **n12** 115
Wakefield, Ne., U.S. **B9** 120
Wakefield, R.I., U.S. **F3** 132
Wakefield, Va., U.S. **D6** 139
Wake Forest, N.C., U.S. . . . **B4** 126
Wake Island, dep., Oc. . . . **C10** 58
Wakema, Myan. **C3** 34
Wakeman, Oh., U.S. **A3** 128
Wakkanai, Japan **B16** 28
Waku Kungo, Ang. **F3** 54
Wakulla, co., Fl., U.S. **B2** 102
Walachia, hist. reg., Rom. . **G8** 20
Walbridge, Oh., U.S. **e6** 128
Wałbrzych, Pol. **D4** 20
Walcott, Ia., U.S. **C7** 108
Walcott, Lake, res., Id., U.S. **G5** 105
Wałcz, Pol. **C4** 20
Walden, Can. **A3** 89
Walden, Co., U.S. **A4** 99
Walden, N.Y., U.S. **D6** 125
Waldenburg see Wałbrzych,
  Pol. **D4** 20

Walden Ridge, mtn., Tn.,
  U.S. **D8** 135
Waldheim, Sk., Can. **E2** 91
Waldo, Ar., U.S. **D2** 97
Waldoboro, Me., U.S. **D3** 112
Waldo Lake, l., Ma., U.S. . . **h11** 114
Waldo Lake, l., Or., U.S. . . **D4** 130
Waldport, Or., U.S. **C2** 130
Waldron, Ar., U.S. **C1** 97
Waldron, In., U.S. **F6** 107
Waldwick, N.J., U.S. **A4** 123
Wales, prov., U.K. **E4** 12
Waleska, Ga., U.S. **B2** 103
Walgett, Austl. **G4** 62
Walgreen Coast, Ant. . . . **D30** 67
Walhalla, N.D., U.S. **A8** 127
Walhalla, S.C., U.S. **B1** 133
Walhonding, stm., Oh., U.S. **B3** 128
Walikale, D.R.C. **D5** 54
Walker, Ia., U.S. **B6** 108
Walker, La., U.S. **g10** 111
Walker, Mi., U.S. **E5** 115
Walker, Mn., U.S. **C4** 116
Walker, co., Al., U.S. **B2** 94
Walker, co., Ga., U.S. **B1** 103
Walker, co., Tx., U.S. **D5** 136
Walker, stm., Nv., U.S. . . . **D3** 121
Walker Lake, l., Nv., U.S. . . **E3** 121
Walker River Indian
  Reservation, Nv., U.S. . **D3** 121
Walkersville, Md., U.S. . . . **B3** 113
Walkerton, On., Can. **C3** 89
Walkerton, In., U.S. **B5** 107
Walkertown, N.C., U.S. . . . **A2** 126
Walkerville, Mt., U.S. **D4** 119
Wall, S.D., U.S. **D3** 134
Wallace, Id., U.S. **B3** 105
Wallace, N.C., U.S. **B4** 126
Wallace, co., Ks., U.S. **D2** 109
Wallaceburg, On., Can. . . . **E2** 89
Wallace Lake, res., La., U.S. **B2** 111
Walla Walla, Wa., U.S. . . . **C7** 140
Walla Walla, co., Wa., U.S. **C7** 140
Walla Walla, stm., U.S. . . . **C7** 140
Walled Lake, Mi., U.S. . . . **o15** 115
Wallen, In., U.S. **B7** 107
Wallenpaupack, Lake, l.,
  Pa., U.S. **D11** 131
Waller, Tx., U.S. **q14** 136
Waller, co., Tx., U.S. **E4** 136
Wallingford, Ct., U.S. **D4** 100
Wallingford, Vt., U.S. **E3** 138
Wallington, N.J., U.S. **h8** 123
Wallis, Îles, is., Wal./F. . . **F12** 58
Wallis and Futuna, dep.,
  Oc. **F12** 58
Wallkill, N.Y., U.S. **D6** 125
Wallkill, stm., N.Y., U.S. . . . **D6** 125
Wall Lake, Ia., U.S. **B2** 108
Wall Lake, l., Ia., U.S. **B4** 108
Walloomsac, stm., U.S. . . . **F2** 138
Walloon Lake, l., Mi., U.S. . **C6** 115
Wallowa, Or., U.S. **B9** 130
Wallowa, co., Or., U.S. . . . **B9** 130
Wallowa Mountains, mts.,
  Or., U.S. **B9** 130
Wallula, Lake, res., U.S. . . **C7** 140
Wallum Lake, l., R.I., U.S. . **A1** 132
Walnut, Ia., U.S. **C2** 108
Walnut, Il., U.S. **B4** 106
Walnut, stm., Ks., U.S. . . . **E6** 109
Walnut Canyon National
  Monument, Az., U.S. . . **B4** 96
Walnut Cove, N.C., U.S. . . **A2** 126
Walnut Creek, Ca., U.S. . . **h8** 98
Walnut Creek, stm., Ks.,
  U.S. **D4** 109
Walnut Grove, Al., U.S. . . . **A3** 94
Walnut Grove, Mn., U.S. . . **F3** 116
Walnutport, Pa., U.S. **E10** 131
Walnut Ridge, Ar., U.S. . . . **A5** 97
Walpole, Austl. **H2** 60
Walpole, Ma., U.S. **B5** 114
Walpole, N.H., U.S. **D2** 122
Walsall, Eng., U.K. **D6** 12
Walsenburg, Co., U.S. **D6** 99
Walsh, Co., U.S. **D8** 99
Walsh, co., N.D., U.S. **A8** 127
Walterboro, S.C., U.S. **F6** 133
Walter F. George Dam, U.S. **D4** 94
Walter F. George Lake, res.,
  U.S. **D4** 94
Walters, Ok., U.S. **C3** 129
Walthall, co., Ms., U.S. . . . **D3** 117
Waltham, Ma., U.S. **B5** 114
Walthill, Ne., U.S. **B9** 120
Walthourville, Ga., U.S. . . . **E5** 103
Walton, In., U.S. **C5** 107
Walton, Ky., U.S. **B5** 110
Walton, N.Y., U.S. **C5** 125
Walton, co., Fl., U.S. **u15** 102
Walton, co., Ga., U.S. **C3** 103
Walvis Bay, Nmb. **C1** 56
Walvis Bay, b., Nmb. **C1** 56
Walvis Ridge **K14** 66
Walworth, Wi., U.S. **F5** 142
Walworth, co., S.D., U.S. . . **B5** 134
Walworth, co., Wi., U.S. . . . **F5** 142
Wamac, Il., U.S. **E4** 106
Wamba, D.R.C. **C5** 54
Wamba, Nig. **E6** 50
Wamba, stm., Afr. **E3** 54
Wamego, Ks., U.S. **C7** 109
Wamesit, Ma., U.S. **A5** 114

Wamsutter, Wy., U.S. **E5** 143
Wanaka, N.Z. **p12** 63c
Wanamingo, Mn., U.S. . . . **F6** 116
Wanapum Dam, Wa., U.S. . **C6** 140
Wanapum Lake, res., Wa.,
  U.S. **B6** 140
Wanaque, N.J., U.S. **A4** 123
Wanaque Reservoir, res.,
  N.J., U.S. **A4** 123
Wanatah, In., U.S. **B4** 107
Wanchese, N.C., U.S. **B7** 126
Wando, stm., S.C., U.S. . . . **F8** 133
Wando Woods, S.C., U.S. . **k11** 133
Wanfoxia, China **A7** 30
Wanganui, N.Z. **p13** 63c
Wangaratta, Austl. **H4** 62
Wangiwangi, Pulau, i.,
  Indon. **E6** 36
Wangqing, China **B1** 31
Wanigela, Pap. N. Gui. . . **H12** 32
Wanneroo, Austl. **G2** 60
Wanning, China **F3** 30
Wanxian, China **E9** 28
Wanyuan, China **C2** 30
Wanzai, China **D3** 30
Wapakoneta, Oh., U.S. . . . **B1** 128
Wapato, Wa., U.S. **C5** 140
Wapawekka Lake, l., Sk.,
  Can. **D7** 118
Wapello, Ia., U.S. **C6** 108
Wapello, co., Ia., U.S. **C5** 108
Wapiti, stm., Can. **B1** 84
Wappapello, Lake, res.,
  Mo., U.S. **D7** 118
Wappingers Falls, N.Y., U.S. **D7** 125
Wapsipinicon, stm., Ia., U.S. **B6** 108
War, W.V., U.S. **D3** 141
Waramaug, Lake, l., Ct.,
  U.S. **C2** 100
Warangal, India **F3** 40
Ward, Ar., U.S. **B4** 97
Ward, co., N.D., U.S. **A4** 127
Ward, co., Tx., U.S. **D1** 136
Warden, Wa., U.S. **C6** 140
Wardha, India **E3** 40
Ward Mountain, mtn., Mt.,
  U.S. **D2** 119
Ware, Ma., U.S. **B3** 114
Ware, co., Ga., U.S. **E4** 103
Ware, stm., Ma., U.S. **B3** 114
War Eagle Mountain, mtn.,
  Id., U.S. **G2** 105
Wareham, Ma., U.S. **C6** 114
Warehouse Point, Ct., U.S. **B5** 100
Waren, Indon. **G10** 32
Ware Shoals, S.C., U.S. . . . **C3** 133
Warfield, B.C., Can. **E9** 85
Wargla, Alg. **B6** 48
Warialda, Austl. **F5** 62
Warin Chamrap, Thai. **C4** 34
Warmbad, Nmb. **D2** 56
Warmbad, S. Afr. **C4** 56
Warminster, Pa., U.S. . . . **F11** 131
Warm Springs Indian
  Reservation, Or., U.S. . **C5** 130
Warm Springs Reservoir,
  res., Or., U.S. **D8** 130
Warner, N.H., U.S. **D3** 122
Warner, Ok., U.S. **B6** 129
Warner, stm., N.H., U.S. . . **D3** 122
Warner Mountains, mts.,
  Ca., U.S. **B3** 98
Warner Peak, mtn., Or.,
  U.S. **E7** 130
Warner Robins, Ga., U.S. . . **D3** 103
Warr Acres, Ok., U.S. **B4** 129
Warracknabeal, Austl. **H3** 62
Warragul, Austl. **H4** 62
Warren, Ar., U.S. **D3** 97
Warren, Il., U.S. **A4** 106
Warren, In., U.S. **C7** 107
Warren, Ma., U.S. **B3** 114
Warren, Mi., U.S. **F7** 115
Warren, Mn., U.S. **B2** 116
Warren, Oh., U.S. **A5** 128
Warren, Or., U.S. **B4** 130
Warren, Pa., U.S. **C3** 131
Warren, R.I., U.S. **D5** 132
Warren, Vt., U.S. **C3** 138
Warren, co., Ga., U.S. **C4** 103
Warren, co., Ia., U.S. **C4** 108
Warren, co., Il., U.S. **C3** 106
Warren, co., In., U.S. **D3** 107
Warren, co., Ky., U.S. **C3** 110
Warren, co., Mo., U.S. **C6** 118
Warren, co., N.C., U.S. . . . **A4** 126
Warren, co., N.J., U.S. **B3** 123
Warren, co., N.Y., U.S. . . . **B7** 125
Warren, co., Oh., U.S. **C1** 128
Warren, co., Pa., U.S. **C3** 131
Warren, co., Tn., U.S. **D8** 135
Warren, co., Va., U.S. **B4** 139
Warren, stm., U.S. **D5** 132
Warren Park, In., U.S. . . . **k10** 107
Warren Peaks, mts., Wy.,
  U.S. **B8** 143
Warrensburg, Il., U.S. **D4** 106
Warrensburg, Mo., U.S. . . . **C4** 118
Warrensburg, N.Y., U.S. . . **B7** 125
Warrensville Heights, Oh.,
  U.S. **h9** 128
Warrenton, S. Afr. **D3** 56
Warrenton, Ga., U.S. **C4** 103
Warrenton, Mo., U.S. **C6** 118

Warrenton, N.C., U.S. **A4** 126
Warrenton, Or., U.S. **A3** 130
Warrenton, Va., U.S. **B5** 139
Warrenville, Il., U.S. **k8** 106
Warrenville, S.C., U.S. . . . **D4** 133
Warri, Nig. **E6** 50
Warrick, co., In., U.S. **H3** 107
Warrington, Fl., U.S. **u14** 102
Warrior, Al., U.S. **B3** 94
Warrior Lake, res., Al., U.S. **C2** 94
Warrnambool, Austl. **H3** 62
Warroad, Mn., U.S. **B3** 116
Warsaw see Warszawa, Pol. **C6** 20
Warsaw, Il., U.S. **C2** 106
Warsaw, In., U.S. **B6** 107
Warsaw, Ky., U.S. **B5** 110
Warsaw, Mo., U.S. **C4** 118
Warsaw, N.C., U.S. **B4** 126
Warsaw, N.Y., U.S. **C2** 125
Warsaw, Va., U.S. **C6** 139
Warszawa (Warsaw), Pol. . **C6** 20
Wartburg, Tn., U.S. **C9** 135
Warwick, Austl. **F5** 62
Warwick, P.Q., Can. **D6** 90
Warwick, Md., U.S. **B6** 113
Warwick, N.Y., U.S. **D6** 125
Warwick, R.I., U.S. **D4** 132
Wasaga Beach, On., Can. . **C4** 89
Wasatch, co., Ut., U.S. . . . **C4** 137
Wasco, Ca., U.S. **E4** 98
Wasco, co., Or., U.S. **B5** 130
Waseca, Mn., U.S. **F5** 116
Waseca, co., Mn., U.S. . . . **F5** 116
Washakie, co., Wy., U.S. . . **C5** 143
Washakie Needles, mts.,
  Wy., U.S. **C3** 143
Washburn, Il., U.S. **C4** 106
Washburn, Me., U.S. **B4** 112
Washburn, N.D., U.S. **B5** 127
Washburn, Wi., U.S. **B3** 142
Washburn, co., Wi., U.S. . . **C2** 142
Washburn, Mount, mtn.,
  Wy., U.S. **B2** 143
Wāshīm, India **E3** 40
Washington, D.C., U.S. . . . **C3** 113
Washington, Ga., U.S. **C4** 103
Washington, Ia., U.S. **C6** 108
Washington, Il., U.S. **C4** 106
Washington, In., U.S. **G3** 107
Washington, Ks., U.S. **C6** 109
Washington, Ky., U.S. **B6** 110
Washington, La., U.S. **D3** 111
Washington, Mo., U.S. **C6** 118
Washington, Ms., U.S. **D2** 117
Washington, N.C., U.S. . . . **B5** 126
Washington, N.J., U.S. . . . **B3** 123
Washington, Pa., U.S. **F1** 131
Washington, Ut., U.S. **F2** 137
Washington, co., Al., U.S. . **D1** 94
Washington, co., Ar., U.S. . **A1** 97
Washington, co., Co., U.S. . **B7** 99
Washington, co., Fl., U.S. . **u16** 102
Washington, co., Ga., U.S. . **C4** 103
Washington, co., Ia., U.S. . **C6** 108
Washington, co., Id., U.S. . **E2** 105
Washington, co., Il., U.S. . . **E4** 106
Washington, co., In., U.S. . **G5** 107
Washington, co., Ks., U.S. . **C6** 109
Washington, co., Ky., U.S. . **C4** 110
Washington, co., La., U.S. . **D5** 111
Washington, co., Md., U.S. **A2** 113
Washington, co., Me., U.S. **D5** 112
Washington, co., Mn., U.S. **E6** 116
Washington, co., Mo., U.S. **D7** 118
Washington, co., Ms., U.S. **B3** 117
Washington, co., N.C., U.S. **B6** 126
Washington, co., Ne., U.S. . **C9** 120
Washington, co., N.Y., U.S. **B7** 125
Washington, co., Oh., U.S. . **C4** 128
Washington, co., Ok., U.S. . **A6** 129
Washington, co., Or., U.S. . **B3** 130
Washington, co., Pa., U.S. . **F1** 131
Washington, co., R.I., U.S. . **E2** 132
Washington, co., Tn., U.S. **C11** 135
Washington, co., Tx., U.S. . **D4** 136
Washington, co., Ut., U.S. . **F2** 137
Washington, co., Va., U.S. . **f9** 139
Washington, co., Vt., U.S. . **C3** 138
Washington, co., Wi., U.S. . **E5** 142
Washington, state, U.S. . . . **B5** 140
Washington, Lake, l., Fl.,
  U.S. **D6** 102
Washington, Lake, l., Mn.,
  U.S. **E4** 116
Washington, Lake, l., Ms.,
  U.S. **B3** 117
Washington, Lake, l., Wa.,
  U.S. **e11** 140
Washington, Mount, mtn.,
  N.H., U.S. **B4** 122
Washington Court House,
  Oh., U.S. **C2** 128
Washington Island, i., Wi.,
  U.S. **C7** 142
Washington Park, Il., U.S. . **E3** 106
Washington Terrace, Ut.,
  U.S. **B4** 137
Washita, co., Ok., U.S. . . . **B3** 129
Washita, stm., Ok., U.S. . . **C4** 129
Washoe, co., Nv., U.S. . . . **C2** 121
Washoe City, Nv., U.S. . . . **D2** 121
Washougal, Wa., U.S. **D3** 140
Washow Bay, b., Mb., Can. **D3** 86
Washtenaw, co., Mi., U.S. . **F7** 115

Wasilla, Ak., U.S. **C10** 95
Wasior, Indon. **D8** 36
Waskom, Tx., U.S. **C5** 136
Waspam, Nic. **C3** 80
Wasque Point, c., Ma., U.S. **D7** 114
Wassookeag, Lake, l., Me.,
  U.S. **C3** 112
Wassuk Range, mts., Nv.,
  U.S. **E3** 121
Wataga, Il., U.S. **B3** 106
Watampone, Indon. **D6** 36
Watansopeng, Indon. **D5** 36
Watauga, co., N.C., U.S. . . **A1** 126
Watauga, stm., Tn., U.S. . **C12** 135
Watauga Lake, res., Tn.,
  U.S. **C12** 135
Watchaug Pond, l., R.I.,
  U.S. **F2** 132
Watch Hill Point, c., R.I.,
  U.S. **G1** 132
Watchung, N.J., U.S. **B4** 123
Waterbury, Ct., U.S. **C3** 100
Waterbury, Vt., U.S. **C3** 138
Waterbury Center, Vt., U.S. **C3** 138
Waterbury Reservoir, res.,
  Vt., U.S. **C3** 138
Wateree, stm., S.C., U.S. . . **D6** 133
Wateree Lake, res., S.C.,
  U.S. **C6** 133
Waterford, Ire. **D3** 12
Waterford, Ct., U.S. **D7** 100
Waterford, N.Y., U.S. **C7** 125
Waterford, Pa., U.S. **C2** 131
Waterford, Wi., U.S. **F5** 142
Waterhen Lake, l., Mb.,
  Can. **C2** 86
Waterloo, Bel. **E9** 12
Waterloo, On., Can. **D4** 89
Waterloo, P.Q., Can. **D5** 90
Waterloo, Ia., U.S. **B5** 108
Waterloo, Il., U.S. **E3** 106
Waterloo, In., U.S. **B7** 107
Waterloo, N.Y., U.S. **C4** 125
Waterloo, Wi., U.S. **E5** 142
Waterman, Il., U.S. **B5** 106
Waterman Reservoir, res.,
  R.I., U.S. **B3** 132
Waterproof, La., U.S. **C4** 111
Watersmeet, Mi., U.S. . . **n12** 115
Waterton Lakes National
  Park, Ab., Can. **E3** 84
Watertown, Ct., U.S. **C3** 100
Watertown, Ma., U.S. . . . **g11** 114
Watertown, N.Y., U.S. **B5** 125
Watertown, S.D., U.S. **C8** 134
Watertown, Tn., U.S. **A5** 135
Watertown, Wi., U.S. **E5** 142
Water Valley, Ms., U.S. . . . **A4** 117
Waterville, Ks., U.S. **C7** 109
Waterville, Me., U.S. **D3** 112
Waterville, Mn., U.S. **F5** 116
Waterville, N.Y., U.S. **C5** 125
Waterville, Oh., U.S. **A2** 128
Waterville, Wa., U.S. **B5** 140
Watervliet, Mi., U.S. **F4** 115
Watervliet, N.Y., U.S. **C7** 125
Watford, On., Can. **E3** 89
Watford City, N.D., U.S. . . **B2** 127
Wathena, Ks., U.S. **C9** 109
Watheroo, Austl. **G2** 60
Watkins, Mn., U.S. **E4** 116
Watkins Glen, N.Y., U.S. . . **C4** 125
Watkinsville, Ga., U.S. . . . **C3** 103
Watling Island see San
  Salvador, i., Bah. **D10** 76
Watonga, Ok., U.S. **B3** 129
Watonwan, co., Mn., U.S. . **F4** 116
Watonwan, stm., Mn., U.S. **G4** 116
Watsa, D.R.C. **C5** 54
Watseka, Il., U.S. **C6** 106
Watsontown, Pa., U.S. . . . **D8** 131
Watsonville, Ca., U.S. **D3** 98
Watts Bar Dam, Tn., U.S. . **D9** 135
Watts Bar Lake, res., Tn.,
  U.S. **D9** 135
Wattsville, S.C., U.S. **B4** 133
Watubela, Kepulauan, is.,
  Indon. **D8** 36
Waubaushene, On., Can. . **C5** 89
Waubay, S.D., U.S. **B8** 134
Waubay Lake, l., S.D., U.S. **B8** 134
Wauchope, Austl. **E5** 60
Wauchula, Fl., U.S. **E5** 102
Wauconda, Il., U.S. **h8** 106
Waugh Mountain, mtn., Id.,
  U.S. **D4** 105
Waukee, Ia., U.S. **C4** 108
Waukegan, Il., U.S. **A6** 106
Waukesha, Wi., U.S. **F5** 142
Waukesha, co., Wi., U.S. . **E5** 142
Waukewan, Lake, l., N.H.,
  U.S. **C3** 122
Waukomis, Ok., U.S. **A4** 129
Waukon, Ia., U.S. **A6** 108
Waunakee, Wi., U.S. **E4** 142
Waungumbaug Lake, l., Ct.,
  U.S. **B6** 100
Waupaca, Wi., U.S. **D4** 142
Waupaca, co., Wi., U.S. . . . **D5** 142
Waupun, Wi., U.S. **E5** 142
Wauregan, Ct., U.S. **C8** 100
Waurika, Ok., U.S. **C4** 129
Waurika Lake, res., Ok.,
  U.S. **C3** 129

Name	Map Ref.	Page

Wausau, Wi., U.S. **D4** 142
Wausau, Lake, res., Wi., U.S. **D4** 142
Wauseon, Oh., U.S. **A1** 128
Waushara, co., Wi., U.S. . . **D4** 142
Wautoma, Wi., U.S. **D4** 142
Wauwatosa, Wi., U.S. . . . **m12** 142
Wave Hill, Austl. **D5** 60
Waveland, Ms., U.S. **E4** 117
Waverley, N.S., Can. **E6** 87
Waverly, Ia., U.S. **B5** 108
Waverly, Il., U.S. **D4** 106
Waverly, Ks., U.S. **D8** 109
Waverly, Mn., U.S. **E5** 116
Waverly, Mo., U.S. **B4** 118
Waverly, Ne., U.S. **D9** 120
Waverly, N.Y., U.S. **C4** 125
Waverly, Oh., U.S. **C3** 128
Waverly, Tn., U.S. **A4** 135
Waverly, Va., U.S. **C5** 139
Waverly, W.V., U.S. **B3** 141
Waverly Hall, Ga., U.S. . . . **D2** 103
Wāw, Sudan **I10** 48
Wāw al-Kabīr, Libya **E8** 48
Wawanesa, Mb., Can. **E2** 86
Wawasee, Lake, l., In., U.S. **B6** 107
Wawayanda Lake, l., N.J., U.S. **A4** 123
Wawota, Sk., Can. **H4** 91
Waxahachie, Tx., U.S. **C4** 136
Waxhaw, N.C., U.S. **C2** 126
Waycross, Ga., U.S. **E4** 103
Wayland, Ia., U.S. **C6** 108
Wayland, Ma., U.S. **g10** 114
Wayland, Mi., U.S. **F5** 115
Wayland, N.Y., U.S. **C3** 125
Waylyn, S.C., U.S. **k12** 133
Waymart, Pa., U.S. **C11** 131
Wayne, Mi., U.S. **p15** 115
Wayne, Ne., U.S. **B8** 120
Wayne, N.J., U.S. **B4** 123
Wayne, W.V., U.S. **C2** 141
Wayne, co., Ga., U.S. **E5** 103
Wayne, co., Ia., U.S. **D4** 108
Wayne, co., Il., U.S. **E5** 106
Wayne, co., In., U.S. **E7** 107
Wayne, co., Ky., U.S. **D5** 110
Wayne, co., Mi., U.S. **F7** 115
Wayne, co., Mo., U.S. . . . **D7** 118
Wayne, co., Ms., U.S. . . . **D5** 117
Wayne, co., N.C., U.S. . . . **B4** 126
Wayne, co., Ne., U.S. **B8** 120
Wayne, co., N.Y., U.S. . . . **B3** 125
Wayne, co., Oh., U.S. **B4** 128
Wayne, co., Pa., U.S. . . . **C11** 131
Wayne, co., Tn., U.S. **B4** 135
Wayne, co., Ut., U.S. **E4** 137
Wayne, co., W.V., U.S. . . . **C2** 141
Wayne City, Il., U.S. **E5** 106
Waynesboro, Ga., U.S. . . . **C4** 103
Waynesboro, Ms., U.S. . . . **D5** 117
Waynesboro, Pa., U.S. . . . **G6** 131
Waynesboro, Tn., U.S. . . . **B4** 135
Waynesboro, Va., U.S. . . . **B4** 139
Waynesburg, Oh., U.S. . . . **B4** 128
Waynesburg, Pa., U.S. . . . **G1** 131
Waynesville, Mo., U.S. . . . **D5** 118
Waynesville, N.C., U.S. . . **f10** 126
Waynesville, Oh., U.S. . . . **C1** 128
Waynetown, In., U.S. **D3** 107
Waynewood, Va., U.S. . . . **g12** 139
Waynoka, Ok., U.S. **A3** 129
Wayzata, Mn., U.S. **n11** 116
Waza, Cam. **D7** 50
We, Pulau, i., Indon. **B1** 36
Weakley, co., Tn., U.S. . . . **A3** 135
Weatherford, Ok., U.S. . . . **B3** 129
Weatherford, Tx., U.S. . . . **C4** 136
Weatherly, Pa., U.S. **E10** 131
Weatogue, Ct., U.S. **B4** 100
Weaver, Al., U.S. **B4** 94
Weaver Mountains, mts., Az., U.S. **C3** 96
Weaverville, Ca., U.S. . . . **B2** 98
Weaverville, N.C., U.S. . . **f10** 126
Webb, Al., U.S. **D4** 94
Webb, Ms., U.S. **B3** 117
Webb, co., Tx., U.S. **F3** 136
Webb City, Mo., U.S. **D3** 118
Webbers Falls, Ok., U.S. . . **B6** 129
Webberville, Mi., U.S. . . . **F6** 115
Webb Lake, l., Me., U.S. . . **D2** 112
Weber, co., Ut., U.S. **B4** 137
Weber City, Va., U.S. **f9** 139
Webster, Ma., U.S. **B4** 114
Webster, N.Y., U.S. **B3** 125
Webster, Pa., U.S. **F2** 131
Webster, S.D., U.S. **B8** 134
Webster, co., Ga., U.S. . . . **D2** 103
Webster, co., Ia., U.S. **B3** 108
Webster, co., Ky., U.S. . . . **C2** 110
Webster, co., La., U.S. . . . **B2** 111
Webster, co., Mo., U.S. . . **D5** 118
Webster, co., Ms., U.S. . . . **B4** 117
Webster, co., Ne., U.S. . . . **D7** 120
Webster, co., W.V., U.S. . . **C4** 141
Webster City, Ia., U.S. . . . **B4** 108
Webster Groves, Mo., U.S. **f13** 118
Webster Reservoir, res., Ks., U.S. **C4** 109
Webster Springs, W.V., U.S. **C4** 141
Websterville, Vt., U.S. . . . **C4** 138
Weda, Indon. **C7** 36
Weddell Sea, Ant. **C1** 67
Wedgeport, N.S., Can. . . . **F4** 87

Wedgewood, Mo., U.S. . . . **f13** 118
Wedowee, Al., U.S. **B4** 94
Weed, Ca., U.S. **B2** 98
Weed Heights, Nv., U.S. . . **E2** 121
Weedon, P.Q., Can. **D6** 90
Weedsport, N.Y., U.S. . . . **B4** 125
Weedville, Pa., U.S. **D5** 131
Weehawken, N.J., U.S. . . . **h8** 123
Weeksbury, Ky., U.S. **C7** 110
Weeping Water, Ne., U.S. . **D9** 120
Weichang, China **A4** 30
Weiden in der Oberpfalz, Ger. **F12** 12
Weifang, China **D11** 28
Weihai, China **D12** 28
Weimar, Ger. **E12** 12
Weimar, Tx., U.S. **E4** 136
Weinan, China **E9** 28
Weiner, Ar., U.S. **B5** 97
Weippe, Id., U.S. **C3** 105
Weir, Ks., U.S. **E9** 109
Weir, Lake, l., Fl., U.S. **C5** 102
Weirsdale, Fl., U.S. **D5** 102
Weirton, W.V., U.S. **A4** 141
Weiser, Id., U.S. **E2** 105
Weiser, stm., Id., U.S. . . . **E2** 105
Weishan Hu, l., China . . . **B4** 30
Weissenburg in Bayern, Ger. **F12** 12
Weissenfels, Ger. **E12** 12
Weiss Lake, res., Al., U.S. . **A4** 94
Weixi, China **A3** 34
Weixian, China **B4** 30
Wejherowo, Pol. **B5** 20
Welbourn Hill, Austl. **F5** 60
Welch, W.V., U.S. **D3** 141
Welcome, Mn., U.S. **G4** 116
Welcome, S.C., U.S. **B3** 133
Weld, co., Co., U.S. **A6** 99
Weldon, N.C., U.S. **A5** 126
Weldon Spring, Mo., U.S. . **f12** 118
Weleetka, Ok., U.S. **B5** 129
Welk'īṭē, Eth. **B7** 54
Welland, On., Can. **E5** 89
Wellesley, On., Can. **D4** 89
Wellesley, Ma., U.S. **B5** 114
Wellesley Islands, is., Austl. **D2** 62
Wellford, S.C., U.S. **B3** 133
Wellington, Austl. **G4** 62
Wellington, On., Can. . . . **D7** 89
Wellington, N.Z. **I11** 58
Wellington, Co., U.S. **A5** 99
Wellington, Ks., U.S. **E6** 109
Wellington, Mo., U.S. . . . **B4** 118
Wellington, Nv., U.S. . . . **E2** 121
Wellington, Oh., U.S. . . . **A3** 128
Wellington, Tx., U.S. **B2** 136
Wellington, Ut., U.S. **D5** 137
Wellington, Isla, i., Chile . **G2** 69
Wellman, Ia., U.S. **C6** 108
Wells, Me., U.S. **E2** 112
Wells, Mi., U.S. **C3** 115
Wells, Mn., U.S. **G5** 116
Wells, Nv., U.S. **B7** 121
Wells, co., In., U.S. **C7** 107
Wells, co., N.D., U.S. **B6** 127
Wells, stm., Vt., U.S. **C4** 138
Wellsboro, Pa., U.S. **C7** 131
Wellsburg, Ia., U.S. **B5** 108
Wellsburg, W.V., U.S. . . . **A4** 141
Wellston, Oh., U.S. **C3** 128
Wellston, Ok., U.S. **B4** 129
Wellsville, Ks., U.S. **D8** 109
Wellsville, Mo., U.S. **B6** 118
Wellsville, N.Y., U.S. **C3** 125
Wellsville, Oh., U.S. **B5** 128
Wellsville, Ut., U.S. **B4** 137
Wellton, Az., U.S. **E1** 96
Wels, Aus. **F13** 12
Welsh, La., U.S. **D3** 111
Wembley, Ab., Can. **B1** 84
Wenatchee, Wa., U.S. . . . **B5** 140
Wenatchee, stm., Wa., U.S. **B5** 140
Wenatchee Lake, l., Wa., U.S. **B5** 140
Wenatchee Mountains, mts., Wa., U.S. **B5** 140
Wenchang, China **F3** 30
Wenchi, Ghana **E4** 50
Wendell, Id., U.S. **G4** 105
Wendell, N.C., U.S. **B4** 126
Wendeng, China **B5** 30
Wendover, Ut., U.S. **C1** 137
Wengyuan, China **E3** 30
Wenham, Ma., U.S. **A6** 114
Wenham Lake, l., Ma., U.S. **f12** 114
Wenling, China **D5** 30
Wenshan, China **G8** 28
Wenshang, China **B4** 30
Wensu, China **A4** 40
Wentworth, Austl. **G3** 62
Wentworth, Lake, l., N.H., U.S. **C4** 122
Wentzville, Mo., U.S. **C7** 118
Wenzhou, China **F12** 28
Weohyakapka, Lake, l., Fl., U.S. **E5** 102
Werda, Bots. **D3** 56
Weri, Indon. **D8** 36
Werribee, Austl. **H3** 62
Wesel, Ger. **E10** 12
Weser, stm., Ger. **D11** 12
Weslaco, Tx., U.S. **F4** 136
Wesleyville, Nf., Can. . . . **D5** 88

Wesleyville, Pa., U.S. **B2** 131
Wessel, Cape, c., Austl. . . **C6** 60
Wessel Islands, is., Austl. . **C6** 60
Wesserunsett Lake, l., Me., U.S. **D3** 112
Wessington Springs, S.D., U.S. **C7** 134
Wesson, Ms., U.S. **D3** 117
West, Tx., U.S. **D4** 136
West, stm., Ct., U.S. **D5** 100
West, stm., Ma., U.S. **h9** 114
West, stm., Vt., U.S. **E3** 138
West Acton, Ma., U.S. . . . **g10** 114
West Alexandria, Oh., U.S. **C1** 128
West Allis, Wi., U.S. **m11** 142
West Alton, Mo., U.S. . . . **f13** 118
West Andover, Ma., U.S. . **A5** 114
West Antarctica, reg., Ant. **E29** 67
West Baden Springs, In., U.S. **G4** 107
West Baton Rouge, co., La., U.S. **D4** 111
West Bay, b., Fl., U.S. . . . **u16** 102
West Bay, b., N.C., U.S. . . **B6** 126
West Bay, b., Tx., U.S. . . . **r15** 136
West Bend, Ia., U.S. **B3** 108
West Bend, Wi., U.S. **E5** 142
West Bengal, prov., India . **E5** 40
West Berlin, N.J., U.S. . . . **D3** 123
West Billerica, Ma., U.S. . . **f10** 114
West Blocton, Al., U.S. . . . **B2** 94
Westborough, Ma., U.S. . . **B4** 114
West Bountiful, Ut., U.S. . . **C4** 137
West Boylston, Ma., U.S. . **B4** 114
West Branch, Ia., U.S. . . . **C6** 108
West Branch, Mi., U.S. . . . **D6** 115
West Branch Reservoir, res., Ct., U.S. **B3** 100
West Bridgewater, Ma., U.S. **B5** 114
Westbrook, Ct., U.S. **D6** 100
Westbrook, Me., U.S. . . . **E2** 112
Westbrook, Mn., U.S. . . . **F3** 116
West Burlington, Ia., U.S. . **D6** 108
West Butte, mtn., Mt., U.S. **B5** 119
Westby, Wi., U.S. **E3** 142
West Cache Creek, stm., Ok., U.S. **C3** 129
West Caldwell, N.J., U.S. . **B4** 123
West Canada Creek, stm., N.Y., U.S. **B6** 125
West Cape Howe, c., Austl. **H2** 60
West Caroline Basin **H16** 64
West Carroll, co., La., U.S. **B4** 111
West Carrollton, Oh., U.S. **C1** 128
West Carthage, N.Y., U.S. . **B5** 125
Westchester, Il., U.S. **k9** 106
West Chester, Pa., U.S. . . **G10** 131
Westchester, co., N.Y., U.S. **D7** 125
West Chicago, Il., U.S. . . . **k8** 106
West Chop, c., Ma., U.S. . . **D6** 114
West College Corner, In., U.S. **E8** 107
West Columbia, S.C., U.S. **D5** 133
West Columbia, Tx., U.S. . **E5** 136
West Concord, Ma., U.S. . **B5** 114
West Concord, Mn., U.S. . **F6** 116
West Concord, N.C., U.S. . **B2** 126
Westconnaug Reservoir, res., R.I., U.S. **C2** 132
West Cote Blanche Bay, b., La., U.S. **E4** 111
West Covina, Ca., U.S. . . **m13** 98
West Crossett, Ar., U.S. . . **D4** 97
West Cumberland, Me., U.S. **E2** 112
West Dennis, Ma., U.S. . . **C7** 114
West Des Moines, Ia., U.S. **C4** 108
West Elk Mountains, mts., Co., U.S. **C3** 99
West Elk Peak, mtn., Co., U.S. **C3** 99
Westerly, R.I., U.S. **F1** 132
Western Australia, state, Austl. **E2** 60
Western Desert, des., Egypt **F9** 14
Western Dvina (Zapadnaja Dvina), stm., Eur. **C4** 22
Western Ghāts, mts., India . **F3** 40
Westernport, Md., U.S. . . **m12** 113
Western Sahara, dep., Afr. . **B2** 50
Western Samoa see Samoa, ctry., Oc. **F12** 58
Western Sayans see Zapadnyj Sajan, mts., Russia **D11** 26
Western Springs, Il., U.S. . . **k9** 106
Westerville, Oh., U.S. . . . **B3** 128
West European Basin . . . **F6** 66
West Falkland, i., Falk. Is. . . **H4** 69
West Falmouth, Ma., U.S. . **C6** 114
West Fargo, N.D., U.S. . . . **C9** 127
West Feliciana, co., La., U.S. **D4** 111
Westfield, N.B., Can. **D3** 87
Westfield, In., U.S. **D5** 107
Westfield, Ma., U.S. **B2** 114
Westfield, N.J., U.S. **B4** 123
Westfield, N.Y., U.S. **C1** 125
Westfield, Pa., U.S. **C6** 131
Westfield, Wi., U.S. **E4** 142
Westfield, stm., Ma., U.S. . **B2** 114
West Fork, Ar., U.S. **B1** 97
West Fork, stm., W.V., U.S. **B4** 141
West Frankfort, Il., U.S. . . **F5** 106
West Freehold, N.J., U.S. . **C4** 123

West Friendship, Md., U.S. **B4** 113
Westgate, Fl., U.S. **F6** 102
West Grand Lake, l., Me., U.S. **C5** 112
West Grove, Pa., U.S. . . . **G10** 131
West Hanover, Ma., U.S. . **h12** 114
West Hartford, Ct., U.S. . . **B4** 100
West Haven, Ct., U.S. . . . **D4** 100
West Hazleton, Pa., U.S. . **E9** 131
West Helena, Ar., U.S. . . . **C5** 97
West Hill Reservoir, res., Ma., U.S. **B4** 114
Westhope, N.D., U.S. . . . **A4** 127
West Ice Shelf, Ant. **C13** 67
West Indies, is. **D11** 76
West Island, i., Ma., U.S. . . **C6** 114
West Jefferson, N.C., U.S. . **A1** 126
West Jefferson, Oh., U.S. . **C2** 128
West Jordan, Ut., U.S. . . . **C3** 137
West Kingston, R.I., U.S. . **F3** 132
West Lafayette, In., U.S. . . **D4** 107
West Lafayette, Oh., U.S. . **B4** 128
Westlake, La., U.S. **D2** 111
Westlake, Oh., U.S. **h9** 128
West Lake, l., Me., U.S. . . . **C4** 112
Westland, Mi., U.S. **F7** 115
West Laramie, Wy., U.S. . . **E7** 143
West Lawn, Pa., U.S. **F10** 131
West Lebanon, In., U.S. . . **D3** 107
West Liberty, Ia., U.S. . . . **C6** 108
West Liberty, Ky., U.S. . . . **C6** 110
West Liberty, Oh., U.S. . . . **B2** 128
West Liberty, W.V., U.S. . . **f8** 141
West Linn, Or., U.S. **B4** 130
Westlock, Ab., Can. **B4** 84
West Long Branch, N.J., U.S. **C4** 123
West Lorne, On., Can. . . . **E3** 89
West Marion, N.C., U.S. . . **f10** 126
West Medway, Ma., U.S. . **B5** 114
West Memphis, Ar., U.S. . **B5** 97
West Miami, Fl., U.S. **s13** 102
West Middlesex, Pa., U.S. . **D1** 131
West Mifflin, Pa., U.S. . . . **F2** 131
West Milton, Oh., U.S. . . . **C1** 128
West Milwaukee, Wi., U.S. **m12** 142
Westminster, Ca., U.S. . . . **n12** 98
Westminster, Co., U.S. . . . **B5** 99
Westminster, Md., U.S. . . **A4** 113
Westminster, S.C., U.S. . . **B1** 133
West Monroe, La., U.S. . . . **B3** 111
Westmont, Il., U.S. **k9** 106
Westmont, N.J., U.S. **D2** 123
Westmont, Pa., U.S. **F4** 131
Westmoreland, Tn., U.S. . **A5** 135
Westmoreland, co., Pa., U.S. **F2** 131
Westmoreland, co., Va., U.S. **B6** 139
Westmorland, Ca., U.S. . . **F6** 98
West Musquash Lake, l., Me., U.S. **C5** 112
West Mystic, Ct., U.S. . . . **D8** 100
West Newton, Pa., U.S. . . **F2** 131
West New York, N.J., U.S. . **h8** 123
West Nicholson, Zimb. . . . **C4** 56
West Nishnabotna, stm., Ia., U.S. **C2** 108
West Norriton, Pa., U.S. . . **o20** 131
Weston, Ct., U.S. **E2** 100
Weston, Ma., U.S. **g10** 114
Weston, Mo., U.S. **B3** 118
Weston, Oh., U.S. **A2** 128
Weston, W.V., U.S. **B4** 141
Weston, co., Wy., U.S. . . . **C8** 143
Weston-super-Mare, Eng., U.K. **E5** 12
West Orange, N.J., U.S. . . **B4** 123
Westover, Md., U.S. **D6** 113
Westover, W.V., U.S. **B5** 141
Westover Air Force Base, mil., Ma., U.S. **B2** 114
West Palm Beach, Fl., U.S. **F6** 102
West Pawlet, Vt., U.S. . . . **E2** 138
West Pearl, stm., La., U.S. . **D6** 111
West Pelzer, S.C., U.S. . . . **B3** 133
West Pensacola, Fl., U.S. . **u14** 102
West Peoria, Il., U.S. **C4** 106
Westphalia, Mi., U.S. **F6** 115
West Pittsburg, Pa., U.S. . **E1** 131
West Pittston, Pa., U.S. . . **m17** 131
West Plains, Mo., U.S. . . . **E6** 118
West Point, Ca., U.S. **C3** 98
West Point, Ga., U.S. **D1** 103
West Point, Ia., U.S. **D6** 108
West Point, Ky., U.S. **C4** 110
West Point, Ms., U.S. . . . **B5** 117
West Point, Ne., U.S. **C9** 120
West Point, N.Y., U.S. . . . **D7** 125
West Point, Va., U.S. **C6** 139
West Point, mtn., Ak., U.S. **C11** 95
Westport, On., Can. **C8** 89
Westport, Ct., U.S. **E2** 100
Westport, In., U.S. **F6** 107
Westport, Wa., U.S. **C1** 140
West Portsmouth, Oh., U.S. **D2** 128
West Quoddy Head, c., Me., U.S. **D6** 112
West Reading, Pa., U.S. . . **F10** 131
West Rutland, Vt., U.S. . . **D2** 138
West Saint Paul, Mn., U.S. **n12** 116
West Salem, Il., U.S. **E5** 106
West Salem, Oh., U.S. . . . **B3** 128

West Salem, Wi., U.S. . . . **E2** 142
West Scarborough, Me., U.S. **E2** 112
West Seneca, N.Y., U.S. . . **C2** 125
West Siberian Lowland see Zapadno-Sibirskaja ravnina, pl., Russia . . . **C9** 26
West Simsbury, Ct., U.S. . **B4** 100
West Slope, Or., U.S. **g12** 130
West Spanish Peak, mtn., Co., U.S. **D6** 99
West Springfield, Ma., U.S. **B2** 114
West Springfield, Va., U.S. **g12** 139
West Swanzey, N.H., U.S. . **E2** 122
West Terre Haute, In., U.S. **F3** 107
West Thompson Lake, res., Ct., U.S. **B8** 100
West Union, Ia., U.S. **B6** 108
West Union, Oh., U.S. . . . **D2** 128
West Union, W.V., U.S. . . **B4** 141
West Unity, Oh., U.S. **A1** 128
West University Place, Tx., U.S. **r14** 136
West Valley City, Ut., U.S. **C4** 137
West Vancouver, B.C., Can. **f12** 85
West Van Lear, Ky., U.S. . . **C7** 110
West View, Pa., U.S. **h13** 131
Westville, Il., U.S. **C6** 106
Westville, In., U.S. **A4** 107
Westville, N.H., U.S. **E4** 122
Westville, N.J., U.S. **D2** 123
Westville, Ok., U.S. **A7** 129
Westville Lake, res., Ma., U.S. **B3** 114
West Virginia, state, U.S. . **C4** 141
West Walker, stm., U.S. . . **E2** 121
West Wareham, Ma., U.S. **C6** 114
West Warwick, R.I., U.S. . . **D3** 132
Westwego, La., U.S. **k11** 111
Westwood, Ca., U.S. **B3** 98
Westwood, Ks., U.S. **k16** 109
Westwood, Ky., U.S. **B7** 110
Westwood, Ma., U.S. **B5** 114
Westwood, N.J., U.S. **B4** 123
Westwood Lakes, Fl., U.S. . **s13** 102
West Wyalong, Austl. **G4** 62
West Wyoming, Pa., U.S. . **n17** 131
West Yarmouth, Ma., U.S. **C7** 114
West Yellowstone, Mt., U.S. **F5** 119
West York, Pa., U.S. **G8** 131
Wetar, Pulau, i., Indon. . . . **E7** 36
Wetar, Selat, strt., Asia . . . **E7** 36
Wetaskiwin, Ab., Can. . . . **C4** 84
Wete, Tan. **D7** 54
Wethersfield, Ct., U.S. . . . **C5** 100
Wet Mountains, mts., Co., U.S. **C5** 99
Wetumka, Ok., U.S. **B5** 129
Wetumpka, Al., U.S. **C3** 94
Wetzel, co., W.V., U.S. . . . **B4** 141
Wetzlar, Ger. **E11** 12
Wewahitchka, Fl., U.S. . . . **B1** 102
Wewak, Pap. N. Gui. **G11** 32
Wewoka, Ok., U.S. **B5** 129
Wexford, Ire. **D3** 12
Wexford, co., Mi., U.S. . . . **D5** 115
Weyauwega, Wi., U.S. . . . **D5** 142
Weymouth, Eng., U.K. . . . **E5** 12
Weymouth, Ma., U.S. . . . **B6** 114
Whakatane, N.Z. **o14** 63c
Whalesville, Md., U.S. . . . **D7** 113
Whangarei, N.Z. **o13** 63c
Wharton, N.J., U.S. **B3** 123
Wharton, Tx., U.S. **E4** 136
Wharton, co., Tx., U.S. . . . **E4** 136
Wharton Basin **J13** 64
What Cheer, Ia., U.S. **C5** 108
Whatcom, co., Wa., U.S. . **A4** 140
Whatcom, Lake, l., Wa., U.S. **A3** 140
Wheatland, In., U.S. **B3** 107
Wheatland, Ia., U.S. **C7** 108
Wheatland, Wy., U.S. . . . **D8** 143
Wheatland, co., Mt., U.S. . **D7** 119
Wheatland Reservoir, res., Wy., U.S. **E7** 143
Wheatley, On., Can. **E2** 89
Wheaton, Il., U.S. **B5** 106
Wheaton, Md., U.S. **B3** 113
Wheaton, Mn., U.S. **E2** 116
Wheaton, Mo., U.S. **E3** 118
Wheat Ridge, Co., U.S. . . **B5** 99
Wheelbarrow Peak, mtn., Nv., U.S. **F5** 121
Wheeler, Ms., U.S. **A5** 117
Wheeler, Tx., U.S. **B2** 136
Wheeler, co., Ga., U.S. . . . **D4** 103
Wheeler, co., Ne., U.S. . . . **C7** 120
Wheeler, co., Or., U.S. . . . **C6** 130
Wheeler, co., Tx., U.S. . . . **B2** 136
Wheeler Air Force Base, mil., Hi., U.S. **g9** 104
Wheeler Lake, res., Al., U.S. **A2** 94
Wheeler Peak, mtn., Ca., U.S. **C4** 98
Wheeler Peak, mtn., N.M., U.S. **A4** 124
Wheeler Peak, mtn., Nv., U.S. **E7** 121
Wheelersburg, Oh., U.S. . **D3** 128
Wheeling, Il., U.S. **h9** 106
Wheeling, W.V., U.S. **A4** 141
Wheeling Creek, stm., W.V., U.S. **f8** 141

Name	Map Ref.	Page
Wheelwright, Ky., U.S.	C7	110
Whetstone, stm., U.S.	E2	116
Whidbey Island, i., Wa., U.S.	A3	140
Whidbey Island Naval Air Station, mil., Wa., U.S.	A3	140
Whigham, Ga., U.S.	F2	103
Whiskey Peak, mtn., Wy., U.S.	D5	143
Whiskeytown-Shasta-Trinity National Recreation Area, Ca., U.S.	B2	98
Whistler, B.C., Can.	D6	85
Whitacres, Ct., U.S.	A5	100
Whitakers, N.C., U.S.	A5	126
Whitbourne, Nf., Can.	E5	88
Whitby, On., Can.	D6	89
Whitchurch-Stouffville, On., Can.	D5	89
White, co., Ar., U.S.	B4	97
White, co., Ga., U.S.	B3	103
White, co., Il., U.S.	E5	106
White, co., In., U.S.	C4	107
White, co., Tn., U.S.	D8	135
White, stm., Az., U.S.	D5	96
White, stm., In., U.S.	H2	107
White, stm., Mi., U.S.	E4	115
White, stm., Nv., U.S.	E6	121
White, stm., Tx., U.S.	C2	136
White, stm., Vt., U.S.	D4	138
White, stm., Wa., U.S.	B5	140
White, stm., Wa., U.S.	B4	140
White, stm., U.S.	C4	97
White, stm., U.S.	D5	134
White, stm., U.S.	C7	137
White Bay, b., Nf., Can.	D3	88
White Bear, stm., Nf., Can.	E3	88
White Bear Lake, Mn., U.S.	E5	116
White Bluff, Tn., U.S.	A4	135
White Butte, mtn., N.D., U.S.	C2	127
White Castle, La., U.S.	D4	111
White Center, Wa., U.S.	e11	140
White City, Or., U.S.	E4	130
White Clay Creek, stm., U.S.	A3	120
White Cliffs, Austl.	F3	60
White Cliffs, Austl.	G3	62
White Cloud, Mi., U.S.	E5	115
Whitecourt, Ab., Can.	B3	84
White Creek, stm., U.S.	E2	138
Whiteday, stm., W.V., U.S.	h10	141
White Deer, Tx., U.S.	B2	136
White Earth Indian Reservation, Mn., U.S.	C3	116
White Earth Lake, l., Mn., U.S.	C3	116
Whiteface, stm., Mn., U.S.	C6	116
Whiteface Mountain, mtn., N.Y., U.S.	f11	125
Whitefield, N.H., U.S.	B3	122
Whitefish, Mt., U.S.	B2	119
Whitefish Bay, Wi., U.S.	m12	142
Whitefish Bay, b., Mi., U.S.	B6	115
Whitefish Lake, l., Mn., U.S.	D4	116
Whitefish Range, mts., Mt., U.S.	B2	119
Whiteford, Md., U.S.	A5	113
White Hall, Al., U.S.	C3	94
White Hall, Ar., U.S.	C3	97
White Hall, Il., U.S.	D3	106
Whitehall, Mi., U.S.	E4	115
Whitehall, Mt., U.S.	E4	119
Whitehall, N.Y., U.S.	B7	125
Whitehall, Oh., U.S.	m11	128
Whitehall, Wi., U.S.	D2	142
Whitehall Reservoir, res., Ma., U.S.	h9	114
Whitehaven, Eng., U.K.	C5	12
White Haven, Pa., U.S.	D10	131
Whitehorn, Point, c., Wa., U.S.	A3	140
Whitehorse, Yk., Can.	F13	82
White Horse, N.J., U.S.	C3	123
Whitehouse, Oh., U.S.	A2	128
White House, Tn., U.S.	A5	135
White Island Shores, Ma., U.S.	C6	114
White Knob Mountains, mts., Id., U.S.	F5	105
White Lake, l., La., U.S.	E3	111
Whiteman Air Force Base, mil., Mo., U.S.	C4	118
White Mesa Natural Bridge, Az., U.S.	A4	96
White Mountain Peak, mtn., Ca., U.S.	D4	98
White Mountains, mts., N.H., U.S.	B3	122
White Mountains, mts., U.S.	D4	98
Whitemouth, stm., Mb., Can.	E4	86
Whitemouth Lake, l., Mb., Can.	E4	86
White Nile see Abyad, Al-Bahr al-, stm., Sudan	H11	48
White Oak, Oh., U.S.	o12	128
White Oak Creek, stm., Oh., U.S.	D2	128
Whiteoak Creek, stm., Tn., U.S.	A4	135
White Oak Lake, res., Ar., U.S.	D2	97
White Pigeon, Mi., U.S.	G5	115
White Pine, Mi., U.S.	m12	115
White Pine, Tn., U.S.	C10	135
White Pine, co., Nv., U.S.	D6	121
White Plains, Md., U.S.	C4	113
White Plains, N.Y., U.S.	D7	125
White River Junction, Vt., U.S.	D4	138
White Rock, B.C., Can.	E6	85
White Russia see Belarus, ctry., Eur.	C9	20
White Salmon, Wa., U.S.	D4	140
White Salmon, stm., Wa., U.S.	D4	140
White Sands Missile Range, mil., N.M., U.S.	E3	124
White Sands National Monument, N.M., U.S.	E3	124
Whitesboro, N.Y., U.S.	B5	125
Whitesboro, Tx., U.S.	C4	136
Whitesburg, Ga., U.S.	C2	103
Whitesburg, Ky., U.S.	C7	110
Whites Creek, stm., Tn., U.S.	g10	135
White Sea see Beloe more, Russia	C5	26
Whiteside, co., Il., U.S.	B3	106
White Sulphur Springs, Mt., U.S.	D6	119
White Sulphur Springs, W.V., U.S.	D4	141
Whitesville, Ky., U.S.	C3	110
White Swan, Wa., U.S.	C5	140
White Tank Mountains, mts., Az., U.S.	k7	96
Whiteville, N.C., U.S.	C4	126
Whiteville, Tn., U.S.	B2	135
White Volta, stm., Afr.	E4	50
Whitewater, Ks., U.S.	E6	109
Whitewater, Wi., U.S.	F5	142
Whitewater, stm., Ks., U.S.	E6	109
Whitewater, stm., U.S.	F7	107
Whitewater Baldy, mtn., N.M., U.S.	D1	124
Whitewater Bay, b., Fl., U.S.	G6	102
Whitewood, S.D., U.S.	C2	134
Whitewright, Tx., U.S.	C4	136
Whitfield, co., Ga., U.S.	B2	103
Whitfield Estates, Fl., U.S.	q10	102
Whiting, Ia., U.S.	B1	108
Whiting, In., U.S.	A3	107
Whiting, Wi., U.S.	D4	142
Whiting Field Naval Air Station, mil., Fl., U.S.	u14	102
Whitinsville, Ma., U.S.	B4	114
Whitley, co., In., U.S.	B6	107
Whitley, co., Ky., U.S.	D5	110
Whitley City, Ky., U.S.	D5	110
Whitman, Ma., U.S.	B6	114
Whitman, W.V., U.S.	D2	141
Whitman, co., Wa., U.S.	B8	140
Whitman Square, N.J., U.S.	D2	123
Whitmire, S.C., U.S.	B4	133
Whitmore Lake, Mi., U.S.	p14	115
Whitmore Mountains, mts., Ant.	E31	67
Whitmore Village, Hi., U.S.	f9	104
Whitney, S.C., U.S.	B4	133
Whitney, Tx., U.S.	D4	136
Whitney, Lake, res., Tx., U.S.	D4	136
Whitney, Mount, mtn., Ca., U.S.	D4	98
Whitney Point Lake, res., N.Y., U.S.	C5	125
Whitsunday Island, i., Austl.	E4	62
Whittier, Ak., U.S.	C10	95
Whittier, Ca., U.S.	F4	98
Whitwell, Tn., U.S.	D8	135
Whyalla, Austl.	G2	62
Wiarton, On., Can.	C3	89
Wibaux, Mt., U.S.	D12	119
Wibaux, co., Mt., U.S.	D12	119
Wichita, Ks., U.S.	E6	109
Wichita, co., Ks., U.S.	D2	109
Wichita, co., Tx., U.S.	B3	136
Wichita Falls, Tx., U.S.	C3	136
Wichita Mountains, mts., Ok., U.S.	C3	129
Wick, Scot., U.K.	A5	12
Wickenburg, Az., U.S.	D3	96
Wickham, Austl.	E2	60
Wickham, Cape, c., Austl.	H3	62
Wickiup Reservoir, res., Or., U.S.	E5	130
Wickliffe, Ky., U.S.	f8	110
Wickliffe, Oh., U.S.	A4	128
Wicklow, Ire.	D3	12
Wicomico, co., Md., U.S.	D6	113
Wicomico, stm., Md., U.S.	D6	113
Wiconisco, Pa., U.S.	E8	131
Widefield, Co., U.S.	C6	99
Widgiemooltha, Austl.	G3	60
Wieluń, Pol.	D5	20
Wien, Aus.	F15	12
Wiener Neustadt, Aus.	G15	12
Wieprz, stm., Pol.	D7	20
Wiesbaden, Ger.	E11	12
Wiggins, Ms., U.S.	E4	117
Wiggins Peak, mtn., Wy., U.S.	C3	143
Wight, Isle of, i., Eng., U.K.	E6	12
Wikwemikong, On., Can.	B3	89
Wilbarger, co., Tx., U.S.	B3	136
Wilber, Ne., U.S.	D9	120
Wilberforce, Oh., U.S.	C2	128
Wilbraham, Ma., U.S.	B3	114
Wilbur, Wa., U.S.	B7	140
Wilburton, Ok., U.S.	C6	129
Wilcannia, Austl.	G3	62
Wilcox, Pa., U.S.	C4	131
Wilcox, co., Al., U.S.	D2	94
Wilcox, co., Ga., U.S.	E3	103
Wild, stm., U.S.	B4	122
Wild Ammonoosuc, stm., N.H., U.S.	B3	122
Wild Branch, stm., Vt., U.S.	B4	138
Wilder, Id., U.S.	F2	105
Wilder, Vt., U.S.	D4	138
Wilder Dam, U.S.	C2	122
Wildhorse Creek, stm., Ok., U.S.	C4	129
Wild Horse Reservoir, res., Nv., U.S.	B6	121
Wildorado, Tx., U.S.	B1	136
Wild Rice, stm., Mn., U.S.	C2	116
Wild Rice, stm., N.D., U.S.	C8	127
Wildwood, Fl., U.S.	D4	102
Wildwood, N.J., U.S.	F3	123
Wildwood Crest, N.J., U.S.	F3	123
Wilhelm, Mount, mtn., Pap. N. Gui.	H12	32
Wilhelmina Peak see Trikora, Puncak, mtn., Indon.	G10	32
Wilhelmshaven, Ger.	D10	12
Wilkes, co., Ga., U.S.	C4	103
Wilkes, co., N.C., U.S.	A1	126
Wilkes-Barre, Pa., U.S.	D10	131
Wilkesboro, N.C., U.S.	A1	126
Wilkes Land, reg., Ant.	D16	67
Wilkin, co., Mn., U.S.	D2	116
Wilkinsburg, Pa., U.S.	F2	131
Wilkinson, W.V., U.S.	D3	141
Wilkinson, co., Ga., U.S.	D3	103
Wilkinson, co., Ms., U.S.	D2	117
Will, co., Il., U.S.	B6	106
Willacoochee, Ga., U.S.	E3	103
Willacy, co., Tx., U.S.	F4	136
Willamette, stm., Or., U.S.	C3	130
Willamette Pass, Or., U.S.	D4	130
Willamina, Or., U.S.	B3	130
Willapa Bay, b., Wa., U.S.	C1	140
Willard, Mo., U.S.	D4	118
Willard, Oh., U.S.	A3	128
Willard, Ut., U.S.	B3	137
Willard Bay, b., Ut., U.S.	B3	137
Willards, Md., U.S.	D7	113
Willard Stream, stm., Vt., U.S.	B5	138
Willcox, Az., U.S.	E6	96
Willcox Playa, l., Az., U.S.	E5	96
Willemstad, Neth. Ant.	C6	80
William Bill Dannelly Reservoir, res., Al., U.S.	C2	94
Williams, Az., U.S.	B3	96
Williams, Ca., U.S.	C2	98
Williams, co., N.D., U.S.	A2	127
Williams, co., Oh., U.S.	A1	128
Williams, co., Vt., U.S.	E3	138
Williams, stm., W.V., U.S.	C4	141
Williams Bay, Wi., U.S.	F5	142
Williamsburg, Ia., U.S.	C5	108
Williamsburg, In., U.S.	E8	107
Williamsburg, Ky., U.S.	D5	110
Williamsburg, Oh., U.S.	C1	128
Williamsburg, Pa., U.S.	F5	131
Williamsburg, Va., U.S.	C6	139
Williamsburg, co., S.C., U.S.	D8	133
Williams Fork, stm., Co., U.S.	A3	99
Williams Lake, B.C., Can.	C6	85
Williamson, N.Y., U.S.	B3	125
Williamson, W.V., U.S.	D2	141
Williamson, co., Il., U.S.	F4	106
Williamson, co., Tn., U.S.	B5	135
Williamson, co., Tx., U.S.	D4	136
Williamsport, In., U.S.	D3	107
Williamsport, Md., U.S.	A2	113
Williamsport, Pa., U.S.	D7	131
Williamston, Mi., U.S.	F6	115
Williamston, N.C., U.S.	B5	126
Williamston, S.C., U.S.	B3	133
Williamstown, Ky., U.S.	B5	110
Williamstown, Ma., U.S.	A1	114
Williamstown, N.J., U.S.	D3	123
Williamstown, Pa., U.S.	E8	131
Williamstown, Vt., U.S.	C3	138
Williamstown, W.V., U.S.	B3	141
Williamsville, Il., U.S.	D4	106
Williamsville, N.Y., U.S.	C2	125
Willimantic, Ct., U.S.	B6	100
Willimantic, stm., Ct., U.S.	B6	100
Willimantic Reservoir, res., Ct., U.S.	C7	100
Willingboro, N.J., U.S.	C3	123
Willis, Tx., U.S.	D5	136
Willis Group, is., Austl.	D5	62
Williston, S. Afr.	E3	56
Williston, Fl., U.S.	C4	102
Williston, N.D., U.S.	A2	127
Williston, S.C., U.S.	E5	133
Williston Lake, res., B.C., Can.	B6	85
Willits, Ca., U.S.	C2	98
Willmar, Mn., U.S.	E3	116
Willoughby, Oh., U.S.	A4	128
Willoughby, Lake, l., Vt., U.S.	B4	138
Willoughby Hills, Oh., U.S.	A4	128
Willow, Ak., U.S.	g17	95
Willow Creek, stm., Nv., U.S.	E5	121
Willow Creek, stm., Ut., U.S.	D6	137
Willow Creek, stm., Wy., U.S.	C6	143
Willow Grove Naval Air Station, mil., Pa., U.S.	F11	131
Willowick, Oh., U.S.	A4	128
Willowmore, S. Afr.	E3	56
Willow Reservoir, res., Wi., U.S.	C3	142
Willow Run, De., U.S.	i7	101
Willow Run, Mi., U.S.	p14	115
Willows, Ca., U.S.	C2	98
Willow Springs, Il., U.S.	k9	106
Willow Springs, Mo., U.S.	E6	118
Wilmar, Ar., U.S.	D4	97
Wilmerding, Pa., U.S.	k14	131
Wilmette, Il., U.S.	A6	106
Wilmington, De., U.S.	B3	101
Wilmington, Il., U.S.	B5	106
Wilmington, Ma., U.S.	A5	114
Wilmington, N.C., U.S.	C5	126
Wilmington, Oh., U.S.	C2	128
Wilmington, Vt., U.S.	F3	138
Wilmington Manor, De., U.S.	i7	101
Wilmore, Ky., U.S.	C5	110
Wilmot, Ar., U.S.	D4	97
Wilson, Ar., U.S.	B5	97
Wilson, Ks., U.S.	D5	109
Wilson, La., U.S.	D4	111
Wilson, N.C., U.S.	B5	126
Wilson, Ok., U.S.	C4	129
Wilson, Pa., U.S.	E11	131
Wilson, Wy., U.S.	C2	143
Wilson, co., Ks., U.S.	E8	109
Wilson, co., N.C., U.S.	B5	126
Wilson, co., Tn., U.S.	A5	135
Wilson, co., Tx., U.S.	E3	136
Wilson, Mount, mtn., Az., U.S.	B1	96
Wilson, Mount, mtn., Ca., U.S.	m12	98
Wilson, Mount, mtn., Co., U.S.	D2	99
Wilson, Mount, mtn., Nv., U.S.	E7	121
Wilson, Mount, mtn., Or., U.S.	B5	130
Wilson Creek, stm., Wa., U.S.	B5	140
Wilson Creek, stm., Wa., U.S.	B6	140
Wilson Lake, res., Al., U.S.	A2	94
Wilson Lake, res., Ks., U.S.	D4	109
Wilsons Beach, N.B., Can.	E3	87
Wilsons Promontory, pen., Austl.	H4	62
Wilsonville, Al., U.S.	B3	94
Wilsonville, Or., U.S.	h12	130
Wilton, Al., U.S.	B3	94
Wilton, Ct., U.S.	E2	100
Wilton, Ia., U.S.	C6	108
Wilton, Me., U.S.	D2	112
Wilton, N.D., U.S.	B5	127
Wilton, N.H., U.S.	E3	122
Wiluna, Austl.	F3	60
Wimauma, Fl., U.S.	E4	102
Wimico, Lake, l., Fl., U.S.	C1	102
Winamac, In., U.S.	B4	107
Winburg, S. Afr.	D4	56
Wincheck Pond, l., R.I., U.S.	E1	132
Winchendon, Ma., U.S.	A3	114
Winchester, On., Can.	B9	89
Winchester, Eng., U.K.	E6	12
Winchester, Il., U.S.	D3	106
Winchester, In., U.S.	D8	107
Winchester, Ks., U.S.	k15	109
Winchester, Ma., U.S.	g11	114
Winchester, N.H., U.S.	E2	122
Winchester, Nv., U.S.	G6	121
Winchester, Oh., U.S.	D2	128
Winchester, Tn., U.S.	B5	135
Winchester, Va., U.S.	A4	139
Winchester Bay, Or., U.S.	D2	130
Wind, stm., Wa., U.S.	D4	140
Wind, stm., Wy., U.S.	C4	143
Windber, Pa., U.S.	F4	131
Wind Cave National Park, S.D., U.S.	D2	134
Winder, Ga., U.S.	C3	103
Windfall, In., U.S.	D6	107
Windgap, Pa., U.S.	E11	131
Windham, Ct., U.S.	C7	100
Windham, Oh., U.S.	A4	128
Windham, co., Ct., U.S.	B7	100
Windham, co., Vt., U.S.	F3	138
Windhoek, Nmb.	C2	56
Wind Lake, Wi., U.S.	F5	142
Wind Lake, l., Wi., U.S.	n11	142
Windmill Point, c., Va., U.S.	C6	139
Windom, Mn., U.S.	G3	116
Windom Peak, mtn., Co., U.S.	D3	99
Window Rock, Az., U.S.	B6	96
Wind Point, Wi., U.S.	n12	142
Wind River Indian Reservation, Wy., U.S.	C4	143
Wind River Peak, mtn., Wy., U.S.	D3	143
Wind River Range, mts., Wy., U.S.	C3	143
Windsor (part of Grand Falls-Windsor), Nf., Can.	D4	88
Windsor, On., Can.	E1	89
Windsor, P.Q., Can.	D5	90
Windsor, Co., U.S.	A6	99
Windsor, Ct., U.S.	B5	100
Windsor, Il., U.S.	D5	106
Windsor, Mo., U.S.	C4	118
Windsor, N.C., U.S.	A6	126
Windsor, Pa., U.S.	G8	131
Windsor, Va., U.S.	D6	139
Windsor, Vt., U.S.	E4	138
Windsor, co., Vt., U.S.	D3	138
Windsor Heights, Ia., U.S.	e8	108
Windsor Locks, Ct., U.S.	B5	100
Windward Islands, is., N.A.	F12	76
Windward Passage, strt., N.A.	E10	76
Windy Hill, S.C., U.S.	C8	133
Windy Peak, mtn., Wa., U.S.	A6	140
Winefred Lake, l., Ab., Can.	B5	84
Winfield, Al., U.S.	B2	94
Winfield, Ia., U.S.	C6	108
Winfield, Ks., U.S.	E7	109
Winfield, Mo., U.S.	C7	118
Winfield, W.V., U.S.	C3	141
Wing, stm., Mn., U.S.	D3	116
Wingate, N.C., U.S.	C2	126
Wingham, On., Can.	D3	89
Winifrede, W.V., U.S.	m12	141
Winisk, stm., On., Can.	n18	89
Wink, Tx., U.S.	D1	136
Winkelman, Az., U.S.	E5	96
Winkler, Mb., Can.	E3	86
Winkler, co., Tx., U.S.	D1	136
Winlock, Wa., U.S.	C3	140
Winn, co., La., U.S.	C3	111
Winneba, Ghana	E4	50
Winnebago, Il., U.S.	A4	106
Winnebago, Mn., U.S.	G4	116
Winnebago, Ne., U.S.	B9	120
Winnebago, Wi., U.S.	h8	142
Winnebago, co., Ia., U.S.	A4	108
Winnebago, co., Il., U.S.	A4	106
Winnebago, co., Wi., U.S.	D5	142
Winnebago, stm., Ia., U.S.	A4	108
Winnebago, Lake, l., Wi., U.S.	E5	142
Winnebago Indian Reservation, Ne., U.S.	B9	120
Winneconne, Wi., U.S.	D5	142
Winnemucca, Nv., U.S.	C4	121
Winnemucca Lake, l., Nv., U.S.	C2	121
Winner, S.D., U.S.	D6	134
Winneshiek, co., Ia., U.S.	A6	108
Winnetka, Il., U.S.	A6	106
Winnfield, La., U.S.	C3	111
Winnibigoshish, Lake, l., Mn., U.S.	C4	116
Winnipeg, Mb., Can.	E3	86
Winnipeg, stm., Can.	D4	86
Winnipeg, Lake, l., Mb., Can.	C4	86
Winnipeg Beach, Mb., Can.	D3	86
Winnipegosis, Mb., Can.	D2	86
Winnipegosis, Lake, l., Mb., Can.	C2	86
Winnipesaukee, Lake, l., N.H., U.S.	C4	122
Winnisquam, N.H., U.S.	C3	122
Winnisquam Lake, l., N.H., U.S.	C3	122
Winnsboro, La., U.S.	B4	111
Winnsboro, S.C., U.S.	C5	133
Winnsboro, Tx., U.S.	C5	136
Winnsboro Mills, S.C., U.S.	C5	133
Winona, Mn., U.S.	F7	116
Winona, Mo., U.S.	D6	118
Winona, Ms., U.S.	B4	117
Winona, co., Mn., U.S.	F7	116
Winona Lake, In., U.S.	B6	107
Winona Lake, l., Vt., U.S.	C2	138
Winooski, Vt., U.S.	C2	138
Winooski, stm., Vt., U.S.	C3	138
Winslow, Az., U.S.	C5	96
Winslow, In., U.S.	H3	107
Winslow, Me., U.S.	D3	112
Winsted, Ct., U.S.	B3	100
Winsted, Mn., U.S.	F4	116
Winston, Fl., U.S.	D4	102
Winston, Or., U.S.	D3	130
Winston, co., Al., U.S.	A2	94
Winston, co., Ms., U.S.	B4	117
Winston-Salem, N.C., U.S.	A2	126
Winter Garden, Fl., U.S.	D5	102
Winter Harbor, Me., U.S.	D4	112
Winter Haven, Fl., U.S.	D5	102
Winter Park, Fl., U.S.	D5	102
Winter Park, N.C., U.S.	C5	126
Winterport, Me., U.S.	D4	112
Winter Ridge, mtn., Or., U.S.	E6	130
Winters, Ca., U.S.	C2	98
Winters, Tx., U.S.	D3	136
Winterset, Ia., U.S.	C4	108
Wintersville, Oh., U.S.	B5	128
Winterthur, Switz.	G11	12
Winterton, Nf., Can.	E5	88
Winterville, Ga., U.S.	C3	103
Winterville, N.C., U.S.	B5	126

Name	Map Ref.	Page
Winthrop, Ia., U.S.	B6	108
Winthrop, Ma., U.S.	B6	114
Winthrop, Me., U.S.	D3	112
Winthrop, Mn., U.S.	F4	116
Winthrop, Lake, l., Ma., U.S.	h10	114
Winthrop Harbor, Il., U.S.	A6	106
Wintinna, Austl.	F5	60
Winton, Austl.	E3	62
Winton, N.C., U.S.	A6	126
Winton, N.Z.	q12	63c
Winton Lake, res., Oh., U.S.	o12	129
Winyah Bay, b., S.C., U.S.	E9	133
Wirt, co., W.V., U.S.	B3	141
Wiscasset, Me., U.S.	D3	112
Wisconsin, state, U.S.	D4	142
Wisconsin, stm., Wi., U.S.	E3	142
Wisconsin, Lake, res., Wi., U.S.	E4	142
Wisconsin Dells, Wi., U.S.	E4	142
Wisconsin Rapids, Wi., U.S.	D4	142
Wise, Va., U.S.	f9	139
Wise, co., Tx., U.S.	C4	136
Wise, co., Va., U.S.	e9	139
Wishek, N.D., U.S.	C6	127
Wishram, Wa., U.S.	D4	140
Wisła, stm., Pol.	C5	20
Wismar, Ger.	D12	12
Wisner, La., U.S.	C4	111
Wisner, Ne., U.S.	C9	120
Wissota, Lake, res., Wi., U.S.	D2	142
Wister, Ok., U.S.	C7	129
Wister Lake, res., Ok., U.S.	C7	129
Witbank, S. Afr.	D4	56
Withamsville, Oh., U.S.	C1	128
Witherspoon, Mount, mtn., Ak., U.S.	g18	95
Withlacoochee, stm., Fl., U.S.	C4	102
Withlacoochee, stm., U.S.	B3	102
Witless Bay, Nf., Can.	E5	88
Witt, Il., U.S.	D4	106
Wittenberg, Wi., U.S.	D4	142
Wittenberge, Ger.	D12	12
Wittenoom, Austl.	E2	60
Wittlich, Ger.	E10	12
Wittman, Md., U.S.	C5	113
Wittmann, Az., U.S.	D3	96
Witu Islands, is., Pap. N. Gui.	G12	32
Wixom, Mi., U.S.	o14	115
Wixom Lake, res., Mi., U.S.	E6	115
Włocławek, Pol.	C5	20
Woburn, Ma., U.S.	B5	114
Wodonga, Austl.	H4	62
Wokam, Pulau, i., Indon.	H9	32
Wolcott, Ct., U.S.	C4	100
Wolcott, In., U.S.	C3	107
Wolcottville, In., U.S.	A7	107
Woleai, atoll, Micron.	D8	58
Wolf, stm., Ms., U.S.	E4	117
Wolf, stm., Tn., U.S.	e9	135
Wolf, stm., Wi., U.S.	C5	142
Wolf, Volcán, vol., Ec.	C1	70
Wolf Creek, Or., U.S.	E3	130
Wolf Creek, stm., W.V., U.S.	m13	141
Wolf Creek, stm., U.S.	A2	129
Wolf Creek Pass, Co., U.S.	D3	99
Wolfe, co., Ky., U.S.	C6	110
Wolfeboro, N.H., U.S.	C4	122
Wolfeboro Falls, N.H., U.S.	C4	122
Wolfe City, Tx., U.S.	C4	136
Wolfen, Ger.	E13	12
Wolf Lake, Mi., U.S.	E4	115
Wolf Lake, l., Il., U.S.	k9	106
Wolf Mountain, mtn., Ak., U.S.	B9	95
Wolf Point, Mt., U.S.	B11	119
Wolfsberg, Aus.	G14	12
Wolfsburg, Ger.	D12	12
Wolf Swamp, sw., N.C., U.S.	C5	126
Wollaston, Islas, is., Chile	I3	69
Wollaston Lake, l., Sk., Can.	m8	91
Wollongong, Austl.	G5	62
Wolmaransstad, S. Afr.	D4	56
Wolverhampton, Eng., U.K.	D5	12
Woman Lake, l., Mn., U.S.	D4	116
Womelsdorf, Pa., U.S.	F9	131
Wonder Lake, Il., U.S.	A5	106
Wondinong, Austl.	F2	60
Wonewoc, Wi., U.S.	E3	142
Wŏnsan, N. Kor.	D13	28
Wonthaggi, Austl.	H4	62
Wood, co., Oh., U.S.	A2	128
Wood, co., Tx., U.S.	C5	136
Wood, co., W.V., U.S.	B3	141
Wood, co., Wi., U.S.	D3	142
Wood, stm., Sk., Can.	H2	91
Wood, stm., R.I., U.S.	F2	132
Wood, stm., Wy., U.S.	C3	143
Wood, Mount, mtn., Mt., U.S.	E7	119
Woodall Mountain, mtn., Ms., U.S.	A5	117
Woodbine, Ga., U.S.	F5	103
Woodbine, Ia., U.S.	C2	108
Woodbine, Ky., U.S.	D5	110
Woodbine, N.J., U.S.	E3	123
Woodbridge, Ct., U.S.	D3	100
Woodbridge, Va., U.S.	B5	139
Woodbridge [Township], N.J., U.S.	B4	123
Woodburn, In., U.S.	B8	107
Woodburn, Or., U.S.	B4	130
Woodbury, Ct., U.S.	C3	100
Woodbury, Ga., U.S.	D2	103
Woodbury, Mn., U.S.	F6	116
Woodbury, N.J., U.S.	D2	123
Woodbury, Tn., U.S.	B5	135
Woodbury, co., Ia., U.S.	B1	108
Woodcliff Lake, N.J., U.S.	g8	123
Woodcliff Lake, l., N.J., U.S.	g8	123
Wood Dale, Il., U.S.	k9	106
Wood End, spit, Ma., U.S.	B7	114
Woodfield, S.C., U.S.	C6	133
Woodford, co., Il., U.S.	C4	106
Woodford, co., Ky., U.S.	B5	110
Woodhull, Il., U.S.	B3	106
Woodlake, Ca., U.S.	D4	98
Woodland, Ca., U.S.	C3	98
Woodland, Me., U.S.	C5	112
Woodland, N.C., U.S.	A5	126
Woodland, Wa., U.S.	D3	140
Woodland Acres, Co., U.S.	D6	99
Woodland Park, Co., U.S.	C5	99
Woodlawn, Ky., U.S.	e9	110
Woodlawn, Md., U.S.	g10	113
Woodlawn, Oh., U.S.	n13	128
Woodlawn, Va., U.S.	D2	139
Woodmont, Ct., U.S.	E4	100
Woodmoor, Md., U.S.	B4	113
Woodridge, Il., U.S.	k8	106
Wood-Ridge, N.J., U.S.	h8	123
Wood River, Il., U.S.	E3	106
Wood River, Ne., U.S.	D7	120
Woodroffe, Mount, mtn., Austl.	F5	60
Woodruff, S.C., U.S.	B3	133
Woodruff, Wi., U.S.	C4	142
Woodruff, co., Ar., U.S.	B4	97
Woods, co., Ok., U.S.	A3	129
Woods, Lake, res., Tn., U.S.	B5	135
Woods, Lake of the, l., N.A.	B9	92
Woodsboro, Tx., U.S.	E4	136
Woods Cross, Ut., U.S.	C4	137
Woodsfield, Oh., U.S.	C4	128
Woods Hole, Ma., U.S.	C6	114
Woodson, Ar., U.S.	C3	97
Woodson, co., Ks., U.S.	E8	109
Woodstock, N.B., Can.	C2	87
Woodstock, On., Can.	D4	89
Woodstock, Ga., U.S.	B2	103
Woodstock, Il., U.S.	A5	106
Woodstock, Md., U.S.	B4	113
Woodstock, N.Y., U.S.	C6	125
Woodstock, Va., U.S.	B4	139
Woodstock, Vt., U.S.	D3	138
Woodstown, N.J., U.S.	D2	123
Woodsville, N.H., U.S.	B2	122
Woodville, Fl., U.S.	B2	102
Woodville, Ms., U.S.	D2	117
Woodville, Oh., U.S.	A2	128
Woodville, Tx., U.S.	D5	136
Woodville, Wi., U.S.	D1	142
Woodward, Ia., U.S.	C4	108
Woodward, Ok., U.S.	A2	129
Woodward, co., Ok., U.S.	A2	129
Woodworth, La., U.S.	C3	111
Woolmarket, Ms., U.S.	E5	117
Woolrich, Pa., U.S.	D7	131
Woolsey Peak, mtn., Az., U.S.	D3	96
Woomera, Austl.	G2	62
Woonsocket, R.I., U.S.	A3	132
Woonsocket, S.D., U.S.	C7	134
Woonsocket Reservoir Number Three, res., R.I., U.S.	B3	132
Wooster, Oh., U.S.	B4	128
Worcester, S. Afr.	E2	56
Worcester, Eng., U.K.	D5	12
Worcester, Ma., U.S.	B4	114
Worcester, co., Ma., U.S.	A3	114
Worcester, co., Md., U.S.	D7	113
Worden, Il., U.S.	E4	106
Worden Pond, l., R.I., U.S.	F3	132
Worland, Wy., U.S.	B5	143
Worms, Ger.	F11	12
Worth, Il., U.S.	k9	106
Worth, co., Ga., U.S.	E3	103
Worth, co., Ia., U.S.	A4	108
Worth, co., Mo., U.S.	A3	118
Worthing, Eng., U.K.	E6	12
Worthington, In., U.S.	F4	107
Worthington, Ky., U.S.	B7	110
Worthington, Mn., U.S.	G3	116
Worthington, Oh., U.S.	B2	128
Worthington Peak, mtn., Nv., U.S.	F6	121
Wosu, Indon.	D6	36
Wour, Chad	B8	50
Wowoni, Pulau, i., Indon.	D6	36
Woy Woy, Austl.	G5	62
Wrangel Island see Vrangelja, ostrov, i., Russia	B20	26
Wrangell, Ak., U.S.	D13	95
Wrangell, Cape, c., Ak., U.S.	E2	95
Wrangell, Mount, mtn., Ak., U.S.	f19	95
Wrangell Island, i., Ak., U.S.	m24	95
Wrangell Mountains, mts., Ak., U.S.	C11	95
Wrangell-Saint Elias National Park, Ak., U.S.	C11	95
Wrath, Cape, c., Scot., U.K.	A4	12
Wray, Co., U.S.	A8	99
Wrens, Ga., U.S.	C4	103
Wrentham, Ma., U.S.	B5	114
Wrexham, Wales, U.K.	D5	12
Wright, co., Ia., U.S.	B4	108
Wright, co., Mn., U.S.	E4	116
Wright, co., Mo., U.S.	D5	118
Wright, Mount, mtn., Mt., U.S.	C4	119
Wright Brothers National Memorial, hist., N.C., U.S.	A7	126
Wright City, Mo., U.S.	C8	118
Wright City, Ok., U.S.	C6	129
Wright Patman Lake, res., Tx., U.S.	A6	78
Wright-Patterson Air Force Base, mil., Oh., U.S.	C1	128
Wrightson, Mount, mtn., Az., U.S.	F5	96
Wrightstown, N.J., U.S.	C3	123
Wrightstown, Wi., U.S.	D5	142
Wrightsville, Ar., U.S.	C3	97
Wrightsville, Ga., U.S.	D4	103
Wrightsville, Pa., U.S.	F8	131
Wrightsville Beach, N.C., U.S.	C5	126
Wrightsville Reservoir, res., Vt., U.S.	C3	138
Wrocław, Pol.	D4	20
Wu, stm., China	F9	28
Wuchang, China	E3	30
Wuchuan, China	A3	30
Wuda, China	B2	30
Wudaoliang, China	D6	28
Wudi, China	B4	30
Wuding, China	A4	34
Wudu, China	E8	28
Wugang, China	F10	28
Wuhai, China	D9	28
Wuhan, China	E10	28
Wuhe, China	C4	30
Wuhu, China	E11	28
Wüjang, China	E3	28
Wukari, Nig.	E6	50
Wuliang Shan, mts., China	G8	28
Wuming, China	B5	34
Wupatki National Monument, Az., U.S.	B4	96
Wuppertal, Ger.	E10	12
Wuqi, China	B2	30
Wuqing, China	B4	30
Wurno, Nig.	D6	50
Würzburg, Ger.	F12	12
Wushan, China	C2	30
Wushenqi, China	D9	28
Wusuli (Ussuri), stm., Asia	E15	26
Wutai Shan, mtn., China	D10	28
Wutongqiao, China	F8	28
Wuvulu Island, i., Pap. N. Gui.	G11	32
Wuwei, China	D8	28
Wuwei, China	C4	30
Wuxi, China	E12	28
Wuyi Shan, mts., China	F11	28
Wuyuan, China	C9	28
Wuzhi Shan, mtn., China	H9	28
Wuzhong, China	D9	28
Wuzhou, China	G10	28
Wyaconda, stm., Mo., U.S.	A6	118
Wyandot, co., Oh., U.S.	B2	128
Wyandotte, Mi., U.S.	F7	115
Wyandotte, co., Ks., U.S.	C9	109
Wyanet, Il., U.S.	B4	106
Wye, stm., U.K.	D5	12
Wylie, Lake, res., U.S.	A5	133
Wyman Lake, res., Me., U.S.	C3	112
Wymore, Ne., U.S.	D9	120
Wyndham, Austl.	D4	60
Wynndel, B.C., Can.	E9	85
Wynne, Ar., U.S.	B5	97
Wynnewood, Ok., U.S.	C4	129
Wynoochee, stm., Wa., U.S.	B2	140
Wyoming, On., Can.	E2	89
Wyoming, De., U.S.	D3	101
Wyoming, Ia., U.S.	B6	108
Wyoming, Il., U.S.	B4	106
Wyoming, Mi., U.S.	F5	115
Wyoming, Mn., U.S.	E6	116
Wyoming, Oh., U.S.	o13	128
Wyoming, Pa., U.S.	n17	131
Wyoming, R.I., U.S.	E2	132
Wyoming, co., N.Y., U.S.	C2	125
Wyoming, co., Pa., U.S.	D9	131
Wyoming, co., W.V., U.S.	D3	141
Wyoming, state, U.S.	C5	143
Wyoming Peak, mtn., Wy., U.S.	D2	143
Wyoming Range, mts., Wy., U.S.	D2	143
Wyomissing, Pa., U.S.	F10	131
Wyong, Austl.	G5	62
Wysocking Bay, b., N.C., U.S.	B7	126
Wythe, co., Va., U.S.	D1	139
Wytheville, Va., U.S.	D1	139

X

Name	Map Ref.	Page
Xaafuun, Raas, c., Som.	H15	48
Xaçmaz, Azer.	B13	44
Xaidulla, China	D3	28
Xainza, China	E5	28
Xai-Xai, Moz.	D5	56
Xalapa, Mex.	D5	78
Xam Nua, Laos	B4	34
Xá-Muteba, Ang.	E3	54
Xangongo, Ang.	B2	56
Xankändi, Azer.	C12	44
Xánthi, Grc.	D10	18
Xanxerê, Braz.	D7	72
Xapuri, Braz.	F6	70
Xàtiva, Spain	H6	16
Xau, Lake, pl., Bots.	C3	56
Xenia, Oh., U.S.	C2	128
Xi, stm., China	G10	28
Xiachuan Dao, i., China	E3	30
Xiamen, China	G11	28
Xi'an, China	E9	28
Xianfeng, China	D2	30
Xiang, stm., China	D3	30
Xiangfan, China	E10	28
Xianggang (Hong Kong), China	E3	30
Xiangkhoang, Laos	C4	34
Xiangride, China	D7	28
Xiangtan, China	F10	28
Xianju, China	D5	30
Xianning, China	D3	30
Xianyang, China	C2	30
Xianyou, China	F11	28
Xiaogan, China	E10	28
Xiao Hinggan Ling, mts., China	A1	31
Xiaojin, China	C1	30
Xiapu, China	F12	28
Xiayi, China	C4	30
Xichang, China	F8	28
Xigazê, China	F5	28
Ximiao, China	C8	28
Xin'anjiang Shuiku, res., China	D4	30
Xinavane, Moz.	C5	56
Xincai, China	C4	30
Xing'an, China	F10	28
Xingcheng, China	A5	30
Xinghe, China	A3	30
Xingren, China	D2	30
Xingtai, China	D10	28
Xingu, stm., Braz.	D9	70
Xingxian, China	B3	30
Xingyi, China	F8	28
Xinhua, China	D3	30
Xining, China	D8	28
Xinji, China	B4	30
Xinjiang Uygur Zizhiqu (Sinkiang), prov., China	C5	28
Xinjin, China	C1	30
Xinjin, China	B5	30
Xinjiulong (New Kowloon), China	E3	30
Xinning, China	D3	30
Xinwen, China	B4	30
Xinxian, China	B3	30
Xinxiang, China	D10	28
Xinyang, China	E10	28
Xique-Xique, Braz.	D3	74
Xisha Qundao (Paracel Islands), is., China	C6	34
Xiushan, China	D2	30
Xiushui, China	D3	30
Xixiang, China	C2	30
Xizang Zizhiqu (Tibet), prov., China	E5	28
Xuancheng, China	E11	28
Xuanhan, China	C2	30
Xuanhua, China	A4	30
Xuanwei, China	D1	30
Xuchang, China	E10	28
Xupu, China	D3	30
Xuwen, China	G10	28
Xuyong, China	F9	28
Xuzhou, China	E11	28

Y

Name	Map Ref.	Page
Yaan, China	E8	28
Yablonovy Range see Jablonovyj hrebet, mts., Russia	D13	26
Yabrīn, Sau. Ar.	F5	42
Yacolt, Wa., U.S.	D3	140
Yacuiba, Bol.	C5	72
Yādgīr, India	F3	40
Yadkin, co., N.C., U.S.	A2	126
Yadkin, stm., N.C., U.S.	B2	126
Yadkinville, N.C., U.S.	A2	126
Yadong, China	A1	34
Yafran, Libya	E6	14
Yagoua, Cam.	A3	54
Yagradagzê Shan, mtn., China	D7	28
Yahyalı, Tur.	C6	44
Yainax Butte, mtn., Or., U.S.	E5	130
Yakima, Wa., U.S.	C5	140
Yakima, co., Wa., U.S.	C4	140
Yakima, stm., Wa., U.S.	C6	140
Yakima Indian Reservation, Wa., U.S.	C5	140
Yako, Burkina	D4	50
Yakoma, D.R.C.	C4	54
Yakumo, Japan	B3	31
Yaku-shima, i., Japan	E14	28
Yakutat, Ak., U.S.	D12	95
Yakutat Bay, b., Ak., U.S.	D11	95
Yakutia see Jakutija, state, Russia	C14	26
Yakutsk see Jakutsk, Russia	C14	26
Yakymivka, Ukr.	F13	20
Yala, Thai.	E4	34
Yale, Mi., U.S.	E8	115
Yale, Ok., U.S.	A5	129
Yale, Mount, mtn., Co., U.S.	C5	99
Yale Lake, res., Wa., U.S.	D3	140
Yalgoo, Austl.	F2	60
Yalinga, C.A.R.	B4	54
Yalobusha, co., Ms., U.S.	A4	117
Yalobusha, stm., Ms., U.S.	B4	117
Yalong, stm., China	E7	28
Yalova, Tur.	B3	44
Yalta, Ukr.	G13	20
Yalu, stm., Asia	C13	28
Yalvaç, Tur.	C4	44
Yamachiche, P.Q., Can.	C5	90
Yamagata, Japan	D16	28
Yamaguchi, Japan	D2	31
Yamal Peninsula see Jamal, poluostrov, pen., Russia	B8	26
Yambio, Sudan	J10	48
Yamdena, Pulau, i., Indon.	E8	36
Yamethin, Myan.	B3	34
Yamhill, Or., U.S.	h11	130
Yamhill, co., Or., U.S.	B3	130
Yamoussoukro, C. Iv.	E3	50
Yampa, stm., Co., U.S.	A2	99
Yampil', Ukr.	E10	20
Yamsay Mountain, mtn., Or., U.S.	E5	130
Yamuna, stm., India	D4	40
Yamunānagar, India	C3	40
Yamzho Yumco, l., China	F6	28
Yana see Jana, stm., Russia	C15	26
Yanam, India	F4	40
Yan'an, China	D9	28
Yanbu' al-Bahr, Sau. Ar.	F3	38
Yancey, co., N.C., U.S.	f10	126
Yanceyville, N.C., U.S.	A3	126
Yancheng, China	E12	28
Yanchi, China	D9	28
Yanfolila, Mali	D3	50
Yangambi, D.R.C.	C4	54
Yangchun, China	E3	30
Yanggao, China	A3	30
Yangjiang, China	G10	28
Yangliuqing, China	B4	30
Yangon (Rangoon), Myan.	C3	34
Yangquan, China	D10	28
Yangshan, China	E3	30
Yangshuo, China	E3	30
Yangtze see Chang, stm., China	E9	28
Yangxian, China	C2	30
Yangxin, China	D4	30
Yangzhou, China	E11	28
Yanji, China	C13	28
Yankton, S.D., U.S.	E8	134
Yankton, co., S.D., U.S.	D8	134
Yanqi, China	C5	28
Yantai, China	D12	28
Yantic, stm., Ct., U.S.	C7	100
Yanting, China	C2	30
Yanyuan, China	A4	34
Yanzhou, China	B4	30
Yaoundé, Cam.	B2	54
Yap, i., Micron.	E10	32
Yapen, Pulau, i., Indon.	D8	32
Yaqui, stm., Mex.	B3	78
Yardley, Pa., U.S.	F12	131
Yardville, N.J., U.S.	C3	123
Yarīm, Yemen	H4	38
Yarkand see Shache, China	D3	28
Yarkant see Yarkant, stm., China	B3	40
Yarkant, stm., China	B3	40
Yarloop, Austl.	G2	60
Yarmouth, Me., U.S.	E2	112
Yarnell, Az., U.S.	C3	96
Yaroslavl' see Jaroslavl', Russia	D6	26
Yarumal, Col.	B4	70
Yass, Austl.	G4	62
Yatağan, Tur.	D3	44
Yaté, N. Cal.	I9	62a
Yates, co., N.Y., U.S.	C3	125
Yates Center, Ks., U.S.	E8	109
Yates City, Il., U.S.	C3	106
Yatsushiro, Japan	E14	28
Yatta Plateau, plat., Kenya	D7	54
Yavapai, co., Az., U.S.	C3	96
Yavarí (Javari), stm., S.A.	D5	70
Yavatmāl, India	E3	40
Yaví, Cerro, mtn., Ven.	B6	70
Yawgoog Pond, l., R.I., U.S.	E1	132
Yazd, Iran	D6	42
Yazoo, co., Ms., U.S.	C3	117
Yazoo, stm., Ms., U.S.	C3	117
Yazoo City, Ms., U.S.	C3	117
Ye, Myan.	C3	34
Yeadon, Pa., U.S.	p21	131
Yeagertown, Pa., U.S.	E6	131
Yecheng, China	D3	28
Yecla, Spain	H6	16
Yeeda, Austl.	D3	60
Yei, Sudan	J11	48
Yélimané, Mali	C2	50
Yell, co., Ar., U.S.	B2	97
Yellow see Huang, stm., China	D11	28
Yellow, stm., In., U.S.	B4	107
Yellow, stm., Wi., U.S.	C3	142

Name	Map Ref.	Page
Yellow, stm., Wi., U.S.	D3	142
Yellow, stm., U.S.	u15	102
Yellow Creek, stm., Tn., U.S.	A4	135
Yellowhead Pass, Can.	C1	84
Yellowjacket Mountains, mts., Id., U.S.	D4	105
Yellowknife, Can.	F17	82
Yellow Lake, l., Wi., U.S.	C1	142
Yellow Medicine, co., Mn., U.S.	F2	116
Yellow Sea, Asia	D12	28
Yellow Springs, Oh., U.S.	C2	128
Yellowstone, co., Mt., U.S.	D8	119
Yellowstone, stm., U.S.	D10	119
Yellowstone Lake, l., Wy., U.S.	B2	143
Yellowstone National Park, co., Mt., U.S.	E6	119
Yellowstone National Park, U.S.	B2	143
Yellville, Ar., U.S.	A3	97
Yelm, Wa., U.S.	C3	140
Yemassee, S.C., U.S.	F6	133
Yemen, ctry., Asia	G5	38
Yenagoa, Nig.	F6	50
Yenakiieve, Ukr.	E15	20
Yenangyaung, Mya.	B2	34
Yen Bai, Viet.	B4	34
Yendéré, Burkina	D4	50
Yendi, Ghana	E4	50
Yengisar, China	D3	28
Yenice, stm., Tur.	B5	44
Yenişehir, Tur.	B3	44
Yenisey see Enisej, stm., Russia	C10	26
Yentna, stm., Ak., U.S.	f16	95
Yerevan, Arm.	B11	44
Yerington, Nv., U.S.	E2	121
Yerington Indian Reservation, Nv., U.S.	D2	121
Yerköy, Tur.	C6	44
Yermo, Ca., U.S.	E5	98
Yerupaja, Nevado, mtn., Peru	F4	70
Yerushalayim, Isr.	D3	42
Yeşilhisar, Tur.	C6	44
Yetti, reg., Afr.	A3	50
Yeu, Île d', i., Fr.	D5	16
Yevpatoriia, Ukr.	G12	20
Ygatimí, Para.	C6	72
Yi'an, China	B13	28
Yibin, China	F8	28
Yichang, China	E10	28
Yichuan, China	B3	30
Yichun, China	D3	30
Yichun, China	B13	28
Yidu, China	B4	30
Yidu, China	C3	30
Yilan, China	B13	28
Yıldızeli, Tur.	C7	44
Yiliang, China	G8	28
Yinchuan, China	D9	28
Yingde, China	E3	30
Yingkou, China	C12	28
Yingtan, China	F11	28
Yining, China	C4	28
Yinmabin, Mya.	B2	34
Yirga 'Alem, Eth.	B7	54
Yirol, Sudan	B6	54
Yishan, China	E2	30
Yitulihe, China	A12	28
Yiyang, China	F10	28
Yiyang, China	D4	30
Yizhang, China	D3	30
Yli-Kitka, l., Fin.	C13	10
Yoakum, Tx., U.S.	E4	136
Yoakum, co., Tx., U.S.	C1	136
Yockanookany, stm., Ms., U.S.	C4	117
Yocona, stm., Ms., U.S.	A4	117
Yogyakarta, Indon.	E4	36
Yoho National Park, B.C., Can.	D9	85
Yokadouma, Cam.	C2	54
Yoko, Cam.	B2	54
Yokohama, Japan	D15	28
Yokosuka, Japan	C3	31
Yokote, Japan	C4	31
Yola, Nig.	E7	50
Yolo, co., Ca., U.S.	C2	98
Yom, stm., Thai.	C3	34
Yomba Indian Reservation, Nv., U.S.	D4	121
Yonago, Japan	D14	28
Yoncalla, Or., U.S.	D3	130
Yonezawa, Japan	C3	31
Yong'an, China	F11	28
Yongchang, China	B1	30
Yongchuan, China	D2	30
Yongding, China	E4	30
Yongfeng, China	A7	34
Yongkang, China	D5	30
Yongping, China	A3	34
Yongren, China	F8	28
Yongshan, China	F8	28
Yongxiu, China	D4	30
Yongzhou, China	F10	28
Yonkers, N.Y., U.S.	E7	125
Yonne, stm., Fr.	C8	16
Yopal, Col.	D5	80
Yopurga, China	B3	40
York, Austl.	G2	60
York, stm., On., Can.	B7	89
York, On., Can.	D5	89
York, Eng., U.K.	C6	12
York, Al., U.S.	C1	94
York, Me., U.S.	E2	112
York, co., Me., U.S.	E2	112
York, Ne., U.S.	D8	120
York, co., Ne., U.S.	D8	120
York, Pa., U.S.	G8	131
York, co., Pa., U.S.	G8	131
York, S.C., U.S.	B5	133
York, co., S.C., U.S.	A5	133
York, stm., Va., U.S.	C6	139
York, co., Va., U.S.	C6	139
York, Cape, c., Austl.	C3	62
York, Kap, c., Grnld.	C26	82
York Beach, Me., U.S.	E2	112
Yorke Peninsula, pen., Austl.	G2	62
York Harbor, Me., U.S.	E2	112
Yorklyn, De., U.S.	A3	101
Yorktown, In., U.S.	D7	107
Yorktown, Tx., U.S.	E4	136
Yorktown, Va., U.S.	C6	139
Yorktown Manor, R.I., U.S.	E4	132
Yorkville, Il., U.S.	B5	106
Yorkville, N.Y., U.S.	B5	125
Yorkville, Oh., U.S.	B5	128
Yoro, Hond.	B2	80
Yoron-jima, i., Japan	g6	31a
Yosemite National Park, Ca., U.S.	D4	98
Yos Sudarso, Pulau, i., Indon.	H10	32
Yotaú, Bol.	B5	72
You, stm., China	G9	28
Youbou, B.C., Can.	g11	85
Youghiogheny, stm., U.S.	F2	131
Youghiogheny River Lake, res., U.S.	G3	131
Young, Austl.	G4	62
Young, Az., U.S.	C5	96
Young, co., Tx., U.S.	C3	136
Young Harris, Ga., U.S.	B3	103
Youngs, Lake, l., Wa., U.S.	f11	140
Youngstown, N.Y., U.S.	B1	125
Youngstown, Oh., U.S.	A5	128
Youngsville, La., U.S.	D3	111
Youngsville, Pa., U.S.	C3	131
Youngtown, Az., U.S.	k8	96
Youngwood, Pa., U.S.	F2	131
Youxian, China	D3	30
Youyang, China	F9	28
Yozgat, Tur.	C6	44
Ypacarai, Para.	D6	72
Ypsilanti, Mi., U.S.	F7	115
Yreka, Ca., U.S.	B2	98
Ystad, Swe.	I5	10
Yuanling, China	F10	28
Yuanmou, China	F8	28
Yuba, stm., Ca., U.S.	C3	98
Yuba, co., Ca., U.S.	C3	98
Yuba City, Ca., U.S.	C3	98
Yūbari, Japan	C16	28
Yucatán, state, Mex.	C7	78
Yucatan Channel, strt., N.A.	A2	80
Yucatan Peninsula, pen., N.A.	B2	80
Yucca Lake, l., Nv., U.S.	F5	121
Yucca Mountain, mtn., Nv., U.S.	G5	121
Yucheng, China	B4	30
Yudu, China	D4	30
Yueqing, China	D5	30
Yuexi, China	A4	34
Yueyang, China	F10	28
Yugoslavia, ctry., Eur.	C8	18
Yukon, ter., Can.	F12	82
Yukon, stm., N.A.	F7	82
Yukon, Ok., U.S.	B4	129
Yulee, Fl., U.S.	B5	102
Yulin, China	G10	28
Yulin, China	D9	28
Yuma, Az., U.S.	E1	96
Yuma, co., Az., U.S.	E1	96
Yuma, co., Co., U.S.	A8	99
Yuma, Co., U.S.	A8	99
Yuma Marine Corps Air Station, mil., Az., U.S.	E1	96
Yumbi, D.R.C.	D3	54
Yumbo, Col.	E4	80
Yumen, China	D7	28
Yuncheng, China	D10	28
Yunnan, prov., China	G8	28
Yunxian, China	E10	28
Yunxiao, China	E4	30
Yunyang, China	C2	30
Yurimaguas, Peru	E4	70
Yuruá see Juruá, stm., S.A.	E6	70
Yushan, China	D4	30
Yü Shan, mtn., Tai.	E5	30
Yushu, China	E7	28
Yutan, Ne., U.S.	C9	120
Yutian, China	D4	28
Yuyao, China	C5	30
Yvetot, Fr.	C7	16

Z

Name	Map Ref.	Page
Žabasak, Kaz.	D11	22
Zabīd, Yemen	H4	38
Zābol, Iran	D8	42
Zacapa, Guat.	B2	80
Zacapu, Mex.	D4	78
Zacatecas, state, Mex.	C4	78
Zacatecas, Mex.	C4	78
Zachary, La., U.S.	D4	111
Zadar, Cro.	B5	18
Zadoi, China	C7	40
Zadonsk, Russia	C15	20
Zafer Burnu, c., N. Cyp.	E6	44
Zafra, Spain	H3	16
Zagazig, Egypt	E10	14
Zagora, Mor.	E2	14
Zagreb, Cro.	B5	18
Zāgros, Kūhhā-ye (Zagros Mountains), mts., Iran	D6	42
Zagros Mountains see Zāgros, Kūhhā-ye, mts., Iran	D6	42
Zāhedān, Iran	E8	42
Zahīrābād, India	F3	40
Zahlah, Leb.	F6	44
Zaire see Congo, Democratic Republic of the, ctry., Afr.	D4	54
Zaire see Congo, stm., Afr.	D2	54
Zaječar, Yugo.	C9	18
Zajsan, Kaz.	E10	26
Zajsan, ozero, l., Kaz.	E10	26
Zakamensk, Russia	D12	26
Zakho, Iraq	D10	44
Zákinthos, i., Grc.	F8	18
Zákinthos, Grc.	F8	18
Zakopane, Pol.	E6	20
Zakouma, Chad	A3	54
Zalaegerszeg, Hung.	F4	20
Zalău, Rom.	F7	20
Zalishchyky, Ukr.	E8	20
Zamantı, stm., Tur.	D6	44
Zambeze (Zambezi), stm., Afr.	A3	56
Zambezi (Zambeze), stm., Afr.	B5	56
Zambezi, Zam.	A3	56
Zambia, ctry., Afr.	E5	52
Zamboanga, Phil.	E8	34
Zamboanga Peninsula, pen., Phil.	E8	34
Zambrów, Pol.	C7	20
Zâmbuè, Moz.	B5	56
Žambyl, Kaz.	E9	26
Zamora, Spain	G4	16
Zamora de Hidalgo, Mex.	D4	78
Zamość, Pol.	D7	20
Zanaga, Congo	D2	54
Zanesville, Oh., U.S.	C4	128
Zanjān, Iran	C5	42
Zante see Zákinthos, i., Grc.	F8	18
Zanthus, Austl.	G3	60
Zanzibar, Tan.	E7	54
Zanzibar, i., Tan.	E7	54
Zanzibar Channel, strt., Tan.	E7	54
Zaozhuang, China	C4	30
Zapadno-Sibirskaja ravnina, pl., Russia	C9	26
Zapadnyj Sajan, mts., Russia	D11	26
Zapala, Arg.	E2	69
Zapata, co., Tx., U.S.	F3	136
Zapata, Tx., U.S.	F3	136
Zapopan, Mex.	C4	78
Zaporizhzhia, Ukr.	F13	20
Zaqatala, Azer.	B12	44
Zara, Tur.	C7	44
Zaragoza, Spain	G6	16
Zarajsk, Russia	B15	20
Zaranj, Afg.	D8	42
Zarasai, Lith.	I12	10
Zárate, Arg.	E6	72
Zarembo Island, i., Ak., U.S.	m23	95
Zarghon Shahr, Afg.	D9	42
Zaria, Nig.	D6	50
Žarkamys, Kaz.	E10	22
Žarma, Kaz.	B4	28
Žary, Pol.	D3	20
Zāskār Mountains, mts., Asia	C3	40
Zavala, co., Tx., U.S.	E3	136
Zave, Zimb.	B5	56
Zavitinsk, Russia	A13	28
Zawiercie, Pol.	D5	20
Zāwiyat Masūs, Libya	E8	14
Zaysan, Lake see Zajsan, ozero, l., Kaz.	E10	26
Zdolbuniv, Ukr.	D9	20
Zduńska Wola, Pol.	D5	20
Zearing, Ia., U.S.	B4	108
Zebulon, Ga., U.S.	C2	103
Zebulon, N.C., U.S.	B4	126
Zeehan, Austl.	I4	62
Zeeland, Mi., U.S.	F5	115
Zeerust, S. Afr.	D4	56
Zeigler, Il., U.S.	F4	106
Zeja, Russia	D14	26
Zeja, stm., Russia	D14	26
Zejskoe vodohranilišče, res., Russia	D14	26
Zelenogorsk, Russia	F13	10
Zelenokumsk, Russia	B4	42
Železnodorožnyj, Russia	B9	22
Železnogorsk, Russia	C13	20
Železnogorsk-Ilimskij, Russia	D12	26
Zelienople, Pa., U.S.	E1	131
Zell am See, Aus.	G13	12
Zémio, C.A.R.	B5	54
Zenica, Bos.	B6	18
Zenith, Wa., U.S.	f11	140
Zenobia Peak, mtn., Co., U.S.	A2	99
Zenza do Itombe, Ang.	E2	54
Zephyr Cove, Nv., U.S.	E2	121
Zephyrhills, Fl., U.S.	D4	102
Zestafoni, Geor.	A10	44
Zeya see Zeja, stm., Russia	D14	26
Zeya Reservoir see Zejskoe vodohranilišče, res., Russia	D14	26
Žezkazgan, Kaz.	E8	26
Zgierz, Pol.	D5	20
Zhalun, China	C4	40
Zhangjiakou, China	C10	28
Zhangping, China	F11	28
Zhangpu, China	E4	30
Zhangye, China	D8	28
Zhangzhou, China	G11	28
Zhanhua, China	D4	28
Zhanjiang, China	G10	28
Zhao'an, China	G11	28
Zhaojue, China	D1	30
Zhaoqing, China	G10	28
Zhaotong, China	F8	28
Zhashkiv, Ukr.	E11	20
Zhaxigang, China	E3	28
Zhdanov see Mariupol', Ukr.	F14	20
Zhejiang, prov., China	F11	28
Zhenghe, China	D4	30
Zhenglan Qi, China	A4	30
Zhengzhou, China	D10	28
Zhenjiang, China	C4	30
Zhenning, China	D2	30
Zhenping, China	E10	28
Zhenxiong, China	D1	30
Zhenyuan, China	F9	28
Zhidoi, China	C6	40
Zhijiang, China	D2	30
Zhmerynka, Ukr.	E10	20
Zhob, stm., Pak.	D9	42
Zhob, Pak.	D9	42
Zhongba, China	E4	28
Zhongdian, China	F7	28
Zhongning, China	D9	28
Zhongshan, China	B6	34
Zhongwei, China	B2	30
Zhongxian, China	C2	30
Zhongxiang, China	E10	28
Zhoushan Qundao, is., China	E12	28
Zhovtneve, Ukr.	F12	20
Zhuanghe, China	B5	30
Zhucheng, China	B4	30
Zhumadian, China	C3	30
Zhuolu, China	A4	30
Zhuozhou, China	D11	28
Zhushan, China	E10	28
Zhuzhou, China	F10	28
Zhytomyr, Ukr.	D10	20
Zia Indian Reservation, N.M., U.S.	h7	124
Zibo, China	D11	28
Ziebach, co., S.D., U.S.	C4	134
Zielona Góra, Pol.	D3	20
Žigalovo, Russia	D12	26
Žigansk, Russia	C14	26
Zigong, China	F8	28
Ziguinchor, Sen.	D1	50
Zihuatanejo, Mex.	D4	78
Zile, Tur.	B6	44
Žilina, Slvk.	E5	20
Zillah, Libya	E8	48
Zillah, Wa., U.S.	C5	140
Zilwaukee, Mi., U.S.	E7	115
Zima, Russia	D12	26
Zimbabwe, ctry., Afr.	B4	56
Zimi, S.L.	E2	50
Zimmerman, Mn., U.S.	E5	116
Zinder, Niger	D6	50
Zion, Il., U.S.	A6	106
Zion National Park, Ut., U.S.	F3	137
Zion Reservoir, res., Az., U.S.	C6	96
Zionsville, In., U.S.	E5	107
Zipaquirá, Col.	D5	80
Zirkel, Mount, mtn., Co., U.S.	A4	99
Zitong, China	C2	30
Zittau, Ger.	E14	12
Zitundo, Moz.	D5	56
Ziway Hāyk', l., Eth.	B7	54
Ziyun, China	D2	30
Zlatoust, Russia	D7	26
Zlīţan, Libya	D7	48
Złobin, Bela.	C11	20
Złotów, Pol.	C4	20
Zmeinogorsk, Russia	A4	28
Znam'ianka, Ukr.	E12	20
Znojmo, Czech Rep.	E4	20
Žodzina, Bela.	B10	20
Zolfo Springs, Fl., U.S.	E5	102
Zomba, Mwi.	B6	56
Zonguldak, Tur.	B4	44
Zouar, Chad	B8	50
Zouérat, Maur.	B2	50
Zrenjanin, Yugo.	B8	18
Žuantobe, Kaz.	B9	42
Zug, Switz.	A2	18
Zugdidi, Geor.	A9	44
Zugspitze, mtn., Eur.	G12	12
Žukovka, Russia	C12	20
Zumbo, Moz.	B5	56
Zumbro, stm., Mn., U.S.	F6	116
Zumbrota, Mn., U.S.	F6	116
Zuni (Zuni Pueblo), N.M., U.S.	B1	124
Zuni, stm., U.S.	C6	96
Zuni Indian Reservation, N.M., U.S.	B1	124
Zuni Mountains, mts., N.M., U.S.	B1	124
Zunyi, China	F9	28
Zūrābād, Iran	C11	44
Zurich, On., Can.	D3	89
Zürich, Switz.	A2	18
Zurich, Lake see Zürichsee, l., Switz.	A2	18
Zürichsee, l., Switz.	A2	18
Zuru, Nig.	D6	50
Zuwārah, Libya	E6	14
Zvishavane, Zimb.	C4	56
Zvolen, Slvk.	E5	20
Zwedru, Lib.	E3	50
Zwickau, Ger.	E13	12
Zwolle, Neth.	D10	12
Zwolle, La., U.S.	C2	111
Żyrardów, Pol.	C6	20
Zyrjanka, Russia	C17	26
Zyrjanovsk, Kaz.	E10	26
Żywiec, Pol.	E5	20